MARKETING

Concepts and Strategies

Twelfth Edition

William M. Pride

Texas A&M University

O.C. Ferrell

Colorado State University

Houghton Mifflin Company   Boston   New York

Executive Editor: George Hoffman
Senior Development Editor: Susan M. Kahn
Senior Project Editor: Cathy Labresh Brooks
Editorial Assistant: Lindsay Frost
Senior Production/Design Coordinator: Jill Haber
Senior Manufacturing Coordinator: Priscilla Bailey
Marketing Manager: Steven W. Mikels
Senior Designer: Henry Rachlin

Custom Publishing Editor: Dan Luciano
Custom Publishing Production Manager: Kathleen McCourt
Project Coordinator: Kayla Whittet

Cover design: Sarah Melhado Bishins
Cover Image: Michael Doret

Credits for advertisements and photographs begin on page G-38.

ISBN: 0-618-27254-2
N01203

1 2 3 4 5 6 7 8 9 – DS – 04 03 02

 Houghton Mifflin
                      Custom Publishing

222 Berkeley Street • Boston, MA 02116

Address all correspondence and order information to the above address.

BRIEF CONTENTS

CONTENTS

Note: Each chapter concludes with a Summary, Important Terms, Discussion and Review Questions, Application Questions, and Internet Exercise & Resources.

Part Four   Distribution Decisions   349

14   Marketing Channels and Supply Chain Management   350

15   Wholesaling and Physical Distribution   373

16   Retailing   401

Part Five   Promotion Decisions   431

17   Integrated Marketing Communications   432

18   Advertising and Public Relations   459

19   Personal Selling and Sales Promotion   487

Part Six   Pricing Decisions   517

20   Pricing Concepts   518

23   Marketing on the Internet   601

24   e-Marketing   631

Appendix A   Careers in Marketing   A-1

Appendix B   Financial Analysis in Marketing   B-1

Appendix C   Sample Marketing Plan   C-1

PREFACE

Marketing: Concepts and Strategies has become the most widely adopted introductory marketing textbook in the world. We appreciate the confidence that adopters have placed in our textbook and continue to work hard to make sure that, as in previous editions, this edition keeps pace with changes. This edition provides new marketing knowledge, and a complete balanced approach to teaching this important course. We feel that our book has been successful because it focuses on a comprehensive framework and provides complete coverage of marketing's best practices validated by the latest research. In fact, nearly three-quarters of all of the references used in this edition are from 2000 and 2001. This indicates our desire to reflect the latest changes reshaping the development and implementation of marketing strategies.

While we provide cutting-edge marketing knowledge, there are many marketing issues that all students should learn. Therefore, we provide many new real-world examples, cases, and boxed features that make the traditional content come alive. Our reviewers tell us that we have done an excellent job in presenting marketing in an engaging, readable way that connects students to the realities of marketing. We emphasize emerging developments in the field of marketing such as information technology, customer relationship management, marketing on the Internet, and social issues. But we also provide balance in our coverage, avoiding overemphasis of trendy topics. For example, the role of the Internet in marketing is still evolving. We provide a completely revised chapter on this topic as well as an online chapter on e-marketing to stay current. Most of the issues related to customer relationship management are integrated throughout our textbook, making it clear to students that although this term is now more widely used, marketers have been doing most of these activities for many years. Our book and the online Pride/Ferrell Marketing Learning Center provide all of the resources instructors and students need to maximize learning in introductory marketing courses.

We have also been careful to retain the strengths that have made this the most successful introductory marketing text in the United States and throughout the world. Primary among those strengths is a dedication to customer value and customer relationships—two crucial aspects of today's competitive environment. We listen closely to the feedback of both students and instructors, in order to continue to provide exceptional student value and the most complete, usable, and relevant teaching package available today.

Building on Established Strengths

Features of the Book

As with previous editions, we are providing a comprehensive and practical introduction to marketing that is both easy to teach and to learn. The entire text is structured to excite students about the subject and to help them learn completely and efficiently.

- An *organizational model* at the beginning of each part provides a "roadmap" of the text and a visual tool for understanding the connection between concepts.

- *Learning objectives* at the start of each chapter present concrete expectations about what students are to learn as they read the chapter.

- An *opening vignette* about a particular organization or current market trend introduces the topic for each chapter. Vignettes in this edition include interesting anecdotes about the marketing issues surrounding a variety of products and services from diverse organizations such as FedEx, Nokia, McDonald's, and eBay. Through these vignettes, students are exposed to contemporary marketing realities and are better prepared to understand and apply the concepts they will explore in the text.

- *Key term definitions* appear in the margin to help students build their marketing vocabulary.

- Numerous *figures, tables, photographs, advertisements,* and *Snapshot* and *Net Sights* features increase comprehension and stimulate interest.

- Four types of *boxed features* reinforce students' awareness of the particular issues affecting marketing and the types of choices and decisions marketers must make.

 Tech*know boxes include discussions about the impact of technological advances on products and how they are marketed. Examples of topics are online co-branding, traditional versus online retailing, and using software to set prices.

 Marking Citizenship boxes raise students' awareness of social responsibility and ethical issues and the types of ethical choices that marketers face every day. Some of the organizations on which we focus are Wal-Mart, Royal Caribbean, and TRUSTe.

 Global Marketing boxed features examine the challenges of marketing in widely diverse cultures for companies such as Universal Studios, Heinz, and De Beers.

 Building Customer Relationships boxes look at how organizations try to build long-term relationships with their customers. Examples include Home Depot, NASCAR, and Great Harvest Bread Company.

- A complete *chapter summary* reviews the major topics discussed, and the list of *important terms* provides another end-of-chapter study aid to expand students' marketing vocabulary.

- *Discussion and review questions* at the end of each chapter encourage further study and exploration of chapter content, and *application questions* enhance students' comprehension of important topics.

- An *Internet exercise* at the end of each chapter asks students to examine a website and assess one or more strategic issues associated with the site. *E-Center Resources* points students to the various learning tools that are available on the text's website, the Marketing Learning Center.

- Two in-depth *cases* at the end of each chapter help students understand the application of chapter concepts. One of the end-of-chapter cases is related to a video segment. Some examples of companies highlighted in the cases are New Belgium Brewing Company, Build-A-Bear, JetBlue, VIPdesk.com, and PETsMART.

- A *strategic case* at the end of each part helps students integrate the diverse concepts that have been discussed within the related chapters. Some of the organizations highlighted in these cases include *USA Today,* The American Dairy Industry, and DoubleClick.

- *Appendixes* discuss marketing career opportunities, explore financial analysis in marketing, and present a sample marketing plan.

- A comprehensive *glossary* defines more than 625 important marketing terms.

Text Organization

We have organized the seven parts of *Marketing: Concepts and Strategies* to give students a theoretical and practical understanding of marketing decision making. Part 1 presents an overview of marketing and examines strategic market planning, marketing environment forces, social responsibility and ethics, and international marketing. Part 2 considers information systems and marketing research, target market analysis, and consumer and business buying behavior. Part 3 focuses on the conceptualization, development, management, and branding and packaging, of goods and services. Part 4 deals with marketing channels and supply chain management, wholesaling and physical distribution, and retailing. Part 5 covers integrated marketing communications and promotion methods including advertising, personal selling, sales promotion, and public relations. Part 6 is devoted to pricing decisions. Part 7 discusses implementation and control, e-commerce, and marketing and the Internet.

What's New to This Edition?

To stay on top of the fast-paced changes in the practice of marketing—and new developments in teaching and learning about it—we have added a number of new features to this edition of *Marketing*.

- All the videos are new! A brand new video package accompanies this new edition. Each video (one per chapter) provides the student with an opportunity to put to use the information learned within the context of issues discussed in the chapter.

- A new boxed feature in each chapter, Net Sights, highlights websites that students can visit to learn more about the concepts, companies, and issues that are relevant to the topics discussed in the chapter.

- A brand new text design for this edition makes this book even more reader friendly. A stronger pedagogical use of colors, additional photos, and examples all come together to help students make the connection between concepts discussed in the book and examples taken from a variety of real-world businesses.

- All the boxed features are new or updated. Over half the cases are new and the others have been revised.

- Throughout the text the authors evaluated recent research and best practices to update key concepts presented in the text. Nearly three-quarters of the citations used in this edition of *Marketing* are taken from 2000 and 2001 academic and trade sources. These revisions represent a ground-up rebuilding of cutting-edge concepts and examples.

- Customer relationship management (CRM) is introduced in Chapter 1 and integrated throughout the text at appropriate discussion points. CRM examines how companies acquire customer-related information and how they use it to develop long-term relationships with customers. CRM examines how companies use various sources, including the Internet, to better understand their customers.

- The text presents the latest understanding and role of information technology. Information technology managers rank customer relationship management as their most important issue. New innovations such as streaming video, wireless communication, and the expansion of broadband continue to provide new marketing opportunities. This coverage is integrated into the text at appropriate discussion points in Chapters 1, 3, 6, and 23.

- Coverage of e-marketing (Chapter 24) has been significantly revised and rewritten to reflect current trends including the latest perspectives on the future of e-marketing and the demise of the dot-coms. This chapter continues to appear online on the Pride/Ferrell Marketing Learning Center.

- Over half of the Internet Exercises are new and the others have been revised.

- Global marketing (Chapter 5) material has been updated and rewritten to include the latest coverage of global trade agreements, issues, and trends in global marketing, and the latest research in the area.

- Ethics and social responsibility (Chapter 4) coverage has been expanded to include the latest information on how domestic and international companies contributed support efforts in the aftermath of the September 11 terrorist attacks.

- The pricing chapters (20 and 21) have been reorganized to provide a clearer presentation of this topic. Discussion of demand, elasticity, and costs has been moved to the first pricing chapter.

A Comprehensive Instructional Resource Package

For instructors, this edition of *Marketing* includes an exceptionally comprehensive package of teaching materials.

- *Instructor's website.* This continually updated, password-protected site includes valuable tools to help design and teach the course. Contents include sample syllabi, downloadable text files from the *Instructor's Resource Manual*, role-play exercises, PowerPoint® slides, and suggested answers to questions posed on the student website. New to this edition is a downloadable game, *Who Wants to Be an "A" Student?*, by John Drea, Western Illinois University. This easy-to-use game makes in-class review challenging and fun, and has been proven to increase students' test scores.

- *PowerPoint® slide presentations.* For each chapter, over 25 slides related to the learning objectives have been specially developed for this edition. The slides are original representations of the concepts in the book, providing a complete lecture for each chapter. These slides include key figures and tables from the textbook as well as additional data and graphics. These slides, along with a PowerPoint® reader, are available on the website.

- *HMClassPrep™ CD.* This new software package provides all the tools instructors need to create customized multimedia lecture presentations for display on computer-based projection systems. The software makes available lecture outlines from the *Instructor's Resource Manual,* figures and tables from the text and transparencies, the PowerPoint® slides, and a link to the Web. Instructors can quickly and easily select from and integrate all of these components, and prepare a seamless customized classroom presentation.

- *Online/distance learning support.* Instructors can create and customize online course materials to use in distance learning, distributed learning, or as a supplement to traditional classes. The *Blackboard Course Cartridge* and *WebCT e-Pack* include a variety of study aids for students as well as course-management tools for instructors.

- *Test Bank.* The *Test Bank* provides more than 3,000 test items including true/false, multiple-choice, and essay questions. Each objective test item is accompanied by the correct answer, a main text page reference, and a key to whether the question tests knowledge, comprehension, or application. The *Test Bank* also provides difficulty and discrimination ratings derived from actual class testing for most of the multiple-choice questions. Lists of author-selected questions that facilitate quick construction of tests or quizzes appear in an appendix. These author-selected lists of multiple-choice questions are representative of chapter content. An outside consultant working with the authors was used to review, improve, and test this edition of the *Test Bank.*

- *HMTesting.* This computerized version of the *Test Bank* allows instructors to select, edit, and add questions, or generate randomly selected questions to produce a test master for easy duplication. An Online Testing System and Gradebook function allows instructors to administer tests via a network system, modem, or personal computer; and sets up a new class, records grades from tests or assignments, analyzes grades, and produces class and individual statistics. This program is available for use on IBM, IBM-compatible, and Macintosh computers.

- *Marketing videos.* This series contains all new videos for use with the end-of-chapter video cases. The *Instructor's Resource Manual* provides specific information about each video segment.

- *Color transparencies.* A set of over 250 color transparencies offers the instructor visual teaching assistance. About half of these are illustrations from the text. The rest are figures, tables, and diagrams that can be used as additional instructional aids.

- *Call-in test service.* This service lets instructors select items from the *Test Bank* and call our toll-free number to order printed tests.

- *Instructor's Resource Manual.* Written by the text's authors, the *Instructor's Resource Manual* includes a complete set of teaching tools. For each chapter of the text, there is (1) a teaching resources quick reference guide, (2) a purpose and perspective statement, (3) a guide for using the transparencies, (4) a comprehensive lecture outline, (5) special class exercises, (6) a debate issue, (7) a chapter quiz, (8) answers to discussion and review questions, (9) comments on the end-of-chapter cases, and (10) video information. In addition, the *Instructor's Resource Manual* includes comments on the end-of-part strategic cases and answers to the questions posed at the end of Appendix B, Financial Analysis in Marketing.

- *Role-play exercises.* Three role-play exercises that allow students to assume various roles within an organization are available in the *Instructor's Resource Manual* and instructor's website. The exercises are designed to help students understand the real-world challenges of decision making in marketing. Decisions require a strategic response from a class group or team. These exercises simulate a real-world experience, and give students an opportunity to apply the marketing concepts covered in the text. The *Instructor's Resource Manual* provides indepth information concerning the implementation and evaluation of these exercises.

A Complete Package of Student Supplements

The complete package available with *Marketing: Concepts and Strategies* includes numerous support materials that facilitate student learning.

- *Pride/Ferrell Marketing Learning Center.* Our student website at **http://www.prideferrell.com** contains the following:

■ *Chapter 24, e-Marketing.* This chapter, which appears online at the Pride/Ferrell Marketing Learning Center, explores the world of online marketing, and will be updated as needed to incorporate the latest developments.

■ *Internet Exercises.* Including the text exercises with updates as necessary, these reinforce chapter concepts by guiding students through specific websites and asking them to assess the information from a marketing perspective.

■ *ACE online self-tests.* Written by the text authors, these questions allow students to practice taking tests and get immediate scoring results.

■ *General Resources.* This comprehensive list, which will be continually updated, provides links to numerous authoritative marketing information resources, categorized in a way that makes them accessible and helpful to both students and instructors.

■ *Company links.* Hot links to companies featured in the text are provided so that students can further their research and understanding of the marketing practices of these companies.

■ *Online glossary* and *chapter summary.* These sections help students review key concepts and definitions.

■ *Marketing plan worksheets.* These worksheets take students step-by-step through the process of creating their own marketing plan. Along with the text discussion and sample marketing plan, this is a project that will help students apply their knowledge of marketing theories.

■ *Career center.* Downloadable "Personal Career Plan Worksheets" and links to various marketing careers websites will help students explore their options and plan their job search.

● *Real Deal UpGrade CD.* This self-study aid includes information and exercises on time management, muscle reading, note taking, and testing to help students improve their overall study skills. It also includes practice tests for every chapter in the textbook.

● *Study Guide.* Written by the text's authors, this printed supplement helps students to review and integrate key marketing concepts. The *Study Guide* contains questions different from those in the online study aids and *Real Deal UpGrade CD,* and includes chapter outlines as well as matching, true/false, multiple-choice, and minicase sample test items with answers.

Your Comments and Suggestions Are Valued

Bill Pride and O.C. Ferrell have been coauthors of *Marketing: Concepts and Strategies* for the past 25 years. Their major focus has been on teaching and preparing learning material for introductory marketing students. They have both traveled extensively to work with students and understand the needs of professors of introductory marketing courses. Both authors teach this marketing course on a regular basis and test the materials included in the book, *Test Bank,* and other ancillary materials to make sure they are effective in the classroom.

Through the years, professors and students have sent us many helpful suggestions for improving the text and ancillary components. We invite your comments, questions, and criticisms. We want to do our best to provide materials that enhance the teaching and learning of marketing concepts and strategies. Your suggestions will be sincerely appreciated. Please write us, or e-mail us at w-pride@tamu.edu or oferrell@lamar.colostate.edu, or call 909-845-5857 (Pride) or 970-491-4398 (Ferrell). You can also send a feedback message through the website at http://www.prideferrell.com.

Acknowledgments

Like most textbooks, this one reflects the idea of many academicians and practitioners who have contributed to the development of the marketing discipline. We appreciate the opportunity to present their ideas in this book.

A special faculty advisory board assisted us in making decisions during the development of the text and the instructional package. For being "on-call" and available to answer questions and make valuable suggestions, we are grateful to those who participated:

David Andrus
Kansas State University

Jenell Bramlage
University of Northwestern Ohio

Renée Florsheim
Loyola Marymount University

Richard C. Hansen
Ferris State University

Manoj Hastak
American University

Joan M. Inzinga
Bay Path College

Marilyn Lavin
University of Wisconsin—Whitewater

Monle Lee
Indiana University—South Bend

Lalita A. Manrai
University of Delaware

Martin Meyers
*University of Wisconsin—
Stevens Point*

Carolyn Y. Nicholson
Stetson University

David P. Paul, III
Monmouth University

Edna J. Ragins
North Carolina A&T State University

Mohammed Rawwas
University of Northern Iowa

Morris A. Shapero
Schiller International University

Eric R. Spangenberg
Washington State University

Scott J. Vitell
The University of Mississippi

George W. Wynn
James Madison University

A number of individuals have made helpful comments and recommendations in their reviews of this and earlier editions. We appreciate the generous help of these reviewers:

Zafar U. Ahmed
Minot State University

Thomas Ainscough
*University of Massachusetts—
Dartmouth*

Joe F. Alexander
University of Northern Colorado

Mark I. Alpert
University of Texas at Austin

David M. Ambrose
University of Nebraska

Linda K. Anglin
Minnesota State University

George Avellano
Central State University

Emin Babakus
University of Memphis

Julie Baker
University of Texas—Arlington

Siva Balasabramanian
Southern Illinois University

Joseph Ballenger
Stephen F. Austin State University

Guy Banville
Creighton University

Joseph Barr
Framingham State College

Thomas E. Barry
Southern Methodist University

Charles A. Bearchell
*California State University—
Northridge*

Richard C. Becherer
*University of Tennessee—
Chattanooga*

Walter H. Beck, Sr.
Reinhardt College

Russell Belk
University of Utah

W.R. Berdine
California State Polytechnic Institute

Karen Berger
Pace University

Bob Berl
University of Memphis

Stewart W. Bither
Pennsylvania State University

Roger Blackwell
Ohio State University

Peter Bloch
University of Missouri—Columbia

Wanda Blockhus
San Jose State University

Paul N. Bloom
University of North Carolina

James P. Boespflug
Arapahoe Community College

Joseph G. Bonnice
Manhattan College

John Boos
Ohio Wesleyan University

James Brock
Susquehanna College

John R. Brooks, Jr.
Houston Baptist University

William G. Browne
Oregon State University

John Buckley
Orange County Community College

Gul T. Butaney
Bentley College

James Cagley
University of Tulsa

Pat J. Calabro
University of Texas—Arlington

Linda Calderone
State University of New York College of Technology at Farmingdale

Joseph Cangelosi
University of Central Arkansas

William J. Carner
University of Texas—Austin

James C. Carroll
University of Central Arkansas

Terry M. Chambers
Westminster College

Lawrence Chase
Tompkins Cortland Community College

Larry Chonko
Baylor University

Barbara Coe
University of North Texas

Ernest F. Cooke
Loyola College—Baltimore

Robert Copley
University of Louisville

John I. Coppett
University of Houston—Clear Lake

Robert Corey
West Virginia University

Deborah L. Cowles
Virginia Commonwealth University

Melvin R. Crask
University of Georgia

William L. Cron
Southern Methodist University

Gary Cutler
Dyersburg State Community College

Bernice N. Dandridge
Diablo Valley College

Lloyd M. DeBoer
George Mason University

Sally Dibb
University of Warwick

Ralph DiPietro
Montclair State University

Paul Dishman
Idaho State University

Suresh Divakar
State University of New York—Buffalo

Casey L. Donoho
Northern Arizona University

Peter T. Doukas
Westchester Community College

Lee R. Duffus
Florida Gulf Coast University

Robert F. Dwyer
University of Cincinnati

Roland Eyears
Central Ohio Technical College

Thomas Falcone
Indiana University of Pennsylvania

James Finch
University of Wisconsin—La Crosse

Letty C. Fisher
SUNY/Westchester Community College

Charles W. Ford
Arkansas State University

John Fraedrich
Southern Illinois University, Carbondale

David J. Fritzsche
University of Washington

Donald A. Fuller
University of Central Florida

Terry Gable
California State University—Northridge

Ralph Gaedeke
California State University, Sacramento

Cathy Goodwin
University of Manitoba

Geoffrey L. Gordon
Northern Illinois University

Robert Grafton-Small
University of Strathclyde

Harrison Grathwohl
California State University—Chico

Alan A. Greco
North Carolina A&T State University

Blaine S. Greenfield
Bucks County Community College

Thomas V. Greer
University of Maryland

Sharon F. Gregg
Middle Tennessee University

Jim L. Grimm
Illinois State University

Charles Gross
University of New Hampshire

Joseph Guiltinan
University of Notre Dame

Nancy Hanson-Rasmussen
University of Wisconsin—Eau Claire

Robert R. Harmon
Portland State University

Mary C. Harrison
Amber University

Lorraine Hartley
Franklin University

Michael Hartline
Samford University

Timothy Hartman
Ohio University

Salah S. Hassan
George Washington University

Del I. Hawkins
University of Oregon

Dean Headley
Wichita State University

Esther Headley
Wichita State University

Debbora Heflin-Bullock
California State Polytechnic University—Pomona

Merlin Henry
Rancho Santiago College

Lois Herr
Elizabethtown College

Charles L. Hilton
Eastern Kentucky University

Elizabeth C. Hirschman
Rutgers, State University of New Jersey

George C. Hozier
University of New Mexico

John R. Huser
Illinois Central College

Ron Johnson
Colorado Mountain College

Theodore F. Jula
Stonehill College

Peter F. Kaminski
Northern Illinois University

Yvonne Karsten
Minnesota State University

Jerome Katrichis
Temple University

James Kellaris
University of Cincinnati

Alvin Kelly
Florida A&M University

Philip Kemp
DePaul University

Sylvia Keyes
Bridgewater State College

William M. Kincaid, Jr.
Oklahoma State University

Roy Klages
State University of New York at Albany

Douglas Kornemann
Milwaukee Area Technical College

Patricia Laidler
Massasoit Community College

Bernard LaLonde
Ohio State University

Richard A. Lancioni
Temple University

Irene Lange
California State University—Fullerton

Geoffrey P. Lantos
Stonehill College

Charles L. Lapp
University of Texas—Dallas

Virginia Larson
San Jose State University

John Lavin
Waukesha County Technical Institute

Hugh E. Law
East Tennessee University

Debbie McAlister
Southwest Texas State University

Ron Lennon
Barry University

Richard C. Leventhal
Metropolitan State College

Marilyn Liebrenz-Himes
The George Washington University

Jay D. Lindquist
Western Michigan University

Terry Loe
Baylor University

Mary Logan
Southwestern Assemblies of God College

Paul Londrigan
Mott Community College

Anthony Lucas
Community College of Allegheny County

George Lucas
U.S. Learning, Inc.

William Lundstrom
Cleveland State University

Rhonda Mack
College of Charleston

Stan Madden
Baylor University

Patricia M. Manninen
North Shore Community College

Gerald L. Manning
Des Moines Area Community College

Franklyn Manu
Morgan State University

Allen S. Marber
University of Bridgeport

Gayle J. Marco
Robert Morris College

James McAlexander
Oregon State University

Donald McCartney
University of Wisconsin—Green Bay

Anthony McGann
University of Wyoming

Jack McNiff
State University of New York College of Technology at Farmingdale

Lee Meadow
Eastern Illinois University

Carla Meeske
University of Oregon

Jeffrey A. Meier
Fox Valley Technical College

James Meszaros
County College of Morris

Brian Meyer
Minnesota State University

Martin Meyers
University of Wisconsin—Stevens Point

Stephen J. Miller
Oklahoma State University

William Moller
University of Michigan

Kent B. Monroe
University of Illinois

Carlos W. Moore
Baylor University

Carol Morris-Calder
Loyola Marymount University

David Murphy
Madisonville Community College

Keith Murray
Bryant College

Sue Ellen Neeley
University of Houston—Clear Lake

Francis L. Notturno, Sr.
Owens Community College

Terrence V. O'Brien
Northern Illinois University

James R. Ogden
Kutztown University of Pennsylvania

Mike O'Neill
California State University—Chico

Robert S. Owen
State University of New York—Oswego

Allan Palmer
University of North Carolina at Charlotte

Teresa Pavia
University of Utah

John Perrachione
Truman State University

Michael Peters
Boston College

Linda Pettijohn
Southwest Missouri State University

Lana Podolak
Community College of Beaver County

Raymond E. Polchow
Muskingum Area Technical College

Thomas Ponzurick
West Virginia University

William Presutti
Duquesne University

Kathy Pullins
Columbus State Community College

Daniel Rajaratnam
Baylor University

James D. Reed
Louisiana State University—Shreveport

William Rhey
University of Tampa

Glen Riecken
East Tennessee State University

Winston Ring
University of Wisconsin—Milwaukee

Ed Riordan
Wayne State University

Robert A. Robicheaux
University of Alabama

Robert H. Ross
Wichita State University

Vicki Rostedt
The University of Akron

Michael L. Rothschild
University of Wisconsin—Madison

Bert Rosenbloom
Drexel University

Kenneth L. Rowe
Arizona State University

Elise Sautter
New Mexico State University

Ronald Schill
Brigham Young University

Bodo Schlegelmilch
Vienna University of Economics and Business Administration

Edward Schmitt
Villanova University

Thomas Schori
Illinois State University

Donald Sciglimpaglia
San Diego State University

Stanley Scott
University of Alaska—Anchorage

Harold S. Sekiguchi
University of Nevada—Reno

Gilbert Seligman
Dutchess Community College

Richard J. Semenik
University of Utah

Beheruz N. Sethna
Lamar University

Terence A. Shimp
University of South Carolina

Mark Siders
Southern Oregon University

Carolyn F. Siegel
Eastern Kentucky University

Dean C. Siewers
Rochester Institute of Technology

Lyndon Simkin
University of Warwick

Roberta Slater
Cedar Crest College

Paul J. Solomon
University of South Florida

Robert Solomon
Stephen F. Austin State University

Sheldon Somerstein
City University of New York

Rosann L. Spiro
Indiana University

William Staples
University of Houston—Clear Lake

Bruce Stern
Portland State University

Claire F. Sullivan
Metropolitan State University

Carmen Sunda
University of New Orleans

Robert Swerdlow
Lamar University

Steven A. Taylor
Illinois State University

Hal Teer
James Madison University

Ira Teich
Long Island University—C. W. Post

Dillard Tinsley
Stephen F. Austin State University

Sharynn Tomlin
Angelo State University

Hale Tongren
George Mason University

James Underwood
University of Southwest Louisiana

Barbara Unger
Western Washington University

Tinus Van Drunen
University Twente (Netherlands)

Dale Varble
Indiana State University

R. Vish Viswanathan
University of Northern Colorado

Charles Vitaska
Metropolitan State College

Kirk Wakefield
University of Mississippi

Harlan Wallingford
Pace University

Jacquelyn Warwick
Andrews University

James F. Wenthe
Georgia College

Sumner M. White
Massachusetts Bay Community College

Alan R. Wiman
Rider College

Ken Wright
West Australia College of Advanced Education—Churchland Campus

George Wynn
James Madison University

Poh-Lin Yeoh
Bentley College

Irvin A. Zaenglein
Northern Michigan University

We deeply appreciate the assistance of Barbara Gilmer and Marian Wood for providing editorial suggestions, technical assistance, and support. Gwyneth Walters assisted in research, editing, and content development for the text, supplements, and the Pride/Ferrell Marketing Learning Center. For assistance in completing numerous tasks associated with the text and supplements, we express appreciation to Dana Schubert, Robyn Smith, Adele Lewis, Clarissa Sims, Colette Williams, Reagen Ladd, Niki Manning, Marian Wood, Karen Guessford, and Patricia Thomas.

We especially want to thank Linda Ferrell, University of Northern Colorado, who participated in all aspects of content and supplement development. Daniel Sherrell, University of Memphis, developed the framework used in Chapter 23. We especially appreciate his work in developing the six major characteristics of marketing on the Internet. Michael Hartline, Samford University, helped in the development of the marketing plan outline and the sample marketing plan in Appendix C as well as the career worksheets on the website. Debbie McAlister, Southwest Texas State University, provided assistance with Marketing Citizenship content and boxes.

We appreciate Charlie Cook, the University of West Alabama, for developing the PowerPoint® slide presentations. We also wish to thank Kirk Wakefield, University of Memphis, for developing the class exercises included in the *Instructor's Resource Manual,* and John Drea, Western Illinois University, for developing the *"A" Student* game. We especially thank Jim L. Grimm, Illinois State University, for drafting the financial analysis appendix.

We express appreciation for the support and encouragement given to us by our colleagues at Texas A&M University and Colorado State University. We are also grateful for the comments and suggestions we receive from our own students, student focus groups, and student correspondents who provide ongoing feedback through the website.

A number of talented professionals at Houghton Mifflin have contributed to the development of this book. We are especially grateful to Charlie Hartford, George Hoffman, Steve Mikels, Susan Kahn, Cathy Brooks, Lindsay Frost, Julia Perez, Lisa Boden, Henry Rachlin, Marcy Kagan, and Penny Peters. Their inspiration, patience, support, and friendship are invaluable.

William M. Pride

O. C. Ferrell

Marketing and Its Environment

PART ONE

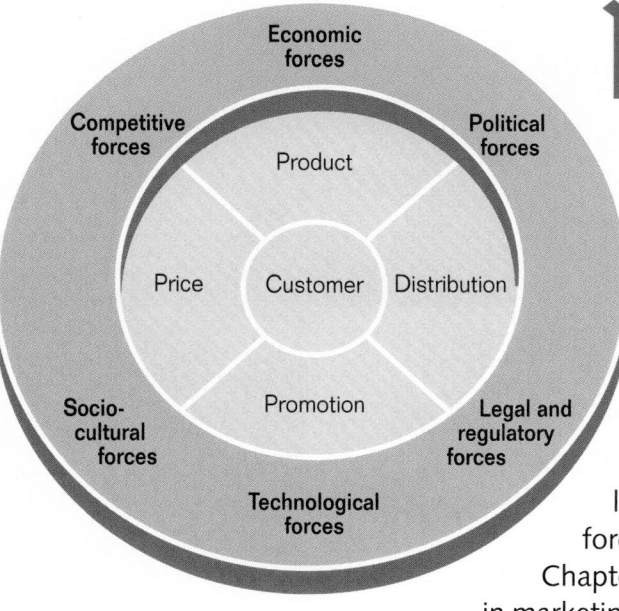

Part 1 introduces the field of marketing and offers a broad perspective from which to explore and analyze various components of the marketing discipline. Chapter 1 defines *marketing* and explores some key concepts, including customers and target markets, the marketing mix, relationship marketing, the marketing concept, and value. Chapter 2 provides an overview of strategic marketing issues, such as the effect of organizational resources and opportunities on the planning process; the role of the mission statement; corporate, business-unit, and marketing strategies; and the creation of the marketing plan. These issues are profoundly affected by competitive, economic, political, legal and regulatory, technological, and sociocultural forces in the marketing evironment, the focus of Chapter 3. Chapter 4 deals with the role of social responsibility and ethics in marketing decisions. Chapter 5 discusses the nature, opportunities, and challenges of marketing in a global economy.

1

An Overview of Strategic Marketing

OBJECTIVES

- To be able to define **marketing** as focused on customers
- To identify some important marketing terms, including **target market, marketing mix, marketing exchanges,** and **marketing environment**
- To become aware of the marketing concept and marketing orientation
- To understand the importance of building customer relationships
- To learn about the process of marketing management
- To recognize the role of marketing in our society

The video game industry is getting hotter every day. In 2000, sales of video game consoles more than doubled, fueled largely by the success of Sony's PlayStation 2. With new game consoles from Nintendo and Microsoft, the environment for this $20 billion industry has become extremely competitive.

Sony has long led the video game industry with its hugely successful PlayStation game platform, and its newest PlayStation 2 console continues to set the standard for the industry. The company will sell 10 million PlayStation 2s in the United States by the end of 2001. With a one-year head start on the competition, Sony planned to woo consumers to its platform by focusing on hardware and software features. The PlayStation 2 already plays music and DVD movies, and future consoles will include a 40-gigabyte hard drive, a narrowband and broadband network connector, and a compatible LCD monitor, keyboard, mouse, and software from America Online and RealNetworks. But despite its leadership, Sony faces a serious challenge from Nintendo and Microsoft.

Video Game Wars

Although its portable GameBoy devices are best sellers, with more than 100 million units sold since 1989, Nintendo has not competed directly against Sony—until now. Launched in 2001, Nintendo's GameCube console, which retails for $100 less than Sony's PlayStation 2 and Microsoft's Xbox, will focus exclusively on video game technology. Nintendo has traditionally developed games in-house, but that may change as the company enters the competitive market for game players older than its traditional under-17 market. Games available for the GameCube include *Luigi's Mansion, Wave Race, Blue Storm, Rogue Squadron II,* and *Madden NFL 2002.* In addition, the company is working on making its GameBoy and GameCube systems cross-compatible so that the new GameBoy Advance can serve as a controller for the GameCube.

The "new kid on the block" in the video game industry is Microsoft, which launched the Xbox game console in 2001. Microsoft developed the Xbox to compete directly with Sony's PlayStation 2 on price, speed, and other features. Although the Xbox can play music and DVD, these functions require the separate purchase of a remote control. However, the Xbox has double the graphic and central processing power and random-access memory available in the PlayStation 2. Best known for its computer software, it's no surprise that Microsoft planned to focus its marketing efforts on the Xbox's available games and user-friendly interface rather than on its hardware capabilities. Microsoft planned to spend $500 million to market the new game console in its first 18 months, twice what the company spent to launch Windows 95 six years earlier.

Fueled by the improving technology of these new game consoles, consumers are snatching up new games like *Tomb Raider, Tony Hawk Pro Skater,* and *Zelda Oracle.* These improvements will continue to affect how Sony, Nintendo, and Microsoft compete for video game afficionados. Can Sony's PlayStation platform maintain its dominance with the entry of these tough competitors? Can Nintendo succeed at marketing a video game system for older consumers without sacrificing its lead in games for the under-17 market? Will Microsoft's marketing prowess and software know-how give it an edge in this competitive arena? Regardless of the outcome, one clear winner will emerge. Game fanatics will certainly benefit from lower prices, faster speeds, and more realistic graphics.[1]

Like all organizations, Microsoft, Nintendo, and Sony must develop products that customers want, communicate useful information about them to excite interest, price them appropriately, and make them available when and where customers may want to buy them. Even if they do these things well, competition from other entertainment product marketers, economic conditions, and other factors may affect the companies' success. Such factors influence the decisions that all organizations must make in strategic marketing.

This chapter introduces the strategic marketing concepts and decisions covered throughout the text. First, we develop a definition of *marketing* and explore each element of the definition in detail. Next, we introduce the marketing concept and consider several issues associated with implementing it. We also take a brief look at the concept of value, which customers are demanding today more than ever before. We then explore the process of marketing management, which includes planning, organizing, implementing, and controlling marketing activities to encourage marketing exchanges. Finally, we examine the importance of marketing in our global society.

Defining Marketing

If you ask several people what *marketing* is, you are likely to hear a variety of descriptions. Marketing encompasses many more activities than most people realize. In this book, we define **marketing** as the process of creating, distributing, promoting, and pricing goods, services, and ideas to facilitate satisfying exchange relationships with customers in a dynamic environment. Let's take a closer look at selected parts of this definition.

marketing The process of creating, distributing, promoting, and pricing goods, services, and ideas to facilitate satisfying exchange relationships with customers in a dynamic environment

customers The purchasers of organizations' products; the focal point of all marketing activities

Marketing Focuses on Customers

As the purchasers of the products that organizations develop, promote, distribute, and price, **customers** are the focal point of all marketing activities (see Figure 1.1). Organizations have to define their products not as what the companies make or produce but as what they do to satisfy customers. The Walt Disney Company is not in the business of establishing theme parks; it is in the business of making people happy. At Disney World, customers are guests, the crowd is an audience, and employees are cast

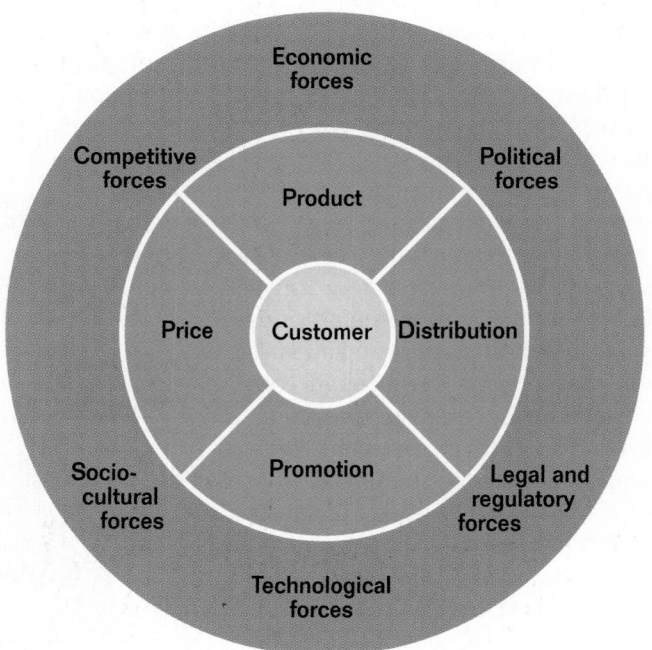

FIGURE 1.1   Components of Strategic Marketing

Appealing to Target Markets
Target provides products that appeal to diverse markets.

members. Customer satisfaction and enjoyment can come from anything received when buying and using a product. For example, Procter & Gamble's Folger's Cafe Latte instant coffees—in flavors such as Mocha Fusion, Vanilla Vibe, and Chocolate Mint Mambo—provide an alternative to standing in line at the coffee shop, while its newly formulated Tide HE helps keep clothes looking new even with today's high-efficiency washing machines.

The essence of marketing is to develop satisfying exchanges from which both customers and marketers benefit. The customer expects to gain a reward or benefit in excess of the costs incurred in a marketing transaction. The marketer expects to gain something of value in return, generally the price charged for the product. Through buyer-seller interaction, a customer develops expectations about the seller's future behavior. To fulfill these expectations, the marketer must deliver on promises made. Over time, this interaction results in interdependencies between the two parties. Fast-food restaurants such as Wendy's and Burger King depend on repeat purchases from satisfied customers—many often live or work a few miles from these restaurants—while customer expectations revolve around good food, value, and dependable service.

Organizations generally focus their marketing efforts on a specific group of customers, or **target market.** PepsiCo, for example, targets its Mountain Dew Code Red soft drink at teenagers looking for an extra jolt in a high-caffeine soda.[2] Marketing managers may define a target market as a vast number of people or a relatively small group. Rolls-Royce, for example, targets its automobiles at a small, very exclusive

target market   A specific group of customers on whom an organization focuses its marketing efforts

market: wealthy people who want the ultimate in prestige in an automobile. Cidco's Mailstation, a small, portable Internet device, is targeted primarily at senior citizens who want to stay in touch with family via e-mail but do not want to invest in a complete personal computer. Other companies target multiple markets, with different products, promotion, prices, and distribution systems for each one. Nike uses this strategy, marketing different types of shoes to meet specific needs of cross-trainers, rock climbers, basketball players, aerobics enthusiasts, and other athletic-shoe buyers. Global Marketing highlights one firm that targets customers around the world. We explore the concept of target markets in more detail in Chapter 7.

GLOBAL MARKETING

Chupa Chups: Sweetening the World, One Country at a Time

What's your favorite flavor of lollipop? Cherry? Root beer? How about blue raspberry? These are viable options—if you live in the United States. But if you live in the Netherlands, you might have picked licorice as your favorite flavor. In China lichee nut and tea are favorite flavors, while *tarte tatin,* a type of apple pie, is popular in France. Like many companies, Chupa Chups Group is working to serve more markets around the world.

In 1958, Barcelona-based Chupa Chups decided to drop more than 200 products and focus exclusively on lollipops. Now the company produces more than 4 billion suckers annually and distributes them in 270 countries. With more than $455 million in sales, it is the sixth largest seller of hard candy in the world. Sales have been increasing as much as 40 percent a year, and 92 percent of sales now come from outside of Spain.

Chupa Chup's international success can be attributed to two key marketing strategies: tailoring its product to meet different flavor preferences and understanding and respecting the various cultures to which it markets. This explains why the company markets so many different and seemingly unusual flavors: to satisfy different consumer taste preferences in each country. In an advertising campaign in Germany, the company successfully used *leck mich,* which means "lick me." However, a similar campaign, in partnership with M&M/Mars in the United States, was rejected because of its risqué nature. In China, research indicated that eating candy without offering to share with other children is considered rude. Chupa Chups addressed the issue so children could feel comfortable eating suckers in public. The firm is also looking to take advantage of the Chinese cultural practice of handing out candy at weddings.

Chupa Chups also faced difficulty marketing lollipops to teenage girls in Middle Eastern countries, where eating a sucker in public is viewed as an attempt to be seductive and therefore frowned on within the Muslim culture. Thus, the company is emphasizing lollipop consumption in private places like homes, movie theaters, and cafés. Chupa Chups achieved great publicity in Europe by giving free candy to a well-known soccer coach who was trying to quit smoking. During stressful moments, the coach was shown on television pacing the field and sucking on a Chupa Chups lollipop. The company is also working to adapt this concept to an American lifestyle. Although most Americans are not soccer fans, many may appreciate the need to cope with stress and cravings while trying to quit smoking. Marketing lollipops as a nicotine substitute may prove to be an effective strategy in a country that is increasingly frowning on the consumption of tobacco.

By striving to understand the cultures in which it does business, Chupa Chups has successfully entered many foreign countries and gained market share. In Spain, Chupa Chups has practically become synonymous with the word *lollipop.* The company hopes that its customizing marketing efforts will make the brand name a household term around the world.

Marketing Deals with Products, Distribution, Promotion, and Price

Marketing is more than simply advertising or selling a product; it involves developing and managing a product that will satisfy customer needs. It focuses on making the product available in the right place and at a price acceptable to buyers. It also requires communicating information that helps customers determine if the product will satisfy their needs. These activities are planned, organized, implemented, and controlled to meet the needs of customers within the target market. Marketers refer to these activities—product, distribution, promotion, and pricing—as the **marketing mix** because they decide what type of each element to use and in what amounts. A primary goal of a marketing manager is to create and maintain the right mix of these elements to satisfy customers' needs for a general product type. Note in Figure 1.1 that the marketing mix is built around the customer.

Marketing managers strive to develop a marketing mix that matches the needs of customers in the target market. The marketing mix for Ralph Lauren's Polo brand of clothing, for example, combines a specific level of product design and quality with coordinated distribution, promotion, and price appropriate for the target market. The marketing mix for Ralph Lauren's Chaps clothing line differs from that for Polo, with lower prices and broader distribution.

Before marketers can develop a marketing mix, they must collect in-depth, up-to-date information about customer needs. Such information might include data about the age, income, ethnicity, gender, and educational level of people in the target market, their preferences for product features, their attitudes toward competitors' products, and the frequency with which they use the product. Such research helped convince Apple Computer of the need for a low-cost, easy-to-connect, Internet-ready computer, and it responded by developing the iMac. Demand for the iMac remains strong, indicating that Apple's research was on target. Apple's success with the iMac led to the opening of its first retail stores in 2001. In Chapter 6, we explore how organizations gather marketing research data. Armed with such data, marketing managers are better able to develop a marketing mix that satisfies a specific target market.

Let's look more closely at the decisions and activities related to each marketing mix variable.

The Product Variable. Successful marketing efforts result in products that become a part of everyday life. Consider the satisfaction customers have had over the years from Coca-Cola, Levi's jeans, Visa credit cards, Tylenol pain relievers, and 3M Post-it notepads. The product variable of the marketing mix deals with researching customers' needs and wants and designing a product that satisfies them. A **product** can be a good, a service, or an idea. A *good* is a physical entity you can touch. A Ford Focus, a Britney Spears compact disc, a Duracell battery, and a kitten in a pet store are examples of goods. A *service* is the application of human and mechanical efforts to people or objects to provide intangible benefits to customers. Air travel, dry cleaning, haircuts, banking, medical care, and day care are examples of services. *Ideas* include concepts, philosophies, images, and issues. For instance, a marriage counselor, for a fee, gives spouses ideas to help improve their relationship. Other marketers of ideas include political parties, churches, and schools. Note, however, that the actual production of tangible goods is not a marketing activity.

The product variable also involves creating or modifying brand names and packaging, and may include decisions regarding warranty and repair services. Even the world's greatest golfer is a global brand. Tiger Woods, who has sparked a renewed interest in golf among teens and young adults, has endorsed products from American Express, Buick, and General Mills, as well as his own product line from Nike.

Product variable decisions and related activities are important because they are directly involved with creating products that address customers' needs and wants. To maintain an assortment of products that helps an organization achieve its goals, marketers must develop new products, modify existing ones, and eliminate those that no longer satisfy enough buyers or that yield unacceptable profits. Ford Motor Company, for example, reintroduced its classic Thunderbird with a "vintage" redesign that

marketing mix Four marketing activities—product, distribution, promotion, and pricing—that a firm can control to meet the needs of customers within its target market

product A good, a service, or an idea

A Product Can Be an Idea
The National Civil Rights Museum in Memphis promotes equality.

appeals to customers' nostalgia for the original model, popular in the 1950s. Limited supplies and overwhelming demand made this "new" car an instant success. We consider such product issues and many more in Chapters 10 through 13.

The Distribution Variable.   To satisfy customers, products must be available at the right time and in convenient locations. In dealing with the distribution variable, a marketing manager makes products available in the quantities desired to as many target market customers as possible, keeping total inventory, transportation, and storage costs as low as possible. With these objectives in mind, McDonald's expanded distribution by opening restaurants in Wal-Mart stores and in Amoco and Chevron service stations. This practice permits the fast-food giant to share costs with its partners and to reach more customers when and where hunger strikes. McDonald's now operates more than 28,700 restaurants in 120 countries, which ring up annual sales of more than $40 billion.[3] A marketing manager may also select and motivate intermediaries (wholesalers and retailers), establish and maintain inventory control procedures, and develop and manage transportation and storage systems. The advent of the Internet and electronic commerce has also dramatically influenced the distribution variable. Companies can now make their products available throughout the world without maintaining facilities in each country. The Great Southern Sauce Company, a small firm in Little Rock, Arkansas, for example, sells salsa, barbecue sauce, and other sauces through its website to buyers all over the United States and as far away as London and Saudi Arabia.[4] We examine distribution issues in Chapters 14 through 16.

The Promotion Variable.   The promotion variable relates to activities used to inform individuals or groups about the organization and its products. Promotion can aim to increase public awareness of the organization and of new or existing products. Schering-Plough, for example, is using New York Mets catcher Mike Piazza to tout the benefits of its allergy medicine, Claritin, through television commercials.[5] Promotional activities can also educate customers about product features or urge people to take a particular stance on a political or social issue, such as smoking or drug abuse. Promotion can help sustain interest in established products that have been available for decades, such as Arm & Hammer baking soda or Ivory soap. Many companies are using the Internet and the World Wide Web to communicate information about themselves and their products. Ragu's website, for example, offers Italian phrases, recipes, and a sweepstakes, while Southwest Airlines' website enables customers to make flight reservations. In Chapters 17 through 19, we take a detailed look at promotion activities.

The Price Variable.   The price variable relates to decisions and actions associated with establishing pricing objectives and policies and determining product prices. Price is a critical component of the marketing mix because customers are concerned about the value obtained in an exchange. Price is often used as a competitive tool. For example, gardening products available at Lowe's home improvement stores cost 5 to 50 percent less than comparable products available at nurseries and small garden centers.[6] Intense price competition sometimes leads to price wars, but high prices can also be used competitively to establish a product's image. Waterman and Mont Blanc pens, for example, have an image of high quality and high price that has given them significant status. We explore pricing decisions in Chapters 20 and 21.

The marketing mix variables are often viewed as controllable because they can be modified. However, there are limits to how much marketing managers can alter them. Economic conditions, competitive structure, or government regulations may prevent a manager from adjusting prices frequently or significantly. Making changes in the size, shape, and design of most tangible goods is expensive; therefore, such product features cannot be altered very often. In addition, promotional campaigns and methods used to distribute products ordinarily cannot be rewritten or revamped overnight.

Marketing Builds Satisfying Exchange Relationships

exchange The provision or transfer of goods, services, or ideas in return for something of value

Individuals and organizations engage in marketing to facilitate **exchanges,** the provision or transfer of goods, services, or ideas in return for something of value. Any product (good, service, or even idea) may be involved in a marketing exchange. We assume only that individuals and organizations expect to gain a reward in excess of the costs incurred.

For an exchange to take place, four conditions must exist. First, two or more individuals, groups, or organizations must participate, and each must possess something of value that the other party desires. Second, the exchange should provide a benefit or satisfaction to both parties involved in the transaction. Third, each party must have confidence in the promise of the "something of value" held by the other. If you go to a Sting concert, for example, you go with the expectation of a great performance. Finally, to build trust, the parties to the exchange must meet expectations.

Figure 1.2 depicts the exchange process. The arrows indicate that the parties communicate that each has something of value available to exchange. An exchange will not necessarily take place just because these conditions exist; marketing activities can occur even without an actual transaction or sale. You may see an ad for a Viking refrigerator, for instance, but you might never buy the product. When an exchange occurs, products are traded for other products or for financial resources.

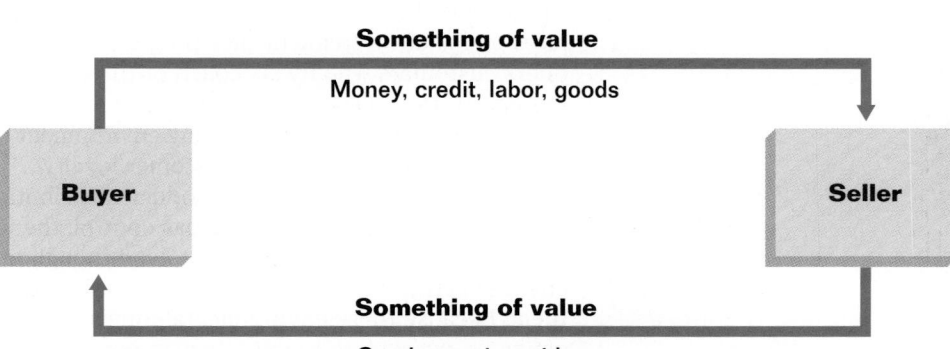

FIGURE 1.2
Exchange Between Buyer and Seller

Marketing activities should attempt to create and maintain satisfying exchange relationships. To maintain an exchange relationship, buyers must be satisfied with the obtained good, service, or idea, and sellers must be satisfied with the financial reward or something else of value received. A dissatisfied customer who lacks trust in the relationship often searches instead for alternative organizations or products.

Marketing Occurs in a Dynamic Environment

marketing environment The competitive, economic, political, legal and regulatory, technological, and sociocultural forces that surround the customer and affect the marketing mix

Marketing activities do not take place in a vacuum. The **marketing environment,** which includes competitive, economic, political, legal and regulatory, technological, and sociocultural forces, surrounds the customer and affects the marketing mix (see Figure 1.1). The effects of these forces on buyers and sellers can be dramatic and difficult to predict. They can create threats to marketers, but can also generate opportunities for new products and new methods of reaching customers.

The forces of the marketing environment affect a marketer's ability to facilitate exchanges in three general ways. First, they influence customers by affecting their lifestyles, standards of living, and preferences and needs for products. Because a marketing manager tries to develop and adjust the marketing mix to satisfy customers, effects of environmental forces on customers also have an indirect impact on marketing mix components. The merging of telecommunications and computer technologies, for example, allows FedEx Corporation to interact with customers via the World Wide Web. FedEx customers can track packages from their home or office computers and send e-mail feedback to FedEx about its services. This technology thus enables FedEx to gather marketing research information directly from customers. Second, marketing environment forces help determine whether and how a marketing manager can perform certain marketing activities. Third, environmental forces may affect a marketing manager's decisions and actions by influencing buyers' reactions to the firm's marketing mix.

Marketing environment forces can fluctuate quickly and dramatically, which is one reason marketing is so interesting and challenging. Because these forces are closely interrelated, changes in one may cause changes in others. For example, because of evidence linking children's consumption of soft drinks to health issues such as obesity, diabetes, and osteoporosis, Coca-Cola has experienced negative publicity and calls for legislation regulating the sale of soft drinks in public schools. In response, the company recently announced it will work with schools to make available a greater variety of beverages in school vending machines, including water, juices, and sugar- and caffeine-free drinks. Although Coca-Cola will continue to profit from the sales of vending machine beverages, other companies, including archrival PepsiCo, will almost certainly move to match Coca-Cola's plans, rendering the latter's advantage in this area short-lived.[7]

Even though changes in the marketing environment produce uncertainty for marketers and at times hurt marketing efforts, they also create opportunities. Marketers who are alert to changes in environmental forces can not only adjust to and influence these changes but also capitalize on the opportunities such changes provide. Most airlines offer frequent flier miles as rewards to loyal customers who make a commitment to fly their airline. AirTran Airlines took the concept a step further by developing a frequent flier program that offers free trips on *other* airlines. The discount air carrier launched the program after recognizing that competitors were matching its low fares and that its frequent flier program did not give it a competitive edge. Now it offers customers who fly six coach or three business-class round trips on AirTran by the end of the calendar year a free ticket on another carrier. AirTran's response to competitive forces in the marketing environment helped give the company a competitive advantage by increasing customer loyalty.[8]

Marketing mix elements—product, distribution, promotion, and price—are factors over which an organization has control; the forces of the environment, however, are subject to far less control. But even though marketers know they cannot predict changes in the marketing environment with certainty, they must nevertheless plan for them. Because these environmental forces have such a profound effect on marketing activities, we explore each of them in considerable depth in Chapter 3.

Understanding the Marketing Concept

Some firms have sought success by buying land, building a factory, equipping it with people and machines, and then making a product they believe buyers need. However, these firms frequently fail to attract customers with what they have to offer because they defined their business as "making a product" rather than as "helping potential customers satisfy their needs and wants." For example, when compact discs became more popular than vinyl records, turntable manufacturers had an opportunity to develop new products to satisfy customers' needs for home entertainment. Companies that did not pursue this opportunity, such as Dual and Empire, are no longer in business. Such organizations have failed to implement the marketing concept.

marketing concept A philosophy that an organization should try to satisfy customers' needs through a coordinated set of activities that also allows the organization to achieve its goals

According to the **marketing concept,** an organization should try to provide products that satisfy customers' needs through a coordinated set of activities that also allows the organization to achieve its goals. Customer satisfaction is the major focus of the marketing concept. To implement the marketing concept, an organization strives to determine what buyers want and uses this information to develop satisfying products. It focuses on customer analysis, competitor analysis, and integration of the firm's resources to provide customer value and satisfaction, as well as long-term profits.[9] The firm must also continue to alter, adapt, and develop products to keep pace with customers' changing desires and preferences. Ben & Jerry's, for example, constantly assesses customer demand for ice cream and sorbet. On its website, it maintains a "flavor graveyard" listing combinations that were tried and ultimately failed. It also notes its top ten flavors each month. Pharmaceutical companies such as Merck and Pfizer continually strive to develop new products to fight infectious diseases, viruses, cancer, and other medical problems. Drugs that lower cholesterol, control diabetes, alleviate depression, or improve the quality of life in other ways also provide huge profits for the drug companies. When new products—like Rogaine, a hair growth product—are developed, the companies must develop marketing activities to reach customers and communicate the products' benefits and side effects. Thus, the marketing concept emphasizes that marketing begins and ends with customers.

The marketing concept is not a second definition of marketing. It is a management philosophy guiding an organization's overall activities. This philosophy affects all organizational activities, not just marketing. Production, finance, accounting, human resources, and marketing departments must work together.

The marketing concept is also not a philanthropic philosophy aimed at helping customers at the expense of the organization. A firm that adopts the marketing concept must satisfy not only its customers' objectives but also its own, or it will

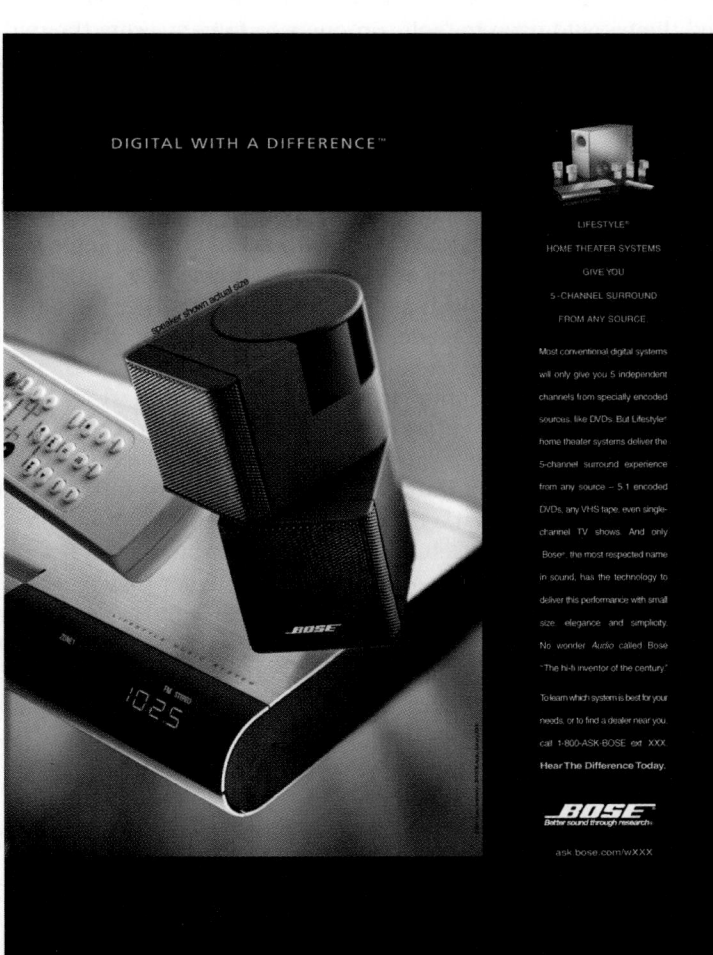

The Marketing Concept
Bose continually develops new audio products to meet changing consumer needs and to stay ahead of the competition.

not stay in business long. The overall objectives of a business might relate to increasing profits, market share, sales, or a combination of all three. The marketing concept stresses that an organization can best achieve these objectives by being customer oriented. Thus, implementing the marketing concept should benefit the organization as well as its customers.

It is important for marketers to consider not only their current buyers' needs but also the long-term needs of society. Striving to satisfy customers' desires by sacrificing society's long-term welfare is unacceptable. For example, while many parents want disposable diapers that are comfortable, absorbent, and safe for their babies, society in general does not want nonbiodegradable disposable diapers that create tremendous landfill problems now and for the future. Marketers are expected to act in a socially responsible manner, an idea we discuss in more detail in Chapter 4.

Evolution of the Marketing Concept

The marketing concept may seem like an obvious approach to running a business. However, businesspeople have not always believed that the best way to make sales and profits is to satisfy customers. (See Figure 1.3.)

The Production Orientation.   During the second half of the nineteenth century, the Industrial Revolution was in full swing in the United States. Electricity, rail transportation, division of labor, assembly lines, and mass production made it possible to produce goods more efficiently. With new technology and new ways of using labor, products poured into the marketplace, where demand for manufactured goods was strong.

The Sales Orientation.   In the 1920s, strong demand for products subsided, and businesses realized they would have to "sell" products to buyers. From the mid-1920s to the early 1950s, businesses viewed sales as the major means of increasing profits, and this period came to have a sales orientation. Businesspeople believed the most important marketing activities were personal selling, advertising, and distribution. Today some people incorrectly equate marketing with a sales orientation.

The Marketing Orientation.   By the early 1950s, some businesspeople began to recognize that efficient production and extensive promotion did not guarantee that customers would buy products. These businesses, and many others since, found that they must first determine what customers want and then produce it rather than making the products first and then trying to persuade customers that they need them. As more organizations realized the importance of satisfying customers' needs, U.S. businesses entered the marketing era, one of marketing orientation.

marketing orientation
An organizationwide commitment to researching and responding to customer needs

A **marketing orientation** requires the "organizationwide generation of market intelligence pertaining to current and future customer needs, dissemination of the intelligence across departments, and organizationwide responsiveness to it."[10] Top management, marketing managers, nonmarketing managers (those in production, finance, human resources, and so on), and customers are all important in developing and carrying out a marketing orientation. Unless marketing managers provide continuous customer-focused leadership with minimal interdepartmental conflict, achieving a marketing orientation will be difficult. Nonmarketing managers must communicate with marketing managers to share information important to understanding the customer. Finally, a marketing orientation involves being responsive to ever-changing

FIGURE 1.3
The Evolution of the Marketing Concept

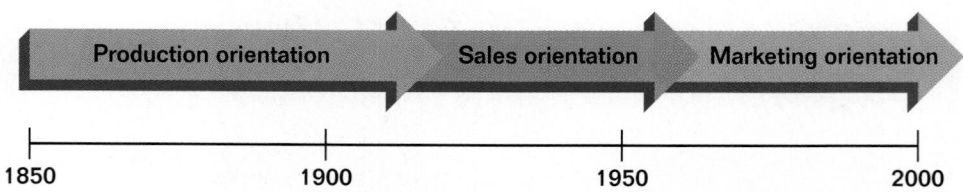

| Production orientation | Sales orientation | Marketing orientation |

| 1850 | 1900 | 1950 | 2000 |

customer needs and wants. To accomplish this, Amazon.com, the online provider of books and compact discs, follows buyers' online purchases and recommends related topics. Trying to assess what customers want, difficult to begin with, is further complicated by the speed with which fashions and tastes can change. Today businesses want to satisfy customers and build meaningful long-term buyer-seller relationships.

Implementing the Marketing Concept

A philosophy may sound reasonable and look good on paper, but that does not mean it can be put into practice easily. To implement the marketing concept, a marketing-oriented organization must accept some general conditions and recognize and deal with several problems. Consequently, the marketing concept has yet to be fully accepted by all American businesses.

Management must first establish an information system to discover customers' real needs and then use the information to create satisfying products. When M&M/Mars asked customers to choose a new M&M color to replace tan, 10.2 million people voted by mail, phone, fax, and e-mail. Blue received 54 percent of the vote, with purple, pink, and "no change" losing.[11] Within months, blue joined red, green, yellow, orange, and dark brown in the M&M lineup. Similarly, Parker Brothers encouraged customers to vote online for a new Monopoly piece (a biplane, bag of money, or piggy bank). These examples illustrate one technique marketers can use to obtain information about customers' desires and to respond in a way that forges a positive marketing relationship. An information system is usually expensive; management must commit money and time for its development and maintenance. But without an adequate information system, an organization cannot be marketing oriented.

To satisfy customers' objectives as well as its own, a company must also coordinate all its activities. This may require restructuring the internal operations and overall objectives of one or more departments. If the head of the marketing unit is not a member of the organization's top-level management, he or she should be. Some departments may have to be abolished and new ones created. Implementing the marketing concept demands the support not only of top management but of managers and staff at all levels.

Managing Customer Relationships

Achieving the full profit potential of each customer relationship should be the fundamental goal of every marketing strategy. Marketing relationships with customers are the lifeblood of all businesses. At the most basic level, profits can be obtained through relationships in the following ways: (1) by acquiring new customers, (2) by enhancing the profitability of existing customers, and (3) by extending the duration of customer relationships. Implementing the marketing concept means optimizing the exchange relationship, which is the relationship between a company's financial investment in customer relationships and the return generated by customers responding to that investment.[12]

Maintaining positive relationships with customers is an important goal for marketers. The term **relationship marketing** refers to "long-term, mutually beneficial arrangements in which both the buyer and seller focus on value enhancement through the creation of more satisfying exchanges."[13] Relationship marketing continually deepens the buyer's trust in the company, and, as the customer's confidence grows, this in turn increases the firm's understanding of the customer's needs. Successful marketers respond to customer needs and strive to increase value to buyers over time. Eventually this interaction becomes a solid relationship that allows for cooperation and mutual dependency. For example, customers depend on the Coca-Cola Company to provide a standardized, reliable, satisfying soft drink anyplace in the world. Due to its efforts to expand distribution to every possible location, Coca-Cola sells 30 percent of its volume in North America, 26 percent in Latin America, 21 percent in Europe, 16 percent in the Asian/Pacific region, and 7 percent in Africa and the Middle East.[14] The company continues to expand distribution and to maintain a

relationship marketing
Establishing long-term, mutually satisfying buyer-seller relationships

high-quality product. Coca-Cola is also a good "corporate citizen," donating millions of dollars to education and health and human services each year.

To build these long-term customer relationships, marketers are increasingly turning to marketing research and information technology. **Customer relationship management (CRM)** focuses on using information about customers to create marketing strategies that develop and sustain desirable customer relationships. By increasing customer value over time, organizations try to retain and increase long-term profitability through customer loyalty.[15] For example, AmSouth Bank, a financial institution with branches throughout the southeastern United States, promotes itself as "The Relationship Bank" and offers every financial service a business or consumer could conceivably need. Instead of focusing on acquiring new customers, AmSouth strives to serve all the financial needs of each individual customer, thereby acquiring a greater share of each customer's financial business.[16]

Managing customer relationships requires identifying patterns of buying behavior and using that information to focus on the most promising and profitable customers.[17] Building Customer Relationships examines how Home Depot has modified its strategy to address the needs of particular target markets. Companies must be sensitive to

BUILDING CUSTOMER RELATIONSHIPS

Home Depot Develops Relationships with Its Customers

When Bernie Marcus and Arthur Blank opened the first Home Depot store in Atlanta in 1979, they altered the hardware and home improvement business forever. Marcus and Blank envisioned huge, warehouse-style stores stocked with extensive selections of low-priced products. Today do-it-yourselfers and building contractors can browse among 50,000 products for the home and yard, from kitchen and bathroom fixtures to lumber, tools, and plants. Some Home Depot stores are open 24 hours a day. Customers can also order products online and pick them up at a nearby store or have them delivered. The company offers free home improvement clinics to teach customers how to "do it yourself," but for those customers who prefer using professionals, most stores offer installation services. Well-trained employees, easily recognizable in their orange aprons, help customers find just the right product or demonstrate the proper use of a particular tool. With more than 1,100 stores in North and South America generating annual sales of $46 billion, Home Depot has become one of the most successful startup firms in the last 20 years.

Home Depot continually evaluates who its customers are and what they want from a home improvement store. After one such "audit," the company recognized that it could provide more services to contractors; it is now upgrading services for professional builders in about 500 stores. The company is also launching new, smaller stores in some suburban locations for those customers who have limited needs and hate to wade through a large store. These new stores, roughly half the size of a traditional Home Depot, will be customized to match the needs of the neighborhoods in which they operate.

Home Depot has adopted a customer orientation in crafting each element of its marketing strategy. In terms of product selection, Home Depot provides expansive depth in product lines and continually adjusts the product mix to meet changing market needs. Many Home Depot stores offer appliances and have increased their offerings in the home decorating and remodeling areas with greater selections of lighting, tile, and cabinetry, as well as Ralph Lauren paints. The company's pricing strategy allows it to satisfy customers with competitive prices as well as high quality and informed service. Customer service employees are experts trained to communicate with building contractors, plumbers, electricians, and novice do-it-yourselfers alike.

With new leadership from Bob Nardelli, previously from General Electric, Home Depot is poised to continue responding to customer needs. Nardelli acknowledges that two important keys to the company's continuing success are expanding services and service quality and continuing to retain, attract, and motivate some of the best employees in the business. Nardelli firmly believes that success in retailing depends on motivating employees. With increased competition from Lowe's, the number two home improvement retailer, Home Depot continues to feel pressure to remain in touch with its customers. Given its past record of success and commitment to both customers and employees, Home Depot is set to capitalize on its key strengths.

customers' requirements and desires and establish communication to build their trust and loyalty. Consider that the lifetime value of a Taco Bell customer is approximately $12,000, while a lifelong Lexus customer is worth about $600,000.[18] Because the loss of a loyal potential lifetime customer could result in lower profits, managing customer relationships has become a major focus of strategic marketing today.

Through the use of Internet-based marketing strategies (e-marketing), companies can personalize customer relationships on a nearly one-on-one basis. A wide range of products, such as computers, jeans, golf clubs, cosmetics, and greeting cards, can be tailored for specific customers. At Priceline.com, for example, customers can specify the price they are willing to pay for a particular product and then find companies that are willing to sell at that price.[19] Customer relationship management provides a strategic bridge between information technology and marketing strategies aimed at long-term relationships with high-revenue customers.[20] This involves finding and retaining customers using information to improve customer value and satisfaction. For example, Amazon.com uses e-mail to inform customers about books, music, or videos that may be of interest. Amazon analyzes each e-mail campaign to determine which strategies yield the greatest response rates and additional purchases. When the company offered a $5 or $10 gift certificate to 1 million new customers, 150,000 customers purchased again.[21] Thus, information technology helps Amazon manage customer relationships to build value and increase sales and satisfaction. We take a closer look at some of these e-marketing strategies in Chapter 23.

Value-Driven Marketing

Value is an important element of managing long-term customer relationships and implementing the marketing concept. We view **value** as a customer's subjective assessment of benefits relative to costs in determining the worth of a product (customer value = customer benefits − customer costs).

value A customer's subjective assessment of benefits relative to costs in determining the worth of a product

Customer benefits include anything a buyer receives in an exchange. Hotels and motels, for example, basically provide a room with a bed and bathroom, but each firm provides a different level of service, amenities, and atmosphere to satisfy its guests. Hampton Inns offers the minimum services necessary to maintain a quality, efficient, low-price overnight accommodation. In contrast, the Ritz Carlton provides every imaginable service a guest might desire and strives to ensure that all service is of the highest quality. Customers judge which type of accommodation offers the best value according to the benefits they desire and their willingness and ability to pay for the costs associated with the benefits.

Customer costs include anything a buyer must give up to obtain the benefits the product provides. The most obvious cost is the monetary price of the product, but nonmonetary costs can be equally important in a customer's determination of value. Two nonmonetary costs are the time and effort customers expend to find and purchase desired products. To reduce time and effort, a company can increase product availability, thereby making it more convenient for buyers to purchase the firm's products. Another nonmonetary cost is risk, which can be reduced by offering good basic warranties or extended warranties for an additional charge.[22] Another risk reduction strategy is the offer of a 100 percent satisfaction guarantee. This strategy is increasingly popular in today's catalog/telephone/Internet shopping environment. L.L. Bean, for example, uses such a guarantee to reduce the risk involved in ordering merchandise from its catalogs.

The process people use to determine the value of a product is not highly scientific. All of us tend to get a feel for the worth of products based on our own expectations and previous experience. We can, for example, compare the value of tires, batteries, and computers directly with the value of competing products. We evaluate movies, sporting events, and performances by entertainers on the more subjective basis of personal preferences and emotions. For most purchases, we do not consciously try to calculate the associated benefits and costs. It becomes an instinctive feeling that Kellogg's Corn Flakes are a good value or that McDonald's is a good place

On the surface, low-cost home DSL looks like a great idea for business. But you get what you pay for. After all, home DSL is asymmetric. So it only moves at a high rate of speed when downloading, or receiving information from the Internet. Its upload speed is limited. That means slower service when you're e-mailing clients, sending out large files or trading stocks online. All of which can be incredibly time sensitive. Fortunately, Covad has a solution: symmetric DSL. It provides your business with a consistent high-speed connection to and from the Internet. And it's one of the ways Covad gives you the edge you need to succeed. Find out more at 1-877-872-0502. Or visit covad.com/sdsl1.

COVAD
1-877-872-0502

Value-Driven Marketing
Covad understands that businesses want DSL service that quickly uploads and downloads information.

to take children for a quick lunch. The purchase of an automobile or a mountain bike may have emotional components, but more conscious decision making may also figure in the process of determining value.

In developing marketing activities, it is important to recognize that customers receive benefits based on their experiences. For example, many computer buyers consider services such as fast delivery, ease of installation, technical advice, and training assistance to be important elements of the product. Customers also derive benefits from the act of shopping and selecting products. These benefits can be affected by the atmosphere or environment of a store, such as Red Lobster's nautical/seafood theme. Even the ease of navigating a website can have a tremendous impact on perceived value. For this reason, General Motors has developed a user-friendly way to navigate its website for researching and pricing vehicles. Using the Internet to compare a Saturn with a Mercedes could result in different customers viewing different automobiles as an excellent value. The Saturn has been highly rated by owners as providing low-cost, reliable transportation and having dealers who provide outstanding service. A Mercedes may cost twice as much but has the advantage of being rated as a better-engineered automobile that also has a higher social status than the Saturn. Different customers may view each car as being an exceptional value for their own personal satisfaction.

The marketing mix can be used to enhance perceptions of value. A product that demonstrates value usually has a feature or an enhancement that provides benefits. Promotional activities can also help create an image and prestige characteristics that customers consider in their assessment of a product's value. In some cases, value may simply be perceived as the lowest price. Many customers may not care about the quality of the paper towels they buy; they simply want the cheapest ones for use in cleaning up spills because they plan to throw them in the trash anyway. On the other hand, more people are looking for the fastest, most convenient way to achieve a goal and therefore become insensitive to pricing. For example, many busy customers are buying more prepared meals in supermarkets to take home and serve quickly even though these meals cost considerably more than meals prepared from scratch. In such cases, the products with the greatest convenience may be perceived as having the greatest value. The availability or distribution of products can also enhance their value. Taco Bell wants to have its Mexican fast-food products available at any time and any place people are thinking about consuming food. It has therefore introduced Taco Bell products into supermarkets, vending machines, college campuses, and other convenient locations. Thus, the development of an effective marketing strategy requires understanding the needs and desires of customers and designing a marketing mix to satisfy them and provide the value they want.

Marketing Management

marketing management The process of planning, organizing, implementing, and controlling marketing activities to facilitate exchanges effectively and efficiently

Marketing management is the process of planning, organizing, implementing, and controlling marketing activities to facilitate exchanges effectively and efficiently. Effectiveness and efficiency are important dimensions of this definition. *Effectiveness* is the degree to which an exchange helps achieve an organization's objectives. *Efficiency* refers to minimizing the resources an organization must spend to achieve a specific level of desired exchanges. Thus, the overall goal of marketing management is to facilitate highly desirable exchanges and to minimize the costs of doing so.

Planning is a systematic process of assessing opportunities and resources, determining marketing objectives, and developing a marketing strategy and plans for implementation and control. Planning determines when and how marketing activities are performed and who performs them. It forces marketing managers to think ahead, establish objectives, and consider future marketing activities and their impact on society. Effective planning also reduces or eliminates daily crises. We take a closer look at marketing strategies and plans in the next chapter.

Organizing marketing activities involves developing the internal structure of the marketing unit. The structure is the key to directing marketing activities. The marketing unit can be organized by functions, products, regions, types of customers, or a combination of all four.

Proper implementation of marketing plans hinges on coordination of marketing activities, motivation of marketing personnel, and effective communication within the unit. Marketing managers must motivate marketing personnel, coordinate their activities, and integrate their activities both with those in other areas of the company and with the marketing efforts of personnel in external organizations, such as advertising agencies and research firms. If McDonald's runs a promotion advertising Big Macs for 99 cents, proper implementation of this plan requires that each of the company's restaurants have enough staff and product on hand to handle the increased demand. An organization's communication system must allow the marketing manager to stay in contact with high-level management, with managers of other functional areas within the firm, and with personnel involved in marketing activities both inside and outside the organization.

The marketing control process consists of establishing performance standards, comparing actual performance with established standards, and reducing the difference between desired and actual performance. An effective control process has four requirements. It should ensure a rate of information flow that allows the marketing manager to detect quickly any differences between actual and planned levels of performance. It must accurately monitor various activities and be flexible enough to accommodate changes. The costs of the control process must be low relative to costs that would arise without controls. Finally, the control process should be designed so that both managers and subordinates can understand it. In Chapter 22, we examine the organizing, implementing, and controlling of marketing strategies in greater detail.

The Importance of Marketing in Our Global Economy

Our definition of marketing and discussion of marketing activities reveal some of the obvious reasons the study of marketing is relevant in today's world. In this section, we look at how marketing affects us as individuals and at its role in our increasingly global society.

Marketing Costs Consume a Sizable Portion of Buyers' Dollars

Studying marketing will make you aware that many marketing activities are necessary to provide satisfying goods and services. Obviously, these activities cost money. About one-half of a buyer's dollar goes for marketing costs. If you spend $17.00 on a new compact disc, about $8.50 goes toward activities related to distribution and the retailer's expenses and profit margins. The production (pressing) of the CD represents about $1, or 6 percent of its price. A family with a monthly income of $3,000 that allocates $600 to taxes and savings spends about $2,400 for goods and services. Of this amount, $1,200 goes for marketing activities. If marketing expenses consume that much of your dollar, you should know how this money is used.

SNAPSHOT

Average U.S. family earned $63,410

The average family earned $63,410 during the previous 12 months, according to Census 2000. A breakdown of what the U.S.'s 70.8 million families earned in the previous year:

Less than $15,000 — 10.4%
$15,000–$34,999 — 23.3%
$35,000–$49,999 — 16.8%
$50,000–$74,999 — 22.0%
$75,000–$99,999 — 12.3%
$100,000–$149,999 — 9.7%
$150,000+ — 5.5%

Source: *USA Today*, August 24, 2001, p. 1A. Copyright 2001, *USA Today*. Reprinted with permission.

Marketing Is Used in Nonprofit Organizations

Although the term *marketing* may bring to mind advertising for McDonald's, Chevrolet, and IBM, marketing is also important in organizations working to achieve goals other than ordinary business objectives such as profit. Government agencies at the federal, state, and local levels engage in marketing activities to fulfill their mission and goals. The U.S. Army, for example, uses promotion, including television advertisements and event sponsorships, to communicate the benefits of enlisting to potential recruits. Universities and colleges engage in marketing activities to recruit new students as well as donations from alumni and businesses. Rensselaer Polytechnic Institute, for example, launched a $1 million marketing campaign to strengthen its image and broaden its appeal. The campaign, which featured print advertisements and television commercials with the tag line "Why not change the World?", ran for two years. Subsequent research found that 86 percent of those polled now rate the school as excellent, and an anonymous donor recently gave the school $360 million, the largest donation ever given to any U.S. university for unlimited use.[23]

In the private sector, nonprofit organizations also employ marketing activities to create, distribute, promote, and even price programs that benefit particular segments of society. Habitat for Humanity, for example, must promote its philosophy of low-income housing to the public to raise funds and donations of supplies to build or renovate housing for low-income families who contribute "sweat equity" to the construction of their own homes. Such activities helped nonprofit organizations raise $190 billion in philanthropic contributions to assist them in fulfilling their missions.[24]

Marketing Is Important to Business and the Economy

Businesses must sell products to survive and grow, and marketing activities help sell their products. Financial resources generated from sales can be used to develop innovative products. New products allow a firm to better satisfy customers' changing needs, which in turn enables the firm to generate more profits. Even nonprofit businesses need to "sell" to survive.

Marketing activities help produce the profits that are essential not only to the survival of individual businesses but also to the health and ultimate survival of the global economy. Profits drive economic growth because without them businesses find it difficult, if not impossible, to buy more raw materials, hire more employees, attract more capital, and create additional products that in turn make more profits. Without profits, marketers cannot continue to provide jobs and contribute to social causes.

Marketing Fuels Our Global Economy

Profits from marketing products contribute to the development of new products and technologies. Advances in technology, along with falling political and economic barriers and the universal desire for a higher standard of living, have made marketing across national borders commonplace while stimulating global economic growth. As a result of worldwide communications and increased international travel, many American brands have achieved widespread acceptance around the world. At the same time, customers in the United States have greater choices among the products they buy, as foreign brands such as Toyota (Japan), Bayer (Germany), and British Petroleum now sell alongside American brands such as General Motors, Tylenol, and Chevron. People around the world watch CNN and MTV on Toshiba and Sony televisions they purchased at Wal-Mart. Electronic commerce via the Internet now enables businesses of all sizes to reach buyers around the world. We explore the international markets and opportunities for global marketing in Chapter 5.

Marketing and the Growth of Technology
Accenture notes the growing use of wireless devices and Visor produces just such a product.

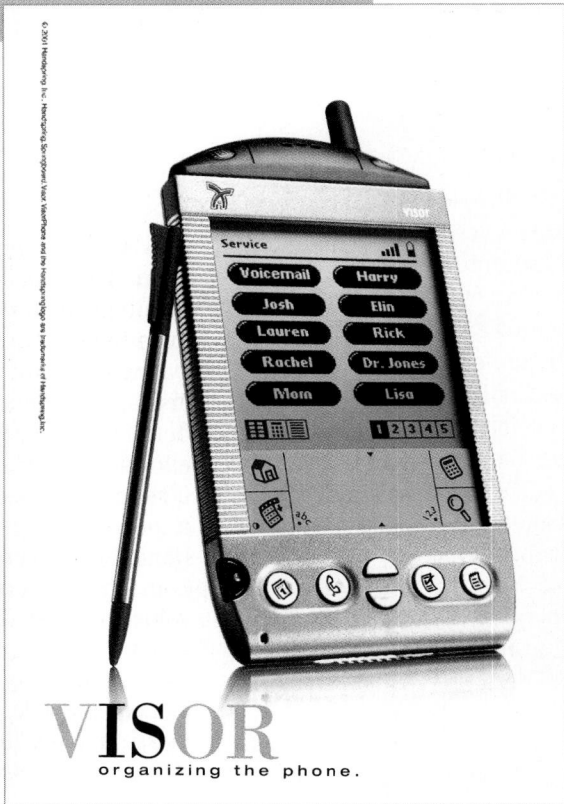

Meet Your New Best Friend!

Hog the remote. Gain five pounds. Drink from the carton. Tell dumb jokes.

He won't mind.

Find your new best friend at an MSPCA animal shelter! Look for him online at:

www.MSPCA.org

(Lots of great pet-care and seasonal tips, too!)

Carol Lundeen

Marketing Knowledge Enhances Consumer Awareness

Besides contributing to the well-being of our economy, marketing activities help improve the quality of our lives. Studying marketing allows us to assess a product's value and flaws more effectively. We can determine which marketing efforts need improvement and how to attain that goal. For example, an unsatisfactory experience with a warranty may make you wish for stricter law enforcement so that sellers would fulfill their promises. You may also wish that you had more accurate information about a product before you purchased it. Understanding marketing enables us to evaluate corrective measures (such as laws, regulations, and industry guidelines) that could stop unfair, damaging, or unethical marketing practices. Thus, understanding how marketing activities work can help you be a better consumer.

Marketing Connects People Through Technology

New technology, especially technology related to computers and telecommunications, helps marketers understand and satisfy more customers than ever before. Through toll-free telephone numbers, customers can provide feedback about their experiences with a company's products. Even bottled water products, such as Dannon Natural Spring Water, provide toll-free telephone numbers for questions or comments. This information can help marketers refine and improve their products to better satisfy consumer needs. The Internet, especially the World Wide Web, also allows companies to provide tremendous amounts of information about their products to consumers and to interact with them through e-mail. A consumer shopping for a personal digital assistant, for example, can visit the websites of Palm and Handspring to compare the features of the PalmPilot and Visor, respectively. Although consumers are often reluctant to purchase products directly via the Internet, many value the Internet as a significant source of information for making purchasing decisions.

The Internet has also become a vital tool for marketing to other businesses. In fact, online sales are expected to account for 42 percent of all business-to-business marketing by 2005 while currently 1 percent of all retail sales occur completely online.[25] Successful companies are using technology in their marketing strategies to develop profitable relationships with these customers. We look more closely at marketing on the Internet in Chapter 23.

Net Sights

The World Wide Web has become a very useful information tool for consumers and marketers alike. Marketers can now turn to numerous websites for the latest information about consumer trends, industry news, economic data, competitors' products and prices, and much, much more. We will highlight some of these sites in each chapter in a Net Sights box. One of the most useful sites is the Marketing Learning Center site for this textbook at **http://www.prideferrell. com.** There you will find chapter summaries, self-tests, and exercises, as well as career information and links to many more useful marketing-related websites.

Socially Responsible Marketing Can Promote the Welfare of Customers and Society

The success of our economic system depends on marketers whose values promote trust and cooperative relationships in which customers are treated with respect. The public is increasingly insisting that social responsibility and ethical concerns be considered in planning and implementing marketing activities. Although some marketers' irresponsible or unethical activities end up on the front pages of *USA Today* or *The Wall Street Journal,* more firms are working to develop a responsible approach to developing long-term relationships with customers *and* society. For example, Bristol-Myers Squibb Company and Merck & Company, two of the largest pharmaceutical firms in the United States, recently announced they would lower the prices charged for their AIDS treatment medicines in developing countries in Africa. Although the companies' action came in response to international criticism of their pricing strategies for AIDS treatments in nations with high rates of poverty, many international and AIDS activist organizations hailed the move for reducing the high cost of treating AIDS patients in African nations.[26] By managing concern about the impact of marketing on society, a firm can protect the interests of the general public and the natural environment. We examine these issues and many others as we develop a framework for understanding more about marketing in the remainder of this book.

Marketing Offers Many Exciting Career Prospects

From 25 to 33 percent of all civilian workers in the United States perform marketing activities. The marketing field offers a variety of interesting and challenging career opportunities throughout the world, such as personal selling, advertising, packaging, transportation, storage, marketing research, product development, wholesaling, and retailing. In addition, many individuals working for nonbusiness organizations engage in marketing activities to promote political, educational, cultural, church, civic, and charitable activities. Whether a person earns a living through marketing activities or performs them voluntarily for a nonprofit group, marketing knowledge and skills are valuable personal and professional assets.

Summary

Marketing is the process of creating, distributing, promoting, and pricing goods, services, and ideas to facilitate satisfying exchange relationships with customers in a dynamic environment. As the purchasers of the products that organizations develop, promote, distribute, and price, customers are the focal point of all marketing activities. The essence of marketing is to develop satisfying exchanges from which both customers and marketers benefit. Organizations generally focus their marketing efforts on a specific group of customers, or target market.

Marketing involves developing and managing a product that will satisfy customer needs, making the product available in the right place and at a price acceptable to customers, and communicating information that helps customers determine if the product will satisfy their needs. These activities—product, distribution, promotion, and pricing—are known as the marketing mix because marketing managers decide what type of each element to use and in what amounts. Marketing managers strive to develop a marketing mix that matches the needs of customers in the target market. Before marketers can develop a marketing mix, they must collect in-depth, up-to-date information about customer needs. The product variable of the marketing mix deals with researching customers' needs and wants and designing a product that satisfies them. A product can be a good, a service, or an idea. In dealing with the distribution variable, a marketing manager tries to make products available in the quantities desired to as many customers as possible. The promotion variable relates to activities used to inform individuals or groups about the organization and its products. The price variable relates to decisions and actions associated with establishing pricing policies and determining product prices. These marketing mix variables are often viewed as controllable because they can be changed, but there are limits to how much they can be altered.

Individuals and organizations engage in marketing to facilitate exchanges—the provision or transfer of goods, services, and ideas in return for something of value. Four conditions must exist for an exchange to occur: (1) two or more individuals, groups, or organizations must partici-pate, and each must possess something of value that the other party desires; (2) the exchange should provide a benefit or satisfaction to both parties involved in the transaction; (3) each party must have confidence in the promise of the "something of value" held by the other; and (4) to build trust, the parties to the exchange must meet expectations. Marketing activities should attempt to create and maintain satisfying exchange relationships.

The marketing environment, which includes competi-tive, economic, political, legal and regulatory, technologi-cal, and sociocultural forces, surrounds the customer and the marketing mix. These forces can create threats to mar-keters, but they also generate opportunities for new prod-ucts and new methods of reaching customers. These forces can fluctuate quickly and dramatically.

According to the marketing concept, an organization should try to provide products that satisfy customers' needs through a coordinated set of activities that also allows the organization to achieve its goals. Customer sat-isfaction is the marketing concept's major objective. The philosophy of the marketing concept emerged in the United States during the 1950s after the production and sales eras. Organizations that develop activities consistent with the marketing concept become marketing-oriented organiza-tions. To implement the marketing concept, a marketing-oriented organization must establish an information sys-tem to discover customers' needs and use the information to create satisfying products. It must also coordinate all its activities and develop marketing mixes that create value for customers in order to satisfy their needs.

Relationship marketing involves establishing long-term, mutually satisfying buyer-seller relationships. Customer relationship management (CRM) focuses on using information about customers to create marketing strategies that develop and sustain desirable customer relationships. Managing customer relationships requires identifying patterns of buying behavior and using that information to focus on the most promising and profitable customers.

Value is a customer's subjective assessment of bene-fits relative to costs in determining the worth of a prod-uct. Benefits include anything a buyer receives in an exchange, while costs include anything a buyer must give up to obtain the benefits the product provides. The mar-keting mix can be used to enhance perceptions of value.

Marketing management is the process of planning, organizing, implementing, and controlling marketing activities to facilitate effective and efficient exchanges. Planning is a systematic process of assessing opportuni-ties and resources, determining marketing objectives, developing a marketing strategy, and preparing for imple-mentation and control. Organizing marketing activities involves developing the marketing unit's internal struc-ture. Proper implementation of marketing plans depends on coordinating marketing activities, motivating market-ing personnel, and communicating effectively within the unit. The marketing control process consists of establish-ing performance standards, comparing actual perform-ance with established standards, and reducing the differ-ence between desired and actual performance.

Marketing is important in our society in many ways. Marketing costs absorb about half of each buyer's dollar. Marketing activities are performed in both business and nonprofit organizations. Marketing activities help business organizations generate profits, and they help fuel the increasingly global economy. A knowledge of marketing enhances consumer awareness. New technology improves marketers' ability to connect with customers. Socially responsible marketing can promote the welfare of cus-tomers and society. Finally, marketing offers many exciting career opportunities.

Important Terms

Marketing
Customers
Target market
Marketing mix
Product
Exchange
Marketing environment
Marketing concept

Marketing orientation
Relationship marketing
Customer relationship
  management (CRM)
Value
Marketing management

Discussion and Review Questions

1. What is marketing? How did you define the term before you read this chapter?
2. What is the focus of all marketing activities? Why?
3. What are the four variables of the marketing mix? Why are these elements known as variables?

4. What conditions must exist before a marketing exchange can occur? Describe a recent exchange in which you participated.
5. What are the forces in the marketing environment? How much control does a marketing manager have over these forces?
6. Discuss the basic elements of the marketing concept. Which businesses in your area use this philosophy? Explain why.
7. How can an organization implement the marketing concept?
8. What is customer relationship management? Why is it so important to "manage" this relationship?
9. What is value? How can marketers use the marketing mix to enhance the perception of value?
10. What types of activities are involved in the market-ing management process?
11. Why is marketing important in our society? Why should *you* study marketing?

Application Questions

1. Identify several businesses in your area that have not adopted the marketing concept. What characteristics of these organizations indicate nonacceptance of the marketing concept?
2. Identify possible target markets for the following products:
   a. Kellogg's Corn Flakes
   b. Wilson tennis rackets
   c. Disney World
   d. Diet Pepsi
3. Discuss the variables of the marketing mix (product, price, promotion, and distribution) as they might relate to each of the following:
   a. a trucking company
   b. a men's clothing store
   c. a skating rink
   d. a campus bookstore

Internet Exercise & Resources

Visit **www.prideferrell.com** for resources to help you master the material in this chapter, plus materials that will help you expand your marketing knowledge, including: Internet exercise updates, ACE self-tests, hotlinks to companies featured in this chapter, and much more.

Online with the American Marketing Association

The American Marketing Association (AMA) is the marketing discipline's primary professional organization. In addition to sponsoring academic research, publishing marketing literature, and organizing meetings of local businesspeople with student members, it helps individual members find employment in member firms. To see what the AMA has to offer you, visit the AMA website at

www.marketingpower.com

1. What type of information is available on the AMA website to assist students in planning their careers and finding jobs?

2. If you joined a student chapter of the AMA, what benefits would you receive?

3. What marketing mix variable does the AMA's Internet marketing efforts exemplify?

VIDEO CASE 1.1
Harte-Hanks Provides Customer Relationship Management Services

Harte-Hanks was founded as a West Texas newspaper publisher in the 1920s by Houston Harte and Bernard Hanks. By the 1970s, the San Antonio–based firm had grown into a diversified communications company with newspapers, television stations, radio stations, and other media businesses. In 1997, however, Harte-Hanks divested most of these news outlets to transform itself into a global marketing firm focusing on customer relationship management services. Now a buzzword in marketing, customer relationship management (CRM) involves using information about customers to create marketing strategies that build and sustain long-term

customer relationships. The goal of CRM is to build satisfying exchange relationships between buyers and sellers by gathering useful data at all customer-contact points and analyzing those data to better identify customers' needs and desires. Understanding how a customer subjectively assesses a product's benefits relative to its costs is important in developing any corporate CRM program.

To help client companies create and sustain customer relationships, Harte-Hanks employs the latest information technology to acquire, analyze, and communicate data about existing and prospective customers from every possible point of customer interaction. This information helps clients plan and implement marketing strategies to facilitate effective exchanges and thereby build long-term relationships with the most profitable customers. Harte-Hanks therefore offers complete CRM solutions to help companies drive customers to their stores, websites, and call/contact centers.

Harte-Hanks markets its services to client companies from a variety of industries ranging from high-technology, retail, and finance to pharmaceutical, health care, and insurance. For example, Harte-Hanks revamped the website strategy for promoting the arthritis drug Celebrex for Pfizer and Pharmacia Corporation. The redesigned site not only promotes Celebrex but also provides information for customers. For The Sports Authority, a sporting-goods retailer, Harte-Hanks coordinates multimedia contacts with customers. This CRM program helps The Sports Authority manage customer acquisition, cross-selling, and customer retention by integrating customers' companywide activity to develop a profile of each customer. This helps the retailer analyze interactions and transactions to recognize significant events and respond quickly to customer needs and sales opportunities. For example, after The Sports Authority ran a regional campaign offering holiday shoppers an incentive for making additional purchases, it used Harte-Hanks' CRM services to analyze daily transactions, leverage customer information resources, and facilitate distribution services through a Harte-Hanks regional center.

To help clients improve their marketing efforts, Harte-Hanks offers a five-step CRM module. The first step involves constructing and updating current marketing practices. The second step includes identifying and creating the tools needed to access relevant information. The third step focuses on analyzing data to derive beneficial customer information. In the fourth step, clients learn how to apply the knowledge they have gained from data analysis. This step also includes customer service and using different methods of interaction. Finally, Harte-Hanks shows the client how to execute the entire solution through direct mail, a call center, or some combination of services that best suits the client's needs.

Although Harte-Hanks' CRM module generates a large amount of the company's total revenue, the firm also maintains several targeted advertising publications, including the *Penny Saver* in California and *The Flyer* in Florida. The zoned editions of these publications allow advertisers to target customers by geographic area, demographics, and even lifestyle and language. The company has also formed a number of strategic alliances to achieve its objective of providing high-quality services to help clients meet their own goals. One of these alliances is with Xchange, a provider of campaign management software, which helps Harte-Hanks offer web-based customer relationship management services. The alliance will give Harte-Hanks' clients more control over their direct marketing campaigns. The company also joined with E-Dialog, an e-mail marketing firm, to integrate e-mail with other media to enhance clients' direct and interactive marketing programs.

Harte-Hanks defines marketing by concentrating on the customer, the central focus of all marketing activities. As Chet Dalzell, Harte-Hanks' director of public relations, says, customer confidence, once shaken, can be difficult to regain. Harte-Hanks therefore has established several customer-focused systems to address customer relationship issues internally before they become external problems. For example, the company might create a system that avoids sending e-mails that recipients might perceive as spam (unsolicited commercial e-mail) or sending sensitive customer information that has not been encrypted. Such steps are important not only for improving clients' customer relationships but for preventing any customer contact that might be perceived as negative.[27]

QUESTIONS FOR DISCUSSION

1. Define Harte-Hanks' target market. How can Harte-Hanks' CRM products help companies build satisfying exchange relationships?
2. What forces from the marketing environment provide opportunities for Harte-Hanks? What forces might threaten the firm's marketing strategy?
3. Does Harte-Hanks appear to be implementing the marketing concept? How can the company help its clients implement the marketing concept?

CASE 1.2
Montgomery Ward: The Rise and Fall of an American Retailing Icon

On December 28, 2000, some 3,700 people learned they no longer had jobs when their employer, Montgomery Ward, announced it was filing for bankruptcy. This news came as a complete shock because the 128-year-old company had recently emerged from Chapter 11 bankruptcy proceedings and was implementing new strategies to restore its reputation as a trusted retailer. Indeed, the venerable company had essentially originated the concept of mail-order shopping in the United States (Montgomery Ward had been publishing a general merchandise catalog for 14 years when its rival, Sears, Roebuck, was founded in 1886). The oldest privately held department store chain in the United States, Montgomery Ward had already updated one-fifth of its stores and rung up sales of $3.2 billion in 1999. However, according to CEO and chairman Roger Goddu, "Overall weak holiday sales and a very difficult retail environment simply did not permit us to complete the turnaround that might have been possible in an otherwise thriving economy. Sadly, today's action is unavoidable." After the announcement, the company began the difficult process of shutting 250 stores and 10 distribution centers. To understand how such a respected com-

pany failed requires examining more than a century of retailing history.

In 1872, Aaron Montgomery Ward was a 28-year-old traveling salesman for a St. Louis dry goods company. Ward had a dream: a business in which customers from across the country sent their hard-earned money to him in exchange for goods he advertised in a catalog. Although many people thought Ward's idea was foolish, Ward was confident he could prosper by simply keeping his promises to customers. He also knew the rapid growth of railroad lines across the country would help him market goods at affordable prices and deliver them promptly. This confidence sustained him through the loss of his first batch of goods in the Great Chicago Fire, his two partners quitting, and skepticism from the press.

Working in a room above a stable, Ward sent out his first one-page catalog and hired a youngster to help him fill the orders that he knew would come flowing in. Ward promptly answered all customer questions, and by 1875 he began to promote his company with the motto "Satisfaction Guaranteed or Your Money Back," a truly novel concept in the burgeoning nineteenth-century American retail

industry. By 1878, the company achieved $300,000 in sales; by 1887, it realized $1 million.

The catalog grew to 500 pages by the turn of the nineteenth century, and more than 1 million customers pored over its pages, knowing they could count on the company's money-back guarantee. The catalog served as a store without walls or boundaries, stocking just about everything imaginable (except for wives, despite repeated customer requests). Ward's catalog allowed rural Americans to purchase the same goods people in the big cities were buying. In the South, African Americans, barred by segregation policies from trying on clothes in stores, quickly became loyal customers. To handle all the orders, Ward built the biggest skyscraper west of New York City on Chicago's Michigan Avenue in 1899. Aaron Ward retired in 1901 and devoted the rest of his life to philanthropic and environmental endeavors.

Of course, other businesses quickly caught on to Montgomery Ward's success and opened their own mail-order businesses and, eventually, stores where people could see and try out the goods advertised in catalogs. In the face of this growing competition, Montgomery Ward opened its first stores in the 1920s. To further distinguish Ward's from Sears and other general merchandise rivals, executives decided in 1939 to give away a coloring book as a Christmas sales promotion. They asked a company copywriter, R. L. May, to create a story to accompany the coloring book. After visiting the Lincoln Park Zoo and consulting his 4-year-old daughter, May wrote a tale about a reindeer with an unusual deformity. Montgomery Ward gave away 2.4 million copies of the coloring book that year, and Rudolph the Red-Nosed Reindeer became a perennial Christmas favorite of children everywhere.

Based on the precedent established by its founder, the company also gave some of the profits from its success back to the community. When Aaron Ward ran the company in the late nineteenth century, he was appalled by the sight of sprawling shanties and factories outside his window. Ward began a life-long crusade to keep Chicago's lakefront open to the public, using his money and power to fight would-be developers of the land. He even sent out company employees to pick up trash along the shore of what eventually became Grant Park. When Ward died in 1913, he left millions of dollars to build what is now the Field Museum of Natural History. Ward money also helped to endow the medical and dental schools at Northwestern University.

For the first half of the twentieth century, Montgomery Ward prospered, ultimately building nine mail-order warehouses to service customer orders. After the Second World War, however, the company seemed to lose its edge. Savvy competitors were quick to open large stores along the nation's new interstate highway system, but Montgomery Ward failed to follow suit. After years of floundering, Mobil Corporation acquired the company in 1976, but Montgomery Ward continued to struggle. In 1988, former chairman Bernard F. Brennan engineered a management-led buyout for $3.8 billion, but that effort also failed to produce a true turnaround. Besieged by stiff competition from specialty retailers like the Gap, Home Depot, and Best Buy, as well as discount retailers such as Target and Wal-Mart, Montgomery Ward declared bankruptcy in 1997 in an effort to stave off closure.

By the time Montgomery Ward emerged from Chapter 11 bankruptcy in 1999, it was in the midst of implementing a new strategy to revitalize the firm yet again. The company had updated one-fifth of its stores, closed another 48 stores, and slashed the payroll by 3,800 jobs. However, it soon became apparent that even these efforts were simply too little, too late for the venerable retailer to survive in the fiercely competitive U.S. retail market. The company had hoped for 9 percent sales growth during 2000, but never exceeded 2 percent. According to Kurt Barnard, an industry analyst, Montgomery Ward "failed to establish an identity for themselves, a niche, and that makes it difficult to stand out. They never gave shoppers a reason for preferring it to any one of its rivals. It was just there, like soaking corn flakes."

Montgomery Ward was not the only retail casualty in 2000; Bradlee's, a discount chain, also filed for Chapter 11 and announced it was shutting down for good. As companies all over the nation began to tighten their belts in response to a slowing economy, layoffs mounted in many industries. This was little consolation for those Montgomery Ward employees who lost their jobs when the company failed. As Sid Doolittle, a 28-year Ward employee and vice president and head of the catalog division when he left the company, said, "When a company that old that had employed that many people for that many years closes, you feel a sense of loss."[28]

QUESTIONS FOR DISCUSSION

1. Did Aaron Montgomery Ward understand the marketing concept?
2. Describe the marketing mix of Montgomery Ward at the turn of the nineteenth century.
3. What other steps might Montgomery Ward executives have taken to turn around the company instead of closing it?

Strategic Planning

2

OBJECTIVES

- To describe the strategic planning process
- To explain how organizational resources and opportunities affect the planning process
- To understand the role of the mission statement in strategic planning
- To examine corporate, business-unit, and marketing strategies
- To understand the process of creating the marketing plan

Cleaning Up the Paper Towel Market

In 1907, Scott Paper Company introduced the first paper towel—the Sanitowel—to the United States to help keep children from spreading the common cold in their classrooms. The company premiered the first paper towel for use in the kitchen in 1931. Over the years, Scott continued to improve the mundane paper towel, becoming the first company to offer pastel colors in 1956 and the first to introduce designer prints in 1966. By the time the company was acquired by rival Kimberly-Clark in 1995, however, Scott's paper products were languishing, with barely 5 percent of customers choosing Scott Towels over Procter & Gamble's Bounty. Today the 35-year-old Bounty brand dominates the $2.7 billion market for paper towels. Sensing an opportunity, Kimberly-Clark launched a new marketing strategy to resuscitate the aging Scott Towels.

Kimberly-Clark began by revamping the product, introducing softer, more absorbent Scott Towels "with Ridges." The improved product required 20 percent less paper pulp, thus reducing production costs. The company also boosted advertising spending by 15.6 percent to $3.5 million during 2000. During the same period, rival Procter & Gamble slashed its advertising budget for Bounty by more than 30 percent, yet still outspent Kimberly-Clark by more than $25 million. However, while Bounty advertisements ran on national network television, Kimberly-Clark focused its promotional efforts on local television ads targeting specific markets as it rolled out the improved towels in different parts of the country. The company also exploited Procter & Gamble's decision to decrease its in-store presence at supermarkets during this period, reducing its full-time sales force to part time and later contracting out much of this promotional task. In contrast, Kimberly-Clark sales representatives increased their store visits, meeting with store managers and observing whether Scott brands were getting sufficient shelf space. For slow-growing products like paper towels, such efforts can make a big difference. According to a grocery manager at a Chicago Treasure Island supermarket, the Kimberly-Clark representative stops by twice a month, but "We don't see anyone from P&G. I'm more inclined to give [the Kimberly-Clark sales representative] the shelf location she wants."

When rising pulp prices in 2000 forced manufacturers to raise prices, Procter & Gamble increased Bounty's wholesale price by 9 percent. Kimberly-Clark, which produces two-thirds of its pulp, was able to limit its price increase to just 6 percent. And, because the company employed frequent discounts off the price of Scott Towels, customers could regularly find Scott Towels on sale for 69 or 79 cents instead of the regular price of $1.19. Procter & Gamble, however, did not match this strategy, and Bounty continued to sell for $1.29 most of the time. As the marketing director of one supermarket chain points out, "I don't care how loyal you are, most people aren't going to pass up a 50 cent price difference."

Kimberly-Clark's marketing strategy to improve Scott Towels, boost promotional efforts, limit price increases, and target the right customers paid off with a 24 percent sales increase to $197 million, up from $150 million the year before. During the same period, Bounty's sales grew by just $18 million, or 1.7 percent. Scott's share of the paper towel market grew from 5.9 percent to 7.2 percent, while Bounty's share fell 1.8 percent to 39 percent of the market. Although Bounty clearly continues to dominate the paper towel market, Kimberly-Clark's nimble marketing strategy allowed the company to exploit weaknesses in Procter & Gamble's strategy to bring new life to a not so glamorous product.[1]

With competition increasing, Kimberly-Clark and many other companies are spending more time and resources on strategic planning, that is, on determining how to use their resources and abilities to achieve their objectives. Although most of this book deals with specific marketing decisions and strategies, this chapter focuses on "the big picture," on all the functional areas and activities—finance, production, human resources, and research and development, as well as marketing—that must be coordinated to reach organizational goals. Effectively implementing the marketing concept of satisfying customers and achieving organizational goals requires that all organizations engage in strategic planning.

We begin this chapter with an overview of the strategic planning process. Next, we examine how organizational resources and opportunities affect strategic planning and the role played by the organization's mission statement. After discussing the development of both corporate and business-unit strategy, we explore the nature of marketing strategy and the creation of the marketing plan. These elements provide a framework for the development and implementation of marketing strategies, as we will see throughout the remainder of this book.

Understanding the Strategic Planning Process

Through the process of **strategic planning,** a firm establishes an organizational mission and formulates goals, corporate strategy, marketing objectives, marketing strategy, and, finally, a marketing plan.[2] A marketing orientation should guide the process of strategic planning to ensure that a concern for customer satisfaction is an integral part of the process. Figure 2.1 shows the components of strategic planning.

strategic planning The process of establishing an organizational mission and formulating goals, corporate strategy, marketing objectives, marketing strategy, and a marketing plan

The process begins with a detailed analysis of the organization's strengths and weaknesses and identification of opportunities and threats within the marketing environment. Based on this analysis, the firm can establish or revise its mission and goals, and then develop corporate strategies to achieve these goals. Next, each functional

FIGURE 2.1
Components of Strategic Planning
Source: Figure adapted from *Marketing Strategy* by O. C. Ferrell, Michael Hartline, and George Lucas, Jr. Copyright © 2002 by Harcourt Brace & Company, reproduced by permission of the publisher.

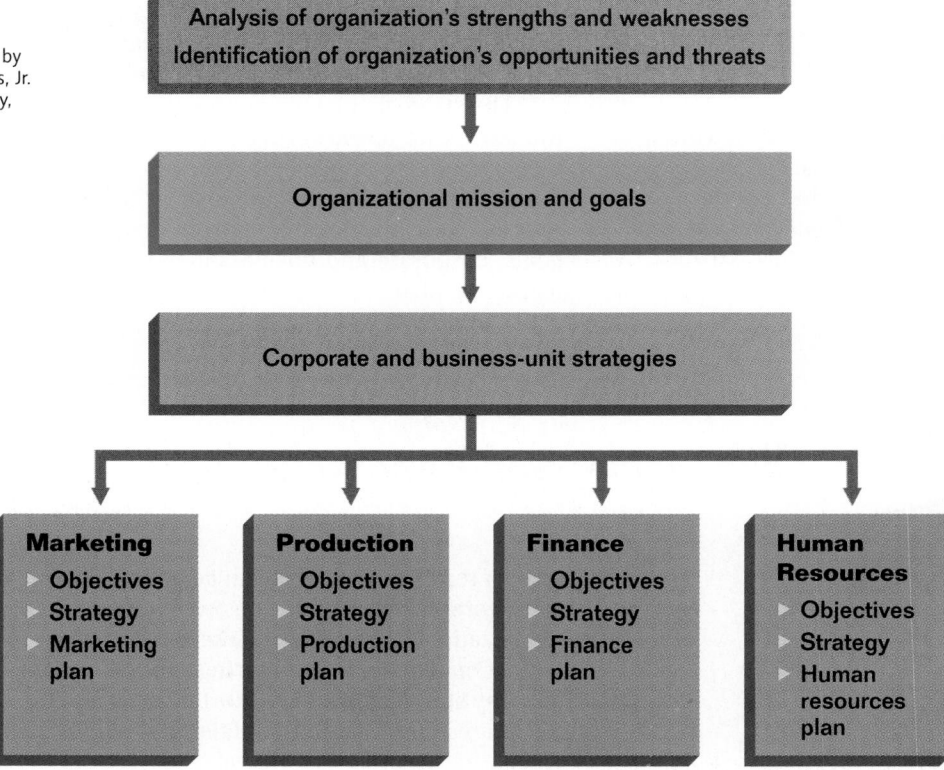

area of the organization (marketing, production, finance, human resources, etc.) establishes its own objectives and develops strategies to achieve them.[3] The objectives and strategies of each functional area must support the organization's overall goals and mission. The strategies of each functional area should also be coordinated with a focus on marketing orientation. For example, developing an organizational culture in which the firm's human resource focus is on marketing orientation is an important requirement for an effective marketing strategy and has been linked to successful organizational performance.[4] The use of cross-functional teams for decision making can significantly reduce conflict between marketers and members of other functional areas, including manufacturing, finance, and research and development.[5] At Southwest Airlines, for example, employees work in a culture where the company's vaunted sense of warmth, friendliness, personal pride, and fun is linked to a customer orientation in its marketing strategy.

marketing strategy A strategy for identifying and analyzing a target market and developing a marketing mix to meet the needs of that market

Because our focus is marketing, we are, of course, most interested in the development of marketing objectives and strategies. Marketing objectives should be designed so that their achievement will contribute to the corporate strategy and they can be accomplished through efficient use of the firm's resources. To achieve its marketing objectives, an organization must develop a **marketing strategy,** which includes identifying and analyzing a target market and developing a marketing mix to satisfy individuals in that market. Thus, a marketing strategy includes a plan of action for developing, distributing, promoting, and pricing products that meet the needs of the target market. Marketing strategy is best formulated when it reflects the overall direction of the organization and is coordinated with all the firm's functional areas. When properly implemented and controlled, a marketing strategy will contribute to the achievement not only of marketing objectives but also of the organization's overall goals. General Motors' Saturn division, for example, represents an innovative effort by a U.S. automaker to define and serve a target market by offering value, quality, reliability, and service, as well as an image of being "a different kind of company." This strategy has resulted in Saturn being named the top brand in customer satisfaction according to J.D. Power & Associates. About three-fourths of Saturn customers say they would not have purchased a GM vehicle if there were no Saturn.[6] These efforts also helped create a community of loyal Saturn owners, which in turn helped Saturn fulfill its goals and objectives as part of General Motors' overall corporate strategy. Even with satisfied customers and dealers, however, Saturn has had to adjust its marketing strategy to address aging products and factories operating at half capacity. Part of its new marketing plan includes the VUE, a small sport-utility vehicle.[7]

marketing plan A written document that specifies the activities to be performed to implement and control an organization's marketing activities

The strategic planning process ultimately yields a marketing strategy that is the framework for a **marketing plan,** a written document that specifies the activities to be performed to implement and control the organization's marketing activities. In the remainder of this chapter, we discuss the major components of the strategic planning process: organizational opportunities and resources, organizational mission and goals, corporate and business-unit strategy, marketing strategy, and the role of the marketing plan.

Assessing Organizational Resources and Opportunities

The strategic planning process begins with an analysis of the marketing environment. Economic, competitive, political, legal and regulatory, sociocultural, and technological forces can constrain an organization and influence its overall goals; they also affect the amount and type of resources the firm can acquire. However, these environmental forces can create favorable opportunities as well, opportunities that can be translated into overall organizational goals and marketing objectives. We examine these forces and their impact on the strategic planning process in detail in Chapter 3.

Any strategic planning effort must assess the organization's available financial and human resources and capabilities, as well as how the level of these factors is likely to change in the future. Additional resources may be needed to achieve the organization's

Often forgets it's a camera. The new Spectra.

Polaroid click instantly.

Core Competency
Polaroid maintains its core
competency in the instant
camera market.

goals and mission.[8] Resources can also include good-will, reputation, and brand names. The reputations and well-known brand names of Rolex watches and Cross pens, for example, are resources that give these firms an advantage over their competitors. Such strengths also include **core competencies,** things a firm does extremely well—sometimes so well that they give the company an advantage over its competition. For example, the Chili's Grill & Bar restaurant chain, owned by Brinker International, has built an advantage over competitors such as Bennigan's and Houlihan's through superior menus and service, resulting in good food at moderate prices in a casual atmosphere.[9]

Analysis of the marketing environment involves not only an assessment of resources but also identification of opportunities in the marketplace. When the right combination of circumstances and timing permits an organization to take action to reach a particular target market, a **market opportunity** exists. Advances in computer technology and the growth of the Internet have made it possible for real estate firms to provide prospective home buyers

core competencies   Things a firm does extremely well, which sometimes give it an advantage over its competition

market opportunity   A combination of circumstances and timing that permits an organization to take action to reach a target market

strategic window   A temporary period of optimal fit between the key requirements of a market and a firm's capabilities

competitive advantage   The result of a company's matching a core competency to opportunities in the marketplace

with databases of homes for sale all over the country. At www.realtor.com, the website of the National Association of Realtors, buyers have access to a wealth of online information about homes for sale, including photos, floor plans, and details about neighborhoods, schools, and shopping. The World Wide Web represents a great market opportunity for real estate firms because its visual nature is perfectly suited to the task of shopping for a home. Opportunities like these are often called **strategic windows,** temporary periods of optimal fit between the key requirements of a market and the particular capabilities of a firm competing in that market.[10]

Marketers need to be able to recognize and analyze market opportunities and strategic windows. An organization's very survival depends on developing products that satisfy its target market(s). Few organizations can assume that products popular today will interest buyers in five years or even next year. In fact, research indicates that U.S. corporations lose half their customers every five years.[11] To remain competitive, a company can modify existing products (as Oscar Mayer and Frito-Lay did when they reduced the fat content of some products to address increasing health concerns among consumers), introduce new products (such as Procter & Gamble's Swiffer electrostatic dust mop), or eliminate those that no longer contribute to profits (such as the Oldsmobile and Plymouth automobile brands).

When a company matches a core competency to opportunities it has discovered in the marketplace, it is said to have a **competitive advantage.** In some cases, a company may possess manufacturing, technical, or marketing skills that it can match to market opportunities to create a competitive advantage. Microsoft, for example, used its marketing and technical skills to create the Windows operating system to make computers easier to use. Although most personal computers are now sold with Windows already installed, Microsoft strives to maintain its competitive advantage by improving Windows and introducing Windows-compatible software, such as its web browser, Internet Explorer.

Establishing an Organizational Mission and Goals

mission statement A long-term view of what the organization wants to become

Once an organization has assessed its resources and opportunities, it can begin to establish goals and strategies to take advantage of those opportunities. The goals of any organization should derive from its **mission statement,** a long-term view, or vision, of what the organization wants to become. Herbal tea marketer Celestial Seasonings, for example, says that its mission is "To create and sell healthful, naturally oriented products that nurture people's bodies and uplift their souls."[12]

When an organization decides on its mission, it really answers two questions: Who are our customers? and What is our core competency? (*Core competencies* define the focus of a firm's knowledge and resources from a customer perspective.) Although these questions seem very simple, they are two of the most important questions any firm must answer. Defining these customers' needs and wants gives direction to what the company must do to satisfy them.

Creating or revising a mission statement is quite challenging because of the many complex variables to be considered. Nonetheless, having a mission statement can benefit an organization in many ways. A mission statement gives the organization a clear purpose and direction, distinguishes it from competitors, provides direction for strategic planning, and fosters a marketing orientation. A mission statement provides anyone associated with the organization, anywhere in the world, with an understanding of what the organization is about.

An organization's goals, derived from its mission statement, guide the remainder of its planning efforts. Goals focus on the end results the organization seeks. Southwest Airlines's mission statement, for example, incorporates the company's goals of striving for a high-quality product, a sound financial position, and community responsibility.

Organizations can have both short-term and long-term goals. Companies experiencing a crisis or a situation involving negative publicity may be forced to focus

Mission Statement
Southwest Airlines communicates its mission.

Customer Service Commitment

Our Mission Statement

The mission of Southwest Airlines is dedication to the highest quality of Customer Service delivered with a sense of warmth, friendliness, individual pride, and Company Spirit.

SOUTHWEST AIRLINES®
A SYMBOL OF FREEDOM

Revised August 1, 2001

At Southwest Airlines, our Mission Statement has always governed the way we conduct our business. It highlights our desire to serve our Customers and gives us direction when we have to make service-related decisions. It is another way of saying, "we always try to do the right thing!" Our Mission Statement has also led the way to the airline industry's best cumulative consumer satisfaction record, according to statistics accumulated and published by the U.S. Department of Transportation. That is why we are sharing it with you.

In keeping with the spirit and intent of our Mission Statement, and as evidence of our wish to continually meet the expectations of our valued Customers, Southwest wants you to have a basic understanding of how we operate. We want you to have confidence in our airline and Employees, and we want you to be aware that there are, or may be, circumstances that can have an impact on your travel plans, purchase decisions, or your overall expectations.

solely on the short-term decisions necessary to stay in business, such as increasing cash flow by lowering prices or selling off parts of the business. Mattel, for example, attempted to stem three years of anemic sales by refocusing on classic toys, including Barbie Dolls and Hot Wheels cars, and divesting itself of the Learning Company, a poorly performing chain of computer game stores.[13] Other organizations have more optimistic, long-term goals. McDonald's, for example, is focusing on repositioning the company in the highly competitive fast-food business through new and improved products, including new stores under its Chipotle Grill and McCafe brand names. In many cases, companies that pursue long-term goals have to sacrifice short-term results to achieve them. Best Buy, the giant electronics retailer, sacrificed profits for a number of years so that it could expand and build larger stores than its competition to boost sales and gain a greater share of consumer spending on electronics. This strategy paid off as Best Buy became more profitable.

Developing Corporate and Business-Unit Strategies

In any organization, strategic planning begins at the corporate level and proceeds downward to the business-unit and marketing levels. Corporate strategy is the broadest of these three levels and should be developed with the organization's overall mission in mind. Business-unit strategy should be consistent with the corporate strategy, and marketing strategy should be consistent with both the business-unit and corporate strategies. Figure 2.2 shows the relationships among these planning levels. Before we examine marketing strategy, we must first discuss the broader topics of corporate and business-unit strategy.

Corporate Strategy

corporate strategy A strategy that determines the means for utilizing resources in the various functional areas to reach the organization's goals

Corporate strategy determines the means for utilizing resources in the functional areas of marketing, production, finance, research and development, and human resources to reach the organization's goals. A corporate strategy determines not only the scope of the business but also its resource deployment, competitive advantages, and overall coordination of functional areas. It addresses the two questions posed in

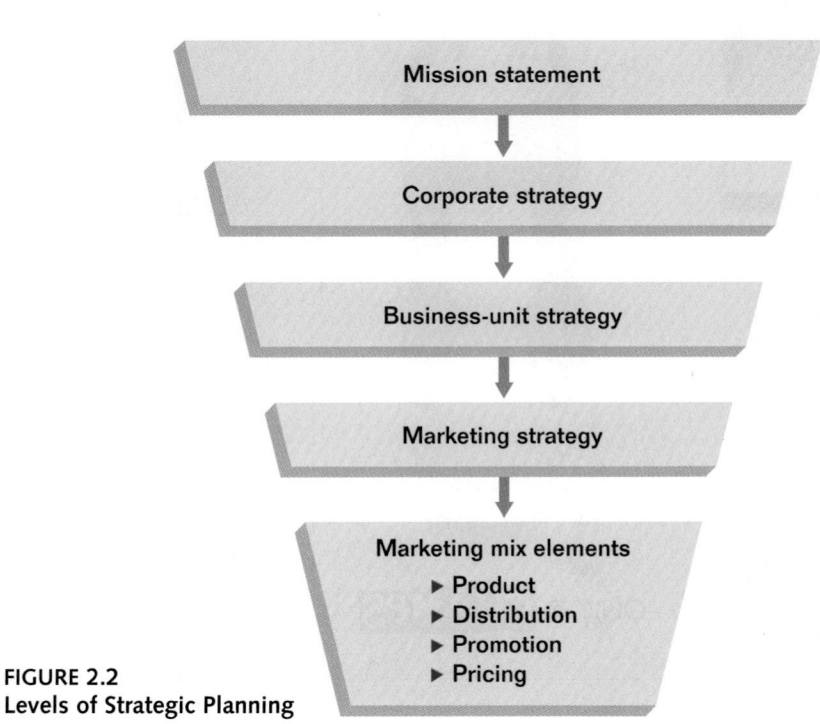

FIGURE 2.2
Levels of Strategic Planning

SNAPSHOT

Executives note hot business topics

The most discussed topics at conference board meetings in recent months (% of meetings in which a topic has been addressed):

e-Business privacy issues	64%
Using technology effectively to enhance decision-making and competitiveness	56%
Leadership	54%
Making cultural changes to respond more quickly to competitive challenge	51%
Strategic planning	51%

Source: *USA Today*, July 26, 2001, p. 1B. Copyright 2001, *USA Today*. Reprinted with permission.

the organization's mission statement: Who are our customers? and What is our core competency? The term *corporate* in this context does not apply solely to corporations; corporate strategy is used by all organizations, from the smallest sole proprietorship to the largest multinational corporation.

Corporate strategy planners are concerned with broad issues such as corporate culture, competition, differentiation, diversification, interrelationships among business units, and environmental and social issues. They attempt to match the resources of the organization with the opportunities and threats in the environment. Corporate strategy planners are also concerned with defining the scope and role of the firm's business units so that they are coordinated to reach the ends desired. Ford Motor Company, for example, plans to spend $500 million a year to revamp Jaguar, which it acquired in 1989, and turn it into a high-volume luxury car brand. To achieve this objective, Ford is applying its marketing and manufacturing resources to introduce new, lower-priced models, including the X-type, which the company hopes will bring in new buyers with its sleek styling and competitive price.[14]

Corporate Strategy
Reebok makes its athletic shoes available at many mass retailers and provides special designs exclusively for Champs Sports. Datek positions itself as providing fair, accurate trading to the individual investor.

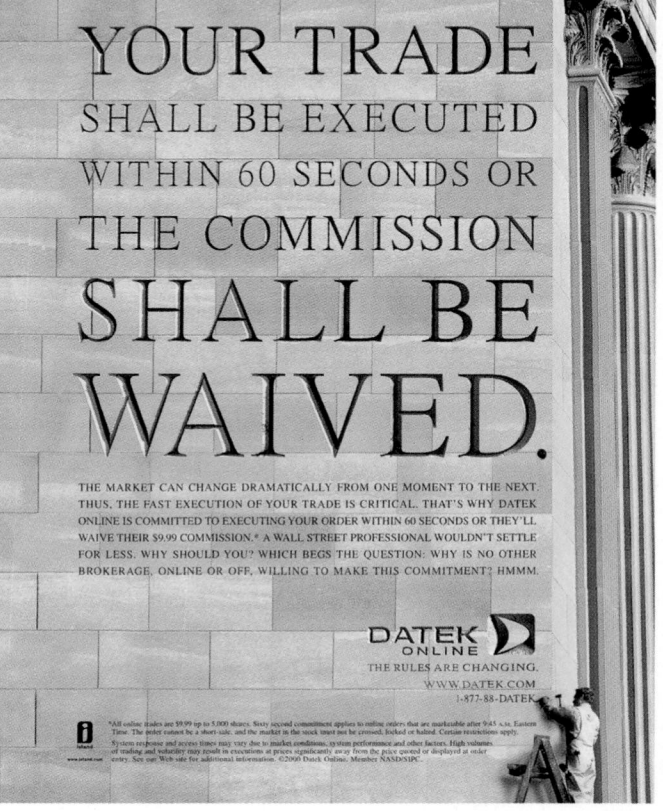

Business-Unit Strategy

After analyzing corporate operations and performance, the next step in strategic planning is to determine future business directions and develop strategies for individual business units. A **strategic business unit (SBU)** is a division, product line, or other profit center within the parent company. Borden's strategic business units, for example, consist of dairy products, snacks, pasta, niche grocery products like ReaLemon juice and Cremora coffee creamer, and other units such as glue and paints. Each of these units sells a distinct set of products to an identifiable group of customers, and each competes with a well-defined set of competitors. The revenues, costs, investments, and strategic plans of each SBU can be separated from those of the parent company and evaluated. SBUs operate in a variety of markets, which have differing growth rates, opportunities, degrees of competition, and profit-making potential. From the perspective of corporate strategy, an SBU needs to be developed according to how well the company's skills and expertise fit with that unit's needs and success. In other words, can the corporate strategy contribute to the critical success factors of that unit?[15]

strategic business unit (SBU) A division, product line, or other profit center within a parent company

Portfolio Analysis. Strategic planners should recognize the different performance capabilities of each SBU and carefully allocate scarce resources among those divisions. Several tools allow a firm's portfolio of strategic business units, or even individual products, to be classified and visually displayed according to the attractiveness of various markets and the business's relative market share within those markets. A **market** is a group of individuals and/or organizations that have needs for products in a product class and have the ability, willingness, and authority to purchase those products. The percentage of a market that actually buys a specific product from a particular company is referred to as that product's (or business unit's) **market share.** Palm Inc., for example, controls 59 percent of the market for handheld organizers with its PalmPilot family, while rival Handspring's Visor system has grown to 28 percent.[16]

market A group of individuals and/or organizations that have needs for products in a product class and have the ability, willingness, and authority to purchase those products

market share The percentage of a market that actually buys a specific product from a particular company

One of the most helpful tools is the **market-growth/market-share matrix,** the Boston Consulting Group (BCG) approach, which is based on the philosophy that a product's market growth rate and its market share are important considerations in determining its marketing strategy. All the firm's SBUs and products should be integrated into a single, overall matrix and evaluated to determine appropriate strategies for individual products and overall portfolio strategies. Managers can use this model to determine and classify each product's expected future cash contributions and future cash requirements. Generally, managers who use this model should examine the competitive position of a product (or SBU) and the opportunities for improving that product's contribution to profitability and cash flow.[17] The BCG analytical approach is more of a diagnostic tool than a guide for making strategy prescriptions.

market-growth/market-share matrix A strategic planning tool based on the philosophy that a product's market growth rate and market share are important in determining marketing strategy

Figure 2.3, which is based on work by the BCG, enables the strategic planner to classify a firm's products into four basic types: stars, cash cows, dogs, and question marks.[18] *Stars* are products with a dominant share of the market and good prospects for growth. However, they use more cash than they generate to finance growth, add capacity, and increase market share. An example of a star might be Apple's Internet-friendly iMac computer. *Cash cows* have a dominant share of the market but low prospects for growth; typically, they generate more cash than is required to maintain market share. Bounty, the best-selling paper towels in the United States, represents a cash cow for Procter & Gamble. *Dogs* have a subordinate share of the market and low prospects for growth; these products are often found in

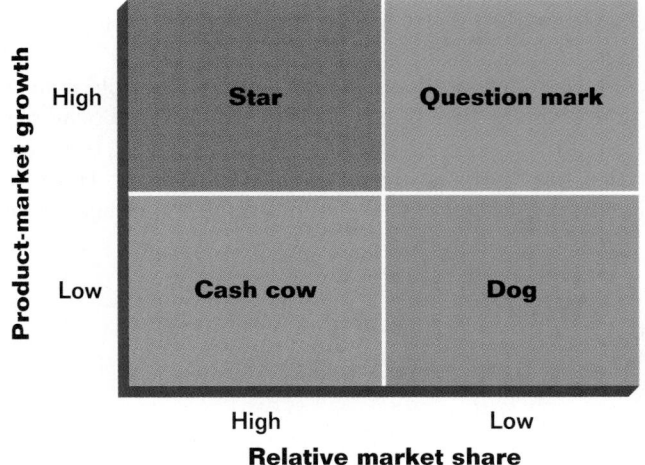

FIGURE 2.3
Growth-Share Matrix Developed by the Boston Consulting Group

Source: *Perspectives,* No. 66, "The Product Portfolio." Reprinted by permission from The Boston Consulting Group, Inc., Boston, MA. Copyright © 1970.

established markets. Checkers, a fast-food chain that features twin drive-through lanes, is experiencing declining profits and market share and may be considered a dog relative to other fast-food chains with different formats. *Question marks,* sometimes called "problem children," have a small share of a growing market and generally require a large amount of cash to build market share. Mercedes mountain bikes, for example, are a question mark relative to Mercedes' automobile products.

The long-term health of an organization depends on having some products that generate cash (and provide acceptable profits) and others that use cash to support growth. Among the indicators of overall health are the size and vulnerability of the cash cows; the prospects for the stars, if any; and the number of question marks and dogs. Particular attention should be paid to those products with large cash appetites. Unless the company has an abundant cash flow, it cannot afford to sponsor many such products at one time. If resources, including debt capacity, are spread too thin, the company will end up with too many marginal products and will be unable to finance promising new-product entries or acquisitions in the future.

Growth Strategies for Business Units.
Based on the analyses of each product or business unit, a firm may choose one or more competitive strategies, including intensive growth or diversified growth. Figure 2.4 shows these competitive strategies on a product-market matrix. This matrix can help in determining growth that can be implemented through marketing strategies.

Intensive growth can occur when current products and current markets have the potential for increasing sales. There are three main strategies for intensive growth: market penetration, market development, and product development. *Market penetration* is a strategy of increasing sales in current markets with current products. America Online (AOL), for example, increased its customer base from less than 1 million to 30 million by offering free service for limited time periods. *Market development* is a strategy of increasing sales of current products in new markets. Arm & Hammer, for instance, successfully introduced its baking soda, the firm's basic product, into new markets for use as a carpet deodorizer, as a freshener for litter boxes, and as a toothpaste. Market development also occurs whenever a company introduces its products into international markets for the first time. Although General Motors had to make minor modifications to the Saturn when it introduced the brand in Japan, the basic strategy was market development. Finally, *product development* is a strategy of increasing sales by improving present products or developing new products for current markets. Kimberly-Clark, for example, improved Scott Towels by making them softer and giving them ridges.[19] Perhaps the most common example of product development occurs in the automobile industry, in which car manufacturers regularly introduce redesigned or completely new models to their current markets. The 2002 Jeep Cherokee was redesigned and renamed the Liberty with a number of new performance features that significantly differentiate it from the 2001 model.

Diversified growth occurs when new products are developed to be sold in new markets. Firms have become increasingly diversified since the 1960s. The Coca-Cola Company, for example, diversified by acquiring Mad River Traders, giving the soft-drink giant entry into the market for "New Age" beverages like Mad River Traders' premium teas, sodas, and juice drinks.[20] Diversification offers some advantages over

Net Sights

Corporate executives and marketing managers must stay informed to develop successful corporate, business-unit, and marketing strategies. In addition to regularly reading local, national, and international industry-related newspapers and journals, many busy executives turn to CEO Express. This website, **http://www.ceoexpress.com,** provides online access to daily newspapers from all over the nation and beyond. It has links to alternative weekly newspapers, local and regional business journals, special-interest publications, and syndicated news services. Visitors to the site can also track stocks, access government agencies, and search the Web for the latest industry news.

intensive growth Growth occurring when current products and current markets have the potential for increasing sales

diversified growth Growth occurring when new products are developed to be sold in new markets

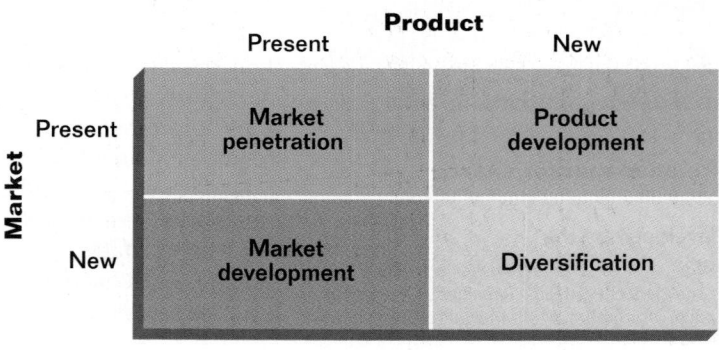

FIGURE 2.4
Competitive Growth Strategies
Source: H. I. Ansoff, *New Corporate Strategy* (New York: Wiley, 1988), p. 109.

single-business firms because it allows firms to spread their risk across a number of markets. Philip Morris has spread risk by diversifying with SBUs that include beer and food products, as well as cigarettes. More important, diversification allows firms to make better and wider use of their managerial, technical, and financial resources. Marketing expertise can be applied across businesses, which may also share advertising themes, distribution channels, warehouse facilities, and even sales forces.[21] Kimberly-Clark, which markets Kleenex tissues and Huggies diapers, was able to take advantage of this when it acquired Scott Paper.[22]

Developing a Marketing Strategy

The next phase in strategic planning is the development of sound strategies for each functional area of the organization. Within the marketing area, a strategy is typically designed around two components: (1) the selection of a target market and (2) the creation of a marketing mix that will satisfy the needs of the chosen target market. A marketing strategy articulates the best use of the firm's resources and tactics to achieve its marketing objectives. It should also match customers' desire for value with the organization's distinctive capabilities. Internal capabilities should be used to maximize external opportunities. The planning process should be guided by a marketing-oriented culture and processes in the organization.[23] When properly implemented, a good marketing strategy also enables a company to achieve its business-unit and corporate objectives. Although corporate, business-unit, and marketing strategies all overlap to some extent, the marketing strategy is the most detailed and specific of the three.

Target Market Selection

Selecting an appropriate target market may be the most important decision a company has to make in the planning process. This is so because the target market must be chosen before the organization can adapt its marketing mix to meet this market's needs and preferences. Defining the target market and developing an appropriate marketing mix are the keys to strategic success. Alamo Rent-A-Car, for example, grew from a small regional company to the nation's fourth-largest daily car rental company by defining its market as leisure travelers, while its major competitors focused on business travelers. Alamo introduced unlimited mileage and developed strong ties to travel agents and tour operators to dominate the leisure traveler market. If a company selects the wrong target market, all other marketing decisions will be a waste of time. The Gap, for example, experienced poor sales in Japan, perhaps in part because it used English-language tags on clothing, store employees greeted customers too informally, and prices were not competitive with similar merchandise sought by Japanese consumers.[24]

An organization should also examine whether it possesses the resources and skills necessary to create a marketing mix that will satisfy the needs of its target market. Organizations that do not possess the resources or skills to meet the needs of a particular

Target Market Selection
Luxury product manufacturers such as BMW target high-income families and individuals.

Love knows no limits.

M Power

With 333 horses, the power is Herculean. The handling, telepathic. And the brakes, breathtaking. Add a roof that disappears as swiftly as its taillights, and you have pure, unremitting love.

The New BMW M3 convertible

The Ultimate Driving Machine

target market are usually better off finding a different market to serve. Gateway Computers, for example, found that it did not have the resources to compete effectively with Dell Computer in the large corporate computer market, so it focused its resources on home and small-business computer buyers. Gateway attempted to reach this market through its own retail stores and an exclusive distribution agreement with OfficeMax retail stores. When this strategy failed to achieve the desired results, Gateway withdrew from the OfficeMax relationship and scaled back its stores. The computer company now focuses on direct sales to its target market.[25]

Accurate target market selection is crucial to productive marketing efforts. Products and even companies sometimes fail because marketers do not identify appropriate customer groups at whom to aim their efforts. Organizations that try to be all things to all people rarely satisfy the needs of any customer group very well. An organization's management therefore should designate which customer groups the firm is trying to serve and gather adequate information about those customers. Building Customer Relationships looks at how one small business created a successful marketing strategy by targeting a tiny market segment. Identification and analysis of a target market provide a foundation on which the firm can develop a marketing mix.

BUILDING CUSTOMER RELATIONSHIPS

Renaissance Pen Company: Developing the Write Marketing Strategy

Most of us get by with an inexpensive Bic, Pentel, or Write Brothers pen, or even a free pen with an organization's logo. Some people, however, desire a high-quality, high-fashion, high-status writing instrument. Renaissance Pen Company has chosen to target this tiny segment of the pen market by marketing pens that sell for as much as $80,000. Although this may seem an outrageous price to pay for a pen, sales have been brisk enough to generate revenues of $1.3 million a year.

In 1995, Patrick H. Pinkston got the idea to market prestige pens after observing airline passengers using plastic $150 Montblanc pens. He sold his business, Horizon Healthcare, and plowed the funds into launching Renaissance Pen Company. Pinkston defined the firm's target market as very-high-income customers interested in limited-edition fountain pens. Initially the firm offered three jewel-encrusted pens in blue, green, or red for $2,700 to $3,400. Nervous at first about the high price, Pinkston was amazed when customers made multiple purchases. One customer purchased ten green pens because they matched the color of his Bentley and he wanted to hand them out as holiday gifts. Pinkston saw this as an indication that there were enough wealthy customers to support a strategy based on high-priced designer pens.

The company's next step was to enter the very exclusive, high-end market by producing solid-gold pens. This strategy was risky, as a single pen had a price tag of $44,000. Nonetheless, the strategy paid off and the inventory sold out in eight months. The company also employed a focused branding strategy, marketing the most expensive pens under the name Michel Perchin because, as Pinkston commented, "The names of all expensive watches are French-sounding." The exclusive brand name added value to the pens and gave them an exclusive image.

Despite their high price tags, Renaissance pens are not the most expensive in the world. Renaissance competes against 35 other firms for this exclusive market. Caran D'Ache, for example, offers a $230,000 pen with 5,072 tiny diamonds. Montblanc markets a $130,000 pen with 4,810 diamonds. Perhaps the most unique pen producer is Krone LLC, which incorporates fine materials and even artifacts into its pens. The Abraham Lincoln Limited Edition pen includes Lincoln's birthstone, a cabochon amethyst, and even Lincoln's DNA in the form of porous glass powder. Lincoln's signature is engraved on the pen, and the pen's .925 silver clip holds a small 18 karat gold portrait. Krone produced just 1,008 of these pens, which sell for $1,650. The company offers another limited-edition pen that includes fragments from one of Babe Ruth's bats; its price tag is $2,800.

Do people actually use these prestige pens? In fact, most become collectors' items valued as art rather than mere utensils. Few of these high-end pens actually contain ink; they are intended to be seen or collected as investments, not used for writing. Retailers have convinced Patrick Pinkston that his company's reputation for innovation and high-quality pens can be transferred to other products. Even with such strong competition, Renaissance has expanded the product line with limited-edition vases, napkin holders, and candlesticks for $6,000 and up.

Organizations should also choose their target markets carefully because of changes taking place in the U.S. population. Companies that have targeted baby boomers are finding that their market is aging. As they age, baby boomers are buying fewer products like homes and home furnishings and more products like financial services (for retirement) and health-related products. Coach, which markets upscale leather handbags, is therefore introducing new products in an effort to attract younger customers. Although these younger buyers may not want to spend (or be able to afford) $200 for a leather handbag, the company hopes they will embrace its less expensive but equally high-quality offerings, including headbands, key fobs, and related leather products.[26]

When exploring possible target markets, marketing managers try to evaluate how entering them would affect the company's sales, costs, and profits. Marketing information should be organized to facilitate a focus on the chosen target customers. Accounting and information systems, for example, can be used to track revenues and costs by customer (or group of customers). In addition, managers and employees need to be rewarded for focusing on profitable customers. Teamwork skills can be developed with organizational structures that promote a customer orientation that allows quick responses to changes in the marketing environment.[27]

Marketers should also assess whether the company has the resources to develop the right mix of product, price, promotion, and distribution to meet the needs of a particular target market. In addition, they determine if satisfying those needs is consistent with the firm's overall objectives and mission. When Amazon.com, the number one Internet bookseller, began selling music CDs on its website, it made the decision that efforts to target music buyers would increase profits and be consistent with its objectives in the book market.[28] The size and number of competitors already marketing products in possible target markets are of concern as well.

Creating the Marketing Mix

The selection of a target market serves as the basis for creating a marketing mix to satisfy the needs of that market. The decisions made in creating a marketing mix are only as good as the organization's understanding of the target market. This understanding typically comes from careful, in-depth research into the characteristics of the target market. Thus, while demographic information is important, the organization should also analyze customer needs, preferences, and behavior with respect to product design, pricing, distribution, and promotion. For example, most customer transactions at mutual fund companies no longer involve a sales representative. Companies like Fidelity and Vanguard therefore developed easy-to-navigate websites that provide customers with information and allow them to conduct transactions online. This not only lowers the prices charged for transactions and the cost of promotion but also makes product information and services more accessible.

Marketing mix decisions should have two additional characteristics: consistency and flexibility. All marketing mix decisions should be consistent with the business-unit and corporate strategies. Such consistency allows the organization to achieve its objectives on all three levels of planning. Flexibility, on the other hand, permits the organization to alter the marketing mix in response to changes in market conditions, competition, and customer needs. Marketing strategy flexibility has a positive influence on organizational performance. Marketing orientation and strategic flexibility complement each other to help the organization manage varying environmental conditions.[29]

Table 2.1 offers some examples of how the marketing mix can be altered to match business-unit and marketing strategies for intensive growth. In market penetration, the goal of all marketing efforts is to increase sales of a particular brand or to increase sales within a specific target market segment. Some of the most common marketing mix decisions aimed at increasing sales volume include making the product more desirable, lowering prices, expanding the product's distribution, and engaging in promotion activities.

Different elements of the marketing mix can be adapted to accommodate different marketing strategies. The strategy of market development, for example, often involves

Table 2.1 — Matching the Marketing Mix to Intensive Growth Strategies

Business-Unit Strategy	Marketing Strategy	Marketing Mix			
		Product	Pricing	Distribution	Promotion
Market Penetration	Increase sales of brand X	Increase quality	Lower prices	Make available at more outlets	Offer coupons; advertise new prices
	Increase sales in the 18–29 age group	Add features desired by this segment	Lower prices	Make available at outlets visited by this segment	Target advertising to this group via media selection
Market Development	Find new uses for the product; seek out new markets; move into global markets	Conduct research to discover new uses; add features desired by new markets	Changes will depend on new uses and new markets	Seek distribution outlets in new markets; find global distribution partners	Educate consumers on new uses via advertising; create new advertising appeals for new markets
Product Development	Improve existing products or develop new products	Invest in consumer research and product development	Increase prices on improved products	Obtain shelf space for new products; gain the cooperation of retailers	Educate consumers on improvements; use advertising sales promotion to introduce new products

moving into global markets in an effort to expand market share. One of the most important marketing decisions in global markets is the choice of distribution channels. In some cases, U.S. companies create partnerships with foreign companies to gain access to distribution networks.

Organizations should always strive to create very strong marketing mixes. The success of the marketing mix depends on the combination of all four elements. Each marketing mix element must work together with the others. Pricing efforts, for example, should complement the overall marketing strategy by sending a message that reinforces the company's desired product image. Automobile companies have used large rebates or coupons for $1,000 off the sticker price of a new car to boost sales. The impact of such discounts on long-term customer relationships and coordination with other elements of the marketing unit is a major consideration in marketing strategy.[30] A company needs to assess its customers to discover how they value its product in order to make sound pricing, promotion, and distribution decisions.[31] If one marketing mix element is improperly matched to the others or to the target market, the product is likely to fail.

Creating the Marketing Plan

A major concern in the strategic planning process is **marketing planning,** the systematic process of assessing marketing opportunities and resources, determining marketing objectives, defining marketing strategies, and establishing guidelines for implementation and control of the marketing program. The outcome of marketing planning is the development of a marketing plan. As noted earlier, a marketing plan is a written document that outlines and explains all the activities necessary to implement marketing strategies. It describes the firm's current position or situation, establishes marketing objectives for the product or product group, and specifies how the organization will attempt to achieve these objectives.

marketing planning The process of assessing opportunities and resources, determining objectives, defining strategies, and establishing guidelines for implementation and control of the marketing program

Marketing plans vary with respect to the time period they cover. Generally, short-range plans are for one year or less. Moderate-range plans cover periods of more than one year but less than five years. Both types of plans are usually quite detailed. Long-range plans cover periods of more than five years, perhaps up to fifteen years, and are usually not as specific. Marketing managers may have short-, medium-, and long-range plans all at the same time. Long-range plans are relatively rare. However, as the marketing environment continues to change and business decisions become more complex, profitability and survival will depend more and more on the development of long-range plans.[32]

The extent to which marketing managers develop and use plans also varies. A firm should have a plan for each marketing strategy it develops. Because such plans must be modified as forces in the firm and in the environment change, marketing planning is a continuous process. Figure 2.5 illustrates the marketing planning cycle, which is a circular process. As the feedback lines in the figure indicate, planning is not unidirectional. Feedback is used to coordinate and synchronize all stages of the planning cycle.

Developing a clear, well-written marketing plan, though time consuming, is important. The plan is the basis for internal communication among employees. It covers the assignment of responsibilities and tasks, as well as schedules for implementation. It presents objectives and specifies how resources are to be allocated to achieve those objectives. Finally, it helps marketing managers monitor and evaluate the performance of a marketing strategy.

Marketing planning and implementation are inextricably linked in successful companies. The marketing plan provides a framework to stimulate thinking and provide strategic direction, while implementation occurs as an adaptive response to day-to-day issues, opportunities, and unanticipated situations—for example, increasing interest rates or an economic slowdown—that cannot be incorporated into marketing plans. Implementation-related adaptations directly affect an organization's marketing orientation, rate of growth, and strategic effectiveness.[33]

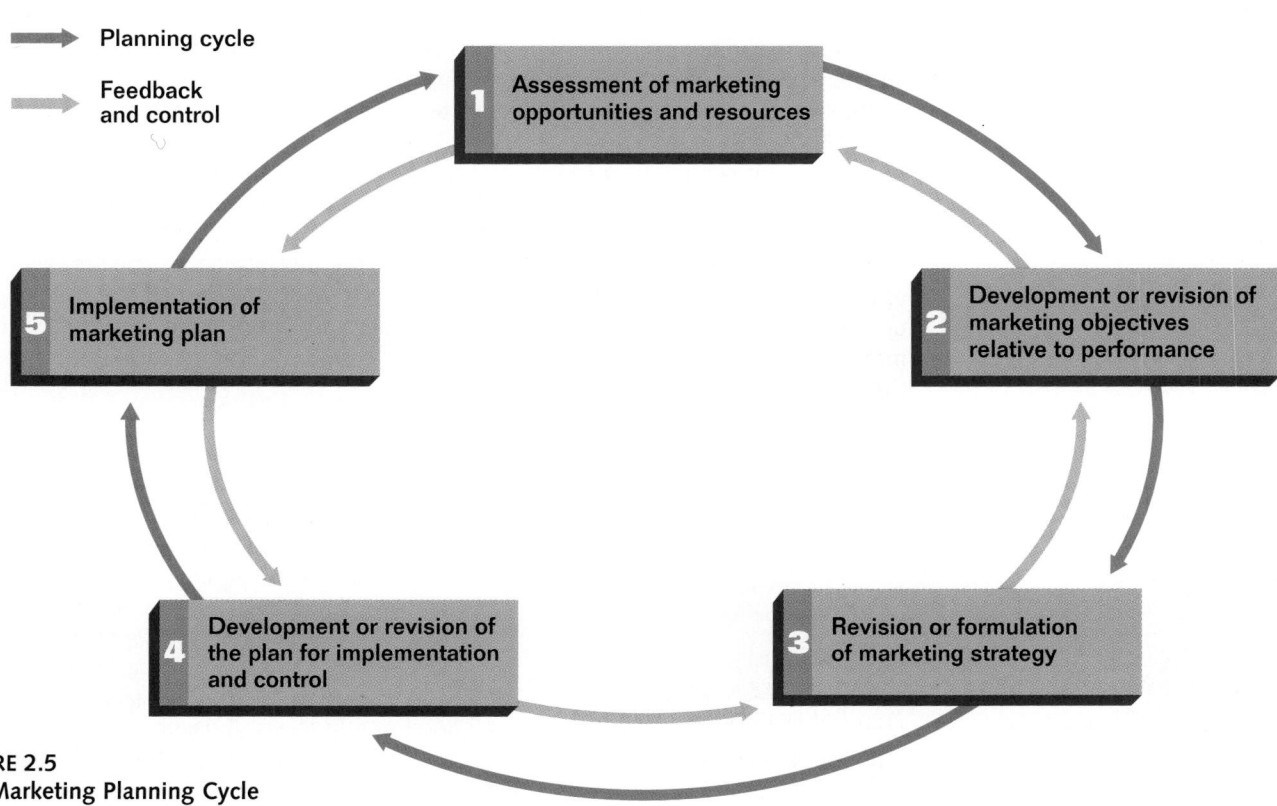

FIGURE 2.5
The Marketing Planning Cycle

Although planning provides numerous benefits, some managers do not use formal marketing plans because they spend almost all their time focusing on daily problems, many of which would be eliminated by adequate planning. However, planning is becoming more important as marketing managers realize that planning is necessary to develop, coordinate, and control marketing activities effectively and efficiently. When formulating a marketing plan, a new enterprise or a firm with a new product does not have current performance to evaluate or an existing plan to revise. Therefore, its marketing planning centers on analyzing available resources and options to assess opportunities. Managers can then develop marketing objectives and a strategy for achieving them. In addition, many firms recognize the need to include information systems in their plans so they can have continuous feedback and keep their marketing activities oriented toward objectives. When Barnes & Noble developed a website for selling books online, its information system had to provide adequate feedback on opportunities, the resources needed for entering the online market, and the impact of online sales on store sales. (Information systems are discussed in Chapter 6.)

Components of the Marketing Plan

Organizations use many different formats when devising marketing plans. Plans may be written for strategic business units, product lines, individual products or brands, or specific markets. Most plans share some common ground, however, by including many of the same components (see Table 2.2). In the following sections, we consider the major parts of a typical marketing plan and the purpose each part serves.

Executive Summary. The executive summary is a synopsis (often just one or two pages) of the entire marketing plan. It includes an introduction, an explanation of the major aspects of the plan, and a statement about the costs of implementing the plan. The executive summary does not provide detailed information; rather, it gives an overview of the plan so that readers can identify key issues pertaining to their roles in the planning and implementation process.[34]

The executive summary is one of the most important parts of the marketing plan because it is often furnished to people outside the organization. It may, for example, be useful to the organization's financial institution when that party becomes involved in the financial aspects of the marketing plan. Suppliers or investors who play a pivotal role in implementing the plan may also be given access to the executive summary.

Environmental Analysis. The environmental analysis supplies information about the company's current situation with respect to the marketing environment, the target market, and the firm's current objectives and performance. The first section of

Table 2.2	Components of the Marketing Plan	
I. Executive Summary		V. Marketing Strategies
		A. Target market
II. Environmental Analysis		B. Marketing mix
A. The marketing environment		
B. Target market(s)		VI. Marketing Implementation
C. Current marketing objectives and performance		A. Marketing organization
		B. Activities and responsibilities
III. SWOT Analysis		C. Implementation timetable
A. Strengths and weaknesses		
B. Opportunities and threats		VII. Evaluation and Control
		A. Performance standards
IV. Marketing Objectives		B. Financial controls
		C. Monitoring procedures (audits)

DEAR MR. FORGETFUL:
YOU MIGHT NEED
THE PRODUCT FOR
THE PRODUCT DEMO.

Anna (your assistant)
Palo Alto, CA

UNITED STATES
POSTAL SERVICE

Express Mail Service & Priority Mail Service:
☑ fleets of planes   ☑ dedicated cargo space   ☑ call 1-800-222-1811 for pickup

The U.S. Postal Service is everywhere so you can be anywhere"
www.usps.com

Environmental Analysis: Assessing the Target Market's Needs
The United States Postal Service promotes its services to target business customers.

the environmental analysis is an assessment of all the external environmental factors—competitive, economic, political, legal and regulatory, technological, and sociocultural—that can affect marketing activities. (We examine the complexities and interactions of these factors in Chapter 3.) In addition, this section should include information about such internal environmental matters as the firm's current culture, the availability and deployment of human resources, the age and capacity of equipment or technology, and the availability of financial resources.

In the second section of the environmental analysis, the organization should examine the current status of its target markets. This section assesses the current needs of each target market, anticipated changes in those needs, and how well the organization's products are meeting those needs. In assessing its target markets, the firm should try to understand all relevant customer behavior variables and product usage statistics. Knowing, for example, that about 90 percent of children's product requests to a parent are by brand name helps marketers to better understand the potential influence of children on their parents' spending.[35] Marketing-oriented organizations should know their customers well enough to have access to this type of information. Organizations that do not have this information may have to conduct marketing research to fully understand their current target markets.

The final aspect of environmental analysis is a critical evaluation of the firm's current marketing objectives and performance. All organizations should periodically examine their marketing objectives to ensure these objectives remain consistent with the changing marketing environment. This analysis yields important input for later stages of the marketing plan. The organization should also evaluate its current performance with respect to changes in the environment and the target markets. Poor or declining performance may be the result of holding on to marketing objectives that fail to consider the current realities of the marketing environment. Apple Computer, for example, experienced a major decline in its market share for personal computers when it established objectives that were not realistic in the dynamic environment of the computer industry. Consumer acceptance of Microsoft's Windows operating system advanced rapidly, and this competitive force made Apple's objective of increasing the market for its own operating system impossible to fulfill. Apple's objectives for the iMac computer may prove more realistic.

The information needed for environmental analysis is obtained from both the internal and external environments, usually through the firm's marketing information system. However, if the required information is not available, it may have to be collected through marketing research. The environmental analysis phase is one of the most difficult parts of the marketing plan and often illustrates the need for an ongoing effort to collect and organize environmental data. Having this sort of information readily available makes the other parts of the marketing plan easier to develop.

SWOT analysis Assessment of an organization's strengths, weaknesses, opportunities, and threats

strengths Competitive advantages or core competencies that give a firm an advantage in meeting the needs of its target markets

weaknesses Any limitations a company faces in developing or implementing a marketing strategy

opportunities Favorable conditions in the environment that could produce rewards for an organization if acted on properly

threats Conditions or barriers that may prevent a firm from reaching its objectives

SWOT Analysis. The **SWOT analysis** assesses an organization's strengths, weaknesses, opportunities, and threats (SWOT). These factors are derived from the environmental analysis in the preceding portion of the marketing plan.

The analysis of strengths and weaknesses focuses on internal factors that give an organization certain advantages and disadvantages in meeting the needs of its target markets. **Strengths** refer to competitive advantages or core competencies that give the firm an advantage in meeting the needs of its target markets. Any analysis of company strengths should be customer focused because strengths are meaningful only when they assist the firm in meeting customer needs. For instance, a company may possess a highly trained and capable sales force, which would be considered a major strength in many industries. However, if product quality is poor relative to competitors', a good sales force may do little to help satisfy customer needs. Strengths are usually related to core competencies that provide a competitive advantage. John Deere, for example, promotes its service, experience, and reputation in the farm equipment business to emphasize the craftsmanship it uses in its lawn tractors and mowers for city dwellers.

Weaknesses refer to any limitations a company faces in developing or implementing a marketing strategy. PepsiCo, with fewer resources than Coca-Cola Company, has found it difficult to expand in the fountain market, which includes restaurants, theaters, and sports arenas, where Coca-Cola holds two-thirds of the market.[36] Weaknesses should also be examined from a customer perspective because customers often perceive weaknesses that a company cannot see. Apple Computer's operating system became a weakness when the computer industry went to a Windows standard, but the strong loyalty of Apple's customers remains a key strength.

Taking a customer-oriented approach toward the analysis of strengths and weaknesses does not mean strengths and weaknesses that are not customer oriented should be forgotten. Rather, it suggests that all firms should tie their strengths and weaknesses to customer requirements. Only those strengths that relate to satisfying customers should be considered true competitive advantages. Likewise, weaknesses that directly affect customer satisfaction should be considered competitive disadvantages.

The second section of the SWOT analysis examines the opportunities and threats that exist in the environment. Both opportunities and threats exist independently of the firm. They can, however, greatly affect its operations. The way to differentiate a strength or weakness from an opportunity or threat is to ask: Would this issue exist if the company did not exist? If the answer is yes, the issue should be considered external to the firm.[37] Because opportunities and threats are external to the firm, they represent issues to be considered by all organizations, even those that do not compete with the firm.

Opportunities refer to favorable conditions in the environment that could produce rewards for the organization if acted on properly. That is, opportunities are situations that exist but must be acted on if the firm is to benefit from them. Amazon.com, for example, acted quickly when new technology made it possible to sell books on the Internet. **Threats,** on the other hand, refer to conditions or barriers that may prevent the firm from reaching its objectives. For instance, Barnes & Noble's launching of a website to sell books represented a threat to Amazon.com. Like opportunities, threats must be acted on to prevent them from limiting the organization's capabilities.

Opportunities and threats can stem from many sources within the environment. When a competitor's introduction of a new product threatens a firm, a defensive strategy may be required. If the firm can develop and launch a new product that meets or exceeds the competition's offering, it can transform the threat into an opportunity.[38]

Figure 2.6 depicts a four-cell SWOT matrix that can help managers in the planning process. When an organization matches internal strengths to external opportunities, it creates competitive advantages in meeting the needs of its customers. In addition, an organization should act to convert internal weaknesses into strengths and external

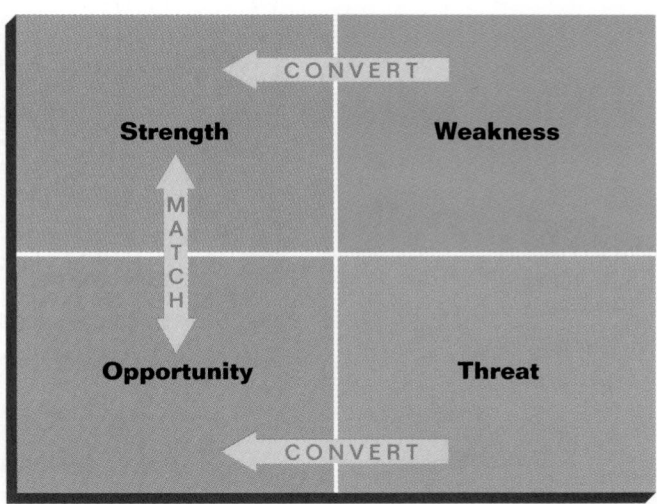

FIGURE 2.6
The Four-Cell SWOT Matrix
Source: Adapted from Nigel F. Piercy, *Market-Led Strategic Change.* Copyright
© 1992 Butterworth-Heinemann Ltd., p. 371. Used with permission.

threats into opportunities. General Motors' Saturn, for instance, converted the threats posed by sports-utility vehicles from Ford and other carmakers into opportunities when it introduced the Vue, a compact SUV. A firm that lacks adequate marketing skills can hire outside consultants to help convert a weakness into a strength.

The SWOT analysis framework has gained widespread acceptance because it is both a simple and powerful tool for marketing strategy development. However, like any planning tool, SWOT is only as good as the information it contains. Thorough marketing research and accurate information systems are essential for the SWOT analysis to identify key issues in the environment.

Marketing Objectives.   This section of the marketing plan delineates the marketing objectives that underlie the plan. A **marketing objective** states what is to be accomplished through marketing activities. A marketing objective of Ritz Carlton Hotels, for example, is to have 92 percent of its customers indicate they had a memorable experience at the hotel.[39] Marketing objectives should be based on a careful study of the SWOT analysis and should relate to matching strengths to opportunities and/or the conversion of weaknesses or threats. These objectives can be stated in terms of product introduction, product improvement or innovation, sales volume, profitability, market share, pricing, distribution, advertising, or employee training activities.

Marketing objectives should possess certain characteristics. First, a marketing objective should be expressed in clear, simple terms so that all marketing personnel understand exactly what they are trying to achieve. Second, an objective should be written so that it can be measured accurately. This allows the organization to determine if and when the objective has been achieved. If an objective is to increase market share by 10 percent, the firm should be able to measure market share changes accurately. Third, a marketing objective should specify a time frame for its accomplishment. A firm that sets an objective of introducing a new product should state the time period in which to do this. Finally, a marketing objective should be consistent with both business-unit and corporate strategy. This ensures that the firm's mission is carried out at all levels of the organization. General Motors, for example, may have an overall marketing objective of maintaining a 31 percent share of the U.S. auto market. To achieve this objective, some GM divisions may have to increase market share while the shares of other divisions decline.

marketing objective
A statement of what is to be accomplished through marketing activities

sustainable competitive advantage   An advantage that the competition cannot copy

Marketing Strategies.   This section of the marketing plan outlines how the firm will achieve its marketing objectives. As already noted, marketing strategy consists of target market selection and the development of a marketing mix. In a broader sense, however, marketing strategy refers to how the firm will manage its relationships with customers so that it gains an advantage over the competition.

Target market selection is the first stage of this process. The marketing plan should clearly define target markets in terms of demographics, geography, psychological profiles, product usage, and so on. This step is crucial because to develop a marketing mix that can satisfy customer needs, a marketer must understand those needs. In developing a marketing mix, the firm should determine how the elements of the mix—product, distribution, promotion, and price—will work together to satisfy the needs of the target market.

It is at the marketing mix level that a firm details how it will achieve a competitive advantage. To gain an advantage, the firm must do something better than its competition. In other words, its products must be of higher quality, its prices must be consistent with the level of quality (value), its distribution methods must be efficient and cost as little as possible, and its promotion must be more effective than the competition's. It is also important that the firm attempt to make these advantages sustainable. A **sustainable competitive advantage** is one that the competition cannot copy. Wal-Mart, for example, maintains a sustainable competitive advantage over Kmart because of its very efficient and low-cost distribution system. This advantage allows Wal-Mart to offer lower prices. However, Kmart has a sustainable advantage over Wal-Mart in terms of store locations. Since Kmart stores were in most urban areas before Wal-Mart began moving from rural areas, they are typically in better and more convenient locations. In fact, location is often referred to as the most sustainable competitive advantage because it is almost impossible for competitors to change or copy it.

Marketing Implementation.   This section of the marketing plan outlines how the marketing strategies will be implemented by answering many of the questions about the marketing activities outlined in the preceding section: What specific actions will be taken? How will these activities be performed? When will these activities be performed? Who is responsible for the completion of these activities? How much will these activities cost? Without a workable plan for implementation, the success of the marketing strategy is in jeopardy. For this reason, the implementation phase of the marketing plan is as important as any previous phase. Building Customer Relationships looks at how one organization implemented a new marketing strategy.

BUILDING CUSTOMER RELATIONSHIPS

Pro Bowling Goes High-Tech

In 1999, the Professional Bowlers Association (PBA) was $3 million in debt and rapidly losing members. Although the league had no marketing plan and ran few promotions, its program consistently ranked among the top ten television shows on cable and outperformed programming by the National Hockey League and National Women's Basketball Association. Its website, though rather bland, attracted a million visitors a month. Despite the popularity of bowling, the association did not generate enough money to support its operations; it was even borrowing funds from the pension plan to meet payroll expenses. Just when the nonprofit thought it was finished, three high-tech knights came to the rescue.

Chris Peters, former vice president of development for Microsoft Office, initiated a deal in 2000 to purchase the league for about $5 million. His partners in the deal included RealNetworks CEO Rob Glaser and Starwave CEO Mike Slade. Beyond their interest in the sport, the trio recognized a potential for profit. The new owners immediately set about making changes to revitalize the league. They changed its status from nonprofit to for-profit and officially changed its name to PBA to be consistent with other major sports associations. They then began devising a marketing strategy to change the way people look at bowling.

In planning a marketing strategy, they determined that two factors would be essential to the PBA's success. First, the PBA had to help fans understand the sport. Although bowling has been played for a century, many viewers don't understand the game's subtleties. Thus, the PBA will not only provide information about bowling's rules and regulations but will also educate fans about the fine points of the game, such as how hand position, amount of oil in the lane, or ball placement in the lane can affect the way the ball curves or pins fall. Second, the PBA had to get fans to be involved with and care about the players. Many Americans stereotype bowlers as overweight, beer-guzzling males in bowling shirts; now the PBA is making efforts to show that many bowlers are physically fit, subdued, and introverted, much like many tennis players. The association's new owners also upped the stakes: players will compete for $4.3 million in prize money, up from $1.8 million. Changing the format to pit the player with the highest individual game score against the traditional finalists with the highest averages will help develop new rivalries. Given its new owners' association with high-tech firms, it's no surprise that the PBA plans to use technology to implement these strategies. The organization's website (www.pba.com) provides a wealth of information, including stats on each player. Viewers can even watch tournaments online: bowling is the first sport to be webcast.

After implementing these changes, the PBA won a multiyear contract with Miller High Life and Miller Lite, the league's first sponsorship since its acquisition by the high-tech team. With its new strategy, the PBA is demonstrating that it can attract and retain viewers in the United States as well as in Europe and Asia, where bowling is becoming increasingly popular. By combining the technological strengths of its new owners with a well-implemented marketing strategy, the PBA is set to roll a perfect strike.

Because implementation is so important, we devote all of Chapter 22 to issues in marketing implementation. In that discussion, we examine how the organization of the marketing function affects the implementation of marketing strategy. We also consider the importance of employees to marketing implementation. When discussing implementation, it is important to remember this fact: organizations do not implement strategies; people do. Thus, Chapter 22 addresses employee motivation, communication, and training as key factors in the implementation of marketing strategy.

Evaluation and Control.   The final section of the marketing plan details how the results of the plan will be measured and evaluated. The control phase of this section includes the actions to take to reduce the differences between planned and actual performance. First, standards for assessing the actual performance need to be established. These standards can be based on increases in sales volume, profitability, or market share. They can even be advertising standards, such as brand name recognition or recall. The second part of the control process deals with the financial data that can be used to evaluate whether the marketing plan is working. If the marketing plan is not living up to expectations, the firm can use a number of monitoring procedures to pinpoint potential causes for the discrepancies. One such procedure is the marketing audit, which can help isolate weaknesses in the marketing plan and recommend actions to help improve performance. Because evaluation and control procedures are directly related to marketing implementation, they are discussed in detail in Chapter 22.

Using the Marketing Plan

The creation and implementation of a complete marketing plan will allow the organization to achieve not only its marketing objectives but its business-unit and corporate goals as well. However, a marketing plan is only as good as the information it contains and the effort and creativity that went into its development. Thus, the importance of having a good marketing information system cannot be overstated. Equally important is the role of managerial judgment throughout the strategic planning process. Managers should always weigh any information against its accuracy and their own intuition when making marketing decisions. To succeed, a company must have a plan that is closely followed yet flexible enough to allow for adjustments to reflect changes in the marketing environment.[40]

Note that the marketing plan outline in Table 2.2 should serve as a structure for the written document rather than as a series of sequential planning steps. In practice, many of the elements in the outline are decided on simultaneously. For example, the actual development of marketing strategies should take into account how those strategies will be implemented. This is one of the realities of marketing planning discussed in Chapter 22. It is also important to realize that most organizations have their own unique format and terminology to describe the marketing plan. For that reason, the outline in Table 2.2 should not be regarded as the only correct format for the creation of a marketing plan. Every marketing plan is and should be unique to the organization for which it was created.

While the creation of a marketing plan is an important milestone in strategic planning, it is by no means the final step. Some of the information used to create the plan may turn out to be inaccurate. Many of the managerial assumptions or projections used in the analysis often turn out differently when the plan is put into practice. These realities underscore the need to make the marketing plan flexible enough to be adjusted on a daily basis. They also highlight the need for good environmental analysis, to which we turn in the next chapter.

Summary

Through the process of strategic planning, a firm establishes an organizational mission and goals, corporate strategy, marketing objectives, marketing strategy, and, finally, a marketing plan. To achieve its marketing objectives, an organization must develop a marketing strategy, which includes identifying and analyzing a target market and developing a marketing mix that meets the needs of customers in that market. The strategic planning process ultimately yields the framework for a marketing plan, a written document that specifies the activities to be performed to implement and control the organization's marketing activities.

The strategic planning process begins with an analysis of the marketing environment, including economic, competitive, political, legal and regulatory, sociocultural, and technological forces. These forces can affect the resources a firm can acquire and create favorable opportunities. Resources include core competencies, things a firm does extremely well—sometimes so well that it gives the company an advantage over its competition. When the right combination of circumstances and timing permits an organization to take action to reach a particular target market, a market opportunity exists. Strategic windows are temporary periods of optimal fit between the key requirements of a market and the particular capabilities of a firm competing in that market. When a company matches a core competency to opportunities it has discovered in the marketplace, it gains a competitive advantage.

The goals of any organization should derive from its mission statement, a long-term view, or vision, of what the organization wants to become. The mission statement answers two questions: Who are our customers? and What is our core competency? A well-formulated mission statement gives an organization a clear purpose and direction, distinguishes it from competitors, provides direction for strategic planning, and fosters an organizationwide focus on customers. An organization's short- and long-term goals, which focus on the end results sought, guide the remainder of its planning efforts.

Corporate strategy determines the means for utilizing resources in the functional areas of production, finance, research and development, human resources, and marketing to reach the firm's goals. Corporate strategy planners are concerned with broad issues such as corporate culture, competition, differentiation, diversification, interrelationships among business units, and environmental and social issues.

The next step in strategic planning is a consideration of strategic business units (SBUs), which are divisions, product lines, or other profit centers within the parent company. A market is a group of individuals and/or organizations that have needs for products in a product class and have the ability, willingness, and authority to purchase those products. The percentage of a market that actually buys a specific product from a particular company is referred to as that product's market share. The market-growth/market-share matrix is a strategic planning tool that integrates a firm's products or SBUs into a single, overall matrix and evaluates them to determine appropriate strategies for individual products and overall portfolio strategies. Strategies for intensive growth, which occurs when current products and current markets have the potential for increasing sales, include market penetration, market development, and product development. Diversified growth occurs when new products are developed to be sold in new markets.

While corporate, business-unit, and marketing strategies all overlap to some extent, the marketing strategy is the most detailed and specific of the three. Marketing strategy is typically composed of two elements: the selection of a target market and the creation of a marketing mix that will satisfy the needs of the chosen target market. Selecting an appropriate target market may be the most important decision a company makes in the planning process because it serves as the basis for creating a marketing mix to satisfy the needs of that market. Marketing mix decisions should be consistent with business-unit and corporate strategies; they should also be flexible enough to respond to changes in market conditions, competition, and customer needs. Different elements of the marketing mix can be changed to accommodate different marketing strategies.

Marketing planning is the systematic process of assessing marketing opportunities and resources, determining marketing objectives, defining marketing strategies, and establishing guidelines for implementation and control of the marketing program. The outcome of marketing planning is the marketing plan, which outlines and explains all the activities necessary to implement marketing strategies. A firm should have a plan for each marketing strategy it develops. The marketing plan fosters internal communication among employees, assigns responsibilities and schedules, presents objectives, specifies how resources are to be allocated to achieve objectives, and helps marketing managers monitor and evaluate the performance of a marketing strategy.

Most marketing plans include many of the same components. The executive summary is a synopsis of the entire plan. The environmental analysis supplies information about the company's current situation with respect to the marketing environment, the target market, and the firm's current objectives and performance. The SWOT analysis assesses an organization's strengths, weaknesses, opportunities, and threats. The marketing objectives section states what is to be accomplished through marketing activities. The section on marketing strategies outlines how the firm will achieve its marketing objectives and achieve a competitive advantage, preferably a sustainable one that the competition cannot copy. The implementation section specifies how marketing strategies will be carried out by answering many of the questions about the marketing activities outlined in the marketing strategies section. Most marketing plans also detail how the results of the plan will be measured and evaluated.

A marketing plan is only as good as the information it contains and the effort and creativity that went into its development. Therefore, good marketing information systems and managerial judgment are important factors in creating a complete and workable marketing plan. Every marketing plan should be unique to the organization for which it is created. It should also be flexible enough to be adjusted on a daily basis.

Important Terms

Strategic planning
Marketing strategy
Marketing plan
Core competencies
Market opportunity
Strategic window
Competitive advantage
Mission statement
Corporate strategy
Strategic business unit (SBU)
Market
Market share
Market-growth/market-share matrix
Intensive growth
Diversified growth
Marketing planning
SWOT analysis
Strengths
Weaknesses
Opportunities
Threats
Marketing objective
Sustainable competitive advantage

Discussion and Review Questions

1. Identify the major components of strategic planning, and explain how they are interrelated.
2. What are the two major parts of a marketing strategy?
3. What are some issues to consider in analyzing a firm's resources and opportunities? How do these issues affect marketing objectives and marketing strategy?
4. Describe the benefits of a good mission statement. What role does the mission statement play in strategic planning?
5. Explain how an organization can create a competitive advantage at the corporate, business-unit, and marketing strategy levels.

6. Give examples of intensive and diversified growth strategies being used by today's firms. Which strategy appears to be the most effective in today's environment? Why?
7. Describe the role of the marketing plan in developing marketing strategy. How important is the SWOT analysis to the marketing planning process?
8. How should organizations set marketing objectives?
9. Refer to question 5. How can an organization make its competitive advantages sustainable over time? How difficult is it to create sustainable competitive advantages?
10. What benefits do marketing managers gain from planning? Is planning necessary for long-run survival? Why or why not?

Application Questions

1. Organizational goals are necessary for a firm to achieve success in a dynamic marketing environment. Contact three organizations that appear to be successful. Talk with one of the managers or executives in the company, and ask if he or she would share with you the company's mission statement or organizational goals. Obtain as much information as possible about the statement and the organizational goals. Discuss how the statement matches the criteria outlined in the text.
2. Short-term goals help a firm reach its long-term goals. Assume you own a new family-style restaurant that will open for business in the coming year. Formulate a long-term goal for the company, and then develop short-term goals that will assist you in achieving the long-term goal.
3. Amazon.com identified an opportunity to capitalize on a desire of many consumers to shop at home. This strategic window gave Amazon.com a very competitive position in a new market. Consider the opportunities that may be present in your city, region, or the United States as a whole. Identify a strategic window, and discuss how a company could take advantage of this opportunity. What kind of core competencies are necessary?
4. The selection of a target market may be one of the most important decisions a marketer makes. McDonald's has been very successful in identifying and satisfying the needs of its target market. Identify the target market of each of the following companies:
   a. American Express
   b. Nike
   c. Walt Disney
   d. CompuServe

Internet Exercise & Resources

Sony: The Internet and Corporate Strategy

Internet analysts have praised Sony's website as one of the best organized and most informative on the Internet. See why by accessing

www.sony.com

1. Based on the information provided at the website, describe Sony's strategic business units.

2. Based on your existing knowledge of Sony as an innovative leader in the consumer electronics industry, describe the company's primary competitive advantage. How does Sony's online home page support this competitive advantage?

3. Assess the quality and effectiveness of Sony's home page. Specifically, perform a preliminary SWOT analysis comparing Sony's home page with other high-quality web pages you have visited.

VIDEO CASE 2.1

Buzzsaw.com: Building Strategically on the Web

Construction projects are collaborative efforts among property owners, architects, engineers, general contractors, and subcontractors. However, with hundreds of people working in disparate teams, such projects can be plagued by miscommunications and mistakes that result in costly overruns, lost time, and other difficulties. A group of construction engineers and software industry leaders came up with a vision to address these issues by using the World Wide Web to manage building projects. Their vision became Buzzsaw.com, a website that functions as a virtual storehouse and conference room where everyone involved in a construction project can "meet" and view one another's work. By collaborating online, building professionals can reduce project cycle times and costs, thereby boosting profits.

Through Buzzsaw.com, project team members can monitor every step in the construction process, often without ever leaving their desks. They can transmit, store, and share blueprints, forms, change orders, and loan and legal documents. For example, Buzzsaw's Project Folders enable team members to post drawings and discuss them online with other members of the project team. General contractors can use Bid Manager to invite qualified subcontractors to bid on specific jobs. The site's Construction Manager consolidates work orders and helps team

members address design and building problems that inevitably arise on any project. A recently introduced application, Plans and Specs, allows architects and contractors to download blueprints and plans to their own computers, make real-time design changes, and communicate these changes with others as the project takes shape.

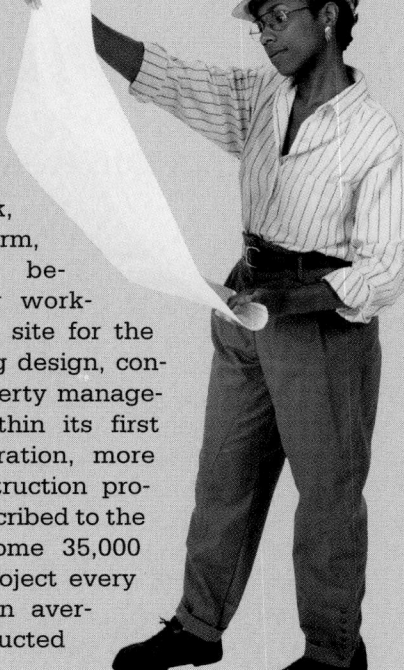

Initially spun off from Autodesk, Inc., a software firm, Buzzsaw.com has become the premier workspace collaboration site for the $3.9 trillion building design, construction, and property management industry. Within its first two years of operation, more than 125,000 construction professionals had subscribed to the site to manage some 35,000 projects—a new project every twenty minutes, on average. A survey conducted by Zwieg White & Associates found that 45 percent of industry professionals had used Buzzsaw's project management and collaboration services; its closest competitor had attracted just 16 percent of the companies surveyed. Buzzsaw captured such a large share of the market by offering a secure online workspace for a highly fragmented process, allowing project teams to share information quickly while simultaneously increasing profitability. Among the firms that have benefited from the service are The Walt Disney Company, Dow Corning, and Toys "R" Us.

For Toys "R" Us, Buzzsaw helped manage the conversion of two former Times Square (New York) theaters into a 10,000-square-foot flagship store, complete with a 30-foot-tall mechanical dinosaur, a 50-foot-tall ferris wheel, and a 2-story Barbie townhouse. Through Buzzsaw, Tracy LeBlanc, the project's senior architectural manager, was able to monitor the project from his office 20 miles away in Paramus, New Jersey. LeBlanc and the project's architects, consultants, and contractors shared and updated documents electronically. They also observed the project's progress through digital photographs uploaded weekly as well as via webcams LeBlanc installed inside and outside the construction site. In previous projects LeBlanc managed, construction team members could share documents only by printing out each new draft and sending it to others via messenger; ensuring that everyone worked from the most recent set of plans was a challenge in itself. Toys "R" Us paid $2,000 a month to subscribe to the service, which LeBlanc estimated saved $100,000 in messenger, printing, and photo-processing charges in one year alone.

When Buzzsaw.com was spun off from Autodesk, Inc., as an independent company in 1999, it was funded by Autodesk, Morgan Stanley Dean Witter and Real Estate Equity Groups, Bank of America, and Impact Venture Partners. Just two years later, however, Autodesk announced that it had reacquired Buzzsaw for $15 million because of its ability to extend its business into new markets. Moreover, executives expected Buzzsaw to become profitable by the end of its second year, at a time when many dot-com companies were failing and only a few were profitable.[41]

QUESTIONS FOR DISCUSSION

1. Describe the marketing strategy Buzzsaw.com used to successfully serve building industry professionals.
2. How has Buzzsaw succeeded as an online facilitator of communications among members of construction project teams while so many Internet-based companies have failed?
3. What changes in Buzzsaw's marketing strategy might be appropriate for continued success under Autodesk?

CASE 2.2
Saturn: "A Different Kind of Company. A Different Kind of Car"

In 1985, General Motors (GM) began a grand experiment when it launched Saturn as a separate, independent subsidiary with an investment of $5 billion. Former GM chairman Robert B. Smith envisioned Saturn as a "laboratory" to find better ways to manufacture and market cars. GM's share of the U.S. passenger car market had been declining since 1985, falling 11 points to 33 percent. Moreover, a J. D. Power & Associates study had indicated that 42 percent of new-car shoppers didn't even consider a GM car. Saturn's mission, therefore, was to sell 80 percent of its cars to drivers who otherwise would not have bought a GM car. GM believed that Saturn was the key to its long-term competitiveness and survival.

Saturn managers spent years developing the new company from scratch. They viewed partnerships as a key element of Saturn's future relationships between management and labor and between company and supplier, with everyone sharing the risks and rewards. To truly separate Saturn from the traditional Detroit auto-building mindset, GM built Saturn in Spring Hill, Tennessee. It also provided the latest technology, manufacturing methods, pacesetting labor relations, and participatory management ideas. Saturn represented the largest single construction project in the history of GM. While other GM plants merely assemble parts, Saturn manufactures almost everything, including power trains, moldings, and instrument panels, at the Spring Hill facility.

From the beginning, the United Auto Workers Union (UAW) and General Motors both wanted Saturn to succeed and, in a partnership unprecedented in the auto industry, the two entities joined hands and decided to work side by side. As a result, all decisions at Saturn are reached by consensus. UAW members, for example, helped select Saturn "partners" such as suppliers, dealers, and even the advertising agency. All employees, blue and white collar alike, must be approved by both union members and management. New employees at Saturn's Tennessee plant also face extensive training to learn how to work in teams and keep track of costs.

The first Saturns arrived at dealerships in 1990. Initially Saturn offered just four models: the SC1 and SC2 coupes and the SL1 and SL2 sedans. An entry-level coupe (the SL) and the SW1 and SW2 station wagons were introduced in 1993. These were followed by the EV1, a limited-production electric car, in 1996 and innovative three-door versions of the SC1 and SC2 in 1998. Saturn rolled out its first mid-size sedan and station wagon, the L-Series, in 1999. The next addition to the Saturn line, the VUE sport-utility vehicle, arrived at dealerships in late 2001. Saturn's fundamental philosophy required the cars to have a higher level of quality than other General Motors vehicles.

The story of Saturn is inseparable from its advertising history because Saturn involved all marketing entities, from the advertising agency to the dealers, in every decision. After a lengthy search and review process, Saturn managers—with input from a panel of company executives, dealers, and UAW representatives—chose San Francisco's Hal Riney & Partners to handle what would become a more than $100 million advertising account. Riney contributed to many Saturn decisions. Keeping in mind the target market of college-educated men and women ages 25 to 49, the agency adopted a "straight-talk," people-oriented philosophy that would be applied to many aspects of the Saturn brand. For example, all Saturn retail stores would be called "Saturn of (Geographic Location)" to stress the Saturn name rather than the dealer's. Car models were given simple names, and even vehicle color descriptions were kept simple—"red" rather than "raspberry red," for example. Riney applied the people-oriented philosophy in advertising by stressing Saturn the company rather than the car, with the tag line "A different kind of company. A different kind of car." The first commercials highlighted the Spring Hill heartland and Saturn employees. Later ads featured stories of Saturn customers, focusing on buyers' lifestyles and playing up product themes that baby boomers hold dear, such as safety, utility, and value. One commercial

highlighted a recall order Saturn issued to fix a seat problem and showed a Saturn representative traveling to Alaska to fix a customer's car. The result of Riney's folksy, straight-talk campaign was a sharply focused brand image for Saturn.

With marketing and distribution expenses accounting for 30 to 35 percent of a new car's cost, Saturn planned its distribution very carefully. The company gives dealers large territories so that each competes with rival brands rather than with one another. Saturn generally has only one dealership in a metropolitan area. The first dealerships were set up in areas with high import-car sales, and most were located on the East and West coasts to avoid cannibalizing sales of other GM cars. In addition, Saturn chose dealers that know how to appeal to import-car buyers. Most dealers have salespeople working in teams and avoid high-pressure sales techniques. Salespeople usually split commissions and cooperate to provide a relaxed, inviting showroom environment, allowing customers to browse and offering service and advice only as customers seek them.

The revolutionary ideas employed at Saturn continued with its pricing strategy. Initially base prices ranged from $9,000 to $12,000, competitive with import-car prices. Saturn's prices remain very competitive today, ranging from $11,000 for a basic SL sedan to $23,000 for an LW300 station wagon. At most dealers, there are no rebates or promotions and no haggling over price. Although Saturn cannot set prices or control the one-price policy because of legal considerations, dealers have found the one-price policy very appealing because of tight profit margins and the high-integrity sales approach required by Saturn's marketing strategy. Potential buyers can also access the iShowroom, an interactive buying center, from Saturn's web page (www.saturn.com) to obtain pricing information for all models, as well as "build" their own Saturn, starting with a base car and adding options.

The marketing mix developed by Saturn was a resounding success in the first half of the 1990s. Initial sales of Saturn cars were tremendous; however, the company encountered problems meeting demand, with many customers waiting more than six weeks for their automobiles. Saturn officials said part of the problem was due to the fact that they were unwilling to compromise on quality. Despite these problems, Saturn sold 170,495 cars in the 1992 model year, giving it a 2.1 percent share of the U.S. auto market and leapfrogging over Hyundai, Subaru, Volkswagen, and Mitsubishi. More important, Saturn ranked third in J. D. Power & Associates' measurement of new-car buyer satisfaction, a position the company maintained or exceeded behind only Lexus and Infiniti. May 1993 was the first profitable month for Saturn Corporation since its first car was produced.

Until 1996, Saturn was able to sustain sales momentum by developing a cultlike following with its down-home ads and successful picnics in Spring Hill to which all Saturn owners were invited. Since then, however, even high-profile customer events and Riney's creative advertising failed to overcome declining sales in the subcompact market. Overall sales peaked in 1994 at 286,000 vehicles, and sales have been declining ever since even though the industry has experienced record sales.

By the mid-1990s, people were questioning Saturn's decision to focus on small cars, leaving it vulnerable when demand shifted toward bigger vehicles, especially minivans, pickup trucks, and sport-utility vehicles. Some analysts wondered whether the company had missed an opportunity to capitalize on its success as a respected, high-quality, small-car manufacturer. Even Saturn workers, watching Honda and Toyota sell all the CR-Vs and RAV4s they could make, suggested in 1996 that the company should offer a small SUV. By the time Saturn launched the VUE in 2001, however, the SUV market had peaked under the threat of a weakening economy and rising gasoline prices.

Saturn's struggles in recent years cannot be blamed solely on leadership within the division. Although having General Motors, with its vast resources, as a corporate parent is a potential plus, by the late 1990s GM appeared to hesitate in its support of Saturn. Instead of strengthening the young Saturn brand, GM executives made heavy investments to revitalize the Oldsmobile and Cadillac brands. Not until 2000 did GM announced that it would invest $1.5 billion into Saturn for the development of new products. About $1 billion went into development and production of the VUE SUV and a new sedan. Another $500 million was invested in the Spring Hill plant to build a 450,000-square-foot facility to manufacture GM's new global four-cylinder engine.

Although Saturn's sales have been declining, it continues to have a devoted customer following and a strong reputation for quality. The company ranked first in J. D. Power & Associates 2000 and 2001 Sales Satisfaction Surveys, ahead of import luxury vehicles such as Lexus and Infiniti. As Saturn moves into its second decade of production, it faces the challenge of maintaining its identity and building on the unique marketing strategy it developed in its first decade while continuing to rely on the resources of its parent company.[42]

QUESTIONS FOR DISCUSSION

1. Have Saturn's strategic marketing planning efforts been successful? Why or why not?
2. What should Saturn do as competitors attempt to copy its unique brand image and pricing and dealer service policies?
3. Briefly describe the target market and marketing mix used by Saturn.

The Marketing Environment

3

OBJECTIVES

- To recognize the importance of environmental scanning and analysis
- To understand how competitive and economic factors affect organizations' ability to compete and customers' ability and willingness to buy products
- To identify the types of political forces in the marketing environment
- To understand how laws, government regulations, and self-regulatory agencies affect marketing activities
- To explore the effects of new technology on society and on marketing activities
- To analyze sociocultural issues that marketers must deal with as they make decisions

55

FedEx Moves with the Marketplace

Founded by Frederick W. Smith as Federal Express, FedEx Corporation pioneered the concept of overnight package delivery and launched a new industry in 1973. Indeed, when asked to think of global express services, most people immediately recall FedEx's purple-and-orange logo. However, the company faces intense competition from United Parcel Service, the U.S. Postal Service, and other companies that serve global customers desiring overnight delivery services.

To continue to provide the best customer service worldwide, FedEx recently reorganized its corporate operations into four independent operating companies. FedEx Ground Package system, formerly RPS, will focus on delivering small packages for the business-to-business and business-to-residential markets. FedEx Custom Critical will concentrate on time-critical shipments, while FedEx Global Logistics will provide integrated logistics, technology, and transportation solutions. FedEx Express, probably the best known of the divisions, will continue to emphasize global express delivery.

Despite its renown for three decades of strong customer service, FedEx continues to face new challenges. One issue involved the need to generate greater sales revenue to support the company's fleet of more than 660 planes, and particularly to minimize excessive idle time. To meet this challenge, the company turned to an unlikely source: a competitor. In 2001, FedEx entered into a two-part agreement with the U.S. Postal Service that will likely generate $6.3 billion in revenue for FedEx over seven years. One part of the deal requires that FedEx carry all of the postal service's express and priority mail between airports. The second part allows FedEx to place drop-off boxes in 10,000 post offices across the country, with an option for 38,000 more boxes if the first phase is successful. FedEx will not deliver U.S. mail, and the post office will not accept or deliver FedEx packages. Prior to the deal, the postal service had an arrangement with Emory Worldwide Airlines, which was deemed too costly because it required the postal service to pay for full airplane loads of shipments even when planes were not filled to capacity. With the FedEx deal, the postal service will pay only for the aircraft space it needs. By filling nearly thirty DC-10 aircraft a day, this business will minimize FedEx's unused aircraft capacity.

To continue to compete successfully against United Parcel Service and other firms, FedEx must continually evaluate its marketing environment and respond to changing conditions. Although it has traditionally viewed the U.S. Postal Service as a competitor, the two companies have formed an alliance to work together for their mutual benefit. This alliance should increase revenues and help both firms operate more efficiently, a major key in today's competitive global environment.[1]

Companies like FedEx and the U.S. Postal Service are modifying marketing strategies in response to customers' changing desires. Because recognizing and addressing such changes in the marketing environment are crucial to marketing success, we will focus on the forces that contribute to these changes in some detail.

This chapter explores the competitive, economic, political, legal and regulatory, technological, and sociocultural forces that constitute the marketing environment. First, we define the marketing environment and consider why it is critical to scan and analyze it. Next, we discuss the effects of competitive forces and explore the influence of general economic conditions: prosperity, recession, depression, and recovery. We also examine buying power and forces that influence consumers' willingness to spend. We then discuss the political forces that generate government actions affecting marketing activities and examine the effect of laws and regulatory agencies on these activities. After analyzing the major dimensions of the technological forces in the environment, we consider the impact of sociocultural forces on marketing efforts.

Examining and Responding to the Marketing Environment

The marketing environment consists of external forces that directly or indirectly influence an organization's acquisition of inputs (human, financial, and natural resources and raw materials, and information) and creation of outputs (goods, services, or ideas). As indicated in Chapter 1, the marketing environment includes six such forces: competitive, economic, political, legal and regulatory, technological, and sociocultural.

Whether fluctuating rapidly or slowly, environmental forces are always dynamic. Changes in the marketing environment create uncertainty, threats, and opportunities for marketers. Although the future is not very predictable, marketers try to predict what may happen. We can say with certainty that marketers continue to modify their marketing strategies and plans in response to dynamic environmental forces. Consider how technological changes have affected the products offered by computer companies and how the public's growing emphasis on health and fitness has influenced the products of clothing, food, exercise equipment, and health care companies. Marketing managers who fail to recognize changes in environmental forces leave their firms unprepared to capitalize on marketing opportunities or cope with threats created by changes in the environment. Monitoring the environment is crucial to an organization's survival and to the long-term achievement of its goals.

Environmental Scanning and Analysis

environmental scanning The process of collecting information about forces in the marketing environment

To monitor changes in the marketing environment effectively, marketers engage in environmental scanning and analysis. **Environmental scanning** is the process of collecting information about forces in the marketing environment. Scanning involves observation; secondary sources such as business, trade, government, and general-interest publications; and marketing research. The Internet has become a popular scanning tool, since it makes data more accessible and allows companies to gather needed information quickly. Environmental scanning gives companies an edge over competitors in taking advantage of current trends. However, simply gathering information about competitors and customers is not enough; companies must know *how* to use that information in the strategic planning process. Managers must be careful not to gather so much information that sheer volume makes analysis impossible.

environmental analysis The process of assessing and interpreting the information gathered through environmental scanning

Environmental analysis is the process of assessing and interpreting the information gathered through environmental scanning. A manager evaluates the information for accuracy, tries to resolve inconsistencies in the data, and, if warranted, assigns significance to the findings. By evaluating this information, the manager should be able to identify potential threats and opportunities linked to environmental changes. Understanding the current state of the marketing environment and recognizing threats and opportunities arising from changes within it help companies with strategic planning. In particular, it can help marketing managers assess the performance of current marketing efforts and develop future marketing strategies.

Responding to Environmental Forces

Marketing managers take two general approaches to environmental forces: accepting them as uncontrollable or attempting to influence and shape them.[2] An organization that views environmental forces as uncontrollable remains passive and reactive toward the environment. Instead of trying to influence forces in the environment, its marketing managers adjust current marketing strategies to environmental changes. They approach with caution market opportunities discovered through environmental scanning and analysis. On the other hand, marketing managers who believe that environmental forces can be shaped adopt a more proactive approach. For example, if a market is blocked by traditional environmental constraints, proactive marketing managers may apply economic, psychological, political, and promotional skills to gain access to and operate within it. Once they identify what is blocking a market opportunity, they assess the power of the various parties involved and develop strategies to overcome the obstructing environmental forces. Microsoft and Intel, for example, have responded to political, legal, and regulatory concerns about their power in the computer industry by communicating the value of their competitive approaches to various publics. The computer giants contend that their competitive success results in superior products for their customers. Global Marketing looks at an Indian firm's effort to respond to a changing marketing environment.

A proactive approach can be constructive and bring desired results. To exert influence on environmental forces, marketing managers seek to identify market oppor-

GLOBAL MARKETING

India 3.0

India, a country famous for its surplus of engineers, benefited from a booming American economy in the last decade. Fueled by the rapid growth of the Internet, many U.S. companies searching for competitive advantage chose to outsource their technology functions, often to Indian companies that could provide quality services at 40 percent of their cost in the United States. However, when the dot-com boom ended in the early 2000s, many American firms were forced to scale back operations, laying off employees and limiting outsource contracts. Many Indian high-tech companies, especially software firms, saw their stock prices plummet as much as 60 to 70 percent. But despite the downturn, many of these firms have survived and even thrived with triple-digit growth. One such company is Wipro Technologies, based in Bangalore. Under the leadership of Vivek Paul, Wipro morphed from a trader of vegetable and edible oils into one of India's largest software service providers. Wipro recently ranked 87th out of the top 100 global technology companies and 16th among the best software service and distribution companies. It aspires to be among the top ten global information technology (IT) companies by 2004.

To achieve its goal, Wipro must outperform competitors such as IBM Global Consulting, Electronic Data Services, PricewaterhouseCoopers, and Accenture. Wipro must keep several environmental factors under control to best these savvy competitors. First, it must monitor all competition, including U.S. firms desiring to enter the low-margin coding industry as well as new entrants from low-cost countries such as China, the Philippines, and Vietnam. Second, Wipro must find a way to reduce its dependence on short-term outsource contracts in favor of building long-term customer relationships. Third, the company must address a sudden shortage of local engineering and nonengineering professionals, which limits its ability to provide well-rounded consulting services without seeking expertise externally. Finally, Wipro, like many Indian companies, needs to diversify its revenue sources to minimize the effects of regional downturns such as that experienced in the United States in the early 2000s.

Wipro has adopted a three-step process to address these challenges. The first step involves building industry verticals, which are organizations that unite the talents of engineers with other business professionals in marketing, operations, management, and other functions. Next, the company must recruit professionals who meet its needs. Wipro expects to add 30,000 employees by 2004, and the firm plans to shift a number of employees abroad so they can be closer to the firm's customers. Finally, Wipro has shifted its focus to reduce its dependence on customers in the U.S., who accounted for 61 percent of its 2001 revenues. By scanning its environment and making necessary adjustments to its marketing strategies, Wipro has positioned itself to better compete in today's changing business world.

Responding to Environmental Forces
Honda produced the first gasoline-electric hybrid automobile, responding to consumer demand for more functional environment-friendly cars.

It's an environmental movement all by itself.

How many cars does it take to change the world? Just one, perhaps. Introducing the Honda Insight. It's America's first gasoline-electric hybrid automobile.

Nothing short of an engineering breakthrough, the new Insight achieves an astounding 68 miles per gallon on the highway, 61 miles per gallon in the city, and a phenomenal 700-mile range on one tank of fuel. How? Simply by combining an efficient three-cylinder gasoline engine with an electric motor that's powered by nickel-metal hydride batteries which never need to be plugged in. Then add a lightweight body, and a world-class aerodynamic design, and you have the ultra-low-emission Insight. It's the result of years of research and development into lighter, more fuel-efficient, cleaner cars. In other words, technology with a conscience. Then again, what else would you expect from a car powered by Honda?

HONDA
The power of dreams.

tunities or to extract greater benefits relative to costs from existing market opportunities. For example, a firm losing sales to competitors with lower-priced products may develop a technology that makes its production processes more efficient, thus allowing it to lower prices of its own products. Political action is another way to affect environmental forces. The pharmaceutical industry, for example, has lobbied very effectively for fewer restrictions on prescription drug marketing. However, managers must recognize that there are limits on how much environmental forces can be shaped. Although an organization may be able to influence legislation through lobbying, it is unlikely that a single organization can significantly increase the national birthrate or move the economy from recession to prosperity.

We cannot say whether a reactive or a proactive approach to environmental forces is better. For some organizations the passive, reactive approach is more appropriate, but for others the aggressive approach leads to better performance. Selection of a particular approach depends on an organization's managerial philosophies, objectives, financial resources, customers, and human skills, as well as on the environment within which the organization operates. Both organizational factors and managers' personal characteristics affect the variety of responses to changing environmental conditions. These adaptive changes range from strategic to tactical.[3] Microsoft, for example, can take a proactive approach because of its financial resources and the highly visible image of its founder, Bill Gates.

The remainder of this chapter explores in greater detail each of the six environmental forces—competitive, economic, political, legal and regulatory, technological, and sociocultural—that interact to create opportunities and threats that must be considered in strategic planning.

Competitive Forces

Few firms, if any, operate free of competition. In fact, for most goods and services, customers have many alternatives from which to choose. Thus, when marketing managers define the target market(s) their firm will serve, they simultaneously establish a set of competitors.[4] In addition, marketing managers must consider the type of competitive structure in which the firm operates. In this section, we examine types of competition and competitive structures, as well as the importance of monitoring competitors' actions.

60

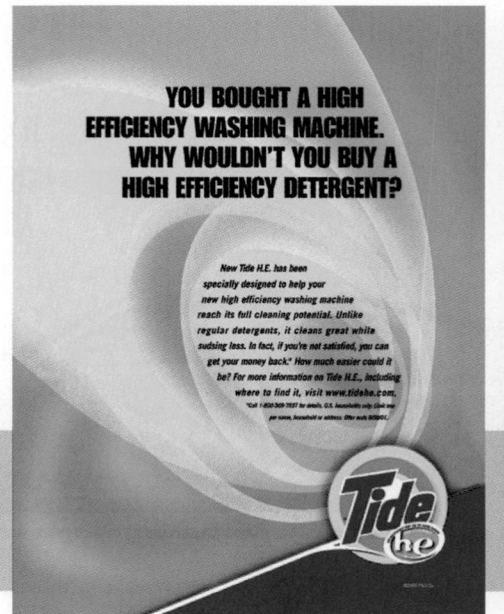

Brand Competitors
Tide and Cheer would be brand competitors in the laundry detergent market if they were marketed by different companies.

Types of Competition

competition Other organizations that market products that are similar to or can be substituted for a marketer's products in the same geographic area

brand competitors Firms that market products with similar features and benefits to the same customers at similar prices

product competitors Firms that compete in the same product class but have products with different features, benefits, and prices

generic competitors Firms that provide very different products that solve the same problem or satisfy the same basic customer need

total budget competitors Firms that compete for the limited financial resources of the same customers

monopoly A competitive structure in which an organization offers a product that has no close substitutes, making that organization the sole source of supply

Broadly speaking, all firms compete with one another for customers' dollars. More practically, however, a marketer generally defines **competition** as other firms that market products that are similar to or can be substituted for its products in the same geographic area. These competitors can be classified into one of four types. **Brand competitors** market products with similar features and benefits to the same customers at similar prices. For example, a thirsty, calorie-conscious customer may choose a diet soda, such as Diet Coke, Diet Pepsi, or Diet RC, from the soda machine. However, these sodas face competition from other types of beverages. **Product competitors** compete in the same product class, but their products have different features, benefits, and prices. The thirsty dieter, for instance, might purchase iced tea, juice, or bottled water instead of a soda. **Generic competitors** provide very different products that solve the same problem or satisfy the same basic customer need. Our customer, for example, might simply have a glass of water from the kitchen tap to satisfy her thirst. **Total budget competitors** compete for the limited financial resources of the same customers.[5] Total budget competitors for Diet Coke, for example, might include gum, a candy bar, or a newspaper. Although all four types of competition can affect a firm's marketing performance, brand competitors are the most significant because buyers typically see the different products of these firms as direct substitutes for one another. Consequently, marketers tend to concentrate environmental analyses on brand competitors.

Types of Competitive Structures

The number of firms that supply a product may affect the strength of competitors. When just one or a few firms control supply, competitive factors exert a different sort of influence on marketing activities than when many competitors exist. Table 3.1 presents four general types of competitive structures: monopoly, oligopoly, monopolistic competition, and pure competition.

A **monopoly** exists when a firm offers a product that has no close substitutes, making that organization the sole source of supply. Because the organization has no competitors, it controls supply of the product completely and, as a single seller, can erect barriers to potential competitors. In actuality, most monopolies surviving today are local utilities, which are heavily regulated by local, state, or federal agencies. These monopolies are tolerated because of the tremendous financial resources needed to develop and operate them. For example, few organizations can obtain the financial or political resources to mount any competition against a local water supplier. On the other hand, competition is increasing in the electric and cable television industries.

Table 3.1	Selected Characteristics of Competitive Structures			
Type of Structure	Number of Competitors	Ease of Entry into Market	Product	Example
Monopoly	One	Many barriers	Almost no substitutes	Fort Collins (Colorado) Water Utilities
Oligopoly	Few	Some barriers	Homogeneous or differentiated (with real or perceived differences)	General Motors (autos)
Monopolistic competition	Many	Few barriers	Product differentiation, with many substitutes	Levi Strauss (jeans)
Pure competition	Unlimited	No barriers	Homogeneous products	Vegetable farm (sweet corn)

oligopoly A competitive structure in which a few sellers control the supply of a large proportion of a product

monopolistic competition A competitive structure in which a firm has many potential competitors and tries to develop marketing strategy to differentiate its product

pure competition A market structure characterized by an extremely large number of sellers, none strong enough to influence price or supply significantly

An **oligopoly** exists when a few sellers control the supply of a large proportion of a product. In this case, each seller considers the reactions of other sellers to changes in marketing activities. Products facing oligopolistic competition may be homogeneous, such as aluminum, or differentiated, such as automobiles. Usually barriers of some sort make it difficult to enter the market and compete with oligopolies. For example, because of the enormous financial outlay required, few companies or individuals could afford to enter the oil-refining or steel-producing industries. Moreover, some industries demand special technical or marketing skills, a qualification that deters entry of many potential competitors.

Monopolistic competition exists when a firm with many potential competitors attempts to develop a marketing strategy to differentiate its product. For example, Levi Strauss has established an advantage for its blue jeans through a well-known trademark, design, advertising, and a reputation for quality. Although many competing brands of blue jeans are available, this firm has carved out a market niche by emphasizing differences in its products.

Pure competition, if it existed at all, would entail a large number of sellers, not one of which could significantly influence price or supply. Products would be homogeneous, and entry into the market would be easy. The closest thing to an example of pure competition is an unregulated farmers' market, where local growers gather to sell their produce.

Pure competition is an ideal at one end of the continuum; monopoly is at the other end. Most marketers function in a competitive environment somewhere between these two extremes.

Monitoring Competition

Marketers need to monitor the actions of major competitors to determine what specific strategies competitors are using and how those strategies affect their own. Price is one of the marketing strategy variables that most competitors monitor. When AirTran or Southwest Airlines lowers the fare on a route, most major airlines attempt to match the price. Monitoring guides marketers in developing competitive advantages and aids them in adjusting current marketing strategies and planning new ones.

In monitoring competition, it is not enough to analyze available information; the firm must develop a system for gathering ongoing information about competitors. Understanding the market and what customers want, as well as what the competition is providing, will assist in maintaining a marketing orientation.[6] Information about competitors allows marketing managers to assess the performance of their own marketing efforts and to recognize the strengths and weaknesses in their own marketing strategies. In addition, organizations are rewarded for taking risks and dealing with the uncertainty created by inadequate information.[7] Data about market shares, product movement, sales volume, and expenditure levels can be useful. However, accurate information on these matters is often difficult to obtain. We explore how marketers collect and organize such data in Chapter 6.

Economic Forces

Economic forces in the marketing environment influence both marketers' and customers' decisions and activities. In this section, we examine the effects of general economic conditions as well as buying power and the factors that affect people's willingness to spend.

Economic Conditions

The overall state of the economy fluctuates in all countries. Changes in general economic conditions affect (and are affected by) supply and demand, buying power, willingness to spend, consumer expenditure levels, and the intensity of competitive behavior. Therefore, current economic conditions and changes in the economy have a broad impact on the success of organizations' marketing strategies.

Fluctuations in the economy follow a general pattern, often referred to as the **business cycle.** In the traditional view, the business cycle consists of four stages: prosperity, recession, depression, and recovery. From a global perspective, different regions of the world may be in different stages of the business cycle during the same period. Throughout much of the last decade, for example, the United States experienced booming growth (prosperity). The U.S. economy began to slow in 2000, with a brief recession, especially in high-technology industries, in 2001. Japan, however, endured a recession during most of the last decade and into the 2000s. Economic variation in the global marketplace creates a planning challenge for firms that sell products in multiple markets around the world.

During **prosperity,** unemployment is low and total income is relatively high. Assuming a low inflation rate, this combination ensures high buying power. If the economic outlook remains prosperous, consumers generally are willing to buy. In the prosperity stage, marketers often expand their product offerings to take advantage of increased buying power. They can sometimes capture a larger market share by intensifying distribution and promotion efforts.

Because unemployment rises during a **recession,** total buying power declines. Pessimism accompanying a recession often stifles both consumer and business spending. As buying power decreases, many customers may become more price and value conscious and look for basic, functional products. During a recession, some firms make the mistake of drastically reducing their marketing efforts, thus damaging their ability to survive. Obviously, however, marketers should consider some revision of their marketing activities during a recessionary period. Because consumers are more concerned about the functional value of products, a company should focus its marketing research on determining precisely what functions buyers want and make sure these functions become part of its products. Promotional efforts should emphasize value and utility. For example, during a recent economic slowdown, online florist FTD.com adapted its marketing strategy to focus equally on acquiring new customers and retaining current ones, including reminding shoppers about special occasions that call for flowers.[8]

A prolonged recession may become a **depression,** a period in which unemployment is extremely high, wages are very low, total disposable income is at a minimum, and consumers lack confidence in the economy. A depression usually lasts for an extended period of time, often years, and has been experienced by Russia, Mexico, and Brazil in the last decade. During the economic turmoil in Mexico, Coca-Cola Company chose to continue its marketing efforts while most of its competitors cut back or even abandoned the Mexican market. By maintaining a high level of marketing, Coca-Cola increased its share of the Mexican market by 4 to 6 percent. Although evidence supports maintaining or even increasing spending during economic slowdowns, marketing budgets will more likely be cut in the face of an economic downturn.[9]

During **recovery,** the economy moves from depression or recession to prosperity. During this period, high unemployment begins to decline, total disposable income increases, and the economic gloom that reduced consumers' willingness to buy subsides. Both the ability and willingness to buy rise. Marketers face some problems during recovery, for example, difficulty in ascertaining how quickly and to what level

business cycle A pattern of economic fluctuations that has four stages: prosperity, recession, depression, and recovery

prosperity A stage of the business cycle characterized by low unemployment and relatively high total income, which together cause buying power to be high (provided the inflation rate stays low)

recession A stage of the business cycle during which unemployment rises and total buying power declines, stifling both consumer and business spending

depression A stage of the business cycle when unemployment is extremely high, wages are very low, total disposable income is at a minimum, and consumers lack confidence in the economy

recovery A stage of the business cycle in which the economy moves from recession or depression toward prosperity

prosperity will return. In this stage, marketers should maintain as much flexibility in their marketing strategies as possible so that they can make the needed adjustments.

Buying Power

buying power Resources, such as money, goods, and services, that can be traded in an exchange

income For an individual, the amount of money received through wages, rents, investments, pensions, and subsidy payments for a given period

disposable income After-tax income

discretionary income Disposable income available for spending and saving after an individual has purchased the basic necessities of food, clothing, and shelter

wealth The accumulation of past income, natural resources, and financial resources

The strength of a person's **buying power** depends on economic conditions and the size of the resources—money, goods, and services that can be traded in an exchange—that enable the individual to make purchases. The major financial sources of buying power are income, credit, and wealth. For an individual, **income** is the amount of money received through wages, rents, investments, pensions, and subsidy payments for a given period, such as a month or a year. Normally this money is allocated among taxes, spending for goods and services, and savings. The median annual household income in the United States is approximately $38,885.[10] However, because of differences in people's educational levels, abilities, occupations, and wealth, income is not equally distributed in this country.

Marketers are most interested in the amount of money left after payment of taxes because this **disposable income** is used for spending or saving. Because disposable income is a ready source of buying power, the total amount available in a nation is important to marketers. Several factors determine the size of total disposable income. One is the total amount of income, which is affected by wage levels, the rate of unemployment, interest rates, and dividend rates. Because disposable income is income left after taxes are paid, the number and amount of taxes directly affect the size of total disposable income. When taxes rise, disposable income declines; when taxes fall, disposable income increases.

Disposable income that is available for spending and saving after an individual has purchased the basic necessities of food, clothing, and shelter is called **discretionary income.** People use discretionary income to purchase entertainment, vacations, automobiles, education, pets, furniture, appliances, and so on. Changes in total discretionary income affect sales of these products, especially automobiles, furniture, large appliances, and other costly durable goods.

Credit enables people to spend future income now or in the near future. However, credit increases current buying power at the expense of future buying power. Several factors determine whether people use or forgo credit. First, credit must be available. Interest rates too affect buyers' decisions to use credit, especially for expensive purchases such as homes, appliances, and automobiles. When interest rates are low, the total cost of automobiles and houses becomes more affordable. Low interest rates in the United States over the past ten years induced many buyers to take on the high level of debt necessary to own a home, fueling a tremendous boom in the construction of new homes and the sale of older homes. In contrast, when interest rates are high, consumers are more likely to delay buying such expensive items. Use of credit is also affected by credit terms, such as size of the down payment and amount and number of monthly payments.

Wealth is the accumulation of past income, natural resources, and financial resources. It exists in many forms, including cash, securities, savings accounts, jewelry, and real estate. Like income, wealth is unevenly distributed. A person can have a high income and very little wealth. It is also possible, but not likely, for a person to have great wealth but little income. The significance of wealth to marketers is that as people become wealthier, they gain buying power in three ways: they can use their wealth to make current purchases, to generate income, and to acquire large amounts of credit.

Income, credit, and wealth equip consumers with buying power to purchase goods and services. Marketing managers need to be aware of current levels and expected changes in buying power in their own markets because buying power directly affects the types and quantities of goods and services that customers purchase. Information about buying power is available from government sources, trade associations, and research agencies. One of the most current and comprehensive sources of buying power data is the *Sales & Marketing Management Survey of Buying Power,* published annually by *Sales & Marketing Management* magazine. Having buying power, however, does not mean consumers will buy. They must also be willing to use their buying power.

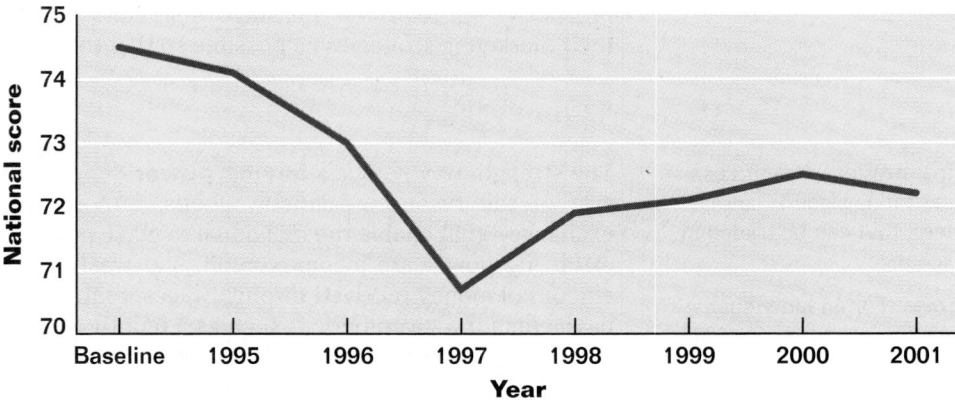

Willingness to Spend

willingness to spend
An inclination to buy because
of expected satisfaction from a
product, influenced by the ability
to buy and numerous psychological and social forces

People's **willingness to spend**—their inclination to buy because of expected satisfaction from a product—is, to some degree, related to their ability to buy. That is, people are sometimes more willing to buy if they have the buying power. However, a number of other elements also influence willingness to spend. Some elements affect
specific products; others influence spending in general. A product's price and value
influence almost all of us. Cross pens, for example, appeal to customers who are willing to spend more for fine writing instruments even when lower-priced pens are readily available. The amount of satisfaction received from a product already owned may
also influence customers' desire to buy other products. Satisfaction depends not only
on the quality of the currently owned product but also on numerous psychological
and social forces. The American Customer Satisfaction Index, computed by the
National Quality Research Center at the University of Michigan (see Figure 3.1) offers
an indicator of customer satisfaction with a wide variety of businesses. Among other
things, the index suggests that if customers become more dissatisfied, they may curtail their overall spending, which could stifle economic growth.[11]

Factors that affect customers' general willingness to spend are expectations
about future employment, income levels, prices, family size, and general economic
conditions. Willingness to spend ordinarily declines if people are unsure whether or
how long they will be employed, and usually increases if people are reasonably certain of higher incomes in the future. Expectations of rising prices in the near future
may also increase willingness to spend in the present. For a given level of buying
power, the larger the family, the greater the willingness to spend. One reason for this
relationship is that as the size of a family increases, more dollars must be spent to provide the basic necessities to sustain family members.

Political Forces

Political, legal, and regulatory forces of the
marketing environment are closely interrelated. Legislation is enacted, legal decisions
are interpreted by courts, and regulatory agencies are created and operated, for the
most part, by elected or appointed officials. Legislation and regulations (or their lack)
reflect the current political outlook. Consequently the political forces of the marketing environment have the potential to influence marketing decisions and strategies.

Marketing organizations strive to maintain good relations with elected political
officials for several reasons. Political officials well disposed toward particular firms or
industries are less likely to create or enforce laws and regulations unfavorable to
those companies. For example, political officials who believe oil companies are making honest efforts to control pollution are unlikely to create and enforce highly restric-
tive pollution control laws. In addition, governments are big buyers, and political officials can influence how much a government agency purchases and from whom.

Finally, political officials can play key roles in helping organizations secure foreign markets.

Many marketers view political forces as beyond their control and simply adjust to conditions arising from those forces. Some firms, however, seek to influence the political process. In some cases, organizations publicly protest the actions of legislative bodies. More often, organizations help elect to political offices individuals who regard them positively. Much of this help is in the form of campaign contributions. Although laws restrict direct corporate contributions to campaign funds, corporate influence may be channeled into campaigns through executives' or stockholders' personal contributions. Such actions violate the spirit of corporate campaign contribution laws. A sizable donation to a campaign fund may carry an implicit understanding that the elected official will perform political favors for the executive's firm. Occasionally some businesses find it so important to ensure favorable treatment that they make illegal corporate contributions to campaign funds.

Although laws limit corporate contributions to campaign funds for specific candidates, it is legal for businesses and other organizations to contribute to political parties. Some companies even choose to donate to more than one party. Marketers can also influence the political process through political action committees (PACs) that solicit donations from individuals and then contribute those funds to candidates running for political office. Companies are barred by federal law from donating directly to candidates for federal offices or to political action committees, but they can organize PACs to which their executives, employees, and stockholders can make significant donations as individuals. Companies can also participate in the political process through lobbying to persuade public and/or government officials to favor a particular position in decision making. Many companies concerned about the threat of legislation or regulation that may negatively affect their operations employ lobbyists to communicate their concerns to elected officials. Microsoft, for example, established a Washington office with a staff of 14 lobbyists and spent $4.6 million to persuade federal officials that breaking up the company for antitrust violations would harm the computer industry and the U.S. economy.[12]

Combating Cigarette Company Advertising and Lobbying
To counter the influence of cigarette company advertising and political lobbying, organizations such as the Centers for Disease Control create messages to communicate the negative effects of smoking.

Legal and Regulatory Forces

A number of federal laws influence marketing decisions and activities. Table 3.2 lists some of the most significant of these. In addition to discussing these laws, which deal with competition and consumer protection, this section examines the effects of regulatory agencies and self-regulatory forces on marketing efforts.

Table 3.2	**Major Federal Laws Affecting Marketing Decisions**
Act (Date Enacted)	**Purpose**
Sherman Antitrust Act (1890)	Prohibits contracts, combinations, or conspiracies to restrain trade; establishes as a misdemeanor monopolizing or attempting to monopolize
Clayton Act (1914)	Prohibits specific practices such as price discrimination, exclusive dealer arrangements, and stock acquisitions whose effect may noticeably lessen competition or tend to create a monopoly
Federal Trade Commission Act (1914)	Created the Federal Trade Commission; also gives the FTC investigatory powers to be used in preventing unfair methods of competition
Robinson-Patman Act (1936)	Prohibits price discrimination that lessens competition among wholesalers or retailers; prohibits producers from giving disproportionate services of facilities to large buyers
Wheeler-Lea Act (1938)	Prohibits unfair and deceptive acts and practices regardless of whether competition is injured; places advertising of foods and drugs under the jurisdiction of the FTC
Lanham Act (1946)	Provides protections and regulation of brand names, brand marks, trade names, and trademarks
Celler-Kefauver Act (1950)	Prohibits any corporation engaged in commerce from acquiring the whole or any part of the stock or other share of the capital assets of another corporation when the effect substantially would lessen competition or tend to create a monopoly
Fair Packaging and Labeling Act (1966)	Makes illegal the unfair or deceptive packaging or labeling of consumer products
Magnuson-Moss Warranty (FTC) Act (1975)	Provides for minimum disclosure standards for written consumer product warranties; defines minimum consent standards for written warranties; allows the FTC to prescribe interpretive rules in policy statements regarding unfair or deceptive practices
Consumer Goods Pricing Act (1975)	Prohibits the use of price maintenance agreements among manufacturers and resellers in interstate commerce
Antitrust Improvements Act (1976)	Requires large corporations to inform federal regulators of prospective mergers or acquisitions so they can be studied for any possible violations of the law
Trademark Counterfeiting Act (1980)	Provides civil and criminal penalties against those who deal in counterfeit consumer goods or any counterfeit goods that can threaten health or safety
Trademark Law Revision Act (1988)	Amends the Lanham Act to allow brands not yet introduced to be protected through registration with the Patent and Trademark Office
Nutrition Labeling and Education Act (1990)	Prohibits exaggerated health claims; requires all processed foods to contain labels with nutritional information
Telephone Consumer Protection Act (1991)	Establishes procedures to avoid unwanted telephone solicitations; prohibits marketers from using an automated telephone dialing system or an artificial or prerecorded voice to certain telephone lines
Federal Trademark Dilution Act (1995)	Grants trademark owners the right to protect trademarks and requires relinquishment of names that match or parallel existing trademarks
Digital Millennium Copyright Act (1996)	Refined copyright laws to protect digital versions of copyrighted materials, including music and movies
Children's Online Privacy Protection Act (2000)	Regulates the collection of personally identifiable information (name, address, e-mail address, hobbies, interests, or information collected through cookies) online from children under age 13

Procompetitive Legislation

Procompetitive laws are designed to preserve competition. Most of these laws were enacted to end various antitrade practices deemed unacceptable by society. The Sherman Antitrust Act, for example, was passed in 1890 to prevent businesses from restraining trade and monopolizing markets. A request that a competitor agree to fix prices or divide markets would, if accepted, result in a violation of the Sherman Act.[13]

Other examples of illegal competitive trade practices include stealing trade secrets or obtaining other confidential information from a competitor's employees, trademark and copyright infringement, price fixing, false advertising, and deceptive selling methods such as "bait and switch" and false representation of products. For example, the Lanham Act (1946) and the Federal Trademark Dilution Act (1996) help companies protect their trademarks (brand names, logos, and other registered symbols) against infringement. The latter also requires users of names that match or parallel existing trademarks to relinquish them to prevent confusion among consumers. Antitrust laws also authorize the government to punish companies that engage in such anticompetitive practices. For example, the U.S. Department of Justice fined Anchor Industrial Products, Inc., $600,000 after the firm pleaded guilty to charges of conspiring to fix the price of carbon cathode block, a product used in aluminum smelters.[14]

Consumer Protection Legislation

Consumer protection legislation is not a recent development. During the mid-1800s, lawmakers in many states passed laws to prohibit adulteration of food and drugs. However, consumer protection laws at the federal level mushroomed in the mid-1960s and early 1970s. A number of them deal with consumer safety, such as the food and drug acts, designed to protect people from actual and potential physical harm caused by adulteration or mislabeling. Other laws prohibit the sale of various hazardous products, such as flammable fabrics and toys that may injure children. Others concern automobile safety. Congress has also passed several laws concerning information disclosure. Some require that information about specific products, such as textiles, furs, cigarettes, and automobiles, be provided on labels. Other laws focus on particular marketing activities: product development and testing, packaging, labeling, advertising, and consumer financing. For example, concerns about companies' online collection and use of personal information, especially about children, resulted in the passage of the Children's Online Privacy Protection Act of 2000, which prohibits websites and Internet providers from seeking personal information from children under age 13 without parental consent.[15]

Regulatory Forces
The government requires that all automobiles, such as Mercedes-Benz's SUVs, pass rigorous crash tests.

The only SUV that is built, and destroyed, like a Mercedes-Benz.

Built: Roof pillars are engineered to support the weight of the vehicle. Air bags help protect in both front and side impacts. Every advanced M-Class safety feature comes standard on all models. Bumper height is positioned for greater crash compatibility with smaller cars – an SUV first. Destroyed: Head-on collision. Rollover. Side impact. Offset impact. A safety testing regimen of 24 different types of testing. More than any government requires. This is not just an SUV. This is a Mercedes-Benz. For more information, call 1-800-FOR-MERCEDES or visit us at www.MBUSA.com. The M-Class starts at $35,300.

Mercedes-Benz

Encouraging Compliance with Laws and Regulations

Marketing activities are often at the forefront of organizational misconduct, with fraud and antitrust violations the most frequently sentenced organizational crimes. Legal violations usually begin when marketers develop programs that unknowingly or unwittingly overstep legal bounds. Many marketers lack experience in dealing with complex legal actions and decisions. Some test the limits of certain laws by operating in a legally questionable way to see how far they can get with certain practices before being prosecuted. Other marketers, however, interpret regulations and statutes strictly to avoid violating a vague law. When marketers interpret laws in relation to specific marketing practices, they often analyze recent court decisions both to better understand what the law is intended to do and to predict future court interpretations. Marketing Citizenship looks at one company's efforts to resolve its legal issues.

To ensure that marketers comply with the law, the federal government is moving toward greater organizational accountability for misconduct. The U.S. Sentencing Commission (USSC) introduced a detailed set of guidelines to regulate the sentencing of companies convicted of breaking the law. The basic philosophy of the Federal Sentencing Guidelines for Organizations is that companies are responsible for crimes committed by their employees. These guidelines were designed not only to hold companies as well as employees accountable for illegal actions but also to streamline the sentencing and fine structures for offenses. (Previously laws punished only those

MARKETING CITIZENSHIP

Legal Issues at Wal-Mart

When you're the world's largest retailer, with more than 1,660 stores, you can expect a few legal issues with the 100 million customers who flock to your stores each week. Wal-Mart's enormous success—profits reached $6.3 billion in 2001—may account for some of the lawsuits against the company. In one year, Wal-Mart was involved in more than 4,800 lawsuits, roughly 12 per day, or one every two hours. Indeed, Wal-Mart may be the most-sued organization after the U.S. government. Several websites even collect information on suits against the retail giant and offer advice on how to proceed in litigation.

As Wal-Mart has grown, so have the types of lawsuits filed against the company. Suits have involved store parking lot security, customers slipping on store floors, and products falling off shelves and injuring customers. Others relate to the sale of hunting weapons or customers being injured while stampeding the store for a "hot" toy like the Furbies that went on sale just before Christmas 1998. The plaintiffs in the Furby lawsuit believed Wal-Mart should have been responsible for controlling the crowd and providing enough security to ensure customer safety. In addition, Wal-Mart regularly faces lawsuits related to pricing, packaging, advertising, and labeling issues.

Wal-Mart does not take its position as an "easy target" lightly. Based on the philosophy of company founder Sam Walton, the retailer is taking a stand against "frivolous" lawsuits. Under Walton, Wal-Mart settled any dispute in which the company was at fault and admitted guilt.

If the company was not responsible, Walton insisted that the claim be heard in court to defend the company's reputation. Today Wal-Mart's attorneys vigorously fight many cases that might have been cheaper to settle out of court. The rules for settling lawsuits involving major corporations are often more in tune with an accounting analysis than with a strict ethical or legal overview. If an average case costs $12,000 to defend and can be settled for $8,000, it may make sense to settle out of court to minimize loss of time and potential for bad press.

Wal-Mart continues to express a desire to be a good corporate citizen, but some critics complain the company rarely admits guilt. Because many of the firm's legal disputes are with customers, the company now appeals fewer cases and publicizes examples of disputes that it is resolving. Considering the out-of-pocket costs as well as the potential for negative publicity, Wal-Mart's strategy seems to be paying off: the number of lawsuits against the company has stabilized over the past five years.

An increasing number of lawsuits against major corporations (e.g., Eli Lilly for Prozac, Allstate and other insurance companies) has prompted a backlash against plaintiff lawyers who get a percentage of settlements and more support for corporations facing such litigation. Experts believe that in the end, consumers will be the ultimate judges of whether Wal-Mart is a responsible corporate citizen by voting "with their dollars" to continue as Wal-Mart customers or take their business elsewhere.

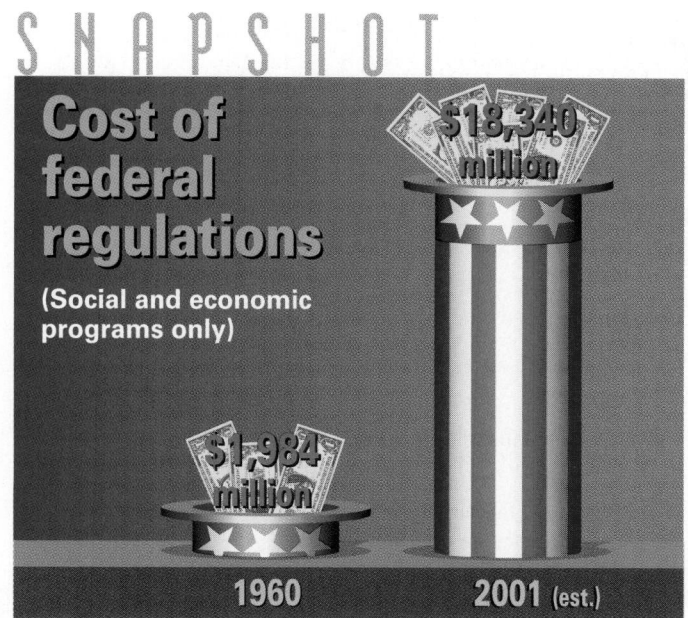

Cost of federal regulations
(Social and economic programs only)

$18,340 million

$1,984 million

1960   2001 (est.)

employees directly responsible for an offense, not the company.) The underlying assumption is that "good citizen corporations" maintain compliance systems and internal controls to prevent misconduct and to educate employees about questionable activities. Thus, the new guidelines focus on crime prevention and detection by mitigating penalties for firms that have chosen to develop such compliance programs should one of their employees be involved in misconduct.

The bottom line is that unless a marketer works in a company with an effective compliance program that meets the minimum requirements of the U.S. Sentencing Commission's recommendations, both the individual and the company face severe penalties if the marketer violates the law. Daiwa Bank, for example, was hit with a $340 million fine for misrepresenting financial information, while Archer Daniels Midland received a $100 million fine for price fixing. Further, the Federal Sentencing Guidelines for individuals often mandate substantial prison sentences even for first-time offenders convicted of a felony, such as antitrust, fraud, import/export violations, or environmental crimes.

Regulatory Agencies

Federal regulatory agencies influence many marketing activities, including product development, pricing, packaging, advertising, personal selling, and distribution. Usually these bodies have the power to enforce specific laws, as well as some discretion in establishing operating rules and regulations to guide certain types of industry practices. Because of this discretion and overlapping areas of responsibility, confusion or conflict regarding which agencies have jurisdiction over which marketing activities is common.

Federal Trade Commission (FTC) An agency that regulates a variety of business practices and curbs false advertising, misleading pricing, and deceptive packaging and labeling

Of all the federal regulatory units, the **Federal Trade Commission (FTC)** influences marketing activities most. Although the FTC regulates a variety of business practices, it allocates a large portion of resources to curbing false advertising, misleading pricing, and deceptive packaging and labeling. When it receives a complaint or otherwise has reason to believe a firm is violating a law, the commission issues a complaint stating that the business is in violation. If the company continues the questionable practice, the FTC can issue a cease-and-desist order demanding that the business stop doing whatever caused the complaint. The firm can appeal to the federal courts to have the order rescinded. However, the FTC can seek civil penalties in court, up to a maximum penalty of $10,000 a day for each infraction if a cease-and-desist order is violated.

The commission can also require companies to run corrective advertising in response to previous ads considered misleading. This mandated corrective advertising is proving to be costly to many companies. For example, the FTC filed a formal complaint against Enforma Natural Products for deceptive advertising of its weight loss products. Among the company's claims for the Enforma System, which was promoted through 30-minute infomercials and a website, was that "you can eat what you want and never, ever, ever have to diet again." The FTC's complaint charged that such claims were false and could not be substantiated. To settle the charges, Enforma agreed to make no more deceptive claims and to pay the FTC $10 million in reparation.[16] The FTC has also emerged as the leading enforcement agency for consumer protection issues on the Internet.[17]

The FTC also assists businesses in complying with laws, and it evaluates new marketing methods every year. For example, the agency has held hearings to help firms establish guidelines for avoiding charges of price fixing, deceptive advertising, and questionable telemarketing practices. It has also held conferences and hearings on

Table 3.3	Major Federal Regulatory Agencies
Agency	**Major Areas of Responsibility**
Federal Trade Commission (FTC)	Enforces laws and guidelines regarding business practices; takes action to stop false and deceptive advertising, pricing, packaging, and labeling
Food and Drug Adminstration (FDA)	Enforces laws and regulations to prevent distribution of adulterated or misbranded foods, drugs, medical devices, cosmetics, veterinary products, and potentially hazardous consumer products
Consumer Product Safety Commission (CPSC)	Ensures compliance with the Consumer Product Safety Act; protects the public from unreasonable risk of injury from any consumer product not covered by other regulatory agencies
Federal Communications Commission (FCC)	Regulates communication by wire, radio, and television in interstate and foreign commerce
Environmental Protection Agency (EPA)	Develops and enforces environmental protection standards and conducts research into the adverse effects of pollution
Federal Power Commission (FPC)	Regulates rates and sales of natural gas producers, thereby affecting the supply and price of gas available to consumers; also regulates wholesale rates for electricity and gas, pipeline construction, and U.S. imports and exports of natural gas and electricity

electronic (Internet) commerce. When general sets of guidelines are needed to improve business practices in a particular industry, the FTC sometimes encourages firms within that industry to establish a set of trade practices voluntarily. The FTC may even sponsor a conference bringing together industry leaders and consumers for this purpose.

Unlike the FTC, other regulatory units are limited to dealing with specific products, services, or business activities. For example, the Food and Drug Administration (FDA) enforces regulations prohibiting the sale and distribution of adulterated, misbranded, or hazardous food and drug products. Table 3.3 outlines the areas of responsibility of six federal regulatory agencies.

In addition, all states, as well as many cities and towns, have regulatory agencies that enforce laws and regulations regarding marketing practices within their states or municipalities. State and local regulatory agencies try not to establish regulations that conflict with those of federal regulatory agencies. They generally enforce laws dealing with the production and sale of particular goods and services. Utility, insurance, financial, and liquor industries are commonly regulated by state agencies. Among these agencies' targets are misleading advertising and pricing. Recent legal actions suggest that states are taking a firmer stance against perceived deceptive pricing practices and are using basic consumer research to define deceptive pricing.

Self-Regulatory Forces

In an attempt to be good corporate citizens and to prevent government intervention, some businesses try to regulate themselves. A number of trade associations have developed self-regulatory programs. Though these programs are not a direct outgrowth of laws, many were established to stop or stall the development of laws and governmental regulatory groups that would regulate the associations' marketing practices. Sometimes trade associations establish ethics codes by which their members must abide or risk censure or exclusion from the association. For example, the Water Quality Association has developed a comprehensive code of ethics to help companies that sell water purification equipment avoid illegal and unethical activities.

Perhaps the best-known nongovernmental regulatory group is the **Better Business Bureau,** a local regulatory agency supported by local businesses. More than 140 bureaus help settle problems between consumers and specific business firms. Each bureau also acts to preserve good business practices in a locality, although it usually lacks strong enforcement tools for dealing with firms that employ

Better Business Bureau
A local, nongovernmental regulatory agency, supported by local businesses, that helps settle problems between customers and specific business firms

questionable practices. When a firm continues to violate what the Better Business Bureau believes to be good business practices, the bureau warns consumers through local newspapers or broadcast media. If the offending organization is a BBB member, it may be expelled from the local bureau. The membership of Priceline.com, for example, was revoked by a Connecticut Better Business Bureau after the online retailer failed to address numerous complaints related to misrepresentation of products, failure to provide promised refunds, and failure to correct billing problems.[18] The BBB has also developed a "BBBOnLine" site to help consumers recognize websites that handle the collection of personal information in an ethical manner. BBB members that use the site agree to binding arbitration with regard to online privacy issues.

The Council of Better Business Bureaus is a national organization composed of all local Better Business Bureaus. The National Advertising Division (NAD) of the Council of Better Business Bureaus operates a self-regulatory program that investigates claims regarding alleged deceptive advertising. For example, after investigating complaints about Kal Kan Foods' advertising of Whiskas Homestyle Favorites cat food, the NAD asked the pet food maker to modify the advertising to avoid making unsubstantiated claims about the product's performance.[19]

National Advertising Review Board (NARB) A self-regulatory unit that considers challenges to issues raised by the National Advertising Division (an arm of the Council of Better Business Bureaus) about an advertisement

Another self-regulatory entity, the **National Advertising Review Board (NARB),** considers cases in which an advertiser challenges issues raised by the National Advertising Division about an advertisement. Kal Kan, for example, has appealed to the NARB the NAD's decision that its advertising of Whiskas Homestyle Favorites cat food contains unsubstantiated claims.[20] Cases are reviewed by panels drawn from NARB members representing advertisers, agencies, and the public. The NARB, sponsored by the Council of Better Business Bureaus and three advertising trade organizations, has no official enforcement powers. However, if a firm refuses to comply with its decision, the NARB may publicize the questionable practice and file a complaint with the FTC.

Self-regulatory programs have several advantages over governmental laws and regulatory agencies. Establishment and implementation are usually less expensive, and guidelines are generally more realistic and operational. In addition, effective self-regulatory programs reduce the need to expand government bureaucracy. However, these programs have several limitations. When a trade association creates a set of industry guidelines for its members, nonmember firms do not have to abide by them. Furthermore, many self-regulatory programs lack the tools or authority to enforce guidelines. Finally, guidelines in self-regulatory programs are often less strict than those established by government agencies.

Technological Forces

The word *technology* brings to mind scientific advances such as computers, DVDs, cellular phones, cloning, robots, lifestyle drugs, lasers, space shuttles, the Internet, and more. Such developments make it possible for marketers to operate ever more efficiently and to provide an exciting array of products for consumers. However, even though these innovations are outgrowths of technology, none of them *is* technology. **Technology** is the application of knowledge and tools to solve problems and perform tasks more efficiently. Technology grows out of research performed by businesses, universities, government agencies, and nonprofit organizations. More than half of this research is paid for by the federal government, which supports research in such diverse areas as health, defense, agriculture, energy, and pollution.

technology The application of knowledge and tools to solve problems and perform tasks more efficiently

The rapid technological growth of the last several decades is expected to accelerate in the twenty-first century. It has transformed the U.S. economy into the most productive in the world and provided Americans with an ever-higher standard of living and tremendous opportunities for sustained business expansion. Technology and technological advancements clearly influence buyers' and marketers' decisions, so let's take a closer look at the impact of technology and its use in the marketplace.

Impact of Technology

Technology determines how we, as members of society, satisfy our physiological needs. In various ways and to varying degrees, eating and drinking habits, sleeping patterns, sexual activities, health care, and work performance are all influenced by both existing technology and changes in technology. Because of the technological revolution in communications, for example, marketers can now reach vast numbers of people more efficiently through a variety of media. Electronic mail, voice mail, cellular phones, pagers, and notebook computers help marketers stay in touch with clients, make appointments, and handle last-minute orders or cancellations. Telecommuting—using telecommunications technology to work from home or other nontraditional areas—is becoming an increasingly popular use of computer technology. About 16 million employees telecommute for at least part of their workweek, and marketing has become a significant telecommuting job.[21]

Personal computers are now in 50 percent of all U.S. consumers' homes, and millions of them include broadband or modems for accessing the Internet. Although we enjoy the benefits of communicating through the Internet, we are increasingly concerned about protecting our privacy and intellectual property. Likewise, although health and medical research has created new drugs that save lives, cloning and genetically modified foods have become controversial issues to many segments of society. In various ways and to varying degrees, home environments, health care, leisure, and work performance are all influenced by both current technology and advances in technology.[22]

The effects of technology relate to such characteristics as dynamics, reach, and the self-sustaining nature of technological progress. The *dynamics* of technology involve the constant change that often challenges the structures of social institutions, including social relationships, the legal system, religion, education, business, and leisure. *Reach* refers to the broad nature of technology as it moves through society. Consider the impact of cellular and wireless telephones. The ability to call from almost any location has many benefits but also negative side effects, including increases in traffic accidents, increased noise pollution, and fears about potential health risks.[23]

The *self-sustaining* nature of technology relates to the fact that technology acts as a catalyst to spur even faster development. As new innovations are introduced, they stimulate the need for more advancements to facilitate further development. For example, the Internet has created the need for ever-faster transmission of signals through broadband connections such as high-speed phone lines (DSL), satellites,

SONY.

DREAM ON®

FIRST IT ELIMINATED VINYL.
THE PHOTO ALBUM IS NEXT.

CD Mavica

The Impact of Technology
Sony focuses on research and development to provide technological advances.

and cable. Broadband allows connections to the Internet to be 50 times faster than through a traditional phone modem, permits users to download large files, and creates opportunities for rich multimedia experiences.[24] However, broadband has been slow to reach areas outside of major cities, and just 6 percent of U.S. households currently have some type of broadband access. Until broadband services become more universally available, their promise to further accelerate technological advances will be limited.[25] Technology initiates a change process that creates new opportunities for new technologies in every industry segment or personal life experience that it touches. At some point, there is even a multiplier effect that causes still greater demand for more change to improve performance.[26]

The expanding opportunities for e-commerce, the sharing of business information, and the ability to maintain business relationships and conduct business transactions via telecommunications networks are already changing the relationship between businesses and consumers.[27] More and more people are turning to the Internet to purchase computers and related peripherals, software, books, music, and even furniture. Consumers are increasingly using the Internet to book travel reservations, transact banking business, and trade securities. The forces unleashed by the Internet are particularly important in business-to-business relationships, where uncertainties are being reduced by improving the quantity, reliability, and timeliness of information. Consider the alliance among Ford, General Motors, DaimlerChrysler, Renault, Nissan, Oracle, and Commerce One, which makes parts from suppliers available through a competitive online auction, compacting months of negotiations into a single day. The goal of the alliance is to reduce the time it takes to bring a new vehicle to market from 54 months to 18.[28] In many cases, companies are moving toward making most of their purchases online. Business-to-business Internet sales are expected to exceed $1.33 trillion by 2003, with computer and electronics sales contributing nearly $400 billion.[29] By 2005, online sales are expected to account for 42 percent of all business-to-business transactions.[30]

Adoption and Use of Technology

Many companies do not remain market leaders because they fail to keep up with technological changes. It is important for firms to determine when a technology is changing the industry and to define the strategic influence of the new technology. For example, wireless devices in use today include radios, cell phones, TVs, pagers, and car keys. In the future, most long-distance communication will likely occur through fiber optics, and short-distance communication will be wireless.[31] Demand for wireless technology is accelerating, with 50 percent of *Fortune* 1000 companies expected to commit 15 percent of all network spending to wireless voice and data technology.[32] Figure 3.2 depicts the most popular activities on wireless web devices. In the future, refrigerators, medicine cabinets, and even product packaging may contain wireless micro devices that broadcast product characteristics, features, expiration dates, and other information.[33] To remain competitive, companies today must keep up with and adapt to these technological advances.

The extent to which a firm can protect inventions stemming from research also influences its use of technology. How secure a product is from imitation depends on how easily others can copy it without violating its patent. If ground-breaking products

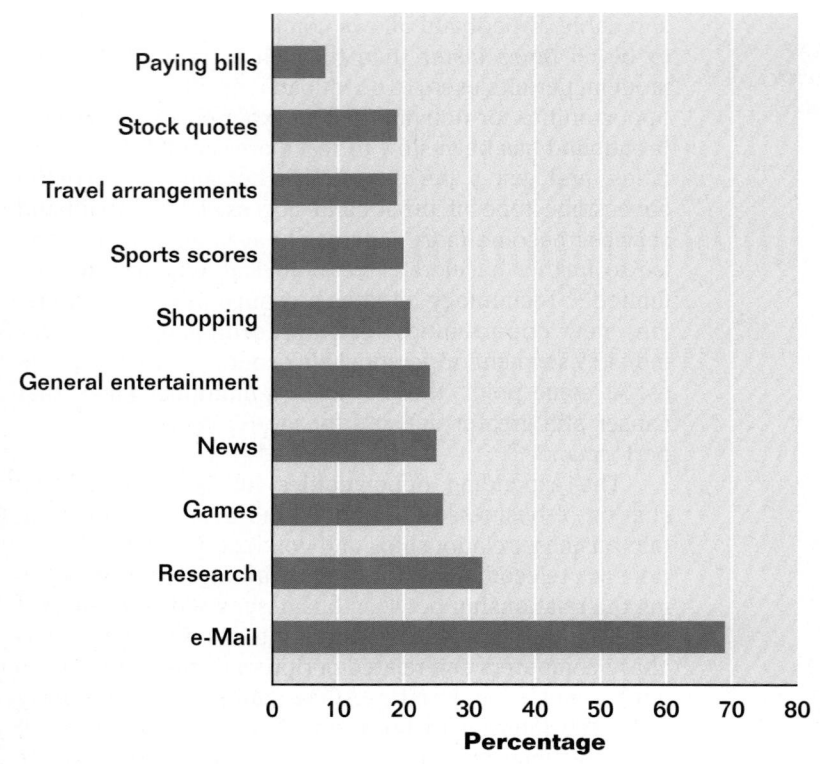

FIGURE 3.2
Top Ten Activities for Wireless Web Device Users
Source: "New Survey Indicates Wireless Web Penetration Highest among Young Affluent Males," TNS Intersearch, press release, Feb. 7, 2001, http://www.intersearch.tnsofres.com/.

and processes cannot be protected through patents, a company is less likely to market them and make the benefits of its research available to competitors.

Through a procedure known as *technology assessment,* managers try to foresee the effects of new products and processes on their firm's operation, on other business organizations, and on society in general. With information obtained through a technology assessment, management tries to estimate whether benefits of adopting a specific technology outweigh costs to the firm and to society at large. The degree to which a business is technologically based also influences its managers' response to technology.

Sociocultural Forces

Sociocultural forces are the influences in a society and its culture(s) that bring about changes in attitudes, beliefs, norms, customs, and lifestyles. Profoundly affecting how people live, these forces help determine what, where, how, and when people buy products. Like the other environmental forces, sociocultural forces present marketers with both challenges and opportunities. For a closer look at sociocultural forces, we examine three major issues: demographic and diversity characteristics, cultural values, and consumerism. We further explore the effects of culture and subcultures on buying behavior in Chapter 8.

sociocultural forces The influences in a society and its culture(s) that change people's attitudes, beliefs, norms, customs, and lifestyles

Demographic and Diversity Characteristics

Changes in a population's demographic characteristics—age, gender, race, ethnicity, marital and parental status, income, and education—have a significant bearing on relationships and individual behavior. These shifts lead to changes in how people live and ultimately in their consumption of such products as food, clothing, housing, transportation, communication, recreation, education, and health services. We look at a few of the changes in demographics and diversity that are affecting marketing activities.

One demographic change affecting the marketplace is the increasing proportion of older consumers. According to the U.S. Bureau of the Census, the number of people age 65 and older is expected to more than double by the year 2050, reaching 82 million.[34] Consequently, marketers can expect significant increases in the demand for health care services, recreation, tourism, retirement housing, and selected skin care products. Del Webb Development Company is one firm taking advantage of this opportunity by creating several Sun City retirement communities for mature adults. In addition to providing housing, facilities, and activities designed for older residents, Del Webb's newest Sun City is located to take advantage of the scenic beauty and moderate climate of the Texas Hill Country, as well as close proximity to cultural events in nearby Austin. To reach older customers effectively, of course, marketers must understand the diversity within the mature market with respect to geographic location, income, marital status, and mobility and self-care limitations.

The number of singles is also on the rise. Nearly 40 percent of U.S. adults are single, and many plan to remain that way. Moreover, single men living alone comprise 11 percent of all households (up from 3.5 percent in 1970), and single women living alone make up nearly 15 percent (up from 7.3 percent in 1970).[35] Single people have quite different spending patterns than couples and families with children. They are less likely to own homes and so buy less furniture and fewer appliances. They spend more heavily on convenience foods, restaurants, travel, entertainment, and recreation. In addition, they tend to prefer smaller packages, whereas families often buy bulk goods and products packaged in multiple servings.

The United States is entering another baby boom, with 74 million Americans age 18 or younger. The new baby boom represents 29 percent of the total population; the original baby boomers, now ages 35 to 54, account for nearly 30 percent.[36] The children of the original baby boomers differ from one another radically in terms of race, living arrangements, and socioeconomic class. Thus, the newest baby boom is much more diverse than previous generations.

Another noteworthy population trend is the increasingly multicultural nature of U.S. society. The number of immigrants into the United States has steadily risen during the last 40 years. In the 1960s, 3.3 million people immigrated to the United States; in the 1970s, 4.5 million came here; in the 1980s, 7.6 million arrived; and in the 1990s, the United States received 7.3 million legal immigrants.[37]

In contrast to earlier immigrants, very few recent ones are of European origin. Another reason for the increasing cultural diversification of the United States is that most recent immigrants are relatively young, whereas U.S. citizens of European origin are growing older. These younger immigrants tend to have more children than their older counterparts, further shifting the population balance. By the turn of the twentieth century, the U.S. population had shifted from one dominated by whites to one consisting largely of three racial and ethnic groups: whites, blacks, and Hispanics. The U.S. government projects that by the year 2025, nearly 61 million Hispanics, 47 million blacks, 22 million Asians, and 3 million Native Americans will call the United States home.[38] Figure 3.3 depicts how experts believe the U.S. population will change over the next 50 years.

Net Sights

The U.S. government compiles a staggering amount of demographic data on American citizens that marketers can mine for information about specific target markets. Much of this information is available in the annual *Statistical Abstract of the United States* (**http://www.census.gov/statab/www/**).

In addition, marketers eagerly await the latest results of the decennial U.S. census survey, much of which is accessible at **http://www.census.gov**.

FIGURE 3.3
U.S. Population Projections by Race

Source: Bureau of the Census, *Statistical Abstract of the United States, 2000* (Washington, DC: Government Printing Office, 2001), p. 17.

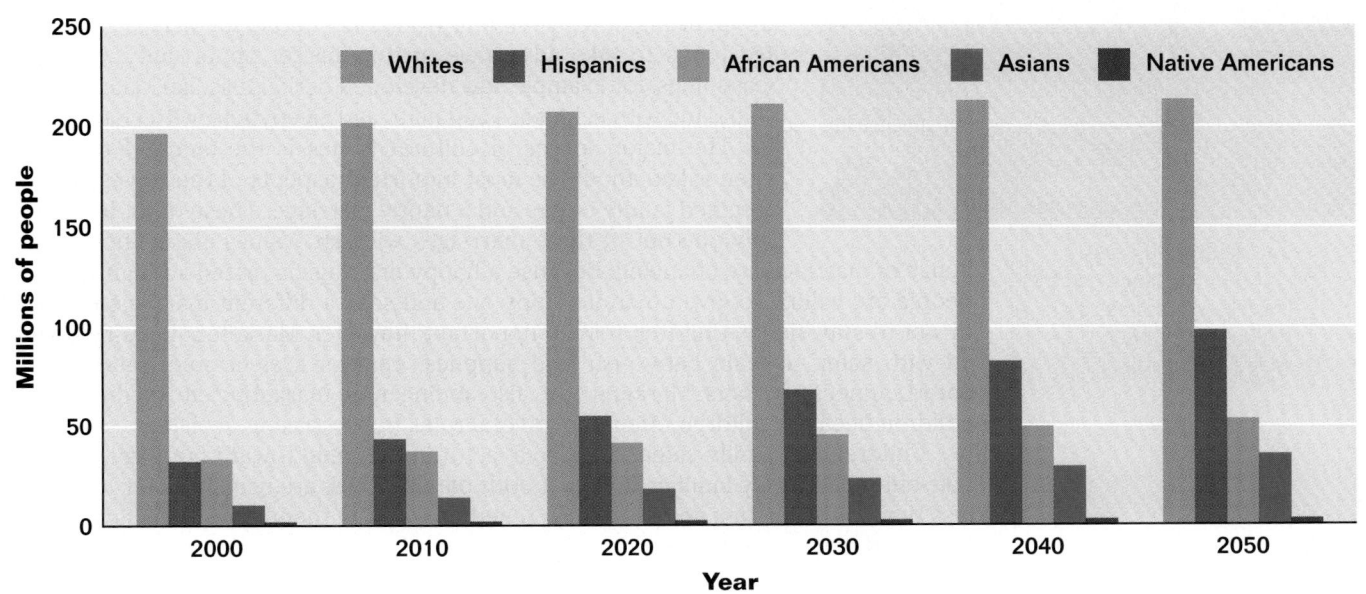

Sociocultural Forces
AARP understands that the lifestyles of its members require that it offer a variety of services.

Marketers recognize that these profound changes in the U.S. population bring unique problems and opportunities. Hispanics, for example, generate nearly $560 billion in annual buying power.[39] But a diverse population means a more diverse customer base, and marketing practices must be modified—and diversified—to meet its changing needs. Sears, for example, modifies its promotional strategy for stores located in urban areas with large Asian American populations. To kick off the fall retailing season, these stores have tied promotions to the Asia Moon Festival, a September harvest-time celebration, by hosting cultural events such as performances by local dancers, as well as offering a free gift for any purchase over $10. The giant retailer has also tied promotions to Black History Month in February and Mexican Independence Day in September.[40] Procter & Gamble, which spends more than $46 million a year to promote its products to Hispanic customers through advertisements on the Univision and Telemundo networks, is one of many companies that recognize the growing buying power of ethnically diverse customers.[41]

Cultural Values

Changes in values have dramatically influenced people's needs and desires for products. Although cultural values do not shift overnight, they do change at varying speeds. Marketers try to monitor these changes knowing this information can equip them to predict changes in consumers' needs for products at least in the near future.

Starting in the late 1980s, issues of health, nutrition, and exercise grew in importance. People today are more concerned about the foods they eat and thus are choosing more low-fat, nonfat, and no-cholesterol products. Compared with Americans in the previous two decades, Americans today are more likely to favor smoke-free environments and reduced consumption of alcohol. They have also altered their sexual behavior to reduce the risk of contracting sexually transmitted diseases. Marketers have responded with a proliferation of foods, beverages, and exercise products that fit this new lifestyle, as well as with programs to help people quit smoking and contraceptives that are safer and more effective. Americans are also becoming increasingly open to alternative medicines and nutritionally improved foods. As a result, sales of herbs and herbal remedies, vitamins, and dietary supplements have escalated. More marketers are investing in research into traditional herbal medicines and fortified foods to take advantage of this market opportunity. Celestial Seasonings, for example, has developed herbal teas like Mama Bear's Cold Care, with echinacea and mint, and Sleepytime, with chamomile.

The major source of cultural values is the family. For years, when asked about the most important aspects of their lives, adults specified family issues and a happy marriage. These days, however, only one out of three marriages will last. Values about the permanence of marriage are changing. Because a happy marriage is prized so highly, more people are willing to give up an unhappy one and seek a different marriage partner or opt to stay single. Children remain important, however. Marketers have responded with safer, upscale baby gear and supplies, children's electronics, and family entertainment products. Marketers are also aiming more marketing efforts directly at children because children often play pivotal roles in purchasing decisions.

Children and family values are also a factor in the trend toward more eat-out and take-out meals. Busy families in which both parents work are usually eager to spend less time in the kitchen and more time together enjoying themselves. Beneficiaries of this trend have primarily been fast-food and casual restaurants like McDonald's, Taco Bell, Boston Market, and Applebee's, but 75 percent of grocery stores have added more ready-to-cook or ready-to-serve meal components to meet the needs of busy customers. For example, a Virginia firm, Ukrop's Super Markets, offers healthy, ready-to-serve meals at its deli counters.[42]

Today's consumers are more and more concerned about the natural environment. One of society's environmental hurdles is proper disposal of waste, especially of non-degradable materials such as disposable diapers and polystyrene packaging. Companies have responded by developing more environmentally sensitive products and packaging. Procter & Gamble, for example, uses recycled materials in some of its packaging and sells environment-friendly refills. Raytheon has developed a new Amana refrigerator that does not use chlorofluorocarbons (CFCs), which harm the earth's ozone layer. A number of marketers sponsor recycling programs and encourage their customers to take part in them. Many organizations, including America's Electric Utility Companies and Phillips Petroleum, take pride in their efforts to protect the environment.

Consumerism

consumerism Organized efforts by individuals, groups, and organizations to protect consumers' rights

Consumerism is a varied array of individuals, groups, and organizations seeking to protect consumers' rights. The movement's major forces are individual consumer advocates, consumer organizations and other interest groups, consumer education, and consumer laws.

To achieve their objectives, consumers and their advocates write letters or send e-mail to companies, lobby government agencies, broadcast public service announcements, and boycott companies whose activities they deem irresponsible. For example, several organizations evaluate children's products for safety, often announcing dangerous products before Christmas so parents can avoid them. Other actions by the consumer movement have resulted in seat belts and air bags in automobiles, dolphin-safe tuna, the banning of unsafe three-wheel motorized vehicles, and numerous laws regulating product safety and information. We will take a closer look at consumerism in the next chapter.

Summary

The marketing environment consists of external forces that directly or indirectly influence an organization's acquisition of inputs (personnel, financial resources, raw materials, information) and generation of outputs (goods, services, ideas). The marketing environment includes competitive, economic, political, legal and regulatory, technological, and sociocultural forces.

Environmental scanning is the process of collecting information about forces in the marketing environment; environmental analysis is the process of assessing and interpreting information obtained in scanning. This information helps marketing managers predict opportunities and threats associated with environmental fluctuation. Marketing managers may assume either a passive, reactive approach or a proactive, aggressive approach in responding to these environmental fluctuations. The choice depends on the organization's structures and needs and on the composition of environmental forces that affect it.

All businesses compete for customers' dollars. A marketer, however, generally defines competition as other firms that market products that are similar to or can be substituted for its products in the same geographic area. These competitors can be classified into one of four types: Brand competitors; Product competitors; Generic competitors; Total budget competitors. The number of firms controlling the supply of a product may affect the strength of competitors. The four general types of competitive structures are monopoly, oligopoly, monopolistic competition, and pure competition. Marketers monitor what competitors are currently doing and assess changes occurring in the competitive environment.

General economic conditions, buying power, and willingness to spend can strongly influence marketing decisions and activities. The overall state of the economy fluctuates in a general pattern known as the business cycle. The stages of the business cycle are prosperity, recession, depression, and recovery. Consumers' goods, services, and financial holdings make up their buying power, or ability to purchase. Financial sources of buying power are income, credit, and wealth. After-tax income used for spending or saving is disposable income. Disposable income left after an individual purchases the basic necessities of food, clothes, and shelter is discretionary income. Factors affecting buyers' willingness to spend include product price, level of satisfaction obtained from currently used products, family size, and expectations about future employment, income, prices, and general economic conditions.

The political, legal, and regulatory forces of the marketing environment are closely interrelated. The political environment may determine what laws and regulations affecting specific marketers are enacted and how much the government purchases and from which suppliers. It can also be important in helping organizations secure foreign markets.

Federal legislation affecting marketing activities can be divided into procompetitive legislation—laws designed to preserve and encourage competition—and consumer protection laws that generally relate to product safety and information disclosure. Actual effects of legislation are determined by how marketers and courts interpret the laws. Federal guidelines for sentencing violations of these laws represent an attempt to force marketers to comply with the law.

Federal, state, and local regulatory agencies usually have power to enforce specific laws and some discretion in establishing operating rules and drawing up regulations to guide certain types of industry practices. Industry self-regulation represents another regulatory force; marketers view this type of regulation more favorably than government action because they have more opportunity to take part in creating guidelines. Self-regulation may be less expensive than government regulation, and its guidelines are generally more realistic. However, such regulation generally cannot ensure compliance as effectively as government agencies.

Technology is the application of knowledge and tools to solve problems and perform tasks more efficiently. Consumer demand, product development, packaging, promotion, prices, and distribution systems are all influenced directly by technology.

Sociocultural forces are the influences in a society and its culture that result in changes in attitudes, beliefs, norms, customs, and lifestyles. Major sociocultural issues directly affecting marketers include demographic and diversity characteristics, cultural values, and consumerism. Changes in a population's demographic characteristics, such as age, income, race, and ethnicity, can lead to changes in that population's consumption of products. Changes in cultural values, such as those relating to health, nutrition, family, and the natural environment, have had striking effects on people's needs for products and therefore are closely monitored by marketers. Consumerism refers to the efforts of individuals, groups, and organizations to protect consumers' rights. Consumer rights organizations inform and organize other consumers, raise issues, help businesses develop consumer-oriented programs, and pressure lawmakers to enact consumer protection laws.

Important Terms

Environmental scanning
Environmental analysis
Competition
Brand competitors
Product competitors
Generic competitors
Total budget competitors
Monopoly
Oligopoly
Monopolistic competition
Pure competition
Business cycle
Prosperity
Recession
Depression
Recovery
Buying power
Income
Disposable income
Discretionary income
Wealth
Willingness to spend
Federal Trade Commission (FTC)
Better Business Bureau
National Advertising Review Board (NARB)
Technology
Sociocultural forces
Consumerism

Discussion and Review Questions

1. Why are environmental scanning and analysis important to marketers?
2. What are the four types of competition? Which is most important to marketers?
3. In what ways can each of the business cycle stages affect consumers' reactions to marketing strategies?
4. What business cycle stage are we experiencing currently? How is this stage affecting business firms in your area?
5. Define *income, disposable income,* and *discretionary income.* How does each type of income affect consumer buying power?
6. How is consumer buying power affected by wealth and consumer credit?
7. What factors influence a buyer's willingness to spend?
8. Describe marketers' attempts to influence political forces.
9. What types of problems do marketers experience as they interpret legislation?
10. What are the goals of the Federal Trade Commission? List the ways in which the FTC affects marketing activities. Do you think a single regulatory agency should have such broad jurisdiction over so many marketing practices? Why or why not?
11. Name several nongovernmental regulatory forces. Do you believe self-regulation is more or less effective than governmental regulatory agencies? Why?
12. What does the term *technology* mean to you? Do the benefits of technology outweigh its costs and potential dangers? Defend your answer.
13. Discuss the impact of technology on marketing activities.
14. What factors determine whether a business organization adopts and uses technology?
15. What is the evidence that cultural diversity is increasing in the United States?
16. In what ways are cultural values changing? How are marketers responding to these changes?
17. Describe consumerism. Analyze some active consumer forces in your area.

Application Questions

1. Assume you are opening *one* of the following retail stores. Identify publications at the library or online that provide information about the environmental forces likely to affect the store. Briefly summarize the information each provides.
   a. Convenience store   d. Fast-food restaurant
   b. Women's clothing store   e. Furniture store
   c. Grocery store

2. For each of the following products, identify brand competitors, product competitors, generic competitors, and total budget competitors:
   a. Dodge Caravan minivan   c. America Online
   b. Levi's jeans

3. Technological advances and sociocultural forces have a great impact on marketers. Identify at least one technological advancement and one sociocultural change that has affected you as a consumer. Explain the impact of each on your needs as a customer.

Internet Exercise & Resources

Visit **www.prideferrell.com** for resources to help you master the material in this chapter, plus materials that will help you expand your marketing knowledge, including: Internet exercise updates, ACE self-tests, hotlinks to companies featured in this chapter, and much more.

The Federal Trade Commission Online

To learn more about the Federal Trade Commission and its functions, look at the FTC's website at

www.ftc.gov

1. Based on information on the website, describe the FTC's impact on marketing.

2. Examine the sections entitled "News Releases, Publications & Speeches" and "Formal Actions, Opinions & Activities." Describe three recent incidents of illegal or inappropriate marketing activities and the FTC's response to those actions.

3. How could the FTC's website assist a company in avoiding misconduct?

VIDEO CASE 3.1

Netscape Navigates a Changing Environment

One of the earliest players in the Internet-driven "New Economy" is Netscape Communications, which markets web-browsing software as well as business software solutions. The firm is also behind an award-winning web search engine and Netscape NetCenter, a popular web portal. At one time, Netscape was the fastest-growing software company in history until a bitter fight with Microsoft forced it to reinvent itself.

Netscape was founded in 1994 by Marc Andreessen and Jim Clark. When he was a computer science student at the University of Illinois, Andreessen had come up with the idea for a World Wide Web browser with a graphical user interface (GUI). At that time, the Internet was essentially accessible only to scientists, researchers, govern-

ment engineers, and a few students with strong computer skills using text-based software; the World Wide Web was still in its infancy. Together with a team of UI students, Andreessen translated his vision into Mosaic, the first GUI web browser, which was distributed by the university for noncommercial use. Mosaic represented a major technological breakthrough that not only permitted multimedia applications but, for the first time, allowed people with limited computer skills to access the Internet. After Andreessen left the university, he joined forces with Jim Clark, who shared his excitement about the commercial opportunities promised by the Internet.

Within months of the company's founding, the team launched its first product, a new GUI browser called Netscape Navigator. Because of its ease of use and ability to tap into the growing volume and variety of information on the Web, Navigator became an overnight success and a media star. Within a year, Netscape Communications had become the world's fastest-growing software firm, with $45 million in revenues from licensing the browser technology to other companies. Propelled in part by Netscape's easy-to-use browser, the Internet quickly exploded into a global marketplace for the trading of goods, services, and information, from automobiles and airline tickets to collectibles, books, and music. During Netscape's first year, the number of Internet users grew from 2 million to 15 million.

Netscape continued to upgrade its browser and develop new products to allow consumers and businesses to harness the potential of this rapidly growing medium. The growth of Netscape also facilitated Sun Microsystems's development of the Java programming language, which allowed software companies to create applications to run on any computer operating system, including Microsoft's Windows. Because Java enhanced user flexibility and ease of use, it further expanded the commercial and informational potential of the World Wide Web.

Like many other companies, Microsoft had also observed the dramatic growth of the Internet and saw its potential for commercial uses. By 1995, Microsoft had developed its own web browser, Internet Explorer, which it bundled into Windows 95. Microsoft executives viewed Netscape as a serious threat because of the success of the Navigator product. According to James Barksdale, Netscape's CEO, Microsoft's strategy for Windows and Internet Explorer involved nothing short of eliminating Netscape. Together with executives from other firms, Barksdale complained that Microsoft's strategy for marketing Windows 95—including bundling Internet Explorer into the software, restricting computer manufacturers' ability to install competing browsers (e.g., Netscape Navigator), offering Internet service providers (ISPs) financial incentives to make Internet Explorer their "preferred" browser, and other actions Barksdale labeled "predatory"—was anticompetitive and violated federal antitrust laws.

The effect of Microsoft's strategy was dramatic. In early 1996, Netscape held a 70 percent share of the web browser market and derived about 70 percent of its revenue from licenses. By fall of 1998, Netscape's share of the market had declined to less than 50 percent, and the company had stopped generating revenues from licensing browsers because it had to literally give the product away to

compete with Microsoft. Among home Internet users, Netscape's market share declined from 51 percent in 1996 to 35 percent in 1998. These figures were cited as evidence of "Microsoft's Monopoly" in a lawsuit the federal government and 20 states filed against the software giant in 1998. Microsoft was eventually found guilty of violating federal antitrust laws and ordered to be split in two; Microsoft has appealed the penalty.

Before the trial ended, however, Netscape was acquired by America Online (AOL), the largest Internet service provider in the United States. According to Steve Case, AOL's chairman and CEO, "With the Netscape acquisition, we have dramatically improved America Online's ability to make the interactive medium more and more central to the lives of people around the world—especially enhancing our reach into the workplace. This acquisition will greatly accelerate our business momentum by advancing our multiple-brand, multiple-product strategy and helping us take e-commerce to a new level." Soon after, AOL merged with Time Warner, creating one of the largest media companies in the world. For AOL Time Warner, Netscape remains a strong brand, and its technologies and business relationships will help the media giant continue to expand the goods and services it markets.

Although its share of the browser market declined as a result of the bitter battle with Microsoft, Netscape retains a fiercely loyal group of customers who insist that its browser products are the best on the market. Netscape continues to flourish, expanding existing products, including Navigator and Communicator browsers, and developing new ones to provide Internet solutions for corporate customers. By transforming itself into a software enterprise, Netscape is helping businesses build internal networks accessible by suppliers, distributors, customers, and partners around the world. Such "extranets" help companies cut costs and improve their bottom lines. Netscape also helps companies establish "intranets," internal networks accessible only to widespread employees, including one for the U.S. Department of Defense. The company also launched a NetBusiness website for registered business users; the site includes an online small-business journal, *NetBusiness,* featuring content from Time Warner publications as well as from other NetBusiness partners.

The dynamics of technology involve constant change that can profoundly alter the marketing environment. To remain competitive, companies like Netscape must remain vigilant in assessing environmental forces to recognize opportunities as well as threats that can erase a firm's hard-won competitive advantage seemingly overnight.[43]

QUESTIONS FOR DISCUSSION

1. What factors in the marketing environment helped Netscape achieve success in such a short time? What factors later harmed the company?

2. Assess AOL Time Warner's strategy for expanding the Netscape brand. How can the firm minimize further competitive threat from Microsoft?

3. During much of Netscape's life, the U.S. economy was experiencing great prosperity. The economy began to slow at the turn of the century, however, and many Internet-based companies failed. What actions should AOL Time Warner executives take to ensure that Netscape survives this business cycle?

CASE 3.2
Microsoft Versus the U.S. Government

Few companies have had the kind of impact Microsoft Corporation has in its 25 years of operation. Founded by William ("Bill") H. Gates and Paul G. Allen, Microsoft's innovative products and marketing prowess have made it the world's leading marketer of computer software, including operating systems for personal computers (PCs), network servers, and other devices; office productivity software; software development tools; and Internet products, such as the MSN online network. Microsoft also sells computer hardware, provides consulting services, licenses consumer software, and continues to research and develop new products and technologies for the future. Based in Redmond, Washington, the company has grown to 39,100 employees and reached annual sales of nearly $23 billion. Despite its phenomenal success, the company has also been the subject of considerable controversy as a result of its competitive practices.

In 1990, the Federal Trade Commission (FTC) began investigating Microsoft for possible violations of the Sherman and Clayton Antitrust acts, which prohibit restraint of trade by businesses, especially monopolists. When the FTC deadlocked on a decision in 1993, it passed the case on to the U.S. Department of Justice. Microsoft eventually settled the charges without admitting any wrongdoing. Among other provisions, the settlement required the company to end its practice of selling its MS-DOS operating system to computer manufacturers at a 60 percent discount. Microsoft had granted the discount to manufacturers that agreed to pay the company for every computer they sold instead of paying for every computer sold with MS-DOS preinstalled. Critics had labeled this discount unfair to both consumers and computer companies because most manufacturers had to pay Microsoft regardless of whether they installed MS-DOS or some other operating system. Competitors had accused Microsoft of being anticompetitive because the practice made it uneconomical for a computer manufacturer to give up a 60 percent discount to install a competing operating system on some computers.

After various companies, particularly Netscape Communications and Sun Microsystems, continued to complain about Microsoft's competitive practices, the federal government took an aggressive stand, charging Microsoft with creating a monopolistic environment that substantially lessened competition in the industry. The company settled the charges in 1995 and consented to a decree that barred it from imposing anticompetitive licensing terms on PC manufacturers.

In 1997, however, the Justice Department asked a federal court to hold Microsoft in civil contempt for violating the terms of the consent decree and to impose a $1-million-a-day fine. This time the issue was Microsoft's bundling of its Internet Explorer web browser into the Windows 95 operating system. Microsoft argued that Internet Explorer was an integrated, inseparable part of Windows 95 and that it had not incorporated the browser technology into Windows solely to disadvantage rivals such as Netscape. The company denied government allegations that it had attempted to "illegally divide the browser market" with Netscape and that it had entered into exclusionary contracts with Internet service and content providers. Finally, Microsoft argued that it did not illegally restrict the ability of computer manufacturers to alter the Windows desktop screen that users see when they turn on their computers for the first time. A U.S. district court judge disagreed and issued an injunction prohibiting the company from requiring Windows 95 licensees to include Internet Explorer with Windows. While Microsoft waited for its appeal to be heard, it supplied PC makers with either an older version of Windows 95 without Internet Explorer or a current version stripped of all Internet Explorer files. The product would not boot up, however, a fact that Microsoft later admitted it knew beforehand. Consequently the Justice Department asked the court to hold Microsoft in contempt. At the same time, Microsoft's stock began to drop. Possibly fearing further stock devaluation, Microsoft consented to provide vendors with the most up-to-date version of Windows 95 without the Internet Explorer desktop icon.

After two years of negotiations, the federal government, along with 20 states (one later dropped out), formally charged Microsoft with abusing its monopoly in the computer software business. At the heart of these charges were three primary issues: (1) bundling the Internet Explorer web browser with Windows 98 to damage competition, particularly Netscape; (2) using cross-promotional deals with Internet providers to extend Microsoft's monopoly; and (3) illegally preventing PC makers from customizing the Windows opening screen.

The trial began on October 19, 1998, in the U.S. district court of Judge Thomas Penfield Jackson. By the time Microsoft began its defense in January 1999, its credibility had been severely damaged by federal prosecutors. Jim Allchin, a long-time Microsoft employee often referred to as "Microsoft's lord of Windows," was called in to prove that separating the Internet Explorer browser from Windows would be detrimental. However, his videotaped demonstration did exactly the opposite when icons on the computer screen mysteriously appeared at a moment's notice throughout the tape.

Microsoft attempted to settle the case, but the two sides could not reach an agreement. One remedy suggested by the government was for Microsoft to agree to seat government-appointed people on its board of directors, a solution Microsoft rejected as a government takeover. By 2000, the government had begun to talk about splitting the company into two. Judge Jackson then appointed Richard Posner, a respected member of the Seventh Circuit Court, to negotiate another settlement, but the gap between the two sides remained insurmountable.

Without a settlement agreement, Judge Jackson issued his final decision in the case on June 7, 2000. He ruled that Microsoft had indeed violated federal antitrust laws and ordered the company split into two independent corporations, one to sell Windows software and the other to sell other Microsoft products. Jackson offered several grounds for his dramatic decision, the first being simply that Microsoft had refused to admit any wrongdoing. He also stated that the ruling was intended to prevent Microsoft from insulting the government by refusing to comply with federal antitrust laws. Jackson said he found Microsoft to be "untrustworthy" because of its past behavior, including selling defective Windows software after being ordered to unbundle Internet Explorer from Windows. Jackson further indicated that his decision was intended to prevent Microsoft from bullying its competitors. In splitting up Microsoft, Jackson expressed a hope to reignite competition in the computer industry and spur innovation and creativity that the software giant had stifled.

Microsoft didn't see it that way. Gates and other company executives protested that splitting the firm in two was the equivalent of a "corporate death sentence." They also countered that it would not spur innovation but stifle it. The split would make software development more complex and make it difficult to effectively integrate two or more programs across two businesses. The company also argued that separate marketing of software would drive up prices for consumers. Microsoft appealed the decision.

A little more than a year later, the U.S. Court of Appeals for the District of Columbia affirmed Jackson's ruling that Microsoft had illegally operated as a monopoly in the market for computer operating systems. However, the court rejected Jackson's order to split the company and ordered a new judge to assess a penalty against the computer giant for violating federal antitrust laws. The Justice Department hailed the decision as a victory because it upheld the government's core argument that Microsoft had acted monopolistically. Microsoft also claimed victory because the decision "removes the cloud of breakup" hanging over the company and stifling marketing strategy. Nonetheless, Microsoft appealed the decision to the Supreme Court. However, a decision had not been issued as of the writing of this case. By the time you read this, both sides will likely have negotiated a settlement requiring the computer giant to modify some of its business practices.[44]

QUESTIONS FOR DISCUSSION

1. What are the legal issues in this case as they relate to Microsoft's marketing strategy? What laws did Microsoft break?
2. Although ultimately overturned, Judge Jackson's order to split the company would have made Microsoft only the fourth company to be broken up as a result of violations of U.S. antitrust laws. Why would the judge have ordered such an extreme penalty for illegal monopolistic activities?
3. What role has Microsoft played in today's technological revolution?

Social Responsibility and Ethics in Marketing

4

OBJECTIVES

- To understand the concept and dimensions of social responsibility
- To define and describe the importance of marketing ethics
- To become familiar with ways to improve ethical decisions in marketing
- To understand the role of social responsibility and ethics in improving marketing performance

83

Helping the World, One Can at a Time

What substance can fill the Georgia Dome 27 times each year? Unfortunately, the answer is the aluminum cans and beverage bottles that get thrown into landfills instead of being recycled. But what is the big deal? Why is recycling so important? First, recyclable waste is an unnecessary burden on the already full landfills. This type of waste alone has increased more than 50 percent in the past decade; 2.5 million plastic bottles are used every hour in America. Moreover, tin requires 100 years to biodegrade, aluminum 500 years, and glass 1 million years. Second, recycling conserves energy. Recycling aluminum requires 90 to 95 percent less energy than mining and processing bauxite ore, the source of aluminum. Recycling one aluminum can can generate the energy to run a television for 3 hours or a 100-watt light bulb for 20 hours. However, recycling is declining because only 44 percent of Americans have access to a roadside recycling center, and many consider these centers to be dirty and unsafe.

Tomra, a company based in Norway, wants to change the way Americans view recycling. The company began this effort in southern California, where it installed 50 rePlanet recycling centers. These centers are clean, brightly lit, conveniently located at grocery stores, and accessible at all hours. An attendant runs each station from 10:00 A.M. to 5:00 P.M. Tuesdays through Saturdays. Consumers can recycle even when an attendant is not present by using the company's reverse vending machines. Designed much like an ATM, these machines employ a moving conveyor belt with cameras that take digital pictures to identify the container. The machine then computes the customer's refund and dispenses a voucher, which can be redeemed inside the store for cash or food items. Based on early use, Tomra's rePlanet centers increased the volume of recycled containers over previous centers by 60 percent. Tomra intends to process more than 150,000 containers per month—about 200 per hour—through its California centers. California is currently considered Tomra's single largest market, where organic growth has increased by more than 153 percent.

In addition to accepting containers for recycling, Tomra's rePlanet centers promote conservation of the natural environment in other ways. When customers drop off materials, the on-site attendants can offer tips about how to improve the environment. They also distribute sunflower and other seed samples so customers can add vegetation and color to their yards. In addition to flowers, Tomra is actively donating larger plant specimens. For every 200,000 containers deposited, the company plants one tree in the neighborhood surrounding the center. The company has already planted 36 trees.

Through its rePlanet recycling centers and other activities, Tomra is proving that it cares about maximizing its positive impact and minimizing its negative impact on society, especially the natural environment. As the centers continue to prove successful, Tomra intends to open 150 more in southern California and to begin negotiations with grocers in the northern portion of the state. After California, the company plans to open recycling centers throughout the United States, beginning in states that heavily promote recycling through deposits, such as New York, Michigan, and Iowa. Tomra has taken something once considered dirty and inconvenient and made it a pleasant experience, while proving that a business can be environmentally responsible and still make a profit.[1]

By taking an environmentally responsible, customer-focused approach to marketing, Tomra has grown into a successful marketing firm. Like Tomra, most marketers operate responsibly and within the limits of the law. Some companies, however, choose to engage in activities that customers, other marketers, and society in general deem unacceptable. Such activities include questionable selling practices, bribery, price discrimination, deceptive advertising, misleading packaging, and the marketing of defective products. For example, 37 percent of the software programs used by businesses worldwide are illegally pirated copies.[2] Practices of this kind raise questions about marketers' obligations to society. Inherent in these questions are the issues of social responsibility and marketing ethics.

Because social responsibility and ethics can have a profound impact on the success of marketing strategies, we devote this chapter to their role in marketing decision making. We begin by defining social responsibility and exploring its dimensions. We also discuss social responsibility issues, such as the natural environment and the marketer's role as a member of the community. Next, we define and examine the role of ethics in marketing decisions. We consider ethical issues in marketing, the ethical decision-making process, and ways to improve ethical conduct in marketing. Finally, we incorporate social responsibility and ethics into strategic market planning.

The Nature of Social Responsibility

social responsibility
An organization's obligation to maximize its positive impact and minimize its negative impact on society

In marketing, **social responsibility** refers to an organization's obligation to maximize its positive impact and minimize its negative impact on society. Social responsibility thus deals with the total effect of all marketing decisions on society. Ample evidence demonstrates that ignoring society's demands for responsible marketing can destroy customers' trust and even prompt government regulations. Irresponsible actions that anger customers, employees, or competitors may not only jeopardize a marketer's financial standing but have legal repercussions as well. For instance, Mitsubishi Motors, Japan's number four automaker, faced criminal charges and negative publicity after executives admitted the company had systematically covered up customer complaints about tens of thousands of defective automobiles for 20 years to avoid expensive and embarrassing product recalls.[3] In contrast, socially responsible activities can generate positive publicity and boost sales. The Breast Cancer Awareness Crusade sponsored by Avon Products, for example, has raised nearly $110 million to help fund community-based breast cancer education and early detection services. Within the first few years of the Awareness Crusade, hundreds of stories about Avon's efforts appeared in major media, which contributed to an increase in company sales. Avon, a marketer of women's cosmetics, is also known for employing a large number of women and promoting them to top management; the firm has more female top managers (86 percent) than any other *Fortune* 500 company.[4]

Socially responsible efforts like Avon's have a positive impact on local communities; at the same time, they indirectly help the sponsoring organization by attracting goodwill, publicity, and potential customers and employees. Thus, while social responsibility is certainly a positive concept in itself, most organizations embrace it in the expectation of indirect long-term benefits. Our own research suggests that a marketing-oriented culture is conducive to social responsibility, which in turn is associated with greater employee commitment and improved business performance.[5] Table 4.1 provides a sampling of companies that have chosen to make social responsibility a strategic long-term objective.

The Dimensions of Social Responsibility

marketing citizenship
The adoption of a strategic focus for fulfilling the economic, legal, ethical, and philanthropic social responsibilities expected by stakeholders

stakeholders Constituents who have a "stake" or claim in some aspect of a company's products, operations, markets, industry, and outcomes

Socially responsible organizations strive for **marketing citizenship** by adopting a strategic focus for fulfilling the economic, legal, ethical, and philanthropic social responsibilities that their stakeholders expect of them. **Stakeholders** include those constituents who have a "stake," or claim, in some aspect of a company's products,

Table 4.1	A Sampling of Socially Responsible Marketers
CitySoft Inc. (Watertown, MA)	Provides web development services with a work force recruited from urban neighborhoods
Honest Tea Inc. (Bethesda, MD)	Produces and markets bottled teas and biodegradable tea bags
New Leaf Paper LLC (San Francisco, CA)	Produces and markets recycled paper products
Sustainable Harvest Inc. (Emeryville, CA)	Markets organic, shade-grown coffee supplied by small family farms and cooperatives
Village Real Estate Services (Nashville, TN)	Specializes in urban home sales and revitalizing neighborhoods and communities
Wild Planet Toys Inc. (San Francisco, CA)	Produces and markets gender-neutral, nonviolent toys
WorldWise Inc. (San Rafael, CA)	Produces and markets garden, home, and pet products made from recycled or organic materials

Source: Thea Singer, "Can Business Still Save the World?" *Inc.*, Apr. 2001, pp. 58–71.

operations, markets, industry, and outcomes; these include customers, employees, investors and shareholders, suppliers, governments, communities, and many others. Companies that consider the diverse perspectives of stakeholders in their daily operations and strategic planning are said to have a *stakeholder orientation,* an important element of corporate citizenship.[6] For example, British home improvement retailer B&Q secured stakeholder input on issues ranging from child labor, fair wages, and equal opportunity to environmental impact. Based on consultations with store managers, employees, suppliers, and government representatives, the retailer now recognizes and measures its progress on all four dimensions of corporate social responsibility.[7] As Figure 4.1 shows, these dimensions can be viewed as a pyramid.[8] The economic and legal aspects have long been acknowledged, but philanthropic and ethical issues have gained recognition more recently.

RESPONSIBILITIES

FIGURE 4.1
The Pyramid of Corporate Social Responsibility
Source: Archie B. Carroll, "The Pyramid of Corporate Social Responsibility: Toward the Moral Management of Organizational Stakeholders," adaptation of Figure 3, p. 42. Reprinted from *Business Horizons*, July/Aug. 1991. Copyright © 1991 by the Foundation for the School of Business at Indiana University. Used with permission.

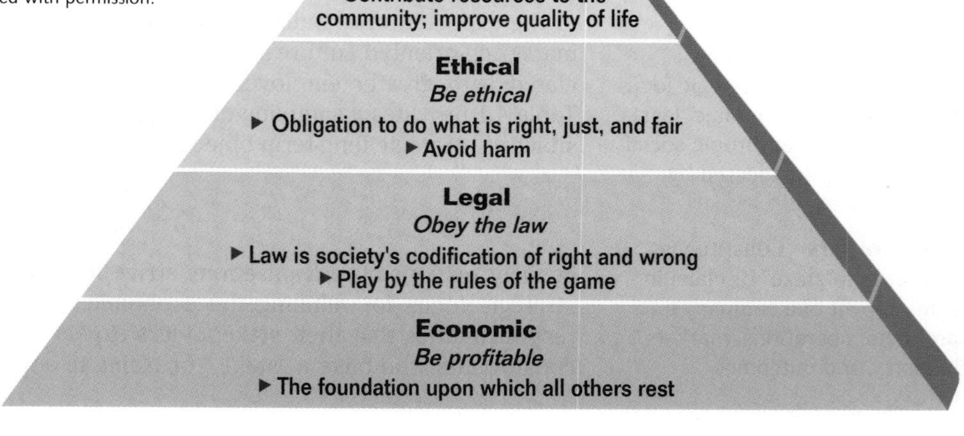

Philanthropic
Be a good corporate citizen
▶ Contribute resources to the community; improve quality of life

Ethical
Be ethical
▶ Obligation to do what is right, just, and fair
▶ Avoid harm

Legal
Obey the law
▶ Law is society's codification of right and wrong
▶ Play by the rules of the game

Economic
Be profitable
▶ The foundation upon which all others rest

Building Relationships . . .

A Special Look at a Company in Transformation

Around the world and in everything we do, Ford Motor Company is learning to look ahead even farther. Our work is not simply about making a single sale, or completing a hire or generating this quarter's "buy" recommendation. Important as those things are, they are part of a bigger process: the process of building deep and lasting bonds between our company and customers, suppliers, dealers, society, investors, and our employees – every single one of our principal stakeholder groups. Those bonds add up to loyalty, and loyalty is the key to realizing our goal of being the world's leading consumer company for automotive products and services.

The Nature of Social Responsibility
Ford recognizes the importance of all stakeholders in addressing ethical and social responsibility issues.

At the most basic level, all companies have an economic responsibility to be profitable so they can provide a return on investment to their owners and investors, create jobs for the community, and contribute goods and services to the economy. How organizations relate to stockholders, employees, competitors, customers, the community, and the natural environment affects the economy. When economic downturns or poor decisions lead companies to lay off employees, communities often suffer as they attempt to absorb the displaced employees. Customers may also experience diminished levels of service as a result of fewer experienced employees. Stock prices often decline when layoffs are announced, affecting the value of stockholders' investment portfolios. Moreover, stressed-out employees facing demands to reduce expenses may make poor decisions that affect the natural environment, product quality, employee rights, and customer service. An organization's sense of economic responsibility is especially significant for employees, raising such issues as equal job opportunities, workplace diversity, job safety, health, and employee privacy. Economic responsibilities require finding a balance between society's demand for social responsibility and investors' desire for profits. Aaron Lamstein, founder and CEO of WorldWise, says, "You can't put one in front of the other. You can't be successful if you can't do both." Lamstein's company, which markets home, garden, and pet care products made of recycled or organic materials, is profiled in Marketing Citizenship on page 88.[9]

Marketers also have an economic responsibility to compete fairly. Size frequently gives companies an advantage over others. Large firms can often generate economies of scale that allow them to put smaller firms out of business. Consequently, small companies and even whole communities may resist the efforts of firms like Wal-Mart, Home Depot, and Best Buy to open stores in their vicinity. These firms are able to operate at such low costs that small, local firms cannot compete. Though consumers appreciate lower prices, the failure of small businesses creates unemployment for some members of communities.[10] Such issues create concerns about social responsibility for organizations, communities, and consumers.

Marketers are also expected, of course, to obey laws and regulations. The efforts of elected representatives and special-interest groups to promote responsible corporate behavior have resulted in laws and regulations designed to keep U.S. companies' actions within the range of acceptable conduct. When customers, interest groups, or businesses become outraged over what they perceive as irresponsibility on the part of a marketing organization, they may urge their legislators to draft new legislation to regulate the behavior, or they may engage in litigation to force the organization to "play by the rules." For example, Fruit of the Loom sued Gildan Activewear, accusing its Canadian rival of using confidential documents obtained from a former Fruit of the Loom manager to steal market share and gain a competitive edge in the fiercely competitive underwear market. With *Fortune* 1000 companies losing an estimated $45 billion a year due to corporate espionage, managers are particularly anxious to prevent such incidents.[11]

Economic and legal responsibilities are the most basic levels of social responsibility for a good reason: failure to consider them may mean that a marketer is not around long enough to engage in ethical or philanthropic activities. Beyond these dimensions is **marketing ethics,** principles and standards that define acceptable conduct in marketing as determined by various stakeholders, including the public, government regulators, private-interest groups, consumers, industry, and the organization itself. The most basic of these principles have been codified as laws and regulations to encourage marketers to conform to society's expectations of conduct. However, marketing ethics goes beyond legal issues. Ethical marketing decisions foster trust, which helps to build long-term marketing relationships. We take a more detailed look at the ethical dimension of social responsibility later in this chapter.

At the top of the pyramid are philanthropic responsibilities. These responsibilities, which go beyond marketing ethics, are not required of a company, but they promote human welfare or goodwill, as do the economic, legal, and ethical dimensions of

marketing ethics Principles and standards that define acceptable marketing conduct as determined by various stakeholders

MARKETING CITIZENSHIP

WorldWise, Inc., Turns Green into Green

Founded in 1990, WorldWise, Inc., markets pet, lawn and garden, and hearth products made primarily from recycled, reclaimed, or sustainably harvested materials. With a staff of just 15, the company has grown slowly and selectively, gaining customers that include some of North America's largest retail chains, such as Home Depot, Wal-Mart, Target, Petco, and Ace Hardware. The company also markets to regular retail customers, who appreciate the company's environmentally friendly focus. Despite its small size, WorldWise has a very ambitious mission: to change the world by making "environmentally responsible products that work as well or better, look as good or finer and cost the same or less as the competition."

Based in San Rafael, California, WorldWise was founded by Aaron Lamstein (now CEO) and Phil Genet (chairman of the board). After researching thousands of products, Lamstein decided to launch the company by marketing environmentally friendly products already selling in niche markets under the WorldWise brand. From the beginning, the company was very selective about the items it chose to carry the WorldWise name. Its first product was an exotic fruit-and-nut mix whose ingredients came from the Amazon rain forest. This strategy armed the company with tremendous marketing intelligence about the types of environmentally friendly products that interested consumers and helped the firm begin to research and develop its own products.

WorldWise now markets more than 25 products in three categories. One of its newest products is the Terra Notta, an unbreakable planter made from recycled plastics and rubber. One of the company's most popular offerings is the award-winning Cat Scratcher, a scratching post and lounge for cats made from recycled cardboard and enhanced with organic catnip. The company also makes products from reclaimed materials, including discarded bottle caps and abandoned tree stumps, and from recycled materials ranging from cardboard to plastics. By purchasing these products, consumers kept more than 1 million pounds of materials out of landfills and prevented half a million pounds of greenhouse gases from entering the atmosphere in 2000.

WorldWise's founders' desire to build an environmentally responsible firm has helped the company gain new customers who appreciate its environmental focus and reputation for quality. Charlie Rossi, garden center manager for Home Depot in San Rafael, is enthusiastic about WorldWise and its products: "They are good, first-quality products. They have tip-top service, the products are always there, and we have never had a problem." These characteristics have also helped the company win a number of awards for its environmentally friendly products, and Aaron Lamstein was recently named to the environmental advisory board of Wal-Mart.

Philanthropic Responsibilities
Franchises such as TOGO's, Dunkin' Donuts, and Baskin Robbins responded quickly to the disastrous events of September 11, 2001 by donating coffee, food, and supplies for volunteers, as well as by contributing to national fundraising efforts.

cause-related marketing
The practice of linking products to a particular social cause on an ongoing or short-term basis

strategic philanthropy The synergistic use of organizational core competencies and resources to address key stakeholders' interests and achieve both organizational and social benefits

social responsibility. That many companies have demonstrated philanthropic responsibility is evidenced by the nearly $11 billion in annual corporate donations and contributions to environmental and social causes.[12] Many corporations immediately made significant contributions to the victims and families of the September 11, 2001 attack on the United States. For example, Coca Cola Company contributed $12 million, DaimlerChrysler $10 million, and Microsoft $10 million to assist victims.[13] Companies such as Home Depot and Starbucks contributed $1 million and were also involved in other activities to help the victims. For example, Home Depot supplied rescue materials and Starbucks collected donations in its stores for the September 11th Fund established by the New York Community Fund and the United Way.[14] Even small companies participate in philanthropy through donations and volunteer support of local causes and national charities, such as the Red Cross and the United Way.

More companies than ever are adopting a strategic approach to corporate philanthropy. Many firms link their products to a particular social cause on an ongoing or short-term basis. One of the first companies to apply this practice, known as **cause-related marketing,** was American Express, which donated to the Statue of Liberty restoration fund every time customers used their American Express card. The promotion was extraordinarily successful, generating new customers and increasing the use of credit cards dramatically. Customers tend to like such cause-related programs because they provide an additional reason to "feel good" about a particular purchase. Marketers like the programs because well-designed ones increase sales and create feelings of respect and admiration for the companies involved. Some companies are beginning to extend the concept of corporate philanthropy beyond financial contributions by adopting a **strategic philanthropy** approach, the synergistic use of organizational core competencies and resources to address key stakeholders' interests and achieve both organizational and social benefits. Strategic philanthropy involves employees, organizational resources and expertise, and the ability to link these assets to the concerns of key stakeholders, including employees, customers, suppliers, and social needs. Strategic philanthropy involves both financial and nonfinancial contributions to stakeholders (employee time, goods and services, and company technology and equipment, as well as facilities), but it also benefits the company.[15] Home Depot, for example, has been progressive in aligning its expertise and resources to address community needs. Its relationship with Habitat for Humanity gives employees a chance to improve their skills and bring direct knowledge back into the workplace to benefit customers. It also enhances Home Depot's image of expertise as the "do-it-yourself" center. Home Depot also responds to customers' needs during disasters such as hurricanes. Many home building supply and hardware stores have taken advantage of customers by inflating prices on emergency materials, but Home Depot opens its stores 24 hours a day and makes materials available at reduced costs to help customers survive the disaster.[16]

Table 4.2	Social Responsibility Issues	
Issue	**Description**	**Major Social Concerns**
Natural environment	Consumers insisting not only on the quality of life but also on a healthful environment so they can maintain a high standard of living during their lifetimes	Conservation Water pollution Air pollution Land pollution
Consumerism	Activities undertaken by independent individuals, groups, and organizations to protect their rights as consumers	The right to safety The right to be informed The right to choose The right to be heard
Community relations	Society anxious to have marketers contribute to its well-being, wishing to know what marketers do to help solve social problems	Equality issues Disadvantaged members of society Safety and health Education and general welfare

Social Responsibility Issues

Although social responsibility may seem to be an abstract ideal, managers make decisions related to social responsibility every day. To be successful, a business must determine what customers, government regulators, and competitors, as well as society in general, want or expect in terms of social responsibility. Table 4.2 summarizes three major categories of social responsibility issues: the natural environment, consumerism, and community relations.

The Natural Environment. One of the more common ways marketers demonstrate social responsibility is through programs designed to protect and preserve the natural environment. A recent survey indicated that 83.5 percent of *Fortune* 500 companies have a written environmental policy, 74.7 percent engage in recycling activities, and 69.7 percent have made investments in waste reduction efforts.[17] Many companies are making contributions to environmental protection organizations, sponsoring and participating in clean-up events, promoting recycling, retooling manufacturing processes to minimize waste and pollution, and generally reevaluating the effects of their products on the natural environment. Wal-Mart, for example, provides on-site recycling for customers and encourages its suppliers to reduce wasteful packaging. Procter & Gamble uses recycled materials in some of its packaging and markets refills for some products, which reduces packaging waste. Marketing Citizenship on page 93 describes another firm's efforts to be more environmentally responsible. Such efforts generate positive publicity and often increase sales for the companies involved.

green marketing The specific development, pricing, promotion, and distribution of products that do not harm the natural environment

Green marketing refers to the specific development, pricing, promotion, and distribution of products that do not harm the natural environment. General Motors, for example, is developing new "hybrid" pickup trucks and buses that use electric motors to augment their internal-combustion engines, improving the vehicles' fuel economy without a reduction in power.[18] Herman Miller, Inc., has replaced a number of the glues and finishes used in its ergonomic furniture with more environmentally friendly compounds and chooses woods carefully to ensure they come from renewable sources. The company also encourages its suppliers to switch to reusable packaging materials and designs its production facilities to function as efficiently as possible, thereby reducing waste and energy use.[19]

Many products have been certified as "green" by environmental organizations such as Green Seal and carry a special logo identifying them as such. Lumber products at Home Depot and U.K.-based B&Q may carry a seal from the Forest Stewardship Council to indicate they were harvested from sustainable forests using environmen-

Green Marketing
The Nature Conservancy works with businesses and communities to preserve our natural resources. DTE Energy works to minimize its emission of greenhouse gases.

FIGURE 4.2
The European Eco-label

tally friendly methods.[20] Likewise, most Chiquita bananas are certified through the Better Banana Project as having been grown with more environmentally and labor-friendly practices.[21] In Europe, companies can voluntarily apply for an Eco-label to indicate that their products are less harmful to the environment than competing products, based on scientifically determined criteria (see Figure 4.2).

Although demand for economic, legal, and ethical solutions to environmental problems is widespread, the environmental movement in marketing includes many different groups whose values and goals often conflict. Some environmentalists and marketers believe that companies should work to protect and preserve the natural environment by implementing the following goals:

1. *Eliminate the concept of waste.* Recognizing that pollution and waste usually stem from inefficiency, the question is not what to do with waste but how to make things without waste.

2. *Reinvent the concept of a product.* Products should be reduced to only three types and eventually just two. The first type is consumables, which are eaten or, when placed in the ground, turn into soil with few harmful side effects. The second type is durable goods—such as cars, televisions, computers, and refrigerators—which

Recycling
Environmental Defense promotes the idea that buying recycled products is good for the environment.

should be made, used, and returned to the manufacturer within a closed-loop system. Such products should be designed for disassembly and recycling. The third category is unsalables and includes such products as radioactive materials, heavy metals, and toxins. These products should always belong to the original makers, who should be responsible for them and their full life cycle effects. Reclassifying products in this way encourages manufacturers to design products more efficiently.

3. *Make prices reflect the cost.* Every product should reflect or at least approximate its actual cost—not only the direct cost of production but also the cost of air, water, and soil. For example, the cost of a gallon of gasoline, according to the World Resources Institute in Washington, DC, is approximately $4.50 when pollution, waste disposal, health effects, and defense expenditures like those of the Persian Gulf War are factored in.

4. *Make environmentalism profitable.* Consumers are beginning to recognize that competition in the marketplace should not occur between companies harming the environment and those trying to save it.[22]

Consumerism. Another significant issue in socially responsible marketing is consumerism, which we defined in Chapter 3 as the efforts of independent individuals, groups, and organizations to protect the rights of consumers. A number of interest groups and individuals have taken action against companies they consider irresponsible by lobbying government officials and agencies, engaging in letter-writing campaigns and boycotts, and making public service announcements. The consumer movement has been helped by news-format television programs, such as "Dateline," "60 Minutes," and "Prime Time Live," as well as by 24-hour news coverage from CNN and MSNBC. The Internet too has changed the way consumers obtain information about companies' goods, services, and activities.

Ralph Nader, one of the best-known consumer activists, continues to crusade for consumer rights. Consumer activism by Nader and others has resulted in

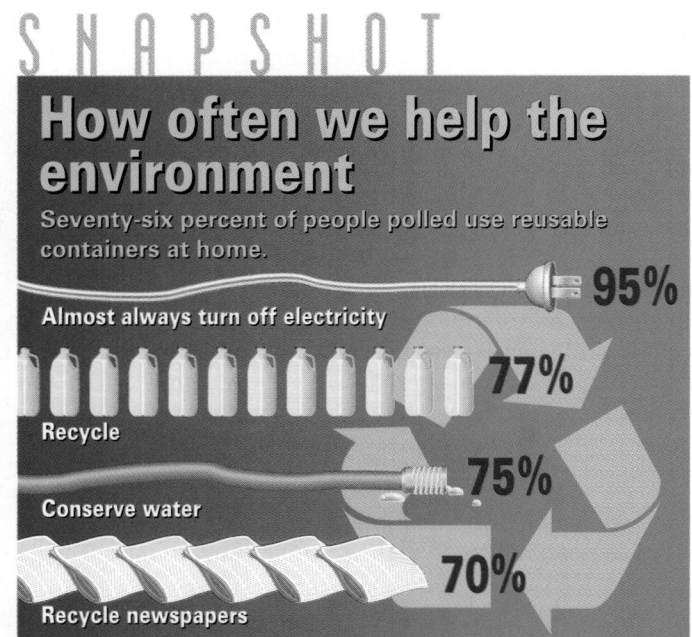

How often we help the environment
Seventy-six percent of people polled use reusable containers at home.

Almost always turn off electricity   95%
Recycle   77%
Conserve water   75%
Recycle newspapers   70%

Source: *USA Today*, May 9, 2000. www.usatoday.com. Copyright 2000, *USA Today*. Reprinted with permission.

legislation requiring many features that make cars safer: seat belts, air bags, padded dashboards, stronger door latches, head restraints, shatterproof windshields, and collapsible steering columns. Activists' efforts have also helped facilitate the passage of several consumer protection laws, including the Wholesome Meat Act of 1967, the Radiation Control for Health and Safety Act of 1968, the Clean Water Act of 1972, and the Toxic Substance Act of 1976.

Also of great importance to the consumer movement are four basic rights spelled out in a consumer "bill of rights" drafted by President John F. Kennedy. These rights include the right to safety, the right to be informed, the right to choose, and the right to be heard.

Ensuring consumers' *right to safety* means marketers have an obligation not to market a product that they know could harm consumers. This right can be extended to imply that all products must be safe for their intended use, include thorough and explicit instructions for proper and safe use, and have been tested to ensure reliability and quality.

Consumers' *right to be informed* means consumers should have access to and the opportunity to review all relevant information about a product before buying it. Many laws require specific labeling on product packaging to satisfy this right. In addition, labels on alcoholic and tobacco products inform consumers that these products may cause illness and other problems.

MARKETING CITIZENSHIP

Royal Caribbean Cleans Up

In the early 1990s, federal investigators accused Royal Caribbean Cruise Lines (RCCL) of dumping thousands of gallons of oily bilge, photo-developing chemicals, and dry-cleaning fluids into Caribbean waters, New York Harbor, Alaska's Inside Passage, and the Port of Miami. Although it initially fought the charges, the Miami-based company eventually pleaded guilty to 22 federal charges. It was fined $27 million—$2 million more than Exxon was fined for the *Valdez* oil spill—and placed on five years of corporate probation. Recognizing that consumers might not want to patronize a cruise line with a reputation for environmental misconduct, Jack Williams, the company's new president, apologized to the public for Royal Caribbean's crimes and set the company on a new course.

Today Royal Caribbean is actively working to become more environmentally responsible. The company has adopted a new advertising slogan, "Save the Waves," and its turquoise logo is displayed on every employee's name badge and on every ship. All RCCL cruise ships now have environmental officers, and one of the company's board members is a former administrator of the Environmental Protection Agency. The company is also building new ships with gas turbines instead of diesel, which will dramatically reduce airborne exhaust. RCCL's newest ship, the *Voyager of the Sea*, three times the size of the *Titanic* and 75 percent bigger than the rest of Royal Caribbean's ships, is not only the largest cruise ship ever built but also one of the most efficient and environmentally friendly.

The ship can turn completely around without moving forward or backward. When winds become too gusty, its on-deck restaurants are closed down to prevent trash from blowing into the ocean.

To promote and recognize environmental innovation and improvement throughout the firm, Royal Caribbean is sponsoring internal annual awards. The company presented its first Environmental Ship of the Year award to the *Enchantment of the Seas* on the basis of seven criteria: environmental performance, effectiveness of corrective actions, completion of corrective action to clear audit findings, reports of near-incidents, weekly and monthly environmental reports, performance of environmental equipment, and innovative thinking. The first Best Environmental Innovation of the Year award, designed to reward ships and crews that think "outside of the box," went to the *Monarch of the Seas*. These winners were selected by independent external auditors from Haley and Aldrich according to which ship most closely adhered to RCCL's new Environmental Compliance Plan.

By communicating its commitment to be environmentally responsible to both the public—including potential customers—and internally, Royal Caribbean hopes to leave the past behind and boost passenger revenue. The company may have needed a wake-up call to become environmentally responsible, but it now serves as a lesson for other cruise lines. This new social and environmental awareness should pay off handsomely in the marketplace.

There's a reason we'll never run out of trees. We put them back after we use them.

Most of the natural resources people rely on aren't being replaced. In fact, they can't be replaced. Fortunately, that's not the case with trees. This year, like every year, Weyerhaeuser planted over 100 million seedlings to replenish forests that provide products people need every day, like wood to build homes, packaging to ship food and paper for books. That's especially meaningful when you realize we harvest only a small portion of the timberlands in our care—about 2 to 3 percent a year, depending on growing cycles.

We understand that managing a resource as precious as trees isn't just a business. It's a special responsibility. So we never forget a simple lesson most of us learned as children: If you always put things back, they'll always be there when you need them.

Weyerhaeuser
The future is growing
www.weyerhaeuser.com

Environmental Responsibility
Weyerhaeuser communicates environmental responsibility by leading and promoting reforestation.

The *right to choose* means consumers should have access to a variety of products and services at competitive prices. They should also be assured of satisfactory quality and service at a fair price. Activities that reduce competition among businesses in an industry might jeopardize this right.

The *right to be heard* ensures that consumers' interests will receive full and sympathetic consideration in the formulation of government policy. The right to be heard also promises consumers fair treatment when they complain to marketers about products. This right benefits marketers too, because when consumers complain about a product, the manufacturer can use this information to modify the product and make it more satisfying.

Community Relations.   Social responsibility also extends to marketers' roles as community members. Individual communities expect marketers to make philanthropic contributions to civic projects and institutions and to be "good corporate citizens." While most charitable donations come from individuals, corporate philanthropy is on the rise. Target, for example, contributes significant resources to education, including direct donations of $14 million to schools as well as fundraising and scholarship programs that assist teachers and students. Through the retailer's Take Charge of Education program, customers using a Target Guest Card can designate a specific school to which Target donates 1 percent of their total purchase. This program is designed to make customers feel that their purchases are benefiting their community while increasing the use of Target Guest Cards.[23] Smaller firms can also make positive contributions to their communities. For example, Colorado-based New Belgium Brewing Company donates $1 for every barrel of beer brewed to charities within the markets it serves. The brewery divides the funds among states in proportion to interests and needs, considering environmental, social, drug and alcohol awareness, and cultural issues.[24] From a positive perspective, a marketer can significantly improve its community's quality of life through employment opportunities, economic development, and financial contributions to educational, health, cultural, and recreational causes.[25]

The Nature of Ethics

As noted earlier, marketing ethics is a dimension of social responsibility involving principles and standards that define acceptable conduct in marketing. Acceptable standards of conduct in making individual and group decisions in marketing is determined by various stakeholders and by an organization's ethical climate.

Marketers should be aware of ethical standards for acceptable conduct from several viewpoints—company, industry, government, customers, special-interest groups, and society at large. When marketing activities deviate from accepted standards, the exchange process can break down, resulting in customer dissatisfaction, lack of trust, and lawsuits. In fact, 78 percent of consumers say they avoid certain businesses or products because of negative perceptions about them.[26] For example, after 174 deaths and more than 700 injuries resulted from traffic accidents involving Ford Explorers equipped with Firestone tires, Bridgestone/Firestone and Ford Motor Company faced numerous lawsuits and much negative publicity. Ford claimed that defective Firestone tires were to blame for the accidents, while Bridgestone/Firestone contended that design flaws in Ford's best-selling Explorer made it more likely to roll over than other sport-utility vehicles. Many consumers, concerned more for their own safety than for the corporate blame game, lost confidence in both companies and turned to competitors' products.[27] When managers engage in activities that deviate from accepted principles, continued marketing exchanges become difficult, if not impossible. The best time to deal with such problems is during the strategic planning process, not after major problems materialize.

As we have already noted, marketing ethics goes beyond legal issues. Marketing decisions based on ethical considerations foster mutual trust in marketing relationships. Although we often try to draw a boundary between legal and ethical issues, the distinction between the two is frequently blurred in decision making. Marketers operate in an environment in which overlapping legal and ethical issues color many decisions. To separate legal and ethical decisions, one must assume that marketing managers can instinctively differentiate legal and ethical issues. However, while the legal ramifications of some issues and problems may be obvious, others are not. Questionable decisions and actions often result in disputes that must be resolved through litigation. The legal system therefore provides a formal venue for marketers to resolve ethical disputes as well as legal ones. For example, four African Americans sued Ford Motor Credit Company, accusing the nation's largest automobile finance firm of charging black buyers higher interest rates for auto loans than white customers with similar credit histories. The suit alleged that the company empowers dealers to inflate loan costs to buyers they think will pay higher rates. Ford has denied the allegations.[28] Indeed, most ethical disputes reported in the media involve the legal system at some level. In many cases, however, settlements are reached without requiring the decision of a judge or jury.

Before we proceed with our discussion of ethics in marketing, it is important to state that it is not our purpose to question anyone's ethical beliefs or personal convictions. Nor is it our purpose to examine the conduct of consumers, although some do behave unethically (engaging, for instance, in coupon fraud, shoplifting, returning clothing after wearing it, and other abuses). Instead, our goal here is to underscore the importance of resolving ethical issues in marketing and to help you learn about marketing ethics.

Ethical Issues in Marketing

ethical issue An identifiable problem, situation, or opportunity requiring a choice among several actions that must be evaluated as right or wrong, ethical or unethical

An **ethical issue** is an identifiable problem, situation, or opportunity requiring an individual or organization to choose from among several actions that must be evaluated as right or wrong, ethical or unethical. Any time an activity causes marketing managers or customers in their target market to feel manipulated or cheated, a marketing ethical issue exists, regardless of the legality of that activity. For example, organizational objectives that call for increased profits or market share may pressure marketers to knowingly bring an unsafe product to market. Such pressures represent ethical issues. Regardless of the reasons behind specific ethical issues, marketers must be able to identify these issues and decide how to resolve them. To do so requires familiarity with the many kinds of ethical issues that may arise in marketing. Some examples of ethical issues related to product, promotion, price, and distribution (the marketing mix) appear in Table 4.3.

Table 4.3	Typical Ethical Issues Related to the Marketing Mix
Product Issue	
Product information	Covering up defects in products that could cause harm to a consumer; withholding critical performance information that could affect a purchase decision.
Distribution Issue	
Counterfeiting	Counterfeit products are widespread, especially in the areas of computer software, clothing, and audio and video products. The Internet has facilitated the distribution of counterfeit products.
Promotion Issue	
Advertising	Deceptive advertising or withholding important product information in a personal selling situation.
Pricing Issue	
Deceptive pricing	Indicating that an advertised sale price is a reduction below the regular list price when in fact that is not the case.

Product-related ethical issues generally arise when marketers fail to disclose risks associated with a product or information regarding the function, value, or use of a product. Most automobile companies have experienced negative publicity associated with design or safety issues that resulted in a government-required recall of specific models. Pressures can build to substitute inferior materials or product components to reduce costs. Ethical issues also arise when marketers fail to inform customers about existing conditions or changes in product quality; this failure is a form of dishonesty about the nature of the product. Consider the introduction of a new size of candy bar, labeled with a banner touting its "new larger size." However, when placed in vending machines alongside older candy bars of the same brand, it was apparent that the product was actually slightly *smaller* than the candy bar it replaced. Although this could have been a mistake, the firm still has to defend and deal with the consequences of its actions.

Promotion can create ethical issues in a variety of ways, among them false or misleading advertising and manipulative or deceptive sales promotions, tactics, and publicity. A major ethical issue in promotion pertains to the marketing of video games that have been accused of promoting violence and weapons to children. Many other ethical issues are linked to promotion, including the use of bribery in personal selling situations. Even when a bribe is offered to benefit the organization, it is usually considered unethical. Because it jeopardizes trust and fairness, it hurts the organization in the long run.

In pricing, common ethical issues are price fixing, predatory pricing, and failure to disclose the full price of a purchase. The emotional and subjective nature of price creates many situations in which misunderstandings between the seller and buyer cause ethical problems. Marketers have the right to price their products to earn a reasonable profit, but ethical issues may crop up when a company seeks to earn high profits at the expense of its customers. Some pharmaceutical companies, for example, have been accused of pricing products at exorbitant levels and taking advantage of customers who must purchase the medicine to survive or to maintain their quality of life.

Ethical issues in distribution involve relationships among producers and marketing middlemen. Marketing middlemen, or intermediaries (wholesalers and retailers), facilitate the flow of products from the producer to the ultimate customer. Each intermediary performs a different role and agrees to certain rights, responsibilities, and rewards associated with that role. For example, producers expect wholesalers and retailers to honor agreements and keep them informed of inventory needs. Other serious ethical issues with regard to distribution include manipulating a product's availability for purposes of exploitation and using coercion to force intermediaries to behave in a specific manner.

The Ethical Decision-Making Process

To grasp the significance of ethics in marketing decision making, it is helpful to examine the factors that influence the ethical decision-making process. As Figure 4.3 shows, individual factors, organizational relationships, and opportunity interact to determine ethical decisions in marketing.

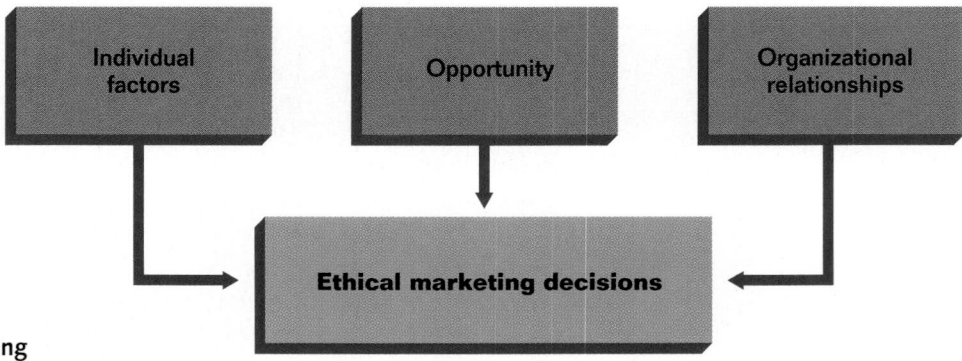

FIGURE 4.3
Factors That Influence the Ethical Decision-Making Process in Marketing

Individual Factors.   When people need to resolve ethical conflicts in their daily lives, they often base their decisions on their own values and principles of right or wrong. For example, a study by the Josephson Institute of Ethics reported that seven out of ten students admitted to cheating on a test at least once in the past year, and 92 percent admitted to lying to their parents in the past year. One out of six students confessed to showing up for class drunk in the same period.[29] People learn values and principles through socialization by family members, social groups, religion, and formal education. In the workplace, however, research has established that an organization's values often have more influence on marketing decisions than do a person's own values.[30]

Organizational Factors.   Although people can and do make ethical choices pertaining to marketing decisions, no one operates in a vacuum.[31] Ethical choices in marketing are most often made jointly, in work groups and committees or in conversations and discussions with coworkers. Marketers resolve ethical issues not only on the basis of what they learned from their backgrounds but also based on what they learn from others in the organization. The outcome of this learning process depends on the strength of each individual's personal values, opportunity for unethical behavior, and exposure to others who behave ethically or unethically. Superiors, peers, and subordinates in the organization influence the ethical decision-making process. Although people outside the organization, such as family members and friends, also influence decision makers, organizational culture and structure operate through organizational relationships to influence ethical decisions.

organizational, or **corporate, culture**   A set of values, beliefs, goals, norms, and rituals that members of an organization share

   Organizational, or **corporate, culture** is a set of values, beliefs, goals, norms, and rituals that members of an organization share. These values also help shape employees' satisfaction with their employer, which may affect the quality of the service they provide to customers. Figure 4.4 indicates that at least 92 percent of surveyed employees who see trust, respect, and honesty applied frequently in their organizations express satisfaction with their employers.[32] A firm's culture may be expressed formally through codes of conduct, memos, manuals, dress codes, and ceremonies, but it is also conveyed informally through work habits, extracurricular activities, and anecdotes. An organization's culture gives its members meaning and suggests rules for how to behave and deal with problems within the organization.

   With regard to organizational structure, most experts agree that the chief executive officer or vice president of marketing sets the ethical tone for the entire organization. Lower-level managers obtain their cues from top managers, but they too impose some of their personal values on the company. This interaction between corporate culture and executive leadership helps determine the ethical value system of the firm.

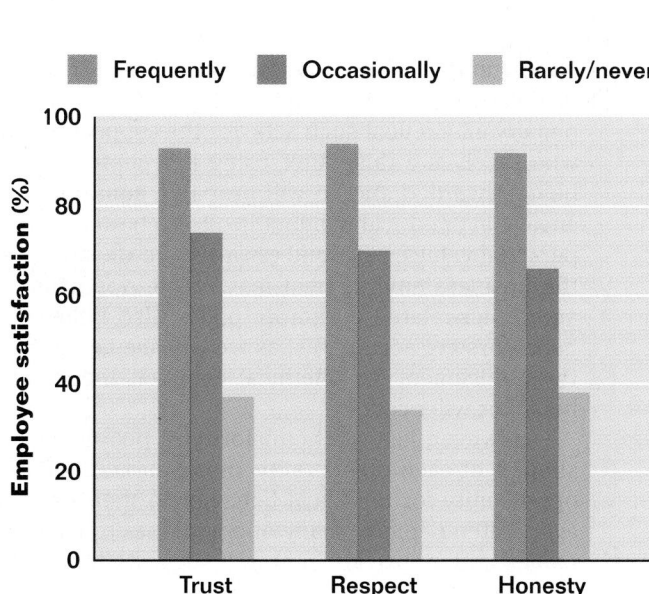

FIGURE 4.4
The Relationship of Organizational Values to Employee Satisfaction
Source: Ethics Resource Center, *The Ethics Resource Center's 2000 National Business Ethics Survey: How Employees Perceive Ethics at Work* (Washington, D.C.: Ethics Resource Center, 2000), p. 85. Reprinted with permission.

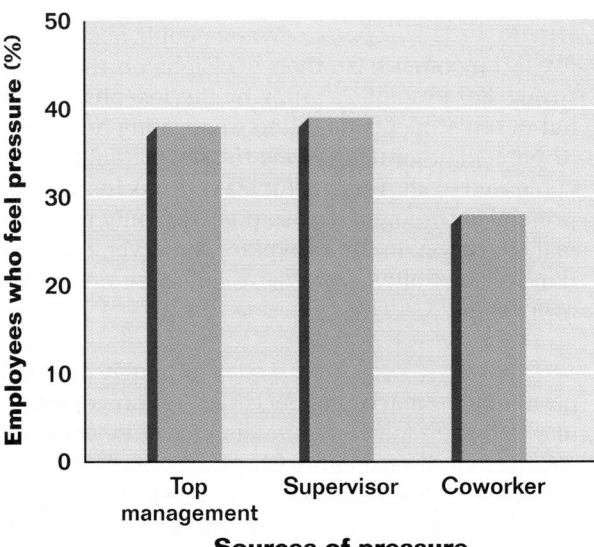

FIGURE 4.5
Sources of Pressure to Compromise Ethics Standards at Work

Source: Ethics Resource Center, *The Ethics Resource Center's 2000 National Business Ethics Survey: How Employees Perceive Ethics at Work* (Washington, D.C.: Ethics Resource Center, 2000), p. 38. Reprinted with permission.

Coworkers' influence on ethical choices depends on the person's exposure to unethical behavior. Especially in gray areas, the more a person is exposed to unethical activity by others in the organizational environment, the more likely he or she is to behave unethically. Most marketers take their cues from coworkers in learning how to solve problems, including ethical problems.[33] Moreover, research suggests that marketing employees who perceive their work environment as ethical experience less role conflict and ambiguity, are more satisfied with their jobs, and are more committed to their employer.[34]

Organizational pressure plays a key role in creating ethical issues. For example, because of pressure to meet a schedule, a salesperson may be asked by a superior to lie to a customer over the phone about a late product shipment. Similarly, pressure to meet a sales quota may result in overly aggressive sales tactics. Research in this area indicates that superiors and coworkers can create organizational pressure, which plays a key role in creating ethical issues. In a study by the Ethics Resource Center, 60 percent of respondents said they had experienced pressure from superiors or coworkers to compromise ethical standards to achieve business objectives.[35] Figure 4.5 shows the sources of pressure reported by employees. Nearly all marketers face difficult issues whose solutions are not obvious or that present conflicts between organizational objectives and personal ethics.

Opportunity. Another factor that may shape ethical decisions in marketing is opportunity, that is, conditions that limit barriers or provide rewards. A marketer who takes advantage of an opportunity to act unethically and is rewarded or suffers no penalty may repeat such acts as other opportunities arise. For example, a salesperson who receives a raise after using a deceptive sales presentation to increase sales is being rewarded and so will probably continue the behavior. Indeed, opportunity to engage in unethical conduct is often a better predictor of unethical activities than are personal values.[36] Beyond rewards and the absence of punishment, other elements in the business environment may create opportunities. Professional codes of conduct and ethics-related corporate policy also influence opportunity by prescribing what behaviors are acceptable, as we will see later. The larger the rewards and the milder the punishment for unethical conduct, the greater is the likelihood that unethical behavior will occur.

However, just as the majority of people who go into retail stores do not try to shoplift at each opportunity, most marketers do not try to take advantage of every opportunity for unethical behavior in their organizations. Although marketing managers often perceive many opportunities to engage in unethical conduct in their companies and industries, research suggests that most refrain from taking advantage of such opportunities. Moreover, most marketing managers do not believe that unethical conduct in general results in success.[37] Individual factors as well as organizational culture may influence whether an individual becomes opportunistic and tries to take advantage of situations unethically.

Improving Ethical Conduct in Marketing

It is possible to improve ethical conduct in an organization by hiring ethical employees and eliminating unethical ones, and by improving the organization's ethical standards. One way to approach improvement of an organization's ethical standards is to use a "bad apple–bad barrel" analogy. Some people always do things in their own self-interest, regardless of organizational goals or accepted moral standards; they are sometimes called "bad apples." To eliminate unethical conduct, an organization must rid itself of bad apples through screening techniques and enforcement of the firm's ethical standards. However, organizations sometimes become "bad barrels," not because the individuals within them are bad but because the pressures to survive and succeed create conditions (opportunities) that reward unethical behavior. One way to resolve the problem of the bad barrel is to redesign the organization's image and culture so that it conforms to industry and societal norms of ethical conduct.[38]

If top management develops and enforces ethics and legal compliance programs to encourage ethical decision making, it becomes a force to help individuals make better decisions. When marketers understand the policies and requirements for ethical conduct, they can more easily resolve ethical conflicts. However, marketers can never fully abdicate their personal ethical responsibility in making decisions. Claiming to be an agent of the business ("the company told me to do it") is not accepted as a legal excuse and is even less defensible from an ethical perspective.[39]

Codes of Conduct.   Without compliance programs and uniform standards and policies regarding conduct, it is hard for employees to determine what conduct is acceptable within the company. In the absence of such programs and standards, employees will generally make decisions based on their observations of how their peers and superiors behave. To improve ethics, many organizations have developed **codes of conduct** (also called *codes of ethics*) consisting of formalized rules and standards that describe what the company expects of its employees. Most large corporations have formal codes of conduct. Codes of conduct promote ethical behavior by reducing opportunities for unethical behavior; employees know both what is expected of them and what kind of punishment they face if they violate the rules. Codes help marketers deal with ethical issues or dilemmas that develop in daily operations by prescribing or limiting specific activities. Codes of conduct have also made companies that subcontract manufacturing operations abroad more aware of the ethical issues associated with supporting facilities that underpay and even abuse their work force. The American Apparel Manufacturers Association, for example, has endorsed the principles and certification program of Worldwide Responsible Apparel Production (WRAP), a nonprofit organization dedicated to promoting and certifying "lawful, human, and ethical manufacturing throughout the world." Companies that endorse the principles are expected to allow independent monitoring to ensure their contractors are complying with the principles.[40]

Codes of conduct do not have to be so detailed that they take every situation into account, but they should provide guidelines that enable employees to achieve organizational objectives in an ethical, acceptable manner. The American Marketing Association Code of Ethics, reprinted in Table 4.4, does not cover every possible ethical issue, but it *does* provide a useful overview of what marketers believe are sound principles for guiding marketing activities. This code serves as a helpful model for structuring an organization's code of conduct.

Ethics Officers.   Organizational compliance programs must also have oversight by high-ranking persons in the organization known to respect legal and ethical standards. Ethics officers are typically responsible for creating and distributing a code of

codes of conduct   Formalized rules and standards that describe what the company expects of its employees

Table 4.4   Code of Ethics of the American Marketing Association

Members of the American Marketing Association (AMA) are committed to ethical professional conduct. They have joined together in subscribing to this Code of Ethics embracing the following topics:

Responsibilities of the Marketer

Marketers must accept responsibility for the consequences of their activities and make every effort to ensure that their decisions, recommendations, and actions function to identify, serve, and satisfy all relevant publics: consumers, organizations and society. Marketers' professional conduct must be guided by:

1. The basic rule of professional ethics: not knowingly to do harm;
2. The adherence to all applicable laws and regulations;
3. The accurate representation of their education, training and experience; and
4. The active support, practice and promotion of this Code of Ethics.

Honesty and Fairness

Marketers shall uphold and advance the integrity, honor, and dignity of the marketing profession by:

1. Being honest in serving consumers, clients, employees, suppliers, distributors and the public;
2. Not knowingly participating in conflict of interest without prior notice to all parties involved; and
3. Establishing equitable fee schedules including the payment or receipt of usual, customary and/or legal compensation for marketing exchanges.

Rights and Duties of Parties in the Marketing Exchange Process

Participants in the marketing exchange process should be able to expect that:

1. Products and services offered are safe and fit for their intended uses;
2. Communications about offered products and services are not deceptive;
3. All parties intend to discharge their obligations, financial and otherwise, in good faith; and
4. Appropriate internal methods exist for equitable adjustment and/or redress of grievances concerning purchases.

It is understood that the above would include, but is not limited to, the following responsibilities of the marketer:

In the area of product development management:
- Disclosure of all substantial risks associated with product or service usage
- Identification of product component substitution that might materially change the product or affect the buyer's purchase decision
- Identification of extra-cost added features

In the area of promotions:
- Avoidance of false and misleading advertising
- Rejection of high pressure manipulations, or misleading sales tactics
- Avoidance of sales promotions that use deception or manipulation

In the area of distribution:
- Not manipulating the availability of a product for purpose of exploitation
- Not using coercion in the marketing channel
- Not exerting undue influence over the resellers' choice to handle a product

In the area of pricing:
- Not engaging in price fixing
- Not practicing predatory pricing
- Disclosing the full price associated with any purchase

In the area of marketing research:
- Prohibiting selling or fund raising under the guise of conducting research
- Maintaining research integrity by avoiding misrepresentation and omission of pertinent research data
- Treating outside clients and suppliers fairly

Organizational Relationships

Marketers should be aware of how their behavior may influence or impact on the behavior of others in organizational relationships. They should not demand, encourage or apply coercion to obtain unethical behavior in their relationships with others, such as employees, suppliers or customers.

1. Apply confidentiality and anonymity in professional relationships with regard to privileged information;
2. Meet their obligations and responsibilities in contracts and mutual agreements in a timely manner;
3. Avoid taking the work of others, in whole, or in part, and representing this work as their own or directly benefit from it without compensation or consent of the originator or owner; and
4. Avoid manipulation to take advantage of situations to maximize personal welfare in a way that unfairly deprives or damages the organization or others.

Any AMA members found to be in violation of any provision of this Code of Ethics may have his or her Association membership suspended or revoked.

Source: Reprinted by permission of the American Marketing Association.

conduct, enforcing the code, and meeting with organizational members to discuss or provide advice about ethical issues. Many ethics officers also employ toll-free telephone "hotlines" to provide advice, anonymously when desired, to employees who believe they face an ethical issue. Sears, for example, maintains a 24-hour, toll-free "assist line" on which employees may express any concerns they have to a company representative. This tool gives the company the opportunity to listen to and counsel employees, clarify its policies, and receive reports of misconduct.[41] Hotlines can also provide a mechanism for employees to report misconduct by others.[42]

Implementing Ethics and Legal Compliance Programs. To nurture ethical conduct in marketing, open communication and coaching on ethical issues are essential. This requires providing employees with ethics training, clear channels of communication, and follow-up support throughout the organization.

It is important that companies consistently enforce standards and impose penalties or punishment on those who violate codes of conduct. In addition, the company must take reasonable steps in response to violations of standards and, as appropriate, revise the compliance program to diminish the likelihood of future misconduct. To succeed, a compliance program must be viewed as a part of the overall marketing strategy implementation. If ethics officers and other executives are not committed to the principles and initiatives of marketing ethics and social responsibility, the program's effectiveness will be in question. On the other hand, ethics officers still must focus most of their attention on the development of the organization's culture. While the Federal Sentencing Guidelines for Organizations may have been the chief motivating factor in the creation of ethics offices, a survey of ethics officers reported that 76 percent believe the purpose of their ethics office is to "insure commitment to corporate values," and 68 percent said they were motivated by the need to establish a better corporate culture. Today the purpose of most compliance programs is not to check off boxes corresponding to the Federal Sentencing Guidelines' seven requirements for a compliance program but to create a values-based corporate culture.[43]

Although the virtues of honesty, fairness, and openness are often assumed to be self-evident and universally accepted, marketing strategy decisions involve complex and detailed matters in which correctness may not be so clear-cut. A high level of personal morality may not be sufficient to prevent an individual from violating the law in an organizational context in which even experienced lawyers debate the exact meaning of the law. Because it is impossible to train all members of an organization as lawyers, the identification of ethical issues and implementation of compliance programs and codes of conduct that incorporate both legal and ethical concerns constitute the best approach to preventing violations and avoiding litigation. Codifying ethical standards into meaningful policies that spell out what is and is not acceptable gives marketers an opportunity to reduce the probability of behavior that could create legal problems. Without proper ethical training and guidance, it is impossible for the average marketing manager to understand the exact boundaries of illegality in the areas of price fixing, copyright violations, fraud, export/import violations, and so on. A corporate focus on ethics helps create a buffer zone around issues that could potentially trigger serious legal complications for the company.

Net Sights

The E-Center for Business Ethics (**http://e-businessethics.com**) offers a wealth of information about business ethics, corporate citizenship, organizational compliance, and related topics. In addition to specific resources on Internet privacy and corporate codes of conduct, this comprehensive site offers articles, case studies, and games, as well as links to numerous organizations and agencies that support ethics and compliance in business.

Implementing Ethics Programs
Business Ethics magazine makes annual awards to organizations that have excellent ethical performance.

Incorporating Social Responsibility and Ethics into Strategic Planning

Although the concepts of marketing ethics and social responsibility are often used interchangeably, it is important to distinguish between them. *Ethics* relates to individual and group decisions—judgments about what is right or wrong in a particular decision-making situation—whereas *social responsibility* deals with the total effect of marketing decisions on society. The two concepts are interrelated because a company that supports socially responsible decisions and adheres to a code of conduct is likely to have a positive effect on society. Because ethics and social responsibility programs can be profitable as well, an increasing number of companies are incorporating them into their overall strategic market planning.

As we have emphasized throughout this chapter, ethics is one dimension of social responsibility. Being socially responsible relates to doing what is economically sound, legal, ethical, and socially conscious. One way to evaluate whether a specific activity is ethical and socially responsible is to ask other persons in the organization if they approve of it. Contact with concerned consumer groups and industry or government regulatory groups may be helpful. A check to see whether there is a specific company policy about an activity may help resolve ethical questions. If other organization members approve of the activity and it is legal and customary within the industry, chances are the activity is acceptable from both an ethical and a social responsibility perspective. Table 4.5 provides an audit of mechanisms to help control ethics and social responsibility in marketing.

A rule of thumb for resolving ethical and social responsibility issues is that if an issue can withstand open discussion that results in agreement or limited debate, an acceptable solution may exist. Nevertheless, even after a final decision is reached, different viewpoints on the issue may remain. Openness is not the end-all solution to the ethics problem. However, it does create trust and facilitates learning relationships.[44]

Table 4.5	**Organizational Audit of Social Responsibility and Ethics Control Mechanisms**

Answer True or False for each statement.

T   F   1. No mechanism exists for top management to detect social responsibility and ethical issues relating to employees, customers, the community, and society.

T   F   2. There is no formal or informal communication within the organization about procedures and activities that are considered acceptable behavior.

T   F   3. The organization fails to communicate its ethical standards to suppliers, customers, and groups that have a relationship with the organization.

T   F   4. There is an environment of deception, repression, and cover-ups concerning events that could be embarrassing to the company.

T   F   5. Compensation systems are totally dependent on economic performance.

T   F   6. The only concerns about environmental impact are those that are legally required.

T   F   7. Concern for the ethical value systems of the community with regard to the firm's activities is absent.

T   F   8. Products are described in a misleading manner, with no information on negative impact or limitations communicated to customers.

True answers indicate a lack of control mechanisms, which, if implemented, could improve ethics and social responsibility.

Social Responsibility Improves Marketing Performance
American Airlines supports a socially responsible cause—finding a cure for cystic fibrosis—by sponsoring a celebrity ski weekend. Merck makes parents aware of the dangers associated with chickenpox.

Being Socially Responsible and Ethical Is Not Easy

To promote socially responsible and ethical behavior while achieving organizational goals, marketers must monitor changes and trends in society's values. For example, companies around the world are developing and marketing more nutritious, healthful products in response to increasing public concern about cancer and heart disease. When Frito-Lay introduced WOW potato chips with 50 percent less fat than regular chips, retailers could barely maintain enough inventory to meet demand. Furthermore, marketers must develop control procedures to ensure that daily decisions do not damage their company's relations with the public. An organization's top management must assume some responsibility for employees' conduct by establishing and enforcing policies.

After determining what society wants, marketers must attempt to predict the long-term effects of decisions pertaining to those wants. Specialists outside the company, such as doctors, lawyers, and scientists, are often consulted, but sometimes there is a lack of agreement within a discipline as to what is an acceptable marketing decision. Forty years ago, for example, tobacco marketers promoted cigarettes as being good for one's health. Now, years after the discovery that cigarette smoking is linked to cancer and other medical problems, society's attitude toward smoking has changed, and marketers are confronted with new social responsibilities, such as providing a smoke-free atmosphere for customers. Most major hotel chains allocate at least some of their rooms to nonsmokers, many rental car companies provide smoke-free cars, and most other businesses within the food, travel, and entertainment industries provide smoke-free environments or sections.

Many of society's demands impose costs. For example, society wants a cleaner environment and the preservation of wildlife and their habitats, but it also wants low-priced products. Consider the plight of the gas station owner who asked his customers if they would be willing to spend an additional 1 cent per gallon if he instituted an air filtration system to eliminate harmful fumes. The majority indicated they supported his plan. However, when the system was installed and the price increased, many customers went to a competitor across the street for the cost savings. Thus, companies must carefully balance the costs of providing low-priced products against the costs of manufacturing, packaging, and distributing their products in an environmentally responsible manner.

In trying to satisfy the desires of one group, marketers may dissatisfy others. In the smoking debate, for example, marketers must balance nonsmokers' desire for a smoke-free environment against smokers' desire, or need, to continue to smoke. Some anti-tobacco crusaders call for the complete elimination of tobacco products to ensure a smoke-free world. However, this attitude fails to consider the difficulty smokers have in quitting (now that tobacco marketers have admitted their product is addictive) and the impact on U.S. communities and states that depend on tobacco crops for their economic survival. Thus, this issue, like most ethical and social responsibility issues, cannot be viewed in black and white.

Balancing society's demands to satisfy all members of society is difficult, if not impossible. Marketers must evaluate the extent to which members of society are willing to pay for what they want. For instance, customers may want more information about a product but be unwilling to pay the costs the firm incurs in providing the data. Marketers who want to make socially responsible decisions may find the task a challenge because, ultimately, economic survival must be ensured.

Social Responsibility and Ethics Improve Marketing Performance

Do not think, however, that the challenge is not worth the effort. On the contrary, increasing evidence indicates that being socially responsible and ethical pays off. Research suggests that a relationship exists between a marketing orientation and an organizational climate that supports marketing ethics and social responsibility. This relationship implies that being ethically and socially concerned is consistent with meeting the demands of customers and other stakeholders. By encouraging their employees to understand their markets, companies can help them respond to stakeholders' demands.[45]

A survey of marketing managers found a direct association between corporate social responsibility and profits.[46] In a survey of consumers, nearly 90 percent indicated that when quality, service, and price are equal among competitors, they would be more likely to buy from the company with the best reputation for social responsibility. In addition, 54 percent would pay more for a product that supported a cause they care about, 66 percent would switch brands to support such a cause, and 62 percent would switch retailers.[47]

Thus, recognition is growing that the long-term value of conducting business in a socially responsible manner far outweighs short-term costs.[48] Companies that fail to develop strategies and programs to incorporate ethics and social responsibility into their organizational culture may pay the price with poor marketing performance and the potential costs of legal violations, civil litigation, and damaging publicity when questionable activities are made public.

Because marketing ethics and social responsibility are not always viewed as organizational performance issues, many managers do not believe they need to consider them in the strategic planning process. Individuals also have different ideas as to what is ethical or unethical, leading them to confuse the need for workplace ethics and the right to maintain their own personal values and ethics. While the concepts are undoubtedly controversial, it is possible—and desirable—to incorporate ethics and social responsibility into the planning process.[49]

Summary

Social responsibility refers to an organization's obligation to maximize its positive impact and minimize its negative impact on society. It deals with the total effect of all marketing decisions on society. Although social responsibility is a positive concept, most organizations embrace it in the expectation of indirect long-term benefits.

Marketing citizenship involves adopting a strategic focus for fulfilling the economic, legal, ethical, and philanthropic social responsibilities expected of them by their stakeholders, those constituents who have a "stake," or claim, in some aspect of the company's products, operations, markets, industry, and outcomes. At the most basic level, companies have an economic responsibility to be profitable so they can provide a return on investment to their stockholders, create jobs for the community, and contribute goods and services to the economy. Marketers are also expected to obey laws and regulations. Marketing ethics refers to principles and standards that define acceptable conduct in marketing as determined by various stakeholders, including the public, government regulators, private-interest groups, industry, and the organization itself. Philanthropic responsibilities go beyond marketing ethics; they are not required of a company, but they promote human welfare or goodwill. Many firms use cause-related marketing, the practice of linking products to a social cause on an ongoing or short-term basis. Strategic philanthropy refers to the synergistic use of organizational core competencies and resources to address key stakeholders' interests and achieve both organizational and social benefits.

Three major categories of social responsibility issues are the natural environment, consumerism, and community relations. One of the more common ways marketers demonstrate social responsibility is through programs designed to protect and preserve the natural environment. Green marketing refers to the specific development, pricing, promotion, and distribution of products that do not harm the environment. Consumerism consists of the efforts of independent individuals, groups, and organizations to protect the rights of consumers. Consumers expect to have the right to safety, the right to be informed, the right to choose, and the right to be heard. Many marketers view social responsibility as including contributions of resources (money, products, time) to community causes, such as the natural environment, arts and recreation, disadvantaged members of the community, and education.

Whereas social responsibility is achieved by balancing the interests of all stakeholders in an organization, ethics relates to acceptable standards of conduct in making individual and group decisions. Marketing ethics goes beyond legal issues. Ethical marketing decisions foster mutual trust in marketing relationships.

An ethical issue is an identifiable problem, situation, or opportunity requiring an individual or organization to choose from among several actions that must be evaluated as right or wrong, ethical or unethical. A number of ethical issues relate to the marketing mix (product, promotion, price, and distribution).

Individual factors, organizational relationships, and opportunity interact to determine ethical decisions in marketing. Individuals often base their decisions on their own values and principles of right or wrong. However, ethical choices in marketing are most often made jointly, in work groups and committees or in conversations and discussions with coworkers. Organizational culture and structure operate through organizational relationships (with superiors, peers, and subordinates) to influence ethical decisions. Organizational, or corporate, culture is a set of values, beliefs, goals, norms, and rituals that members of an organization share. The more a person is exposed to unethical activity by others in the organizational environment, the more likely he or she is to behave unethically. Organizational pressure plays a key role in creating ethical issues, as does opportunity, that is, conditions that limit barriers or provide rewards.

It is possible to improve ethical behavior in an organization by hiring ethical employees and eliminating unethical ones, and by improving the organization's ethical standards. If top management develops and enforces ethics and legal compliance programs to encourage ethical decision making, it becomes a force to help individuals make better decisions. To improve company ethics, many organizations have developed codes of conduct, formalized rules and standards that describe what the company expects of its employees. A marketing compliance program must have oversight by a high-ranking person in the organization known to abide by legal and common ethical standards; this person is usually called an ethics officer. To nurture ethical conduct in marketing, open communication and coaching on ethical issues are essential. This requires providing employees with ethics training, clear channels of communication, and follow-up support throughout the organization. Companies must consistently enforce standards and impose penalties or punishment on those who violate codes of conduct.

An increasing number of companies are incorporating ethics and social responsibility programs into their overall strategic market planning. To promote socially responsible and ethical behavior while achieving organizational goals, marketers must monitor changes and trends in society's values. They must determine what society wants and attempt to predict the long-term effects of their decisions. Costs are associated with many of society's demands, and balancing these demands to satisfy all of society is difficult. However, increasing evidence indicates that being socially responsible and ethical provides good benefits: an enhanced public reputation, which can increase market share, costs savings, and profits.

Important Terms

Social responsibility
Marketing citizenship
Stakeholders
Marketing ethics
Cause-related marketing
Strategic philanthropy

Green marketing
Ethical issue
Organizational (corporate) culture
Codes of conduct

Discussion and Review Questions

1. What is social responsibility, and why is it important?
2. What are stakeholders? What role do they play in strategic marketing decisions?
3. What are four dimensions of social responsibility? What impact do they have on marketing decisions?
4. What is strategic philanthropy? How does it differ from more traditional philanthropic efforts?
5. What are some major social responsibility issues? Give an example of each.
6. What is the difference between ethics and social responsibility?
7. Why is ethics an important consideration in marketing decisions?
8. How do the factors that influence ethical or unethical decisions interact?
9. What ethical conflicts could exist if business employees fly on certain airlines just to receive benefits for their personal "frequent flier" program?
10. Give an example of how each component of the marketing mix can be affected by ethical issues.
11. How can the ethical decisions involved in marketing be improved?
12. How can people with different personal values work together to make ethical decisions in organizations?

13. What tradeoffs might a company have to make to be socially responsible and responsive to society's demands?
14. What evidence exists that being socially responsible and ethical is worthwhile?

Application Questions

1. Some organizations promote their social responsibility. These companies often claim that being ethical is good business and that it pays to be a good citizen of the community. Identify an organization in your community that has a reputation for being ethical and socially responsible. What activities account for this image? Is the company successful? Why or why not?
2. If you had to conduct a social audit of your organization's ethics and social responsibility, what information would most interest you? What key stakeholders would you want to communicate with? How could such an audit assist the company in improving its ethics and social responsibility?
3. Suppose that in your job you face situations that require you to make decisions about what is right or wrong, and then you have to act on these decisions. Describe such a situation. Without disclosing your actual decision, explain what you based it on. What and whom did you think of when you were considering what to do? Why did you consider them?
4. Consumers interact with many businesses daily and weekly. Not only do companies in an industry acquire a reputation for being ethical or unethical; entire industries also become known as ethical or unethical. Identify two types of businesses with which you or others you know have had the most conflict involving ethical issues. Describe these ethical issues.

Internet Exercise & Resources

Visit **www.prideferrell.com** for resources to help you master the material in this chapter, plus materials that will help you expand your marketing knowledge, including: Internet exercise updates, ACE self-tests, hotlinks to companies featured in this chapter, and much more.

Business for Social Responsibility (BSR) is a nonprofit organization for companies desiring to operate responsibly and demonstrate respect for ethical values, people, communities, and the natural environment. Founded in 1992, BSR offers members practical information, research, educational programs, and technical assistance as well as the opportunity to network with peers on current social responsibility issues. To learn more about this organization and access its many resources, visit

http://www.bsr.org

1. What types of businesses join BSR, and why?
2. Pick three recent articles in BSR's "News Archives" that deal with social responsibility issues in marketing. For each article, explain how these issues relate to a concept covered in Chapter 4.
3. Peruse the "Global Resource Center" and find the report on ethics codes. Using this report, list some examples of corporate codes of ethics and describe the benefits of establishing a code of ethics.

VIDEO CASE 4.1
New Belgium Brewing Company

The idea for New Belgium Brewing Company (NBB) began with a bicycling trip through Belgium, where some of the world's finest ales have been brewed for centuries. As Jeff Lebesch, an American electrical engineer, cruised around the country on a fat-tired mountain bike, he wondered if he could produce such high-quality ales in his home state of Colorado. After returning home, Lebesch began to experiment in his Fort Collins basement. When his home-brewed experiments earned rave reviews from friends, Lebesch and his wife, Kim Jordan, decided to open the New Belgium Brewing Company in 1991. They named their first brew Fat Tire Amber Ale in honor of Lebesch's Belgian biking adventure.

Today New Belgium markets a variety of permanent and seasonal ales and pilsners. The standard line includes Sunshine Wheat, Blue Paddle Pilsner, Abbey Ale, Trippel Ale, and 1554 Black Ale, as well as the firm's number one seller, the original Fat Tire Amber Ale. NBB also markets seasonal beers, such as Frambozen and Abbey Grand Cru—released at Thanksgiving—and Christmas and Farmhouse Ale, which are sold during the early fall months. The firm also occasionally offers one-time-only brews—such as LaFolie, a wood-aged beer—that are sold only until the batch runs out. Bottle label designs employ "good ol' days" nostalgia. The Fat Tire label, for example, features an old-style cruiser bike with fat tires, a padded seat, and a basket hanging from the handlebars. All the label and packaging designs were created by the same watercolor artist, Jeff Lebesch's next-door neighbor.

Although Fat Tire was initially sold only in Fort Collins, distribution quickly expanded throughout the rest of Colorado. Customers can now find Fat Tire and other New Belgium offerings in ten western states, including Washington, Montana, Texas, New Mexico, and Arizona. The brewery regularly receives e-mails and telephone inquiries as to when New Belgium beers will be available elsewhere.

Since its founding, NBB's most effective promotion has been via word-of-mouth advertising by devoted customers. The company avoids mass advertising because it doesn't fit the image NBB wants to project. Instead the brewery relies on small-scale, local promotions, such as print advertisements in alternative magazines, participation in local festivals, and sponsorship of alternative sports events. Through event sponsorships, such as the Tour de Fat and Ride the Rockies, NBB has raised thousands of dollars for various environmental, social, and cycling nonprofit organizations.

New Belgium beers are priced to reflect their quality at about $7 per six-pack. This pricing strategy conveys the message that the products are special and of consistently higher quality than macrobrews, such as Budweiser and Coors, but also keeps them competitive with other microbrews, such as Pete's Wicked Ale, Pyramid Pale Ale, and Sierra Nevada. To demonstrate its appreciation for its retailers and business partners, New Belgium does not sell beer to consumers on-site at the brewhouse for less than the retailers charge.

New Belgium's marketing strategy involves pairing the quality of its products, as well as their names and looks, with a concern for how the company's activities affect the natural environment. The brewery looks for cost-efficient, energy-saving alternatives to conducting business and reducing its impact on the environment. Thus, the company's employee-owners unanimously agreed to invest in a wind turbine, making New Belgium the first fully wind-powered brewery in the United States. Since the switch from coal power, New Belgium has reduced its CO_2 emissions by 1,800 metric tons per year. The company further reduces its energy use with a steam condenser that captures and reuses the hot water from boiling the barley and hops in the production process to start the next brew; the steam is redirected to heat the floor tiles and de-ice the loading docks in cold weather. New Belgium also strives to recycle as many supplies as possible, including cardboard boxes, keg caps, office materials, and the amber glass used in bottling. New Belgium has recycled tons of amber glass, cardboard, and shrink-wrap. The brewery also stores spent barley and hop grains in an on-premise silo and invites local farmers to pick up the grains, free of charge, to feed their pigs. Another way NBB conserves energy is through the use of "sun tubes," which provide natural daytime lighting throughout the brewhouse all year long. NBB also encourages employees to reduce air pollution through alternative transportation. As an incentive, NBB gives each employee a "cruiser bike"—just like the one on the Fat Tire Amber Ale label—after one year of employment to encourage biking to work.

Beyond its use of environment-friendly technologies and innovations, New Belgium Brewing Company strives to improve communities and enhance lives through corporate giving, event sponsorship, and philanthropic involvement. The company donates $1 per barrel of beer sold to various cultural, social, environmental, and drug and alcohol awareness programs across the ten western states in which it distributes beer. Typical grants range from $2,500 to $5,000. Involvement is spread equally among the ten states, unless a special need requires greater participation or funding. The brewhouse also maintains a community board where organizations can post community involvement activities and proposals. This board allows tourists and employees to see opportunities to help out the community, and it provides nonprofit organizations with a forum for making their needs known. Organizations can also apply for grants through the New Belgium Brewing Company website, which has a link designated for this purpose.

New Belgium's commitment to quality, the environment, and its employees and customers is clearly expressed in its stated purpose: "To operate a profitable brewery which makes our love and talent manifest." This dedication has been well rewarded with loyal customers and industry awards. The company received an award for best mid-size brewing company of the year and best mid-size brewmaster at the Great American Beer Festival in 1999. New Belgium also took home medals for three different brews: Abbey Belgian Style Ale, Blue Paddle Pilsner, and LaFolie specialty ale. Jeff Lebesch and Kim Jordan were named the recipients of the Rocky Mountain Region Entrepreneur of the Year Award for manufacturing. In

2000 NBB received the Better Business Bureau's Marketplace Ethics Award.

From cutting-edge environmental programs and high-tech industry advancements to employee-ownership programs and a strong belief in giving back to the community, New Belgium demonstrates its desire to create a living, learning community. According to David Edgar, director of the Institute for Brewing Studies, "They've created a very positive image for their company in the beer-consuming public with smart decision-making." Although some members of society do not believe a brewery can be socially responsible, New Belgium has set out to prove that for those who make the choice to drink responsibly, the company can do everything possible to contribute to society.[50]

QUESTIONS FOR DISCUSSION
1. What steps has New Belgium Brewing Company taken to be socially responsible?
2. As a smaller business, how can New Belgium justify donating $1 per barrel of beer sold to environmental and community causes?
3. Some segments of society contend that companies that sell alcoholic beverages cannot be socially responsible organizations because of the inherent nature of their products. Do you believe New Belgium Brewing Company's actions and initiatives make it a socially responsible business? Why or why not?

CASE 4.2
Danger on the Highway: Bridgestone/Firestone's Tire Recall

Bridgestone/Firestone, Inc., based in Nashville, Tennessee, has been in the business of making tires since 1900, when Harvey Firestone founded Firestone Tire & Rubber Company in Akron, Ohio. Firestone was acquired by Bridgestone USA, Inc., a subsidiary of Tokyo-based Bridgestone Corporation, in 1990 for $2.6 billion. Today the company markets 8,000 different types and sizes of tires and a host of other products. The company has also enjoyed a long and prosperous relationship with Ford Motor Company, which began in 1906 when Henry Ford purchased 2,000 sets of tires from Harvey Firestone.

Despite emerging as a leader in the tire industry, Bridgestone/Firestone has faced several crises related to its tires' safety. In 1978, Firestone recalled 14.5 million tires—the largest tire recall ever at the time—after excess application of the adhesives binding the rubber and steel resulted in 500 tread separations and blowouts. The company also paid a $500,000 fine for concealing safety problems. However, this incident paled in comparison to problems the company faced in the late 1990s, which quickly grew to affect its relationship with Ford as well.

In July 1998, a State Farm Insurance researcher advised the National Highway Traffic Safety Administration (NHTSA) that he had found 20 cases of tread failure associated with Firestone tires dating back to 1992. He was politely thanked, but no action resulted. In January 2000, Houston television station KHOU aired a nine-minute story on tread-separation accidents in Texas. After the story aired, many people called the station to relate their own experiences with Firestone tire failures, most of them on Ford Explorer sport-utility vehicles. These examples were relayed to Joan Claybrook, former chief of the NHTSA. Finally, Sean Kane, a former employee of the Center for Auto Safety and the founder of Strategic Safety, a research organization, also tried to alert the NHTSA about problems with tread separation on Firestone tires. After learning about similar problems in Venezuela, Strategic Safety, together with Public Citizen, another consumer watchdog group, issued a press release on August 1 asking Ford to issue a vehicle recall.

Despite the evidence compiled by these sources, the NHTSA was slow to respond. In March 2000, investigators Steve Beretzky and Rob Wahl found 22 tread-separation complaints that they marked for "initial evaluation." The number of complaints skyrocketed between March and May, and by May 2 the NHTSA had elevated their status to "preliminary investigation." Days later, the NHTSA requested that Bridgestone/Firestone supply production data and complaint files, which the company produced on July 27.

Upon obtaining a copy of the report, Ford immediately began analyzing the data. Of the 2,498 complaints logged by that time, 81 percent involved P235/75R15 Firestone tires. Of the 1,699 complaints about tread separation, 84 percent involved Ford's Explorer and Bronco SUVs and its Ranger and F-150 trucks. On August 5, agents of Ford and Bridgestone/Firestone met in Dearborn, Michigan to discuss the issue. By this time, the NHTSA was investigating 21 deaths possibly related to tread separation on Firestone tires. Within days, the investigation had grown to include 46 possible deaths, and Ford and Bridgestone/Firestone met with NHTSA officials to discuss a plan of action. The next day, August 9, the companies issued a recall of 6.5 million tires.

The recall included 3.8 million P235/75R15 radial ATX and ATXII tires and 2.7 million Wilderness AT tires, all made in Firestone's Decatur, Illinois, plant. Bridgestone/Firestone organized the official recall by state, giving priority to Arizona, California, Florida, and Texas, where the greatest percentage of casualties had occurred. Based on NHTSA data, Florida and Texas each accounted for 22 percent of complaints, followed by California with 20 percent, Arizona with 5 percent, and Georgia with 4 percent. Bridgestone/Firestone issued letters to customers detailing the recall procedure: customers could take their tires to Firestone retailers, Ford dealerships, or other tire retail outlets and receive a similar Bridgestone/Firestone tire or an equivalent competitor's model.

After continued investigations, the NHTSA encouraged Bridgestone/Firestone to expand the recall to include other sizes and models of tires, but the company refused. On September 1, the NHTSA issued a consumer advisory warning of potential problems with other sizes of Firestone tires.

During Senate hearings about the growing number of complaints and accidents, evidence surfaced that Bridgestone/Firestone had known about potential tread-separation problems dating back to 1994. The company also admitted increasing production to dilute the failure rate. Executives stated they had not investigated further because failure rates as determined by warranty claims had not demonstrated significant patterns. Bridgestone/Firestone officials accepted full responsibility and admitted the company had made "bad tires." Masatoshi Ono stepped down as CEO, and John Lampe, former executive vice president, took over Bridgestone USA.

Although many have been quick to point a blaming finger at Bridgestone/Firestone, evidence suggesting that Ford was not entirely blameless also emerged. The design of the Ford Explorer and Ford's recommendations for tire pressure for the vehicle have been scrutinized to determine whether they contributed to the rate of tire separations and rollover accidents. In July 2001, Bridgestone/Firestone formally asked the U.S. secretary of transportation to investigate whether the design of the Ford Explorer may have contributed to the growing number of complaints. The company charged that the design of the Explorer may cause the vehicle to roll over easily.

Since the recall announcement, both companies' stock prices have declined, and Bridgestone/Firestone suffered a $750 million loss in 2000. Opinion polls suggested that the public had lost faith in the companies and that consumers were quite worried about the safety of Ford Explorers with Firestone tires. Moreover, both companies face an estimated 300 lawsuits stemming from deaths and injuries resulting from tread-separation incidents. The first of these suits, which went to trial in Texas in August 2001, was settled out of court for $7.85 million. Ford, which also was named in the suit, settled for $6 million before the trial began. By the time of the settlement, federal regulators had recorded more than 203 deaths and 700 injuries in vehicles—primarily Ford Explorers—equipped with Firestone tires.

The ultimate question is not where this crisis will leave Ford and Bridgestone/Firestone but how it will affect the ethical and legal responsibilities of the government, regulatory agencies, and businesses. Consumers can now research all aspects of vehicle quality except tires, so one suggestion has been to create consumer reports on tire durability, traction, strength, and other important traits. It is up to consumers to determine whether Ford, Bridgestone/Firestone, and the NHTSA acted ethically and responsibly based on the information available. Did they try to hide information? Did they act quickly enough? Will the public forgive and forget? Only time will tell.[51]

QUESTIONS FOR DISCUSSION

1. To what extent do companies need to make a proactive effort to collect and analyze data concerning possible safety issues?
2. What mistakes did Ford, Bridgestone/Firestone, and the NHTSA each make in early attempts to handle the tire recall crisis?
3. What ethical implications might be involved in accepting responsibility versus blaming others?

Global Markets and International Marketing

5

- To understand the nature of global markets and international marketing
- To analyze the environmental forces affecting international marketing efforts
- To identify several important regional trade alliances, markets, and agreements
- To examine methods of involvement in international marketing activities
- To recognize that international marketing strategies fall along a continuum from customization to globalization

111

Shakira Unplugged: En Inglés

When 23-year-old Shakira performed "Ojos Asi" ("Eyes Like These"), an unusual blend of her Latin and Lebanese heritage with a dance-rock beat, at the first-ever Latin Grammy Awards show in Los Angeles in 2000, she received a standing ovation. The young Colombian woman went on to collect two Latin Grammys, for Best Female Pop Vocal Performance ("Ojos Asi") and for Best Female Rock Vocal Performance ("Octavo Dia") at the ceremony. She earned a Grammy Award for Best Latin Pop Album (*Shakira: MTV Unplugged*) a few months later. Although American audiences, particularly teenagers, are buying CDs by U.S.-born Hispanic artists, including the late Selena, Ricky Martin, and Christina Aguilera, few non-Latin music buyers have heard of the artist known in her own country as the "Colombian Madonna" and elsewhere in Latin America as a "Latina Alanis Morissette" due to her unique voice and song-writing talents. Sony Music Entertainment, a subsidiary of Tokyo-based Sony Corporation, hopes all that will change with the release of Shakira's first English-language album in 2001.

Shakira (born Shakira Isabel Mebarak Ripoll) has been writing and recording songs since she was 13 and has sold more than 8 million albums worldwide. While growing up, Shakira was stimulated by a variety of musical influences, including the pop and folk music of her native Colombia, the Arabic music her Lebanese father brought home, and the American rock 'n' roll she heard on local radio stations. Although her first two albums failed to click, her third, *Pies Descalzos (Bare Feet)*, took off, and some of its cuts, including "Estoy Aqui," "Donde Estas Corazon?", and "Antologia," climbed to the tops of charts all across Latin America.

Recognizing the young woman's talent and potential star power, Frank Welzer, president of Sony Latin America, championed Shakira throughout the Sony empire and encouraged the company to invest in her future. Another mentor was Emilio Estefan, a member of the Cuban American band Miami Sound Machine and husband of Gloria Estefan. While producing Shakira's next album, *Donde Estan Los Ladrones? (Where Are the Thieves?)*, Estefan encouraged her to mix her Latin, Lebanese, and American influences, which yielded the hit song "Ojos Asi." Estefan also prompted Shakira to take greater control of her career and to learn English. Shakira's third champion was Freddy DeMann, who had previously managed Michael Jackson and Madonna. In 1999, DeMann began booking Shakira in the United States in areas with large Hispanic populations. She quickly sold out shows in Anaheim (California), San Diego, and Miami. After seeing the audience response to her performances there and at the Latin Grammy Awards, Sony committed to expanding her audience.

Shakira had been working on her English and soon became comfortable enough to begin writing songs in her new language with a little help from Gloria Estefan. She spent the fall of 2000 in the Bahamas and on an exclusive farm in Argentina, writing 15 songs in English for the new album. After going over the songs with Shakira, Gloria Estefan told her, "Don't change a thing." Will these efforts turn Shakira into the next Selena or Madonna in the United States? Only time will tell, but her unique voice and strong stage presence have already resonated with audiences all over the world.[1]

Before picking up an Egg McMuffin at McDonald's this morning, a young woman in Hong Kong may have brightened her smile with Colgate toothpaste and highlighted her eyes with Avon eye shadow. Her brother, on business that same day in Frankfurt, may cash a check in a local Citicorp branch bank. Elsewhere that day, a Polish office worker may lunch on a pizza from Pizza Hut, fried chicken from KFC, or a taco from Taco Bell. An Australian mother shopping for a birthday present in Melbourne may drop in at Daimaru, a Japanese department store, while a New Yorker in Syracuse may shop for a train set for his 2-year-old at the Lost Forest, an Australian toy boutique. The earth is now populated by more than 6 billion people whose lives are intertwined in one tremendous global marketplace. In fact, global trade in goods and services reached $7.2 trillion in 2000, up from $5.5 trillion in 1999.[2]

Because of the increasingly global nature of marketing, we devote this chapter to the unique features of global markets and international marketing. We begin by exploring the environmental forces that create opportunities and threats for international marketers. Next, we consider several regional trade alliances, markets, and agreements. Finally, we examine the levels of commitment U.S. firms have to international marketing and their degree of involvement in it. These represent significant factors that must be considered in any marketing plan that includes an international component.

The Nature of International Marketing

international marketing
Developing and performing marketing activities across national boundaries

Technological advances and rapidly changing political and economic conditions are making it easier than ever for companies to market their products overseas as well as at home. **International marketing** involves developing and performing marketing activities across national boundaries. For example, Wal-Mart has more than 1 million employees and operates 3,400 stores around the world, including the United States, Canada, Mexico, Argentina, Brazil, China, and Germany, while McDonald's serves 45 million customers a day at 29,000 restaurants in 120 countries.[3]

Many U.S. firms are finding that international markets provide tremendous opportunities for growth. For example, Yahoo!, an Internet portal service, was the first portal in France to offer French-language content. This helped the U.S. company to reach 63 percent of the French people who access the Internet and to remain competitive even after France Télecom launched its own portal services, Wanadoo and Voilá.[4] Indeed, most of the world's population and two-thirds of its total purchasing power are outside the United States. Accessing these markets can promote innovation, while intensifying global competition spurs companies to market better, less expensive products. Most automobile marketers, for instance, are developing products for use by customers worldwide. In the future, just ten auto brands may be recognized globally. Some of these are likely to be from General Motors, whose many globally recognized brands include Saab, Opel, Chevrolet, and Cadillac. Global Marketing looks at the brands Heinz markets around the world.

rien n'est jamais
ni tout noir, ni tout blanc

Prêt pour l'accès à Internet*

Vos infos
personnelles
sous la main

Façades amovibles

Nouvel ordinateur de poche Palm™ m105

Avoir accès, où que vous soyez, à toutes vos informations personnelles (rendez-vous, carnet d'adresses...), envoyer un e-mail* au bout du monde, consulter les horaires de ciné dans un train, accéder au net* dans un jardin grâce aux applications web clipping et même changer de couleur avec votre humeur... le Palm™ m105 vous donne le feu vert. Simplement extraordinaire. Simplement Palm.

©2001 Palm, Inc. Tous droits réservés. Palm, Simply Palm et le logo Palm sont des marques commerciales de Palm, Inc ou de ses filiales. Certains logiciels sont disponibles et vendus séparément. L'ordinateur de poche m105 est livré avec une façade amovible noire ; les autres façades de couleur sont vendues séparément.
*Pour accéder à l'e-mail et à l'internet mobile, un téléphone mobile ou un modem compatible est nécessaire.

Simply Palm™
www.palm.com/fr

Adapting Products and Promotion
Palm adapts its products and promotion for France.

Environmental Forces in International Markets

Firms that enter foreign markets often find they must make significant adjustments in their marketing strategies. The environmental forces that affect foreign markets may differ dramatically from those affecting domestic markets. Thus, a successful international marketing strategy requires a careful environmental analysis. Conducting research to understand the needs and desires of foreign customers is crucial to international marketing success. Many firms have demonstrated that such efforts can generate tremendous financial rewards, increase market share, and heighten customer awareness of their products around the world. In this section, we explore how differences in the sociocultural, economic, political, legal, and technological forces of the marketing environment in other countries can profoundly affect marketing activities.

GLOBAL MARKETING

Heinz's Global Success

When you think of Heinz, you probably think of ketchup and Heinz 57 steak sauce. Indeed, Heinz sells 650 million bottles of ketchup a year in 140 countries, as well as 11 billion individual ketchup packets marketed to restaurants and food service companies—at least two packets for each person on earth. But you may not realize that this 130-year-old company owns 150 of the world's number one and number two brands, including StarKist, Ore-Ida, 9-Lives, Bagel Bites, and Kibbles 'n Bits. With annual sales of more than $9 billion, Heinz can attribute much of its success to catering its 50 subsidiaries' products to the 200 countries in which it does business. Heinz's strategy for growth is global category management to support core businesses in key markets: the United States, Canada, the United Kingdom, Italy, Australia, and New Zealand, as well as in new markets such as Japan, India, Indonesia, Poland, the Philippines, and China.

In many countries, Heinz is known for soup, beans, and pasta meals, which account for $1.1 billion in sales each year. In the United Kingdom, where Heinz controls 60 percent of the soup market, many believe that Heinz is a British firm. Tuna, which the company markets around the world under the brand names StarKist, John West, Petit Navire, and Greenseas, contributes another $1 billion in sales. Through Ore-Ida, the company dominates 50 percent of the processed-potato market in the United States. Frozen entrees also contribute to Heinz's bottom line, with worldwide sales of $1.4 billion from Smart Ones, the Budget Gourmet, and Weight Watchers. Heinz recently acquired U.K. brands such as Go Ahead! Pizza, McVitie's American Dream and Jane Asher desserts, Linda McCartney's vegetarian/meat-free products, and San Marco pizzas.

Heinz also sells more than $1 billion of baby foods, cereals, juices, and biscuits a year. In Italy, Canada, and Australia, 90 percent of infants consume Heinz baby foods. In the United Kingdom, Heinz's Farley brand holds 60 percent of the market. Emerging markets for Heinz infant foods include India, where sales are growing more than 30 percent each year, and China.

Pet food represents the fastest-growing product category in the United States. With global pet food sales of $1.3 billion, Heinz continues to develop new products and product-line extensions of its successful 9-Lives and Kibbles 'n Bits brands. In Australia and New Zealand, Heinz markets Pup-Peroni Nawsomes dog snacks.

Ketchup, of course, remains the firm's cash cow. With the successful introduction of Blastin' Green and Funky Purple ketchup, Heinz controls more than 51 percent of the ketchup market in the United States. To keep up with demand for these new products, Heinz factories had to work 24 hours a day, 7 days a week. Early in its introduction, Blastin' Green ketchup was in such short supply that consumers were bidding for bottles on eBay.

Heinz has been a successful global marketer because it knows how to deliver value in each country in which it operates. Heinz focuses on profitable market segments and reducing costs while building a world-class supply chain with superior customer service. The bottom line is introducing many successful new products while simultaneously improving gross margins. Understanding regional, political, and cultural differences has been essential to Heinz's global marketing strategy and success.

Only eight percent
of the world
speaks English.

LEMONADE

LEMONADE
น้ำมะนาว
LIMONADA
レモネード
LIMONATA
निम्बू का रस
LIMONADE
檸檬
ZITRONENLIMONADE

The other
92 percent is going
to your competitor.

Is your web site multilingual? Creating and managing web content in one language is difficult enough. Now imagine trying to do so in Japanese, Spanish, French and German. With Uniscape.com's web-based translation management solution, multilingual web sites have just become a whole lot easier. Now human translators are alerted automatically to changes in your web content, making ongoing updates to your site a cinch in 42 different languages.

**Visit us at www.uniscape.com
Or call 1–888–464–4186.**

www.
uniscape
.com

Cultural Differences
Uniscape creates multilingual websites.

Cultural, Social, and Ethical Forces

Cultural, social, and ethical differences among nations can have significant effects on marketing activities. Because marketing activities are primarily social in purpose, they are influenced by beliefs and values regarding family, religion, education, health, and recreation. For example, in Greece, where sunbathing is a common form of recreation, American products such as Johnson & Johnson Baby Sunblock have a large target market. By identifying major sociocultural deviations among countries, marketers lay groundwork for an effective adaptation of marketing strategy. For instance, when Little Caesars opened new franchise pizza outlets abroad, it made some menu changes to accommodate local tastes and social norms. In Japan, Little Caesars' pizzas are garnished with asparagus, potatoes, squid, or seaweed. Turkish menus include a local pastry for dessert, while Middle Eastern menus exclude pork.[5] Although football is a popular sport in the United States and a major opportunity for many television advertisers, soccer is the most popular televised sport in Europe. And, of course, marketing communications often must be translated into other languages. For example, New Horizons Computer Learning Centers, the world's largest computer training firm, has translated course materials into 14 languages and adapted marketing campaigns to serve customers in 45 countries.[6]

It can be difficult to transfer marketing symbols, trademarks, logos, and even products to international markets, especially if these are associated with objects that have profound religious or cultural significance in a particular culture. For example, when Big Boy opened a new restaurant in Bangkok, it quickly became popular with European and American tourists, but the local Thais refused to eat there. Instead, they placed gifts of rice and incense at the feet of the Big Boy statue—a chubby boy holding a hamburger—which reminded them of Buddha. In Japan, customers were forced to tiptoe around a logo painted on the floor at the entrance to an Athlete's Foot store because in Japan it is taboo to step on a crest. On the other hand, A&W's Great Root Beer is an American icon that has been successfully translated around the world—it appeals to customers everywhere.[7]

Cultural differences may also affect marketing negotiations and decision-making behavior. For example, although Americans and Taiwanese sales agents are equally sensitive to customer interests, research suggests that Taiwanese are more sensitive to the interests of their company and competitors and less sensitive to the interests of colleagues. Identifying such differences in work-related values of employees across different nationalities helps companies design more effective sales management practices.[8] Table 5.1 offers a sampling of behaviors that may be viewed as rude, insensitive, or offensive in business negotiations. Research has shown that when marketers use a problem-solving approach—that is, gain information about a particular client's needs and tailor goods or services to meet those needs—customer satisfaction in marketing negotiations increases in France, Germany, the United Kingdom, and the United States. However, the attractiveness of the salesperson and his or her similarity to the customer increase satisfaction only for Americans; the role and status of the seller are more important in both the United Kingdom and France.[9] Cultural differences in the emphasis placed on personal relationships, status, decision-making styles, and approaches to bidding have been known to complicate business dealings between Americans and Japanese.[10] In the Far East, a gift may

Table 5.1	A Sampling of Cross-Cultural Behavioral Differences
Country	**Behaviors Viewed as Rude or Otherwise Unacceptable**
Japan	Talking about price during negotiations
Finland	Standing with your arms folded across your chest
Belgium	Talking with your hands in your pockets
Egypt	Showing the sole of your shoe (as when legs are crossed)
Zambia	Pointing directly at someone or something
France	Chewing gum, yawning, or conversing loudly in public
Hong Kong	Blinking conspicuously during conversation
India	Expressing anger
New Zealand	Using toothpicks or chewing gum in public
England	Pushing your way in front of others standing in a line
Sri Lanka	Touching, leaning on, or sitting on an image of Buddha
Thailand	Stepping on a doorsill when entering a building

Source: "Gestures Around the World," Web of Culture, www.webofculture.com/worldsmart/gestures.html, July 5, 2001.

be considered a necessary introduction before negotiation, but in the United States or Canada, a gift may be misconstrued as an illegal bribe.

Buyers' perceptions of other countries can influence product adoption and use. For example, research indicates that Japanese consumers evaluate products from Japan more favorably than those from other countries regardless of product superiority. Americans, however, evaluate domestic products more favorably than foreign ones only when the U.S. products are superior to products from other countries.[11] When people are unfamiliar with products from another country, their perceptions of the country itself may affect their attitude toward the product and help determine whether they will buy it. If a country has a reputation for producing quality products and therefore has a positive image in consumers' minds, marketers of products from that country will want to make the country of origin well known. For example, a generally favorable image of Western computer technology has fueled sales of American personal computers and Microsoft software in Japan. On the other hand, marketers may want to dissociate themselves from a particular country. Because the world has not always viewed Mexico as producing quality products, Volkswagen may not want to advertise that some of the models it sells in the United States, including the Beetle, are made in Mexico.

When products are introduced from one nation into another, acceptance is far more likely if similarities exist between the two cultures. Due to a new global sensitivity about food, middle-class U.S. families are eating more like their counterparts in Japan, France, and Canada. For international marketers, cultural differences have implications for product development, advertising, packaging, and pricing. Schlotzsky's, for example, experienced slower than expected sales when it opened a new restaurant in Beijing. Although the Texas-based sandwich chain has enjoyed great success in the United States, the Chinese are less accustomed to eating foods with their hands, and they often like to share their meals with companions, which is difficult to do with a sandwich. The company hopes that training staff and placing pictures on restaurant tables to demonstrate how to hold and eat the sandwiches will help Chinese customers appreciate the large sandwiches and thus increase sales.[12]

Differences in ethical standards can also affect marketing efforts. China and Vietnam, for example, have different standards regarding intellectual property than the United States. This creates an issue for marketers of computer software, music CDs, and books. Because of differences in cultural and ethical standards, many companies are working both individually and collectively to establish ethics programs and standards for international business conduct.[13] Levi Strauss's code of ethics, for example, bars the firm from manufacturing in countries where workers are known to be abused. Starbucks' global code of ethics strives to protect agricultural workers who harvest coffee. Many companies choose to standardize their ethical behavior across national boundaries to maintain a consistent and well-integrated corporate culture.

Economic Forces

Global marketers need to understand the international trade system, particularly the economic stability of individual nations, as well as trade barriers that may stifle marketing efforts. Economic differences among nations—differences in standards of living, credit, buying power, income distribution, national resources, exchange rates, and the like—dictate many of the adjustments that must be made in marketing abroad.

The United States and Western Europe are more stable economically than many other regions of the world. In recent years, a number of countries, including Russia, Japan, Korea, Thailand, and Singapore, have experienced such economic problems as depression, high unemployment, corporate bankruptcies, instability in currency markets, trade imbalances, and financial systems that need major reforms. Even more stable developing countries, such as Mexico and Brazil, tend to have greater fluctuations in their business cycles than the United States does. Economic instability can disrupt the markets for U.S. products in places that otherwise might be great marketing opportunities.

Economic Differences
Ernst & Young provides advice in navigating economic differences between countries. Xporta assists in determining the costs of international trade.

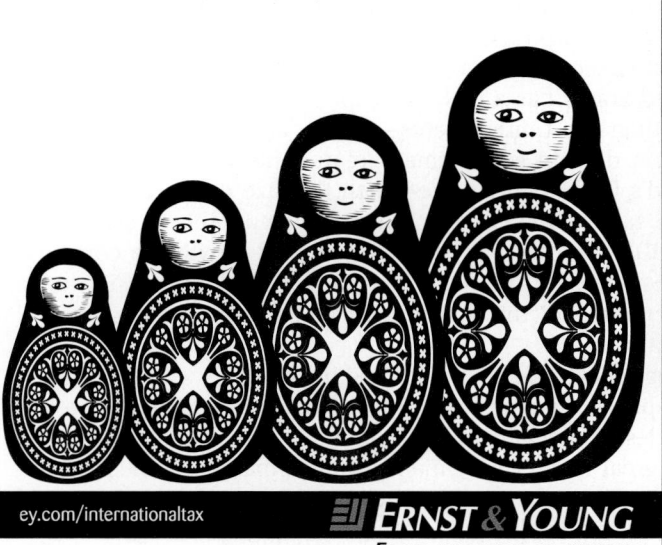

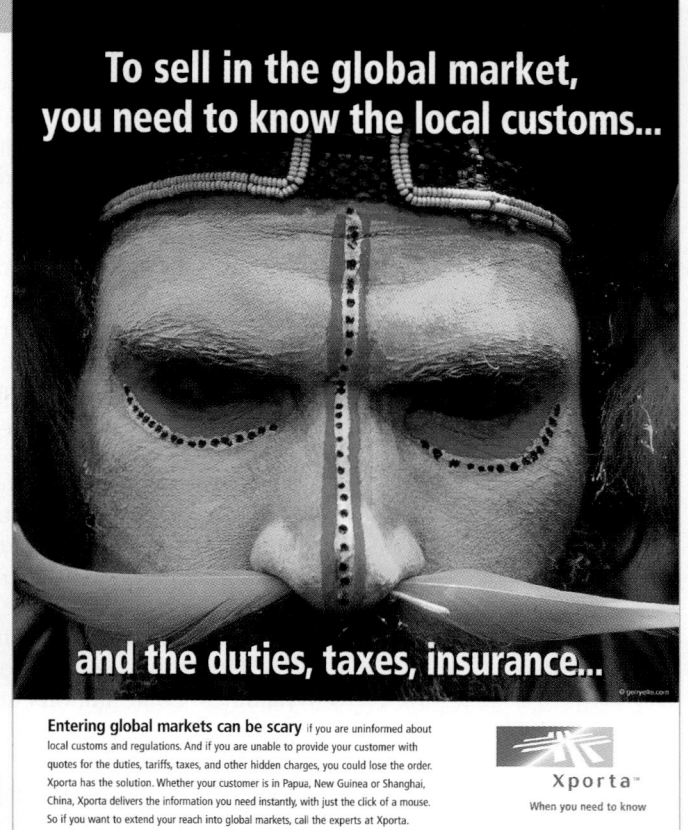

import tariff   A duty levied by a nation on goods bought outside its borders and brought in

quota   A limit on the amount of goods an importing country will accept for certain product categories in a specific time period

embargo   A government's suspension of trade in a particular product or with a given country

exchange controls
Government restrictions on the amount of a particular currency that can be bought or sold

balance of trade   The difference in value between a nation's exports and its imports

gross domestic product (GDP)   The market value of a nation's total output of goods and services for a given period; an overall measure of economic standing

Beyond assessing the stability of a nation's economy, marketers should also consider whether the nation imposes trade restrictions, such as tariffs. An **import tariff** is any duty levied by a nation on goods bought outside its borders and brought in. Because they raise the prices of foreign goods, tariffs impede free trade between nations. Tariffs are usually designed either to raise revenue for a country or to protect domestic products.

Nontariff trade barriers include quotas and embargoes. A **quota** is a limit on the amount of goods an importing country will accept for certain product categories in a specific time period. An **embargo** is a government's suspension of trade in a particular product or with a given country. Embargoes are generally directed at specific goods or countries and are established for political, health, or religious reasons. For example, the United States forbids the importation of cigars from Cuba for political reasons. However, demand for Cuban cigars is so strong that many enter the U.S. market illegally. Laws regarding pricing policies may also serve as trade barriers. Great Britain, for example, has weaker antitrust laws than the United States and is generally more accepting of price collusion. Consequently many products cost much more in Britain than in the United States. Because customers may not be able to afford the higher prices of imported products, such policies effectively create barriers to foreign trade.

Exchange controls, government restrictions on the amount of a particular currency that can be bought or sold, may also limit international trade. They can force businesspeople to buy and sell foreign products through a central agency, such as a central bank. On the other hand, to promote international trade, some countries have joined together to form free trade zones—multinational economic communities that eliminate tariffs and other trade barriers. Such regional trade alliances are discussed later in the chapter. Foreign currency exchange rates also affect the prices marketers can charge in foreign markets. Fluctuations in the international monetary market can change the prices charged across national boundaries on a daily basis. Consequently these fluctuations must be considered in any international marketing strategy.

Countries may limit imports to maintain a favorable balance of trade. The **balance of trade** is the difference in value between a nation's exports and its imports. When a nation exports more products than it imports, a favorable balance of trade exists because money is flowing into the country. The United States has a negative balance of trade for goods and services of $369 billion, the largest deficit since 1988. A negative balance of trade is considered harmful because it means U.S. dollars are supporting foreign economies at the expense of U.S. companies and workers.[14]

In terms of the value of all products produced by a nation, the United States has the largest gross domestic product in the world, more than $9 trillion. **Gross domestic product (GDP)** is an overall measure of a nation's economic standing; it is the market value of a nation's total output of goods and services for a given period. However, it does not take into account the concept of GDP in relation to population (GDP per capita). The United States has a GDP per capita of $33,357. Switzerland is roughly 230 times smaller than the United States—a little larger than the state of Maryland—but its population density is six times greater than that of the United States. Although Switzerland's GDP is about one-fourth the size of the U.S. GDP, its GDP per capita is about the same. Even Canada, which is comparable in size to the United States, has a lower GDP and GDP per capita.[15] Table 5.2 provides a comparative economic analysis of Switzerland, Canada, and the United States. Knowledge about per capita income, credit, and the distribution of income provides general insights into market potential.

Opportunities for international trade are not limited to countries with the highest incomes. Some nations are progressing at a much faster rate than they were a few years ago, and these countries—especially in Latin America, Africa, Eastern Europe, and the Middle East—have great market potential. However, marketers must understand the political and legal environment before they can convert buying power of customers in these countries into actual demand for specific products.

Table 5.2	**A Comparative Economic Analysis of Canada, Switzerland, and the United States**		
	Canada	**Switzerland**	**United States**
Land area (sq. mi.)	3,560,219	15,355	3,539,227
Population (millions)	31.28	7.26	284.8
Population density (persons per sq. mi.)	8	472	78
GDP, 2000 ($ billions)	$688.8	$241.2	$9,896
GDP per capita	$20,302	$35,665	$33,357

Source: Bureau of the Census, *Statistical Abstract of the United States, 2000* (Washington, D.C.: Government Printing Office, 2001), pp. 822–824, 832 and www.census.gov.

Political and Legal Forces

A nation's political system, laws, regulatory bodies, special-interest groups, and courts all have great impact on international marketing. A government's policies toward public and private enterprise, consumers, and foreign firms influence marketing across national boundaries. Some countries have established import barriers. Many nontariff barriers, such as quotas and minimum price levels set on imports, port-of-entry taxes, and stringent health and safety requirements, still make it difficult for American companies to export their products.[16] For example, the collectivistic nature of Japanese culture and the high-context nature of Japanese communication make some types of direct marketing messages less effective there and may predispose many Japanese to support greater regulation of direct marketing practices.[17] A government's attitude toward importers has a direct impact on the economic feasibility of exporting to that country.

Differences in national standards of ethics are illustrated by what the Mexicans call *la mordida,* "the bite." The use of payoffs and bribes is deeply entrenched in many governments. Because U.S. trade and corporate policy, as well as U.S. law, prohibits direct involvement in payoffs and bribes, American companies may have a hard time competing with foreign firms that do engage in these practices. Some U.S. businesses that refuse to make payoffs are forced to hire local consultants, public relations firms, or advertising agencies, which results in indirect payoffs. The ultimate decision about whether to give small tips or gifts where they are customary must be based on a company's code of ethics. However, under the Foreign Corrupt Practices Act of 1977, it is illegal for U.S. firms to attempt to make large payments or bribes to influence policy decisions of foreign governments. Nevertheless, facilitating payments, or small payments to support the performance of standard tasks, are often acceptable. The act also subjects all publicly held U.S. corporations to rigorous internal controls and recordkeeping requirements for their overseas operations.

Technological Forces

Advances in technology have made international marketing much easier. Voice mail, e-mail, fax, cellular phones, and the Internet make international marketing activities more affordable and convenient. Internet use has accelerated dramatically within the United States and abroad. In Europe, 50 percent of households have Internet access at home or work, pushing e-commerce revenues to $16.4 billion.[18] In Japan, 47 million are logging on to the Internet, and 22.5 million Chinese have Internet access.[19]

Can you buy it
in Hoboken?

Can you make it
in Nepal?

Can you ship it
into Lisbon,

in time to
stock the mall?

MOVE GOODS BETWEEN GLOBAL MARKETS
FASTER AND MORE PROFITABLY THAN EVER BEFORE.

VASTERA
Opening the world to e-business

www.vastera.com

Information Technology
Vastera provides high-tech international communication solutions.

In many developing countries that lack the level of technological infrastructure found in the United States and Japan, marketers are beginning to capitalize on opportunities to "leapfrog" existing technology. For example, cellular and wireless phone technology is reaching many countries at less expense than traditional hard-wired telephone systems. In China, few households have a private phone line, partly because it costs as much as $440 to install and requires a wait of several months. Many customers have bypassed expensive private lines in favor of wireless communications. With the Chinese market for mobile phones expected to rise to 250 million units by 2005, many firms, including Motorola, Nokia, Ericsson, and Vodafone, are anxious to target the growing Chinese marketplace.[20] Hewlett-Packard also hopes to bring new technologies to less developed countries. The company has launched World e-Inclusion, an economic development initiative that seeks to apply technology-based solutions to empower people in developing countries. Pilot programs for the initiative have already yielded high-speed Internet connections for remote villages in Central America and specialized software for coffee growers in Sumatra.[21]

Regional Trade Alliances, Markets, and Agreements

Although many more firms are beginning to view the world as one huge marketplace, various regional trade alliances and specific markets affect companies engaging in international marketing: Some create opportunities, others impose constraints. In this section we examine several regional trade alliances, markets, and changing conditions affecting markets, including the North American Free Trade Agreement among the United States, Canada, and Mexico; the European Union; the Common Market of the Southern Cone; Asia-Pacific Economic Cooperation; the General Agreement on Tariffs and Trade; and the World Trade Organization.

The North American Free Trade Agreement (NAFTA)

North American Free Trade Agreement (NAFTA)
An alliance that merges Canada, Mexico, and the United States into a single market

The **North American Free Trade Agreement (NAFTA),** implemented in 1994, effectively merged Canada, Mexico, and the United States into one market of more than 400 million consumers. NAFTA will eliminate virtually all tariffs on goods produced and traded among Canada, Mexico, and the United States to create a free trade area by 2009. The estimated annual output for this trade alliance is $6 trillion.

NAFTA makes it easier for U.S. businesses to invest in Mexico and Canada; provides protection for intellectual property (of special interest to high-technology and entertainment industries); expands trade by requiring equal treatment of U.S. firms in both countries; and simplifies country-of-origin rules, hindering Japan's use of Mexico as a staging ground for further penetration into U.S. markets. Although most tariffs on products coming to the United States will be lifted, duties on more sensitive products, such as household glassware, footware, and some fruits and vegetables, will be phased out over a 15-year period.

Canada's 31 million consumers are relatively affluent, with a per capita GDP of $20,302.[22] Trade between the United States and Canada totals about $408 billion.[23]

Currently exports to Canada support approximately 1.5 million U.S. jobs. Canadian investments in U.S. companies are also increasing, and various markets, including air travel, are opening as regulatory barriers dissolve.[24]

With a per capita GDP of $5,741, Mexico's 100 million consumers are less affluent than Canadian consumers. However, they bought $111 billion worth of U.S. products last year. In fact, Mexico has become the United States' second-largest trading market, after Canada.[25] Many U.S. companies, including Hewlett-Packard, IBM, and General Motors, have taken advantage of Mexico's low labor costs and close proximity to the United States to set up production facilities, sometimes called *maquiladoras.* Production at the *maquiladoras,* especially in the automotive, electronics, and apparel industries, tripled between 1994 and 2000 as companies as diverse as Ford, John Deere, Motorola, Sara Lee, Kimberly-Clark, and VF Corporation set up facilities in north-central Mexican states. With the *maquiladoras* accounting for roughly half of Mexico's exports, Mexico has risen to become the world's eighth-largest exporter.[26] Although Mexico experienced financial instability throughout the 1990s, privatization of some government-owned firms and other measures instituted by the Mexican government and businesses, along with a booming U.S. economy, have helped Mexico's economy. Moreover, increasing trade between the United States and Canada constitutes a strong base of support for the ultimate success of NAFTA. Mexico's membership in NAFTA also links the United States with other Latin American countries, providing additional opportunities to integrate trade among all the nations in the Western Hemisphere. Chile, for example, is expected to become the fourth member of NAFTA, but political forces may delay its entry into the agreement for several years.

Although NAFTA has been controversial, it has become a positive factor for U.S. firms wishing to engage in international marketing. Because licensing requirements have been relaxed under the pact, smaller businesses that previously could not afford to invest in Mexico and Canada will be able to do business in those markets without having to locate there. NAFTA's long phase-in period provides ample time for adjustment by those firms affected by reduced tariffs on imports. Furthermore, increased competition should lead to a more efficient market, and the long-term prospects of including most countries in the Western Hemisphere in the alliance promise additional opportunities for U.S. marketers.

Net Sights

One excellent source for country-specific information may be somewhat surprising: the U.S. Central Intelligence Agency (CIA). For years, the CIA has published an annual *World Fact Book* (**http://www.cia.gov/cia/publications/factbook/index.html**), which profiles every country in the world. This useful guide offers detailed information on each country's geography (including maps and climate information), population, government and military, economy, infrastructure, and significant transnational issues. Before doing business in a specific country, marketers will need to conduct further research, and *The World Fact Book* can be an excellent place to begin.

The European Union (EU)

European Union (EU)
An alliance that promotes trade among its member countries in Europe

The **European Union (EU),** also called the *European Community* or *Common Market,* was established in 1958 to promote trade among its members, which initially included Belgium, France, Italy, West Germany, Luxembourg, and the Netherlands. In 1991 East and West Germany united, and by 1995 the United Kingdom, Spain, Denmark, Greece, Portugal, Ireland, Austria, Finland, and Sweden had joined as well. (Cyprus, Poland, Hungary, the Czech Republic, Slovenia, and Estonia have begun formal negotiations to join the EU; Latvia, Lithuania, Romania, Bulgaria, the Slovak Republic, Malta, Turkey, and Ukraine have requested membership as well.[27]) Until 1993 each nation functioned as a separate market, but at that time the members officially unified into one of the largest single world markets, which today includes 390 million consumers.

To facilitate free trade among members, the EU is working toward standardization of business regulations and requirements, import duties, and value-added taxes; the elimination of customs checks; and the creation of a standardized currency for use by all members. Many European nations (Austria, Belgium, Finland, France, Germany, Ireland, Italy, Luxembourg, the Netherlands, Portugal, and Spain) link their exchange rates together to a common currency, the *euro*. The common currency requires many marketers to modify their pricing strategies and will subject them to increased competition. However, the use of a single currency frees companies that sell goods among European countries from the nuisance of dealing with complex exchange rates.[28] The long-term goals are to eliminate all trade barriers within the EU, improve the economic efficiency of the EU nations, and stimulate economic growth, thus making the union's economy more competitive in global markets, particularly against Japan and other Pacific Rim nations, and North America. However, several disputes and debates still divide the member nations, and many barriers to completely free trade remain. Consequently it may take many years before the EU is truly one deregulated market.

As the EU nations attempt to function as one large market, consumers in the EU may become more homogeneous in their needs and wants. Marketers should be aware, however, that cultural differences among the nations may require modifications in the marketing mix for customers in each nation. Differences in taste and preferences in these diverse markets are significant for international marketers. The British, for example, prefer front-loading washing machines, whereas the French prefer top-loaders. Consumers in Spain eat far more poultry products than Germans do.[29] Such differences may exist even within the same country, depending on the geographic region. Gathering information about these distinct tastes and preferences is likely to remain a very important factor in developing marketing mixes that satisfy the needs of European customers.

The Common Market of the Southern Cone (MERCOSUR)

Common Market of the Southern Cone (MERCOSUR)
An alliance that promotes the free circulation of goods, services, and production factors, and has a common external tariff and commercial policy among member nations in South America

The **Common Market of the Southern Cone (MERCOSUR),** was established in 1991 under the Treaty of Asunción to unite Argentina, Brazil, Paraguay, and Uruguay as a free trade alliance; Bolivia and Chile joined as associates in 1996. The alliance represents 215 million consumers—63 percent of South America's population—with a combined gross domestic product of (US) $1.4 trillion, making it the third-largest trading bloc behind NAFTA and the European Union. Like NAFTA, MERCOSUR promotes "the free circulation of goods, services and production factors among the countries" and established a common external tariff and commercial policy.[30]

Asia-Pacific Economic Cooperation (APEC)

Asia-Pacific Economic Cooperation (APEC)
An alliance that promotes open trade and economic and technical cooperation among member nations throughout the world

The **Asia-Pacific Economic Cooperation (APEC),** established in 1989, promotes open trade and economic and technical cooperation among member nations, which initially included Australia, Brunei Darussalam, Canada, Indonesia, Japan, Korea, Malaysia, New Zealand, the Philippines, Singapore, Thailand, and the United States. Since then the alliance has grown to include China, Hong Kong, Chinese Taipei, Mexico, Papua New Guinea, Chile, Peru, Russia, and Vietnam. The 21-member alliance represents 2.5 billion consumers, has a combined gross domestic product of (US) $18 trillion, and accounts for nearly 44 percent of global trade. APEC differs from other international trade alliances in its commitment to facilitating business and its practice of allowing the business/private sector to participate in a wide range of APEC activities.[31]

Despite economic turmoil and a recession in Asia in recent years, companies of the APEC have become increasingly competitive and sophisticated in global business in the last three decades. Moreover, the markets of the APEC offer tremendous opportunities to marketers who understand them.

The Japanese in particular have made tremendous inroads on world markets for automobiles, motorcycles, watches, cameras, and audio and video equipment. Products from Sony, Sanyo, Toyota, Mitsubishi, Canon, Suzuki, and Toshiba are sold all over the world and have set standards of quality by which other products are often judged. Despite the high volume of trade between the United States and Japan, the two economies are less integrated than the U.S. economy is with Canada's and Western Europe's. If Japan imported goods at the same rate as other major nations, the United States would sell billions of dollars more each year to Japan. The United States and Japan continually struggle with cultural and political differences and are, in general, at odds over how to do business with each other. Global Marketing describes one firm's efforts to penetrate the Japanese market.

The People's Republic of China, a country of 1.3 billion people, has launched a program of economic reform to stimulate its economy by privatizing many industries, restructuring its banking system, and increasing public spending on infrastructure (including railways and telecommunications).[32] The potential of China's consumer

GLOBAL MARKETING

Universal Studios Goes to Japan

Theme parks such as Six Flags, Sea World, Disneyland and DisneyWorld, and Universal Studios have long been a favorite vacation destination for American families and tourists from abroad. Theme parks outside the United States are becoming increasingly popular with the success of EuroDisney (France) and Disneyland Tokyo. Now Japanese families have another opportunity for fun at Universal Studios Japan, which opened in Osaka in 2001.

Universal Studios began exploring the possibility of opening an overseas park in the early 1990s. As one of the highest movie-consuming countries outside the United States, Japan was a prime target. The Japanese also tend to be more welcoming and embracing of Western cultures. When Tokyo Disneyland opened in 1983, it drew crowds of 17 million, making it the most heavily visited theme park in the world. Situated on 140 acres in Osaka, Universal Studios Japan is expected to attract 8 million visitors a year, including 400,000 tourists from abroad.

Universal Studio Japan's main draw will be 18 attractions, 5 of which will be unique to Japan. Motion Picture Magic highlights the latest production technology and moviemaking magic, while Animation Celebration shows off some of Universal Studio's favorite cartoon characters. Hollywood Magic is a nighttime phenomenon featuring fireworks, lasers, and spouting water above the park's central lake. Other exhibits include a 40-foot-tall Tyrannosaurus Rex robot from *Jurassic Park* and a human-attacking shark from *Jaws*.

The greatest challenge Universal Studios faced was adapting an American experience to develop a uniquely Japanese theme park. Before designing the park, the company interviewed Japanese guests at its California and Florida parks to find out what they did and didn't like. This research indicated that Japanese tourists were

impressed by the parks' open expanses, but were turned off by their large meal portions. Japanese and American chefs therefore were asked to combine foods to create typical American dishes with a Japanese twist, such as seafood pizza and a gumbolike soup. All scripts were written in English, translated to Japanese, and then edited to remove any offensive lines or untranslatable puns or references. But Universal not only blended the two cultures; it also created features to appeal strictly to the Japanese, including a park layout that reflects their preference for a systematic, clockwise traffic flow, a shop that sells edible souvenirs like dinosaur-shaped bean cakes, and Japanese-style toilets. Early plans for the park included a gigantic primeval octopus living in the local harbor, but the idea was dropped due to feedback that the Japanese consider octopuses to be friendly and tasty, and monsters in general to be outdated. Other ideas that were panned included samurai warriors, geisha dancers, and the concept of a restaurant called Shakin's, which originated from a 1906 California earthquake.

The grand opening of Universal Studios Japan highlighted famous Universal Studios characters, including Snoopy, Marilyn Monroe, Charlie Chaplin, and even Arnold Schwarzenegger as The Terminator. If the park becomes as successful as hoped, it will not only generate profits for its owners but also potentially infuse (US) $2.41 billion into the Japanese economy through associated transportation, lodging, and other tourism revenue.

Airlines Take Advantage of NAFTA
AeroMexico uses its website to reach U.S. and Canadian customers and has an alliance with Delta to expand markets in North America.

market is so vast that it is almost impossible to measure, but doing business in China also entails many risks. Political and economic instability, especially inflation, corruption, and erratic policy shifts, have undercut marketers' efforts to stake a claim in what could become the world's largest market. Moreover, piracy is a major issue, and protecting a brand name in China is difficult. Because copying is a tradition in China and laws protecting copyrights and intellectual property are weak and minimally enforced, the country is flooded with counterfeit videos, movies, compact discs, computer software, furniture, and clothing. For example, Bo Concepts, a Danish retail chain, has suffered declining sales in China as a result of domestic firms offering "knockoffs" of the firm's furniture at discounted prices and misappropriating the firm's catalog and brand name.[33]

China's trade surplus with the United States reached nearly $100 billion in 2000.[34] Nike and Adidas have shifted most of their shoe production to China, and recently China has become a major producer of compact disc players, cellular phones, portable stereos, and personal computers. It is apparent that the Chinese intend to use American and European investments to accelerate their export of automobiles, automobile parts, semiconductors, and telecommunications products.

Less visible and sometimes less stable Pacific Rim regions, such as South Korea, Thailand, Singapore, Taiwan, and Hong Kong, have become major manufacturing and financial centers. Even before Korean brand names such as Samsung, Daewoo, and Hyundai became household words, these products prospered under U.S. company labels, including GE, GTE, RCA, and J. C. Penney. Singapore boasts huge global markets for rubber goods and pharmaceuticals. Hong Kong is still a strong commercial center after being transferred to Chinese control. Vietnam is becoming one of Asia's fastest-growing markets for U.S. businesses, but Taiwan may have the most promising future of all the Pacific Rim nations as a strong local economy and low import barriers draw increasing imports. Firms from Thailand and Malaysia are also thriving, carving out niches in the world markets for a variety of products from toys to automobile parts.

General Agreement on Tariffs and Trade (GATT) and World Trade Organization (WTO)

General Agreement on Tariffs and Trade (GATT) An agreement among nations to reduce worldwide tariffs and increase international trade

dumping Selling products at unfairly low prices

World Trade Organization (WTO) An entity that promotes free trade among member nations

Like NAFTA and the European Union, the **General Agreement on Tariffs and Trade (GATT)** is based on negotiations among member countries to reduce world wide tariffs and increase international trade. Originally signed by 23 nations in 1947, GATT provides a forum for tariff negotiations and a place where international trade problems can be discussed and resolved. GATT negotiations currently involve some 124 nations and have had far-reaching ramifications for the international marketing strategies of U.S. firms.

GATT sponsors rounds of negotiations aimed at reducing trade restrictions. Seven rounds of GATT negotiations have reduced the average worldwide tariffs on manufactured goods from 45 percent to 5 percent, and negotiators have been able to eliminate or ease nontariff trade restrictions such as import quotas, red tape in customs procedures, and "buy national" agreements. The most recent round, the Uruguay Round (1988–1994), further reduced trade barriers for most products and provided new rules to prevent **dumping,** the selling of products at unfairly low prices.

The most significant outcome of the Uruguay Round was the establishment of the **World Trade Organization (WTO)** to promote free trade among member nations. Fulfilling this purpose requires eliminating trade barriers; educating individuals, companies, and governments about trade rules around the world; and assuring global markets that no sudden changes of policy will occur. The WTO also serves as a forum for trade negotiations and dispute resolution. At the heart of the WTO are agreements that provide legal ground rules for international commerce and trade policy.[35]

International Involvement

Marketers engage in international marketing activities at several levels of involvement covering a wide spectrum, as Figure 5.1 shows. Domestic marketing involves marketing strategies aimed at markets within the home country; at the other extreme, global marketing entails developing marketing strategies for major regions or for the entire world. Many firms with an international presence start out as small companies serving local and regional markets and expand to

FIGURE 5.1
Levels of Involvement in Global Marketing

national markets before considering opportunities in foreign markets. Limited exporting may occur even if a firm makes little or no effort to obtain foreign sales. Foreign buyers may seek out the company and/or its products, or a distributor may discover the firm's products and export them. The level of commitment to international marketing is a major variable in international marketing strategies. In this section, we examine importing and exporting, trading companies, licensing and franchising, contract manufacturing, joint ventures, direct ownership, and other approaches to international involvement.

Importing and Exporting

importing   The purchase of products from a foreign source

exporting   The sale of products to foreign markets

Importing and exporting require the least amount of effort and commitment of resources. **Importing** is the purchase of products from a foreign source. **Exporting,** the sale of products to foreign markets, enables businesses of all sizes to participate in global business. A firm may find an exporting intermediary to take over most marketing functions associated with selling to other countries. This approach entails minimal effort and cost. Modifications in packaging, labeling, style, or color may be the major expenses in adapting a product for the foreign market.

Export agents bring together buyers and sellers from different countries and collect a commission for arranging sales. Export houses and export merchants purchase products from different companies and then sell them abroad. They are specialists at understanding foreign customers' needs. Using exporting intermediaries involves limited risk because no direct investment in the foreign country is required.

Information for Importers
The Real Yellow Pages® from BellSouth publishes the *BellSouth Guía Export,* a directory of U.S. exporters that is distributed to over 400,000 importers in Latin America and the Caribbean. UPS provides detailed information on import billing.

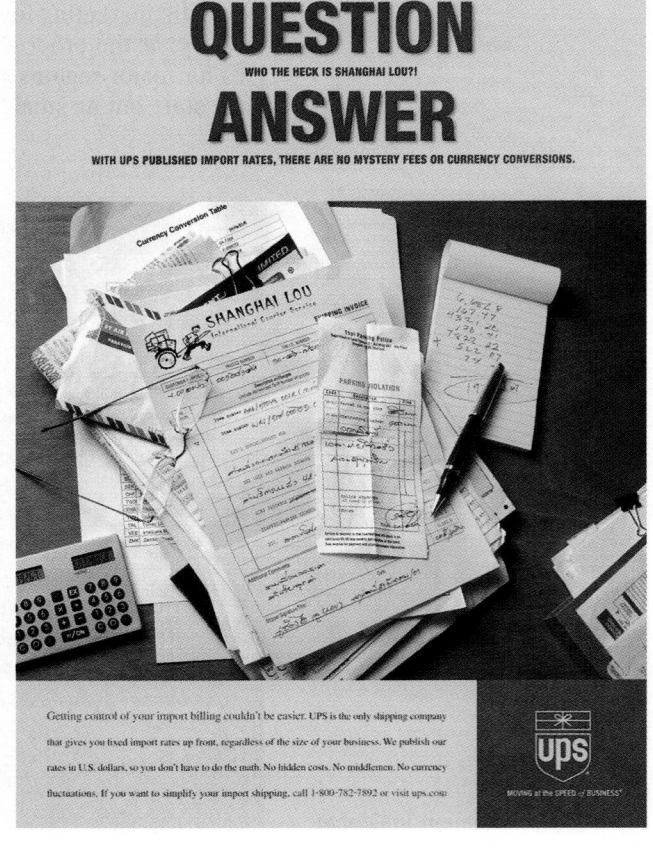

SNAPSHOT

Top U.S. cigarette importers (billions of cigarettes)

Japan 70.9

Lebanon 10.9

Saudi Arabia 8.7

Russia and Singapore are among those who receive the least amount of cigarettes from the U.S.

Source: *USA Today*, http://usatoday.com/snapshot/money/msnap102.htm. Copyright 2000, *USA Today*. Reprinted with permission.

trading company A company that links buyers and sellers in different countries

licensing An alternative to direct investment requiring a licensee to pay commissions or royalties on sales or supplies used in manufacturing

Buyers from foreign companies and governments provide a direct method of exporting and eliminate the need for an intermediary. These buyers encourage international exchange by contacting overseas firms about their needs and the opportunities available in exporting to them. Indeed, research suggests that many small firms tend to rely heavily on such native contacts, especially in developed markets, and remain production oriented rather than marketing oriented in their approach to international marketing.[36] Domestic firms that want to export with minimal effort and investment should seek out export intermediaries. Once a company becomes involved in exporting, it usually develops a more positive image of its country and more optimistic about its competitiveness.[37]

Trading Companies

Marketers sometimes employ a **trading company** which links buyers and sellers in different countries but is not involved in manufacturing and does not own assets related to manufacturing. Trading companies buy goods in one country at the lowest price consistent with quality and sell them to buyers in another country. The best-known U.S. trading company is Sears World Trade, which specializes in consumer goods, light industrial items, and processed foods. A trading company acts like a wholesaler, taking on much of the responsibility of finding markets while facilitating all marketing aspects of a transaction. An important function of trading companies is taking title to products and performing all the activities necessary to move the products from the domestic country to a foreign country. For example, large grain-trading companies operating out of home offices in both the United States and overseas control a major portion of the world's trade in basic food commodities. These trading companies sell homogeneous agricultural commodities that can be stored and moved rapidly in response to market conditions.

Trading companies reduce risk for firms seeking to get involved in international marketing. A trading company provides producers with information about products that meet quality and price expectations in domestic and international markets. Additional services a trading company may provide include consulting, marketing research, advertising, insurance, product research and design, legal assistance, warehousing, and foreign exchange.

Licensing and Franchising

When potential markets are found across national boundaries, and when production, technical assistance, or marketing know-how is required, **licensing** is an alternative to direct investment. The licensee (the owner of the foreign operation) pays commissions or royalties on sales or supplies used in manufacturing. The licensee may also pay an initial down payment or fee when the licensing agreement is signed. Exchanges of management techniques or technical assistance are primary reasons for licensing agreements. Yoplait is a French yogurt that is licensed for production in the United States; the Yoplait brand tries to maintain a French image.

Licensing is an attractive alternative to direct investment when the political stability of a foreign country is in doubt or when resources are unavailable for direct investment. Licensing is especially advantageous for small manufacturers wanting to launch a well-known brand internationally. For example, Questor Corporation owns the Spalding name but produces not a single golf club or tennis ball itself; all Spalding sporting products are licensed worldwide. Lowenbrau has used licensing agreements, including one with Miller in the United States, to increase sales worldwide without committing capital to building breweries.

franchising A form of licensing in which a franchiser, in exchange for a financial commitment, grants a franchisee the right to market its product in accordance with the franchiser's standards

Franchising is a form of licensing in which a company (the franchiser) grants a franchisee the right to market its product, using its name, logo, methods of operation, advertising, products, and other elements associated with the franchiser's business, in return for a financial commitment and an agreement to conduct business in accordance with the franchiser's standard of operations. This arrangement allows franchisers to minimize the risks of international marketing in four ways: (1) the franchiser does not have to put up a large capital investment; (2) the franchiser's revenue stream is fairly consistent because franchisees pay a fixed fee and royalties; (3) the franchiser retains control of its name and increases global penetration of its product; and (4) franchise agreements ensure a certain standard of behavior from franchisees, which protects the franchise name.[38] Kentucky Fried Chicken, Wendy's, McDonald's, Holiday Inn, and Marriott are well-known franchisers with international visibility.

Contract Manufacturing

contract manufacturing The practice of hiring a foreign firm to produce a designated volume of product to specification

Contract manufacturing occurs when a company hires a foreign firm to produce a designated volume of the firm's product to specification, and the final product carries the domestic firm's name. The Gap, for example, relies on contract manufacturing for some of its apparel; Reebok uses Korean contract manufacturers to manufacture many of its athletic shoes. Marketing may be handled by the contract manufacturer or by the contracting company.

Joint Ventures

joint venture A partnership between a domestic firm and a foreign firm or government

In international marketing, a **joint venture** is a partnership between a domestic firm and a foreign firm or government. Joint ventures are especially popular in industries that call for large investments, such as natural resources extraction or automobile manufacturing. Control of the joint venture may be split equally, or one party may control decision making. Joint ventures are often a political necessity because of nationalism and government restrictions on foreign ownership. They also provide legitimacy in the eyes of the host country's citizens. Local partners have firsthand knowledge of the economic and sociopolitical environment and of distribution networks, and they may have privileged access to local resources (raw material, labor management, and so on). Entrepreneurs in many less developed countries actively seek associations with a foreign partner as a ready means of implementing their own corporate strategy.[39]

Joint ventures are assuming greater global importance because of cost advantages and the number of inexperienced firms entering foreign markets. They may be the result of a tradeoff between a firm's desire for completely unambiguous control of an enterprise and its quest for additional resources. They may occur when acquisition or internal development is not feasible or when the risks and constraints leave no other alternative. As project sizes increase in the face of global competition and firms attempt to spread the huge costs of technological innovation, the impetus to form joint ventures is stronger.[40]

strategic alliance A partnership formed to create a competitive advantage on a worldwide basis

Strategic alliances, the newest form of international business structure, are partnerships formed to create competitive advantage on a worldwide basis. They are very similar to joint ventures. What distinguishes international strategic alliances from other business structures is that partners in the alliance may have been traditional rivals competing for market share in the same product class.[41] An example of such an alliance is New United Motor Manufacturing, Inc. (NUMMI), formed by Toyota and General Motors to make automobiles for both firms. This alliance united the quality engineering of Japanese cars with the marketing expertise and market access of General Motors. Partners in international strategic alliances often retain their distinct identities, and each brings a core competency to the union.

The success rate of international alliances could be higher if there were a better fit between the companies. A strategic alliance should focus on a joint market opportunity from which all partners can benefit.[42] In the automobile, computer, and airline industries, strategic alliances are becoming the predominant means of competing. International competition is so fierce and the costs of competing on a global basis are so high that few firms have all the resources needed to do it alone. Firms that lack the internal resources essential for international success may seek to collaborate with other companies. A shared mode of leadership among partner corporations combines joint abilities and allows collaboration from a distance. Focusing on customer value and implementing innovative ways to compete create a winning strategy.[43] One such collaboration is a partnership of Northwest Airlines, KLM, Air China, Alitalia, Japan Air System, Kenya Airways, and Malaysia Airlines, designed to improve customer service among the seven firms.

Direct Ownership

direct ownership A situation in which a company owns subsidiaries or other facilities overseas

Once a company makes a long-term commitment to marketing in a foreign nation that has a promising political and economic environment, **direct ownership** of a foreign subsidiary or division is a possibility. Mexico's Gigante grocery chain, for example, has opened stores in Los Angeles and southern California, where it hopes its name will appeal to the large Hispanic population there.[44] Most foreign investment covers only manufacturing equipment or personnel because the expenses of developing a separate foreign distribution system can be tremendous. The opening of retail stores in Europe, Canada, or Mexico can require a staggering financial investment in facilities, research, and management.

multinational enterprise A firm that has operations or subsidiaries in many countries

The term **multinational enterprise** refers to firms that have operations or subsidiaries in many countries. Often the parent company is based in one country and carries on production, management, and marketing activities in other countries. The firm's subsidiaries may be mostly autonomous so they can respond to the needs of individual international markets. Table 5.3 lists the ten largest global corporations.

A wholly owned foreign subsidiary may be allowed to operate independently of the parent company to give its management more freedom to adjust to the local environment. Cooperative arrangements are developed to assist in marketing efforts, production, and management. A wholly owned foreign subsidiary may export products to the home country. Some U.S. automobile manufacturers, for example, import cars built by their foreign subsidiaries. A foreign subsidiary offers important tax, tariff, and other operating advantages. One of the greatest advantages is the cross-cultural approach. A subsidiary usually operates under foreign management so that it can develop a local identity. The greatest danger in such an arrangement comes from political uncertainty: a firm may lose its foreign investment.

Table 5.3   The Ten Largest Global Corporations

Rank	Company	Country	Industry	Revenues (in millions)
1	Exxon Mobil	U.S.	Petroleum refining	$210,392
2	Wal-Mart Stores	U.S.	General merchandiser	$193,295
3	General Motors	U.S.	Motor vehicles	$184,632
4	Ford Motor	U.S.	Motor vehicles	$180,598
5	DaimlerChrysler A.G.	Germany	Motor vehicles	$150,070
6	Royal Dutch/Shell Group	Britain/Netherlands	Petroleum refining	$149,146
7	BP	Britain	Petroleum refining	$148,062
8	General Electric	U.S.	Diversified financials	$129,853
9	Mitsubishi	Japan	Trading	$126,579
10	Toyota Motor Corporation	Japan	Motor vehicles	$121,416

Source: "Global 500: The World's Largest Corporations," *Fortune,* www.fortune.com, July 15, 2001.

Customization Versus Globalization of International Marketing Strategies

Like domestic marketers, international marketers develop marketing strategies to serve specific target markets. Traditionally international marketing strategies have customized marketing mixes according to cultural, regional, and national differences. Many soap and detergent manufacturers, for example, adapt their products to local water conditions, equipment, and washing habits. Colgate-Palmolive even devised an inexpensive, plastic, hand-powered washing machine for use in households that have no electricity in less developed countries. Ford Motor Company has customized its F-series truck to accommodate global differences in roads, product use, and economic conditions. The strategy has been quite successful, with millions of Ford trucks sold around the world. Ford's strategy may best be described as *mass customization,* the use of standard platforms with custom applications. This practice dissolves the oxymoron of efficiency of mass production with effectiveness of customization of a product or service.[45]

globalization The development of marketing strategies that treat the entire world (or its major regions) as a single entity

At the other end of the spectrum, **globalization** of marketing involves developing marketing strategies as though the entire world (or its major regions) were a single entity; a globalized firm markets standardized products in the same way everywhere.[46] Nike and Adidas shoes, for example, are standardized worldwide. Other examples of globalized products include electronic communications equipment, Western American clothing, movies, soft drinks, rock and alternative music CDs, cosmetics, and toothpaste. Sony televisions, Levi jeans, and American cigarette brands post year-to-year gains in the world market.

For many years, organizations have attempted to globalize their marketing mixes as much as possible by employing standardized products, promotion campaigns, prices, and distribution channels for all markets. The economic and competitive payoffs for globalized marketing strategies are certainly great. Brand name, product characteristics, packaging, and labeling are among the easiest marketing mix variables to standardize; media allocation, retail outlets, and price may be more difficult. In the end, the degree of similarity among the various environmental and market conditions determines the feasibility and degree of globalization. A successful globalization strategy often depends on the extent to which a firm is able to implement the idea of "think globally, act locally."[47] Even take-out food lends itself to globalization: McDonald's, KFC, and Taco Bell restaurants seem to satisfy hungry customers in every hemisphere, although menus may be customized to some degree to satisfy local tastes.

International marketing demands some strategic planning if a firm is to incorporate foreign sales into its overall marketing strategy. International marketing activities often require customized marketing mixes to achieve the firm's goals. Globalization requires a total commitment to the world, regions, or multinational areas

Global Super Power.

Suddenly, 40 million international companies are within your grasp.

Until now, there was no way to perform an international online company search without jumping from one country directory to another, each with its own search method, content quality and classification system.

Now, WorldAtOnce gives you the entire world in a single stroke. It's the first and only online database that lets you access 40 million companies across 200 countries and 3 thousand business headings with one seamless search.

**40 Million Companies
200 Countries
3000 Headings
1 Friendly Database**

ONE WORLD · ONE SEARCH

WorldAtOnce.com

Log on to www.worldatonce.com for a test search today.

worldatonce.com is a service of WorldFinder Corp. of Santa Barbara, CA

©2001 WorldFinder Corp.

Globalization
WorldAtOnce provides an online global company search of 40 million companies.

as an integral part of the firm's markets; world or regional markets become as important as domestic ones. Regardless of the extent to which a firm chooses to globalize its marketing strategy, extensive environmental analysis and marketing research are necessary to understand the needs and desires of the target market(s) and successfully implement the chosen marketing strategy. A global presence does not automatically result in a global competitive advantage. However, a global presence generates five opportunities for creating value: (1) to adapt to local market differences, (2) to exploit economies of global scale, (3) to exploit economies of global scope, (4) to mine optimal locations for activities and resources, and (5) to maximize the transfer of knowledge across locations.[48] To exploit these opportunities, marketers need to conduct marketing research, the topic of the next chapter.

Summary

International marketing involves developing and performing marketing activities across national boundaries. International markets can provide tremendous opportunities for growth.

A detailed analysis of the environment is essential before a company enters a foreign market. Environmental aspects of special importance include cultural, social, ethical, economic, political, legal, and technological forces. Because marketing activities are primarily social in purpose, they are influenced by beliefs and values regarding family, religion, education, health, and recreation. Cultural differences may affect marketing negotiations, decision-making behavior, and product adoption and use. A nation's economic stability and trade barriers can affect marketing efforts. Significant trade barriers include import tariffs, quotas, embargoes, and exchange controls. Gross domestic product (GDP) and GDP per capita are common measures of a nation's economic standing. Political and legal forces include a nation's political system, laws, regulatory bodies, special-interest groups, and courts. Advances in technology have greatly facilitated international marketing.

Various regional trade alliances and specific markets create both opportunities and constraints for companies engaged in international marketing. These include the North American Free Trade Agreement, the European Union, the Common Market of the Southern Cone, Asia-Pacific Economic Cooperation, the General Agreement on Tariffs and Trade, and the World Trade Organization.

There are several ways to get involved in international marketing. Importing (the purchase of products from a foreign source) and exporting (the sale of products to foreign markets) are the easiest and most flexible methods. Marketers may employ a trading company, which links buyers and sellers in different countries but is not involved in manufacturing and does not own assets related to manufacturing. Licensing and franchising are arrangements whereby one firm pays fees to another for the use of its name, expertise, and supplies. Contract manufacturing occurs when a company hires a foreign firm to produce a designated volume of the firm's product to specification and the final product carries the domestic firm's name. Joint ventures are partnerships between a domestic firm and a foreign firm or a government; strategic alliances are partnerships formed to create competitive advantage on a worldwide basis. Finally, a firm can build its own marketing or production facilities overseas. When companies have direct ownership of facilities in many countries, they may be considered multinational enterprises.

Although most firms adjust their marketing mixes for differences in target markets, some firms standardize their marketing efforts worldwide. Traditional full-scale international marketing involvement is based on products customized according to cultural, regional, and national differences. Globalization, however, involves developing marketing strategies as if the entire world (or regions of it) were a single entity; a globalized firm markets standardized products in the same way everywhere. International marketing demands some strategic planning if a firm is to incorporate foreign sales into its overall marketing strategy.

Important Terms

International marketing	General Agreement on
Import tariff	Tariffs and Trade
Quota	(GATT)
Embargo	Dumping
Exchange controls	World Trade Organization
Balance of trade	(WTO)
Gross domestic product	Importing
(GDP)	Exporting
North American Free	Trading company
Trade Agreement	Licensing
(NAFTA)	Franchising
European Union (EU)	Contract manufacturing
Common Market of	Joint venture
the Southern Cone	Strategic alliance
(MERCOSUR)	Direct ownership
Asia-Pacific Economic	Multinational enterprise
Cooperation (APEC)	Globalization

Discussion and Review Questions

1. How does international marketing differ from domestic marketing?
2. What factors must marketers consider as they decide whether to become involved in international marketing?
3. Why are the largest industrial corporations in the United States so committed to international marketing?
4. Why do you think this chapter focuses on an analysis of the international marketing environment?
5. A manufacturer recently exported peanut butter with a green label to a nation in the Far East. The product failed because it was associated with jungle sickness. How could this mistake have been avoided?
6. If you were asked to provide a small tip (or bribe) to have a document approved in a foreign nation where this practice is customary, what would you do?
7. How will NAFTA affect marketing opportunities for U.S. products in North America (the United States, Mexico, and Canada)?
8. In marketing dog food to Latin America, what aspects of the marketing mix would a U.S. firm need to alter?
9. What should marketers consider as they decide whether to license or enter into a joint venture in a foreign nation?
10. Discuss the impact of strategic alliances on marketing strategies.
11. Contrast globalization with customization of marketing strategies. Is one practice better than the other? Explain.

Application Questions

1. Understanding the complexities of the marketing environment is necessary for a marketer to successfully implement marketing strategies in the international marketplace. Which environmental forces (sociocultural, economic, political/legal, and technological) might a marketer need to consider when marketing the following products in the international marketplace, and why?
   a. Barbie dolls   c. Financial services
   b. Beer   d. Television sets
2. Many firms, including Procter & Gamble, FedEx, and Occidental Petroleum, wish to do business in Eastern Europe and in the countries that were once part of the Soviet Union. What events could occur that would make marketing in these countries more difficult? What events might make it easier?
3. This chapter discusses various organizational approaches to international marketing. Which would be the best arrangements for international marketing of the following products, and why?
   a. Construction equipment manufacturing
   b. Cosmetics
   c. Automobiles
4. Procter & Gamble has made a substantial commitment to foreign markets, especially in Latin America. Its actions may be described as a "globalization of marketing." Describe how a shoe manufacturer would go from domestic marketing, to limited exporting, to international marketing, and finally to a globalization of marketing. Give examples of some activities that might be involved in this process.

Internet Exercise & Resources

Visit **www.prideferrell.com** for resources to help you master the material in this chapter, plus materials that will help you expand your marketing knowledge, including: Internet exercise updates, ACE self-tests, hotlinks to companies featured in this chapter, and much more.

FTD Online

Founded in 1910 as "Florists' Telegraph Delivery," FTD was the first company to offer a "flowers-by-wire" service. FTD does not itself deliver flowers but depends on local florists to provide this service. In 1994, FTD expanded its toll-free telephone-ordering service by establishing a website. Visit the site at

www.ftd.com

1. Click on International. Select a country to which you would like to send flowers. Summarize the delivery and pricing information that would apply to that country.

2. Determine the cost of sending fresh-cut seasonal flowers to Germany.

3. What are the benefits of this global distribution system for sending flowers worldwide? What other consumer products could be distributed globally through the Internet?

VIDEO CASE 5.1
The Global Expansion of Subway Restaurants

The Subway story began in 1965 when Dr. Peter Buck loaned Fred DeLuca $1,000 to open a sandwich shop in Bridgeport, Connecticut, which DeLuca hoped would help fund his college education. Since that time, Subway Sandwich Shops has grown to more than 15,000 restaurants in 75 countries, ranking it second behind only McDonald's in number of outlets and making its founder a billionaire. Subway remains a 100 percent franchised organization, and all Subway restaurants are individually owned and operated. Opening a Subway franchise store requires a $10,000 franchise fee to acquire the Subway name and $65,000 to $175,000 to build a store, depending on location. The company has been named the number one franchise opportunity in every category by *Entrepreneur* Magazine, won a Restaurants and Institutions (Choice and Chains) Gold Award in the sandwich category, and received a *Nation's Restaurant News* Menu Masters Award for the best menu/line extension.

More than 2,500 Subway stores have opened outside the United States. For example, in Australia, where the first Subway opened in 1988, the company's goal is to make Subway the number one chain. More than 300 Subway shops have opened since 1988. Initially Subway did not seek to expand internationally, but when an entrepreneur from Bahrain approached the company about opening a sandwich shop on the Persian Gulf island, Subway decided to accept the challenge of global expansion.

Expanding a food venture into a foreign country involves many issues, such as finding quality supplies for use in making sandwiches. Subway insists on a "gold standard of quality" when adapting to international environments. To properly train new franchise owners in locations around the globe, Subway has had to adapt to different languages and cultures. Initially international franchisees were trained in English in the United States; now the company has training facilities in Puerto Rico, Australia, and China.

When Subway enters a new market, the first issues it faces are building brand awareness and learning about potential customers' eating preferences and customs. Rather than second-guessing cultural differences, Subway attempts to adapt quickly to a new restaurant's immediate service area. In Israel, for example, the company omits pork items from its menu to avoid violating religious dietary customs. In other countries where people are not used to eating sandwiches, Subway has had to educate consumers about this uniquely American product.

In addition to established markets, Subway is expanding into developing nations. In 2001, Subway opened its first restaurant in Croatia. Located in a 1929 building shared with the Capital Hotel Dubrovnik, the restaurant's entrance faces a busy pedestrian street with many shops and open terraces in one of the most beautiful areas of Zagreb. The franchisees chose to open a Subway because they wanted to offer Croatians something new and they recognized an opportunity in the dynamic Croatian market to serve a need for affordable fast food with friendly service. The company plans to open additional shops in other major Croatian cities.

Subway also opened its first restaurant in Oman in 2001, where it joins other fast-food restaurants such as Fuddruckers, McDonald's, and Pizza Hut. Oman is one of the fastest-growing economies in the Middle East, with many international businesses in operation. Subway hopes to fill a void for those in the market for health-conscious food. In Oman, Subway offers its traditional menu and plans to include specialized items to meet local preferences.

France became the twenty-third European country to have a Subway sandwich shop in 2001. France's first Subway is situated near the Bastille in Paris. By day, the area's rich history attracts many tourists; at night, the area is renowned for its night life. The French are passionate about food, and they like submarine sandwiches. Subway believes the restaurant will fill a void in the area for those looking for more health-conscious food choices. Although both Oman and France were slow to embrace the Subway concept, it appears that the brand's healthy attributes have been a major factor in this expansion.

Subway began positioning its menu as a more health-conscious choice after learning about the unique weight loss plan of one of its customers. Jared S. Fogle had been a regular Subway customer, but after reaching 425 pounds, he noticed the store's "7 under 6" promotion, which highlighted seven sandwiches with less than 6 grams of fat. Fogle began to eat a 6-inch turkey sandwich (no oil, mayo, condiments, or cheese) for lunch and a 12-inch veggie sandwich (no condiments or cheese) for dinner every day. His initial weight loss reinforced his commitment to eating more of the low-fat sandwiches. After a year on his exclusive "Subway diet," Jared Fogle lost 235 pounds. His weight loss story turned Fogle into a national celebrity, with appearances on "Oprah" and NBC's "Today" with Katie Couric, an article in *USA Today,* and numerous TV commercials for Subway. Subway's TV ads make it clear that Fogle's diet was his own creation and may not be appropriate for everyone. Fogle, who has maintained his weight loss, continues to do TV commercials for Subway.

Subway has translated the Jared Fogle commercials into other languages for some international markets. The message is that Subway sandwiches are not only tasty but also healthier than offerings from competing fast-food restaurants. For example, one quarter-pound hamburger at another leading fast-food restaurant contains more than 62 grams of fat, whereas Subway offers a number of items with less than 10 grams of fat. Promoting the healthy benefits of its products has helped Subway develop its concept into the largest submarine sandwich franchise in the world.[49]

QUESTIONS FOR DISCUSSION

1. Why has Subway been able to expand so quickly into international markets?
2. What are some advantages and disadvantages of using franchised owner-operators to expand internationally?
3. Is Subway's health-conscious positioning the best promotional platform to expand stores internationally? Why or why not?

CASE 5.2
Dat'l Do-It Cooks Up Hot Exports

In the early 1980s, Christopher Way started cooking up spicy-hot datil pepper sauces for his Barnacle Bill's Seafood House restaurant in St. Augustine, Florida. The sauces proved so popular that the jars he put on the restaurants' tables kept disappearing. Way reasoned that if his customers liked the sauce enough to steal it, they would pay for it if given the opportunity. So in 1983, Way founded Dat'l Do-It to create and market hot sauces and relishes. Little did he know that in just a few years, his fledgling company would have a global presence.

The timing of Dat'l Do-It's launch was just right, as consumer interest in spicier foods was beginning to heat up. Way's sauces were uniquely positioned to capitalize on this trend since they contain datil peppers—one of the hottest peppers in the world, just slightly less blistering than the habañero pepper—as a primary ingredient. The potent peppers, grown only in the St. Augustine area, flavor Way's products in a range of heat intensities, from Dat'l Do-It Pepper Jelly on the mild end of the scale to Devil Drops at the volcanic end.

Way initially cooked up the sauces in the kitchen of Barnacle Bill's, but he soon had a food chemist adapt the recipes for mass production. The adapted formulas were designed both to taste good and have a longer shelf life. Way then contracted with a commercial food manufacturing plant to produce the sauces on a large scale. He also hired local farmers to grow hundreds of bushels of peppers each season to supply the producer with enough datils to cook up truckloads of sauce. Within a few short years, however, Way established a Dat'l Do-It farm, which has the capacity to produce up to 20,000 pounds of peppers per season. The Dat'l Do-It farm grows the peppers outside on platforms, where they are drip-watered and naturally pest-controlled by a legion of ladybugs.

Way soon developed a whole line of datil-based products, including Hot Sauce, Hot Vinegar, BBQ Sauce, Salsa, Wing Sauce, Pepper Jelly, Hellish Relish, Minorcan Mustard, Devil Drops, and GargOils flavored oils. With a full line of products ready for market, Way needed to get them to customers, a task that proved both time consuming and costly for a start-up firm. Even though a vice president of the giant Winn-Dixie supermarket chain loved Dat'l Do-It's sauces and wanted to carry the line, Way was able to get his products onto the shelves of only a few of the stores. "The 'gourmet' or specialized food arena is still a really difficult market to get into," Way says.

Despite these challenges, Dat'l Do-It's sales continued to grow. By 1993, the company was breaking even with sales just below $500,000. Way decided it was time to set up a Dat'l Do-It Hot Shop to sell his sauces in St. Augustine, and he made plans to franchise similar shops throughout the South. He also opened small kiosks in high-traffic shopping malls during the Christmas season and started a mail-order operation to reach customers all over the United States.

Soon after, Kodo Matsumoto, an exporter based in St. Petersburg, Florida, encouraged Way to export Dat'l Do-It products to Japan. Matsumoto pointed out that studies indicate Japanese people enjoy spicy foods, and Matsumoto had successfully marketed a variety of products to the Japanese market. However, Way couldn't simply put his products into boxes and ship them to Japan. He first had to modify the ingredients and labels to comply with stringent Japanese regulations. He had to rely on Matsumoto for guidance in navigating the complex customs and practices of the Japanese distribution system, which traditionally has been geared toward protecting locally made products.

Thanks to Matsumoto's expert knowledge of the Japanese market, Way continues to expand his exports year after year. In fact, Way is so excited about prospects for international sales that he recently changed the sign at the Dat'l Do-It farm to read "World Headquarters." He also launched a website (www.datldoit.com) through which customers around the world can reorder their favorite spicy condiments. No doubt Dat'l Do-It will continue to expand globally as Way cooks up new plans for his company in the coming years.[50]

QUESTIONS FOR DISCUSSION

1. Trade restrictions required Christopher Way to make changes to his product in order to export his products to Japan. What other changes might be required as Dat'l Do-It expands into other foreign countries?
2. What economic forces might affect the cost of Dat'l Do-It products in Japan, thereby influencing demand?
3. As Dat'l Do-It expands its global distribution, it may want to consider a higher level of involvement. What level of involvement would be most appropriate? Defend your answer.

STRATEGIC CASE 1

USA Today: The Nation's Newspaper

USA Today debuted in 1982 as the first national general-interest daily newspaper in the United States. The paper was the brainchild of Allen H. Neuharth, then chairman of Gannett Company, Inc., a diversified global news and communications company that owns newspapers and television stations and operates commercial printing, newswire, data, and news programming services. Gannett is the largest U.S. newspaper firm, with 98 daily newspapers with a combined daily paid circulation of 7.8 million.

The Launch of USA Today

In February 1980, Neuharth met with members of a task force to discuss his vision for a unique nationally distributed daily newspaper. He believed a national newspaper could capitalize on two seemingly disparate trends: an increasingly short attention span among a generation nurtured on television and a growing public hunger for more information. Thus, *USA Today*'s primary mission would be to provide more news about more subjects in less time. Research suggested that *USA Today* should target primarily achievement-oriented men in professional and managerial positions who are heavy newspaper readers and frequent travelers. Whereas newspapers like *The New York Times* and *The Wall Street Journal* are targeted at the nation's intellectual elite and business leaders, *USA Today* would be edited for "Middle America": young, well-educated Americans who are on the move and care about what is going on in the world.

By early 1982, a team of news, advertising, and production personnel from Gannett's daily newspapers had developed and printed three different prototypes, which were sent to nearly 5,000 professional people. Although the prototypes had similar content, they differed in layout and graphic presentations. Readers were also sent response cards asking what they liked best and least about the proposed paper and whether or not they would buy it. After receiving a positive response, Gannett's board of directors unanimously approved the paper's launch.

On September 15, 1982, 155,000 copies of the first edition of *USA Today* hit the newsstands. On page one, Neuharth summarized *USA Today*'s mission statement, explaining that he wanted to make the newspaper enlightening and enjoyable to the public, informative to national leaders, and attractive to advertisers. The first issue sold out. Barely a month after its debut, *USA Today*'s circulation hit

362,879, double the original year-end projection, and topped the 1 million mark just seven months after its introduction. The typical reader turned out to be a well-educated, 40-year-old professional, usually a manager, with an annual income of about $60,000.

For a newspaper, *USA Today* was truly unique. It was a paper created for the TV generation, an idea reflected in its distinctive coin box, designed to look like a television set. The paper's motto was "An economy of words. A wealth of information." Each issue included four sections: News, Money, Life, and Sports. A prospective reader could grasp the top news of the day on page one just by viewing it in the coin box. For time-pressed readers, *USA Today* layered news for easy access and quick comprehension, and it made extensive use of briefs columns, secondary headlines, subheads, breakouts, at-a-glance boxes, and informational graphics.

After research indicated that many readers brought the paper home instead of reading it on their commute or at work, Gannett launched a home delivery subscription service in 1984. Home delivery caused problems at first, because the in-house computer technology could not handle subscription mailing lists efficiently, and the postal service did not always deliver the paper on its publication day. Nevertheless, subscriptions grew, and by 1991 nearly half of *USA Today*'s distribution was via home and office delivery.

Critics were quick to pan the unconventional paper. Some labeled it "McPaper"—the fast food of the newspaper business—due to its terse, brash writing style and its short coverage of complex issues. Among their criticisms were that the paper was loaded with "gimmicks," such as tight, short stories that did not jump from page to page (except for the cover story); splashy, colorful graphics, including a national weather map; a distinctive, casual writing style; a brief roundup of news items from each state; summary boxes; charts and statistics-laden sports coverage; and a focus on celebrities and sports, with more detailed sports stories than almost any other paper in the nation. There was no foreign staff and little coverage of the world beyond the United States. Nevertheless, readers seemed to admire the paper for its balance and focus on brevity and clarity. Circulation surpassed 1.4 million by late 1985.

By the end of its third year, *USA Today* had become the second-largest paper in the country, with a circulation topped only by *The Wall Street*

Journal. However, Neuharth's early predictions that *USA Today* would turn a profit within a few years of launch proved overly optimistic. It took about five years to move from the red to the black, but by 1993 profits were approximately $5 million, and the following year they doubled to about $10 million.

Marketing Mix Changes

Although *USA Today* competed primarily against weekly news magazines and business newspapers rather than with daily local papers, many dailies began to borrow from *USA Today*'s style. Even old-line newspapers, such as *The New York Times*, began to add more color, shorten their stories, and beef up circulation campaigns to compete with "The Nation's Newspaper." In the face of this increasing competition, along with a recognition of changing reader needs, it was time for *USA Today* to respond to those needs and evolve in the late 1980s.

To stay ahead of imitators, *USA Today* continued to innovate and began a move toward becoming a more serious newspaper with improved journalism. The shift to harder news began with the space shuttle *Challenger* disaster in 1986, when major coverage of the tragedy helped circulation skyrocket. Starting in the late 1980s, Gannett also began incorporating less traditional value-added features to keep readers interested. The paper added 1–800 and 1–900 hotline numbers that readers could call for expert information on financial planning, college admissions, minority business development, taxes, and other subjects. Thousands of readers responded to opinion polls and write-in surveys on political and current-event issues. In 1991, the editorial pages were redesigned to provide more room for guest columnists and to encourage debate. Gannett also initiated a high school Academic All Star program that it later expanded to include colleges and universities. The year 2000 saw the first major redesign in *USA Today*'s history as the paper moved from a 54-inch to a 50-inch width to make it easier to read and cleaner in design. The pages were slimmer and easier to handle, especially in tight spaces like airplanes, trains, buses, and subways, and it fit more readily into briefcases, a need that Gannett had learned about from focus groups.

USA Today has also been innovative in its promotional activities. Historically the paper limited its promotions primarily to outdoor advertising and television. In the late 1980s, however, Neuharth launched a BusCapade promotion tour, traveling to all 50 states and talking with all kinds of people, including the governors of each state, to raise public awareness of the paper. Encouraged by the tour's success, Neuharth soon followed up with a JetCapade promotion in which he and a small news team traveled to 30 countries in 7 months, stimulating global demand for the paper. During a visit to the troops of Operation Desert Storm in the Persian Gulf in 1991, General Norman Schwarzkopf expressed a need for news from home, and *USA Today* arranged for delivery of 18,000 copies a day. The overseas success of *USA Today* led to the publication of *USA Today International,* now available in more than 90 countries in Western Europe, the Middle East, North Africa, and Asia.

Gannett's first strategy for enlisting advertisers was called the Partnership Plan, which offered six months of free space to those who purchased six months of paid advertising. In 1987, *USA Today* began to accept regional advertising for a wide variety of categories, including regional travel, retailing, tourism, and economic development. The paper also moved aggressively into "blue-chip circulation," offering bulk quantities of *USA Today* at discounted prices to hotels, airlines, and restaurants, which in turn provided the paper free to their customers. Today more than 500,000 copies of *USA Today* are distributed through blue-chip circulation every day.

In 1991, *USA Today* broke one of the most sacred practices of daily newspapers when it began offering advertising space on page one. The company sold one-inch color strips across the entire width of the bottom of the page through one-year contracts for $1 million to $1.2 million each, with each advertiser taking one day a week. As has been true for so many of *USA Today*'s innovations, critics were quick to criticize this move, claiming the paper had "besmirched" its front page with advertising.

Rapid delivery has always been crucial to *USA Today*'s success. By the mid-1990s, the paper was earning kudos for its ability to deliver timely news, thanks to its late deadlines. For instance, in many parts of the country, *USA Today* prints later sports scores than local or regional papers. To speed distribution, the paper added printing sites around the world. Additional technological advances allowed Gannett to make production of *USA Today* totally digital, providing newsrooms with later deadlines and readers with earlier delivery times.

USA Today Online

A decade after its launch, *USA Today* had become the most widely read newspaper in the country, with daily readership of more than 6.5 million. In an era when nearly all major national media were experiencing declines in readership or viewing audience, *USA Today* continued to grow. Rising distribution and promotion costs, however, were beginning to cut into the newspaper's profits. To reverse this trend, *USA Today* created several spin-offs, including its first special-interest publication, *Baseball Weekly*. *USA Today* also joined with Cable News Network to produce a football TV program, and it launched SkyRadio to provide live radio on commercial airline flights. In 2000, Gannett launched a new broadcast and Internet initiative known as *USA Today Live* to provide news stories to Gannett television stations.

The major spin-off, however, was *USA Today Online*, which the company introduced in 1995. Like its print sibling, the website (www.usatoday.com) is organized into News, Sports, Money, and Life sections that allow readers to receive up-to-the-moment news with colorful graphics and crisp audio. It represents one of the most extensive sites on the World Wide Web, with more than 140,000 pages of up-to-the-minute general, sports, business, and technology news, as well as 5-day weather forecasts and travel information, all available free 24 hours a day.

Although the website's daily news content is free, Gannett has left open the option to charge site users in the future. Currently advertising provides revenue streams. Another revenue generator, launched in response to frequent reader requests for archived material, was a pay-per-view archives service (http://archives.usatoday.com) launched in 1998. This service allows readers to conduct a free, unlimited search of all the paper's articles that have run since April 1987. Articles may be downloaded for $1 per story, with payments handled by credit card.

Like its print sibling, *USA Today Online* has evolved to meet consumers' changing desires. In 1997 the website launched an online classifieds area, giving readers the opportunity to buy the goods and services of 24 companies in 6 online Marketplaces: Classifieds, Travel, Financial, Tech-nology, Entertainment, and Flowers and Gifts. Since its inception, the website has studied computer logs to make decisions about editorial content, staff, and even budgetary expenditures. In 1998, it adopted custom software developed by Intelligent Environments to create a real-time system for surveying online readers. The resulting Quick Question gauges the opinions of *USA Today Online* readers on newsworthy events and issues.

Looking Ahead

USA Today has been remarkably successful, with 17 years of continuous circulation growth in a time when overall newspaper readership was on the decline. More than 5.4 million consumers read *USA Today* daily, and approximately 2.3 million subscribe to the paper. *USA Today Online,* one of the few profitable websites, was the world's most visited website, according to Media Metrix, with more than 15 million people accessing the site each month. At the corporate level, Gannett's 2000 revenues advanced more than 20 percent to approximately $6.2 billion, fueled by strong advertising demand, the Olympics, election-related ad spending, and strategic acquisitions.

To remain competitive, *USA Today* continues to upgrade and innovate, keeping several priorities in mind. One priority is to hold the price at 50 cents despite cost pressures. Another is to continue updating both the print and web products to ensure they are providing a complete "read" that people can trust. A third priority is to push technology so the print product can provide the latest sports scores and news ahead of competitors. Adopting a value-added strategy can help *USA Today* continue to differentiate itself from other national news providers. In the future, the key will be to ensure that both the print and online versions of *USA Today* provide content that readers cannot find anywhere else.

QUESTIONS FOR DISCUSSION

1. Describe Gannett's target market for *USA Today.* How did the firm's marketing strategy appeal to this market?
2. What forces in the marketing environment created opportunities for a successful national daily newspaper? What forces have created challenges for the newspaper?
3. Evaluate *USA Today*'s decision to enter the online news market. In light of this decision, should the marketing strategy for the print version of *USA Today* be changed?

Buyer Behavior and Target Market Selection

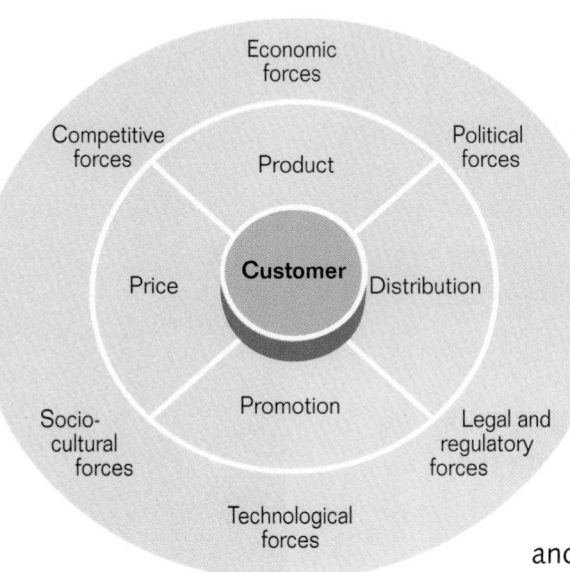

Part 2 focuses on the buyer. The development of a marketing strategy begins with the buyer. Chapter 6 provides a foundation for analyzing buyers through a discussion of marketing information systems and the basic steps in the marketing research process. Understanding elements that affect buying decisions enables marketers to better analyze customers' needs and evaluate how specific marketing strategies can satisfy those needs. Chapter 7 focuses on one of the major steps in the development of a marketing strategy: selecting and analyzing target markets. Chapter 8 examines consumer buying decision processes and factors that influence buying decisions. Chapter 9 stresses business markets, organizational buyers, the buying center, and the organizational buying decision process.

6

Marketing Research and Information Systems

OBJECTIVES

- To describe the basic steps in conducting marketing research
- To explore the fundamental methods of gathering data for marketing research
- To describe the nature and role of information systems in marketing decision making
- To understand how such tools as databases, decision support systems, and the Internet facilitate marketing research
- To identify key ethical and international considerations in marketing research

Imagine waking up in the morning, stumbling to the bathroom sink, loading your toothbrush with Crest toothpaste, and looking up to see the fuzzy reflection of a video camera in the mirror. Forget that you signed up for MTV's "The Real World"? No, it's just the Procter & Gamble (P&G) research crew you allowed into your home to observe how you perform your daily activities. Although marketing research has traditionally focused on problems consumers already recognize, P&G researchers hope this direct observation approach will help them identify and address problems that consumers don't even know they have.

Although 98 percent of U.S. consumers purchase Crest, Charmin, Comet, and many other P&G brands, just 33 percent of the world population buys products made by the Cincinnati-based firm. With sales growth languishing at 2.5 percent a year, P&G hopes to boost its revenues by capitalizing on growth opportunities overseas. To achieve this goal, many of P&G's marketing research efforts are now targeted toward international markets like the United Kingdom, Italy, Germany, and China.

Reality TV or Marketing Research?

Compared to other research methods, direct observation of consumers provides several benefits. Video clips can be placed on a secure website for viewing by 150 P&G employees. A bigger audience gives the company greater potential for valuable feedback. More problems can be identified and solutions found to address those issues. Direct observation can also generate information that participants might normally forget or choose not to disclose when being interviewed or surveyed. For example, many people say they brush their teeth twice a day because they believe that is the correct and expected response. But the reality is that many people don't brush twice daily because of interference from external sources. Direct observation of consumers can uncover such information. Another advantage of this approach is that it contributes to insights gained through coordinated and integrated research efforts. P&G can cross-reference these results with any of 4,000 to 5,000 research studies it conducts annually or to its existing database of 50,000 studies. Finally, P&G can get a global perspective on the wants and needs of its target market.

But this new form of research also has some drawbacks, especially concerns about privacy. Although participants in these studies willingly allow themselves to be videotaped, the company must avoid recording certain behaviors, inform any visitors about the situation, and guarantee the videos will be viewed only internally for research purposes. Another issue is reactivity, which occurs when participants modify normal behaviors because they know they are being observed. For example, a participant might increase his or her daily intake of vegetables during the observation period to appear more in line with social norms or expectations. Another drawback is that it is not practical to pore through hours of videotape for just a few clues about human behavior. Although the information gained may be interesting, not all of it will be useful or result in a successful new product. Finally, such research doesn't guarantee that any new product innovation will result.

Recently P&G conducted a study to determine why consumers dread washing dishes after cooking meals at home. More than 42 percent said the reason they dislike it is that it is time consuming. Such research will become more valuable if P&G can confirm it through direct observation studies. The company also runs a research project in Cincinnati at a local laundromat that allows its researchers to conduct interviews while consumers wash their clothes. Valuable insight will be gained by comparing the behaviors at a public laundromat with how consumers use products at home.[1]

The marketing research conducted by Procter & Gamble illustrates that to implement the marketing concept, marketers require information about the characteristics, needs, and desires of target market customers. When used effectively, such information facilitates relationship marketing by helping marketers focus their efforts on meeting and even anticipating the needs of their customers. Marketing research and information systems that can provide practical and objective information to help firms develop and implement marketing strategies therefore are essential to effective marketing.

In this chapter, we focus on how marketers gather information needed to make marketing decisions. First, we define marketing research and examine the individual steps of the marketing research process, including various methods of collecting data. Next, we look at how technology aids in collecting, organizing, and interpreting marketing research data. Finally, we consider ethical and international issues in marketing research.

The Importance of Marketing Research

marketing research The systematic design, collection, interpretation, and reporting of information to help marketers solve specific marketing problems or take advantage of marketing opportunities

Marketing research is the systematic design, collection, interpretation, and reporting of information to help marketers solve specific marketing problems or take advantage of marketing opportunities. As the word *research* implies, it is a process for gathering information not currently available to decision makers. The purpose of marketing research is to inform an organization about customers' needs and desires, marketing opportunities for particular goods and services, and changing attitudes and purchase patterns of customers. Detecting shifts in buyers' behaviors and attitudes helps companies stay in touch with the ever-changing marketplace. Marketers of pet supplies, for example, would be very interested to know that 93 percent of pet owners buy at least one present a year for their furry companions, and most buy four or more. One-quarter of pet owners surveyed by the American Animal Hospital Association admitted to purchasing outfits for their pets, 44 percent had bought souvenirs for their pets while on vacation,

The Value of Marketing Research
Pine Company and JRP assist organizations in collecting and analyzing data to help them better understand the needs of their target markets and improve their overall performance.

and 74 percent said they would go into debt to provide for their pets' well-being. The $23 billion consumers spend to satisfy their pets' perceived needs and wants every year represents a tremendous opportunity for those companies willing to invest the resources to understand this indulgent market.[2] Strategic planning requires marketing research to facilitate the process of assessing such opportunities or threats.

Marketing research can help a firm better understand market opportunities, ascertain the potential for success for new products, and determine the feasibility of a particular marketing strategy. Pizza Hut, for example, conducted research to learn more about its most profitable group of customers: high school and college students. The research involved asking a carefully selected group of 350 students to refrain from consuming pizza products for 30 days and record their cravings for pizza and feelings about going without during the study period. The company, owned by Tricon Global Restaurants, hopes this research will help it better understand the effects of "pizza deprivation," food cravings, and food desires among this desirable market, which may result in modifications in its marketing strategy.[3]

All sorts of organizations use marketing research to help them develop marketing mixes to match the needs of customers. Supermarkets, for example, have learned from marketing research that roughly half of all Americans prefer to have their dinners ready in 15 to 30 minutes. Such information highlights a tremendous opportunity for supermarkets to offer high-quality "heat and eat" meals to satisfy this growing segment of the food market. Political candidates also depend on marketing research to understand the scope of issues their constituents view as important. Both George W. Bush and Al Gore spent millions surveying voters to better understand issues in the last U.S. presidential election.

The real value of marketing research is measured by improvements in a marketer's ability to make decisions. Marketers should treat information in the same manner as they use other resources, and they must weigh the costs of obtaining information against the benefits derived. Information should be judged worthwhile if it results in marketing activities that better satisfy the firm's target customers, lead to increased sales and profits, or help the firm achieve some other goal.

The Marketing Research Process

To maintain the control needed to obtain accurate information, marketers approach marketing research as a process with logical steps: (1) locating and defining problems or issues, (2) designing the research project, (3) collecting data, (4) interpreting research findings, and (5) reporting research findings (Figure 6.1). These steps should be viewed as an overall approach to conducting research rather than as a rigid set of rules to be followed in each project. In planning research projects, marketers must consider each step carefully and determine how they can best adapt them to resolve the particular issues at hand.

Locating and Defining Problems or Research Issues

The first step in launching a research study is problem or issue definition, which focuses on uncovering the nature and boundaries of a situation or question related to marketing strategy or implementation. The first sign of a problem is typically a departure from some normal function, such as failure to attain objectives. If a corporation's

FIGURE 6.1
The Five Steps of the Marketing Research Process

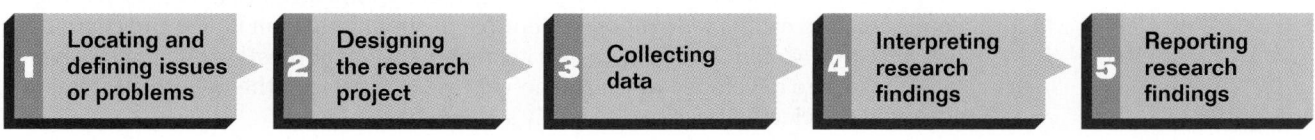

1 Locating and defining issues or problems   2 Designing the research project   3 Collecting data   4 Interpreting research findings   5 Reporting research findings

objective is a 12 percent sales increase and the current marketing strategy resulted in a 6 percent increase, this discrepancy should be analyzed to help guide future marketing strategies. Declining sales, increasing expenses, and decreasing profits also signal problems. Customer relationship management (CRM) is frequently based on analysis of existing customers. However, research indicates that this information could be biased and therefore misleading when making decisions related to identifying and acquiring new customers.[4] Armed with this knowledge, a firm could define a problem as finding a way to adjust for biases stemming from existing customers when gathering data or to develop methods for gathering information to help find new customers. Conversely, when an organization experiences a dramatic rise in sales or some other positive event, it may conduct marketing research to discover the reasons and maximize the opportunities stemming from them.

Marketing research often focuses on identifying and defining market opportunities or changes in the environment. When a firm discovers a market opportunity, it may need to conduct research to understand the situation more precisely so it can craft an appropriate marketing strategy. For example, Lowe's Companies, Inc., the second-largest home improvement retail chain, discovered that 75 percent of its sales come from retail customers, who account for 50 percent of the $400 billion home improvement market. On the other hand, 25 percent of Lowe's sales come from contractors and other commercial business customers, who spend $175 billion on home improvement products. Armed with this information, the company can focus its efforts on specific target markets and refine its marketing strategy to maximize its customer orientation.[5]

To pin down the specific boundaries of a problem or an issue through research, marketers must define the nature and scope of the situation in a way that requires probing beneath the superficial symptoms. The interaction between the marketing manager and the marketing researcher should yield a clear definition of the research need. Researchers and decision makers should remain in the problem or issue definition stage until they have determined precisely what they want from marketing research and how they will use it. Deciding how to refine a broad, indefinite problem or issue into a precise, researchable statement is a prerequisite for the next step in the research process.

Designing the Research Project

Once the problem or issue has been defined, the next step is **research design,** an overall plan for obtaining the information needed to address it. This step requires formulating a hypothesis and determining what type of research is most appropriate for testing the hypothesis to ensure the results are reliable and valid.

Developing a Hypothesis.   The objective statement of a marketing research project should include hypotheses based on both previous research and expected research findings. A **hypothesis** is an informed guess or assumption about a certain problem or set of circumstances. It is based on all the insight and knowledge available about the problem or circumstances from previous research studies and other sources. As information is gathered, a researcher can test the hypothesis. For example, a food marketer like H. J. Heinz might propose the hypothesis that children today have considerable influence on their families' buying decisions regarding ketchup and other grocery products. A marketing researcher would then gather data, perhaps through surveys of children and their parents, and draw conclusions as to whether the hypothesis is correct. Supermarkets concerned about shoplifting would be interested in the findings of a research study in which 40 percent of supermarket managers surveyed reported cigarettes and alcoholic beverages as their most frequently shoplifted items.[6] If a supermarket manager had hypothesized that smaller packaged goods, such as candy, were more susceptible to shoplifting than liquor and cigarettes, this research would lead him or her to reject that hypothesis. Sometimes several hypotheses are developed during an actual research project; the hypotheses that are accepted or rejected become the study's chief conclusions.

Copyright © Houghton Mifflin Company. All rights reserved.

Net Sights

Perhaps one of the best-known pollsters and research firms, the Gallup Organization has been conducting public opinion surveys and providing other management consulting services since 1935. The company is frequently called on to survey the public about political issues—especially during election campaigns—as well as business and economic issues, social issues, and lifestyle topics. To view the company's latest survey results, visit

http://www.gallup.com/

research design   An overall plan for obtaining the information needed to address a research problem or issue

hypothesis   An informed guess or assumption about a certain problem or set of circumstances

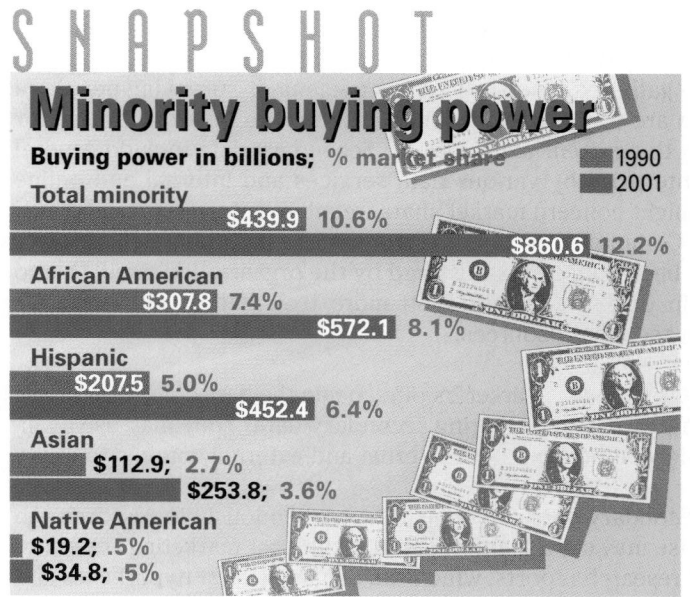

SNAPSHOT

Minority buying power

Buying power in billions; % market share   ■1990 ■2001

Total minority
$439.9 10.6%
$860.6 12.2%

African American
$307.8 7.4%
$572.1 8.1%

Hispanic
$207.5 5.0%
$452.4 6.4%

Asian
$112.9; 2.7%
$253.8; 3.6%

Native American
$19.2; .5%
$34.8; .5%

Source: Jeffrey M. Humphreys, Selig Center for Economic Growth, University of Georgia, reported in *Marketing News*, July 2, 2001, p. 17.

exploratory research
Research conducted to gather more information about a problem or to make a tentative hypothesis more specific

descriptive research
Research conducted to clarify the characteristics of certain phenomena to solve a particular problem

causal research   Research in which it is assumed that a particular variable X causes a variable Y

reliability   A condition existing when a research technique produces almost identical results in repeated trials

validity   A condition existing when a research method measures what it is supposed to measure

Types of Research.   The hypothesis being tested determines whether an exploratory, descriptive, or causal approach will be used to gather data. When marketers need more information about a problem or want to make a tentative hypothesis more specific, they may conduct **exploratory research.** For instance, they may review the information in the firm's own records or examine publicly available data. Questioning knowledgeable people inside and outside the organization may yield new insights into the problem. Information available on the Internet about industry trends or demographics may also be an excellent source for exploratory research. For example, finding data online indicating that Hispanic buying power increased 118 percent between 1990 and 2001, accounting for 6.4 percent of all U.S. buying power, could be quite useful to consider in marketing plans to serve specific market segments.[7]

If marketers need to understand the characteristics of certain phenomena to solve a particular problem, **descriptive research** can aid them. Such studies may range from general surveys of customers' education, occupation, or age to specifics on how often teenagers eat at fast-food restaurants after school or how often customers buy new pairs of athletic shoes. For example, if Nike and Reebok want to target more young women, they might ask 15-to-35-year-old females how often they work out, how frequently they wear athletic shoes for casual use, and how many pairs of athletic shoes they buy in a year. Such descriptive research can be used to develop specific marketing strategies for the athletic-shoe market. Descriptive studies generally demand much prior knowledge and assume the problem or issue is clearly defined. Some descriptive studies require statistical analysis and predictive tools. The marketer's major task is to choose adequate methods for collecting and measuring data.

Hypotheses about causal relationships call for a more complex approach than a descriptive study. In **causal research,** it is assumed that a particular variable X causes a variable Y. Marketers must plan the research so that the data collected prove or disprove that X causes Y. To do so, marketers must try to hold constant all variables except X and Y. For example, to determine whether new carpeting, pet-friendly policies, or outside storage increases the number of rentals in an apartment complex, researchers need to keep all variables constant except one of these three variables in a specific time period.

Research Reliability and Validity.   In designing research, marketing researchers must ensure that research techniques are both reliable and valid. A research technique has **reliability** if it produces almost identical results in repeated trials. But a reliable technique is not necessarily valid. To have **validity,** the research method must measure what it is supposed to measure, not something else. For example, although a group of customers may express the same level of satisfaction based on a rating scale, the individuals may not exhibit the same repurchase behavior because of different personal characteristics. This result might cause the researcher to question the validity of the satisfaction scale if the purpose of rating satisfaction was to estimate potential repurchase behavior.[8] A study to measure the effect of advertising on sales would be valid if advertising could be isolated from other factors or variables that affect sales. The study would be reliable if replications of it produced the same results.

Collecting Data

The next step in the marketing research process is collecting data to help prove (or disprove) the research hypothesis. The research design must specify what types of data to collect and how they will be collected.

primary data   Data observed and recorded or collected directly from respondents

secondary data   Data compiled both inside and outside the organization for some purpose other than the current investigation

Types of Data.   Marketing researchers have two types of data at their disposal. **Primary data** are observed and recorded or collected directly from respondents. This type of data must be gathered by observing phenomena or surveying people of interest. **Secondary data** are compiled both inside and outside the organization for some purpose other than the current investigation. Secondary data include general reports supplied to an enterprise by various data services and internal and online databases. Such reports might concern market share, retail inventory levels, and customers' buying behavior. Commonly, secondary data are already available in private or public reports or have been collected and stored by the organization itself. Due to the opportunity to obtain data via the Internet, more than half of all marketing research now comes from secondary sources.

Sources of Secondary Data.   Marketers often begin the data collection phase of the marketing research process by gathering secondary data. They may use available reports and other information from both internal and external sources to study a marketing problem.

Internal sources of secondary data can contribute tremendously to research. An organization's own database may contain information about past marketing activities, such as sales records and research reports, which can be used to test hypotheses and pinpoint problems. From sales reports, for example, a firm may be able to determine not only which product sold best at certain times of the year but also which colors and sizes customers preferred. Such information may have been gathered for management or financial purposes.[9] Table 6.1 lists some commonly available internal company information that may be useful for marketing research purposes.

Accounting records are also an excellent source of data but, strangely enough, are often overlooked. The large volume of data an accounting department collects does not automatically flow to other departments. As a result, detailed information about costs, sales, customer accounts, or profits by product category may not be easily accessible to the marketing area. This condition develops particularly in organizations that do not store marketing information on a systematic basis.

External sources of secondary data include periodicals, government publications, unpublished sources, and online databases. Periodicals such as *Business Week, The Wall Street Journal, Sales & Marketing Management, American Demographics, Marketing Research,* and *Industrial Marketing* publish general information that can help marketers define problems and develop hypotheses. *Survey of Buying Power,* an annual supplement to *Sales & Marketing Management,* contains sales data for major industries on a county-by-county basis. Many marketers also consult federal government publications such as the *Statistical Abstract of the United States,* the *Census of Business,* the *Census of Agriculture,* and the *Census of Population;* some of these government publications are available through online information services or the Internet. Data from the 2000 U.S. census helped Hyundai Motor America pinpoint communities and neighborhoods with specific demographics matching Hyundai vehicle buyer profiles. This information allowed the company to target its promotional efforts at specific zip codes with promising demographics rather than at entire cities. As a result, the number of customers taking test drives and ultimately purchasing Hyundai vehicles like the Sonata and Santa Fe jumped, and the company's costs per vehicle was slashed by half.[10]

Table 6.1   **Internal Sources of Secondary Data**
• Daily, weekly, monthly, and annual sales reports, which may be broken down by geographical area, by product line, or even by product
• Accounting information, such as expenses and profits
• Competitive information gathered by the sales force
Source: "Internal Secondary Market Research," Small Business Owner's Toolkit, www.lycos.com/business/cch/guidebook.html?lpv=1&docNumber=P03_3020, June 23, 2001.

Table 6.2	**External Sources of Secondary Data**

- Trade associations
- Industry publications and databases
- Government databases (e.g., Bureau of the Census)
- Sales, volume, and brand market share measurement systems (e.g., ACNielsen Company and Information Resources, Inc.)

Source: "External Secondary Market Research," CCH Business Owner's Toolkit, www.lycos.com/business/cch/guidebook.html?lpv=1&docNumber=P03_3011, June 23, 2001.

In addition, companies may subscribe to services, such as ACNielsen or Information Resources, Inc., that track retail sales and other information. Small businesses may be unable to afford such services, but they can still find a wealth of information through industry publications and trade associations.[11] Table 6.2 summarizes the major external sources of secondary data, excluding syndicated services.

Methods of Collecting Primary Data.   The collection of primary data is a more lengthy, expensive, and complex process than the collection of secondary data. To gather primary data, researchers use sampling procedures, survey methods, observation, and experimentation. These efforts can be handled in-house by the firm's own research department or contracted to a private research firm such as ACNielsen, Information Resources, Inc., IMS International, and Quality Controlled Services.

population All the elements, units, or individuals of interest to researchers for a specific study

Sampling   Because the time and resources available for research are limited, it is almost impossible to investigate all the members of a target market or other population. A **population,** or "universe," includes all the elements, units, or individuals of interest to researchers for a specific study. For a Gallup poll designed to predict the results of a presidential election, all registered voters in the United States would constitute the population. By systematically choosing a limited number of units—a **sample**—to represent the characteristics of a total population, researchers can project the reactions of a total market or market segment. (In the case of the presidential poll, a representative national sample of several thousand registered voters would be selected and surveyed to project the probable voting outcome.) **Sampling** in marketing research, therefore, is the process of selecting representative units from a total population. Sampling techniques allow marketers to predict buying behavior fairly accurately on the basis of the responses from a representative portion of the population of interest. Most types of marketing research employ sampling techniques.

sample A limited number of units chosen to represent the characteristics of a total population

sampling The process of selecting representative units from a total population

probability sampling A sampling technique in which every element in the population being studied has a known chance of being selected for study

There are two basic types of sampling: probability sampling and nonprobability sampling. With **probability sampling,** every element in the population being studied has a known chance of being selected for study. Random sampling is a kind of probability sampling. When marketers employ **random sampling,** all the units in a population have an equal chance of appearing in the sample. The various events that can occur have an equal or known chance of taking place. For example, a specific card in a regulation deck should have a 1/52 probability of being drawn at any one time. Sample units are ordinarily chosen by selecting from a table of random numbers statistically generated so that each digit, 0 through 9, will have an equal probability of occurring in each position in the sequence. The sequentially numbered elements of a population are sampled randomly by selecting the units whose numbers appear in the table of random numbers.

random sampling A type of probability sampling in which all units in a population have an equal chance of appearing in the sample

stratified sampling A type of probability sampling in which the population is divided into groups according to a common attribute and a random sample is then chosen within each group

Another kind of probability sampling is **stratified sampling,** in which the population of interest is divided into groups according to a common attribute and a random sample is then chosen within each group. The stratified sample may reduce some of the error that could occur in a simple random sample. By ensuring that each major

Primary Data Collection
Walker Information assists companies in collecting data directly from customers and then analyzing it.

group or segment of the population receives its proportionate share of sample units, investigators avoid including too many or too few sample units from each group. Samples are usually stratified when researchers believe there may be variations among different types of respondents. For example, many political opinion surveys are stratified by gender, race, age, and/or geographic location.

The second type of sampling, **nonprobability sampling,** is more subjective than probability sampling because there is no way to calculate the likelihood that a specific element of the population being studied will be chosen. Quota sampling, for example, is highly judgmental because the final choice of participants is left to the researchers. In **quota sampling,** researchers divide the population into groups and then arbitrarily choose participants from each group. A study of people who wear eyeglasses, for example, may be conducted by interviewing equal numbers of men and women who wear eyeglasses. In quota sampling, there are some controls—usually limited to two or three variables, such as age, gender, or race—over the selection of participants. The controls attempt to ensure that representative categories of respondents are interviewed. Because quota samples are not probability samples, not everyone has an equal chance of being selected, and sampling error therefore cannot be measured statistically. Quota samples are used most often in exploratory studies, when hypotheses are being developed. Often a small quota sample will not be projected to the total population, although the findings may provide valuable insights into a problem. Quota samples are useful when people with some common characteristic are found and questioned about the topic of interest. A probability sample used to study people allergic to cats would be highly inefficient.

Survey Methods   Marketing researchers often employ sampling to collect primary data through mail, telephone, online, or personal interview surveys. The results of such surveys are used to describe and analyze buying behavior. Selection of a survey method depends on the nature of the problem or issue, the data needed to test the hypothesis, and the resources, such as funding and personnel, available to the researcher. Table 6.3 summarizes and compares the advantages of the various survey methods.

Gathering information through surveys is becoming increasingly difficult because fewer people are willing to participate. Many people believe responding to surveys takes up too much scarce personal time, especially as surveys become longer and more detailed. Others have concerns about how much information marketers are gathering and whether their privacy is being invaded. The unethical use of selling techniques disguised as marketing surveys has also led to decreased cooperation. These factors contribute to nonresponse rates for any type of survey.

In a **mail survey,** questionnaires are sent to respondents, who are encouraged to complete and return them. Mail surveys are used most often when the individuals in the sample are spread over a wide area and funds for the survey are limited. A mail survey is the least expensive survey method as long as the response rate is high

nonprobability sampling
A sampling technique in which there is no way to calculate the likelihood that a specific element of the population being studied will be chosen

quota sampling   A nonprobability sampling technique in which researchers divide the population into groups and then arbitrarily choose participants from each group

mail survey   A research method in which respondents answer a questionnaire sent through the mail

Table 6.3	Comparison of the Four Basic Survey Methods			
	Mail Surveys	**Telephone Surveys**	**Online Surveys**	**Personal Interview Surveys**
Economy	Potentially lower in cost per interview than telephone or personal surveys if there is an adequate response rate.	Avoids interviewers' travel expenses; less expensive than in-home interviews.	The least expensive method if there is an adequate response rate.	The most expensive survey method; shopping mall and focus-group interviews have lower costs than in-home interviews.
Flexibility	Inflexible; questionnaire must be short and easy for respondents to complete.	Flexible because interviewers can ask probing questions, but observations are impossible.	Less flexible; survey must be easy for online users to receive and return; short, dichotomous, or multiple-choice questions work best.	Most flexible method; respondents can react to visual materials; demographic data are more accurate; in-depth probes are possible.
Interviewer bias	Interviewer bias is eliminated; questionnaires can be returned anonymously.	Some anonymity; may be hard to develop trust in respondents.	Interviewer bias is eliminated, but e-mail address on the return eliminates anonymity.	Interviewers' personal characteristics or inability to maintain objectivity may result in bias.
Sampling and respondents' cooperation	Obtaining a complete mailing list is difficult; nonresponse is a major disadvantage.	Sample limited to respondents with telephones; devices that screen calls, busy signals, and refusals are a problem.	Sample limited to respondents with computer access; the available e-mail address list may not be a representative sample for some purposes.	Not-at-homes are a problem, which may be overcome by focus-group and shopping mall interviewing.

enough to produce reliable results. The main disadvantages of this method are the possibility of a low response rate and of misleading results if respondents differ significantly from the population being sampled.

Premiums or incentives that encourage respondents to return questionnaires have been effective in developing panels of respondents who are interviewed regularly by mail. Such mail panels, selected to represent a target market or market segment, are especially useful in evaluating new products and providing general information about customers, as well as records of their purchases (in the form of purchase diaries). Mail panels and purchase diaries are much more widely used than custom mail surveys, but both panels and purchase diaries have shortcomings. Research indicates that the people who take the time to fill out a diary have higher incomes and more education than the general population. But if researchers include less educated consumers in the panel, they risk lower response rates.[12]

In a **telephone survey,** an interviewer records respondents' answers to a questionnaire over a phone line. A telephone survey has some advantages over a mail survey. The rate of response is higher because it takes less effort to answer the telephone and talk than to fill out and return a questionnaire. If there are enough interviewers, a telephone survey can be conducted very quickly. Thus, political candidates or organizations seeking an immediate reaction to an event may choose this method. In addition, a telephone survey permits interviewers to gain rapport with respondents and ask probing questions.

However, only a small proportion of the population likes to participate in telephone surveys. More than three-fourths of Americans feel indifferent toward telephone surveys or don't like them at all.[13] This poor image can significantly limit participation and distort representation in a telephone survey. Moreover, telephone surveys are lim-

telephone survey A research method in which respondents' answers to a questionnaire are recorded by interviewers on the phone

ited to oral communication; visual aids or observation cannot be included. Interpreters of results must make adjustments for individuals who are not at home or do not have telephones. Many households are excluded from telephone directories by choice (unlisted numbers) or because the residents moved after the directory was published. Potential respondents often use telephone answering machines, voice mail, or Caller ID to screen or block calls. These issues have serious implications for the use of telephone samples in conducting surveys. Some adjustment must be made for groups of respondents that may be undersampled because of a smaller than average incidence of telephone listings. Nondirectory telephone samples can overcome such bias. Various methods are available, including random-digit dialing (adding random numbers to the telephone prefix) and plus-one telephone sampling (increasing the last digit of a directory number by 1). These methods make it feasible to dial any working number, whether or not it is listed in a directory.

online survey A research method in which respondents answer a questionnaire via e-mail or on a website

Online surveys are evolving as an alternative to telephone surveys. In an **online survey,** questionnaires can be transmitted to respondents who have agreed to be contacted and have provided their e-mail addresses. Because e-mail is semi-interactive, recipients can ask for clarification of specific questions or pose questions of their own. The potential advantages of e-mail surveys are quick response and lower cost than traditional mail and telephone surveys, but these advantages have not yet been realized because of limited access to respondents and unreliable response rates.[14] In addition, more firms are using their websites to conduct surveys. Evolving technology and the interactive nature of the Internet allow for considerable flexibility in designing online questionnaires.

Given the growing number of households that have computers with Internet access, marketing research is likely to rely heavily on online surveys in the future. Indeed, experts predict that Internet-based marketing research will account for about 50 percent, or around $3 billion, of marketing research spending by 2005 compared to just 2 percent of marketing research revenues in 1998.[15] Furthermore, as negative atti-

Collecting Data Through Surveys
RDD, Inc.'s specialty is creating and executing telephone surveys for clients who want to know more about their customers. Similarly, Fieldwork helps with data collection by conducting focus-group interviews.

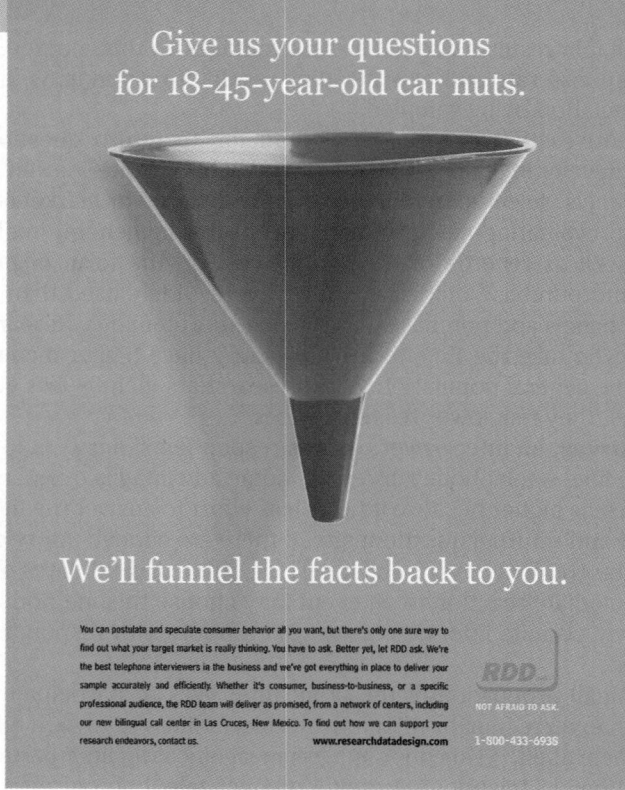

tudes toward telephone surveys render that technique less representative and more expensive, the integration of e-mail, fax, and voice mail functions into one computer-based system provides a promising alternative for survey research. E-mail surveys have especially strong potential within organizations whose employees are networked and for associations that publish members' e-mail addresses. College students in particular are often willing to provide their e-mail address and other personal information in exchange for incentives such as T-shirts and other giveaways.[16] However, there are some ethical issues to consider when using e-mail for marketing research, such as "spam" (unsolicited e-mail) and privacy.

In a **personal interview survey,** participants respond to questions face to face. Various audiovisual aids—pictures, products, diagrams, or prerecorded advertising copy—can be incorporated in a personal interview. Rapport gained through direct interaction usually permits more in-depth interviewing, including probes, follow-up questions, or psychological tests. In addition, because personal interviews can be longer, they may yield more information. Finally, respondents can be selected more carefully, and reasons for nonresponse can be explored. One study found that respondents in personal interviews had the most favorable attitudes toward survey research in general. They liked seeing the person asking the questions and having the personal contact characteristic of the interview.[17]

One such research technique is the **in-home (door-to-door) interview.** The in-home interview offers a clear advantage when thoroughness of self-disclosure and elimination of group influence are important. In an in-depth interview of 45 to 90 minutes, respondents can be probed to reveal their real motivations, feelings, behaviors, and aspirations.

The object of a **focus-group interview** is to observe group interaction when members are exposed to an idea or a concept. Often these interviews are conducted informally, without a structured questionnaire, in small groups of 8 to 12 people. They allow customer attitudes, behavior, lifestyles, needs, and desires to be explored in a flexible and creative manner. Questions are open-ended and stimulate respondents to answer in their own words. Researchers can ask probing questions to clarify something they do not fully understand or something unexpected and interesting that may help explain buying behavior. For example, Ford may use focus groups to determine whether to change its advertising to emphasize a vehicle's safety features rather than its style and performance. It may be necessary to use separate focus groups for each major market segment studied—men, women, and age groups—and experts recommend the use of at least two focus groups per segment in case one group is unusually idiosyncratic.[18]

Still another option is the **telephone depth interview,** which combines the traditional focus group's ability to probe with the confidentiality provided by telephone surveys. This type of interview is most appropriate for qualitative research projects among a small targeted group that is difficult to bring together for a traditional focus group because of members' profession, location, or lifestyle. Respondents can choose the time and day for the interview. Although this method is difficult to implement, it can yield revealing information from respondents who otherwise would be unwilling to participate in marketing research.[19]

The nature of personal interviews has changed. In the past, most personal interviews, which were based on random sampling or prearranged appointments, were conducted in the respondent's home. Today most personal interviews are conducted in shopping malls. **Shopping mall intercept interviews** involve interviewing a percentage of individuals passing by certain "intercept" points in a mall. Like any face-to-face interviewing method, mall intercept interviewing has many advantages. The interviewer is in a position to recognize and react to respondents' nonverbal indications of confusion. Respondents can be shown product prototypes, videotapes of commercials, and the like, and asked for their reactions. The mall environment lets the researcher deal with complex situations. For example, in taste tests, researchers know that all the respondents are reacting to the same product, which can be prepared and monitored from the mall test kitchen. In addition to the ability to conduct tests requiring bulky equipment, lower cost and greater control make shopping mall intercept interviews popular.

personal interview survey
A research method in which participants respond to survey questions face to face

in-home (door-to-door) interview   A personal interview that takes place in the respondent's home

focus-group interview
A research method involving observation of group interaction when members are exposed to an idea or a concept

telephone depth Interview
interview that combines the traditional focus group's ability to probe with the confidentiality provided by telephone surveys

shopping mall intercept interview   A research method that involves interviewing a percentage of persons passing by "intercept" points in a mall

on-site computer interview
A variation of the shopping mall intercept interview in which respondents complete a self-administered questionnaire displayed on a computer monitor

An **on-site computer interview** is a variation of the mall intercept interview in which respondents complete a self-administered questionnaire displayed on a computer monitor. A computer software package can be used to conduct such interviews in shopping malls. After a brief lesson on how to operate the software, respondents can proceed through the survey at their own pace. Questionnaires can be adapted so that respondents see only those items (usually a subset of an entire scale) that may provide useful information about their attitudes.[20]

Questionnaire Construction   A carefully constructed questionnaire is essential to the success of any survey. Questions must be clear, easy to understand, and directed toward a specific objective; that is, they must be designed to elicit information that meets the study's data requirements. Researchers need to define the objective before trying to develop a questionnaire because the objective determines the substance of the questions and the amount of detail. A common mistake in constructing questionnaires is to ask questions that interest the researchers but do not yield information useful in deciding whether to accept or reject a hypothesis. Finally, the most important rule in composing questions is to maintain impartiality.

The questions are usually of three kinds: open-ended, dichotomous, and multiple-choice.

Open-Ended Question

What is your general opinion about broadband Internet access for your computer?

_____

_____

_____

Dichotomous Question

Do you presently have broadband access at home, work, or school?

Yes _____ No _____

Multiple-Choice Question

What age group are you in?

　　　Under 20 _____

　　　20–29 _____

　　　30–39 _____

　　　40–49 _____

　　　50–59 _____

　　　60 and over _____

Researchers must be very careful about questions that a respondent might consider too personal or that might require an admission of activities that other people are likely to condemn. Questions of this type should be worded to make them less offensive.

Observation Methods   In using observation methods, researchers record individuals' overt behavior, taking note of physical conditions and events. Direct contact with them is avoided; instead, their actions are examined and noted systematically. For instance, researchers might use observation methods to answer the question "How long does the average McDonald's restaurant customer have to wait in line before being served?" Observation may include the use of ethnographic techniques, such as watching customers interact with a product in a real-world environment. Bissell, Inc., employed ethnographic techniques when it observed how a very small sample of consumers used its Steam Gun, a hot-water-based cleaning appliance, in the home. Based on this research, the company made a number of changes to the product, including its name, before launching the Steam N Clean.[21] Building Customer Relationships explores ethnographic research in greater detail.

Observation may also be combined with interviews. For example, during a personal interview, the condition of a respondent's home or other possessions may be observed and recorded. The interviewer can also directly observe and confirm such demographic information as race, approximate age, and sex.

Data gathered through observation can sometimes be biased if the person is aware of the observation process. However, an observer can be placed in a natural market environment, such as a grocery store, without biasing or influencing shoppers' actions. If the presence of a human observer is likely to bias the outcome or if human sensory abilities are inadequate, mechanical means may be used to record behavior. Mechanical observation devices include cameras, recorders, counting machines, scanners, and equipment that records physiological changes. A special camera can be used to record the eye movements of people as they look at an advertisement; the camera detects the sequence of reading and the parts of the advertisement that receive greatest attention. The electronic scanners used in supermarkets are very useful in marketing research. They provide accurate data on sales and cus-

BUILDING CUSTOMER RELATIONSHIPS

Anthropologists Unearth Marketing Secrets

Although not a new research technique, the use of corporate anthropologists has escalated in recent years. Anthropologists, who study humans, are being used to help marketers better understand the motives behind consumer behavior. Because the term *anthropology* is often associated with tasks, these researchers prefer to call themselves *knowledge liaisons, ethnographers,* or *evaluators.* Ethnographic research combines observation and interviewing methods to determine the essence of consumers' purchasing decisions and how products are used in everyday life. These studies cost between $5,000 and $800,000, depending on the depth of the research, but many corporations consider them invaluable.

Best Western is one company using this research technique to learn more about its customers and product offerings. One question the company sought to answer through ethnographic research was: Would boosting the senior discount above 10 percent stimulate increased demand in that market segment? Couples over age 50 were paid to record their stay so the company could learn more about their views toward the hotel's rooms and services. Through the study, researchers learned that many over-50 couples enjoyed the challenge of convincing hotel clerks to give them a higher discount rate. With the money saved on the hotel room, the couples enjoyed a more expensive dinner in town. Based on this information, Best Western opted not to increase the senior discount.

The National Cattlemen's Beef Association (NCBA) also wanted to learn more about its customer base. Throughout the 1990s, the NCBA observed an increase in total beef sales but a decline in the preference for varied cuts. To uncover the reason behind the shift, researchers interviewed random shoppers and observed participants in grocery stores and at home preparing meals. The results suggested that consumers were confused about the distinctions among cuts of meat and the best method for cooking each cut. Now the NCBA plans to organize the meat by cooking method, include recipes, and provide cooking instructions.

Still another firm using ethnographic research is Colgate-Palmolive Company. In New York, consumers were videotaped at the grocery store as they selected a brand of toothbrush. Surprisingly, many consumers spent a great deal of time reading about the new features and attempting to examine the brush through the package. Based on the results, the company redesigned toothbrush packages to include more see-through plastic.

Many companies are turning to ethnographic research to improve current products and packaging, and even to identify new product ideas for the future. In the end, the goal is to find products that meet consumers' needs rather than developing a product and then trying to convince consumers to purchase it. Thus, ethnographic research is helping to bring companies closer to their target markets.

tomers' purchase patterns, and marketing researchers may buy such data from the supermarkets.

Observation is straightforward and avoids a central problem of survey methods: motivating respondents to state their true feelings or opinions. However, observation tends to be descriptive. When it is the only method of data collection, it may not provide insights into causal relationships. Another drawback is that analyses based on observation are subject to the biases of the observer or the limitations of the mechanical device.

experiment A research method that attempts to maintain certain variables while measuring the effects of experimental variables

Experimentation   Another method for gathering primary data is experimentation. In an **experiment,** marketing researchers attempt to maintain certain variables while measuring the effects of experimental variables. Experimentation requires that an independent variable (one not influenced by or dependent on other variables) be manipulated and the resulting changes in a dependent variable (one contingent on, or restricted to, one value or set of values assumed by the independent variable) be measured. For example, when Houghton Mifflin introduces a new edition of its *American Heritage Dictionary,* it may want to estimate the number of dictionaries that could be sold at various levels of advertising expenditure and price. The dependent variable would be sales, and the independent variable would be advertising expenditure and price. Researchers would design the experiment so that other independent variables that might influence sales, such as distribution and variations of the product, would be controlled. Experimentation is used in marketing research to improve hypothesis testing.

Interpreting Research Findings

statistical interpretation Analysis of what is typical or what deviates from the average

After collecting data to test their hypotheses, marketers need to interpret the research findings. Interpretation of the data is easier if marketers carefully plan their data analysis methods early in the research process. They should also allow for continual evaluation of the data during the entire collection period. They can then gain valuable insight into areas that should be probed during the formal interpretation.

The first step in drawing conclusions from most research is to display the data in table format. If marketers intend to apply the results to individual categories of the things or people being studied, cross-tabulation may be quite useful, especially in tabulating joint occurrences. For example, using the two variables gender and purchase rates of automobile tires, a cross-tabulation could show how men and women differ in purchasing automobile tires.

After the data are tabulated, they must be analyzed. **Statistical interpretation** focuses on what is typical or what deviates from the average. It indicates how widely responses vary and how they are distributed in relation to the variable being measured. When marketers interpret statistics, they must take into account estimates of expected error or deviation from the true values of the population. The analysis of data may lead researchers to accept or reject the hypothesis being studied.

Interpreting Data
Triversity interprets consumer data to help businesses make full use of the information.

Data require careful interpretation by the marketer. If the results of a study are valid, the decision maker should take action; if it is discovered that a question has been incorrectly worded, the results should be ignored. For example, if a survey of 1,200 hypothetical online consumers reveals that 75 percent belong to some form of online loyalty program, is that finding good, bad, or indifferent? Yielding information useful for decision making required a follow-up question to elicit the fact that just 22 percent of those consumers believed their loyalty programs had any impact on their actual purchasing behavior.[22] Likewise, knowing that a majority of consumers support cause-related marketing does not provide enough information to guide marketing strategy decisions. Further research, however, found that at least 65 percent of surveyed consumers had participated in a cause-related marketing campaign. Of those, three-quarters indicated they had either switched brands, tried a product, or increased their product usage, and four out of five said they felt more positive about these purchases, more loyal to the company or brand, and more inclined to seek out future cause-related campaigns.[23] Managers must understand the research results and relate the results to a context that permits effective decision making.

Reporting Research Findings

The final step in the marketing research process is to report the research findings. Before preparing the report, the marketer must take a clear, objective look at the findings to see how well the gathered facts answer the research question or support or negate the initial hypotheses. In most cases, it is extremely doubtful that the study can provide everything needed to answer the research question. Thus, the researcher must point out the deficiencies, and the reasons for them, in the report.

The report of research results is usually a formal, written document. Researchers must allow time for the writing task when they plan and schedule the project. Because the report is a means of communicating with the decision makers who will use the research findings, researchers need to determine beforehand how much detail and supporting data to include. They should keep in mind that corporate executives prefer reports that are short, clear, and simply expressed. Researchers often give their summary and recommendations first, especially if decision makers do not have time to study how the results were obtained. A technical report allows its users to analyze data and interpret recommendations because it describes the research methods and procedures and the most important data gathered. Thus, researchers must recognize the needs and expectations of the report user and adapt to them.

Bias and distortion can be a major problem if the researcher is intent on obtaining favorable results. Consider that research analyzing consumers' reports of their frequency of using long-distance telephone calls, letters, cards, and visits for personal communication found that some groups underreport their usage, whereas other groups overreport it. In particular, researchers found that consumers underestimate the duration of lengthy telephone calls but overestimate the length of short ones; in general, people tend to overestimate both the frequency and duration of their telephone calls. Without this information, companies relying on survey results may get a distorted view of the market for long-distance telephone services by mistakenly judging it to be larger and more homogeneous than it really is.[24]

Marketing researchers want to know about behavior and opinions, and they want accurate data to help in making decisions. Careful wording of questions is very important because a biased or emotional word can change the results tremendously. Marketing research and marketing information systems can provide an organization with accurate and reliable customer feedback, which a marketer must have to understand the dynamics of the marketplace. As managers recognize the benefits of marketing research, they assign it a much larger role in decision making.

Using Technology to Improve Marketing Information Gathering and Analysis

Technology is making information for marketing decisions increasingly accessible. The ability of marketers to track customer buying behavior and to better discern what buyers want is changing the nature of marketing. Customer relationship management is being enhanced by integrating data from all customer contacts and combining that information to improve customer retention. Information technology permits internal research and quick information gathering to better understand and satisfy customers. For example, company responses to e-mail complaints as well as to communications through mail, telephone, and personal contact can be used to improve customer satisfaction, retention, and value.[25] Armed with such information, marketers can fine-tune marketing mixes to satisfy the needs of their customers.

The integration of telecommunications and computer technologies is allowing marketers to access a growing array of valuable information sources related to industry forecasts, business trends, and customer buying behavior. Electronic communication tools can be effectively utilized to gain accurate information with minimal customer interaction. Most marketing researchers have e-mail, voice mail, teleconferencing, and fax machines at their disposal. In fact, many firms use marketing information systems to network all these technologies and organize all the marketing data available to them. In this section, we look at marketing information systems and specific technologies that are helping marketing researchers obtain and manage marketing research data.

Marketing Information Systems

marketing information system (MIS) A framework for the management and structuring of information gathered regularly from sources inside and outside an organization

A **marketing information system (MIS)** is a framework for the day-to-day management and structuring of information gathered regularly from sources both inside and outside an organization. As such, an MIS provides a continuous flow of information about prices, advertising expenditures, sales, competition, and distribution expenses. Kraft General Foods, for example, operates one of the largest marketing information systems in the food industry, maintaining, using, and sharing information with others to increase the value of what the company offers customers. Kraft seeks to develop a dialogue with customers by providing toll-free numbers. It receives hundreds of thousands of calls annually from customers who ask questions and express concerns about products.

The main focus of the marketing information system is on data storage and retrieval, as well as on computer capabilities and management's information requirements. Regular reports of sales by product or market categories, data on inventory levels, and records of sales people's activities are examples of information that is useful in making decisions. In the MIS, the means of *gathering* data receive less attention than do the procedures for expediting the *flow* of information.

An effective marketing information system starts by determining the objective of the information, that is, by identifying decision needs that require certain information. The firm can then specify an information system for continuous monitoring to provide regular, pertinent information on both the external and internal environment. FedEx, for example, has developed interactive marketing systems to provide instantaneous communication between the company and its customers. Through the telephone and Internet, customers can track their packages and receive immediate feedback concerning delivery. The company's website provides valuable information about customer usage, and it allows customers to express directly what they think about company services. The evolving telecommunications and computer technology is allowing marketing information systems to cultivate one-to-one relationships with customers.

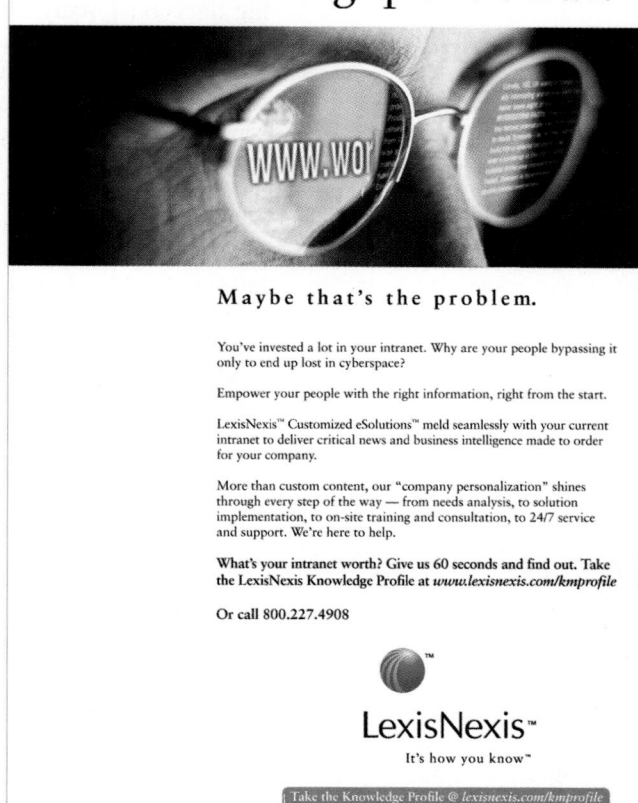

Databases

database A collection of information arranged for easy access and retrieval

Most marketing information systems include internal databases. A **database** is a collection of information arranged for easy access and retrieval. Databases allow marketers to tap into an abundance of information useful in making marketing decisions: internal sales reports, newspaper articles, company news releases, government economic reports, bibliographies, and more, often accessed through a computer system. Information technology has made it possible to develop databases to guide strategic planning and help improve customer services. Wal-Mart, for example, maintains one of the largest corporate databases in the United States, with data about sales and inventory levels as well as data mined from customer receipts from all its stores. These data help Wal-Mart pinpoint purchasing patterns, which helps the firm manage inventory levels and determine effective product placement. Wal-Mart's database may be more accurately described as a data warehouse; this is discussed further in Tech*know. Many commercial websites require consumers to register and provide personal information to access the site or make a purchase. Frequent flier programs permit airlines to ask loyal customers to participate in surveys about their needs and desires, and the airlines can track their best customers' flight patterns by time of day, week, month, and year. Grocery stores gain a significant amount of data through checkout scanners tied to store discount cards.

Marketing researchers can also use commercial databases developed by information research firms, such as LEXIS-NEXIS, to obtain useful information for marketing decisions. Many of these commercial databases are accessible online for a fee. They can also be obtained in printed form or on computer compact discs (CD-ROMs). In most commercial databases, the user typically does a computer search by key word, topic, or company, and the database service generates abstracts, articles, or reports that can then be printed out. Accessing multiple reports or a complete article may cost extra.

single-source data
Information provided by a single marketing research firm

Information provided by a single firm on household demographics, purchases, television viewing behavior, and responses to promotions such as coupons and free samples is called **single-source data.**[26] For example, Behavior Scan, offered by Information Resources, Inc., screens about 60,000 households in 26 U.S. markets. This single-source information service monitors consumer household televisions and records the programs and commercials watched. When buyers from these households shop in stores equipped with scanning registers, they present Hotline cards (similar to credit cards) to cashiers. This enables each customer's identification to be

TECH*KNOW

Mining Data

Thanks to advances in information technology, especially data storage and processing, marketers have available an ever-growing quantity of data about customer buying behavior. To extract from this mound of data potentially useful information to guide marketing decisions, marketers are developing methods of mining data. *Data mining* refers to the discovery of patterns hidden in databases that have the potential to contribute to marketers' understanding of customers and their needs. Data mining employs computer technology to extract data from internal and external sources; translate and format the data; analyze, substantiate, and assign meaning to data; organize databases; and build and implement decision support systems to make data-mining results accessible to decision makers. Effective data mining can help firms acquire new customers, retain profitable customers and identify unprofitable ones, and pinpoint potential relationships between product purchases in point-of-sale transactions.

Many firms are building data warehouses and data marts to facilitate data mining. A *data warehouse* is an organizationwide data collection and storage system that draws data from all of a firm's critical operation systems and from selected external data sources. Such systems require a substantial investment ($10 million or more and one to three years to develop) and therefore demand significant planning and commitment to ensure useful results. In contrast, a *data mart* is a subject-area or division-based data repository that collects data from a department or division's critical systems and from selected external sources. Because of the reduced scale of involvement, data marts can often be developed and implemented for $10,000 to $1 million within six months. Regardless of scale, both systems combine data storage, data analysis, and computer processing technology to help marketers make sense of the vast quantity of data collected in their marketing information systems.

Building a data warehouse, however, is no guarantee that a firm will gain significant insights into its customers. Many companies have established expensive systems that generate overwhelming amounts of data but little information useful for effective decision making. But a number of firms, including Empire Blue Cross and Blue Shield, Safeway Stores PLC, Wal-Mart Stores, and Burlington Coat Factories have built data warehouses or data marts that have produced amazing results and enhanced decision making. Burlington Coat Factories, for example, set up a data warehouse to track sales and guide the buying of the coats and apparel it resells in retail outlets. The system enables Burlington to monitor the effects of the weather on individual store sales and to conservatively stock and restock each store as appropriate. Thus, a well-planned data-mining system can improve marketing decisions and strategies and contribute to the bottom line.

electronically coded so the firm can track each product purchased and store the information in a database. It is important to gather longitudinal (long-term) information on customers to maximize single-source data.[27]

Marketing Decision Support Systems

A **marketing decision support system (MDSS)** is customized computer software that aids marketing managers in decision making by helping them anticipate the effects of certain decisions. Some decision support systems have a broader range and offer greater computational and modeling capabilities than spreadsheets; they let managers explore a greater number of alternatives. For example, a decision support system can determine how sales and profits might be affected by higher or lower interest rates or how sales forecasts, advertising expenditures, production levels, and the like might affect overall profits. For this reason, decision support system software is often a major component of a company's marketing information system. For example, both Oracle and Ford Motor Company use a software product called NeuroServer that acts as a customer interface to solve problems and answer questions for customers. Based on customized parameters, it allows marketers to acquire specific information on customers that can go into the decision support system.[28] Some decision support systems incorporate artificial intelligence and other advanced computer technologies.

The Internet and Online Information Services

The Internet has evolved as a most powerful communication medium, linking customers and companies around the world via computer networks with e-mail, forums, web pages, and more. Growth of the Internet, and especially the World Wide Web, has launched an entire industry that is working to make marketing information easily accessible to both marketing firms and customers.

Table 6.4 lists a number of websites that can be valuable resources for marketing research. The Bureau of the Census, for example, uses the World Wide Web to disseminate information that may be useful to marketing researchers, particularly through the *Statistical Abstract of the United States* and data from the most recent census. Among the companies that exploit census data for marketing decisions are Starbucks, which analyzes the data to assess potential coffee shop sites, and

Table 6.4	Resources for Marketing Information
Government Sources	
U.S. Bureau of the Census	www.census.gov
U.S. Department of State	www.state.gov
FedWorld	www.fedworld.gov
Chamber of Commerce	chamber-of-commerce.com
Commercial Sources	
ACNielsen	www.acnielsen.com
Information Resources, Inc.	www.infores.com
Gallup	www.gallup.com
Arbitron	www.arbitron.com
Periodicals and Books	
American Demographics	www.americandemographics.com
Advertising Age	www.adage.com
Sales & Marketing Management	www.salesandmarketing.com
Fortune	www.fortune.com
Inc.	www.inc.com
Business Week	www.businessweek.com
Bloomberg Report	www.bloomberg.com

Internet Research
Common Knowledge collects data for its customers through Internet surveys as well as other means.

Blockbuster, which mines the data to help determine how many copies of a particular movie or video game to offer at each store.[29]

Companies can also mine their own websites for useful information. Amazon.com, for example, has built a relationship with its customers by tracking the types of books and music they purchase. Each time a customer logs onto the website, the company can offer recommendations based on the customer's previous purchases. Such a marketing system helps the company track the changing desires and buying habits of its most valued customers.

Marketing researchers can also subscribe to online services such as CompuServe, MSN, Prodigy, DIALOG, and NEXIS. These services typically offer their subscribers such specialized services as databases, news services, and forums, as well as access to the Internet itself. Marketers can subscribe to "mailing lists" that periodically deliver electronic newsletters to their computer screens, and they can participate in on-screen discussions with thousands of network users. This enhanced communication with a firm's customers, suppliers, and employees provides a high-speed link that boosts the capabilities of the firm's marketing information system.

While most web pages are open to anyone with Internet access, big companies like Cisco Systems also maintain internal web pages, called "intranets," that allow employees to access such internal data as customer profiles and product inventory—information once hidden in databases only technicians could unlock. Such sensitive corporate information can be protected from outside users of the World Wide Web by special security software called *firewalls*. Turner Broadcasting System uses intranets to test products during the development phase. Marketing department employees view animated clips and listen to sound bites from popular cartoon talk shows. They then express their opinions by e-mailing the animators directly. The animators use this feedback to revise the cartoon before it appears on the firm's public cartoon site on America Online. Most marketers who get in the habit of accessing their companies' internal web pages often move on to seek information externally as well as via the rest of the World Wide Web.[30]

Issues in Marketing Research

The Importance of Ethical Marketing Research

Marketing managers and other professionals are relying more and more on marketing research, marketing information systems, and new technologies to make better decisions. It is therefore essential that professional standards be established by which to judge the reliability of such research. Such standards are necessary because of the ethical and legal issues that develop in gathering marketing research data. In addition, the relationships between research suppliers, such as marketing research agencies, and the marketing managers who make strategy decisions require ethical behavior. Organizations like the Marketing Research Association have developed codes of conduct and guidelines to promote ethical marketing research. To be effective, such guidelines must instruct those who participate in marketing research on how to avoid misconduct. Table 6.5 recommends explicit steps interviewers should follow when introducing a questionnaire.

International Issues in Marketing Research

As we indicated in Chapter 5, sociocultural, economic, political, legal, and technological forces vary in different regions of the world. These variations create challenges for organizations attempting to understand foreign customers through marketing research. The marketing research process we described in this chapter is used

---

Table 6.5   Guidelines for Questionnaire Introduction

Questionnaire introduction should:

- Allow interviewers to introduce themselves by name.
- State the name of the research company.
- Indicate this is a marketing research project.
- Explain there will be no sales involved.
- Note the general topic of discussion (if this is a problem in a "blind" study, a statement such as "consumer opinion" is acceptable).
- State the likely duration of the interview.
- Assure the anonymity of the respondent and confidentiality of all answers.
- State the honorarium if applicable (for many business-to-business and medical studies this is done up front for both qualitative and quantitative studies).
- Reassure the respondent with a statement such as, "There are no right or wrong answers, so please give thoughtful and honest answers to each question" (recommended by many clients).

Source: Reprinted with permission of The Marketing Research Association, P.O. Box 230, Rocky Hill, CT 06067-0230, (860)257-4008.

---

globally, but to ensure that the research is valid and reliable, data-gathering methods may have to be modified to allow for regional differences. For example, the annual Global Airline Performance (GAP) study, which surveys 240,000 air travelers every year about their opinions on 22 airlines departing from 30 North American, European, and Asian airports, can be conducted in English, French, Dutch, German, Swedish, Chinese, or Japanese.[31] To ensure that global and regional differences are satisfactorily addressed, many companies retain a research firm with experience in the country of interest. Most of the largest marketing research firms derive a significant share of their revenues from research conducted outside the United States. As Table 6.6 indicates, ACNielsen, the largest marketing research firm in the world, received 67 percent of its revenues from outside the United States.[32]

Experts recommend a two-pronged approach to international marketing research. The first phase involves a detailed search for and analysis of secondary data to gain greater understanding of a particular marketing environment and to pinpoint issues that must be taken into account in gathering primary research data. Secondary data can be particularly helpful in building a general understanding of the market, including economic, legal, cultural, and demographic issues, as well as in assessing the risks of doing business in that market and in forecasting demand.[33] Marketing researchers often begin by studying country trade reports from the U.S. Department of Commerce as well as country-specific information from local sources, such as a country's website, and trade and general business publications such as *The Wall Street Journal*. These sources can offer insight into the marketing environment in a particular country and can even indicate untapped market opportunities abroad.

The second phase involves field research using many of the methods described earlier, including focus groups and telephone surveys, to refine a firm's understanding

---

Table 6.6   Top Marketing Research Firms

Company	Global Revenues (millions)	Percentage Revenues from Outside the U.S.
1. ACNielsen Corp.	$1,577	67.0
2. IMS Health Inc.	$1,131	62.5
3. Information Resources Inc.	$532	25.0
4. VNU Inc.	$527	2.6
5. NFO WorldGroup	$471	62.4

Source: "Top 50 U.S. Research Organizations," *Marketing News*, June 4, 2001, p. H4.

International Issues in Marketing Research
International Survey Research helps businesses understand a variety of cultural norms and values.

of specific customer needs and preferences. Specific differences among countries can have a profound influence on data gathering. For example, in-home (door-to-door) interviews are illegal in some countries. In China, few people have regular telephone lines, making telephone surveys both impractical and nonrepresentative of the total population. Primary data gathering may have a greater chance of success if the firm employs local researchers who better understand how to approach potential respondents and can do so in their own language.[34] Regardless of the specific methods used to gather primary data, whether in the United States or abroad, the goal is to better understand the needs of specific target markets to craft the best marketing strategy to satisfy the needs of customers in each market, as we will see in the next chapter.

Summary

To implement the marketing concept, marketers need information about the characteristics, needs, and wants of target market customers. Marketing research and information systems that furnish practical, unbiased information help firms avoid assumptions and misunderstandings that could lead to poor marketing performance.

Marketing research is the systematic design, collection, interpretation, and reporting of information to help marketers solve specific marketing problems or take advantage of marketing opportunities. It is a process for gathering information not currently available to decision makers. The value of marketing research is measured by improvements in a marketer's ability to make decisions.

To maintain the control needed to obtain accurate information, marketers approach marketing research as a process with logical steps: (1) locating and defining problems or issues, (2) designing the research project, (3) collecting data, (4) interpreting research findings, and (5) reporting research findings.

The first step in launching a research study, problem or issue definition, focuses on uncovering the nature and boundaries of a situation or question related to marketing strategy or implementation. In the second step, marketing researchers design a research project to obtain the information needed to address it. This step requires formulating a hypothesis and determining what type of research to employ to test the hypothesis so the results are reliable and valid. A hypothesis is an informed guess or assumption about a problem or set of circumstances. The type of hypothesis being tested dictates whether an exploratory, descriptive, or causal approach will be used to gather data. Research is considered reliable if it produces almost

identical results in repeated trials; it is valid if it measures what it is supposed to measure.

For the third step of the research process, collecting data, two types of data are available. Primary data are observed and recorded or collected directly from respondents; secondary data are compiled inside or outside the organization for some purpose other than the current investigation. Sources of secondary data include an organization's own database and other internal sources, periodicals, government publications, unpublished sources, and online databases. Methods of collecting primary data include sampling, surveys, observation, and experimentation. Sampling involves selecting representative units from a total population. In probability sampling, every element in the population being studied has a known chance of being selected for study. Nonprobability sampling is more subjective than probability sampling because there is no way to calculate the likelihood that a specific element of the population being studied will be chosen. Marketing researchers employ sampling to collect primary data through mail, telephone, online, or personal interview surveys. A carefully constructed questionnaire is essential to the success of any survey. In using observation methods, researchers record respondents' overt behavior and take note of physical conditions and events. In an experiment, marketing researchers attempt to maintain certain variables while measuring the effects of experimental variables.

To apply research data to decision making, marketers must interpret and report their findings properly—the final two steps in the marketing research process. Statistical interpretation focuses on what is typical or what deviates from the average. After interpreting the research findings, the researchers must prepare a report on the findings that the decision makers can understand and use. Researchers must also take care to avoid bias and distortion.

Many firms use computer technology to create a marketing information system (MIS), a framework for the management and structuring of information gathered regularly from sources both inside and outside the organization. A database is a collection of information arranged for easy access and retrieval. A marketing decision support system (MDSS) is customized computer software that aids marketing managers in decision making by helping them anticipate the effects of certain decisions. Online information services and the Internet also enable marketers to communicate with customers and obtain information.

Eliminating unethical marketing research practices and establishing generally acceptable procedures for conducting research are important goals of marketing research. Both domestic and international marketing use the same marketing research process, but international marketing may require modifying data-gathering methods to address regional differences.

Important Terms

Marketing research
Research design
Hypothesis
Exploratory research
Descriptive research
Causal research
Reliability
Validity
Primary data
Secondary data
Population
Sample
Sampling
Probability sampling
Random sampling
Stratified sampling
Nonprobability sampling
Quota sampling
Mail survey
Telephone survey
Online survey
Personal interview survey
In-home (door-to-door) interview
Focus-group interview
Telephone depth interview
Shopping mall intercept interview
On-site computer interview
Experiment
Statistical interpretation
Marketing information system (MIS)
Database
Single-source data
Marketing decision support system (MDSS)

Discussion and Review Questions

1. What is marketing research? Why is it important?
2. Describe the five steps in the marketing research process.
3. What is the difference between defining a research problem and developing a hypothesis?
4. Describe the different types of approaches to marketing research and indicate when each should be used.
5. Where are data for marketing research obtained? Give examples of internal and external data.
6. What is the difference between probability sampling and nonprobability sampling? In what situation would it be best to use random sampling? Stratified sampling? Quota sampling?
7. Suggest some ways to encourage respondents to cooperate in mail surveys.
8. If a survey of all homes with listed telephone numbers is conducted, what sampling design should be used?
9. Describe some marketing problems that could be solved through information gained from observation.
10. What is a marketing information system, and what should it provide?
11. Define a database. What is its purpose, and what does it include?
12. How can marketers use online services and the Internet to obtain information for decision making?
13. What role does ethics play in marketing research? Why is it important that marketing researchers be ethical?
14. How does marketing research in other countries differ from marketing research in the United States?

Application Questions

1. After observing customers' traffic patterns, Bashas' Markets repositioned the greeting card section in its stores, and card sales increased substantially. To increase sales for the following types of companies, what information might marketing researchers want to gather from customers?
   a. Furniture stores
   b. Gasoline outlets/service stations
   c. Investment companies
   d. Medical clinics
2. When a company wants to conduct research, it must first identify a problem or possible opportunity to market its goods or services. Choose a company in your city that you think might benefit from a research project. Develop a research question and outline a method to approach this question. Explain why you think the research question is relevant to the organization and why the particular methodology is suited to the question and the company.
3. Input for marketing information systems can come from internal or external sources. ACNielsen Corporation is the largest provider of single-source marketing research in the world. Indicate two firms or companies in your city that might benefit from internal sources and two that would benefit from external sources, and explain why they would benefit. Suggest the type of information each should gather.
4. Suppose you were opening a health insurance brokerage firm and wanted to market your services to small businesses with fewer than 50 employees. Determine which database for marketing information you would use in your marketing efforts, and explain why you would use it.

Visit **www.prideferrell.com** for resources to help you master the material in this chapter, plus materials that will help you expand your marketing knowledge, including: Internet exercise updates, ACE self-tests, hotlinks to companies featured in this chapter, and much more.

American Demographics' Marketing Tools Directory

American Demographics makes an online directory of marketing research tools available to the marketing information industry. Known as the Marketing Tools Directory, it includes numerous resources that are searchable by topic. Visit the site at

www.marketingtools.com

1. What information in the directory could assist in a marketing research project?

2. What resources listed in the directory would be helpful in maintaining an internal marketing information system?

3. What research tools are available through the directory?

VIDEO CASE 6.1

IRI Provides Marketing Research Data from Multiple Sources

Marketing research is a crucial marketing activity because it informs companies about customers' needs, desires, and changes in their attitudes and purchase patterns and helps marketers identify opportunities for particular goods and services. One of today's leading marketing research firms is Information Resources, Inc. (IRI), which provides sales data to customers indicating how much of their products have been sold, where, and at what price. Such information is critical to strategic market planning and managing the movement of products through the supply chain. The Chicago-based firm's customers include manufacturers, retailers, and sales/marketing agencies in the United States and throughout the world. With annual revenues of $531 million, the firm offers these customers vital marketing intelligence to help them make sound strategic marketing decisions.

One of IRI's most renowned research tools is the InfoScan store-tracking service. Through Info-Scan, IRI collects sales data from a system of check-out scanners in supermarkets, drugstores, and mass merchandisers. Every week, data collected from more than 20,000 stores are input into IRI's huge database for analysis. IRI then breaks this information down into client-specific databases. The company then sells the analyzed information to customers, which include manufacturers such as Nestlé, Procter & Gamble, PepsiCo, and Lever

Bros., as well as retailers like Kroger's, Albertson's, Walgreen's, and Target.

Databases developed by IRI allow these marketers to tap into an abundance of information on sales, market share, distribution, pricing, and promotion for hundreds of consumer product categories. For example, InfoScan can track new products to assess their performance and gauge competitors' reactions to their marketing strategy. Once new products are on store shelves, IRI monitors related information such as prices and market share of competing products. This information helps the products' marketers gauge the effect of competitors' tactics so they can adjust their marketing strategies as necessary. InfoScan can also help marketers assess customers' reactions to changes in a product's price, packaging, display, and other marketing mix elements. By tracking a product's sales in relation to promotional efforts, InfoScan data also help marketers assess the effect of their own advertising as well as that of competitors.

Another IRI product, Behavior Scan, provides single-source data on household demographics, television viewing behavior, purchases, and responses to promotions such as coupons and free samples. Through Behavior Scan, IRI screens about 60,000 households in 26 U.S. markets. Behavior Scan monitors participating households' television viewing habits, recording the programs and commercials each household watches. When consumers from these households shop in a store equipped with scanning registers, they present credit-card-size hotline cards, which allow the store to electronically identify them so IRI can track their purchases and store the information in a database for analysis. With this information, IRI can relate the purchases of a household to the commercials viewed on television, further allowing the companies to assess the effects of their promotional strategies.

Although IRI specializes primarily in scanner-based data collection that documents what consumers buy under certain conditions—that is, behavioral research—the company also recognizes the value of attitudinal research to explain the "why behind the buy." To this end, IRI sought an alliance with Sorensen Associates to observe and interview shoppers at the point of purchase in supermarkets and other retail outlets. These in-store research methods provide valuable insights into shopping behavior and attitudes in a real-life retail environment. To further expand its portfolio of client services, IRI has also partnered with Mosaic Group to conduct field surveys. By providing survey research, IRI can introduce new services to help clients make better and more timely marketing decisions. As companies develop databases, the various data sources can be merged to improve efficiency and develop and improve customer satisfaction.

All of IRI's services facilitate customer relationship management using marketing research and information technology to provide profiles of consumers, including behavior and attitudes. IRI is also employing information technology to deliver information over the Internet. In 2000 the company launched CPGNetwork.com, through which cus-

tomers can access marketing intelligence in the form of data-driven analyses, alerts, key performance indicators, "best practices," and case studies via the Web.

In addition to its services to client customers, IRI occasionally provides public relations information to the retail industry. For example, the company recently released a study indicating that 23 percent of online consumers have purchased consumer packaged goods online, and 99 percent of those customers planned to maintain or increase their online spending levels over the next year. Although just 12 percent of online consumer packaged goods shoppers spent more than 25 percent of their budget online, that number is expected to increase by 35 percent. Such information is important to retailers because it indicates that purchases of consumer packaged goods via the Internet are increasing and represent an opportunity for online retailers.

IRI tailors its information services to the unique information needs of each customer. The research it provides arms these customers with marketing intelligence to help them match their marketing mixes to the needs of their customers. With timely and accurate information about what products are selling, where they are selling, the most effective prices, and competitors' activities, marketers can make sound decisions about the marketing strategy for specific products.[35]

QUESTIONS FOR DISCUSSION
1. How are the data gathered by IRI useful in customer relationship management?
2. What is the advantage of integrating scanner data with television viewing behavior?
3. Compare the usefulness of behavioral scanner data with data conducted through surveys.

CASE 6.2
A Look-Look at Youth Trends

Teenagers and young adults have become the trendsetters and taste makers for American society. However, these trends are dynamic, seeming to change overnight, and today's "cool" fashion item quickly becomes "so yesterday." Moreover, the nation's 60 million teenagers command some $140 billion in buying power, and this figure is expected to grow 5 to 10 percent annually. Keeping up with this lucrative yet dynamic market is a challenge

that few marketing research firms have been able to meet with both accuracy and speed. One firm, however, has been able to peer into the minds of today's youth with startling clarity: Look-Look.com, an online information and research firm that offers information, news, and photographs about trends among the 14-to-30-year-old demographic group in near real-time. The firm's reputation has grown rapidly, and its revenues are projected to reach $20 million to $50 million in the next five years.

Look-Look was founded in 1999 by DeeDee Gordon and Sharon Lee, who met while working at Lambesis, a Del Mar, California, advertising agency. Gordon became an astute observer of youth trends while running a Boston store. Lee is the strategist who turns Gordon's observations into successful marketing plans. The two have been labeled "urban archaeologists" because they are able to uncover trends and opportunities that marketers can tap into to satisfy this challenging and energetic market.

To understand the constantly changing trends among 14-to-30–year-olds, Look-Look hand-picked and prescreened more than 10,000 young people from all over the world. The firm chooses forward-thinking trendsetters who are innovative and influential among their peers and pays them to answer surveys; report on their opinions, ideas, styles, and trends; and even photograph fashion trends with digital cameras. Although such trendsetters account for only about 20 percent of youths, they influence the other 80 percent. Gordon and Lee believe that understanding today's young people requires a continuing "e-dialog," not just once- or twice-a-year focus groups or market surveys. Gordon and Lee also make frequent trips to Tokyo and London, which are often breeding grounds for the next hot trend.

Look-Look clients pay $20,000 a year to gain instant access to the results of the firm's online surveys and other research. These clients include firms representing the apparel, cosmetics, beverage, video game, and movie industries. Look-Look provides these clients with information about the latest trends in youth fashion, entertainment, technology, leisure activities, foods and beverages, health and beauty, mindset, and more. Look-Look delivers fast, accurate, and timely information through the Internet and the company's own intranet and database. Clients can even get almost immediate responses to research questions the firm poses to its 10,000 respondents 24 hours a day.

The firm's website offers a variety of information to help clients better understand the tastes and interests of young people today, including photo spreads, news stories, "youth correspondent" reports, survey results, graphics, and top-ten lists of respondents' favorite gadgets, books, celebrities, and music. For example, one recent survey reported that most young people are willing to pay a monthly fee to use websites that allow music downloads, such as Napster, and that their use of these sites has little effect on the number of CDs they actually purchase. Other Look-Look research suggests that young people are sophisticated enough to distinguish between make-believe violence and real-life violence. Indeed, Look-Look's success may stem from the fact that it respects the increasing sophistication of today's young people and does not treat them condescendingly. As Sharon Lee says, "Teen consumers have gotten sophisticated about companies and style. Trends move so quickly, and there are so many choices. Manufacturers and retailers have to listen to get the competitive edge."

The "living research" Look-Look provides continuously listens to and observes young people to ensure the information it supplies is authentic and up to date. Whether it's cropped, cherry-red hair, skin-tight leather hip-hugger pants, tattoos, or body piercing, Look-Look knows what young people like and, for a fee, helps marketers stay on top of these trends to satisfy this very lucrative market.[36]

QUESTIONS FOR DISCUSSION

1. How does the information Look-Look.com supplies help marketers appeal to teenagers and young adults?
2. What advantages do the methods Look-Look employs have over traditional marketing research methods?
3. Some critics claim that Look-Look's core of trendsetting respondents are "too hip" to reflect the tastes of mainstream teens and young adults. How might this be a problem for a company using Look-Look data to develop a marketing strategy?

Target Markets: Segmentation and Evaluation

7

Nokia knows that tech-savvy, fashion-conscious teens around the world use cell phones not only to be in touch but also to be in style. Understanding the tastes and interests of this lucrative target market has kept cash registers ringing for the Helsinki-based communications giant. Despite intense competition from rivals Motorola and Ericsson, Nokia has already captured an impressive 37 percent share of the U.S. mobile phone market. And talk about sales potential: fewer than three in ten U.S. teens now own a cell phone, although ownership is expected to more than double within four years. As a result, Nokia has plenty of room to expand by satisfying the needs of this key segment to create brand-loyal customers who will continue buying its products in future years.

Nokia Answers the Call by Targeting Cell Phones at Teens

With a $2 billion yearly investment in research and development, Nokia carefully studies market trends and incorporates the latest technology to create products for teens and other customer groups. On average, the company launches one new phone every month, providing an ever-changing array of products and features to appeal to teens who want both cutting-edge functionality and individualized fashion touches. One popular model blends updated phone features, such as wireless web messaging and downloadable games, with the style possibilities of customizable ring tones and changeable covers so teens can express themselves in a wide variety of ways. Because teens often spend hours using e-mail and chatting online, "messaging has turned out to be very popular with the entry-level age group," notes a Nokia manager.

Edgy, state-of-the-art products are only the start, however. Nokia also knows how to reach out to the teen market through targeted promotions. The company is especially active in arranging product placements to put its latest cell phones into the hands of film stars in youth-oriented movies. Backing these product placements with tie-in media and web-based advertising helped boost the company's brand preference among teens from 47 to 63 percent in just one year. Nokia recently signed actress Jennifer Love Hewitt to reinforce this brand preference leadership by promoting its phones in a special advertising campaign. In addition, the company has partnered with Cingular and other telecommunications companies to promote cell phones using school posters, ads in entertainment publications, and other promotional activities geared to the teen market.

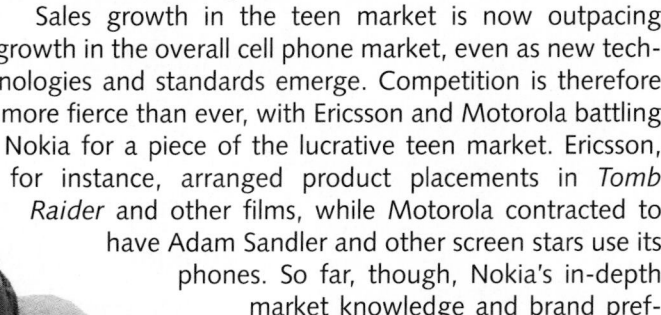

Sales growth in the teen market is now outpacing growth in the overall cell phone market, even as new technologies and standards emerge. Competition is therefore more fierce than ever, with Ericsson and Motorola battling Nokia for a piece of the lucrative teen market. Ericsson, for instance, arranged product placements in *Tomb Raider* and other films, while Motorola contracted to have Adam Sandler and other screen stars use its phones. So far, though, Nokia's in-depth market knowledge and brand preference leadership among teens have helped the company stay on track toward its goal of achieving a 40 percent global market share.[1]

To compete effectively, Nokia has singled out specific customer groups toward which it will direct its marketing efforts. Any organization that wants to succeed must identify its customers and develop and maintain marketing mixes that satisfy the needs of these customers.

In this chapter, we explore markets and market segmentation. Initially we define the term *market* and discuss the major requirements of a market. Then we examine the steps in the target market selection process, including identifying the appropriate targeting strategy; determining which variables to use for segmenting consumer and business markets; developing market segment profiles; evaluating relevant market segments; and selecting target markets. Finally, we discuss various methods for developing sales forecasts.

What Are Markets?

The word *market* has a number of meanings. People sometimes use it to refer to a specific location where products are bought and sold—for example, a flea market. A large geographic area may also be called a market. Sometimes the word refers to the relationship between supply and demand of a specific product, as in the question "How is the market for digital cameras?" *Market* may also be used as a verb, meaning to sell something.

A market is a group of people who, as individuals or as organizations, have needs for products in a product class and have the ability, willingness, and authority to purchase such products. In general use, the term *market* sometimes refers to the total population, or mass market, that buys products. However, our definition is more specific; it refers to persons seeking products in a specific product category. For example, students are part of the market for textbooks, as well as the markets for software, pens, paper, food, music, and other products. Obviously, our complex economy has many different markets.

Requirements of a Market

As stated in our definition, for a market to exist, the people in the aggregate must meet the following four requirements:

1. They must need or desire a particular product. If they do not, that aggregate is not a market.

2. They must have the ability to purchase the product. Ability to purchase is a function of buying power, which consists of resources such as money, goods, and services that can be traded in an exchange situation.

3. They must be willing to use their buying power.

4. They must have the authority to buy the specific products.

Individuals can have the desire, the buying power, and the willingness to purchase certain products but may not be authorized to do so. For example, teenagers may have the desire, the money, and the willingness to buy liquor, but a liquor producer does not consider them a market because teenagers are prohibited by law from buying alcoholic beverages. An aggregate of people that lacks any one of the four requirements thus does not constitute a market.

Types of Markets

Markets fall into one of two categories: consumer markets and business markets (also called business-to-business, industrial, or organizational markets). These categories are based on the characteristics of the individuals and groups that make up a specific market and the purposes for which they buy products. A **consumer market** consists of purchasers and individuals in their households who intend to consume or benefit from the purchased products and do not buy products for the main purpose of making a profit. Each of us belongs to numerous consumer markets. The millions of

consumer market Purchasers and household members who intend to consume or benefit from the purchased products and do not buy products to make profits

Consumer and Business Markets
In the advertisement on the left, Benjamin Moore Paints is aiming its products at consumer markets. On the right, Corbis promotes the fact that it licenses images to customers in business markets.

business market Individuals or groups that purchase a specific kind of product for resale, direct use in producing other products, or use in general daily operations

individuals with the ability, willingness, and authority to buy make up a multitude of consumer markets for such products as housing, food, clothing, vehicles, personal services, appliances, furniture, and recreational equipment.

A **business market** consists of individuals or groups that purchase a specific kind of product for one of three purposes: resale, direct use in producing other products, or use in general daily operations. For example, a lamp producer who buys electrical wire to use in the production of lamps is a part of a business market for electrical wire. This same firm purchases dust mops to clean its office areas. Although the mops are not used in the direct production of lamps, they are used in the operations of the firm; thus, this manufacturer is part of a business market for dust mops. The four categories of business markets are producer, reseller, government, and institutional.

Target Market Selection Process

In Chapter 1 we indicate that the first of two major components for developing a marketing strategy is to select a target market. Although marketers may employ several methods for target market selection, generally they use a five-step process. This process is shown in Figure 7.1, and we discuss it in the following sections.

Step 1: Identify the Appropriate Targeting Strategy

As you may recall from Chapter 1, a target market is a group of people or organizations for which a business creates and maintains a marketing mix specifically designed to satisfy the needs of group members. The strategy used to select a target market is affected by target market characteristics, product attributes, and the organization's objectives and resources. Figure 7.2 illustrates the three basic targeting strategies: undifferentiated, concentrated, and differentiated.

FIGURE 7.1
Target Market Selection Process

1 Identify the appropriate targeting strategy	2 Determine which segmentation variables to use	3 Develop market segment profiles	4 Evaluate relevant market segments	5 Select specific target markets

FIGURE 7.2
Targeting Strategies
The letters in each target market represent potential customers. Customers with the same letters have similar characteristics and similar product needs.

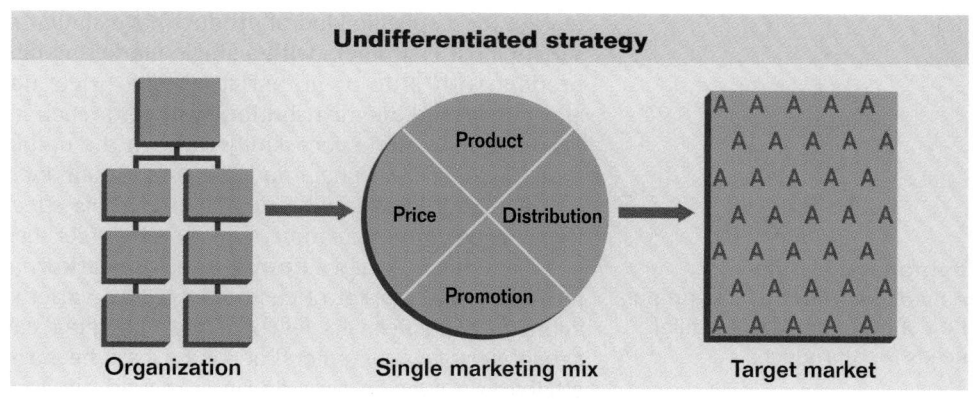

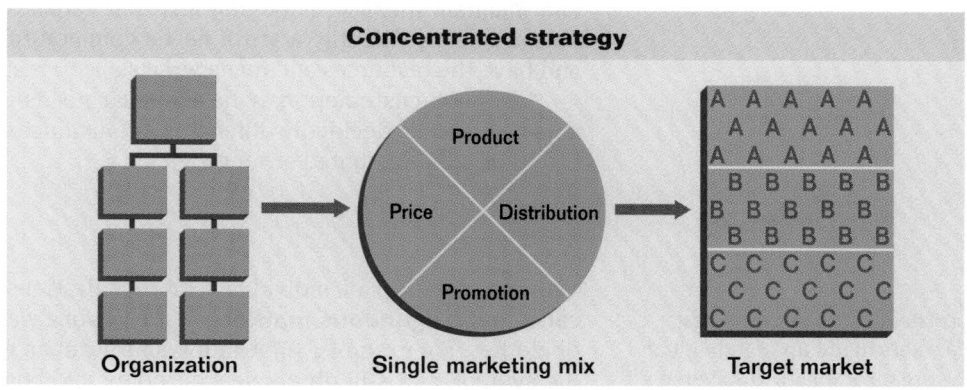

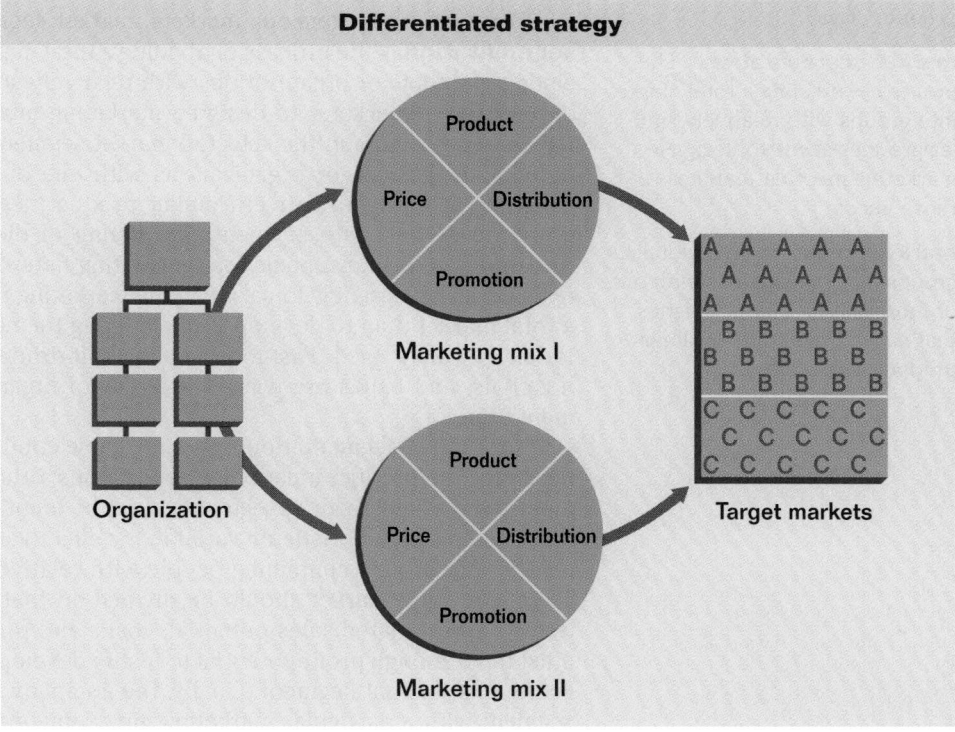

undifferentiated targeting strategy   A strategy in which an organization defines an entire market for a particular product as its target market, designs a single marketing mix, and directs it at that market

Undifferentiated Strategy

An organization sometimes defines an entire market for a particular product as its target market. When a company designs a single marketing mix and directs it at the entire market for a particular product, it is using an **undifferentiated targeting strategy.** As Figure 7.2 shows, the strategy assumes that all customers in the target market for a specific kind of product have similar needs, and so the organization can satisfy most customers with a single marketing mix. This mix consists of one type of product with little or no variation, one price, one promotional program aimed at everybody, and one distribution system to reach most customers in the total market. Products marketed successfully through the undifferentiated strategy include staple food items, such as sugar and salt, and certain kinds of farm produce.

The undifferentiated targeting strategy is effective under two conditions. First, a large proportion of customers in a total market must have similar needs for the product, a situation termed a **homogeneous market.** A marketer using a single marketing mix for a total market of customers with a variety of needs would find that the marketing mix satisfies very few people. A "universal car" meant to satisfy everyone would satisfy very few customers' needs for cars because it would not provide the specific attributes a specific person wants. Second, the organization must be able to develop and maintain a single marketing mix that satisfies customers' needs. The company must be able to identify a set of needs common to most customers in a total market and have the resources and managerial skills to reach a sizable portion of that market.

Although customers may have similar needs for a few products, for most products their needs decidedly differ. In such instances, a company should use a concentrated or a differentiated strategy.

Concentrated Strategy Through Market Segmentation

Markets made up of individuals or organizations with diverse product needs are called **heterogeneous markets.** Not everyone wants the same type of car, furniture, or clothes. For example, some individuals want an economical car, others desire a status symbol, and still others seek a roomy and comfortable vehicle. The automobile market, thus, is heterogeneous.

For such heterogeneous markets, market segmentation is appropriate. **Market segmentation** is the process of dividing a total market into groups, or segments, consisting of people or organizations with relatively similar product needs. The purpose is to enable a marketer to design a marketing mix that more precisely matches the needs of customers in the selected market segment. A **market segment** consists of individuals, groups, or organizations with one or more similar characteristics that cause them to have relatively similar product needs. For instance, the cola market could be divided into segments consisting of diet cola drinkers and regular cola drinkers. The main rationale for segmenting heterogeneous markets is that a company is better able to develop a satisfying marketing mix for a relatively small portion of a total market than to develop a mix meeting the needs of all people. Market segmentation is widely used. Fast-food chains, soft-drink companies, magazine publishers, hospitals, and banks are just a few types of organizations that employ market segmentation.

For market segmentation to succeed, five conditions must exist. First, customers' needs for the product must be heterogeneous; otherwise there is little reason to segment the market. Second, segments must be identifiable and divisible. The company must find a characteristic or variable for effectively separating individuals in a total market into groups containing people with relatively uniform needs for the product. Third, the total market should be divided so that segments can be compared with respect to estimated sales potential, costs, and profits. Fourth, at least one segment must have enough profit potential to justify developing and maintaining a special marketing mix for that segment. Finally, the company must be able to reach the chosen segment with a particular marketing mix. Some market segments may be difficult or impossible to reach because of legal, social, or distribution constraints. For instance, marketers of Cuban rum and cigars cannot sell to U.S. consumers because of political and trade restrictions.

When an organization directs its marketing efforts toward a single market segment using one marketing mix, it is employing a **concentrated targeting strategy.** Porsche focuses on the luxury sports car segment and directs all its marketing efforts toward high-income individuals who want to own high-performance sports cars. Cross

homogeneous market
A market in which a large proportion of customers have similar needs for a product

heterogeneous markets
Markets made up of individuals or organizations with diverse needs for products in a specific product class

market segmentation The process of dividing a total market into groups with relatively similar product needs to design a marketing mix that matches those needs

market segment Individuals, groups, or organizations with one or more similar characteristics that cause them to have similar product needs

concentrated targeting strategy A strategy in which an organization targets a single market segment using one marketing mix

Concentrated Targeting Strategy
Cross uses a concentrated targeting strategy. It aims a single marketing mix at the upscale segment of the writing instrument market.

Pen Company aims its products at the upscale gift segment of the pen market and does not compete with Bic, which focuses on the inexpensive, disposable pen segment. Notice in Figure 7.2 that the organization using the concentrated strategy is aiming its marketing mix only at "B" customers. Similarly, Lionel targets the segment of the toy train market that prefers detailed, large-scale trains—a $250 million segment, but only 25 percent of the overall market for toy trains.[2]

The chief advantage of the concentrated strategy is that it allows a firm to specialize. The firm analyzes characteristics and needs of a distinct customer group and then focuses all its energies on satisfying that group's needs. A firm may generate a large sales volume by reaching a single segment. Also, concentrating on a single segment permits a firm with limited resources to compete with larger organizations that may have overlooked smaller segments.

Specialization, however, means that a company puts all its eggs in one basket, which can be hazardous. If a company's sales depend on a single segment and the segment's demand for the product declines, the company's financial strength also declines. Moreover, when a firm penetrates one segment and becomes well entrenched, its popularity may keep it from moving into other segments. For example, it is very unlikely that Cross could or would want to compete with Bic in the low-end, disposable pen market segment.

Differentiated Strategy Through Market Segmentation

differentiated targeting strategy   A strategy in which an organization targets two or more segments by developing a marketing mix for each

With a **differentiated targeting strategy,** an organization directs its marketing efforts at two or more segments by developing a marketing mix for each (see Figure 7.2). After a firm uses a concentrated strategy successfully in one market segment, it sometimes expands its efforts to include additional segments. For example, Fruit of the Loom underwear has traditionally been aimed at one segment: men. However, the company now markets underwear for women and children as well. Marketing mixes for a differentiated strategy may vary as to product features, distribution methods, promotion methods, and prices.

A firm may increase sales in the aggregate market through a differentiated strategy because its marketing mixes are aimed at more people. For example, the Gap, which established its retail clothes reputation by targeting people under 25, now targets several age groups, from infants to people over 60. A company with excess production capacity may find a differentiated strategy advantageous because the sale of products to additional segments may absorb excess capacity. On the other hand, a differentiated strategy often demands more production processes, materials, and people. Thus, production and costs may be higher than with a concentrated strategy.

Step 2: Determine Which Segmentation Variables to Use

Segmentation variables are the characteristics of individuals, groups, or organizations used to divide a market into segments. For example, location, age, gender, or rate of product usage can all be bases for segmenting markets.

segmentation variables
Characteristics of individuals, groups, or organizations used to divide a market into segments

To select a segmentation variable, several factors are considered. The segmentation variable should relate to customers' needs for, uses of, or behavior toward the product. Stereo marketers might segment the stereo market based on income and age, but not on religion, because people's stereo needs do not differ due to religion. Furthermore, if individuals or organizations in a total market are to be classified accurately, the segmentation variable must be measurable. Age, location, and gender are measurable because such information can be obtained through observation or questioning. But segmenting a market on the basis of, say, intelligence is extremely difficult because this attribute is harder to measure accurately.

A company's resources and capabilities affect the number and size of segment variables used. The type of product and degree of variation in customers' needs also dictate the number and size of segments targeted. In short, there is no best way to segment markets.

Choosing a segmentation variable or variables is a critical step in targeting a market. Selecting an inappropriate variable limits the chances of developing a successful marketing strategy. To help you better understand potential segmentation variables, we examine the major types of variables used to segment consumer markets and the types used to segment business markets.

Variables for Segmenting Consumer Markets

A marketer using segmentation to reach a consumer market can choose one or several variables from an assortment of possibilities. As Figure 7.3 shows, segmentation variables can be grouped into four categories: demographic, geographic, psychographic, and behavioristic.

Demographic Variables. Demographers study aggregate population characteristics such as the distribution of age and gender, fertility rates, migration patterns, and mortality rates. Demographic characteristics that marketers commonly use in segmenting markets include age, gender, race, ethnicity, income, education, occupation, family size, family life cycle, religion, and social class. Marketers rely on these demographic characteristics because they are often closely linked to customers' needs and purchasing behavior and can be readily measured. Like demographers, a few marketers even use mortality rates. Service Corporation International (SCI), the largest U.S. funeral services company, attempts

SNAPSHOT

Marital status of women

More than half the women in the U.S. are married, while 21% have lived only the single life.

11% Widowed
13% Divorced/separated
21% Never married
55% Married

Source: *USA Today*, Oct. 17, 2000, www.usatoday.com/snapshot/life. Copyright 2000, *USA Today*. Reprinted with permission.

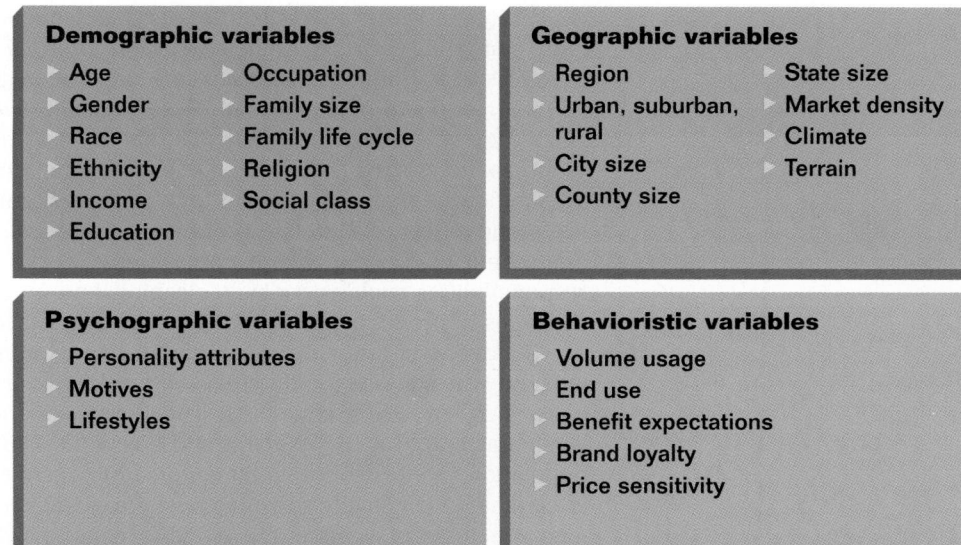

FIGURE 7.3
Segmentation Variables for Consumer Markets

to locate its facilities in higher-income suburban areas with high mortality rates. SCI operates more than 4,000 funeral service locations, cemeteries, and crematoriums.[3]

Age is a commonly used variable for segmentation purposes. For example, knowing that a hipper image would help dealers targeting younger prospects, Toyota recently changed the name of one dealership network in Japan to Netz. By refocusing its sales efforts on entry-level drivers and offering lower-priced cars like the bB hatchback and FunCargo models, Toyota hopes to increase its market share among consumers in their 20s and 30s.[4] Marketers need to be aware of age distribution and how that distribution is changing. All age groups under 55 are expected to decrease by the year 2025, and all age categories 55 and older are expected to increase. In 1970, the average age of a U.S. citizen was 27.9; currently, it is about 35.7. As Figure 7.4 shows, Americans 65 to 74 years old outspend not only customers in the 25-to-34 age group, but also the average U.S. customer for numerous product categories.

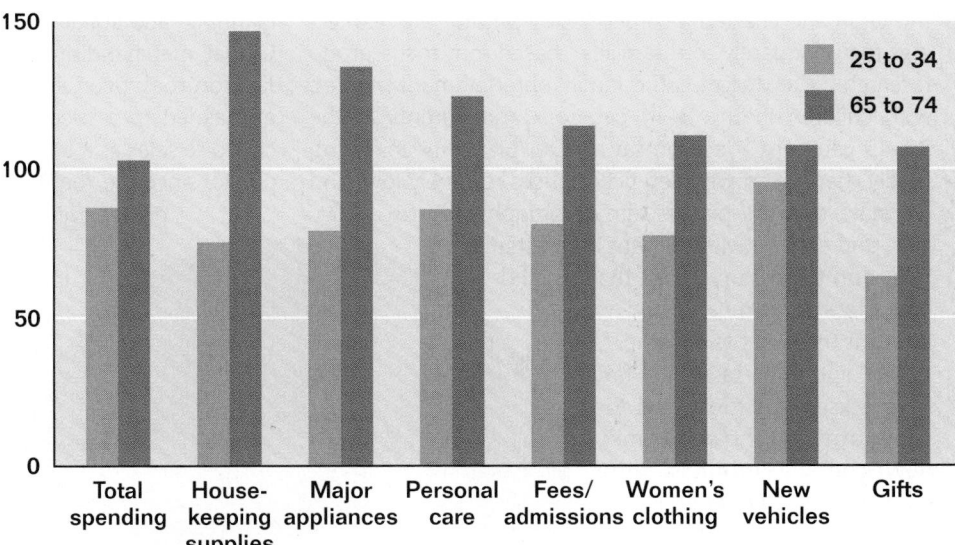

FIGURE 7.4
Spending Levels of Two Age Groups for Selected Product Categories
Index of 100 equals the spending of the average U.S. consumer.
Source: Reprinted from *American Demographics Magazine*, with permission. © 1997 PRIMEDIA Intertec, Stanford, CT.

Many marketers recognize the purchase influence of children and are targeting more marketing efforts at them. As a group, children ages 4 to 12 have annual incomes in excess of $27 billion. Numerous products are aimed specifically at children—toys, clothing, food and beverages, and entertainment such as movies and TV cable channels. They spend approximately $23 billion and save $4 billion. Children in this age group spend more than $7 billion of their own money annually on snacks and beverages and more than $6 billion on toys and entertainment. In addition, children in this age group influence $188 billion of parental spending yearly.[5] In households with only one parent or those in which both parents work, children often take on additional responsibilities such as cooking, cleaning, and grocery shopping and thus influence the types of products and brands that are purchased.

Gender is another demographic variable commonly used to segment markets, including the markets for clothing, soft drinks, nonprescription medications, toiletries, magazines, and even cigarettes. The Bureau of the Census reports that girls and women account for 51.1 percent and boys and men for 48.9 percent of the total U.S. population.[6] Some deodorant marketers utilize gender segmentation: Secret deodorant is marketed specifically to women, whereas Old Spice deodorant is directed toward men. A number of websites are aimed at females, including Cybergirl, Girl Tech, Moms

GLOBAL MARKETING

Harlem Globetrotters Target Families Around the World

Thanks to the effective use of market segmentation, the Harlem Globetrotters are still shooting hoops. First formed in 1926, the team of talented African American basketball players earned an international reputation for its special blend of top-notch entertainment and highly competitive skills. During the 1980s and 1990s, however, the team played to dwindling crowds and its parent company finally filed for bankruptcy. Then Mannie Jackson, a former Globetrotter player turned corporate executive, bought the team and charted a comeback by putting the marketing focus squarely on families, based on focus-group research. "Our target is the family entertainment market, with children in the 8–14 category and parents in the 35–45 category," Jackson says. "Our brand means being family friendly, so we keep ticket prices relatively low, and we make sure our players sign autographs, talk to kids, and engage with the fans in the stands. We don't do anything that would embarrass a mom and dad who've brought their kids to a game."

In line with targeting families, Jackson has revamped the Globetrotters show to mix new comedy routines with hard-driving competition and tricky ball-handling skills. The team sometimes plays against top-ranked college basketball teams, creating excitement among the target market fans and bringing in new audiences. About half of the team's audiences are return customers, but Jackson's goal is to increase that number to 75 percent or higher. He is also expanding the team's geographic targeting by booking shows more frequently in smaller markets like Hutchinson, Kansas, where he perceives growing demand.

True to their name, the Globetrotters play internationally and target families in other countries. Non-U.S. business accounts for 50 percent of its profits, and the team is planning additional tours and dates around the world. Global merchandising sales have also quadrupled since Jackson took over, a sign that the family targeting strategy has led to a successful turnaround. "We follow merchandise sales as a barometer of how we're doing with the public, since we feel that if we're doing the right things, people will want the souvenirs," he says.

The Globetrotters are not only selling more merchandise but are drawing larger crowds and generating higher profits. When Jackson took over, yearly audience attendance was below 300,000 and the team was losing $1 million on annual revenues of roughly $9 million. Today the Globetrotters attract more than 2 million people yearly and generate $6 million in profits on annual revenues of $60 million—a winning performance in any league.

Gender-Based Segmentation
The skates in this catalog spread are definitely designed for, and marketed to, women.

Online, Women's Wire, and Online Women's Business Center. Effective targeting of women online relies heavily on personalization, sense of community, and trust.[7] Jiffy Lube, noted for its speedy oil change services, was surprised when marketing research revealed that women make up at least half of its customer base. The company decided to actively target this segment by remodeling its service centers to include a child-play area, Internet access, and women's magazines.[8]

Marketers also use race and ethnicity as variables for segmenting markets for such products as food, music, clothing, and cosmetics and for services like banking and insurance. The U.S. Hispanic population illustrates the importance of ethnicity as a segmentation variable. Made up of people of Mexican, Cuban, Puerto Rican, and Central and South American heritage, this ethnic group is growing five times faster than the general population. Consequently, Campbell Soup, Procter & Gamble, and other companies target Hispanic consumers, viewing this segment as attractive because of its size and growth potential. However, targeting Hispanic customers is not an easy task. For example, although marketers have long believed that Hispanic consumers are exceptionally brand-loyal and prefer Spanish-language broadcast media, research does not support these assumptions. Not only do advertisers disagree about the merits of using Spanish-language media; they also realize they cannot effectively advertise to Mexicans, Puerto Ricans, and Cubans using a common Spanish language.[9]

Because it strongly influences people's product needs, income often provides a way to divide markets. It affects their ability to buy and their desires for certain lifestyles. Product markets segmented by income include sporting goods, housing, furniture, cosmetics, clothing, jewelry, home appliances, automobiles, and electronics.

Among the factors influencing household income and product needs are marital status and the presence and age of children. These characteristics, often combined and called the *family life cycle,* affect

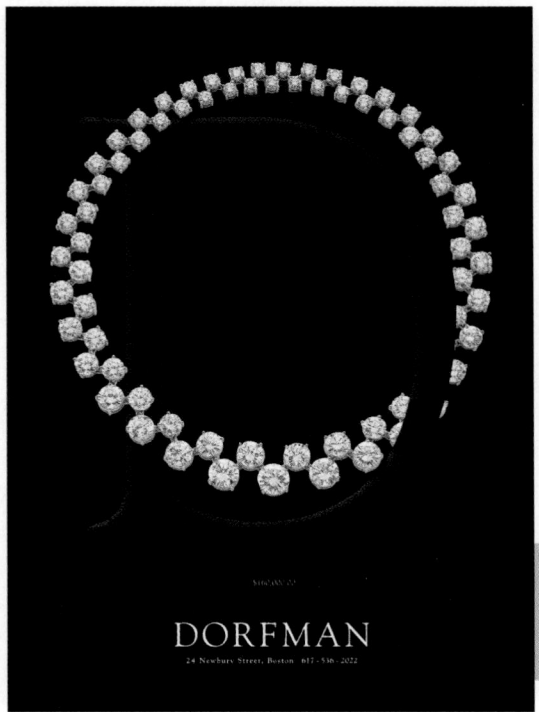

DORFMAN
24 Newbury Street, Boston 617-536-2022

Segmentation Based on Income
Jewelry products are often segmented on the basis of income. The jewelry shown in this advertisement is priced at $160,000 and is aimed at high-income customers.

Table 7.1   Life Cycle Stages Influence Beverage Purchases

Percent of All Dollars Spent Annually in Each Beverage Category, by Life Stage

	Carbonated Beverages	Coffee	Juices, Refrigerated	Soft drinks, Non-carb.	Bottled Water	All Remaining Carb. Bev/Diet	All Remaining Carb. Bev/Reg	Coffee, Liquid
Young singles (age 18–34)	2%	1%	2%	2%	2%	2%	1%	3%
Childless younger couples (two adults, 18–34)	4%	3%	4%	4%	6%	4%	4%	8%
New families (2 adults, 1 or more children <6)	5%	3%	5%	8%	6%	4%	5%	4%
Maturing families (2 adults, 1 or more children, not all <6 or +12)	26%	19%	22%	36%	22%	21%	30%	19%
Established families (1 or more children, all +12)	12%	9%	10%	10%	10%	9%	14%	12%
Middle-aged singles (35–54)	7%	5%	7%	4%	9%	9%	7%	7%
Middle-aged childless couples (2 adults, 35–54)	18%	17%	16%	14%	18%	19%	16%	18%
Empty-nesters (2 adults, +55, no children at home)	20%	32%	24%	17%	20%	24%	17%	21%
Older singles (55+)	7%	11%	10%	6%	7%	8%	6%	8%
Total	100%	100%	100%	100%	100%	100%	100%	100%

Source: *American Demographics,* "Drink Me" by Matthew Grimm. February 2000, pp. 62–63. Reprinted by permission of the publisher.

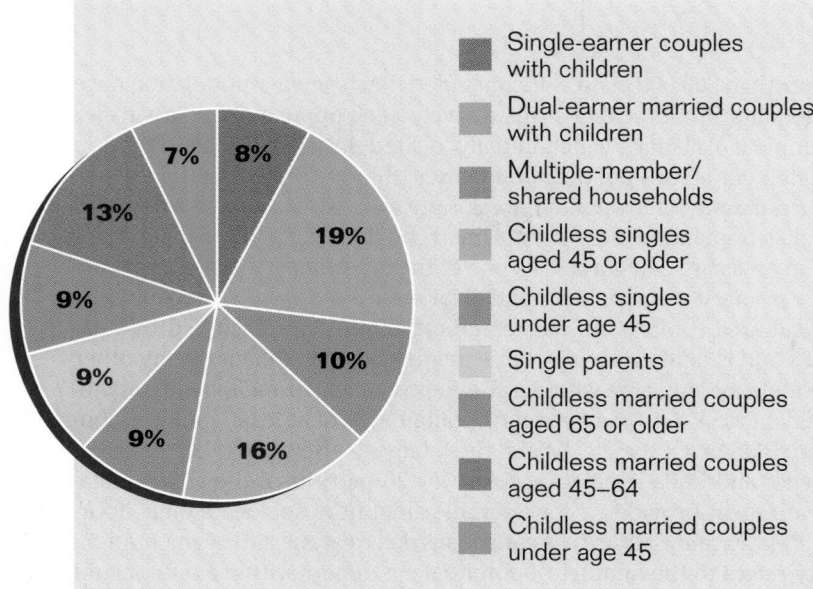

Single-earner couples with children

Dual-earner married couples with children

Multiple-member/ shared households

Childless singles aged 45 or older

Childless singles under age 45

Single parents

Childless married couples aged 65 or older

Childless married couples aged 45–64

Childless married couples under age 45

FIGURE 7.5
Family Life Cycle Stages as a Percentage of All Households

Source: Bureau of the Census, *Current Population Survey.*

needs for housing, appliances, food and beverages, automobiles, and recreational equipment. Using the information in Table 7.1, consider how life cycle stages affect the purchase of beverages.

Family life cycles can be broken down in various ways. Figure 7.5 shows a breakdown into nine categories. The composition of the American household in relation to family life cycle has changed. The "typical" American family of a single-earner married couple with children dropped from 21 percent of all households in 1970 to about 7 percent today, and the number of households in which one person lives alone or with unrelated people has increased from 23 percent to about 38 percent. Childless singles under age 45 headed just 3 percent of households in 1970, but their share has increased to about 10 percent today. People in a particular life cycle stage may have very specific needs that can be satisfied by precisely designed marketing mixes.

Marketers also use many other demographic variables. For instance, dictionary publishing companies segment markets by education level. Some insurance companies segment markets using occupation, targeting health insurance at college students and at younger workers with small employers that do not provide health coverage.

Geographic Variables. Geographic variables—climate, terrain, city size, population density, and urban/rural areas—also influence customer product needs. Markets may be divided into regions because one or more geographic variables can cause customers to differ from one region to another. A company selling products to a national market might divide the United States into the following regions: Pacific, Southwest, Central, Midwest, Southeast, Middle Atlantic, and New England. A firm operating in one or several states might regionalize its market by counties, cities, zip code areas, or other units.

City size can be an important segmentation variable. Some marketers focus efforts on cities of a certain size. For example, one franchised restaurant organization will not

Family Life Cycle Segmentation
Saab aims its Saab 9-5 Wagon at individuals in a specific stage of the family life cycle.

locate in cities of fewer than 200,000 people. It concluded that a smaller population base would result in inadequate profits. Other firms actively seek opportunities in smaller towns. A classic example is Wal-Mart, which initially located only in small towns.

Because cities often cut across political boundaries, the U.S. Bureau of the Census developed a system to classify metropolitan areas (any area with a city or urbanized area of at least 50,000 population and a total metropolitan population of at least 100,000). Metropolitan areas are categorized as one of the following: a metropolitan statistical area (MSA), a primary metropolitan statistical area (PMSA), or a consolidated metropolitan statistical area (CMSA). An MSA is an urbanized area encircled by non-metropolitan counties and is neither socially nor economically dependent on any other metropolitan area. A metropolitan area within a complex of at least 1 million inhabitants can elect to be named a PMSA. A CMSA is a metropolitan area of at least 1 million consisting of two or more PMSAs. Of the 20 CMSAs, the 5 largest—New York, Los Angeles, Chicago, San Francisco, and Philadelphia—account for 20 percent of the U.S. population. The federal government provides a considerable amount of socioeconomic information about MSAs, PMSAs, and CMSAs that can aid market analysis and segmentation.

market density The number of potential customers within a unit of land area

Market density refers to the number of potential customers within a unit of land area, such as a square mile. Although market density relates generally to population density, the correlation is not exact. For example, in two different geographic markets of approximately equal size and population, market density for office supplies would be much higher in one area if it contained a much greater proportion of business customers than the other area. Market density may be a useful segmentation variable because low-density markets often require different sales, advertising, and distribution activities than do high-density markets.

geodemographic segmentation Marketing segmentation that clusters people in zip code areas and smaller neighborhood units based on lifestyle and demographic information

A number of marketers are using geodemographic segmentation. **Geodemographic segmentation** clusters people in zip code areas and even smaller neighborhood units based on lifestyle information and especially demographic data, such as income, education, occupation, type of housing, ethnicity, family life cycle, and level of urbanization. These small, precisely described population clusters help marketers isolate demographic units as small as neighborhoods where the demand for specific products is strongest. Information companies such as Donnelley Marketing Information Services, Claritas, and C.A.C.I., Inc., provide geodemographic data services called Prospect Zone, PRIZM, and Acorn, respectively. PRIZM is based on a classification of the more than 500,000 U.S. neighborhoods into one of 40 cluster types, such as "shotguns and pickups," "money and brains," and "gray power."

micromarketing An approach to market segmentation in which organizations focus precise marketing efforts on very small geographic markets

Geodemographic segmentation allows marketers to engage in micromarketing. **Micromarketing** is the focusing of precise marketing efforts on very small geographic markets, such as community and even neighborhood markets. Providers of financial and health care services, retailers, and consumer products companies use micromarketing. Special advertising campaigns, promotions, retail-site location analyses, special pricing, and unique retail product offerings are a few examples of micromarketing facilitated through geodemographic segmentation.

Climate is commonly used as a geographic segmentation variable because of its broad impact on people's behavior and product needs. Product markets affected by climate include air-conditioning and heating equipment, clothing, gardening equipment, recreational products, and building materials.

Psychographic Variables. Marketers sometimes use psychographic variables, such as personality characteristics, motives, and lifestyles, to segment markets. A psychographic dimension can be used by itself to segment a market or combined with other types of segmentation variables.

Personality characteristics can be useful for segmentation when a product resembles many competing products and consumers' needs are not significantly related to other segmentation variables. However, segmenting a market according to personality traits can be risky. Although marketing practitioners have long believed consumer choice and product use vary with personality, until recently marketing research had indicated only weak relationships. It is hard to measure personality traits accurately, especially since most personality tests were developed for clinical use, not for segmentation purposes.

When appealing to a personality characteristic, marketers almost always select one that many people view positively. Individuals with this characteristic, as well as those who would like to have it, may be influenced to buy that marketer's brand. Marketers taking this approach do not worry about measuring how many people have the positively valued characteristic; they assume a sizable proportion of people in the target market either have or want to have it.

When motives are used to segment a market, the market is divided according to consumers' reasons for making a purchase. Personal appearance, affiliation, status, safety, and health are examples of motives affecting the types of products purchased and the choice of stores in which they are bought. For example, White Wave of Boulder, Colorado, uses health motives to segment the consumer market for Silk, its soy milk product. Sold in the dairy section of some 27,000 U.S. stores, Silk is low-fat, low-cholesterol, and protein-rich, and tastes like milk. Despite being priced much higher than cow's milk, Silk doubled its market share in just one year by targeting health-conscious milk drinkers.[10]

Lifestyle segmentation groups individuals according to how they spend their time, the importance of things in their surroundings (homes or jobs, for example), beliefs about themselves and broad issues, and some demographic characteristics, such as income and education.[11] Lifestyle analysis provides a broad view of buyers because it encompasses numerous characteristics related to people's activities (work, hobbies, entertainment, sports), interests (family, home, fashion, food, technology), and opinions (politics, social issues, education, the future).

One of the more popular programs studying lifestyles is conducted by the Stanford Research Institute's Value and Lifestyle Program (VALS). This program surveys American consumers to select groups with identifiable values and lifestyles. Initially, it identified three broad consumer groups: Outer-Directed, Inner-Directed,

BUILDING CUSTOMER RELATIONSHIPS

Who Is the NASCAR Customer?

The race is on to identify and reach specific groups of customers using lifestyle characteristics such as an interest in sports. In recent years, the National Association for Stock Car Auto Racing (NASCAR) has attracted the attention of major marketers who want to ride the wave of auto racing's growing popularity. McDonald's, Wrangler, Visa, United Parcel Service, Coca-Cola, and Home Depot are just some of the mainstream marketers joining car-related firms such as Goodyear and Pennzoil in working with NASCAR to market to racing fans.

But who exactly is the NASCAR customer? Research shows that 60 percent of NASCAR fans are male and 60 percent are married. Most are employed full time and are more likely than the "average" American to be machine operators or crafts workers. More than half have a household income of more than $50,000, and a whopping 72 percent buy from NASCAR's sponsors. An estimated 7 percent of all Americans consider themselves fiercely dedicated auto racing fans. These consumers invest more than six hours a week watching races and following racing news, and spend nearly $700 on NASCAR-related goods and services every year.

One reason for stock car racing's growing popularity as a sport and as a marketing vehicle is its wholesome family image. "Our drivers are accessible," explains NASCAR's vice president of marketing. "People think, 'These are good role models for my children.'" Fans also like to see the close cooperation and split-second timing needed by drivers and their pit crews. And although many fans may be unable to envision themselves slam-dunking a basketball in the NBA playoffs or slugging a homer in the World Series, they can more easily identify with drivers competing in Winston Cup car races. " "Everybody can drive a car,"' says another NASCAR executive. "It's even a kid's fantasy to drive."

Over the past decade, NASCAR has capitalized on the sport's growth by licensing the rights to put NASCAR logos on selected products. Today fans buy more than $1.2 billion of NASCAR-licensed products. Now NASCAR is seeking to expand its customer base by forging multi-year network television contracts to broadcast racing to 30 million American viewers. Some races are also being broadcast on Spanish radio stations, reaching yet another segment of the population. In turn, these moves have opened up new opportunities for marketers to ride the sport's popularity and reach their target markets through advertising, sponsorship, and licensing arrangements.

RAIN IS MEASURED IN INCHES.

SNOW IS MEASURED IN INCHES.

SO ARE FISH.

SIMMS

Lifestyle Segmentation
Simms fishing products, through advertisements such as the one shown here, are targeted at individuals seeking an outdoor leisure lifestyle.

and Need-Driven consumers. A VALS 2 classification categorizes consumers into five basic lifestyle groups: Strugglers, Action-Oriented, Status-Oriented, Principle-Oriented, and Actualizers. An expanded set of VALS 2 lifestyle groups appears in Figure 7.6, which shows the proportion of each group that participated in selected sports recently. Marketers of products related to inline skating, jet skiing, wave running, water biking, and mountain and rock climbing would most likely focus on the "actualizer" and "experiencer" lifestyle segments.[12] The VALS studies have been used to create products as well as to segment markets.

Many other lifestyle classification systems exist. Several companies, such as Experían's BehaviorBank, collect lifestyle data on millions of consumers.

Behavioristic Variables.   Firms can divide a market according to some feature of consumer behavior toward a product, commonly involving some aspect of product use. For example, a market may be separated into users—classified as heavy, moderate, or light—and nonusers. To satisfy a specific group, such as heavy users, marketers may create a distinctive product, set special prices, or initiate special promotion and distribution activities. Per capita consumption data help to identify different levels of usage. For example, economic census data show that per capita spending on building supplies at building-material stores varies widely across the United States, ranging from $537 per resident in New Hampshire to $29 per resident in Wyoming. This information helps companies like Home Depot plan expansion and resource allocation.

How customers use or apply products may also determine segmentation. To satisfy customers who use a product in a certain way, some feature—say, packaging, size, texture, or color—may be designed precisely to make the product easier to use, safer, or more convenient.

benefit segmentation The division of a market according to benefits that customers want from the product

Benefit segmentation is the division of a market according to benefits that consumers want from the product. Although most types of market segmentation assume a relationship between the variable and customers' needs, benefit segmentation differs in that the benefits customers seek *are* their product needs. For example, a customer

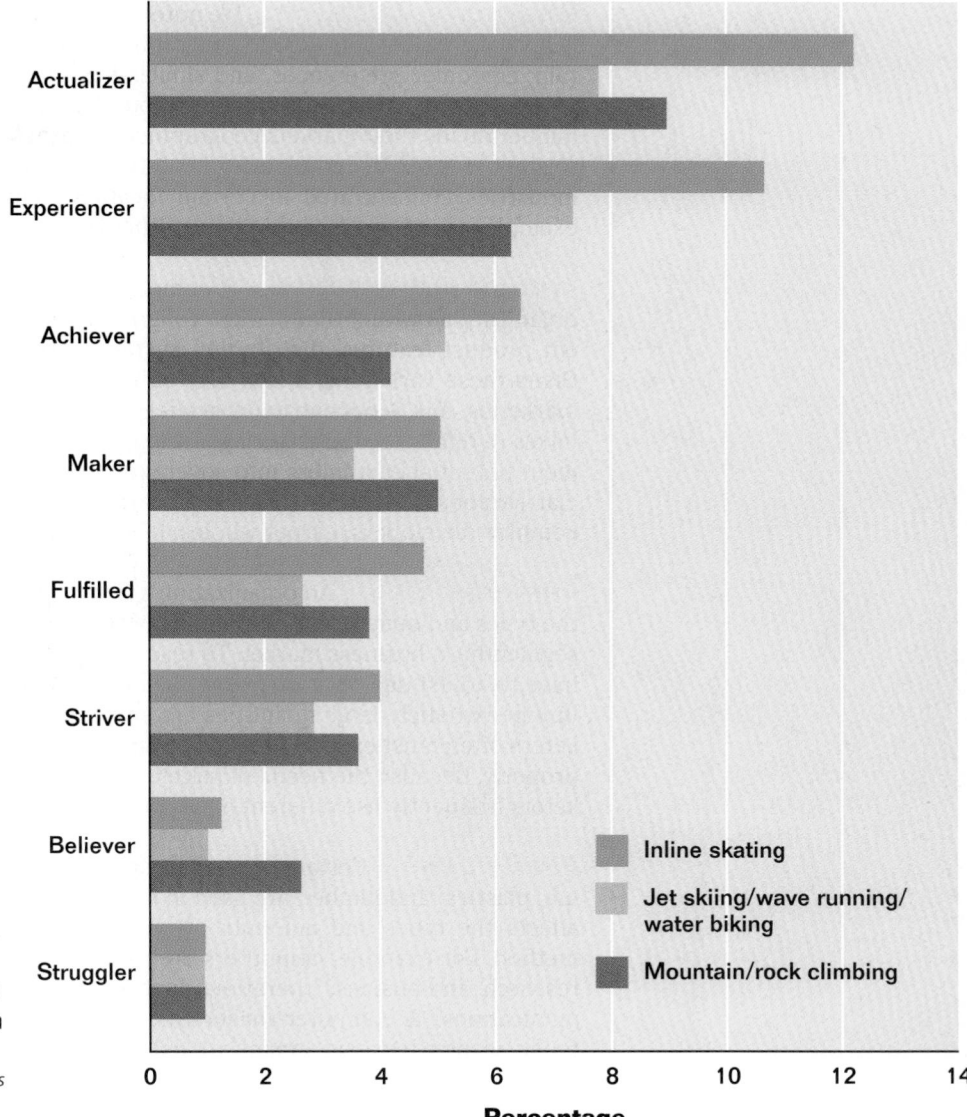

FIGURE 7.6
Percentage of U.S. Adults, Classified by VALS 2 Type, Who Participated in Selected Sports in 1996

Source: Reprinted from *American Demographics Magazine,* with permission. © 1997 PRIMEDIA Intertec, Stanford, CT.

who purchases over-the-counter cold relief medication may be specifically interested in two benefits: stopping a runny nose and relieving chest congestion. Thus, individuals are segmented directly according to their needs. By determining the desired benefits, marketers may be able to divide people into groups seeking certain sets of benefits. The effectiveness of such segmentation depends on three conditions: the benefits sought must be identifiable; using these benefits, marketers must be able to divide people into recognizable segments; and one or more of the resulting segments must be accessible to the firm's marketing efforts. Both Timberland and Avia, for example, segment the foot apparel market based on benefits sought.

As this discussion shows, consumer markets can be divided according to numerous characteristics. Business markets are segmented using different variables, as we will see in the following section.

Variables for Segmenting Business Markets

Like consumer markets, business markets are frequently segmented. Marketers segment business markets according to geographic location, type of organization, customer size, and product use.

Geographic Location.   We noted that the demand for some consumer products can vary considerably among geographic areas because of differences in climate, terrain, customer preferences, and similar factors. Demand for business products also varies according to geographic location. For example, producers of certain types of lumber divide their markets geographically because their customers' needs vary from region to region. Geographic segmentation may be especially appropriate for reaching industries concentrated in certain locations. Furniture and textile producers, for example, are concentrated in the Southeast.

Type of Organization.   A company sometimes segments a market by types of organizations within that market. Different types of organizations often require different product features, distribution systems, price structures, and selling strategies. Given these variations, a firm may either concentrate on a single segment with one marketing mix (concentration strategy) or focus on several groups with multiple mixes (a differentiated targeting strategy). A carpet producer, for example, could segment potential customers into several groups, such as automobile makers, commercial carpet contractors (firms that carpet large commercial buildings), apartment complex developers, carpet wholesalers, and large retail carpet outlets.

Customer Size.   An organization's size may affect its purchasing procedures and the types and quantities of products it wants. Size can thus be an effective variable for segmenting a business market. To reach a segment of a particular size, marketers may have to adjust one or more marketing mix components. For example, customers who buy in extremely large quantities are sometimes offered discounts. In addition, marketers often must expand personal selling efforts to serve large organizational buyers properly. Because the needs of large and small buyers tend to be quite distinct, marketers frequently use different marketing practices to reach various customer groups.

Product Use.   Certain products, especially basic raw materials like steel, petroleum, plastics, and lumber, are used in numerous ways. How a company uses products affects the types and amounts of products purchased, as well as the purchasing method. For example, computers are used for engineering purposes, basic scientific research, and business operations such as word processing, accounting, and telecommunications. A computer maker therefore may segment the computer market by types of use because organizations' needs for computer hardware and software depend on the purpose for which products are purchased.

Step 3: Develop Market Segment Profiles

A market segment profile describes the similarities among potential customers within a segment and explains the differences among people and organizations in different segments. A profile may cover such aspects as demographic characteristics, geographic factors, product benefits sought, lifestyles, brand preferences, and usage rates. Individuals and organizations within segments should be quite similar with respect to several characteristics and product needs and differ considerably from those within other market segments. Marketers use market segment profiles to assess the degree to which the organization's possible products can match or fit potential customers' product needs. Market segment profiles help marketers understand how a business can use its capabilities to serve potential customer groups.

The use of market segment profiles benefits marketers in several ways. Such profiles help a marketer determine which segment or segments are most attractive to the organization relative to the firm's strengths, weaknesses, objectives, and resources. While marketers may initially believe certain segments are quite attractive, development of market segment profiles may yield information that indicates the opposite. For the market segment or segments chosen by the organization, the information included in market segment profiles can be highly useful in making marketing decisions.

Step 4: Evaluate Relevant Market Segments

After analyzing the market segment profiles, a marketer is likely to identify several relevant market segments that require further analysis and eliminate certain segments from consideration. To further assess relevant market segments, several important factors, including sales estimates, competition, and estimated costs associated with each segment, should be analyzed.

Sales Estimates

Potential sales for a segment can be measured along several dimensions, including product level, geographic area, time, and level of competition.[13] With respect to product level, potential sales can be estimated for a specific product item (for example, Diet Coke) or an entire product line (Coca-Cola Classic, Caffeine-Free Coke, Diet Coke, Caffeine-Free Diet Coke, Cherry Coca-Cola, and Diet Cherry Coca-Cola comprise one product line). A manager must also determine the geographic area to be included in the estimate. In relation to time, sales estimates can be short range (one year or less), medium range (one to five years), or long range (longer than five years). The competitive level specifies whether sales are being estimated for a single firm or for an entire industry.

Market potential is the total amount of a product, for all firms in an industry, that customers will purchase within a specified period at a specific level of industry-wide marketing activity. Market potential can be stated in terms of dollars or units. A segment's market potential is affected by economic, sociocultural, and other environmental forces. Marketers must assume a certain general level of marketing effort in the industry when they estimate market potential. The specific level of marketing effort varies from one firm to another, but the sum of all firms' marketing activities equals industrywide marketing efforts. A marketing manager must also consider whether and to what extent industry marketing efforts will change.

Company sales potential is the maximum percentage of market potential that an individual firm within an industry can expect to obtain for a specific product. Several factors influence company sales potential for a market segment. First, the market potential places absolute limits on the size of the company's sales potential. Second, the magnitude of industrywide marketing activities has an indirect but definite impact on the company's sales potential. Those activities have a direct bearing on the size of the market potential. When Domino's Pizza advertises home-delivered pizza, for example, it indirectly promotes pizza in general; its commercials may indirectly help sell Pizza Hut's and other competitors' home-delivered pizza. Third, the intensity and effectiveness of a company's marketing activities relative to those of its competitors affect the size of the company's sales potential. If a company spends twice as much as any of its competitors on marketing efforts and if each dollar spent is more effective in generating sales, the firm's sales potential will be quite high compared to its competitors'.

There are two general approaches to measuring company sales potential: breakdown and buildup. In the **breakdown approach,** the marketing manager first develops a general economic forecast for a specific time period. Next, market potential is estimated on the basis of this economic forecast. The company's sales potential is then derived from the general economic forecast and estimate of market potential. In the **buildup approach,** the marketing manager begins by estimating how much of a product a potential buyer in a specific geographic area, such as a sales territory, will purchase in a given period. The manager then multiplies that amount by the total number of potential buyers in that area. The manager performs the same calculation for each geographic area in which the firm sells products and then adds the totals for each area to calculate market potential. To determine company sales potential, the manager must estimate, based on planned levels of company marketing activities, the proportion of the total market potential the company can obtain.

market potential The total amount of a product that customers will purchase within a specified period at a specific level of industry-wide marketing activity

company sales potential The maximum percentage of market potential that an individual firm can expect to obtain for a specific product

breakdown approach Measuring company sales potential based on a general economic forecast for a specific period and the market potential derived from it

buildup approach Measuring company sales potential by estimating how much of a product a potential buyer in a specific geographic area will purchase in a given period, multiplying the estimate by the number of potential buyers, and adding the totals of all the geographic areas considered

Competitive Assessment

Besides obtaining sales estimates, it is crucial to assess competitors already operating in the segments being considered. Without competitive information, sales estimates may be misleading. A market segment that seems attractive based on sales estimates may prove to be much less so following a competitive assessment. Such an assessment should ask several questions about competitors: How many exist? What are their strengths and weaknesses? Do several competitors have major market shares and together dominate the segment? Can our company create a marketing mix to compete effectively against competitors' marketing mixes? Is it likely that new competitors will enter this segment? If so, how will they affect our firm's ability to compete successfully? Answers to such questions are important for proper assessment of the competition in potential market segments.

The actions of a national food company that considered entering the dog food market illustrate the importance of competitive assessment. Through a segmentation study, the food company determined that dog owners can be divided into three segments according to how they view their dogs and dog foods. One group saw their dogs as performing a definite utilitarian function, such as protecting family members, playing with children, guarding the property, or herding farm animals. These people wanted a low-priced, nutritional dog food and were not interested in a wide variety of flavors. The second segment of dog owners treated their dogs as companions and family members. These individuals were willing to pay relatively high prices for dog foods and wanted a variety of types and flavors so their dogs would not get bored. Dog owners in the third segment were found to actually hate their dogs. These people wanted the cheapest dog food they could buy and were not concerned with nutrition, flavor, or variety. The food company examined the extent to which competitive brands were serving all these dog owners and found that each segment contained at least three well-entrenched competing brands, which together dominated the segment. The food company's management decided not to enter the dog food market because of the strength of the competing brands.

Cost Estimates

To fulfill the needs of a target segment, an organization must develop and maintain a marketing mix that precisely meets the wants and needs of individuals and organizations in that segment. Developing and maintaining such a mix can be expensive. Distinctive product features, attractive package design, generous product warranties, extensive advertising, attractive promotional offers, competitive prices, and high-quality personal service consume considerable organizational resources. Indeed, to reach certain segments, the costs may be so high that a marketer may see the segment as inaccessible. Another cost consideration is whether the organization can effectively reach a segment at costs equal to or below competitors' costs. If the firm's costs are likely to be higher, it will be unable to compete in that segment in the long run.

Step 5: Select Specific Target Markets

An important initial issue to consider in selecting a target market is whether customers' needs differ enough to warrant the use of market segmentation. If segmentation analysis shows customer needs to be fairly homogeneous, the firm's management may decide to use the undifferentiated approach, discussed earlier. However, if customer needs are heterogeneous, which is much more likely, one or more target markets must be selected. On the other hand, marketers may decide not to enter and compete in any of the segments.

Assuming one or more segments offer significant opportunities for the organization to achieve its objectives, marketers must decide in which segments to participate.

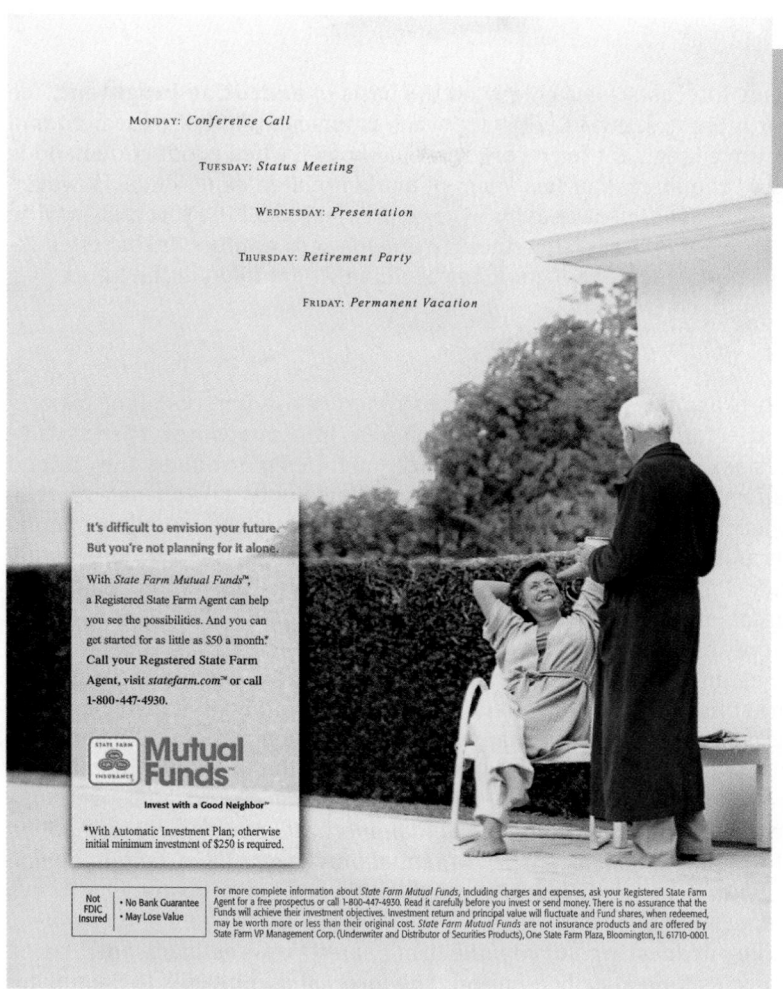

MONDAY: *Conference Call*

TUESDAY: *Status Meeting*

WEDNESDAY: *Presentation*

THURSDAY: *Retirement Party*

FRIDAY: *Permanent Vacation*

It's difficult to envision your future.
But you're not planning for it alone.

With *State Farm Mutual Funds*™,
a Registered State Farm Agent can help
you see the possibilities. And you can
get started for as little as $50 a month.*
Call your Registered State Farm
Agent, visit *statefarm.com*™ or call
1-800-447-4930.

Mutual Funds™

Invest with a Good Neighbor™

*With Automatic Investment Plan; otherwise
initial minimum investment of $250 is required.

Not FDIC Insured • No Bank Guarantee • May Lose Value

For more complete information about *State Farm Mutual Funds*, including charges and expenses, ask your Registered State Farm Agent for a free prospectus or call 1-800-447-4930. Read it carefully before you invest or send money. There is no assurance that the Funds will achieve their investment objectives. Investment return and principal value will fluctuate and Fund shares, when redeemed, may be worth more or less than their original cost. *State Farm Mutual Funds* are not insurance products and are offered by State Farm VP Management Corp. (Underwriter and Distributor of Securities Products), One State Farm Plaza, Bloomington, IL 61710-0001.

Selecting Specific Target Markets
State Farm carefully selected the target market for its Mutual Funds—adults with specific financial planning needs.

Ordinarily, information gathered in the previous step—about sales estimates, competitors, and cost estimates—requires careful consideration in this final step to determine long-term profit opportunities. Also, the firm's management must investigate whether the organization has the financial resources, managerial skills, employee expertise, and facilities to enter and compete effectively in selected segments. Furthermore, the requirements of some market segments may be at odds with the firm's overall objectives, and the possibility of legal problems, conflicts with interest groups, and technological advancements could make certain segments unattractive. In addition, when prospects for long-term growth are taken into account, some segments may appear very attractive and others less desirable.

Selecting appropriate target markets is important to an organization's adoption and use of the marketing concept philosophy. Identifying the right target market is the key to implementing a successful marketing strategy, whereas failure to do so can lead to low sales, high costs, and severe financial losses. A careful target market analysis places an organization in a better position to both serve customers' needs and achieve its objectives.

Developing Sales Forecasts

sales forecast   The amount of a product a company expects to sell during a specific period at a specified level of marketing activities

A **sales forecast** is the amount of a product the company actually expects to sell during a specific period at a specified level of marketing activities. The sales forecast differs from the company sales potential. It concentrates on what actual sales will be at a certain level of company marketing effort, whereas the company sales potential assesses what sales are possible at various levels of marketing activities, assuming certain environmental conditions will exist. Businesses use the sales forecast for planning, organizing, implementing, and controlling their activities. The success of numerous activities depends on this forecast's accuracy. Common problems in companies that fail are improper planning and lack of realistic sales forecasts. Overly ambitious sales forecasts can lead to overbuying, overinvestment, and higher costs.

To forecast sales, a marketer can choose from a number of forecasting methods, some arbitrary and others more scientific, complex, and time consuming. A firm's choice of method or methods depends on the costs involved, type of product, market characteristics, time span of the forecast, purposes of the forecast, stability of the historical sales data, availability of required information, managerial preferences, and forecasters' expertise and experience.[14] Common forecasting techniques fall into five categories: executive judgment, surveys, time series analysis, regression analysis, and market tests.

Executive Judgment

executive judgment Sales forecasting based on the intuition of one or more executives

At times, a company forecasts sales chiefly on the basis of **executive judgment,** the intuition of one or more executives. This approach is unscientific but expedient and inexpensive. Executive judgment may work reasonably well when product demand is relatively stable and the forecaster has years of market-related experience. However, because intuition is swayed most heavily by recent experience, the forecast may be overly optimistic or overly pessimistic. Another drawback to intuition is that the forecaster has only past experience as a guide for deciding where to go in the future.

Surveys

customer forecasting survey A survey of customers regarding the quantities of products they intend to buy during a specific period

Another way to forecast sales is to question customers, sales personnel, or experts regarding their expectations about future purchases. In a **customer forecasting survey,** marketers ask customers what types and quantities of products they intend to buy during a specific period. This approach may be useful to a business with relatively few customers. For example, Intel, which markets to a limited number of companies (primarily computer manufacturers), could conduct customer forecasting surveys effectively. PepsiCo, in contrast, has millions of customers and could not feasibly use a customer survey to forecast future sales.

Customer surveys have several drawbacks. Customers must be able and willing to make accurate estimates of future product requirements. Although some organizational buyers can estimate their anticipated purchases accurately from historical buying data and their own sales forecasts, many cannot make such estimates. In addition, customers may not want to take part in a survey. Occasionally a few respondents give answers they know are incorrect, making survey results inaccurate. Moreover, customer surveys reflect buying intentions, not actual purchases. Customers' intentions may not be well formulated, and even when potential purchasers have definite buying intentions, they do not necessarily follow through on them. Finally, customer surveys consume much time and money.

In a **sales force forecasting survey,** the firm's salespeople estimate anticipated sales in their territories for a specified period. The forecaster combines these territorial estimates to arrive at a tentative forecast. A marketer may survey the sales staff for several reasons. The most important is that the sales staff is closer to customers on a daily basis than other company personnel and therefore should know more about customers' future product needs. Moreover, when sales representatives assist in developing the forecast, they are more likely to work toward its achievement. Another advantage of this method is that forecasts can be prepared for single territories, divisions consisting of several territories, regions made up of multiple divisions, and the total geographic market. Thus, the method provides sales forecasts from the smallest geographic sales unit to the largest.

sales force forecasting survey A survey of a firm's sales force regarding anticipated sales in their territories for a specified period

A sales force survey also has limitations. Salespeople may be too optimistic or pessimistic because of recent experiences. In addition, salespeople tend to underestimate sales potential in their territories when they believe their sales goals will be determined by their forecasts. They also dislike paperwork because it takes up time that could be spent selling. If preparation of a territorial sales forecast is time consuming, the sales staff may not do the job adequately.

Nonetheless, sales force surveys can be effective under certain conditions. The salespeople as a group must be accurate, or at least consistent, estimators. If the aggregate forecast is consistently over or under actual sales, the marketer who develops the final forecast can make the necessary adjustments. Assuming the survey is well administered, the sales force can have the satisfaction of helping to establish reasonable sales goals and the assurance that its forecasts are not being used to set sales quotas.

expert forecasting survey Sales forecasts prepared by experts such as economists, management consultants, advertising executives, college professors, or other persons outside the firm

When a company wants an **expert forecasting survey,** it hires professionals to help prepare the sales forecast. These experts are usually economists, management consultants, advertising executives, college professors, or other persons outside the firm with solid experience in a specific market. Drawing on this experience and their analyses of available information about the company and the market, experts prepare and present forecasts or answer questions regarding a forecast. Using experts is expedient and relatively inexpensive. However, because they work outside the firm, these forecasters may be less motivated than company personnel to do an effective job.

A more complex form of the expert forecasting survey incorporates the Delphi technique. The **Delphi technique** is a procedure in which experts create initial forecasts, submit them to the company for averaging, and have the results returned to them so that they can make individual refined forecasts. The premise is that the experts will use the averaged results when making refined forecasts and that these forecasts will be in a narrower range. The procedure may be repeated several times until the experts, each working separately, reach a consensus on the forecasts. The ultimate goal in using the Delphi technique is to develop a highly accurate sales forecast.

Time Series Analysis

With **time series analysis,** the forecaster uses the firm's historical sales data to discover a pattern or patterns in the firm's sales over time. If a pattern is found, it can be used to forecast sales. This forecasting method assumes that past sales patterns will continue in the future. The accuracy, and thus usefulness, of time series analysis hinges on the validity of this assumption.

In a time series analysis, a forecaster usually performs four types of analyses: trend, cycle, seasonal, and random factor. **Trend analysis** focuses on aggregate sales data, such as the company's annual sales figures, covering a period of many years to determine whether annual sales are generally rising, falling, or staying about the same. Through **cycle analysis,** a forecaster analyzes sales figures (often monthly sales data) from a period of three to five years to ascertain whether sales fluctuate in a consistent, periodic manner. When performing **seasonal analysis,** the analyst studies daily, weekly, or monthly sales figures to evaluate the degree to which seasonal factors, such as climate and holiday activities, influence sales. In a **random factor analysis,** the forecaster attempts to attribute erratic sales variations to random, nonrecurrent events, such as a regional power failure, a natural disaster, or political unrest in a foreign market. After performing each of these analyses, the forecaster combines the results to develop the sales forecast. Time series analysis is an effective forecasting method for products with reasonably stable demand, but not for products with highly erratic demand.

Regression Analysis

Like time series analysis, regression analysis requires the use of historical sales data. In **regression analysis,** the forecaster seeks to find a relationship between past sales (the dependent variable) and one or more independent variables, such as population, per capita income, or gross domestic product. Simple regression analysis uses one independent variable, whereas multiple regression analysis includes two or more independent variables. The objective of regression analysis is to develop a mathematical formula that accurately describes a relationship between the firm's sales and one or more variables; however, the formula indicates only an association, not a causal relationship. Once an accurate formula is established, the analyst plugs the necessary information into the formula to derive the sales forecast.

Regression analysis is useful when a precise association can be established. However, a forecaster seldom finds a perfect one. Furthermore, this method can be used only when available historical sales data are extensive. Thus, regression analysis is futile for forecasting sales of new products.

Market Tests

A **market test** involves making a product available to buyers in one or more test areas and measuring purchases and consumer responses to distribution, promotion, and price. Test areas are often cities with populations of 200,000 to 500,000, but can be larger metropolitan areas or towns with populations of 50,000 to 200,000. A market test provides information about consumers' actual, rather than intended, purchases.

Delphi technique A procedure in which experts create initial forecasts, submit them to the company for averaging, and then refine the forecasts

time series analysis A forecasting method that uses historical sales data to discover patterns in the firm's sales over time and generally involves trend, cycle, seasonal, and random factor analyses

trend analysis An analysis that focuses on aggregate sales data over a period of many years to determine general trends in annual sales

cycle analysis An analysis of sales figures for a period of three to five years to ascertain whether sales fluctuate in a consistent, periodic manner

seasonal analysis An analysis of daily, weekly, or monthly sales figures to evaluate the degree to which seasonal factors influence sales

random factor analysis An analysis attempting to attribute erratic sales variation to random, nonrecurrent events

regression analysis A method of predicting sales based on finding a relationship between past sales and one or more variables, such as population or income

market test Making a product available to buyers in one or more test areas and measuring purchases and consumer responses

In addition, purchase volume can be evaluated in relation to the intensity of other marketing activities—advertising, in-store promotions, pricing, packaging, and distribution. Forecasters base their sales estimate for larger geographic units on customer response in test areas.

Because it does not require historical sales data, a market test is effective for forecasting sales of new products or sales of existing products in new geographic areas. A market test also gives a marketer an opportunity to test various elements of the marketing mix. However, these tests are often time consuming and expensive. In addition, a marketer cannot be certain that consumer response during a market test represents the total market response or that such a response will continue in the future.

Using Multiple Forecasting Methods

Although some businesses depend on a single sales forecasting method, most firms use several techniques. Sometimes a company is forced to use several methods when marketing diverse product lines, but even for a single product line several forecasts may be needed, especially when the product is sold to different market segments. Thus, a producer of automobile tires may rely on one technique to forecast tire sales for new cars and on another to forecast sales of replacement tires. Variation in the length of needed forecasts may call for several forecasting methods. A firm that employs one method for a short-range forecast may find it inappropriate for long-range forecasting. Sometimes a marketer verifies results of one method by using one or more other methods and comparing outcomes.

Summary

A market is an aggregate of people who, as individuals or as organizations, have needs for products in a product class and have the ability, willingness, and authority to purchase such products.

In general, marketers employ a five-step process when selecting a target market. Step 1 is to identify the appropriate targeting strategy. When a company designs a single marketing mix and directs it at the entire market for a particular product, it is using an undifferentiated targeting strategy. The undifferentiated strategy is effective in a homogeneous market, whereas a heterogeneous market needs to be segmented through a concentrated targeting strategy or a differentiated targeting strategy. Both these strategies divide markets into segments consisting of individuals, groups, or organizations that have one or more similar characteristics and so can be linked to similar product needs. When using a concentrated strategy, an organization directs marketing efforts toward a single market segment through one marketing mix. With a differentiated targeting strategy, an organization directs customized marketing efforts at two or more segments.

Certain conditions must exist for effective market segmentation. First, customers' needs for the product should be heterogeneous. Second, the segments of the market should be identifiable and divisible. Third, the total market should be divided so that segments can be compared with respect to estimated sales, costs, and profits. Fourth, at least one segment must have enough profit potential to justify developing and maintaining a special marketing mix for that segment. Fifth, the firm must be able to reach the chosen segment with a particular marketing mix.

Step 2 is determining which segmentation variables to use. Segmentation variables are the characteristics of individuals, groups, or organizations used to divide a total market into segments. The segmentation variable should relate to customers' needs for, uses of, or behavior toward the product. Segmentation variables for consumer markets can be grouped into four categories: demographic (e.g., age, gender, income, ethnicity, family life cycle), geographic (population, market density, climate), psychographic (personality traits, motives, lifestyles), and behavioristic (volume usage, end use, expected benefits, brand loyalty, price sensitivity). Variables for segmenting business markets include geographic location, type of organization, customer size, and product use.

Step 3 in the target market selection process is to develop market segment profiles. Such profiles describe the similarities among potential customers within a segment and explain the differences among people and organizations in different market segments. Step 4 is evaluating relevant market segments, which requires that several important factors—including sales estimates, competition, and estimated costs associated with each segment—be determined and analyzed. Step 5 involves the actual selection of specific target markets. In this final step, the company considers whether customers' needs differ enough to warrant segmentation and which segments to focus on.

A sales forecast is the amount of a product the company actually expects to sell during a specific period at a specified level of marketing activities. To forecast sales, marketers can choose from a number of methods. The choice depends on various factors, including the costs involved, type of product, market characteristics, and time span and purposes of the forecast. There are five categories of forecasting techniques: executive judgment, surveys, time series analysis, regression analysis, and market tests. Executive judgment is based on the intuition of one or more executives. Surveys include customer, sales force, and expert forecasting surveys. Time series analysis uses the firm's historical sales data to discover

patterns in the firm's sales over time and employs four major types of analyses: trend, cycle, seasonal, and random factor. With regression analysis, forecasters attempt to find a relationship between past sales and one or more independent variables. Market testing involves making a product available to buyers in one or more test areas and measuring purchases and consumer responses to distribution, promotion, and price. Many companies employ multiple forecasting methods.

Important Terms

Consumer market
Business market
Undifferentiated targeting
  strategy
Homogeneous market
Heterogeneous market
Market segmentation
Market segment
Concentrated targeting
  strategy
Differentiated targeting
  strategy
Segmentation variables
Market density
Geodemographic
  segmentation
Micromarketing
Benefit segmentation
Market potential

Company sales potential
Breakdown approach
Buildup approach
Sales forecast
Executive judgment
Customer forecasting
  survey
Sales force forecasting
  survey
Expert forecasting survey
Delphi technique
Time series analysis
Trend analysis
Cycle analysis
Seasonal analysis
Random factor analysis
Regression analysis
Market test

Discussion and Review Questions

1. What is a market? What are the requirements for a market?
2. In your local area, identify a group of people with unsatisfied product needs who represent a market. Could this market be reached by a business organization? Why or why not?
3. Outline the five major steps in the target market selection process.
4. What is an undifferentiated strategy? Under what conditions is it most useful? Describe a present market situation in which a company is using an undifferentiated strategy. Is the business successful? Why or why not?
5. What is market segmentation? Describe the basic conditions required for effective segmentation. Identify several firms that use market segmentation.
6. List the differences between concentrated and differentiated strategies, and describe the advantages and disadvantages of each.
7. Identify and describe four major categories of variables that can be used to segment consumer markets. Give examples of product markets that are segmented by variables in each category.

8. What dimensions are used to segment business markets?
9. Define geodemographic segmentation. Identify several types of firms that might employ this type of market segmentation, and explain why.
10. What is a market segment profile? Why is it an important step in the target market selection process?
11. Describe the important factors that marketers should analyze to evaluate market segments.
12. Why is a marketer concerned about sales potential when trying to select a target market?
13. Why is selecting appropriate target markets important to an organization that wants to adopt the marketing concept philosophy?
14. What is a sales forecast? Why is it important?
15. What are the two primary types of surveys a company might use to forecast sales? Why would a company use an outside expert forecasting survey?
16. Under what conditions are market tests useful for sales forecasting? Discuss the advantages and disadvantages of market tests.
17. Discuss the benefits of using multiple forecasting methods.

Application Questions

1. MTV Latino targets the growing Hispanic market in the United States. Identify another product marketed to a distinct target market. Describe the target market, and explain how the marketing mix appeals specifically to that group.
2. Generally, marketers use one of three basic targeting strategies to focus on a target market: (1) undifferentiated, (2) concentrated, or (3) differentiated. Locate an article that describes the targeting strategy of a particular organization. Describe the target market, and explain the strategy being used to reach that market.
3. The stereo market may be segmented according to income and age. Name two ways the market for each of the following products might be segmented.
   a. Candy bars
   b. Travel agency services
   c. Bicycles
   d. Hair spray
4. If you were using a time series analysis to forecast sales for your company for the next year, how would you use the following sets of sales figures?

a.

1993	$145,000	1998	$149,000
1994	$144,000	1999	$148,000
1995	$147,000	2000	$180,000
1996	$145,000	2001	$191,000
1997	$148,000	2002	$227,000

b.

	2000	2001	2002
Jan.	$12,000	$14,000	$16,000
Feb.	$13,000	$14,000	$15,500
Mar.	$12,000	$14,000	$17,000
Apr.	$13,000	$15,000	$17,000
May	$15,000	$17,000	$20,000
June	$18,000	$18,000	$21,000
July	$18,500	$18,000	$21,500
Aug.	$18,500	$19,000	$22,000
Sep.	$17,000	$18,000	$21,000
Oct.	$16,000	$15,000	$19,000
Nov.	$13,000	$14,000	$19,000
Dec.	$14,000	$15,000	$18,000

c. 2000 sales increased 21.2 percent (opened an additional store in 2000)
2000 sales increased 18.8 percent (opened another store in 2002)

Internet Exercise & Resources

Visit **www.prideferrell.com** for resources to help you master the material in this chapter, plus materials that will help you expand your marketing knowledge, including: Internet exercise updates, ACE self-tests, hotlinks to companies featured in this chapter, and much more.

iExplore

iExplore is an Internet company that offers a variety of travel and adventure products. Learn more about its goods, services, and travel advice through its website at

http://www.iexplore.com

1. Based on the information provided at the website, what are some of iExplore's basic products?

2. What market segments does iExplore appear to be targeting with its website? What segmentation variables are being used to segment these markets?

3. How does iExplore appeal to comparison shoppers?

VIDEO CASE 7.1

BuyandHold.com Is Bullish on Smaller Investors

Whether the financial markets go up or down, BuyandHold.com's strategy of targeting smaller, more cost-conscious investors is paying dividends. Headed by CEO and cofounder Peter E. Breen, New York-based BuyandHold.com launched its online brokerage site in 1999 with the goal of offering consumers affordable access to stocks and mutual funds. "Wall Street put up a lot of different barriers for people," Breen notes. "BuyandHold.com came along and took all those barriers down."

The financial barriers are all but gone, thanks to Buyandhold.com's bargain pricing: low even when compared with the commissions charged by deep-discount Web-only brokers. Customers pay as little as $1.99 per trade when they buy or sell securities, and they can open an account with just $20.

Moreover, customers can buy securities according to the amount they have to invest, even if this means buying a fraction of a share. In contrast, traditional brokerages prefer trades made in 100-share blocks or at least full-share lots.

Pricing isn't the only difference between BuyandHold.com and other brokerage firms. The company also focuses on an unusual target market. Merrill Lynch and other full-service firms generally target investors with larger portfolios who want considerable investment advice and personal assistance; DirecTrade and competing online brokers target day traders and other active investors who frequently buy and sell. In contrast, BuyandHold.com aims for lower-income consumers who can afford to build a portfolio only little by little and see investing as a way to meet a long-term need such as financing a child's college education or saving for retirement. "Most of our customers embrace the BuyandHold philosophy of investing," explains CEO Breen. "They invest regularly, adding to their portfolios weekly, monthly, or quarterly, regardless of market conditions." In fact, during a recent market dip, BuyandHold.com's customers kept right on buying, even as customers of other firms, concerned about short-term losses, frantically sold their holdings.

The only way BuyandHold.com can offer rock-bottom pricing to serve its target segment is to keep costs as low as possible. One way it does this is by bundling all the orders it receives and going into the market to buy and sell just twice a day, once in mid-morning and again in mid-afternoon. Although this process minimizes trading costs, it also limits the customer's ability to take advantage of changing market conditions and place trades at specific prices. Another way BuyandHold.com keeps costs down is by limiting its selection of stocks and mutual funds. Unlike mainstream brokers, which allow investors to choose from a much wider selection of securities, BuyandHold.com offers stock from fewer than 5,000 public companies.

However, low cost doesn't mean no service. BuyandHold.com maintains an online library for customers who want to learn more about investing and to investigate particular securities. It also promotes an automated plan that enables customers to electronically transfer funds and make small investments on a set schedule throughout the year. And the company has won several "Best of the Web" awards from business and financial services publications.

By targeting just one consumer segment, BuyandHold.com's management has the opportunity to learn a great deal about its market. Breen and his senior managers, for example, found out through feedback that some customers wanted a pricing alternative for more active trading. As a result, the firm changed its pricing strategy to add a $9.99 flat monthly fee covering unlimited trades.

Management also realized that many cost-conscious investors were saving money by buying shares directly from public companies rather than through brokers. In response, the firm established the Virtual Direct Stock Purchase Plan. Under this plan, participating companies like Walt Disney post an online link to a special BuyandHold.com webpage where consumers can set up accounts and buy stock. The companies save money because they don't have to prepare and mail customer statements, and consumers can stick with their investment choices or trade in additional securities at a low price.

Through careful targeting and ongoing innovation, BuyandHold.com attracted 200,000 accounts in its first 15 months of operation. However, the firm now faces increased competitive pressures. ShareBuilder.com, which also targets buy-and-hold investors, offers low buying commissions and more securities. On the other hand, it charges much more for sell orders and executes trades just once a week, further limiting customers' flexibility. Other rivals are entering the market with their own versions of affordable investment services. In the coming years, BuyandHold.com will have to use all its marketing savvy to continue attracting cost-conscious consumers who want to invest for the long term.[15]

QUESTIONS FOR DISCUSSION

1. What type of general targeting strategy is BuyandHold.com using? Explain.
2. What segmentation variables does BuyandHold.com use?
3. As more competitors start marketing to the cost-conscious segment, would you recommend that BuyandHold.com change its targeting strategy? Why or why not?

CASE 7.2

LifeSpring Targets Seniors with a Taste for Nutrition

Once upon a time, seniors with diabetes or heart disease had no choice but to settle for bland, boring meals. How times change! Now people with chronic heart conditions can order tasty and nutritionally balanced frozen meals, spiced with sound dietary advice, for delivery direct to their doorsteps.

The culinary mastermind behind these special meals is LifeSpring Nutrition Solutions, a California-based company with financial backing from the Monsanto life sciences division of Pharmacia. At LifeSpring—formerly known as LifeSource—chefs, physicians, gerontologists, and nutritionists collaborate on mouth-watering prepared foods to tempt the palates of seniors who have diabetes, congestive heart failure, and heart disease. These ready-to-heat meals taste good and pack a huge nutritional punch, exceeding the requirements set by the American Heart Association, National Institutes of

Health, and American Diabetes Association. A study by Tufts New England Medical Center confirms that the LifeSpring program does lower cholesterol and other heart disease risk factors.

Like an upscale version of Meals on Wheels, LifeSpring delivers such elegant entrees as Grilled Chicken Broccoli Alfredo, Roast Turkey with Cranberry Wild Rice Pilaf, and Salmon Ravioli with Artichokes, Spinach, and Tomatoes, all in microwavable containers. To start the meal, LifeSpring offers hearty soups, such as Tortellini Minestrone and Creamy Chicken Soup with Spring Vegetables. For dessert, it offers "smoothies" (choices include fruit flavors and chocolates) that are both healthy and satisfying. By design, LifeSpring foods minimize fat, sodium, and calories while maximizing flavor and nutritional value.

LifeSpring's segmentation strategy is to divide the market using a blend of demographic, geographic, psychographic, and behavioristic variables. The key demographic variables are age (people over 50) and income (affluent seniors able to afford a $5.50 meal). According to the company's research, some 56 million U.S. seniors have heart disease, and around 14 million have diabetes. By 2005, the U.S. senior population will grow to 85 million, with more than three-quarters of those over 65 suffering from serious chronic illnesses. This fast-growing senior segment is also relatively well off, collectively holding about 70 percent of the net worth of the country's households, or almost $9 million. Moreover, seniors' spending on health care tops $525 billion, mostly for chronic health conditions like heart disease, which hints at the enormous potential for sales of health-related products such as vitamin-rich prepared foods.

The key geographic variable in LifeSpring's recipe is location. To ensure that its meals arrive without the defrosting and refreezing problems that can damage food quality, LifeSpring has uniformed drivers in refrigerated trucks delivering orders to each customer's home or office. This personal delivery service is available in San Francisco, Los Angeles, southeastern Florida, Cleveland, and Akron. Customers outside those areas can order on the Web and receive meals overnight via FedEx.

LifeSpring's key psychographic variable is lifestyle, which is directly connected to the health of its customers. Seniors with heart conditions or diabetes often have less active lifestyles. Those who lack "the energy or the means to get to a conventional grocery store," notes John Hale, LifeSpring's chief operating officer, appreciate home delivery of meals.

In addition, the company is segmenting the senior market using the behavioristic variable of benefit expectations. This segmentation strategy

allows LifeSpring to target seniors who want what COO Hale calls "diet freedom," a compelling benefit for those who have medical conditions that dictate certain dietary restrictions. "We're offering customization of diets to reach individuals' health goals, and if they want to substitute 15, 20, or 50 percent of their diet, it's up to them," Hale says.

LifeSpring uses a value-added approach in that it delivers more than meals: it also delivers easy access to free information and advice about nutrition. When customers call the firm's toll-free number to order meals, they have the option to speak with a registered dietician about menu planning, dietary needs, and other concerns. LifeSpring's information systems track each customer's ordering patterns, thus speeding reorders. Even the product's packaging has been specially designed for this market segment, with larger type on the heating instructions and a microwavable container that stays cool as the contents heat up.

To gauge interest in its products and develop accurate sales forecasts, LifeSpring started test marketing its meals in the San Francisco area. To support this test, the company planned public relations events such as tasting parties in retirement communities. It also used direct-response marketing to stimulate demand and encourage trial usage. Once the brand was established in California, the company selected additional markets for home delivery and developed an Internet-based order system to reach national markets. The company recently expanded its menu by acquiring McDougall's Right Foods, which makes organic, low-fat one-cup meals. With an appetite for growth, LifeSpring is using effective targeting to take advantage of demographic trends that suggest higher demand is still ahead.[16]

QUESTIONS FOR DISCUSSION

1. What kind of targeting strategy is LifeSpring using?
2. How can LifeSpring use micromarketing to focus on geographic markets?
3. If LifeSpring formulates plans to do business with 1.75 percent of San Francisco–area seniors, does this sales estimate refer to market potential or company sales potential?

Consumer Buying Behavior

8

195

McDonald's Chews over Changes in Consumer Behavior

McDonald's, by far the world's largest restaurant chain, popularized the concept of fast food by understanding what, when, where, and how people like to eat. Its mainstay menu of burgers, fries, and soft drinks beefed up its bottom line for decades. Now worldwide sales are sputtering, forcing the company to seriously look at changes in consumer behavior and come up with a menu that will jumpstart global growth as fast food slows down, new tastes emerge, and burgers take a back seat.

Based in Oak Brook, Illinois, McDonald's continues to attract young families and teenage burger fans to its units around the world. However, U.S. baby boomers are increasingly trading up to mid-level restaurants and cafés offering varied menus, more service, and trendier décor—chains like Applebee's, Chili's, and Starbucks. Many office workers who used to pop into downtown and suburban McDonald's locations for a quick, inexpensive lunch break are switching to sandwiches, soups, and salads served up by specialized chains such as Au Bon Pain and Subway. And health-conscious consumers are eating much more chicken than ever before.

Aware of these shifts in consumer behavior, McDonald's has been gobbling up nonburger food chains and experimenting with new formats and menus to achieve its goal of doubling U.S. sales within five years. It recently purchased the bankrupt Boston Market chain, which focuses on chicken and home-style meals, as well as the U.K. Pret A Manger chain, which is known for sandwiches. Other nonburger businesses include Chipotle Mexican Grill, Donatos Pizza, and Aroma Café. In the testing stage are new "Mac" twists such as McCafé (featuring coffee and desserts), McDiner (offering meat loaf and other classic diner fare), and McSnack (featuring a scaled-down menu and limited seating space). Some Latin American McDonald's units are also opening stand-alone kiosks that sell only ice cream and desserts.

On top of these long-term changes in consumer eating habits, sales of beef products in many European countries have been hurt by livestock health issues such as mad cow disease and foot-and-mouth disease. In response, McDonald's conducted focus-group research to hear what customers had to say about these concerns. "We asked our customers and they told us that they trusted us and that they just wanted us to reassure them that they should trust us," explains the chain's European controller. "We have the highest beef and food safety standards. Customers trust us because they know of our standards."

Based on this research, McDonald's has taken a number of steps to reassure European consumers about the safety of its burgers. In France, the company invited customers to tour its kitchens and learn firsthand about the chain's food suppliers and its food preparation methods. It also broadened the menu to add new pork dishes in many countries and stepped up promotion of nonbeef offerings. Meanwhile some outlets began putting more emphasis on breakfast offerings to raise sales of nonbeef menu items. With ongoing research and responsive marketing, McDonald's is working hard to meet the challenges that short-term and long-term changes in consumer behavior are bringing, now and in the future.[1]

Marketers at successful organizations like McDonald's go to great efforts to understand their customers' needs and gain a better grasp of customers' buying behavior. A firm's ability to establish and maintain satisfying customer relationships requires an understanding of buying behavior. **Buying behavior** is the decision processes and acts of people involved in buying and using products. **Consumer buying behavior** refers to the buying behavior of ultimate consumers, those who purchase products for personal or household use and not for business purposes. Marketers attempt to understand buying behavior for several reasons. First, buyers' reactions to a firm's marketing strategy have a great impact on the firm's success. Second, as indicated in Chapter 1, the marketing concept stresses that a firm should create a marketing mix that satisfies customers. To find out what satisfies buyers, marketers must examine the main influences on what, where, when, and how consumers buy. Third, by gaining a better understanding of the factors that affect buying behavior, marketers are in a better position to predict how consumers will respond to marketing strategies.

In this chapter, we first examine how the customer's level of involvement affects the type of problem solving employed and discuss the types of consumer problem-solving processes. Then we analyze the major stages of the consumer buying decision process, beginning with problem recognition, information search, and evaluation of alternatives and proceeding through purchase and postpurchase evaluation. Next, we examine situational influences—surroundings, time, purchase reason, and buyer's mood and condition—that affect purchasing decisions. We go on to consider psychological influences on purchasing decisions: perception, motives, learning, attitudes, personality and self-concept, and lifestyles. We conclude with a discussion of social influences that affect buying behavior, including roles, family, reference groups and opinion leaders, social classes, and culture and subcultures.

Level of Involvement and Consumer Problem-Solving Processes

buying behavior The decision processes and acts of people involved in buying and using products

consumer buying behavior Buying behavior of people who purchase products for personal or household use and not for business purposes

level of involvement An individual's intensity of interest in a product and the importance of the product for that person

routinized response behavior A type of consumer problem-solving process used when buying frequently purchased, low-cost items that require very little search-and-decision effort

limited problem solving A type of consumer problem-solving process that buyers use when purchasing products occasionally or need information about an unfamiliar brand in a familiar product category

Consumers generally try to acquire and maintain an assortment of products that satisfy their current and future needs. To do so, consumers engage in problem solving. When purchasing such products as food, clothing, shelter, medical care, education, recreation, and transportation, people engage in different types of problem-solving processes. The amount of effort, both mental and physical, that buyers expend in solving problems varies considerably. A major determinant of the type of problem-solving process employed depends on the customer's **level of involvement,** the degree of interest in a product and the importance the individual places on this product. High-involvement products tend to be those visible to others (such as clothing, furniture, or automobiles) and that are expensive. Expensive bicycles, for example, are usually high-involvement products. High-importance issues, such as health care, are associated with high levels of involvement. Low-involvement products tend to be those that are less expensive and have less associated social risk, such as many grocery items. When a person's interest in a product category is ongoing and long term, it is referred to as *enduring involvement.* In contrast, *situational involvement* is temporary and dynamic, and results from a particular set of circumstances. Involvement level, as well as other factors, affects a person's selection of one of three types of consumer problem solving: routinized response behavior, limited problem solving, or extended problem solving.

A consumer uses **routinized response behavior** when buying frequently purchased, low-cost items needing very little search-and-decision effort. When buying such items, a consumer may prefer a particular brand but is familiar with several brands in the product class and views more than one as being acceptable. Typically, low-involvement products are bought through routinized response behavior, that is, almost automatically. For example, most buyers spend little time or effort selecting a soft drink or a brand of cereal.

Buyers engage in **limited problem solving** when buying products occasionally or when they need to obtain information about an unfamiliar brand in a familiar product category. This type of problem solving requires a moderate amount of time for

Eat my voltage.

Introducing a work of pure genius. Prius, the world's first production car to combine a super-efficient gasoline engine with an advanced electric motor that never needs to be plugged in. No recharging stations. No plugs. No compromises. Powered by the revolutionary Toyota Hybrid System, Prius stores the energy produced during deceleration and converts it into electric power. It's fast, fun to drive and produces up to 90% fewer harmful emissions. Prius. This changes everything.

The new Prius. Starting at $19,995. Destination Charge $485. Total MSRP $20,480.**
Visit www.toyota.com/prius or call 800-GO-TOYOTA.

TOYOTA PRIUS | genius

Levels of Involvement
Buying decisions about numerous grocery products, such as dishwashing detergent, are associated with low levels of involvement. Buying decisions regarding automobiles, especially one that is powered by both gas and electricity, are associated with high levels of involvement.

extended problem solving
A type of consumer problem-solving process employed when purchasing unfamiliar, expensive, or infrequently bought products

impulse buying An unplanned buying behavior resulting from a powerful urge to buy something immediately

information gathering and deliberation. For example, if Procter & Gamble introduces an improved Tide laundry detergent, buyers will seek additional information about the new product, perhaps by asking a friend who has used it or watching a commercial about it, before making a trial purchase.

The most complex type of problem solving, **extended problem solving,** occurs when purchasing unfamiliar, expensive, or infrequently bought products—for instance, a car, home, or college education. The buyer uses many criteria to evaluate alternative brands or choices and spends much time seeking information and deciding on the purchase. Extended problem solving is frequently used for purchasing high-involvement products.

Purchase of a particular product does not always elicit the same type of problem-solving process. In some instances, we engage in extended problem solving the first time we buy a certain product but find that limited problem solving suffices when we buy it again. If a routinely purchased, formerly satisfying brand no longer satisfies us, we may use limited or extended problem solving to switch to a new brand. Thus, if we notice that the brand of pain reliever we normally buy is not working, we may seek out a different brand through limited problem solving. Most consumers occasionally make purchases solely on impulse, and not on the basis of any of these three problem-solving processes. **Impulse buying** involves no conscious planning but results from a powerful urge to buy something immediately.

Consumer Buying Decision Process

consumer buying decision process A five-stage purchase decision process that includes problem recognition, information search, evaluation of alternatives, purchase, and postpurchase evaluation

The **consumer buying decision process,** shown in Figure 8.1, includes five stages: problem recognition, information search, evaluation of alternatives, purchase, and postpurchase evaluation. Before we examine each stage, consider these important points. First, the actual act of purchasing is only one stage in the process, and usually not the first stage. Second, even though we indicate that a purchase occurs, not all decision processes lead to a purchase; individuals may end the process at any stage. Finally, not all consumer decisions include all five stages. People engaged in extended problem solving usually go through all stages of this decision process, whereas those engaged in limited problem solving and routinized response behavior may omit some stages.

Possible influences on the decision process

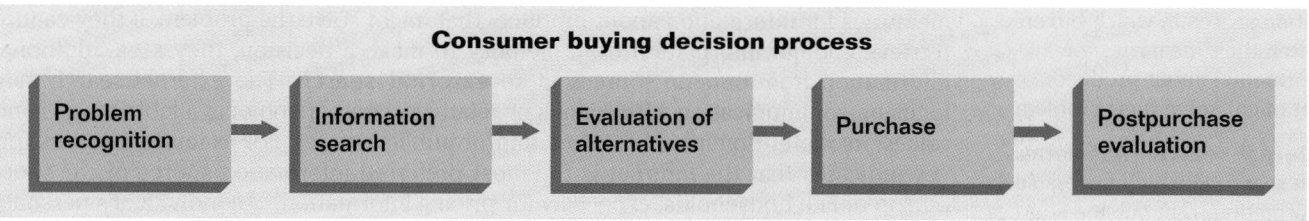

Situational influences	**Psychological influences**	**Social influences**
▸ Physical surroundings ▸ Social surroundings ▸ Time ▸ Purchase reason ▸ Buyer's mood and condition	▸ Perception ▸ Motives ▸ Learning ▸ Attitudes ▸ Personality and self-concept ▸ Lifestyles	▸ Roles ▸ Family ▸ Reference groups and opinion leaders ▸ Social classes ▸ Culture and subcultures

Consumer buying decision process

Problem recognition → Information search → Evaluation of alternatives → Purchase → Postpurchase evaluation

FIGURE 8.1
Consumer Buying Decision Process and Possible Influences on the Process

Problem Recognition

Problem recognition occurs when a buyer becomes aware of a difference between a desired state and an actual condition. Consider a student who owns a nonprogrammable calculator and learns she needs a programmable one for her math course. She recognizes that a difference exists between the desired state—having a programmable calculator—and her actual condition. She therefore decides to buy a new calculator.

The speed of consumer problem recognition can be quite rapid or rather slow. Sometimes a person has a problem or need but is unaware of it. Marketers use sales personnel, advertising, and packaging to help trigger recognition of such needs or

Problem Recognition
The maker of Carbona cleaning products employs advertising to encourage problem recognition that certain stains are difficult to remove and that its product will remove them.

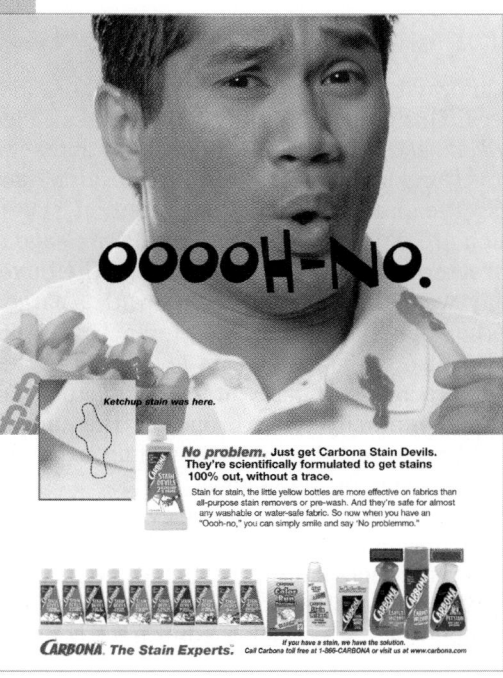

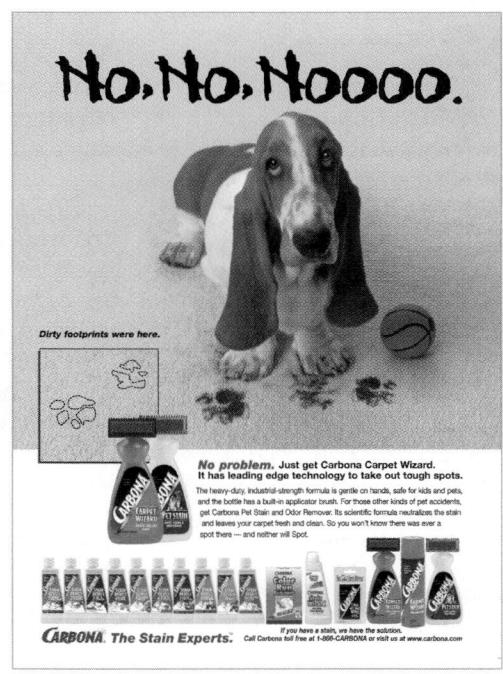

problems. For example, a university bookstore may advertise programmable calculators in the school newspaper at the beginning of the term. Students who see the advertisement may recognize that they need these calculators for their course work.

Information Search

After recognizing the problem or need, a buyer (if continuing the decision process) searches for product information that will help resolve the problem or satisfy the need. For example, the above-mentioned student, after recognizing the need for a programmable calculator, may search for information about different types and brands of calculators. She acquires information over time from her surroundings. However, the information's impact depends on how she interprets it.

An information search has two aspects. In an **internal search,** buyers search their memories for information about products that might solve the problem. If they cannot retrieve enough information from memory to make a decision, they seek additional information from outside sources in an **external search.** The external search may focus on communication with friends or relatives, comparison of available brands and prices, marketer-dominated sources, and/or public sources. For example, a recent survey indicates that the Internet is the most preferred information source of car shoppers in online households, especially for pricing information.[2] An individual's personal contacts—friends, relatives, associates—often are influential sources of information because the person trusts and respects them. Utilizing marketer-dominated sources of information, such as salespeople, advertising, package labeling, and in-store demonstrations and displays, typically requires little effort on the consumer's part. Buyers also obtain information from public sources—for instance, government reports, news presentations, publications such as *Consumer Reports,* and reports from product-testing organizations. Consumers frequently view information from public sources as highly credible because of its factual and unbiased nature.

Repetition, a technique well known to advertisers, increases consumers' learning of information. When seeing or hearing an advertising message for the first time, recipients may not grasp all its important details but learn more details as the message is repeated. Nevertheless, even when commercials are initially effective, repetition eventually may cause wearout, meaning consumers pay less attention to the commercial and respond to it less favorably than they did at first.

Information can be presented verbally, numerically, or visually. Marketers pay great attention to the visual components of their advertising materials.

Evaluation of Alternatives

A successful information search yields a group of brands that a buyer views as possible alternatives. This group of brands is sometimes called a **consideration set** (also called an *evoked set*). For example, a consideration set of calculators might include those made by Texas Instruments, Hewlett-Packard, Sharp, and Casio.

To assess the products in a consideration set, the buyer uses **evaluative criteria,** which are objective (such as an EPA mileage rating) and subjective (such as style) characteristics that are important to the buyer. For example, one calculator buyer may want a rechargeable unit with a large display and large buttons, whereas another may have no size preferences but dislikes rechargeable calculators. The buyer also assigns a certain level of importance to each criterion; some features and characteristics carry more weight than others. Using the criteria, the buyer rates and eventually ranks brands in the consideration set. The evaluation stage may yield no brand the buyer is willing to purchase. In that case, a further information search may be necessary.

Marketers may influence consumers' evaluations by *framing* the alternatives, that is, by describing the alternatives and their attributes in a certain manner. Framing can make a characteristic seem more important to a consumer and facilitate its recall from memory. For example, by stressing a car's superior comfort and safety features over those of a competitor's, a carmaker can direct consumers' attention toward these

internal search An information search in which buyers search their memories for information about products that might solve their problem

external search An information search in which buyers seek information from outside sources

consideration set A group of brands that a buyer views as alternatives for possible purchase

evaluative criteria Objective and subjective characteristics that are important to a buyer

points of superiority. Framing probably influences the decision processes of inexperienced buyers more than those of experienced ones. If the evaluation of alternatives yields one or more brands the consumer is willing to buy, then he or she is ready to move on to the next stage of the decision process: the purchase.

Purchase

In the purchase stage, the consumer chooses the product or brand to be bought. Selection is based on the outcome of the evaluation stage and on other dimensions. Product availability may influence which brand is purchased. For example, if the brand ranked highest in evaluation is unavailable, the buyer may purchase the brand ranked second. If a consumer wants a black pair of Nikes and cannot find them in her size, she might buy a black pair of Reeboks.

During this stage, buyers also pick the seller from whom they will buy the product. The choice of seller may affect final product selection—and so may the terms of sale, which, if negotiable, are determined at this stage. Other issues, such as price, delivery, warranties, maintenance agreements, installation, and credit arrangements, are also settled. Finally, the actual purchase takes place during this stage, unless the consumer decides to terminate the buying decision process.

Postpurchase Evaluation

After the purchase, the buyer begins evaluating the product to ascertain if its actual performance meets expected levels. Many criteria used in evaluating alternatives are applied again during postpurchase evaluation. The outcome of this stage is either satisfaction or dissatisfaction, which influences whether the consumer complains, communicates with other possible buyers, and repurchases the brand or product.

cognitive dissonance
A buyer's doubts shortly after a purchase about whether the decision was the right one

Shortly after purchase of an expensive product, evaluation may result in **cognitive dissonance,** doubts in the buyer's mind about whether purchasing the product was the right decision. For example, after buying a pair of $169 inline skates, a person may feel guilty about the purchase or wonder whether she purchased the right brand and quality. Cognitive dissonance is most likely to arise when a person has recently bought an expensive, high-involvement product that lacks some of the desirable features of competing brands. A buyer experiencing cognitive dissonance may attempt to return the product or seek positive information about it to justify choosing it. Marketers sometimes attempt to reduce cognitive dissonance by having salespeople telephone recent purchasers to make sure they are satisfied with their new purchases. At times, recent buyers are sent results of studies showing that other consumers are very satisfied with the brand.

As Figure 8.1 shows, three major categories of influences are believed to affect the consumer buying decision process: situational, psychological, and social. In the remainder of this chapter, we focus on these influences. Although we discuss each major influence separately, their effects on the consumer decision process are interrelated.

Situational Influences on the Buying Decision Process

Situational influences result from circumstances, time, and location that affect the consumer buying decision process. For example, buying an automobile tire after noticing while washing your car that the tire is badly worn is a different experience from buying a tire right after a blowout on the highway derails your vacation. Situational factors can influence the buyer during any stage of the consumer buying decision process and may cause the individual to shorten, lengthen, or terminate the process.

situational influences
Influences resulting from circumstances, time, and location that affect the consumer buying decision process

Situational factors can be classified into five categories: physical surroundings, social surroundings, time perspective, reason for purchase, and the buyer's momentary mood and condition.[3] Physical surroundings include location, store atmosphere, aromas, sounds, lighting, weather, and other factors in the physical environment in which the decision process occurs. Marketers at some banks, department stores, and specialty stores go to considerable trouble and expense to create physical settings conducive to making purchase decisions. Numerous restaurant chains, such as Olive Garden and Chili's, invest heavily in facilities, often building from the ground up, to provide special surroundings that enhance customers' dining experiences.

Clearly, in some settings, dimensions, such as weather, traffic sounds, and odors, are beyond marketers' control; instead they must try to make customers more comfortable. General climatic conditions, for example, may influence a customer's decision to buy a specific type of vehicle (such as an SUV) and certain accessories (such as four-wheel drive). Current weather conditions, depending on whether they are favorable or unfavorable, may either encourage or discourage consumers to go shopping and to seek out specific products.

Social surroundings include characteristics and interactions of others who are present when a purchase decision is being made, such as friends, relatives, salespeople, and other customers. Buyers may feel pressured to behave in a certain way because they are in public places such as restaurants, stores, or sports arenas. Thoughts about who will be around when the product is used or consumed is also a dimension of the social setting. An overcrowded store or an argument between a customer and a salesperson may cause consumers to stop shopping or even leave the store.

The time dimension, too, influences the buying decision process in several ways, such as the amount of time required to become knowledgeable about a product, to search for it, and to buy it. Time plays a major role in that the buyer considers the possible frequency of product use, the length of time required to use the product, and the length of the overall product life. Other time dimensions that influence purchases include time of day, day of the week or month, seasons, and holidays. The amount of time pressure a consumer is under affects how much time is devoted to purchase decisions. A customer under severe time constraints is likely either to make quick purchase decisions or to delay them.

The purchase reason raises the questions of what exactly the product purchase should accomplish and for whom. Generally, consumers purchase an item for their own use, for household use, or as a gift. For example, people who are buying a gift may buy a different product than if they were purchasing the product for themselves. If you own a Cross pen, for example, it is unlikely that you bought it for yourself.

The buyer's momentary moods (such as anger, anxiety, contentment) or momentary conditions (fatigue, illness, being flush with cash) may have a bearing on the consumer buying decision process. These moods or conditions immediately precede the current situation and are not chronic. Any of these moods or conditions can affect a person's ability and desire to search for information, receive information, or seek and evaluate alternatives. They can also significantly influence a consumer's postpurchase evaluation.

Psychological Influences on the Buying Decision Process

Psychological **influences** partly determine people's general behavior and thus influence their behavior as consumers. Primary psychological influences on consumer behavior are perception, motives, learning, attitudes, personality and self-concept, and lifestyles. Even though these psychological factors operate internally, they are very much affected by social forces outside the individual.

psychological influences
Factors that in part determine people's general behavior, thus influencing their behavior as consumers

Perception

Different people perceive the same thing at the same time in different ways. When you first look at the illustration below, do you see the fish changing into birds or the birds changing into fish? Similarly, an individual at different times may perceive the same item in a number of ways. **Perception** is the process of selecting, organizing, and interpreting information inputs to produce meaning. **Information inputs** are sensations received through sight, taste, hearing, smell, and touch. When we hear an advertisement, see a friend, smell polluted air or water, or touch a product, we receive information inputs.

perception The process of selecting, organizing, and interpreting information inputs to produce meaning

information inputs
Sensations received through the sense organs

selective exposure
The process of selecting inputs to be exposed to our awareness while ignoring others

As the definition indicates, perception is a three-step process. Although we receive numerous pieces of information at once, only a few reach our awareness. We select some inputs and ignore others because we do not have the ability to be conscious of all inputs at one time. This phenomenon is sometimes called **selective exposure** because an individual selects which inputs will reach awareness. If you are concentrating on this paragraph, you probably are not aware that cars outside are making noise, that the room light is on, or that you are touching this page. Even though you receive these inputs, they do not reach your awareness until they are pointed out.

Fish or Birds?
Do you see the fish changing into birds or the birds changing into fish?

An individual's current set of needs affects selective exposure. Information inputs that relate to one's strongest needs at a given time are more likely to be selected to reach awareness. It is not by random chance that many fast-food commercials are aired near mealtimes. Customers are more likely to tune in to these advertisements at these times.

The selective nature of perception may result not only in selective exposure but also in two other conditions: selective distortion and selective retention. **Selective distortion** is changing or twisting currently received information; it occurs when a person receives information inconsistent with personal feelings or beliefs. For example, on seeing an advertisement promoting a disliked brand, a viewer may distort the information to make it more consistent with prior views. This distortion substantially lessens the effect of the advertisement on the individual. In **selective retention,** a person remembers information inputs that support personal feelings and beliefs and forgets inputs that do not. After hearing a sales presentation and leaving a store, a customer may forget many selling points if they contradict personal beliefs.

selective distortion An individual's changing or twisting of information when it is inconsistent with personal feelings or beliefs

selective retention Remembering information inputs that support personal feelings and beliefs and forgetting inputs that do not

TECH * KNOW

Makeover for Online Beauty Sites

Eve.com expected customers to buy fragrances without sniffing them first; iBeauty.com thought lipstick buyers cared only about color, not brand. These are just some of the misconceptions that have hobbled the online cosmetics industry and thinned its ranks. In the late 1990s, nearly 200 websites sold beauty products; today fewer than 3 dozen are operating. Eve.com, one of the most popular and best-financed sites, lasted less than 18 months. Now the survivors, and some newcomers, are working hard to adapt their sites to the way consumers prefer to buy cosmetics.

Consumers rely heavily on sensory impressions when comparing beauty products, so it's not surprising that a minuscule 2 percent have recently purchased cosmetics online. Color is a particularly important decision factor for makeup and nail polish products. Yet 60 percent of online shoppers mistrust the colors shown on the screen. This is a legitimate concern, because colors can vary on different computer screens. Even when shoppers make a cosmetics purchase, 15 percent wind up returning products because the actual color didn't match what they saw on the site.

Responding to this concern, E-Color has created software that automatically adjusts the screen display of colors as shown on consumer monitors. This means that visitors to the L'Oréal site and other participating sites will be able to see truer, color-corrected versions of each product. And because many consumers consider brand as well as color when buying cosmetics, iBeauty and other sites now offer the option to browse by brand as well as by color.

Fragrance is an important consideration for perfumes and soaps. Consumers are generally reluctant to buy a scented product without experiencing the aroma. Digiscents is addressing this issue by selling the iSmell Personal Scent Synthesizer. When plugged into a computer, the device will emit fragrances based on codes transmitted by participating cosmetics sites. Reflect.com, backed by Procter & Gamble, takes a different approach: the site invites online shoppers to select ingredients and mix a custom fragrance, then buy a $5 sample to try. To sweeten the deal, those who buy a sample receive a $5 credit toward their purchase.

Finally, cosmetics sites are easing consumers' doubts by making it easier to return or exchange products purchased online. Customers of Sephora.com, for example, can return unwanted items to any of Sephora's 64 stores. Such consumer-friendly policies, coupled with technological changes and a better understanding of consumer buying behavior, are putting a new face on web-based cosmetics retailing.

The second step in the process of perception is perceptual organization. Information inputs that reach awareness are not received in an organized form. To produce meaning, an individual must mentally organize and integrate new information with what is already stored in memory. People use several methods to organize. One method, called *closure,* occurs when a person mentally fills in missing elements in a pattern or statement. In an attempt to draw attention to its brand, an advertiser will capitalize on closure by using incomplete images, sounds, or statements in its advertisements.

Interpretation, the third step in the perceptual process, is the assignment of meaning to what has been organized. A person bases interpretation on what he or she expects or what is familiar. For this reason, a manufacturer that changes a product or its package faces a major problem. When people are looking for the old, familiar product or package, they may not recognize the new one. For instance, when Smucker's redesigned its packaging, marketers told designers that although they wanted a more contemporary package design, they also wanted a classic look so that customers would perceive their products to be the familiar ones they had been buying for years. Unless a product or package change is accompanied by a promotional program that makes people aware of the change, an organization may suffer a sales decline.

Although marketers cannot control buyers' perceptions, they often try to influence them through information. Several problems may arise from such attempts, however. First, a consumer's perceptual process may operate such that a seller's information never reaches that person. For example, a buyer may block out a salesperson's presentation. Second, a buyer may receive a seller's information but perceive it differently than was intended. For example, when a toothpaste producer advertises that "35 percent of the people who use this toothpaste have fewer cavities," a customer might infer that 65 percent of users have more cavities. Third, a buyer who perceives information inputs to be inconsistent with prior beliefs is likely to forget the information quickly.

Motives

motive An internal energizing force that directs a person's behavior toward satisfying needs or achieving goals

A **motive** is an internal energizing force that orients a person's activities toward satisfying needs or achieving goals. Buyers' actions are affected by a set of motives rather than by just one motive. At a single point in time, some of a person's motives are stronger than others. For example, a person's motives for having a cup of coffee are much stronger right after waking up than just before going to bed. Motives also affect the direction and intensity of behavior. Some motives may help an individual achieve his or her goals, whereas others create barriers to goal achievement.

Maslow's hierarchy of needs The five levels of needs that humans seek to satisfy, from most to least important

Abraham Maslow, an American psychologist, conceived a theory of motivation based on a hierarchy of needs. According to Maslow, humans seek to satisfy five levels of needs, from most important to least important, as shown in Figure 8.2. This sequence is known as **Maslow's hierarchy of needs.** Once needs at one level are met, humans seek to fulfill needs at the next level up in the hierarchy.

FIGURE 8.2
Maslow's Hierarchy of Needs
Maslow believed that people seek to fulfill five categories of needs.

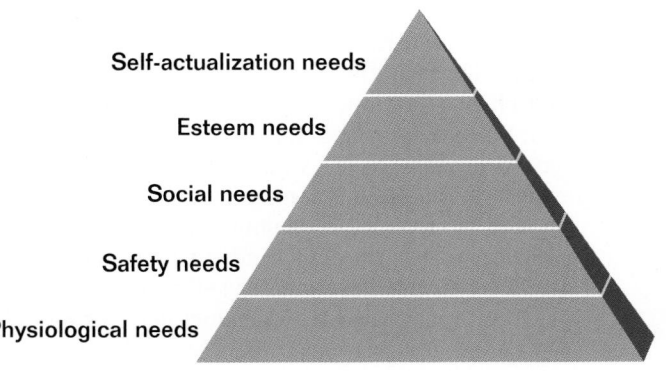

At the most basic level are *physiological needs,* requirements for survival such as food, water, sex, clothing, and shelter, which people try to satisfy first. Food and beverage marketers often appeal to physiological needs. Marketers of whitening toothpastes, such as Ultrabrite, sometimes promote their brands based on sex appeal.

At the next level are *safety needs,* which include security and freedom from physical and emotional pain and suffering. Life insurance, automobile air bags, carbon monoxide detectors, vitamins, and decay-fighting toothpastes are products that consumers purchase to meet safety needs.

Next are *social needs,* the human requirements for love and affection and a sense of belonging. Advertisements frequently appeal to social needs. Ads for cosmetics and other beauty products, jewelry, and even cars often suggest that purchasing these products will bring love. Certain types of trendy clothing, such as Gap khakis, Nike athletic shoes, or T-shirts imprinted with logos or slogans, appeal to the customer's need to belong.

At the level of *esteem needs,* people require respect and recognition from others as well as self-esteem, a sense of their own worth. Owning a Lexus automobile, having a beauty makeover, or flying first class can satisfy esteem needs. Slim-Fast Foods uses motivational research to design more effective marketing programs. After learning that dieters who regularly received encouraging e-mail messages lost weight more quickly than those who did not, the company designed a Buddy Program to match dieters according to age, food preferences, and other characteristics. More than 14,000 dieters have signed up, an indication of the motivational power of recognition and respect from others. "Our club members wanted someone they could share stories with—about their successes, their hurdles, how they prepare menus," says a Slim-Fast spokesperson.[4]

At the top of the hierarchy are *self-actualization needs.* These refer to people's need to grow and develop and to become all they are capable of becoming. Some products that satisfy these needs include fitness center memberships, education, self-improvement workshops, and skiing lessons. In its recruiting advertisements, the U.S. Army tells potential enlistees to "be all that you can be in the Army." These messages imply that people can reach their full potential by enlisting in the U.S. Army.

Motives that influence where a person purchases products on a regular basis are called **patronage motives.** A buyer may shop at a specific store because of such patronage motives as price, service, location, product variety, or friendliness of salespeople. To capitalize on patronage motives, marketers try to determine why regular customers patronize a particular store and to emphasize these characteristics in the store's marketing mix.

patronage motives Motives that influence where a person purchases products on a regular basis

Learning

learning Changes in an individual's thought processes and behavior caused by information and experience

Learning refers to changes in a person's thought processes and behavior caused by information and experience. Consequences of behavior strongly influence the learning process. Behaviors that result in satisfying consequences tend to be repeated. For example, a consumer who buys a Snickers candy bar and enjoys the taste is more likely to buy a Snickers again. In fact, the individual will probably continue to purchase that brand until it no longer provides satisfaction. When effects of the behavior are no longer satisfying, the person may switch brands or stop eating candy bars altogether.

When making purchasing decisions, buyers process information. Individuals have differing abilities in this regard. The type of information inexperienced buyers use may differ from the type used by experienced shoppers familiar with the product and purchase situation. Thus, two potential purchasers of an antique desk may use different types of information in making their purchase decisions. The inexperienced buyer may judge the desk's value by price, whereas the more experienced buyer may seek information about the manufacturer, period, and place of origin to judge the desk's quality and value. Consumers lacking experience may seek information from others when making a purchase and even take along an informed "purchase pal." More experienced buyers have greater self-confidence and more knowledge about the product and can recognize which product features are reliable cues to product quality.

Marketers help customers learn about their products by helping them gain experience with them. Free samples, sometimes coupled with coupons, can successfully encourage trial and reduce purchase risk. For example, because some consumers may be wary of exotic menu items, restaurants sometimes offer free samples. In-store demonstrations foster knowledge of product uses. A software producer may use point-of-sale product demonstrations to introduce a new product. Test drives give potential new-car purchasers some experience with the automobile's features.

Consumers also learn by experiencing products indirectly through information from salespeople, advertisements, friends, and relatives. Through sales personnel and advertisements, marketers offer information before (and sometimes after) purchases to influence what consumers learn and to create more favorable attitudes toward the product. Yet their efforts are seldom fully successful. Marketers encounter problems in attracting and holding consumers' attention, in providing consumers with important information for making purchase decisions, and in convincing them to try the product.

Attitudes

attitude An individual's enduring evaluation of, feelings about, and behavioral tendencies toward an object or idea

An **attitude** is an individual's enduring evaluation of, feelings about, and behavioral tendencies toward an object or idea. The objects toward which we have attitudes may be tangible or intangible, living or nonliving. For example, we have attitudes toward sex, religion, politics, and music, just as we do toward cars, football, and breakfast cereals. Although attitudes can change, they tend to generally remain stable and do not vary from moment to moment. However, all of a person's attitudes do not have equal impact at any one time; some are stronger than others. Individuals acquire attitudes through experience and interaction with other people.

MARKETING CITIZENSHIP

Battling Unethical Consumer Behavior

Shouldn't marketing citizenship be a two-way street? This question is even more urgent as the Internet and other powerful technologies transform the way marketers and consumers interact. In particular, marketers are concerned about the impact of three types of unethical consumer behavior:

- *Unauthorized copying.* Consumers enjoy the convenience of buying or downloading music, videos, software, and other products—and for awhile, Napster and similar sites made swapping music files a snap. But when people make copies to share with others, they are violating the intellectual property rights of the companies that market those products. In a recent consumer survey, 20 percent of respondents said they know someone who has downloaded music without paying, and 14 percent said they know someone who has illegally copied a videotape. The recording industry is cracking down on file-sharing sites, but some consumers continue to freely exchange unauthorized copies. Is this practice ethical?

- *Payment fraud.* Online retailers and payment sites have been hit by hackers who break in, steal credit card numbers, and manipulate the accounts to get cash or buy goods. PayMe, PayPlace, and other electronic payment sites have either limited operations or closed down after being victimized by payment fraud

schemes. PayPal, one of the largest and most popular sites, chose to fight back using software designed to detect fraudulent activity. Instead of working quietly behind the scenes, the company has taken a very public stand against payment fraud and helps authorities gather evidence to prosecute hackers. Should hackers who are caught get off easy?

- *Shoplifting.* Shoplifting and other store theft cost retailers $29 billion per year. Federated Department Stores, one of the nation's largest retail chains, spends an estimated $250 million annually to cover shoplifting losses and prevent theft. With the rising cost of goods, the average value of merchandise stolen in a single shoplifting incident is $128. Now even honest shoppers must put up with the inconvenience of antitheft tags on merchandise and electronic surveillance equipment scanning store and parking lot locations. Should all consumers feel under suspicion when shopping, even though only a few behave unethically?

Other types of unethical consumer behavior include returning used or broken products as if they were new and lying on credit account applications. In the end, such behaviors result in higher prices for all and stricter preventive measures that can frustrate honest consumers.

An attitude consists of three major components: cognitive, affective, and behavioral. The cognitive component is the person's knowledge and information about the object or idea. The affective component comprises feelings and emotions toward the object or idea. The behavioral component manifests itself in the person's actions regarding the object or idea. Changes in one of these components may or may not alter the other components. Thus, a consumer may become more knowledgeable about a specific brand without changing the affective or behavioral components of his or her attitude toward that brand.

Consumer attitudes toward a company and its products greatly influence success or failure of the firm's marketing strategy. When consumers have strong negative attitudes toward one or more aspects of a firm's marketing practices, they may not only stop using its products but also urge relatives and friends to do likewise.

Because attitudes play such an important part in determining consumer behavior, marketers should measure consumer attitudes toward prices, package designs, brand names, advertisements, salespeople, repair services, store locations, features of existing or proposed products, and social responsibility efforts. Several methods help marketers gauge these attitudes. One of the simplest ways is to question people directly. Knowing that negative attitudes can keep shoppers away, Kmart, for example, sought to pinpoint problems by asking customers to call a telephone hotline and answer a few questions to rate their experience. Within six months, 20 million shoppers had responded, helping the discount retailer to identify and change practices that were dampening satisfaction ratings. Kmart's satisfaction rating already is on the rise as the chain aims to boost sales by encouraging more visits by current customers.[5]

attitude scale Means of measuring consumer attitudes by gauging the intensity of individuals' reactions to adjectives, phrases, or sentences about an object

Marketers also evaluate attitudes through attitude scales. An **attitude scale** usually consists of a series of adjectives, phrases, or sentences about an object. Respondents indicate the intensity of their feelings toward the object by reacting to the adjectives, phrases, or sentences in a certain way. For example, a marketer measuring people's attitudes toward shopping might ask respondents to indicate the extent to which they agree or disagree with a number of statements, such as "Shopping is more fun than watching television." By using an attitude scale, a marketing research company was able to identify and classify six major types of clothing purchasers. The scale was based on such attributes as demographics, media use, and purchase behavior.

When marketers determine that a significant number of consumers have negative attitudes toward an aspect of a marketing mix, they may try to change those attitudes to make them more favorable. This task is generally lengthy, expensive, and difficult, and may require extensive promotional efforts. For example, the California Prune Growers, an organization of prune producers, has tried to use advertising to change consumers' attitudes toward prunes by presenting them as a nutritious snack high in potassium and fiber. To alter consumers' responses so that more of them buy a given brand, a firm might launch an information-focused campaign to change the cognitive component of a consumer's attitude or a persuasive (emotional) campaign to influence the affective component. Distributing free samples might help change the behavioral component. Both business and nonbusiness organizations try to change people's attitudes about many things, from health and safety to prices and product features.

Personality and Self-Concept

personality A set of internal traits and distinct behavioral tendencies that result in consistent patterns of behavior

Personality is a set of internal traits and distinct behavioral tendencies that result in consistent patterns of behavior in certain situations. An individual's personality arises from hereditary characteristics and personal experiences that make the person unique. Personalities typically are described as having one or more characteristics such as compulsiveness, ambition, gregariousness, dogmatism, authoritarianism, introversion, extroversion, and competitiveness. Marketing researchers look for relationships between such characteristics and buying behavior. Even though a few links between several personality traits and buyer behavior have been determined, results

Self-Concept
Steve Madden, maker of sportswear, footwear, and accessories, appeals to individuals whose self-concept includes being fashionable.

of many studies have been inconclusive. The weak association between personality and buying behavior may be the result of unreliable measures rather than a lack of a relationship. A number of marketers are convinced that consumers' personalities do influence types and brands of products purchased. For example, the type of clothing, jewelry, or automobile a person buys may reflect one or more personality characteristics.

At times marketers aim advertising at certain types of personalities. For example, ads for certain cigarette brands are directed toward specific personality types. Marketers focus on positively valued personality characteristics, such as security consciousness, sociability, independence, or competitiveness, rather than on negatively valued ones like insensitivity or timidity.

A person's self-concept is closely linked to personality. **Self-concept** (sometimes called *self-image*) is a person's view or perception of himself or herself. Individuals develop and alter their self-concepts based on an interaction of psychological and social dimensions. Research shows that a buyer purchases products that

self-concept Perception or view of oneself

reflect and enhance the self-concept and that purchase decisions are important to the development and maintenance of a stable self-concept. Consumers' self-concepts may influence whether they buy a product in a specific product category and may affect brand selection as well as where they buy. For example, home improvement retailer Lowe's is targeting women—who make 90 percent of household decisions about home decor and home improvement—using self-concept as the basis of its advertising message. "Only Lowe's has everything and everyone to help your house tell the story about who you really are," says the company's advertising tag line.[6]

Lifestyles

lifestyle An individual's pattern of living expressed through activities, interests, and opinions

A **lifestyle** is an individual's pattern of living expressed through activities, interests, and opinions. Lifestyle patterns include the ways people spend time, the extent of their interaction with others, and their general outlook on life and living. People partially determine their own lifestyles, but the pattern is also affected by personality, as well as by demographic factors such as age, education, income, and social class. Lifestyles are measured through a lengthy series of questions.

Lifestyles have a strong impact on many aspects of the consumer buying decision process, from problem recognition to postpurchase evaluation. Lifestyles influence consumers' product needs, brand preferences, types of media used, and how and where they shop.

Social Influences on the Buying Decision Process

Forces that other people exert on buying behavior are called **social influences.** As Figure 8.1 shows, they are grouped into five major areas: roles, family, reference groups and opinion leaders, social classes, and culture and subcultures.

social influences The forces other people exert on one's buying behavior

role Actions and activities that a person in a particular position is supposed to perform based on expectations of the individual and surrounding persons

Roles

All of us occupy positions within groups, organizations, and institutions. Associated with each position is a **role,** a set of actions and activities a person in a particular position is supposed to perform based on expectations of both the individual and surrounding persons. Because people occupy numerous positions, they have many roles. For example, a man may perform the roles of son, husband, father, employee or employer, church member, civic organization member, and student in an evening college class. Thus, multiple sets of expectations are placed on each person's behavior.

An individual's roles influence both general behavior and buying behavior. The demands of a person's many roles may be diverse and even inconsistent. Consider the various types of clothes that you buy and wear depending on whether you are going to class, to work, to a party, to church or synagogue, or to an aerobics class. You and others involved in these settings have expectations about what is acceptable clothing for these events. Thus, the expectations of those around us affect our purchases of clothing and many other products.

Family Influences

Family influences have a very direct impact on the consumer buying decision process. Parents teach children how to cope with a variety of problems, including those dealing with purchase decisions. **Consumer socialization** is the process through which a person acquires the knowledge and skills to function as a consumer. Often children gain this knowledge and set of skills by observing parents and older siblings in purchase situations, as well as through their own purchase experiences. Children observe brand preferences and buying practices in their families and, as adults, maintain some of these brand preferences and buying practices as they establish and raise their own families. Buying decisions made by a family are a combination of group and individual decision making.

Although female roles continue to change, women still make buying decisions related to many household items, including health care products, laundry supplies, paper products, and foods. Spouses participate jointly in the purchase of a variety of products, especially durable goods. Due to changes in men's roles, a significant proportion of men are major grocery shoppers. Children make many purchase decisions and influence numerous household purchase decisions. Knowing that children wield considerable influence over food brand preferences, H.J. Heinz is targeting them with EZ Squirt green ketchup in a squeeze bottle. Kids like squeezing squiggly green patterns on their hamburgers, and parents like the ketchup's extra vitamin C. Demand has been so strong that the company achieved its initial year's sales projections in the first 90 days after the product was launched.[7]

The extent to which either one or both of the two adult family members take part in family decision making varies among families and product categories. Traditionally family decision-making processes have been grouped into four categories: autonomic, husband-dominant, wife-dominant, and syncratic. Autonomic decision making means that an equal number of decisions are made by each adult household member. In husband-dominant or wife-dominant decision making, the husband or the wife makes most of the family decisions. Syncratic decision making means most decisions concerning

WORK

HOME

HEAVEN

Allen Edmonds
For All Walks of Life™

Almost any place feels like paradise in Allen-Edmonds shoes. They come in styles from business to casual. Not to mention the widest selection available, from size 5-18, widths AAAA to EEE. Plus, our exclusive Recrafting™ process is the next best thing to life everlasting. For a catalog and nearest dealer, call 1-800-235-2348.

Shoes from top to bottom: Bradley, Quincy, Devonshire   www.allenedmonds.com   Made in USA

Role Influences
Allen Edmonds provides many styles of men's shoes. The influences of multiple roles affect the buying decision process of many products, including shoes.

consumer socialization The process through which a person acquires the knowledge and skills to function as a consumer

SNAPSHOT

Frugality begins at home

Adults admit many of the views they have about money were formed at an early age.

77%
80%
85%
50% off

Budget money   **Donation to charity/church**   **Shop for best buy**

Source: *USA Today*, www.usatoday.com/snapshot. Copyright 2001, *USA Today*. Reprinted with permission.

purchases are made jointly by both partners. The type of family decision making employed depends on the values and attitudes of family members.

When two or more family members participate in a purchase, their roles may dictate that each is responsible for performing certain purchase-related tasks, such as initiating the idea, gathering information, determining if the product is affordable, deciding whether to buy the product, or selecting the specific brand. The specific purchase tasks performed depend on the types of products being considered, the kind of family purchase decision process typically employed, and the amount of influence children have in the decision process. Thus, different family members may play different roles in the family buying process. To develop a marketing mix that precisely meets the needs of target market members, marketers must know not only who does the actual buying but also which other family members perform purchase-related tasks.

The family life cycle stage affects individual and joint needs of family members. (Family life cycle stages were discussed in Chapter 7.) For example, consider how the car needs of recently married "twenty-somethings" differ from those of the same couple when they are "forty-somethings" with a 13-year-old daughter and a 17-year-old son. Family life cycle changes can affect which family members are involved in purchase decisions and the types of products purchased.

Reference Groups and Opinion Leaders

reference group Any group that positively or negatively affects a person's values, attitudes, or behavior

A **reference group** is any group that positively or negatively affects a person's values, attitudes, or behavior. Reference groups can be large or small. Most people have several reference groups, such as families, work-related groups, fraternities or sororities, civic clubs, professional organizations, or church-related groups.

In general, there are three major types of reference groups: membership, aspirational, and disassociative. A membership reference group is one to which an individual actually belongs; the individual identifies with group members strongly enough to take on the values, attitudes, and behaviors of people in that group. An aspirational reference group is a group to which one aspires to belong; one desires to be like those group members. A group that a person does not wish to be associated with is a disassociative reference group; the individual does not want to take on the values, attitudes, and behavior of group members.

A reference group may serve as an individual's point of comparison and source of information. A customer's behavior may change to be more in line with actions and beliefs of group members. For example, a person might stop buying one brand of shirts and switch to another based on reference group members' advice. An individual may also seek information from the reference group about other factors regarding a prospective purchase, such as where to buy a certain product.

The extent to which a reference group affects a purchase decision depends on the product's conspicuousness and on the individual's susceptibility to reference group influence. Generally, the more conspicuous a product, the more likely that the purchase decision will be influenced by reference groups. A product's conspicuousness is determined by whether others can see it and whether it can attract attention. Reference groups can affect whether a person does or does not buy a product at all, buys a type of product within a product category, or buys a specific brand.

A marketer sometimes tries to use reference group influence in advertisements by suggesting that people in a specific group buy a product and are highly satisfied with it. In this type of appeal, the advertiser hopes that many will accept the suggested group as a reference group and buy (or react more favorably to) the product. Whether this kind of advertising succeeds depends on three factors: how effectively the advertisement communicates the message, the type of product, and the individual's susceptibility to reference group influence.

opinion leader A reference group member who provides information about a specific sphere that interests reference group participants

In most reference groups, one or more members stand out as opinion leaders. An **opinion leader** provides information about a specific sphere that interests reference group participants who seek information. Opinion leaders are viewed by other group members as being well informed about a particular area and as easily accessible. An opinion leader is not the foremost authority on all issues. However, because such individuals know they are opinion leaders, they feel a responsibility to remain informed about their sphere of interest and thus seek out advertisements, manufacturers' brochures, salespeople, and other sources of information.

An opinion leader is likely to be most influential when consumers have high product involvement but low product knowledge, when they share the opinion leader's values and attitudes, and when the product details are numerous or complicated.

Social Classes

social class An open group of individuals with similar social rank

In all societies, people rank others into higher or lower positions of respect. This ranking results in social classes. A **social class** is an open group of individuals with similar social rank. A class is referred to as "open" because people can move into and out of it. Criteria for grouping people into classes vary from one society to another. In the United States, we take into account many factors, including occupation, education, income, wealth, race, ethnic group, and possessions. A person who is ranking someone does not necessarily apply all of a society's criteria. Sometimes, too, the role of income in social class determination tends to be overemphasized. Although income does help determine social class, the other factors also play a role. Within social classes, both incomes and spending habits differ significantly among members.

Analyses of social class in the United States commonly divide people into three to seven categories. Social scientist Richard P. Coleman suggests that for purposes of consumer analysis the population be divided into the four major status groups shown in Table 8.1, but he cautions marketers that considerable diversity exists in people's life situations within each status group.

To some degree, individuals within social classes develop and assume common behavioral patterns. They may have similar attitudes, values, language patterns, and possessions. Social class influences many aspects of people's lives. For example, it affects their chances of having children and their children's chances of surviving infancy. It influences their childhood training, choice of religion, selection of occupation, and leisure time activities. Because social class has a bearing on so many aspects of a person's life, it also affects buying decisions.

Social class influences people's spending, saving, and credit practices. It determines to some extent the type, quality, and quantity of products a person buys and uses. For example, it affects purchases of clothing, foods, financial and health care services, travel, recreation, entertainment, and home furnishings. Social class also affects an individual's shopping patterns and types of stores patronized. In some instances, marketers attempt to focus on certain social classes through store location and interior design, product design and features, pricing strategies, personal sales efforts, and advertising.

Culture and Subcultures

culture The values, knowledge, beliefs, customs, objects, and concepts of a society

Culture is the accumulation of values, knowledge, beliefs, customs, objects, and concepts that a society uses to cope with its environment and passes on to future generations. Examples of objects are foods, furniture, buildings, clothing, and tools. Concepts include education, welfare, and laws. Culture also includes core values and the degree of acceptability of a wide range of behaviors in a specific society. For example, in our culture customers as well as businesspeople are expected to behave ethically.

Culture influences buying behavior because it permeates our daily lives. Our culture determines what we wear and eat and where we reside and travel. Society's

Table 8.1	Social Class Behavioral Traits and Purchasing Characteristics	
Class (% of Population)	**Behavioral Traits**	**Buying Characteristics**
Upper (14%); includes upper-upper, lower-upper, upper-middle	Income varies among the groups, but goals are the same Various lifestyles: preppy, conventional, intellectual, etc. Neighborhood and prestigious schooling important	Prize quality merchandise Favor prestigious brands Products purchased must reflect good taste Invest in art Spend money on travel, theater, books, tennis, golf, and swimming clubs
Middle (32%)	Often in management Considered white collar Prize good schools Desire an attractive home in a nice, well-maintained neighborhood Often emulate the upper class Enjoy travel and physical activity Often very involved in children's school and sports activities	Like fashionable items Consult experts via books, articles, etc. before purchasing Spend for experiences they consider worthwhile for their children (e.g., ski trips, college education) Tour packages, weekend trips Attractive home furnishings
Working (38%)	Emphasis on family, especially for economic and emotional supports (e.g., job opportunity tips, help in times of trouble) Blue collar Earn good incomes Enjoy mechanical items and recreational activities Enjoy leisure time after working hard	Buy vehicles and equipment related to recreation, camping, and selected sports Strong sense of value Shop for best bargains at off-price and discount stores Purchase automotive equipment for making repairs Enjoy local travel, recreational parks
Lower (16%)	Often unemployed due to situations beyond their control (e.g., layoffs, company takeovers) Can include individuals on welfare and homeless individuals Often have strong religious beliefs May be forced to live in less desirable neighborhoods In spite of their problems, often good-hearted toward others Enjoy everyday activities when possible	Most products purchased are for survival Ability to convert good discards into usable items

Source: Adapted with permission from Richard P. Coleman, "The Continuing Significance of Social Class to Marketing," *Journal of Consumer Research,* Dec. 1983, pp. 265–280, with data from J. Paul Peter and Jerry C. Olson, *Consumer Behavior: Marketing Strategy Perspective* (Homewood, IL.: Irwin, 1987), p. 433.

interest in the healthfulness of food affects food companies' approaches to developing and promoting their products. Culture also influences how we buy and use products and our satisfaction from them. In the U.S. culture, makers of furniture, cars, and clothing strive to understand how people's color preferences are changing.

Because culture to some degree determines product purchases and uses, cultural changes affect product development, promotion, distribution, and pricing. Food marketers, for example, have made a multitude of changes in their marketing efforts. Thirty years ago, most families in our culture ate at least two meals a day together, and the mother spent four to six hours a day preparing those meals. Today, more than 75 percent of women between ages 25 and 54 work outside the home, and average family incomes have risen considerably. These shifts, along with scarcity of time, have resulted in dramatic changes in the national per capita consumption of certain foods, such as take-out foods, frozen dinners, and shelf-stable foods.

When U.S. marketers sell products in other countries, they realize the tremendous impact those cultures have on product purchases and use. Global marketers find that people in other regions of the world have different attitudes, values, and needs, which call for different methods of doing business as well as different types of marketing mixes. Some international marketers fail because they do not or cannot adjust to cultural differences.

A culture consists of various subcultures. **Subcultures** are groups of individuals whose characteristic values and behavior patterns are similar and differ from those of the surrounding culture. Subcultural boundaries are usually based on geographic designations and demographic characteristics, such as age, religion, race, and ethnicity. Our culture is marked by a number of different subcultures, among them West Coast, teenage, Asian American, and college students. Within subcultures, greater similarities exist in people's attitudes, values, and actions than within the broader culture. Relative to other subcultures, individuals in one subculture may have stronger preferences for specific types of clothing, furniture, or foods. It is important to understand that a person can be a member of more than one subculture and that the behavioral patterns and values attributed to specific subcultures do not necessarily apply to all group members.

The percentage of the American population comprising ethnic and racial subcultures is expected to grow. By 2050, about one-half of the people of the United States will be members of racial and ethnic minorities. The Bureau of the Census reports that the three largest and fastest-growing ethnic U.S. subcultures are African Americans, Hispanics, and Asians. The population growth of these subcultures interests marketers. To target these groups more precisely, marketers are striving to become increasingly sensitive to and knowledgeable about their differences. Businesses recognize that to succeed, their marketing strategies will have to take into account the values, needs, interests, shopping patterns, and buying habits of various subcultures.

African American Subculture. In the United States, the largest racial or ethnic subculture is African American. Research reveals that African American consumers possess distinct buying patterns. For example, African American consumers shop as often as four times a week and spend more on boys' clothing, athletic footwear, personal care services, and automobile rentals than do white consumers. Compared with other consumers, African Americans use coupons less often. In addition, research reveals that African Americans respond positively to advertising and products that reflect their heritage and prefer promotional messages appearing in media that target them specifically. They most commonly learn about products from television advertisements, salespeople, and information provided by calling manufacturers' toll-free numbers.

Increasingly, organizations are directing marketing efforts toward African American consumers. More African Americans are featured in advertisements for a wide array of products, including automobiles, athletic shoes, clothing, cosmetics, fast foods, soft drinks, and telecommunication services. In 1987, Hallmark Cards launched its Afrocentric brand, Mahogany, with 16 cards. Today Mahogany's selection includes hundreds of different cards. State Farm Insurance recently recruited film director Spike Lee to appear in an ad campaign aimed at increasing awareness of State Farm Insurance among African Americans.[8] Major cereal companies such as General Mills, Kellogg, and Kraft Foods aim special marketing efforts at African Americans because of their high consumption of cereals. More than 82 percent of African American households have ready-to-eat cereals in their pantries.[9]

Hispanic Subculture. In the next ten years, Hispanics will become the largest ethnic group in the United States.[10] Because of its growth and purchasing power, understanding the Hispanic subculture is critical to marketers. In general, Hispanics have strong family values, a need for respect, concern for product quality, and strong brand loyalty. Studies reveal that the majority of Hispanic consumers not only are brand loyal but also will pay more for a well-known brand. They tend to spend more time shopping in grocery stores than other consumers but use far fewer coupons. Promotions using Hispanic celebrities are effective in getting marketing messages across to Hispanic audiences. Incorporating prominent members of the Hispanic community, such as athletes and performers, into promotions is often successful. For

subculture A group of individuals whose characteristic values and behavior patterns are similar and differ from those of the surrounding culture

many adult Hispanics, the language of choice is Spanish. Studies reveal that Hispanics respond strongly to ads on Spanish television and radio. Shopping is more likely to be a family event in Hispanic households. When considering the buying behavior of Hispanics, marketers must keep in mind that this subculture is really composed of nearly two dozen nationalities, including Cuban, Mexican, Puerto Rican, Caribbean, Spanish, and Dominican. Each has its own history and unique culture that affect consumer preferences and buying behavior.

To attract this powerful subculture, marketers are taking Hispanic values and preferences into account when developing products and creating advertising and promotions. Recognizing that Hispanics are family oriented and fond of eating out, McDonald's, Denny's, and Churchs Chicken actively market to Hispanics. Recently Burger King launched campaigns directed at this subculture. Kmart focuses major marketing efforts on Hispanics; it expects Hispanics to emerge as its number one core shoppers by 2020.[11]

Asian American Subculture.   Asian Americans are the fastest-growing, most affluent, and perhaps most diverse American subculture. The term *Asian American* includes people from more than 15 ethnic groups, including Filipinos, Chinese, Japanese, Indians, Koreans, and Vietnamese. The individual language, religion, and value system of each group influences its members' purchasing decisions. Some traits of this subculture, however, carry across ethnic divisions, including an emphasis on hard work, strong family ties, and a high value placed on education. Asian Americans prefer to communicate and to read and listen to media in their native languages. With respect to buying behavior, marketers recognize that Asians are generally willing to pay more for distinct, well-known brands.

Retailers with a large population of Chinese shoppers have begun to capitalize on this group's celebration of the Chinese Lunar New Year. For example, during this time in the Los Angeles area, supermarkets stock traditional Chinese holiday foods and items used in the celebration, such as candles, greeting cards, and party goods. One ethnic characteristic of Asian Americans, especially Chinese, is that they like to gamble. Some Las Vegas casinos target specific marketing efforts at Asian Americans, especially in San Francisco, Los Angeles, and even New York.[12]

Subculture
Within subcultures, great similarities exist in people's attitudes, values, and actions. In the United States, the fastest growing subculture is Asian American.

Summary

Buying behavior is the decision processes and acts of people involved in buying and using products. Consumer buying behavior is the buying behavior of ultimate consumers.

An individual's level of involvement—the importance and intensity of interest in a product in a particular situation—affects the type of problem-solving process used. Enduring involvement is an ongoing interest in a product class because of personal relevance, whereas situational involvement is a temporary interest stemming from the particular circumstance or environment in which buyers find themselves. There are three kinds of consumer problem solving: routinized response behavior, limited problem solving, and extended problem solving. Consumers rely on routinized response behavior when buying frequently purchased, low-cost items requiring little search-and-decision effort. Limited problem solving is used for products purchased occasionally or when buyers need to acquire information about an unfamiliar brand in a familiar product category. Consumers engage in extended problem solving when purchasing an unfamiliar, expensive, or infrequently bought product. Purchase of a certain product does not always elicit the same type of decision making. Impulse buying is not a consciously planned buying behavior but involves a powerful urge to buy something immediately.

The consumer buying decision process includes five stages: problem recognition, information search, evaluation of alternatives, purchase, and postpurchase evaluation. Not all decision processes culminate in a purchase, nor do all consumer decisions include all five stages. Problem recognition occurs when buyers become aware of a difference between a desired state and an actual condition. After recognizing the problem or need, buyers search for information about products to help resolve the problem or satisfy the need. In the internal search, buyers search their memories for information about products that might solve the problem. If they cannot retrieve from memory enough information for a decision, they seek additional information through an external search. A successful search yields a group of brands, called a consideration set, that a buyer views as possible alternatives. To evaluate the products in the consideration set, the buyer establishes certain criteria by which to compare, rate, and rank different products. Marketers can influence consumers' evaluation by framing alternatives.

In the purchase stage, consumers select products or brands on the basis of results from the evaluation stage and on other dimensions. Buyers also choose the seller from whom they will buy the product. After the purchase, buyers evaluate the product to determine if its actual performance meets expected levels. Shortly after the purchase of an expensive product, for example, the postpurchase evaluation may result in cognitive dissonance, dissatisfaction brought on by the consumer's doubts as to whether he or she should have bought the product in the

first place or would have been better off buying another desirable brand.

Three major categories of influences affect the consumer buying decision process: situational, psychological, and social. Situational influences are external circumstances or conditions existing when a consumer makes a purchase decision. Situational influences include surroundings, time, reason for purchase, and the buyer's mood and condition.

Psychological influences partly determine people's general behavior, thus influencing their behavior as consumers. The primary psychological influences on consumer behavior are perception, motives, learning, attitudes, personality and self-concept, and lifestyles. Perception is the process of selecting, organizing, and interpreting information inputs (sensations received through sight, taste, hearing, smell, and touch) to produce meaning. The three steps in the perceptual process are selection, organization, and interpretation. Individuals have numerous perceptions of packages, products, brands, and organizations, which affect their buying decision processes. A motive is an internal energizing force that orients a person's activities toward satisfying needs or achieving goals. Learning refers to changes in a person's thought processes and behavior caused by information and experience. Marketers try to shape what consumers learn to influence what they buy. An attitude is an individual's enduring evaluation, feelings, and behavioral tendencies toward an object or idea and consists of three major components: cognitive, affective, and behavioral. Personality is the set of traits and behaviors that make a person unique. Self-concept, closely linked to personality, is a person's view or perception of himself or herself. Research indicates that buyers purchase products that reflect and enhance their self-concept. Lifestyle is an individual's pattern of living expressed through activities, interests, and opinions. Lifestyles influence consumers' needs, brand preferences, and how and where they shop.

Social influences are forces that other people exert on buying behavior. They include roles, family, reference groups and opinion leaders, social class, and culture and subcultures. Everyone occupies positions within groups, organizations, and institutions, and each position has a role—a set of actions and activities that a person in a particular position is supposed to perform based on expectations of both the individual and surrounding persons. In a family, children learn from parents and older siblings how to make decisions, such as purchase decisions. Consumer socialization is the process through which a person acquires the knowledge and skills to function as a consumer. The consumer socialization process is partially accomplished through family influences. A reference group is any group that positively or negatively affects a person's values, attitudes, or behavior. The three major types of reference groups are membership, aspirational, and disassociative. In most reference groups, one or more members stand out as opinion leaders by furnishing requested information to reference group participants. A social class is an open group of individuals with similar social rank. Social class influences people's spending, saving, and credit practices. Culture is the accumulation of values, knowledge, beliefs, customs, objects, and concepts that a society uses to cope with its environment and passes on to future generations. A culture is made up of subcultures. A subculture is a group of individuals whose characteristic values and behavior patterns are similar and differ from those of the surrounding culture. U.S. marketers focus on three major ethnic subcultures: African American, Hispanic, and Asian American.

Important Terms

Buying behavior
Consumer buying
   behavior
Level of involvement
Routinized response
   behavior
Limited problem solving
Extended problem solving
Impulse buying
Consumer buying decision
   process
Internal search
External search
Consideration set
Evaluative criteria
Cognitive dissonance
Situational influences
Psychological influences
Perception
Information inputs
Selective exposure

Selective distortion
Selective retention
Motive
Maslow's hierarchy of
   needs
Patronage motives
Learning
Attitude
Attitude scale
Personality
Self-concept
Lifestyle
Social influences
Role
Consumer socialization
Reference group
Opinion leader
Social class
Culture
Subculture

Discussion and Review Questions

1. How does a consumer's level of involvement affect his or her choice of problem-solving process?
2. Name the types of consumer problem-solving processes. List some products you have bought using each type. Have you ever bought a product on impulse? If so, describe the circumstances.
3. What are the major stages in the consumer buying decision process? Are all these stages used in all consumer purchase decisions? Why or why not?
4. What are the categories of situational factors that influence consumer buying behavior? Explain how each of these factors influences buyers' decisions.
5. What is selective exposure? Why do people engage in it?
6. How do marketers attempt to shape consumers' learning?
7. Why are marketers concerned about consumer attitudes?
8. In what ways do lifestyles affect the consumer buying decision process?
9. How do roles affect a person's buying behavior? Provide examples.

10. What are family influences, and how do they affect buying behavior?
11. What are reference groups? How do they influence buying behavior? Name some of your own reference groups.
12. How does an opinion leader influence the buying decision process of reference group members?
13. In what ways does social class affect a person's purchase decisions?
14. What is culture? How does it affect a person's buying behavior?
15. Describe the subcultures to which you belong. Identify buying behavior that is unique to one of your subcultures.

Application Questions

1. Consumers use one of three problem-solving processes when purchasing goods or services: routinized response behavior, limited problem solving, or extended problem solving. Describe three buying experiences you have had (one for each type of problem solving), and identify which problem-solving type you used. Discuss why that particular process was appropriate.
2. The consumer buying process consists of five stages: problem recognition, information search, evaluation of alternatives, purchase, and post-purchase evaluation. Not every buying decision goes through all five stages, and the process does not necessarily conclude in a purchase. Interview a classmate about the last purchase he or she made. Report the stages used and those skipped, if any.
3. Attitudes toward products or companies often affect consumer behavior. The three components of an attitude are cognitive, affective, and behavioral. Briefly describe how a beer company might alter the cognitive and affective components of consumer attitudes toward beer products and toward the company.
4. An individual's roles influence that person's buying behavior. Identify two of your roles and give an example of how they have influenced your buying decisions.
5. Select five brands of toothpaste and explain how the appeals used in advertising these brands relate to Maslow's hierarchy of needs.

Internet
Exercise & Resources

Visit **www.prideferrell.com** for resources to help you master the material in this chapter, plus materials that will help you expand your marketing knowledge, including: Internet exercise updates, ACE self-tests, hotlinks to companies featured in this chapter, and much more.

Amazon.com

Some mass-market e-commerce sites, such as Amazon.com Inc., have extended the concept of customization to their customer base. Amazon has created an affinity group by drawing upon certain users' likes and dislikes to make product recommendations to other users. Check out this pioneering online retailer at:

www.amazon.com

1. What might motivate some consumers to read a "Top Selling" list?

2. Is the consumer's level of involvement with online book purchase likely to be high or low?

3. Discuss the consumer buying decision process as it relates to a decision to purchase from Amazon.com.

VIDEO CASE 8.1
Understanding Consumer Behavior Builds Sales at Build-A-Bear

How many retail empires are built by chief executive bears—especially CEBs with a keen sense of consumer behavior? So far, just one: the Build-A-Bear Workshop, a store chain that turns the point-of-sale buying process into a hands-on, interactive experience.

The CEB behind Build-A-Bear is Maxine Clark, who spent 25 years as an executive with May Department Stores before leaving the corporate world to become an entrepreneur in 1997. Thinking back to her much-loved teddy bear and to the magic she remembered in special shopping trips as a child, Clark focused her new business on a very smart niche: entertainment retailing designed to please children of all ages. "I felt there was a need for more creative retail," she notes. "My strength is in merchandising and marketing, and I knew that kids require you to be creative. I loved retailing and wanted to try something different."

Clark was determined to make memories, not simply sell an everyday, off-the-shelf product. So she created a store-based workshop environment and invited buyers to actively participate in crafting their own stuffed animals. Master Bear Builders (store employees) help buyers choose the types of animals they want. Bears, bunnies, dogs, ponies, and frogs, available in small or large sizes, are just some of the choices. Next, buyers select the fake-fur color and the amount of stuffing, insert the

heart, help stitch the seams, gently fluff the fur, and name their new friends. Finally, they get to dress their animals in miniature cowboy gear, angel wings, or dozens of other whimsical outfits and pick out cute accessories to create one-of-a-kind, personalized stuffed animals that express their interests and dreams. The stuffed animal alone costs $10 or more. Outfits and accessories, priced at $2 and up, round out the total purchase price. Each animal goes home in a house-shaped package, complete with a birth certificate signed by Clark as CEB.

As part of the buying procedure, customers enter their animals' names and their own names and addresses, e-mail addresses, gender, and birth dates at computer stations in each store. This information is used to generate a birth certificate for every toy. Then the information is pooled with sales data and other details, carefully analyzed, and used to plan newsletters and other communications and promotions. In addition, because each animal contains a unique bar-coded tag, the company can send lost toys back to their owners by consulting the database to determine ownership.

Before opening the first Build-A-Bear store—in St. Louis, Missouri—Clark tested the idea on the 10-year-old daughter of a friend, who was enthusiastic about the concept. As the chain grows, she continues to stay in touch with changes in her market's needs and behavior through a Cub Advisory Board composed of 20 children, ages 6 to 14. The group meets every three months to discuss new programs and review proposals for new stuffed animals, fur colors, accessories, and fashions. Between meetings, Clark requests feedback from the board on specific questions via mail and e-mail, and combs through customer letters and e-mail messages to learn more about what customers like and don't like. Looking ahead to global expansion, the CEB is forming a webbased advisory board to tap the ideas of a broader cross-section of customers.

The special retail atmosphere Clark wants to create requires lots of behind-the-scenes planning. Build-A-Bear's retail employees must complete an intensive three-week training course at World Bearquarters in St. Louis before they start work in a store. Yet the company doesn't take itself too seriously. The organization weaves a "bear" theme throughout its official activities. For example, managers hold titles such as "bearitory leader," and employees are entitled to "honey days," 15 days of paid vacation and personal time off every year.

Although Build-A-Bear began as a one-store business, it has quickly grown into a bear-size success story. Yearly sales through the chain of more than 50 stores exceed $50 million, and Clark expects to be operating more than 250 stores by 2007. Each store rings up about $700 per square foot in annual sales, an impressive achievement for a relatively new retail concept. In the future, the company hopes to expand into a variety of multimedia entertainment products such as books, television programs, and movies. Customers can already buy CDs and audiocassettes featuring fun songs like "Ready Teddy." No matter what innovations Clark implements in the coming years, she will continue to put on a great show for her customers. "Retail is entertainment, and the store is a stage," Clark says. "When customers have fun, they spend more money."[13]

QUESTIONS FOR DISCUSSION

1. Which situational influences would you expect to be most important for customers in a Build-A-Bear Workshop?
2. What role does learning play in shaping the buying behavior of Build-A-Bear's customers?
3. How does Build-A-Bear influence the level of involvement that customers might attach to stuffed animals? Does level of involvement depend on whether the customer is a child or a parent?

CASE 8.2

Marketing to Women: A Lucrative Direction for Automakers

Automakers are noticing that women are definitely in the driver's seat when it comes to vehicle purchases. Surveys show that women make or influence eight out of ten U.S. car or truck purchases. This means American women are spending an estimated $83 billion on cars and trucks every year. Sales of sport-utility vehicles (SUVs), minivans, and light trucks make up more than half of all new-vehicle purchases, a national craze fueled largely by women's huge purchasing power. These developments explain why car manufacturers are building up their knowledge of consumer buying behavior to compete more aggressively for a larger share of this lucrative and influential market.

A "tremendous buying force" is the way one top official of DaimlerChrysler characterizes women's influence on vehicle purchases, especially vehicles other than cars. He notes that most women "don't want to return to a car after driving a light truck such as a minivan" because they like the higher vantage point, a sharp contrast to the seats in today's low-slung cars.

Clearly lifestyles and life stages are powerful influences on women's buying decisions. Women with families find minivans, SUVs, and light trucks roomier and more convenient than cars for ferrying children, pets, and possessions, which is why almost 20 percent of all women own such vehicles. Subaru, for example, is targeting women in an ongoing ad campaign featuring tennis great Martina Navratilova, who previously drove the company's Outback SUV and now drives its Forester model. "I am the hired gun for the active-lifestyle woman," Navratilova says. "I'm the epitome of it. My car looks like a sporting goods store, with a tennis racket, a basketball, etc. I'm always throwing things in it." Acura also targets active women through its sponsorship of the Acura Women's Cycle Team, women's tennis tournaments, and other events.

Cindy Hess, vice president of small-car platform engineering at DaimlerChrysler, had women's lifestyles in mind when designing the PT Cruiser, a roomy, nostalgic vehicle that handles like a passenger car. "One of the things we find is that people get to the point where they want to carry a lot of stuff or friends," she comments. "They're saying, 'I don't want the minivan, I don't want the look,' but they need space and a little cargo room. And they see that this is stylish." So stylish, in fact, that demand has far outstripped supply, creating lengthy waiting lists and inspiring local PT Cruiser clubs as well as an online PT Cruiser Women's Network.

Another dimension of women's car-buying behavior is catching the eye of automakers. U.S. women tend to be highly brand loyal, and nearly 75 percent choose American car brands. The story is very different for U.S. men, who are increasingly steering toward purchasing imports. "*Vive la différence,*" say automakers as they step up their targeting of women with special marketing programs such as educational events, sports sponsorships, and scholarships. DaimlerChrysler, for example, has begun offering special Women's Day events at industry showcases such as the North America International Auto Show, Chicago Auto Show, and New York Auto Show. Company experts present DaimlerChrysler's newest models and lead semi-

nars on off-road driving, vehicle maintenance, child safety seats, and other topics of interest to women.

General Motors puts the marketing spotlight on women through the Chevrolet Recognizing Excellence of Women in Academics and Rewarding Dynamic Student-athletes (REWARDS) scholarship program. Championship figure skater Michelle Kwan promotes and presents these scholarships, which go to college-bound women who excel academically and are active in sports ranging from basketball and kayaking to track and, of course, figure skating.

As U.S. automakers put new emphasis on women's buying behavior, their European counterparts are moving more cautiously. For example, a top executive of Peugeot's European ad agency stresses that corporate fleet buyers and men are the most important targets for many Peugeot models: "We are not going to target a Peugeot 406 directly at women, because the vast majority who buy these cars are men, and are going to be alienated."

In the United Kingdom, many car commercials show women in small, practical cars rather than larger or more glamorous ones, a custom that, research shows, antagonizes half of all women ages 18 to 44—not a good foundation on which to build customer relationships. Still, women are clearly part of the European marketing plans made by multinational automakers like Ford. "We always ensure women's views are taken on board and made to count because they are an important audience," confirms the brand manager for Mondeo, a Ford model sold in Europe. "Whoever is within the buying audience of a car, we will target, and women are counted within every category now."[14]

QUESTIONS FOR DISCUSSION

1. Which of the needs in Maslow's hierarchy do women seem to be satisfying when they buy a car or light truck?
2. How do women's lifestyles influence their vehicle-buying decisions?
3. When planning marketing efforts, why should automakers take into account the various roles women play?

Business Markets and Buying Behavior

9

OBJECTIVES

- To become familiar with the various types of business markets
- To identify the major characteristics of business customers and transactions
- To understand several attributes of demand for business products
- To become familiar with the major components of a buying center
- To understand the stages of the business buying decision process and the factors that affect this process
- To describe industrial classification systems and explain how they can be used to identify and analyze business markets

Sodexho Marriott Stirs Up the Food-Service Industry

Cooking for a crowd is all in a day's work for Sodexho Marriott Services. With more than $4.5 billion in annual sales, Sodexho Marriott competes with Aramark and others to operate food service facilities for corporations, stadiums, hospitals, colleges, and other organizations. A key ingredient in Sodexho's marketing recipe is its focus on the education food service market, where industrywide annual sales are approaching $30 billion. This market covers full-service management of dining facilities on college campuses across the United States.

Sodexho is always cooking up new ways to help its institutional customers better serve their own customers. Its latest innovation is a segmentation program called LifeSTYLING. This program enables Sodexho to adjust its offerings from campus to campus based on students' eating behaviors and preferences. The company started by hiring segmentation specialists to analyze student lifestyle research and identify distinct segments within the overall market based on taste differences and ability to pay. Out of this analysis came six segments: Trend Setters—like ethnic and innovative foods and have a large food budget; Metro Fusion—like ethnic and innovative foods and have a small food budget; Fun Express—prefer ethnic and innovative foods and have a medium-size food budget; Main Streamers—enjoy traditional foods and have a small food budget; Time Liners—prefer traditional foods and have a medium-size food budget; and Star Gazers—like traditional, ethnic, and innovative foods and have a medium to high food budget.

Next, the company surveyed thousands of students on campuses where it operates food service facilities to assess their reactions to many different facets of the offering. By researching preferences for brand name foods and beverages, hours of service, take-out options, atmospherics, portion size, and other features, Sodexho was able to profile each segment in much more detail. Then it began testing the segmentation process at dozens of U.S. campuses. At each test site, employees asked students for their ZIP codes and added this information to the database so the student body could be segmented. Finally, Sodexho analyzed the data for each campus and began adjusting its offering based on the preferences of the predominant segments. For example, at Western Washington University in Bellingham, Washington, Sodexho found there was a big market for take-out food. Says Dawn Perry, senior director of marketing for the education division, "Portability was important to these students. So we implemented our Cafe Fresca program and have seen about a 20 percent increase in sales in the take-out category."

Each campus turned out to have a unique blend of segments. At Huntington College in Indiana, 24 percent of the students were classified as Trend Setters, so the company began serving more ethnic and innovative foods such as shrimp jambalaya with jalapeño cornbread. At Plattsburgh State University in New York, Sodexho turned the dining hall into a restaurant-style facility, complete with an open kitchen. More changes are ahead as Sodexho rolls out its segmentation program and stirs up the education food service industry.[1]

Serving business markets effectively requires understanding those markets. Marketers at Sodexho Marriott go to considerable lengths to understand their customers so they can provide better services and develop and maintain long-term customer relationships. Like consumer marketers, business marketers are concerned about satisfying their customers.

In this chapter, we look at business markets and business buying decision processes. We first discuss various kinds of business markets and the types of buyers making up these markets. Next, we explore several dimensions of business buying, such as characteristics of transactions, attributes and concerns of buyers, methods of buying, and distinctive features of demand for products sold to business purchasers. We then examine how business buying decisions are made and who makes the purchases. Finally, we consider how business markets are analyzed.

Business Markets

business markets Individuals or groups that purchase a specific kind of product for resale, direct use in producing other products, or use in general daily operations

A **business market** (also called a *business-to-business market*) consists of individuals or groups that purchase a specific kind of product for one of three purposes: resale, direct use in producing other products, or use in general daily operations. The four categories of business markets are producer, reseller, government, and institutional. In the remainder of this section, we discuss each of these types of markets.

Producer Markets

producer markets Individuals and business organizations that purchase products to make profits by using them to produce other products or using them in their operations

Individuals and business organizations that purchase products for the purpose of making a profit by using them to produce other products or using them in their operations are classified as **producer markets.** Producer markets include buyers of raw materials, as well as purchasers of semifinished and finished items used to produce other products. For example, manufacturers buy raw materials and component parts for direct use in product production. Grocery stores and supermarkets are part of producer markets for numerous support products such as paper and plastic bags, counters, and scanners. Farmers are part of producer markets for farm machinery, fertilizer, seed, and livestock. Producer markets include a broad array of industries, ranging from agriculture, forestry, fisheries, and mining to construction, transportation, communications, and utilities. As Table 9.1 indicates, the number of business establishments in national producer markets is enormous.

Manufacturers are geographically concentrated. More than half are located in only seven states: New York, California, Pennsylvania, Illinois, Ohio, New Jersey, and

Table 9.1	Number of Establishments in Industry Groups
Industry	**Number of Establishments**
Agriculture, forestry, fishing	117,000
Mining	27,000
Construction	667,000
Manufacturing	398,000
Transportation, public utilities	301,000
Finance, insurance, real estate	677,000
Services	2,544,000

Source: Bureau of the Census, *Statistical Abstract of the United States* (Washington, DC: Government Printing Office, 2000), p. 544.

Aiming at Producer Markets
Both Baldor and Engelhard market their products to companies that would be a part of producer markets.

Michigan. This concentration sometimes enables businesses that sell to producer markets to serve them more efficiently. Within certain states, production in a specific industry may account for a sizable proportion of that industry's total production.

Reseller Markets

reseller markets
Intermediaries who buy finished goods and resell them for profit

Reseller markets consist of intermediaries, such as wholesalers and retailers, who buy finished goods and resell them for profit. Aside from making minor alterations, resellers do not change the physical characteristics of the products they handle. Except for items that producers sell directly to consumers, all products sold to consumer markets are first sold to reseller markets.

Wholesalers purchase products for resale to retailers, to other wholesalers, and to producers, governments, and institutions. Of the 530,000 wholesalers in the United States, a large percentage are located in New York, California, Illinois, Texas, Ohio, Pennsylvania, and New Jersey.[2] Although some products are sold directly to end users, many manufacturers sell their products to wholesalers, who in turn sell the products to other firms in the distribution system. Thus, wholesalers are very important in helping producers get a product to customers. Professional buyers and buying committees make wholesalers' initial purchase decisions. Reordering is often automated.

Retailers purchase products and resell them to final customers. There are approximately 1.6 million retailers in the United States, employing more than 22 million people and generating more than $2.3 trillion in annual sales.[3] Some retailers carry a large number of items. Supermarkets may handle as many as 30,000 different products. In small, individually owned retail stores, owners or managers make purchasing decisions. In chain stores, a central office buyer or buying committee frequently decides whether a product will be made available for selection by store managers. For most products, however, local management makes the actual buying decisions for a particular store.

When making purchase decisions, resellers consider several factors. They evaluate the level of demand for a product to determine in what quantity and at what prices the product can be resold. Retailers assess the amount of space required to handle a

Even with grips you won't be able to hold on to them.

The BIC Matic Grip® and Cristal Grip®...
two updates of two best sellers
that will sell even better with the
added value of soft comfort grips.
Just try to keep them on the shelves.

The best loved name in writing.

BIC®

Marketing to Resellers
In this advertisement Bic is attempting to reach organizations that would be classified as being in reseller markets.

product relative to its potential profit. In fact, they sometimes evaluate products on the basis of sales per square foot of selling area. Because customers often depend on resellers to have products available when needed, resellers typically appraise a supplier's ability to provide adequate quantities when and where wanted. Resellers also take into account the ease of placing orders and the availability of technical assistance and training programs from the producer. When resellers consider buying a product not previously carried, they try to determine whether the product competes with or complements products the firm currently handles. These types of concerns distinguish reseller markets from other markets.

Government Markets

Federal, state, county, and local governments make up **government markets.** These markets spend billions of dollars annually for a variety of goods and services to support their internal operations and provide citizens with such products as highways, education, water, energy, and national defense. The federal government spends about $274 billion annually on national defense alone.[4] Government expenditures annually account for about 19 percent of the U.S. gross domestic product.

Besides the federal government, there are 50 state governments, 3,043 county governments, and 84,410 local governments.[5] The amount spent by federal, state, and local units during the last 30 years has increased rapidly because the total number of government units and the services they provide have both increased. Costs of providing these services have also risen. As Table 9.2 notes, the federal government spends more than half the total amount spent by all governments.

government markets
Federal, state, county, and local governments that buy goods and services to support their internal operations and provide products to their constituencies

Table 9.2	Annual Expenditures by Government Units for Selected Years (in billions of dollars)		
Year	Total Government Expenditures	Federal Government Expenditures	State and Local Expenditures
1975	560	292	268
1980	959	526	432
1985	1,581	1,032	658
1990	2,369	1,393	976
1995	2,820	1,704	1,116
2000*	3,360	2,084	1,276

*Estimates

Source: Bureau of the Census, *Statistical Abstract of the United States* (Washington, D.C.: Government Printing Office, 2000), p. 301.

The types and quantities of products bought by government markets reflect societal demands on various government agencies. As citizens' needs for government services change, so does demand for products by government markets. Although it is common to hear of large corporations being awarded government contracts, in fact businesses of all sizes market to government agencies. For example, over the last five years, Infinity Technologies, a small firm in Huntsville, Alabama, has been awarded government contracts with the U.S. Army, the U.S. Navy, NASA, the U.S. Air Force, and the General Services Administration. [6]

Because government agencies spend public funds to buy the products needed to provide services, they are accountable to the public. This accountability explains their relatively complex set of buying procedures. Some firms do not even try to sell to government buyers because they want to avoid the tangle of red tape. However, many marketers have learned to deal efficiently with government procedures and do not find them a stumbling block. For certain products, such as defense-related items, the government may be the only customer. The U.S. Government Printing Office publishes and distributes several documents explaining buying procedures and describing the types of products various federal agencies purchase.

Governments make purchases through bids or negotiated contracts. Although companies may be reluctant to approach government markets because of the complicated bidding process, once they understand the rules of this process, some firms routinely penetrate government markets. To make a sale under the bid system, firms must apply for and be approved to be placed on a list of qualified bidders. When a government unit wants to buy, it sends out a detailed description of the products to qualified bidders. Businesses wishing to sell such products submit bids. The government unit is usually required to accept the lowest bid.

When buying nonstandard or highly complex products, a government unit often uses a negotiated contract. Under this procedure, the government unit selects only a few firms and then negotiates specifications and terms; it eventually awards the contract to one of the negotiating firms. Most large defense-related contracts, once held by such companies as McDonnell Douglas and General Dynamics, traditionally were negotiated in this fashion. However, as the number and size of such contracts have declined, these companies have had to strengthen their marketing efforts and look to other markets. Although government markets can impose intimidating requirements, they can also be very lucrative.

Institutional Markets

institutional markets
Organizations with charitable, educational, community, or other nonbusiness goals

Organizations with charitable, educational, community, or other nonbusiness goals constitute **institutional markets.** Members of institutional markets include churches, some hospitals, fraternities and sororities, charitable organizations, and private colleges. Institutions purchase millions of dollars' worth of products annually to provide goods, services, and ideas to congregations, students, patients, and others. Because institutions often have different goals and fewer resources than other types of organizations, marketers may use special marketing efforts to serve them. For example, Hussey Seating in Maine sells bleacher stadium seating to schools, colleges, and other institutions, as well as to sports arenas. The family-owned business shows its support for institutional customers through assistance with school funding and reduced-cost construction of local economic development projects.[7]

Dimensions of Marketing to Business Customers

Having considered different types of business customers, we now look at several dimensions of marketing to business customers. We examine several characteristics of transactions with business customers, and then discuss attributes of business customers and some of their primary concerns when making purchase decisions. Next, we consider buying methods and major types of purchases. Finally, we discuss the characteristics of demand for business products.

Characteristics of Transactions with Business Customers

Transactions between businesses differ from consumer sales in several ways. Orders by business customers tend to be much larger than individual consumer sales. Suppliers often must sell products in large quantities to make profits; consequently, they prefer not to sell to customers who place small orders. For example, Airborne Express competes successfully against FedEx and UPS by providing low-cost overnight delivery services primarily to businesses that buy such services in high volume.

Some business purchases involve expensive items, such as computers. Other products, such as raw materials and component items, are used continuously in production, and the supply may need frequent replenishing. The contract regarding terms of sale of these items is likely to be a long-term agreement.

Discussions and negotiations associated with business purchases can require considerable marketing time and selling effort. Purchasing decisions are often made by committee; orders are frequently large and expensive; and products may be custom built. Several people or departments in the purchasing organization will probably be involved. One department might express a need for a product, a second department might develop the specifications, a third might stipulate maximum expenditures, and a fourth might place the order.

reciprocity   An arrangement unique to business marketing in which two organizations agree to buy from each other

One practice unique to business markets is **reciprocity,** an arrangement in which two organizations agree to buy from each other. Reciprocal agreements that threaten competition are illegal. The Federal Trade Commission and the Justice Department take actions to stop anticompetitive reciprocal practices. Nonetheless, a certain amount of reciprocal activity occurs among small businesses and, to a lesser extent, among larger companies. Because reciprocity influences purchasing agents to deal only with certain suppliers, it can lower morale among agents and lead to less than optimal purchases.

Attributes of Business Customers

Business customers differ from consumers in their purchasing behavior in that they are better informed about the products they purchase. They demand detailed information about products' functional features and technical specifications to ensure that the products meet the organization's needs. Personal goals, however, may also influence business buying behavior. Most purchasing agents seek the psychological satisfaction that comes with organizational advancement and financial rewards. Agents who consistently exhibit rational business buying behavior are likely to attain these personal goals because they help their firms achieve organizational objectives. Today many suppliers and their customers build and maintain mutually beneficial relationships, sometimes called *partnerships.*

Building Long-Term Relationships with Business Customers
Like many other companies, Hertz attempts to develop long-term relationships with small businesses by offering special rates and packages of special services designed to meet the needs of small businesses.

Primary Concerns of Business Customers

When making purchasing decisions, business customers take into account a variety of factors. Among their chief considerations are price, product quality, and service. Price matters greatly to business customers because it influences operating costs and costs of goods sold, which in turn affect selling price, profit margin, and ultimately the ability to compete. When purchasing major equipment, a business customer views price as the amount of investment necessary to obtain a certain level of return or savings. A business customer is likely to compare the price of a product with the benefits the product will provide to the organization.

Most business customers try to achieve and maintain a specific level of quality in the products they buy. To achieve this goal, most firms establish standards (usually stated as a percentage of defects allowed) for these products and buy them on the basis of a set of expressed characteristics, commonly called *specifications*. A customer evaluates the quality of the products being considered to determine whether they meet specifications. If a product fails to meet specifications or malfunctions for the ultimate consumer, the customer may drop that product's supplier and switch to a different one. On the other hand, customers are ordinarily cautious about buying products that exceed specifications because such products often cost more, thus increasing the organization's overall costs. Specifications are designed to meet a customer's wants, and anything that does not contribute to meeting those wants is considered wasteful.

Business buyers value service. Services offered by suppliers directly and indirectly influence customers' costs, sales, and profits. In some instances, the mix of customer services is the major means by which marketers gain a competitive advantage. Typical services desired by customers are market information, inventory maintenance, on-time delivery, and repair services. Business buyers are likely to need technical product information, data regarding demand, information about general economic conditions, or supply and delivery information. Maintaining adequate inventory is critical because it helps make products accessible when a customer

TECH*KNOW

Digging Deeper into Buying Behavior

Who, what, when, where, why, and *how*—marketers targeting business markets are always looking for new ways to track and analyze buying behavior. One approach is to use sophisticated software to comb through customer data and search out details about buyers' needs, likes, and dislikes. Honeywell International did this when it used customer management software to track its interactions with the airlines that buy jet engines and other products from its air transport division. While studying the data, Honeywell learned that some airlines were complaining about problems with parts inventories. In response, the company began offering customers a new inventory management service.

Flexjet, owned by Canadian plane manufacturer Bombardier Aerospace, uses a different approach to collecting data about business customers. Companies pay $400,000 and up to share ownership of a plush Flexjet plane for use by corporate executives and clients. Knowing that quality service is vital to customer satisfaction, Flexjet designed a brief questionnaire for customers to complete after each flight using a Palm handheld computer. Crew members also input information about the flight and then transmit everything to Flexjet headquarters for overnight analysis. As a result, Flexjet can quickly identify and address any problems to keep its business customers satisfied and continue gaining ground against its main competitor, market leader NetJets.

Permaboss.com, which makes industrial machinery for embossing and fusing, listened carefully when buyers expressed concerns about keeping machines running after installation. The company realized that letting machines sit idle while waiting for repair or supplies would be costly for customers. Its solution? Equip each machine with web-based streaming audio and video technology. Now technicians at Permaboss.com headquarters can easily diagnose problems and talk customers through the repair process. The machines also gather data on usage patterns so Permaboss.com can send reminders about scheduled maintenance.

Mimeo.com carved out a significant position in the printing business by analyzing business buying behavior and responding to the need for after-hours printing. Although the company is based in New York, it maintains a facility close to FedEx's Memphis sorting hub so it can accept late-day print jobs and send shipments to customers overnight. Currently more than one-third of its orders arrive after most printers have gone home. "Unlike a corporate copy center, which may close at 5 o'clock, we're able to take orders up to 10 o'clock," explains the CEO. "That's five hours that we're open and able to service our corporate clients."

needs them and reduces the customer inventory requirements and costs. Since business customers are usually responsible for ensuring that products are on hand and ready for use when needed, on-time delivery is crucial. Furthermore, reliable, on-time delivery saves business customers money because it enables them to carry less inventory. Purchasers of machinery are especially concerned about obtaining repair services and replacement parts quickly because inoperable equipment is costly. Caterpillar Inc., manufacturer of earth-moving, construction, and materials-handling machinery, has built an international reputation, as well as a competitive advantage, by providing prompt service and replacement parts for its products around the world.

Quality of service is a critical issue because customer expectations about service have broadened. Using traditional service quality standards based only on traditional manufacturing and accounting systems is not enough. Communication channels that allow customers to ask questions, voice complaints, submit orders, and trace shipments are indispensable components of service. Marketers should strive for uniformity of service, simplicity, truthfulness, and accuracy. They should also develop customer service objectives and monitor customer service programs. Firms can monitor service by formally surveying customers or informally calling on customers and asking questions about the service they receive. Expending the time and effort to ensure that customers are happy can greatly benefit marketers by increasing customer retention. One study found that boosting customer retention by 5 percent could double a small firm's profitability.[8]

Methods of Business Buying

Although no two business buyers do their jobs the same way, most use one or more of the following purchase methods: *description, inspection, sampling,* and *negotiation.* When products are standardized according to certain characteristics (such as size, shape, weight, and color) and graded using such standards, a business buyer may be able to purchase simply by describing or specifying quantity, grade, and other attributes. Agricultural products often fall into this category. Sometimes buyers specify a particular brand or its equivalent when describing the desired product. Purchases on the basis of description are especially common between a buyer and seller with an ongoing relationship built on trust.

Certain products, such as industrial equipment, used vehicles, and buildings, have unique characteristics and may vary with regard to condition. For example, a particular used truck may have a bad transmission. Consequently, business buyers of such products must base purchase decisions on inspection.

Sampling entails taking a specimen of the product from the lot and evaluating it on the assumption that its characteristics represent the entire lot. This method is appropriate when the product is homogeneous—for instance, grain—and examining the entire lot is not physically or economically feasible.

Some purchases by businesses are based on negotiated contracts. In certain instances, buyers describe exactly what they need and ask sellers to submit bids. They then negotiate with the suppliers who submit the most attractive bids. This approach may be used when acquiring commercial vehicles, for example. In other cases, the buyer may be unable to identify specifically what is to be purchased but can provide only a general description, as might be the case for a piece of custom-made equipment. A buyer and seller might negotiate a contract that specifies a base price and provides for the payment of additional costs and fees. These contracts are most commonly used for one-time projects such as buildings, capital equipment, and special projects.

Purchases Through Negotiating Contracts
Commercial vehicles are sometimes purchased through negotiated contracts.

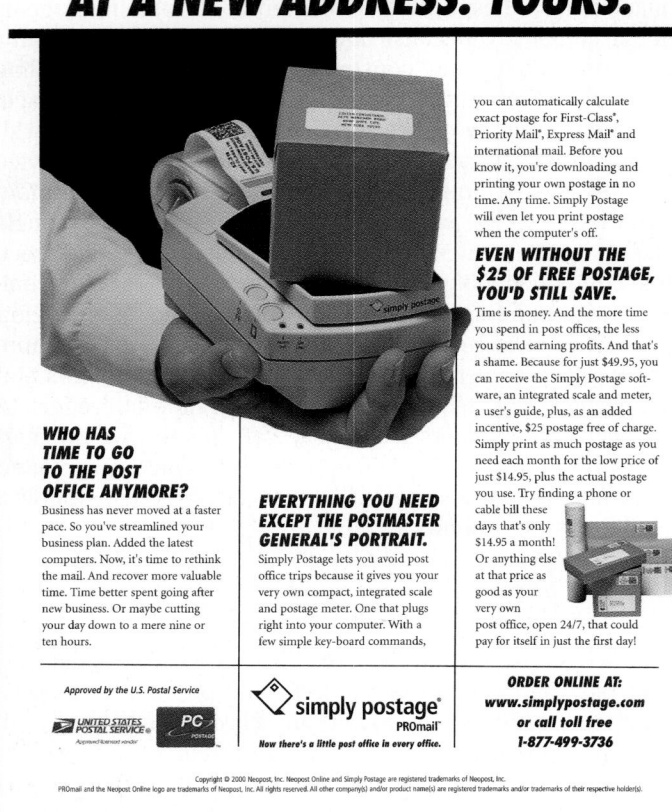

A New-Task Purchase
The initial purchase of postage equipment and software by a company is an example of a new-task purchase.

Types of Business Purchases

Most business purchases are one of three types: new-task, straight rebuy, or modified rebuy purchase. In a **new-task purchase,** an organization makes an initial purchase of an item to be used to perform a new job or solve a new problem. A new-task purchase may require development of product specifications, vendor specifications, and procedures for future purchases of that product. To make the initial purchase, the business buyer usually needs much information. New-task purchases are important to suppliers, for if business buyers are satisfied with the products, suppliers may be able to sell buyers large quantities of them for many years.

A **straight rebuy purchase** occurs when buyers purchase the same products routinely under approximately the same terms of sale. Buyers require little information for these routine purchase decisions and tend to use familiar suppliers that have provided satisfactory service and products in the past. These suppliers try to set up automatic reordering systems to make reordering easy and convenient for business buyers. A supplier may even monitor the business buyer's inventories and indicate to the buyer what should be ordered and when.

In a **modified rebuy purchase,** a new-task purchase is changed the second or third time it is ordered or requirements associated with a straight rebuy purchase are modified. A business buyer might seek faster delivery, lower prices, or a different quality level of product specifications. A modified rebuy situation may cause regular suppliers to become more competitive to keep the account, since other suppliers could obtain the business. For example, when a firm buys a slightly different set of communication services, it has made a modified purchase.

Demand for Business Products

Unlike consumer demand, demand for business products (also called *industrial demand*) can be characterized as (1) derived, (2) inelastic, (3) joint, or (4) fluctuating.

Derived Demand. Because business customers, especially producers, buy products for direct or indirect use in the production of goods and services to satisfy consumers' needs, the demand for business products derives from the demand for consumer products; it is therefore called **derived demand.** In the long run, no demand for business products is totally unrelated to the demand for consumer products. The derived nature of demand is usually multilevel. Business marketers at different levels are affected by a change in consumer demand for a particular product. For instance, consumers have become concerned with health and good nutrition, and as a result are purchasing more products with less fat, cholesterol, and sodium. When consumers reduced their purchases of high-fat foods, a change occurred in the demand for products marketed by food processors, equipment manufacturers, and

---

new-task purchase   An initial purchase by an organization of an item to be used to perform a new job or solve a new problem

straight rebuy purchase A routine purchase of the same products by a business buyer

modified rebuy purchase A new-task purchase that is changed on subsequent orders or when the requirements of a straight rebuy purchase are modified

derived demand   Demand for industrial products that stems from demand for consumer products

Source: *USA Today*, May 30, 2001, p. 1B. Copyright 2001, *USA Today.* Reprinted with permission.

inelastic demand   Demand that is not significantly altered by a price increase or decrease

joint demand   Demand involving the use of two or more items in combination to produce a product

suppliers of raw materials associated with these products. When consumer demand for a product changes, a wave is set in motion that affects demand for all firms involved in the production of that product.

Inelastic Demand.
Inelastic demand means that a price increase or decrease will not significantly alter demand for a business product. Because some business products contain a number of parts, price increases affecting only one or two parts may yield only a slightly higher per-unit production cost. When a sizable price increase for a component represents a large proportion of the product's cost, demand may become more elastic because the price increase in the component causes the price at the consumer level to rise sharply. For example, if aircraft engine manufacturers substantially increase the price of engines, forcing Boeing to raise the prices of the aircraft it manufactures, the demand for airliners may become more elastic as airlines reconsider whether they can afford to buy new aircraft. An increase in the price of windshields, however, is unlikely to greatly affect either the price of or the demand for airliners.

Inelasticity applies only to industry demand for business products, not to the demand curve an individual firm faces. Suppose a spark plug producer increases the price of spark plugs sold to manufacturers of small engines, but its competitors continue to maintain lower prices. The spark plug company will probably experience reduced unit sales because most small-engine producers will switch to lower-priced brands. A specific firm is vulnerable to elastic demand, even though industry demand for a specific business product is inelastic.

Joint Demand.
Demand for certain business products, especially raw materials and components, is subject to joint demand. **Joint demand** occurs when two or more items are used in combination to produce a product. For example, a firm that manufactures axes needs the same number of ax handles as it does ax blades. These two products thus are demanded jointly. If a shortage of ax handles exists, the producer buys fewer ax blades. Understanding the effects of joint demand is particularly important for a marketer selling multiple jointly demanded items. Such a marketer realizes that when a customer begins purchasing one of the jointly demanded items, a good opportunity exists to sell related products.

Fluctuating Demand.
Because it is derived from consumer demand, the demand for business products may fluctuate enormously. In general, when particular consumer products are in high demand, their producers buy large quantities of raw materials and components to ensure meeting long-run production requirements. In addition, these producers may expand production capacity, which entails acquiring new equipment and machinery, more workers, and more raw materials and component parts. Conversely, a decline in demand for certain consumer goods significantly reduces demand for business products used to produce those goods.

Marketers of business products may notice changes in demand when customers change inventory policies, perhaps because of expectations about future demand. For example, if several dishwasher manufacturers that buy timers from one producer increase their inventory of timers from a two-week to a one-month supply, the timer producer will have a significant, immediate increase in demand.

Sometimes price changes lead to surprising temporary changes in demand. A price increase for a business product may initially cause business customers to buy more of the item because they expect the price to rise further. Similarly, demand for a business product may be significantly lower following a price cut because buyers are waiting for further price reductions. Fluctuations in demand can be substantial in industries in which prices change frequently.

Business Buying Decisions

Business (organizational) buying behavior refers to the purchase behavior of producers, government units, institutions, and resellers. Although several factors affecting consumer buying behavior (discussed in the previous chapter) also influence business buying behavior, a number of factors are unique to the latter. We first analyze the buying center to learn who participates in business purchase decisions. We then focus on the stages of the buying decision process and the factors affecting it.

The Buying Center

Relatively few business purchase decisions are made by just one person; mostly they are made through a buying center. The **buying center** is the group of people within the organization who make business purchase decisions. They include users, influencers, buyers, deciders, and gatekeepers.[9] One person may perform several roles. These participants share some goals and risks associated with their decisions.

Users are the organization members who actually use the product being acquired. They frequently initiate the purchase process and/or generate purchase specifications. After the purchase, they evaluate product performance relative to the specifications.

Influencers are often technical personnel, such as engineers, who help develop the specifications and evaluate alternative products. Technical personnel are especially important influencers when products being considered involve new, advanced technology.

Buyers select suppliers and negotiate terms of purchase. They may also become involved in developing specifications. Buyers are sometimes called purchasing agents or purchasing managers. Their choices of vendors and products, especially for new-task purchases, are heavily influenced by people occupying other roles in the buying center. For straight rebuy purchases, the buyer plays a major role in vendor selection and negotiations.

Deciders actually choose the products. Although buyers may be deciders, it is not unusual for different people to occupy these roles. For routinely purchased items, buyers are commonly deciders. However, a buyer may not be authorized to make purchases exceeding a certain dollar limit, in which case higher-level management personnel are deciders.

Finally, gatekeepers, such as secretaries and technical personnel, control the flow of information to and among people occupying other roles in the buying center. Buyers who deal directly with vendors also may be gatekeepers because they can control information flows. The flow of information from a supplier's sales representatives to users and influencers is often controlled by personnel in the purchasing department.

The number and structure of an organization's buying centers are affected by the organization's size and market position, the volume and types of products being purchased, and the firm's overall managerial philosophy regarding exactly who should be involved in purchase decisions. The size of a buying center is influenced by the stage of the buying decision process and the type of purchase (new-task, straight rebuy, or modified rebuy).[10] Varying goals among members of a buying center can have both positive and negative effects on the purchasing process.

A marketer attempting to sell to a business customer should determine who is in the buying center, the types of decisions each individual makes, and which individuals are most influential in the decision process. Because in some instances many people make up the buying center, marketers cannot feasibly contact all participants. Instead, they must be certain to contact a few of the most influential.

Stages of the Business Buying Decision Process

Like consumers, businesses follow a buying decision process. This process is summarized in the lower portion of Figure 9.1. In the first stage, one or more individuals recognize that a problem or need exists. Problem recognition may arise under a variety of circumstances—for instance, when machines malfunction or a firm modifies an

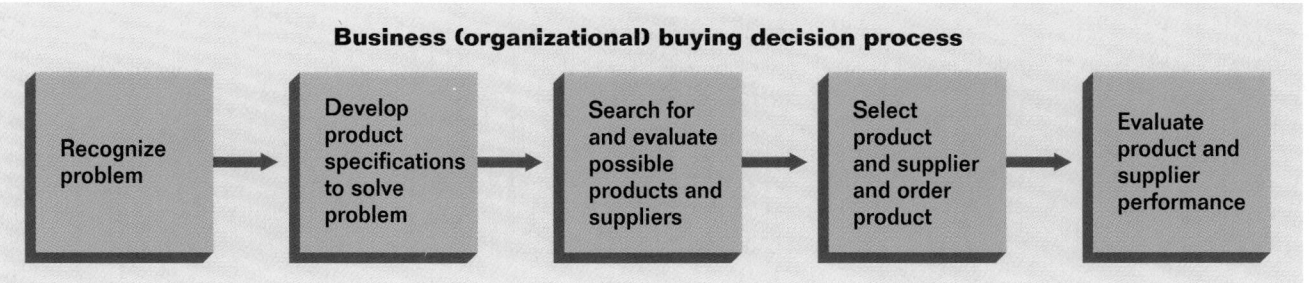

Possible influences on the decision process

Environmental	Organizational	Interpersonal	Individual
▸ Competitive factors ▸ Economic factors ▸ Political forces ▸ Legal and regulatory forces ▸ Technological changes ▸ Sociocultural issues	▸ Objectives ▸ Purchasing policies ▸ Resources ▸ Buying center structure	▸ Cooperation ▸ Conflict ▸ Power relationships	▸ Age ▸ Education level ▸ Personality ▸ Tenure ▸ Position in organization

Business (organizational) buying decision process

Recognize problem → Develop product specifications to solve problem → Search for and evaluate possible products and suppliers → Select product and supplier and order product → Evaluate product and supplier performance

FIGURE 9.1
Business (Organizational) Buying Decision Process and Factors That May Influence It

existing product or introduces a new one. Individuals in the buying center, such as users, influencers, or buyers, may be involved in problem recognition, but it may be stimulated by external sources, such as sales representatives or advertisements.

The second stage of the process, development of product specifications, requires that buying center participants assess the problem or need and determine what is necessary to resolve or satisfy it. During this stage, users and influencers, such as engineers, often provide information and advice for developing product

Problem Recognition
GERS is aiming this advertisement at company managers in an effort to stimulate problem recognition.

Our suppliers have many things in common,
but none of them are the same.

We believe our supplier base should be
as diverse as the policyholders we serve.
For more information please contact
State Farm's Purchasing Division at
(309) 766-2342 to speak with a supplier
diversity representative.

STATE FARM
INSURANCE

Like a good neighbor State Farm is there.*
statefarm.com®

State Farm Insurance Companies • Home Offices: Bloomington, Illinois

Vendor Search
State Farm enhances its vendor search by promoting its supplier diversity programs, which demonstrates its willingness to establish partnerships with vendors run by women and minorities.

specifications. By assessing and describing needs, the organization should be able to establish product specifications.

Searching for and evaluating potential products and suppliers is the third stage in the decision process. Search activities may involve looking in company files and trade directories, contacting suppliers for information, soliciting proposals from known vendors, and examining websites, catalogs, and trade publications. To facilitate vendor search, some organizations, such as Wal-Mart, advertise their desire to build partnerships with specific types of vendors, such as those owned by women or by minorities. During this stage some organizations engage in **value analysis,** an evaluation of each component of a potential purchase. Value analysis examines quality, designs, materials, and possibly item reduction or deletion to acquire the product in the most cost-effective way. Some vendors may be deemed unacceptable because they are not large enough to supply needed quantities; others may be excluded because of poor delivery and service records. Sometimes the product is not available from any existing vendor and the buyer must find an innovative company, like 3M, to design and make the product. Products are evaluated to make sure they meet or exceed product specifications developed in the second stage. Usually suppliers are judged according to multiple criteria. A number of firms employ **vendor analysis,** a formal, systematic evaluation of current and potential vendors focusing on such characteristics as price, product quality, delivery service, product availability, and overall reliability.

Results of deliberations and assessments in the third stage are used during the fourth stage to select the product to be purchased and the supplier from which to buy it. In some cases, the buyer selects and uses several suppliers, a process known as **multiple sourcing.** In others, only one supplier is selected, a situation known as **sole sourcing.** Firms with federal government contracts are required to have several sources for an item. Sole sourcing has traditionally been discouraged except when a product is available from only one company. Sole sourcing is much more common today, however, partly because such an arrangement means better communications between buyer and supplier, stability and higher profits for suppliers, and often lower prices for buyers. However, many organizations still prefer multiple sourcing because this approach lessens the possibility of disruption caused by strikes, shortages, or bankruptcies. The actual product is ordered in this fourth stage, and specific details regarding terms, credit arrangements, delivery dates and methods, and technical assistance are finalized.

value analysis An evaluation of each component of a potential purchase

vendor analysis A formal, systematic evaluation of current and potential vendors

multiple sourcing An organization's decision to use several suppliers

sole sourcing An organization's decision to use only one supplier

During the fifth stage, the product's performance is evaluated by comparing it with specifications. Sometimes the product meets the specifications, but its performance does not adequately solve the problem or satisfy the need recognized in the first stage. In that case, product specifications must be adjusted. The supplier's performance is also evaluated during this stage. If supplier performance is inadequate, the business purchaser seeks corrective action from the supplier or searches for a new one. Results of the evaluation become feedback for the other stages in future business purchase decisions.

This business buying decision process is used in its entirety primarily for new-task purchases. Several stages, but not necessarily all, are used for modified rebuy and straight rebuy situations.

Influences on the Business Buying Decision Process

Figure 9.1 also lists four major categories of factors that influence business buying decisions: environmental, organizational, interpersonal, and individual.

Environmental factors include competitive and economic factors, political forces, legal and regulatory forces, technological changes, and sociocultural issues.

GLOBAL MARKETING

Developing Business in Developing Countries

Where others see low incomes and low-tech infrastructure, Hewlett-Packard's senior managers see plenty of long-term business opportunities in India, Senegal, Bangladesh, and other developing countries. Through a program called World e-Inclusion, the California-based, $49 billion computer and printer giant is reaching out to entrepreneurs and organizations in developing countries that have yet to log onto the online-business boom. The idea is to foster future business development while advancing a social agenda of bringing technology resources to underserved regions of the world.

World e-Inclusion has put together a network of local development groups, nonprofit organizations, and government agencies to buy, lease, or receive donated Hewlett-Packard goods and services. In turn, these partners are arranging to put the products into the hands of farmers, entrepreneurs, and small-business owners. Many of these businesspeople will receive off-the-shelf personal computers; others will receive specially designed solar-powered models capable of wireless or satellite communication. All recipients will learn how they can use the technology to make faster, more convenient connections with local suppliers and buyers.

Hewlett-Packard is supporting this ambitious global initiative in a variety of ways. First, it has opened new research laboratories in India to investigate product innovations suitable for business and consumer use in developing nations. These labs will create products that are economically and culturally sustainable as well as technically advanced. Second, the company is boosting its service, sales, and operations presence in India and elsewhere to meet the needs of the new business customers it has targeted. Third, Hewlett-Packard is working with lenders on programs to funnel small loans to budding entrepreneurs in developing countries. Finally, it is stimulating community development efforts by joining with AOL Time Warner to donate computers, modems, printers, and Internet access to Peace Corps volunteers in 15 countries.

Despite the social mission attached to the World e-Inclusion programs, Hewlett-Packard management stresses that the long-term purpose is business development, not charity. "There's a big difference between creating a sustainable business model around products and services that raise the standard of living and aid or philanthropy money pouring in on an ongoing basis," the CEO says. "In the former, you can make money. In the latter, you make none."

These factors generate considerable uncertainty for an organization, which can make individuals in the buying center apprehensive about certain types of purchases. Changes in one or more environmental forces can create new purchasing opportunities and threats. For example, changes in competition and technology can make buying decisions difficult in the case of products like software, computers, and telecommunications equipment.

Business factors influencing the buying decision process include the company's objectives, purchasing policies, and resources, as well as the size and composition of its buying center. An organization may have certain buying policies to which buying center participants must conform. For instance, a firm's policies may mandate long-term contracts, perhaps longer than most sellers desire. An organization's financial resources may require special credit arrangements. Any of these conditions could affect purchase decisions.

Interpersonal factors are the relationships among people in the buying center. Use of power and level of conflict among buying center participants influence business buying decisions. Certain individuals in the buying center may be better communicators than others and may be more persuasive. Often these interpersonal dynamics are hidden, making them difficult for marketers to assess.

Individual factors are personal characteristics of participants in the buying center, such as age, education, personality, and tenure and position in the organization. For example, a 55-year-old manager who has been in the organization for 25 years may affect decisions made by the buying center differently than a 30-year-old person employed only two years. How influential these factors are depends on the buying situation, the type of product being purchased, and whether the purchase is new-task, modified rebuy, or straight rebuy. Negotiating styles of people vary within an organization and from one organization to another. To be effective, marketers must know customers well enough to be aware of these individual factors and the effects they may have on purchase decisions.

Using Industrial Classification Systems

Marketers have access to a considerable amount of information about potential business customers, since much of this information is available through government and industry publications and websites. Marketers use this information to identify potential business customers and to estimate their purchase potential.

Identifying Potential Business Customers

Standard Industrial Classification (SIC) system The federal government system for classifying selected economic characteristics of industrial, commercial, financial, and service organizations

North American Industry Classification System (NAICS) An industry classification system that will generate comparable statistics among the United States, Canada, and Mexico

Much information about business customers is based on industrial classification systems. In the United States, marketers traditionally have relied on the **Standard Industrial Classification (SIC) system,** which the federal government developed to classify selected economic characteristics of industrial, commercial, financial, and service organizations. However, the SIC system is being replaced by a new industry classification system called the **North American Industry Classification System (NAICS).** NAICS is a single industry classification system that all three NAFTA partners (the United States, Canada, and Mexico) will use to generate comparable statistics among all three countries. The NAICS classification is based on the types of production activities performed.[11] NAICS is similar to the International Standard Industrial Classification (ISIC) system used in Europe and many other parts of the world. Whereas the SIC system divides industrial activity into 10 divisions, NAICS divides it into 20 sectors. NAICS contains 1,172 industry classifications, compared with 1,004 in the SIC system. NAICS is more comprehensive and will be more up to date; all three countries have agreed to update it every five years. In addition, NAICS will provide considerably more information about service industries and high-tech products. A comparison of the SIC system and NAICS appears in Table 9.3. Over the next few years, all three NAFTA countries will convert from previously used industrial classification systems to NAICS.

Table 9.3	Comparison of the SIC System and NAICS for Manufacturers of Magnetic and Optical Media		
SIC Hierarchy		**NAICS Hierarchy**	
Division D	Manufacturing	Sector 31–33	Manufacturing
Major Group 36	Manufacturers of electronic and other electrical equipment, except computer equipment	Subsector 334	Computer and electronic manufacturing
Industry Subgroup 369	Manufacturers of miscellaneous electrical machinery, equipment, and supplies	Industry Group 3346	Manufacturing and reproduction of and optical media
Detailed Industry 3695	Manufacturers of magnetic and optical recording media	Industry 33461	Manufacturing and reproduction of magnetic and optical media
		U.S. Industry 334611	U.S. specific—reproduction of software

Source: Copyright © 1998, Manufacturers' Agents National Association, 23016 Mill Creek Road, P.O. Box 3467, Laguna Hills, CA 92654-3467. Phone (949) 859-4040; fax (949) 855-2973. All rights reserved. Reproduction without permission is strictly prohibited.

Industrial classification systems are ready-made tools that allow marketers to divide organizations into groups based mainly on the types of goods and services provided. Although an industrial classification system is a vehicle for segmentation, it is most appropriately used in conjunction with other types of data to determine exactly how many and which customers a marketer can reach.

input-output data
Information that tells what types of industries purchase the products of a particular industry

Input-output analysis works well in conjunction with an industrial classification system. This type of analysis is based on the assumption that the output, or sales, of one industry are the input, or purchases, of other industries. **Input-output data** tell what types of industries purchase products of a particular industry. A major source of national input-output data is the *Survey of Current Business,* published by the Office of Business Economics, U.S. Department of Commerce. After learning which industries purchase the major portion of an industry's output, the next step is finding the industrial classification numbers for those industries. Because firms are grouped differently in input-output tables and industrial classification systems, ascertaining industrial classification numbers can be difficult. However, the Office of Business Economics provides some limited conversion tables with input-output data. These tables can help marketers assign classification numbers to industry categories used in input-output analysis.

Having determined the classification numbers of industries that buy the firm's output, a marketer is in a position to ascertain the number of organizations that are potential buyers. Government sources, such as the *Census of Business,* the *Census of Manufacturers,* and *County Business Patterns,* report the number of establishments, the

Net Sights

The Thomas Register of Manufacturers (**www.thomasregister. com**) is an online database of nearly 160,000 U.S. and Canadian manufacturers. This website allows quick searches by company name, product, or brand name. Results include links to company websites, fax-back literature, and online commerce when available. Registration is required and free.

value of industry shipments, the number of employees, the percentage of imports and exports, and industry growth rates within classifications. Commercial sources also provide information about organizations categorized by industrial classifications.

A marketer can take several approaches to determine the identities and locations of organizations in specific groups. One approach is to use state directories or commercial industrial directories, such as *Standard & Poor's Register* and Dun & Bradstreet's *Million Dollar Directory.* These sources contain such information about a firm as its name, industrial classification, address, phone number, and annual sales. By referring to one or more of these sources, marketers isolate business customers with industrial classification numbers, determine their locations, and develop lists of potential customers by desired geographic area. A more expedient, although more expensive, approach is to use a commercial data service. Dun & Bradstreet, for example, can provide a list of organizations that fall into a particular industrial classification group. For each company on the list, Dun & Bradstreet gives the name, location, sales volume, number of employees, type of products handled, names of chief executives, and other pertinent information. Either method can effectively identify and locate a group of potential customers. However, a marketer probably cannot pursue all organizations on the list. Because some companies have greater purchasing potential than others, marketers must determine which customer or customer group to pursue.

Estimating Purchase Potential

To estimate the purchase potential of business customers or groups of customers, a marketer must find a relationship between the size of potential customers' purchases and a variable available in industrial classification data, such as the number of employees. For example, a paint manufacturer might attempt to determine the average number of gallons purchased by a specific type of potential customer relative to the number of employees. A marketer with no previous experience in this market segment will probably have to survey a random sample of potential customers to establish a relationship between purchase sizes and numbers of employees. Once this relationship is established, it can be applied to potential customer groups to estimate their purchases. After deriving these estimates, the marketer is in a position to select the customer groups with the most sales and profit potential.

Despite their usefulness, industrial classification data pose several problems. First, a few industries do not have specific designations. Second, because a transfer of products from one establishment to another is counted as a part of total shipments, double counting may occur when products are shipped between two establishments within the same firm. Third, because the Bureau of the Census is prohibited from providing data that identify specific business organizations, some data, such as value of total shipments, may be understated. Finally, because government agencies provide industrial classification data, a significant lag usually exists between data collection time and the time the information is released.

Summary

Business markets consist of individuals and groups that purchase a specific kind of product for resale, direct use in producing other products, or use in day-to-day operations. Producer markets include those individuals and business organizations purchasing products for the purpose of making a profit by using them to produce other products or as part of their operations. Intermediaries that buy finished products and resell them to make a profit are classified as reseller markets. Government markets consist of federal, state, county, and local governments, which spend billions of dollars annually for goods and services to support internal operations and to provide citizens with needed services. Organizations with charita-ble, educational, community, or other not-for-profit goals constitute institutional markets.

Transactions involving business customers differ from consumer transactions in several ways. Such transactions tend to be larger, and negotiations occur less frequently, though they are often lengthy. They often involve more than one person or department in the purchasing organization. They may also involve reciprocity, an arrangement in which two organizations agree to buy from each other. Business customers are usually better informed than ultimate consumers and more likely to seek information about a product's features and technical specifications.

When purchasing products, business customers are particularly concerned about quality, service, and price. Quality is important because it directly affects the quality of products the buyer's firm produces. To achieve an exact level of quality, organizations often buy products on the basis of a set of expressed characteristics, called specifications. Because services have such a direct influence on a firm's costs, sales, and profits, such matters as market information, on-time delivery, and availability of parts are crucial to a business buyer. Although business customers do not depend solely on price to decide which products to buy, price is of prime concern because it directly influences profitability.

Business buyers use several purchasing methods, including description, inspection, sampling, and negotiation. Most organizational purchases are new-task, straight rebuy, or modified rebuy. In a new-task purchase, an organization makes an initial purchase of items to be used to perform new jobs or to solve new problems. In a modified rebuy purchase, a new-task purchase is changed the second or third time it is ordered or requirements associated with a straight rebuy purchase are modified. A straight rebuy purchase occurs when a buyer purchases the same products routinely under approximately the same terms of sale.

Industrial demand differs from consumer demand along several dimensions. Industrial demand derives from demand for consumer products. At the industry level, industrial demand is inelastic. If an industrial item's price changes, product demand will not change as much proportionally. Some industrial products are subject to joint demand, which occurs when two or more items are used in combination to make a product. Finally, because organizational demand derives from consumer demand, the demand for business products can fluctuate widely.

Business, or organizational, buying behavior refers to the purchase behavior of producers, resellers, government units, and institutions. Business purchase decisions are made through a buying center, the group of people involved in making such purchase decisions. Users are those in the organization who actually use the product. Influencers help develop specifications and evaluate alternative products for possible use. Buyers select suppliers and negotiate purchase terms. Deciders choose the products. Gatekeepers control the flow of information to and among individuals occupying other roles in the buying center.

The stages of the business buying decision process are problem recognition, development of product specifications to solve problems, search for and evaluation of products and suppliers, selection and ordering of the most appropriate product, and evaluation of the product's and supplier's performance.

Four categories of factors influence business buying decisions: environmental, organizational, interpersonal, and individual. Environmental factors include political forces, laws and regulations, sociocultural factors, economic conditions, competitive forces, and technological changes. Business factors include the company's objectives, purchasing policies, and resources, as well as the size and composition of its buying center. Interpersonal factors are the relationships among people in the buying center. Individual factors are personal characteristics of members of the buying center, such as age, education, personality, tenure, and position in the organization.

Business marketers have a considerable amount of information available for use in planning marketing strategies. Much of this information is based on an industrial classification system, which categorizes businesses into major industry groups, industry subgroups, and detailed industry categories. An industrial classification system provides marketers with information needed to identify business customer groups. Currently the United States is converting from the traditional SIC system to NAICS. It can best be used for this purpose in conjunction with other information, such as input-output data. After identifying target industries, a marketer can obtain the names and locations of potential customers by using government and commercial data sources. Marketers then must estimate potential purchases of business customers by finding a relationship between a potential customer's purchases and a variable available in industrial classification data.

Important Terms

Business markets
Producer markets
Reseller markets
Government markets
Institutional markets
Reciprocity
New-task purchase
Straight rebuy purchase
Modified rebuy purchase
Derived demand
Inelastic demand
Joint demand
Business (organizational) buying behavior

Buying center
Value analysis
Vendor analysis
Multiple sourcing
Sole sourcing
Standard Industrial Classification (SIC) system
North American Industry Classification System (NAICS)
Input-output data

Discussion and Review Questions

1. Identify, describe, and give examples of the four major types of business markets.
2. Regarding purchasing behavior, why might business customers generally be considered more rational than ultimate consumers?
3. What are the primary concerns of business customers?
4. List several characteristics that differentiate transactions involving business customers from consumer transactions.
5. What are the commonly used methods of business buying?
6. Why do buyers involved in a straight rebuy purchase require less information than those making a new-task purchase?

7. How does demand for business products differ from consumer demand?

8. What are the major components of a firm's buying center?

9. Identify the stages of the business buying decision process. How is this decision process used when making straight rebuys?

10. How do environmental, business, interpersonal, and individual factors affect business purchases?

11. What function does an industrial classification system help marketers perform?

12. List some sources that a business marketer can use to determine the names and addresses of potential customers.

Application Questions

1. Identify organizations in your area that fit each business market category—producer, reseller, government, and institutional. Explain your classifications.

2. Indicate the method of buying (description, inspection, sampling, negotiation) an organization would be most likely to use when purchasing each of the following items. Defend your selection.
   a. A building for the home office of a light bulb manufacturer
   b. Wool for a clothing manufacturer
   c. An Alaskan cruise for a company retreat, assuming a regular travel agency is used
   d. One-inch nails for a building contractor

3. Purchases by businesses may be described as new-task, modified rebuy, or straight rebuy. Categorize the following purchase decisions and explain your choice.
   a. Bob has purchased toothpicks from Smith Restaurant Supply for 25 years and recently placed an order for yellow toothpicks rather than the usual white ones.
   b. Jill's investment company has been purchasing envelopes from AAA Office Supply for a year and now needs to purchase boxes to mail year-end portfolio summaries to clients. Jill calls AAA to purchase these boxes.
   c. Reliance Insurance has been supplying its salespeople with small personal computers to assist in their sales efforts. The company recently agreed to begin supplying them with faster, more sophisticated computers.

4. Identifying qualified customers is important to the survival of any organization. NAICS provides helpful information about many different businesses. Find the NAICS manual at the library and identify the NAICS code for the following items:
   a. Chocolate candy bars
   b. Automobile tires
   c. Men's running shoes

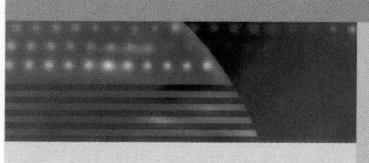

Visit **www.prideferrell.com** for resources to help you master the material in this chapter, plus materials that will help you expand your marketing knowledge, including: Internet exercise updates, ACE self-tests, hotlinks to companies featured in this chapter, and much more.

Internet Exercise & Resources

General Electric Company

General Electric Company is a highly diversified, global corporation with many divisions. GEPolymerland.com is the online site for GE's resins business. Visit the site at

www.GEPolymerland.com

1. At what type of business markets are GE's resin products targeted?

2. How does GEPolymerland address some of the concerns of business customers?

3. What environmental factors do you think affect demand for GE resin products?

VIDEO CASE 9.1

Oracle Meets the Challenges of Serving Business Customers

Database technology is a necessity for many businesses, and Oracle is putting its considerable marketing muscle behind a push to retain dominance of this $8.8 billion sector. Based in California with an e-business center in Virginia, Oracle is going head to head against IBM and Microsoft as it competes for customers in the producer, reseller, government, and institutional markets.

Oracle made its name in database systems, but its newer e-commerce applications are emerging as the foundation for future growth and profits. Off the Internet, more than half of all *Fortune* 500 firms rely on Oracle technology. On the Internet, all ten of the top e-business sites use Oracle e-commerce software, including E*Trade, eBay, and Amazon.com. The U.S. government is also a big customer, buying different Oracle packages for use in the Department of Defense, Department of Transportation, and numerous other agencies. And institutions such as HealthSouth use Oracle technology to centralize and streamline recordkeeping and provide authorized personnel with instant wireless access to mountains of data. In all, 100,000 business customers use one or more Oracle products.

Software is only part of Oracle's portfolio, however. The company also provides training, troubleshooting, and consulting services to help business customers get the most out of their Oracle systems. In fact, Oracle has become the world's largest information technology trainer, teaching half a million people annually to use its software. At the same time, it derives more than 60 percent of its revenues from the sale of consulting services to businesses that buy its systems.

Oracle recognizes that selecting, customizing, and installing a new database or e-commerce system is a major undertaking for any business—among the most complex technology purchases these customers will ever make. "People are building worldwide databases and global computer systems and moving their business processes onto the Internet," observes Oracle CEO Larry Ellison. "The larger a database becomes, the more important it becomes."

To attract new customers and reassure current ones, Oracle constantly looks for ways to show that its software is cutting-edge, secure, reliable, and easy to use. Its communications cite specific benefits, quote from customer testimonials, and point to the lengthy and distinguished customer list. Detailed feature-by-feature comparisons and online demonstrations invite customers to see why Oracle's products are better than those of IBM and other rivals. Customers can also download sample

software and then arrange payment for their purchases through the Oracle site.

Oracle places a high value on customer input. The company has long followed a policy of asking customers what they want and following up by creating technology that delivers the desired benefits. Several years ago, corporate managers told Oracle they wanted a single, integrated system to manage their e-business operations rather than the patchwork of applications available at the time. Based on this information, Oracle created a seamless suite of applications that allows customers to effectively handle diverse e-business tasks while tracking and sharing data among internal functions. The company doesn't just conduct internal tests; it relies entirely on its own software for all e-commerce operations. Over time, Oracle has reaped impressive time and cost savings from its e-business software and improved its profit margins—results it often trumpets in its advertising campaigns.

Now Oracle is moving beyond traditional software by putting e-commerce and other software online and allowing customers access through its e-business portal. Online access relieves customers of the headaches and expense of maintaining existing systems or upgrading to new ones, and reduces the potential for costly downtime. It also allows customers to choose and use a wider variety of software applications from Oracle as well as from selected other suppliers.

Always a fierce competitor, Oracle is determined to stay one byte ahead of Microsoft and other rivals. It also faces competition from makers of specialized software, such as Siebel Systems (which focuses on sales and related systems) and i2 Technologies (which has made a name in e-commerce systems). Despite the pressure, CEO Ellison is expertly building his company's brand by aggressively promoting the firm's breakthrough technologies, making numerous industry appearances, staying in touch with the media, and—just as important—reaching out to key customers.[12]

QUESTIONS FOR DISCUSSION

1. What does Oracle do to address buyer needs and concerns throughout the buying decision process?
2. What might Oracle say to customers who express concerns about sole sourcing of a single, integrated e-commerce suite?
3. How would you describe the demand for Oracle's e-commerce software? Is it derived? Inelastic? Joint? Fluctuating? Explain your answers.

CASE 9.2

Resellers Sweet on Jo's Candies

The customer list of Jo's Candies reads like a *Who's Who* of upscale retailing. Neiman Marcus, Starbucks, Norm Thompson, Williams-Sonoma, and Borders are just some of the top-drawer chains that are sweet on the confectioner's hand-dipped, chocolate-covered graham crackers. Jo's Candies, which began as a small chocolate shop in southern California, has expanded over the past decade. It now sells 500,000 graham treats every month in more than 3,000 gourmet shops, specialty stores, and coffee bars on four continents. Though the company often sells directly to larger retailers, it sells through Fralick and other wholesalers to reach smaller retailers. While moving the company toward its goal of $15 million in annual sales by 2005, CEO Tom King has learned some important lessons about the tricky but profitable business of marketing to resellers.

The first lesson is that buyers for large chains want something unique. No retail giant wants to place an order if the same product, in identical packaging, is available in competing stores. For this reason, Jo's Candies readily customizes its packaging and its products to each chain's specifications. For example, the company puts its chocolate grahams in three-packs with Borders labeling for the book chain. No matter what the request, Jo's Candies stands ready to go along. When Starbucks requested a special product for the coffee chain's mail-order catalog and Williams-Sonoma wanted a different product for its gourmet kitchen catalog, CEO King said yes, then got busy behind the scenes making sure the orders were filled and the buyers were satisfied.

Second, the company has found that personal attention is important for building trust and strengthening relationships with resellers. "I always try to communicate with major customers once a week—by fax, phone, or e-mail—and try to meet with my largest accounts face-to-face every four to six weeks," explains CEO King. Even small gestures are important. Retail buyers hear from Jo's Candies when their birthdays and anniversaries roll around. But they also know that King is willing to hop on a jet and meet with them when problems arise. And Jo's Candies guarantees every sale, offering to buy back its chocolate grahams if resellers are unhappy after three months of selling them. The only time the company had to make good on this guarantee was when a customer asked to return a case of cookies that had been inadvertently left in the sun.

The third lesson about doing business with resellers has been painful and expensive. The Nordstrom chain, the largest of Jo's Candies' retail accounts, was buying more than $200,000 worth of chocolate grahams every year. Then, one by one, various Nordstrom stores decided it was cheaper to cook up their own chocolate grahams than to keep buying from an outside source. Soon all but six Nordstrom stores stopped selling Jo's Candies, a loss that hit the company quite hard. This episode taught the CEO the need to constantly expand the customer base so that the company does not become overly dependent on any one reseller. In fact, Jo's Candies now has a strict rule whereby no single customer is allowed to account for more than 60 percent of overall sales.

Still, because every order from a retail chain represents a major profit opportunity for a small manufacturer like Jo's Candies, the company continues focusing on larger resellers. In reseller markets, size matters. National chains have many shelves to fill, so they buy tremendous quantities, which makes them an attractive target for many suppliers. On the other hand, these big buyers are often tough negotiators that look closely at the terms of every sale, especially price. In addition, they sometimes request a period of exclusivity, asking Jo's Candies not to sell the same product to a competitor for several months or more. King has accepted this condition on occasion, but sometimes he will agree only if the reseller says it will guarantee a certain volume of purchases for that period. "Usually, they can't make the guarantee, so they back down," says King.

While the large resellers never lose sight of the enormous buying power they wield, they also know they need suppliers who can provide them with good products for their stores. Product quality, service, and timing are important concerns for these chains. So, as Jo's Candies continues to grow, it is paving the way for more and bigger orders by following the pattern of establishing a relationship with a reseller and then proving it can deliver as promised. "You're selling a product," observes CEO King, "but you're also selling your reputation."

The success of Jo's Candies, as well as its awards and rave reviews in *Food & Wine* and other magazines, has attracted imitators. With six or more rivals bringing out their own versions of chocolate-covered grahams, King has had to don his apron and go back into the kitchen to experiment with chocolate and other ingredients. In his words, the challenge is "to create new combinations to be one jump ahead." King says he already has "at least three proven winners [that] I will roll out in the next three years." Two recent innovations are Dr. Peter's Lemon Breeze and Dr. Peter's Peppermint Crunch, both chocolate-covered confections. In some cases, Jo's Candies markets new products online and by mail order before making them available to resellers in large volume.

The final lesson King has learned in a decade of marketing to resellers is to respect their time. Before meeting with a reseller, the CEO does his homework, reviewing information about the account and writing a short agenda to guide the discussion. Some small suppliers may quake at the thought of pitching a product to the buyer for a well-known chain, but not King: "I am never, ever intimidated, because I go in there prepared."[13]

QUESTIONS FOR DISCUSSION

1. If you were a buyer for a large reseller, what information would you request from Jo's Candies before you decided to order for the first time?
2. If you were Tom King, what information would you research about a large reseller in advance of your first sales call?
3. Tom King spends considerable time and effort developing and maintaining long-term customer relationships. Do business customers such as resellers care about having long-term relationships with suppliers? Explain.

STRATEGIC CASE 2

Palm: Computing Power in the Palm of Your Hand

A computer in the palm of your hand? Apple Computer tried it with the Newton—which the company dubbed a PDA (personal digital assistant)—and failed miserably, spending an estimated $500 million in the process. In 1994, just two months after Newton's debut, Palm, Inc., founded by Jeff Hawkins, introduced the Zoomer PDA for the Radio Shack chain. Zoomer was also a flop. But Hawkins and his technoteam learned enough from these two flawed products to create the Palm handheld, a pocket-size device that lets users track appointments, access an address book, write memos, and even surf the Net and send messages via wireless communications. The Palm handheld quickly became the fastest-selling computer product in history; well over 13 million have been sold.

Who Was Buying the Zoomer— and Why?

Although humbled by the failure of the Zoomer PDA, Hawkins and his colleagues were not ready to give up. Instead they used in-depth surveys to find out exactly who had bought the Zoomer and, just as important, why. The results completely contradicted their assumptions about who would want a PDA and what it would be used for. Palm, Inc. had been targeting the consumer market, but it turned out that businesses were the biggest buyers. The company had envisioned the PDA as competition for a personal computer, but users saw it as complementary, more like a substitute for paper and pencil with which they could take notes and juggle appointments on the fly.

A New Approach for Palm

Armed with these findings, Hawkins took some time to rethink the PDA concept and emerged with two critical conclusions. First, Hawkins concluded that trying to make a device that can decipher anyone's handwriting was asking too much from a device as small as a PDA. That had been the main problem for Apple's Newton. Hawkins envisioned an entirely new approach: rather than have the PDA learn the user's handwriting, the user would learn the PDA's writing system. "People like learning," he explains. "People can learn to work with tools. Computers are tools. People like to learn how to use things that work." On the basis of this

insight, Palm developed Graffiti, a system of simplified pen strokes representing letters. Once users mastered the Graffiti system, the PDA would be able to decode their handwritten messages every time.

Hawkin's second conclusion was that size matters. To be convenient, the PDA had to fit in a shirt pocket—no small feat for a multifunctional computer product. Once again the Palm Computing team rose to the challenge, crafting a 6-ounce, pocket-size computer powered by AAA batteries and designed to sell for less than $300. Even more amazing, the entire new-product development effort involved just 28 employees and cost a relatively modest $3 million, a small price tag in the big-spending computer world.

A New Parent for Palm, Then Independence

Needing deeper pockets to fund production of its new product, Palm, Inc. approached U.S. Robotics and agreed to be acquired for $44 million in stock. (Later 3Com acquired U.S. Robotics and, after several years, set Palm free as a separate company.) With its parent's backing, Palm launched its first two products in April 1996. The PalmPilot 1000 was a basic PDA model; the PalmPilot 5000 was a memory-enhanced one. Computer magazines raved about the new gadgets, and customers started buying them in droves. In short order, PalmPilots were seen tucked into shirt pockets at business meetings all over the United States.

New Uses for Palm

"By midsummer, we couldn't build enough of them," remembers Palm's marketing manager. "Customers were stamping their feet. And we weren't just selling to geeks in Silicon Valley. We were selling all over the place." As the research had indicated, business customers were the primary purchasers, pushing sales to heady levels as they found many everyday uses for Palm handhelds. At Harley-Davidson in York, Pennsylvania, for example, engineers and technicians began using Palm handhelds to collect quality control data and statistical information about motorcycle products on the assembly line. At Outreach Health Services in Austin, Texas, home health care workers learned to use Palm handhelds to record patient data and schedule work activities. More and more business users found that Palm handhelds were convenient and simple to use, fueling sales.

New Competition for Palm

Palm Computing's success has attracted more competition over time. Philips, Casio, Compaq, and other manufacturers now offer higher-end palm-size computers based on the Microsoft PocketPC operating system. This could be a significant competitive threat because Microsoft wields so much power in the marketplace. Also, Palm earns considerably more profit from its pricier models than from its low-end ones, so diminished share in the high end of the market would certainly hurt profit margins. The onslaught of competition has already pushed prices ever lower and dented Palm's overall revenues and profitability.

Although Palm does not use Microsoft's operating system, it enjoys the support of 145,000 independent developers who have committed to creating new software and add-on gadgets for Palm handhelds. To cope with increased competition, it has also incorporated wireless communication capabilities, improved the viewing screen, and reduced the size, all while keeping prices reasonable. But the company has struggled with new-product introductions and was slow to add an expansion slot that would extend the Palm handhelds' functionality, a key feature of the popular PDAs marketed by rival Handspring.

New Company, New Targets

Palm's most innovative competitor is Handspring, a company headed by former Palm executives Jeff Hawkins and Donna Dubinsky. Handspring's products are geared toward the consumer market and use a licensed version of the Palm operating system rather than the Microsoft system. More colorful and lower priced than the original Palm handhelds, the Handspring PDAs were the first to sport an expansion slot enabling users to plug in an MP3 music player, a digital camera, a cell phone, or dozens of other devices.

Just as the Palm handhelds touched off a buying frenzy among business customers, the new Handspring devices have sparked a similar frenzy among consumers and won over some business users as well. After less than a year on the market, the Handspring Visor had a 21 percent share of the market, sending Palm's share below 65 percent. Handspring's success has been bittersweet for Palm, which collects approximately $9 in licensing fees for every Visor sold. However, Handspring also has the right to develop PDAs using Microsoft's system or

other systems, which would cut into Palm's licensing fees. In the end, Palm earns more from the sale of its own PDAs than from its licensing fees, so Handspring's speedy ascent poses more of a threat than an opportunity for Palm.

Reading Palm's Future

Now Palm is looking for growth overseas by targeting the tech-savvy Japanese market. Amid intense competition from local PDA makers NEC, Toshiba, Sony, Sharp, and Casio, Palm has introduced a wireless PDA to help Japanese buyers stay connected. Wireless communication capability is the only way Palm can compete with the population's habitual use of web-enabled cell phones, already in the hands of more than 30 million Japanese consumers. Handspring, Casio, and other PDA makers are fighting back by providing adapters for wireless cards made by NTT DoCoMo, Japan's leading cell phone company.

Meanwhile, sensing convergence ahead, Microsoft has developed a combination cell phone and PDA to be offered in the United States and Europe by wireless communications carriers Vodafone and VoiceStream. In Japan, Kyocera is licensing the Palm system for a wireless phone-organizer combination. Kyocera says that Handspring and Nokia, not Palm, are emerging as its main competitors. The battle lines are drawn. Will Palm answer the call?

QUESTIONS FOR DISCUSSION

1. What type of targeting strategy is Palm, Inc. using for the Palm handheld? What segmentation variables did it use for the Palm handheld? Explain your answers.
2. What issues are likely to be most important for a company that is considering the purchase of PDAs for its sales force?
3. How would you recommend that Palm use marketing research to support its introduction of a PDA in Japan?
4. Which influences on the consumer buying decision process seem to be most important for Palm's customers?

Product Decisions

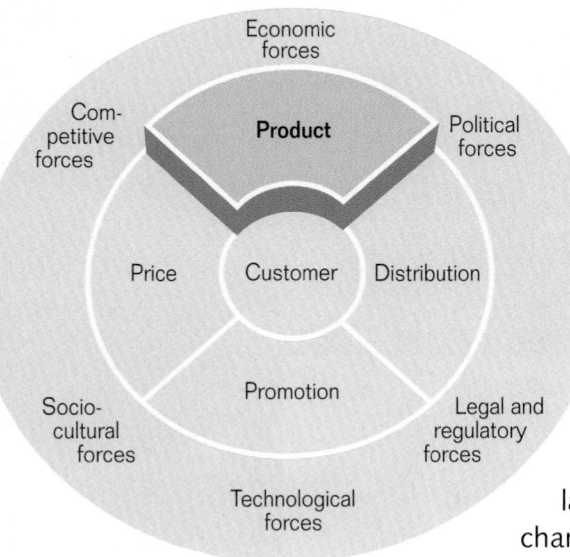

We are now prepared to analyze the decisions and activities associated with developing and maintaining effective marketing mixes. In Parts 3 through 6, we focus on the major components of the marketing mix: product, distribution, promotion, and price. Part 3 explores the product ingredient of the marketing mix. Chapter 10 introduces basic concepts and relationships that must be understood if one is to make effective product decisions. Chapter 11 analyzes a variety of dimensions regarding product management, including line extensions and product modification, new-product development, and product deletions. Chapter 12 discusses branding, packaging, and labeling. Chapter 13 explores the nature, importance, and characteristics of services.

10 Product Concepts

OBJECTIVES

- To understand the concept of a product
- To explain how to classify products
- To examine the concepts of product item, product line, and product mix and understand how they are connected
- To understand the product life cycle and its impact on marketing strategies
- To describe the product adoption process
- To understand why some products fail and some succeed

ew people are fortunate enough to turn their passion for a hobby into a successful business, but entrepreneur Randy King is one of the lucky handful who have
done just that. Fueled by his passion for kites, King, together with co-owner Ken
Garrett, founded Windy Conditions Kite Systems in 1997 to market kites as well as
flags, banners, and windsocks.

Sales of kites total about $100 million a year, and kite afi-
cionados are often willing to invest big money in their hobby.
Sporting kites typically cost between $1,500 and $2,000,
while hobby kite owners generally spend between $100 and
$5,000 on their kites. Windy Conditions focuses on market-
ing kites that allow customers to express themselves by incorporating their own banners or flags into a frame. Sports fans,
for example, can fly kites promoting their favorite team. Other kite fliers can make
a statement by showing off the American flag or their state flag, eagles, smiley faces,
rainbows, cartoon characters, seasonal themes, or ethnic images. Windy Conditions
is currently the only firm that markets these banner and flag kits.

Windy Conditions markets two different sizes of frame systems that can accommodate most flags and banners on the market. Customers can even make their own
cloth banners to use in a Windy Conditions frame; they can also customize their kites
with their own tails. Both flag and banner kites can be controlled with a single line,
although the company says banner kites may perform better with dual lines.

Since founding the company, King and Garrett have greatly refined their flag
and banner kites, making them much lighter and easier to fly. The partners are
confident that their product is durable, versatile, high quality, and
reasonably priced ($35 to $60). The kites are sold in
specialty stores in Colorado, Arizona, and
Nebraska, as well as online at
www.windyconditions.
com. King and Garrett
promote their kites as
a fun alternative to
installing a flagpole to
demonstrate national
pride. With interest in
kite flying soaring, King
and Garrett hope their
passion will help Windy
Conditions capture as
much of the kite market as
possible.[1]

Turning a Passion for Kite Flying into Profits

The product is an important variable in the marketing mix. Products such as Windy Conditions Kites can be a firm's most important asset and visible contact with buyers. If a company's products do not meet customers' desires and needs, the company will fail unless it makes adjustments. Developing successful products like kites requires knowledge of fundamental marketing and product concepts.

In this chapter, we first define a product and discuss how buyers view products. Next, we examine the concepts of product line and product mix. We then explore the stages of the product life cycle and the effect of each life cycle stage on marketing strategies. Next, we outline the product adoption process. Finally, we discuss the factors that contribute to a product's failure or success.

What Is a Product?

As defined in Chapter 1, a *product* is a good, a service, or an idea received in an exchange. It can be either tangible or intangible and includes functional, social, and psychological utilities or benefits. It also includes supporting services, such as installation, guarantees, product information, and promises of repair or maintenance. Thus, the 5-year/60,000-mile warranty that covers most new automobiles is part of the product itself. A **good** is a tangible physical entity, such as a Dell personal computer or a Big Mac. A **service** in contrast, is intangible; it is the result of the application of human and mechanical efforts to people or objects. Examples of services include a performance by Britney Spears, online travel agencies, medical examinations, child day care, real estate services, and martial arts lessons. (Chapter 13 provides a detailed discussion of services.) An **idea** is a concept, philosophy, image, or issue. Ideas provide the psychological stimulation that aids in solving problems or adjusting to the environment. For example, MADD (Mothers Against Drunk Driving) promotes safe consumption of alcohol and stricter enforcement of laws against drunk driving.

When buyers purchase a product, they are really buying the benefits and satisfaction they think the product will provide. A Rolex watch, for example, is purchased to make a statement of success, not just for telling time. Services in particular are purchased on the basis of expectations. Expectations, suggested by images, promises,

good   A tangible physical entity

service   An intangible result of the application of human and mechanical efforts to people or objects

idea   A concept, philosophy, image, or issue

What Is a Product?
By encouraging parents to speak with their children about drugs, the National Youth Anti-Drug Media Campaign is marketing the idea that communication helps to keep kids off drugs. Similarly, by promoting the harmful ingredients in cigarettes, the Centers for Disease Control markets the idea that smoking is bad for your health.

In five minutes they will be on a school bus. Somebody on the bus may ask them if they want to try drugs.

Now would be a good time to talk to them.

Who is your child's best friend? What does your child do for fun? What did your child do at school today? Does your child know about drugs? These are a few simple things that a parent should know about their child. Take the time to become involved with your children and communicate to our youth that drugs are not part of our Native cultures. For more information on talking to your kids about drugs, please call 1.800.788.2800.

Communication. The Anti-Drug.
Office of National Drug Control Policy
www.theantidrug.com

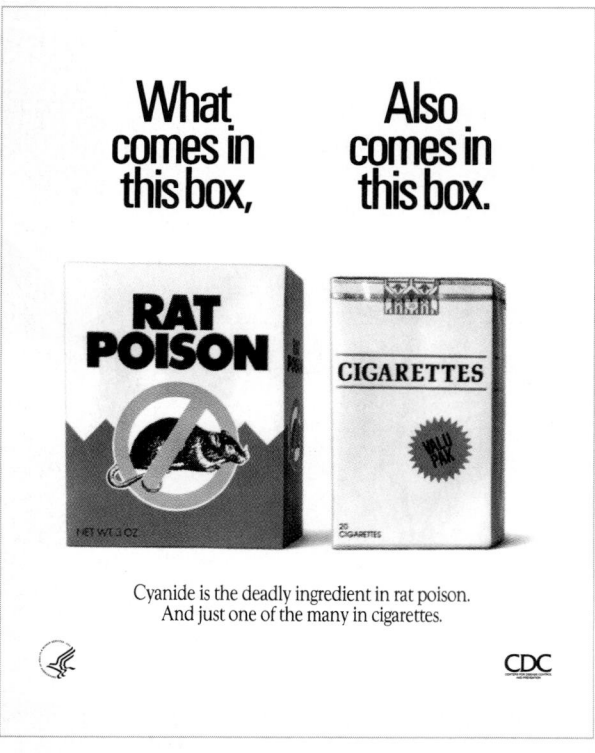

What comes in this box,   **Also comes in this box.**

RAT POISON   CIGARETTES

Cyanide is the deadly ingredient in rat poison.
And just one of the many in cigarettes.

CDC

and symbols, as well as processes and delivery, help consumers make judgments about tangible and intangible products. Products are formed by the activities and processes that help satisfy expectations. CNN, for example, did not invent network news, but it did make national and international news available worldwide 24 hours a day. Likewise, Starbucks did not originate the coffee shop, but it did develop standardized and inviting stores with high-quality coffee beverages that became a stylish way to enjoy what traditionally was a commodity product.[2] Often symbols and cues are used to make intangible products more tangible, or real, to the consumer. Allstate Insurance Company, for example, uses giant hands to symbolize security, strength, and friendliness.

Classifying Products

Products fall into one of two general categories. Products purchased to satisfy personal and family needs are **consumer products.** Those bought to use in a firm's operations, to resell, or to make other products are **business products.** Consumers buy products to satisfy their personal wants, whereas business buyers seek to satisfy the goals of their organizations.

consumer products Products purchased to satisfy personal and family needs

business products Products bought to use in an organization's operations, to resell, or to make other products

The same item can be both a consumer product and a business product. For example, when a consumer buys a computer disk for a home computer, it is classified as a consumer product. However, when an organization purchases a computer disk for office use, it is considered a business product because it is used in daily operations. Thus, the buyer's intent—or the ultimate use of the product—determines whether an item is classified as a consumer or a business product.

Product classifications are important because classes of products are aimed at particular target markets, and this affects distribution, promotion, and pricing decisions. Furthermore, appropriate marketing strategies vary among the classes of consumer and business products. In short, how a product is classified can affect the entire marketing mix. In this section, we examine the characteristics of consumer and business products and explore the marketing activities associated with some of these products.

Consumer Products

The most widely accepted approach to classifying consumer products is based on characteristics of consumer buying behavior. It divides products into four categories: convenience, shopping, specialty, and unsought products. However, not all buyers behave in the same way when purchasing a specific type of product. Thus, a single product can fit into several categories. To minimize this problem, marketers think in terms of how buyers *generally* behave when purchasing a specific item. In addition, they recognize that the "correct" classification can be determined only by considering a particular firm's intended target market. Examining the four traditional categories of consumer products can provide further insight.

convenience products Relatively inexpensive, frequently purchased items for which buyers exert minimal purchasing effort

Convenience Products. **Convenience products** are relatively inexpensive, frequently purchased items for which buyers exert only minimal purchasing effort. They range from bread, soft drinks, and chewing gum to gasoline and newspapers. The buyer spends little time planning the purchase or comparing available brands or sellers. Even a buyer who prefers a specific brand will readily choose a substitute if the preferred brand is not conveniently available.

Classifying a product as a convenience product has several implications for a firm's marketing strategy. A convenience product is normally marketed through many retail outlets. Because sellers experience high inventory turnover, per-unit gross margins can be relatively low. Producers of convenience products, such as Altoid mints, expect little promotional effort at the retail level and thus must provide it themselves with advertising and sales promotion. Packaging is also an important element of the marketing mix for convenience products. The package may have to sell the product because many convenience items are available only on a self-service basis at the retail level.

shopping products Items for which buyers are willing to expend considerable effort in planning and making purchases

Shopping Products. **Shopping products** are items for which buyers are willing to expend considerable effort in planning and making the purchase. Buyers spend much time comparing stores and brands with respect to prices, product features, qualities, services, and perhaps warranties. Appliances, bicycles, furniture, stereos, cameras, and shoes exemplify shopping products. These products are expected to last a fairly long time and thus are purchased less frequently than convenience items. Even though shopping products are more expensive than convenience products, few buyers of shopping products are particularly brand-loyal. Most consumers, for example, are not brand-loyal for computers and clothing. If they were, they would be unwilling to shop and compare among brands. Even when they are brand-loyal, they still may spend considerable time comparing the features of different models of a brand. A consumer looking for a new Maytag washing machine, for example, may explore the company's website to compare the features of different washers before talking to a salesperson. Regardless of the number of brands of interest, buyers may also consult buying guides such as *Consumer Reports* or visit consumer information websites such as epinions.com to view others' opinions or ratings of brands and models before making an actual purchase.

To market a shopping product effectively, a marketer considers several key issues. Shopping products require fewer retail outlets than convenience products. Because shopping products are purchased less frequently, inventory turnover is lower, and marketing channel members expect to receive higher gross margins. Although large sums of money may be required to advertise shopping products, an even larger percentage of resources is likely to be used for personal selling. Usually the producer and the marketing channel members expect some cooperation from one another with respect to providing parts and repair services and performing promotional activities.

specialty products Items with unique characteristics that buyers are willing to expend considerable effort to obtain

Specialty Products. **Specialty products** possess one or more unique characteristics, and generally buyers are willing to expend considerable effort to obtain them. Buyers actually plan the purchase of a specialty product; they know exactly what they want and will not accept a substitute. Examples of specialty products include a Mont Blanc pen and a one-of-a-kind piece of baseball memorabilia, such as

Example of a Specialty Product
Graff's diamond rings are an example of a specialty product.

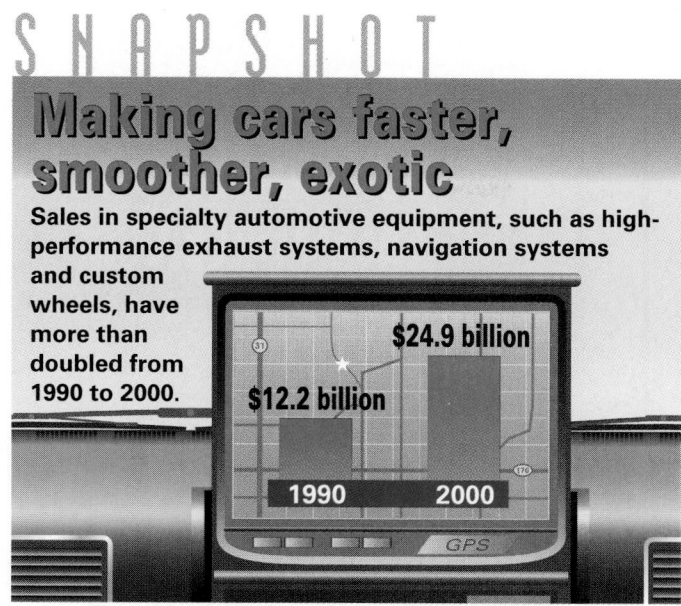

SNAPSHOT

Making cars faster, smoother, exotic

Sales in specialty automotive equipment, such as high-performance exhaust systems, navigation systems and custom wheels, have more than doubled from 1990 to 2000.

$12.2 billion — 1990
$24.9 billion — 2000

GPS

Source: *USA Today*, August 20, 2001, p. 1B. Copyright 2001, *USA Today*. Reprinted with permission.

unsought products Products purchased to solve a sudden problem, products of which customers are unaware, and products that people do not necessarily think about buying

installations Facilities and nonportable major equipment

accessory equipment Equipment used in production or office activities

a ball signed by Babe Ruth. When searching for specialty products, buyers do not compare alternatives; they are concerned primarily with finding an outlet that has the preselected product available. Bentley automobiles, for example, are very expensive, ranging from $215,000 to $360,000. Bentley dealers may invite prospective buyers to test-drive a vehicle at a race track. If the prospect decides to make a purchase, he or she has a Bentley "personally commissioned" and typically flies to the automaker's plant in Crewe, England, to observe its manufacture.[3]

The fact that an item is a specialty product can affect a firm's marketing efforts in several ways. Specialty products are often distributed through a limited number of retail outlets. Like shopping products, they are purchased infrequently, causing lower inventory turnover and thus requiring relatively high gross margins.

Unsought Products. **Unsought products** are products purchased when a sudden problem must be solved, products of which customers are unaware, and products that people do not necessarily think of purchasing. Emergency medical services and automobile repairs are examples of products needed quickly to solve a problem. A consumer who is sick or injured has little time to plan to go to an emergency medical center or hospital. Likewise, in the event of a broken fan belt on the highway, a consumer will likely seek out the nearest auto repair facility to get back on the road as quickly as possible. In such cases, speed and problem resolution are far more important than price and other features buyers might normally consider if they had more time for decision making.

Business Products

Business products are usually purchased on the basis of an organization's goals and objectives. Generally the functional aspects of the product are more important than the psychological rewards sometimes associated with consumer products. Business products can be classified into seven categories according to their characteristics and intended uses: installations, accessory equipment, raw materials, component parts, process materials, MRO supplies, and business services.

Installations. **Installations** include facilities, such as office buildings, factories, and warehouses, and major equipment that is nonportable, such as production lines and very large machines. Major equipment usually is used for production purposes. Some major equipment is custom made to perform specific functions for a particular organization, but other items are standardized and perform similar tasks for many types of firms. Normally installations are expensive and intended to be used for a considerable length of time. Because they are so expensive and typically involve a long-term investment of capital, purchase decisions are often made by high-level management. Marketers of installations frequently must provide a variety of services, including training, repairs, maintenance assistance, and even aid in financing such purchases.

Accessory Equipment. **Accessory equipment** does not become a part of the final physical product but is used in production or office activities. Examples include file cabinets, fractional-horsepower motors, calculators, and tools. Compared with major equipment, accessory items are usually much cheaper, purchased routinely with less negotiation, and treated as expense items rather than capital items because they are not expected to last as long. Accessory products are standardized items that can be used in several aspects of a firm's operations. More

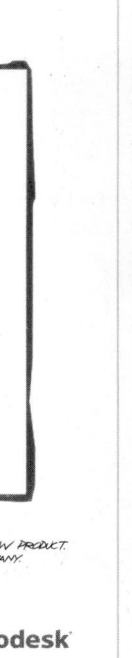

Business Services
Companies such as Autodesk and Salesforce.com provide services to businesses to improve product design and customer relationship management.

outlets are required for distributing accessory equipment than for installations, but sellers do not have to provide the multitude of services expected of installations marketers.

raw materials Basic natural materials that become part of a physical product

Raw Materials.
Raw materials are the basic natural materials that actually become part of a physical product. They include minerals, chemicals, agricultural products, and materials from forests and oceans. They are usually bought and sold according to grades and specifications, and in relatively large quantities. Rose oil and jasmine are examples of raw materials in making perfume.

component parts Items that become part of the physical product and are either finished items ready for assembly or items that need little processing before assembly

Component Parts.
Component parts become a part of the physical product and are either finished items ready for assembly or products that need little processing before assembly. Although they become part of a larger product, component parts often can be easily identified and distinguished. Spark plugs, tires, clocks, and switches are all component parts of the automobile. Buyers purchase such items according to their own specifications or industry standards. They expect the parts to be of specified quality and delivered on time so that production is not slowed or stopped. Producers that are primarily assemblers, such as most lawn mower and computer manufacturers, depend heavily on suppliers of component parts.

process materials Materials that are used directly in the production of other products but are not readily identifiable

Process Materials.
Process materials are used directly in the production of other products. Unlike component parts, however, process materials are not readily identifiable. For example, a salad dressing manufacturer includes vinegar in its salad dressing. The vinegar is a process material because it is included in the salad dressing but is not identifiable. As with component parts, process materials are purchased according to industry standards or the purchaser's specifications.

MRO supplies Maintenance, repair, and operating items that facilitate production and operations but do not become part of the finished product

MRO Supplies.
MRO supplies are maintenance, repair, and operating items that facilitate production and operations but do not become part of the finished product. Paper, pencils, oils, cleaning agents, and paints are in this category. MRO supplies are commonly sold through numerous outlets and are purchased routinely. To ensure supplies are available when needed, buyers often deal with more than one seller.

business services The intangible products that many organizations use in their operations

Business Services. **Business services** are the intangible products that many organizations use in their operations. They include financial, legal, marketing research, information technology, and janitorial services. Firms must decide whether to provide their own services internally or obtain them from outside the organization. This decision depends on the costs associated with each alternative and how frequently the services are needed.

Product Line and Product Mix

Marketers must understand the relationships among all the products of their organization to coordinate the marketing of the total group of products. The following concepts help describe the relationships among an organization's products. A **product item** is a specific version of a product that can be designated as a distinct offering among an organization's products. An L.L. Bean flannel shirt represents a product item. A **product line** is a group of closely related product items that are considered to be a unit because of marketing, technical, or end-use considerations. For example, there are 9 kinds of Kleenex tissue, 16 flavors of Eggo waffles, and 19 varieties of Colgate toothpaste. Each year more than 31,000 new consumer products come out with multiple items for almost every product line.[4] The exact boundaries of a product line (although sometimes blurred) are usually indicated by using descriptive terms such as "frozen dessert" product line or "shampoo" product line. To come up with the optimal product line, marketers must understand buyers' goals. In the personal computer industry, for example, companies are likely to expand their product lines when industry barriers are low or perceived market opportunities exist. Firms with high market share are likely to expand their product lines aggressively, as are marketers with relatively high prices or limited product lines.[5] Specific product items in a product line usually reflect the desires of different target markets or the different needs of consumers.

product item A specific version of a product

product line A group of closely related product items viewed as a unit because of marketing, technical, or end-use considerations

A **product mix** is the composite, or total, group of products that an organization makes available to customers. For example, all the health care, beauty care, laundry and cleaning, food and beverage, paper, cosmetic, and fragrance products that Procter & Gamble manufactures constitute its product mix. The **width of product mix** is measured by the number of product lines a company offers. The **depth of product mix** is the average number of different products offered in each product line. Figure 10.1 shows the width and depth of a part of Procter & Gamble's product mix. Procter & Gamble is known for using distinctive branding, packaging,

product mix The total group of products that an organization makes available to customers

width of product mix The number of product lines a company offers

depth of product mix The average number of different products offered in each product line

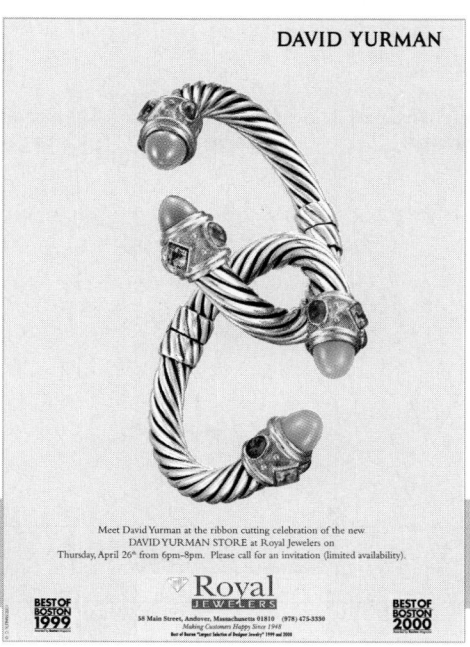

Product Line
David Yurman markets a variety of jewelry in his product line.

Laundry detergents	Toothpastes	Bar soaps	Deodorants	Shampoos	Tissue/Towel
Ivory Snow 1930	Gleem 1952	Ivory 1879	Old Spice 1948	Pantene 1947	Charmin 1928
Dreft 1933	Crest 1955	Camay 1926	Secret 1956	Head & Shoulders 1961	Puffs 1960
Tide 1946		Zest 1952	Sure 1972	Vidal Sassoon 1974	Bounty 1965
Cheer 1950		Safeguard 1963		Pert Plus 1979	Kids' Fresh Wipes 1998
Bold 1965		Oil of Olay 1993		Ivory 1983	
Gain 1966				Physique 2000	
Era 1972					
Febreze Clean Wash 2000					

Depth

Width

FIGURE 10.1
The Concepts of Product Mix Width and Depth Applied to Selected United States Procter & Gamble Products
Source: Reprinted by permission of Procter & Gamble.

and consumer advertising to promote individual items in its detergent product line. Tide, Bold, Gain, Cheer, and Era—all Procter & Gamble detergents—share the same distribution channels and similar manufacturing facilities, yet each is promoted as a distinctive product adding depth to the product line.

Product Life Cycles and Marketing Strategies

Just as biological cycles progress from birth through growth and decline, so do product life cycles. As Figure 10.2 shows, a **product life cycle** has four major stages: introduction, growth, maturity, and decline. As a product moves through its cycle, the strategies relating to competition, promotion, distribution, pricing, and market information must be periodically evaluated and possibly changed. Astute marketing managers use the life cycle concept to make sure the introduction, alteration, and termination of a product are timed and executed properly. By understanding the typical life cycle pattern, marketers are better able to maintain profitable products and drop unprofitable ones.

product life cycle The progression of a product through four stages: introduction, growth, maturity, and decline

FIGURE 10.2
The Four Stages of the Product Life Cycle

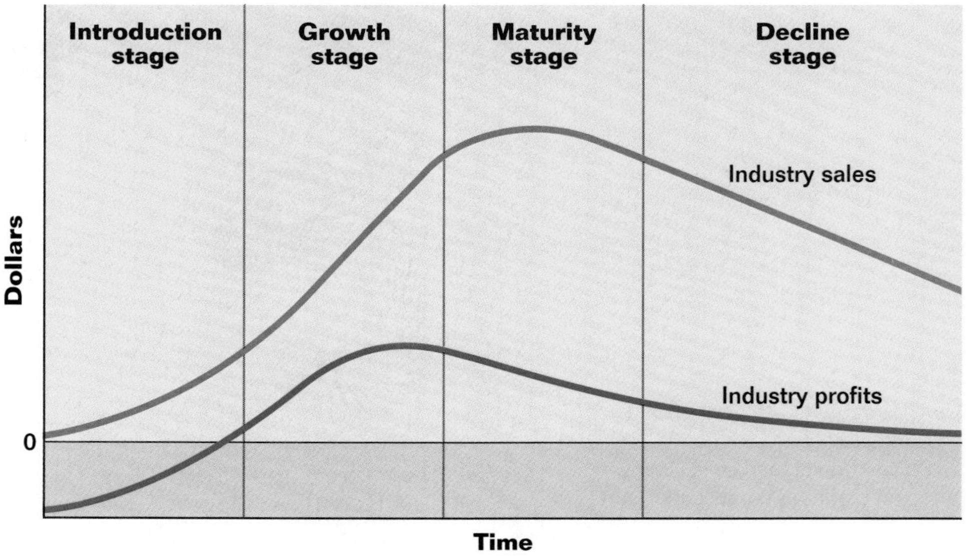

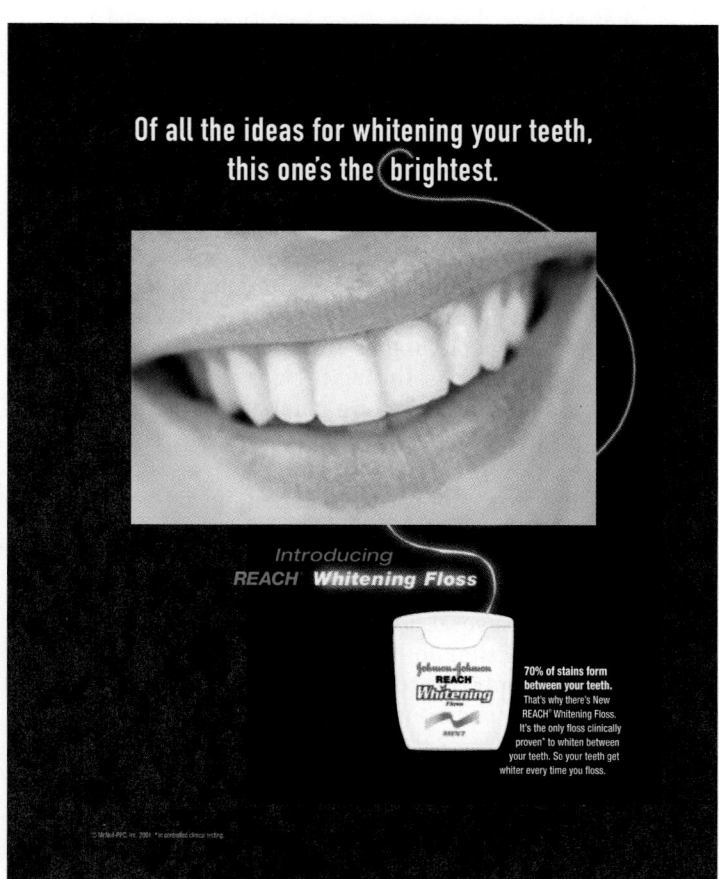

Of all the ideas for whitening your teeth, this one's the brightest.

Introducing
REACH **Whitening Floss**

70% of stains form between your teeth.
That's why there's New REACH Whitening Floss. It's the only floss clinically proven* to whiten between your teeth. So your teeth get whiter every time you floss.

Introduction Stage
Johnson & Johnson promotes the introduction of its whitening dental floss.

Introduction

The **introduction stage** of the product life cycle begins at a product's first appearance in the marketplace, when sales start at zero and profits are negative. Profits are below zero because initial revenues are low, and the company generally must cover large expenses for promotion and distribution. Notice in Figure 10.2 how sales should move upward from zero, and profits should also move upward from a position in which they are negative because of high expenses.

Developing and introducing a new product can mean an outlay of $100 million or more. Colgate-Palmolive derives 38 percent of its global revenues from products introduced within the last five years. For revenues from the U.S. market, the figure is even higher—61 percent.[6] Although the importance of new products is significant, the risk of new-product failure is quite high, depending on the industry and how product failure is defined. Because of high risks and costs, few product introductions represent revolutionary inventions. More typically, product introductions involve a new packaged convenience food, a new model of automobile, or a new fashion in clothing rather than a major product innovation. The more marketing oriented the firm, the more likely it will be to launch innovative, new-to-the-market products.[7]

Potential buyers must be made aware of the new product's features, uses, and advantages. Two difficulties may arise at this point. First, sellers may lack the resources, technological knowledge, and marketing know-how to launch the product successfully. Second, the initial product price may have to be high to recoup expensive marketing research or development costs. Given these difficulties, it is not surprising that many products never get beyond the introduction stage.

Most new products start off slowly and seldom generate enough sales to bring immediate profits. As buyers learn about the new product, marketers should be alert for product weaknesses and make corrections quickly to prevent the product's early demise. Marketing strategy should be designed to attract the segment that is most interested and has the fewest objections. As the sales curve moves upward and the breakeven point is reached, the growth stage begins.

introduction stage The initial stage of a product's life cycle —its first appearance in the marketplace—when sales start at zero and profits are negative

Net Sights

Founded in 1976, the Product Development & Management Association (PDMA) is a nonprofit organization of product developers, academics, and service providers dedicated to the support of product development research. PDMA sponsors an annual international conference on new-product development, highlighting the latest academic research, and offers members several publications devoted to product innovation. Many of these publications and other information related to new-product development and management are available on the organization's website at **http://www.pdma. org/.**

Growth

During the **growth stage,** sales rise rapidly and profits reach a peak and then start to decline (see Figure 10.2). The growth stage is critical to a product's survival because competitive reactions to the product's success during this period will affect the product's life expectancy. For example, Palm successfully marketed the first personal digital assistant (PDA), the PalmPilot, but today competes against numerous other brands such as Handspring, Casio, and Hewlett-Packard.

Profits begin to decline late in the growth stage as more competitors enter the market, driving prices down and creating the need for heavy promotional expenses. At this point, a typical marketing strategy encourages strong brand loyalty and competes with aggressive emulators of the product. During the growth stage, the organization tries to strengthen its market share and develop a competitive niche by emphasizing the product's benefits. Aggressive pricing, including price cuts, is also typical during this stage.

As sales increase, management must support the momentum by adjusting the marketing strategy. The goal is to establish and fortify the product's market position by encouraging brand loyalty. To achieve greater market penetration, segmentation may have to be used more intensely. That would require developing product variations to satisfy the needs of people in several different market segments. Palm, for example, markets many versions of its PalmPilot digital assistant, as well as related software and accessories, to satisfy different customer groups. Marketers should also analyze the competing brands' product positions relative to their own brands and take corrective actions.

Gaps in geographic market coverage should be filled during the growth period. As a product gains market acceptance, new distribution outlets usually become easier to obtain. Marketers sometimes move from an exclusive or a selective exposure to a more intensive network of dealers to achieve greater market penetration. Marketers must also make sure the physical distribution system is running efficiently so that customers' orders are processed accurately and delivered on time.

Promotion expenditures may be slightly lower than during the introductory stage but are still quite substantial. As sales increase, promotion costs should drop as a percentage of total sales. A falling ratio between promotion expenditures and sales should contribute significantly to increased profits. The advertising messages should stress brand benefits. Coupons and samples may be used to increase market share.

After recovering development costs, a business may be able to lower prices. As sales volume increases, efficiencies in production can result in lower costs. These savings may be passed on to buyers. If demand remains strong and there are few competitive threats, prices tend to remain stable. If price cuts are feasible, they can help a brand gain market share and discourage new competitors from entering the market.

Maturity

During the **maturity stage,** the sales curve peaks and starts to decline and profits continue to fall (see Figure 10.2). This stage is characterized by intense competition, as many brands are now in the market. Competitors emphasize improvements and differences in their versions of the product. As a result, during the maturity stage, weaker competitors are squeezed out or lose interest in the product. For example, some brands of DVDs will perish as the DVD reaches the maturity stage.

During the maturity phase, the producers who remain in the market are likely to change their promotional and distribution efforts. Advertising and dealer-oriented promotions are typical during this stage of the product life cycle. Marketers must also take into account that as the product reaches maturity, buyers' knowledge of it attains a high level. Consumers of the product are no longer inexperienced generalists; instead they are experienced specialists. Marketers of mature products sometimes expand distribution into global markets. Often the products have to be adapted to more precisely fit differing needs of global customers.

Maturity Stage
To create interest in its mature product, Masterfoods USA—a Mars, Incorporated Company—highlights its "M&M's"® Candies and suggests new uses such as "M&M's" Mores.™

Because many products are in the maturity stage of their life cycles, marketers must know how to deal with these products and be prepared to adjust their marketing strategies. As Table 10.1 shows, there are many approaches to altering marketing strategies during the maturity stage. As noted there, to increase the sales of mature products, marketers may suggest new uses for them. Arm & Hammer has boosted demand for its baking soda by this method. Likewise, as AOL's subscription growth leveled off in the United States, the Internet service provider's life cycle was extended through aggressive expansion into Europe as well as Asia and Latin America.[8]

Table 10.1	Selected Approaches for Managing Products in the Maturity Stage
Approaches	**Examples**
Develop new product uses	Knox gelatin used as a plant food
	Arm & Hammer baking soda marketed as a refrigerator deodorant
	Cheez Whiz promoted as a microwavable cheese sauce
Increase product usage among current users	Multiple packaging used for products in which a larger supply at the point of consumption actually increases consumption (such as for soft drinks or beer)
Increase number of users	Global markets or small niches in domestic markets pursued
Add product features	Cell phones that can access the Internet
	Global positioning systems in automobiles
Change package sizes	Single-serving sizes introduced
	Travel-size packages of personal care products introduced
Increase product quality	Life of light bulbs increased
	Reliability and durability of U.S.-made automobiles increased
Change nonproduct marketing mix variables—promotion, price, distribution	Focus of Dr Pepper advertisements shifted from teenagers to people ages 18 to 54
	A package of dishwasher detergent containing one-third more product offered for the same price
	Computer hardware marketed through mail-order outlets

Building Customer Relationships describes Cadillac's efforts to extend the venerable brand's life cycle. As customers become more experienced and knowledgeable about products during the maturity stage (particularly about business products), the benefits they seek may change as well, necessitating product modifications.

Three general objectives can be pursued during the maturity stage:

1. *Generate cash flow.* This is essential for recouping the initial investment and generating excess cash to support new products.

BUILDING CUSTOMER RELATIONSHIPS

Revitalizing a Maturing Brand

If someone told you he drove a car that resembled the Batmobile, would you have imagined he owned a Cadillac? Although the new Cadillac designs were sketched in a Detroit studio, their sharp angles and sleek body make them appear to have been computer generated. This new look represents a $4 billion gamble at reviving this once popular luxury vehicle.

The century-old Cadillac brand gained momentum in the 1950s when Cadillac became the top-selling luxury vehicle for the first time. The brand held that position from 1950 to 1998 with memorable models such as the Coupe deVille and Eldorado convertible. During their introduction and growth phases, Cadillac products were known for their innovative styling and cutting-edge technology. Examples of these features include the popular tail fins, a mass-produced V-8 engine, and the first sun roofs.

Sales peaked in 1978 at 350,813. During its maturity phase, Cadillac held 46 percent of the market for luxury vehicles. However, after the twin oil shocks of the 1970s, Americans began seeking smaller, more fuel-efficient vehicles. In response, Cadillac may have overcompensated in drastically reducing the size of its cars. To respond quickly, the firm fancied up comparable Chevrolets by adding chrome and leather. Quality also declined as many cars suffered from leaky roofs, poorly built engines, and an array of other defects. Over the next 20 years, Cadillac faced a reputation for poor reliability and inconsistent quality.

By the 1990s, the company recognized that a major overhaul was necessary to pull the brand out of decline and avoid the fate of Oldsmobile. In 2000 only

199,918 vehicles were sold, slightly more than half the number sold during Cadillac's peak year. The company fell to sixth, behind Lexus, BMW, Mercedes-Benz, Acura, and Lincoln models, commanding just 12 percent of the current market share. Many customers switched brands because Cadillac no longer met their needs for performance, speed, size, and reliability. Cadillac also failed to notice the trend toward sports-utility vehicles. It wasn't until the 2001 models that Cadillac introduced a newly designed SUV to sport the Cadillac name. Because it failed to appeal to a younger affluent crowd, Cadillac now finds its average customer is older, less educated, and earning less than customers of competitors like Lexus, BMW, Acura, Mercedes, and Lincoln.

To revitalize the brand and attract the more desirable market segment, Cadillac is drastically revamping its products. The effort to invigorate sales relies on two concepts from its historic success: art and science. Evoq, Imaj, and Vizon were concept cars built to showcase the new sleek, artsy look of expected models like the $65,000 roadster and $50,000 pickup truck (EXT). The new science being incorporated includes night vision and satellite communications. The company is building a new factory in Lansing, Michigan, modeled after operations in Thailand and Poland, that will be used exclusively to manufacture Cadillacs. With a capacity of 160,000 vehicles, the plant is the first built by General Motors, Cadillac's corporate parent, in more than 15 years.

Cadillac is focusing all its energy to create a new product that appeals to consumers. Will the current technology and sleek design win over a younger crowd or drive away current customers? With its popularity waning for 25 years, Cadillac must act quickly to pull its product out of the decline phase. This $4 billion arts-and-science campaign is the critical success factor that will determine Cadillac's fate. Will Cadillac be thrust to a higher position or quietly retired?

2. *Maintain share of market.* Companies with marginal market share must decide whether they have a reasonable chance to improve their position or whether they should drop out.

3. *Increase share of customer.* Whereas *market share* refers to the percentage of total customers held by a firm, *share of customer* relates to the percentage of each customer's needs being met by the firm. For example, many banks have added new services (brokerage, financial planning, auto leasing, etc.) to gain more of each customer's financial services business. Likewise, many supermarkets are seeking to increase share of customer by adding services such as restaurants, video rentals, and dry cleaning to provide one-stop shopping for their customers' household needs.[9]

During the maturity stage, marketers actively encourage dealers to support the product. Dealers may be offered promotional assistance in lowering their inventory costs. In general, marketers go to great lengths to serve dealers and to provide incentives for selling their brands.

Maintaining market share during the maturity stage requires moderate, and sometimes large, promotion expenditures. Advertising messages focus on differentiating a brand from the field of competitors, and sales promotion efforts are aimed at both consumers and resellers.

A greater mixture of pricing strategies is used during the maturity stage. Strong price competition is likely and may ignite price wars. Firms also compete in other ways than price, such as through product quality or service. In addition, marketers develop price flexibility to differentiate offerings in product lines. Markdowns and price incentives are common. Prices may have to be increased, however, if distribution and production costs rise.

Decline

decline stage   The stage of a product's life cycle when sales fall rapidly

During the **decline stage,** sales fall rapidly (see Figure 10.2). When this happens, the marketer considers pruning items from the product line to eliminate those not earning a profit. The marketer may also cut promotion efforts, eliminate marginal distributors, and, finally, plan to phase out the product. Although Procter & Gamble's Oxydol detergent had been around for 86 years, the company phased it out and sold the brand name to Redox Brands for $7 million. Sales had declined from $64 million in 1950 to $5.5 million when the product was terminated.[10]

An organization can justify maintaining a product as long as it contributes to profits or enhances the overall effectiveness of a product mix. Unilever, which markets diverse products ranging from Dove soap to Lipton tea, has slashed its product mix from 1,600 to 970 items and plans to eliminate another 250. The firm believes too many choices can frustrate consumers. Other retailers are cutting back on the number of items carried in a product category.[11]

In this stage, marketers must determine whether to eliminate the product or try to reposition it to extend its life. Usually a declining product has lost its distinctiveness because similar competing products have been introduced. Competition engenders increased substitution and brand switching as buyers become insensitive to minor product differences. For these reasons, marketers do little to change a product's style, design, or other attributes during its decline. New technology or social trends, product substitutes, or environmental considerations may also indicate that the time has come to delete the product.

During a product's decline, outlets with strong sales volumes are maintained and unprofitable outlets are weeded out. An entire marketing channel may be eliminated if it does not contribute adequately to profits. An outlet not previously used, such as a factory outlet, will sometimes be used to liquidate remaining inventory of an obsolete product. As sales decline, the product becomes more inaccessible, but loyal buyers seek out dealers who still carry it.

Spending on promotion efforts is usually considerably reduced. Advertising of special offers may slow the rate of decline. Sales promotions, such as coupons and premiums, may temporarily regain buyers' attention. As the product continues to decline, the sales staff shifts its emphasis to more profitable products.

The marketing manager has two options during the decline stage: attempt to postpone the decline or accept its inevitability. Many firms lack the resources to renew a product's demand and are forced to consider harvesting or divesting the product or the strategic business unit (SBU). The *harvesting* approach employs a gradual reduction in marketing expenditures and a less resource-intensive marketing mix. DaimlerChrysler, for example, has moved into a position for harvesting its Plymouth brand, which probably will be eliminated from the company's product mix. Harvesting the Plymouth brand will enable the company to funnel extra resources into its more prosperous Dodge and Chrysler brands. A company adopting the *divesting* approach withdraws all marketing support from the declining product or SBU. It may continue to sell the product until losses are sustained or arrange for another firm to acquire the product. Home Depot, for example, made the tough decision to divest its Crossroads stores for farm dwellers and move human and financial resources to Home Depot Expo, a chain for upscale consumers doing significant renovations or remodeling projects.[12]

Because most businesses have a product mix consisting of multiple products, a firm's destiny is rarely tied to one product. A composite of life cycle patterns forms when various products in the mix are at different cycle stages. As one product is declining, other products are in the introduction, growth, or maturity stage. Marketers must deal with the dual problem of prolonging the lives of existing products and introducing new products to meet organizational sales goals.

Product Adoption Process

Acceptance of new products—especially new-to-the-world products—usually doesn't happen overnight. In fact, it can take a very long time. People are sometimes cautious or even skeptical about adopting new products, as indicated by some of the remarks quoted in Table 10.2. Customers who eventually accept a new product do so through an adoption process. The stages of the **product adoption process** are as follows:

product adoption process
The stages buyers go through in accepting a product

1. *Awareness.* The buyer becomes aware of the product.

2. *Interest.* The buyer seeks information and is receptive to learning about the product.

3. *Evaluation.* The buyer considers the product's benefits and decides whether to try it.

4. *Trial.* The buyer examines, tests, or tries the product to determine if it meets his or her needs.

5. *Adoption.* The buyer purchases the product and can be expected to use it again whenever the need for this general type of product arises.[13]

In the first stage, when individuals become aware that the product exists, they have little information about it and are not concerned about obtaining more. For example, one might be aware that Polaroid offers a talking camera that has built-in recorded comic messages to evoke smiles, but have no plans to gather more information about it. Consumers enter the interest stage when they are motivated to get information about the product's features, uses, advantages, disadvantages, price, or

Encouraging Product Trial
Snickers® Brand encourages trial of its new product by offering a free coupon.

Table 10.2	Most New Ideas Have Their Skeptics

"I think there is a world market for maybe five computers."
—Thomas Watson, chairman of IBM, 1943

"This 'telephone' has too many shortcomings to be seriously considered as a means of communication. The device is inherently of no value to us."
—Western Union internal memo, 1876

"The wireless music box has no imaginable commercial value. Who would pay for a message sent to nobody in particular?"
—David Sarnoff's associates in response to his urgings for investment in the radio in the 1920s

"The concept is interesting and well-formed, but in order to earn better than a 'C,' the idea must be feasible."
—A Yale University management professor in response to Fred Smith's paper proposing reliable overnight delivery service (Smith went on to found Federal Express Corp.)

"Who the hell wants to hear actors talk?"
—H. M. Warner, Warner Brothers, 1927

"A cookie store is a bad idea. Besides, the market research reports say America likes crispy cookies, not soft and chewy cookies like you make."
—Banker's response to Debbie Fields's idea of starting Mrs. Fields' Cookies

"We don't like their sound, and guitar music is on the way out."
—Decca Recording Co. rejecting the Beatles, 1962

location. During the evaluation stage, individuals consider whether the product will satisfy certain criteria that are crucial to meeting their specific needs. In the trial stage, they use or experience the product for the first time, possibly by purchasing a small quantity, taking advantage of free samples, or borrowing the product from someone. Supermarkets, for instance, frequently offer special promotions to encourage consumers to taste products. During this stage, potential adopters determine the usefulness of the product under the specific conditions for which they need it.

Individuals move into the adoption stage by choosing a specific product when they need a product of that general type. However, entering the adoption process does not mean the person will eventually adopt the new product. Rejection may occur at any stage, including the adoption stage. Both product adoption and product rejection can be temporary or permanent.

This adoption model has several implications when a new product is being launched. First, the company must promote the product to create widespread awareness of its existence and its benefits. Samples or simulated trials should be arranged to help buyers make initial purchase decisions. At the same time, marketers should emphasize quality control and provide solid guarantees to reinforce buyer opinion during the evaluation stage. Finally, production and physical distribution must be linked to patterns of adoption and repeat purchases.

When an organization introduces a new product, people do not begin the adoption process at the same time, nor do they move through the process at the same speed. Of those who eventually adopt the product, some enter the adoption process rather quickly, whereas others start considerably later. For most products, there is also a group of nonadopters who never begin the process.

Depending on the length of time it takes them to adopt a new product, consumers fall into one of five major adopter categories: innovators, early adopters, early majority, late majority, and laggards.[14] Figure 10.3 illustrates each adopter category and the percentage of total adopters it typically represents. **Innovators** are the first to adopt a new product; they enjoy trying new products and tend to be venturesome. **Early adopters** choose new products carefully and are viewed as "the people to check

innovators   First adopters of new products

early adopters   Careful choosers of new products

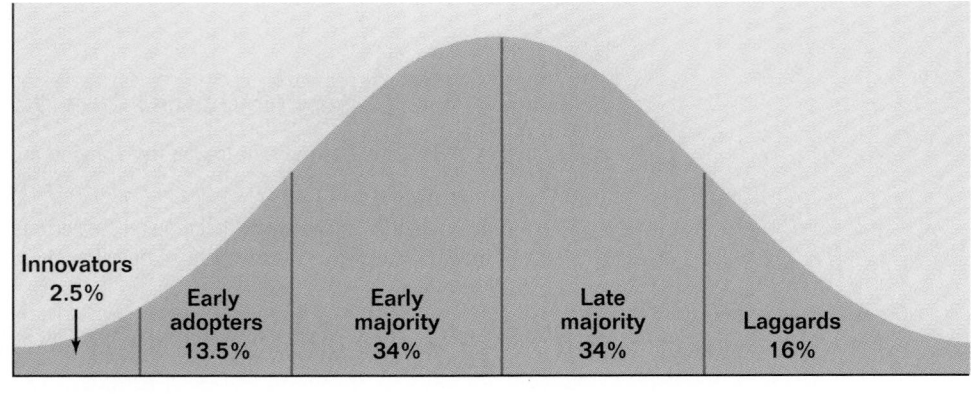

FIGURE 10.3
Distribution of Product Adopter Categories

Source: Excerpt from *Diffusion of Innovations,* Fourth Edition by Everett M. Rogers. Reprinted with permission of The Free Press, a division of Simon & Schuster, Inc. Copyright © 1995 by Everett M. Rogers. Copyright © 1962, 1971, 1983 by The Free Press.

early majority Those adopting new products just before the average person

late majority Skeptics who adopt new products when they feel it is necessary

laggards The last adopters, who distrust new products

with" by those in the remaining adopter categories. People in the **early majority** adopt just prior to the average person; they are deliberate and cautious in trying new products. Individuals in the **late majority** are quite skeptical of new products, but eventually adopt them because of economic necessity or social pressure. **Laggards,** the last to adopt a new product, are oriented toward the past. They are suspicious of new products, and when they finally adopt the innovation, it may already have been replaced by a new product.

Why Some Products Fail and Others Succeed

Thousands of new products are introduced annually, and many of them fail. Statistical bureaus, consulting firms, and trade publications estimate that one in three new products fail each year; others report an annual new-product failure rate as high as 80 to 90 percent. The annual cost of product failures to American firms can reach $100 billion. Failure and success rates vary from organization to organization, but in general consumer products fail more often than business products. Being one of the first brands launched in a product category is no guarantee of success. One study found that in 50 product categories, only half of the pioneers survived.[15] Table 10.3 shows examples of recent product successes and failures. Marketing Citizenship profiles one company with a good track record for successful products.

Products fail for many reasons. One of the most common reasons is the company's failure to match product offerings to customer needs. When products do not offer value and lack the features customers want, they fail in the marketplace. For example, Thirsty Cat! and Thirsty Dog! bottled waters for pets failed because consumers saw no

Table 10.3	**Product Successes and Failures**
Product Successes	**Product Failures**
Smith Kline Beecham Nicoderm CQ	R.J. Reynolds Premier smokeless cigarettes
Canon Elph digital camera	Polaroid instant cameras
PalmPilot PDAs	Apple Lisa personal computer
Coca-Cola Dasani water	Coca-Cola New Coke
Starbucks coffee shops	Nestlé Panache coffee
Procter & Gamble Pantene shampoos	Gillette For Oily Hair shampoo
Tide High Efficiency laundry detergent	Drel Home Dry Cleaning Kits
Procter & Gamble Swiffer mop and dusting cloths	S.C. Johnson Allercare aerosol spray, carpet powder, and dust mite powder
Bacardi Breezers	Miller Clear Beer

reason to buy fish- or beef-flavored bottled water for their pets.[16] Ineffective or inconsistent branding has also been blamed for product failures. Examples of products that failed because their brands failed to convey the right message or image include Gerber Singles (gourmet food for adults packaged in baby food jars), Microsoft's Bob (a "social interface" cartoon character that many users perceived as juvenile), and Gillette's For Oily Hair Only shampoo.[17] Other reasons cited for new-product failure include technical or design problems, poor timing, overestimation of market size, ineffective promotion, and insufficient distribution.

When examining the problem of product failure, it is important to distinguish the degree of failure. Absolute failure occurs when an organization loses money on a new product because it is unable to recover development, production, and marketing costs. This product usually is deleted from the product mix. Relative product failure occurs when a product returns a profit but does not meet a company's profit or market share objectives. If a company repositions or improves a relative product failure, that product may become a successful member of the product line. Some products experience relative product failure after years of success. Campbell Soup, for example, has been growing slowly for many years. The company continues to focus on its condensed-soup product line but has done little to improve packaging, promotion, or

MARKETING CITIZENSHIP

From a Joke to a Successful Product

Often people venture into marketing without putting much thought into their expected enterprises. When such ventures are poorly planned or miss a major trend in marketing, failure often results. Sometimes, however, the timing is right, the market is ready, and the business is a raving success. Newman's Own is an example of a business that was started halfheartedly and expected to fail by outsiders, yet managed to surpass all expectations.

Newman's Own was founded in 1982 by actor Paul Newman and author A. E. Hotchner. For years, the pair had given a homemade oil-and-vinegar salad dressing packaged in old wine bottles as gifts to friends and family during the holidays. The dressing always received rave reviews and requests for an encore. Almost as a joke, Newman and Hotchner decided to start a business to market their dressing, figuring if their friends liked it so much, the general public would too. Experts warned they should expect to lose $1 million in their first year of business. Instead, they made $1 million.

Paul Newman attributes the firm's success to two factors. First, he adamantly insists on only the freshest ingredients. The company never uses artificial preservatives or ingredients in the dressing or in newer products including ice cream, pasta sauces, salsas, popcorn, lemonade, and steak sauce. Second, Newman's Own donates all after-tax profits to educational and charitable organizations in the countries in which its products are marketed. These include Canada, Australia, Iceland, Japan, England, Germany, France, and Israel. The company has donated more than $100 million to organizations that often go unnoticed by the public and larger companies. Among these groups are The Flying Doctors, which provides specialty surgical procedures in isolated parts of Africa.

Newman's Own also sponsors competitions and gives awards to recognize outstanding individuals, groups, and organizations. One example is the Newman's Own Award for Military Community Excellence. Instead of hosting car washes or other traditional moneymakers, organizations on various military bases are encouraged to develop innovative programs to improve the quality of life for military families worldwide. Another example is the PEN/Newman's Own First Amendment Award, established in 1992 to acknowledge individuals who stand up for their freedom of speech. A recent winner was a college president in Texas who supported an independent theater that intended to produce a controversial play. When local officials threatened to withhold a funding grant, Newman's Own stepped in and gave $18,000, on top of the $25,000 prize, to ensure the theater would not be underfunded and forced to close. The Newman's Own/George Award is still another example; it donates $250,000 to a charity selected by the winner—the organization demonstrating the most innovative and significant corporate philanthropy.

What began as a joke has grown into a very serious business venture with successful products. Through its corporate citizenship, Newman's Own has helped thousands of people with donations to educational and charitable organizations. But Newman and Hotchner don't consider themselves heroic. They just wanted to create great-tasting, all-natural products that put consumers in a charitable frame of mind.

distribution. This leaves Campbell Soup with a core product whose market has fallen 21 percent in the last four years.[18]

Despite this gloomy picture of new-product failure, some new products are very successful. Perhaps the most important ingredient for success is the product's ability to provide a significant and perceivable benefit to a sizable number of customers. New products with an observable advantage over similar available products, such as more features, ease of operation, or improved technology, have a greater chance to succeed. The Nintendo GameBoy Advance, for example, which has a screen that is 50 percent larger and has greater resolution than previous GameBoy versions, has proven very popular among preteens. Critical to launching a product that will achieve market success is effective planning and management. Companies that follow a systematic, customer-focused plan for new-product development, such as Procter & Gamble, Gillette, and 3M, are well positioned to launch successful products.

Summary

A product is a good, a service, or an idea received in an exchange. It can be either tangible or intangible and includes functional, social, and psychological utilities or benefits. A product can be an idea, a service, a good, or any combination of the three. When consumers purchase a product, they are buying the benefits and satisfaction they think the product will provide.

Products can be classified on the basis of the buyer's intentions. Consumer products are those purchased to satisfy personal and family needs. Business products are purchased for use in a firm's operations, to resell, or to make other products. Consumer products can be subdivided into convenience, shopping, specialty, and unsought products. Business products can be classified as installations, accessory equipment, raw materials, component parts, process materials, MRO supplies, and business services.

A product item is a specific version of a product that can be designated as a distinct offering among an organization's products. A product line is a group of closely related product items that are considered a unit because of marketing, technical, or end-use considerations. The composite, or total, group of products that an organization makes available to customers is called the product mix. The width of the product mix is measured by the number of product lines the company offers. The depth of a product mix is the average number of different products offered in each product line.

The product life cycle describes how product items in an industry move through four stages: introduction, growth, maturity, and decline. The life cycle concept is used to ensure that the introduction, alteration, and termination of a product are timed and executed properly. The sales curve is at zero at introduction, rises at an increasing rate during growth, peaks at maturity, and then

declines. Profits peak toward the end of the growth stage of the product life cycle. The life expectancy of a product is based on buyers' wants, the availability of competing products, and other environmental conditions. Most businesses have a composite of life cycle patterns for various products. It is important to manage existing products and develop new ones to keep the overall sales performance at a desired level.

When customers accept a new product, they usually do so through a five-stage adoption process. The first stage is awareness, when buyers become aware that a product exists. Interest, the second stage, occurs when buyers seek information and are receptive to learning about the product. The third stage is evaluation; buyers consider the product's benefits and decide whether to try it. The fourth stage is trial; during this stage, buyers examine, test, or try the product to determine if it meets their needs. The last stage is adoption, when buyers actually purchase the product and use it whenever a need for this general type of product arises.

Of the thousands of new products introduced every year, many fail. Absolute failure occurs when an organization loses money on a new product. Absolute failures are usually removed from the product mix. Relative failure occurs when a product returns a profit but fails to meet a company's objectives. Some reasons for product failure include failure to match product offerings to customer needs, poor timing, and ineffective or inconsistent branding. Some new products do succeed, especially those that provide significant and observable benefits to customers. Products that have perceivable advantages over similar products also have a better chance to succeed. Effective marketing planning and product management are important factors in a new product's chances of success.

Important Terms

Good	Consumer products	Shopping products	Raw materials
Service	Business products	Specialty products	Component parts
Idea	Convenience products	Unsought products	Process materials
		Installations	MRO supplies
		Accessory equipment	Business services

Product item
Product line
Product mix
Width of product mix
Depth of product mix
Product life cycle
Introduction stage
Growth stage

Maturity stage
Decline stage
Product adoption process
Innovators
Early adopters
Early majority
Late majority
Laggards

and how do they affect the commercialization phase?

10. What are the five major adopter categories describing the length of time required for a consumer to adopt a new product, and what are the characteristics of each?

11. In what ways does the marketing strategy for a mature product differ from the marketing strategy for a growth product?

12. What are the major reasons for new-product failure?

Discussion and Review Questions

1. List the tangible and intangible attributes of a pair of Nike athletic shoes. Compare the benefits of the Nike shoes with those of an intangible product such as a hairstyling in a salon.
2. A product has been referred to as a "psychological bundle of satisfaction." Is this a good definition of a product? Why or why not?
3. Is a personal computer sold at a retail store a consumer product or a business product? Defend your answer.
4. How do convenience products and shopping products differ? What are the distinguishing characteristics of each type of product?
5. In the category of business products, how do component parts differ from process materials?
6. How does an organization's product mix relate to its development of a product line? When should an enterprise add depth to its product lines rather than width to its product mix?
7. How do industry profits change as a product moves through the four stages of its life cycle?
8. What is the relationship between the concepts of product mix and product life cycle?
9. What are the stages in the product adoption process,

Application Questions

1. Choose a familiar clothing store. Describe its product mix, including its depth and width. Evaluate the mix and make suggestions to the owner.
2. Tabasco pepper sauce is a product that has entered the maturity stage of the product life cycle. Name products that would fit into each of the four stages (introduction, growth, maturity, and decline). Describe each product and explain why it fits in that stage.
3. Generally buyers go through a product adoption process before becoming loyal customers. Describe your experience in adopting a product you now use consistently. Did you go through all the stages?
4. Identify and describe a friend or family member who fits into each of the following adopter categories. How would you use this information if you were product manager for a fashion-oriented, medium-priced clothing retailer such as J. Crew or JC Penney?
   a. Innovator
   b. Early adopter
   c. Early majority
   d. Late majority
   e. Laggard

Internet Exercise & Resources

Visit **www.prideferrell.com** for resources to help you master the material in this chapter, plus materials that will help you expand your marketing knowledge, including: Internet exercise updates, ACE self-tests, hotlinks to companies featured in this chapter, and much more.

Goodyear Tire & Rubber Company

In addition to providing information about the company's products, Goodyear's website helps consumers find the exact products they want and will even direct them to the nearest Goodyear retailer. Visit the Goodyear site at

www.goodyear.com

1. How does Goodyear use its website to communicate information about the quality of its tires?
2. How does Goodyear's website demonstrate product design and features?
3. Based on what you learned at the website, describe what Goodyear has done to position its tires.

VIDEO CASE 10.1

PlayStation 2 Provides a New Product Experience

Every year there seems to be one must-have item on every child's wish list, and for the 2000 holiday season, that item was Sony's PlayStation 2 video game console. Video game aficionados of all ages couldn't wait to get their hands on the new game player to enjoy their favorite games with cutting-edge graphics and accessories. Stoked by advancing computer technology and consumer demand for better, more realistic graphics and high-quality games, the $13 billion video game industry has become very competitive. Arcadia Investments estimates that worldwide sales of video game hardware and software topped $13 billion in 2001. Indeed, Americans spent almost as much money ($5.6 billion) on video games as they did on going to the movies ($7.7 billion) in 2000.

Sony has long led the industry with its hugely successful PlayStation game platform. The company continues to set the standard for the industry with the PlayStation 2, which was launched just in time for the 2000 holiday shopping season. Sony promoted the new system by focusing on its hardware and software features. The PlayStation 2 not only plays the latest games with 128-bit graphics (up from 64 in the PlayStation 1) but can also play music CDs and movies on DVDs. The PlayStation 2 console has 300 megahertz of central processing power, a 150 MHZ graphics processor, 38 megabytes of random access memory, and an 8 megabyte storage card. Sony expected to sell 10 million PlayStation 2s in the United States by the end of 2001, giving the firm a 14 percent share of the market. Although targeted primarily at 16-to-24 year-olds, the PlayStation 2 has been very popular among adult gamers as well.

In addition to the PlayStation 2 console, Sony later introduced more accessories, including a 40 gigabyte hard drive; a narrowband and broadband network connector; and a compatible LCD monitor, keyboard, mouse, and new software from America Online and RealNetworks. Sales of older systems, including the original PlayStation (now called PSOne), continue to climb as well, doubling to $1 billion in 2000.

The launch of Sony's PlayStation 2 created mayhem among consumers obsessed with the latest video game hardware, software, and accessories. Sony hit a snag early, however, when it had to slash the number of machines available on the first day of sales due to shortages of parts. The shortage could have proven disastrous for Sony at a time when competitors were announcing their own product advancements and new competitors had begun to enter the market. However, Sony's strong reputation among hard-core gamers helped the firm weather the crisis, and most customers patiently waited for their names to reach the tops of waiting lists for the next available units.

Sony's marketing strategy for the PlayStation 2 faced challenges from new entrants into the video game market. Nintendo's GameCube console, launched a year after the PlayStation 2, retailed for $100 less than the Sony system. Although its portable GameBoy devices have been best sellers for years, with more than 100 million units sold since 1989, Nintendo has not competed directly against Sony before. Nintendo is also working on making its GameBoy and GameCube systems cross-compatible so the new GameBoy Advance can serve as a controller for the GameCube.

Microsoft, another new entrant into the video game market, launched its Xbox game console in late 2001. Microsoft developed the Xbox to compete directly with Sony's PlayStation 2 on price, speed, and other features. The Xbox has double the graphics, central processing power, and random access memory, but it cannot play CDs and DVDs without a separate remote control. Like the PlayStation 2, the Xbox system is priced at around $300 and targeted at 16-to-24-year-olds. Microsoft, well known for its computer software, planned to focus its marketing efforts on the Xbox's available games and user-friendly interface rather than its hardware capabilities. The company planned to spend $500 million to market the Xbox, twice what it had spent to launch Windows 95.

Video games represent a product that is more intangible than tangible. Buyers search for performance and functional benefits. Every time the game is played, a different game experience results. The experience and the excitement associated with playing the game are the ultimate product. It is also possible to make the product more tangible through packaging and graphics used in branding and the instructions associated with the game. The important thing for PlayStation 2 is that potential buyers be made aware of the new product's features, uses, and advantages. The marketing strategy for PlayStation 2 was designed to attract the segment that is most interested and has the fewest objections to purchase.

Fueled by the technological advances in the new game consoles, consumers are snatching up new games like *Tomb Raider, Tony Hawk Pro Skater,* and *Zelda Oracle.* Despite the marketing muscle and strong brand recognition wielded by new products from Nintendo and Microsoft, industry analysts recognize that the highly competitive video game industry has seen its share of failures, including such pioneers as Atari, 3DO, and, more recently, Sega. Although competitors may introduce lower-priced game players or players with more advanced technology, consumers' ultimate decision about which system is best will be based on experience.[19]

Copyright © Houghton Mifflin Company. All rights reserved.

QUESTIONS FOR DISCUSSION

1. Classify Sony's PlayStation 2 as to type of product. Defend your classification.
2. At what point in the product life cycle is Sony's PlayStation 2 game console? How does this life cycle stage affect Sony's marketing strategies for this product?
3. To which product adopter categories is Sony most likely to promote the PlayStation 2?

CASE 10.2

Schwinn: Reviving a Classic American Brand

For decades American children yearned for Schwinn bicycles, and kids who rode Schwinn Excelsiors, Phantoms, and Sting-Rays were the envy of their neighborhoods. Today, however, if you ask people under 30 to name a popular brand of bicycle, they will probably mention Trek or Cannondale, but not Schwinn. When consumer tastes changed from sturdy, low-cost bikes to trendy, high-priced ones, Schwinn's sales plummeted. Unwilling to let Schwinns disappear along with Underwood typewriters, the venerable bicycle maker launched an all-out effort to bring back the best-known brand name on two wheels. With Americans spending approximately $2 billion a year to buy 17 million bicycles, the market for bikes clearly had room to grow.

More than 100 years ago, Iganz Schwinn founded his bicycle company and built it into the most prestigious in the industry. For years Schwinn ruled as the number one U.S. bicycle brand, and in the 1970s the Schwinn brand name ranked number three in the United States, behind only Coca-Cola and United Airlines. In the late 1970s and early 1980s, however, cyclists got serious. To pedal off sidewalks and roads and into mountains and woods, they wanted upright handlebars, fat tires, and additional climbing gears. They also wanted the state-of-the-art technology provided by Cannondale, Giant, Waterloo, and market-leading Trek. Schwinn, however, wasn't paying attention and continued to focus on the shrinking market for ten-speed bikes through most of the 1980s. By 1993 two-thirds of all bikes sold were mountain bikes, and the once mighty Schwinn filed for bankruptcy. Believing in Schwinn's name and reputation, Sam Zell bought the company, moved its headquarters to Boulder, Colorado, and formulated a strategy to take Schwinn back to the top of a crowded bicycle market.

Zell's goal was to get the Schwinn name on everything from $100 children's bicycles to $2,500 mountain bikes. The first step toward achieving that goal was to upgrade Schwinn's entire product line. To make its bicycles stronger and lighter, for example, Schwinn turned to EMF Industries, a company whose new electromagnetic process turns out aluminum that makes bicycle frames much stronger. Schwinn also

restyled all 48 of its models to make them attractive to today's customers.

Zell's strategy worked. Between 1993 and 1997, Schwinn rose from ninth to second in the market, selling more than 350,000 bicycles and fitness products a year. Stated the owner of a bicycle shop in Boulder, "Two years ago we said, 'There is no way we would ever sell a Schwinn mountain bike.' Now they're responsible for about one-third of our annual sales." By 2001, Schwinn dominated the independent bike dealer market for both mountain and BMX bikes, according to the Sports Marketing Survey.

Schwinn continued to build on its momentum by introducing new products. One of its hottest new products is a retro-style model: the Cruiser Deluxe, a one-speed model with a wide seat, chrome fenders, authentic 1950s pedals, and balloon tires, which sells for about $480. For those nostalgic cyclists who don't mind spending a bit more, there is the Black Phantom. Built from the 1949 blueprints, this model has faux-wood grain trim and exact replicas of the original fenders, horn, tires, and chrome—and, of course, the coaster breaks. In fact, the only difference between the original and the reproduction is the price. In the old days, the bike cost about $80; today the price is about $3,000.

It wasn't easy for Schwinn to transform its image from stodgy to stylish. The company launched a $10 million advertising campaign and several creative promotional efforts. Print ads featured enthusiasts mountain biking and racing on Schwinn bicycles, and Schwinn's professional mountain bike team raced every weekend between April and September. To generate positive word of mouth about its products, Schwinn developed Project Underground, through which the company began selling its elite models at lower-than-cost prices to employees of Schwinn dealers before the models' general release. Thanks to this program, bike store employees could rave about Schwinn bikes based on personal experience.

By 1997, Schwinn's new products and intense promotions had revived the company. The bicycle maker had not, however, achieved its goal of becoming the number one bicycle company in the world. To continue to work toward that goal, Zell sold Schwinn to Questor's Partners L.P., an organization with the finances and vision to complete the rebirth begun in 1993. A year later, Questor acquired rival bikemaker GT and consolidated the operations of the two firms. Schwinn/GT focused on building international sales, increasing sales of parts and accessories, and capitalizing on the growing popularity of its retro-style 1950s models. Despite the turnaround achieved by Zell, Schwinn/GT again filed for Chapter 11 bankruptcy in 2001, and the cycling division was sold to Pacific Cycle LLC for $86 million. Pacific Cycle, which markets the Mongoose, Pacific, and Roadmaster brand bicycles, plans to continue maintaining Schwinn's strong dealer network as well as the brand's essence and positioning. According to Chris Hornung, Pacific Cycle's chief executive officer, "The Schwinn name is an American icon. It is the brand that many Americans grew up with and aspired to own. We feel that we offer the best opportunity in a generation to restore vitality to the Schwinn brand."[20]

QUESTIONS FOR DISCUSSION

1. How would Schwinn mountain bikes be classified as a product?
2. In what stage of the product life cycle is the bicycle industry? Explain.
3. Evaluate Schwinn management's decision to launch the Black Phantom.

Developing and Managing Products

11

OBJECTIVES

- To understand how companies manage existing products through line extensions and product modifications

- To describe how businesses develop a product idea into a commercial product

- To understand the importance of product differentiation and the elements that differentiate one product from another

- To explore how products are positioned and repositioned in the customer's mind

- To understand how product deletion is used to improve product mixes

- To describe organizational structures used for managing products

271

Revitalizing a Familiar Brand: Campbell Soup Company

With 132 years of success in the soup business, 20 market-leading businesses, and annual sales of $6.7 billion, you might think Campbell Soup Company has little to worry about. This is not the case, however. Last year, although sales increased modestly, Campbell lost market share and profits declined. Moreover, sales of condensed soups have fallen 21 percent since 1998. The company must now strive to adapt products to meet changing needs and develop new products to remain competitive.

To be more competitive, Campbell Soup is investing in upgrading the quality of its soups. This is due mainly to pressure from the Progresso brand, which recently was acquired by General Mills, giving Progresso access to greater funds for research and development and advertising. Campbell has also increased advertising spending, in part to challenge Progresso head to head. In promotions for Chunky New England Clam Chowder, Campbell's Select Grilled Chicken with Sundried Tomato, and Campbell's Red & White Minestrone soups, Campbell is directly comparing the soups to Progresso's.

In addition, Campbell has boosted investments in research to develop new forms of soup for consumption away from home and introduced new packaging with "easy-open" lids across its entire line of condensed soups. However, the company recognizes that its future success is no longer wholly tied to soups. Campbell is now introducing Supper Bakes, boxes of shelf-stable ingredients including everything needed to produce a home-cooked meal except for the meat. The entrees require just 5 minutes to prepare and approximately 30 minutes to bake. Supper Bake flavors include Savory Pork Chops with Herb Stuffing and Garlic Chicken with Pasta. Campbell has also expanded its Prego line of sauces with Prego Pasta Bakes, a line of complete pasta entrees.

This initiative to revitalize Campbell Soup comes after many years of taking a conservative approach to marketing, reacting to competitors' strategies more than undertaking innovation. For example, the company was slow to recognize consumer interest in healthy as well as ready-to-serve soups. As a former Campbell Soup executive stated, "It's definitely a risk-averse, control-oriented culture. It's all about two things: financial control and how much profit you can squeeze out of a tomato."

Although it may be accused of complacency, Campbell remains a strong presence in global soup markets. It markets the Campbell's brand of soups worldwide, as well as Erasco soups in Germany, Liebig soups in France, and dry soups and sauces in Europe under the Batchelors, Oxo, Lesieur, Royco, Liebig, Heisse Tasse, Bla Band, and McDonnels brands. The company wants to innovate and expand these brands, but it must exercise care in doing so to avoid harming its core business: condensed soups. Retailers may be reluctant to make room on their shelves for new Campbell products, especially given the strong demand for alternative, higher-end brands such as Progresso and Wolfgang Puck's line of restaurant-quality, gourmet soups. Campbell's ability to successfully introduce new products that match consumers' lifestyles and tastes will ultimately determine its success.[1]

To compete effectively and achieve their goals, organizations like the Campbell Soup Company must be able to adjust their product mixes in response to changes in customers' needs. A firm often has to introduce new products, modify existing products, or delete products that were successful perhaps only a few years ago. To provide products that satisfy target markets and achieve the organization's objectives, a marketer must develop, alter, and maintain an effective product mix. An organization's product mix may need several types of adjustments. Because customers' attitudes and product preferences change over time, their desire for certain products may wane.

In some cases, a company needs to alter its product mix for competitive reasons. A marketer may have to delete a product from the mix because a competitor dominates the market for that product. Similarly, a firm may have to introduce a new product or modify an existing one to compete more effectively. A marketer may expand the firm's product mix to take advantage of excess marketing and production capacity.

In this chapter, we examine several ways to improve an organization's product mix, including management of existing products, development of new products, product differentiation, positioning and repositioning of products, and elimination of weak products from the product mix. First, we discuss managing existing products through effective line extension and product modification. Next, we examine the stages of new-product development. Then we go on to discuss the ways companies differentiate their products in the marketplace and follow with a discussion of product positioning and repositioning. Next, we examine the importance of deleting weak products and the methods companies use to eliminate them. Finally, we look at the organizational structures used to manage products.

Managing Existing Products

An organization can benefit by capitalizing on its existing products. By assessing the composition of the current product mix, a marketer can identify weaknesses and gaps. This analysis can then lead to improvement of the product mix through line extension and through product modification.

line extension Development of a product that is closely related to existing products in the line but meets different customer needs

Line Extensions

A **line extension** is the development of a product closely related to one or more products in the existing product line but designed specifically to meet somewhat different customer needs. For example, Nabisco extended its cookie line to include Reduced Fat Oreos and Double Stuffed Oreos. Hyundai introduced the Elantra GT as a line extension of its best-selling Elantra model. The Elantra GT has five doors and offers more functionality than the basic Electra model.[2]

Many of the so-called new products introduced each year are in fact line extensions. Line extensions are more common than new products because they are a less expensive, lower-risk alternative for increasing sales. A line extension may focus on a different market segment or may be an attempt to increase sales within the same market segment by more precisely satisfying the needs of people in that segment. Line extensions also are used to take market share from competitors. The Elantra GT, for example, was introduced to compete directly with the Mazda Protégé S five-door hatchback wagon.[3] However, one side effect of employing a line extension is that it may result in a more negative evaluation of the core product.[4] In the case of Hyundai's new line extension, the firm's objective was for the Elantra GT to comprise 15 to

introducing new sour skittles.

Line Extensions
The Skittles® Brand introduces a new line extension—Sour Skittles® Bite Size Candies—to manage its existing products.

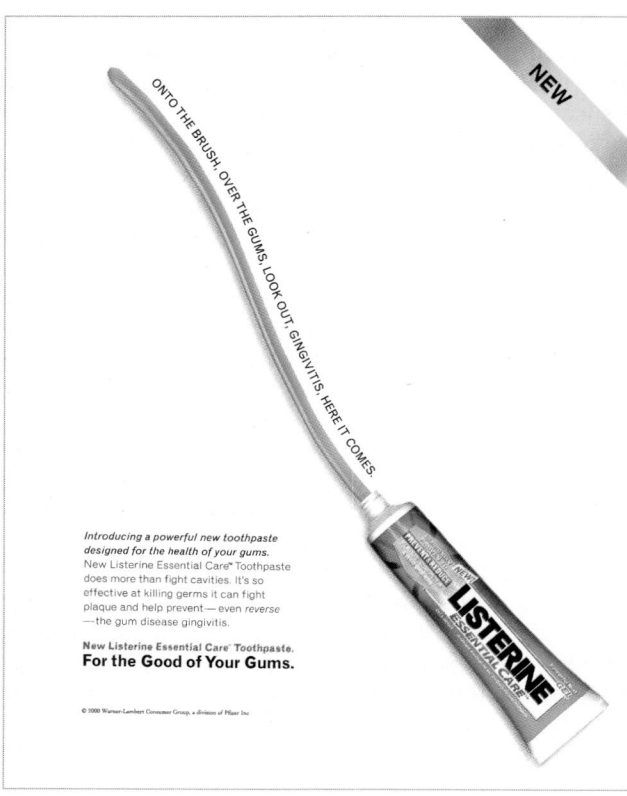

ONTO THE BRUSH. OVER THE GUMS, LOOK OUT GINGIVITIS, HERE IT COMES.

NEW

Introducing a powerful new toothpaste designed for the health of your gums.
New Listerine Essential Care® Toothpaste does more than fight cavities. It's so effective at killing germs it can fight plaque and help prevent—even reverse —the gum disease gingivitis.

New Listerine Essential Care® Toothpaste.
For the Good of Your Gums.

© 2000 Warner-Lambert Consumer Group, a division of Pfizer Inc.

Product Modifications
Listerine provides a functional product improvement.

20 percent of all Elantra sales.[5] Some customers may ultimately view the basic Elantra more negatively because of the functional advantages of the GT five-door model.

Product Modifications

product modification
Change in one or more characteristics of a product

Product modification means changing one or more characteristics of a product. A product modification differs from a line extension in that the original product does not remain in the line. For example, U.S. automakers use product modifications annually when they create new models of the same brand. Once the new models are introduced, the manufacturers stop producing last year's model. Like line extensions, product modifications entail less risk than developing new products.

Product modification can indeed improve a firm's product mix, but only under certain conditions. First, the product must be modifiable. Second, customers must be able to perceive that a modification has been made. Third, the modification should make the product more consistent with customers' desires so it provides greater satisfaction. There are three major ways to modify products: quality, functional, and aesthetic modifications.

quality modifications
Changes relating to a product's dependability and durability

Quality Modifications. **Quality modifications** are changes relating to a product's dependability and durability. The changes usually are executed by altering the materials or the production process. For example, Energizer increased its product's durability by using better materials—a larger cathode and anode interface—that make batteries last longer.

Reducing a product's quality may allow an organization to lower its price and direct the item at a different target market. In contrast, increasing the quality of a product may give a firm an advantage over competing brands. In fact, over the last 20 years, increased global competition, rapid technological changes, and more demanding customers have forced marketers to improve product integrity to remain competitive.[6] Higher quality may enable a company to charge a higher price by creating customer loyalty and lowering customer sensitivity to price. However, higher quality may require the use of more expensive components and processes, thus forcing the organization to cut costs in other areas. Some firms, such as Caterpillar, are finding ways to increase quality while reducing costs.

functional modifications
Changes affecting a product's versatility, effectiveness, convenience, or safety

Functional Modifications. Changes that affect a product's versatility, effectiveness, convenience, or safety are called **functional modifications;** they usually require that the product be redesigned. Product categories that have undergone considerable functional modification include office and farm equipment, appliances, cleaning products, and telecommunications services. For example, telephone companies have offered Caller ID services, which reveal the telephone numbers of most callers, for more than ten years. However, customers still complain that many calls show up as "anonymous" or "out of area." In response, some telephone companies have enhanced the service to allow customers to screen out such unidentified calls. Other companies offer Privacy Manager, a Caller ID add-on service that requires unidentified callers to record their names so the recipient can decide whether to answer the call.[7]

Functional modifications can make a product useful to more people and thus enlarge its market. They can place a product in a favorable competitive position by providing benefits that competing brands do not offer. They can also help an organization achieve and maintain a progressive image. Finally, functional modifications are sometimes made to reduce the possibility of product liability lawsuits.

aesthetic modifications
Changes to the sensory appeal of a product

Aesthetic Modifications. **Aesthetic modifications** change the sensory appeal of a product by altering its taste, texture, sound, smell, or appearance. A buyer making a purchase decision is swayed by how a product looks, smells, tastes, feels, or sounds. Procter & Gamble, for example, added a new Caribbean flavor to its Sunny Delight orange beverage product line. Thus, an aesthetic modification may strongly affect purchases. For years, automobile makers have relied on aesthetic modifications such as new colors or headlight designs.

Through aesthetic modifications, a firm can differentiate its product from competing brands and thus gain a sizable market share. The major drawback in using aesthetic modifications is that their value is determined subjectively. Although a firm may strive to improve the product's sensory appeal, customers may actually find the modified product less attractive, as shown in Building Customer Relationships.

BUILDING CUSTOMER RELATIONSHIPS

Modifying Trucks with a Woman's Touch

Product modification is widely used in the automobile industry to ensure that auto brands satisfy customers' needs and desires. In the highly competitive truck market, more automakers are recognizing that women are increasingly buying trucks. Although women account for only about 11 percent of pickup truck buyers, their numbers are growing. Moreover, research indicates that women are playing a greater role in deciding what options should be on the family pickup. Many women are also buying sport-utility vehicles (SUVs) and minivans, which are classified as trucks as well. Modifications to these products are increasingly being credited to female engineers and designers. With women influencing more than 80 percent of all new-vehicle purchases—about half of which are trucks in the United States—it makes sense to enlist women to help design product modifications on trucks, SUVs, and minivans.

Female engineers recognize that women drivers want trucks that are more comfortable, ergonomic, and driver friendly. Thus, to attract more women drivers, automakers are moving to blend function and personal use, especially to accommodate smaller women and shorter men. Some of the new features that women engineers have incorporated into trucks include adjustable brake and gas pedals, smoother automatic transmissions, better-insulated passenger cabins, larger cabins for families, and smoother, more carlike rides. Diane Allen, one of the designers who worked on Nissan's Frontier pickup, spent weeks learning about the "truck culture" and the desires and ideas of pickup owners by visiting construction sites.

Most automakers not only have female engineers on their staff but also use several informal teams made up of nonengineering female workers. These teams are impor-tant in evaluating new concepts and features in vehicle design that women may want. Ford Motor Company, for example, created a development team of 30 female engineers, called the Windstar Moms, to make its Windstar minivans more user friendly for women with children. Ford has continued to rely on its team of Windstar Moms over the years; this team was instrumental in developing the new Solutions minivan, which is outfitted with a refrigerator, a microwave, a washer-dryer, a vacuum cleaner, and other home appliances. Similarly, DaimlerChrysler recruited an informal group of female engineers, the Women's Product Advocate Team, to provide a voice for female customers in the development of more women-friendly vehicles. Kate Zak, brand character design manager for Saturn, designed Saturn's first SUV, the VUE. These companies believe that using more women engineers brings a feminine perspective that will provide an advantage in understanding what women expect in a vehicle.

Although many factors affect a product's versatility, effectiveness, convenience, and safety, women engineers are also focusing on aesthetic modifications. Modifying truck designs to better match women's personalities, as well as providing larger, more comfortable cabins and soft-ride vehicles, is important. Such aesthetic modifications are evaluated subjectively with the recognition that sensory appeal may be the ultimate characteristic that triggers purchases. These modifications have brought to trucks family-friendly interior and exterior designs while deemphasizing sharp edges and "macho" styles. Product modifications entail less risk than developing new products, and the new truck designs may result in increasing sales among the many women buyers looking for trucks that fit their lifestyles.

Developing New Products

A firm develops new products as a means of enhancing its product mix and adding depth to a product line. Developing and introducing new products is frequently expensive and risky. For example, Maxwell House introduced Maxwell House Brewed Coffee in a 48-ounce package resembling a milk carton with a handy screw-on plug. This ready-to-microwave, instantly recognizable product, located in supermarket refrigerated sections, failed because customers did not value the benefits it provided.[8] New-product failures are not uncommon, as discussed in the previous chapter. They can create major financial problems for organizations, sometimes even causing them to go out of business.

Failure to introduce new products is also risky. For example, the makers of Timex watches gained a large share of the U.S. watch market through effective marketing strategies during the 1960s and early 1970s. In the 1980s, Timex's market share slipped considerably, in part because Timex had failed to introduce new products. In recent times, however, Timex has introduced technologically advanced new products and has regained market share.

The term *new product* can have more than one meaning. A genuinely new product offers innovative benefits. But products that are different and distinctly better are often viewed as new. The following items (listed in no particular order) are product innovations of the last 30 years: Post-it notes, fax machines, cell phones, personal computers, PDAs, disposable razors, Caller ID, and DVDs. Thus, a new product can be an innovative product that has never been sold by any organization, such as the digital camera when it was introduced for the first time. A radically new product involves a complex developmental process, including an extensive business analysis to determine the possibility of success.[9] It can also be a product that a given firm has not marketed previously, although similar products may have been available from other companies, such as Crayola School Glue. Eddie Bauer, best known for its rugged outdoor wear, extended this image with the introduction of a new line of men's cologne. It was considered a new product because Eddie Bauer had not previously marketed cologne or cosmetics. Finally, a product can be viewed as new when it is brought to one or

Examples of New Products
Toro introduces a new robotic mower to provide a unique consumer benefit. OFF!™ introduces a new attractive mosquito lamp, which promises to provide improved protection.

Introducing the revolutionary Toro iMow™ Robotic Mower.

Introducing the attractive repellent.

New OFF!® Mosquito Lamp. It works hard, repelling mosquitoes and keeping them far away. And, it looks great, glowing softly in the dark. The heat of the candle activates an innovative repellent pad that protects an area 15 times greater than a citronella candle. It's effective. It's attractive. It's new OFF!® Mosquito Lamp.

KEEPS BUGS OFF!®

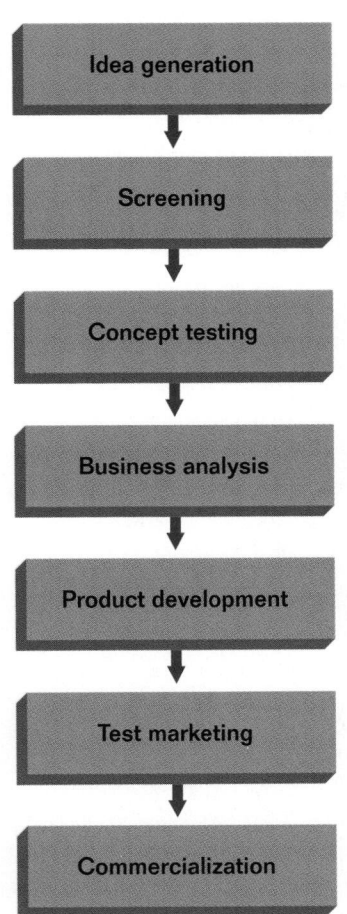

FIGURE 11.1
Phases of New-Product Development

new-product development process A seven-phase process for introducing products

idea generation Seeking product ideas to achieve objectives

screening Choosing the most promising ideas for further review

concept testing Seeking potential buyers' responses to a product idea

more markets from another market. For example, making the Saturn VUE SUV available in Japan is viewed as a new-product introduction in Japan.

Before a product is introduced, it goes through the seven phases of the **new-product development process** shown in Figure 11.1: (1) idea generation, (2) screening, (3) concept testing, (4) business analysis, (5) product development, (6) test marketing, and (7) commercialization. A product may be dropped, and many are, at any stage of development. In this section, we look at the process through which products are developed, from idea inception to fully commercialized product.

Idea Generation

Businesses and other organizations seek product ideas that will help them achieve their objectives. This activity is **idea generation.** The fact that only a few ideas are good enough to be commercially successful underscores the difficulty of the task. Although some organizations get their ideas almost by chance, firms that try to manage their product mixes effectively usually develop systematic approaches for generating new-product ideas. Indeed, there is a relationship between the amount of market information gathered and the number of ideas generated by work groups in organizations.[10] At the heart of innovation is a purposeful, focused effort to identify new ways to serve a market.

New-product ideas can come from several sources. They may come from internal sources—marketing managers, researchers, sales personnel, engineers, or other organizational personnel. Brainstorming and incentives or rewards for good ideas are typical intrafirm devices for stimulating development of ideas. For example, the idea for 3M Post-it adhesive-backed notes came from an employee. As a church choir member, he used slips of paper to mark songs in his hymnal. Because the pieces of paper fell out, he suggested developing an adhesive-backed note. New-product ideas may also arise from sources outside the firm, such as customers, competitors, advertising agencies, management consultants, and private research organizations. Consultants are often used as sources for stimulating new-product ideas. The Eureka Ranch, also known as the "idea factory," charges clients as much as $150,000 for a three-day creativity session.[11] Developing new-product alliances with other firms has also been found to enhance the acquisition and utilization of information useful for creating new-product ideas.[12] A significant portion of this money is used to assess customers' needs. Asking customers what they want from products and organizations has helped many firms become successful and remain competitive.

Screening

In the process of **screening,** the ideas with the greatest potential are selected for further review. During screening, product ideas are analyzed to determine whether they match the organization's objectives and resources. If a product idea results in a product similar to the firm's existing products, marketers must assess the degree to which the new product could cannibalize the sales of current products. The company's overall abilities to produce and market the product are also analyzed. Other aspects of an idea to be weighed are the nature and wants of buyers and possible environmental changes. At times a checklist of new-product requirements is used when making screening decisions. This practice encourages evaluators to be systematic and thus reduces the chances of overlooking some pertinent fact. Compared with other phases, the largest number of new-product ideas are rejected during the screening phase.

Concept Testing

To evaluate ideas properly, it may be necessary to test product concepts. In **concept testing,** a small sample of potential buyers is presented with a product idea through a written or oral description (and perhaps a few drawings) to determine their attitudes and initial buying intentions regarding the product. For a single product idea, an organization can test one or several concepts of the same product. Concept testing is a low-

Product description

An insecticide company is considering the development and introduction of a new tick and flea control product for pets. This product would consist of insecticide and a liquid dispensing brush for applying the insecticide to dogs and cats. The insecticide is in a cartridge that is installed in the handle of the brush. The insecticide is dispensed through the tips of the bristles when they touch the pet's skin (which is where most ticks and fleas are found). The actual dispensing works very much like a felt-tip pen. Only a small amount of insecticide actually is dispensed on the pet because of this unique dispensing feature. Thus, the amount of insecticide that is placed on your pet is minimal compared to conventional methods of applying a tick and flea control product. One application of insecticide will keep your pet free from ticks and fleas for fourteen days.

Please answer the following questions:

1. In general, how do you feel about using this type of product on your pet?

2. What are the major advantages of this product compared with the existing product that you are currently using to control ticks and fleas on your pet?

3. What characteristics of this product do you especially like?

4. What suggestions do you have for improving this product?

5. If it is available at an appropriate price, how likely are you to buy this product?

        Very likely   Semi-likely   Not likely

6. Assuming that a single purchase would provide 30 applications for an average-size dog or 48 applications for an average-size cat, approximately how much would you pay for this product?

FIGURE 11.2
Concept Test for a Tick and Flea Control Product

cost procedure that lets the organization determine customers' initial reactions to a product idea before it invests considerable resources in research and development. The results of concept testing can help product development personnel better understand which product attributes and benefits are most important to potential customers.

Figure 11.2 shows a concept test for a proposed tick and flea control product. Notice that the concept is briefly described, then a series of questions is presented. The questions vary considerably depending on the type of product being tested. Typical questions are: In general, do you find this proposed product attractive? Which benefits are especially attractive to you? Which features are of little or no interest to you? Do you feel this proposed product would work better for you than the product you currently use? Compared with your current product, what are the primary advantages of the proposed product? If this product were available at an appropriate price, would you buy it? How often would you buy this product? How could this proposed product be improved?

Business Analysis

business analysis Assessing the potential of a product idea for the firm's sales, costs, and profits

During the **business analysis** stage, the product idea is evaluated to determine its potential contribution to the firm's sales, costs, and profits. In the course of a business analysis, evaluators ask a variety of questions: Does the product fit in with the organization's existing product mix? Is demand strong enough to justify entering the market, and will the demand endure? What types of environmental and competitive changes can be expected, and how will these changes affect the product's future sales, costs, and profits? Are the organization's research, development, engineering, and production capabilities adequate to develop the product? If new facilities must be constructed, how quickly can they be built, and how much will they cost? Is the necessary financing for development and commercialization on hand or obtainable at terms consistent with a favorable return on investment?

In the business analysis stage, firms seek market information. The results of consumer polls, along with secondary data, supply the specifics needed to estimate potential sales, costs, and profits. For example, in the 2000 census, nearly one-fourth of the population identified themselves to be of a race other than white. Evidence indicates that future marketing research and market tests must reflect the interests and preferences of diverse potential markets.[13]

For many products in this stage (when they are still just product ideas), forecasting sales accurately is difficult. This is especially true for innovative and completely new products. Organizations sometimes employ breakeven analysis to determine how many units they would have to sell to begin making a profit. At times an organization also uses payback analysis, in which marketers compute the time period required to recover the funds that would be invested in developing the new product. Because breakeven and payback analyses are based on estimates, they are usually viewed as useful but not particularly precise during this stage.

Product Development

product development
Determining if producing a product is feasible and cost effective

Product development is the phase in which the organization determines if it is technically feasible to produce the product and if it can be produced at costs low enough to make the final price reasonable. To test its acceptability, the idea or concept is converted into a prototype, or working model. The prototype should reveal tangible and intangible attributes associated with the product in consumers' minds. The product's design, mechanical features, and intangible aspects must be linked to wants in the marketplace. Through marketing research and concept testing, product attributes important to buyers are identified. These characteristics must be communicated to customers through the design of the product.

After a prototype is developed, its overall functioning must be tested. Its performance, safety, convenience, and other functional qualities are tested both in a laboratory and in the field. Functional testing should be rigorous and lengthy enough to test the product thoroughly.

A crucial question that arises during product development is how much quality to build into the product. For example, a major dimension of quality is durability. Higher quality often calls for better materials and more expensive processing, which increase production costs and, ultimately, the product's price. In determining the specific level of quality, a marketer must ascertain approximately what price the target market views as acceptable. In addition, a marketer usually tries to set a quality level consistent with that of the firm's other products. Obviously, the quality of competing brands is also a consideration. For example, Nike's market share has declined to 42 percent from 48 percent in 1997, in part because the firm focused on high-quality but high-end traditional athletic shoes while competitors such as Skechers and New Balance introduced trendier and more mid-priced shoes, which account for the majority of domestic athletic shoe sales.[14]

The development phase of a new product is frequently lengthy and expensive; thus, a relatively small number of product ideas are put into development. If the product appears sufficiently successful during this stage to merit test marketing, then, during the latter part of the development stage, marketers begin to make decisions regarding branding, packaging, labeling, pricing, and promotion for use in the test marketing stage.

Test Marketing

test marketing   Introducing a product on a limited basis to measure the extent to which potential customers will actually buy it

A limited introduction of a product in geographic areas chosen to represent the intended market is called **test marketing.** Its aim is to determine the extent to which potential customers will buy the product. Test marketing is not an extension of the development stage; it is a sample launching of the entire marketing mix. Test marketing should be conducted only after the product has gone through development and initial plans regarding the other marketing mix variables have been made.

Companies use test marketing to lessen the risk of product failure. The dangers of introducing an untested product include undercutting already profitable products and, should the new product fail, loss of credibility with distributors and customers. Anheuser-Busch, for example, has unsuccessfully test marketed a number of non-alcoholic and trace-alcoholic beverages, including Root 66 (late 1970s), Chelsea (late 1980s), and Zeltzer Seltzer (late 1980s). The brands were dropped during testing because of distribution problems, poor demand and profits, or criticism that the beer company was inappropriately targeting its products at youngsters. Now the company is test marketing a new, non-alcoholic energy drink, 180 Degrees, which will compete directly with Red Bull and other "New Age" beverages.[15]

Test marketing provides several benefits. It lets marketers expose a product in a natural marketing environment to measure its sales performance. While the product is being marketed in a limited area, the company can strive to identify weaknesses in the product or in other parts of the marketing mix. A product weakness discovered after a nationwide introduction can be expensive to correct. Moreover, if consumers' early reactions are negative, marketers may be unable to persuade consumers to try the product again. Thus, making adjustments after test marketing can be crucial to the success of a new product. On the other hand, testing results may be positive enough to accelerate the introduction of a new product. Test marketing also allows marketers to experiment with variations in advertising, pricing, and packaging in different test areas and to measure the extent of brand awareness, brand switching, and repeat purchases resulting from these alterations in the marketing mix.

Selection of appropriate test areas is very important because the validity of test market results depends heavily on selecting test sites that provide accurate representation of the intended target market. Table 11.1 lists some of the most popular test market cities. The criteria used for choosing test cities depend on the product's attributes, the target market's characteristics, and the firm's objectives and resources.

Test marketing is not without risks. It is expensive, and competitors may try to interfere. A competitor may attempt to "jam" the test program by increasing its own advertising or promotions, lowering prices, and offering special incentives, all to combat the recognition and purchase of the new brand. Any such tactics can invalidate test results. Sometimes, too, competitors copy the product in the testing stage and rush to introduce a similar product. It is therefore desirable to move to the commercialization phase as soon as possible after successful testing. On the other hand, some firms have been known to heavily promote new products long before they are ready for the market to discourage competitors from developing similar new products. When the product introduction is delayed to the point where the public begins to doubt its existence, such products may become known as "vaporware," particularly in the computer software industry.[16]

Because of these risks, many companies use alternative methods to measure customer preferences. One such method is simulated test marketing. Typically consumers at shopping centers are asked to view an advertisement for a new product and are given a free sample to take home. These consumers are subsequently interviewed over the phone and asked to rate the product. The major advantages of simulated test marketing are greater speed, lower costs, and tighter security, which reduce the flow of information to competitors and reduce jamming. Gillette's Personal Care Division spends less than $200,000 for a simulated test that lasts three to five months. A live test market costs Gillette $2 million, counting promotion and distribution, and takes one to two years to complete. Several marketing research firms, such as ACNielsen

Test Marketing
Crest Whitestrips were test marketed on the Internet before they were made available in stores.

Table 11.1	Popular Test Markets in the United States		
Tulsa, OK	Wichita, KS	Longview, TX	Pittsfield, MA
Charleston, WV	Bloomington, IL	Lafayette, LA	Jacksonville, FL
Midland, TX	Oklahoma City, OK	Omaha, NE	Edmond, OK
Springfield, IL	Indianapolis, IN	Phoenix, AZ	High Point, NC
Lexington-Fayette, KY	Rockford, IL	Gastonia, NC	Salt Lake City, UT
Eau Claire, WI	Grand Junction, CO	Rome, GA	Marion, IN
Cedar Rapids, IA	Visalia, CA		

Sources: Strategic Mapping, Inc., Santa Clara, CA; and Betsy Spethmann, "Test Market USA," *Brandweek*, May 8, 1995, p. 42.

Company, offer test marketing services to help provide independent assessment of proposed products.

Clearly not all products that are test marketed are launched. At times problems discovered during test marketing cannot be resolved. Procter & Gamble, for example, test marketed a new plastic wrap product called Impress in Grand Junction, Colorado, but decided not to launch the brand nationally.[17]

Commercialization

commercialization Deciding on full-scale manufacturing and marketing plans and preparing budgets

During the **commercialization** phase, plans for full-scale manufacturing and marketing must be refined and settled and budgets for the project prepared. Early in the commercialization phase, marketing management analyzes the results of test marketing to find out what changes in the marketing mix are needed before the product is introduced. The results of test marketing may tell marketers to change one or more of the product's physical attributes, modify the distribution plans to include more retail outlets, alter promotional efforts, or change the product's price. However, as more and more changes are made based on test marketing findings, the test marketing projections may become less valid.

During the early part of this stage, marketers must not only gear up for larger-scale production but also make decisions about warranties, repairs, and replacement parts. The type of warranty a firm provides can be a critical issue for buyers, especially when expensive, technically complex goods like appliances are involved. Maytag, for example, provides a money-back guarantee on its refrigerators. Establishing an effective system for providing repair services and replacement parts is necessary to maintain favorable customer relationships. Although the producer may furnish these services directly to buyers, it is more common for the producer to provide such services through regional service centers. Regardless of how services are provided, it is important to customers that they be performed quickly and correctly.

The product enters the market during the commercialization phase. When introducing a product, a firm may spend enormous sums for advertising, personal selling, and other types of promotion, as well as for plant and equipment. Such expenditures may not be recovered for several years. Smaller organizations may find commercializing of a product especially difficult.

Products are not usually launched nationwide overnight but are introduced through a process called a *roll-out*. Through a roll-out, a product is introduced in stages, starting in one set of geographic areas and gradually expanding into adjacent areas. It may take several years to market the product nationally. Sometimes the test cities are used as initial marketing areas, and the introduction of the product becomes a natural extension of test marketing. A product test marketed in Sacramento, Fort Collins, Abilene, Springfield, and Jacksonville, as the map in Figure 11.3 shows, could be introduced first in those cities. After the stage 1 introduction is complete, stage 2 could include market coverage of the states where the test cities are located. In stage

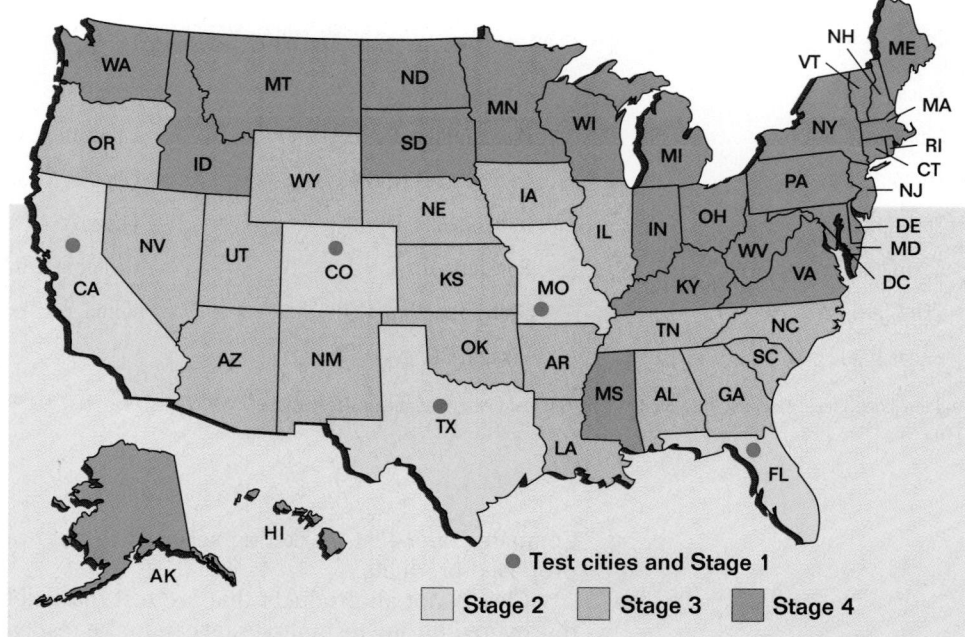

FIGURE 11.3
Stages of Expansion into a National Market During Commercialization

Source: Adapted from Herbert G. Hicks, William M. Pride, and James D. Powell, *Business: An Involvement Approach.* Copyright © 1975. Reproduced with permission of The McGraw-Hill Companies.

3, marketing efforts might be extended into adjacent states. All remaining states would then be covered in stage 4. Gradual product introductions do not always occur state by state; other geographic combinations, such as groups of counties that overlap across state borders, are sometimes used. Products destined for multinational markets may also be rolled out one country or region at a time. Procter & Gamble test marketed its new Circ line of men's hair coloring products in several cities in the United Kingdom, gradually expanding the areas for the product's distribution.[18]

Gradual product introduction is desirable for several reasons. It reduces the risks of introducing a new product. If the product fails, the firm will experience smaller losses if it introduced the item in only a few geographic areas than if it marketed the product nationally. Furthermore, a company cannot introduce a product nationwide overnight because a system of wholesalers and retailers necessary to distribute the product cannot be established so quickly. The development of a distribution network may take considerable time. Also, the number of units needed to satisfy national demand for a successful product can be enormous, and a firm usually cannot produce the required quantities in a short time.

Despite the good reasons for introducing a product gradually, marketers realize this approach creates some competitive problems. A gradual introduction allows competitors to observe what the firm is doing and to monitor results, just as the firm's own marketers are doing. If competitors see that the newly introduced product is successful, they may quickly enter the same target market with similar products. In addition, as a product is introduced region by region, competitors may expand their marketing efforts to offset promotion of the new product.

Product Differentiation Through Quality, Design, and Support Services

product differentiation
Creating and designing products so that customers perceive them as different from competing products

Some of the most important characteristics of products are the elements that distinguish them from one another. **Product differentiation** is the process of creating and designing products so that customers perceive them as different from competing products. Customer perception is critical in differentiating products. Perceived differences might include quality, features, styling, price, or image. A crucial element used to differentiate one product from another is the brand, discussed in the next chapter. In this section, we examine three aspects of product differentiation that companies must consider when creating and offering products for sale: product quality, product design and features, and product support services. These aspects involve the company's attempt to create real differences among products. Later in this chapter, we discuss how companies position their products in the marketplace based on these three aspects.

Product Quality

quality The overall characteristics of a product that allow it to perform as expected in satisfying customer needs

Quality refers to the overall characteristics of a product that allow it to perform as expected in satisfying customer needs. The words *as expected* are very important to this definition because quality usually means different things to different customers. For some, durability signifies quality. Among the most durable products on the market today is the Craftsman line of tools at Sears; indeed, Sears provides a lifetime guarantee on the durability of these tools. For other consumers, a product's ease of use may indicate quality.

The concept of quality also varies between consumer and business markets. According to one study, American consumers consider high-quality products to have these characteristics (in order): reliability, durability, ease of maintenance, ease of use, a known and trusted brand name, and a reasonable price.[19] For business markets, technical suitability, ease of repair, and company reputation are important characteristics. Unlike consumers, most organizations place far less emphasis on price than on product quality.

level of quality The amount of quality a product possesses

consistency of quality The degree to which a product has the same level of quality over time

One important dimension of quality is **level of quality,** the amount of quality a product possesses. The concept is a relative one; that is, the quality level of one product is difficult to describe unless it is compared with that of other products. For example, most consumers would consider the quality level of Timex watches to be good, but when they compare Timex with Rolex, most consumers would say a Rolex's level of quality is higher. How high should the level of quality be? It depends on the product. A 99.9 percent accuracy rate would mean that 1,314 phone calls would be misplaced every minute, 500 incorrect surgical procedures would be performed daily, and 22,000 checks would be deducted from the wrong accounts each hour. Is 99.9 percent accuracy good enough?[20]

A second important dimension is consistency. **Consistency of quality** refers to the degree to which a product has the same level of quality over time. Consistency means giving consumers the quality they expect every time they purchase the product. Like level of quality, consistency is a relative concept; however, it implies a quality comparison within the same brand over time. The quality level of McDonald's French fries is generally consistent from one location to another. If FedEx delivers more than 99 percent of overnight packages on time, its service has consistent quality.

The consistency of product quality can also be compared across competing products. It is at this stage that consistency becomes critical to a company's success. Companies that can provide

Differentiation Through Product Quality
Century 21 promotes its consistent high level of quality in assisting in the purchase of a luxury home.

quality on a consistent basis have a major competitive advantage over rivals. FedEx, for example, is viewed as more consistent in delivery schedules than the U.S. Postal Service. In simple terms, no company has ever succeeded by creating and marketing low-quality products. Many companies have taken major steps, such as implementing total quality management (TQM), to improve the quality of their products. (TQM is discussed further in Chapter 22.)

By and large, higher product quality means marketers will charge a higher price for the product. This fact forces marketers to consider quality carefully in their product-planning efforts. Not all customers want or can afford the highest-quality products available. Thus, many companies offer a range of products that vary widely in quality.

BUILDING CUSTOMER RELATIONSHIPS

Weaving Product Quality: Longaberger Company

Rated by *Forbes* as one of the top privately held companies in the United States, Longaberger Company is a $1 billion direct-sales firm based in Newark, Ohio. The company employs more than 8,200 people to craft handmade baskets, wrought iron, pottery, fabric liners, and accessories, which it markets through nearly 70,000 independent associates. Like Avon and Tupperware, Longaberger baskets are marketed through home shows at which a trained sales associate demonstrates the craftsmanship of each product and offers suggestions for using it in the home. In 2000 the company sold 36.8 million products, including 9.3 million of its increasingly popular baskets. The company-sponsored Longaberger Collectors Club has grown to 175,000 members, making it the nation's fourth-largest collector's club.

Longaberger's mission statement—"to stimulate a better quality of life"—reflects the company's entrepreneurial founder, Dave Longaberger. The fifth of 12 children growing up in the foothills of the Appalachian Mountains, Longaberger was economically disadvantaged; he also stuttered and suffered from epilepsy. These challenges, however, did not stand in the way of his ambition. He worked in a grocery store, shoveled snow, delivered newspapers, mowed grass, and hauled trash. His family called him the "25-cent millionaire" because he was always working to earn money.

Eventually Longaberger noticed that handmade baskets were becoming fashionable. He opened J.W.'s Handwoven Baskets in 1973 in the hope that consumers would appreciate the craftsmanship and quality of the baskets his father made. The shop later became Longaberger Company and was selling more than 1 million baskets a year by the late 1980s. In 1990, the company began to add pottery, wrought iron, fabrics, and other home and lifestyle products to its product mix.

Today Longaberger is the premier marketer of handmade baskets in the United States. Although Dave Longaberger died in 1999, his daughter Tami continues to run the family business much as her father did. Through the Longaberger Foundation, the company contributes 30 percent of its profits to charity. The company's hardwood maple baskets still employ the precise, tight weaving style Longaberger's father learned while employed at the Dresden Basket factory in the 1920s. The high-quality baskets have an average price tag of $50; the most expensive is $250. The company does virtually no advertising, relying instead on word-of-mouth praise from customers and its well-trained sales associates to communicate its products' benefits. The company has been asked to provide gift baskets for the Blockbuster Entertainment Awards, the Academy Awards, the NAACP Image Awards, Christmas in Washington, D.C., and the Joni Mitchell Tribute. The Longaberger name has become synonymous with quality, and its baskets are made to be collected and handed down from one generation to the next.

Going strong.

No for kids who'd rather jump around than sit still, there's Dannon Fluoride to Go. Fluoridated spring water that's already "kid-size" to take everywhere. And the fluoride inside? That'll help them build strong teeth every day. *Spring to life.*

DANNON
Fluoride
to go

From the makers of
Dannon Natural Spring Water.

Differentiation Through Product Features
Dannon differentiates its product through the addition of fluoride—a new feature—to its bottled water.

Product Design and Features

Product design refers to how a product is conceived, planned, and produced. Design is a very complex topic because it involves the total sum of all the product's physical characteristics. Many companies are known for the outstanding designs of their products: Sony for personal electronics, Hewlett-Packard for laser printers, Levi Strauss for clothing, and JanSport for backpacks. Good design is one of the best competitive advantages any brand can possess.

One component of design is **styling,** or the physical appearance of the product. The style of a product is one design feature that can allow certain products to sell very rapidly. Good design, however, means more than just appearance; it also involves a product's functioning and usefulness. For example, a pair of jeans may look great, but if they fall apart after three washes, clearly the design was poor. Most consumers seek out products that both look good and function well.

Product features are specific design characteristics that allow a product to perform certain tasks. By adding or subtracting features, a company can differentiate its products from those of the competition. Chrysler promotes its line of minivans as having more features related to passenger safety—dual air bags, steel-reinforced doors, and integrated child safety seats—than any other auto company. Product features can also be used to differentiate products within the same company. For example, Nike offers both a walking shoe and a run-walk shoe for specific consumer needs. In these cases, the company's products are sold with a wide range of features, from low-priced "base" or "stripped-down" versions to high-priced and prestigious "feature-packed" ones. The automotive industry regularly sells products with a wide range of features. In general, the more features a product has, the higher its price and, often, the higher the perceived quality.

For a brand to have a sustainable competitive advantage, marketers must determine the product designs and features that customers desire. Information from marketing research efforts and from databases can help in assessing customers' product design and feature preferences. Samsonite Corporation, the Denver-based luggage manufacturer, uses three databases to determine what customers do and don't like about its own brands and competing brands. Samsonite shares this information with its dealers so they can better serve customers.[21] Being able to meet customers' desires for product design and features at prices they can afford is crucial to a product's long-term success.

Product Support Services

Many companies differentiate their product offerings by providing support services. Usually referred to as **customer services,** these services include any human or mechanical efforts or activities a company provides that add value to a product.[22] Examples of customer services include delivery and installation, financing arrangements, customer training, warranties and guarantees, repairs, layaway plans, convenient hours of operation, adequate parking, and information through toll-free numbers. For example, many hotel chains, including Marriott International, Hilton Hotels,

product design How a product is conceived, planned, and produced

styling The physical appearance of a product

product features Specific design characteristics that allow a product to perform certain tasks

customer services Human or mechanical efforts or activities that add value to a product

We gave it the once-over. 300 times.

Audi Assured®
Certified Pre-Owned Cars

Backed by an Audi 2 year or 100,000 mile limited warranty.†

Winner of *Car and Driver's* 10Best Award 1996, 1997 and 1998 • Available with legendary quattro® all-wheel drive • Extensive multi-point inspection • Luxurious interior of fine fabrics, leather, wood and aluminum • A rare opportunity to drive an Audi A4 at a remarkable price.

Visit your Audi dealer or www.audiusa.com/preowned to search our national vehicle locator.

†See dealer for details. "Audi," "Audi Assured," "quattro," "A4" and the four rings emblem are registered trademarks of AUDI AG. To find out more about Audi and Audi Assured vehicles and warranty, call 1-800-FOR-AUDI or visit us at www.audiusa.com/preowned.

Differentiation Through Product Support Services
Audi provides a 2-year or 100,000-mile warranty on pre-owned cars as a support service to buyers.

and Starwood Hotels & Resorts Worldwide, offer Web-based reservation services for the convenience of their customers. The companies' websites also provide information on hotels' prices, amenities, and frequent-guest programs.[23]

Whether as a major or minor part of the total product offering, all marketers of goods sell customer services. Providing good customer service may be the only way a company can differentiate its products when all products in a market have essentially the same quality, design, and features. This is especially true in the computer industry. When buying a laptop computer, for example, consumers shop more for fast delivery, technical support, warranties, and price than for product quality and design. Through research, a company can discover the types of services customers want and need. For example, some customers are more interested in financing, whereas others are more concerned with installation and training. The level of customer service a company provides can profoundly affect customer satisfaction. The American Customer Satisfaction Index compiled by the National Quality Research Center at the University of Michigan ranks customer satisfaction among a wide variety of businesses. Recent surveys suggest that dissatisfied customers may curtail their overall spending, which could stifle economic growth.[24] Among the industries rated as doing a poor job of satisfying customers are phone companies, airlines, and utilities.[25]

Product Positioning and Repositioning

product positioning refers to the decisions and activities intended to create and maintain a certain concept of the firm's product (relative to competitive brands) in customers' minds. When marketers introduce a product, they try to position it so that it seems to possess the characteristics the target market most desires. This projected image is crucial. Crest is positioned as a fluoride toothpaste that fights cavities, and Close-Up is positioned as a whitening toothpaste that enhances the user's sex appeal.

product positioning Creating and maintaining a certain concept of a product in customers' minds

Product position is the result of customers' perceptions of a product's attributes relative to those of competitive brands. Buyers make numerous purchase decisions on a regular basis. To avoid a continuous reevaluation of numerous products, buyers tend to group, or "position," products in their minds to simplify buying decisions. Rather than allowing customers to position products independently, marketers often try to influence and shape consumers' concepts or perceptions of products through advertising. Marketers sometimes analyze product positions by developing perceptual maps, as shown in Figure 11.4. Perceptual maps are created by questioning a sample of consumers about their perceptions of products, brands, and organizations with respect to two or more dimensions. To develop a perceptual map like the one in Figure 11.4, respondents would be asked how they perceive selected pain relievers in regard to price and type of pain for which the products are used. Also, respondents would be asked about their preferences for product features to establish "ideal points" or "ideal clusters," which represent a consensus about what a specific group of customers

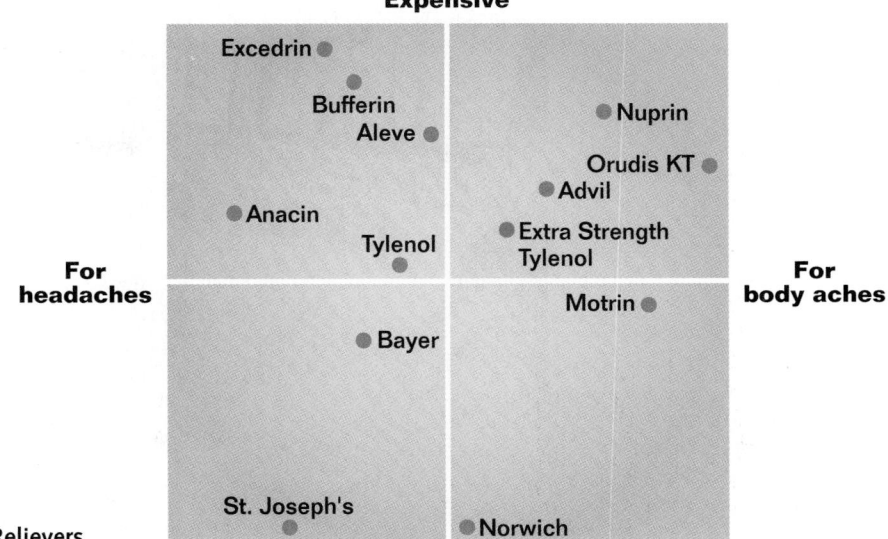

FIGURE 11.4
Hypothetical Perceptual Map for Pain Relievers

desires in terms of product features. Then marketers can compare how their brand is perceived compared with the ideal points.

Product positioning is part of a natural progression when market segmentation is used. For example, the Chico's retail chain targets 35- to 55-year-old, overweight women with its stylish, moderately priced clothing.[26] Segmentation lets the firm aim a given brand at a portion of the total market. Effective product positioning helps serve a specific market segment by creating an appropriate concept in the minds of customers in that segment. A firm can position a product to compete head-on with another brand, as PepsiCo has done against Coca-Cola, or to avoid competition, as 7Up has done relative to other soft-drink producers. Head-to-head competition may be a marketer's positioning objective if the product's performance characteristics are at least equal to those of competitive brands and if the product is priced lower. Head-to-head positioning may be appropriate even when the price is higher if the product's performance characteristics are superior. Conversely, positioning to avoid competition may be best when the product's performance characteristics do not differ significantly from competing brands. Moreover, positioning a brand to avoid competition may be appropriate when that brand has unique characteristics that are important to some buyers. Volvo, for example, has for years positioned itself away from competitors by focusing on the safety characteristics of its cars. Whereas some auto companies mention safety issues in their advertisements, many are more likely to focus on style, fuel efficiency, performance, or terms of sale. Avoiding competition is critical when a firm introduces a brand into a market in which it already has one or more brands. Marketers usually want to avoid cannibalizing sales of their existing brands, unless the new brand generates substantially larger profits.

Net Sights

Because quality can be used to position and differentiate a product, measuring customers' assessments of quality has become a crucial issue in marketing strategy. The University of Michigan's Business School has established the National Quality Research Center (NQRC) to focus on measuring customer satisfaction and studying its relationship to quality, customer retention, profitability, and productivity for business and government organizations, specific industries, and even national economies. NQRC (**http://www.bus.umich.edu/research/nqrc/**) also tracks the quality of goods and services from the consumer's perspective and releases this information to companies and countries as an economic indicator, the American Customer Satisfaction Index, available at **http://www.bus.umich.edu/research/nqrc/acsi.html.**

Product Positioning
Wheaties positions its Energy Crunch™ cereal for active, health-conscious consumers.

If a product has been planned properly, its features and brand image will give it the distinct appeal needed. Style, shape, construction, quality of work, and color help create the image and the appeal. If buyers can easily identify the benefits, they are, of course, more likely to purchase the product. When the new product does not offer certain preferred attributes, there is room for another new product.

Positioning decisions are not just for new products. Evaluating the positions of existing products is important because a brand's market share and profitability may be strengthened by product repositioning. For example, several years ago Kraft was on the verge of discontinuing Cheez Whiz because its sales had declined considerably. After Kraft marketers repositioned Cheez Whiz as a fast, convenient, microwavable cheese sauce, its sales rebounded to new heights. When introducing a new product into a product line, one or more existing brands may have to be repositioned to minimize cannibalization of established brands and assure a favorable position for the new brand.

Repositioning can be accomplished by physically changing the product, its price, or its distribution. Rather than making any of these changes, marketers sometimes reposition a product by changing its image through promotional efforts. For example, to compete more effectively with Visa and MasterCard, American Express is using promotion to shift its elite credit card image to a broader, more accessible image. This image repositioning has been facilitated by forging acceptance deals at retailers where customers frequently shop, including supermarkets, gas stations, and even Wal-Mart.[27]

Product Deletion

Generally a product cannot satisfy target market customers and contribute to the achievement of an organization's overall goals indefinitely. **Product deletion** is the process of eliminating a product from the product mix, usually because it no longer satisfies a sufficient number of customers. A declining product reduces an organization's profitability and drains resources that could be used to modify other products or develop new ones. A marginal product may require shorter production runs, which can increase per-unit production costs. Finally, when a dying product completely loses favor with customers, the negative feelings may transfer to some of the company's other products.

Most organizations find it difficult to delete a product. A decision to drop a product may be opposed by managers and other employees who believe the product is necessary to the product mix. Salespeople who still have some loyal customers are especially upset when a product is dropped. Considerable resources and effort are

product deletion Eliminating a product from the product mix

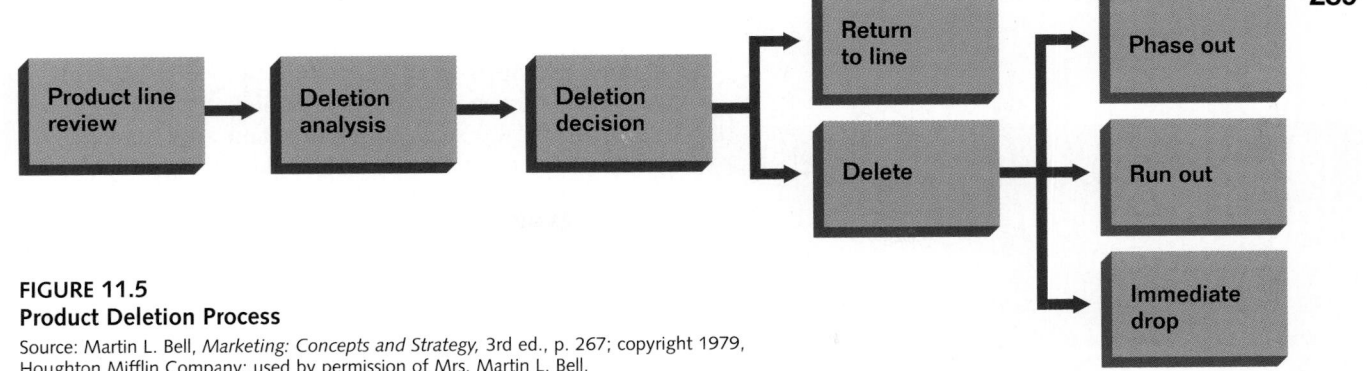

FIGURE 11.5
Product Deletion Process
Source: Martin L. Bell, *Marketing: Concepts and Strategy*, 3rd ed., p. 267; copyright 1979, Houghton Mifflin Company; used by permission of Mrs. Martin L. Bell.

sometimes spent trying to change a slipping product's marketing mix to improve its sales and thus avoid having to eliminate it.

Some organizations delete products only after the products have become heavy financial burdens. A better approach is some form of systematic review in which each product is evaluated periodically to determine its impact on the overall effectiveness of the firm's product mix. Such a review should analyze the product's contribution to the firm's sales for a given period, as well as estimate future sales, costs, and profits associated with the product. It should also gauge the value of making changes in the marketing strategy to improve the product's performance. A systematic review allows an organization to improve product performance and ascertain when to delete products. Procter & Gamble, for example, discontinued its White Cloud brand of toilet tissue in the early 1990s after determining the product did not match customer needs. However, after Wal-Mart acquired the rights to the name, White Cloud was repositioned as a premium private label brand and expanded to include laundry detergent, fabric softener, and dryer sheets. Ironically, these products now compete head to head with Procter & Gamble's Tide laundry detergent and Downy fabric softener in Wal-Mart stores.[28]

Basically there are three ways to delete a product: phase it out, run it out, or drop it immediately (see Figure 11.5). A *phase-out* allows the product to decline without a change in the marketing strategy; no attempt is made to give the product new life. A *run-out* exploits any strengths left in the product. Intensifying marketing efforts in core markets or eliminating some marketing expenditures, such as advertising, may cause a sudden jump in profits. This approach is commonly taken for technologically obsolete products, such as older models of computers and calculators. Often the price is reduced to get a sales spurt. The third alternative, an *immediate drop* of an unprofitable product, is the best strategy when losses are too great to prolong the product's life.

Organizing to Develop and Manage Products

After reviewing the concepts of product line and mix, life cycles, positioning, and repositioning, it should be obvious that managing products is a complex task. Often the traditional functional form of organization, in which managers specialize in such business functions as advertising, sales, and distribution, does not fit a company's needs. In this case, management must find an organizational approach that accomplishes the tasks necessary to develop and manage products. Alternatives to functional organization include the product or brand manager approach, the market manager approach, and the venture team approach.

A **product manager** is responsible for a product, a product line, or several distinct products that make up an interrelated group within a multiproduct organization. A **brand manager** is responsible for a single brand. General Foods, for example, has one brand manager for Maxim coffee and one for Maxwell House coffee. A product or brand manager operates cross-functionally to coordinate the activities, information, and strategies involved in marketing an assigned product. Product managers and

product manager The person within an organization responsible for a product, a product line, or several distinct products that make up a group

brand manager The person responsible for a single brand

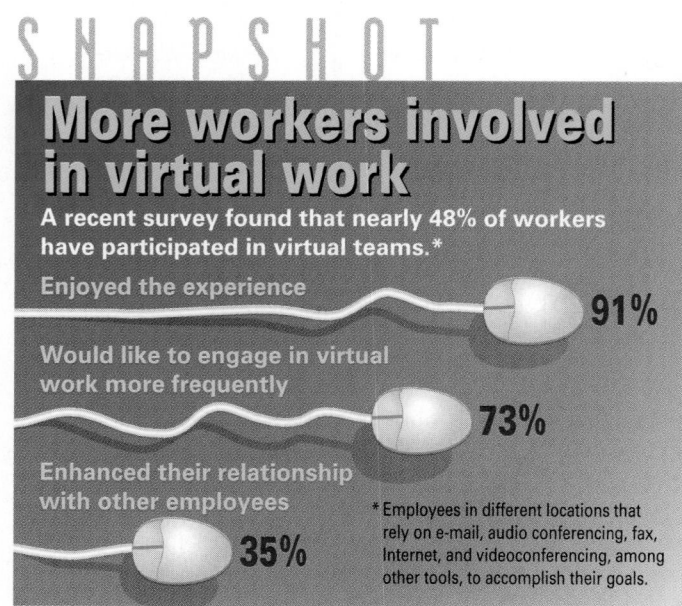

SNAPSHOT

More workers involved in virtual work

A recent survey found that nearly 48% of workers have participated in virtual teams.*

Enjoyed the experience

91%

Would like to engage in virtual work more frequently

73%

Enhanced their relationship with other employees

35%

* Employees in different locations that rely on e-mail, audio conferencing, fax, Internet, and videoconferencing, among other tools, to accomplish their goals.

Source: *USA Today*, April 26, 2001, p. 1B. Copyright 2001, *USA Today*. Reprinted with permission.

market manager The person responsible for managing the marketing activities that serve a particular group of customers

venture team A cross-functional group that creates entirely new products that may be aimed at new markets

brand managers plan marketing activities to achieve objectives by coordinating a mix of distribution, promotion (especially sales promotion and advertising), and price. They must consider packaging and branding decisions and work closely with personnel in research and development, engineering, and production. Marketing research helps product managers understand consumers and find target markets. The product or brand manager approach to organization is used by many large, multiple-product companies in the consumer packaged-goods business.

A **market manager** is responsible for managing the marketing activities that serve a particular group of customers. This organizational approach is particularly effective when a firm engages in different types of marketing activities to provide products to diverse customer groups. A company might have one market manager for business markets and another for consumer markets. These broad market categories might be broken down into more limited market responsibilities.

A **venture team** creates entirely new products that may be aimed at new markets. Unlike a product or market manager, a venture team is responsible for all aspects of developing a product: research and development, production and engineering, finance and accounting, and marketing. Venture team members are brought together from different functional areas of the organization. In working outside of established divisions, venture teams have greater flexibility to apply inventive approaches to develop new products that can take advantage of opportunities in highly segmented markets. Companies are increasingly using such cross-functional teams for product development in an effort to boost product quality. Quality may be positively related to information integration within the team, customers' influence on the product development process, and a quality orientation within the firm.[29] When a new product has demonstrated commercial potential, team members may return to their functional areas, or they may join a new or existing division to manage the product.

Summary

Organizations must be able to adjust their product mixes to compete effectively and achieve their goals. A product mix can be improved through line extension and through product modification. A line extension is the development of a product closely related to one or more products in the existing line but designed specifically to meet different customer needs. Product modification is the changing of one or more characteristics of a product. This approach can be effective when the product is modifiable, when customers can perceive the change, and when customers want the modification. Quality modifications relate to a product's dependability and durability. Functional modifications affect a product's versatility, effectiveness, convenience, or safety. Aesthetic modifications change the sensory appeal of a product.

Developing new products can enhance a firm's product mix and add depth to the product line. A new product may be an innovation that has never been sold by any organization; a product that a given firm has not marketed previously, although similar products may have been available from other organizations; or a product brought from one market to another.

Before a product is introduced, it goes through a seven-phase new-product development process. In the idea generation phase, new-product ideas may come from internal or external sources. In the process of screening, ideas are evaluated to determine whether they are consistent with the firm's overall objectives and resources. Concept testing, the third phase, involves having a small sample of potential customers review a brief description of the product idea to determine their initial perceptions of the proposed product and their early buying intentions. During the business analysis stage, the product idea is evaluated to determine its potential contribution to the firm's sales, costs, and profits. In the product development stage, the organization determines if it is technically feasible to produce the product and if it can be produced at a cost low enough to make the final price reasonable. Test marketing is a limited introduction of a product in areas chosen to represent the intended market. Finally, in the commercialization phase, full-scale production of the product begins and a complete marketing strategy is developed.

Product differentiation is the process of creating and designing products so that customers perceive them as different from competing products. Product quality, product design and features, and product support services are three aspects of product differentiation that companies consider when creating and marketing products. Product quality includes the overall characteristics of a product that allow it to perform as expected in satisfying customer needs. The level of quality is the amount of quality a product possesses. Consistency of quality is the degree to which a product has the same level of quality over time. Product design refers to how a product is conceived, planned, and produced. Components of product design include styling (the physical appearance of the product) and product features (the specific design characteristics that allow a product to perform certain tasks). Companies often differentiate their products by providing support services, usually called customer services. Customer services are human or mechanical efforts or activities that add value to a product.

Product positioning refers to the decisions and activities that create and maintain a certain concept of the firm's product in the customer's mind. Product position is the result of customers' perceptions of the product's attributes relative to competitive brands. Product positioning plays a role in market segmentation. Organizations can position a product to compete head to head with another brand if the product's performance is at least equal to the competitive brand's and if the product is priced lower. When a brand possesses unique characteristics that are important to some buyers, positioning it to avoid competition is appropriate. It is important to avoid positioning a product so that it competes with sales of the company's existing products. Companies can also increase an existing brand's market share and profitability through product repositioning. Repositioning can be accomplished by making physical changes in the product, changing its price or distribution, or changing its image.

Product deletion is the process of eliminating a product that no longer satisfies a sufficient number of customers. Although a firm's personnel may oppose product deletion, weak products are unprofitable, consume too much time and effort, may require shorter production runs, and can create an unfavorable impression of the firm's other products. A product mix should be systematically reviewed to determine when to delete products. Products to be deleted can be phased out, run out, or dropped immediately.

Often the traditional functional form of organization does not lend itself to the complex task of developing and managing products. Alternative organizational forms include the product or brand manager approach, the market manager approach, and the venture team approach. A product manager is responsible for a product, a product line, or several distinct products that make up an interrelated group within a multiproduct organization. A brand manager is a product manager who is responsible for a single brand. A market manager is responsible for managing the marketing activities that serve a particular group or class of customers. A venture team is sometimes used to create entirely new products that may be aimed at new markets.

Important Terms

Line extension
Product modification
Quality modifications
Functional modifications
Aesthetic modifications
New-product development
 process
Idea generation
Screening
Concept testing
Business analysis
Product development
Test marketing
Commercialization

Product differentiation
Quality
Level of quality
Consistency of quality
Product design
Styling
Product features
Customer services
Product positioning
Product deletion
Product manager
Brand manager
Market manager
Venture team

Discussion and Review Questions

1. What is a line extension, and how does it differ from a product modification?
2. Compare and contrast the three major approaches to modifying a product.
3. Identify and briefly explain the seven major phases of the new-product development process.
4. Do small companies that manufacture just a few products need to be concerned about developing and managing products? Why or why not?
5. Why is product development a cross-functional activity within an organization? That is, why must finance, engineering, manufacturing, and other functional areas be involved?
6. What is the major purpose of concept testing, and how is it accomplished?
7. What are the benefits and disadvantages of test marketing?
8. Why can the process of commercialization take a considerable amount of time?
9. What is product differentiation, and how can it be achieved?
10. Explain how the term *quality* has been used to differentiate products in the automobile industry in recent years. What are some makes and models of automobiles that come to mind when you hear the terms *high quality* and *poor quality*?
11. What is product positioning? Under what conditions would head-to-head product positioning be appropriate? When should head-to-head positioning be avoided?
12. What types of problems does a weak product cause in a product mix? Describe the most effective approach for avoiding such problems.
13. What type of organization might use a venture team to develop new products? What are the advantages and disadvantages of such a team?

Application Questions

1. When developing a new product, a company often test markets the proposed product in a specific area or location. Suppose you wish to test market your new revolutionary SuperWax car wax, which requires only one application for a lifetime finish. Where and how would you test market your new product?

2. Product positioning aims to create a certain concept of a product in consumers' minds relative to its competition. Pepsi is positioned in direct competition with Coca-Cola, whereas Volvo has traditionally positioned itself away from competitors by emphasizing its safety features. Following are several distinct positions in which an organization may place its product. Identify a product that would fit into each position.
   a. High-price/high-quality
   b. Low-price
   c. Convenience
   d. Uniqueness

3. Select an organization that you think should reposition itself in the consumer's eye. Identify where it is currently positioned, and make recommendations for repositioning. Explain and defend your suggestions.

4. A product manager may make quality, functional, or aesthetic modifications when modifying a product. Identify a familiar product that recently was modified, categorize the modification (quality, functional, or aesthetic), and describe how you would have modified it differently.

5. Phasing out a product from the product mix often is difficult for an organization. Visit a retail store in your area, and ask the manager what products he or she has had to discontinue in the recent past. Find out what factors influenced the decision to delete the product and who was involved in the decision. Ask the manager to identify any products that should be but have not been deleted, and try to ascertain the reason.

Internet Exercise & Resources

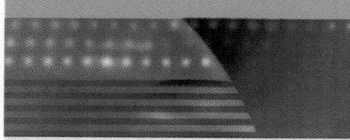

Visit **www.prideferrell.com** for resources to help you master the material in this chapter, plus materials that will help you expand your marketing knowledge, including: Internet exercise updates, ACE self-tests, hotlinks to companies featured in this chapter, and much more.

Merck & Company

Merck, a leading global pharmaceutical company, develops, manufactures, and markets a broad range of health care products. In addition, the firm's Merck-Medco Managed Care Division manages pharmacy benefits for more than 40 million Americans. The company has established a website to serve as an educational and informational resource for Internet users around the world. To learn more about the company and its research, visit its award-winning site at

www.merck.com

1. What products has Merck developed and introduced recently?

2. What role does research play in Merck's success? How does research facilitate new-product development at Merck?

3. Find Merck's mission statement. Is Merck's focus on research consistent with the firm's mission and values?

 ## VIDEO CASE 11.1
Cali Cosmetics Positions Products with Olive Oil

Competition in the $39.9 billion U.S. cosmetics and personal care market is very intense. Companies like Procter & Gamble, L'Oréal, Unilever, and Estée Lauder compete fiercely with many brands, but no company controls more than 11 percent of the market. In 2000 6,168 personal care products were introduced in the United States, and these were as

likely to have been launched by lesser-known firms such as Hearts and Roses, Love Thy Hair, and Matahari as by market leaders like Procter & Gamble and L'Oréal. In this highly competitive industry, product differentiation is crucial. Typically this is accomplished through brand name, product design, and styling, as well as specific product features and ingredients. For example, cosmetics companies have incorporated fruits, vegetables, herbs, vitamins, and just about anything else imaginable that can be safely applied to skin.

A recent innovation in modern beauty products is the use of olive oil—the same ingredient favored by professional chefs and home cooks alike, which the ancient Romans called "liquid gold" and "nectar of the gods." The healthful benefits of olive oil for human skin and hair have long been recognized: ancient Egyptians used it as a moisturizer, Roman gladiators as a salve for wounds, and the Spanish as a primary ingredient of Castile soap. Although olive oil has not been used for such purposes in modern times, it has recently experienced a resurgence in the cosmetics industry, as part of a trend toward using more botanical ingredients in beauty products. Experts believe that the olive offers many cosmetic benefits: the skin, pulp, and oil contain glycerides and fatty acids that clean and moisturize, while the pits and bark make excellent exfoliants. Research also suggests that olive oil may have anti-aging and cancer-fighting properties. Japanese researchers, for example, found that olive oil extracts slowed the development of harmful skin lesions on mice exposed to radiation from sunlamps. They concluded that olives may contain ingredients that destroy the free radicals that lead to skin damage.

With the growing recognition of the benefits of olives and olive oil, many established companies are including olive oil as an ingredient, and even the primary essence, in a variety of personal care products, including lip balms, shampoos, bath oils, hand lotions, nail soaks, massage oils, and more. Some companies offer just one item infused with olive extracts, such as Philosophy's Amazing Grace perfumed olive oil body scrub and Bibo's O-live a Little hand and body lotion. Australia's Aesop line now includes an olive facial cleanser, Greece's Korres Athens offers an olive pit scrub, and Britain's Body Shop markets an olive moisturizer. Other companies are marketing entire collections of olive oil–based cosmetics, including The Thymes, which introduced Olive Leaf, a product line that incorporates every part of the olive into products designed to improve the skin's texture and protect it from environmental damage.

An Italian firm, Cali Cosmetics, has joined the competition with its Olivia line of beauty products. Founded by Italy's Baronessa Consuelo Cali, Cali's extensive cosmetics collection features vitamin-enriched extracts of Italian olive oil whose ingredients work together to protect and soften skin. Cali Cosmetics grew out of the Cali family's olive orchard and spa. Legend has it that the area, on the outskirts of Rome overlooking the Mediterranean Sea, was discovered by Roman nobles who enjoyed olive oil treatments there in the nineteenth century. The Cali Beauty Farm, housed in the Cali family's ancestral castle, has since relied on olive-based food recipes and beauty treatments to appeal to customers. The baroness became the primary owner of the spa in the late 1980s; in the late 1990s, she began to concentrate on adapting old family recipes passed down from generation to generation and perfected them with the help of modern technology to develop the Olivia line for use at home. The key ingredient of Olivia products is olive oil, not the olive itself.

The Olivia line includes cleansers, moisturizers, and scrubs for the hair, face, body, and feet. The firm extracts all the vitamins from the olive oil to create a nongreasy beauty product promoted as having regenerating power and a moisture-balancing attribute. With prices ranging from $7 for bar soap to $24 for eye cream, the Cali line is more affordable than some competing olive-based products. Due to their unusual ingredients, Olivia beauty products can be sold not only in department stores but also in grocery stores and florist shops. The products are now sold in 1,000 stores in seven countries.

In millions of stores around the globe, Cali Cosmetics is competing in a market saturated with products that smell good, feel good, and claim to promote healthy skin. With the Olivia line, Cali Cosmetics is trying to position its olive oil–based products as superior to thousands of competing beauty products. With sales of more than $1 million a year in just three years, the benefits and image of Cali's Olivia line may give it the distinctive appeal required to succeed in this highly competitive market.[30]

QUESTIONS FOR DISCUSSION

1. Are Olivia beauty products line extensions, modified products, or new products for the Cali family?
2. Describe the positioning of Olivia beauty products.
3. Assess Cali Cosmetics' strategy for differentiating its products from those of competitors.

CASE 11.2

Can Pepsi Make Pepsi One the One?

During the 1980s and early 1990s, PepsiCo acquired a reputation as a well-run company, and industry experts extolled its ability and willingness to launch new products. Customers thought its ads were fun and creative. By the early 1990s, however, the company seemed to have lost its focus. For example, in 1992 PepsiCo introduced what it thought would be the next soft-drink sensation, Crystal Pepsi, with much hoopla. The product proved a dismal failure, however.

Now Pepsi has introduced a new low-calorie soft drink, Pepsi One, the first domestic soft drink made with the artificial sweetener acesulfame potassium (ace K). As you might expect from its name, Pepsi One has 1 calorie and, according to its marketer, tastes just like regular Pepsi. Why would PepsiCo risk another product flop? PepsiCo executives believe the company must continually innovate, move fast, and introduce new products to remain competitive. They hope, of course, that Pepsi One will become the soft drink of the century—the one that will steal market share from archrival Coca-Cola, the number one soft-drink maker.

On the day the federal Food and Drug Administration (FDA) approved ace K for use in soft drinks, PepsiCo announced plans to launch Pepsi One, a blend of aspartame and Sunett, the ace K brand. Within hours of FDA approval, PepsiCo made sure that its bottlers were trying samples of the new drink. Industry experts and the media noted the lightning speed with which the soft-drink maker acted. But for more than ten years, while waiting for FDA approval of ace K, PepsiCo's researchers had spent much time and resources developing a better-tasting diet cola, one that would taste "more like regular cola." The vice president of PepsiCo research believes Pepsi One is it, stating, "It's the most regular tasting diet product on the market."

Although PepsiCo was quick to announce its plans to introduce Pepsi One, it did not actually launch the product until testing indicated consumers liked its taste as much as its creators did. As one PepsiCo executive described it, these test results were "extraordinary" and "the best we've seen in twenty years." In extensive home-use tests, almost 70 percent of Pepsi One tasters reported they would purchase the product again. Those results were good enough for PepsiCo, which had a $100 million marketing plan in place.

To differentiate Pepsi One from the horde of diet soft drinks, PepsiCo focused on the product's taste, which is almost indistinguishable from the taste of sugared soft drinks. Understating the diet aspect of Pepsi One helped attract an unusual market segment for a diet drink: cola-loving males in their 20s and 30s. PepsiCo executives insisted that Pepsi One would not compete head to head with Diet Pepsi, citing steps the company has taken to differentiate Pepsi One from the older brand. For example, the new soft drink omits the word *diet* in its name, and even the word *Pepsi* is secondary to the thick, black lettering of the word *One*. Remarked one of PepsiCo's marketing directors, "We'd be thrilled if consumers just call it "One.""

Pepsi One's launch—backed by radio, print, outdoor, and in-store advertising, as well as massive sampling—ranks as the most expensive ever for the number-two cola company. Ads with the tagline "Only ONE has it all" featuring actor Cuba Gooding, Jr., aired almost around the clock on virtually every television network in the United States. To lure impulse buyers, PepsiCo set up more than 11,000 supermarket end-of-aisle displays. At shopping malls all over the country, the company set up "lounges" with inflatable couches where shoppers could sit down for a taste of Pepsi One. In addition, customers ordering home-delivered pizza from Pizza Hut received cans of Pepsi One, and sandwich buyers at 7-Eleven stores got free samples. Even greeters at Wal-Mart handed out little cups of Pepsi One with each "hello." A joint effort with MTV featured actor "master sampler" Tom Green, who turned up at gas stations and libraries to encourage consumers to try the new drink.

Within a year, PepsiCo modified the promotion mix for Pepsi One, comparing its taste to Coca-Cola and adopting a new tagline, "Too good to be one calorie. But it is." At the same time, the company employed a brandwide advertising campaign, the "Joy of Cola," featuring many celebrities. PepsiCo also resurrected a tactic from the 1970s with the "Pepsi Challenge," which encouraged consumers to compare Pepsi products against Coca-Cola in blind taste tests.

Did PepsiCo's gamble on Pepsi One pay off? In its first full year of sales, Pepsi One secured a 1.2 percent share of the soft-drink market, while Diet Coke's share declined slightly to 8.5 percent. In drugstores, sales of Pepsi One tripled, reaching $8.6 million. Although it is far too early in Pepsi One's launch to determine whether it will become the soft drink of the century, it may be stealing market share from archrival Coca-Cola's best-selling diet soft drink. Only time will tell whether PepsiCo's intensive product development efforts and careful product management will make Pepsi One the product that proves Pepsi is back.[31]

QUESTIONS FOR DISCUSSION

1. Is Pepsi One a new product, a modified product, or a line extension? Explain your answer.
2. In what way is Pepsi One positioned?
3. Over the years, PepsiCo has had a number of product failures. Evaluate PepsiCo management's decision to introduce Pepsi One.

Branding and Packaging

12

OBJECTIVES

- To explain the value of branding
- To understand brand loyalty
- To analyze the major components of brand equity
- To recognize the types of brands and their benefits
- To understand how to select and protect brands
- To examine three types of branding policies
- To understand co-branding and brand licensing
- To describe the major packaging functions and design considerations and how packaging is used in marketing strategies
- To examine the functions of labeling and its legal issues

295

Nike Swings Away from the Swoosh

Few trademarks are as recognizable as the Nike swoosh. In years past, the Oregon-based maker of athletic footwear and clothing prominently plastered its swoosh across every product, advertisement, and sponsorship. With top athletes such as Michael Jordan wearing the swoosh, audiences all over the world grew familiar with the Nike brand and the products it represents.

Then the fashion world changed, as did the sports world. More adventuresome sports, such as snowboarding and mountain biking, became popular. Women's soccer and basketball teams drew ever-larger crowds. Suddenly a new mix of products was in demand, and Nike was caught flatfooted. Faster than a speeding swoosh, its brand cooled off while competing brands, sporting up-to-the-minute styling and features, became red-hot. As Nike's sales and profits dropped, Skechers, New Balance, and other rivals raced into the spotlight, capturing buyers' imaginations and higher market share.

Nike moved quickly to battle back, expanding its focus on products more in tune with the lifestyles of targeted segments. First, it assigned a team of specialists to create shoes, boots, and clothing for skateboarding and other fast-growing sports favored by younger buyers. Next, it put more emphasis on upscale casual apparel for men and women, and linked many items to fast-selling shoe lines in an effort to reduce dependence on footwear by expanding its sale of clothing. The company also brought back past classics like its best-selling Air Jordan sneakers and rolled out expensive new shoes like the Shox line.

Meanwhile, in a radical break from tradition, Nike reduced its use of the swoosh, hoping to recapture the brand's cachet. The swoosh still appears on many Nike items, but it's often smaller and subtler. In the upscale apparel line, for instance, the swoosh appears mainly on labels, not on the front of the garment or in other in-your-face locations. Nike CEO Philip Knight explains, "If you blast [the swoosh] on every T-shirt, every sign in the soccer match, you dilute it." Now, he says, "There's more thought given to how we use it."

Further, Nike has redesigned the logo for its line of Tiger Woods golf clothing and footwear, a top seller in high-end resort and pro shops. Like the swoosh, this special logo is discreetly positioned on labels, inside shoes, and in other less conspicuous places. However, brand decisions are complex, and sometimes Nike makes a move that mystifies industry observers. After it bought Bauer Sports to enter the hockey equipment segment, for instance, the company went ahead and launched a new Nike brand of hockey skates, potentially cutting into established sales of the Bauer products it had just acquired.

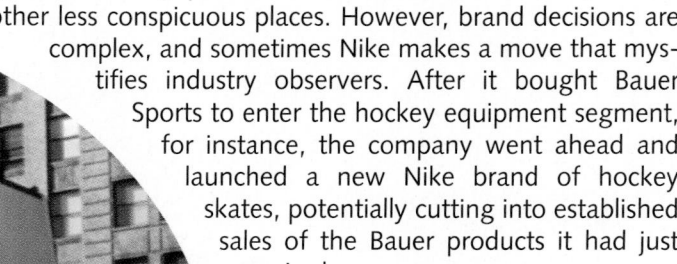

The swoosh is still very much alive and visible in Nike's advertisements, on its website, and on its products. But behind-the-scenes changes are still to come as the company keeps a closer eye on its markets, its competitors, and its brand's future.[1]

Packages, brands, and components of brands, such as the Nike swoosh, are part of a product's tangible features, the verbal and physical cues that help customers identify the products they want and influence their choices when they are unsure. As such, branding and packaging play an important role in marketing strategy. A good brand is distinct and memorable; without one, a firm could not differentiate its products, and shoppers' choices would essentially be arbitrary. A good package design is cost effective, safe, environmentally responsible, and valuable as a promotional tool.

In this chapter, we discuss branding, its value to customers and marketers, brand loyalty, and brand equity. Next, we examine the various types of brands. We then consider how companies choose and protect brands, the various branding policies employed, co-branding, and brand licensing. We look at packaging's critical role as part of the product. We then explore the functions of packaging, issues to consider in packaging design, how the package can be a major element in marketing strategy, and packaging criticisms. We conclude with a discussion of labeling.

Branding

brand   An identifying name, term, design, or symbol

brand name   The part of a brand that can be spoken

brand mark   The part of a brand not made up of words

trademark   A legal designation of exclusive use of a brand

trade name   Full legal name of an organization

Marketers must make many decisions about products, including choices about brands, brand names, brand marks, trademarks, and trade names. A **brand** is a name, term, design, symbol, or any other feature that identifies one seller's good or service as distinct from those of other sellers. A brand may identify one item, a family of items, or all items of that seller.[2] A **brand name** is the part of a brand that can be spoken—including letters, words, and numbers—such as 7Up. A brand name is often a product's only distinguishing characteristic. Without the brand name, a firm could not differentiate its products. To consumers, a brand name is as fundamental as the product itself. Indeed, many brand names have become synonymous with the product, such as Scotch Tape and Xerox copiers. Through promotional activities, the owners of these brand names try to protect them from being used as generic names for tape and photocopiers.

The element of a brand that is not made up of words—often a symbol or design—is a **brand mark.** One example is the Golden Arches, which identify McDonald's restaurants and can be seen on patches worn by athletic teams—from U.S. Olympic teams to Little League softball teams—sponsored by McDonald's. A **trademark** is a legal designation indicating that the owner has exclusive use of a brand or a part of a brand and others are prohibited by law from using it. To protect a brand name or brand mark in the United States, an organization must register it as a trademark with the U.S. Patent and Trademark Office. In 2000, the Patent and Trademark Office registered 127,794 trademarks.[3] Finally, a **trade name** is the full and legal name of an organization, such as Ford Motor Company, rather than the name of a specific product.

Value of Branding

Both buyers and sellers benefit from branding. Brands help buyers identify specific products that they do and do not like, which in turn facilitates the purchase of items that satisfy their needs and reduces the time required to purchase the product. Without brands, product selection would be quite random because buyers could have no assurance they were purchasing what they preferred. The purchase

Brand Mark
The Swiss Army shield in this advertisement is an example of a brand mark.

of certain brands can be a form of self-expression. For example, clothing brand names are important to many teenage boys. Names such as Tommy Hilfiger, Polo, Champion, Guess, and Nike give manufacturers an advantage in the marketplace. A brand also helps buyers evaluate the quality of products, especially when they are unable to judge a product's characteristics. That is, a brand may symbolize a certain quality level to a customer, and in turn the person lets that perception of quality represent the quality of the item. A brand helps reduce a buyer's perceived risk of purchase. In addition, a psychological reward may come from owning a brand that symbolizes status. The Mercedes-Benz brand in the United States is an example.

Sellers benefit from branding because each company's brands identify its products, which makes repeat purchasing easier for customers. Branding helps a firm introduce a new product that carries the name of one or more of its existing products because buyers are already familiar with the firm's existing brands. Branding also facilitates promotional efforts because the promotion of each branded product indirectly promotes all other similarly branded products. Coca-Cola's brand extensions—additional products marketed under the Coca-Cola brand—improved its market share from 36 percent in the early 1980s to 42 percent in the 1990s. Branding also fosters brand loyalty. To the extent that buyers become loyal to a specific brand, the company's market share for that product achieves a certain level of stability, allowing the firm to use its resources more efficiently. Once a firm develops some degree of customer loyalty for a brand, it can maintain a fairly consistent price rather than continually cutting the price to attract customers. A brand is just as much of an asset as the company's building or machinery. When marketers increase their brand's value, they also raise the total asset value of the organization. (We discuss brand value in more detail later in this chapter.) At times marketers must decide whether to change a brand name. This is a difficult decision because the value in the existing brand name must be given up to gain the potential to build a higher value in a new brand name.

SNAPSHOT

Kids' top brand picks

Kids 7 to 14 years old in the U.S. and U.K. chose their favorite brands in six product categories:

Chocolate: **Snickers**

Cereals: **Cinnamon Toast Crunch**

Fast food: **McDonald's**

TV media: **MTV**

Sports clothing: **Nike**

Soft drinks: **Sprite**

Source: "A Quantitative Look at the Best Brands," *Selling to Kids,* June 14, 2000.

Brand Loyalty

As we just noted, creating and maintaining customer loyalty toward a brand is a major benefit of branding. **Brand loyalty** is a customer's favorable attitude toward a specific brand. If brand loyalty is strong enough, customers may consistently purchase this brand when they need a product in that product category. Although brand loyalty may not result in a customer's purchasing a specific brand all the time, the brand is at least viewed as a potentially viable choice in the set of brands being considered for purchase. Development of brand loyalty in a customer reduces his or her risks and shortens the time spent buying the product. However, the degree of brand loyalty for products varies from one product category to another. For example, it is challenging to develop brand loyalty for most products because customers can usually judge its quality and do not need to refer to a brand as an indicator of quality. Brand loyalty also varies by country. Customers in France, Germany, and the United Kingdom tend to be less brand-loyal than U.S. customers.

There are three degrees of brand loyalty: recognition, preference, and insistence. **Brand recognition** occurs when a customer is aware that the brand exists and views it as an alternative purchase if the preferred brand is unavailable or if the other available brands are unfamiliar. This is the mildest form of brand loyalty. The term *loyalty* clearly is being used very loosely here. One of the initial objectives of a marketer introducing a new brand is to create widespread awareness of the brand to generate brand recognition.

Brand preference is a stronger degree of brand loyalty: a customer definitely prefers one brand over competitive offerings and will purchase this brand if available.

brand loyalty   A customer's favorable attitude toward a specific brand

brand recognition   A customer's awareness that a brand exists and is an alternative purchase

brand preference   The degree of brand loyalty in which a customer prefers one brand over competitive offerings

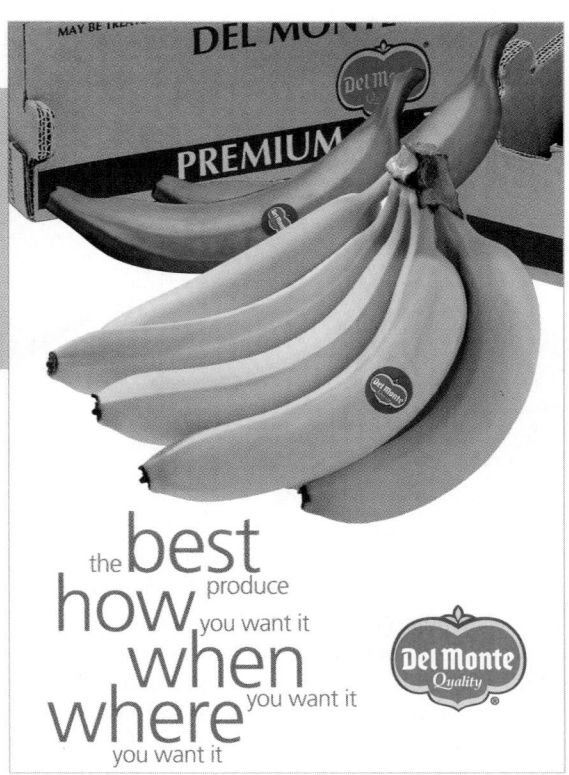

Branding Challenge
Developing brand loyalty for products such as produce can be challenging because customers can often judge the product quality for themselves. Del Monte uses its well-respected brand name to convince customers that its produce is high quality.

However, if the brand is not available, the customer will accept a substitute brand rather than expending additional effort finding and purchasing the preferred brand. A marketer is likely to be able to compete effectively in a market when a number of customers have developed brand preference for its specific brand.

brand insistence The degree of brand loyalty in which a customer strongly prefers a specific brand and will accept no substitute

When **brand insistence** occurs, a customer strongly prefers a specific brand, will accept no substitute, and is willing to spend a great deal of time and effort to acquire that brand. If a brand-insistent customer goes to a store and finds the brand unavailable, he or she will seek the brand elsewhere rather than purchase a substitute brand. Brand insistence is the strongest degree of brand loyalty; it is a brander's dream. However, it is the least common type of brand loyalty. Customers vary considerably regarding the product categories for which they may be brand-insistent. Can you think of products for which you are brand-insistent? Perhaps a brand of deodorant, soft drink, jeans, or even pet food (if your pet is brand-insistent).

Brand loyalty in general seems to be declining, partly because of marketers' increased reliance on sales, coupons, and other short-term promotions and partly because of the sometimes overwhelming array of similar new products from which customers can choose. Several recent studies indicate that brand loyalty is declining for all age groups and especially among consumers age 50 and older.[4]

Building brand loyalty is a major challenge for many marketers. It is an extremely important issue. The creation of brand loyalty significantly contributes to an organization's ability to achieve a sustainable competitive advantage.

Brand Equity

A well-managed brand is an asset to an organization. The value of this asset is often referred to as brand equity. **Brand equity** is the marketing and financial value associated with a brand's strength in a market. Besides the actual proprietary brand assets, such as patents and trademarks, four major elements underlie brand equity: brand name awareness, brand loyalty, perceived brand quality, and brand associations (see Figure 12.1).[5]

brand equity The marketing and financial value associated with a brand's strength in a market

Being aware of a brand leads to brand familiarity, which in turn results in a level of comfort with the brand. A familiar brand is more likely to be selected than an

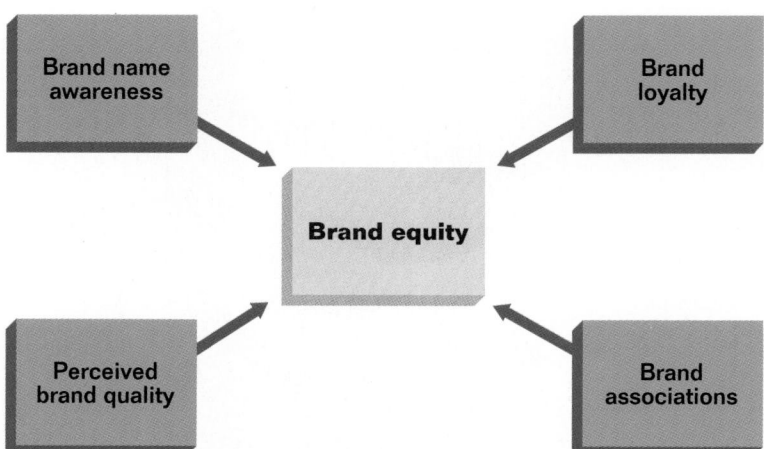

FIGURE 12.1
Major Elements of Brand Equity
Source: Adapted with the permission of The Free Press, a division of Simon & Schuster, Inc., from *Managing Brand Equity: Capitalizing on the Value of a Brand Name* by David A. Aaker. Copyright © 1991 by David A. Aaker.

unfamiliar brand because the familiar brand often is viewed as more reliable and of more acceptable quality. The familiar brand is likely to be in a customer's consideration set, whereas the unfamiliar brand is not.

Brand loyalty is an important component of brand equity because it reduces a brand's vulnerability to competitors' actions. Brand loyalty allows an organization to keep its existing customers and avoid spending an enormous amount of resources gaining new ones. Loyal customers provide brand visibility and reassurance to potential new customers. And because customers expect their brands to be available when and where they shop, retailers strive to carry the brands known for their strong customer following.

Customers associate a particular brand with a certain level of overall quality. A brand name may be used as a substitute for actual judgment of quality. In many cases, customers can't actually judge the quality of the product for themselves and instead must rely on the brand as a quality indicator. Perceived high brand quality helps support a premium price, allowing a marketer to avoid severe price competition. Also, favorable perceived brand quality can ease the introduction of brand extensions, as the high regard for the brand will likely translate into high regard for the related products.

The set of associations linked to a brand is another key component of brand equity. At times a marketer works to connect a particular lifestyle or, in some instances, a certain personality type with a specific brand. For example, customers associate Michelin tires with protecting family members, a De Beers diamond with a loving, long-lasting relationship ("A Diamond Is Forever"), and Dr Pepper with a unique taste. These types of brand associations contribute significantly to the brand's equity. Brand associations are sometimes facilitated by using trade characters, such as the Jolly Green Giant, Pillsbury Dough Boy, and Charlie the Tuna. Placing these trade characters in advertisements and on packages helps consumers link the ads and packages to the brands.

Although difficult to measure, brand equity represents the value of a brand to an organization. An organization may buy a brand from another company at a premium price because outright brand purchase may be less expensive and less risky than creating and developing a brand from scratch. For example, PepsiCo purchased Quaker Oats Company for $13.4 billion primarily to acquire the Gatorade brand, which at that time had 78 percent of the sports drink market.[6] Brand equity helps give a brand the power to capture and maintain a consistent market share, which provides stability to the organization's sales volume.

Table 12.1 lists the 25 brands with the highest economic value. Any company that owns a brand listed in Table 12.1 would agree that the economic value of that brand is likely to be the greatest single asset in the organization's possession. A brand's overall economic value rises and falls with the brand's profitability, brand awareness, brand loyalty, and perceived brand quality, and the strength of positive brand associations.

Table 12.1	The World's Most Valuable Brands		
Rank	**Brand**	**Country**	**Brand Value (in billions $)**
1	Coca-Cola	U.S.	72.5
2	Microsoft	U.S.	70.2
3	IBM	U.S.	53.2
4	Intel	U.S.	39.0
5	Nokia	Finland	38.5
6	General Electric	U.S.	38.1
7	Ford	U.S.	36.4
8	Disney	U.S.	33.6
9	McDonald's	U.S.	27.9
10	AT&T	U.S.	25.5
11	Marlboro	U.S.	22.1
12	Mercedes	Germany	21.1
13	Hewlett-Packard	U.S.	20.6
14	Cisco Systems	U.S.	20.0
15	Toyota	Japan	18.9
16	Citibank	U.S.	18.9
17	Gillette	U.S.	17.4
18	Sony	Japan	16.4
19	American Express	U.S.	16.1
20	Honda	Japan	15.2
21	Compaq	U.S.	14.6
22	Nescafé	Switzerland	13.7
23	BMW	Germany	13.0
24	Kodak	U.S.	11.9
25	Heinz	U.S.	11.8

Source: "Billion Dollar Brand," *Financial Times*, July 17, 2000.

Types of Brands

manufacturer brands Brands initiated by producers

There are three categories of brands: manufacturer, private distributor, and generic. **Manufacturer brands** are initiated by producers and ensure that producers are identified with their products at the point of purchase—for example, Green Giant, Compaq Computer, and Levi's jeans. A manufacturer brand usually requires a producer to become involved in distribution, promotion, and, to some extent, pricing decisions. Brand loyalty is encouraged by promotion, quality control, and guarantees; it is a valuable asset to a manufacturer. The producer tries to stimulate demand for the product, which tends to encourage sellers and resellers to make the product available.

private distributor brands Brands initiated and owned by resellers

Private distributor brands (also called *private brands, store brands,* or *dealer brands*) are initiated and owned by resellers—wholesalers or retailers. The major characteristic of private brands is that the manufacturers are not identified on the products. Retailers and wholesalers use private distributor brands to develop more efficient promotion, generate higher gross margins, and change store image. Miller's Outpost, a chain of apparel stores in 14 western states, has launched a private brand of jeans called Anchor Blue. Like the Gap, Miller's Outpost started out as a Levi Strauss brand retailer and hopes to be as successful as the Gap by focusing on its own private labeled products.[7] Private distributor brands give retailers or wholesalers freedom to purchase products of a specified quality at the lowest cost without disclosing the identity of the manufacturer. Wholesaler brands include IGA (Independent Grocers' Alliance) and Topmost (General Grocer). Familiar retailer brand names include Sears' Kenmore and J. C. Penney's Arizona. Many successful private brands are distributed nationally. Kenmore washers are as well known as most manufacturer brands. Sometimes retailers with successful private distributor brands start manufacturing their own products to gain more control over product costs, quality, and design with the hope of increasing profits. Private brands account for more than 16 percent of dollar volume sales and is approximately 20 percent of unit volume sales in supermarkets.[8] Supermarket private brands are popular globally, too. In the United Kingdom, private brand products generate more than 30 percent of supermarket revenues; in France, 25 percent; in Belgium and Germany, more than 22 percent; in Holland, 18 percent; and in Spain, 10 percent. Boots, the largest drugstore chain in Great Britain, has earned such a wide reputation for high-quality store brands that its private label suntan lotion and painkiller are the nation's top sellers in their product categories.[9]

Types of Brands
Shown here are examples of store brands, generic brands, and manufacturer brands.

Competition between manufacturer brands and private distributor brands (sometimes called "the battle of the brands") is ongoing. To compete against manufacturer brands, retailers have tried to strengthen consumer confidence in private brands. Results of a recent study on consumer perceptions of private and manufacturer brands appear in Figure 12.2. For manufacturers, developing multiple manufacturer brands and distribution systems has been an effective means of combating the increased competition from private brands. By developing a new brand name, a producer can adjust various elements of a marketing mix to appeal to a different target market. The growth of private brands has been steady. One reason is that retailers advertise the manufacturer brands, which brings customers to their stores, but sell the private brands, especially to price-sensitive customers. Another reason is that retailers with private labels negotiate better prices from producers of manufacturer brands.[10] To compete against private brands, some manufacturer brand makers have stopped increasing prices or even cut their prices, which has narrowed the price gap, the major advantage of buying a private brand. Traditionally, private brands have appeared in packaging that directly imitates the packaging of competing manufacturers' brands without significant legal ramifications. However, the legal risks of using look-alike packaging are increasing for private branders.

Some private distributor brands are produced by companies that specialize in making only private distributor brands; others are made by producers of manufacturer brands. Producers of both types of brands find it difficult at times to ignore the opportunities that arise from producing private distributor brands. If a producer decides not to produce a private brand for a reseller, a competitor probably will. Moreover, the production of private distributor brands allows the producer to use excess capacity during periods when its own brands are at nonpeak production. The ultimate decision of whether to produce a private or a manufacturer brand depends on a company's resources, production capabilities, and goals.

Some marketers of traditionally branded products have embarked on a policy of not branding, often called *generic branding*. **Generic brands** indicate only the product category (such as aluminum foil) and do not include the company name or other identifying terms. Generic brands are usually sold at lower prices than comparable

generic brands Brands indicating only the product category

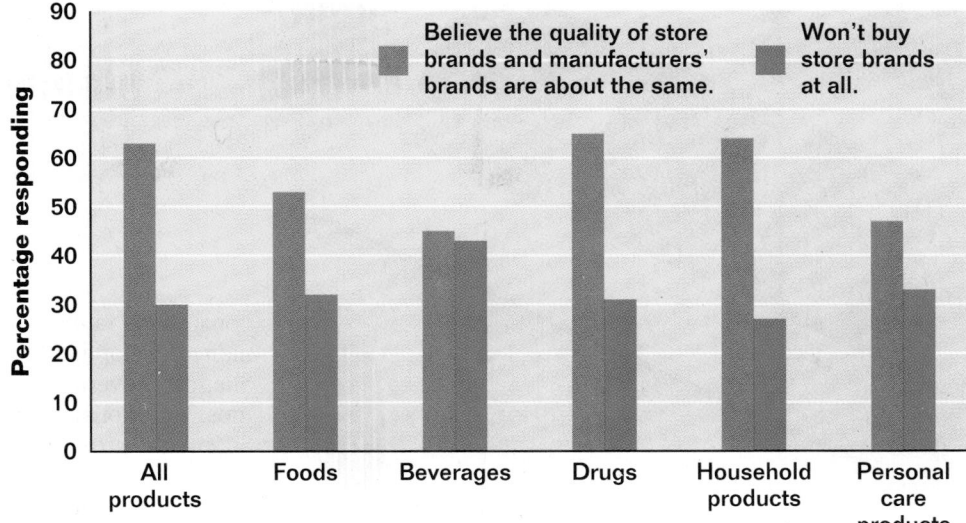

FIGURE 12.2
Consumers' Perceptions of Store and Manufacturers' Brands for Selected Product Groups

Source: "Store Brands at the Turning Point," Consumer Research Network, 3624 Market Street, Philadelphia, PA.

branded items. Although at one time generic brands may have represented as much as 10 percent of all retail grocery sales, today they account for less than a half of a percent.

Selecting a Brand Name

Marketers consider a number of factors in selecting a brand name. First, the name should be easy for customers (including foreign buyers, if the firm intends to market its products in other countries) to say, spell, and recall. Short, one-syllable names, such as Cheer, often satisfy this requirement. Second, the brand name should indicate the product's major benefits and, if possible, should suggest in a positive way the product's uses and special characteristics; negative or offensive references should be avoided. For example, the brand names of such household cleaning products as Ajax dishwashing liquid, Vanish toilet bowl cleaner, Formula 409 multipurpose cleaner, Cascade dishwasher detergent, and Wisk laundry detergent connote strength and effectiveness. Third, to set it apart from competing brands, the brand should be distinctive. If a marketer intends to use a brand for a product line, that brand must be compatible with all products in the line. Finally, a brand should be designed so that it can be used and recognized in all types of media. Finding the right brand name has become a challenging task because many obvious product names have already been used.

How are brand names devised? Brand names can be created from single or multiple words—for example, Bic or Dodge Grand Caravan. Letters and numbers are used to create such brands as IBM PC or Z71. Words, numbers, and letters are combined to yield brand names like Mazda RX7 or Mitsubishi 3000GT. To avoid terms that have negative connotations, marketers sometimes use fabricated words that have absolutely no meaning when created—for example, Kodak and Exxon. Occasionally a brand is simply brought out of storage and used as is or modified. Firms often maintain banks of registered brands, some of which may have been used in the past. Cadillac, for example, has a bank of approximately 360 registered trademarks. The LaSalle brand, used in the 1920s and 1930s, could be called up for a new Cadillac model in the future. Possible brand names sometimes are tested in focus groups or in other settings to assess customers' reactions.

Who actually creates brand names? Brand names can be created internally by the organization. Sometimes a name is suggested by individuals who are close to the development of the product. Some organizations have committees that participate in brand name creation and approval. Large companies that introduce numerous new products annually are likely to have a department that develops brand names. At times, outside

Rocco Strongarm

Pat Combs

Bertha Beastly

(Our name never quite fit us either.)

CIC Applicant Background Checks has changed its name to HireCheck.
Now, our company carries the same name as America's leading employment screening software.
Same quality services. Same rapid, flexible delivery. Same nationwide reach. Better name.

HIRE**CHECK**
The power you need for the decisions you make.

New Corporate Headquarters:
805 executive center drive west, suite 300, st. petersburg, florida 33702
800.321.4473

A Member of The First American Family of Companies NYSE: FAF

consultants and companies that specialize in brand name development are used. When Triarc named a new Snapple beverage, its brand team sought ideas from most traditional sources of brand names, including all of Snapple's promotional agencies, all individuals who worked on the Snapple brand, and their friends and relatives. The company ran a contest offering prizes to employees for the best brand suggestions. In addition, three agencies that specialize in brand naming were used. In total, about 1,000 names were generated. Eventually "Whipper Snapple" was selected.[11]

Even though most of the important branding considerations apply to both goods and services, branding a service has some additional dimensions. The service brand is usually the same as the company name. Financial companies, such as Fidelity Investments and Charles Schwab Discount Brokerage, have established strong brand recognition. These companies have used their names to create an image of value and friendly, timely, responsible, accurate, and knowledgeable customer assistance. Service providers (such as United Air Lines) are perceived by customers as having one brand name, even though they offer multiple products (first class, business class, and coach). Because the service brand name and company name are so closely interrelated, a service brand name must be flexible enough to encompass a variety of current services, as well as new ones the company might offer in the future. Geographical references like *western* and descriptive terms like *trucking* limit the scope of possible associations with the brand name. Because Southwest Airlines now flies to many parts of the country, its name has become too limited in its scope of associations. *Humana,* with its connotations of kindness and compassion, is flexible enough to encompass all services that a hospital, insurance plan, or health care facility offers. Frequently a service marketer will employ a symbol along with its brand name to make the brand distinctive and to communicate a certain image. For example, Wausau Insurance Company's advertising of its distinctive name and brand logo (a train station) has increased both its response rates to direct mail and general consumer acceptance of the company.[12]

Protecting a Brand

A marketer should also design a brand so that it can be protected easily through registration. A series of court decisions has created a broad hierarchy of protection based on brand type. From most protectable to least protectable, these brand types are fanciful (Exxon), arbitrary (Dr Pepper), suggestive (Spray 'n Wash), descriptive (Minute Rice), and generic (aluminum foil). Generic brands are not protectable. Surnames and descriptive, geographic, or functional names are difficult to protect.[13] However, research shows that overall, consumers prefer descriptive and suggestive brand names and find them easier to recall compared with fanciful and arbitrary brand names.[14] Because of their designs, some brands can be legally infringed on more easily than others. Although registration protects trademarks domestically for ten years and trademarks can be renewed indefinitely, a firm should develop a system for ensuring that its trademarks are renewed as needed.

To protect its exclusive rights to a brand, a company must make certain the brand is not likely to be considered an infringement on any brand already registered with the U.S. Patent and Trademark Office. This task may be complex because infringement is determined by the courts, which base their decisions on whether a brand causes consumers to be confused, mistaken, or deceived about the source of the product. McDonald's is one company that aggressively protects its trademarks against infringement; it has brought charges against a number of companies with "Mc" names because it fears the use of that prefix will give consumers the impression that these companies are associated with or owned by McDonald's. Auto Shack changed its name to AutoZone when faced with legal action from Tandy Corporation, owner of Radio Shack. Tandy maintained that it owned the name *Shack.* After research showed that virtually every auto supply store in the country used *auto* in its name, *zone* was deemed the best word to pair with *auto.*

BUILDING CUSTOMER RELATIONSHIPS

3Com Reboots Its Brand

How does a computer networking company reboot a well-known brand? That was the challenge facing 3Com. The 3Com brand, which doubles as the company name, was based on the founders' original vision of "computer, communication, and compatibility." Now, more than two decades after the California-based company was born, top management was planning a major change in marketing strategy and wanted to reinforce the new direction by relaunching the brand.

Although most of 3Com's revenues come from electronic connectivity devices and software, it had also marketed a variety of other products over the years, ranging from PC modems to PalmPilot personal digital assistants (PDAs). The company had even tried selling stand-alone Internet appliances made for the consumer market. But once 3Com decided to exit the consumer market and refocus on technology for business customers, CEO Bruce Claflin knew it was time to take a fresh look at the brand.

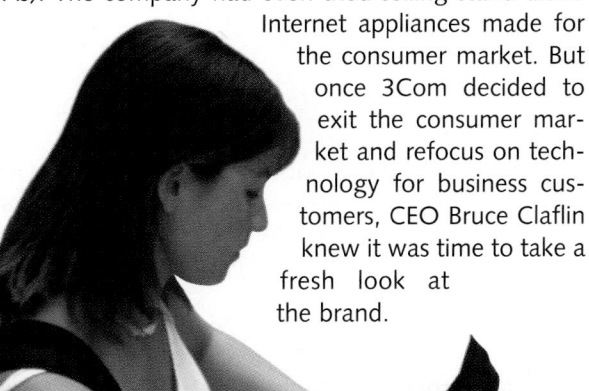

The company conducted marketing research to find out how customers viewed the brand. "Our research confirmed that our customers believe that 3Com excels at simplifying the use of technology and, in the process, simplifying their lives," Claflin notes. "As a happy coincidence, there is a major backlash underway against unnecessarily complex technology in all sectors of our lives. In 3Com's efforts to rebrand our company, we also ended up riding a wave that is sweeping across the nation."

Following up on the research results, the company planned its rebranding campaign, rallying around "Radical Simplicity" as the new advertising tag line. Management developed a one-day branding "boot camp" to bring the relaunch message to the field. "We had camps at six locations and hit employees from all areas—marketing, sales, manufacturing, IT [information technology], finance," says James Peters, 3Com's brand assets manager. During these meetings, employees learned branding basics, discussed the implications of the new tag line, and shared ideas about ways to fulfill the brand's promise.

To keep up the brand-building momentum, 3Com created a Brand Council with representation from all functions. Council members convene on a regular basis to evaluate the results of the rebranding effort and identify areas for improvement. In addition, 3Com has established a Marketing Tool Kit website where employees can check official branding guidelines, download logos, or search for other marketing materials. Now, if the company changes its tag line or tinkers with brand graphics, employees will be able to find the latest information on the Tool Kit site—a radically simple idea.

A marketer should guard against allowing a brand name to become a generic term used to refer to a general product category. Generic terms cannot be protected as exclusive brand names. For example, *aspirin, escalator,* and *shredded wheat*—all brand names at one time—eventually were declared generic terms that refer to product classes. Thus, they could no longer be protected. To keep a brand name from becoming a generic term, the firm should spell the name with a capital letter and use it as an adjective to modify the name of the general product class, as in Kool-Aid Brand Soft Drink Mix.[15] Including the word *brand* just after the brand name is also helpful. An organization can deal with this problem directly by advertising that its brand is a trademark and should not be used generically. The firm can also indicate that the brand is a registered trademark by using the symbol ®.

In the interest of strengthening trademark protection, Congress enacted the Trademark Law Revision Act in 1988, the only major federal trademark legislation since the Lanham Act of 1946. The purpose of this more recent legislation is to increase the value of the federal registration system for U.S. firms relative to foreign competitors and to better protect the public from counterfeiting, confusion, and deception.[16]

A U.S. firm that tries to protect a brand in a foreign country frequently encounters problems. In many countries, brand registration is not possible; the first firm to use a brand in such a country automatically has the rights to it. In some instances, U.S. companies actually have had to buy their own brand rights from a firm in a foreign country because the foreign firm was the first user in that country.

Marketers trying to protect their brands must also contend with brand counterfeiting. In the United States, for instance, one can purchase counterfeit General Motors parts, Cartier watches, Louis Vuitton handbags, Walt Disney character dolls, Warner Brothers clothing, Mont Blanc pens, and a host of other products illegally marketed by manufacturers that do not own the brands. Annual losses caused by counterfeit products are estimated to be between $250 billion and $350 billion annually. Many counterfeit products are manufactured overseas—in Turkey, China, Thailand, Italy, and Colombia, for example—but some are counterfeited in the United States. Counterfeit products are often hard to distinguish from the real brands. Products most likely to be counterfeited are well-known brands that appeal to a mass market and products for which the physical materials are inexpensive compared with the products' prices. Microsoft estimates that its revenues would double if counterfeiting of its brand name products were eliminated. Some $40 billion a year are lost in the computer software business because of counterfeit and pirated products. Brand fraud not only results in lost revenue for the brand's owner, it also means a low-quality product for customers, distorts competition, affects investment levels, reduces tax revenues and legitimate employment, creates safety risks, affects international relations. It also likely affects customers' perceptions of the brand due to the counterfeit product's inferior quality.

Branding Policies

Before establishing branding policies, a firm must decide whether to brand its products at all. If a company's product is homogeneous and similar to competitors' products, it may be difficult to brand. Raw materials such as coal, sand, and farm produce are hard to brand because of the homogeneity of such products and their physical characteristics.

individual branding A policy of naming each product differently

If a firm chooses to brand its products, it may opt for one or more of the following branding policies: individual, family, and brand-extension branding. **Individual branding** is a policy of naming each product differently. For example, Unilever relies on an individual branding policy for its line of detergents, which includes Wisk, Persil, and All. The company has organized its products into three branding tiers: "power" brands marketed across national borders, products marketed under different brands in different countries, and local brands sold only in specific markets.[17] A major advantage of individual branding is that if an organization introduces a poor product, the

History
of
Excellence

Pro-Line International promises to continue to bring you the
quality products you and your family expect and deserve.

Pro-Line International ©2000 Visit our web site at www.proline-intl.com

Family Branding
Pro-Line uses a family branding
policy. Some of its brands are
shown in this advertisement.

family branding Branding all
of a firm's products with the
same name

brand-extension branding
Using an existing brand name for
an improved or new product

negative images associated with it do not contaminate
the company's other products. An individual branding
policy may also facilitate market segmentation when a
firm wishes to enter many segments of the same market.
Separate, unrelated names can be used, and each brand
can be aimed at a specific segment. Sara Lee utilizes
individual branding among its many divisions, which
include Coach luggage, Hanes underwear, L'eggs panty-
hose, Champion sportswear, and other vastly different
brands.

In **family branding,** all of a firm's products are
branded with the same name or at least part of the name,
such as Kellogg's Frosted Flakes, Kellogg's Rice Krispies,
and Kellogg's Corn Flakes. In some cases, a company's
name is combined with other words to brand items. Arm
& Hammer uses its name on all its products, along with
a generic description of the item, such as Arm & Hammer
Heavy Duty Detergent, Arm & Hammer Pure Baking Soda,
and Arm & Hammer Carpet Deodorizer. Unlike individual
branding, family branding means the promotion of one
item with the family brand promotes the firm's other
products. Other major companies that use family branding include Mitsubishi, Kodak,
and Fisher-Price.

In **brand-extension branding,** a firm uses one of its existing brand names as
part of a brand for an improved or new product, which is often in the same product
category as the existing brand. McNeil Consumer Products, the makers of Tylenol and
Extra Strength Tylenol, also introduced Extra Strength Tylenol P.M., thus extending
the Tylenol brand. Marketers share a common concern that if a brand is extended too
many times or extended too far outside its original product category, the brand can
be significantly weakened. For example, Miller Brewing Company has extended its
brand to Miller Lite, Genuine Draft, Draft Lite, Ice, Ice Lite, Milwaukee's Best, Ice
House, and Red Dog, but so many extensions may confuse customers and encourage
them to do considerable brand switching. The Nabisco Snackwell brand initially
appeared only on crackers, cookies, and snack bars, all of which fall into the baked
snack category. However, extending the brand to yogurts and gelatin mixes goes further afield. Although some experts might caution Nabisco against extending the
Snackwell brand to this degree, some evidence suggests that brands can be successfully extended to less related product categories through the use of advertisements
that extend customers' perceptions of the original product category. For example,
Waterford, an upscale Irish brand of crystal, extended its name to writing instruments
when seeking sales growth beyond closely related product categories, such as china,
cutlery, and table linens.[18]

An organization is not limited to a single branding policy. A company that uses
primarily individual branding for many of its products may also use brand extensions.
Branding policy is influenced by the number of products and product lines the company produces, the characteristics of its target markets, the number and types of competing products available, and the size of the firm's resources.

Co-Branding

co-branding Using two or more brands on one product

Co-branding is the use of two or more brands on one product. Marketers employ co-branding to capitalize on the brand equity of multiple brands. Co-branding is popular in a number of processed food categories and in the credit card industry. The brands used for co-branding can be owned by the same company. For example, Kraft's Lunchables product teams the Kraft cheese brand with Oscar Mayer lunchmeats, another Kraft-owned brand. The brands may also be owned by different companies. Credit card companies like American Express, Visa, and MasterCard, for instance, team up with other brands like General Motors, AT&T, and many airlines. Currently 21 airline–credit card co-brand programs operate in the United States. It is predicted that in just a few years, credit card purchases will outstrip flying as the number one way to earn frequent flier miles.[19]

Effective co-branding capitalizes on the trust and confidence customers have in the brands involved. The brands should not lose their identities, and it should be clear to customers which brand is the main brand. For example, it is fairly obvious that Kellogg owns the brand and is the main brander of Kellogg's Healthy Choice Cereal. It is important for marketers to understand that when a co-branded product is unsuccessful, both brands are implicated in the product failure. To gain customer acceptance, the brands involved must represent a complementary fit in the minds of buyers. Trying to link a brand like Harley-Davidson with a brand like Healthy Choice will not achieve co-branding objectives because customers are not likely to perceive these brands as compatible.

Co-branding can help an organization differentiate its products from those of competitors. By using the product development skills of a co-branding partner, an organization can create a distinctive product. For example, Hiram Walker partnered

TECH*KNOW

The Tricky Art of Online Co-Branding

During the heady days of dot-com delirium just a few years ago, offline companies eagerly jumped on the Internet bandwagon by setting up co-branding deals with startup e-businesses. Kellogg, for example, joined with e-tailer Toysmart.com to co-brand cereal boxes as part of an online frequent buyer program dubbed Eet and Ern. A different kind of arrangement brought the Athlete's Foot chain together with Internet service provider NetZero in a promotion offering free co-branded web access to the retailer's customers.

With more consumers surfing the Web every day and experts predicting explosive growth in e-commerce, co-branding looked, at the time, like a good way for offline firms to reach the apparently lucrative and largely untapped online market. For their part, e-businesses believed that linking with established offline companies would gain them credibility and expand their market beyond the Internet.

Fast-forward to reality. Toysmart became one of the many dot-com casualties littering the online landscape, going out of business just three weeks after Kellogg's co-branded cereal packages started appearing on supermarket shelves. Luckily Kellogg had lined up other co-branding partners, so the loyalty program continued without interruption. The Athlete's Foot–NetZero deal also ran into problems after NetZero experienced financial difficulties. The co-branded free Internet offer, once highly touted, has disappeared from the Athlete's Foot website.

Some online co-branding agreements have proven profitable for both partners, however. Amazon.com and Toys "R" Us are involved with two co-branded sites. Toysrus.com is a co-branded toy retailing site, and Babiesrus.com is a co-branded site selling products for newborns and infants. Toysrus.com has been highly successful, reporting higher sales and profits even as eToys, Toysmart, Toytime, Redrocket, and other toy e-tailers were shutting down.

To minimize problems, experts say that co-branding agreements should allow for some flexibility so the partners can make changes as the environment evolves. Also, offline companies should protect their rights to trademarks and copyrights, ensure that customer data and other information will remain safe and confidential even if the deal collapses, and monitor fulfillment and other activities that can affect performance as well as influence the public image of the brands involved.

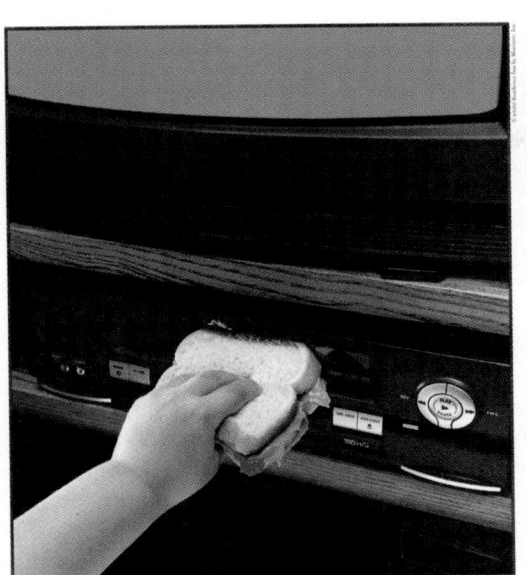

With Residence Inn® and AT&T, you can keep up with all the news from home.

AT&T
www.att.com

Sure you miss the family. But you won't miss the news. Because every suite has reliable AT&T communications® to help you keep in touch on extended business trips. It's just what you'd expect from Marriott's flagship all-suite hotel. Where you earn Marriott Rewards® points or miles toward a free vacation. To learn more or make a reservation, visit residenceinn.com, call your travel agent or call us at 800-331-3131.

*Available at most locations

Marriott
Residence Inn®
Room to work, room to relax, room to breathe.™

Co-Branding
This advertisement promotes co-branded products.

brand licensing An agreement whereby a company permits another organization to use its brand on other products for a licensing fee

with Sara Lee to produce a Kahlua White Russian Brownie; a Hiram Walker gift package includes an eight-ounce serving of these special brownies, along with a bottle of Kahlua. Co-branding also can take advantage of the distribution capabilities of co-branding partners. For example, Polaroid Corporation entered into a co-branding agreement with Nike to introduce the Nike Runamok Pic, a special shoe with a clear display window for the postage-stamp-size photo stickers from the top-selling iZone Instant Pocket Camera. These shoes will be sold at Niketown, select Foot Locker stores, and Journeys.[20]

While co-branding has been used for a number of years, it began to grow in popularity in the 1980s when Monsanto aggressively promoted its NutraSweet product as an ingredient in such well-known brands as Diet Coke. The company also used this approach with lesser-known brands to instill trust and confidence in buyers' minds. Intel, too, has capitalized on ingredient co-branding through its "Intel Inside" program. The effectiveness of ingredient co-branding relies heavily on continued promotional efforts by the ingredient's producer.

Brand Licensing

A popular branding strategy involves **brand licensing,** an agreement in which a company permits another organization to use its brand on other products for a licensing fee. Royalties may be as low as 2 percent of wholesale revenues or higher than 10 percent. Mattel, for example, licensed Warner Brothers' Harry Potter brand for use on board games and toys to tie in with the first movie based on the wildly popular book series. Warner was guaranteed royalties of $20 million from Mattel's licensing fee of 15 percent of gross revenues earned on these branded products.[21] The licensee is responsible for all manufacturing, selling, and advertising functions and bears the costs if the licensed product fails. Not long ago, only a few firms licensed their corporate trademarks, but today licensing is a multi-billion-dollar business. The top U.S. licensing company is Walt Disney Company. The NFL, the NCAA, NASCAR, and Major League Baseball are all in the top ten in retail sales of licensed products, each with at least $2 billion in sales in 2000.[22]

The advantages of licensing range from extra revenues and low-cost or free publicity to new images and trademark protection. For example, Coca-Cola has licensed its trademark for use on glassware, radios, trucks, and clothing in the hope of protecting its trademark. However, brand licensing has drawbacks. The major disadvantages are a lack of manufacturing control, which could hurt the company's name, and bombarding consumers with too many unrelated products bearing the same name. Licensing arrangements can also fail because of poor timing, inappropriate distribution channels, or mismatching of product and name.

Packaging

Packaging involves the development of a container and a graphic design for a product. A package can be a vital part of a product, making it more versatile, safer, and easier to use. Like a brand name, a package can influence customers' attitudes toward a product and so affect their purchase decisions. For example, several producers of jellies, sauces, and ketchups have packaged their products in squeezable containers to make use and storage more convenient. Package characteristics help shape buyers' impressions of a product at the time of purchase or during use. In this section, we examine the main functions of packaging and consider several major packaging decisions. We also analyze the role of the package in a marketing strategy.

Innovation Isn't for Everyone.
Just the Profit-Minded.

The Garden Party® Grape Clamshell and Hefty® Slide-Rite® Grape Bags:

* EASE OF MERCHANDISING—simplify merchandising, help manage costs and sell more grapes.
* SHRINK REDUCTION—reduce retail shrink by as much as 25 to 50%.
* RISK MANAGEMENT—secure closure keeps grapes where they belong—in the package.

1-877-PACTIV-1

Product Protection
This advertisement, aimed at the grocery industry, promotes the protective qualities of Pactiv's packaging materials. Not only does this packaging material protect the product from damage, but also it protects the product from customers' "grazing" in retail grocery stores.

Packaging Functions

Effective packaging means more than simply putting products in containers and covering them with wrappers. First, packaging materials serve the basic purpose of protecting the product and maintaining its functional form. Fluids like milk, orange juice, and hair spray need packages that preserve and protect them. The packaging should prevent damage that could affect the product's usefulness and thus lead to higher costs. Since product tampering has become a problem, several packaging techniques have been developed to counter this danger. Some packages are also designed to deter shoplifting.

Another function of packaging is to offer convenience to consumers. For example, small aseptic packages—individual-size boxes or plastic bags that contain liquids and do not require refrigeration—strongly appeal to children and young adults with active lifestyles. The size or shape of a package may relate to the product's storage, convenience of use, or replacement rate. Small, single-serving cans of vegetables, for instance, may prevent waste and make storage easier. A third function of packaging is to promote a product by communicating its features, uses, benefits, and image. Sometimes a reusable package is developed to make the product more desirable. For example, the Cool Whip package doubles as a food-storage container.

Major Packaging Considerations

As they develop packages, marketers must take many factors into account. Obviously, one major consideration is cost. Although a variety of packaging materials, processes, and designs are available, costs vary greatly. In recent years, buyers have shown a willingness to pay more for improved packaging, but there are limits. Marketers should conduct research to determine exactly how much customers are willing to pay for effective and efficient package designs.

As already mentioned, developing tamper-resistant packaging is very important for certain products. Although no package is tamper-proof, marketers can develop packages that are difficult to tamper with. At a minimum, all packaging must comply with the Food and Drug Administration's packaging regulations. However, packaging should also make any product tampering evident to resellers and consumers. Although effective tamper-resistant packaging may be expensive to develop, when balanced against the costs of lost sales, loss of consumer confidence and company reputation, and potentially expensive product liability lawsuits, the costs of ensuring consumer safety are minimal.

Marketers should also consider how much consistency is desirable among an organization's package designs. No consistency may be the best policy, especially if a

family packaging Using similar packaging for all of a firm's products or packaging that has one common design element

firm's products are unrelated or aimed at vastly different target markets. To promote an overall company image, a firm may decide that all packages should be similar or include one major element of the design. This approach is called **family packaging.** Sometimes it is used only for lines of products, as with Campbell's soups, Weight Watcher's foods, and Planter's nuts.

A package's promotional role is an important consideration. Through verbal and nonverbal symbols, the package can inform potential buyers about the product's content, features, uses, advantages, and hazards. A firm can create desirable images and associations by its choice of color, design, shape, and texture. Many cosmetics manufacturers, for example, design their packages to create impressions of richness, luxury, and exclusiveness. A package performs a promotional function when it is designed to be safer or more convenient to use if such characteristics help stimulate demand.

To develop a package that has a definite promotional value, a designer must consider size, shape, texture, color, and graphics. Beyond the obvious limitation that the package must be large enough to hold the product, a package can be designed to appear taller or shorter. Light-colored packaging may make a package appear larger, whereas darker colors may minimize the perceived size.

Colors on packages are often chosen to attract attention, and color can positively influence customers' emotions. People associate specific colors with certain feelings and experiences. For example,

Blue is soothing; it is also associated with wealth, trust, and security.

Gray is associated with strength, exclusivity, and success.

Orange can stand for low cost.

Red connotes excitement and stimulation.

Purple is associated with dignity and stateliness.

Yellow connotes cheerfulness and joy.

Black is associated with being strong and masterful.[23]

Distinctive Packaging Shapes
Distinctive package shapes provide enhanced brand identities.

When opting for color on packaging, marketers must judge whether a particular color will evoke positive or negative feelings when linked to a specific product. Rarely, for example, do processors package meat or bread in green materials because customers may associate green with mold. Marketers must also determine whether a specific target market will respond favorably or unfavorably to a particular color. Cosmetics for women are more likely to be sold in pastel packaging than are personal-care products for men. Packages designed to appeal to children often use primary colors and bold designs. A relatively recent trend in packaging is colorless packages. Clear products and packaging connote a pure, natural product.

Packaging must also meet the needs of resellers. Wholesalers and retailers consider whether a package facilitates transportation, storage, and handling. Resellers may refuse to carry certain products if their packages are cumbersome. Concentrated versions of laundry detergents and fabric softeners aid retailers in offering more product diversity within the existing shelf space.

A final consideration is whether to develop packages that are environmentally responsible. Nearly one-half of all garbage consists of discarded plastic packaging, such as polystyrene containers, plastic soft-drink bottles, and carryout bags. Plastic packaging material does not biodegrade, and paper requires the destruction of valuable forests. Consequently a number of companies have changed to environmentally sensitive packaging; they are also recycling more materials. Procter & Gamble markets several cleaning products in a concentrated form, which requires less packaging than the ready-to-use version. H. J. Heinz is looking for alternatives to its plastic ketchup squeeze bottles. Other companies are also searching for alternatives to environmentally harmful packaging. In some instances, however, customers have objected to such switches because the newer environmentally responsible packaging may be less effective or more inconvenient. Therefore, marketers must carefully balance society's desire to preserve the environment against customers' desire for convenience.

Packaging and Marketing Strategy

Packaging can be a major component of a marketing strategy. A new cap or closure, a better box or wrapper, or a more convenient container may give a product a competitive advantage. The right type of package for a new product can help it gain market recognition very quickly. In the case of existing brands, marketers should reevaluate packages periodically. Especially for consumer convenience products, marketers should view packaging as a major strategic tool. For instance, in the food industry, jumbo and large package sizes for such products as hot dogs, pizzas, English muffins, frozen dinners, and biscuits have been very successful. When considering the strategic uses of packaging, marketers must also analyze the cost of packaging and package changes. The biggest packaging spenders are listed in Table 12.2. In this section, we examine several ways in which packaging can be used strategically.

Table 12.2	Companies That Spend the Most on Packaging	
	Anheuser-Busch	Kraft General Foods
	Campbell Soup	Kraft USA
	Coca-Cola	Miller Brewing
	Coca-Cola Foods	PepsiCo
	General Mills	Procter & Gamble

Altering the Package.   At times a marketer changes a package because the existing design is no longer in style, especially when compared with the packaging of competitive products. Arm & Hammer now markets a refillable plastic shaker for its baking soda. Quaker Oats hired a package design company to redesign its Rice-A-Roni package to give the product the appearance of having evolved with the times while retaining its traditional taste appeal. Rice-A-Roni had been experiencing a lag in sales because of increased competition. An overhaul of the product packaging to a refreshing and more up-to-date look was credited with a 20 percent increase in sales over the previous year. Similarly, Del Monte introduced a contemporary look for its tomato products and experienced a double-digit gain in the first year.

A package may be redesigned because new product features need to be highlighted or because new packaging materials have become available. An organization may decide to change a product's packaging to reposition the product or to make the product safer or more convenient to use. Nestlé USA, for example, changed its Coffee Mate package to a new, easy-to-grip plastic container that features a portable spout, eliminating the need to unscrew the lid and spoon out the creamer. Nestlé expects the new, more convenient package to give its powdered-creamer product a boost in the marketplace.[24]

Innovative Packaging
Evian employs innovative packaging as a part of its marketing strategy.

Secondary-Use Packaging.   A secondary-use package is one that can be reused for purposes other than its initial function. For example, a margarine container can be reused to store leftovers, and a jelly container can serve as a drinking glass. Customers often view secondary-use packaging as adding value to products, in which case its use should stimulate unit sales.

Category-Consistent Packaging.   With category-consistent packaging, the product is packaged in line with the packaging practices associated with a particular product category. Some product categories—for example, mayonnaise, mustard, ketchup, and peanut butter—have traditional package shapes. Other product categories are characterized by recognizable color combinations, such as red and white for soup, and red, white, and blue for Ritz-like crackers. When an organization introduces a brand in one of these product categories, marketers will often use traditional package shapes and color combinations to ensure customers will recognize the new product as being in that specific product category.

Innovative Packaging.   Sometimes a marketer employs a unique cap, design, applicator, or other feature to make a product distinctive. Such packaging can be effective when the innovation makes the product safer or easier to use, or provides better protection for the product. In some instances, marketers use innovative or unique packages that are inconsistent with traditional packaging practices to make the brand stand out from its competitors. To distinguish their products, marketers in the beverage industry have long used innovative shapes and packaging materials. Unusual packaging sometimes requires expending considerable resources, not only on package design but also on making customers aware of the unique package and its benefit.

Multiple Packaging.   Rather than packaging a single unit of a product, marketers sometimes use twin packs, tri-packs, six-packs, or other forms of multiple packaging. For certain types of products, multiple packaging may increase demand because it increases the amount of the product available at the point of consumption (in one's house, for example). It may also increase consumer acceptance of the product by encouraging the buyer to try the product several times. Multiple packaging can make products easier to handle and store, as in the case of six-packs for soft drinks; it can also facilitate special price offers, such as two-for-one sales. However, multiple packaging does not work for all types of products. One would not use additional table salt, for example, simply because an extra box is in the pantry.

Handling-Improved Packaging. A product's packaging may be changed to make it easier to handle in the distribution channel—for example, by changing the outer carton or using special bundling, shrink-wrapping, or pallets. In some cases, the shape of the package is changed. An ice cream producer, for instance, may change from a cylindrical package to a rectangular one to facilitate handling. In addition, at the retail level, the ice cream producer may be able to get more shelf facings with a rectangular package than with a round one. Outer containers for products are sometimes changed so they will proceed more easily through automated warehousing systems.

Criticisms of Packaging

The last several decades have brought a number of improvements in packaging. However, some packaging problems still need to be resolved.

Some packages suffer from functional problems in that they simply do not work well. The packaging for flour and sugar is, at best, poor. Both grocers and consumers are very much aware that these packages leak and are easily torn. Can anyone open and close a bag of flour without spilling at least a little bit? Certain packages, such as refrigerated biscuit cans, milk cartons with foldout spouts, and potato chip bags, are frequently difficult to open. The traditional shapes of packages for products like ketchup and salad dressing make the product inconvenient to use. Have you ever wondered when tapping on a ketchup bottle why the producer didn't put the ketchup in a mayonnaise jar?

Although many steps have been taken to make packaging safer, critics still focus on the safety issues. Containers with sharp edges and easily broken glass bottles are sometimes viewed as a threat to safety. Certain types of plastic packaging and aerosol containers represent possible health hazards.

At times packaging is viewed as being deceptive. Package shape, graphic design, and certain colors may be used to make a product appear larger than it actually is. The inconsistent use of certain size designations, such as giant, economy, family, king, and super, can lead to customer confusion.

Finally, although customers in this country traditionally prefer attractive, effective, convenient packaging, the cost of such packaging is high.

Labeling

Labeling is very closely interrelated with packaging and is used for identification, promotional, and informational and legal purposes.

labeling Providing identifying, promotional, or other information on package labels

Labels can be small or large relative to the size of the product and carry varying amounts of information. The sticker on a Chiquita banana, for example, is quite small and displays only the brand name of the fruit. A label can be part of the package itself or a separate feature attached to the package. The label on a can of Coke is actually part of the can, whereas the label on a two-liter bottle of Coke is separate and can be removed. Information presented on a label may include the brand name and mark, the registered trademark symbol, package size and content, product features, nutritional information, type and style of the product, number of servings, care instructions, directions for use and safety precautions, the name and address of the manufacturer, expiration dates, seals of approval, and other facts.

universal product code (UPC) A series of electronically readable lines identifying a product and containing inventory and pricing information

For many products, the label includes a **universal product code (UPC),** a series of thick and thin electronically readable lines identifying the product and providing inventory and pricing information for producers and resellers. The UPC is electronically read at the retail checkout counter.

Distinctive Labeling
Heinz employs its unique crown-shaped label to make its brands easy to identify on the shelf.

Labels can facilitate the identification of a product by displaying the brand name in combination with a unique graphic design. For example, Heinz ketchup is easy to identify on a supermarket shelf because the brand name is easy to read and the label has a distinctive crownlike shape. By drawing attention to products and their benefits, labels can strengthen an organization's promotional efforts. Labels may contain such promotional messages as the offer of a discount or a larger package size at the same price, or information about a new or improved product feature.

A number of federal laws and regulations specify information that must be included on the labels of certain products. Garments must be labeled with the name of the manufacturer, country of manufacture, fabric content, and cleaning instructions. Labels on nonedible items like shampoos and detergents must include both safety precautions and directions for use. In 1966, Congress passed the Fair Packaging and Labeling Act, one of the most comprehensive pieces of labeling and packaging legislation. This law focuses on mandatory labeling requirements, voluntary adoption of packaging standards by firms within industries, and the provision of power to the Federal Trade Commission and the Food and Drug Administration to establish and enforce packaging regulations.

The Nutrition Labeling Act of 1990 requires the FDA to review food labeling and packaging, focusing on nutrition content, label format, ingredient labeling, food descriptions, and health messages. This act regulates much of the labeling on more than 250,000 products made by 17,000 U.S. companies. Any food product for which a nutritional claim is made must have nutrition labeling that follows a standard format. Food product labels must state the number of servings per container, serving size, number of calories per serving, number of calories derived from fat, number of carbohydrates, and amounts of specific nutrients such as vitamins. Although consumers have responded favorably to this type of information on labels, evidence as to whether they actually use it has been mixed.

The use of new technology in the production and processing of food has led to additional food labeling issues. The FDA now requires that a specific irradiation logo be used when labeling irradiated food products. In addition, the FDA also has issued voluntary guidelines for food companies to follow if they choose to label foods as biotech-free or promote biotech ingredients.[25] Despite legislation to make labels as accurate and informative as possible, questionable labeling practices persist. The Center for Science in the Public Interest questions the practice of naming a product "Strawberry Frozen Yogurt Bars" when it contains strawberry flavoring but no strawberries, or of calling a breakfast cereal "lightly sweetened" when sugar makes up 22 percent of its ingredients. Many labels on vegetable oils say "no cholesterol," but many of these oils contain saturated fats that can raise cholesterol levels. The Food and Drug Administration amended its regulations to forbid producers of vegetable oil from making "no cholesterol" claims on their labels.

Another area of concern is the issue of "green labeling." Consumers who are committed to making environmentally responsible purchasing decisions are sometimes fooled by labels. The U.S. Public Interest Research Group accused several manufacturers of "greenwashing" customers, using misleading claims to sell products by playing on customers' concern for the environment. For example, some manufacturers put a recycling symbol on labels for products made of polyvinyl chloride plastic, which cannot be recycled in the vast majority of American communities.

Of concern to many manufacturers are the Federal Trade Commission's guidelines regarding "Made in U.S.A." labels, a growing problem due to the increasingly global nature of manufacturing. The FTC requires that "all or virtually all" of a product's components be made in the United States if the label says "Made in U.S.A." Although the FTC recently considered changing its guidelines to read "substantially all," it rejected this idea and maintains the "all or virtually all" standard. In light of this decision, the FTC ordered New Balance to stop making that claim on its athletic shoe labels because some components (rubber soles) are made in China. The "Made in U.S.A." labeling issue has not been totally resolved. The FTC criteria for using "Made in U.S.A." are likely to be challenged and subsequently changed.[26]

Summary

A brand is a name, term, design, symbol, or any other feature that identifies one seller's good or service and distinguishes it from those of other sellers. A brand name is the part of a brand that can be spoken. A brand mark is the element that cannot be spoken. A trademark is a legal designation indicating that the owner has exclusive use of a brand or part of a brand and others are prohibited by law from using it. A trade name is the legal name of an organization. Branding helps buyers identify and evaluate products, helps sellers facilitate product introduction and repeat purchasing, and fosters brand loyalty.

Brand loyalty is a customer's favorable attitude toward a specific brand. If brand loyalty is strong enough, customers may consistently purchase a particular brand when they need a product in this product category. The three degrees of brand loyalty are brand recognition, preference, and insistence. Brand recognition exists when a customer is aware that the brand exists and views it as an alternative purchase if the preferred brand is unavailable. Brand preference is the degree of brand loyalty in which a customer prefers one brand over competing brands and will purchase it if available. Brand insistence is the degree of brand loyalty in which a customer will accept no substitute.

Brand equity is the marketing and financial value associated with a brand's strength. It represents the value of a brand to an organization. The four major elements underlying brand equity include brand name awareness, brand loyalty, perceived brand quality, and brand associations.

A manufacturer brand, initiated by the producer, ensures that the firm is associated with its products at the point of purchase. A private distributor brand is initiated and owned by a reseller, sometimes taking on the name of the store or distributor. Manufacturers combat growing competition from private distributor brands by developing multiple brands. A generic brand indicates only the product category and does not include the company name or other identifying terms.

When selecting a brand name, a marketer should choose one that is easy to say, spell, and recall and that alludes to the product's uses, benefits, or special characteristics. Brand names can be devised from words, letters, numbers, nonsense words, or a combination of these. Brand names are created inside an organization by individuals, committees, or branding departments, and by outside consultants. Services as well as products are branded, often with the company name and an accompanying symbol that makes the brand distinctive or conveys a desired image.

Producers protect ownership of their brands through registration with the U.S. Patent and Trademark Office. A company must make certain the brand name it selects does not infringe on an already registered brand by confusing or deceiving consumers about the source of the product. In most foreign countries, brand registration is on a first-come, first-serve basis, making protection more difficult. Brand counterfeiting is becoming increasingly common and can undermine consumers' confidence in a brand.

Companies brand their products in several ways. Individual branding designates a unique name for each of a company's products. Family branding identifies all of a firm's products with a single name, and brand-extension branding applies an existing name to a new or improved product. Co-branding is the use of two or more brands on one product. It is a popular branding method in a number of processed food categories and in the credit card industry. The brands may be owned by the same company or by different companies. Effective co-branding profits from the trust and confidence customers have in the brands involved. To avoid confusion, marketers must ensure that customers understand which brand is the main brand. Co-brands must have a complementary fit in buyers' minds. Co-branding sometimes allows an organization to differentiate its products from those of competitors. It can also take advantage of the distribution capabilities of the co-branding partners. Finally, through a licensing agreement and for a licensing fee, a firm may permit another organization to use its brand on other products. Brand licensing enables producers to earn extra revenue, receive low-cost or free publicity, and protect their trademarks.

Packaging involves development of a container and a graphic design for a product. Effective packaging offers protection, economy, safety, and convenience. It can influence a customer's purchase decision by promoting features, uses, benefits, and image. When developing a package, marketers must consider the value to the customer of efficient and effective packaging, offset by the price the customer is willing to pay. Other considerations include making the package tamper resistant, whether to use multiple packaging and family packaging, how to design the package as an effective promotional tool, how best to accommodate resellers, and whether to develop environmentally responsible packaging. Firms choose particular colors, designs, shapes, and textures to create desirable images and associations. Packaging can be an important part of an overall marketing strategy and can be used to target certain market segments. Modifications in packaging can revive a mature product and extend its product life cycle. Producers alter packages to convey new features or to make them safer or more convenient. If a package has a secondary use, the product's value to the consumer may increase. Category-consistent packaging makes products more easily recognized by consumers.

Innovative packaging enhances a product's distinctiveness. Consumers may criticize packaging that does not work well, poses health or safety problems, is deceptive in some way, or is not biodegradable or recyclable.

Labeling is closely interrelated with packaging and is used for identification, promotional, and informational and legal purposes. The labels of many products include a universal product code, a series of electronically readable lines identifying a product and containing inventory and pricing information. Various federal laws and regulations require that certain products be labeled or marked with warnings, instructions, nutritional information, manufacturer's identification, and the like. Despite legislation, questionable labeling practices persist, including misleading information about fat content and cholesterol, freshness, and recyclability of packaging.

Important Terms

Brand	Generic brands
Brand name	Individual branding
Brand mark	Family branding
Trademark	Brand-extension
Trade name	branding
Brand loyalty	Co-branding
Brand recognition	Brand licensing
Brand preference	Family packaging
Brand insistence	Labeling
Brand equity	Universal product code
Manufacturer brands	(UPC)
Private distributor brands	

Discussion and Review Questions

1. What is the difference between a brand and a brand name? Compare and contrast the terms *brand mark* and *trademark*.
2. How does branding benefit consumers and marketers?
3. What are the three major degrees of brand loyalty?
4. What is brand equity? Identify and explain the major elements of brand equity.
5. Compare and contrast manufacturer brands, private distributor brands, and generic brands.
6. Identify the factors a marketer should consider in selecting a brand name.
7. The brand name Xerox is sometimes used generically to refer to photocopying, and Kleenex is used to refer to tissues. How can the manufacturers protect their brand names, and why would they want to?
8. What is co-branding? What major issues should be considered when using co-branding?
9. What are the major advantages and disadvantages of brand licensing?
10. Describe the functions a package can perform. Which function is most important? Why?
11. What are the main factors a marketer should consider when developing a package?
12. In what ways can packaging be used as a strategic tool?
13. What are the major criticisms of packaging?
14. What are the major functions of labeling?
15. In what ways do regulations and legislation affect labeling?

Application Questions

1. Identify two brands for which you are brand insistent. How did you begin using these brands? Why do you no longer use other brands?
2. General Motors introduced the subcompact Geo with a name that appeals to a world market. Invent a brand name for a line of luxury sports cars that also would appeal to an international market. Suggest a name that implies quality, luxury, and value.
3. When a firm decides to brand its products, it may choose one of several strategies. Name one company that utilizes each of the following strategies. How does each strategy help the company?
   a. Individual branding
   b. Family branding
   c. Brand-extension branding
4. For each of the following product categories, choose an existing brand. Then, for each selected brand, suggest a co-brand and explain why the co-brand would be effective.
   a. Cookies
   b. Pizza
   c. Long-distance telephone service
   d. A sports drink
5. Packaging provides product protection, customer convenience, and promotion of image, key features, and benefits. Identify a product that utilizes packaging in each of these ways, and evaluate the effectiveness of the package for that function.
6. Identify a package that you believe to be inferior. Explain why you think the package is inferior, and discuss your recommendations for improving it.

Internet Exercise & Resources

Visit **www.prideferrell.com** for resources to help you master the material in this chapter, plus materials that will help you expand your marketing knowledge, including: Internet exercise updates, ACE self-tests, hotlinks to companies featured in this chapter, and much more.

Pillsbury

Like other marketers of consumer products, Pillsbury has set up a website to inform and entertain consumers. Catering to the appeal of its most popular product spokesperson, Pillsbury has given its Dough Boy his own site. Visit him at

http://www.doughboy.com

1. What branding policy does Pillsbury seem to be using with regard to the products it presents on this site?

2. How does this Pillsbury website promote brand loyalty?

3. What degree of consistency exists in Pillsbury's packaging of its products displayed on the website?

VIDEO CASE 12.1

PlumpJack Winery Pours Out Cork Controversy

PlumpJack Winery has embarked on a highly public and controversial experiment in wine packaging. Instead of using corks to seal its upscale Napa Valley Reserve Cabernet Sauvignon wine bottles, the winery is sealing half of the bottles with metal screw-tops. To call attention to this unusual method of closing bottles of premium wines, the winery is packaging the bottles in a twin-pack, one with a cork (priced at $125) and one with a screw-top (priced at $135). Only time will tell whether this unorthodox packaging approach sells more wine, but it certainly generates media coverage and provides a distinctive marketing angle for the brand.

PlumpJack is owned by composer Gordon Getty, his son Bill Getty, and San Francisco politician Gavin Newsom. Named after an opera that the elder Getty wrote, which features the Jack Falstaff character from Shakespeare's *Henry IV,* the winery is set on 50 acres in Oakville, deep in California's Napa Valley wine country. The vineyards of Robert Mondavi and other famous wine brands are nearby, but so far PlumpJack is the only one to embrace screw-tops for high-end wines.

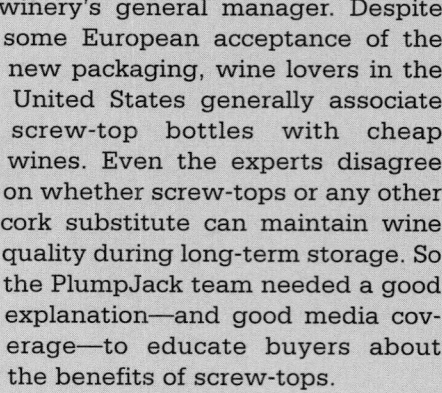

Gordon Getty devised the screw-top idea out of concern for the environmental impact of the dwindling worldwide supply of cork. He also disliked the musty character that natural cork occasionally imparts to bottled wine and the tiny bits of broken cork that often fall into newly uncorked bottles. Getty knew that a few wineries were testing synthetic corks as replacements for natural corks. Even though synthetic corks have been available for more than a decade, they have managed to replace only 2 percent of the world's 14 billion corks. So Getty and his partners, working with winery management, decided to explore other alternatives.

"In researching the idea, we found that there are premium Swiss and European wines with screw-tops," recalls John Conover, the winery's general manager. Despite some European acceptance of the new packaging, wine lovers in the United States generally associate screw-top bottles with cheap wines. Even the experts disagree on whether screw-tops or any other cork substitute can maintain wine quality during long-term storage. So the PlumpJack team needed a good explanation—and good media coverage—to educate buyers about the benefits of screw-tops.

Their first step was to invite the University of California at Davis to study the quality of the wine from both corked and screw-top bottles. This close scrutiny by a respected institution would, over time, confirm or disprove the winery's theory that screw-top packaging was at least as effective as natural cork for maintaining wine quality. Simply announcing the university study showed wine buyers (and competitors) how serious PlumpJack's owners were about their innovative packaging. Next, the partners came up with the twin-pack concept as a way to encourage buyers to personally compare the wines from the corked bottle and the screw-top bottle.

Once their packaging plans were in place, the PlumpJack partners kicked off a media campaign to announce the screw-top innovation. CNN picked up the story, a national morning television program showcased the wine, and reporters from Europe and Asia interviewed winery management. Meanwhile industry publications debated the appeal and effectiveness of screw-tops and quoted the views of different experts.

The internationalization of wine marketing is also working in PlumpJack's favor. "The marketplace for premium California wine is now global," remarks Conover. "Where we once had a market that was basically west of the Rockies, we are now selling wine into Germany, Japan, New York, and other places where California wines were not featured before. The playing field for premium wines is now bigger than it has ever been." Because wine buyers outside the United States may be more familiar with screw-top bottles, they may be more willing to give the screw-top PlumpJack wine an objective taste test.

Another trend is helping PlumpJack, according to Mary Pisor, the winery's associate winemaker: "The consumer's ability to buy ultra-premium wines has increased dramatically since the early 1990s," she says. "As I travel around the country, I find wine collectors in their 20s and 30s who have the fiscal ability to pay the kind of prices we now see for our wines." PlumpJack's luxury wines usually retail for $100-plus per bottle, even without the added expense of capping with screw tops.

This initial experiment involved only 133 cases of wine packaged with screw-tops, but future releases may be larger still. "This has been a long time coming, as anyone who follows the wine industry knows," comments Gordon Getty. "The technology is in place, we believe the market is prepared, and all that remains is for someone to break the barrier of tradition."[27]

QUESTIONS FOR DISCUSSION

1. Can PlumpJack's screw-top bottles be considered category-consistent packaging? Explain.
2. PlumpJack is using screw-top caps to improve the quality and perhaps make its premium wine more distinctive. But since screw-top caps are used for inexpensive wines in the United States, will customers view PlumpJack wines as cheaper, lower-quality wines even though the screw-top cap may actually improve PlumpJack wines' quality? Explain.
3. Would you recommend that PlumpJack sell its screw-top wines singly instead of in a twin-pack with corked wines? Explain.
4. How might PlumpJack use labeling to promote its innovative packaging?

CASE 12.2
Hearts on Fire: Branding the Symbol of Commitment

How can a gem company convince customers that its diamonds are a cut above the rest? Increasingly the answer is branding. People are often very particular about the brands of shampoo or deodorant they buy, but when they shop for a diamond, they probably don't have a specific brand in mind. Although an engaged couple may have done some homework regarding the "Four Cs" of diamond value (carat weight, color, clarity, and cut), they are unlikely to walk into a jewelry store and ask for a diamond by name—unless they want a Hearts on Fire.

Boston-based diamond wholesaler Hearts on Fire, formerly known as Di-Star, has put major marketing power behind its Hearts on Fire brand name diamond. Complete with a logo and marketing plan, the Hearts on Fire diamond is cut with 58 fiery facets and designed to give the extra sparkle that inspired the brand's slogan, "The difference is perfection. It's a difference you can see."

Glenn Rothman, owner of Hearts on Fire, went into the diamond wholesaling business in 1972, but it wasn't until 22 years later that he decided to boost his profit margin by creating a branded diamond backed by a full-fledged marketing campaign. On a business trip to Belgium, he saw the diamonds he wanted to brand, stones that had been perfected and sold in Japan for years under the name Hearts and Arrows. With fewer than one in a million diamonds cut to their level of perfection, these stones looked more brilliant than other diamonds of comparable size. Rothman renamed them Hearts on Fire, brought the diamond cut back to the United States, and began planning a marketing strategy.

At the time, many industry experts were skeptical about marketing diamonds by cut, which they asserted was too subjective a measure, especially considering there was no accepted international grading system for diamond cut. In 1996, however, the American Gem Society, which represents some 1,500 jewelers, opened an independent laboratory to certify the cut. Hearts on Fire received its highest cut grade. That same year, Rothman test marketed Hearts on Fire in 26 markets during the holiday season. First-year sales were promising, and by the end of 1997, diamond shoppers were asking for and purchasing Hearts on Fire diamonds in 200 stores in 42 states and at Harrod's department store in London.

Branded diamonds are not a new concept. The Keepsake Diamonds brand was popular in the 1960s and 1970s, but it died out after the company was sold. Lazare Kaplan International has been promoting and selling its brand since 1986. Marketers at organizations that brand diamonds believe the brand enhances credibility, conveys an exclusive image, and differentiates their diamonds from those sold by high-volume discounters such as Zales and Service Merchandise. "Ideal cut" brands such as Hearts on Fire project an upscale image and bring shoppers into high-end stores. According to Rothman, however, branding a diamond does not guarantee success. Diamond companies also must be good marketers, using marketing tools to build the right brand associations and brand familiarity.

Toward that end, Hearts on Fire has developed a comprehensive marketing program that includes public relations, promotional support, sales training, and incentives. The company's public relations strategy focuses on publicity that maintains the visibility of the Hearts on Fire brand name. Promotional support includes brochures, displays, prepared print ads, posters, counter cards, and special-event and seasonal promotions. With the help of an advertising agency experienced in building high-end consumer brands, the company promotes its brand in targeted radio and television advertising campaigns. Two recent campaigns used the themes "The Difference Is Perfection" and "How to Tell Your Heart's on Fire." These ads, says the company's marketing director, educate consumers and make them more aware of the Hearts on Fire diamond. The firm also provides comprehensive, free training for all its retailers and their employees to enhance their knowledge of and improve their ability to sell the Hearts on Fire brand. Salespeople can earn cash incentives and prizes ranging from hats and T-shirts to diamonds and trips to Asia or Europe.

To make sure customers remember that its brand name diamonds are different from any others they may have considered, Hearts on Fire employs some untraditional marketing tools. The company laser-inscribes a unique identification number on an edge at the middle of each stone. Of course, customers can't see this mark with the naked eye. To overcome that difficulty, Hearts on Fire provides retailers with a "proportion scope" that magnifies stones while filtering out white light. When shoppers gaze at a Hearts on Fire diamond through this mechanism, they see eight perfect hearts and eight arrows, thus assuring them they are purchasing the brand they want. When a buyer leaves the jewelry store with a Hearts on Fire diamond, the jewelry piece is wrapped in a Japanese silk box and comes with a guarantee in a velvet folder.

Asserts one jeweler, "Hearts on Fire is the best diamond program I have ever seen, one that is a role model for all lines of branded diamonds." The program appears to be working. Even though Hearts on Fire diamonds cost about 20 percent more than ordinary diamonds of similar size, the company's sales continue to rise. It now rings up nearly $50 million in annual sales to 400 jewelry retailers around the United States. Rothman is currently creating a flashy retail display to showcase the beauty of his branded diamond—in his words, "giving consumers an experience around the purchase of the brand." The brand has even attracted the attention of the American Museum of Natural History in New York City, which included Hearts on Fire diamonds in its Nature of Diamonds exhibit because they "exemplify the perfecting of the modern day round brilliant cut."[28]

QUESTIONS FOR DISCUSSION

1. Why would a customer have an interest in a branded diamond?
2. Evaluate the phrase "Hearts on Fire" as a brand name.
3. In what ways can Glenn Rothman and his marketers build brand equity for Hearts on Fire diamonds?

Services Marketing

13

O B J E C T I V E S

- To understand the nature and importance of services
- To identify the characteristics of services that differentiate them from goods
- To describe how the characteristics of services influence the development of marketing mixes for services
- To understand the importance of service quality and explain how to deliver exceptional service quality
- To explore the nature of nonprofit marketing

Royal Caribbean's Smooth-Sailing Service

Climb a rock wall, skate across the ice, or putt a few balls without leaving the cruise ship. Forget shuffleboard: Royal Caribbean, based in Miami, Florida, is setting sail with new ships and new services to please younger cruise customers. Nearly 44 million Americans would like to take a cruise vacation, say researchers, but haven't yet set sail because they worry about being bored or inactive during the voyage. In fact, Generation Xers and baby boomers claim they crave new experiences and activities when they travel. These are the kind of vacationers who will enjoy the food, facilities, and service on Royal Caribbean's newest cruise ships: *Explorer of the Seas, Adventure of the Seas,* and *Voyager of the Seas.*

Explorer of the Seas is a giant ocean liner that can carry more than 3,000 passengers. Despite its size, the ship has many cozy corners and unique touches, such as the gas-lit loft disco; the Aquarium Bar, with giant fish tanks; and the Royal Promenade, dotted with European-style cafés and pubs. Its sister ship, the equally large *Voyager of the Seas,* boasts such trail-blazing innovations as a full-size ice skating rink, an in-line skating track, and a climbing wall. *Adventure of the Seas,* launched in 2002, is also a megaliner, with glitzy, upscale restaurants, a state-of-the-art video arcade, a teen disco, and a sports bar.

Although much of the competition among cruise lines focuses on food, facilities, amenities, and destinations, Royal Caribbean knows that the quality of the overall experience is what vacationers will remember. This is why the company created a total guest satisfaction program called Anchored in Excellence. "We wanted a point of responsibility for the door-to-door vacation experience," explains Adam Goldstein, Royal Caribbean's senior vice president. "The job requires us to consider all the elements of the guests' experience, from the moment they walk out the door until the time they get back at the end of the vacation."

Royal Caribbean helps prospective vacationers envision the cruise experience even before they book passage on a ship. Its television commercials, for example, highlight the beautiful scenery and exciting activities of different ports of call. Its website includes written descriptions of 1,500 shore excursions plus brief video snippets of particularly interesting destinations. Customers can also use the website to sign up in advance for shore excursions and indicate a language preference for their tours.

When a cruise is disrupted by mechanical difficulties or other unforeseen problems, Royal Caribbean takes special care of its passengers. Depending on the length of the disruption, passengers may receive onboard credit or a discount on a future cruise. If the entire cruise is canceled at the last minute, passengers receive a full refund plus a free future cruise. Such customer-sensitive policies, coupled with an ever-expanding list of new destinations, new ships, and new services, are helping Royal Caribbean attract younger, first-time passengers as well as older customers who want to set sail again.[1]

Many of the products offered by Royal Caribbean and other cruise lines are services rather than tangible goods. This chapter presents concepts that apply specifically to products that are services. The organizations that market service products include for-profit firms, such as those offering financial, personal, and professional services, and nonprofit organizations, such as educational institutions, churches, charities, and governments.

We begin this chapter with a focus on the growing importance of service industries in our economy. We then address the unique characteristics of services. Next, we deal with the challenges these characteristics pose in developing and managing marketing mixes for services. We then discuss customers' judgment of service quality and the importance of delivering high-quality services. Finally, we define nonprofit marketing and examine the development of nonprofit marketing strategies.

The Nature and Importance of Services

service An intangible product involving a deed, performance, or effort that cannot be physically possessed

All products, whether goods, services, or ideas, are to some extent intangible. A **service** is an intangible product involving a deed, a performance, or an effort that cannot be physically possessed.[2] Services are usually provided through the application of human and/or mechanical efforts directed at people or objects. For example, a service like education involves the efforts of service providers (teachers) directed at people (students), whereas janitorial and interior decorating services direct their efforts at objects. Services can also involve the use of mechanical efforts directed at people (air transportation) or objects (freight transportation). A wide variety of services, such as health care and landscaping, involve both human and mechanical efforts. Although many services entail the use of tangibles like tools and machinery, the primary difference between a service and a good is that a service is dominated by the intangible portion of the total product.

Services as products should not be confused with the related topic of customer services. Customer service involves any human or mechanical activity that adds value to the product.[3] While customer service is a part of the marketing of goods, service marketers also provide customer services. For example, many service companies offer guarantees to their customers in an effort to increase value. Hampton Inns, a national chain of mid-price hotels, gives its guests a free night if they are not 100 percent satisfied with their stay (fewer than .5 percent of Hampton customers ask for a refund). In some cases, a 100 percent satisfaction guarantee or similar service commitment may motivate employees to provide high-quality service, not because failure to do so leads to personal penalties but because they are proud to be part of an organization that is so committed to good service.

The increasing importance of services in the U.S. economy has led many people to call the United States the world's first service economy. Service industries account for more than half of the country's gross domestic product (GDP) and about 80 percent of its nonfarm jobs.[4] More than one-half of new businesses are service businesses, and service employment is expected to continue to grow. These industries have absorbed much of the influx of women and minorities into the work force.

One major catalyst in the growth of consumer services has been long-term economic growth in the United States, which has led to increased interest in financial services, travel, entertainment, and personal care. Lifestyle changes have similarly encouraged expansion of the service sector. In the past 40 years, the number of women in the work force has more than doubled. With a

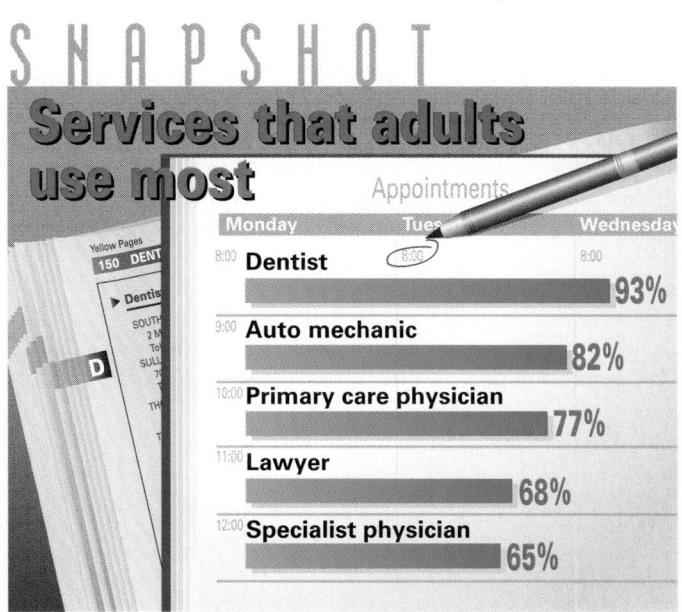

Services that adults use most

Appointments

	Monday	Tuesday	Wednesday
8:00	**Dentist**		

Dentist 93%

Auto mechanic 82%

Primary care physician 77%

Lawyer 68%

Specialist physician 65%

Source: *USA Today*, March 29, 2001, p. 1D. Copyright © 2001 *USA Today*. Reprinted with permission.

high proportion of women now working, the need for child care, domestic services, and other time-saving services has increased. Consumers want to avoid such tasks as meal preparation, house cleaning, yard maintenance, and tax preparation; consequently, franchise operations such as Subway, Merry Maids, ChemLawn, and H&R Block have experienced rapid growth. Also, because Americans have become more fitness and recreation oriented, the demand for exercise and recreational facilities has escalated. In terms of demographics, the U.S. population is growing older, and this change has promoted tremendous expansion of health care services. Finally, the increasing number and complexity of high-tech goods have spurred demand for repair services.

Business services have prospered as well. Business services include repairs and maintenance, consulting, installation, equipment leasing, marketing research, advertising, temporary office personnel, and janitorial services. Expenditures for business services have risen even faster than expenditures for consumer services. A contributing factor has been the recent trend in downsizing among many U.S. companies, which has dramatically raised the demand for temporary office personnel. The growth in business services has been attributed to the increasingly complex, specialized, and competitive business environment.

Characteristics of Services

The issues associated with marketing service products are not exactly the same as those associated with marketing goods. To understand these differences, it is first necessary to understand the distinguishing characteristics of services. Services have six basic characteristics: intangibility, inseparability of production and consumption, perishability, heterogeneity, client-based relationships, and customer contact.[5]

Intangibility

intangibility A service that is not physical and cannot be touched

As already noted, the major characteristic that distinguishes a service from a good is intangibility. **Intangibility** means a service is not physical and therefore cannot be touched. For example, it is impossible to touch the education that students derive from attending classes; the intangible benefit is becoming more knowledgeable. In addition, services cannot be physically possessed. Students obviously cannot physically possess knowledge as they can a stereo or a car.

Figure 13.1 depicts a tangibility continuum from pure goods (tangible) to pure services (intangible). Pure goods, if they exist at all, are rare since practically all marketers of goods also provide customer services. Even a tangible product like sugar must be delivered to the store, priced, and placed on a shelf before a customer can purchase it. Intangible, service-dominant products like education or health care are clearly service products. But what about products near the center of

HOW WORLD TRAVELERS
SURVIVE
SHIPPING AND HANDLING.

FOUR SEASONS
Hotels and Resorts

FIFTY HOTELS, TWENTY-TWO COUNTRIES, ONE PHILOSOPHY.

Inseparability of Production and Consumption
The production and consumption of hotel-related services, such as those provided by Four Seasons Hotels and Resorts, are inseparable. Both production and consumption occur simultaneously.

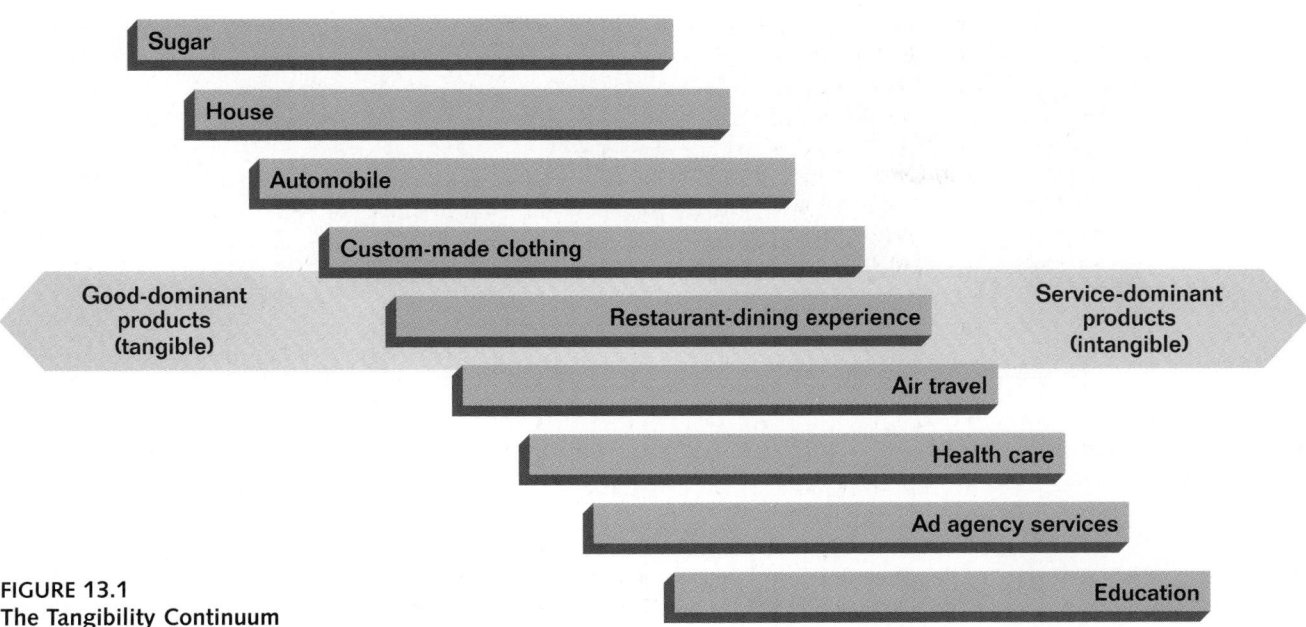

FIGURE 13.1
The Tangibility Continuum

the continuum? Is a restaurant like Chili's a goods marketer or a service marketer? Services like airline flights have something tangible to offer, such as drinks and meals. Knowing where the product lies on the continuum is important in creating marketing strategies for service-dominant products.

Inseparability of Production and Consumption

inseparability Being produced and consumed at the same time

Another important characteristic of services that creates challenges for marketers is **inseparability,** which refers to the fact that the production of a service cannot be separated from its consumption by customers. For example, air passenger service is produced and consumed simultaneously. In other words, services are often produced, sold, and consumed at the same time. In goods marketing, a customer can purchase a good, take it home, and store it until ready to use it. The manufacturer of the good may never see an actual customer. Customers, however, often must be present at the production of a service (such as investment consulting or surgery) and cannot take the service home. Because of inseparability, customers not only want a specific type of service but expect it to be provided in a specific way by a specific individual. For example, the production and consumption of a medical exam occur simultaneously, and the patient knows in advance who the physician is and generally understands how the exam will be done.

Perishability

perishability The inability of unused service capacity to be stored for future use

Services are characterized by **perishability** in that the unused service capacity of one time period cannot be stored for future use. For example, empty seats on an air flight today cannot be stored and sold to passengers at a later date. Other examples of service perishability include unsold basketball tickets, unscheduled dentists' appointment times, and empty hotel rooms. Although some goods, such as meat, milk, and produce, are perishable, goods generally are less perishable than services. If a pair of jeans has been sitting on a department store shelf for a week, someone can still buy them the next day. Goods marketers can handle the supply-demand problem through production scheduling and inventory techniques. Service marketers do not have the same advantage, and they face several hurdles in trying to balance supply and demand. They can, however, plan for demand that fluctuates according to day of the week, time of day, or season.

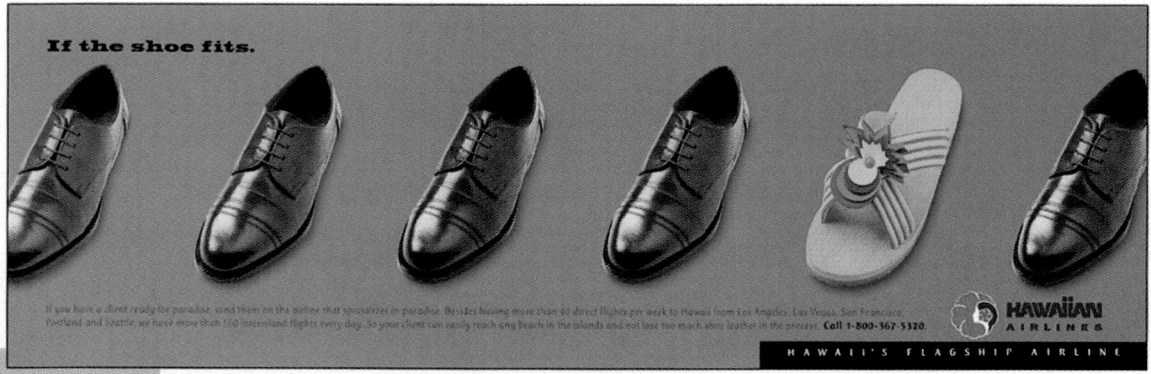

Perishability
The inventories of service providers, such as Hawaiian Airlines, are time sensitive and cannot be stored for later use. Unsold inventory perishes and thus has no value.

heterogeneity Variation in quality

Heterogeneity

Services delivered by people are susceptible to **heterogeneity,** or variation in quality. Quality of manufactured goods is easier to control with standardized procedures, and mistakes are easier to isolate and correct. Because of the nature of human behavior, however, it is very difficult for service providers to maintain a consistent quality of service delivery. This variation in quality can occur from one organization to another, from one service person to another within the same service facility, and from one service facility to another within the same organization. For example, one bank may provide more convenient hours and charge fewer fees than the one next door, or the retail clerks in one bookstore may be more knowledgeable and therefore more helpful than those in another bookstore owned by the same chain. In addition, the service a single employee provides can vary from customer to customer, day to day, or even hour to hour. Although many service problems are one-time events that cannot be predicted or controlled ahead of time, training and establishment of standard procedures can help increase consistency and reliability.

Heterogeneity usually increases as the degree of labor intensiveness increases. Many services, such as auto repair, education, and hairstyling, rely heavily on human labor. Other services, such as telecommunications, health clubs, and public transportation, are more equipment intensive. People-based services are often prone to fluctuations in quality from one time period to the next. For example, the fact that a hairstylist gives a customer a good haircut today does not guarantee that customer a haircut of equal quality from the same hairstylist at a later date or even a later hour. A morning customer may receive a better haircut than an end-of-the-day customer from the same stylist. Equipment-based services, in contrast, suffer from this problem to a lesser degree than people-based services. For instance, automated teller machines have reduced inconsistency in the quality of teller services at banks, and bar code scanning has improved the accuracy of service at the checkout counters in grocery stores.

Client-Based Relationships

client-based relationships
Interactions that result in satisfied customers who use a service repeatedly over time

The success of many services depends on creating and maintaining **client-based relationships,** interactions with customers that result in satisfied customers who use a service repeatedly over time.[6] In fact, some service providers, such as lawyers, accountants, and financial advisers, call their customers *clients* and often develop and maintain close, long-term relationships with them. For such service providers, it is not enough to attract customers. They are successful only to the degree to which they can maintain a group of clients who use their services on an ongoing basis. For example, a doctor may serve a family in his or her area for decades. If the members of this family like the quality of the doctor's services, they are likely to recommend the doctor to other families. If several families repeat this positive word-of-mouth communication, the doctor will likely acquire a long list of satisfied clients before long. This process is the key to creating and maintaining client-based relationships. To ensure that it actually occurs, the service provider must take steps to build trust, demonstrate customer commitment, and satisfy customers so well that they become very loyal to the provider and unlikely to switch to competitors.

Customer Contact

customer contact   The level of interaction between provider and customer needed to deliver the service

Not all services require a high degree of customer contact, but many do. **Customer contact** refers to the level of interaction between the service provider and the customer that is necessary to deliver the service. High-contact services include health care, real estate, and legal and hair care services. Examples of low-contact services are tax preparation, auto repair, and dry cleaning. Note that high-contact services generally involve actions directed toward people, who must be present during production. A hairstylist's customer, for example, must be present during the styling process.

MARKETING CITIZENSHIP

Is It Ethical to Market Sex-Selection Services?

The Genetics & IVF Institute in Fairfax, Virginia, is at the forefront of a new dilemma in marketing citizenship: the ethics of marketing a highly controversial—and largely unregulated—service. The Genetics & IVF Institute holds the exclusive license to market the patented MicroSort method of sex selection for babies. Parents-to-be who sign up for the MicroSort method, invented by the U.S. Department of Agriculture (USDA) for use in breeding livestock, can choose, with a significant degree of success, whether to have a boy or a girl. Since the Genetics & IVF Institute first announced the results of a clinical trial in which 13 out of 14 parents conceived the baby girls they wanted, publicity has generated intense interest and boosted demand for the sex-selection service, which is still in the trial stage.

The institute says it is marketing a "family balancing" service. Ed Fugger, one of the institute's MicroSort specialists, says the service helps parents conceive the children they dream of. He also notes that this method saves parents the financial pressure of continuing to have children until they have the son or daughter they have been waiting for. "It's just a win-win situation for families that want to use this," Fugger comments.

The U.S. market for sex-selection services is estimated at between $200 million and $400 million annually. Couples who use the MicroSort

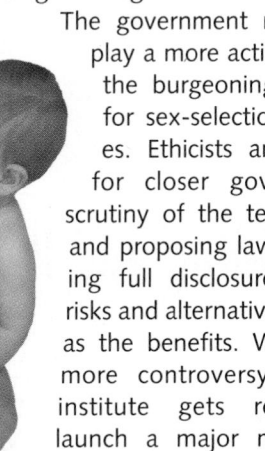

method generally try three times, at $3,200 each, before they conceive or decide to stop trying. Despite the expense, the institute already has a lengthy waiting list and receives more than 250 parent inquiries from all around the world every month. The USDA license doesn't restrict the institute from applying the sex-selection services outside the United States. "Literally we could open a site tomorrow anywhere we wanted," explains Fugger. "We are developing a strategy to provide access to this to patients not only in the U.S. but in many other countries."

Once the trials are complete and the institute can prove MicroSort is safe as well as effective, it will face more decisions about how to ethically market the sex-selection service. What customer groups should be targeted? What types of marketing communications would be most appropriate? What media would agree to carry advertising messages for this service? The government may also play a more active role in the burgeoning market for sex-selection services. Ethicists are calling for closer government scrutiny of the technology and proposing laws requiring full disclosure of the risks and alternatives as well as the benefits. Watch for more controversy as the institute gets ready to launch a major marketing effort in the near future.

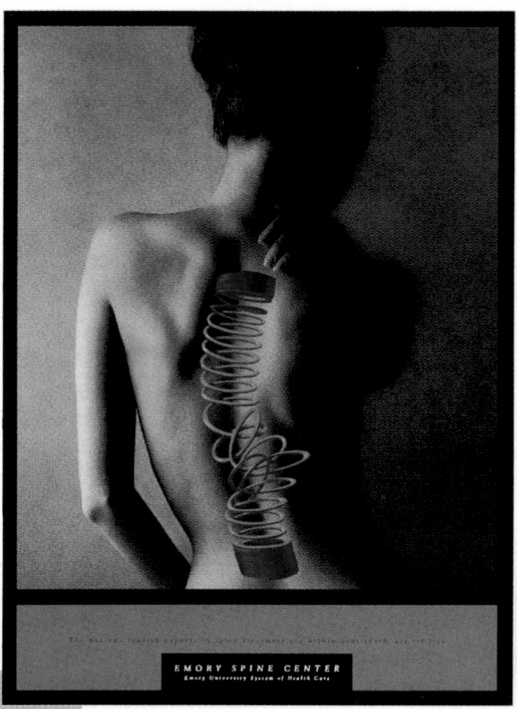

1 inch = four hours stuck in traffic.

Luckily, there's Kinko's Pickup and Delivery Service.

FREE PICKUP AND DELIVERY SERVICE. The way it works is simple: You call us and we drive over to your business and pick up your hard copies or digital files. When your documents are ready, we bring them back. Basically, the only trip you take is to the phone. To find out more, give us a call at 1-800-2-KINKOS.

kinko's
we're doing more:

POSTERS, SIGNS & BANNERS • FULL-COLOR COPIES • VOLUME PRICING • DIGITAL PRINTING • BINDING • TABS
Open 24 hours • www.kinkos.com • America Online Keyword: Kinko's • 1-800-2-KINKOS

Products, services and hours vary by location. See store for details. Minimum order may apply. America Online is a registered trademark of America Online, Inc. Kinko's and we're doing more are proprietary marks of Kinko's Ventures, Inc. and are used by permission. ©2001 Kinko's, Inc. All rights reserved.

Customer Contact
The services provided by Emory Spine Center require high customer contact whereas many of the services provided by Kinko's require very little customer contact.

Because the customer must be present, the process of production may be just as important as its final outcome. Although it is sometimes possible for the service provider to go to the customer, high-contact services typically require that the customer go to the production facility. Thus, the physical appearance of the facility may be a major component of the customer's overall evaluation of the service. While low-contact services do not require the physical presence of the customer during delivery, he or she will likely need to be present to initiate and terminate the service. For example, customers of tax preparation services must bring in all necessary documents but often do not remain during the preparation process.

Employees of high-contact service providers are a very important ingredient in creating satisfied customers. A fundamental precept of customer contact is that satisfied employees lead to satisfied customers. In fact, research indicates that employee satisfaction is the single most important factor in providing high service quality. Thus, to minimize the problems that customer contact can create, service organizations must take steps to understand and meet the needs of employees by adequately training them, empowering them to make more decisions, and rewarding them for customer-oriented behavior.[7] To provide the quality of customer service that has made it the fastest-growing coffee retailer in the world, Starbucks provides extensive employee training. Employees receive about 25 hours of initial training, which includes memorizing recipes and learning the differences among a variety of coffees, proper coffee-making techniques, and many other skills that stress Starbucks' dedication to customer service. Starbucks has 3,500 stores and about 50,000 employees.[8]

Developing and Managing Marketing Mixes for Services

The characteristics of services discussed in the previous section create a number of challenges for service marketers (see Table 13.1). These challenges are especially evident in the development and management of marketing mixes for services. Although such mixes contain the four major marketing mix variables—product, distribution, promotion, and price—the characteristics of services require that marketers consider additional issues.

Table 13.1	Service Characteristics and Marketing Challenges
Service Characteristics	**Resulting Marketing Challenges**
Intangibility	Difficult for customer to evaluate Customer does not take physical possession Difficult to advertise and display Difficult to set and justify prices Service process is usually not protectable by patents
Inseparability of production and consumption	Service provider cannot mass-produce services Customer must participate in production Other consumers affect service outcomes Services are difficult to distribute
Perishability	Services cannot be stored Very difficult to balance supply and demand Unused capacity is lost forever Demand may be very time sensitive
Heterogeneity	Service quality is difficult to control Difficult to standardize service delivery
Client-based relationships	Success depends on satisfying and keeping customers over the long term Generating repeat business is challenging Relationship marketing becomes critical
Customer contact	Service providers are critical to delivery Requires high levels of service employee training and motivation Changing a high-contact service into a low-contact service to achieve lower costs without reducing customer satisfaction

Sources: K. Douglas Hoffman and John E. G. Bateson, *Essentials of Services Marketing* (Ft. Worth, TX: Dryden Press, 1997), pp. 25–38; Valarie A. Zeithaml, A. Parasuraman, and Leonard L. Berry, *Delivering Quality Service: Balancing Customer Perceptions and Expectations* (New York: Free Press, 1990); Leonard L. Berry and A. Parasuraman, *Marketing Services: Competing through Quality* (New York: Free Press, 1991), p. 5.

Development of Services

A service offered by an organization generally is a package, or bundle, of services consisting of a core service and one or more supplementary services. A core service is the basic service experience or commodity that a customer expects to receive. A supplementary service is a supportive one related to the core service and is used to differentiate the service bundle from that of competitors. For example, Hampton Inns provides a room as a core service. Bundled with the room are such supplementary services as free local phone calls, cable television, and a complimentary continental breakfast.

As discussed earlier, heterogeneity results in variability in service quality and makes it difficult to standardize service delivery. However, heterogeneity provides one advantage to service marketers: it allows them to customize their services to match the specific needs of individual customers. Health care is an example of an extremely customized service; the services provided differ from one patient to the next. Such customized services can be expensive for both provider and customer, and some service marketers therefore face a dilemma: how to provide service at an acceptable level of quality in an efficient and economic manner and still satisfy individual customer needs. To cope with this problem, some service marketers offer standardized packages. For example, a lawyer may offer a divorce package at a specified

Car insurance with
no State Farm Agent?
I'm not that brave.

State Farm Customer Janet Babb

Volcanologist Janet Babb will get within inches of red-hot molten lava. But ask her about car insurance without a State Farm Agent, and she'll freely admit, "I wouldn't get within a mile of that." Want to play it safe with your car insurance? Be like Janet, and go with the reliable service and competitive rates you get with a State Farm Agent.

Like a good neighbor, State Farm is there.

State Farm Mutual Automobile Insurance Company (not in NJ) • Home Office: Bloomington, Illinois • statefarm.com™ • AOL Keyword: State Farm

Maintaining a Positive National Image
State Farm Insurance, like a number of other service providers, uses significant levels of advertising to maintain a strong, favorable national image for its brand.

price for an uncontested divorce. When service bundles are standardized, the specific actions and activities of the service provider usually are highly specified. Automobile quick-lube providers frequently offer a service bundle for a single price; the specific actions to be taken are quite detailed about what will be done to a customer's car. Various other equipment-based services are also often standardized into packages. For instance, cable television providers frequently offer several packages, such as "Basic," "Standard," "Premier," and "Hollywood."

The characteristic of intangibility makes it difficult for customers to evaluate a service prior to purchase. A customer who is shopping for a pair of jeans can try them on before buying them, but how does she or he evaluate a haircut before the service is performed? Intangibility requires service marketers like hairstylists to market promises to customers. The customer is forced to place some degree of trust in the service provider to perform the service in a manner that meets or exceeds these promises. Service marketers must guard against making promises that raise customer expectations beyond what they can provide.

To cope with the problem of intangibility, marketers employ tangible cues, such as well-groomed, professional-appearing contact personnel and clean, attractive physical facilities, to help assure customers about the quality of the service. Life insurance companies sometimes try to make the quality of their policies more tangible by putting them on very-high-quality paper and enclosing them in leather sheaths. Since customers often rely on brand names as an indicator of product quality, service marketers at organizations whose names are the same as their service brand names should strive to build a strong national image for their companies. For example, American Express, McDonald's, American Life, and America Online try to maintain strong, positive national company images because these names are the brand names of the services they provide.

The inseparability of production and consumption and the level of customer contact also influence the development and management of services. The fact that customers take part in the production of a service means other customers can affect the outcome of the service. For instance, if a nonsmoker dines in a restaurant without a no-smoking section, the overall quality of service experienced by the nonsmoking customer declines. For this reason, many restaurants have no-smoking sections or prohibit smoking anywhere on their premises. Service marketers can reduce these problems by encouraging customers to share the responsibility of maintaining an environment that allows all participants to receive the intended benefits of the service.

Some of the challenges of service design may be overcome by relying on the behavioral sciences. Using the results of behavioral studies, Richard Chase and Sriram Dasu have identified five major guidelines to consider when designing a service. The first guideline is to segment the pleasure and to combine the pain. For example, when gambling, people prefer to win $5 twice rather than $10 just one time and to lose only one time rather than twice. Cruise lines have picked up on this idea; a look at any cruise's agenda will reveal how the vacation is packed with fun events. Yet, cruise customers pay only one time. The second guideline is to get the bad experiences out of the way as soon as possible. For example, during a doctor's appointment, unpleasant events such as injections should be completed quickly because the patient usually dreads these activities. The third guideline is to build commitment through choice. When a physician allows patients to participate in decisions about their treatments, patients feel like they have some control over their lives and are more likely to come back to the same clinic. Choice seems to ease the pain and discomfort of unpleasant events. The fourth guideline is that the service provider give customers rituals and stick to them. Since people are creatures of habit, they include many rituals in their daily lives. These rituals are especially significant in longer-term professional services; deviation from them can even be considered a sign of failure. Finally, service providers should finish strong. For example, the final evenings of most cruises include lavish meals with extravagant desserts and spectacular shows.[9]

Distribution of Services

Marketers deliver services in a variety of ways. In some instances, customers go to a service provider's facility. For example, most health care, dry cleaning, hair care, and tanning services are delivered at service providers' facilities. Some services are provided at the customer's home or business. Lawn care, air conditioning and heating repair, and carpet cleaning are examples. Some services are delivered primarily at "arm's length," meaning no face-to-face contact occurs between the customer and the service provider. A number of equipment-based services are delivered at arm's length, including telephone, electric, online, and cable television services.

BUILDING CUSTOMER RELATIONSHIPS

USAA's Personalized Service Keeps Customers Loyal

How does a financial services company build a legendary reputation for personalized service without seeing any of its customers in person? For Texas-based USAA, the answer is to use sophisticated technology to better serve its 4.3 million customers, mainly active or retired U.S. military personnel and their families. USAA retains an astounding 98 percent of its customers, and about 5 percent have been customers for 40 years or more. Behind the scenes, USAA encourages this extraordinary loyalty by harnessing technology to help employees understand customer needs and personalize appropriate solutions.

Because it serves customers located in many states and countries, USAA handles most transactions by mail, phone, and the Internet. Its computerized call distribution system routes 50,000 customer calls daily to USAA representatives in different call centers. Every representative can tap into USAA's comprehensive database to examine customer profiles, see which insurance or banking products customers have purchased, look at the history of customer contacts, and enter changes or updates. In addition, USAA's technology is designed to accommodate the special needs of a highly mobile customer base. Military personnel often move on short notice, so the USAA sys-

tem is set up to recalculate customer premiums and fees retroactively. "Very few in the industry will do that," comments Steve Yates, president of USAA Information Technology. "We try to make it easy for them."

Another unique use of technology is USAA's ECHO (Every Contact Has Opportunity) program. Although the company tries to resolve complaints immediately, more complex issues occasionally require special handling. Representatives use the ECHO system to pass on difficult complaints to a dedicated team of employees who work on solving the problems as quickly as possible.

When the company established the USAA.com website to serve customers around the world, it completely overhauled its systems so that any change in a customer's account would be immediately reflected in the centralized database. The company also updates its database by periodically surveying customers about changes in status such as marriage, children, and retirement. Based on these surveys, USAA can tailor its services for each customer's circumstances. For example, if a customer has a college-age child, USAA sends out literature about the wise use of credit cards. Such personalized service demonstrates why USAA has been named a "customer care superstar."

Marketing channels for services are usually short and direct, meaning the producer delivers the service directly to the end user. Some services, however, use intermediaries. For example, travel agents facilitate the delivery of airline services, independent insurance agents participate in the marketing of a variety of insurance policies, and financial planners market investment services. While the brokerage firm E*Trade relies mainly on direct online distribution of its services to customers, it also maintains a consumer financial service center in New York City. In addition, the firm distributes its services through other channels consisting of automated teller machines and customer service centers in Target stores around the United States.[10]

Service marketers are less concerned with warehousing and transportation than are goods marketers. They are, however, very concerned about inventory management, especially balancing supply and demand for services. The service characteristics of inseparability and level of customer contact contribute to the challenges of demand management. In some instances, service marketers use appointments and reservations as approaches for scheduling the delivery of services. Health care providers, attorneys, accountants, auto mechanics, and restaurants often use reservations or appointments to plan and pace the delivery of their services. To increase the supply of a service, marketers use multiple service sites and also increase the number of contact service providers at each site. National and regional eye care and hair care services are examples.

To make delivery more accessible to customers and to increase the supply of a service, as well as reduce labor costs, some service providers have decreased the use of contact personnel and replaced them with equipment. In other words, they have changed a high-contact service into a low-contact one. The banking industry is an example. By installing ATMs, banks have increased production capacity and reduced customer contact. In addition, a number of automated banking services are now available by telephone 24 hours a day. Such services have helped lower costs by reducing the need for customer service representatives. Changing the delivery of services from human to equipment has created some problems, however.

Some customers complain that automated services are less personal. When designing service delivery, marketers must pay attention to the degree of personalization customers desire. The SkiMall website, for example, offers information about winter sports equipment and attractions. Although most online customers browse the site without expecting personalized service, customer service specialists use instant-messenger capabilities to proactively approach customers or immediately respond to customers' questions. Providing for high-contact services at a low-contact site has helped SkiMall triple its business and draw 100,000 visitors every month.[11]

Promotion of Services

The intangibility of services results in several promotion-related challenges to service marketers. Since it may not be possible to depict the actual performance of a service in an advertisement or display it in a store, explaining a service to customers can be a difficult task. Promotion of services typically includes tangible cues that symbolize the service. For example, Trans America uses its pyramid-shaped building to symbolize strength, security, and reliability, important features associated with insurance and other financial services. Similarly, the hands Allstate uses in its ads symbolize personalized service and trustworthy, caring representatives. Although these symbols have nothing to do with the actual services, they make it much easier for customers to understand the intangible attributes associated with insurance services. To make a service more tangible, advertisements for services often show pictures of facilities, equipment, and service personnel. Marketers may also promote their services as a tangible expression of consumers' lifestyles.

Compared with goods marketers, service providers are more likely to promote price, guarantees, performance documentation, availability, and training and certification of contact personnel. When preparing advertisements, service marketers are careful to use concrete, specific language to help make services more tangible in the minds of customers. They are also careful not to promise too much regarding their services so that customer expectations do not rise to unattainable levels.

Through their actions, service contact personnel can be directly or indirectly involved in the personal selling of services. Personal selling is often important because personal influence can help the customer visualize the benefits of a given service.

As noted earlier, intangibility makes experiencing a service prior to purchase difficult, if not impossible. A car can be test-driven, a snack food can be sampled in a supermarket, and a new brand of bar soap can be mailed to customers as a free sample. Some services also can be offered on a trial basis at little or no risk to the customer, but a number of services cannot be sampled before purchase. Promotional programs that encourage trial use of insurance, health care, or auto repair are difficult to design because even after purchase of such services, assessing their quality may require a considerable length of time. For example, an individual may purchase auto insurance from the same provider for ten years before filing a claim, yet the quality of auto insurance coverage is based primarily on how the customer is treated and protected when a claim is made.

Because of the heterogeneity and intangibility of services, word-of-mouth communication is important in service promotion. What other people say about a service provider can have a tremendous impact on whether an individual decides to use that provider. Some service marketers attempt to stimulate positive word-of-mouth communication by asking satisfied customers to tell their friends and associates about the service and may even provide incentives for doing so.

Pricing of Services

Prices for services can be established on several different bases. The prices of pest control services, dry cleaning, carpet cleaning, and a physician's consultation are usually based on the performance of specific tasks. Other service prices are based on time. For example, attorneys, consultants, counselors, piano teachers, and plumbers often charge by the hour or day.

Some services use demand-based pricing. When demand for a service is high, the price also is high; when demand for a service is low, so is the price. The perishability of services means that when demand is low, the unused capacity cannot be stored and is therefore lost forever. Every empty seat on an airline flight or in a movie theater represents lost revenue. Some services are very time sensitive in that a significant number of customers desire the service at a particular time. This point in time is called *peak demand.* A provider of time-sensitive services brings in most of its revenue during peak demand. For an airline, peak demand is usually early and late in the day; for cruise lines, peak demand occurs in the winter for Caribbean cruises and in the summer for Alaskan cruises. Providers of time-sensitive services often use demand-based pricing to manage the problem of balancing supply and demand. They charge top prices during peak demand and lower prices during off-peak demand to encourage more customers to use the service. This is why the price of a matinee movie is often half the price of the same movie shown at night. Major airlines maintain sophisticated databases to help them adjust ticket prices to fill as many seats as possible on every flight. On a single day, each airline makes thousands of fare changes to maximize the use of its seating capacity and thus maximize its revenues. To accomplish this objective, these airlines have to overbook flights and discount fares.

When services are offered to customers in a bundle, marketers must decide whether to offer the services at one price, price them separately, or use a combination of the two methods. For example, some hotels offer a package of services at one price, while others charge separately for the room, phone service, breakfast, and even in-room safes. Some service

Pricing Services
Cell phone service providers, such as Nextel, AT&T Digital, and Sprint PCS, often offer plans consisting of bundles of minutes for specific prices.

providers offer a one-price option for a specific bundle of services and make add-on bundles available at additional charges. For example, a number of cable television companies offer a standard package of channels for one price and offer add-on channel packages for additional charges. Telephone services, such as call waiting and caller ID, are frequently bundled and sold as a package for one price. Procter & Gamble is testing a laundry service under the Juvian brand. Customers can choose the basic package—wash, fold, and return laundry—at a single price and can also opt for additional service bundles, such as aromatherapy treatments, fragrance-free laundering, or color preservation treatments, at an extra charge.[12]

Because of the intangible nature of services, customers rely heavily at times on price as an indicator of quality. If customers perceive the available services in a service category as being similar in quality, and if the quality of such services is difficult to judge even after these services are purchased, customers may seek out the lowest-priced provider. For example, many customers seek auto insurance providers with the lowest rates. If the quality of different service providers is likely to vary, customers may rely heavily on the price-quality association. For example, if you have to have an appendectomy, will you choose the surgeon who charges an average price of $1,500 or the surgeon who will take your appendix out for $399?

For certain types of services, market conditions may limit how much can be charged for a specific service, especially if the services in this category are perceived as generic in nature. For example, the prices charged by a self-serve laundromat are likely to be limited by the going price for laundromat services in a given community. Also, state and local government regulations may reduce price flexibility. The prices charged for auto insurance, utilities, cable television service, and even housing rentals may be significantly controlled by such regulations.

Service Quality

The delivery of high-quality services is one of the most important and most difficult tasks any service organization faces. Because of their characteristics, services are very difficult to evaluate. Hence customers must look closely at service quality when comparing services. **Service quality** is defined as customers' perceptions of how well a service meets or exceeds their expectations.[13] Note that service quality is judged by customers, not by the organization. This distinction is critical because it forces service marketers to examine quality from the customer's viewpoint. For example, a bank may view service quality as having friendly and knowledgeable employees. However, the customers of this bank may be more concerned with waiting time, ATM access, security, and statement accuracy. Thus, it is important for service organizations to determine what customers expect and then develop service products that meet or exceed those expectations.

service quality Customers' perception of how well a service meets or exceeds their expectations

Customer Evaluation of Service Quality

The biggest obstacle for customers in evaluating service quality is the intangible nature of the service. How can customers evaluate something they cannot see, feel, taste, smell, or hear? The evaluation of a good is much easier because all goods possess **search qualities,** tangible attributes such as color, style, size, feel, or fit that can be evaluated prior to purchase. Trying on a new coat and taking a car for a test drive are examples of how customers evaluate search qualities. Services, on the other hand, have very few search qualities; instead, they abound in experience and credence qualities. **Experience qualities,** such as taste, satisfaction, or pleasure, are attributes that can be assessed only during the purchase and consumption of a service.[14] Restaurants and vacations are examples of services high in experience qualities. **Credence qualities** are attributes that customers may be unable to evaluate even after the purchase and consumption of the service. Examples of services high in credence qualities are surgical operations, automobile repairs, consulting, and legal representation. Most consumers lack the knowledge or skills to evaluate the quality of

search qualities Tangible attributes that can be judged before the purchase of a product

experience qualities Attributes assessable only during purchase and consumption of a service

credence qualities Attributes that customers may be unable to evaluate even after purchasing and consuming a service

these types of services. Consequently they must place a great deal of faith in the integrity and competence of the service provider.

Despite the difficulties in evaluating quality, service quality may be the only way customers can choose one service over another. For this reason, service marketers live or die by understanding how consumers judge service quality. Table 13.2 defines five dimensions consumers use when evaluating service quality: tangibles, reliability, responsiveness, assurance, and empathy. Note that all of these dimensions have links to employee performance. Of the five, reliability is the most important in determining customer evaluations of service quality.[15]

Service marketers pay a great deal of attention to the tangibles of service quality. Tangible elements, such as the appearance of facilities and employees, are often the only aspects of a service that can be viewed before purchase and consumption. Therefore, service marketers must ensure that these tangible elements are consistent with the overall image of the service.

Except for the tangibles dimension, the criteria that customers use to judge service quality are intangible. For instance, how does a customer judge reliability? Since dimensions like reliability cannot be examined with the senses, customers must rely on other ways of judging service. One of the most important factors in customer judgments of service quality is service expectations. Service expectations are influenced by past experiences with the service, word-of-mouth communication from other customers, and the service company's own advertising. For example, customers are usually eager to try a new restaurant, especially when friends recommend it. These same

Table 13.2	Dimensions of Service Quality	
Dimension	**Evaluation Criteria**	**Examples**
Tangibles: Physical evidence of the service	Appearance of physical facilities Appearance of service personnel Tools or equipment used to provide the service	A clean and professional-looking doctor's office A clean and neatly attired repairperson The quality of food in a restaurant The equipment used in a medical exam
Reliability: Consistency and dependability in performing the service	Accuracy of billing or recordkeeping Performing services when promised	An accurate bank statement A confirmed hotel reservation An airline flight departing and arriving on time
Responsiveness: Willingness or readiness of employees to provide the service	Returning customer phone calls Providing prompt service Handling urgent requests	A server refilling a customer's cup of tea without being asked An ambulance arriving within 3 minutes
Assurance: Knowledge/competence of employees and ability to convey trust and confidence	Knowledge and skills of employees Company name and reputation Personal characteristics of employees	A highly trained financial adviser A known and respected service provider A doctor's bedside manner
Empathy: Caring and individual attention provided by employees	Listening to customer needs Caring about customers' interests Providing personalized attention	A store employee listening to and trying to understand a customer's complaint A nurse counseling a heart patient

Sources: Adapted from Leonard L. Berry and A. Parasuraman, *Marketing Services: Competing through Quality* (New York: Free Press, 1991); Valarie A. Zeithaml, A. Parasuraman, and Leonard L. Berry, *Delivering Quality Service: Balancing Customer Perceptions and Expectations* (New York: Free Press, 1990); A. Parasuraman, Leonard L. Berry, and Valarie A. Zeithaml, "An Empirical Examination of Relationships in an Extended Service Quality Model," *Marketing Science Institute Working Paper Series,* Report no. 90-122 (Cambridge, MA: Marketing Science Institute, 1990), p. 29.

customers may have also seen advertisements placed by the restaurant. As a result, they have an idea of what to expect when they visit the restaurant for the first time. When they finally dine there, the quality they experience will change the expectations they have for their next visit. That is why providing consistently high service quality is important. If the quality of a restaurant, or of any service, begins to deteriorate, customers will alter their own expectations and change their word-of-mouth communication to others accordingly.

Delivering Exceptional Service Quality

Providing high-quality service on a consistent basis is very difficult. All consumers have experienced examples of poor service: late flight departures and arrivals, inattentive restaurant servers, rude bank employees, long lines. Obviously it is impossible for a service organization to ensure exceptional service quality 100 percent of the time. However, an organization can take many steps to increase the likelihood of providing high-quality service. First, though, the service company must consider the four factors that affect service quality: (1) analysis of customer needs, (2) service quality specifications, (3) employee performance, and (4) management of service expectations (see Figure 13.2).[16]

Analysis of Customer Expectations. Providers need to understand customer expectations when designing a service to meet or exceed those expectations. Only then can they deliver good service. Customers usually have two levels of expectations: desired and acceptable. The desired level of expectations is what the customer really wants. If this level of expectations is provided, the customer will be very satisfied. The acceptable level of expectations is what the customer views as being adequate. The difference between these two levels of expectations is called the customer's *zone of tolerance*.[17]

Service companies sometimes use marketing research, such as surveys and focus groups, to discover customer needs and expectations. For instance, Ritz-Carlton Hotels conducted focus group research to find out the level of service expected by high-tech executives and entrepreneurs, the target audience for its Silicon Valley resort hotel. Based on this analysis, the resort began offering guests around-the-clock tech support as well as high-speed web access, in-room video game consoles, safes to store laptop computers, and cell phone rentals.[18] Other service marketers, especially restaurants, use comment cards on which customers can complain or provide suggestions. Still another approach is to ask employees. Because customer-contact

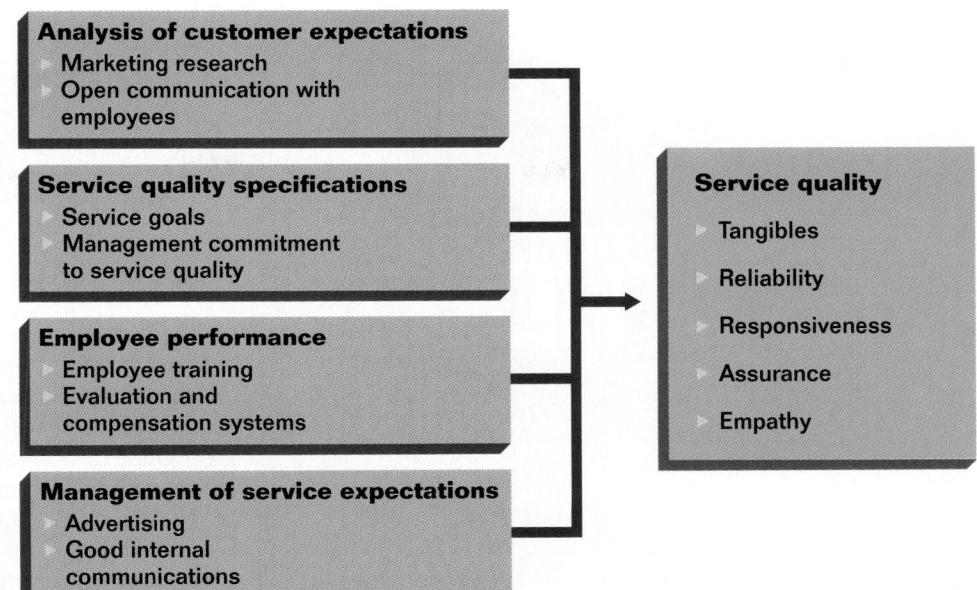

FIGURE 13.2
Service Quality Model

Source: "Service Quality Model," adapted from A. Parasuraman, Leonard L. Berry, and Valarie A. Zeithaml, "An Empirical Examination of Relationships in an Extended Service Quality Model," *Marketing Science Institute Working Paper Series,* Report no. 90-112 (Cambridge, MA: Marketing Science Institute, 1990). Used with permission.

employees interact daily with customers, they are in a good position to know what customers want from the company. Service managers should regularly interact with their employees by asking their opinions on the best way to serve customers.

Service Quality Specifications. Once an organization understands its customers' needs, it must establish goals to help ensure good service delivery. These goals, or service specifications, are typically set in terms of employee or machine performance. For example, a bank may require its employees to conform to a dress code. Likewise, the bank may require that all incoming phone calls be answered by the third ring. Specifications like these can be very important in providing quality service as long as they are tied to the needs expressed by customers.

Perhaps the most critical aspect of service quality specifications is managers' commitment to service quality. Service managers who are committed to quality become role models for all employees in the organization. Such commitment motivates customer-contact employees to comply with service specifications. It is crucial that all managers within the organization embrace this commitment, especially frontline managers, who are much closer to customers than higher-level managers.

Employee Performance. Once an organization sets service quality standards and managers are committed to them, the organization must find ways to ensure that customer-contact employees perform their jobs well. Contact employees in most service industries (bank tellers, flight attendants, servers, sales clerks, etc.) are often the least trained and lowest-paid members of the organization. Service organizations must realize that contact employees are the most important link to the customer, and thus their performance is critical to customer perceptions of service quality. The way to ensure that employees perform well is to train them well so they understand how to do their jobs. Providing information about customers, service specifications, and the organization itself during the training promotes this understanding.

The evaluation and compensation system the organization uses also plays a part in employee performance. Many service employees are evaluated and rewarded on the basis of output measures, such as sales volume (automobile salespeople) or a low error rate (bank tellers). But systems using output measures overlook other major aspects of job performance: friendliness, teamwork, effort, and customer satisfaction. These customer-oriented measures of performance may be a better basis for evaluation and reward. In fact, a number of service marketers use customer satisfaction ratings to determine a portion of service employee compensation.

THE HOSPITALITY TALENT IS
OUT THERE

Find and hire top talent with HotJobs—the smarter solution.

Let a HotJobs Desktop Package deliver hospitality talent to your company, with:

Custom-built packages—**post jobs, search our résumé database, or both**

Refreshable job postings—**change, edit, or update postings at no additional cost**

Versatile searching—**search our database or have résumés e-mailed directly to you**

Easy-to-use tools—**manage the whole process online, even pre-screen applicants**

Extensive access—**thousands of newly-registered hospitality candidates added to our database each month**

We'll tailor our affordable Desktop Packages to fit your recruiting time frames, job volume and budget—so you save money. Call today and discover the smarter recruiting solution.

Call now for a FREE demonstration.
Toll-Free: 1-866-6HOTJOBS (1-866-646-8562)
(mention code P10-N)

© 2001 HotJobs, Ltd. All rights reserved.

hotjobs.com™

ONWARD. UPWARD.

Management of Service Expectations.

Because expectations are so significant in customer evaluations of service quality, service companies recognize they must set realistic expectations about the service they can provide. They can set these expectations through advertising and good internal communication. In their advertisements, service companies make promises about the kind of service they will deliver. As already noted, a service company is forced to make promises because the intangibility of services prevents the organization from showing the benefits in the advertisement. However, the advertiser should not promise more than it can deliver. Doing so may mean disappointed customers.

To deliver on promises made, a company needs to have good internal communication among its departments, especially management, advertising, and store operations. Assume, for example, that a restaurant's radio advertisements guaranteed service within five minutes or the meal would be free. If top management or the advertising department failed to inform store operations about the five-minute guarantee, the restaurant very likely would fail to meet its customers' service expectations. Even though customers might appreciate a free meal, the restaurant would lose some credibility as well as revenue.

As mentioned earlier, word-of-mouth communication from other customers also shapes customer expectations. However, service companies cannot manage this "advertising" directly. The best way to ensure positive word-of-mouth communication is to provide exceptional service quality. It has been estimated that customers tell four times as many people about bad service as they do about good service.

Nonprofit Marketing

nonprofit marketing
Marketing conducted to achieve some goal other than ordinary business goals of profit, market share, or return on investment

Nonprofit marketing includes marketing activities conducted by individuals and organizations to achieve some goal other than ordinary business goals of profit, market share, or return on investment. Nonprofit marketing can be divided into two categories: nonprofit-organization marketing and social marketing. Nonprofit-organization marketing is the use of marketing concepts and techniques by organizations whose goals do not include making profits. Social marketing promotes social causes, such as AIDS research and recycling.

Most of the previously discussed concepts and approaches to service products also apply to nonprofit organizations. Indeed, many nonprofit organizations provide mainly service products. In this section, we examine the concept of nonprofit marketing to determine how it differs from marketing activities in for-profit business organizations. We also explore the marketing objectives of nonprofit organizations and the development of their product strategies.

How Is Nonprofit Marketing Different?

Many nonprofit organizations strive for effective marketing activities. Charitable organizations and supporters of social causes are major nonprofit marketers in this country. Political parties, unions, religious sects, and fraternal organizations also perform marketing activities, yet they are not considered businesses. Whereas the chief beneficiary of a business enterprise is whoever owns or holds stock in it, in theory the only beneficiaries of a nonprofit organization are its clients, its members, or the public at large. The American Museum of Natural History, for example, is a nonprofit service organization.

Nonprofit organizations have greater opportunities for creativity than most for-profit business organizations, but trustees or board members of nonprofit organizations are likely to have trouble judging the performance of the trained professionals they oversee. It is harder for administrators to evaluate the performance of professors or social workers than it is for sales managers to evaluate the performance of salespeople in a for-profit organization.

Another way in which nonprofit marketing differs from for-profit marketing is that nonprofit marketing is sometimes quite controversial. Nonprofit organizations like Greenpeace, the National Rifle Association, and the National Organization for Women spend lavishly on lobbying efforts to persuade Congress, the White House, and even the courts to support their interests, in part because not all of society agrees with their aims. However, marketing as a field of study does not attempt to state what an organization's goals should be or to debate the issue of nonprofit versus for-profit business goals. Marketing tries only to provide a body of knowledge and concepts to help further an organization's goals. Individuals must decide whether they approve or

Nonprofit Organizations That Provide Services
Bethany College and the sponsors of the National Bone Health Campaign (Centers for Disease Control and Prevention, Department of Health and Human Services' Office on Women's Health, and National Osteoporosis Foundation) are nonprofit organizations that provide services.

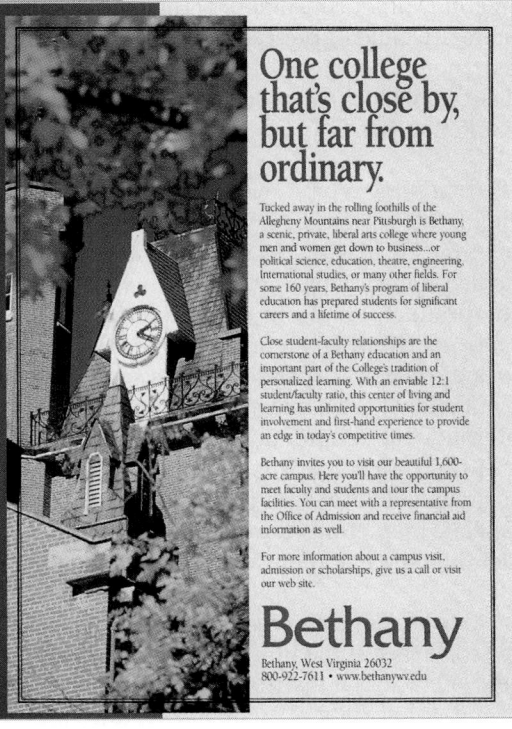

disapprove of a particular organization's goal orientation. Most marketers would agree that profit and consumer satisfaction are appropriate goals for business enterprises, but would probably disagree considerably about the goals of a controversial nonprofit organization.

Nonprofit Marketing Objectives

The basic aim of nonprofit organizations is to obtain a desired response from a target market. The response could be a change in values, a financial contribution, the donation of services, or some other type of exchange. Nonprofit marketing objectives are shaped by the nature of the exchange and the goals of the organization. These objectives should state the rationale for an organization's existence. An organization that defines its marketing objective as providing a product can be left without a purpose if the product becomes obsolete. However, servicing and adapting to the perceived needs and wants of a target public, or market, enhances an organization's chance to survive and achieve its goals.

Developing Nonprofit Marketing Strategies

Nonprofit organizations develop marketing strategies by defining and analyzing a target market and creating and maintaining a total marketing mix that appeals to that market.

target public People interested in or concerned about an organization, a product, or a social cause

Target Markets. We must revise the concept of target markets slightly to apply it to nonprofit organizations. Whereas a business seeks out target groups that are potential purchasers of its product, a nonprofit organization may attempt to serve many diverse groups. For our purposes, a **target public** is a collective of individuals who have an interest in or concern about an organization, a product, or a social cause. The terms *target market* and *target public* are difficult to distinguish for many nonprofit organizations. The target public of the Partnership for a Drug Free America consists of parents, adults, and concerned teenagers. However, the target market for the organization's advertisements consists of potential and current drug users. When an organization is concerned about changing values or obtaining a response from the public, it views the public as a market.[19]

client publics Direct consumers of a product

general publics Indirect consumers of a product

In nonprofit marketing, direct consumers of the product are called **client publics** and indirect consumers are called **general publics.**[20] For example, the client public for a university is its student body, and its general public includes parents, alumni, and trustees. The client public usually receives most of the attention when an organization develops a marketing strategy.

Developing a Marketing Mix. A marketing mix strategy limits alternatives and directs marketing activities toward achieving organizational goals. The strategy should include a blueprint for making decisions about product, distribution, promotion, and price. These decision variables should be blended to serve the target market.

In developing the product, nonprofit organizations usually deal with ideas and services. Problems may evolve when an organization fails to define what it is providing. What product does the Peace Corps provide? Its services include vocational training, health services, nutritional assistance, and community development. It also markets the ideas of international cooperation and the implementation of U.S. foreign policy. The product of the Peace Corps is more difficult to define than the average business product. As indicated in the first part of this chapter, services are intangible and therefore need special marketing efforts. The marketing of ideas and concepts is likewise more abstract than the marketing of tangibles, and much effort is required to present benefits.

Distribution decisions in nonprofit organizations relate to how ideas and services will be made available to clients. If the product is an idea, selecting the right media to communicate the idea will facilitate distribution. By nature, services consist of assistance, convenience, and availability. Availability is thus part of the total service.

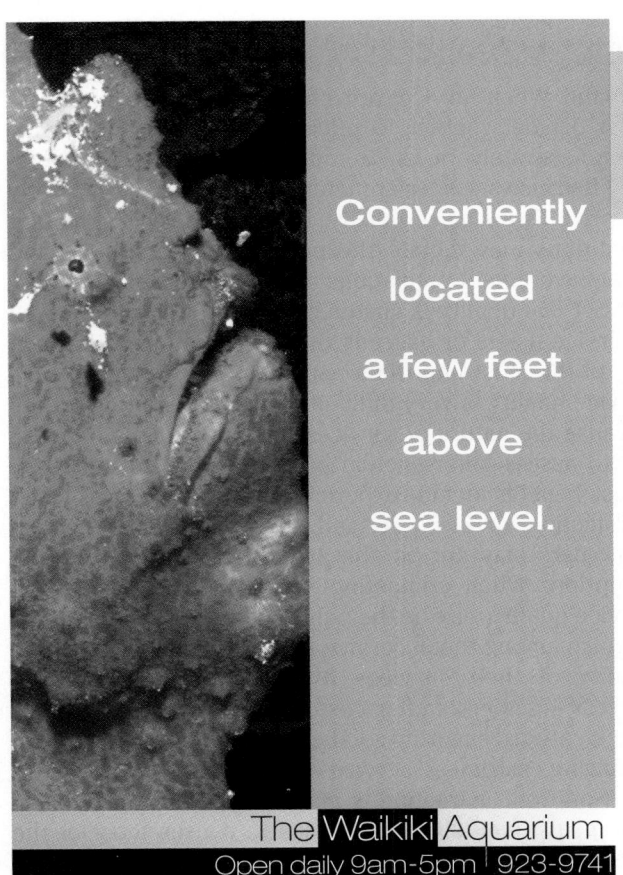

Conveniently located a few feet above sea level.

The Waikiki Aquarium
Open daily 9am-5pm | 923-9741

Promotion of a Nonprofit Organization
The Waikiki Aquarium, like many other nonprofit organizations, employs advertising to raise customer awareness of its services, locations, and prices.

Making a product like health services available calls for knowledge of such retailing concepts as site location analysis.

Developing a channel of distribution to coordinate and facilitate the flow of nonprofit products to clients is a necessary task, but in a nonprofit setting, the traditional concept of the marketing channel may need to be revised. The independent wholesalers available to a business enterprise do not exist in most nonprofit situations. Instead, a very short channel—nonprofit organization to client—is the norm because production and consumption of ideas and services are often simultaneous.

Making promotional decisions may be the first sign that a nonprofit organization is performing marketing activities. Nonprofit organizations use advertising and publicity to communicate with clients and the public. Direct mail remains the primary means of fundraising for social services, such as those provided by the Red Cross and Special Olympics. Many nonprofit organizations also use personal selling, although they may call it by another name. Churches and charities rely on personal selling when they send volunteers to recruit new members or request donations. The U.S. Army uses personal selling when its recruiting officers attempt to persuade men and women to enlist. Special events to obtain funds, communicate ideas, or provide services are also effective promotional activities. Amnesty International, for example, has held worldwide concert tours featuring well-known musical artists to raise funds and increase public awareness of political prisoners around the world.

Although product and promotional techniques may require only slight modification when applied to nonprofit organizations, pricing is generally quite different and the decision making is more complex. The different pricing concepts that the nonprofit organization faces include pricing in user and donor markets. Two types of monetary pricing exist: *fixed* and *variable*. There may be a fixed fee for users, or the price may vary depending on the user's ability to pay. When a donation-seeking organization will accept a contribution of any size, it is using variable pricing.

The broadest definition of price (valuation) must be used to develop nonprofit marketing strategies. Financial price, an exact dollar value, may or may not be charged for a nonprofit product. Economists recognize the giving up of alternatives as a cost.

opportunity cost The value of the benefit given up by choosing one alternative over another

Opportunity cost is the value of the benefit given up by selecting one alternative rather than another. This traditional economic view of price means that if a nonprofit organization can persuade someone to donate time to a cause or to change his or her behavior, the alternatives given up are a cost to (or a price paid by) the individual. Volunteers who answer phones for a university counseling service or a suicide hotline, for example, give up the time they could spend studying or doing other things and the income they might earn from working at a for-profit business organization.

For other nonprofit organizations, financial price is an important part of the marketing mix. Nonprofit organizations today are raising money by increasing the prices of their services or are starting to charge for services if they have not done so before. They are using marketing research to determine what kinds of products people will pay for. Pricing strategies of nonprofit organizations often stress public and client welfare over equalization of costs and revenues. If additional funds are needed to cover costs, the organization may solicit donations, contributions, or grants.

Summary

Services are intangible products involving deeds, performances, or efforts that cannot be physically possessed. They are the result of applying human or mechanical efforts to people or objects. Services are a growing part of the U.S. economy. They have six fundamental characteristics: intangibility, inseparability of production and consumption, perishability, heterogeneity, client-based relationships, and customer contact. Intangibility means that a service cannot be seen, touched, tasted, or smelled. Inseparability refers to the fact that the production of a service cannot be separated from its consumption by customers. Perishability means unused service capacity of one time period cannot be stored for future use. Heterogeneity is variation in service quality. Client-based relationships are interactions with customers that lead to the repeated use of a service over time. Customer contact is the interaction between providers and customers needed to deliver a service.

Core services are the basic service experiences customers expect; supplementary services are those that relate to and support core services. Because of the characteristics of services, service marketers face several challenges in developing and managing marketing mixes. To address the problem of intangibility, marketers use cues that help assure customers about the quality of services. The development and management of service products are also influenced by the service characteristics of inseparability and level of customer contact. Some services require that customers come to the service provider's facility; others are delivered with no face-to-face contact. Marketing channels for services are usually short and direct, but some services do employ intermediaries. Service marketers are less concerned with warehousing and transportation than are goods marketers, but they are very concerned about inventory management and balancing supply and demand for services. Intangibility of services poses several promotion-related challenges. Advertisements with tangible cues that symbolize the service and depict facilities, equipment, and personnel help address these challenges. Service providers are likely to promote price, guarantees, performance documentation, availability, and training and certification of contact personnel. Through their actions, service personnel can be involved directly or indirectly in the personal selling of services.

Intangibility makes it difficult to experience a service before purchasing it. Heterogeneity and intangibility make word-of-mouth communication an important means of promotion. The prices of services are based on task performance, time required, or demand. Perishability creates difficulties in balancing supply and demand because unused capacity cannot be stored. The point in time when a significant number of customers desire a service is called peak demand. Demand-based pricing results in higher prices being charged for services during peak demand. When services are offered in a bundle, marketers must decide whether to offer them at one price, price them separately, or use a combination of the two methods. Because services are intangible, customers may rely on price as a sign of quality. For some services, market conditions may dictate the price; for others, state and local government regulations may limit price flexibility.

Service quality is customers' perception of how well a service meets or exceeds their expectations. Although one of the most important aspects of service marketing, service quality is very difficult for customers to evaluate because the nature of services renders benefits impossible to assess before actual purchase and consumption. These benefits include experience qualities, such as taste, satisfaction, or pleasure, and credence qualities, which customers may not be able to evaluate even after consumption. When competing services are very similar, service quality may be the only way for customers to distinguish among them. Service marketers can increase the quality of their services by following the four-step process of understanding customer needs, setting service specifications, ensuring good employee performance, and managing customers' service expectations.

Nonprofit marketing is marketing aimed at nonbusiness goals, including social causes. It uses most of the same concepts and approaches that apply to business situations. Whereas the chief beneficiary of a business enterprise is whoever owns or holds stock in it, the beneficiary of a nonprofit enterprise should be its clients, its members, or its public at large. The goals of a nonprofit organization reflect its unique philosophy or mission. Some nonprofit organizations have very controversial goals, but many organizations exist to further generally accepted social causes.

The marketing objective of nonprofit organizations is to obtain a desired response from a target market. Developing a nonprofit marketing strategy consists of defining and analyzing a target market and creating and maintaining a marketing mix. In nonprofit marketing, the product is usually an idea or a service. Distribution is aimed at the communication of ideas and the delivery of services. The result is a very short marketing channel. Promotion is very important to nonprofit marketing. Nonprofit organizations use advertising, publicity, and personal selling to communicate with clients and the public. Direct mail remains the primary means of fundraising for social services. Price is more difficult to define in nonprofit marketing because of opportunity costs and the difficulty of quantifying the values exchanged.

Important Terms

Service
Intangibility
Inseparability
Perishability
Heterogeneity
Client-based relationships
Customer contact
Service quality

Search qualities
Experience qualities
Credence qualities
Nonprofit marketing
Target public
Client publics
General publics
Opportunity cost

Discussion and Review Questions

1. How important are services in the U.S. economy?
2. Identify and discuss the major service characteristics.
3. For each marketing mix element, which service characteristics are most likely to have an impact?
4. What is service quality? Why do customers experience difficulty in judging service quality?
5. Identify and discuss the five components of service quality. How do customers evaluate these components?
6. What is the significance of tangibles in service marketing?
7. How do search, experience, and credence qualities affect the way customers view and evaluate services?
8. What steps should a service company take to provide exceptional service quality?
9. How does nonprofit marketing differ from marketing in for-profit organizations?
10. What are the differences among clients, publics, and customers? What is the difference between a target public and a target market?
11. Discuss the development of a marketing strategy for a university. What marketing decisions must be made as the strategy is developed?

Application Questions

1. Imagine you are the owner of a new service business. What is your service? Be creative. What are some of the most important considerations in developing the service, training salespeople, and communicating about your service to potential customers?
2. As discussed in this chapter, the characteristics of services affect the development of marketing mixes for services. Choose a specific service and explain how each marketing mix element could be affected by these service characteristics.
3. In advertising services, a company often must use symbols to represent the offered product. Identify three service organizations you see in outdoor, television, or magazine advertising. What symbols are used to represent their services? What message do the symbols convey to potential customers?
4. Delivering consistently high-quality service is difficult for service marketers. Describe an instance when you received high-quality service and an instance when you experienced low-quality service. What contributed to your perception of high quality? Of low quality?

Internet Exercise & Resources

Visit **www.prideferrell.com** for resources to help you master the material in this chapter, plus materials that will help you expand your marketing knowledge, including: Internet exercise updates, ACE self-tests, hotlinks to companies featured in this chapter, and much more.

Matchmaker.com

The Internet is full of dating sites, but few offer as much information on their members as Matchmaker.com. Matchmaker profiles are gleaned from a survey of some 60 question and essay responses. Check out the site at

www.matchmaker.com

1. Classify Matchmaker.com's product in terms of its position on the service continuum.
2. How does Matchmaker.com enhance customer service and foster better client-based relationships through its Internet marketing efforts?
3. Discuss the degree to which experience and credence qualities exist in the services offered by Matchmaker.com and other "matchmakers."

VIDEO CASE 13.1
Merrill Lynch Direct Logs on to Online Trading

The stylized Merrill Lynch bull, one of the most recognized logos in the financial services industry, has gone digital. Recently launched Merrill Lynch Direct is the bull's answer to online brokerage firms that have revolutionized the buying and selling of investments. Founded in 1914 by bond salesperson Charles Merrill and his partner Edmund Lynch, the firm differentiated itself from the start on the basis of personalized service. Now Merrill Lynch Direct (known as ML Direct) is continuing that tradition by offering services tailored to the needs of do-it-yourself investors.

The ML Direct site offers a comprehensive package of trading, research, and support services. Customers can buy or sell a vast array of stocks, bonds, mutual funds, and other investments with just a few clicks. They can also download mountains of research material from Merrill Lynch's 900 experts or from outside sources. In fact, the ML Direct site features streaming audio and video of company analysts interviewing corporate executives and discussing global economic news, allowing customers to stay abreast of the latest developments in New York, Hong Kong, London,

and other major markets. Soon ML Direct will expand its content to include a broader selection of industry-specific interviews and briefings.

Because customers do not go through live brokers to research their investments or place their trades, ML Direct can charge much lower fees than the full-service side of Merrill Lynch. Online fees start at $29.95 per trade, depending on the quantity and type of security being bought or sold. In contrast, customers of E*Trade and other Internet-only rivals pay even less, but they lack ML Direct's brand strength and research reputation.

Online trading has grown rapidly in recent years and now accounts for nearly 40 percent of all securities transactions. Competition has also become more intense as brokerage firms battle for customers and trading volume. Net-only startups such as E*Trade have staked out the low-price niche. Discount brokers such as Charles Schwab have branched out into web-based trading. Full-service brokers—Merrill Lynch's traditional rivals—have introduced some online services to avoid losing tech-savvy customers.

The ML Direct site is packed with user-friendly features. Visitors can preview the site by taking a virtual tour of its highlights. If they choose, they can sign up for a limited free trial of the company's research reports. Once they open an online account and are ready to trade, customers can even sign up for the initial public offerings of companies that are just issuing stock, a service few online brokers can match. With the ML Direct site up and running all the time, customers can log on at any hour to check their portfolios, look for research reports, or use some of the online calculators to plan their financial future.

Although Merrill Lynch does not disclose exact figures, the marketing budget for ML Direct is far lower than that of top competitors. E*Trade spends more than $500 million annually to promote its services; Charles Schwab spends more than $250 million. Small wonder, then, that ML Direct has a relatively small customer base compared to big-budget rivals. Schwab, for instance, has signed up millions of customers, whereas ML Direct has fewer than 1 million, including the Merrill Lynch full-service customers who use ML Direct when they want to trade without a broker's assistance.

Even with its limited marketing budget, ML Direct has found ways to get its message out to investors. For example, the company recently introduced Merrill Mobile, which allows customers to use wireless handheld computers to obtain securities quotes, news highlights, market data, and other information while on the go. By launching this service at a popular Internet trade show, ML Direct reinforced its online savvy and captured the attention of e-commerce professionals seeking mobile trading capabilities.

Recent changes within Merrill Lynch may alter ML Direct's future direction. The company has laid off 2,000 U.S. brokers and directed the remaining 13,000 brokers to go after customers with $1 million or more in financial assets. Investors with smaller portfolios are being assigned to Merrill call centers. By offering more sophisticated services to wealthier customers, the company is boosting its profit margin. Yet ML Direct is a good way to introduce the Merrill Lynch brand to new investors and younger customers just building their nest eggs.[21]

QUESTIONS FOR DISCUSSION

1. What criteria are ML Direct's customers most likely to use when evaluating service quality?
2. How does the brokerage service ML Direct offers illustrate the inseparability of production and consumption?
3. What elements of perishability must ML Direct take particular care to control? Why?
4. How does Merrill Lynch cope with the issue of intangibility?

CASE 13.2
AARP Uses New Name To Reach Broader Target Market

AARP is the name, and baby boomers are the target of its new marketing efforts. Formerly known as the American Association of Retired Persons, AARP is a membership and advocacy organization for people in the 50-and-over age group. The organization offers group discount programs, consumer education, and other services, in addition to lobbying on behalf of its 34 million members. However, AARP isn't just for retired people anymore, which is why the organization has changed its name and is in the process of completing a major makeover.

The first of 78 million U.S. baby boomers turned 50 years old in 1996, but many are determined to remain youthful regardless of chronological age. One of AARP's challenges is to show this new generation of seniors that its services are relevant and valuable. Fewer than one in three baby boomers join AARP when they first receive its invitation during the year they turn 50, although some join when they are a bit older. So AARP has planned new marketing approaches to appeal to this giant segment.

The decision to give special attention to baby boomers has led to AARP's second challenge: to balance its outreach to 50-year-olds with its commitment to older members. "We have to be very careful that we point out that in trying to reach out more to the boomer generation, we are intensifying our efforts to serve all of our members," observes AARP's executive director.

Before making any changes, AARP conducted extensive marketing research to learn what baby boomers thought of the organization. Data collected in 33 focus groups, two national surveys, and various other studies indicated that "Boomers right now think of AARP as more for their parents," says one AARP official, "but we think we can change this." In fact, when AARP researchers explained the organization's services, potential members responded positively. "So we don't need to reinvent AARP and come up with a bunch of new programs," concludes AARP's executive director. "We have things they value."

With this background, AARP started its makeover by adopting the association's acronym as its name. This softened any negative reaction baby boomers might have to joining a group for "retired persons." Then management launched a $100 million, five-year advertising campaign to position AARP as the organization for active boomers and older seniors, using the tag line "Today's AARP: Your choice. Your voice. Your attitude."

Next, AARP revamped its publications in line with the new target segments. "We realized that there are real challenges in producing a lifestyle magazine that is appropriate for everybody who is age 50 and above," says the director of publications. So AARP split its *Modern Maturity* magazine into two separate editions: one with articles for members ages 56 to 65 and one for members over 65. In addition, the association created a new magazine, *My Generation,* for members under 55—the new boomer target.

AARP is also going out into the community to reach its target market. Its *Modern Maturity* and *My Generation* magazines are sponsoring summertime mall tours featuring dance and yoga exhibitions by seniors, golf games, giveaways, and family entertainment. Few mall events are geared toward the 50-plus segment, so AARP has succeeded in attracting numerous co-sponsors for this annual event. The ten-city promotional tours reach 1 million people every year, spreading the AARP name and building goodwill among members and nonmembers alike.

Bill Novelli, associate executive director for public affairs, says that AARP's long-term marketing objective is to attract half of all Americans age 50 and older as members. Although approximately 47 percent are currently members, achieving the overall goal will not be easy because the senior segment continues to grow quite rapidly: more than 10,000 baby boomers turn 50 every day. Still, AARP is continually finding new ways to reach out to boomers.[22]

QUESTIONS FOR DISCUSSION
1. What dimensions of service quality are being addressed by AARP's new marketing efforts?
2. How is AARP coping with the challenges of marketing an intangible service?
3. What other steps might AARP take to demonstrate reliability, responsiveness, assurance, or empathy?

STRATEGIC CASE 3

Barbie Stays Young and Successful Forever

By the time Barbie celebrated her forty-third birthday, she had long ago claimed the coveted title of most successful toy brand name ever sold. In an industry where last year's hit is this year's loser, Mattel's Barbie sells on and on; to date, more than 1 billion have been sold in 140 countries. Initially dismissed as a passing fad, the glamorous doll has outlasted her critics, selling enough units to circle the earth more than three-and-a-half times if laid head to pointed toe. What is the secret of Mattel's enduring success in this age of high-tech toys? By continually reinventing the product and introducing imaginative brand extensions, Mattel is keeping Barbie forever young—and forever contributing to the company's annual sales of $4.67 billion.

The Birth of Barbie

Founded in 1945 by Harold Matson and Elliot Handler, who combined their names as well as their ideas, Mattel began making toy furniture in a garage workshop in California. Within seven years, Mattel had expanded into burp guns and musical toys, ringing up annual sales of more than $5 million. In 1959, Mattel forever changed the way little girls play with dolls when it introduced a golden-haired doll named after the owner's daughter. The first Barbie sported a ponytail and wore open-toed shoes with her zebra-striped bathing suit, accessorized with sunglasses and earrings. Although buyers at the annual Toy Fair in New York expressed little interest in the Barbie doll, preteen girls of the time certainly did. Along with her extensive, fashionable wardrobe and countless accessories, Barbie was an instant hit. Soon after, Mattel gave the doll a boyfriend, Ken, named for the owner's son. More Barbies and friends followed as the foot-high doll with the improbable figure catapulted Mattel to the top of the toy industry.

A Barbie for Everyone

If Barbie suffers from an "identity crisis," blame Mattel, which has turned out more than 500 variations of the doll over the years. Barbie has dabbled in 75 careers, always stylishly outfitted whether working as a television news reporter, a veterinarian, an astronaut, a doctor, a basketball star, an air force officer, or even a presidential candidate. Indeed, Barbie's fortieth anniversary celebration was promoted with a "Be Anything" campaign, which focused on girls being anything from athletes to computer hackers to dreamers. Barbie has also become a world traveler. Barbies in the Dolls of the World collection represent 45 nationalities, including Jamaican, Japanese, Austrian, and Peruvian. The best-selling Barbie in history remains Totally Hair Barbie, whose tresses stretch from head to toe and turn pink when sprayed.

In her travels Barbie has picked up a string of friends, including Midge, Skipper, Christie, and Share a Smile Becky, who comes with a wheelchair. Some of her friends were modeled after such celebrities as Rosie O'Donnell, Hammer, and Elvis. Barbie also has her own line of dollhouses, sports cars, grocery stores, fast-food restaurants, and motor homes complete with camping equipment and glow-in-the-dark adhesive stars. Customers can even use Barbie Fashion Designer software to print patterns on fabric, cut them out, stitch the seams, and dress their favorite Barbies. With so many dolls and accessories available, F.A.O. Schwarz and other toy stores have created separate Barbie Boutiques to display and sell Barbie products. Mattel also showcases the brand in its own Barbie store in Beverly Hills, California.

Barbie Gets a Makeover, Over and Over

After conquering the hearts of preteen girls in the United States and Western Europe, Barbie went to Asia. Before introducing Barbie in Japan, Mattel made some changes in the all-American doll. Her face was too sophisticated and her makeup too heavy for Japanese tastes, so Barbie received a facelift, acquiring a more wide-eyed, innocent look that appealed to Japanese consumers.

In the late 1990s, Mattel decided Barbie needed more radical plastic surgery to keep up with the latest cultural trends. The biggest change was made to Barbie's exaggerated hourglass figure, which was resculpted into a more naturally proportioned bust, waist, and hip size. This move was applauded by critics who worried that Barbie's original figure contributed to girls' self-image problems. The makeover continued above the neckline, where a closed mouth, less makeup, and softer hair replaced the toothy smile, made-up look, and platinum tresses the doll had sported since her last major makeover in 1977. "In the '80s, Barbie's world was more blond, targeted to glamour and beauty and activities that were right then," says the head of Mattel's Barbie division. "Now she'll have a contemporary look that's more natural and today."

Collectible Barbie

Surprisingly, the fastest-growing segment of the Barbie empire is the adult market for collectibles. Although fans have snapped up vintage Barbies and accessories for years through collectors' networks, only recently did Mattel make a point of targeting adults. Now, in a bid for a piece of the $9.1 billion collectibles market, Mattel has created a series of dolls for collectors, ranging from NASCAR Barbie and Fashion Savvy Barbie to the Hollywood Legends Collection and the Grand Ole Opry Collection.

More upscale are the limited-edition Barbies, such as Fabergé Imperial Elegance Barbie, Presidential Porcelain Barbie, and the Barbie Couture Collection. Evidently they are in great demand. When Bloomingdale's offered limited-edition Donna Karan designer Barbies, its stores sold 30,000 of them in just three weeks. Some of the limited-edition Barbies are even numbered, enhancing their value as collectibles.

Mattel adds several dolls to the Barbie collections every year, giving collectors more choices. Many of the collectibles sport porcelain heads with hand-painted faces and specially designed clothing and accessories. As adaptable as ever, collectible Barbie might be a singing star, sports lover, or motorcycle enthusiast. The Harley-Davidson Barbie, available only at Toys "R" Us, has long, red hair, a helmet, sporty sunglasses, and realistic leatherlike riding gear.

Barbie in the Twenty-First Century

Just as Barbie sports the latest fashions, she keeps up with the latest technology. Barbie's website (www.barbie.com) invites girls to participate in interactive activities such as voting for their favorite Barbie styles and attending special online birthday parties. Mattel also sells Barbie dolls and related software on the site. And, for less than $50, customers can order a customized My Design doll, selecting the face, hairstyle and hair color, eye color, fashions, name, and personality they prefer. Barbie's website draws 1 million visitors every week—and 16 percent of them are male.

As lucrative as the Barbie franchise has been (accounting for 50 percent of the firm's sales), Mattel wants to reduce its dependence on the golden-haired doll. Although Barbie remains its best-known brand, the company also markets Fisher-Price toys; the Disney entertainment lines; Hot Wheels and Matchbox cars; Tyco Toys; Cabbage Patch Kids; and many popular games, including Scrabble. To gain a toehold in catalog retailing, Mattel recently acquired Pleasant Company, which markets the highly successful American Girl line of historical dolls, books, and accessories by mail. The Pleasant Company acquisition will also help Mattel diversify into Barbie magazines, books, videos, and similar spinoffs. The company has also expanded the Barbie name into children's clothing.

After more than 40 years, Barbie's appeal still spans generations. Mattel continues to sell two Barbie dolls every second of the day. According to research studies, 98 percent of American households recognize the Barbie name. A doting 200,000 collectors hold conventions, join clubs, publish Barbie magazines, and exchange ideas on the Internet. What accounts for Barbie's perennial appeal? "It's about fantasy and dreaming," says one Mattel official. Some things never change, not even for the new millennium.

QUESTIONS FOR DISCUSSION

1. What actions have Mattel's marketers taken to extend Barbie's life cycle and maintain the product's success in the marketplace?
2. Describe how Mattel has positioned and differentiated Barbie.
3. Evaluate Barbie's brand equity.
4. In terms of the four categories of consumer products, how would you classify the basic Barbie doll? The My Design doll? Collectible Barbie dolls? What implications do these categories have for marketing the dolls?

Distribution Decisions

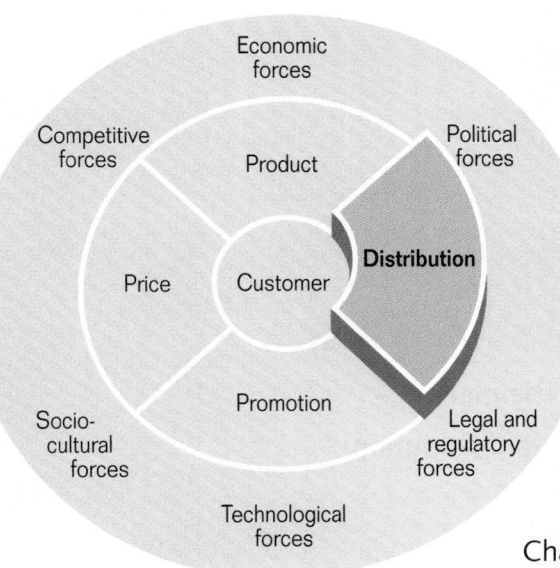

D eveloping products that satisfy customers is important, but it is not enough to guarantee successful marketing strategies. Products must also be available in adequate quantities in accessible locations at the times when customers desire them. Part 4 deals with the distribution of products and the marketing channels and institutions that help to make products available. Chapter 14 discusses the structure and functions of marketing channels and presents an overview of institutions that make up these channels. Chapter 15 analyzes the types of wholesalers and their functions, as well as the decisions and activities associated with the physical distribution of products, such as order processing, materials handling, warehousing, inventory management, and transportation. Chapter 16 focuses on retailing and retailers, including types of retailers, nonstore retailing, franchising, and strategic retailing issues.

14

Marketing Channels and Supply Chain Management

OBJECTIVES

- To describe the nature and functions of marketing channels
- To explain how supply chain management can facilitate distribution for the benefit of all channel members, especially customers
- To identify the types of marketing channels
- To examine the major levels of marketing coverage
- To explore the concepts of leadership, cooperation, and conflict in channel relationships
- To specify how channel integration can improve channel efficiency
- To examine the legal issues affecting channel management

Polo Ralph Lauren Goes Online in Style

Polo Ralph Lauren does everything in style. Its upscale stores showcase the company's tailored fashions, fragrances, gifts, and home furnishings in an elegant, refined atmosphere. The company also markets its luxury products through leading department and specialty stores around the world. So when founder Ralph Lauren and his management team decided to supplement the firm's retail and wholesale channels with a new retail website, they faced the added challenge of translating the company's signature style and well-known brand for the online marketplace.

Lauren's vision involves more than simply posting apparel photos and filling orders at Polo.com. "My goal is not just to have a website," he states. "I want to build a media company—incorporating television, books, movies—and expand our horizons." To make this vision a reality, Lauren formed Ralph Lauren Media in partnership with NBC and two affiliates, NBC Internet and ValueVision International. Building on Lauren's fashion brand and the technical savvy of the NBC affiliates, this joint venture created a distinctive lifestyle environment for Polo.com just as Polo's stores provide a classy and entertaining shopping experience.

"It's not just about clothing, it's about telling stories and creating a gorgeous online store environment that you can literally step into," says David Lauren, Ralph Lauren's son and Polo.com's chief creative officer. Online visitors are treated to views of Polo fashions in luxurious settings with detailed product descriptions and—the special Lauren touch—links to lifestyle trappings such as expensive artworks, vintage accessories, and even high-end vacation hideaways. Other unique features include an online magazine with celebrity interviews, brief audio and video snippets about fashion and entertainment, and an "Ask Ralph" question-and-answer column about fashion.

"Polo has always been about creating worlds and inviting customers to be part of our dream," remarks Ralph Lauren. "We were the first to create multi-page ads that tell a story. We were the first to create stores that enable customers to interact with that lifestyle. Now we're creating another first—Polo.com—a website that allows people to more fully interact and participate in the dreams and the worlds we've created."

Like the Polo stores, Polo.com pampers its customers. Shoppers are treated to free gift wrap and free returns, or they can return products to local Polo stores. Despite all the media content, Polo.com is clearly positioned as a retail site: its toll-free phone number appears on every web page, inviting customers to order by phone if they don't want to order online. So far, Polo.com has not cannibalized sales from other Polo channels. In fact, the company expects the site to generate hundreds of millions of dollars in sales revenues within five years.[1]

distribution The activities that make products available to customers when and where they want to purchase them

Polo Ralph Lauren has achieved success in a competitive industry by choosing to distribute its products through multiple avenues. Such decisions relate to the **distribution** component of the marketing mix, which focuses on the decisions and actions involved in making products available to customers when and where they want to purchase them. Choosing which channels of distribution to use is a major decision in the development of marketing strategies.

In this chapter, we focus on marketing channels. First, we discuss the nature of marketing channels and the need for intermediaries and then analyze the primary functions they perform. Next, we outline the types of marketing channels and explore how marketers determine the appropriate intensity of market coverage for a product. We then consider supply chain management, including behavioral patterns within marketing channels and forms of channel integration. Finally, we look at several legal issues affecting channel management.

The Nature of Marketing Channels

marketing channel A group of individuals and organizations directing products from producers to customers

A **marketing channel** (also called a *channel of distribution* or *distribution channel*) is a group of individuals and organizations that directs the flow of products from producers to customers. The major role of marketing channels is to make products available at the right time at the right place in the right quantities. Providing customer satisfaction should be the driving force behind marketing channel decisions. Buyers' needs and behavior are therefore important concerns of channel members.

marketing intermediary A middleman linking producers to other middlemen or ultimate consumers through contractual arrangements or through the purchase and resale of products

Some marketing channels are direct—from producer straight to customer—but most channels of distribution have marketing intermediaries. A **marketing intermediary** (or *middleman*) links producers to other intermediaries or to ultimate consumers through contractual arrangements or through the purchase and reselling of products. Marketing intermediaries perform the activities described in Table 14.1. Wholesalers and retailers are examples of intermediaries. Wholesalers buy and resell products to other wholesalers, to retailers, and to industrial customers. Retailers purchase products and resell them to ultimate consumers. For example, your local supermarket probably purchased the Tylenol or Advil on its shelves from a wholesaler, which purchased that product, along with other over-the-counter and prescription

Table 14.1	Marketing Channel Activities Performed by Intermediaries
Category of Marketing Activities	**Possible Activities Required**
Marketing information	Analyze sales data and other information in databases and information systems Perform or commission marketing research
Marketing management	Establish strategic plans for developing customer relationships and organizational productivity
Facilitating exchanges	Choose product assortments that match the needs of customers Cooperate with channel members to develop partnerships
Promotion	Set promotional objectives Coordinate advertising, personal selling, sales promotion, publicity, and packaging
Price	Establish pricing policies and terms of sales
Physical distribution	Manage transportation, warehousing, materials handling, inventory control, and communication

drugs, from manufacturers like McNeil Consumer Labs and Whitehall-Robins. Chapters 15 and 16 discuss the functions of wholesalers and retailers in marketing channels in greater detail.

Marketing intermediaries, or channel members, share certain significant characteristics. Each member has different responsibilities within the overall structure of the channel. Mutual profit and success for channel members are attained most readily when channel members cooperate to deliver satisfying products to customers.

Although distribution decisions need not precede other marketing decisions, they are a powerful influence on the rest of the marketing mix. Channel decisions are critical because they determine a product's market presence and buyers' accessibility to the product. For example, because small businesses are more likely to purchase computers from office supply stores like Office Depot or warehouse clubs like Sam's, computer companies may be at a disadvantage without distribution through these outlets. Channel decisions have additional strategic significance because they entail long-term commitments. Thus, it is usually easier to change prices or promotional strategies than to change marketing channels.

Marketing channels serve many functions, including creating utility and facilitating exchange efficiencies. Although some of these functions may be performed by a single channel member, most functions are accomplished through both independent and joint efforts of channel members. When managed effectively, the relationships among channel members can also form supply chains that benefit all members of the channel, including the ultimate consumer.

Marketing Channels Create Utility

Marketing channels create three types of utility: time, place, and possession. *Time utility* is having products available when the customer wants them. *Place utility* is created by making products available in locations where customers wish to purchase them. *Possession utility* means the customer has access to the product to use or to store for future use. Possession utility can occur through ownership or through arrangements that give the customer the right to use the product, such as a lease or rental agreement. Channel members sometimes create from utility by assembling, preparing, or otherwise refining the product to suit individual customer needs.

Marketing Channels Facilitate Exchange Efficiencies

Marketing intermediaries can reduce the costs of exchanges by efficiently performing certain services or functions. Even if producers and buyers are located in the same city, there are costs associated with exchanges. As Figure 14.1 shows, when 4 buyers seek products from 4 producers, 16 transactions are possible. If one intermediary serves both producers and buyers, the number of transactions can be reduced to 8. Intermediaries are specialists in facilitating exchanges. They provide valuable assistance because of their access to and control over important resources used in the proper functioning of marketing channels.

Nevertheless, the press, consumers, public officials, and other marketers freely criticize intermediaries, especially wholesalers. Critics accuse wholesalers of being inefficient and parasitic. Buyers often wish to make the distribution channel as short as possible, assuming the fewer the intermediaries, the lower the price will be. Because suggestions to eliminate them come from both ends of the marketing channel, wholesalers must be careful to perform only those marketing activities that are truly desired. To survive, they must be more efficient and more customer focused than other marketing institutions.

Critics who suggest that eliminating wholesalers would lower customer prices do not recognize that this would not eliminate the need for services that wholesalers provide. Although wholesalers can be eliminated, the functions they perform cannot. Other channel members would have to perform those functions, and customers would still have to pay for them. In addition, all producers would have to deal directly with retailers or customers, meaning every producer would have to keep voluminous

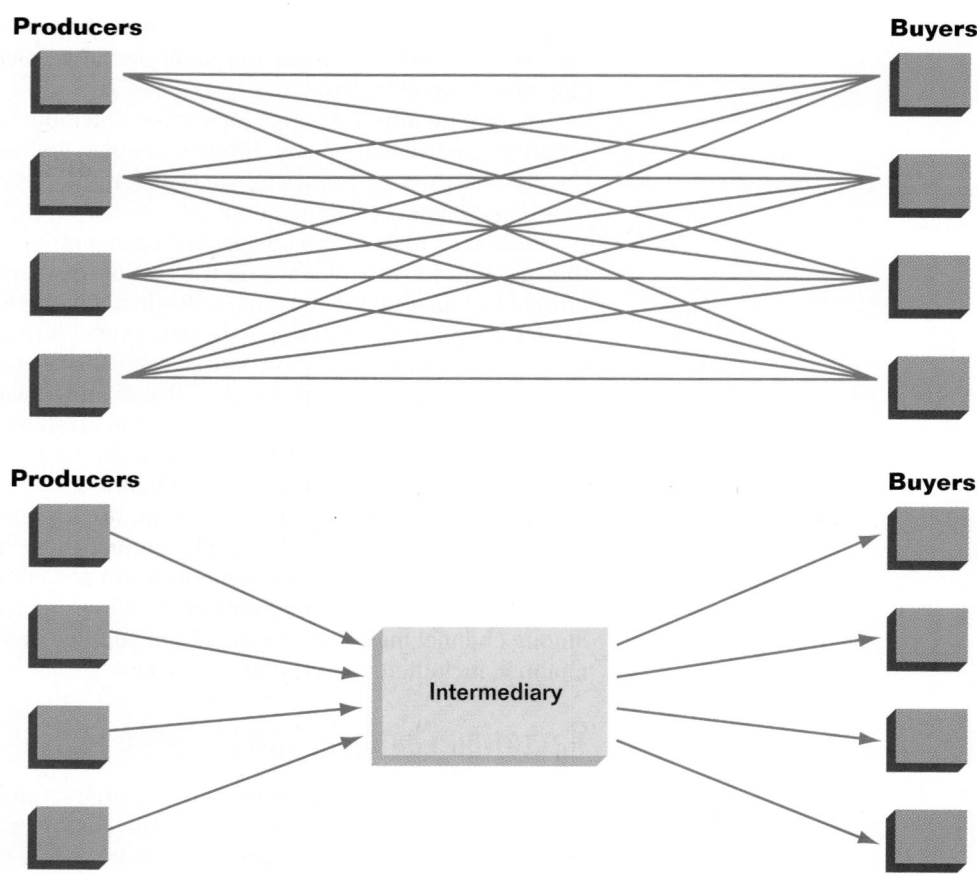

FIGURE 14.1
Efficiency in Exchanges Provided by an Intermediary

records and hire enough personnel to deal with a multitude of customers. Customers might end up paying a great deal more for products because prices would reflect the costs of less efficient channel members.

To illustrate the efficiency of wholesalers' services, assume all wholesalers have been eliminated. Because more than 1.5 million retail stores exist, a widely purchased consumer product—say, candy—would require an extraordinary number of sales contacts, possibly more than a million, to maintain the current level of product exposure. For example, Mars, Inc., would have to deliver candy, purchase and service thousands of vending machines, establish warehouses all over the country, and maintain fleets of trucks. Selling and distribution costs for candy would skyrocket. Instead of a few contacts with food brokers, large retail organizations, and merchant wholesalers, candy manufacturers would have to make thousands of expensive contacts with and shipments to smaller retailers. Such an operation would be highly inefficient, and costs would be passed on to consumers. Candy bars would cost more and be harder to find. Wholesalers are often more efficient and less expensive.

Marketing Channels Form a Supply Chain

An important function of the marketing channel is the joint effort of all channel members to create a supply chain, a total distribution system that serves customers and creates a competitive advantage. **Supply chain management** refers to long-term partnerships among marketing channel members that reduce inefficiencies, costs, and redundancies in the marketing channel and develop innovative approaches to satisfy customers.

Supply chain management involves manufacturing, research, sales, advertising, shipping, and, most of all, cooperation and understanding of tradeoffs throughout the whole channel to achieve the optimal level of efficiency and service. Table 14.2 outlines the key tasks involved in supply chain management. Whereas traditional mar-

supply chain management
Long-term partnerships among marketing channel members that reduce inefficiencies, costs, and redundancies and develop innovative approaches to satisfy customers

Table 14.2	**Key Tasks in Supply Chain Management**
Planning	Organizational and systemwide coordination of marketing channel partnerships to meet customers' product needs
Sourcing	Purchasing of necessary resources, goods, and services from suppliers to support all supply chain members
Facilitating delivery	All activities designed to move the product through the marketing channel to the end user
Relationship building	All marketing activities related to selling, service, and the development of long-term customer relationships

keting channels tend to focus on producers, wholesalers, retailers, and customers, the supply chain is a broader concept that includes facilitating agencies such as shipping companies, communication companies, and other organizations that indirectly take part in marketing exchanges. Thus, the supply chain includes all entities that facilitate product distribution and benefit from cooperative efforts. Toyota, for example, had long relied on a hand-picked group of 213 suppliers to provide low-cost parts and components. Under the pressure of increased global competition, the automaker began encouraging some of its suppliers to work more closely by combining manufacturing operations, attracting more orders to improve economies of scale, and cooperating to create less expensive but high-quality standardized parts.[2]

Supply chain management is helping more firms realize that optimizing supply chain costs through partnerships will improve all members' profits. All parties should focus on cooperating to reduce the costs of all affected channel members. Supply chains start with the customer and require the cooperation of channel members to satisfy customer requirements. When the buyer, the seller, marketing intermediaries, and facilitating agencies work together, the cooperative relationship results in compromise and adjustments that meet customers' needs regarding delivery, scheduling, packaging, or other requirements.

Most companies do not set out to develop a supply chain. Typically they see a need to rework the way they serve their customers. Often they need to increase the

Technology Facilitates Supply Chain Management
Frontstep provides supply chain management tools to assist its customers in improving efficiency and coordination.

quality of a good or service, which results in such goals as reducing the time from production to customer purchase, reducing transportation costs, or lowering information management or administrative costs. Achieving these goals to attain a more competitive position often requires that channel members cooperate and share information as well as accommodate one another's needs.

Technology has dramatically improved the capability of supply chain management on a global basis. The information technology revolution, in particular, has created a virtually seamless distribution process for matching inventory needs to customers' requirements. With integrated information sharing among channel members, costs can be reduced, service can be improved, and value provided to the customer enhanced. For example, one key to Wal-Mart's success is the use of bar code and electronic data interchange (EDI) technology, extending from the firm's suppliers to the warehouse to the customer at the store checkout. Tools like electronic billing, purchase order verification, bar code technology, and image processing integrate needed data into the supply chain and improve overall performance. Intensely competitive industries, such as the telecommunications, computer, apparel, and retail industries, operate the most sophisticated systems of supply chain management.[3] Several companies provide supply chain management software to assist customers in managing sales orders, procurement, warehousing, transportation, and customer service.

Supply chain management should not be considered just a buzzword. Reducing inventory and transportation costs, speeding order cycle times, cutting administrative and handling costs, and improving customer service are all improvements that provide rewards for *all* channel members. The rewards will come as companies determine their positions in the supply chain, identify their partners and their roles, and establish partnerships that focus on customer relationships.

BUILDING CUSTOMER RELATIONSHIPS

Using Supply Chain Management at Barnes & Noble

In the course of operating more than 1,000 stores across the United States plus a popular website featuring 4 million book titles, Barnes & Noble has become expert at supply chain management. The largest U.S. bookstore operator made retailing history when it opened the first category-killer bookstore in the late 1980s. At that time, the store was five times the size of a typical bookstore. Today Barnes & Noble routinely opens massive 100,000-square-foot stores while managing hundreds of smaller mall-based stores, a fast-growing Internet business, and a network of gigantic warehouses. This multipronged distribution strategy has helped the chain boost annual sales to $3.5 billion.

For years, Barnes & Noble managed inventory by having suppliers and wholesalers send book and music orders directly to individual stores. However, as the company opened larger stores, each stocked with up to 200,000 books, it needed a new system to ensure the right items would be available in the right quantities at the right time and in the right place. To accomplish this, Barnes & Noble built three warehouses totaling 1 million square feet to receive and store products until they are shipped to the stores. Once the website came online,

even this huge expanse of warehouse space proved too small to accommodate the amount of merchandise needed to keep up with the surge in sales. Now, after a round of expansion, the warehouses can hold an inventory of 20 million items, ready to go out to Barnes & Noble stores and to web customers in more than 200 countries.

To effectively manage all the intricate details of store and Internet sales, orders, and shipments, Barnes & Noble has forged close relationships with book publishers, wholesalers, and other supply chain partners. Sophisticated Internet-based systems help the retailer capture and communicate customer demand data to improve sales forecasting and help suppliers plan ahead for production. The system also gathers and communicates supplier information about product availability to help Barnes & Noble's buyers plan ahead for ordering. Finally, the system analyzes location-by-location inventory levels to help managers time shipments to stores and customers. "To live up to our promise to the consumer, we want to have everything that's in print available from our facilities," says William F. Duffy, Barnes & Noble's vice president of operations. "The trick is in the appropriate quantities."

Types of Marketing Channels

Because marketing channels appropriate for one product may be less suitable for others, many different distribution paths have been developed. The various marketing channels can be classified generally as channels for consumer products and channels for business products.

Channels for Consumer Products

Figure 14.2 illustrates several channels used in the distribution of consumer products. Channel A depicts the direct movement of goods from producer to consumers. Producers that sell goods directly from their factories to end users are using direct-marketing channels, as are companies that sell their own products over the Internet, such as Dell Computer. In fact, with Internet purchases projected to increase significantly over the next several years, direct channels via the Internet are likely to become important components of many companies' distribution strategies. Although direct-marketing channels are the simplest, they are not necessarily the most effective distribution method. Faced with the strategic choice of going directly to the customer or using intermediaries, a firm must evaluate the benefits to customers of going direct versus the transaction costs involved in using intermediaries.

Channel B, which moves goods from the producer to a retailer and then to customers, is a frequent choice of large retailers, since it allows them to buy in quantity from manufacturers. Retailers like Kmart and Wal-Mart sell clothing, stereos, and many other items purchased directly from producers. New automobiles and new college textbooks are also sold through this type of marketing channel. Primarily nonstore retailers, such as L.L. Bean and J. Crew, also use this type of channel.

A long-standing distribution channel, especially for consumer products, channel C takes goods from the producer to a wholesaler, then to a retailer, and finally to consumers. It is a practical option for producers that sell to hundreds of thousands of customers through thousands of retailers. A single producer finds it hard to do business directly with thousands of retailers. Consider the number of retailers marketing

FIGURE 14.2
Typical Marketing Channels for Consumer Products

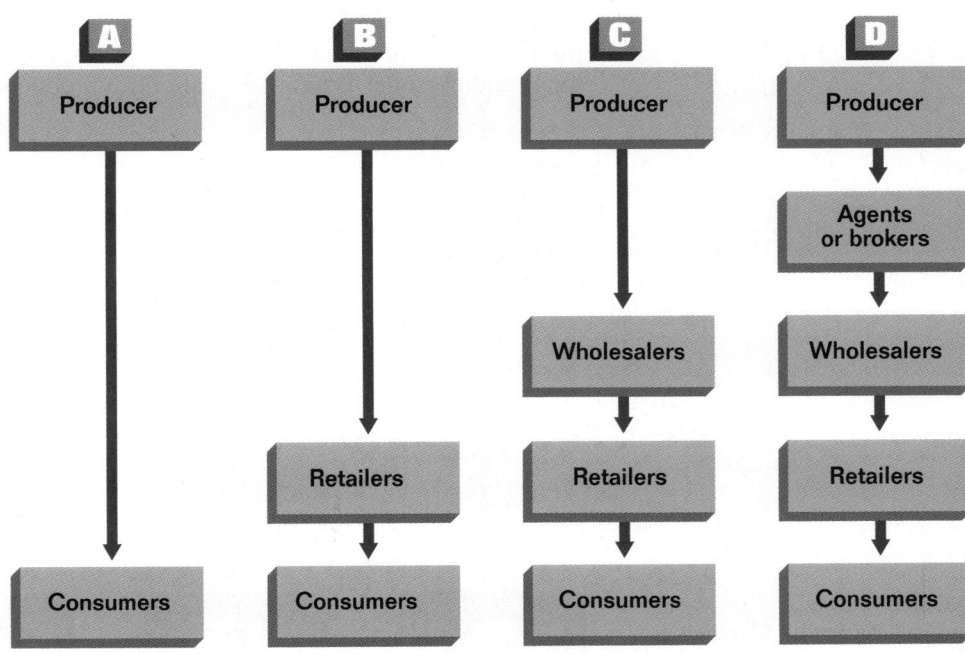

SNAPSHOT

Where books were purchased in 2000

34% Bookstores
24% Book clubs/mail order/ book fairs
9% Mass merchandisers
8% Discount/variety store
6% Internet
5% Warehouse/price clubs
4% Food/drugstores

Source: *USA Today,* April 11, 2001, p. 1D. Copyright © 2001 *USA Today.* Reprinted with permission.

Wrigley's chewing gum. It would be extremely difficult, if not impossible, for Wrigley to deal directly with each retailer that sells its brand of gum. Manufacturers of tobacco products, some home appliances, hardware, and many convenience goods sell their products to wholesalers, which then sell to retailers, which in turn do business with individual consumers.

Channel D, through which goods pass from producer to agents to wholesalers to retailers and then to consumers, is frequently used for products intended for mass distribution, such as processed foods. For example, to place its cracker line in specific retail outlets, a food processor may hire an agent (or a food broker) to sell the crackers to wholesalers. Wholesalers then sell the crackers to supermarkets, vending machine operators, and other retail outlets.

Contrary to popular opinion, a long channel may be the most efficient distribution channel for some consumer goods. When several channel intermediaries perform specialized functions, costs may be lower than when one channel member tries to perform them all.

Channels for Business Products

Figure 14.3 shows four of the most common channels for business products. As with consumer products, manufacturers of business products sometimes work with more than one level of wholesalers.

Channel E illustrates the direct channel for business products. In contrast to consumer goods, more than half of all business products, especially expensive equipment, are sold through direct channels. Handspring initially distributed its Visor handheld computing devices via online and offline electronics retailers, such as Staples, that cater to consumers and small businesses. Once it decided to target buyers in the corporate market, however, Handspring created and trained a sales force to sell direct to corporations.[4] Business customers like to communicate directly with producers, especially when expensive or technically complex products are involved. For this reason, business buyers prefer to purchase expensive and highly complex mainframe computers directly from IBM, Cray, and other mainframe producers. Intel has established direct-marketing channels for selling its microprocessor chips to computer manufacturers. In these circumstances, a customer wants the technical assistance and personal assurances that only a producer can provide.

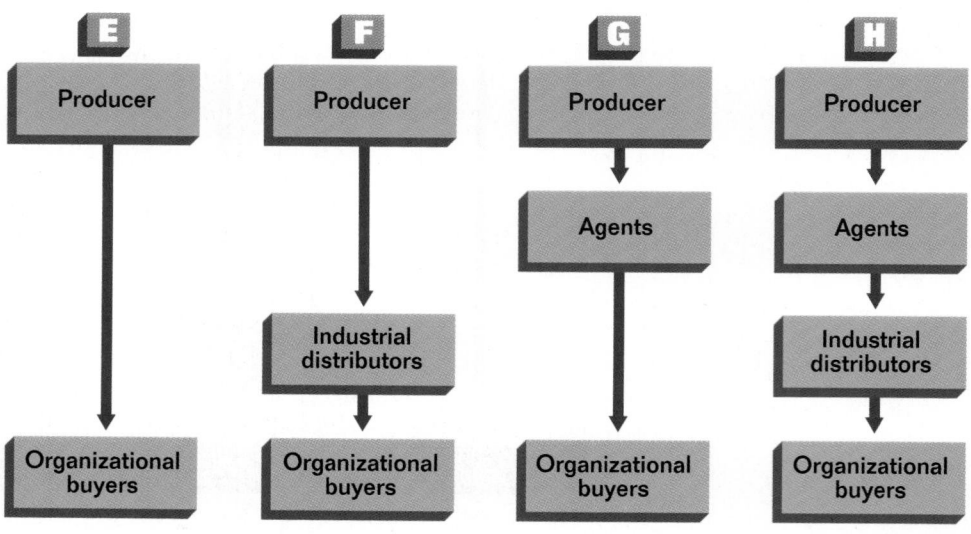

FIGURE 14.3
Typical Marketing Channels for Business Products

In the second business products channel, channel F, an industrial distributor facilitates exchanges between the producer and the customer. An **industrial distributor** is an independent business that takes title to products and carries inventories. Industrial distributors usually sell standardized items such as maintenance supplies, production tools, and small operating equipment. Some industrial distributors carry a wide variety of product lines. Others specialize in one or a small number of lines.

industrial distributor   An independent business that takes title to business products and carries inventories

Industrial distributors are carrying an increasing percentage of business products. Due to mergers and acquisitions, they have become larger and more powerful.[5] Industrial distributors can be most effectively used when a product has broad market appeal, is easily stocked and serviced, is sold in small quantities, and is needed on demand to avoid high losses.

Industrial distributors offer sellers several advantages. They can perform the needed selling activities in local markets at a relatively low cost to a manufacturer and reduce a producer's financial burden by providing customers with credit services. Also, because industrial distributors usually maintain close relationships with their customers, they are aware of local needs and can pass on market information to producers. By holding adequate inventories in their local markets, industrial distributors reduce producers' capital requirements.

Using industrial distributors has several disadvantages, however. Industrial distributors may be difficult to control since they are independent firms. Because they often stock competing brands, a producer cannot depend on them to sell its brand aggressively. Furthermore, since industrial distributors maintain inventories, they incur numerous expenses; consequently they are less likely to handle bulky or slow-selling items or items that need specialized facilities or extraordinary selling efforts. In some cases, industrial distributors lack the technical knowledge necessary to sell and service certain products.

What big distributors really mean when they say you're a big part of their business plan.

The problem with mega-distributors is that they tend to think mega-thoughts: the next stock split, the last quarterly sales chart, that kind of thing. Your design, your pricing and delivery—in fact, everything you need—seems to get wedged in almost as an afterthought. If you'd rather work with a distributor that knows how to put first things first, try Pioneer-Standard Electronics on for size. We're big enough to deliver the best technology, engineering and supply chain services in the business. But we're not too big to know whose plans really count. Get in touch at 800-664-7365 or MyPioneer.com/not2big/one on the web.

pioneer STANDARD   Anything. Anytime. Anywhere.

Industrial Distributor
Pioneer-Standard Electronics is an industrial distributor.

The third channel for business products, channel G, employs a manufacturers' agent, an independent businessperson who sells complementary products of several producers in assigned territories and is compensated through commissions. Unlike an industrial distributor, a manufacturers' agent does not acquire title to the products and usually does not take possession. Acting as a salesperson on behalf of the producers, a manufacturers' agent has little or no latitude in negotiating prices or sales terms.

Using manufacturers' agents can benefit an organizational marketer. These agents usually possess considerable technical and market information and have an established set of customers. For an organizational seller with highly seasonal demand, a manufacturers' agent can be an asset because the seller does not have to support a year-round sales force. The fact that manufacturers' agents are paid on a commission basis may also be an economical alternative for a firm that has highly limited resources and cannot afford a full-time sales force.

Certainly the use of manufacturers' agents is not problem free. Even though straight commissions may be cheaper, the seller may have little control over manufacturers' agents. Because of the compensation method, manufacturers' agents generally want to concentrate on their larger accounts. They are often reluctant to spend time following up sales, putting forth special selling efforts, or providing sellers with market information when such activities reduce the amount of productive selling time. Because they rarely maintain inventories, manufacturers' agents have a limited ability to provide customers with parts or repair services quickly.

Finally, channel H includes both a manufacturers' agent and an industrial distributor. This channel may be appropriate when the producer wishes to cover a large geographic area but maintains no sales force because of highly seasonal demand or because it cannot afford a sales force. This type of channel can also be useful for a business marketer that wants to enter a new geographic market without expanding its existing sales force.

Multiple Marketing Channels and Channel Alliances

dual distribution The use of two or more channels to distribute the same product to the same target market

To reach diverse target markets, manufacturers may use several marketing channels simultaneously, with each channel involving a different group of intermediaries. For example, a manufacturer uses multiple channels when the same product is directed to both consumers and business customers. When Del Monte markets ketchup for household use, it is sold to supermarkets through grocery wholesalers, or, in some cases, directly to retailers, whereas ketchup going to restaurants or institutions follows a different distribution channel. In some instances, a producer may prefer **dual distribution,** the use of two or more marketing channels to distribute the same products to the same target market. An example of dual distribution is a firm that sells products through retail outlets and its own mail-order catalog or website. For

TECH * KNOW

Office Depot Links Multiple Channels

Stores, website, catalogs, Internet kiosks, wireless ordering—Office Depot is using technology to link multiple channels as it markets office supplies to consumers and business customers. The company operates more than 800 stores across North America, selling everything for the office from staples and stationery to paper and printers. Competing against Staples, OfficeMax, and other retail chains, the company maintains its market leadership by constantly expanding into new marketing channels.

The company's fastest-growing channel is its Officedepot.com site, which sells every product available in the stores. In addition, through alliances with Microsoft, Intuit, and other companies, the site offers a wide range of customer-valued online services, such as sales force automation and tax preparation services. Even corporate customers such as Bank of America enjoy the convenience of having employees order supplies directly from Officedepot.com rather than using a cumbersome paper-based ordering system.

Officedepot.com's sales have grown so rapidly that the site was ringing up nearly $1 billion in sales within two years of its launch. The company is now the second-largest Internet retailer in the world, behind Amazon.com, far outdistancing Staples.com and other online rivals. Within a few years, the site is expected to achieve annual sales of $2.5 billion.

The online operation is linked electronically to all the other Office Depot channels, allowing the company to efficiently manage customer relationships, ordering, and inventory across multiple channels. Through the catalog division, Viking Office Products, Office Depot reaches an international customer base of smaller businesses interested in buying discounted office supplies by mail. In addition, it has installed Internet kiosks in its stores so customers can place online orders when they can't find what they want on store shelves. The firm's latest channel, Office Depot Anywhere, allows business customers to order products through wireless handheld Internet access devices.

Is Office Depot's multiple channel strategy simply spreading the same amount of sales over more channels? No, says Monica Luechtefeld, Officedepot.com's chief of e-commerce, citing research indicating that catalog customers who try the online channel actually spend up to one-third more with the company. The bottom line, says Luechtefeld: "Our share of their wallet only increases."

Using Multiple Marketing Channels
Hershey distributes its products through several different marketing channels simultaneously.

example, the upscale cosmetics manufacturer Estée Lauder is diversifying its marketing channels to fuel growth. In addition to selling through department stores, the company is selling through online retailers such as Gloss.com and selling its Aveda, MAC, and Origins products through single-brand cosmetics stores and websites.[6] Gateway sells its computers through a toll-free number, a website, and company-owned retail outlets called Country Stores. Kellogg sells its cereals directly to large retail grocery chains and to food wholesalers that, in turn, sell them to retailers. Dual distribution can cause dissatisfaction among wholesalers and smaller retailers when they must compete with large retail grocery chains that make direct purchases from manufacturers like Kellogg. The practice of dual distribution has been challenged as being anticompetitive. The legal dimensions of dual distribution are discussed later in this chapter.

A **strategic channel alliance** exists when the products of one organization are distributed through the marketing channels of another. The products of the two firms are often similar with respect to target markets or uses, but they are not direct

strategic channel alliance
An agreement whereby the products of one organization are distributed through the marketing channels of another

competitors. For example, a brand of bottled water might be distributed through a marketing channel for soft drinks, or a domestic cereal producer might form a strategic channel alliance with a European food processor. Alliances can provide benefits for both the organization that owns the marketing channel and the company whose brand is being distributed through the channel.

Intensity of Market Coverage

In addition to deciding which marketing channels to use to distribute a product, marketers must determine the intensity of coverage that a product should get, that is, the number and kinds of outlets in which it will be sold. This decision depends on the characteristics of the product and the target market. To achieve the desired intensity of market coverage, distribution must correspond to behavior patterns of buyers. In Chapter 10 we divided consumer products into four categories—convenience products, shopping products, specialty products, and unsought products—according to how consumers make purchases. In considering products for purchase, consumers take into account replacement rate, product adjustment (services), duration of consumption, time required to find the product, and similar factors.[7] These variables directly affect the intensity of market coverage. Three major levels of market coverage are intensive, selective, and exclusive distribution.

Intensive Distribution

intensive distribution   Using all available outlets to distribute a product

Intensive distribution uses all available outlets for distributing a product. Intensive distribution is appropriate for convenience products like bread, chewing gum, soft drinks, and newspapers. Convenience products have a high replacement rate and require almost no service. To meet these demands, intensive distribution is necessary, and multiple channels may be used to sell through all possible outlets. For example, soft drinks, snacks, laundry detergent, and aspirin are available at convenience

Selective Distribution Versus Exclusive Distribution
Brown Cow yogurt, sold primarily in health food stores, is distributed through selective distribution, and HUMMER® automobiles are distributed through exclusive distribution.

stores, service stations, supermarkets, discount stores, and other types of retailers. To consumers, availability means a store is located nearby and minimum time is necessary to search for the product at the store. Sales may have a direct relationship to product availability. The successful sale of such products as bread and milk at service stations or of gasoline at convenience grocery stores illustrates that availability of these products is more important than the nature of the outlet. Producers of consumer packaged items, such as Procter & Gamble, rely on intensive distribution for many of their products (for example, soaps, detergents, food and juice products, and personal care products) because consumers want availability provided quickly.

Selective Distribution

selective distribution
Using only some available outlets to distribute a product

Selective distribution uses only some available outlets in an area to distribute a product. Selective distribution is appropriate for shopping products; durable goods like television sets and stereos usually fall into this category. These products are more expensive than convenience goods, and consumers are willing to spend more time visiting several retail outlets to compare prices, designs, styles, and other features.

Selective distribution is desirable when a special effort, such as customer service from a channel member, is important. Shopping products require differentiation at the point of purchase. To motivate retailers to provide adequate presale service, selective distribution and company-owned stores are often used. Many business products are sold on a selective basis to maintain some control over the distribution process. For example, agricultural herbicides are distributed on a selective basis because dealers must offer services to buyers such as instructions about how to apply herbicides safely or the option of having the dealer apply the herbicide. Evinrude outboard motors are also sold by dealers on a selective basis.

Exclusive Distribution

exclusive distribution Using a single outlet in a fairly large geographic area to distribute a product

Exclusive distribution uses only one outlet in a relatively large geographic area. Exclusive distribution is suitable for products purchased infrequently, consumed over a long period of time, or requiring service or information to fit them to buyers' needs. It is also used for expensive, high-quality products, such as Porsche automobiles. It is not appropriate for convenience products and many shopping products.

Exclusive distribution is often used as an incentive to sellers when only a limited market is available for products. For example, automobiles like the Bentley, made by Rolls-Royce, are sold on an exclusive basis, and Patek Philippe watches, which may sell for $10,000 or more, are available in only a few select locations. A producer using exclusive distribution generally expects dealers to carry a complete inventory, send personnel for sales and service training, participate in promotional programs, and provide excellent customer service. Some products are appropriate for exclusive distribution when first introduced, but as competitors enter the market and the product moves through its life cycle, other types of market coverage and distribution channels often become necessary. A problem that can arise with exclusive distribution (and selective distribution) is that unauthorized resellers acquire and sell products, violating the agreement between a manufacturer and its exclusive authorized dealers. This has been a problem for Rolex, another manufacturer of prestige watches.

Supply Chain Management

To fulfill the potential of effective supply chain management and ensure customer satisfaction, marketing channels require leadership, cooperation, and management of channel conflict. They may also require consolidation of marketing channels through channel integration.

Channel Leadership, Cooperation, and Conflict

Each channel member performs a different role in the system and agrees (implicitly or explicitly) to accept certain rights, responsibilities, rewards, and sanctions for non-conformity. Moreover, each channel member holds certain expectations of other channel members. Retailers, for instance, expect wholesalers to maintain adequate inventories and deliver goods on time. Wholesalers expect retailers to honor payment agreements and keep them informed of inventory needs.

Channel partnerships facilitate effective supply chain management when partners agree on objectives, policies, and procedures for physical distribution efforts associated with the supplier's products. Such partnerships eliminate redundancies and reassign tasks for maximum systemwide efficiency. One of the best-known partnerships is that between Wal-Mart and Procter & Gamble. Procter & Gamble locates some of its staff near Wal-Mart's purchasing department in Bentonville, Arkansas, to establish and maintain the supply chain. Sharing information through a cooperative computer system, Procter & Gamble monitors Wal-Mart's inventory and additional data to determine production and distribution plans for its products. The results are increased efficiency, decreased inventory costs, and greater satisfaction for the customers of both companies.

Net Sights

The Stanford Global Supply Chain Management Forum website (**www.stanford.edu/group/ scforum/Welcome/index.html**) promotes excellence in global supply chain management. It is an example of cooperation between industry and academia to improve the way business is conducted on an international scale.

Wal-Mart believes these efforts provide it with a significant competitive advantage.[8] At this point, many suppliers have been unwilling or unable to make this level of commitment. In this section, we discuss channel member behavior, including leadership, cooperation, and conflict, that marketers must understand to make effective channel decisions.

channel captain The dominant member of a marketing channel or supply chain

channel power The ability of one channel member to influence another member's goal achievement

Channel Leadership. Many marketing channel decisions are determined by consensus. Producers and intermediaries coordinate efforts for mutual benefit. Some marketing channels, however, are organized and controlled by a single leader, or **channel captain** (also called *channel leader*). The channel captain may be a producer, wholesaler, or retailer. Channel captains may establish channel policies and coordinate development of the marketing mix. Wal-Mart, for example, dominates the supply chain for its retail stores by virtue of the magnitude of its resources (especially information management) and strong, nationwide customer base. To become a captain, a channel member must want to influence overall channel performance. To attain desired objectives, the captain must possess **channel power,** the ability to influence another channel member's goal achievement. The member that becomes the channel captain will accept the responsibilities and exercise the power associated with this role.

When a manufacturer's large-scale production efficiency demands increasing sales volume, the manufacturer may exercise power by giving channel members financing, business advice, ordering assistance, advertising, sales and service training, and support materials. For example, U.S. automakers provide these services to retail automobile dealerships. However, these manufacturers also place numerous requirements on their retail dealerships with respect to sales volume, sales and service training, and customer satisfaction.

As already noted, retailers may also function as channel captains. With the rise in power of national chain stores and private brand merchandise, many large retailers such as Wal-Mart are doing so. Small retailers, too, may assume leadership roles when they gain strong customer loyalty in local or regional markets. These retailers control many brands and sometimes replace uncooperative producers. Increasingly, leading retailers are concentrating their buying power with fewer suppliers and, in the process, improving their marketing effectiveness and efficiency. Single-source supply relationships are often successful, whereas multiple-source supply relationships based on price competition are decreasing. Long-term commitments enable retailers to place smaller and more frequent orders as needed rather than waiting for large volume discounts or placing huge orders early in the season and assuming the risks associated with carrying a larger inventory.

Wholesalers assume channel leadership roles as well, although they were more powerful decades ago, when many manufacturers and retailers were smaller, underfinanced, and widely scattered. Today wholesaler leaders may form voluntary chains with several retailers, which they supply with bulk buying or management services; these chains may also market their own brands. In return, the retailers shift most of their purchasing to the wholesaler leader. The Independent Grocers' Alliance (IGA) is one of the best-known wholesaler leaders in the United States. IGA's power is based on its expertise in advertising, pricing, and purchasing knowledge that it makes available to independent business owners. Other wholesaler leaders help retailers with store layouts, accounting, and inventory control.

Channel Leadership
Automobile manufacturers such as General Motors, maker of the Chevy Tahoe Z71, provide channel leadership in the marketing channels for their brands of new cars.

Channel Cooperation.   Channel cooperation is vital if each member is to gain something from other members. By cooperating, retailers, wholesalers, and suppliers can speed up inventory replenishment, improve customer service, and cut the costs of bringing products to the consumer.[9] Without cooperation, neither overall channel goals nor member goals can be realized. All channel members must recognize and understand that the success of one firm in the channel depends, in part, on other member firms. Thus, marketing channel members should make a coordinated effort to satisfy market requirements. Channel cooperation leads to greater trust among channel members and improves the overall functioning of the channel. It also leads to more satisfying relationships among channel members.

There are several ways to improve channel cooperation. If a marketing channel is viewed as a unified supply chain competing with other systems, individual members will be less likely to take actions that create disadvantages for other members. Similarly, channel members should agree to direct efforts toward common objectives so channel roles can be structured for maximum marketing effectiveness, which in turn can help members achieve individual objectives. Heineken, for example, was having difficulty with its 450 distributors; at one point, the time between order and delivery reached 12 weeks. A cooperative system of supply chain management, with Internet-based communications, decreased the lead time from order to delivery to four weeks, and Heineken's sales increased 24 percent.[10] A critical component in cooperation is a precise definition of each channel member's tasks. This provides a basis for reviewing the intermediaries' performance and helps reduce conflicts because each channel member knows exactly what is expected of it.

Channel Conflict.   Although all channel members work toward the same general goal—distributing products profitably and efficiently—members may sometimes disagree about the best methods for attaining this goal. However, if self-interest creates misunderstanding about role expectations, the end result is frustration and conflict for the whole channel. For individual organizations to function together, each channel member must clearly communicate and understand role expectations. Communication difficulties are a potential form of channel conflict because ineffective communication leads to frustration, misunderstandings, and ill-coordinated strategies, jeopardizing further coordination.

The increased use of multiple channels of distribution, driven partly by new technology, has increased the potential for conflict between manufacturers and intermediaries. For example, Hewlett-Packard makes products available directly to consumers through its website (www.hewlett-packard.com), thereby directly competing with existing distributors and retailers.[11] Channel conflicts also arise when intermediaries overemphasize competing products or diversify into product lines traditionally handled by other intermediaries. Sometimes conflict develops because producers strive to increase efficiency by circumventing intermediaries. Such conflict is occurring in marketing channels for computer software. A number of software-only stores are establishing direct relationships with software producers, bypassing wholesale distributors altogether.

When a producer that traditionally used franchised dealers broadens its retailer base to include other types of retail outlets, considerable conflict can arise. When Goodyear intensified its market coverage by allowing Sears and Discount Tire to market Goodyear tires, 2,500 independent Goodyear dealers became very angry.

Although there is no single method for resolving conflict, partnerships can be reestablished if two conditions are met. First, the role of each channel member must be specified. To minimize misunderstanding, all members must be able to expect unambiguous, agreed-on performance levels from one another. Second, members of channel partnerships must institute certain measures of channel coordination, which requires leadership and benevolent exercise of control. To prevent channel conflict from arising, producers or other channel members may provide competing resellers with different brands, allocate markets among resellers, define policies for direct sales to avoid potential conflict over large accounts, negotiate territorial issues among regional distributors, and provide recognition to certain resellers for their importance in distributing to others.

Channel Integration

Channel members can either combine and control most activities or pass them on to another channel member. Channel functions may be transferred between intermediaries and to producers and even customers. However, a channel member cannot eliminate functions; unless buyers themselves perform the functions, they must pay for the labor and resources needed to perform the functions.

Various channel stages may be combined under the management of a channel captain either horizontally or vertically. Such integration may stabilize supply, reduce costs, and increase coordination of channel members.

vertical channel integration
Combining two or more stages of the marketing channel under one management

Vertical Channel Integration.   **Vertical channel integration** combines two or more stages of the channel under one management. This may occur when one member of a marketing channel purchases the operations of another member or simply performs the functions of another member, eliminating the need for that intermediary.

Whereas members of conventional channel systems work independently, participants in vertical channel integration coordinate efforts to reach a desired target market. In this more progressive approach to distribution, channel members regard other members as extensions of their own operations. Vertically integrated channels are often more effective against competition because of increased bargaining power and the sharing of information and responsibilities. At one end of a vertically integrated channel, a manufacturer might provide advertising and training assistance, and the retailer at the other end might buy the manufacturer's products in large quantities and actively promote them.

vertical marketing system (VMS)   A marketing channel managed by a single channel member

Integration has been successfully institutionalized in marketing channels called **vertical marketing systems (VMSs),** in which a single channel member coordinates or manages channel activities to achieve efficient, low-cost distribution aimed at satisfying target market customers. Vertical integration brings most or all stages of the marketing channel under common control or ownership. The Limited, a retail clothing chain, uses a wholly owned subsidiary, Mast Industries, as its primary supply source. Radio Shack operates as a vertical marketing system, encompassing both wholesale and retail functions. Because efforts of individual channel members are combined in a VMS, marketing activities can be coordinated for maximum effectiveness and economy, without duplication of services. Vertical marketing systems are competitive, accounting for a share of retail sales in consumer goods.

Most vertical marketing systems take one of three forms: corporate, administered, or contractual. A *corporate VMS* combines all stages of the marketing channel, from producers to consumers, under a single owner. For example, The Limited established a corporate VMS that operates corporate-owned production facilities and retail stores. Supermarket chains that own food-processing plants and large retailers that purchase wholesaling and production facilities are other examples of corporate VMSs.

In an *administered VMS*, channel members are independent but a high level of interorganizational management is achieved through informal coordination. Members of an administered VMS may, for example, adopt uniform accounting and ordering procedures and cooperate in promotional activities for the benefit of all partners. Although individual channel members maintain autonomy, as in conventional marketing channels, one channel member (such as a producer or large retailer) dominates the administered VMS so that distribution decisions take the whole system into account. Because of its size and power, Intel exercises a strong influence over distributors and manufacturers in its marketing channels, as do Kellogg (cereal) and Magnavox (television and other electronic products).

Under a *contractual VMS,* the most popular type of vertical marketing system, channel members are linked by legal agreements spelling out each member's rights and obligations. Franchise organizations, such as McDonald's and KFC, are contractual VMSs. Other contractual VMSs include wholesaler-sponsored groups, such as IGA (Independent Grocers' Alliance) stores, in which independent retailers band together under the contractual leadership of a wholesaler. Retailer-sponsored cooperatives, which own and operate their own wholesalers, are a third type of contractual VMS.

horizontal channel integration
Combining organizations at the same level of operation under one management

Horizontal Channel Integration.   Combining organizations at the same level of operation under one management constitutes **horizontal channel integration.** An organization may integrate horizontally by merging with other organizations at the same level in the marketing channel. The owner of a dry cleaning firm, for example, might buy and combine several other existing dry cleaning establishments. Horizontal integration may enable a firm to generate sufficient sales revenue to integrate vertically as well.

Although horizontal integration permits efficiencies and economies of scale in purchasing, marketing research, advertising, and specialized personnel, it is not always the most effective method of improving distribution. Problems of size often follow, resulting in decreased flexibility, difficulties in coordination, and the need for additional marketing research and large-scale planning. Unless distribution functions for the various units can be performed more efficiently under unified management than under the previously separate managements, horizontal integration will neither reduce costs nor improve the competitive position of the integrating firm.

Legal Issues in Channel Management

The multitude of federal, state, and local laws governing channel management are based on the general principle that the public is best served by protecting competition and free trade. Under the authority of such federal legislation as the Sherman Antitrust Act and the Federal Trade Commission Act, courts and regulatory agencies determine under what circumstances channel management practices violate this underlying principle and must be restricted. Although channel managers are not expected to be legal experts, they should be aware that attempts to control distribution functions may have legal repercussions. The following practices are among those frequently subject to legal restraint.

Legal Issues
In this notice, Street Flyers states that it is the exclusive distributor in the United States and Canada for Sneaker Skates. This company states its intention to enforce its exclusive distribution agreement.

Dual Distribution

Earlier we said that some companies may use dual distribution by utilizing two or more marketing channels to distribute the same products to the same target market. Compaq, for example, sells computers directly to consumers through a toll-free telephone line and a website, as well as through electronics retailers such as Best Buy. Courts do not consider this practice illegal when it promotes competition. A manufacturer can also legally open its own retail outlets. But the courts view as a threat to competition a manufacturer that uses company-owned outlets to dominate or drive out of business independent retailers or distributors that handle its products. In such cases, dual distribution violates the law. To avoid this interpretation, producers should use outlet prices that do not severely undercut independent retailers' prices.

Restricted Sales Territories

To tighten control over distribution of its products, a manufacturer may try to prohibit intermediaries from selling its products outside designated sales territories. Intermediaries themselves often favor this practice because it gives them exclusive territories, allowing them to avoid competition for the producer's brands within these territories. In recent years, the courts have adopted conflicting positions in regard to restricted sales territories. Although the courts have deemed restricted sales territories a restraint of trade among intermediaries handling the same brands (except for small or newly established companies), they have also held that exclusive territories can actually promote competition among dealers handling different brands. At present, the producer's intent in establishing restricted territories and the overall effect of doing so on the market must be evaluated for each individual case.

Tying Agreements

tying agreement An agreement requiring a channel member to buy other products from a supplier besides the one it wants

When a supplier (usually a manufacturer or franchiser) furnishes a product to a channel member with the stipulation that the channel member must purchase other products as well, a **tying agreement** exists. Suppliers may institute tying arrangements to move weaker products along with more popular items, or a franchiser may tie purchase of equipment and supplies to the sale of franchises, justifying the policy as necessary for quality control and protection of the franchiser's reputation.

A related practice is *full-line forcing*, in which a supplier requires that channel members purchase the supplier's entire line to obtain any of the supplier's products. Manufacturers sometimes use full-line forcing to ensure that intermediaries accept new products and that a suitable range of products is available to customers.

The courts accept tying agreements when the supplier alone can provide products of a certain quality, when the intermediary is free to carry competing products as well, and when a company has just entered the market. Most other tying agreements are considered illegal.

Exclusive Dealing

exclusive dealing Forbidding an intermediary to carry products of a competing manufacturer

When a manufacturer forbids an intermediary to carry products of competing manufacturers, the arrangement is called **exclusive dealing.** Manufacturers receive considerable market protection in an exclusive-dealing arrangement and may cut off shipments to intermediaries who violate the agreement.

The legality of an exclusive-dealing contract is generally determined by applying three tests. If the exclusive dealing blocks competitors from as much as 10 percent of the market, if the sales revenue involved is sizable, and if the manufacturer is much larger (and thus more intimidating) than the dealer, the arrangement is considered anticompetitive.[12] If dealers and customers in a given market have access to similar products or if the exclusive-dealing contract strengthens an otherwise weak competitor, the arrangement is allowed.

Refusal to Deal

For more than 75 years, the courts have held that producers have the right to choose channel members with which they will do business (and the right to reject others). Within existing distribution channels, however, suppliers may not legally refuse to deal with wholesalers or dealers just because these wholesalers or dealers resist policies that are anticompetitive or in restraint of trade. Suppliers are further prohibited from organizing some channel members in refusal-to-deal actions against other members that choose not to comply with illegal policies.

Summary

A marketing channel, or channel of distribution, is a group of individuals and organizations that directs the flow of products from producers to customers. The major role of marketing channels is to make products available at the right time at the right place, and in the right amounts. In most channels of distribution, producers and consumers are linked by marketing intermediaries, or middlemen. Of the two major types of intermediaries, retailers purchase products and resell them to ultimate consumers, and wholesalers buy and resell products to other wholesalers, retailers, and business customers.

Marketing channels serve many functions. They create time, place, and possession utility by making products available when and where customers want them and providing customers with access to product use through sale or rental. Marketing intermediaries facilitate exchange efficiencies, often reducing the costs of exchanges by performing certain services and functions. Although critics suggest eliminating wholesalers, someone must perform their functions in the marketing channel. Because intermediaries serve both producers and buyers, they reduce the total number of transactions that otherwise would be needed to move products from producer to ultimate users.

Marketing channels also form a supply chain, a total distribution system that serves customers and creates a competitive advantage. Supply chain management refers to long-term partnerships among channel members working together to reduce inefficiencies, costs, and redundancies and to develop innovative approaches to satisfy customers. The supply chain includes all entities—shippers and other firms that facilitate distribution, as well as producers, wholesalers, and retailers—that distribute products and benefit from cooperative efforts. Supply chains start with the customer and require the cooperation of channel members to satisfy customer requirements.

Channels of distribution are broadly classified as channels for consumer products and channels for business products. Within these two broad categories, different marketing channels are used for different products. Although consumer goods can move directly from producer to consumers, consumer product channels that include wholesalers and retailers are usually more economical and efficient. Distribution of business products differs from that of consumer products in the types of channels used. A direct distribution channel is common in business marketing. Also used are channels containing industrial distributors, manufacturers' agents, and a combination of agents and distributors. Most producers have multiple or dual channels so the distribution system can be adjusted for various target markets.

A marketing channel is managed such that products receive appropriate market coverage. In choosing intensive distribution, producers strive to make a product available to all possible dealers. In selective distribution, only some outlets in an area are chosen to distribute a product. Exclusive distribution usually gives one dealer exclusive rights to sell a product in a large geographic area.

Each channel member performs a different role in the system and agrees to accept certain rights, responsibilities, rewards, and sanctions for nonconformance. Although many marketing channels are determined by consensus, some are organized and controlled by a single leader, or channel captain. A channel captain may be a producer, wholesaler, or retailer. Channels function most effectively when members cooperate; when they deviate from their roles, channel conflict can arise.

Integration of marketing channels brings various activities under one channel member's management. Vertical integration combines two or more stages of the channel under one management. The vertical marketing system (VMS) is managed centrally for the mutual benefit of all channel members. Vertical marketing systems may be corporate, administered, or contractual. Horizontal integration combines institutions at the same level of channel operation under a single management.

Federal, state, and local laws regulate channel management to protect competition and free trade. Courts may prohibit or permit a practice depending on whether it violates this underlying principle. Various procompetitive legislation applies to distribution practices. Channel management practices frequently subject to legal restraint include dual distribution, restricted sales territories, tying agreements, exclusive dealing, and refusal to deal. When these practices strengthen weak competitors or increase competition among dealers, they may be permitted; in most other cases, when competition may be weakened considerably, they are deemed illegal.

Important Terms

Distribution
Marketing channel
Marketing intermediary
Supply chain management
Industrial distributor
Dual distribution
Strategic channel alliance
Intensive distribution
Selective distribution
Exclusive distribution

Channel captain
Channel power
Vertical channel integration
Vertical marketing system (VMS)
Horizontal channel integration
Tying agreement
Exclusive dealing

Discussion and Review Questions

1. Describe the major functions of marketing channels. Why are these functions better accomplished through combined efforts of channel members?
2. Can one channel member perform all the channel functions? Explain your answer.
3. "Shorter channels are usually a more direct means of distribution and therefore are more efficient." Comment on this statement.
4. List several reasons consumers often blame intermediaries for distribution inefficiencies.
5. Compare and contrast the four major types of marketing channels for consumer products. Through which type of channel is each of the following products most likely to be distributed?
   a. New automobiles
   b. Saltine crackers
   c. Cut-your-own Christmas trees
   d. New textbooks
   e. Sofas
   f. Soft drinks
6. Outline the four most common channels for business products. Describe the products or situations that lead marketers to choose each channel.
7. Describe an industrial distributor. What types of products are marketed through an industrial distributor?

8. Under what conditions is a producer most likely to use more than one marketing channel?

9. Explain the differences among intensive, selective, and exclusive methods of distribution.

10. "Channel cooperation requires that members support the overall channel goals to achieve individual goals." Comment on this statement.

11. Name and describe firms that use (a) vertical integration and (b) horizontal integration in their marketing channels.

12. Explain the major characteristics of each of the three types of vertical marketing systems (VMSs): corporate, administered, and contractual.

13. Under what conditions are tying agreements, exclusive dealing, and dual distribution judged illegal?

Application Questions

1. *Supply chain management* refers to long-term partnerships among channel members working together to reduce inefficiencies, costs, and redundancies and to develop innovative approaches to satisfy customers. Select one of the following companies and explain how supply chain management could increase marketing productivity.
   a. Dell Computer
   b. FedEx
   c. Nike
   d. Taco Bell

2. Organizations often form strategic channel alliances when they find it more profitable or convenient to distribute their products through the marketing channel of another organization. Find an article in a newspaper or on the Internet that describes such a strategic channel alliance. Briefly summarize the article and indicate the benefits each organization expects to gain.

3. Marketers can select from three major levels of market coverage when determining the number and kinds of outlets in which a product will be sold: intensive, selective, or exclusive. Characteristics of the product and its target market determine the intensity of coverage a product should receive. Indicate the intensity level best suited for the following products, and explain why it is appropriate.
   a. Personal computer
   b. Deodorant
   c. Collector baseball autographed by Mark McGwire
   d. Windows 2000 computer software

4. Describe the decision process you might go through if you were attempting to determine the most appropriate distribution channel for one of the following:
   a. Shotguns for hunters
   b. Women's lingerie
   c. Telephone systems for small businesses
   d. Toy trucks for 2-year-olds

Internet Exercise & Resources

Visit **www.prideferrell.com** for resources to help you master the material in this chapter, plus materials that will help you expand your marketing knowledge, including: Internet exercise updates, ACE self-tests, hotlinks to companies featured in this chapter, and much more.

iSupply

Distribution bottlenecks can be an expensive problem for any business. Trying to prevent such problems is iSupply, an Internet supply chain management tool that links all members of a supply chain from the supplier's system to the retailer's storefront system. Learn more about this innovative tool at

http://www.ie.com.my/html/isupply.html

1. Does iSupply represent a new type of marketing channel? Why or why not?

2. Why would firms be cautious when deciding whether to use iSupply?

3. Do you think iSupply represents the future of supply chain management? Why or why not?

VIDEO CASE 14.1
CommercialWare Powers Multiple Channels for Retailers

Marketing intermediaries are always seeking new ways to improve efficiency and strengthen ties with producers and customers. Today retailers such as J. Jill, Staples, Saks Fifth Avenue, Target, Disney, Starbucks, and Patagonia are using web-based technology from CommercialWare to achieve both goals as they expand and market through multiple channels.

Based in Natick, Massachusetts, Commercial-Ware offers a suite of programs to help retailers maintain tighter control over critical marketing functions such as supply chain management, sales transactions, inventory management, and order fulfillment. Managing these functions can be a challenge when a retailer sells through only one channel. When a retailer adds more channels, it also adds complications that in turn can affect relations with customers.

Consider the concerns of Garnet Hill, a catalog company that recently began selling clothing and furniture on the Internet. "Today, if an order is already packed in the warehouse and an online customer calls to cancel, it's virtually impossible to stop the delivery," notes a Garnet Hill executive. "Staying alive means being a company that customers want to deal with by providing the service levels they expect." That's where CommercialWare really shines. The software not only can help Garnet Hill monitor the progress of each order but can even allow the retailer to exchange information with the suppliers and the shippers it hires to fulfill orders. As a result, Garnet Hill can be more responsive to its customers and, at the same time, do a better job of managing all the behind-the-scenes activities that support sales and customer service.

J. Jill, a women's apparel retailer, tapped CommercialWare's expertise when it planned a major expansion across multiple channels. Originally the company sold only through its catalog. When it decided to sell online and open a chain of stores, it also planned to revamp its supply chain management system. "We wanted to consistently extend the brand across the web, the physical stores, and the catalog and continue to enhance customer service," explains Randy Dow, a J. Jill vice president. "We also wanted to reduce the cost of order taking and customer service and enhance customer loyalty." Working with CommercialWare, J. Jill installed web-based software to allow the stores, the catalog call-in center, the online division, and the automated distribution center to handle inventory management, shipping functions, and customer relationship management. With all inventory and order data in a single system, J. Jill can track both sales and returns

and update inventory records every five minutes. When a catalog or online customer places an order, J. Jill can immediately and accurately confirm whether the product is in stock and ready to be shipped. Then it uses the technology to track every product in every order, ensuring that customers receive what they bought, and on time. Now sales growth is outstripping projections, and J. Jill management gives the credit to its multiple channel strategy and the new distribution technology.

Saks Fifth Avenue is another satisfied CommercialWare customer. Robert Dykman, chief technology officer of the Saks Direct division, says the upscale retailer uses the technology to maintain a consistent shopping experience for customers across all channels. The retailer's goal is to deliver the same high-quality service whether customers shop in the store, order from the catalog, or use the website. Using CommercialWare's technology allows Saks to keep its focus squarely on the customer rather than being distracted by back-office distribution details.

More than 80 retailers have hired CommercialWare to streamline their distribution systems. CEO Amish Mehta observes that his company's flexible web-based technology allows traditional retailers to compete more effectively with online retailers. It also allows retailers to request that suppliers ship certain products directly to customers rather than having all products move through the retailer's distribution center on the way to customers. "We think the future distribution model will be a hybrid in which retailers stock eighty percent of the goods they sell and deliver the rest directly through suppliers," says Rohit Agarwal, vice president of CommercialWare. That future is nearly here as online retailers gear up for ever-higher sales volume and traditional retailers add more channels to allow customers more shopping choices.[13]

QUESTIONS FOR DISCUSSION

1. The headline on one of the promotional pieces CommercialWare sends to prospects in the retailing industry reads, "The Nightmare That Is Christmas (Or, Welcome to the World of Retailing)." What does this communicate to prospects about CommercialWare's benefits?
2. How does CommercialWare's technology help retailers strengthen relationships with customers? With suppliers?
3. How is CommercialWare's technology likely to affect channel cooperation and channel integration?

CASE 14.2

Grainger Wires the Channel for Business Products

Need an electric motor or a hard hat? W. W. Grainger has dozens for sale among the 5 million products showcased in its voluminous catalogs and on its website. Grainger is an industrial distributor offering virtually one-stop shopping for producer, government, and institutional markets seeking to buy a wide range of maintenance, repair, and operating (MRO) supplies. With more than 560 distribution branches spread across North America, the company can time shipments to arrive quickly when business customers place orders.

William W. Grainger founded the Illinois-based company in the 1920s as a wholesaler of electric motors. To build sales, Grainger mailed out postcards about his offerings and compiled a catalog titled *MotorBook*. In less than a decade, he was operating 15 U.S. sales branches to serve business customers from coast to coast. By 1949, he had expanded his branch network to 30 states.

Son David Grainger, now senior chairperson, continued the founder's expansion strategy. In the 1980s and 1990s, the company opened high-tech regional distribution centers in Kansas, Georgia, and Texas to supplement its Chicago-area facilities and slash fulfillment time for orders placed by customers around the country. Grainger also expanded its geographic reach by buying Acklands Ltd., a Canadian distributor of automotive and industrial safety products.

By the mid-1990s, Grainger was getting wired. Recognizing that the Internet could bring in many more business customers at a lower cost, management created Grainger.com as a comprehensive online catalog site. Over the years, the company continued to refine its web presence by posting informative resources, adding live-chat customer assistance, a virtual tour of the site for new customers, special international services, and web-only price promotions to bring customers back to the site again and again. Within the first three years of operation, annual web sales grew from $3 million to $267 million as customers flocked to the online catalog, which features many more items than the 80,000 products shown in a typical printed Grainger catalog.

Not all of Grainger's Internet initiatives have been as successful, however. The company had high hopes for its Material Logic division covering three web-based distribution sites. TotalMRO.com was designed as an industrywide portal with catalogs from Grainger and competing distributors. MROverstocks.com was created as an auction site for discontinued or excess industrial products. FindMRO.com was designed as a search site for specialized and hard-to-find industrial products. After launching the three sites, Grainger tried to interest competing distributors and outside investors in buying a stake in Material Logic. The company had spent more than $100 million on its web operations and sought outside funding to support its aggressive movement into electronic procurement. But when no one stepped forward to invest, Grainger quickly shut down the unprofitable division. At the same time, FindMRO.com was becoming popular, so it was merged into the existing Grainger.com operation.

Today Grainger sells $5 billion worth of industrial products every year. Just under 10 percent of total sales revenues come from the profitable Grainger.com site, and the percentage continues to rise as more customers switch from paper-based to electronic purchasing.[14]

QUESTIONS FOR DISCUSSION

1. Why would a competing industrial distributor even consider investing in a portal designed by Grainger?
2. Is Grainger in a position to be a channel captain? Explain.
3. Why would a hospital buy from Grainger instead of buying directly from producers?

Wholesaling and Physical Distribution

15

OBJECTIVES

- To understand the nature of wholesaling in the marketing channel
- To explain wholesalers' functions
- To understand how wholesalers are classified
- To recognize how physical distribution activities are integrated into marketing channels and overall marketing strategies
- To examine the major physical distribution functions of order processing, inventory management, materials handling, warehousing, and transportation
- To discuss the strategic implications of physical distribution systems

Homestore.com Doesn't Want to Eliminate Intermediaries

In today's wired environment, many businesses are using the Internet to bypass intermediaries. Stuart Wolff, Homestore.com's founder and CEO, took the opposite approach: he built Homestore.com into the largest real estate website in America by signing up some 368,000 brokers to use his online services. "From the beginning, I wanted to be a partner to the industry, not a threat," says Wolff.

Knowing that a successful real estate site must have listings of homes and apartments for sale or rent—and lots of them—Wolff and his staff spent the early months traveling the country to sell local real estate listing services on the benefits of subscribing to Homestore.com. Over time, they signed up thousands of brokers and posted more than 1 million home and apartment listings drawn from 740 regional listing services. Participating brokers pay an average of about $40 monthly to post their names, phone numbers, and photos next to their real estate listings. The site also collects revenue from mortgage brokers and other firms that post advertisements targeting home buyers.

Because Homestore.com helps bring buyers and sellers together but has no financial stake in the real estate transactions it facilitates, the site's profit margin is extremely high. In just two years the margin has increased from 63 to 74 percent, even though Wolff continues to invest heavily in television, print, and radio advertising. He also struck a deal with America Online to feature Homestore.com within the popular AOL House and Home Channel.

Despite competition from rivals such as HomeAdvisor.com and Homes.com, Homestore.com has emerged as the industry leader. The site lists 95 percent of all online home and apartment listings and has annual revenues exceeding $500 million. Revenues continue to climb as Homestore.com adds more services. In addition to browsing real estate listings, customers can arrange moving services, investigate neighborhoods, download professionally prepared home plans, get mortgage and insurance quotes, look at security systems, and buy a wide range of landscaping and home improvement services. The combination of a giant national listing database and a constantly expanding menu of offerings brings more than 7 million visitors to the site every month.

Wolff is as concerned with satisfying participating brokers as he is with satisfying home buyers. He has 200 salespeople pounding the pavement to meet face to face with brokers around the United States, an unusual and expensive strategy for a company that operates electronically. Wolff has also opened a telephone call center in Arizona, staffed with 400 service representatives ready to help brokers who call when online transactions go awry or when they need other support. These personal touches complement the high-tech side of the business and help Wolff maintain strong relations with the brokers he serves.[1]

SOLD

HOUSE FOR SALE

374

Companies like Homestore.com facilitate the marketing efforts of middlemen who, in turn, help to make products available to customers when and where they want them. Supply chain management provides the coordination and strategic direction to reduce inefficiencies in the marketing channel, thus optimizing customer service. Physical distribution is a crucial function in supply chain management because it includes those activities associated with handling and moving products through the marketing channel. Wholesalers often play a key role in supply chain management, although manufacturers and retailers also can perform wholesaling activities.

In this chapter, we explore the role of wholesaling and physical distribution in supply chain management. First, we examine the importance of wholesalers in marketing channels, including their functions and classifications. Next, we consider critical physical distribution concepts, including order processing, inventory management, materials handling, warehousing, and transportation.

The Nature of Wholesaling

wholesaling Transactions in which products are bought for resale, for making other products, or for general business operations

wholesaler An individual or organization that facilitates and expedites wholesale transactions

Wholesaling refers to all transactions in which products are bought for resale, for making other products, or for general business operations. It does not include exchanges with ultimate consumers. A **wholesaler** is an individual or organization that facilitates and expedites exchanges that are primarily wholesale transactions. In other words, wholesalers buy products and resell them to reseller, government, and institutional users. For example, SYSCO, the nation's number one food-service distributor, supplies restaurants, hotels, schools, industrial caterers, and hospitals with everything from frozen and fresh food and paper products to medical and cleaning supplies. There are approximately 530,000 wholesaling establishments in the United States,[2] and more than half of all products sold in this country pass through these firms.

Table 15.1 lists the major activities wholesalers perform, but individual wholesalers may perform more or fewer functions than the table shows. Distribution of all

Table 15.1	Major Wholesaling Functions
Supply chain management	Creating long-term partnerships among channel members
Promotion	Providing a sales force, advertising, sales promotion, and publicity
Warehousing, shipping, and product handling	Receiving, storing, and stockkeeping Packaging Shipping outgoing orders Materials handling Arranging and making local and long-distance shipments
Inventory control and data processing	Processing orders Controlling physical inventory Recording transactions Tracking sales data for financial analysis
Risk taking	Assuming responsibility for theft, product obsolescence, and excess inventories
Financing and budgeting	Extending credit Borrowing Making capital investments Forecasting cash flow
Marketing research and information systems	Providing information about markets Conducting research studies Managing computer networks to facilitate exchanges and relationships

goods requires wholesaling activities whether or not a wholesaling firm is involved. Wholesaling activities are not limited to goods; service companies, such as financial institutions, also use active wholesale networks. For example, some banks buy loans in bulk from other financial institutions as well as making loans to their own retail customers.

Wholesalers perform services for other organizations in the marketing channel. They bear the primary responsibility for the physical distribution of products from manufacturers to retailers. In addition, they may establish information systems that help producers and retailers better manage the supply chain from producer to customer. Many wholesalers are using information technology and the Internet to allow their employees, customers, and suppliers to share information between intermediaries and facilitating agencies such as trucking companies and warehouse firms. For example, FedEx, which serves as a facilitating agency in providing overnight or even same-day delivery of packages, provides online tracking of packages for the benefit of its customers. Other firms are making their databases and marketing information systems available to their supply chain partners to facilitate order processing, shipping, and product development and to share information about changing market conditions and customer desires. As a result, some wholesalers play a key role in supply chain management decisions.

Services Provided by Wholesalers

Wholesalers provide essential services to both producers and retailers. By initiating sales contacts with a producer and selling diverse products to retailers, wholesalers serve as an extension of the producer's sales force. Wholesalers also provide financial assistance. They often pay for transporting goods; they reduce a producer's warehousing expenses and inventory investment by holding goods in inventory; they extend credit and assume losses from buyers who turn out to be poor credit risks; and when they buy a producer's entire output and pay promptly or in cash, they are a source of working capital. Wholesalers also serve as conduits for information within the marketing channel, keeping producers up to date on market developments and passing along the manufacturers' promotional plans to other intermediaries. Using wholesalers therefore gives producers a distinct advantage because the specialized services wholesalers perform allow producers to concentrate on developing and manufacturing products that match customers' needs and wants.

Many producers would prefer more direct interaction with retailers. Wholesalers, however, are more likely to have closer contact with retailers because of their strategic position in the marketing channel. Although a producer's own sales force is probably more effective at selling, the costs of maintaining a sales force and performing functions normally done by wholesalers are sometimes higher than the benefits received from an independent sales staff. Wholesalers can spread sales costs over many more products than can most producers, resulting in lower

Wholesaler Services
One of the services performed by wholesalers such as TTI is the gathering and holding of inventory.

costs per product unit. For these reasons, many producers shift informational, financing, and physical distribution activities, such as transportation and warehousing, to wholesalers. Thus, the wholesaler often becomes a major link in the supply chain, creating an optimal level of efficiency and customer service.

Wholesalers support retailers by assisting with marketing strategy, especially the distribution component. Wholesalers also help retailers select inventory. They are often specialists on market conditions and experts at negotiating final purchases. In industries in which obtaining supplies is important, skilled buying is indispensable. For example, Atlanta-based Genuine Parts Company (GPC), the nation's top automotive parts wholesaler, has more than 70 years of experience in the auto parts business. This experience helps it serve its customers effectively. GPC supplies more than 225,000 replacement parts (from 150 different suppliers) to 5,800 NAPA Auto Parts stores.[3] Effective wholesalers make an effort to understand the businesses of their customers. They can reduce a retailer's burden of looking for and coordinating supply sources. If the wholesaler purchases for several different buyers, expenses can be shared by all customers. Furthermore, whereas a manufacturer's salesperson offers retailers only a few products at a time, independent wholesalers always have a wide range of products available. Thus, through partnerships, wholesalers and retailers can forge successful relationships for the benefit of customers.

By buying in large quantities and delivering to customers in smaller lots, wholesalers are able to perform physical distribution activities efficiently. These activities (discussed later in this chapter) include order processing, transportation, materials handling, inventory planning, and warehousing. Wholesalers furnish greater service than might be feasible for a producer's or retailer's own physical distribution system. Furthermore, wholesalers offer quick and frequent delivery even when demand fluctuates and can do so at low cost, which lets the producer and the wholesalers' customers avoid risks associated with holding large inventories.

The distinction between services performed by wholesalers and those provided by other businesses has blurred in recent years. Changes in the competitive nature of business, especially the growth of strong retail chains like Wal-Mart, Home Depot, and Best Buy, are changing supply chain relationships. In many product categories, such as electronics, furniture, and even food products, retailers have discovered that they can deal directly with producers, performing wholesaling activities themselves at a lower cost. An increasing number of retailers are relying on computer technology to expedite ordering, delivery, and handling of goods. Technology is thus allowing retailers to take over many wholesaling functions. When a wholesaler is eliminated from a marketing channel, the functions, listed in Table 15.1, still have to be performed by a member of the marketing channel, whether a producer, retailer, or facilitating agency. These wholesaling activities are critical components of supply chain management.

Types of Wholesalers

Wholesalers are classified according to several criteria. Whether a wholesaler is independently owned or owned by a producer influences how it is classified. Wholesalers can also be grouped according to whether they take title to (own) the products they handle. The range of services provided is another criterion used for classification. Finally, wholesalers are classified according to the breadth and depth of their product lines. Using these criteria, we discuss three general types of wholesaling establishments: merchant wholesalers, agents and brokers, and manufacturers' sales branches and offices.

merchant wholesalers
Independently owned businesses that take title to goods, assume ownership risks, and buy and resell products to other wholesalers, business customers, or retailers

Merchant Wholesalers. **Merchant wholesalers** are independently owned businesses that take title to goods, assume risks associated with ownership, and generally buy and resell products to other wholesalers, business customers, or retailers. A producer is likely to rely on merchant wholesalers when selling directly to customers would be economically unfeasible. Merchant wholesalers are also useful for providing market coverage, making sales contacts, storing inventory, handling orders, collecting market information, and furnishing customer support. Some merchant

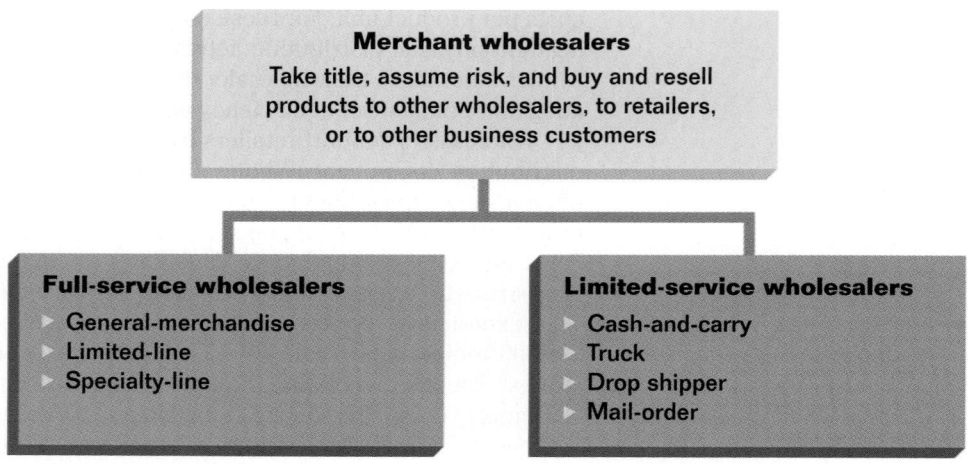

FIGURE 15.1
Types of Merchant Wholesalers

wholesalers are even involved in packaging and developing private brands to help retail customers be competitive. Merchant wholesalers go by various names, including *wholesaler, jobber, distributor, assembler, exporter,* and *importer.* They fall into one of two broad categories: full-service and limited-service (see Figure 15.1).

Full-service wholesalers perform the widest possible range of wholesaling functions. Customers rely on them for product availability, suitable assortments, breaking large quantities into smaller ones, financial assistance, and technical advice and service. Universal Corporation, the world's largest buyer and processor of leaf tobacco, is an example of a full-service wholesaler. Based in Richmond, Virginia, the firm buys, resells, packs, and ships tobacco, and provides financing for its customers, which include cigarette manufacturers like Philip Morris (which accounts for a significant portion of Universal's sales). Universal is also involved in sales of lumber, rubber, tea, nuts, dried fruit, and other products and has operations in 40 countries.[4] Full-service wholesalers handle either consumer or business products and provide numerous marketing services to their customers. Many large grocery wholesalers help retailers with store design, site selection, personnel training, financing, merchandising, advertising, coupon redemption, and scanning. Although full-service wholesalers often earn higher gross margins than other wholesalers, their operating expenses are also higher because they perform a wider range of functions.

Full-service wholesalers are categorized as general-merchandise, limited-line, and specialty-line wholesalers, and as rack jobbers. **General-merchandise wholesalers** carry a wide product mix but offer limited depth within product lines. They deal in such products as drugs, nonperishable foods, cosmetics, detergents, and tobacco. **Limited-line wholesalers** carry only a few product lines, such as groceries, lighting fixtures, or oil-well drilling equipment, but offer an extensive assortment of products within those lines. Bergen Brunswig Corporation, for example, is a limited-line wholesaler of pharmaceuticals and health and beauty aids. Limited-line wholesalers provide a range of services similar to those of general-merchandise wholesalers. **Specialty-line wholesalers** offer the narrowest range of products, usually a single product line or a few items within a product line. Wholesalers that specialize in shellfish, fruit, or other food delicacies are specialty-line wholesalers. **Rack jobbers** are full-service, specialty-line wholesalers that own and maintain display racks in supermarkets, drugstores, and discount and variety stores. They set up displays, mark merchandise, stock shelves, and keep billing and inventory records; retailers need furnish only space. Rack jobbers specialize in nonfood items with high profit margins, such as health and beauty aids, books, magazines, hosiery, and greeting cards.

Limited-service wholesalers provide fewer marketing services than full-service wholesalers and specialize in just a few functions. Producers perform the remaining functions or pass them on to customers or to other intermediaries. Limited-

full-service wholesalers Merchant wholesalers that perform the widest range of wholesaling functions

general-merchandise wholesalers Full-service wholesalers with a wide product mix but limited depth within product lines

limited-line wholesalers Full-service wholesalers that carry only a few product lines but many products within those lines

specialty-line wholesalers Full-service wholesalers that carry only a single product line or a few items within a product line

rack jobbers Full-service, specialty-line wholesalers that own and maintain display racks in stores

limited-service wholesalers Merchant wholesalers that provide some services and specialize in a few functions

Table 15.2   Services That Limited-Service Wholesalers Provide

	Cash-and-Carry	Truck	Drop Shipper	Mail-Order
Physical possession of merchandise	Yes	Yes	No	Yes
Personal sales calls on customers	No	Yes	No	No
Information about market conditions	No	Some	Yes	Yes
Advice to customers	No	Some	Yes	No
Stocking and maintenance of merchandise in customers' stores	No	No	No	No
Credit to customers	No	No	Yes	Some
Delivery of merchandise to customers	No	Yes	No	No

service wholesalers take title to merchandise but often do not deliver merchandise, grant credit, provide marketing information, store inventory, or plan ahead for customers' future needs. Because they offer restricted services, limited-service wholesalers are compensated with lower rates and have smaller profit margins than full-service wholesalers. The decision about whether to use a limited-service or a full-service wholesaler depends on the structure of the marketing channel and the need to manage the supply chain to provide competitive advantage. Although certain types of limited-service wholesalers are few in number, they are important in the distribution of such products as specialty foods, perishable items, construction materials, and coal. Table 15.2 summarizes the services provided by four typical limited-service wholesalers: cash-and-carry wholesalers, truck wholesalers, drop shippers, and mail-order wholesalers.

cash-and-carry wholesalers Limited-service wholesalers whose customers pay cash and furnish transportation

truck wholesalers Limited-service wholesalers that transport products directly to customers for inspection and selection

drop shippers Limited-service wholesalers that take title to products and negotiate sales but never take actual possession of products

mail-order wholesalers Limited-service wholesalers that sell products through catalogs

Cash-and-carry wholesalers are intermediaries whose customers—usually small businesses—pay cash and furnish transportation. Cash-and-carry wholesalers usually handle a limited line of products with a high turnover rate, such as groceries, building materials, and electrical or office supplies. Many small retailers whose accounts are refused by other wholesalers survive because of cash-and-carry wholesalers. **Truck wholesalers,** sometimes called *truck jobbers,* transport a limited line of products directly to customers for on-the-spot inspection and selection. They are often small operators who own and drive their own trucks. They usually have regular routes, calling on retailers and other institutions to determine their needs. **Drop shippers,** also known as *desk jobbers,* take title to goods and negotiate sales but never take actual possession of products. They forward orders from retailers, business buyers, or other wholesalers to manufacturers and arrange for carload shipments of items to be delivered directly from producers to these customers. They assume responsibility for products during the entire transaction, including the costs of any unsold goods. **Mail-order wholesalers** use catalogs instead of sales forces to sell products to retail and business buyers. Wholesale mail-order houses generally feature cosmetics, specialty foods, sporting goods, office supplies, and automotive parts. Mail-order wholesaling enables buyers to choose and order particular catalog items for delivery through United Parcel Service, the U.S. Postal Service, or other carriers. This is a convenient and effective method of selling small items to customers in remote areas that other wholesalers might find unprofitable to serve. The Internet has provided an opportunity for mail-order wholesalers to sell products over their own websites and have the products shipped by the manufacturers.

Agents and Brokers. Agents and brokers negotiate purchases and expedite sales but do not take title to products (see Figure 15.2). Sometimes called *functional middlemen,* they perform a limited number of services in exchange for a commission,

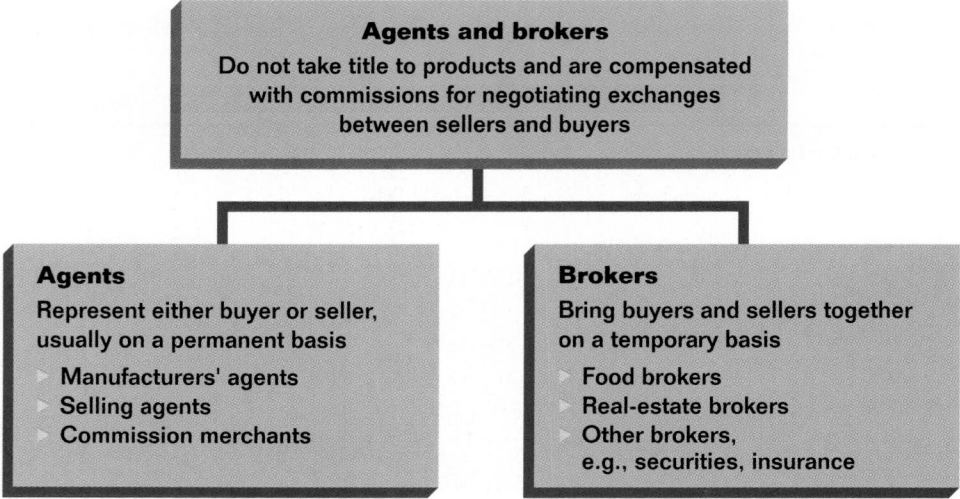

FIGURE 15.2
Types of Agents and Brokers

agents Intermediaries that represent either buyers or sellers on a permanent basis

brokers Intermediaries that bring buyers and sellers together temporarily

which is generally based on the product's selling price. **Agents** represent either buyers or sellers on a permanent basis, whereas **brokers** are intermediaries that buyers or sellers employ temporarily.

Although agents and brokers perform even fewer functions than limited-service wholesalers, they are usually specialists in particular products or types of customers and can provide valuable sales expertise. They know their markets well and often form long-lasting associations with customers. Agents and brokers enable manufacturers to expand sales when resources are limited, to benefit from the services of a trained sales force, and to hold down personal selling costs. Despite the advantages they offer, agents and brokers face increased competition from merchant wholesalers, manufacturers' sales branches and offices, and direct-sales efforts through manufacturer-owned websites. We look here at three types of agents—manufacturers' agents, selling agents, and commission merchants—and at the broker's role in bringing about exchanges between buyers and sellers. Table 15.3 summarizes the services that agents and brokers provide.

manufacturers' agents
Independent intermediaries that represent more than one seller and offer complete product lines

Manufacturers' agents, which account for more than half of all agent wholesalers, are independent intermediaries that represent two or more sellers and usually offer customers complete product lines. They sell and take orders year-round, much as a manufacturer's sales force does. Restricted to a particular territory, a manufacturers' agent handles noncompeting and complementary products. The relationship

Table 15.3	Services That Agents and Brokers Provide			
	Manufacturers' Agents	Selling Agents	Commission Merchants	Brokers
Physical possession of merchandise	Some	Some	Yes	No
Long-term relationship with buyers or sellers	Yes	Yes	Yes	No
Representation of competing product lines	No	No	Yes	Yes
Limited geographic territory	Yes	No	No	No
Credit to customers	No	Yes	Some	No
Delivery of merchandise to customers	Some	Yes	Yes	No

between the agent and the manufacturer is governed by written contracts that outline territories, selling price, order handling, and terms of sale relating to delivery, service, and warranties. Manufacturers' agents have little or no control over producers' pricing and marketing policies. They do not extend credit and may be unable to provide technical advice. They do occasionally store and transport products, assist producers with planning and promotion, and help retailers advertise. Some maintain a service organization; the more services offered, the higher the agent's commission. Manufacturers' agents are commonly used in sales of apparel, machinery and equipment, steel, furniture, automotive products, electrical goods, and certain food items.

selling agents   Intermediaries that market a whole product line or a manufacturer's entire output

Selling agents market either all of a specified product line or a manufacturer's entire output. They perform every wholesaling activity except taking title to products. Selling agents usually assume the sales function for several producers simultaneously and are often used in place of marketing departments. In fact, selling agents are used most often by small producers or by manufacturers that have difficulty maintaining a marketing department because of seasonal production or other factors. In contrast to manufacturers' agents, selling agents generally have no territorial limits and have complete authority over prices, promotion, and distribution. To avoid conflicts of interest, selling agents represent noncompeting product lines. They play a key role in advertising, marketing research, and credit policies of the sellers they represent, at times even advising on product development and packaging.

commission merchants
Agents that receive goods on consignment and negotiate sales in large, central markets

Commission merchants receive goods on consignment from local sellers and negotiate sales in large, central markets. Sometimes called *factor merchants,* these agents have broad powers regarding prices and terms of sale. They specialize in obtaining the best price possible under market conditions. Most often found in agricultural marketing, commission merchants take possession of truckloads of commodities, arrange for necessary grading or storage, and transport the commodities to auction or markets where they are sold. When sales are completed, the agents deduct commission and the expense of making the sale, and then turn over profits to the producer. Commission merchants also offer planning assistance and sometimes extend credit, but usually do not provide promotional support.

A broker's primary purpose is to bring buyers and sellers together. Thus, brokers perform fewer functions than other intermediaries. They are not involved in financing or physical possession, have no authority to set prices, and assume almost no risks. Instead, they offer customers specialized knowledge of a particular commodity and a network of established contacts. Brokers are especially useful to sellers of certain types of products, such as supermarket products and real estate. Food brokers, for example, sell food and general merchandise to retailer-owned and merchant wholesalers, grocery chains, food processors, and business buyers.

Manufacturers' Sales Branches and Offices.

Sometimes called *manufacturers' wholesalers,* manufacturers' sales branches and offices resemble merchant wholesalers' operations.

sales branches   Manufacturer-owned intermediaries that sell products and provide support services to the manufacturer's sales force

Sales branches are manufacturer-owned intermediaries that sell products and provide support services to the manufacturer's sales force. Situated away from the manufacturing plant, they are usually located where large customers are concentrated and demand is high. They offer credit, deliver goods, give promotional assistance, and furnish other services. In many cases, they carry inventory (although this practice often duplicates functions of other channel members and is now declining). Customers include retailers, business buyers, and other wholesalers. Manufacturers of electrical supplies, such as Westinghouse Electric, and of plumbing supplies, such

Net Sights

U.S. Business Reporter devotes a section of its website to wholesaling. Visitors can find a variety of concise, informative articles on the wholesaling environment, relevant statistics, and industry issues, characteristics, and trends. At **www.activemedia-guide.com/wholesaling_industry.htm,** users can search by company name or by industry.

as American Standard, often have branch operations. They are also common in the lumber and automotive parts industries.

Sales offices are manufacturer-owned operations that provide services normally associated with agents. Like sales branches, they are located away from manufacturing plants, but unlike branches, they carry no inventory. A manufacturer's sales office (or branch) may sell products that enhance the manufacturer's own product line. Companies like Campbell Soup provide diverse services to their wholesale and retail customers. Hiram Walker, a liquor producer, imports wine from Spain to increase the number of products its sales offices can offer wholesalers.

Manufacturers may set up these branches or offices to reach their customers more effectively by performing wholesaling functions themselves. A manufacturer may also set up such a facility when specialized wholesaling services are not available through existing intermediaries. A manufacturer's performance of wholesaling and physical distribution activities through its sales branch or office may strengthen supply chain efficiency. In some situations, though, a manufacturer may bypass its sales office or branches entirely—for example, if the producer decides to serve large retailer customers directly.

The Nature of Physical Distribution

Physical distribution, also known as *logistics,* refers to the activities used to move products from producers to consumers and other end users. These activities include order processing, inventory management, materials handling, warehousing, and transportation. Planning an efficient physical distribution system is crucial to developing an effective marketing strategy because it can decrease costs and increase customer satisfaction. Speed of delivery, service, and dependability are often as important to customers as costs. Companies that have the right goods in the right place, at the right time, in the right quantity, and with the right support services are able to sell more than competitors that do not. A construction equipment dealer with a low inventory of replacement parts requires fast, dependable service from component suppliers when it needs parts not in stock. Even when the demand for products is unpredictable, suppliers must be able to respond quickly to inventory needs. In such cases, physical distribution costs may be a minor consideration when compared with service, dependability, and timeliness.

Physical distribution deals with the physical movement and storage of products and supplies both within and among marketing channel members. Physical distribution systems must meet the needs of both the supply chain and customers. Distribution activities are thus an important part of supply chain planning and require the cooperation of all partners. Often one channel member manages physical distribution for all channel members.

Within the marketing channel, physical distribution activities may be performed by a producer, a wholesaler, or a retailer, or they may be outsourced. In the context of distribution, **outsourcing** is the contracting of physical distribution tasks to third parties who do not have managerial authority within the marketing channel. Most physical distribution activities can be outsourced to third-party firms that have special expertise in such areas as warehousing, transportation, and information technology. Cooperative relationships with third-party organizations, such as trucking companies, warehouses, and data-service providers, can help reduce marketing channel costs and boost service and customer satisfaction for all supply chain partners. For example, a number of e-businesses as well as some traditional brick-and-mortar ones have outsourced physical distribution activities, including shipping and warehousing, to build a supply chain of strategic partners to maximize customer service. Such relationships are increasingly being integrated in the supply chain to achieve physical distribution objectives. When choosing companies through which to outsource, marketers must be cautious to use efficient firms that help the outsourcing company provide excellent customer service.

Physical Distribution Objectives

For most companies, the main objectives of physical distribution are to decrease costs and transit time while increasing customer service. However, few distribution systems achieve these goals in equal measure. The large inventories and rapid transportation necessary for good customer service drive up costs. Supply chain managers therefore strive for a reasonable balance among service, costs, and resources. They determine what level of customer service is acceptable and realistic and then develop a "system" outlook to minimize total distribution costs and cycle time.

Meeting Standards of Customer Service.   In physical distribution, availability, timeliness, and accuracy are important dimensions of customer service. Companies set customer service standards based on one, or a combination, of these three dimensions. *Availability* refers to the percentage of orders that can be filled

GLOBAL MARKETING

Selecting Distributors for Global Markets

Every time a company enters a new market, it faces the crucial decision of selecting one or more local distributors. Even in today's wired world, where online groups such as the Global Trading Web Association are setting standards and policies for international e-commerce, producers need distributors to facilitate the actual movement of products to end users.

How should a company plan its international distribution strategy? Experts offer these guidelines:

● *Choose markets first.* In many cases, distributors from other countries make the initial approach, offering to handle the company's products in their markets. A better approach is to decide which countries to enter, then systematically investigate potential distributors before making a decision.

● *Screen distributors carefully.* Loctite, a Connecticut-based adhesives manufacturer, used to work with distributors already handling similar products. Over time, however, the firm found such arrangements unsatisfactory "because the distributors represent the market's status quo, and we are selling a replacement technology and attempting to change the market," says a Loctite executive. Now the company screens distributors on the basis of training, commitment, support, and willingness to partner for mutual success.

● *Build a long-term relationship.* Plan to work with local distributors over the long term rather than as an interim arrangement. This gives distributors more incentive to work together in developing the market.

● *Invest in new markets.* Multinational corporations can demonstrate their commitment to building sales in new

markets by making small investments in the local distribution firms with which they work. This smoothes the way for influencing local distribution activities and enhances the long-term relationship.

● *Participate in strategic distribution decisions.* Take an active role in the distributor's strategic decisions to avoid costly missteps. As one manager notes, "Time and again, we saw distributors cut prices to compensate for failing to target the right customers or to sufficiently train salespeople."

● *Examine detailed data.* Rather than taking a completely hands-off position, producers working with international distributors should request in-depth financial and channel data for each market. This helps management learn about local market conditions and, at the same time, ensures that wholesale pricing and other details are in line with overall strategies and policies.

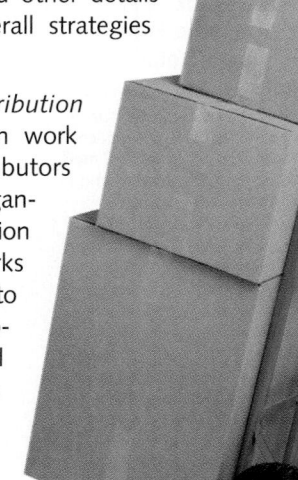

● *Forge regional distribution links.* Producers often work with multiple distributors within a region. Organizing regional distribution councils or networks allows the producer to encourage ongoing coordination of regional distribution strategies for its products.

directly from a company's existing inventory. For example, on average, catalog retailers fill 90.8 percent of their orders from their existing inventories. *Timeliness* refers to how quickly the product is shipped out to the customer. For example, some organizations set a service standard of shipping the product within 24 hours. *Accuracy* refers to whether the product the customer ordered is the product that is shipped to the customer. Some organizations have achieved better than a 99 percent order accuracy rate.[5]

Customers seeking a high level of customer service may also want sizable inventories, efficient order processing, availability of emergency shipments, progress reports, postsale services, prompt replacement of defective items, and warranties. Customers' inventory requirements influence the expected level of physical distribution service. Business customers seeking to reduce their inventory storage and shipping costs may expect wholesalers or third-party firms to take responsibility for maintaining inventory in the marketing channel or to assume the cost of premium transportation. Because service needs vary from customer to customer, companies must analyze—and adapt to—customer preferences. Attention to customer needs and preferences is crucial to increasing sales and obtaining repeat orders. A company's failure to provide the desired level of service may mean loss of customers.

Companies must also examine the service levels competitors offer and match or exceed those standards when the costs of providing the services can be justified by the sales generated. Many companies guarantee service performance to win customers. Services are provided most effectively when service standards are developed and stated in measurable terms, for example, "98 percent of all orders filled within 48 hours." Standards should be communicated clearly to both customers and employees, and diligently enforced. Many service standards outline delivery times and specify provisions for backordering, returning goods, and obtaining emergency shipments.

Reducing Total Distribution Costs. Although physical distribution managers try to minimize the costs associated with order processing, inventory management, materials handling, warehousing, and transportation, decreasing the costs in one area often raises them in another. Figure 15.3 shows the percentage of total costs that physical distribution functions represent. A total-cost approach to physical distribution enables managers to view physical distribution as a system rather than a collection of unrelated activities. This approach shifts the emphasis from lowering the separate costs of individual activities to minimizing overall distribution costs.

The total-cost approach involves analyzing the costs of all distribution alternatives, even those considered too impractical or expensive. Total-cost analyses weigh

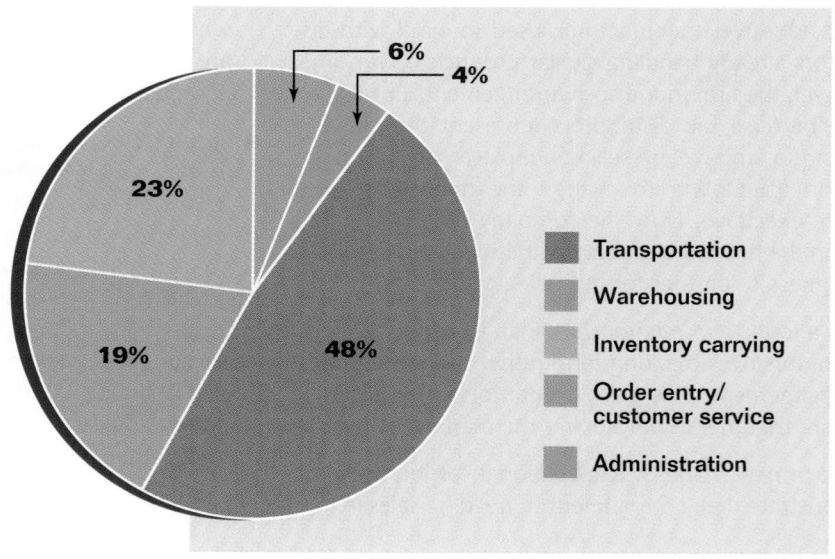

FIGURE 15.3
Proportional Cost of Each Physical Distribution Function as a Percentage of Total Distribution Costs

Source: Herbert W. Davis and Company, Ft. Lee. NJ. "Logistics Cost and Service, 2000," www.establishinc.com. Reprinted by permission of Herbert W. Davis and Company.

6%

4%

23%

19%

48%

Transportation

Warehousing

Inventory carrying

Order entry/
customer service

Administration

inventory levels against warehousing expenses, materials costs against various modes of transportation, and all distribution costs against customer service standards. Costs of potential sales losses from lower performance levels must also be considered. In many cases, accounting procedures and statistical methods are used to figure total costs. When hundreds of combinations of distribution variables are possible, computer simulations are helpful. A distribution system's lowest total cost is never the result of using a combination of the cheapest functions. Instead, it is the lowest overall cost compatible with the company's stated service objectives. For example, Federated Department Stores created a separate division called Federated Logistics and Operations in the mid-1990s to coordinate merchandise distribution, logistics, and vendor technology across the company, including online retail operations and brick-and-mortar retail operations such as Burdine's, Macy's, Rich's/Lazarus, Bloomingdale's, Goldsmith's, Sterns, and The Bon Marché. Through this integrated physical distribution system, Federated has saved more than $150 million over the last five years.[6]

Physical distribution managers must be sensitive to the issue of cost tradeoffs. Higher costs in one functional area of a distribution system may be necessary to achieve lower costs in another. Tradeoffs are strategic decisions to combine (and recombine) resources for greatest cost-effectiveness. When distribution managers regard the system as a network of integrated functions, tradeoffs become useful tools in implementing a unified, cost-effective distribution strategy.

Reducing Cycle Time. Another important goal of physical distribution involves reducing **cycle time,** the time needed to complete a process. Doing so can reduce costs and/or increase customer service. Many companies, particularly overnight delivery firms, major news media, and publishers of books of current interest, are using cycle time reduction to gain a competitive advantage. FedEx believes so strongly in this concept that, in the interest of being the fastest provider of overnight delivery, it conducts research on reducing cycle time and identifying new management techniques and procedures for its employees.

cycle time The time needed to complete a process

Reducing Cycle Time
BAX Global helps its customers reduce cycle time by providing guaranteed overnight delivery.

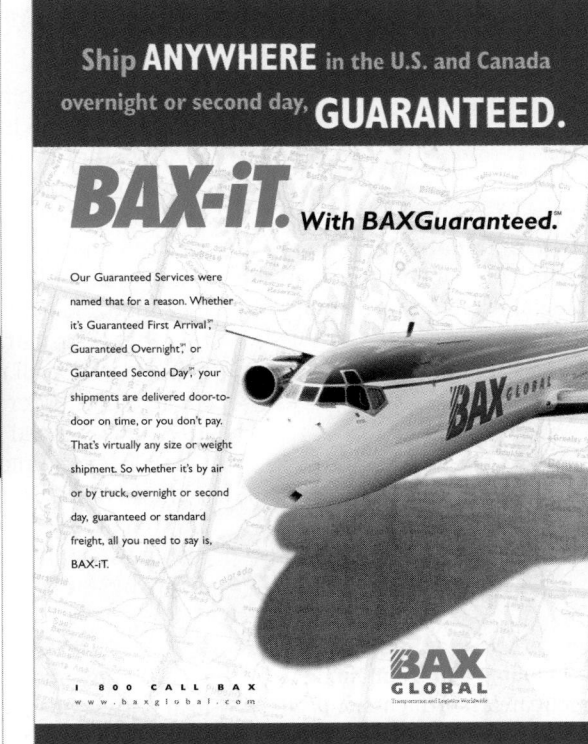

Functions of Physical Distribution

As we saw earlier, physical distribution includes the activities necessary to get products from producers to customers. In this section we take a closer look at these activities, which include order processing, inventory management, materials handling, warehousing, and transportation.

order processing The receipt and transmission of sales order information

Order Processing.
Order processing is the receipt and transmission of sales order information. Although management sometimes overlooks the importance of these activities, efficient order processing facilitates product flow. Computerized order processing provides a database for all supply chain members to increase their productivity. When carried out quickly and accurately, order processing contributes to customer satisfaction, decreased costs and cycle time, and increased profits.

Order processing entails three main tasks: order entry, order handling, and order delivery. Order entry begins when customers or salespeople place purchase orders via telephone, mail, e-mail, or website. Electronic ordering is less time consuming than a manual, paper-based ordering system, and reduces costs. In some companies, sales representatives receive and enter orders personally, and also handle complaints, prepare progress reports, and forward sales order information.

Order handling involves several tasks. Once an order is entered, it is transmitted to a warehouse, where product availability is verified, and to the credit department, where prices, terms, and the customer's credit rating are checked. If the credit department approves the purchase, warehouse personnel (sometimes assisted by automated equipment) pick and assemble the order. If the requested product is not in stock, a production order is sent to the factory or the customer is offered a substitute.

When the order has been assembled and packed for shipment, the warehouse schedules delivery with an appropriate carrier. If the customer pays for rush service, overnight delivery by FedEx, UPS, or another overnight carrier is used. The customer is sent an invoice, inventory records are adjusted, and the order is delivered.

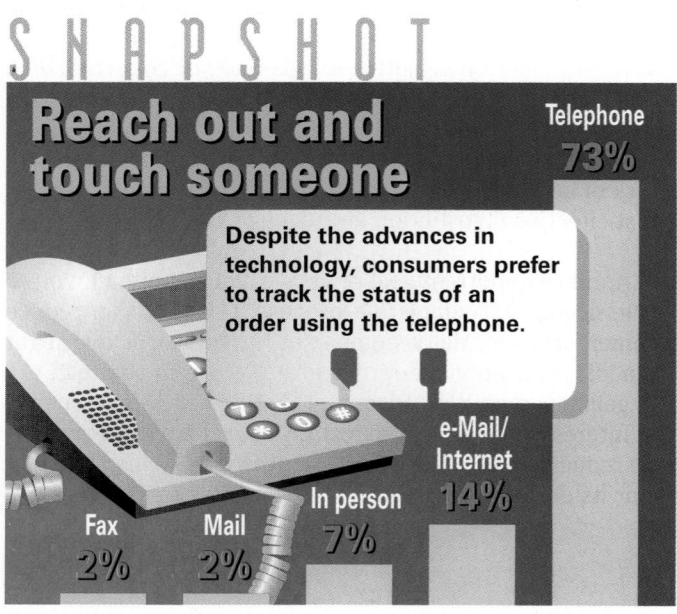

SNAPSHOT

Reach out and touch someone

Despite the advances in technology, consumers prefer to track the status of an order using the telephone.

Telephone **73%**

e-Mail/ Internet **14%**

In person **7%**

Fax **2%** Mail **2%**

Source: *USA Today,* March 26, 2001. Copyright © 2001, *USA Today.* Reprinted with permission.

Whether to use a manual or an electronic order-processing system depends on which method provides the greater speed and accuracy within cost limits. Manual processing suffices for small-volume orders and is more flexible in certain situations. Most companies, however, use **electronic data interchange (EDI),** which uses computer technology to integrate order processing with production, inventory, accounting, and transportation. Within the supply chain, EDI functions as an information system that links marketing channel members and outsourcing firms together. It reduces paperwork for all members of the supply chain and allows them to share information on invoices, orders, payments, inquiries, and scheduling. Consequently many companies have pushed their suppliers toward EDI to reduce distribution costs and cycle times. For example, Dobbs, an airline food service company, has all its merchandising vendors on EDI systems and requests that all other suppliers be EDI-capable. FedEx is another major user of EDI systems. It uses EDI to develop innovative solutions to resolve some of its complex business problems. In addition, a large proportion of its major business customers carry out transactions via EDI.[7]

electronic data interchange (EDI) A computerized means of integrating order processing with production, inventory, accounting, and transportation

Inventory Management.
Inventory management involves developing and maintaining adequate assortments of products to meet customers' needs. Because a firm's investment in inventory usually represents a significant portion of its total assets, inventory decisions have a major impact on physical distribution costs and

inventory management Developing and maintaining adequate assortments of products to meet customers' needs

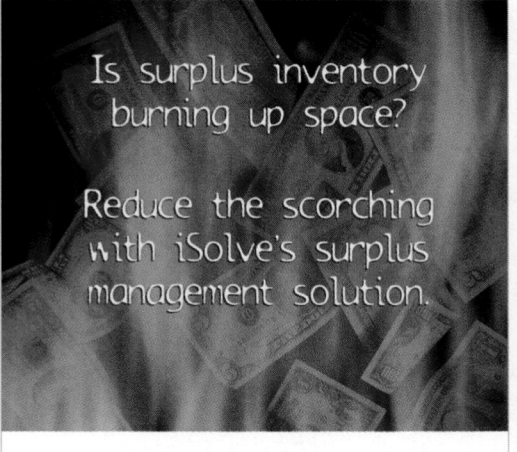

Improving Inventory Management

To properly manage inventory, an organization at times must dispose of excess inventory. Organizations such as iSolve engage in buying, selling, and bartering surplus inventory. Also available to help organizations achieve improved efficiencies in inventory management are a number of software solutions, such as those offered by Manugistics.

the level of customer service provided. When too few products are carried in inventory, the result is *stockouts,* or shortages of products, which in turn result in brand switching, lower sales, and loss of customers. When too many products (or too many slow-moving products) are carried, costs increase, as do risks of product obsolescence, pilferage, and damage. The objective of inventory management is to minimize inventory costs while maintaining an adequate supply of goods to satisfy customers. To achieve this objective, marketers focus on two major issues: when to order and how much to order.

To determine when to order, a marketer calculates the *reorder point,* the inventory level that signals the need to place a new order. To calculate the reorder point, the marketer must know the order lead time, the usage rate, and the amount of safety stock required. The *order lead time* refers to the average time lapse between placing the order and receiving it. The *usage rate* is the rate at which a product's inventory is used or sold during a specific time period. *Safety stock* is the amount of extra inventory a firm keeps to guard against stockouts resulting from above-average usage rates and/or longer-than-expected lead times. The reorder point can be calculated using the following formula:

$$\text{Reorder Point} = (\text{Order Lead Time} \times \text{Usage Rate}) + \text{Safety Stock}$$

Thus, if order lead time is 10 days, usage rate is 3 units per day, and safety stock is 20 units, the reorder point is 50 units.

Efficient inventory management with accurate reorder points is crucial for firms that use a **just-in-time (JIT)** approach, in which supplies arrive just as they are needed for use in production or for resale. When using JIT, companies maintain low inventory levels and purchase products and materials in small quantities whenever they need them. Usually there is no safety stock, and suppliers are expected to provide consistently high-quality products. Just-in-time inventory management requires a high level of coordination between producers and suppliers, but it eliminates waste and reduces inventory costs significantly. This approach has been used successfully by many well-known firms, including Daimler-Chrysler, Harley Davidson, and Dell Computer, to reduce costs and boost customer satisfaction. When a JIT approach is used in a supply chain, suppliers often move close to their customers.

just-in-time (JIT)   An inventory management approach in which supplies arrive just when needed for production or resale

High-Tech Equipment Enhances Materials Handling
Organizations gain considerable efficiencies in materials handling through the use of technologically advanced electronic equipment, such as that offered by the Raymond Corp.

materials handling Physical handling of products

Materials Handling.

Materials handling, the physical handling of products, is an important factor in warehouse operations, as well as in transportation from points of production to points of consumption. Efficient procedures and techniques for materials handling minimize inventory management costs, reduce the number of times a good is handled, improve customer service, and increase customer satisfaction. Systems for packaging, labeling, loading, and movement must be coordinated to maximize cost reduction and customer satisfaction.

Product characteristics often determine handling. For example, the characteristics of bulk liquids and gases determine how they can be moved and stored. Internal packaging is also an important consideration in materials handling; goods must be packaged correctly to prevent damage or breakage during handling and transportation. Most companies employ packaging consultants to help them decide which packaging materials and methods will result in the most efficient handling.

Unit loading and containerization are two common methods used in materials handling. With *unit loading,* one or more boxes are placed on a pallet or skid; these units can then be efficiently loaded by mechanical means such as forklifts, trucks, or conveyer systems. *Containerization* is the consolidation of many items into a single large container, which is sealed at its point of origin and opened at its destination. Containers are usually 8 feet wide, 8 feet high, and 10 to 40 feet long. They can be conveniently stacked and shipped via train, barge, or ship. Once containers reach their destinations, wheel assemblies can be added to make them suitable for ground transportation. Because individual items are not handled in transit, containerization greatly increases efficiency and security in shipping.

warehousing The design and operation of facilities for storing and moving goods

Warehousing.

Warehousing, the design and operation of facilities for storing and moving goods, is another important physical distribution function. Warehousing provides time utility by enabling firms to compensate for dissimilar production and consumption rates. When mass production creates a greater stock of goods than can be sold immediately, companies may warehouse the surplus until customers are ready to buy. Warehousing also helps stabilize prices and availability of seasonal items.

Warehousing is not simply the storage of products. The basic distribution functions warehouses perform include receiving, identifying, sorting, and dispatching goods to storage; holding goods in storage until needed; recalling and assembling stored goods for shipment; and dispatching shipments. When warehouses receive goods by carloads or truckloads, they break down the shipments into smaller quantities for individual customers.

The choice of warehouse facilities is an important strategic consideration. The right type of warehouse allows a company to reduce transportation and inventory costs or improve service to customers. The wrong type of warehouse may drain company resources. Beyond deciding how many facilities to operate and where to locate them, a company must determine which type of warehouse is most appropriate. Warehouses fall into two general categories: private and public. In many cases, a combination of private and public facilities provides the most flexible warehousing approach.

private warehouses
Company-operated facilities for storing and shipping products

Companies operate **private warehouses** for shipping and storing their own products. A firm usually leases or purchases a private warehouse when its warehousing needs in a given geographic market are substantial and stable enough to warrant a long-term commitment to a fixed facility. Private warehouses are also appropriate for firms that require special handling and storage and that want control of warehouse design and operation. Retailers like Sears, Radio Shack, and Kmart find it economical to integrate private warehousing with purchasing and distribution for their retail outlets. When sales volumes are fairly stable, ownership and control of a private warehouse may provide benefits such as property appreciation. Private warehouses, however, face fixed costs such as insurance, taxes, maintenance, and debt expense. They also limit flexibility when firms wish to move inventories to more strategic locations. Before tying up capital in a private warehouse or entering into a long-term lease, a company should consider its resources, level of expertise in warehouse management, and the role of the warehouse in its overall marketing strategy. Many private warehouses are being eliminated by direct links between producers and customers, reduced cycle times, and outsourcing to public warehouses.

public warehouses
Businesses that lease storage space and related physical distribution facilities to other firms

Public warehouses lease storage space and related physical distribution facilities as an outsource service to other companies. They sometimes provide such distribution services as receiving, unloading, inspecting, and reshipping products; filling orders; providing financing; displaying products; and coordinating shipments. They are especially useful to firms that have seasonal production or low-volume storage needs, have inventories that must be maintained in many locations, are testing or entering new markets, or own private warehouses but occasionally require additional storage space. Public warehouses also serve as collection points during product recall programs. Whereas private warehouses have fixed costs, public warehouses offer variable (and often lower) costs because users rent space and purchase warehousing services only as needed.

Many public warehouses furnish security for products being used as collateral for loans, a service provided at either the warehouse or the site of the owner's inventory. *Field public warehouses* are established by public warehouses at the owner's inventory location. The warehouser becomes custodian of the products and issues a receipt that can be used as collateral for a loan. Public warehouses also provide *bonded storage,* a warehousing arrangement in which imported or taxable products are not released until the products' owners pay U.S. customs duties, taxes, or other fees. Bonded warehouses enable firms to defer tax payments on such items until they are delivered to customers.

distribution centers   Large, centralized warehouses that focus on moving rather than storing goods

Distribution centers are large, centralized warehouses that receive goods from factories and suppliers, regroup them into orders, and ship them to customers quickly, the focus being on movement of goods rather than storage.[8] Distribution centers are specially designed for rapid flow of products. They are usually one-story buildings (to eliminate elevators) with access to transportation networks such as major highways or railway lines. Many distribution centers are highly automated, with computer-directed robots, forklifts, and hoists that collect and move products to loading docks. Although some public warehouses offer such specialized services, most distribution centers are privately owned. They serve customers in regional markets and, in some cases, function as consolidation points for a company's branch warehouses. Distribution centers typically are located within 500 miles of half of a company's market.

Distribution centers offer several benefits, the most important being improved customer service. Distribution centers ensure product availability by maintaining full product lines, and the speed of their operations cuts delivery time to a minimum. Distribution centers also reduce costs. Instead of making many smaller shipments to scattered warehouses and customers, factories ship large quantities of goods directly to distribution centers at bulk rates, thus lowering transportation costs. Furthermore, rapid inventory turnover lessens the need for warehouses and cuts storage costs. Federated Department Stores serves more than 400 stores through seven distribution centers, including two in New Jersey, two in California, and one each in Florida, Georgia, and Washington.[9] Some distribution centers facilitate production by receiving and consolidating raw materials and providing final assembly for certain products.

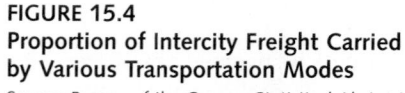

transportation The movement of products from where they are made to where they are used

Transportation.

Transportation, the movement of products from where they are made to where they are used, is the most expensive physical distribution function. Because product availability and timely deliveries depend on transportation functions, transportation decisions directly affect customer service. A firm may even build its distribution and marketing strategy around a unique transportation system if that system can ensure on-time deliveries and thereby give the firm a competitive edge. Companies may build their own transportation fleets (private carriers) or outsource the transportation function to a common or contract carrier.

Transportation Modes   There are five basic transportation modes for moving physical goods: railroads, trucks, waterways, airways, and pipelines. Each mode offers distinct advantages. Many companies adopt physical handling procedures that facilitate the use of two or more modes in combination. Figure 15.4 indicates the percentage of intercity freight carried by each transportation mode; Table 15.4 shows typical transportation modes for various products.

Railroads like Union Pacific and Canadian National carry heavy, bulky freight that must be shipped long distances overland. Railroads commonly haul minerals, sand, lumber, chemicals, and farm products, as well as low-value manufactured goods and an increasing number of automobiles. They are especially efficient for transporting full carloads, which can be shipped at lower rates than smaller quantities because they require less handling. Many companies locate factories or warehouses near major rail lines or on spur lines for convenient loading and unloading.

FIGURE 15.4
Proportion of Intercity Freight Carried by Various Transportation Modes
Source: Bureau of the Census, *Statistical Abstract of the United States* (Washington, D.C.: Government Printing Office, 2000), p. 621.

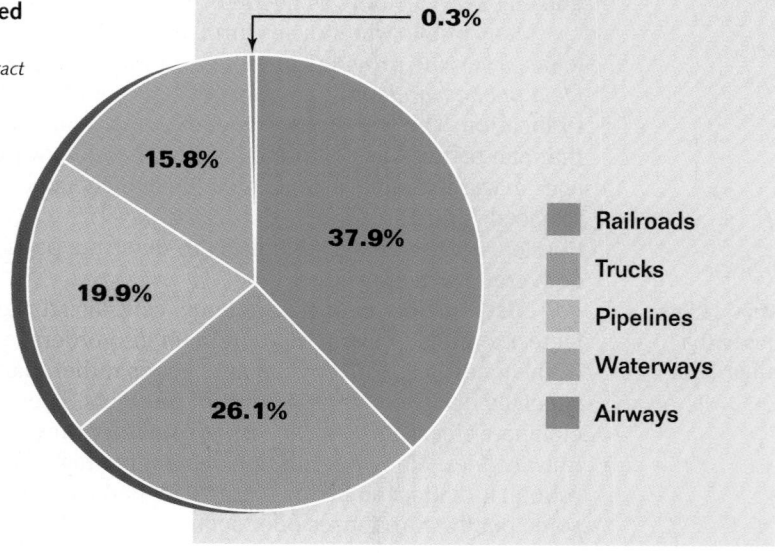

Table 15.4	Typical Transportation Modes for Various Products			
Railroads	**Trucks**	**Waterways**	**Airways**	**Pipelines**
Coal	Clothing	Petroleum	Flowers	Oil
Grain	Paper goods	Chemicals	Perishable food	Processed coal
Chemicals	Computers	Iron ore	Instruments	Natural gas
Lumber	Books	Bauxite	Emergency parts	Water
Automobiles	Livestock	Grain	Overnight mail	Chemicals
Steel				

Trucks provide the most flexible schedules and routes of all major transportation modes because they can go almost anywhere. Because trucks have a unique ability to move goods directly from factory or warehouse to customer, they are often used in conjunction with other forms of transport that cannot provide door-to-door deliveries. Although trucks usually travel much faster than trains, they are more expensive and somewhat more vulnerable to bad weather. They are also subject to size and weight restrictions on the products they carry. Trucks are sometimes criticized for high levels of loss and damage to freight and for delays caused by the rehandling of small shipments. In response, the trucking industry has turned to computerized tracking of shipments and the development of new equipment to speed loading and unloading.

Truck Transportation
Compared to other transportation modes, trucking companies offer the most flexible schedules and are able to go almost anywhere.

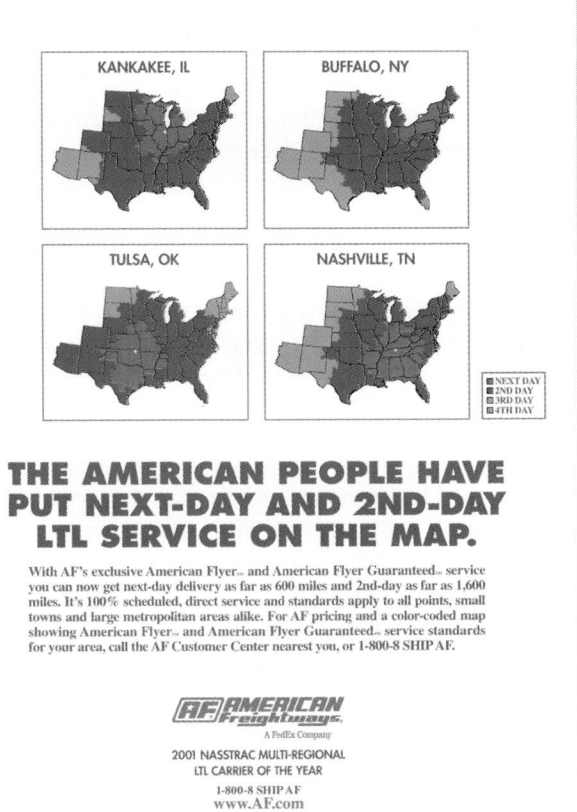

Waterways are the cheapest method of shipping heavy, low-value, nonperishable goods such as ore, coal, grain, and petroleum products. Water carriers offer considerable capacity. Powered by tugboats and towboats, barges that travel along intercoastal canals, inland rivers, and navigation systems can haul at least ten times the weight of one rail car, and ocean-going vessels can haul thousands of containers. However, many markets are inaccessible by water transportation unless supplemented by rail or truck. Furthermore, water transport is extremely slow and sometimes comes to a standstill during freezing weather. Companies depending on waterways may ship their entire inventory during the summer and then store it for winter use. Droughts and floods also create difficulties for users of inland waterway transportation. Nevertheless, the extreme fuel efficiency of water transportation and the continuing globalization of marketing will likely increase its use in the future.

Air transportation is the fastest but most expensive form of shipping. It is used most often for perishable goods; for high-value, low-bulk items; and for products requiring quick delivery over long distances, such as emergency shipments. Some air carriers transport combinations of passengers, freight, and mail. Despite its expense, air transit can reduce warehousing and packaging costs and losses from theft and damage, thus helping to lower total costs (but truck transportation needed for pickup and final delivery adds to cost and transit time). Although air transport accounts for less than 1 percent of total ton-miles carried, its importance as a mode of transportation is growing. In fact, the success of many businesses is now based on the availability of overnight air delivery service provided by such organizations as UPS, Airborne, FedEx, DHL, RPS Air, and the U.S. Postal Service. Amazon.com, for example, ships via UPS many products ordered online within a day

BUILDING CUSTOMER RELATIONSHIPS

FedEx Custom Critical Coddles Customers

FedEx Custom Critical's name highlights its most important customer benefit: meeting critical delivery deadlines. All kinds of customers depend on this FedEx truck and air freight firm to get precious cargo to its destination on time—guaranteed. Oprah Winfrey once hired the company to ship special lighting equipment to Texas on short notice for a live telecast. PPG Ohio, which manufactures glass for building construction, has had only one shipment delivered late during a decade of sending urgent shipments via FedEx Custom Critical.

Weekdays and weekends, at any hour, in any weather, FedEx Custom Critical is ready to pick up a shipment within 90 minutes of a customer's call. Even more important, once the company sets a delivery time, it guarantees to have the cargo at its destination within 15 minutes of that time. If a delivery is two hours late, the customer gets a 25 percent discount; if four hours late, the customer gets a 50 percent discount. But the company rarely has to give discounts because it delivers on schedule 96 percent of the time. Still, with profits—and customer satisfaction—hanging in the balance, FedEx Custom Critical uses technology to keep everything running smoothly.

Trucks are equipped with satellite dishes and computers so the company can track every shipment through every mile of the journey. For especially dangerous or delicate freight, such as hazardous materials or temperature-sensitive commodities, the company rolls out its White Glove Services. Trained operators using specially equipped trucks and tools know exactly how to load, transport, and unload such shipments without damage. For customers who must get a shipment out immediately, regardless of cost, FedEx Custom Critical offers chartered airplanes and dedicated ground transportation.

FedEx Custom Critical also has a new division, UrgentFreight, to serve cost-conscious customers shipping heavier loads for same-day or next-day delivery. Customers simply log on to the UrgentFreight website (http://www.urgentfreight.com) and post their transportation requirements. Carriers have 15 minutes to respond by bidding for the business. Once the price is set, customers and carriers work out the rest of the details by phone. UrgentFreight carefully investigates each carrier's safety ratings and insurance policies before allowing it to post bids, reassuring customers about the level of service they can expect from participating carriers. This is just another way FedEx Custom Critical coddles its customers with top-quality service and on-time performance.

Feeling stranded? Helpless? All alone?

Clearly you didn't use Virgin Atlantic Cargo. Our teams of dedicated professionals ensure that your freight arrives at the right place at the right time. Without incident. So before you say *bon voyage* to your next international shipment, call Virgin Atlantic Cargo. You'll never feel deserted.

See the difference our people make.
Call Virgin Atlantic Cargo today at **1-800-828-6822**,
and visit us online at www.virgin.com/cargo.

North America   Caribbean   United Kingdom   Asia   South Africa   India   Greece

Air Transportation
Although more expensive, air transport offers the fastest mode of transportation. Some organizations use higher-cost air transportation in order to reduce warehousing and inventory costs.

of order. In addition, a number of companies are turning to air freight because they are ordering smaller quantities more frequently and requiring high-speed transportation in an effort to reduce inventory costs.[10]

Pipelines, the most automated transportation mode, usually belong to the shipper and carry the shipper's products. Most pipelines carry petroleum products or chemicals. The Trans-Alaska Pipeline, owned and operated by a consortium of oil companies that includes Exxon, Mobil, and BP-Amoco, transports crude oil from remote oil-drilling sites in central Alaska to shipping terminals on the coast. Slurry pipelines carry pulverized coal, grain, or wood chips suspended in water. Pipelines move products slowly but continuously and at relatively low cost. They are dependable and minimize the problems of product damage and theft. However, contents are subject to as much as 1 percent shrinkage, usually from evaporation. Pipelines have also been a concern to environmentalists, who fear installation and leaks could harm plants and animals.

Choosing Transportation Modes Distribution managers select a transportation mode based on the combination of cost, speed, dependability, load flexibility, accessibility, and frequency that is most appropriate for their products and generates the desired level of customer service. Table 15.5 shows relative ratings of each transportation mode by these selection criteria.

Marketers compare alternative transportation modes to determine whether benefits from a more expensive mode are worth higher costs. Air freight carriers such as FedEx promise many benefits, like speed and dependability, but at much higher costs than other transportation modes. When such benefits are less important, marketers prefer lower costs. Bicycles, for instance, are often shipped by rail because an unassembled bicycle can be shipped more than a thousand miles on a train for as little as $3.60. Bicycle wholesalers plan purchases far enough in advance to capitalize on this cost advantage. Companies such as Accuship can assist marketers in analyzing a variety of transportation options. This Internet firm's software gives corporate users, like Coca-Cola and the Home Shopping Network, information about the speed and cost of different transportation modes and allows them to order shipping and then track shipments online. Accuship processes nearly 1 million shipments every day.[11]

Speed is measured by the total time a carrier has possession of goods, including the time required for pickup and delivery, handling, and movement between points of origin and destination. Speed obviously affects a marketer's ability to provide service, but other, less obvious implications are important as well. Marketers take advantage

Table 15.5	**Relative Ratings of Transportation Modes by Selection Criteria**					
Mode	**Cost**	**Speed**	**Dependability**	**Load Flexibility**	**Accessibility**	**Frequency**
Railroads	Moderate	Average	Average	High	High	Low
Trucks	High	Fast	High	Average	Very high	High
Waterways	Very low	Very slow	Average	Very high	Limited	Very low
Airways	Very high	Very fast	High	Low	Average	Average
Pipelines	Low	Slow	High	Very low	Very limited	Very high

of transit time to process orders for goods en route, a capability especially important to agricultural and raw materials shippers. Some railroads also let carloads in transit be redirected for maximum flexibility in selecting markets. A carload of peaches, for instance, may be shipped to a closer destination if the fruit is in danger of ripening too quickly.

Dependability of a transportation mode is determined by the consistency of service provided. Marketers must be able to count on carriers to deliver goods on time and in an acceptable condition. Along with speed, dependability affects a marketer's inventory costs, including sales lost when merchandise is not available. Undependable transportation necessitates higher inventory levels to avoid stockouts, whereas reliable delivery service enables customers to carry smaller inventories at lower cost. Security problems vary considerably among transportation modes and are a major consideration in carrier selection. A firm does not incur costs directly when goods are lost or damaged because the carrier is usually held liable. Nevertheless, poor service and lack of security indirectly lead to increased costs and lower profits because damaged or lost goods are not available for immediate sale or use.

Load flexibility is the degree to which a transportation mode can provide appropriate equipment and conditions for moving specific kinds of goods, and can be adapted for moving other products. Many products must be shipped under controlled temperature and humidity. Other products, such as liquids or gases, require special equipment or facilities for shipment. A marketer with unusual transport needs can consult the *Official Railway Equipment Register,* which lists the various types of cars and equipment each railroad owns. As Table 15.5 shows, waterways and railroads have the highest load flexibility, whereas pipelines have the lowest.

Accessibility refers to a carrier's ability to move goods over a specific route or network. For example, marketers evaluating transportation modes for reaching Great Falls, Montana, would consider rail lines, truck routes, and scheduled airline service but would eliminate water-borne carriers because Great Falls is inaccessible by water. Some carriers differentiate themselves by serving areas their competitors do not. After deregulation, many large railroad companies sold off or abandoned unprofitable routes, making rail service inaccessible to facilities located on spur lines. Some marketers were forced to buy or lease their own truck fleets to get their products to market. In recent years, small, short-line railroad companies have started buying up track and creating networks of low-cost feeder lines to reach underserved markets.

Frequency refers to how often a company can send shipments by a specific transportation mode. When using pipelines, shipments can be continuous. A marketer shipping by railroad or waterway is limited by the carriers' schedules.

Coordinating Transportation   To take advantage of the benefits offered by various transportation modes and compensate for deficiencies, marketers often combine and coordinate two or more modes. In recent years, **intermodal transportation,** as this integrated approach is sometimes called, has become easier because of new developments within the transportation industry.

Several kinds of intermodal shipping are available. All combine the flexibility of trucking with the low cost or speed of other forms of transport. Containerization facilitates intermodal transportation by consolidating shipments into sealed containers for transport by *piggyback* (shipping that uses both truck trailers and railway flatcars), *fishyback* (truck trailers and water carriers), and *birdyback* (truck trailers and air carriers). As transportation costs have increased, intermodal shipping has gained popularity.

Specialized outsource agencies provide other forms of transport coordination. Known as **freight forwarders,** these firms combine shipments from several organizations into efficient lot sizes. Small loads (less than 500 pounds) are much more expensive to ship than full carloads or truckloads, which frequently requires consolidation. Freight forwarders take small loads from various marketers, buy transport space from carriers, and arrange for goods to be delivered to buyers. Freight forwarders' profits come from the margin between the higher, less-than-carload rates they charge each marketer and the lower carload rates they themselves pay. Because large shipments require less handling, use of freight forwarders can speed delivery.

intermodal transportation
Two or more transportation modes used in combination

freight forwarders
Organizations that consolidate shipments from several firms into efficient lot sizes

Freight forwarders can also determine the most efficient carriers and routes and are useful for shipping goods to foreign markets. Some companies prefer to outsource their shipping to freight forwarders because the latter provide door-to-door service.

megacarriers Freight transportation firms that provide several modes of shipment

Another transportation innovation is the development of **megacarriers,** freight transportation companies that offer several shipment methods, including rail, truck, and air service. CSX, for example, has trains, barges, container ships, trucks, and pipelines, thus offering a multitude of transportation services. In addition, air carriers have increased their ground transportation services. As they expand the range of transportation alternatives, carriers too put greater stress on customer service.

Strategic Issues in Physical Distribution

The physical distribution functions discussed in this chapter—order processing, inventory management, materials handling, warehousing, and transportation—account for about half of all marketing costs. Whether performed by a producer, wholesaler, or retailer, or outsourced to some other firm, these functions have a significant impact on customer service and satisfaction, which are of prime importance to all members of the supply chain.

The strategic importance of physical distribution is evident in all elements of the marketing mix. Product design and packaging must allow for efficient stacking, storage, transport, and tracking. Differentiating products by size, color, and style must take into account additional demands placed on warehousing and shipping facilities. Competitive pricing may depend on a firm's ability to provide reliable delivery or emergency shipments of replacement parts. Firms trying to lower inventory costs may offer quantity discounts to encourage large purchases. Promotional campaigns must be coordinated with distribution functions so that advertised products are available to buyers and order-processing departments can handle additional sales orders efficiently. Channel members must consider warehousing and transportation costs, which may influence a firm's policy on stockouts or its choice to centralize (or decentralize) inventory.

Improving physical distribution starts by closing the gap with customers. The entire supply chain must understand and meet customers' requirements. An effective way to improve physical distribution is to integrate processes across the boundaries of all members of the supply chain. The full scope of the physical distribution process includes suppliers, manufacturers, wholesalers, retailers, transportation firms, and warehouses. To work well, the process requires a formal, integrated plan to balance supply and demand within a defined time period. Physical distribution can also be improved by developing cooperative relationships with suppliers of component parts and services. These relationships should emphasize joint improvement. Cooperation can be enhanced through information technology that allows channel partners to work together to plan production and physical distribution activities, improve the efficiency and safety of product handling and movement, and reduce waste and costs for the benefit of all channel members, including the customer.

No single distribution system is ideal for all situations, and any system must be evaluated continually and adapted as necessary. Pressures to adjust service levels or to reduce costs may lead to a total restructuring of supply chain relationships. The ensuing changes in transportation, warehousing, materials handling, and inventory may affect speed of delivery, reliability, and economy of service. Recognizing that changes in any major distribution function may affect all other functions, marketing strategists consider customers' changing needs and preferences. Customer-oriented marketers analyze the characteristics of their target markets and plan distribution systems to provide products in the right place, at the right time, and at acceptable costs.

Distribution Solutions
Companies such as Roe Logistics can help an organization with a variety of distribution functions, including clearing international customs, freight forwarding, warehousing, and shipping dangerous goods.

Summary

Wholesaling consists of all transactions in which products are bought for resale, for making other products, or for general business operations. Wholesalers are individuals or organizations that facilitate and expedite exchanges that are primarily wholesale transactions. For producers, wholesalers are a source of financial assistance and information; by performing specialized accumulation and allocation functions, they allow producers to concentrate on manufacturing products. Wholesalers provide retailers with buying expertise, wide product lines, efficient distribution, and warehousing and storage.

Merchant wholesalers are independently owned businesses that take title to goods and assume ownership risks. They are either full-service wholesalers, offering the widest possible range of wholesaling functions, or limited-service wholesalers, providing only some marketing services and specializing in a few functions. Full-service merchant wholesalers include general-merchandise wholesalers, which offer a wide but relatively shallow product mix; limited-line wholesalers, which offer extensive assortments within a few product lines; specialty-line wholesalers, which carry only a single product line or a few items within a line; and rack jobbers, which own and service display racks in supermarkets and other stores. Limited-service merchant wholesalers include cash-and-carry wholesalers, which sell to small businesses, require payment in cash, and do not deliver; truck wholesalers, which sell a limited line of products from their own trucks directly to customers; drop shippers, which own goods and negotiate sales but never take possession of products; and mail-order wholesalers, which sell to retail and business buyers through direct-mail catalogs.

Agents and brokers, sometimes called functional middlemen, negotiate purchases and expedite sales in exchange for a commission, but they do not take title to products. Usually specializing in certain products, they can provide valuable sales expertise. Whereas agents represent buyers or sellers on a permanent basis, brokers are intermediaries that buyers and sellers employ on a temporary basis to negotiate exchanges. Manufacturers' agents offer customers the complete product lines of two or more sellers. Selling agents market a complete product line or a producer's entire output and perform every wholesaling function except taking title to products. Commission merchants are agents that receive goods on consignment from local sellers and negotiate sales in large, central markets.

Manufacturers' sales branches and offices are owned by manufacturers. Sales branches sell products and provide support services for the manufacturer's sales force in a given location. Sales offices carry no inventory and function much as agents do.

Physical distribution, or logistics, refers to the activities used to move products from producers to customers and other end users. These activities include order processing, inventory management, materials handling, warehousing, and transportation. An efficient physical distribution system is an important component of an overall marketing strategy because it can decrease costs and increase customer satisfaction. Within the marketing channel, physical distribution activities are often performed by a wholesaler, but they may be performed by a producer or retailer, or outsourced to a third party.

The main objectives of physical distribution are to decrease costs and transit time while increasing customer service. Physical distribution managers strive to balance service, distribution costs, and resources. Because customers' service needs vary, companies must adapt to them. They must also offer service comparable to or better than their competitors' and develop and communicate desirable customer service policies. Costs of providing service are minimized most effectively through the total-cost approach, which evaluates costs of the distribution system as a whole rather than as a collection of separate activities. Reducing cycle time, the time it takes to complete a process, is also important.

Order processing is the receipt and transmission of sales order information. It consists of three main tasks. Order entry begins when customers or salespeople place purchase orders by mail, e-mail, telephone, or computer. Order handling involves verifying product availability, checking customer credit, and preparing products for shipping. Order delivery is provided by the carrier most suitable for a desired level of customer service. Order processing can be done manually, but it is usually accomplished through electronic data interchange (EDI), a computerized system that integrates order processing with production, inventory, accounting, and transportation.

The objective of inventory management is to minimize inventory costs while maintaining a supply of goods adequate for customers' needs. To avoid stockouts without tying up too much capital in inventory, firms must have systematic methods for determining a reorder point, the inventory level that signals the need to place a new order. When firms use the just-in-time approach, products arrive just as they are needed for use in production or resale.

Materials handling, the physical handling of products, is an important factor in warehouse operations, as well as in transportation from points of production to points of consumption. Systems for packaging, labeling, loading, and movement must be coordinated to maximize cost reduction and customer satisfaction. Basic handling systems include unit loading, which entails placing boxes on pallets or skids and using mechanical devices to move them, and containerization.

Warehousing involves the design and operation of facilities for storing and moving goods. Private warehouses are operated by companies for the purpose of distributing their own products. Public warehouses are businesses that lease storage space and related physical distribution facilities to other firms. Distribution centers are large, centralized warehouses specially designed for rapid movement of goods to customers. In many cases, a combination of private and public facilities is the most flexible warehousing approach.

Transportation adds time and place utility to a product by moving it from where it is made to where it is purchased and used. The basic modes of transporting goods are railroads, trucks, waterways, airways, and pipelines. The criteria marketers use when selecting a transportation mode are cost, speed, dependability, load flexibility, accessibility, and frequency. Intermodal transportation allows marketers to combine advantages of two or more modes of transport. Freight forwarders coordinate trans-

port by combining small shipments from several organizations into efficient lot sizes, while megacarriers offer several shipment methods.

Physical distribution functions account for about half of all marketing costs and have a significant impact on customer satisfaction. Effective marketers are therefore actively involved in the design and control of physical distribution systems. Physical distribution affects every element of the marketing mix: product, price, promotion, and distribution. To satisfy customers, marketers consider customers' changing needs and shifts within major distribution functions. They then adapt existing physical distribution systems for greater effectiveness.

Important Terms

Wholesaling
Wholesaler
Merchant wholesalers
Full-service wholesalers
General-merchandise wholesalers
Limited-line wholesalers
Specialty-line wholesalers
Rack jobbers
Limited-service wholesalers
Cash-and-carry wholesalers
Truck wholesalers
Drop shippers
Mail-order wholesalers
Agents
Brokers
Manufacturers' agents
Selling agents

Commission merchants
Sales branches
Sales offices
Physical distribution
Outsourcing
Cycle time
Order processing
Electronic data interchange (EDI)
Inventory management
Just-in-time (JIT)
Materials handling
Warehousing
Private warehouses
Public warehouses
Distribution centers
Transportation
Intermodal transportation
Freight forwarders
Megacarriers

Discussion and Review Questions

1. What is wholesaling?
2. What services do wholesalers provide to producers and retailers?
3. What is the difference between a full-service merchant wholesaler and a limited-service merchant wholesaler?
4. Drop shippers take title to products but do not accept physical possession of them, whereas commission merchants take physical possession of products but do not accept title. Defend the logic of classifying drop shippers as wholesale merchants and commission merchants as agents.
5. Why are manufacturers' sales offices and branches classified as wholesalers? Which independent wholesalers are replaced by manufacturers' sales branch-

es? Which independent wholesalers are replaced by manufacturers' sales offices?
6. Discuss the cost and service tradeoffs involved in developing a physical distribution system.
7. What factors must physical distribution managers consider when developing a customer service mix?
8. What are the main tasks involved in order processing?
9. Discuss the advantages of using an electronic order-processing system. Which types of organizations are most likely to utilize electronic order processing?
10. Explain the tradeoffs inventory managers face when reordering products or supplies. How is the reorder point computed?
11. How does a product's package affect materials handling procedures and techniques?
12. What is containerization? Discuss its major benefits.
13. Explain the major differences between private and public warehouses. What is a field public warehouse?
14. The focus of distribution centers is on the movement of goods. Describe how distribution centers are designed for the rapid flow of products.
15. Compare and contrast the five major transportation modes in terms of cost, speed, dependability, load flexibility, accessibility, and frequency.
16. Discuss ways marketers can combine or coordinate two or more modes of transportation. What is the advantage of doing so?

Application Questions

1. Contact a local retailer with which you do business, and ask the manager to describe the relationship the store has with one of its wholesalers. Using Table 15.1 as a guide, identify the activities performed by the wholesaler. Are any of the functions shared by both the retailer and the wholesaler?
2. Assume you are responsible for the physical distribution of computers at a mail-order company. What would you do to ensure product availability, timely delivery, and quality service for your customers?

3. The type of warehouse facilities used has important strategic implications for a firm. What type of warehouse would be most appropriate for the following situations, and why?

a. A propane gas company recently entered the market in the state of Washington. The company's customers need varied quantities of propane on a timely basis and, at times, on short notice.

b. A suntan lotion manufacturer has little expertise in managing warehouses and needs storage space in several locations in the Southeast.

c. A book publisher must have short cycle time to get its products to customers quickly and needs to send the products to many different retailers.

4. Marketers select a transportation mode based on cost, speed, dependability, load flexibility, accessibility, and frequency (see Table 15.5). Identify a product and then select a mode of transportation based on these criteria. Explain your choice.

Internet Exercise & Resources

FedEx

FedEx has become a critical link in the distribution network of both small and large firms. With its efficient and strategically located super hub in Memphis, FedEx has truly revolutionized the shipping industry. View the company website at

http://www.fedex.com/

1. Comment on how the website's overall design reflects the services the site promotes.

2. Why does FedEx so prominently display a "News" area on its website?

3. Does FedEx differentiate between small and large customers on its website? Why or why not?

Visit **www.prideferrell.com** for resources to help you master the material in this chapter, plus materials that will help you expand your marketing knowledge, including: Internet exercise updates, ACE self-tests, hotlinks to companies featured in this chapter, and much more.

VIDEO CASE 15.1
Quick International Courier Delivers Time-Sensitive Shipments

From delicate biomedical supplies to state-of-the-art integrated circuit boards, Quick International Courier has been speeding time-sensitive shipments to global destinations for more than 20 years. The company, based in New York City, offers round-the-clock pickup of virtually any kind of shipment. Two Quick divisions focus on rapid delivery logistics for specific industries. The QuickSTAT division handles time-sensitive deliveries of biomedical materials, while QuickAerospace transports aircraft components. Depending on the type of product and the urgency of the delivery, Quick and its subsidiaries can arrange for shipment on the very next flight or on a later flight for same-day delivery

nationally and internationally. Business customers value this expedited service because they save precious time and, in turn, are able to offer a higher level of service to their customers.

Starting with a location near the two New York City airports, Quick expanded over the years to better serve the needs of business customers all over North America. The company currently operates in 15 cities across the United States and Canada and is opening additional facilities in Europe. Over time, some of these offices have developed special services geared to the needs of particular industries. The Los Angeles office, for example, offers custom deliveries for the entertainment industry, while the

New York office specializes in deliveries for the financial industry. Some shipments may be large, some small, but all are urgently needed hundreds or thousands of miles away. On any given day, Quick may be arranging for a manufacturer, such as Photronics, to send a new semiconductor photomask from the East Coast to Manchester, England, or helping to rush bone marrow from a donor in Germany to a transplant patient in a Texas medical center.

Michael Montagano, a sourcing specialist in logistics at Photronics, says that Quick's speedy, to-the-minute deliveries keep his customers from experiencing the expensive downtime they would face if products failed to arrive as scheduled. But on-time delivery is just part of the reason Photronics uses Quick: "Because rapid delivery is integral to our clients' success, they need to know exactly where a particular shipment is once it leaves any one of our thirteen manufacturing sites," Montagano says. Quick makes it easy for shippers and their customers to monitor the progress of deliveries at every point from pickup, to cargo loading, to customs processing, to delivery at the final destination.

Now customers can use the company's QuickOnline website to electronically manage all aspects of their urgent shipments. The site allows customers to request courier pickup within 60 minutes, reserve cargo space on a particular airline or flight, review cargo specifications from different airlines, arrange for insurance and documentation, track shipments in progress, look at proof of delivery for shipments already received, request e-mail notification of delivery status, and order specialized shipping supplies. Day or night, customers can log on and find out where and when shipments are moving. "Our goal on track and trace is to update the whereabouts of shipments every thirty minutes all the way, even in the Third World," says CEO Robert Mitzman. Customers can also read about new service enhancements, get shipping tips, and find other information on Quick's latest online newsletter. Looking ahead, Mitzman is planning to offer delivery services to businesses that buy from online exchanges specializing in high-tech products.

Thanks to the worldwide boom in e-commerce, specialized delivery services are in even higher demand today. Quick competes with Sonic Air (owned by shipping giant United Parcel Service) and Sky Courier (owned by UPS rival Airborne Express). Despite this intense competition, Quick's reputation for on-time delivery has attracted some 3,000 business customers, including 75 percent of the largest U.S. companies. Annual revenues top $100 million and continue to grow as Mitzman and his management team offer personalized delivery services to technology firms and other business customers with shipments that can't wait until tomorrow.[12]

QUESTIONS FOR DISCUSSION

1. Is it possible for a company that pays extra for urgent air shipments through Quick International Courier to actually reduce its total distribution costs? Explain.
2. What details about materials handling might Quick have to consider before arranging to pick up specialized cargo such as a shipment of bone marrow or a carton of computer chips?
3. Should Quick expand into air delivery for businesses that serve consumer markets? Why or why not?

CASE 15.2
Wal-Mart Competes Using Efficient, Low-Cost Physical Distribution

How does the world's largest retailer keep the shelves stocked at 4,150 stores while keeping prices low enough to attract 100 million shoppers worldwide every week? Physical distribution is the key. Since the first Wal-Mart opened in Rogers, Arkansas, in 1962, management has carefully balanced its inventory levels, delivery schedules, and transportation costs to ensure products arrive at the right stores at the right time and at the right price. Today the company uses information technology to coordinate the movement of products from suppliers to the loading docks of its 62 distribution centers and on to the chain's Wal-Mart discount stores, SuperCenter combination food/general merchandise outlets, Sam's Club warehouse stores, and Neighborhood Market grocery stores.

Through its Retail Link network, Wal-Mart collaborates with suppliers to forecast sales, plan

future orders, and replenish stock automatically. Here's how the system works. The point-of-sale scanning equipment in each store captures item-by-item, brand-by-brand sales data. Using sophisticated database technology, Wal-Mart analyzes the sales patterns and historical results for the previous 65 weeks with all of its suppliers. Next, retailer and suppliers agree on forecasts for future sales. Then they jointly decide on an order and delivery schedule to ensure inventory levels at each distribution center are appropriate for the forecasted store sales.

Retail Link works. During a pilot test with the maker of Listerine, Wal-Mart was able to boost its in-stock position from 87 percent to 98 percent while cutting the order fulfillment cycle time from 21 to 11 days. The supplier also benefited because it sold the chain an additional $8.5 million of Listerine and was able to better manage its production and delivery activities. Customers benefited because they were able to pick up bottles of Listerine from store shelves when they wanted, and they saved money because low costs allow Wal-Mart to set everyday low prices.

Despite a global roster of 10,000 suppliers, the retailer is always looking for ways to improve its supply chain management and gain flexibility, slash costs, and identify new supply sources. One of its most recent moves was to set up a private procurement website to request and receive supplier bids on contracts, centrally negotiate global purchasing and shipping terms, and increase efficiencies for all participants.

As Wal-Mart has spread farther from its Arkansas base, management has had to plan new distribution centers and arrange truck transportation to bring products to clusters of stores in new areas. The company operates a huge truck fleet to transfer products from distribution centers to stores, but it also contracts with independent trucking firms to transport specialized products, such as food products, in certain areas. In the Northeast, for example, Wal-Mart receives and warehouses shipments of grocery products at an 868,000-square-foot food distribution center in Johnstown, New York. From there, trucks operated by Clarksville Refrigerated Lines fan out to bring orders to Wal-Mart stores across New England, New York, and Pennsylvania. Similarly, a dedicated fleet of refrigerated trucks operated by M.S. Carriers transports perishable food products from Wal-Mart's giant food distribution center in Monroe, Georgia, to Sam's Club warehouse stores in five surrounding states.

Rather than reinvent the wheel for every distribution center and store in North America, Argentina, Brazil, Germany, the United Kingdom, China, and Korea, the company is encouraging each region to share its best distribution practices. As a result, Wal-Mart's German stores are benefiting from the U.S. stores' experience in reducing inventory levels and restocking more rapidly. Its Korean stores are replicating the Mexican operation's popular and profitable web-based grocery delivery program. The world's largest retailer is not finished expanding, and as it opens hundreds of new stores in the coming years, it will continue to hone its distribution skills and keep store shelves stocked at the lowest possible cost.[13]

QUESTIONS FOR DISCUSSION

1. Why is physical distribution so important to Wal-Mart's marketing strategy?
2. Why would Wal-Mart prefer to deal directly with suppliers rather than buying from wholesalers?
3. How does Retail Link help Wal-Mart to better control order processing and inventory management?

Retailing

16

OBJECTIVES

- To understand the purpose and function of retailers in the marketing channel
- To identify the major types of retailers
- To recognize the various forms of nonstore retailing
- To examine major types of franchising and its benefits and weaknesses
- To explore strategic issues in retailing

JCPenney Reaches Out to Traditional and Online Shoppers

In the century since James Cash Penney opened his first dry goods store in Kemmerer, Wyoming, the company he founded has developed into a chain of more than 1,100 stores in the United States, Mexico, and Brazil. Despite head-to-head competition from Sears and price pressure from discounters such as Target, JCPenney's annual sales have grown to $32 billion through acquisitions and aggressive catalog retailing. In recent years, however, the chain has stumbled in the face of a slower economy, a muddled image, outdated stores, and inefficient buying systems. Now, under CEO Allen Questrom, a seasoned turnaround expert, JCPenney is adding more private brands like its popular Arizona label, centralizing purchasing to get updated merchandise to the stores much faster, remodeling older stores, and cutting costs. On top of this ambitious revamping, jcpenney.com is bringing the company's well-known name to a new, younger segment of online shoppers.

JCPenney's traditional strength has been its wide product mix and moderate prices. If shoppers can't find what they want on store shelves, they can head to the catalog sales desk and place an order for fast delivery to store or home. The catalog operation, introduced more than 40 years ago, is the largest on the continent, ringing up $4 billion in merchandise sales every year. In addition to three thick seasonal catalogs, the retailer offers 70 specialty catalogs focusing on domestics, petite women's apparel, and other products. To support the high volume of catalog sales, JCPenney's 14 call centers field 1 million calls during an average week and up to 3 million calls per week during the busy Christmas selling season. Then orders are picked, packed, and shipped from one of the company's five gigantic fulfillment centers around the United States.

Today the call center and fulfillment operations are providing back-office support for jcpenney.com, the company's online retailing venture. The site features a varied and comprehensive merchandise assortment of 250,000 products. Paul Pappajohn, president of e-commerce for JCPenney, notes that "selection is one of the most potent attractions to online customers. We consider ours to be one of the most formidable on the web." He also allows customers to order three ways: on the web, by phone, or through in-store kiosks. In contrast to the fulfillment problems of some web-only retailers, jcpenney.com's proven order-processing system—honed through decades of catalog experience—gets packages on the way to customers within 24 to 48 hours.

Although jcpenney.com's sales are still a fraction of overall sales volume, the site is increasingly popular, thanks to cross-promotions in the stores and the catalogs. "Our three channels have a way of generating sales on each other," Pappajohn comments. In fact, shoppers who buy from all three channels spend an average of $1,000 yearly—four times the amount of average yearly sales compared to shoppers who buy from only one channel. In addition, online shoppers are on average five years younger than store shoppers, as well as more affluent. As a result, JCPenney is making its mark with a new, loyal customer base. Says Pappajohn, "Consumers are still coming to the web, and clearly established brands have the edge."[1]

Retailers like JC Penney, The Gap, and Old Navy are the most visible and accessible channel members to consumers. They are an important link in the marketing channel because they are both marketers for and customers of producers and wholesalers. They perform many marketing functions, such as buying, selling, grading, risk taking, and developing and maintaining information databases about customers. Retailers are in a strategic position to develop relationships with consumers and partnerships with producers and intermediaries in the marketing channel.

In this chapter, we examine the nature of retailing and its importance in supplying consumers with goods and services. We discuss the major types of retail stores and describe several forms of nonstore retailing. We also look at franchising, a retailing form that continues to grow in popularity. Finally, we explore several strategic issues in retailing: location, retail positioning, store image, scrambled merchandising, and the wheel of retailing.

The Nature of Retailing

Retailing includes all transactions in which the buyer intends to consume the product through personal, family, or household use. Buyers in retail transactions are therefore the ultimate consumers. A **retailer** is an organization that purchases products for the purpose of reselling them to ultimate consumers. Although most retailers' sales are directly to the consumer, nonretail transactions occasionally occur when retailers sell products to other businesses. Retailing often takes place in stores or service establishments, but it also occurs through direct selling, direct marketing, and vending machines outside stores.

retailing Transactions in which ultimate consumers are the buyers

retailer An organization that purchases products for the purpose of reselling them to ultimate consumers

Retailing is important to the national economy. Approximately 1.6 million retailers operate in the United States.[2] This number has remained relatively constant for the past 25 years, but sales volume has increased more than fourfold. Most personal income is spent in retail stores, and nearly one out of every seven people employed in the United States works in a retail operation.

Retailers add value, provide services, and assist in making product selections. They can enhance the value of the product by making the shopping experience more convenient, as in home shopping. Through its location, a retailer can facilitate comparison shopping; for example, car dealerships often cluster in the same general vicinity. Product value is also enhanced when retailers offer services, such as technical advice, delivery, credit, and repair services. Finally, retail sales personnel can demonstrate to customers how a product can help address their needs or solve a problem.

The value added by retailers is significant for both producers and ultimate consumers. Retailers are the critical link between producers and ultimate consumers because they provide the environment in which exchanges with ultimate consumers occur. Ultimate consumers benefit through retailers' performance of marketing functions that result in the availability of broader arrays of products. Retailers play a major role in creating time, place, and possession utility and, in some cases, form utility.

Leading retailers such as Wal-Mart, Home Depot, Taco Bell, Macy's, and Toys "R" Us offer consumers a place to browse and compare merchandise to find just what they need. However, such traditional retailing is being challenged by direct marketing channels that provide home shopping through catalogs, television, and the Internet. Traditional retailers are responding to this change in the retail environment in various ways. Wal-Mart has joined forces with fast-food giants like McDonald's and KFC to attract consumers and offer them the added convenience of eating where they shop. In response to competition from Amazon.com, Barnes & Noble developed a website to sell books over the Internet.

New store formats and advances in information technology are making the retail environment highly dynamic and competitive. Instant-messaging technology is helping online retailers converse with customers so they don't click away to another site. Rather than e-mail a retail site and wait for a response, shoppers on Lands' End's website simply click to chat, via keyboard, directly with a customer service representative about sizes, colors, or other product details.[3] This technology has helped the company triple its online sales in just three years. The key to success in retailing is to have a strong customer focus with a retail strategy that provides the level of service, product quality, and innovation that consumers desire. Partnerships among noncompeting retailers and other marketing channel members are providing new opportunities for retailers. For example, airports are leasing space to retailers like Sharper Image, McDonald's, Burger King, and The Body Shop. Kroger and Nordstrom have developed joint co-branded credit cards that offer rebates to customers at participating stores.

Retailers are also finding global opportunities. For example, The Gap is now opening more international stores than domestic ones, a trend that is likely to continue for the foreseeable future. Wal-Mart and Home Depot are opening stores in Canada, Mexico, and South America. McDonald's is growing faster outside the United States than domestically.

Major Types of Retail Stores

Many types of retail stores exist. One way to classify them is by the breadth of products offered. Two general categories include general-merchandise retailers and specialty retailers.

General-Merchandise Retailers

general-merchandise retailer
A retail establishment that offers a variety of product lines that are stocked in depth

A retail establishment that offers a variety of product lines stocked in considerable depth is referred to as a **general-merchandise retailer.** The types of product offerings, mixes of customer services, and operating styles of retailers in this category vary considerably. The primary types of general merchandise retailers are department stores, discount stores, supermarkets, superstores, hypermarkets, warehouse clubs, and warehouse and catalog showrooms (see Table 16.1).

TECH ★ KNOW

How Stores Are Battling Online Rivals

Brick-and-mortar retailers are harnessing technology to fend off competition from online retailers. In book retailing, where web pioneer Amazon.com is challenging the big store chains with low prices, a wide assortment, and fast delivery, Borders Books & Music is fighting back using a high-tech enhancement: computerized in-store kiosks. Through these kiosks, called Title Sleuths, customers can browse and order from the company's entire online inventory instead of being limited to the books on hand in any individual store.

Web-enabled kiosks are becoming increasingly common in all kinds of retail establishments. Sporting goods retailer REI, for example, has installed kiosks in all of its 60 stores. Now in-store shoppers can order any of the company's 78,000 products from any kiosk. Customers like the convenience, and REI is pleased with the results. The total yearly purchases made through the chainwide kiosk system add up to the sales volume of a single store.

The Ohio-based Stambaugh Hardware chain is also using technology to electronically expand in-store access to merchandise. Rather than emulating the strategy of competitors who have built gigantic stores with aisle after aisle of products on display, the company has kept its

stores relatively compact. Customers who want something other than the 18,000 items in stock can use computers, located in each store, to search through 54,000 additional items on Stambaugh's website. For extra convenience, Stambaugh offers a choice of having purchases sent directly to one's home or to the store for pickup when ordering from online inventory.

The technology revolution in retailing is also reaching into car dealerships. Recognizing that customers are surfing the Web for details about cars, features, and pricing, the MotorQuest Automotive Group has outfitted its dealerships in Michigan and Massachusetts with computer stations and high-speed Internet access. Car shoppers are invited to browse vehicle-related Internet sites and use special software to calculate the value of their current vehicles. "The goal is to give the consumer everything on the Net along with all the sources of information that we have at our disposal," says Renny Coe, general manager of one MotorQuest dealership. MotorQuest, Stambaugh, and other retailers with kiosks are on the cutting edge of a trend that is expected to sweep the industry as more stores use technology to compete with online rivals and improve customer service.

Table 16.1	General-Merchandise Retailers	
Type of Retailer	**Description**	**Examples**
Department store	Large organization offering wide product mix and organized into separate departments	Macy's, JC Penney, Sears
Discount store	Self-service, general-merchandise store offering brand name and private brand products at low prices	Wal-Mart, Target, Kmart
Supermarket	Self-service store offering complete line of food products and some nonfood products	Kroger, Albertson's, Winn-Dixie
Superstore	Giant outlet offering all food and nonfood products found in supermarkets, as well as most routinely purchased products	Wal-Mart Supercenters
Hypermarket	Combination supermarket and discount store, larger than a superstore	Carrefour
Warehouse club	Large-scale, members-only establishments combining cash-and-carry wholesaling with discount retailing	Sam's Club, Costco
Warehouse showroom	Facility in a large, low-cost building with large on-premises inventories and minimal service	Ikea
Catalog showroom	Type of warehouse showroom where consumers shop from a catalog and products are stored out of buyers' reach and provided in the manufacturer's carton	Service Merchandise

department stores Large retail organizations characterized by wide product mixes and organized into separate departments to facilitate marketing efforts and internal management

Department Stores.

Department stores are large retail organizations characterized by wide product mixes and employing at least 25 people. To facilitate marketing efforts and internal management in these stores, related product lines are organized into separate departments, such as cosmetics, housewares, apparel, home furnishings, and appliances. Often each department functions as a self-contained business, and buyers for individual departments are fairly autonomous.

Department stores are distinctly service oriented. Their total product may include credit, delivery, personal assistance, merchandise returns, and a pleasant atmosphere. Although some so-called department stores are actually large, departmentalized specialty stores, most department stores are shopping stores. Consumers can compare price, quality, and service at one store with those at competing stores. Along with large discount stores, department stores are often considered retailing leaders in a community and are found in most places with populations of more than 50,000.

Typical department stores, such as Macy's, Sears, Marshall Field's, Dillard's, and Neiman Marcus, obtain a large proportion of sales from apparel, accessories, and cosmetics. Other products these stores carry include gift items, luggage, electronics, home accessories, and sports equipment. Some department stores offer such

Department Stores
Saks Fifth Avenue offers a variety of product lines and customer services.

services as automobile insurance, hair care, income tax preparation, and travel and optical services. In some cases, space for these specialized services is leased out, with proprietors managing their own operations and paying rent to department stores.

discount stores Self-service, general-merchandise stores offering brand name and private brand products at low prices

Discount Stores. **Discount stores** are self-service, general-merchandise outlets that regularly offer brand name and private brand products at low prices. Discounters accept lower margins than conventional retailers in exchange for high sales volume. To keep inventory turnover high, they carry a wide but carefully selected assortment of products, from appliances to housewares and clothing. Major discount establishments also offer food products, toys, automotive services, garden supplies, and sports equipment. Wal-Mart, Target, and Kmart are the three largest discount stores. Many discounters are regional organizations, such as Venture, Bradlees, and Meijer. Most operate in large (50,000 to 80,000 square feet), no-frills facilities. Discount stores usually offer everyday low prices rather than relying on sales events.

Discount retailing developed on a large scale in the early 1950s, when postwar production began catching up with consumer demand for appliances, home furnishings, and other hard goods. Discount stores were often cash-only operations in warehouse districts, offering goods at savings of 20 to 30 percent over conventional retailers. Facing increased competition from department stores and other discount stores, some discounters have improved store services, atmosphere, and location, raising prices and sometimes blurring the distinction between discount stores and department stores. Other discounters continue to focus on price alone.

Discount Stores
Discount stores, like Wal-Mart and Kmart, are self-service, general merchandise retailers that offer both manufacturer's brands and private brands at low prices and low margins.

supermarkets Large, self-service stores that carry a complete line of food products, along with some nonfood products

Supermarkets.

Supermarkets are large, self-service stores that carry a complete line of food products, as well as some nonfood products such as cosmetics and nonprescription drugs. Supermarkets are arranged in departments for maximum efficiency in stocking and handling products but have central checkout facilities. They offer lower prices than smaller neighborhood grocery stores, usually provide free parking, and may also cash checks. Supermarkets must operate efficiently because net profits after taxes are usually less than 1 percent of sales. Supermarkets may be independently owned but are often part of a chain operation. Top U.S. supermarket chains include Kroger, Albertson's, Safeway, and A & P.

Today consumers make more than three-quarters of all grocery purchases in supermarkets. Even so, supermarkets' total share of the food market is declining because consumers now have widely varying food preferences and buying habits, and in many communities shoppers can choose from a number of convenience stores, discount stores, and specialty food stores, as well as a wide variety of restaurants.

superstores Giant retail outlets that carry food and nonfood products found in supermarkets, as well as most routinely purchased consumer products

Superstores.

Superstores, which originated in Europe, are giant retail outlets that carry not only food and nonfood products ordinarily found in supermarkets but also routinely purchased consumer products. Besides a complete food line, superstores sell housewares, hardware, small appliances, clothing, personal care products, garden products, and tires—about four times as many items as supermarkets. Services available at superstores include dry cleaning, automotive repair, check cashing, bill paying, and snack bars.

Superstores combine features of discount stores and supermarkets. Examples include Wal-Mart Supercenters, some Kroger stores, and Super Kmart Centers. To cut handling and inventory costs, they use sophisticated operating techniques and often have tall shelving that displays entire assortments of products. Superstores can have an area of as much as 200,000 square feet (compared with 20,000 square feet in traditional supermarkets). Sales volume is two to three times that of supermarkets, partly because locations near good transportation networks help generate the in-store traffic needed for profitability.

hypermarkets Stores that combine supermarket and discount shopping in one location

Hypermarkets.

Hypermarkets combine supermarket and discount store shopping in one location. Larger than superstores, they range from 225,000 to 325,000 square feet and offer 45,000 to 60,000 different types of low-priced products. They commonly allocate 40 to 50 percent of their space to grocery products and the remainder to general merchandise, including athletic shoes, designer jeans, and other apparel; refrigerators, televisions, and other appliances; housewares; cameras; toys; jewelry; hardware; and automotive supplies. Many lease space to noncompeting businesses such as banks, optical shops, and fast-food restaurants. All hypermarkets focus on low prices and vast selections. Although Kmart, Wal-Mart, and Carrefour (a French retailer) have operated hypermarkets in the United States, most of these stores have been unsuccessful and have closed. Such stores are too big for time-constrained U.S. shoppers. However, hypermarkets are more successful in Europe and South America.

warehouse clubs Large-scale, members-only establishments that combine features of cash-and-carry wholesaling with discount retailing

Warehouse Clubs.

Warehouse clubs, a rapidly growing form of mass merchandising, are large-scale, members-only selling operations combining cash-and-carry wholesaling with discount retailing. For a nominal annual fee (usually about $35), small retailers purchase products at wholesale prices for business use or for resale. Warehouse clubs also sell to ultimate consumers affiliated with government agencies, credit unions, schools, hospitals, and banks, but instead of paying a membership fee, individual consumers may pay about 5 percent more on each item than do business customers.

Sometimes called *buying clubs,* warehouse clubs offer the same types of products as discount stores but in a limited range of sizes and styles. Whereas most discount stores carry around 40,000 items, a warehouse club handles only 3,500 to 5,000 products, usually acknowledged brand leaders. Sam's Club stores, for example, stock about 4,000 items, with 1,400 available most of the time and the rest being one-time

408 Part Four   Distribution Decisions

Warehouse Clubs
A warehouse club, such as Sam's, is a members-only mass merchandiser that engages in both wholesale and retail transactions.

buys. Costco leads the warehouse club industry with sales of $26.98 billion. Sam's Club is second with $24.80 billion in store sales. A third company, BJ's Wholesale Club, which operates in the Northeast and Florida, has a much smaller market.[4] All these establishments offer a broad product mix, including food, beverages, books, appliances, housewares, automotive parts, hardware, and furniture. Warehouse clubs appeal to many price-conscious consumers and small retailers unable to obtain wholesaling services from large distributors. The average warehouse club shopper has more education, a higher income, and a larger household than the average supermarket shopper.

To keep prices lower than those of supermarkets and discount stores, warehouse clubs provide few services. They generally do not advertise, except through direct mail. Their facilities, often located in industrial areas, have concrete floors and aisles wide enough for forklifts. Merchandise is stacked on pallets or displayed on pipe racks. Customers must transport purchases themselves.

warehouse showrooms
Retail facilities in large, low-cost buildings with large on-premise inventories and minimal services

Warehouse and Catalog Showrooms.   **Warehouse showrooms** are retail facilities with five basic characteristics: large, low-cost buildings, warehouse materials handling technology, vertical merchandise displays, large on-premises inventories, and minimal services. IKEA, a Swedish company, sells furniture, household goods, and kitchen accessories in warehouse showrooms and through catalogs around the world, including China and Russia.[5] Wickes Furniture and Levitz Furniture also operate warehouse showrooms. These high-volume, low-overhead operations stress fewer personnel and services. Lower costs are possible because some marketing functions have been shifted to consumers, who must transport, finance, and perhaps store merchandise. Most consumers carry away purchases in the manufacturer's carton, although stores will deliver for a fee.

catalog showrooms   A form of warehouse showroom where consumers shop from a catalog and products are stored out of buyers' reach

In **catalog showrooms,** one item of each product is displayed, often in a locked case, with remaining inventory stored out of the buyer's reach. Using catalogs that have been mailed to their homes or are on store counters, customers order products by phone or in person. Clerks fill orders from the warehouse area, and products are presented in the manufacturer's carton. In contrast to traditional catalog retailers, which offer no discounts and require that customers wait for delivery, catalog showrooms regularly sell below list price and often provide goods immediately.

Catalog showrooms usually sell jewelry, luggage, photographic equipment, toys, small appliances and housewares, sporting goods, and power tools. They advertise extensively and carry established brands and models that are not likely to be discontinued. Because catalog showrooms have higher product turnover, fewer losses through shoplifting, and lower labor costs than department stores, they are able to

Copyright © Houghton Mifflin Company. All rights reserved.

feature lower prices. They offer minimal services, however. Customers may have to stand in line to examine items or place orders. Pressure is being applied to catalog showrooms by the rapid growth of discounters and warehouse clubs. Service Merchandise (the market leader) and Best Products are examples of catalog showroom retailers.

Specialty Retailers

In contrast to general-merchandise retailers with their broad product mixes, specialty retailers emphasize narrow and deep assortments. Despite their name, specialty retailers do not sell specialty items (except when specialty goods complement the overall product mix). Instead, they offer substantial assortments in a few product lines. We examine three types of specialty retailers: traditional specialty retailers, off-price retailers, and category killers.

traditional specialty retailers
Stores that carry a narrow product mix with deep product lines

Traditional Specialty Retailers.   **Traditional specialty retailers** are stores that carry a narrow product mix with deep product lines. Sometimes called *limited-line retailers,* they may be referred to as *single-line retailers* if they carry unusual depth in one main product category. Specialty retailers commonly sell such shopping products as apparel, jewelry, sporting goods, fabrics, computers, and pet supplies. The Limited, Radio Shack, Hickory Farms, The Gap, and Foot Locker are examples of retailers offering limited product lines but great depth within those lines.

Although the number of chain specialty stores is increasing, many specialty stores are independently owned. Florists, bakery shops, and bookstores are among the small, independent specialty retailers that appeal to local target markets, although these stores can be owned and managed by large corporations. Even if this kind of retailer adds a few supporting product lines, the store may still be classified as a specialty store.

Because they are usually small, specialty stores may have high costs in proportion to sales, and satisfying customers may require carrying some products with low turnover rates. However, these stores sometimes obtain lower prices from suppliers by purchasing limited lines of merchandise in large quantities. Successful specialty stores understand their customer types and know what products to carry, thus reducing the risk of unsold merchandise. Specialty stores usually offer better selections and more sales expertise than department stores, their main competitors. By capitalizing

Traditional Specialty Store
Abercrombie & Fitch is a traditional specialty store that specializes in clothing for both men and women.

on fashion, service, personnel, atmosphere, and location, specialty retailers position themselves strategically to attract customers in specific market segments. For example, customers seeking fashion jeans likely would shop at specialty stores. In 2000, 21 percent of U.S. jeans purchases were in traditional specialty stores.[6] They may even become exclusive dealers in their markets for certain products. Through specialty stores, small-business owners provide unique services to match consumers' varied desires. For consumers dissatisfied with the impersonal nature of large retailers, the close, personal contact offered by a small specialty store can be a welcome change.

off-price retailers Stores that buy manufacturers' seconds, overruns, returns, and off-season merchandise for resale to consumers at deep discounts

Off-Price Retailers. **Off-price retailers** are stores that buy manufacturers' seconds, overruns, returns, and off-season production runs at below-wholesale prices for resale to consumers at deep discounts. Unlike true discount stores, which pay regular wholesale prices for goods and usually carry second-line brand names, off-price retailers offer limited lines of national-brand and designer merchandise, usually clothing, shoes, or housewares. The number of off-price retailers has grown since the mid-1980s and now includes such major chains as T.J. Maxx, Stein Mart, Burlington Coat Factory, and Marshalls.

Off-price stores charge 20 to 50 percent less than do department stores for comparable merchandise but offer few customer services. They often feature community dressing rooms, and central checkout counters. Some of these stores do not take returns or allow exchanges. Off-price stores may or may not sell goods with original labels intact. They turn over their inventory nine to twelve times a year, three times as often as traditional specialty stores. They compete with department stores for the same customers: price-conscious, customers who are knowledgeable about brand names.

Another form of off-price retailer is the manufacturer's outlet mall, which makes available manufacturer overstocks and unsold merchandise from other retail outlets. Prices are low, and diverse manufacturers are represented in these malls.

To ensure a regular flow of merchandise into their stores, off-price retailers establish long-term relationships with suppliers that can provide large quantities of goods at reduced prices. Manufacturers may approach retailers with samples, discontinued products, or items that have not sold well. Also, retailers may seek out manufacturers, offering to pay cash for goods produced during the manufacturers' off season. Although manufacturers benefit from such arrangements, they also risk alienating their specialty and department store customers. Department stores tolerate off-price stores as long as they do not advertise brand names, limit merchandise to lower-quality items, and are located away from the department stores. When off-price retailers obtain large stocks of in-season, top-quality merchandise, tension builds between department stores and manufacturers.

category killer A very large specialty store concentrating on a major product category and competing on the basis of low prices and product availability

Category Killers. Over the last 15 years, a new breed of specialty retailer, the category killer, has evolved. A **category killer** is a very large specialty store that concentrates on a major product category and competes on the basis of low prices and enormous product availability. These stores are referred to as category killers because they expand rapidly and gain sizable market shares, taking business away from smaller, high-cost retail outlets. Examples of category killers include Home Depot (building materials), Office Depot (office supplies and equipment), Toys "R" Us (toys), and Best Buy (electronics).

Nonstore Retailing

nonstore retailing The selling of products outside the confines of a retail facility

Nonstore retailing is the selling of products outside the confines of a retail facility. This form of retailing accounts for an increasing percentage of total sales. Three factors are spurring its growth. First, consumers—especially women, because of their increased participation in the work force—have less time to shop in retail stores. Second, some retail store salespeople are poorly informed and, therefore, are less able to assist shoppers. Finally, the number of older consumers, who tend to shop less in large stores, is rising. The three major types of nonstore retailing are direct selling, direct marketing, and automatic vending.

Direct Selling

direct selling The marketing of products to ultimate consumers through face-to-face sales presentations at home or in the workplace

Direct selling is the marketing of products to ultimate consumers through face-to-face sales presentations at home or in the workplace. Traditionally called *door-to-door selling,* direct selling in the United States began with peddlers more than a century ago and has since grown into a sizable industry of several hundred firms. Although direct sellers historically used a cold-canvass, door-to-door approach for finding prospects, many companies today, such as World Book, Kirby, Amway, Mary Kay, and Avon, use other approaches. They initially identify customers through the mail, telephone, Internet, or shopping mall intercepts and set up appointments.

Net Sights

The International eRetail Association website (**http://www.eretailnews.com/Introframe.htm**) provides a host of articles and reports on different aspects of electronic retailing. This site is updated often.

Direct selling sometimes uses the "party plan," which can occur in the customer's home or workplace. With a party plan, a consumer acts as a host and invites a number of friends and associates to view merchandise in a group setting, where a salesperson demonstrates products. The congenial party atmosphere helps to overcome customers' reluctance and encourages them to buy. Direct selling through the party plan requires effective salespeople who can identify potential hosts and provide encouragement and incentives for them to organize a gathering of friends and associates. Companies that commonly use the party plan include Tupperware, Stanley Home Products, and Sarah Coventry.

Direct selling has both benefits and limitations. It gives the marketer an opportunity to demonstrate the product in an environment—usually customers' homes—where it would most likely be used. The door-to-door seller can give the customer personal attention, and the product can be presented to the customer at a convenient time and location. Personal attention to the customer is the foundation on which some direct sellers, such as Mary Kay, have built their businesses. Because commissions for salespeople are so high, ranging from 30 to 50 percent of the sales price, and great effort is required to isolate promising prospects, overall costs of direct selling make it the most expensive form of retailing. Furthermore, some customers view direct selling negatively, owing to unscrupulous and fraudulent practices used by some direct sellers in the past. Some communities even have local ordinances that control or, in some cases, prohibit direct selling.

Direct Marketing

direct marketing The use of the telephone and nonpersonal media to introduce products to consumers, who then can purchase them via mail, telephone, or the Internet

Direct marketing is the use of the telephone and nonpersonal media to communicate product and organizational information to customers, who then can purchase products via mail, telephone, or the Internet. Direct marketing can occur through catalog marketing, direct-response marketing, telemarketing, television home shopping, and online retailing.

catalog marketing A type of marketing in which an organization provides a catalog from which customers make selections and place orders by mail, telephone, or the Internet

Catalog Marketing. In **catalog marketing,** an organization provides a catalog from which customers make selections and place orders by mail, telephone, or the Internet. Catalog marketing began in 1872, when Montgomery Ward issued its first catalog to rural families. Today there are more than 7,000 catalog marketing companies in the United States, as well as a number of retail stores, such as JC Penney, that engage in catalog marketing. Some organizations, including Spiegel and JC Penney, offer a broad array of products spread over multiple product lines. Catalog companies like Lands' End, Pottery Barn, and J. Crew offer considerable depth in one major line of products. Still other catalog companies specialize in only a few products within a single line. Some catalog retailers—for instance, Crate and Barrel and Sharper Image—have stores in major metropolitan areas.

The advantages of catalog retailing include efficiency and convenience for customers. The retailer benefits by being able to locate in remote, low-cost areas, save on expensive store fixtures, and reduce both personal selling and store operating

Nonstore Retailer
Lands' End is primarily a direct marketer engaged in catalog and online retailing.

expenses. On the other hand, catalog retailing is inflexible, provides limited service, and is most effective for a selected set of products.

Catalog sales are about $110 billion annually, and are expected to grow to $155 billion by 2005.[7] Even though the cost of mailing catalogs continues to rise, catalog sales are growing at double the rate of in-store retailing. Williams-Sonoma, for example, sells kitchenware and home and garden products through five catalogs, including Pottery Barn and Gardeners' Eden. Catalog sales have been increasing due to the convenience of catalog shopping. Product quality is often high, and because consumers can call toll-free 24 hours a day, charge the purchase to a credit card, and have the merchandise delivered to their door in one to two days, such shopping is much easier than going to a store. In addition, three-fourths of catalog retailers provide the convenience of shopping online.

Direct-Response Marketing. **Direct-response marketing** occurs when a retailer advertises a product and makes it available through mail or telephone orders. Generally a purchaser may use a credit card, but other forms of payment are acceptable. Examples of direct-response marketing include a television commercial offering a recording artist's musical collection available through a toll-free number, a newspaper or magazine advertisement for a series of children's books available by filling out the form in the ad or calling a toll-free number, and even a billboard promoting floral services available by calling 1-800-Flowers. Direct-response marketing is also conducted by sending letters, samples, brochures, or booklets to prospects on a mailing list and asking that they order the advertised products by mail or telephone. In general, products must be priced above $20 to justify the advertising and distribution costs associated with direct-response marketing.

direct-response marketing
A type of marketing that occurs when a retailer advertises a product and makes it available through mail or telephone orders

Telemarketing. A number of organizations, including Merrill Lynch, Allstate, Avis, Ford, and American Express, use the telephone to strengthen the effectiveness of traditional marketing methods. **Telemarketing** is the performance of marketing-related activities by telephone. Some organizations use a prescreened list of prospective clients, whereas others rely primarily on a cold-canvass approach using telephone directories. Telemarketing can help generate sales leads, improve customer service, speed up payment on past-due accounts, raise funds for nonprofit organizations, and gather marketing data. It is often combined with other marketing efforts, and both nonstore retailers and retailers with establishments use it.

telemarketing The performance of marketing-related activities by telephone

Television Home Shopping. **Television home shopping** presents products to television viewers, encouraging them to order through toll-free numbers and pay with credit cards. Home Shopping Network in Florida originated and popularized this format. There are several home shopping cable channels. A few of these specialize in certain product categories. The most popular products sold through television home shopping are jewelry (40 percent of total sales), clothing, housewares, and electronics.

television home shopping A form of selling in which products are presented to television viewers, who can buy them by calling a toll-free number and paying with a credit card

Home shopping channels have grown so rapidly in recent years that more than 60 percent of U.S. households have access to home shopping programs. Home Shopping Network and QVC are two of the largest home shopping networks. Approximately 60 percent of home shopping sales revenues come from repeat purchasers.

The television home shopping format offers several benefits. Products can be easily demonstrated, and an adequate amount of time can be spent showing the product so that viewers are well informed. The length of time a product is shown depends not only on the time required for doing demonstrations but also on whether the product is selling. Once the calls peak and begin to decline, a new product is shown. Another benefit is that customers can shop at their convenience from the comfort of their homes.

online retailing Retailing that makes products available to buyers through computer connections

Online Retailing. **Online retailing** makes products available to buyers through computer connections. The phenomenal growth of Internet use and online information services like AOL has created new retailing opportunities. Many retailers have set up websites to disseminate information about their companies and products. Although most retailers with websites use them primarily to promote products, a number of companies, including Barnes & Noble, REI, Lands' End, and OfficeMax, sell goods online. Consumers can purchase hard-to-find items, like Pez candy dispensers and Elvis memorabilia, on eBay. They can buy upscale items for their dogs at SitStay.com, a web retailer specializing in high-end dog supplies that carries a carefully screened selection of 1,500 products. "We don't have 10,000 products," explains

GLOBAL MARKETING

Country-by-Country Differences in Online Shopping

Shoppers in France like to pay for their online purchases by check, whereas online shoppers in the United Kingdom prefer to pay by credit card. Online grocery shopping is much more popular in Hong Kong than in Japan, Korea, or the United States. And although the United States is a hotbed of e-commerce activity, only 14 percent of all U.S. shoppers have bought music online compared with 40 percent of all Dutch shoppers.

In the world of online shopping, web-based retailers have to take time to study, understand, and accommodate country-by-country differences in online buying behavior. Online shopping is growing in popularity as people in more nations gain access to Internet technology. Books, recorded music, and computer software—products that shoppers need not examine to be encouraged to buy—are among the best-selling items online.

Established online retailers clearly carry weight among online shoppers, which is why Amazon.com consistently places among the top ten retail sites in the United States, Great Britain, and many other countries. Tesco, a leading U.K. supermarket chain, has parlayed its well-known brand and vast store network into the world's most successful online grocery retailing operation. After

shoppers make their selections online, Tesco.com transmits each order from the website to the store nearest the customer. At the store, an employee handpicks all items aisle by aisle, packages the order, and sets it up for speedy delivery to the customer's door. By linking the site to the locations of existing stores, Tesco can make online grocery shopping available to more than 90 percent of the U.K. population and reassure shoppers that they are getting the same high-quality products sold in the stores.

Payment preferences also vary from country to country, opening opportunities for savvy retailers. For example, 7-Eleven has boosted sales in Japan by recognizing that local customers are wary of paying for online purchases by credit card. The chain's research revealed that 75 percent of online shoppers travel to stores to complete their buying transactions. So the chain has turned its 8,500 stores into payment centers where shoppers can pay in cash for their web purchases and pick up the products when available. In addition, the retailer launched a shopping site, 7dream.com, to sell an assortment of goods and services, such as concert tickets and books, for delivery to local 7-Eleven stores. These web initiatives have increased store traffic and significantly boosted the retailer's sales.

co-founder Kent Krueger. "We have the best of the best."[8] Banks and brokerage firms have established websites to give customers direct access to manage their accounts and enable them to trade online. With advances in computer technology continuing and consumers ever more pressed for time, online retailing will continue to escalate.

Although online retailing represents a major retailing venue, security remains an issue. In a survey conducted by Forrester Research, 53 percent of online merchants cited security as the main reason consumers do not buy from their websites. Most online retailers insist that current encryption technology and the limited liability incurred by credit card users for stolen card numbers make online transactions safe. Nevertheless, a recent consumer survey indicated that 79 percent of non–online shoppers do not like to send credit card or other personal information over the Internet. While this concern ranked high with all non–online shoppers, it was greatest among women with Internet access and among people who have only a high school education.[9] Though security concerns persist, two-thirds of Internet users are planning to purchase over the Web within the next year.[10]

Automatic Vending

automatic vending The use of machines to dispense products

Automatic vending is the use of machines to dispense products. It accounts for less than 2 percent of all retail sales. Video game machines provide an entertainment service, and many banks offer automatic teller machines (ATMs), which dispense cash and perform other services.

Automatic vending is one of the most impersonal forms of retailing. Small, standardized, routinely purchased products (chewing gum, candy, newspapers, cigarettes, soft drinks, coffee) can be sold in machines because consumers usually buy them at the nearest available location. Machines in areas of heavy traffic provide efficient and continuous service to consumers. Such high-volume areas may have more diverse product availability—for example, hot and cold sandwiches, and even cameras. To market its one-time-use Max Cameras, Eastman Kodak is rolling out 10,000 vending machines that allow credit card transactions, are refrigerated to protect the film, and are connected to the Internet. The vending machine's Internet connection will inform Eastman Kodak about who bought each camera, where customers live, the specific location of the machine, and the machine's inventory level. These machines will be located at zoos, stadiums, parks, hotels, and resorts.[11]

Since vending machines need only a small amount of space and no sales personnel, this retailing method has some advantages over stores. The advantages are partly offset, however, by the high costs of equipment and frequent servicing and repairs.

Franchising

franchising An arrangement in which a supplier (franchiser) grants a dealer (franchisee) the right to sell products in exchange for some type of consideration

Franchising is an arrangement whereby a supplier, or franchiser, grants a dealer, or franchisee, the right to sell products in exchange for some type of consideration. The franchiser may receive some percentage of total sales in exchange for furnishing equipment, buildings, management know-how, and marketing assistance to the franchisee. The franchisee supplies labor and capital, operates the franchised business, and agrees to abide by the provisions of the franchise agreement. Table 16.2 lists the top ten fastest-growing U.S. franchises.

Because of changes in the international marketplace, shifting employment options in the United States, the expanding U.S. service economy, and corporate interest in more joint venture activity, franchising is rapidly increasing. In 2000, franchising companies and their franchisees accounted for an estimated $1 trillion in annual U.S. retail sales from 320,000 franchised, small businesses in 75 industries. Franchising accounted for more than 40 percent of all U.S. retail sales and employed more than 8 million people. A new franchise outlet opens somewhere in the United States every 8 minutes, and approximately 8 percent of retail business establishments are franchised businesses.[12] In this section, we look at major types of retail franchises and the advantages and disadvantages of franchising.

Table 16.2	Top Ten Fastest-Growing Franchises in the U.S. for 2001

1. 7-Eleven
2. McDonald's
3. Coverall North America, Inc.
4. Taco Bell Corp.
5. Subway

6. Jani-King
7. Mail Boxes Etc.
8. The Quizno's Corp.
9. Jiffy Lube International, Inc.
10. Curves for Women

Source: *Entrepreneur* magazine's 2001 Franchise 500, www.franchise500.com

Major Types of Retail Franchises

Retail franchise arrangements fall into three general categories. In one type of arrangement, a manufacturer authorizes a number of retail stores to sell a certain brand name item. This franchise arrangement, one of the oldest, is common in sales of cars and trucks, farm equipment, shoes, paint, earth-moving equipment, and petroleum. In the second type of retail franchise, a producer licenses distributors to sell a given product to retailers. This arrangement is common in the soft-drink industry. Most national manufacturers of soft-drink syrups, including Coca-Cola, Dr Pepper, and PepsiCo, grant franchises to bottlers, which in turn serve retailers. In the third type of retail franchise, a franchiser supplies brand names, techniques, or other services instead of complete products. The franchiser may provide certain production and distribution services, but its primary role in the arrangement is careful development and control of marketing strategies. This approach to franchising is very common today and is used by such organizations as Holiday Inn, AAMCO, McDonald's, Dairy Queen, KFC, and H&R Block.

Franchising
While Wendy's has over 6,000 locations, it continues to seek new franchisees, especially minorities and women.

Advantages and Disadvantages of Franchising

Franchising offers several advantages to both the franchisee and the franchiser. It enables a franchisee to start a business with limited capital and to benefit from the business experience of others. Moreover, nationally advertised franchises, such as ServiceMaster and Burger King, are often assured of customers as soon as they open. If business problems arise, the franchisee can obtain guidance and advice from the franchiser at little or no cost. Franchised outlets are generally more successful than independently owned businesses. Fewer than 10 percent of franchised retail businesses fail during the first two years of operation, compared to approximately 50 percent of independent retail businesses. Also, the franchisee receives materials to use in local advertising and can benefit from national promotional campaigns sponsored by the franchiser.

Through franchise arrangements, the franchiser gains fast and selective product distribution without incurring the high cost of constructing and operating its own outlets. The franchiser therefore has more capital for expanding production and advertising. It can also ensure, through the franchise agreement, that outlets are maintained and operated according to its own standards. The franchiser benefits from the fact that the franchisee, being a sole proprietor in most cases, is likely to be very highly motivated to succeed. Success of the franchise means more sales, which translate into higher income for the franchiser.

Despite numerous advantages, franchise arrangements have several drawbacks. The franchiser can dictate many aspects of the business: decor, design of employees' uniforms, types of signs, and numerous details of business operations. In addition, franchisees must pay to use the franchiser's name, products, and assistance. Usually there is a one-time franchise fee and continuing royalty and advertising fees, often collected as a percentage of sales. For example, Subway requires franchisees to come up with $30,000 to $90,000 in startup costs. Franchisees often must work very hard, putting in 10- to 12-hour days, 6 days a week. In some cases, franchise agreements are not uniform. One franchisee may pay more than another for the same services. The franchiser also gives up a certain amount of control when entering into a franchise agreement. Consequently, individual establishments may not be operated exactly the way the franchiser would like.

SNAPSHOT

How often and where do we shop?

Percent of consumers who shopped at the following outlets in the past week.

- 2000
- 1996

Supermarket 54% / 80%
Mass merchandiser 55%
Department store 25% / 35% 27%
Drugstore 22% / 4%
Non-clothing specialty store 18% / 4%
Specialty clothing store 10% / 5%
Warehouse club 7% / 5%

Source: "What's in Store at Retail," *American Demographics*, May 2000, p. 9.

Strategic Issues in Retailing

Consumers often have vague reasons for making retail purchases. Whereas most business purchases are based on economic planning and necessity, consumer purchases may result from social and psychological influences. Because consumers shop for a variety of reasons—to search for specific items, escape boredom, or learn about something new—retailers must do more than simply fill space with merchandise. They must make desired products available, create stimulating shopping environments, and develop marketing strategies that increase store patronage. In this section, we discuss how store location, retail positioning, store image, scrambled merchandising, and the wheel of retailing affect retailing objectives.

Location of Retail Stores

Location, the least flexible of the strategic retailing issues, is one of the most important because location dictates the limited geographic trading area from which a store draws its customers. Retailers consider a variety of factors when evaluating potential locations, including location of the firm's target market within the trading area, kinds of products being sold, availability of public transportation, customer characteristics, and competitors' locations.

In choosing a location, a retailer evaluates the relative ease of movement to and from the site, including such factors as pedestrian and vehicular traffic, parking, and transportation. Most retailers prefer sites with high pedestrian traffic. Preliminary site investigations often include a pedestrian count to determine how many passersby are prospective customers. The nature of the area's vehicular traffic is also analyzed. The customers of certain retailers, such as service stations and many convenience stores, drive to these retail sites, and thus overly congested locations should be avoided. Parking space must be adequate for projected demand, and transportation networks (major thoroughfares and public transit) must accommodate customers and delivery vehicles.

Retailers also evaluate the characteristics of the site itself: types of stores in the area; size, shape, and visibility of the lot or building under consideration; and rental, leasing, or ownership terms. Retailers look for compatibility with nearby retailers because stores that complement one another draw more customers for everyone. When making site location decisions, retailers select from among several general types of locations: free-standing structures, traditional business districts, traditional shopping centers, or nontraditional shopping centers.

Free-Standing Structures.

Free-standing structures are buildings unconnected to other buildings. Organizations may build such structures or lease or buy them. A retailer, for example, may find that its most successful stores are in free-standing structures close to a shopping mall but not in the mall. Use of free-standing structures allows retailers to physically position themselves away from or close to competitors. Quick-service oil change dealers and fast-food restaurants frequently use free-standing structures and locate close to each other. Toys "R" Us and Home Depot also tend to locate in free-standing structures.

Traditional Business Districts.

A traditional business district—"the downtown shopping district"—usually consists of structures attached to one another and located in a central part of a town or city. Often these structures are aging and, in some cities, traditional business districts are decaying and are viewed as nonviable locations for retailers. However, many towns and cities are preserving or revitalizing traditional business districts, thus making them attractive locations for certain types of retailers. Some cities have enclosed walkways, shut off streets from traffic, and provided free parking and trolley systems to help traditional business districts compete with shopping malls more effectively.

Traditional Shopping Centers.

Traditional shopping centers include neighborhood, community, and regional shopping centers. **Neighborhood shopping centers** usually consist of several small convenience and specialty stores, such as small grocery stores, gas stations, and fast-food restaurants. Many of these retailers consider their target markets to be consumers who live within two to three miles of their stores, or ten minutes' driving time. Because most purchases are based on convenience or personal contact, there is usually little coordination of selling efforts within a neighborhood shopping center. Generally product mixes consist of essential products, and depth of the product lines is limited. Convenience stores are most successful when they are closer to consumers than, for example, supermarkets. A good strategy for neighborhood centers is to locate near hotels or interstate highways, or on the route to regional shopping centers.

Community shopping centers include one or two department stores and some specialty stores, as well as convenience stores. They draw consumers looking for shopping and specialty products not available in neighborhood shopping centers. Because these centers serve larger geographic areas, consumers must drive longer distances to community shopping centers than to neighborhood centers. Community shopping centers are planned and coordinated to attract shoppers. Special events, such as art exhibits, automobile shows, and sidewalk sales, stimulate traffic. Overall management of a community shopping center looks for tenants that complement the

neighborhood shopping centers Shopping centers usually consisting of several small convenience and specialty stores

community shopping centers Shopping centers with one or two department stores, some specialty stores, and convenience stores

100 shops, restaurants and theaters, including Neiman Marcus, Tiffany & Co., Gucci and Legal Sea Foods • Located at Huntington Ave. and Dartmouth St. in the Back Bay • Open 10 am-8 pm, Sun 12-6 pm • $6 for three hours of validated parking • 617-369-5000 • shopcopleyplace.com   COPLEY PLACE

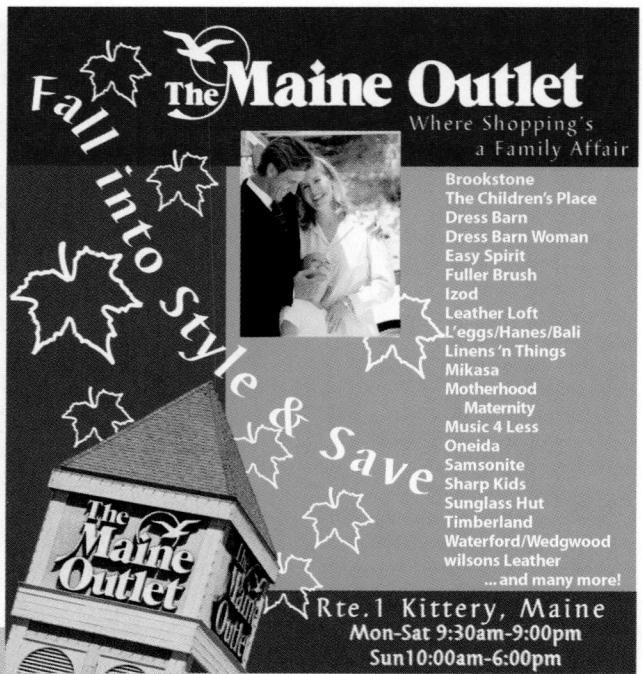

Traditional Versus Nontraditional Shopping Centers
Regional shopping centers, like Copley Place, consist of several department stores, numerous specialty stores, restaurants, and frequently, movie theaters. An outlet mall, such as Maine Outlet, consists of discount factory outlet stores specializing in traditional manufacturers' brands that are available at significantly reduced prices.

regional shopping centers
A type of shopping center with the largest department stores, the widest product mix, and the deepest product lines of all shopping centers

center's total assortment of products. Such centers have wide product mixes and deep product lines.

Regional shopping centers usually have the largest department stores, the widest product mixes, and the deepest product lines of all shopping centers. Many shopping malls are regional shopping centers, although some are community shopping centers. Regional shopping centers carry most products found in a downtown shopping district. With 150,000 or more consumers in their target market, regional shopping centers must have well-coordinated management and marketing activities. Target markets may include consumers traveling from a distance to find products and prices not available in their hometowns.

Because of the expense of leasing space in regional shopping centers, tenants are more likely to be national chains than small, independent stores. Large centers usually advertise, have special events, furnish transportation to some consumer groups, maintain their own security forces, and carefully select the mix of stores. Mall of America, near Minneapolis, is one of the largest shopping malls in the world. It contains about 800 stores, including Nordstrom's and Bloomingdale's, and 100 restaurants and nightclubs. The shopping center features Camp Snoopy, a theme park based on Charlie Brown's famous dog, as well as hotels, miniature golf courses, and water slides. Recently concern has been expressed regarding the possible decline of regional shopping malls. Some regional shopping centers are viewed as being out of touch with the needs of an aging population, struggling with massive debt accumulation, and in need of significant structural repair.[13]

Nontraditional Shopping Centers.   Three new types of shopping centers have emerged that differ significantly from traditional shopping centers. Factory outlet malls feature discount and factory outlet stores carrying traditional manufacturer brands, such as Van Heusen, Levi Strauss, HealthTex, and Wrangler. Manufacturers own these stores and make a special effort to avoid conflict with traditional retailers of their products. Manufacturers claim their stores are in noncompetitive locations, and indeed most factory outlet malls are located outside metropolitan areas. Not all factory outlets stock closeouts and irregulars, but most avoid comparison with discount houses. Factory outlet malls attract customers because of lower prices for quality and major brand names. They operate in much the same way as regional shopping centers, but usually draw traffic from a larger shopping radius. Promotional activity is at the heart of these shopping centers. Craft and antique shows, contests, and special events attract a great deal of traffic.

Another nontraditional shopping center is the miniwarehouse mall. These loosely planned centers sell space to retailers, who operate what are essentially retail stores out of warehouse bays. Developers of the miniwarehouse mall may also sell space to wholesalers or to light manufacturers that maintain a retail facility in their warehouse bays. Some miniwarehouses are located in high-traffic areas and provide ample customer parking, as well as display windows visible from the street. Home improvement materials, specialty foods, pet supplies, and garden and yard supplies are often sold in these malls. Unlike traditional shopping centers, miniwarehouse malls usually do not have coordinated promotional programs and store mixes. This type of nontraditional shopping center comes closest to a neighborhood or community shopping center.

A third type of emerging shopping center is one that does not include a traditional anchor department store. Most malls have one to three main anchor department stores to ensure a continuous stream of mall traffic. With traditional mall sales declining, this new type of shopping mall may be anchored by a store like The Gap. Other likely stores for such malls include Toys "R" Us, Circuit City, PETsMART, and Home Depot. Shopping center developers are combining off-price stores with category killers in "power center" formats. Off-price centers are growing, resulting in a variety of formats vying for the same retail dollar. To compete, regional malls will have to adapt by changing their store mixes.

Retail Positioning

retail positioning Identifying an unserved or underserved market segment and serving it through a strategy that distinguishes the retailer from others in the minds of consumers in that segment

The emergence of new types of stores and expansion of product offerings by traditional stores have intensified retailing competition. Retail positioning is therefore an important consideration. **Retail positioning** involves identifying an unserved or underserved market segment, and serving it through a strategy that distinguishes the retailer from others in the minds of those customers.

The ways in which retailers position themselves vary. A retailer may position itself as a seller of high-quality, premium-priced products and provide many services. Neiman Marcus, for example, specializes in expensive high-fashion clothing and jewelry, sophisticated electronics, and exclusive home furnishings, and provides wrapping and delivery, valet parking, and personal shopping consultants. Another type of retail organization may be positioned as a marketer of reasonable-quality products at everyday low prices. Pizza Hut, for example, has positioned itself as the value alternative by offering a variety of large pizzas at low prices. Its rival, Papa John's, has established a product quality position with the slogan "Better ingredients. Better pizza."

Store Image

To attract customers, a retail store must project an image—a functional and psychological picture in the consumer's mind—that appeals to its target market. Store environment, merchandise quality, and service quality are key determinants of store image.

atmospherics The physical elements in a store's design that appeal to consumers' emotions and encourage buying

Atmospherics, the physical elements in a store's design that appeal to consumers' emotions and encourage buying, help to create an image and position a retailer. McDonald's, for example, is opening McCafés within existing McDonald's restaurants, complete with special café decor and menu items such as gourmet coffee and desserts. Other McDonald's outlets feature distinctly different atmospherics and menu items, such as the diner-style concept being tested in Indiana.[14]

Store Image
A number of organizations, such as Retail Planning Associates, assist retailers in store design to enhance store image and improve store operations.

Exterior atmospheric elements include the appearance of the storefront, display windows, store entrances, and degree of traffic congestion. Exterior atmospherics are particularly important to new customers, who tend to judge an unfamiliar store by its outside appearance and may not enter if they feel intimidated by the building or inconvenienced by the parking lot. Interior atmospheric elements include aesthetic considerations such as lighting, wall and floor coverings, dressing facilities, and store fixtures. Interior sensory elements contribute significantly to atmosphere. Color can attract shoppers to a retail display. Many fast-food restaurants use bright colors, such as red and yellow, because these have been shown to make customers feel hungrier and eat faster, which increases turnover. Sound is another important sensory component of atmosphere and may consist of silence, noise, or music. One study indicated that retail customers shop for a longer period of time when exposed to unfamiliar music than they do when exposed to familiar music.[15] Many retailers believe that shoppers who remain in their stores longer will, in fact, purchase more. A store's layout—arrangement of departments, width of aisles, grouping of products, and location of checkout areas—is another determinant of atmosphere. Department stores, restaurants, hotels, service stations, and specialty stores combine these elements in different ways to create specific atmospheres that may be perceived as warm, fresh, functional, or exciting.

Retailers must assess the atmosphere the target market seeks and then adjust atmospheric variables to encourage desired consumer awareness and action. High-fashion boutiques generally strive for an atmosphere of luxury and novelty. Ralph Lauren's Polo Shops offer limited merchandise in large, open areas with props like saddles or leather chairs adding to the exclusive look and image. On the other hand, discount department stores strive *not* to seem too exclusive and expensive. To appeal to multiple market segments, a retailer may create different atmospheres for different operations within the store; for example, the discount basement, the sports department, the housewares department, and the women's shoe department may each have a unique atmosphere.

Atmospherics
Like many retailers, Crate & Barrel spends considerable resources to make both the external and internal atmospherics attractive and appealing to customers.

Although heavily dependent on atmospherics, a store's image is also shaped by its reputation for integrity, number of services offered, location, merchandise assortments, pricing policies, promotional activities, and community involvement. Characteristics of the target market—social class, lifestyle, income level, and past buying behavior—help form store image as well. How consumers perceive the store can be a major determinant of store patronage. Consumers from lower socioeconomic groups tend to patronize small, high-margin, high-service food stores and prefer small, friendly loan companies over large, impersonal banks, even though the former charge higher interest. Affluent consumers tend to look for exclusive establishments offering high-quality products and prestigious labels. Retailers should be aware of the multiple factors contributing to store image and recognize that perceptions of image vary.

Scrambled Merchandising

scrambled merchandising The addition of unrelated products and product lines to an existing product mix, particularly fast-moving items that can be sold in volume

When retailers add unrelated products and product lines—particularly fast-moving items that can be sold in volume—to an existing product mix, they are practicing **scrambled merchandising.** Retailers adopting this strategy hope to accomplish one or more of the following: (1) convert stores into one-stop shopping centers, (2) generate more traffic, (3) realize higher profit margins, and (4) increase impulse purchases. In scrambled merchandising, retailers must deal with diverse marketing channels. Scrambled merchandising can also blur a store's image in consumers' minds, making it more difficult for a retailer to succeed in today's highly competitive, saturated markets. Finally, scrambled merchandising intensifies competition among traditionally distinct types of stores and forces suppliers to adjust distribution systems to accommodate new channel members.

The Wheel of Retailing

wheel of retailing A hypothesis holding that new retailers usually enter the market as low-status, low-margin, low-price operators but eventually evolve into high-cost, high-price merchants

As new types of retail businesses come into being, they strive to fill niches in a dynamic retailing environment. One hypothesis regarding the evolution and development of new types of retail stores is the **wheel of retailing.** According to this theory, new retailers enter the marketplace with low prices, margins, and status. Their low prices are usually the result of innovative cost-cutting procedures and soon attract imitators. Gradually, as these businesses attempt to broaden their customer base and increase sales, their operations and facilities become more elaborate and more expensive. They may move to more desirable locations, begin to carry higher-quality merchandise, or add services. Eventually, they emerge at the high end of the price, cost, and service scales, competing with newer discount retailers following the same evolutionary process.[16]

Supermarkets, for example, have undergone many changes since their introduction in 1921. Initially, they offered limited services and low food prices. However, over time they developed a variety of new services, including free coffee, gourmet food sections, and children's play areas. Today supermarkets are being challenged by superstores, which offer more product choices and have undercut supermarket prices.

Consider the evolution of department stores, discount stores, warehouse clubs, category killers, and online retailers, shown in Figure 16.1. Department stores like Sears started out as high-volume, low-cost merchants competing with general stores and other small retailers. Discount stores developed later in response to rising expenses of services in department stores. Many discount outlets now appear to be following the wheel of retailing by offering more services, better locations, quality inventories, and therefore higher prices. Some discount stores are almost indistinguishable from department stores. In response have emerged category killers, such as PETsMART and Office Depot, which concentrate on a major product category and offer enormous product depth, in many cases at lower prices than discount stores. Yet even these retailers seem to be following the wheel. Lowe's, a home improvement retailer, has added big-ticket items and more upscale brands, such as Laura Ashley.

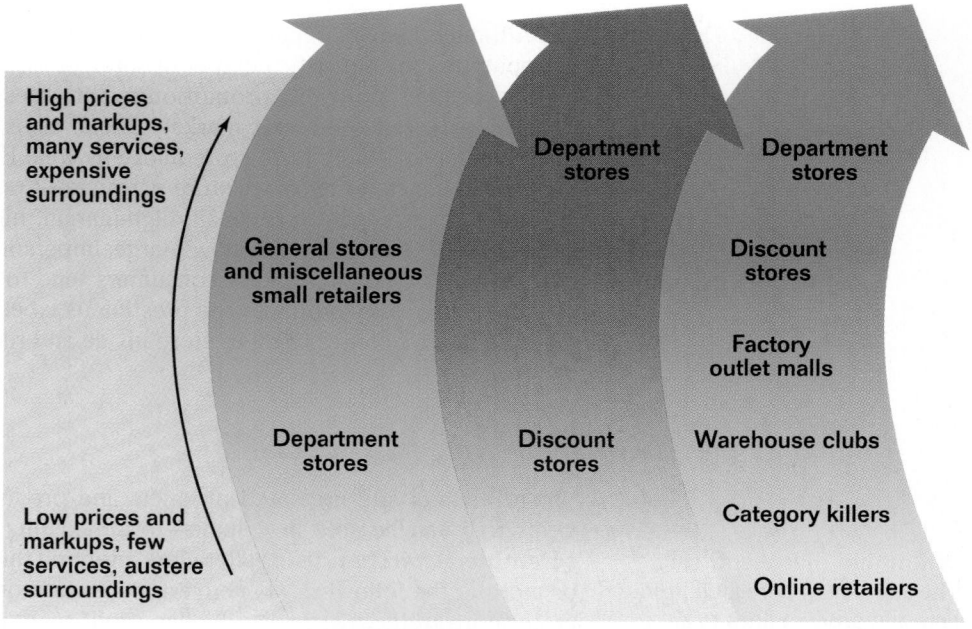

High prices
and markups,
many services,
expensive
surroundings

General stores
and miscellaneous
small retailers

Department
stores

Department
stores

Department
stores

Discount
stores

Factory
outlet malls

Department
stores

Discount
stores

Warehouse clubs

Low prices and
markups, few
services, austere
surroundings

Category killers

Online retailers

1890–1910   1955–1970   1990s

FIGURE 16.1
The Wheel of Retailing
If the "wheel" is considered to be turning slowly in the direction of the arrows, then the department stores around 1900 and the discounters that came later can be viewed as coming on the scene at the low end of the wheel. As it turns slowly, they move with it, becoming higher-price operations and leaving room for lower-price firms to gain entry at the low end of the wheel.
Source: Adapted from Robert F. Hartley, *Retailing: Challenge and Opportunity*, 3rd ed., p. 42. Copyright © 1984 by Houghton Mifflin Company. Used by permission.

The wheel of retailing, along with other changes in the marketing environment and buying behavior itself, requires that retailers adjust in order to survive and compete. Consumers have less time than ever to shop. Shopping today centers on "needs fulfillment" and thus is more utilitarian and work oriented, a fact that many major retailing executives have noticed. As consumers have less time to shop and greater access to more sophisticated technology, retailing venues like catalog retailing, television home shopping, and online retailing will take on greater importance. New retailers will evolve to capitalize on these opportunities, while those that cannot adapt will not survive.

Summary

Retailing includes all transactions in which buyers intend to consume products through personal, family, or household use. Retailers, organizations that sell products primarily to ultimate consumers, are important links in the marketing channel because they are both marketers for and customers of wholesalers and producers. Retailers add value, provide services, and assist in making product selections.

Retail stores can be classified according to the breadth of products offered. Two broad categories are general-merchandise retailers and specialty retailers. The primary types of general-merchandise retailers include department stores, discount stores, supermarkets, super-

stores, hypermarkets, warehouse clubs, and warehouse and catalog showrooms. Department stores are large retail organizations employing at least 25 people and characterized by wide product mixes in considerable depth for most product lines. Their products are organized into separate departments that function like self-contained businesses. Discount stores are self-service, low-price, general-merchandise outlets. Supermarkets are large, self-service food stores that also carry some nonfood products. Superstores are giant retail outlets carrying all the products found in supermarkets and most consumer products purchased on a routine basis. Hypermarkets offer supermarket and discount store shopping at one location. Warehouse clubs are large-scale, members-only discount operations. Warehouse and catalog showrooms are low-cost operations characterized by warehouse methods of materials handling and display, large inventories, and minimal services.

Specialty retailers offer substantial assortments in a few product lines. They include traditional specialty retailers, which carry narrow product mixes with deep product lines; off-price retailers, which sell brand name manufacturers' seconds and production overruns at deep discounts; and category killers, large specialty stores that concentrate on a major product category and compete on the basis of low prices and enormous product availability.

Nonstore retailing is the selling of goods or services outside the confines of a retail facility. The three major types of nonstore retailing are direct selling, direct marketing, and automatic vending. Direct selling is the marketing of products to ultimate consumers through face-to-face sales presentations at home or in the workplace. Direct marketing is the use of telephone and nonpersonal media to communicate product and organizational information to consumers, who then can purchase products by mail or telephone. Forms of direct marketing include catalog marketing, direct-response marketing, telemarketing, television home shopping, and online retailing. Automatic vending is the use of machines to dispense products.

Franchising is an arrangement whereby a supplier grants a dealer the right to sell products in exchange for some type of consideration. Retail franchises are of three general types. A manufacturer may authorize a number of retail stores to sell a certain brand name item; a producer may license distributors to sell a given product to retailers; or a franchiser may supply brand names, techniques,

or other services instead of a complete product. Franchise arrangements have a number of advantages and disadvantages over traditional business forms, and their use is increasing.

To increase sales and store patronage, retailers must consider strategic issues. Location determines the trading area from which a store draws its customers and should be evaluated carefully. When evaluating potential sites, retailers take into account a variety of factors, including the location of the firm's target market within the trading area, kinds of products sold, availability of public transportation, customer characteristics, and competitors' locations. Retailers can choose among several types of locations, including free-standing structures, traditional business districts, traditional shopping centers, or nontraditional shopping centers.

Retail positioning involves identifying an unserved or underserved market segment and serving it through a strategy that distinguishes the retailer from others in those customers' minds. Store image, which various customers perceive differently, derives not only from atmosphere but also from location, products offered, customer services, prices, promotion, and the store's overall reputation. Atmospherics refers to the physical elements of a store's design that can be adjusted to appeal to consumers' emotions and thus induce them to buy. Scrambled merchandising adds unrelated product lines to an existing product mix and is being used by a growing number of stores to generate sales.

The wheel-of-retailing hypothesis holds that new retail institutions start as low-status, low-margin, and low-price operations. As they develop, they increase service and prices and eventually become vulnerable to newer institutions, which enter the market and repeat the cycle.

Important Terms

Retailing
Retailer
General-merchandise retailer
Department stores
Discount stores
Supermarkets
Superstores
Hypermarkets
Warehouse clubs
Warehouse showrooms
Catalog showrooms
Traditional specialty retailers
Off-price retailers
Category killer
Nonstore retailing
Direct selling

Direct marketing
Catalog marketing
Direct-response marketing
Telemarketing
Television home shopping
Online retailing
Automatic vending
Franchising
Neighborhood shopping centers
Community shopping centers
Regional shopping centers
Retail positioning
Atmospherics
Scrambled merchandising
Wheel of retailing

Discussion and Review Questions

1. What value is added to the product by retailers? What value is added by retailers for producers and for ultimate consumers?
2. Differentiate between the two general categories of retail stores based on breadth of product offering.
3. What are the major differences between discount stores and department stores?
4. How does a superstore differ from a supermarket?
5. In what ways are traditional specialty stores and off-price retailers similar? How do they differ?
6. Describe the three major types of nonstore retailing. List some products you have purchased through nonstore retailing in the last six months. Why did you choose this method for making your purchases instead of going to a retail outlet?
7. How is door-to-door selling a form of retailing? Some consumers believe direct-response orders bypass the retailer. Is this true?

8. Evaluate the following statement: "Telemarketing, television home shopping, and online retailing will eventually eliminate the need for traditional forms of retailing."

9. If you were opening a retail business, would you prefer to open an independent store or to own a store under a franchise arrangement? Explain your preference.

10. What major issues should be considered when determining a retail site location?

11. Describe the three major types of traditional shopping centers. Give an example of each type in your area.

12. Discuss the major factors that help determine a retail store's image.

13. How does atmosphere add value to products sold in a store? How important is atmospherics for convenience stores?

14. Is it possible for a single retail store to have an overall image that appeals to sophisticated shoppers, extravagant buyers, and bargain hunters? Why or why not?

15. In what ways does the use of scrambled merchandising affect a store's image?

Application Questions

1. Juanita wants to open a small retail store that specializes in high-quality, high-priced children's clothing. With what types of competitors should she be concerned in this competitive retail environment? Why?

2. Location of retail outlets is an issue in strategic planning. What initial steps would you recommend to Juanita (see question 1) when she considers a location for her store?

3. Different types of stores offer various breadth and depth of assortments. Godiva Chocolate stores, for example, offer a very narrow assortment of products but provide great depth. Visit a discount store, a specialty store, or a department store. Report the number of different product lines offered and the depth within each line. Identify the name and type of store you visited.

4. Atmospherics is an important tool used by retailers in their efforts to position stores. Visit a retail store you shop in regularly or one in which you would like to shop. Identify the store and describe its atmospherics. Be specific about both exterior and interior elements, and indicate how the store is being positioned through its use of atmospherics.

Internet Exercise & Resources

Visit **www.prideferrell.com** for resources to help you master the material in this chapter, plus materials that will help you expand your marketing knowledge, including: Internet exercise updates, ACE self-tests, hotlinks to companies featured in this chapter, and much more.

Walmart.com

Wal-Mart provides a website where customers can shop for products, search for a nearby store, and even pre-order new products. The website lets browsers see what's on sale and view company information. Access Wal-Mart's website at

http://www.walmart.com/

1. How does Wal-Mart attempt to position itself on its website?

2. Compare the atmospherics of Wal-Mart's website to the atmospherics of a traditional Wal-Mart store. Are they consistent? If not, should they be?

3. Read the "Wal-Mart Story" on the website. Relate the firm's history to the wheel-of-retailing concept.

VIDEO CASE 16.1

1-800-Flowers Keeps Its Business in Bloom

Call toll free to send a bouquet anywhere for any reason—that's the simple, customer-friendly idea that transformed a small Manhattan flower shop into the world's largest flower retailer. In the mid-1980s, Jim McCann added a toll-free phone line to his shop, then called Flora Plenty. He chose the phone number 1-800-356-9377 to spell 1-800-Flowers, a number that would be easy for people to remember. Right away, McCann noticed more customers were calling in flower orders for family and friends rather than visiting the store. By 1986, he had operators taking phone orders 24 hours a day, 7 days a week. The phone operation generated so much business that McCann changed the name of his company to 1-800-Flowers and began looking for more ways to make buying as fast and convenient as possible.

As Internet technology emerged in the early 1990s, McCann saw another opportunity to expand by allowing customers to order bouquets with a click of a mouse. He negotiated to get 1-800-Flowers a spot on CompuServe in 1992, making it the first online store. In 1994, McCann arranged to put 1-800-Flowers in a prominent position on the America Online screen. Then he opened a separate website called 1-800-Flowers.com in 1995 and partnered with Microsoft Network, Yahoo!, and thousands of other sites to draw visitors there. In 2001, he began mailing printed catalogs and created a wireless website to allow customers to make purchases using wireless phones or web-enabled handheld computers. Although the company's phone sales are a mainstay, online sales are growing even more rapidly, already topping $100 million per year. In addition, sales of nonflower items have been strong, pushing the company's gross profit margin to a healthy 41 percent.

McCann knows many of his customers buy flowers as gifts for different occasions. Mother's Day remains the busiest day of the year for flower sales, but customers also send bouquets for all kinds of reasons. When a customer orders flowers by phone, on the Web, or from the company's printed catalog, the bouquet is prepared and delivered by one of 1,500 participating florists (including 120 company-owned or franchised shops), depending on the recipient's location.

Because customers can't see the condition of the flowers they order, 1-800-Flowers dispels any misgivings by offering a seven-day freshness guarantee. The company has also added specialty gifts and collectibles, plus fine jewelry, candy, and gourmet food, to give customers a wider range of choices and bring them back again and again for different gift-giving occasions. And they do come back: during one recent quarter, 40 percent of 1-800-Flowers customers made repeat purchases.

After years of handling flower and gift orders, the database at 1-800-Flowers is filled with details about the buying behavior of the company's 10 million customers. Marketing experts use special software to analyze these details and, by adding demographic and psychographic data purchased from external sources, get a well-rounded picture of the customer base. With this background, the company can develop as many as 100 different marketing campaigns to acquire and retain customers in targeted segments. For example, one prime target segment is 18-to-35-year-old men with $60,000-plus in annual income.

1-800-Flowers.com is pioneering online customer service techniques just as 1-800-Flowers pioneered telephone ordering in the flower industry. Originally the company handled online customer inquiries by e-mail or phone. But management quickly realized that customers asking for help wanted answers immediately, not the next day or even a few hours later. So in 1998, management introduced live online customer service chat technology. Now customers can type in their questions and receive typed responses instantly from customer service representatives. This encourages customers to complete their purchases rather than going to competitors, and it reinforces the quality service image of 1-800-Flowers. Just as important, the chat system has sliced the company's customer service e-mail volume in half, saving time and money.

Despite the success of the phone operation and website, McCann knows that some 1-800-Flowers customers really enjoy seeing and smelling the flowers they are buying. For this reason, McCann started Happy Hour on Friday afternoons. During these special events, the company invites local customers to stop by a nearby 1-800-Flowers shop, see some new or unusual flowers, get a special price on featured items, and be inspired to visit, phone, or click on 1-800-Flowers again.[17]

QUESTIONS FOR DISCUSSION

1. Based on breadth of products offered, what type of retailer is 1-800-Flowers?
2. How have Jim McCann's strategic decisions about location affected the development and success of 1-800-Flowers?
3. What is the retail positioning of 1-800-Flowers? How does this positioning differ from the retail positioning of FTD?

CASE 16.2
Whole Foods Grows Up

Beginning with one store in Austin, Texas, Whole Foods Market, Inc., has grown into the nation's largest chain of natural-food supermarkets. The chain specializes in additive-free, preservative-free foods and organically grown produce. With 121 stores in 22 states, operating under the names Whole Foods Market, Fresh Fields, Bread & Circus, and Wellspring Grocery, Whole Foods employs 18,000 people and rings up $1.8 billion in annual sales.

Whole Foods started out in 1978 as Safer Way, a tiny grocery store located in a Victorian house in Austin, Texas. In a progressive city that already had two dozen health food stores, Safer Way was just another market where "hippie" types shopped for natural and organic foods. But Safer Way's owner, John Mackey, had a vision of a natural-foods supermarket that would stock everything from brown rice and soy milk to toilet paper and toothpaste.

With a $50,000 investment from his father and a customer, Mackey went to Mark Skiles and Craig Weller, who ran rival Clarksville Natural Grocery, and pointed out that neither of their enterprises would survive against the bigger grocery chains and health food stores unless they joined forces. The "Tofu Triplets" closed their respective businesses and opened Whole Foods Market in 1980 in a former nightclub. This 11,000-square-foot store offered a much larger selection of products than traditional health food stores, which tended to shun refined sugar, alcohol, red meat, and products containing caffeine. Whole Foods chose to stock those items and many more, along with the usual herbal teas, organic produce, and natural toothpaste. The clean, intimate, and friendly store was an instant success.

By 1985, Whole Foods had expanded to three stores in Austin and one in Houston. However, financial difficulties and differences in management styles caused friction among the three partners. Skiles eventually sold his share of the venture, and Mackey emerged as the chief executive of the growing enterprise. By the early 1990s, the firm had a total of 12 stores located in Texas, California, North Carolina, and Louisiana. When Whole Foods went public in 1992, it raised $23 million and began a spending spree that resulted in the acquisition of Bread & Circus, a six-store chain in New England; Mrs. Gooch's Natural Food Markets, a Los Angeles chain; and Fresh Fields, a supermarket chain in Maryland. It also opened new stores in new markets.

Today Whole Foods targets health-conscious, college-educated city dwellers by opening big, inviting stores in affluent neighborhoods such as the hip Chelsea section of New York City. A typical Whole Foods Market occupies 24,000-plus square feet and has an earth-friendly, feel-good atmosphere. The company's Chelsea store, for example, located in a historic building, offers personalized attention and delivery service. As another example, the Boulder, Colorado, store is "industrial chic" with track lighting on high ceilings. It also offers valet parking and a mountain-view restaurant with a fireplace.

The line between conventional supermarket and natural-food store is blurry in a Whole Foods Market. Alongside natural and organic products, vitamins, and bulk items, shoppers can find well-known brand names like Fritos and Cheerios, as well as Whole Foods' own "365" line of private label products ranging from pet food to olive oil. As Mackey says, "Whole Foods has never been Holy Foods. We didn't want to send people elsewhere to shop." Thus, customers can browse well-stocked shelves of fine wines, ales and stouts, fresh breads, free-range poultry, and filet mignon. They can get a cup of cappuccino, a full meal, or even a massage. At the checkout stand, they can have their purchases packed in beige-and-green canvas shopping bags that have become status symbols in some locales.

Whole Foods is not the only company looking for a bigger piece of the natural-foods retailing market. One major competitor is Wild Oats Markets, which operates 110 supermarkets in the United States and Canada. Trader Joe's, a chain of more than 130 specialty stores that is known for low prices, is another major competitor. Trader Joe's discount pricing is one reason Whole Foods launched its "365" private brand. Of course, all three companies must battle more conventional grocery chains like Kroger, A&P, and Albertson's,

grocery stores operated by Kmart and Wal-Mart, and regional chains like Randall's and H-E-B. H-E-B has proven a particularly savvy competitor in Texas, where it has augmented many of its stores' offerings with some of the organic, natural, and bulk products that attract Whole Foods' customers.

In the face of such strong competition, Whole Foods must carefully plan its retail strategy. Mackey believes the U.S. market can support 500 natural-foods supermarkets and, of course, he would like Whole Foods to own as many of them as possible. One of his expansion plans, an ambitious strategy to sell natural foods and other healthy, environmentally friendly products on the Internet, ended after just three months. Nonetheless, Mackey's emphasis on a balanced product assortment, pleasant atmospherics, and well-chosen locations has helped the chain attract customers and defend its market share in a growing number of U.S. cities.[18]

QUESTIONS FOR DISCUSSION

1. What type of retail store is Whole Foods Market? Who are its target customers?
2. Based on the strategic retailing issues discussed in the chapter, describe Whole Foods' strategy.
3. How can Whole Foods respond to the intense competition it faces? Would franchising be a good option? What other retailing alternatives might the company consider?

STRATEGIC CASE 4

Bass Pro Shops Sport a Strong Channel Strategy

John L. Morris founded Bass Pro Shops when, as a college student, he was unable to persuade a local store to stock new lures and high-tech fishing equipment. More than 30 years later, Bass Pro Shops has become a national leader in retailing equipment and apparel for outdoor sports. Still privately owned, the company reels in $950 million in yearly sales through an extensive catalog operation, 14 Outdoor World superstores, its Tracker Marine boat manufacturing operation, its American Rod & Gun wholesaling company, and an Ozark Mountains resort. Since the beginning, the company has catered to outdoor enthusiasts who are keenly interested in hunting and fishing.

Reaching Customers at Home

Bass Pro's high-volume catalog operation keeps about 500 employees busy around the clock, 7 days a week, answering 170 toll-free phone lines. The company mails about 36 million catalogs a year and ships 400,000 packages a month to a global customer base. Its colorful Outdoor World master catalog lists more than 30,000 items. The company also issues specialty catalogs focusing on hunting, fishing, and boating clothing and equipment. In addition to its catalog, Bass Pro communicates with customers at home through its syndicated radio show, weekly cable television program, and magazine.

Bass Pro Shops has also set up shop on the Internet (http://www.basspro.com). Visitors to the website can browse through thousands of products for fishing, hunting, camping, and marine activities. To build an ongoing connection with customers, Bass Pro offers a free e-mail newsletter with tips about outdoor sports and new-product descriptions. Customers who live far from Outdoor World locations find the catalog and website are convenient for buying products not available in any local stores.

Opening the First Outdoor World Store

In 1981, Bass Pro opened its first Outdoor World store to showcase the thousands of items offered in its catalogs. Bass Pro's founder and CEO, John L. Morris, calls the original Outdoor World the "world's greatest sporting goods store." Four million people visit this store each year—more than the number of visitors to the Gateway Arch in St. Louis—which makes Outdoor World the most popular tourist attraction in Missouri.

Occupying 280,000 square feet, Outdoor World is organized by departments and, because it offers both entertainment and a variety of services, resembles a mall. The departments feature a wide variety of merchandise with many choices within each line. While signs help customers find departments, merchandise lines, and clothing sizes, promotional elements highlight specific merchandise. These elements include flyers announcing special in-store sales and displays of stuffed animals and birds. Northern geese, for example, suspended in mid-air, appear to be landing over the Tracker Marine boat area, while a raccoon raids a box of Cracker Jacks above a display of men's caps.

The store's salespeople have been trained not only to sell products—all of which have a 100 percent satisfaction guarantee—but also to demonstrate the products' proper use and maintenance. Free pamphlets explain how to select such items as baseball bats, bows, camp foods, canoes, golf clubs, rifle scopes, slalom water skis, sleeping bags, and water fowl decoys. Camping equipment, such as tents, is displayed just as it would be used. Outdoor World also provides indoor shooting ranges for testing rifles, handguns, and bows on a variety of targets. About 200 types of bows are available. Seven display cases, each about 6 feet long, hold around 15 handguns each. Golfers can test putters on an indoor putting green and other clubs at an indoor driving range. The store repairs fishing rods and reels, and sharpens knives. Trophy animals can be mounted at Wildlife Creations, the store's award-winning taxidermy shop.

Customers can also visit a trout stream, a live-alligator pit, and six aquariums, one of which contains a 96-pound snapping turtle. At Uncle Buck's 250-seat auditorium on the lower level, they can watch scuba divers hand-feeding freshwater fish. The store has large displays of antique fishing lures and mounted trophy fish and animals, including a 3,247-pound great white shark and a lion poised to leap. For customers who want their pictures taken with the displays, a loaner camera is available.

Taking the stairs or one of two glass-enclosed elevators to the fourth floor, customers have a choice of two restaurants. The Gravel Bar offers cafeteria-style family dining. Hemingway's Blue Water Café is more exotic. Its decorations include a 29,000-gallon aquarium, antique fishing and hunting equipment, mounted animal trophies, and African ritual masks. Near the entrance to Hemingway's, a 4-story waterfall cascades down into a 64,000-gallon reflecting pool stocked with native Missouri fish. Also located on the fourth floor is the Tall Tales Barbershop, where customers can get a haircut while sitting in one of four real "fighting chairs," the kind used on deep-sea fishing boats. They can also have strands of their freshly cut hair made into a fishing lure. The barbershop provides an excellent view of the Tracker Marine boat showroom below.

Special events are an important part of marketing at Outdoor World. The Bass Pro Shops World's Fishing Fair, held in the spring, draws about 50,000 people on each of the 5 days it runs. It features 150 fishing seminars (including fly-fishing demonstrations) and 200 displays. The Fall Hunting Classic attracts about 80,000 visitors over its 4-day run.

Giving Back to the Community

Bass Pro aims to be a good corporate citizen. Outdoor World employees collect coins tossed into the store's aquariums and fountains and donate them to the Ronald McDonald House, which benefits critically ill children and their families. The 400,000 items that Bass Pro ships each month are packed with biodegradable material made from recycled paper rather than less environmentally safe foam "peanuts."

When Berkley, a manufacturer of fishing equipment, promised to stock one fish for each postcard sent in by anglers purchasing its fishing line, Bass Pro CEO Morris promised to match the number of fish stocked by Berkley. As a result, Fellows Lake near Springfield received 5,000 channel catfish from Berkley and 5,000 walleye from Bass Pro. Bass Pro is also a big contributor to Ducks Unlimited, the National Wildlife Federation, and other nonprofit conservation groups.

Expanding the Number of Stores

Bass Pro Shops' brick-and-mortar retail activities were centered on the single Springfield store until 1995, when the company opened a second store, Sportsman's Warehouse, in Atlanta. This store was smaller than Outdoor World but stocked the most popular products in a similar outdoorsy atmosphere. Sales proved so strong, however, that the company replaced it with a much larger Outdoor World store within six years.

Since 1995, CEO Morris has expanded the chain by opening an average of two new Outdoor World stores every year. The striking 160,000-square-foot store in Dania, Florida, recently won top honors in a

retailing magazine's Store of the Year design contest. This Outdoor World is decorated with scenes of local outdoor areas, built with cedar logs and other natural materials, and equipped with a shooting range, putting green, and aquarium. One of the newest stores is another Sportsman's Warehouse, in a 78,000-square-foot building in St. Charles, Missouri. This store, like the larger Outdoor World stores in the chain, skillfully blends in-store entertainment, customer education, and wide selection. It boasts a 25-yard indoor archery range, a video arcade featuring hunting games, educational exhibits on local river life, and a 6,700-gallon aquarium used in fishing demonstrations.

Many Outdoor World stores are located close to family attractions. The store in Grapevine, Texas, for example, is near a megamall, a wilderness-themed hotel, and a new convention center. The Nashville facility is adjacent to a large music-themed shopping center on the site of the former Opryland Theme Park. The Fort Lauderdale store is next to the site of the International Game Fish Association Hall of Fame, built on land donated by the CEO. Morris has also donated $10 million in cash, land, and exhibits for the creation of the Wonders of Wildlife Museum, located near the original Outdoor World store in Springfield, Missouri. Although the Missouri Conservation Commission views this venture as a positive effort to promote conservation and has even donated money toward its completion, some critics see the attraction as a gimmick to boost business for Outdoor World.

Tracker Marine Sets Sail

CEO Morris has always wanted Bass Pro to provide anglers with everything needed to go fishing, including boats. Initially he sold boats obtained from other companies, but in 1978 he established a subsidiary, Tracker Marine, to manufacture Bass Pro's boats. Today Tracker Marine produces 41 different models, including pontoon, aluminum, and fiberglass boats, as well as boat trailers, at 5 plants in Missouri and Florida. Tracker Marine now sells its boats and trailers through a network of about 250 dealers across the United States, as well as 25 in Canada and 1 in Australia. Tracker plans to expand the number of dealerships in Canada and to enter the boat market in Europe and other parts of the world. Tracker Marine's executives believe expansion will help

keep the company's prices competitive. Outdoor World is Tracker Marine's largest customer, and Tracker Marine is the largest advertiser in the Outdoor World master catalog.

Competitive Threats?

Small tackle shops, marine dealers, and other retailers of outdoor products generally cannot match the prices or selection of Bass Pro Shops. Although L.L. Bean sells outdoor products through its large catalog operation and retail stores in Freeport, Maine, its offerings and store location among outlets like Ralph Lauren and London Fog appear to be targeted at a more upscale market. Neither Bass Pro nor L.L. Bean sells firearms through their catalogs because of federal regulations. Outdoor World, however, offers a very large selection of rifles, shotguns, and handguns, whereas L.L. Bean's store offers a smaller selection of rifles and shotguns only. Nonetheless, Bass Pro executives keep an eye on L.L. Bean.

Bass Pro executives say their key operating philosophy has not been to add more and more products, but to stock products that meet the needs of outdoor sports enthusiasts and add value by selling new products that can enhance the experience.

QUESTIONS FOR DISCUSSION

1. Describe the marketing channels Bass Pro Shops uses to distribute outdoor products.
2. What role does physical distribution play in Bass Pro's success with its catalog and retail store operations?
3. What type of retailer does the Outdoor World chain represent?
4. What are the most important dimensions of Bass Pro Shops' retailing strategy?

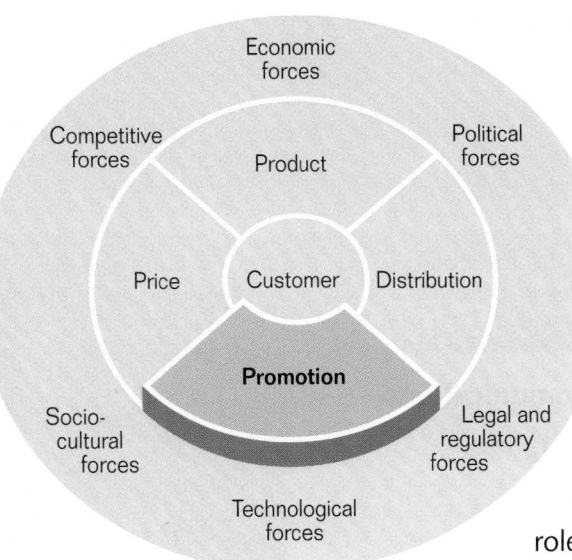

Promotion Decisions

Part five focuses on communication with target market members and, at times, other groups. A specific marketing mix cannot satisfy people in a particular target market unless they are aware of the product and know where to find it. Some promotion decisions relate to a specific marketing mix whereas others are geared toward promoting the entire organization. Chapter 17 discusses integrated marketing communications. It describes the communication process and the major promotional methods that can be included in promotion mixes. Chapter 18 analyzes the major steps in developing an advertising campaign. It also explains what public relations is and how it can be used. Chapter 19 deals with the management of personal selling and the role it can play in a firm's promotional efforts. This chapter also explores the general characteristics of sales promotion and describes sales promotion techniques.

17 Integrated Marketing Communications

OBJECTIVES

- To describe the nature of integrated marketing communications
- To understand the role of promotion in the marketing mix
- To examine the process of communication
- To explain the objectives of promotion
- To explore the elements of the promotion mix
- To look at the major methods of promotion
- To describe factors that affect the choice of promotional methods
- To examine criticisms and defenses of promotion

Sports marketing involves associating a sport, an event, or an athlete with a particular product and communicating that association to a target market through different forms of promotion. Consumers can be very emotional about their favorite sports teams and events, and many marketers hope to transfer those emotions to their products through sponsorships and other promotions. The growing popularity of auto racing is drawing in more corporate sponsors who want to associate their products with strong racing teams and winning racers. Finding the right mix of sponsors can be key to developing a successful, long-term relationship. When Sarah Fisher raced in the Indianapolis 500 as the youngest female Indy driver in history, her main sponsor was Kroger, a large supermarket chain. Some people think Fisher's involvement and success in auto racing has drawn more women to the sport and generated media excitement surrounding the races. Fisher even did TV commercials for Kroger, pushing a shopping cart around a Kroger supermarket.

Winning Communications

Ron Hemelgarn, owner of Hemelgarn Racing, has a long tradition of putting together a strong team of mechanics, drivers, and sponsors. Hemelgarn's sponsors include Taebo (a fitness program), Life Fitness (workout equipment), Team Super Fitness (health clubs), Malibu Naturals (a weight loss product), Delta Faucet, Coors Light, Pennzoil, and Bridgestone/Firestone. It's no coincidence that most of these sponsors target the health- and weight-conscious segment of the market: Hemelgarn owns several hundred health and fitness clubs across the United States.

Success at retaining sponsors is often tied to the success of the racing team. Buddy Lazier won the Indianapolis 500 in 1996 driving for Team Hemelgarn, and he finished fourth in 1997 and second in 1998. In addition, Hemelgarn Racing won the 2000 Indy Racing League Championship. The status associated with winning the Indy 500 is unparalleled in car racing. Sponsors are dazzled by the gold Indy 500 rings each team member receives as a trophy for winning one of the greatest spectator sports in the world. More than 500,000 people attend the Indianapolis 500 each year. Ron Hemelgarn understands the demographics of this target market as well as that of the millions who view the race on television. Upstart teams, new drivers, and bad luck can cost teams sponsor support, making it difficult to retain and attract national sponsors.

Marketing sports such as professional auto racing, basketball, baseball, or golf requires an integrated approach to marketing communications. Indeed promotion is by far the most recognized marketing tool that the general public associates with sports. Displaying logos, advertising, and publicity events are the major sports promotional activities associated with auto racing. For example, Hemelgarn race cars display the Taebo logo, and the entire Hemelgarn team works out exclusively with the Taebo fitness system. When Buddy Lazier wins an Indy Racing League race, he not only appears at media events wearing a Firestone logo on his cap but uses Firestone tires to win the race. This type of promotional relationship with the sponsor's products has proven the most successful.

Ron Hemelgarn knows that getting the right combination of sponsors can be difficult and time consuming. However, without the support of sponsors, it would be impossible for his racing team to be successful. Hemelgarn Racing seems to have the right combination of sponsors, mechanics, drivers, and, perhaps most important, a successful owner who understands the role of promotion in effective sports marketing.[1]

Organizations like Hemelgarn Racing employ a variety of promotional methods to communicate with their target markets. Providing information to customers is vital to initiating and developing long-term customer relationships.

This chapter looks at the general dimensions of promotion. First, we discuss the nature of integrated marketing communications. We then define and examine the role of promotion. Next, we analyze the meaning and process of communication and explore some of the reasons promotion is used. After that, we consider major promotional methods and the factors that influence marketers' decisions to use particular methods. Finally, we examine criticisms and defenses of promotion.

The Nature of Integrated Marketing Communications

integrated marketing communications
Coordination of promotion and other marketing efforts for maximum informational and persuasive impact

Integrated marketing communications refer to the coordination of promotion and other marketing efforts to ensure maximum informational and persuasive impact on customers. Coordinating multiple marketing tools to produce this synergistic effect requires a marketer to employ a broad perspective. A major goal of integrated marketing communications is to send a consistent message to customers. Because various units both inside and outside most companies have traditionally planned and implemented promotional efforts, customers have not always received consistent messages. Integrated marketing communications provide an organization with a way to coordinate and manage its promotional efforts to ensure that customers receive consistent messages. This approach fosters not only long-term customer relationships but also the efficient use of promotional resources.

The concept of integrated marketing communications has been increasingly accepted for several reasons. Mass media advertising, a very popular promotional method in the past, is used less today because of its high cost and unpredictable audiences.[2] Marketers can now take advantage of more precisely targeted promotional tools, such as cable TV, direct mail, CD-ROMs, the Internet, special-interest magazines, and videocassettes. Database marketing is also allowing marketers to more precisely target individual customers. Until recently, suppliers of marketing communications were specialists. Advertising agencies provided advertising campaigns, sales promotion companies provided sales promotion activities and materials, and public relations organizations engaged in publicity efforts. Today a number of promotion-related companies provide one-stop shopping to the client seeking advertising, sales promotion, and public relations, thus reducing coordination problems for the sponsoring company. Because the overall cost of marketing communications has risen significantly, upper management demands systematic evaluations of communication efforts and a reasonable return on investment.

The specific communication vehicles employed and the precision with which they are used are changing as both information technology and customer interests become increasingly dynamic. Today marketers and customers have almost unlimited access to data about each other. Integrating and customizing marketing communications while protecting customer privacy has become a major challenge. However, research conducted for *American Demographics* magazine indicates that 75 percent of adult consumers want products customized to their personal needs, and 70 percent say they would be more loyal to companies that make an effort to discover their needs and tastes.[3] Through the Internet, companies can provide product information and services that are coordinated with traditional promotional activities. Communication relationships with customers can actually determine the nature of the product. For example, Reflect.com, an online cosmetics firm, mixes makeup for different skin types based on information exchanges with customers. Thus, consumers may be willing to exchange personal information for customized products.[4] The sharing of information and use of technology to facilitate communication between buyers and sellers is necessary for successful customer relationship management.

The Role of Promotion

Promotion is communication that builds and maintains favorable relationships by informing and persuading one or more audiences to

promotion Communication to build and maintain relationships by informing and persuading one or more audiences

view an organization more positively and to accept its products. While a company may pursue a number of promotional objectives (discussed later in this chapter), the overall role of promotion is to stimulate product demand. Toward this end, many organizations spend considerable resources on promotion to build and enhance relationships with current and potential customers. For example, the lumber ("Be Constructive"), pork ("Pork: The Other White Meat"), and milk ("Got Milk?") industries promote the use of these products to stimulate demand.[5] Marketers also indirectly facilitate favorable relationships by focusing information about company activities and products on interest groups (such as environmental and consumer groups), current and potential investors, regulatory agencies, and society in general. For example, some organizations promote responsible use of products criticized by society such as tobacco, alcohol, and violent movies. Companies sometimes promote programs that help selected groups. McDonald's, for instance, promotes Ronald McDonald Houses, which aid families of children suffering from cancer. Such *cause-related marketing,* as we discussed in Chapter 4, links the purchase of products to philanthropic efforts for one or more causes. By contributing to causes that its target markets support, cause-related marketing can help marketers boost sales and generate goodwill. Marketing Citizenship examines how one company has expanded the concept of cause-related marketing.

MARKETING CITIZENSHIP

Cause Branding at Timberland

During the 1990s, many companies sought to link sales of a product to a particular cause to gain support from consumers who favor socially responsible companies. Such cause-related marketing typically promoted individual products. The twenty-first century ushered in a new promotional strategy: cause branding, which seeks to heighten cause-related associations with a company and its brands for the long term. One company that has employed this strategy is Timberland, best known for its waterproof hiking boots.

"Pull on your boots and join us. That's all we're asking. It's the best way to understand. You have something to offer and we want you to join us." That is Timberland's plea to get more of its customers and employees involved in their communities. Under the cause-related marketing philosophy, the New Hampshire–based firm would have been satisfied with customers associating Timberland's boots with outdoor conservation activities. However, in promoting its brand, Timberland refused to settle for such a limited amount of community involvement. Instead the company chose a more holistic approach that supports both the name and the image, and draws both customers and employees closer to the brand. To achieve this objective, Timberland ran print ads that included comments about its corporate philosophy along with images of its products. Ads also included a toll-free telephone number for consumers to call to get information about volunteer activities of interest, as well as a list of causes and organizations with which Timberland and its employees are affiliated.

Perhaps Timberland's best-known program is City Year, a national program formed to teach diverse groups of people how to find common ground and accomplish beneficial changes. The program focuses on getting young people to commit to a year of full-time service. In addition to contributing more than $7 million to the program, Timberland provides boots to individuals who participate in City Year. The company has made such a substantial investment in City Year because executives believe it addresses the company's three most important platforms. First, it promotes civic engagement by helping youth develop a strong sense of leadership and volunteerism. Second, City Year endorses diversity by forming unique pairs of volunteers and by working against racism, sexism, and other types of discrimination. Finally, the program emphasizes environmental conservation and preservation.

Timberland also encourages its employees to support their communities. The company offers 40 hours of paid time to perform community service activities such as helping to build homes, renovate day care centers, and clean streets. Timberland employees initially pledged to perform 40,000 hours of community service by 2000, but they achieved this goal more than 16 months early.

By concentrating its promotion efforts on cause branding, Timberland is making a difference, one person at a time. As president and CEO Jeffrey Swartz said, "Our goal is to sell more boots, and we believe that letting consumers know about our values will help strengthen the brand and connect with our consumers on a deeper level."

Marketers also sponsor special events, often leading to news coverage and positive promotion of organizations and their brands. For example, to help launch its Presto line of colorful, stretchy sneakers, Nike rented a studio in Manhattan's trendy meat-packing district to display a wall of nearly 200 Presto shoes. This event stimulated publicity and word-of-mouth communication about the product.[6]

For maximum benefit from promotional efforts, marketers strive for proper planning, implementation, coordination, and control of communications. Effective management of integrated marketing communications is based on information about and feedback from customers and the marketing environment, often obtained from an organization's marketing information system (see Figure 17.1). How successfully marketers use promotion to maintain positive relationships depends largely on the quantity and quality of information the organization receives. Because customers derive information and opinions from many different sources, integrated marketing communications planning also takes into account informal methods of communication such as word of mouth and independent information sources on the Internet. Because promotion is communication that can be managed, we now analyze what communication is and how the communication process works.

FIGURE 17.1
**Information Flows Are Important
in Integrated Marketing Communications**

Promotion and the Communication Process

Communication is essentially the transmission of information. For communication to take place, both the sender and receiver of information must share some common ground. They must have a common understanding of the symbols, words, and pictures used to transmit information. An individual transmitting the following message may believe he or she is communicating with you:

在工廠吾人製造化粧品, 在商店吾人銷售希望。

However, communication has not taken place if you don't understand the language in which the message is written.[7] Thus, we define **communication** as a sharing of meaning.[8] Implicit in this definition is the notion of transmission of information because sharing necessitates transmission.

communication   A sharing of meaning

source   A person, group, or organization with a meaning it tries to share with an audience

As Figure 17.2 shows, communication begins with a source. A **source** is a person, group, or organization with a meaning it attempts to share with an audience. A source could be a salesperson wishing to communicate a sales message or an organization wanting to send a message to thousands of customers through an advertisement. Developing a strategy can enhance the effectiveness of the source's communication. For example, a strategy in which a salesperson attempts to influence a customer's decision by eliminating competitive products from consideration has been found to be effective.[9] A **receiver** is the individual, group, or organization that decodes a coded message, and an *audience* is two or more receivers. The intended receivers or audience of an advertisement for Stouffer's Lean Cuisine, for example, might be consumers who are watching their weight. American dieters tend to be women (66 percent) between ages 55 and 64 and college educated.[10] Stouffer could use this information to target receivers with integrated marketing communications about its products.

receiver   The individual, group, or organization that decodes a coded message

To transmit meaning, a source must convert the meaning into a series of signs or symbols representing ideas or concepts. This is called the **coding process** or *encoding*. When coding meaning into a message, the source must consider certain characteristics of the receiver or audience. To share meaning, the source should use signs or symbols familiar to the receiver or audience. Marketers who understand this realize the importance of knowing their target market and ensuring that an advertisement, for example, uses language the target market understands. Thus, when General Mills advertises Cheerios, it does not mention all the ingredients used to make the cereal because some ingredients would have little meaning to consumers. Some notable problems have occurred in translating English advertisements into other languages to communicate with customers in global markets. For example, Budweiser has been advertised in Spain as the "Queen of Beers," and the Chinese have been encouraged to "eat their fingers off" when receiving KFC's slogan "Finger-Lickin' Good."[11] Clearly it is important that people understand the language used in promotion.

coding process   Converting meaning into a series of signs or symbols

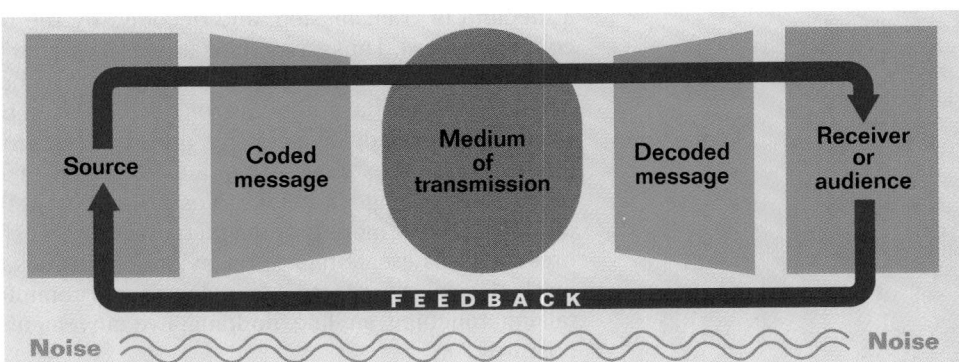

FIGURE 17.2
The Communication Process

When coding a meaning, a source needs to use signs or symbols that the receiver or audience uses for referring to the concepts the source intends to convey. Marketers try to avoid signs or symbols that may have several meanings for an audience. For example, *soda* as a general term for soft drinks might not work well in national advertisements. Although in some parts of the United States the word means "soft drink," in other regions it may connote bicarbonate of soda, an ice cream drink, or something one mixes with Scotch whiskey.

medium of transmission
The means of carrying the coded message from the source to the receiver

To share a coded meaning with the receiver or audience, a source selects and uses a medium of transmission. A **medium of transmission** carries the coded message from the source to the receiver or audience. Transmission media include ink on paper, air wave vibrations produced by vocal cords, chalk marks on a chalkboard, and electronically produced vibrations of air waves (in radio and television signals, for example).

When a source chooses an inappropriate medium of transmission, several problems may arise. The coded message may reach some receivers, but the wrong ones. For example, research indicates that dieters tend to be more culturally sophisticated than the average magazine reader. Their reading choices include *Prevention, Shape, Gourmet, Smart Money,* and *Cycle World,* and they are more likely to look at recipes in *Bon Appétit* and *Martha Stewart Living.*[12] An advertiser attempting to reach this group would need to take this information into account when choosing an appropriate medium of transmission. Coded messages may also reach intended receivers in incomplete form because the intensity of the transmission is weak. For example, radio and broadcast television signals are received effectively only over a limited range, which varies depending on climatic conditions. Members of the target audience living on the fringe of the broadcast area may receive a weak signal; others well within the broadcast area may also receive an incomplete message if, for example, they listen to the radio while driving or studying.

decoding process   Converting signs or symbols into concepts and ideas

In the **decoding process,** signs or symbols are converted into concepts and ideas. Seldom does a receiver decode exactly the same meaning that the source coded. For example, recognizing that one-fourth of the U.S. population is nonwhite, marketers such as Cover Girl, Clairol, Avon, and PepsiCo realize the importance of advertising that includes African Americans and other minority groups, and thus are increasingly turning to African American models. To communicate effectively with black women, appropriate images need to be available in the decoding process.[13] When the result of decoding differs from what was coded, noise exists. **Noise** is anything that reduces the clarity and accuracy of the communication; it has many sources and may affect any or all parts of the communication process. Noise sometimes arises within the medium of transmission itself. Radio static, poor or slow Internet connections, and laryngitis are sources of noise. Noise also occurs when a source uses signs or symbols that are unfamiliar to the receiver or have a different meaning from the one intended. Noise also may originate in the receiver; a receiver may be unaware of a coded message when perceptual processes block it out.

noise   Anything that reduces a communication's clarity and accuracy

feedback   The receiver's response to a message

The receiver's response to a message is **feedback** to the source. The source usually expects and normally receives feedback, although perhaps not immediately. During feedback, the receiver or audience is the source of a message directed toward the original source, which then becomes a receiver. Feedback is coded, sent through a medium of transmission, and decoded by the receiver, the source of the original communication. Thus, communication is a circular process as indicated in Figure 17.2.

During face-to-face communication, such as occurs in personal selling and product sampling, verbal and nonverbal feedback can be immediate. Instant feedback lets communicators adjust messages quickly to improve the effectiveness of their communication. For example, when a salesperson realizes through feedback that a customer does not understand a sales presentation, the salesperson adapts the presentation to make it more meaningful to the customer. This may be why face-to-face sales presentations create higher behavioral intentions to purchase services than do telemarketing sales contacts.[14] In interpersonal communication, feedback occurs through talking, touching, smiling, nodding, eye movements, and other body movements and postures.

When mass communication such as advertising is used, feedback is often slow and difficult to recognize. For example, Nickelodeon, a cable television network, is trying to expand its market by targeting "tweens," children ages 9 to 14, with advertising between programs and commercial-free Nick Jr. programs on CBS on Saturday mornings.[15] However, it may be several years before the effects of this promotion will be known. Feedback does exist for mass communication in the form of measures of changes in sales volume or in consumers' attitudes and awareness levels.

channel capacity The limit on the volume of information a communication channel can handle effectively

Each communication channel has a limit on the volume of information it can handle effectively. This limit, called **channel capacity,** is determined by the least efficient component of the communication process. Consider communications that depend on speech. An individual source can speak only so fast, and there is a limit to how much an individual receiver can take in aurally. Beyond that point, additional messages cannot be decoded; thus, meaning cannot be shared. Although a radio announcer can read several hundred words a minute, a one-minute advertising message should not exceed 150 words because most announcers cannot articulate words into understandable messages at a rate beyond 150 words per minute. Channel capacity can also relate to the types and amounts of information that can be communicated over the Internet. Broadband connections through cable modem, DSL, or satellite can increase the amount of information that can be sent and received.

Objectives of Promotion

Promotional objectives vary considerably from one organization to another and within organizations over time. Large firms with multiple promotional programs operating simultaneously may have quite varied promotional objectives. For the purpose of analysis, we focus on the eight promotional objectives shown in Table 17.1. Although the list is not exhaustive, one or more of these objectives underlie many promotional programs.

Create Awareness

A considerable amount of promotion focuses on creating awareness. For an organization introducing a new product or a line extension, making customers aware of the product is crucial to initiating the product adoption process. A marketer that has invested heavily in product development strives to create product awareness quickly to generate revenues to offset the high costs of product development and introduction. To create awareness of the redesigned 2002 Ford Explorer, Ford Motor Company placed an unusual billboard on top of Manhattan's Jacob Javits Convention Center to promote the new sport-utility vehicle. The ad on the billboard was initially covered with 1,200 pounds of birdseed and was revealed as birds ate the seed.[16]

Table 17.1	**Possible Objectives of Promotion**

- Create awareness
- Stimulate demand
- Encourage product trial
- Identify prospects
- Retain loyal customers
- Facilitate reseller support
- Combat competitive promotional efforts
- Reduce sales fluctuations

www.chick-fil-a.com

Over 30 years ago, the folks at Chick-fil-A® invented the original reason to eat more chicken. Namely, the world's first chicken sandwich. Ever since then, they've been responsible for one tasty chicken creation after another. And because chicken's the healthier choice, one thing's for sure: You'll have no beef with us.

Creating Awareness
Chik-fil-A creates awareness of the health benefits of consuming chicken.

Creating awareness is important for existing products, too. Promotional efforts may aim to increase awareness of brands, product features, image-related issues (such as organizational size or socially responsive behavior), or operational characteristics (such as store hours, locations, and credit availability). Some promotional programs are unsuccessful because marketers fail to generate awareness of critical issues among a significant portion of target market members.

Stimulate Demand

primary demand Demand for a product category rather than for a specific brand

pioneer promotion Promotion that informs consumers about a new product

When an organization is the first to introduce an innovative product, it tries to stimulate **primary demand**—demand for a product category rather than for a specific brand of product—through pioneer promotion. **Pioneer promotion** informs potential customers about the product: what it is, what it does, how it can be used, and where it can be purchased. Because pioneer promotion is used in the introductory stage of the product life cycle, which means there are no competing brands, it neither emphasizes brand names nor compares brands. The first company to introduce the DVD player, for instance, initially attempted to stimulate primary demand by emphasizing the benefits of DVD players in general rather than the benefit of its specific brand.

Primary-demand stimulation is not just for new products. At times an industry trade association rather than a single firm uses promotional efforts to stimulate primary demand. Major League Baseball, for example, spent $250 million to get more consumers to watch major league baseball games. The campaign ranged from a Pepsi $100,000 Grand Slam under-the-cap promotion in 1 billion bottles and a Kraft Foods promotion featuring 56 million trading cards in Post cereals to neighborhood pickup games with Ken Griffey, Jr., and Derek Jeter. Stimulating demand among younger consumers is important because research indicates that of all the major sports, baseball attracts the oldest fans (median age 47), and TV ratings for ballgames have declined in recent years.[17]

selective demand Demand for a specific brand

To build **selective demand,** demand for a specific brand, a marketer employs promotional efforts that point out the strengths and benefits of a specific brand. Building selective demand also requires singling out attributes important to potential buyers. Selective demand can be stimulated by differentiating the product from competing brands in the minds of potential buyers. Microsoft, for example, spent $50 million to lure AOL subscribers to its MSN Internet service after AOL raised its price

SOMETIMES YOU NEED
FREE ADVICE.

This Old House
A Dream Come True
The Ultimate
Shingle-Style House

Build It Better:
Super Lumber, Perfect Walls

Point, Click, Renovate:
The Best Web Sites   Our Guide to
                            Wood Veneers

Affordable Face-Lifts
for Any Room

HERE IT IS.

FREE TRIAL ISSUE! The most popular home improvement
show on public television is also an award-winning magazine.
Call toll-free now to sample an issue — FREE!

1-800-621-6700

www.thisoldhousemagazine.com

THIS OLD HOUSE and the THIS OLD HOUSE Window are registered trademarks of the WGBH Educational Foundation. Used with permission.

Encouraging Product Trial
This Old House magazine
encourages trial by offering a
free issue.

for Internet service, promising not to raise its own already lower rate.[18] It can also be stimulated by increasing the number of product uses and promoting them through advertising campaigns, as well as through price discounts, free samples, coupons, consumer contests and games, and sweepstakes. Promotions for large package sizes or multiple-product packages are directed at increasing consumption, which in turn can stimulate demand. In addition, selective demand can be stimulated by encouraging existing customers to use more of the product.

Encourage Product Trial

When attempting to move customers through the product adoption process, a marketer may successfully create awareness and interest, but customers may stall during the evaluation stage. In this case, certain types of promotion, such as free samples, coupons, test drives or limited free-use offers, contests, and games, are employed to encourage product trial. A magazine publisher, for example, might offer several free issues to entice potential readers to become new subscribers. Whether a marketer's product is the first of a new product category, a new brand in an existing category, or simply an existing brand seeking customers, trial-inducing promotional efforts aim to make product trial convenient and low risk for potential customers. For example, Elizabeth Arden has used special promotions to encourage product trial through a buy-one/get-one-free offer.

Identify Prospects

Certain types of promotional efforts are directed at identifying customers who are interested in the firm's product and are most likely to buy it. A marketer may use a magazine advertisement with a direct-response information form, requesting the reader to complete and mail the form to receive additional information. Some advertisements have toll-free numbers to facilitate direct customer response. Customers who fill out information blanks or call the organization usually have higher interest in the product, which makes them likely sales prospects. The organization can respond with phone calls, follow-up letters, or personal contact by salespeople. Dun & Bradstreet, for example, offered a free article on customer relationship management to businesses that mailed in a card or called a toll-free number. This helped the consulting firm identify prospects to sell data used to develop and maintain customer relationships.

Retain Loyal Customers

Clearly, maintaining long-term customer relationships is a major goal of most marketers. Such relationships are quite valuable. For example, the value of a Taco Bell customer amounts to $12,000.[19] Promotional efforts directed at customer retention can help an organization control its costs because the costs of retaining customers are usually considerably lower than those of acquiring new ones. Frequent-user programs such as those sponsored by airlines, car rental agencies, and hotels, aim to reward loyal customers and encourage them to remain loyal. Some organizations employ special offers that only their existing customers can use. To retain loyal customers, marketers not only advertise loyalty programs but also use reinforcement advertising, which assures current users they have made the right brand choice and tells them how to get the most satisfaction from the product.

Facilitate Reseller Support

Reseller support is a two-way street. Producers generally want to provide support to resellers to maintain sound working relationships, and in turn they expect resellers to support their products. When a manufacturer advertises a product to consumers, resellers should view this promotion as a form of strong manufacturer support. In some instances, a producer agrees to pay a certain proportion of retailers' advertising expenses for promoting its products. When a manufacturer is introducing a new consumer brand in a highly competitive product category, it may be difficult to persuade supermarket managers to carry this brand. However, if the manufacturer promotes the new brand with free sample and coupon distribution in the retailer's area, a supermarket manager views these actions as strong support and is much more likely to handle the product. To encourage wholesalers and retailers to increase their inventories, a manufacturer may provide them with special offers and buying allowances. In certain industries, a producer's salesperson may provide support to a wholesaler by working with the wholesaler's customers (retailers) in the presentation and promotion of the products. Strong relationships with resellers are important to a firm's ability to maintain a sustainable competitive advantage. The use of various promotional methods can help an organization achieve this goal.

Combat Competitive Promotional Efforts

At times a marketer's objective in using promotion is to offset or lessen the effect of a competitor's promotional program. This type of promotional activity does not necessarily increase the organization's sales or market share, but it may prevent a sales or market share loss. A combative promotional objective is used most often by firms in extremely competitive consumer markets, such as the fast-food and automobile industries. When some automakers began advertising their automobiles' ability to withstand collisions, as determined by crash tests conducted by various federal and private agencies, Volkswagen, BMW, Saturn, Mercedes-Benz, Toyota, and other firms quickly followed suit to combat their competitors' advertising. Although these ads were trying to promote safety records, the companies were also trying to prevent market share loss in a very competitive market.[20]

Reduce Sales Fluctuations

Demand for many products varies from one month to another because of such factors as climate, holidays, and seasons. A business, however, cannot operate at peak efficiency when sales fluctuate rapidly. Changes in sales volume translate into changes in production, inventory levels, personnel needs, and financial resources. When promotional techniques reduce fluctuations by generating sales during slow periods, a firm can use its resources more efficiently.

Promotional techniques are often designed to stimulate sales during sales slumps. For example, advertisements promoting price reduction of lawn care equipment can increase sales during fall and winter months. During peak periods, a marketer may refrain from advertising to prevent stimulating sales to the point where the firm cannot handle all the demand. On occasion, an organization advertises that customers can be better served by coming in on certain days. A pizza outlet, for example, might distribute coupons that are valid only Monday through Thursday because on Friday through Sunday the restaurant is extremely busy.

To achieve the major objectives of promotion discussed here, companies must develop appropriate promotional programs. In the next section, we consider the basic components of such programs: the promotion mix elements.

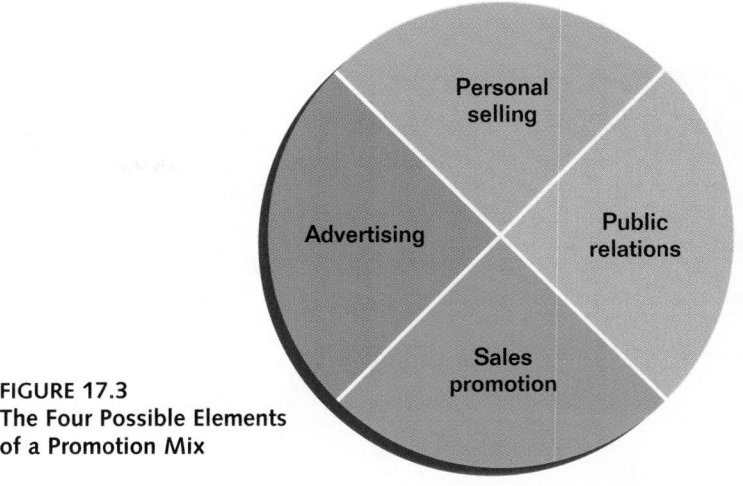

FIGURE 17.3
The Four Possible Elements of a Promotion Mix

The Promotion Mix

Several promotional methods can be used to communicate with individuals, groups, and organizations. When an organization combines specific methods to manage the integrated marketing communications for a particular product, that combination constitutes the promotion mix for that product. The four possible elements of a **promotion mix** are advertising, personal selling, public relations, and sales promotion (see Figure 17.3). For some products, firms use all four ingredients; for others, they use only two or three. Tech*Know on page 445 examines how one company integrated multiple promotional methods to create a highly effective promotion mix.

promotion mix A combination of promotional methods used to promote a specific product

Advertising

Advertising is a paid nonpersonal communication about an organization and its products transmitted to a target audience through mass media, including television, radio, the Internet, newspapers, magazines, direct mail, outdoor displays, and signs on mass transit vehicles. Individuals and organizations use advertising to promote goods, services, ideas, issues, and people. Being highly flexible, advertising can reach an extremely large target audience or focus on a small, precisely defined segment. For instance, Burger King's advertising focuses on a large audience of potential fast-food customers, ranging from children to adults, whereas advertising for Gulfstream jets aims at a much smaller and more specialized target market.

Advertising offers several benefits. It is extremely cost efficient when it reaches a vast number of people at a low cost per person. For example, the cost of a four-color, one-page advertisement in *Time* magazine is $192,000. Because

Advertising
Keebler uses magazine advertising to introduce its new "mini" cookies.

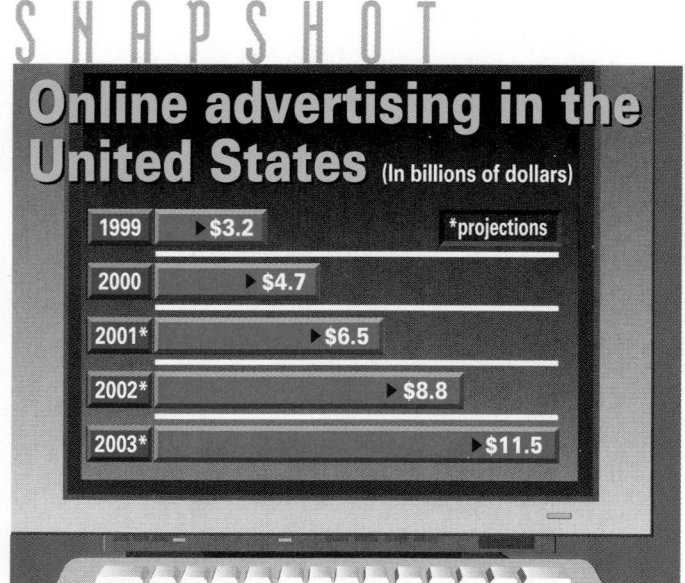

SNAPSHOT

Online advertising in the United States (In billions of dollars)

1999	$3.2
2000	$4.7
2001*	$6.5
2002*	$8.8
2003*	$11.5

*projections

Source: Jupiter Media Matrix, as reported in "Media," *Marketing News,* July 2, 2001, p. 13.

the magazine reaches more than 4 million subscribers, the cost of reaching 1,000 subscribers is only about $47.[21] Advertising also lets the source repeat the message several times. Levi Strauss, for example, advertises on television, in magazines, and in outdoor displays. Advertising repetition has been found to be especially effective for brand name extensions beyond the original product category.[22] Furthermore, advertising a product a certain way can add to its value, and the visibility an organization gains from advertising can enhance its image. At times a firm tries to enhance its own or its product's image by including celebrity endorsers in advertisements. For example, the National Fluid Milk Processor Promotion Board's "milk moustache" campaign has featured Pete Sampras, the Back Street Boys, Britney Spears, and Elton John, as well as animated "celebrities" such as Garfield, the Rugrats, and Blues Clues.[23]

Advertising has disadvantages as well. Even though the cost per person reached may be low, the absolute dollar outlay can be extremely high, especially for commercials during popular television shows. High costs can limit, and sometimes prevent, use of advertising in a promotion mix. Moreover, advertising rarely provides rapid feedback. Measuring its effect on sales is difficult, and it is ordinarily less persuasive than personal selling. In most instances, the time available to communicate a message to customers is limited to seconds, since people look at a print advertisement for only a few seconds and most broadcast commercials are 30 seconds or less. Of course, the use of infomercials can increase exposure time for viewers.

Personal Selling

Personal selling is a paid personal communication that seeks to inform customers and persuade them to purchase products in an exchange situation. The phrase *purchase products* is interpreted broadly to encompass acceptance of ideas and issues. Telemarketing, described in Chapter 16 as direct selling over the telephone, relies heavily on personal selling. However, negative consumer attitudes and pending legislation restricting telemarketing have lessened its effectiveness as a personal selling technique.

Personal selling has both advantages and limitations when compared with advertising. Advertising is general communication aimed at a relatively large target audience, whereas personal selling involves more specific communication directed at one or several persons. Reaching one person through personal selling costs considerably more than through advertising, but personal selling efforts often have greater impact on customers. Personal selling also provides immediate feedback, allowing marketers to adjust their messages to improve communication. It helps them determine and respond to customers' information needs.

When a salesperson and a customer meet face to face, they use several types of interpersonal communication. The predominant communication form is language, both spoken and written. A salesperson and customer frequently use **kinesic communication,** or communication through the movement of head, eyes, arms, hands, legs, or torso. Winking, head nodding, hand gestures, and arm motions are forms of kinesic communication. A good salesperson often can evaluate a prospect's interest in a product or presentation by noting eye contact and head nodding. **Proxemic communication,** a less obvious form of communication used in personal selling situations, occurs when either person varies the physical distance separating them. When a customer backs away from a salesperson, for example, he or she may be displaying a lack of interest in the product or expressing dislike for the salesperson.

kinesic communication Communicating through the movement of head, eyes, arms, hands, legs, or torso

proxemic communication Communicating by varying the physical distance in face-to-face interactions

tactile communication
Communicating through touching

Touching, or **tactile communication,** is also a form of communication, although less popular in the United States than in many other countries. Handshaking is a common form of tactile communication both in the United States and elsewhere.

Management of salespeople is very important in making this component of promotion effective. Salespeople who are directly involved in planning sales activities develop greater trust in their firm and have increased sales performance.[24] More than any other aspect of promotion, the hiring, training, and motivation of the people involved determine its success. Satisfaction with assigned sales territories has also been linked to improved attitudes, motivation, and performance of salespeople.[25]

Public Relations

While many promotional activities are focused on a firm's customers, other stakeholders—suppliers, employees, stockholders, the media, educators, potential investors, government officials, and society in general—are important to an organization as well. To communicate with customers and stakeholders, a company employs

TECH*KNOW

Guerilla Marketing with Buddy Lee

The Lee Company was founded in 1889 by Henry Lee to market overalls, work jackets, and blue denim pants. Over the years, the firm has evolved into a successful marketer of work clothing, western wear, and casual wear. Like many companies today, Lee has not only created websites to promote its products but strives to integrate those sites with its promotional strategies to ensure its communication is both effective and consistent. Now owned by VF Corporation, Lee recently revived a popular promotional character to launch an integrated "guerilla" campaign employing a variety of promotional media.

Lee's promotional campaign involved e-mailing short video clips and links to three websites to more than 200,000 people on an opt-in marketing list. When clicking on the links, visitors met Curry (a race car driver), Super Greg (a DJ), or Roy (a beefy man in caveman clothes). Neither the e-mails nor the websites contained any reference to Lee or its products. During the first week of the mystery campaign, the three websites attracted 100,000 visitors, enough to crash the servers hosting the phony sites. At the same time, Lee blanketed the streets with posters of Curry, Super Greg, and Roy to build awareness of these "bad guys" long before revealing any relationship to Lee Dungarees. Eventually the three characters were exposed as "villains" to be overcome by Buddy Lee, a doll that Lee resurrected as a trademark after a nearly 40-year absence.

Buddy Lee made his first appearance as a "spokes-doll" in the early 1920s. Always decked out in the latest Lee fashions, Buddy hung out in the window of the Dayton Company department store on Nicollet Avenue in Minneapolis, Minnesota. The character proved so popular that Lee began selling plaster likenesses of Buddy in 1923. Buddy Lee was retired in 1960, but the company brought him back in 2000 to boost sales and revive its aging brand.

After introducing consumers to the evil Curry, Super Greg, and Roy, Lee ran television commercials depicting the villains (portrayed by human actors) battling a tiny Buddy Lee doll. Buddy Lee always managed to overcome his foes and win the heart of a lady referee—who, of course, was clad in Lee Dungarees. The commercials directed viewers to Buddy Lee's own website, where they could play Atari-style games and defeat the villains themselves. The catch? Users had to enter the product identification numbers from the tabs of Lee Dungarees in order to play the games.

Since the campaign began, sales of featured Lee products doubled and Lee's market share among young men increased 25 percent. A nationwide tracking study also found a significant change in perception among 17-to-22-year-old consumers. About 64 percent more people indicated they thought it was "cool to wear" Lee products, and 81 percent more perceived Lee Dungarees as "a brand on its way in." The $10 million campaign proved successful enough for Lee to release additional humorous television ads featuring Buddy Lee.

Net Sights

Marketers who use television and radio commercials in their promotion mixes depend on organizations such as ACNielsen Corporation (**http://acnielsen.com/**), the world's leading provider of marketing research, information, and analysis. Although ACNielsen offers many research services, it is best known for its international television audience ratings. Another important rating service is Arbitron(**http://www.arbitron.com/**), which measures radio audiences in local markets across the United States; surveys retail, media, and product patterns of local market consumers; and provides software to analyze media audience and marketing information data. Find out where your favorite TV shows and radio stations rank by visiting these websites.

public relations. Public relations is a broad set of communication efforts used to create and maintain favorable relationships between an organization and its stakeholders. Maintaining a positive relationship with one or more stakeholders can affect a firm's current sales and profits, as well as its long-term survival.

Public relations uses a variety of tools, including annual reports, brochures, event sponsorship, and sponsorship of socially responsible programs aimed at protecting the environment or helping disadvantaged individuals. Other tools arise from the use of publicity, which is a component of public relations. Publicity is nonpersonal communication in news story form about an organization or its products, or both, transmitted through a mass medium at no charge. A few examples of publicity-based public relations tools are news releases, press conferences, and feature articles. Ordinarily, public relations efforts are planned and implemented to be consistent with and support other elements of the promotion mix. Public relations efforts may be the responsibility of an individual or of a department within the organization, or the organization may hire an independent public relations agency. Unpleasant situations and negative events such as product tampering or an environmental disaster may provoke unfavorable public relations for an organization. To minimize the damaging effects of unfavorable coverage, effective marketers have policies and procedures in place to help manage any public relations problems. For example, after Firestone experienced considerable negative publicity due to auto accidents associated with tire tread separation, the company prepared news releases highlighting its efforts to assist in product recalls, as well as its commitment to product quality and availability to answer consumer questions.

Public relations should not be viewed as a set of tools to be used only during crises. To get the most from public relations, an organization should have someone responsible for public relations either internally or externally and should have an ongoing public relations program. Sears, for example, received positive publicity as an official sponsor of the 2002 Winter Olympics and for its initiative to provide home appliances for Olympics-related housing.[26]

Sales Promotion

Sales promotion is an activity or material that acts as a direct inducement, offering added value or incentive for the product, to resellers, salespeople, or consumers.[27] Examples include free samples, games, rebates, sweepstakes, contests, premiums, and coupons. Toyota, for example, teamed up with the Restoration Hardware retail chain in a joint promotion to introduce the Toyota Highlander sports-utility vehicle. This promotion included a sweepstakes to win a $5,000 shopping spree at Restoration Hardware; consumers who purchased a Highlander during a certain period received a $75 gift certificate for Restoration Hardware.[28] *Sales promotion* should not be confused with *promotion;* sales promotion is just one part of the comprehensive area of promotion. Marketers spend more on sales promotion than on advertising, and sales promotion appears to be a faster-growing area than advertising. Coupons are especially important (see Table 17.2).

Generally, when companies employ advertising or personal selling, they depend on them continuously or cyclically. However, a marketer's use of sales promotion tends to be irregular. Many products are seasonal. A company like Toro may offer more sales promotions in August than in the peak selling season of April or May, when more people buy tractors, lawn mowers, and other gardening equipment. Marketers frequently rely on sales promotion to improve the effectiveness of other promotion mix ingredients, especially advertising and personal selling. Decisions to cut sales promotion can have significant negative effects on a company. For example, Clorox decided to cut the promotion budget for Glad branded products two years in a row, in part to compensate for rising plastic resin prices. When competitors did not decrease their promotional budgets, Glad lost significant market share in trash bags (down 10.3 percent), food storage bags (down 10.6 percent), and lawn and leaf bags (down 23.2 percent).[29]

Table 17.2	Characteristics of Coupons and Coupon Redemption
Total number of coupons distributed	248 billion
Total number of coupons redeemed	4.5 billion
Average value of coupon redeemed	79¢
Average duration of coupon from distribution to expiration	14 weeks
Coupons requiring the purchase of more than one product	24 percent
Coupons distributed electronically (online or in supermarkets)	< 0.5 percent
Leading product category for coupons	Disposable diapers
Other popular coupon categories	Paper products, pet treats, cheese, snacks, household cleansers, gravies and sauces, vitamins, toothpaste, canned vegetables

Source: Kate Fitzgerald, "Coupons 2000: Volume Down, Value Up," *Advertising Age,* Mar. 12, 2001, www.adage.com.

An effective promotion mix requires the right combination of components. To see how such a mix is created, we now examine the factors and conditions affecting the selection of promotional methods that an organization uses for a particular product.

Selecting Promotion Mix Elements

Marketers vary the composition of promotion mixes for many reasons. Although a promotion mix can include all four elements, frequently a marketer selects fewer than four. Many firms that market multiple product lines use several promotion mixes simultaneously.

When making decisions about the composition of promotion mixes, marketers should recognize that commercial messages, whether from advertising, personal selling, sales promotion, or public relations, are limited in the extent to which they can inform and persuade customers and move them closer to making purchases. Depending on the type of customers and the products involved, buyers to some extent rely on word-of-mouth communication from personal sources such as family members and friends. More than 40 percent of Americans seek information from friends and family members when buying medical, legal, and auto repair services. Word-of-mouth communication is also very important when people are selecting restaurants and entertainment, and automotive, banking, and personal services like hair care. Effective marketers who understand the importance of word-of-mouth communication attempt to identify advice givers and to encourage them to try their products in the hope they will spread favorable word about them.

Buzz marketing is an attempt to create a trend or acceptance of a product through word-of-mouth communications. For example, Vespa Scooters paid models to ride and park its trendy motorbikes around the right cafes and fashionable retail establishments in Los Angeles. The scooter-riding models were paid by Vespa, which hoped for favorable word-of-mouth communication about the reissued European bikes. The idea is that an accepted member of a social group will always be more credible than any other form of paid communication. Chrysler planted early units of its retro PT Cruiser in rental fleets in Miami hoping to get the grapevine "buzz" going about its new cars.[30] Buzz marketing works best as a part of an integrated marketing communication program that also uses advertising, personal selling, sales promotion, and publicity.

Marketers should not underestimate the importance of both word-of-mouth communication and personal influence, nor should they have unrealistic expectations about the performance of commercial messages.

Viral marketing is a term used to describe a strategy to get users of the Internet to pass on ads and promotions to others. In addition, consumers are increasingly turning to Internet sources for information and opinions about goods and services as well as about the companies. Consumers can go to a number of consumer-oriented websites, such as epinions.com and ConsumerReview.com, to learn about others' feelings about and experiences with specific products. Buyers can also peruse local Internet-based newsgroups and forums to find word-of-mouth information. A consumer looking for a new cell phone service, for example, might inquire in local forums about other participants' experiences and level of satisfaction to gain more information before making a purchase decision.

Promotional Resources, Objectives, and Policies

The size of an organization's promotional budget affects the number and relative intensity of promotional methods included in a promotion mix. If a company's promotional budget is extremely limited, the firm is likely to rely on personal selling because it is easier to measure a salesperson's contribution to sales than to measure the sales effectiveness of advertising. Businesses must have sizable promotional budgets to use regional or national advertising. Organizations with extensive promotional resources generally include more elements in their promotion mixes, but having more promotional dollars to spend does not necessarily mean using more promotional methods.

An organization's promotional objectives and policies also influence the types of promotion selected. If a company's objective is to create mass awareness of a new convenience good, such as a breakfast cereal, its promotion mix probably leans heavily toward advertising, sales promotion, and possibly public relations. If a company hopes to educate consumers about the features of a durable good, such as a home appliance, its promotion mix may combine a moderate amount of advertising, possibly some sales promotion designed to attract customers to retail stores, and a great deal of personal selling because this method is an excellent way to inform customers about such products. If a firm's objective is to produce immediate sales of consumer nondurables, the promotion mix will probably stress advertising and sales promotion. For example, dry cleaners or auto retail firms are more likely to use advertising with a coupon or discount rather than personal selling.

Characteristics of the Target Market

Size, geographic distribution, and demographic characteristics of an organization's target market help dictate the methods to include in a product's promotion mix. To some degree, market size determines composition of the mix. If the size is limited, the promotion mix will probably emphasize personal selling, which can be very effective for reaching small numbers of people. Organizations selling to industrial markets and firms marketing products through only a few wholesalers frequently make personal selling the major component of their promotion mixes. When a product's market consists of millions of customers, organizations rely on advertising and sales promotion because these methods reach masses of people at a low cost per person.

Geographic distribution of a firm's customers also affects the choice of promotional methods. Personal selling is more feasible if a company's customers are concentrated in a small area than if they are dispersed across a vast region. When the company's customers are numerous and dispersed, advertising may be more practical.

Distribution of a target market's demographic characteristics, such as age, income, or education, may affect the types of promotional techniques a marketer selects, as well as the messages and images employed. The 2000 U.S. census found that so-called traditional families—those composed of married couples with children—account for fewer than one-quarter of all U.S. households, down from 30 percent in 1980 and 45 percent in 1960. To reach the three-quarters of households consisting of single parents, unmarried couples, singles, and "empty nesters" (whose children have left home), more companies are modifying the images used in their promotions. Charles Schwab, for example, featured celebrity single mother Sarah Ferguson, the Duchess of York, in commercials for its financial services.

Characteristics of the Product

Generally promotion mixes for business products concentrate on personal selling, whereas advertising plays a major role in promoting consumer goods. This generalization should be treated cautiously, though. Marketers of business products use some advertising to promote products. Advertisements for computers, road-building equipment, and aircraft are fairly common, and some sales promotion is also used occasionally to promote business products. Personal selling is used extensively for consumer durables, such as home appliances, automobiles, and houses, whereas consumer convenience items are promoted mainly through advertising and sales promotion. Public relations appears in promotion mixes for both business and consumer products.

Marketers of highly seasonal products often emphasize advertising, and sometimes sales promotion as well, because off-season sales generally will not support an extensive year-round sales force. Although most toy producers have sales forces to sell to resellers, many of these companies depend chiefly on advertising to promote their products.

A product's price also influences the composition of the promotion mix. High-priced products call for personal selling because consumers associate greater risk with the purchase of such products and usually want information from a salesperson. Few people, for example, are willing to purchase a refrigerator from a self-service establishment. For low-priced convenience items, marketers use advertising rather than personal selling.

A further consideration in creating an effective promotion mix is the stage of the product life cycle. During the introduction stage, much advertising may be necessary for both business and consumer products to make potential users aware of them. For many products, personal selling and sales promotion are also helpful in this stage. In the growth and maturity stages, consumer nondurables require heavy emphasis on advertising, whereas business products often require a concentration of personal selling and some sales promotion. In the decline stage, marketers usually decrease all promotional activities, especially advertising.

Intensity of market coverage is still another factor affecting composition of the promotion mix. When products are marketed through intensive distribution, firms depend strongly on advertising and sales promotion. Many convenience products, such as lotions, cereals, and coffee, are promoted through samples, coupons, and money refunds. When marketers choose selective distribution, promotion mixes vary considerably. Items handled through exclusive distribution, such as expensive watches, furs, and high-quality furniture, typically require a significant amount of personal selling.

A product's use also affects the combination of promotional methods. Manufacturers of highly personal products, such as laxatives, nonprescription contraceptives, and feminine hygiene products, depend on advertising because many customers do not want to talk with salespeople about these products.

Costs and Availability of Promotional Methods

Costs of promotional methods are major factors to analyze when developing a promotion mix. National advertising and sales promotion require large expenditures. However, if these efforts succeed in reaching extremely large audiences, the cost per individual reached may be quite small, possibly a few pennies. Some forms of advertising are relatively inexpensive. Many small, local businesses advertise products through local newspapers, magazines, radio and television stations, outdoor displays, and signs on mass transit vehicles.

Another consideration that marketers explore when formulating a promotion mix is availability of promotional techniques. Despite the tremendous number of media vehicles in the United States, a firm may find that no available advertising medium effectively reaches a certain target market. The problem of media availability becomes more pronounced when marketers advertise in foreign countries. Some media, such as television, simply may not be available, or it may be illegal to advertise on television. Available media may not be open to certain types of advertisements. In some countries, advertisers are forbidden to make brand comparisons on television. Other promotional methods also have limitations. For instance, a firm may wish to increase its sales force but be unable to find qualified personnel.

Push and Pull Channel Policies

push policy Promoting a product only to the next institution down the marketing channel

pull policy Promoting a product directly to consumers to develop strong consumer demand that pulls products through the marketing channel

Another element marketers consider when planning a promotion mix is whether to use a push policy or a pull policy. With a **push policy,** the producer promotes the product only to the next institution down the marketing channel. In a marketing channel with wholesalers and retailers, the producer promotes to the wholesaler because in this case the wholesaler is the channel member just below the producer (see Figure 17.4). Each channel member in turn promotes to the next channel member. A push policy normally stresses personal selling. Sometimes sales promotion and advertising are used in conjunction with personal selling to push the products down through the channel.

As Figure 17.4 shows, a firm using a **pull policy** promotes directly to consumers to develop strong consumer demand for its products. It does so primarily through advertising and sales promotion. Because consumers are persuaded to seek the products in retail stores, retailers in turn go to wholesalers or the producers to buy the products. This policy is intended to pull the goods down through the channel by creating demand at the consumer level. Consumers are told that if the stores don't have it, ask them to get it. For example, when PepsiCo introduced Mountain Dew Code Red, a high-caffeine soda (45 percent more caffeine than most sodas), the product was positioned to appeal to young people, especially teenage boys who like skateboarding and snowboarding. The product launch employed a pull strategy, but instead of blitzing the TV and radio airwaves with commercials, the strategy initially targeted convenience stores and gas stations using colorful banners to promote the new soft drink.[31] Stimulating demand at the consumer level for Mountain Dew Code Red causes the product to be pulled through the channel. Push and pull policies are not mutually exclusive. At times an organization uses both simultaneously.

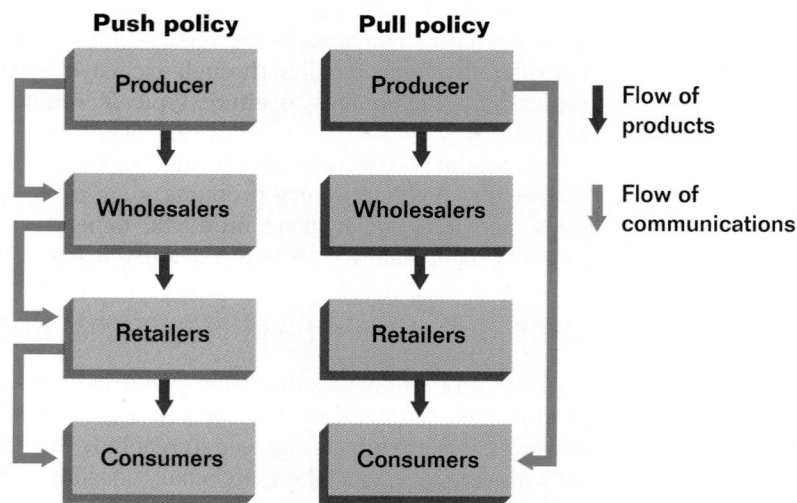

FIGURE 17.4
Comparison of Push and Pull Promotional Strategies

Pull Channel Policy
Coca Cola uses pull advertising to create awareness of its new soft drink and cause consumers to request the product.

Criticisms and Defenses of Promotion

Even though promotional activities can help customers make informed purchasing decisions, social scientists, consumer groups, government agencies, and members of society in general have long criticized promotion. There are two main reasons for such criticism: promotion does have flaws, and it is a highly visible business activity that pervades our daily lives. Although people almost universally complain there is simply too much promotional activity, a number of more specific criticisms have been lodged. In this section, we discuss some of the criticisms and defenses of promotion.

Is Promotion Deceptive?

One common criticism of promotion is that it is deceptive and unethical. During the nineteenth and early twentieth centuries, much promotion was blatantly deceptive. Although no longer widespread, some deceptive promotion still occurs. For example, Publishers Clearing House paid $34 million to settle lawsuits accusing the company of using deceptive sweepstake promotions to get consumers to buy magazines.[32] Questionable weight loss claims are made about various exercise devices and diet programs. Some promotions are unintentionally deceiving; for instance, when advertising to children, it is easy to mislead them because they are more naive than adults and less able to separate fantasy from reality. A promotion may also mislead some receivers because words can have diverse meanings for different people. However, not all promotion should be condemned because a small portion is flawed. Laws, government regulation, and industry self-regulation have helped decrease deceptive promotion.

Does Promotion Increase Prices?

Promotion is also criticized for raising prices, but in fact it often tends to lower them. The ultimate purpose of promotion is to stimulate demand. If it does, the business should be able to produce and market products in larger quantities and thus reduce per-unit production and marketing costs, which can result in lower prices. For example, as demand for personal computers and DVD players has increased, their prices have dropped. When promotion fails to stimulate demand, the price of the promoted product increases because promotion costs must be added to other costs. Promotion also helps keep prices lower by facilitating price competition. When firms advertise prices, their prices tend to remain lower than when they are not promoting prices. Gasoline pricing illustrates how promotion fosters price competition. Service stations with the highest prices seldom have highly visible price signs.

Does Promotion Create Needs?

Some critics of promotion claim that it manipulates consumers by persuading them to buy products they do not need, hence creating "artificial" needs. In his theory of motivation, Abraham Maslow (discussed in Chapter 8) indicates that an individual tries to satisfy five levels of needs: physiological needs, such as hunger, thirst, and sex; safety needs; needs for love and affection; needs for self-esteem and respect from others; and self-actualization needs (that is, the need to realize one's potential).[33] When needs are viewed in this context, it is difficult to demonstrate that promotion creates them. If there were no promotional activities, people would still have needs for food, water, sex, safety, love, affection, self-esteem, respect from others, and self-actualization.

Although promotion may not create needs, it does capitalize on them (which may be why some critics believe promotion creates needs). Many marketers base their appeals on these needs. For example, several mouthwash, toothpaste, and perfume advertisements associate these products with needs for love, affection, and respect. These advertisers rely on human needs in their messages, but they do not create the needs.

Does Promotion Encourage Materialism?

Another frequent criticism of promotion is that it leads to materialism. The purpose of promoting goods is to persuade people to buy them; thus, if promotion works, consumers will want to buy more and more things. Marketers assert that values are instilled in the home and that promotion does not change people into materialistic consumers. However, the behavior of today's children and teenagers contradicts this view; many insist on high-priced, name-brand apparel such as Girbaud, Nike, and Ralph Lauren.

Does Promotion Help Customers Without Costing Too Much?

Every year firms spend billions of dollars for promotion. The question is whether promotion helps customers enough to be worth the cost. Consumers do benefit because promotion informs them about product uses, features, advantages, prices, and locations where the products can be bought. Consumers thus gain more knowledge about available products and can make more intelligent buying decisions. Promotion also informs consumers about services—for instance, health care, educational programs, and day care—as well as about important social, political, and health-related issues. For example, several organizations, such as the California Department of Health Services, inform people about the health hazards associated with tobacco use.

Should Potentially Harmful Products Be Promoted?

Finally, some critics of promotion, including consumer groups and government officials, suggest that certain products should not be promoted at all. Primary targets are products associated with violence and other possibly unhealthy activities, such as handguns, alcohol, and tobacco. Cigarette advertisements, for example, promote smoking, a behavior proven to be harmful and even deadly. Tobacco companies, which spend more than $6 billion annually on promotion, have countered criticism of

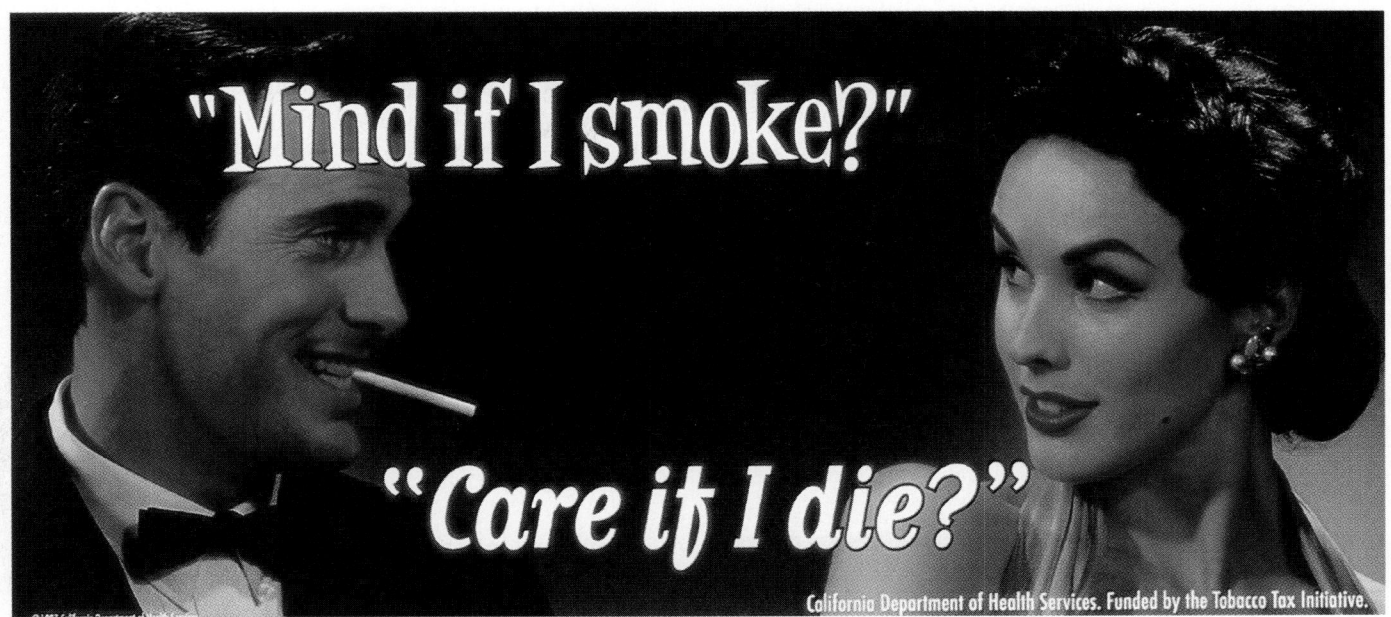

"Mind if I smoke?"

"Care if I die?"

California Department of Health Services. Funded by the Tobacco Tax Initiative.

Promoting Health-Related Issues
Several organizations, such as the California Department of Health Services, provide information about the health hazards associated with tobacco use.

their promotions by pointing out that promoters of butter and red meat are not censured even though their cholesterol-filled products may cause heart disease. Recently a few publishers of newspapers and magazines adopted guidelines stating that they will not publish tobacco-related advertisements with cartoonlike characters if such ads can be interpreted as being targeted at children or teenagers.[34] Those who defend such promotion assert that as long as it is legal to sell a product, promoting that product should be allowed.

Summary

Integrated marketing communications is the coordination of promotion and other marketing efforts to ensure the maximum informational and persuasive impact on customers. Promotion is communication to build and maintain relationships by informing and persuading one or more audiences.

Communication is a sharing of meaning. The communication process involves several steps. First, the source translates meaning into code, a process known as coding or encoding. The source should employ signs or symbols familiar to the receiver or audience. The coded message is sent through a medium of transmission to the receiver or audience. The receiver or audience then decodes the message and usually supplies feedback to the source. When the decoded message differs from the encoded one, a condition called noise exists.

Although promotional objectives vary from one organization to another and within organizations over time, eight primary objectives underlie many promotional programs. Promotion aims to create awareness of a new product, new brand, or existing product; to stimulate primary and selective demand; to encourage product trial through the use of free samples, coupons, limited free-use offers, contests, and games; to identify prospects; to retain loyal customers; to facilitate reseller support; to combat competitive promotional efforts; and to reduce sales fluctuations.

The promotion mix for a product may include four major promotional methods: advertising, personal selling, public relations, and sales promotion. Advertising is paid nonpersonal communication about an organization and its products transmitted to a target audience through a mass medium. Personal selling is paid personal communication that attempts to inform customers and persuade them to purchase products in an exchange situation. Public relations is a broad set of communication efforts used to create and maintain favorable relationships between an organization and its stakeholders. Sales promotion is an activity or material that acts as a direct inducement, offering added value or incentive for the product, to resellers, salespeople, or consumers.

Major determinants of which promotional methods to include in a product's promotion mix are the organization's promotional resources, objectives, and policies; characteristics of the target market; characteristics of the product; and cost and availability of promotional methods. Marketers also consider whether to use a push policy or a pull policy. With a push policy, the producer promotes the product only to the next institution down the marketing channel. Normally, a push policy stresses personal selling. Firms that use a pull policy promote directly to consumers, with the intention of developing strong consumer demand for the products. Once consumers are persuaded to seek the products in retail stores, retailers go to wholesalers or the producer to buy the products.

Promotional activities can help consumers make informed purchasing decisions, but they have also evoked many criticisms. Promotion has been accused of deception. Although some deceiving or misleading promotions

do exist, laws, government regulation, and industry self-regulation minimize deceptive promotion. Promotion has been blamed for increasing prices, but it usually tends to lower them. When demand is high, production and marketing costs decrease, which can result in lower prices. Moreover, promotion helps keep prices lower by facilitating price competition. Other criticisms of promotional activity are that it manipulates consumers into buying products they do not need, that it leads to a more materialistic society, and that consumers do not benefit sufficiently from promotional activity to justify its high cost. Finally, some critics of promotion suggest that potentially harmful products, especially those associated with violence, sex, and unhealthy activities, should not be promoted at all.

Important Terms

Integrated marketing
  communications
Promotion
Communication
Source
Receiver
Coding process
Medium of transmission
Decoding process
Noise
Feedback
Channel capacity
Primary demand
Pioneer promotion
Selective demand
Promotion mix
Kinesic communication
Proxemic communication
Tactile communication
Push policy
Pull policy

Discussion and Review Questions

1. What does *integrated marketing communications* mean?
2. What is the major task of promotion? Do firms ever use promotion to accomplish this task and fail? If so, give several examples.
3. What is communication? Describe the communication process. Is it possible to communicate without using all the elements in the communication process? If so, which ones can be omitted?
4. Identify several causes of noise. How can a source reduce noise?
5. Describe the possible objectives of promotion and discuss the circumstances under which each objective might be used.

6. Identify and briefly describe the four promotional methods an organization can use in its promotion mix.
7. What forms of interpersonal communication besides language can be used in personal selling?
8. How do target market characteristics determine which promotional methods to include in a promotion mix? Assume a company is planning to promote a cereal to both adults and children. Along what major dimensions would these two promotional efforts have to differ from each other?
9. How can a product's characteristics affect the composition of its promotion mix?
10. Evaluate the following statement: "Appropriate advertising media are always available if a company can afford them."
11. Explain the difference between a pull policy and a push policy. Under what conditions should each policy be used?
12. Which criticisms of promotion do you believe are the most valid? Why?
13. Should organizations be allowed to promote offensive, violent, sexual, or unhealthy products that can be legally sold and purchased? Support your answer.

Application Questions

1. The overall objective of promotion is to stimulate demand for a product. Through television advertising, the American Dairy Association promotes the benefits of drinking milk, which is aimed at stimulating primary demand. Advertisements for a specific brand of milk are aimed at stimulating selective demand. Identify two television commercials, one aimed at stimulating primary demand and one aimed at stimulating selective demand. Describe each commercial and discuss how each attempts to achieve its objective.
2. Developing a promotion mix is contingent on many factors, including the type of product and the product's attributes. Which of the four promotional

methods—advertising, personal selling, public relations, or sales promotion—would you emphasize if you were developing the promotion mix for the following products? Explain your answers.

a. Washing machine
b. Cereal
c. Halloween candy
d. Compact disc

3. Suppose marketers at Falcon International Corporation have come to you for recommendations on how they should promote their products. They want to develop a comprehensive promotional campaign and have a generous budget with which to implement their plans. What questions would you ask them, and what would you suggest they consider before developing a promotional program?

4. Marketers must consider whether to use a push or a pull policy when deciding on a promotion mix (see Figure 17.4). Identify a product for which marketers should use each policy and a third product that might best be promoted using a mix of the two policies. Explain your answers.

Internet Exercise & Resources

Visit **www.prideferrell.com** for resources to help you master the material in this chapter, plus materials that will help you expand your marketing knowledge, including: Internet exercise updates, ACE self-tests, hotlinks to companies featured in this chapter, and much more.

University of Iowa Alumni Association Hits the Net

As you will probably discover in a few years, university alumni associations are themselves marketing organizations. Thanks in large part to a popular course related to Internet marketing taught at the University of Iowa and to the Iowa City Chamber of Commerce and a local bank and bookstore, the University of Iowa Alumni Association is now online. Visit its website at

www.biz.uiowa.edu/Iowalum

1. Who are the target markets for the alumni association's Internet marketing efforts?

2. What is being promoted to these individuals?

3. What are the promotional objectives of the website?

VIDEO CASE 17.1
Brainshark Enhances Promotional Messages

Personal selling is paid personal communication that seeks to inform customers and persuade them to purchase products in an exchange situation. Although personal selling efforts cost considerably more than advertising, salespeople often have a greater impact on customers. Of all the promotion mix elements, personal selling is the most precise, enabling marketers to focus on the most promising sales prospects. Marketers are therefore constantly on the lookout for new ways to boost the effectiveness of their sales forces, and many firms have turned to the Internet to improve their sales and communication efforts.

One company that is helping marketers achieve this goal is Brainshark, which employs innovative technology to improve the efficiency of personal selling presentations and communications via the Web. Founded in 1999 by Joseph Gustafson and based in Massachusetts, Brainshark markets a web-based application that allows clients to create, manage, and share business documents enhanced with graphics and audio. The product helps companies communicate faster and more effectively with employees, customers, and partners. It can be used to inform and train customers and partners, introduce new products, and collaborate with employees, partners, and customers. To date, Brainshark's customers include firms in the technology, financial services, training, sales, marketing, customer care, and web communications fields.

Through Brainshark, a client can create a Power-Point presentation and upload it to Brainshark's website along with indexing information. The user then picks up the telephone to record a voiceover to accompany the presentation. Users can also attach documents, including Excel spreadsheets and, eventually, Microsoft Word documents, to the presentation. Once set up, Brainshark clients can e-mail a link to the presentation to customers, employees, and others to view at their leisure. The system can be set up to notify the author whenever the presentation is viewed and by whom. Brainshark employs streaming technology, which allows instant delivery of presentations even to users with low-bandwidth Internet connections. The only tools customers need to access presentations are an industry-standard web browser and a multimedia player. With the latest version of Brainshark, customers don't even need a computer: they can listen to audio presentations via the telephone.

Brainshark's namesake product offers the potential for rich media—the integration of text, voice, and graphics—to make sales pitches more engaging and take advantage of the fact that humans can communicate both aurally and visually. According to the company, attracting and retaining customers and building brand momentum require that communicated messages be received, understood, and retained. On its website, the company highlights the results of a study published in *Cognitive Science* reporting that people retain just 10 percent of information they read but retain 50 percent of information acquired through both seeing and hearing a presentation. When people collaborate with others on information, the retention rate rises to 70 percent. Thus, Brainshark helps clients boost the rate of retention of their communicated messages. According to Gerhard Gschwandtner, publisher of *Selling Power* magazine, "Since many customers prefer to receive product information on the Internet rather than from the salesperson, the salesperson has a greater opportunity to offer customers something much more valuable—guidance and wisdom. As the salesperson becomes a trusted advisor, she or he can fully exploit the power of Brainshark's rich-media, web communications solution to help shape the customer's thought process."

The nature of Brainshark's product also helps companies facilitate internal communications with employees and external communications with part-ners. For example, Brainshark can help train a firm's sales staff and launch new products. The company's recently introduced Fast-Start product extends this ability by combining its rich-media platform with presentation, training, and media communication services to offer event services and support before, during, and after an event. According to Gschwandtner, "By using Brainshark, sales and marketing professionals can consistently and rapidly communicate content throughout their organizations, empowering the sales force to be more productive and to develop customer relationships more effectively."

By the end of its first year, Brainshark had acquired more than 10,000 licensed users, 45 strategic partnerships, and $14 million in venture capital funding. Among its investors are 3i, One Liberty Ventures, SI Ventures, Reach Internet Incubator LLP, and Citizens Capital Corporation. With the successful launch of its web-based communication solution, Brainshark quickly emerged as a leader in the $11 billion market for collaborative service and support technology (CSST), a market that experts project will grow to $43 billion by 2003. Like the marine animal from which it took its name, Brainshark helps clients improve their agility, speed, and competitive advantage.[35]

QUESTIONS FOR DISCUSSION

1. How does Brainshark help companies exploit the communication process to promote their products?
2. How does Brainshark help marketers' promotional messages rise above the "noise" of regular e-mail?
3. How can companies use Brainshark's products to integrate their marketing communications?

CASE 17.2
PETsMART: Reinforcing the Bond Between Humans and Their Pets

More than 60 percent of U.S. households have at least one pet, and more than twice as many have a pet as have a child under age 18. Aging baby boomers and an increasing elderly population are stoking the growth of pet ownership. According to a national survey by the Animal Hospital Association, pet owners spend about $35 billion a year on their furry friends, $12 billion of which goes toward pet health care. These trends in pet ownership have attracted the attention of several retailers and fed the growth of a new form of retail outlet: the pet superstore.

During the early 1980s, 95 percent of pet owners shopped for pet food and other supplies at a supermarket. Although many pet owners still go to a supermarket to buy pet food, the number who do so has declined. When Fluffy, Fido, or Tweety run low on chow, pet owners today are likely to head to the nearest pet superstore. There, in a 25,000-square-foot, warehouselike facility, they can choose from a huge variety of pet foods and more than 10,000 different pet toys and other nonfood items. On-site services include grooming, obedience classes, and even good-health clinics, which are discounted versions of the annual checkups provided by veterinarians.

In the years since the first pet superstores appeared, more than 1,150 such megamarts have opened across the United States, reducing supermarkets' share of total pet food sales to about 55 percent. One pet superstore estimates that nearly half of its food sales are for items not available in supermarkets or other mass merchandise outlets. The superstores' nonfood supplies, such as leashes, shampoos, carriers, toys, and the like, also have traditionally been unavailable in grocery stores.

Phoenix-based PETsMART Inc., one of the leaders of this retailing revolution, wants to be to pet lovers what Home Depot is to homeowners. PETsMART superstores offer more than 12,000 products, including pet foods and a line of pet colognes, shampoos, conditioners, and health maintenance items such as eardrops and eyedrops. Like many of its competitors, PETsMART invites its human customers to bring their furry, feathery, or scaly companions into the stores to browse the aisles with them. With more than 550 superstores throughout North America, PETsMART dominates the pet superstore industry. The firm also operates the Internet's most popular pet-related website (www.PETsMART.com) and markets supplies for traditional household pets and horses through several major branded catalogs and websites. Its sales climbed from $29.3 million in 1990 to nearly $2.25 billion in 2000.

PETsMART was founded in 1987 by Jim and Janice Dougherty as the Pet Food Warehouse, with two stores in Arizona. After growing to seven stores in just two years, the firm began to lose money. In 1990, controlling investors ousted the Doughertys and brought in Sam Parker, a former executive of the Jewel supermarket chain, as chair. Under Parker's guidance, the chain spruced up its stores, widening the aisles, brightening the lighting, and adding more product variety. By the end of 1993, when the company went public, the chain had 106 stores. Since 1994, the company has not only opened hundreds of new superstores but also acquired related firms to enhance its operations, including Petzazz (with 30 superstores throughout the Midwest), Petstuff (52 superstores in the eastern United States and 4 in Ontario, Canada), Sporting Dog Specialties (a pet supply catalog retailer), and Pet Food Giant (10 superstores in New Jersey, Long Island, and Philadelphia). The company also holds a minority ownership position in Banfield, The Pet Hospital, which provides veterinary services in many PETsMART stores.

To achieve its corporate objective of being the dominant retailer of pet foods and supplies in the United States, PETsMART has adopted a step-by-step approach. During its first year of operation, the company's strategy was simply to introduce itself and create an awareness of PETsMART in consumers' minds. Advertising focused on PETsMART's wide selection of products and low prices, hoping to encourage consumers to visit the stores. The chain also capitalized on the strong emotional bond between people and their pets with commercials featuring owner testimonials and such comments as "I'd do anything to keep her happy, anything." Advertising slogans such as "More than low prices, a whole lot more" and "PETsMART has thousands of things to keep your pet happy—for less" reinforced this emotional link.

In its second year of operations, PETsMART began to focus on creating brand loyalty. Its ads emphasized its trademark and encouraged repeat customer visits. In terms of customers' recall of ads, research found PETsMART commercials ranked in the top 5 percent of all filmed advertisements tested. It also indicated that 27 percent of occasional shoppers could be motivated to increase their number of visits. PETsMART continued to focus on the bond between owners and pets with such advertising tag lines as "When is a pet more than a pet? When it's a friend" and "PETsMART—where pets are family."

Unlike traditional pet stores, PETsMART has a policy of not selling puppies or kittens because of the overpopulation of these animals in the United States. Instead it has instituted an Adopt-a-Pet program. Each week, its stores feature several dogs and cats from local animal shelters in the hope of attracting adoptive families. Television commercials touting the program tell viewers, "We don't sell pets, but we help save thousands of them each year." In 2001, the company promoted the one-millionth homeless pet to be adopted through its Adopt-a-Pet program. In addition, together with its nonprofit partner PETsMART Charities, the company has donated more than $14 million to animal welfare programs since 1992.

The estimated 63 million companion pets in the United States have been credited with increasing the health and well-being of their owners, especially by lowering blood pressure and relieving stress. This has prompted PETsMART to target a very special segment of the market, senior citizens, with commercials featuring older pet owners. Advertising slogans strengthen this bond with the tag line, "There's no greater gift than love that's shared."

PETsMART has stated that its number one goal is to be the best in its class: the industry leader. To achieve this goal, the company offers a wider variety of products at lower prices than grocery stores do. To further ensure that it satisfies its customers, PETsMART differentiates itself from other pet stores and mass merchandisers by focusing on emotional, nonprice issues as well.[36]

QUESTIONS FOR DISCUSSION

1. What strategy did PETsMART use during its first year of operation? Its second year? What strategy might it employ next?
2. What elements of the promotion mix has PETsMART used to reach its target market? How could PETsMART employ other promotion mix elements to achieve its goals?
3. What factors affected PETsMART's choice of these promotion mix elements?

Advertising and Public Relations

18

OBJECTIVES

- To describe the nature and types of advertising
- To explore the major steps in developing an advertising campaign
- To identify who is responsible for developing advertising campaigns
- To examine the tools used in public relations
- To analyze how public relations is used and evaluated

459

Big Business Embraces Internet Advertising

What a difference a few years can make! During the 1990s, corporate giants such as PepsiCo, Nike, and McDonald's shied away from banners, buttons, and other early forms of Internet advertising, seeing them as both inefficient and ineffective. Recently, however, more big businesses have launched Internet advertising programs using new, innovative approaches to online promotional efforts. McDonald's, for example, has begun using websites, banners and buttons, instant messaging, online games, pop-up windows, and other online promotional tools to engage customers through interactivity. "We're not going to sell burgers online," explains McDonald's vice president of media, "but we can extend the experience of the brand online and bring McDonald's to life online."

Nike has built a series of special websites to promote specific brands and product categories and to build its brand. The site for Nike Shox, a line of running and basketball shoes, offers entertaining features such as an animated basketball experience "through the eyes of Vince Carter on Nike Shox." By mentioning the site in chatroom messages, Nike drew some 150,000 visitors to the Shox site weekly. Its Play.nike.com site specifically targets teenagers in New York, Chicago, and Los Angeles with sports-oriented video clips, MP3 downloadable soundtracks, personalizable musical e-postcards, and e-mail-ready games. The company also encourages participation and repeat visits by inviting visitors to serve as virtual disk jockeys, click to rate the videos, and register to receive daily game tips via e-mail. "We wanted to tap into the spirit of play as an original expression of sport," says Nike's director of digital brand marketing.

PepsiCo is another giant using the Internet to build its brand and strengthen relationships with customers. Pepsi.com's ever-changing mix of entertainment, promotions, games, merchandise offers, and new-product information draws 200,000 loyal visitors every day. The company has found clever ways to tie its web activities to its television commercials. For example, just hours before debuting a new Britney Spears commercial during the Academy Awards, PepsiCo offered an online sneak preview by posting it on Yahoo! In the next four days, more than 1 million visitors clicked to view the commercial. Building on that response, PepsiCo has continued to preview selected commercials online, along with exclusive behind-the-scenes videos of the stars at work. This strategy, says a top executive at PepsiCo's long-time advertising agency, is effective for "getting the consumer base that much more involved with the brand."[1]

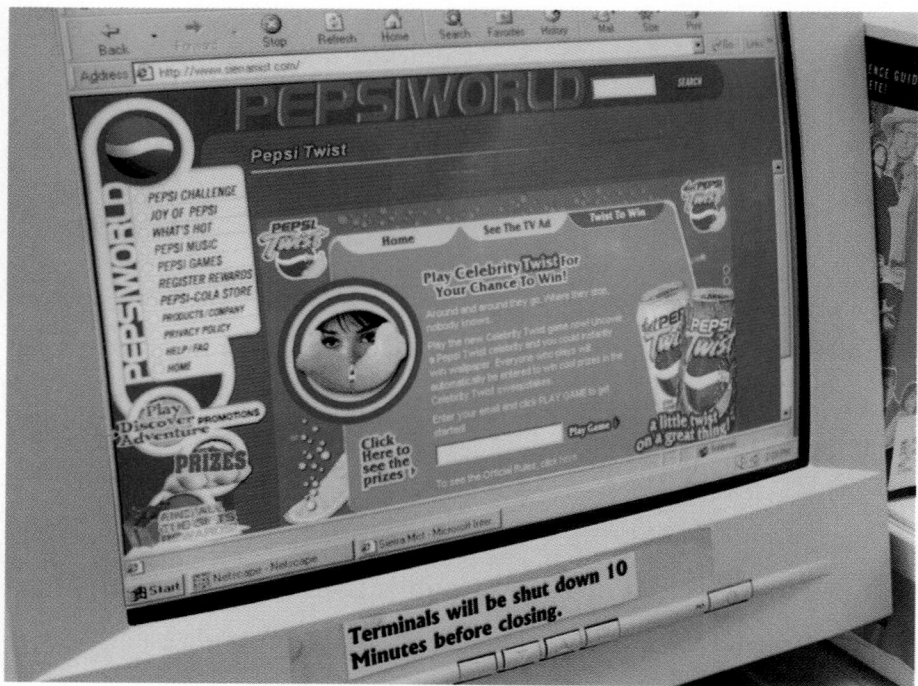

Large organizations like McDonald's, Nike, and Pepsi, as well as smaller companies, use conventional and online promotional efforts, such as advertising, to change the corporate image, launch new products, or promote current brands. In this chapter, we explore several dimensions of advertising and public relations. First, we focus on the nature and types of advertising. Next, we examine the major steps in developing an advertising campaign and describe who is responsible for developing such campaigns. We then discuss the nature of public relations and how public relations is used. We examine various public relations tools and ways to evaluate the effectiveness of public relations. Finally, we focus on how companies deal with unfavorable public relations.

The Nature and Types of Advertising

Advertising permeates our daily lives. At times, we may view it positively; at other times, we avoid it. Some advertising informs, persuades, or entertains us; some bores and even offends us.

advertising Paid nonpersonal communication about an organization and its products transmitted to a target audience through mass media

As mentioned in Chapter 17, **advertising** is a paid form of nonpersonal communication transmitted through mass media, such as television, radio, the Internet, newspapers, magazines, direct mail, outdoor displays, and signs on mass transit vehicles. Organizations use advertising to reach a variety of audiences ranging from small, specific groups, such as stamp collectors in Idaho, to extremely large groups, such as all athletic-shoe purchasers in the United States.

When asked to name major advertisers, most people immediately mention business organizations. However, many nonbusiness types of organizations, including governments, churches, universities, and charitable organizations, take advantage of advertising. In 2000, the U.S. government was the eighteenth largest advertiser in the country, spending approximately $625 billion on advertising.[2] Although we analyze advertising in the context of business organizations here, much of the material applies to all types of organizations.

institutional advertising Promotes organizational images, ideas, and political issues

Advertising is used to promote goods, services, ideas, images, issues, people, and anything else that advertisers want to publicize or foster. Depending on what is being promoted, advertising can be classified as institutional or product advertising. **Institutional advertising** promotes organizational images, ideas, and political issues. It can be used to create or maintain an organizational image. Institutional advertisements may deal with broad image issues, such as organizational strength or the friendliness of employees. They may also aim to create a more favorable view of the organization in the eyes of noncustomer groups such as shareholders, consumer advocacy groups, potential stockholders, or the general public. When a company promotes its position on a public issue—for instance, a tax increase, abortion, gun control, or international trade coalitions—institutional advertising is referred to as **advocacy advertising.** Institutional advertising may be used to promote socially approved behavior like recycling and moderation in consuming alcoholic beverages. This type of advertising not only has societal benefits but also helps build an organization's image.

advocacy advertising Promotes a company's position on a public issue

product advertising Promotes products' uses, features, and benefits

pioneer advertising Tries to stimulate demand for a product category rather than a specific brand by informing potential buyers about the product

competitive advertising Points out a brand's special features, uses, and advantages relative to competing brands

comparative advertising Compares two or more brands on the basis of one or more product characteristics

Product advertising promotes the uses, features, and benefits of products. There are two types of product advertising: pioneer and competitive. **Pioneer advertising** focuses on stimulating demand for a product category (rather than a specific brand) by informing potential customers about the product's features, uses, and benefits. This type of advertising is employed when the product is in the introductory stage of the product life cycle. **Competitive advertising** attempts to stimulate demand for a specific brand by promoting the brand's features, uses, and advantages, sometimes through indirect or direct comparisons with competing brands. To make direct product comparisons, marketers use a form of competitive advertising called **comparative advertising,** which compares two or more brands on the basis of one or more product characteristics. Often the brands promoted through comparative advertisements have low market shares and are compared with competitors that have the highest market shares in the product category. Product categories that commonly use comparative advertising include soft drinks, toothpaste, pain relievers, foods, tires, automobiles, and detergents. Under the provisions of the 1988 Trademark Law Revision Act, marketers using comparative advertisements must not misrepresent the qualities or characteristics of competing products. Other forms of competitive advertising include reminder and reinforcement advertising. **Reminder advertising** tells customers that an established brand is still around and still offers certain characteristics, uses, and advantages. **Reinforcement advertising** assures current users they have made the right brand choice and tells them how to get the most satisfaction from that brand.

reminder advertising
Reminds consumers about an established brand's uses, characteristics, and benefits

reinforcement advertising
Assures users they chose the right brand and tells them how to get the most satisfaction from it

Developing an Advertising Campaign

An **advertising campaign** involves designing a series of advertisements and placing them in various advertising media to reach a particular target audience. As Figure 18.1 indicates, the major steps in creating an advertising campaign are (1) identifying and analyzing the target audience, (2) defining the advertising objectives, (3) creating the advertising platform, (4) determining the advertising appropriation, (5) developing the media plan, (6) creating the advertising message, (7) executing the campaign, and (8) evaluating advertising effectiveness. The number of steps and the exact order in which they are carried out may vary according to an organization's resources, the nature of its product, and the type of target audience to be reached. Nevertheless, these general guidelines for developing an advertising campaign are appropriate for all types of organizations.

advertising campaign
The creation and execution of a series of advertisements to communicate with a particular target audience

Identifying and Analyzing the Target Audience

target audience   The group of people at whom advertisements are aimed

The **target audience** is the group of people at whom advertisements are aimed. Advertisements for Barbie cereal are targeted toward young girls who play with Barbie dolls, whereas those for Special K cereal are directed at health-conscious

Brand Building
Advertising is used to build strong brands.

1   Identify and analyze target audience

2   Define advertising objectives

3   Create advertising platform

4   Determine advertising appropriation

5   Develop media plan

6   Create advertising message

7   Execute campaign

8   Evaluate advertising effectiveness

FIGURE 18.1
**General Steps in Developing and
Implementing an Advertising Campaign**

adults. Identifying and analyzing the target audience are critical processes; the information yielded helps determine other steps in developing the campaign. The target audience may include everyone in the firm's target market. Marketers may, however, direct a campaign at only a portion of the target market. For example, Handspring has started targeting women with ads in *Martha Stewart Living, Country Home,* and *Wired* to position its Visor handheld computing device as a chic fashion accessory.[3]

Advertisers research and analyze advertising targets to establish an information base for a campaign. Information commonly needed includes location and geographic distribution of the target group; the distribution of demographic factors, such as age, income, race, sex, and education; lifestyle information; and consumer attitudes regarding purchase and use of both the advertiser's products and competing products. The exact kinds of information an organization finds useful depend on the type of product being advertised, the characteristics of the target audience, and the type and amount of competition. Generally, the more an advertiser knows about the target audience, the more likely the firm is to develop an effective advertising campaign. When the advertising target is not precisely identified and properly analyzed, the campaign may fail.

Defining the Advertising Objectives

The advertiser's next step is to determine what the firm hopes to accomplish with the campaign. Because advertising objectives guide campaign development, advertisers should define objectives carefully. Advertising objectives should be stated clearly, precisely, and in measurable terms. Precision and measurability allow advertisers to evaluate advertising success at the end of the campaign in terms of whether or not objectives have been met. To provide precision and measurability, advertising objectives should contain benchmarks and indicate how far the advertiser wishes to move from these standards. If the goal is to increase sales, the advertiser should state the current sales level (the benchmark) and the amount of sales increase sought through advertising. An advertising objective should also specify a time frame so that advertisers know exactly how long they have to accomplish the objective. An advertiser with average monthly sales of $450,000 (the benchmark) might set the following objective: "Our primary advertising objective is to increase average monthly sales from $450,000 to $540,000 within 12 months."

If an advertiser defines objectives on the basis of sales, the objectives focus on increasing absolute dollar sales, or unit sales, increasing sales by a certain percentage, or increasing the firm's market share. Even though an advertiser's long-run goal is to increase sales, not all campaigns are designed to produce immediate sales. Some campaigns are designed to increase product or brand awareness, make consumers' attitudes more favorable, or increase consumers' knowledge of product features. If the goal is to increase product awareness, the objectives are stated in terms of communication. A specific communication objective might be to increase product feature awareness from 0 to 40 percent in the target audience by the end of six months.

Creating the Advertising Platform

Before launching a political campaign, party leaders develop a political platform stating major issues that are the basis of the campaign. Like a political platform, an **advertising platform** consists of the basic issues or selling points that an advertiser wishes to include in the advertising campaign. A single advertisement in an advertising campaign may contain one or several issues from the platform. Although the platform sets forth the basic issues, it does not indicate how to present them.

An advertising platform should consist of issues important to customers. One of the best ways to determine those issues is to survey customers about what they consider most important in the selection and use of the product involved. Selling features

advertising platform
Basic issues or selling points to be included in the advertising campaign

Institutional Versus Product Advertising
Toyota uses institutional advertising to improve its overall corporate image by promoting its Supplier Diversity Program. Neutrogena employs product advertising to promote its oil-free acne wash brand and specific product features.

must not only be important to customers, they should also be strongly competitive features of the advertised brand.

Although research is the most effective method for determining what issues to include in an advertising platform, it is expensive. Therefore, an advertising platform is most commonly based on opinions of personnel within the firm and of individuals in the advertising agency, if an agency is used. This trial-and-error approach generally leads to some successes and some failures.

Because the advertising platform is a base on which to build the advertising message, marketers should analyze this stage carefully. A campaign can be perfect in terms of selection and analysis of its target audience, statement of its objectives, its media strategy, and the form of its message. But the campaign will ultimately fail if the advertisements communicate information that consumers do not deem important when selecting and using the product.

Determining the Advertising Appropriation

advertising appropriation
Advertising budget for a specified period

The **advertising appropriation** is the total amount of money a marketer allocates for advertising for a specific time period. It is hard to decide how much to spend on advertising for a specific period because the potential effects of advertising are so difficult to measure precisely.

Many factors affect a firm's decision about how much to appropriate for advertising. Geographic size of the market and the distribution of buyers within the market have a great bearing on this decision. As Table 18.1 shows, both the type of product advertised and the firm's sales volume relative to competitors' sales volumes also play a part in determining what proportion of revenue to spend on advertising. Advertising appropriations for business products are usually quite small relative to product sales, whereas consumer convenience items, such as soft drinks, soaps, and cosmetics, generally have large advertising expenditures relative to sales.

objective-and-task approach
Budgeting for an advertising campaign by first determining its objectives and then calculating the cost of all the tasks needed to attain them

Of the many techniques used to determine the advertising appropriation, one of the most logical is the **objective-and-task approach.** Using this approach, marketers determine the objectives a campaign is to achieve and then attempt to list the

Table 18.1   Twenty Leading National Advertisers

Organization	Advertising Expenditures ($ millions)	Sales ($ millions)	Advertising Expenditures as Percentage of Sales
1. General Motors	3,934.8	136,399	2.9
2. Philip Morris Companies	2,602.9	43,951	5.9
3 Procter & Gamble	2,363.5	20,334	11.6
4. Ford	2,345.2	118,373	2.0
5. Pfizer	2,265.3	17,953	12.6
6. PepsiCo	2,100.7	13,179	15.9
7. DaimlerChrysler	1,984.0	78,622	2.5
8. AOL Time Warner*	1,770.1	36,213	4.9
9. Walt Disney	1,757.5	20,830	8.4
10. Verizon	1,612.9	62,066	2.6
11. Johnson & Johnson	1,601.2	17,000	9.4
12. Sears, Roebuck	1,455.4	36,655	4.0
13. Unilever	1,453.6	10,822	13.4
14. AT&T	1,415.7	65,981	2.1
15. General Electric	1,310.1	90,981	1.4
16. Toyota	1,273.9	43,508	2.9
17. McDonald's	1,273.9	5,259	24.2
18. U.S. government	1,246.3	N/A	N/A
19. Sprint	1,227.3	23,613	5.2
20. Viacom	1,220.9	16,428	7.4

*Based on worldwide sales

Source: Reprinted with permission from the September 24, 2001 issue of *Advertising Age.* Copyright Crain Communications Inc., 2001.

tasks required to accomplish them. The costs of the tasks are calculated and added to arrive at the total appropriation. This approach has one main problem: marketers sometimes have trouble accurately estimating the level of effort needed to attain certain objectives. A coffee marketer, for example, may find it extremely difficult to determine how much of an increase in national television advertising is needed to raise a brand's market share from 8 to 10 percent.

percent-of-sales approach Budgeting for an advertising campaign by multiplying the firm's past and expected sales by a standard percentage

In the more widely used **percent-of-sales approach,** marketers simply multiply the firm's past sales, plus a factor for planned sales growth or decline, by a standard percentage based on both what the firm traditionally spends on advertising and the industry average. This approach, too, has a major flaw: it is based on the incorrect assumption that sales create advertising rather than the reverse. A marketer using this approach during declining sales will reduce the amount spent on advertising, but such a reduction may further diminish sales. Though illogical, this technique has been favored because it is easy to use.

competition-matching approach Determining an advertising budget by trying to match competitors' ad outlays

Another way to determine advertising appropriation is the **competition-matching approach.** Marketers following this approach try to match their major competitors' appropriations in absolute dollars or to allocate the same percentage of sales for advertising that their competitors do. Although a marketer should be aware of what competitors spend on advertising, this technique should not be used alone because the firm's competitors probably have different advertising objectives and different resources available for advertising. Many companies and advertising agencies review competitive spending on a quarterly basis, comparing competitors' dollar expenditures on print, radio, and television with their own spending levels. Competitive tracking of this nature occurs at both the national and regional levels.

arbitrary approach Budgeting for an advertising campaign as specified by a high-level executive in the firm

At times marketers use the **arbitrary approach,** which usually means a high-level executive in the firm states how much to spend on advertising for a certain period. The arbitrary approach often leads to underspending or overspending. Although hardly a scientific budgeting technique, it is expedient.

Deciding how large the advertising appropriation should be is critical. If the appropriation is set too low, the campaign cannot achieve its full potential. When too much money is appropriated, overspending results and financial resources are wasted.

Developing the Media Plan

media plan Specifies media vehicles and schedule for running the advertisements

As Table 18.2 shows, advertisers spend tremendous amounts on advertising media. These amounts have grown rapidly during the past two decades. To derive maximum results from media expenditures, marketers must develop effective media plans. A **media plan** sets forth the exact media vehicles to be used (specific magazines, television stations, newspapers, and so forth) and the dates and times the advertisements will appear. The plan determines how many people in the target audience will be exposed to the message. It also determines, to some degree, the effects of the message on those individuals. Media planning is a complex task requiring thorough analysis of the target audience. Sophisticated computer models have been developed to attempt to maximize the effectiveness of media plans.

To formulate a media plan, the planners select the media for the campaign and prepare a time schedule for each medium. The media planner's primary goal is to reach the largest number of people in the advertising target that the budget will allow. A secondary goal is to achieve the appropriate message reach and frequency for the

Table 18.2	Total Advertising Expenditures (in millions of dollars)							
	1985		**1990**		**1995**		**2000**	
	Total Dollar Amount	Percent of Total	Total Dollar Amount	Percent of Total	Total Dollar Amount	Percent of Total	Total Dollar Amount	Percent of Total
Newspapers	$25,170	26.6%	$ 32,281	25.1%	$ 36,317	22.6%	$ 49,050	20.1%
Magazines	5,341	5.6	6,803	5.3	8,580	5.3	12,370	5.1
Television	20,738	21.8	28,405	22.1	36,246	22.6	59,231	24.3
Radio	6,490	6.9	8,726	6.8	11,338	7.1	19,295	7.9
Yellow pages	6,820*	7.2	8,926	6.9	10,236	6.4	13,228	5.4
Outdoor	945	1.0	1,084	0.8	1,263	0.8	1,758	0.7
Direct mail	15,500	16.4	23,370	18.2	32,866	20.5	44,591	18.3
Business press	2,375	2.5	2,875	2.2	3,559	2.2	4,915	2.0
Internet	NA	0.0	NA	0.0	NA	0.0	4,333	1.8
Miscellaneous	11,438	12.0	16,170	12.6	20,232	12.5	34,919	14.4
TOTAL	$94,718	100.0%	$128,640	100.0%	$160,637	100.0%	$243,680	100.0%

*Estimate

Sources: Robert J. Coen, "U.S. Advertising Volume," *Advertising Age,* May 12, 1986, p. 76; Robert J. Coen, "Coen: Little Ad Growth," *Advertising Age,* May 6, 1991, pp. 1, 16; Robert J. Coen, "U.S. Advertising Volume," *Advertising Age,* May 20, 1996, p. 24; "Coen Cuts Spending Forecast," *Advertising Age,* June 11, 2001, p. 47.

target audience while staying within budget. *Reach* refers to the percentage of consumers in the target audience actually exposed to a particular advertisement in a stated period. *Frequency* is the number of times these targeted consumers are exposed to the advertisement.

Media planners begin with broad decisions but eventually make very specific ones. They first decide which kinds of media to use: radio, television, the Internet, newspapers, magazines, direct mail, outdoor displays, or signs on mass transit vehicles. They assess different formats and approaches to determine which are the most effective. Some media plans are quite focused and use just one medium. The media plans of manufacturers of consumer packaged goods can be quite complex and dynamic.

Media planners take many factors into account when devising a media plan. They analyze location and demographic characteristics of people in the target audience because people's taste in media differ according to demographic groups and locations. There are radio stations especially for teenagers, magazines for men ages 18 to 34, and television cable channels aimed at women in various age groups. Media planners also consider the sizes and types of audiences that specific media reach. Several data services collect and periodically provide information about circulations and audiences of various media.

TECH * KNOW

New Takes on Television Advertising

Now that viewers can avoid commercials by videotaping or digitally recording television programs and then zapping the advertisements, or simply using the remote control to channel-surf during commercial breaks, advertisers are fighting back. Surveys show that 39 percent of U.S. viewers often change channels when commercials come on, and another 19 percent either mute or lower the volume. Faced with widespread avoidance of traditional commercials, many advertisers are adopting an in-your-face approach, using a blend of technology and sponsorship to integrate their products directly into programming.

Princeton Video Image, a New Jersey–based company, digitally inserts products and signage into televised shows and sports events. Cable network ESPN, for example, uses this technology to place advertisers' logos, brands, and signs around the playing field during baseball games and other televised events. The fans in the stands don't see these virtual advertisements, but the ads are clearly visible to viewers at home. Thanks to Princeton's technology, viewers who tuned in to watch celebrities arrive for the Grammy Awards also saw a digitally inserted Ford logo and Denny's banner.

INNX, a television production firm, invites advertisers to sponsor "news-adjacent targeted advertising." Here's how it works. When INNX produces a news segment about a flu epidemic or another health-related development, it attaches a 12-second commercial at the end, including a web address for more information. Procter & Gamble is among the first advertisers to use this approach.

The company recently contracted to feature NyQuil, Crest, and other P&G brands in commercials tacked onto the ends of INNX segments. Distributed to 200 NBC stations and viewed by 9 million people every day, these segments are giving P&G access to a sizable audience.

Many companies are using low-tech product placement to reach television audiences in the context of shows such as "Law & Order," "Who Wants To Be a Millionaire?," and "Survivor." Product placements are prominent on "Survivor," for example, where contestants gaze hungrily at a bag of Doritos and vie for merchandise from Target and cars from Pontiac. Although advertisers like having their products featured in zap-proof programming, such placements "destroy the advertising-entertainment line," complains Gary Ruskin, director of Commercial Alert. "It catches people off-guard and gets them at a time when they're easier to persuade." On the other hand, as "Survivor"'s executive producer notes, "Marketers have to get a benefit for their dollars. As long as you do it in a tasteful way and don't lie to the audience, it's fine."

The content of the message sometimes affects media choice. Print media can be used more effectively than broadcast media to present complex issues or numerous details in single advertisements. If an advertiser wants to promote beautiful colors, patterns, or textures, media offering high-quality color reproduction—magazines or television—should be used instead of newspapers. For example, food can be effectively promoted in full-color magazine advertisements but far less effectively in black and white.

The cost of media is an important but troublesome consideration. Planners try to obtain the best coverage possible for each dollar spent. But there is no accurate way to compare the cost and impact of a television commercial with the cost and impact of a newspaper advertisement. A **cost comparison indicator** lets an advertiser compare the costs of several vehicles within a specific medium (such as two magazines) in relation to the number of people each vehicle reaches. The "cost per thousand" (CPM) is the cost comparison indicator for magazines; it shows the cost of exposing a thousand people to a one-page advertisement.

Table 18.2 shows that the extent to which each medium is used varies and the pattern of use has changed over the years. For example, the proportion of total advertising dollars spent on television has risen since 1985 and surpassed that spent on newspapers by 2000. The proportion of total advertising dollars spent on radio has risen since 1990. Media are selected by weighing the various characteristics, advantages, and disadvantages of each (see Table 18.3 on page 470).

Like media selection decisions, media scheduling decisions are affected by numerous factors, such as target audience characteristics, product attributes, product seasonality, customer media behavior, and size of the advertising budget. There are three general types of media schedules: continuous, flighting, and pulsing. When a *continuous* schedule is used, advertising runs at a constant level with little variation throughout the campaign period. With a *flighting* schedule, advertisements run for set periods of time, alternating with periods in which no ads run. For example, an advertising campaign might have an ad run for two weeks, then suspend it for two weeks, and then run it again for two weeks. A *pulsing* schedule combines continuous and flighting schedules. During the entire campaign, a certain portion of advertising runs continuously, and during specific time periods of the campaign, additional advertising is used to intensify the level of communication with the target audience.

cost comparison indicator
A means of comparing the cost of vehicles in a specific medium in relation to the number of people reached

Creating the Advertising Message

The basic content and form of an advertising message are a function of several factors. A product's features, uses, and benefits affect the content of the message. Characteristics of the people in the target audience—gender, age, education, race, income, occupation, lifestyle, and other attributes—influence both content and form. When Procter & Gamble promotes Crest toothpaste to children, the company emphasizes daily brushing and cavity control. When Crest is marketed to adults, tartar and plaque control are emphasized. To communicate effectively, advertisers use words, symbols, and illustrations that are meaningful, familiar, and attractive to people in the target audience.

An advertising campaign's objectives and platform also affect the content and form of its messages. If a firm's advertising objectives involve large sales increases, the message may include hard-hitting, high-impact language and symbols. When campaign objectives aim at increasing brand awareness, the message may

Television for Women

The #1 Brand
for Women is
The #1 Brand
in Primetime.
Again!

#1 in primetime for 1Q and 2Q
among all basic cable networks!

#1 with all key female demos
in primetime and total day!

... and 23 consecutive months
of ratings growth!

Lifetime
Television for Women

www.lifetimetv.com

Source: Nielsen Media Research
1) Coverage area HH ratings 1Q 01 (1/1-4/1/01) and 2Q 01 (4/2-7/1/01).
2) 2Q 01 coverage area F18-34, F18-49, F25-54, WW18+ ratings among basic cable networks.
3) 6/99-7/01 monthly HH total day ratings vs. prior year.

Promotion by Media Organizations
Organizations such as Lifetime advertise their media capabilities to media planners.

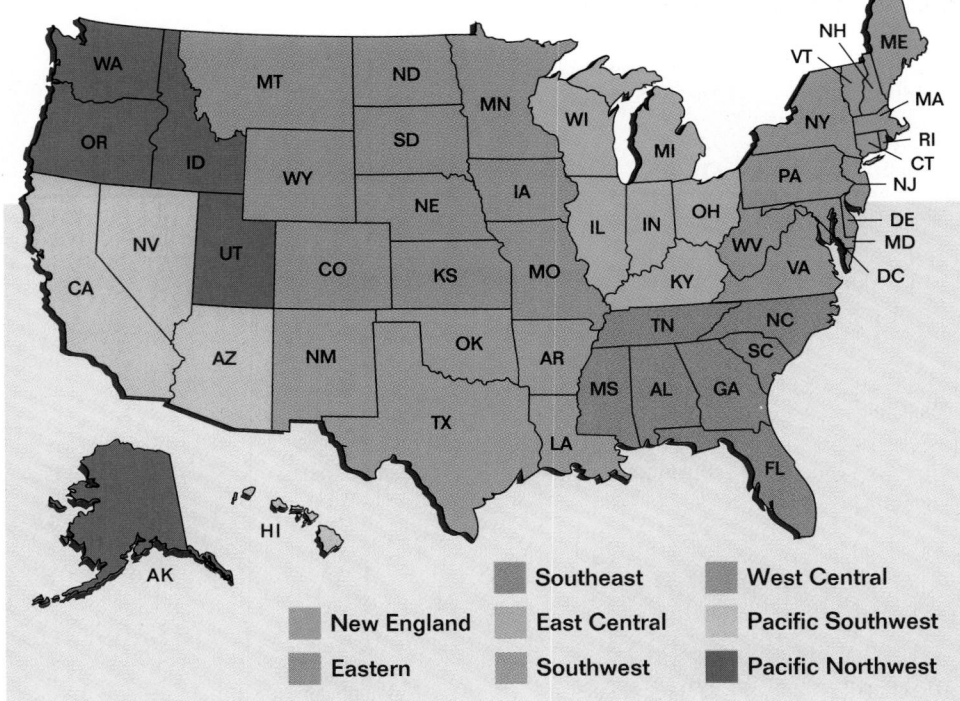

FIGURE 18.2
Geographic Divisions for Time Regional Issues
Source: *Time* magazine.

Legend:
- Southeast
- West Central
- New England
- East Central
- Pacific Southwest
- Eastern
- Southwest
- Pacific Northwest

use much repetition of the brand name and words and illustrations associated with it. Thus, the advertising platform is the foundation on which campaign messages are built.

Choice of media obviously influences the content and form of the message. Effective outdoor displays and short broadcast spot announcements require concise, simple messages. Magazine and newspaper advertisements can include considerable detail and long explanations. Because several kinds of media offer geographic selectivity, a precise message can be tailored to a particular geographic section of the target audience. Some magazine publishers produce **regional issues,** in which advertisements and editorial content of copies appearing in one geographic area differ from those appearing in other areas. As Figure 18.2 shows, *Time* magazine publishes eight regional issues. A company advertising in *Time* might decide to use one message in

regional issues Versions of a magazine that differ across geographic regions

Black and White Versus Color Advertisements
This example highlights the importance of using color in advertising various types of products such as nail polish.

Table 18.3			Characteristics, Advantages, and Disadvantages of Major Advertising Media
Medium	**Types**	**Unit of Sale**	**Factors Affecting Rates**
Newspaper	Morning Evening Sunday Sunday supplement Weekly Special	Agate lines Column inches Counted words Printed lines	Volume and frequency discounts Number of colors Position charges for preferred and guaranteed positions Circulation level Ad size
Magazine	Consumer Farm Business	Pages Partial pages Column inches	Circulation level Cost of publishing Type of audience Volume discounts Frequency discounts Size of advertisement Position of advertisement (covers) Number of colors Regional issues
Direct mail	Letters; catalogs; price lists; calendars; brochures; coupons; circulars; newsletters; postcards; booklets; broadsides; samplers	Not applicable	Cost of mailing lists Postage Production costs
Radio	AM FM	Programs: sole sponsor, co-sponsor, participative sponsor Spots: 5, 10, 20, 30, 60 seconds	Time of day Audience size Length of spot or program Volume and frequency discounts
Television	Network Local CATV	Programs: sole sponsor, co-sponsor, participative sponsor Spots: 5, 10, 15, 30, 60 seconds	Time of day Length of program Length of spot Volume and frequency discounts Audience size
Internet	Websites Banners Buttons Sponsorships Interstitials Classified ads	Not applicable	Length of time Complexity Type of audience Keywords Continuity
Inside transit	Buses Subways	Full, half, and quarter showings sold on monthly basis	Number of riders Multiple-month discounts Production costs Position
Outside transit	Buses Taxicabs	Full, half, and quarter showings; space also rented on per-unit basis	Number of advertisements Position Size
Outdoor	Papered posters Painted displays Spectaculars	Papered posters; sold on monthly basis in multiples called "showings" Painted displays and spectaculars; sold on per-unit basis	Length of time purchased Land rental Cost of production Intensity of traffic Frequency and continuity discounts Location

Cost Comparison Indicator	Advantages	Disadvantages
Milline rate = cost per agate line × 1,000,000 divided by circulation	Reaches large audience; purchased to be read; national geographic flexibility; short lead time; frequent publication; favorable for cooperative advertising; merchandising services	Not selective for socioeconomic groups; short life; limited reproduction capabilities; large advertising volume limits exposure to any one advertisement
Cost per thousand (CPM) = cost per page × 1,000 divided by circulation	Demographic selectivity; good reproduction; long life; prestige; geographic selectivity when regional issues are available; read in leisurely manner	High absolute dollar cost; long lead time
Cost per contact	Little wasted circulation; highly selective; circulation controlled by advertiser; few distractions; personal; stimulates actions; use of novelty; relatively easy to measure performance; hidden from competitors	Expensive; no editorial matter to attract readers; considered junk mail by many; criticized as invasion of privacy
Cost per thousand (CPM) = cost per minute × 1,000 divided by audience size	Reaches 95% of consumers age 12 and older; highly mobile; low-cost broadcast medium; message can be quickly changed; geographic selectivity; demographic selectivity	Provides only audio message; short life of message; listeners' attention limited because of other activities while listening
Cost per thousand (CPM) = cost per minute × 1,000 divided by audience size	Reaches large audience; low cost per exposure; uses audio and video; highly visible; high prestige; geographic and demographic selectivity	High dollar costs; highly perishable message; size of audience not guaranteed; amount of prime time limited
Cost per thousand or by the number of click-throughs	Immediate response; potential to reach a precisely targeted audience; ability to track customers and build databases; very interactive medium	Costs of precise targeting are high; inappropriate ad placement; effects difficult to measure; concerns about security and privacy
Cost per thousand riders	Low cost; "captive" audience; geographic selectivity	Does not reach many professional persons; does not secure quick results
Cost per thousand exposures	Low cost; geographic selectivity; reaches broad, diverse audience	Lacks demographic selectivity; does not have high impact on readers
No standard indicator	Allows for repetition; low cost; message can be placed close to point of sale; geographic selectivity; operable 24 hours a day	Message must be short and simple; no demographic selectivity; seldom attracts readers' full attention; criticized as traffic hazard and blight on countryside

Sources: Information from William F. Arens, *Contemporary Advertising* (Burr Ridge, IL: Irwin/McGraw-Hill, 1999); George E. Belch and Michael Belch, *Advertising and Promotion* (Burr Ridge, IL: Irwin/McGraw-Hill, 1998).

the New England region and another in the rest of the nation. A company may also choose to advertise in only one region. Such geographic selectivity lets a firm use the same message in different regions at different times.

copy The verbal portion of advertisements

Copy.   **Copy** is the verbal portion of an advertisement and may include headlines, subheadlines, body copy, and signature. Not all advertising contains all of these copy elements. The headline is critical because often it is the only part of the copy that people read. It should attract readers' attention and create enough interest to make them want to read the body copy. The subheadline, if there is one, links the headline to the body copy and sometimes is used to explain the headline.

Body copy for most advertisements consists of an introductory statement or paragraph, several explanatory paragraphs, and a closing paragraph. Some copywriters have adopted guidelines for developing body copy systematically: (1) identify a specific desire or problem, (2) recommend the product as the best way to satisfy that desire or solve that problem, (3) state product benefits and indicate why the product is best for the buyer's particular situation, (4) substantiate advertising claims, and (5) ask the buyer to take action. When substantiating claims, it is important to present the substantiation in a credible manner. The proof of claims should help strengthen the image of the product and company integrity.

The signature identifies the advertisement's sponsor. It may contain several elements, including the firm's trademark, logo, name, and address. The signature should be attractive, legible, distinctive, and easy to identify in a variety of sizes.

Components of a Print Advertisement
This advertisement includes all the major components of a print advertisement.

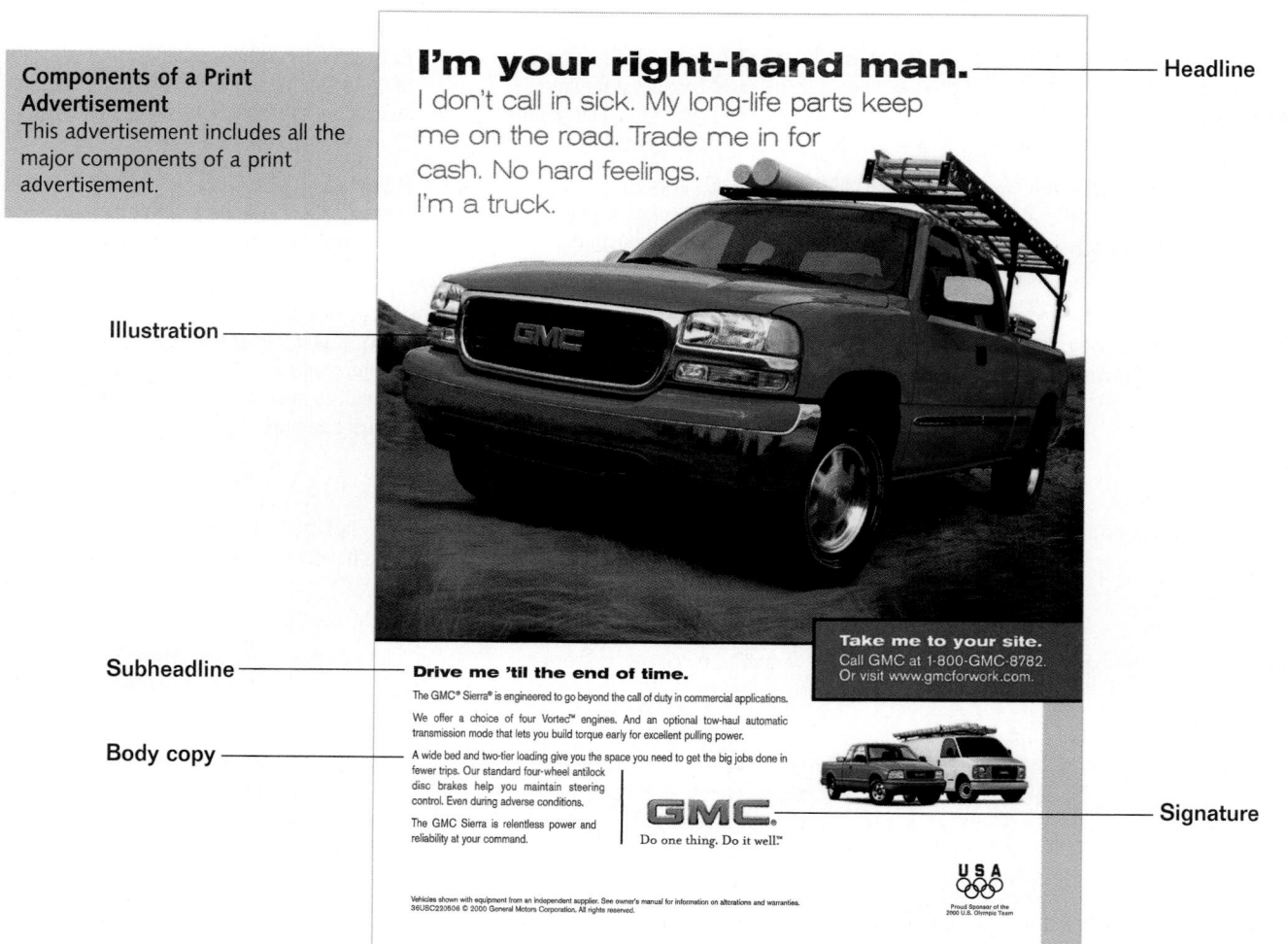

Illustration

Subheadline

Body copy

Headline

Signature

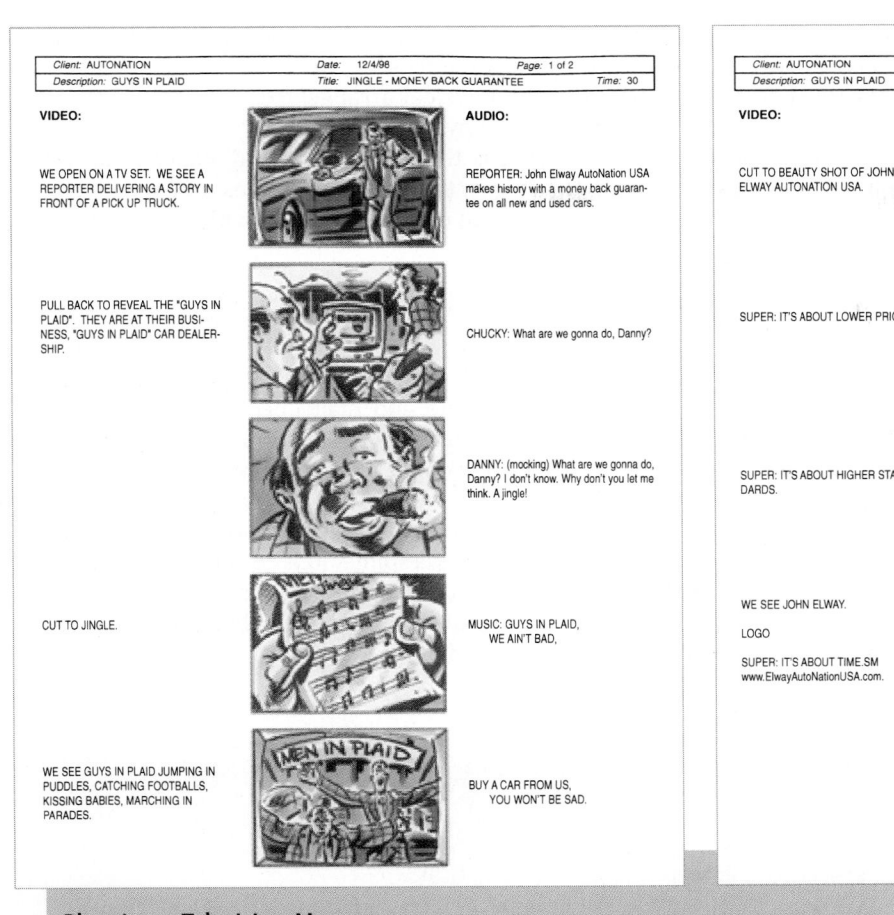

Planning a Television Message
This parallel script was used to create a television advertisement for AutoNation USA.

Because radio listeners often are not fully "tuned in" mentally, radio copy should be informal and conversational to attract listeners' attention, resulting in greater impact. Radio messages are highly perishable and should consist of short, familiar terms. The length should not require a rate of speech exceeding approximately two and one-half words per second.

In television copy, the audio material must not overpower the visual material, and vice versa. However, a television message should make optimal use of its visual portion, which can be very effective for product demonstrations. Copy for a television commercial is sometimes initially written in parallel script form. Video is described in the left column and audio in the right. When the parallel script is approved, the copywriter and artist combine copy with visual material by using a **storyboard,** which depicts a series of miniature television screens showing the sequence of major scenes in the commercial. Beneath each screen is a description of the audio portion to be used with that video segment. Technical personnel use the storyboard as a blueprint when producing the commercial.

storyboard   A mockup combining copy and visual material to show the sequence of major scenes in a commercial

artwork   An ad's illustration and layout

illustrations   Photos, drawings, graphs, charts, and tables used to spark audience interest

Artwork.   Artwork consists of an advertisement's illustrations and layout. Although **illustrations** are often photographs, they can also be drawings, graphs, charts, and tables. Illustrations are used to attract attention, encourage audiences to read or listen to the copy, communicate an idea quickly, or communicate ideas that are difficult to put into words.[4] They are especially important because consumers tend to recall the visual portions of advertisements better than the verbal portions. Advertisers use a variety of illustration techniques. They may show the product

layout The physical arrangement of an ad's illustration and copy

alone, in a setting, in use, or the results of its use. Illustrations can also be in the form of comparisons, contrasts, diagrams, and testimonials.

The **layout** of an advertisement is the physical arrangement of the illustration and the copy—headline, subheadline, body copy, and signature. These elements can be arranged in many ways. The final layout is the result of several stages of layout preparation. As it moves through these stages, the layout promotes an exchange of ideas among people developing the advertising campaign and provides instructions for production personnel.

Executing the Campaign

Execution of an advertising campaign requires extensive planning and coordination because many tasks must be completed on time and many people and firms are involved. Production companies, research organizations, media firms, printers, photo-engravers, and commercial artists are just a few of the people and firms contributing to a campaign.

Implementation requires detailed schedules to ensure that various phases of the work are done on time. Advertising management personnel must evaluate the quality of the work and take corrective action when necessary. In some instances, changes are made during the campaign so it meets objectives more effectively. Sometimes, one firm develops a campaign and another executes it.

BUILDING CUSTOMER RELATIONSHIPS

Is Sex Effective in Advertising?

Does sex sell? According to a recent survey, love is generally more effective than sex in advertising, even though young men are particularly partial to clothing advertisements with sexual content. Yet year after year, advertisers use bare skin and innuendo to get attention. In the process, some attract unwanted publicity that runs counter to their advertising goals.

Consider what happened when the H&M retail chain debuted a new advertisement in upstate New York. The Swedish-based company has long used campaigns with supermodels in name-brand underwear. When it plastered Albany-area buses with posters featuring Claudia Schiffer in a bra and panties, however, it drew some criticism. The mayor said, "I can't and won't advocate for censorship. But I can be an advocate for good taste, which is what this is all about." One local resident complained, "They're not selling the bra, they're selling something else." But H&M refused to pull the posters, saying through a spokesperson: "This is not sex. We sell underwear."

Miller Brewing has also stirred controversy with suggestive television commercials. Its "Never Miss a Genuine Opportunity" campaign for Miller Genuine Draft included one message that some television networks refused to carry. In the commercial, a young woman in an apartment laundry room undresses down to her underwear and stuffs her clothing into a washer. A young man enters, registers surprise, and then produces a Miller six-pack

after he recovers. In response, the woman throws her underwear into the washing machine as a voiceover announces, "Never miss a genuine opportunity." Miller noted that the campaign covered a range of themes, including humor and quality. In the words of Miller's senior vice president of marketing, "We do a better job of defining the camaraderie that exists between people when they share a beer."

Another advertiser using sex in advertising is London-based Virgin Atlantic Airways. In magazine advertisements appearing in *American Lawyer* and other publications, Virgin combines a distinctive visual style with tongue-in-cheek copy to reach business travelers. In one advertisement promoting Virgin's airport lounges, a young man is shown shining the boots of a sexy model. The copy reads, "Now you can take care of the 3 S's right at the airport. Ya know, shower, shave, and shoeshine." A Virgin marketing executive explains his company's advertising strategy: "If there's any campaign where you can put another airline logo on it and it would actually be a valid campaign, that's out automatically. When one of the campaigns can only be done by Virgin, then we know we're onto a winner."

Is using sex in advertising ultimately effective? Sex certainly attracts attention, and controversy over sexual content attracts even more. On the other hand, if love is more effective than sex, should advertisers continue to use sex despite its relatively limited appeal?

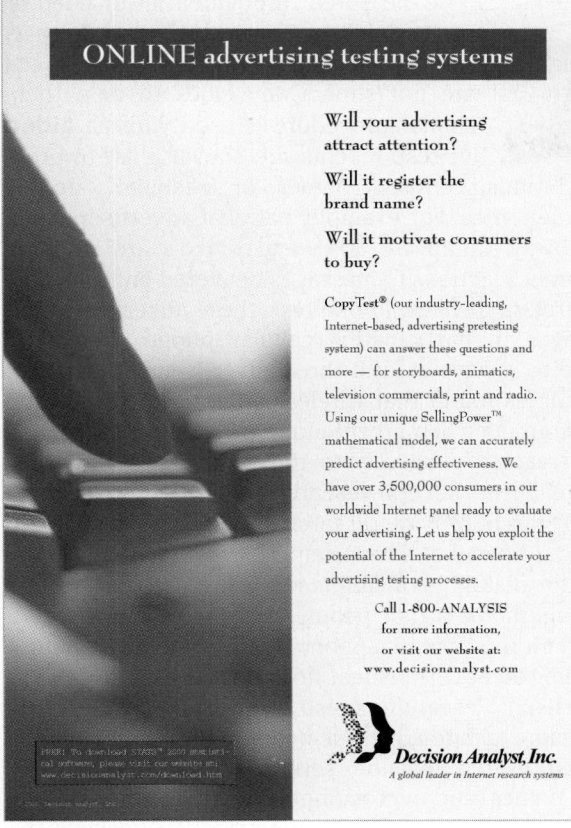

Pretesting Advertisements
Using the Internet, Decision Analyst, Inc. pretests print advertisements as well as radio and television commercials.

Evaluating Advertising Effectiveness

A variety of ways exist to test the effectiveness of advertising. They include measuring achievement of advertising objectives; assessing effectiveness of copy, illustrations, or layouts; and evaluating certain media.

Advertising can be evaluated before, during, and after the campaign. An evaluation performed before the campaign begins is called a **pretest.** A pretest usually attempts to evaluate the effectiveness of one or more elements of the message. To pretest advertisements, marketers sometimes use a **consumer jury,** a panel of actual or potential buyers of the advertised product. Jurors judge one or several dimensions of two or more advertisements. Such tests are based on the belief that consumers are more likely than advertising experts to know what influences them.

To measure advertising effectiveness during a campaign, marketers usually rely on "inquiries." In a campaign's initial stages, an advertiser may use several advertisements simultaneously, each containing a coupon, form, or toll-free phone number through which potential customers can request information. The advertiser records the number of inquiries returned from each type of advertisement. If an advertiser receives 78,528 inquiries from advertisement A, 37,072 from advertisement B, and 47,932 from advertisement C, advertisement A is judged superior to advertisements B and C.

Evaluation of advertising effectiveness after the campaign is called a **posttest.** Advertising objectives often determine what kind of posttest is appropriate. If the objectives focus on communication—to increase awareness of product features or brands or to create more favorable customer attitudes—the posttest should measure changes in these dimensions. Advertisers sometimes use consumer surveys or experiments to evaluate a campaign based on communication objectives. These methods are costly, though.

For campaign objectives stated in terms of sales, advertisers should determine the change in sales or market share attributable to the campaign. However, changes in sales or market share brought about by advertising cannot be measured precisely; many factors independent of advertisements affect a firm's sales and market share. Competitors' actions, government actions, and changes in economic conditions, consumer preferences, and weather are only a few factors that might enhance or diminish a company's sales or market share. By using data about past and current sales and advertising expenditures, advertisers can make gross estimates of the effects of a campaign on sales or market share.

Because it is difficult to determine the direct effects of advertising on sales, many advertisers evaluate print advertisements according to how well consumers can remember them. Posttest methods based on memory include recognition and recall tests. Such tests are usually performed by research organizations through surveys. In a **recognition test,** respondents are shown the actual advertisement and asked whether they recognize it. If they do, the interviewer asks additional questions to determine how much of the advertisement each respondent read. When recall is evaluated, the respondents are not shown the actual advertisement but instead are asked about what they have seen or heard recently.

pretest   Evaluation of ads performed before a campaign begins

consumer jury   A panel of a product's actual or potential buyers who pretest ads

posttest   Evaluation of advertising effectiveness after the campaign

recognition test   A posttest in which individuals are shown the actual ad and asked if they recognize it

SNAPSHOT

Who watches Super Bowl ads?

58% paid more attention than to everyday ads.

ages 18–20   77%

21–24   72%

25–34   68%

35–53   65%

Source: *USA Today*, 2000.

unaided recall test
A posttest in which respondents
identify ads they have recently
seen but are given no recall clues

aided recall test   A posttest
that asks respondents to identify
recent ads and provides clues to
jog their memories

Recall can be measured through either unaided or aided recall methods. In an **unaided recall test,** respondents identify advertisements they have seen recently but are not shown any clues to help them remember. A similar procedure is used with an **aided recall test,** but respondents are shown a list of products, brands, company names, or trademarks to jog their memories. For example, national advertisers such as Subway, CompUSA, KFC, and Kinko's are studying consumer reactions to messages delivered on Web-capable wireless devices. In one test, these advertisers sent messages to participating cellular phone users who agreed to receive at least three advertisements per day. Advertisers found that wireless advertisements scored an encouraging 58 percent aided recall and that participants reacted positively to the products in messages they recalled.[5] Several research organizations, such as Daniel Starch, provide research services that test recognition and recall of advertisements.

The major justification for using recognition and recall methods is that people are more likely to buy a product if they can remember an advertisement about it than if they cannot. However, recalling an advertisement does not necessarily lead to buying the product or brand advertised. Researchers also use a sophisticated technique called *single-source data* to help evaluate advertisements. With this technique, individuals' behaviors are tracked from television sets to checkout counters. Monitors are placed in preselected homes, and microcomputers record when the television set is on and which station is being viewed. At the supermarket checkout, the individual in the sample household presents an identification card. Checkers then record the purchases by scanner, and data are sent to the research facility. Some single-source data companies provide sample households with scanning equipment for use at home to record purchases after returning from shopping trips. Single-source data provide information that links exposure to advertisements with purchase behavior.

Who Develops the Advertising Campaign?

An advertising campaign may be handled by an individual or by a few persons within a firm, by a firm's own advertising department, or by an advertising agency.

In very small firms, one or two individuals are responsible for advertising (and for many other activities as well). Usually these individuals depend heavily on personnel at local newspapers and broadcast stations for copywriting, artwork, and advice about scheduling media.

In certain large businesses—especially large retail organizations—advertising departments create and implement advertising campaigns. Depending on the size of the advertising program, an advertising department may consist of a few multiskilled persons or a sizable number of specialists, such as copywriters, artists, media buyers, and technical production coordinators. Advertising departments sometimes obtain the services of independent research organizations and hire freelance specialists when a particular project requires it.

When an organization uses an advertising agency, the firm and the agency usually develop the advertising campaign jointly. How much each participates in the campaign's total development depends on the working relationship between the firm and the agency. Ordinarily, a firm relies on the agency for copywriting, artwork, technical production, and formulation of the media plan.

Advertising agencies assist businesses in several ways. An agency, especially a large one, can supply the services of highly skilled specialists—not only copywriters, artists, and production coordinators, but also media experts, researchers, and legal advisers. Agency personnel often have broad advertising experience and are usually more objective than a firm's employees about the organization's products.

Because an agency traditionally receives most of its compensation from a 15 percent commission paid by the media from which it makes purchases, firms can obtain some agency services at low or moderate costs. If an agency contracts for $400,000 of television time for a firm, it receives a commission of $60,000 from the television station. Although the traditional compensation method for agencies is changing and now includes other factors, media commissions still offset some costs of using an agency.

Like advertising, public relations can be a vital element in a promotion mix. We turn to it next.

Public Relations

public relations
Communications efforts used to create and maintain favorable relations between an organization and its stakeholders

Public relations is a broad set of communication efforts used to create and maintain favorable relationships between an organization and its stakeholders. An organization communicates with various stakeholders, both internal and external, and public relations efforts can be directed toward any and all of these. A firm's stakeholders can include customers, suppliers, employees, stockholders, the media, educators, potential investors, government officials, and society in general.

Public relations can be used to promote people, places, ideas, activities, and even countries. It focuses on enhancing the image of the total organization. Assessing public attitudes and creating a favorable image are no less important than direct promotion of the organization's products. Because the public's attitudes toward a firm are likely to affect the sales of its products, it is very important for firms to maintain positive public perceptions. In addition, employee morale is strengthened if the public perceives the firm positively.[6] Although public relations can make people aware of a company's products, brands, or activities, it can also create specific company images, such as innovativeness or dependability. Companies like Ben & Jerry's, Patagonia, Sustainable Harvest, and Honest Tea have reputations for being socially responsible not only because they engage in socially responsive behavior but because their actions are reported through news stories and other public relations efforts.[7] By getting the media to report on a firm's accomplishments, public relations helps the company maintain positive public visibility. Some firms use public relations for a single purpose; others use it for several purposes.

Public Relations Tools

Companies use a variety of public relations tools to convey messages and create images. Public relations professionals prepare written materials, such as brochures, newsletters, company magazines, news releases, and annual reports, that reach and influence their various stakeholders.

Annual Report
This annual report (cover shown) created by Cahan & Associates generated considerable public relations value for Maxygen Inc., a biotech company whose products are used in pharmaceuticals, vaccines, chemicals, and agriculture.

▲▲▲▲▲▲

The
Children's
Museum
◆◆◆◆◆◆

FOR IMMEDIATE RELEASE
Contact: Amy Corcoran
(617) 426-6500 ext.213
corcoran@BostonKids.org

ASIAN-AMERICAN DRAGON BOAT FESTIVAL RETURNS TO THE CHARLES

22nd Annual Hong Kong Dragon Boat Festival to be held on
Sunday, June 10, 2001

BOSTON — April 18— Enjoy the festivities at the 22nd Annual Hong Kong Dragon Boat Festival on Sunday, June 10, 2001, from 12:00 p.m.-5:00 p.m., taking place along the Charles River between JFK street and the Western Avenue Bridge. Come marvel at the display of brightly colored dragon boats as they are powered through the Charles River by lively paddlers from Boston and as far away as Canada. The festival is sponsored in part by the Hong Kong Economic and Trade Office, the Hong Kong Dragon Boat Festival in New York, the Dragon Boat Festival Committee of Boston, State Street Corporation, and The Boston Children's Museum.

This year's festival, which is the **largest Asian American celebration in New England**, will include more than 35 teams competing in four categories: open, mixed, corporate and women's. It will also feature traditional Chinese arts and crafts by the Greater Boston Chinese Cultural Association; traditional Japanese festival drummers Odaiko New England; traditional Chinese dance performances by American Chinese Art Society, traditional Cambodian dance performances by Angkor Dance Troupe; contemporary Chinese music; martial arts demonstrations by Wa Lum Martial Arts; and Asian foods. Additionally, the festival will include the highly entertaining Asian Women's Lion Dance by Gund Kwok Asian Women's Lion Dance Troupe.

The Legend of the Dragon Boat Races

Traditionally held on the fifth day of the fifth moon on the lunar calendar (late May to mid June on the solar calendar), the Dragon Boat Festival commemorates the life and death of the Qu Yuan (340-278 BC). A political leader of Chu, Qu Yuan is recognized as China's first distinguished poet. Qu Yuan lost the king's favor and was banished from his homestate of Chu because of his opposition to the prevalent policy of compromise to the powerful state of Qin. In exile, he wrote the poem, "Encountering Sorrow" which shows a great loyalty to his state and its people. In 278, Qu Yuan heard that Chu had been invaded. In despair, he drowned himself in the Mi Lo River. The people of Chu rushed to the river to rescue him. Too late to save Qu Yuan, they splashed furiously and threw *zung-ze* (traditional rice dumplings wrapped in bamboo leaves) into the river as a sacrifice to his spirit and to keep the fishes away from his body.

Today, the Dragon Boat Festivals are popular around the world. The first US Dragon Boat Festival held in Boston was used as a vehicle to promote Asian culture and a chance to bring together diverse communities from Boston and surrounding areas. Last year, more than 20,000 people lined the banks of the Charles to enjoy the festivities and performances.

For more information, check out the Festival website at www.bostondragonboat.org or call (617) 426-6500, x 778.

-end-

300 Congress Street, Boston, MA 02210-1034, (617) 426-6500, TTY 426-5466

Example of a News Release
The Boston Children's Museum issued this information release to publicize an Asian American celebration it was co-sponsoring with several other organizations.

Public relations personnel also create corporate identity materials, such as logos, business cards, stationery, and signs, that make firms immediately recognizable. Speeches are another public relations tool. Because what a company executive says publicly at meetings or to the media can affect the organization's image, his or her speech must convey the desired message clearly.

Event sponsorship, in which a company pays for part or all of a special event, such as a benefit concert or a tennis tournament, is another public relations tool. Examples are Home Depot's sponsorship of NASCAR and the U.S. Olympic team. Sponsoring special events can be an effective means of increasing company or brand recognition with relatively minimal investment. Event sponsorship can gain companies considerable amounts of free media coverage. An organization tries to make sure its product and the sponsored event target a similar audience and that the two are easily associated in customers' minds. For example, United Parcel Service (UPS) has become the official express delivery company of Daytona International Speedway. Daytona International Speedway and the challenges of the Daytona 500 demand that NASCAR teams take speed, technology, and precision to the limit, making the speedway and its events a good match for UPS delivery service standards.[8] Public relations personnel also organize unique events to "create news" about the company. These may include grand openings with celebrities, prizes, hot-air balloon rides, and other attractions that appeal to a firm's publics.

publicity   A news story type of communication transmitted through a mass medium at no charge

Publicity is a part of public relations. **Publicity** is communication in news story form about the organization, its products, or both, transmitted through a mass medium at no charge. Although public relations has a larger, more comprehensive communication function than publicity, publicity is a very important aspect of public relations. Publicity can be used to provide information about goods or services; to announce expansions, acquisitions, research, or new-product launches; or to enhance a company's image.

news release   A short piece of copy publicizing an event or a product

The most common publicity-based public relations tool is the **news release,** sometimes called a *press release,* which is usually a single page of typewritten copy containing fewer than 300 words and describing a company event or product. A news release gives the firm's or agency's name, address, phone number, and contact person. Automakers, as well as other manufacturers, sometimes use news releases when introducing new products. When Wal-Mart made a special effort to carry environmentally safe products and packaging, its public relations department sent out news releases to newspapers, magazines, television contacts, and suppliers, resulting in public relations in the form of magazine articles, newspaper acknowledgments, and television coverage. As Table 18.4 shows, news releases tackle a multitude of specific issues. A **feature article** is a manuscript of up to 3,000 words prepared for a specific publication. A **captioned photograph** is a photograph with a brief description

feature article   A manuscript of up to 3,000 words prepared for a specific publication

captioned photograph A photo with a brief description of its contents

Table 18.4	Possible Issues for Publicity Releases
Changes in marketing personnel	Packaging changes
Support of a social cause	New products
Improved warranties	New slogan
Reports on industry conditions	Research developments
New uses for established products	Company's history and development
Product endorsements	Employment, production, and sales records
Quality awards	Award of contracts
Company name changes	Opening of new markets
Interviews with company officials	Improvements in financial position
Improved distribution policies	Opening of an exhibit
International business efforts	History of a brand
Athletic event sponsorship	Winners of company contests
Visits by celebrities	Logo changes
Reports on new discoveries	Speeches of top management
Innovative marketing activities	Merit awards
Economic forecasts	Anniversary of inventions

press conference A meeting used to announce major news events

explaining the picture's content. Captioned photographs are effective for illustrating new or improved products with highly visible features.

There are several other kinds of publicity-based public relations tools. A **press conference** is a meeting called to announce major news events. Media personnel are invited to a press conference and are usually supplied with written materials and photographs. Letters to the editor and editorials are sometimes prepared and sent to newspapers and magazines. Videos and audiotapes may be distributed to broadcast stations in the hope that they will be aired.

Publicity-based public relations tools offer several advantages, including credibility, news value, significant word-of-mouth communications, and a perception of being endorsed by the media. The public may consider news coverage more truthful and credible than an advertisement because the media are not paid to provide the information. In addition, stories regarding a new-product introduction or a new environmentally responsible company policy, for example, are handled as news items and are likely to receive notice. Finally, the cost of publicity is low compared with the cost of advertising.[9]

Publicity-based public relations tools have some limitations. Media personnel must judge company messages to be newsworthy if the messages are to be published or broadcast at all. Consequently, messages must be timely, interesting, accurate, and in the public interest. Many communications do not qualify. It may take a great deal of time and effort to convince media personnel of the news value of publicity releases. Although public relations personnel usually encourage the media to air publicity releases at certain times, they control neither the content nor the timing of the communication. Media personnel alter length and content of publicity releases to fit publishers' or broadcasters' requirements and may even delete the parts of messages that company personnel view as most important. Furthermore, media personnel use publicity releases in time slots or positions most convenient for them. Thus, messages sometimes appear in locations or at times that may not reach the firm's target audiences. Although these limitations can be frustrating, properly managed publicity-based public relations tools offer an organization substantial benefits.

Evaluating Public Relations Effectiveness

Because of the potential benefits of good public relations, it is essential that organizations evaluate the effectiveness of their public relations campaigns. Research can be conducted to determine how well a firm is communicating its messages or image to its target audiences. *Environmental monitoring* identifies changes in public opinion affecting an organization. A *public relations audit* is used to assess an organization's image among the public or to evaluate the effect of a specific public relations program. A *communications audit* may include a content analysis of messages, a readability study, or a readership survey. If an organization wants to measure the extent to which stakeholders view it as being socially responsible, it can conduct a *social audit.*

One approach to measuring the effectiveness of publicity-based public relations is to count the number of exposures in the media. To determine which releases are published in print media and how often, an organization can hire a clipping service, a firm that clips and sends news releases to client companies. To measure the effectiveness of television coverage, a firm can enclose a card with its publicity releases, requesting that the television station record its name and the dates when the news item is broadcast (although station personnel do not always comply). Though some television and radio tracking services exist, they are extremely costly.

Counting the number of media exposures does not reveal how many people have actually read or heard the company's message or what they thought about the message afterward. However, measuring changes in product awareness, knowledge, and attitudes resulting from the publicity campaign does. To assess these changes, companies must measure these levels before and after public relations campaigns. Although precise measures are difficult to obtain, a firm's marketers should attempt to assess the impact of public relations efforts on the organization's sales.

Dealing with Unfavorable Public Relations

We have thus far discussed public relations as a planned element of the promotion mix. However, companies may have to deal with unexpected and unfavorable public relations resulting from an unsafe product, an accident, controversial actions of employees, or some other negative event or situation. For example, an airline that experiences a plane crash faces a very tragic and distressing situation. Charges of anticompetitive behavior against Microsoft have raised public concern and generated unfavorable public relations for that organization. The public's image of The Body Shop as a socially responsible company diminished considerably when it was reported that the company's actions were not as socially responsible as its promotion promised. Unfavorable coverage can have quick and dramatic effects. A single negative event that produces public relations can wipe out a company's favorable image and destroy positive customer attitudes established through years of expensive advertising campaigns and other promotional efforts. Moreover, today's mass media, including online services and the Internet, disseminate information faster than ever before, and bad news generally receives considerable media attention.

To protect its image, an organization needs to prevent unfavorable public relations or at least lessen its effect if it occurs. First and foremost, the organization should try to prevent negative incidents and events through safety programs, inspections, and effective quality control procedures. However, because negative events can befall even the most cautious firms, an organization should have predetermined plans in place to handle them when they do occur. Firms need to establish policies and procedures for reducing the adverse impact of news coverage of a crisis or controversy. In most cases, organizations should expedite news coverage of negative events rather than trying to discourage or block them. If news coverage is suppressed, rumors and other misinformation may replace facts and be passed along anyway. An unfavorable event can easily balloon into serious problems or public issues and become quite damaging. By being forthright with the press and public and taking prompt action, firms may be able to convince the public of their honest attempts to deal with the situation, and news personnel may be more willing to help explain complex issues to the public. Dealing effectively with a negative event allows an organization to lessen, if not eliminate, the unfavorable impact on its image.

Summary

Advertising is a paid form of nonpersonal communication transmitted to consumers through mass media such as television, radio, the Internet, newspapers, magazines, direct mail, outdoor displays, and signs on mass transit vehicles. Both nonbusiness and business organizations use advertising. Institutional advertising promotes organizational images, ideas, and political issues. When a company promotes its position on a public issue like taxation, institutional advertising is referred to as advocacy advertising. Product advertising promotes uses, features, and benefits of products. The two types of product advertising are pioneer advertising, which focuses on stimulating demand for a product category rather than a specific brand, and competitive advertising, which attempts to stimulate demand for a specific brand by indicating the brand's features,

uses, and advantages. To make direct product comparisons, marketers use comparative advertising, in which two or more brands are compared. Two other forms of competitive advertising are reminder advertising, which tells customers that an established brand is still around, and reinforcement advertising, which assures current users they have made the right brand choice.

Although marketers may vary in how they develop advertising campaigns, they should follow a general pattern. First, they must identify and analyze the target audience, the group of people at whom advertisements are aimed. Second, they should establish what they want the campaign to accomplish by defining advertising objectives. Objectives should be clear, precise, and presented in measurable terms. Third, marketers must create the advertising platform, which contains basic issues to be presented in the campaign. Advertising platforms should consist of issues important to consumers. Fourth, advertisers must decide how much money to spend on the campaign; they arrive at this decision through the objective-and-task approach, percent-of-sales approach, competition-matching approach, or arbitrary approach.

Advertisers must then develop a media plan by selecting and scheduling media to use in the campaign. Some of the factors affecting the media plan are location and demographic characteristics of the target audience, content of the message, and cost of the various media. The basic content and form of the advertising message are affected by product features, uses, and benefits; characteristics of the people in the target audience; the campaign's objectives and platform; and the choice of media. Advertisers use copy and artwork to create the message. The execution of an advertising campaign requires extensive planning and coordination.

Finally, advertisers must devise one or more methods for evaluating advertisement effectiveness. Evaluations performed before the campaign begins are called pretests; those conducted after the campaign are called posttests. Two types of posttests are a recognition test, in which respondents are shown the actual advertisement and asked whether they recognize it, and a recall test. In aided recall tests, respondents are shown a list of products, brands, company names, or trademarks to jog their memories. In unaided tests, no clues are given.

Advertising campaigns can be developed by personnel within the firm or in conjunction with advertising agencies. When a campaign is created by the firm's personnel, it may be developed by one or more individuals or by an advertising department within the firm. Use of an advertising agency may be advantageous because an agency provides highly skilled, objective specialists with broad experience in advertising at low to moderate costs to the firm.

Public relations is a broad set of communication efforts used to create and maintain favorable relationships between an organization and its stakeholders. Public relations can be used to promote people, places, ideas, activities, and countries, and to create and maintain a positive company image. Some firms use public relations for a single purpose; others use it for several purposes. Public relations tools include written materials, such as brochures, newsletters, and annual reports; corporate identity materials, such as business cards and signs; speeches; event sponsorships; and special events. Publicity is communication in news story form about an organization, its products, or both, transmitted through a mass medium at no charge. Publicity-based public relations tools include news releases, feature articles, captioned photographs, and press conferences. Problems that organizations confront in using publicity-based public relations include reluctance of media personnel to print or air releases and lack of control over timing and content of messages.

To evaluate the effectiveness of their public relations programs, companies conduct research to determine how well their messages are reaching their audiences. Environmental monitoring, public relations audits, and counting the number of media exposures are all means of evaluating public relations effectiveness. Organizations should avoid negative public relations by taking steps to prevent negative events that result in unfavorable publicity. To diminish the impact of unfavorable public relations, organizations should institute policies and procedures for dealing with news personnel and the public when negative events occur.

Important Terms

Advertising	Cost comparison
Institutional advertising	indicator
Advocacy advertising	Regional issues
Product advertising	Copy
Pioneer advertising	Storyboard
Competitive advertising	Artwork
Comparative advertising	Illustrations
Reminder advertising	Layout
Reinforcement advertising	Pretest
Advertising campaign	Consumer jury
Target audience	Posttest
Advertising platform	Recognition test
Advertising appropriation	Unaided recall test
Objective-and-task	Aided recall test
approach	Public relations
Percent-of-sales approach	Publicity
Competition-matching	News release
approach	Feature article
Arbitrary approach	Captioned photograph
Media plan	Press conference

Discussion and Review Questions

1. What is the difference between institutional and product advertising?
2. What is the difference between competitive advertising and comparative advertising?
3. What are the major steps in creating an advertising campaign?
4. What is a target audience? How does a marketer analyze the target audience after identifying it?
5. Why is it necessary to define advertising objectives?
6. What is an advertising platform, and how is it used?
7. What factors affect the size of an advertising budget? What techniques are used to determine an advertising budget?
8. Describe the steps in developing a media plan.
9. What is the function of copy in an advertising message?
10. Discuss several ways to posttest the effectiveness of advertising.
11. What role does an advertising agency play in developing an advertising campaign?

12. What is public relations? Who can an organization reach through public relations?
13. How do organizations use public relations tools? Give several examples that you have observed recently.
14. Explain the problems and limitations associated with publicity-based public relations.
15. In what ways is the effectiveness of public relations evaluated?
16. What are some sources of negative public relations? How should an organization deal with unfavorable public relations?

Application Questions

1. An organization must define its objectives carefully when developing an advertising campaign. Which of the following advertising objectives would be most useful for a company, and why?
   a. The organization will spend $1 million to move from second in market share to market leader.
   b. The organization wants to increase sales from $1.2 million to $1.5 million this year to gain the lead in market share.
   c. The advertising objective is to gain as much market share as possible within the next 12 months.
   d. The advertising objective is to increase sales by 15 percent.

2. Copy, the verbal portion of advertising, is used to move readers through a persuasive sequence called AIDA: attention, interest, desire, and action. To achieve this, some copywriters have adopted guidelines for developing advertising copy. Select a print ad and identify how it (1) identifies a specific problem, (2) recommends the product as the best solution to the problem, (3) states the product's advantages and benefits, (4) substantiates the ad's claims, and (5) asks the reader to take action.

3. Advertisers use several types of publicity mechanisms. Look through several recent newspapers and magazines, and identify a news release, a feature article, and a captioned photograph used to publicize a product. Describe the type of product.

4. Negative public relations can harm an organization's marketing efforts if not dealt with properly. Identify a company that recently was the target of negative public relations. Describe the situation and discuss the company's response. What did marketers at this company do well? What, if anything, would you recommend that they change about their response?

Internet Exercise & Resources

Visit **www.prideferrell.com** for resources to help you master the material in this chapter, plus materials that will help you expand your marketing knowledge, including: Internet exercise updates, ACE self-tests, hotlinks to companies featured in this chapter, and much more.

Turbonium.com

For its development of a promotional site for Volkswagen AG's Turbo Beetle, the Arnold Worldwide advertising agency won several awards, including one from *Communication Arts* magazine. See why by visiting the website at

www.turbonium.com/flash/index.html

1. What form of advertising discussed in the chapter best exemplifies the Turbonium website?

2. What advertising objectives is Volkswagen attempting to achieve through this website?

3. Who is the primary target for this Internet advertisement?

VIDEO CASE 18.1

The Ups and Downs of Dot-Com Advertising

The adage "What goes up must come down" is an appropriate description of the short but volatile history of advertising spending by dot-coms. At the height of the dot-com advertising boom, from 1999 into 2000, Internet businesses flush with cash from investors spent lavishly, especially on television advertising, to build their brands and attract web surfers. During the Super Bowl in January 2000, 17 e-commerce companies vied for viewer attention with television commercials. Netpliance.com, maker of the i-opener web appliance, paid more than $3 million—the highest-ever Super Bowl ad price—for just one commercial during the game. Online recruiters Monster.com and HotJobs also bought Super Bowl ads that year.

Other media benefited from the influx of e-commerce ads as well. In the first half of 1999 alone, dot-com advertising in television, radio, print, and outdoor media totaled $775 million. That year, Priceline.com's television and radio ads featuring William Shatner made the name-your-own-price website a household name. Pet.com's sock puppet starred in a series of tongue-in-cheek television ads that made the puppet popular even though the site eventually went out of business. So many dot-coms were crowding the airwaves that Amazon.com tripled its advertising spending during the crucial holiday shopping season at year-end 1999 to rise above the uproar.

By 2001, the situation had changed dramatically. Only three e-commerce companies (the online brokerage firm E*Trade and the recruiting sites HotJobs and Monster.com) aired television commercials during the Super Bowl game in January 2001, amid a general fall-off in advertising spending among Internet businesses. Netpliance stopped selling its i-opener, dropped its advertising campaign, and changed its entire business strategy. As the economy slowed, Pet.com went out of business, Priceline.com struggled financially, Monster.com merged with HotJobs, and the surviving dot-coms started saving their cash for necessities such as payroll.

In addition to tight finances, increased clutter contributed to the downturn in major media advertising. "Two years ago, Yahoo! could advertise on TV and it would stand out," observed one analyst. "Now you watch a half-hour show and you'll see five or six (Internet) ads." Although dot-coms generally cut back on advertising spending to conserve cash, many sought out less traditional promotional techniques to keep their brands in front of target audiences. For example, the Ask Jeeves search site put its best foot forward in the Macy's Thanksgiving Day parade in New York, entering its 16-foot-tall float of the site's butler surrounded by books. Ask Jeeves also arranged to put stickers with questions on apples in New York City grocery stores, directing customers to find the answers on the company's website. Such unusual advertising is generally less costly than television advertising, but it can be risky. "Consumers are getting a little tired of ad messages," said a spokesperson for Ask Jeeves. "The point is not to inundate them every place they are, it's to surprise them but to do it in a way that isn't annoying."

Some dot-coms still see advertising as a vital expenditure for building a new brand and fueling ongoing sales. When a group of airlines launched Orbitz.com, the new travel website spent more than $12 million on online advertising. It also invested millions of dollars in colorful, zany print advertisements to establish the brand and bring customers to the website. Charles Schwab, a major brokerage firm, experienced a significant jump in revenue when it boosted advertising spending

for its web operation. And Amazon.com still sees advertising as a vital tool in its battle with Internet rivals. The online retailer continues to invest millions of dollars monthly in advertising, remaining among the top ten advertisers on the Web nearly every month. With advertising costs on the rise and online competition fiercer than ever, watch for more ups and downs in dot-com advertising.[10]

QUESTIONS FOR DISCUSSION

1. Is the Ask Jeeves campaign an example of selective demand, institutional, or primary-demand advertising?
2. How might Ask Jeeves evaluate the effectiveness of its nontraditional promotion efforts?
3. Should Amazon.com consider using Super Bowl advertisements? Explain.

CASE 18.2
Microsoft: Crafting an Image Through Public Relations

A monopoly and a bully or a champion of free enterprise and high-tech innovation? Different people have different images of Microsoft, the largest and most successful software company in the world, and of Bill Gates, its founder and chair. And image is important to Microsoft, which operates in a highly competitive, high-stakes industry. That's why the company has a team of 150 managers and outside experts dedicated to public relations. Their role is to shape and protect the image of Microsoft and its products, including the Windows operating system, the Internet Explorer web browser, the Xbox game console, and many other products for business and personal use.

Microsoft uses well-honed public relations skills to maintain favorable relationships with its stakeholders and support new-product introductions. For example, in the weeks leading up to the launch of every major update of Windows, computer users are bombarded by media coverage in newspapers, magazines, television, and radio. Many customers also receive newsletters and brochures in the mail or pick these up at local computer stores. By the time the new product finally arrives on store shelves, accompanied by special launch-day events, the enormous anticipatory buzz has created pent-up demand that boosts early sales and generates considerable word-of-mouth communication.

Giving Microsoft a "good-guy" image is another key public relations objective. Targeting students, the company has stepped up giveaways to get its products into grade schools, high schools, and colleges throughout the United States and around the globe. In addition, Bill Gates's charitable foundation is donating millions of dollars' worth of Microsoft software to U.S. public libraries. Such

arrangements allow Microsoft to display its strong support for education publicly while simultaneously building brand equity. As the general manager of Microsoft's education consumer unit has observed, "Today's fifth-grader is tomorrow's business leader. The sooner we have them using our software, the more they carry that brand name forward."

Over time, Microsoft has developed a reputation for extremely aggressive competitive tactics. This combative behavior has long been under regulatory scrutiny, culminating in a lawsuit brought against the company by the Department of Justice and investigations by state attorneys general into violations of antitrust law, which Microsoft vigorously denies. Throughout this protracted legal battle, Microsoft has had its public relations experts working to contain the damage to the company's image and present the company's side most effectively.

Before the trial began, top Microsoft executives traveled around the United States making personal appearances and meeting with reporters. They stressed the message that Microsoft favored technological innovation and wanted customers to have more software choices. Brandishing the results of opinion polls, they also announced that U.S consumers and computer users were giving Microsoft its highest ratings ever.

The company also used the celebrity status of Bill Gates to its advantage during the pretrial period. Rather than keeping his private life private, Gates began talking more about his family life during media interviews. In addition, he scheduled visits to schools and made other public appearances, where he talked about Microsoft products and mingled with audiences. This higher visibility showed

Gates's human side and allowed him to air his views on technology and related topics.

In addition, Microsoft conducted research to determine its standing with business decision makers and information technology professionals, two stakeholder groups that influence Microsoft purchases. Then, through informational ads in major newspapers, the company communicated its message that the antitrust case against Microsoft would only stifle innovation and dampen free choice in the marketplace.

Even as these activities gained momentum, however, Microsoft came under fire after word leaked out about a proposed multimillion-dollar public relations plan targeting 12 states, including those where the company was under investigation. The proposal called for compiling statewide media lists, identifying potential supporters in the academic world, and having people write opinion pieces and letters for placement in local newspapers. A Microsoft spokesperson said the company would probably take some but not all of those actions. "We are particularly interested in telling our story in states where there have been questions about Microsoft," he said.

Ultimately Microsoft was convicted on antitrust violations, but appeals and other legal actions continued for months afterward. Even as the company announced some conciliatory moves, a Microsoft-funded organization called Americans for Technology Leadership was at work behind the scenes. The organization hired professional telemarketers to contact consumers as part of an effort to pressure Congress to halt the Department of Justice's antitrust case. These telemarketers offered to write letters to congressional politicians in each consumer's name—and even pay the postage. "Microsoft's competitors do the same type of thing," explained the organization's president, who said the telemarketing initiative was just one element in "an ongoing effort to reach out to the general public and encourage them to let their opinions be known."

As Microsoft continues to introduce new products and pursue its marketing goals, its executives remain committed to using public relations to polish the company's image among its stakeholders and to keeping the Microsoft brand one of the best known in the world.[11]

QUESTIONS FOR DISCUSSION

1. What major public relations tools does Microsoft use?
2. Who are the stakeholders Microsoft wants to reach with its public relations efforts?
3. How should Microsoft evaluate the results of its public relations programs?
4. How do you think Microsoft should have used public relations to communicate its view during and after the antitrust trial? Explain.

Personal Selling and Sales Promotion

19

O B J E C T I V E S

OBJECTIVES

- To understand the major purposes of personal selling
- To describe the basic steps in the personal selling process
- To identify the types of sales force personnel
- To understand sales management decisions and activities
- To explain what sales promotion activities are and how they are used
- To explore specific consumer and trade sales promotion methods

Whirlpool Puts Salespeople in the "Real Whirled"

How can a multinational company train thousands of retail salespeople in the subtleties of selling 11 brands of household appliances to different customer segments in 170 countries? This was the challenge facing global appliance maker Whirlpool, the U.S. market leader and second in the world behind Electrolux of Sweden. The company manufactures appliances in 13 countries under such well-known brands as Kenmore, KitchenAid, SpeedQueen, and Whirlpool. Looking to build annual sales beyond the current $10.3 billion level, Whirlpool has created a unique training program for the trainers who work with store salespeople at Sears, Home Depot, and other retailers.

The training program, called Real Whirled, puts a cadre of eight trainers together in a home equipped with Whirlpool appliances. The trainers live and work in the specially designed eight-bedroom home for eight weeks, doing daily chores such as laundry, cooking, cleaning, and baking with Whirlpool appliances. In between, they analyze product features and benefits, swap product use tips and frustrations, and critique one another's sales training talks. Whirlpool flies the trainers home twice during the two-month period so they don't lose touch with family and friends during the program.

Because the Real Whirled home is located close to Whirlpool's headquarters in Benton Harbor, Michigan, the trainers sometimes have to show off their knowledge of company products by cooking impromptu dinners for senior managers who arrive without warning. Training directors are also apt to stop by to see how the trainers are progressing. After eight weeks of actually using the different appliances, the trainers sound more knowledgeable—and more credible—when they go on the road to train store salespeople. Brian Clark, a trainer who recently completed the program, found the experience intense but beneficial. "We'd spend a whole day learning about a dishwasher," he recalls, adding, "I have a confidence level that's making a difference in my client contacts."

The purpose of Real Whirled is to keep Whirlpool's trainers and their retail sales trainees focused squarely on how the appliances satisfy customer needs. "It seems like such a no-brainer, but we tend to get away from spending time with the consumer," comments Jackie Seib, the company's national training manager. "The biggest challenge in changing the retail culture is teaching salespeople what the consumer wants." Real Whirled gives the trainers firsthand experience in solving everyday problems using Whirlpool products, so they have real anecdotes and solutions, not just product facts and specifications, to share with the salespeople they train. This innovative sales training program is moving the company closer to achieving its goal of "a Whirlpool product in every home, everywhere."[1]

For many organizations, like Whirlpool, having a well-trained, highly effective sales force plays a major role in maintaining long-term, satisfying customer relationships, which in turn contribute to the company's success. As we saw in Chapter 17, personal selling and sales promotion are two possible elements in a promotion mix. Sales promotion is sometimes a company's sole promotional tool, although it is generally used in conjunction with other promotion mix elements. It is playing an increasingly important role in marketing strategies. Personal selling is becoming more professional and sophisticated, with sales personnel acting more as consultants and advisers.

In this chapter, we focus on personal selling and sales promotion. We first consider the purposes of personal selling and then its basic steps. Next, we look at types of salespeople and how they are selected. We then discuss major sales force management decisions, including setting objectives for the sales force and determining its size; recruiting, selecting, training, compensating, and motivating salespeople; managing sales territories; and controlling and evaluating sales force performance. Then we examine several characteristics of sales promotion, reasons for using sales promotion, and sales promotion methods available for use in a promotion mix.

The Nature of Personal Selling

personal selling Paid personal communication that informs customers and persuades them to buy products

Personal selling is paid personal communication that attempts to inform customers and persuade them to purchase products in an exchange situation. A salesperson describing the benefits of a Kenmore dryer to a customer in a Sears store engages in personal selling. Personal selling gives marketers the greatest freedom to adjust a message to satisfy customers' information needs. Compared with other promotion methods, personal selling is the most precise, enabling marketers to focus on the most promising sales prospects. Other promotion mix elements are aimed at groups of people, some of whom may not be prospective customers. However, personal selling is generally the most expensive element in the promotion mix. The average cost of a sales call is about $170.[2]

Millions of people, including increasing numbers of women, earn their living through personal selling. Sales careers can offer high income, a great deal of freedom, a high level of training, and a high level of job satisfaction. Although personal selling is sometimes viewed negatively, major corporations, professional sales associations, and academic institutions are changing unfavorable stereotypes of salespeople.

Personal selling goals vary from one firm to another. However, they usually involve finding prospects, persuading prospects to buy, and keeping customers satisfied. Identifying potential buyers interested in the organization's products is critical. Because most potential buyers seek information before making purchases, salespeople can ascertain prospects' informational needs and then provide relevant information. To do so, sales personnel must be well trained regarding both their products and the selling process in general.

Salespeople must be aware of their competitors. They must monitor the development of new products and know about competitors' sales efforts in their sales territories, how often and when the competition calls on their accounts, and what the competition is saying about their product in relation to its own. For example, at PowerTV, a California firm that makes software and operating systems for digital cable television boxes, salespeople routinely collect information about competitors' activities and send it to the marketing department for posting on the firm's intranet. This steady flow allows all 240 employees to stay abreast of competitive developments so the company can respond quickly.[3] Salespeople must emphasize the benefits that their products provide, especially when competitors' products do not offer those specific benefits.

Few businesses survive solely on profits from one-time customers. For long-run survival, most marketers depend on repeat sales and thus need to keep their customers satisfied. In addition, satisfied customers provide favorable word-of-mouth communications, attracting new customers. Even though the whole organization is responsible for achieving customer satisfaction, much of the burden falls on salespeople, since they are almost always closer to customers than anyone else in the company and often provide buyers with information and service after the sale. Such contact gives salespeople an opportunity to generate additional sales and offers them a good vantage point for evaluating the strengths and weaknesses of the company's products and other marketing mix components. Their observations help develop and maintain a marketing mix that better satisfies both customers and the firm.

Elements of the Personal Selling Process

The specific activities involved in the selling process vary among salespeople and selling situations. No two salespeople use exactly the same selling methods. Nonetheless, many salespeople move through a general selling process as they sell products. This process consists of seven steps, outlined in Figure 19.1: prospecting, preapproach, approach, making the presentation, overcoming objections, closing the sale, and following up.

Prospecting

Developing a list of potential customers is called **prospecting.** Salespeople seek names of prospects from company sales records, trade shows, commercial databases, newspaper announcements (of marriages, births, deaths, and so on), public records, telephone directories, trade association directories, and many other sources. Sales personnel also use responses to advertisements that encourage interested persons to send in information request forms. Seminars and meetings targeted at particular types of clients, such as attorneys or accountants, may also produce leads.

A number of salespeople prefer to use referrals—recommendations from current customers—to find prospects. Obtaining referrals requires that the salesperson have a good relationship with the current customer and so must have performed well before asking the customer for help. Research shows that one referral is as valuable as twelve cold calls. Also, 80 percent of clients are willing to give referrals, but only 20 percent are ever asked. Sales experts indicate that the advantages of using referrals are that the resulting sales leads are highly qualified, the sales rates are higher, initial transactions are larger, and the sales cycle is shorter.[4]

Consistent activity is critical to successful prospecting. Salespeople must actively search the customer base for qualified prospects who fit the target market profile. After developing the prospect list, a salesperson evaluates whether each prospect is able, willing, and authorized to buy the product. Based on this evaluation, prospects are ranked according to desirability or potential.

Preapproach

Before contacting acceptable prospects, a salesperson finds and analyzes information about each prospect's specific product needs, current use of brands, feelings about available brands, and personal characteristics. The most successful salespeople are thor-

1 Prospecting

2 Preapproach

3 Approach

4 Making the presentation

5 Overcoming objections

6 Closing the sale

7 Following up

FIGURE 19.1
General Steps in the Personal Selling Process

prospecting Developing a list of potential customers

Identifying Prospects
Marketers use a number of sources, such as Salesnet and Zapdata.com, to help in the identification of prospects.

ough in their preapproach, which involves identifying key decision makers, reviewing account histories and problems, contacting other clients for information, assessing credit histories and problems, preparing sales presentations, identifying product needs, and obtaining relevant literature. A salesperson with a lot of information about a prospect is better equipped to develop a presentation that precisely communicates with the prospect.

Approach

approach   The manner in which a salesperson contacts a potential customer

The **approach,** the manner in which a salesperson contacts a potential customer, is a critical step in the sales process. In more than 80 percent of initial sales calls, the purpose is to gather information about the buyer's needs and objectives. Creating a favorable impression and building rapport with prospective clients are important tasks in the approach because the prospect's first impressions of the salesperson are usually lasting ones. During the initial visit, the salesperson strives to develop a relationship rather than just push a product. The salesperson may have to call on a prospect several times before the product is considered. The approach must be designed to deliver value to targeted customers. If the sales approach is inappropriate, the salesperson's efforts are likely to have poor results.

One type of approach is based on referrals: the salesperson approaches the prospect and explains that an acquaintance, associate, or relative suggested the call. The salesperson who uses the "cold canvass" approach calls on potential customers without prior consent. Repeat contact is another common approach: when making the contact, the salesperson mentions a previous meeting. The exact type of approach depends on the salesperson's preferences, the product being sold, the firm's resources, and the prospect's characteristics.

Making the Presentation

During the sales presentation, the salesperson must attract and hold the prospect's attention, stimulate interest, and spark a desire for the product. The salesperson should have the prospect touch, hold, or use the product. If possible, the salesperson should demonstrate the product. Audiovisual equipment and software may also enhance the presentation.

Enhancing Sales Presentations
Salespeople enhance their sales presentations by using audio-visual technology such as InFocus and Sanyo projectors.

During the presentation, the salesperson must not only talk but also listen. The sales presentation gives the salesperson the greatest opportunity to determine the prospect's specific needs by listening to questions and comments and observing responses. Even though the salesperson plans the presentation in advance, she or he must be able to adjust the message to meet the prospect's informational needs.

Overcoming Objections

An effective salesperson usually seeks out a prospect's objections in order to address them. If they are not apparent, the salesperson cannot deal with them, and the prospect may not buy. One of the best ways to overcome objections is to anticipate and counter them before the prospect raises them. However, this approach can be risky because the salesperson may mention objections that the prospect would not have raised. If possible, the salesperson should handle objections as they arise. They also can be addressed at the end of the presentation.

Closing the Sale

closing The stage in the selling process when the salesperson asks the prospect to buy the product

Closing is the stage of the selling process when the salesperson asks the prospect to buy the product. During the presentation, the salesperson may use a "trial close" by asking questions that assume the prospect will buy the product. The salesperson might ask the potential customer about financial terms, desired colors or sizes, or delivery arrangements. Reactions to such questions usually indicate how close the prospect is to buying. Properly asked questions may allow prospects to uncover their own problems and identify solutions themselves. One questioning approach uses broad questions (*what, how, why*) to probe or gather information and focused questions (*who, when, where*) to clarify and close the sale. A trial close allows prospects to indicate indirectly that they will buy the product without having to say those sometimes difficult words, "I'll take it."

A salesperson should try to close at several points during the presentation because the prospect may be ready to buy. One closing strategy involves asking the potential customer to place a low-risk tryout order. An attempt to close the sale may result in objections. Thus, closing can uncover hidden objections, which the salesperson can then address.

Following Up

After a successful closing, the salesperson must follow up the sale. In the follow-up stage, the salesperson determines whether the order was delivered on time and installed properly, if installation was required. He or she should contact the customer to learn if any problems or questions regarding the product have arisen. The follow-up stage is also used to determine customers' future product needs.

Types of Salespeople

To develop a sales force, a marketing manager decides what kind of salesperson will sell the firm's products most effectively. Most business organizations use several different kinds of sales personnel. Based on the functions performed, salespeople can be classified into three groups: order getters, order takers, and support personnel. One salesperson can, and often does, perform all three functions.

Order Getters

order getter The salesperson who sells to new customers and increases sales to current ones

To obtain orders, a salesperson informs prospects and persuades them to buy the product. The **order getter**'s job is to increase sales by selling to new customers and increasing sales to present customers. This task sometimes is called *creative selling*. It requires that salespeople recognize potential buyers' needs and give them necessary information. Order getting is sometimes divided into two categories: current-customer sales and new-business sales.

Current-Customer Sales.   Sales personnel who concentrate on current customers call on people and organizations that have purchased products from the firm before. These salespeople seek more sales from existing customers by following up previous sales. Current customers can also be sources of leads for new prospects.

New-Business Sales.   Business organizations depend to some degree on sales to new customers. New-business sales personnel locate prospects and convert them into buyers. In many organizations, salespeople help generate new business, but organizations that sell real estate, insurance, appliances, heavy industrial machinery, and automobiles depend in large part on new-customer sales.

Order Takers

order taker   The salesperson who primarily seeks repeat sales

Taking orders is a repetitive task salespeople perform to perpetuate long-lasting, satisfying customer relationships. **Order takers** seek repeat sales. One major objective is to be certain customers have sufficient product quantities where and when needed. Most order takers handle orders for standardized products purchased routinely and not requiring extensive sales efforts. The role of order takers is changing, however. In the future, they will probably serve more as identifiers and problem solvers to better meet the needs of their customers. There are two groups of order takers: inside order takers and field order takers.

Inside Order Takers.   In many businesses, inside order takers, who work in sales offices, receive orders by mail, telephone, and the Internet. Certain producers, wholesalers, and retailers have sales personnel who sell from within the firm rather than in the field. This does not mean that inside order takers never communicate with customers face to face. For example, retail salespeople are classified as inside order takers. As more orders are placed through the Internet, the role of the inside order taker will continue to change.

Field Order Takers.   Salespeople who travel to customers are outside, or field, order takers. Often customers and field order takers develop interdependent relationships. The buyer relies on the salesperson to take orders periodically (and sometimes to deliver them), and the salesperson counts on the buyer to purchase a certain quantity of products periodically. Use of small computers has improved the field order taker's inventory and order tracking capabilities.

Field and inside order takers are not passive functionaries who simply record orders in a machinelike manner. Order takers generate the bulk of many organizations' total sales.

Support Personnel

support personnel   Sales staff members who facilitate selling but usually are not involved solely with making sales

Support personnel facilitate selling but usually are not involved solely with making sales. They are engaged primarily in marketing industrial products, locating prospects, educating customers, building goodwill, and providing service after the sale. There are many kinds of sales support personnel; the three most common are missionary, trade, and technical salespeople.

missionary salesperson   A support salesperson who assists the producer's customers in selling to their own customers

Missionary Salespeople.   **Missionary salespeople,** usually employed by manufacturers, assist the producer's customers in selling to their own customers. Missionary salespeople may call on retailers to inform and persuade them to buy the manufacturer's products. When they succeed, retailers purchase products from wholesalers, who are the producer's customers. Manufacturers of medical supplies and pharmaceuticals often use missionary salespeople, called *detail reps,* to promote their products to physicians, hospitals, and retail druggists.

trade salesperson A salesperson involved mainly in helping a producer's customers promote a product

Trade Salespeople.   **Trade salespeople** are not strictly support personnel because they usually take orders as well. However, they direct much effort toward helping customers, especially retail stores, promote the product. They are likely to restock shelves, obtain more shelf space, set up displays, provide in-store demonstrations, and distribute samples to store customers. Food producers and processors commonly employ trade salespeople.

technical salesperson A support salesperson who gives technical assistance to a firm's current customers

Technical Salespeople.   **Technical salespeople** give technical assistance to the organization's current customers, advising them on product characteristics and applications, system designs, and installation procedures. Because this job is often highly technical, the salesperson usually has formal training in one of the physical sciences or in engineering. Technical sales personnel often sell technical industrial products, such as computers, heavy equipment, and steel.

When hiring sales personnel, marketers seldom restrict themselves to a single category because most firms require different types of salespeople. Several factors dictate how many of each type a particular company should have. Product use, characteristics, complexity, and price influence the kind of sales personnel used, as do the number and characteristics of customers. The types of marketing channels and the intensity and type of advertising also affect the composition of a sales force.

Management of the Sales Force

The sales force is directly responsible for generating one of an organization's primary inputs—sales revenue. Without adequate sales revenue, businesses cannot survive. In addition, a firm's reputation is often determined by the ethical conduct of its sales force. The morale and ultimately the success of a firm's sales force depend in large part on adequate compensation, room for advancement, adequate training, and management support—all key areas of sales management. Salespeople who are not satisfied with these elements may leave. Evaluating the input of salespeople is an important part of sales force management because of its strong bearing on a firm's success.

We explore eight general areas of sales management: establishing sales force objectives, determining sales force size, recruiting and selecting salespeople, training sales personnel, compensating salespeople, motivating salespeople, managing sales territories, and controlling and evaluating sales force performance.

Establishing Sales Force Objectives

To manage a sales force effectively, sales managers must develop sales objectives. Sales objectives tell salespeople what they are expected to accomplish during a specified time period. They give the sales force direction and purpose, and serve as standards for evaluating and controlling the performance of sales personnel. Sales objectives should be stated in precise, measurable terms and should specify the time period and geographic areas involved.

Sales objectives are usually developed for both the total sales force and each salesperson. Objectives for the entire force are normally stated in terms of sales volume, market share, or profit. Volume objectives refer to dollar or unit sales. For example, the objective for an electric drill producer's sales force might be to sell $18 million worth of drills, or 600,000 drills annually. When sales goals are stated in terms of market share, they usually call for an increase in the proportion of the firm's sales relative to the total number of products sold by all businesses in that industry. When sales objectives are based on profit, they are generally stated in terms of dollar amounts or return on investment.

Sales objectives, or quotas, for individual salespeople are commonly stated in terms of dollar or unit sales volume. Other bases used for individual sales objectives include average order size, average number of calls per time period, and ratio of orders to calls.

Determining Sales Force Size

Sales force size is important because it influences the company's ability to generate sales and profits. Moreover, size of the sales force affects the compensation methods used, salespeople's morale, and overall sales force management. Sales force size must be adjusted periodically because a firm's marketing plans change along with markets and forces in the marketing environment. One danger in cutting back the size of the sales force to increase profits is that the sales organization may lose strength and resiliency, preventing it from rebounding when growth occurs or better market conditions prevail.

Several analytical methods can help determine optimal sales force size. One method involves determining how many sales calls per year are necessary for the organization to serve customers effectively and then dividing this total by the average number of sales calls a salesperson makes annually. A second method is based on marginal analysis, whereby additional salespeople are added to the sales force until the cost of an additional salesperson equals the additional sales generated by that person. Although marketing managers may use one or several analytical methods, they normally temper decisions with subjective judgments.

Recruiting and Selecting Salespeople

recruiting Developing a list of qualified applicants for sales positions

To create and maintain an effective sales force, sales managers must recruit the right type of salespeople. In **recruiting,** the sales manager develops a list of qualified applicants for sales positions. Costs of hiring and training a salesperson are soaring, reaching more than $60,000 in some industries. Thus, recruiting errors are expensive.

To ensure the recruiting process results in a pool of qualified salespeople from which to hire, a sales manager establishes a set of qualifications before beginning to recruit. Although for years marketers have tried to identify a set of traits characterizing effective salespeople, no set of generally accepted characteristics yet exists. Sales managers must determine what set of traits best fits their companies' particular sales tasks. Two activities help establish this set of required attributes. First, the sales manager should prepare a job description listing specific tasks salespeople are to perform. Second, the manager should analyze characteristics of the firm's successful salespeople, as well as those of ineffective sales personnel. From the job description and analysis of traits, the sales manager should be able to develop a set of specific requirements and be aware of potential weaknesses that could lead to failure.

A sales manager generally recruits applicants from several sources: departments within the firm, other firms, employment agencies, educational institutions, respondents to advertisements, and individuals recommended by current employees. The specific sources depend on the type of salesperson required and the manager's experiences with particular sources.

THE RIGHT SEARCH, THE RIGHT CANDIDATES, THE RIGHT HIRE, THE RIGHT FIT.

Recruiting and Selecting Salespeople
Sales managers sometimes use the specialized services provided by other companies, such as Deploy Solutions, to help them in recruiting and hiring salespeople.

The process of recruiting and selecting salespeople varies considerably from one company to another. Companies intent on reducing sales force turnover are likely to have strict recruiting and selection procedures. State Farm Life Insurance, for example, strives to retain customers by having low sales force turnover. Applicants for the job of State Farm Insurance agent must endure a yearlong series of interviews, tests, and visits with agents before finding out if they have been hired. Approximately 80 percent of State Farm agents are still employed four years after being hired, compared with an industry average of only 30 percent.

Sales management should design a selection procedure that satisfies the company's specific needs. Some organizations use the specialized services of other companies to hire sales personnel. The process should include steps that yield the information required to make accurate selection decisions. However, because each step incurs a certain amount of expense, there should be no more steps than necessary. Stages of the selection process should be sequenced so that the more expensive steps, such as a physical examination, occur near the end. Fewer people will then move through higher-cost stages.

Recruitment should not be sporadic. It should be a continuous activity aimed at reaching the best applicants. The selection process should systematically and effectively match applicants' characteristics and needs with the requirements of specific selling tasks. Finally, the selection process should ensure that new sales personnel are available where and when needed.

Training Sales Personnel

Many organizations have formal training programs; others depend on informal, on-the-job training. Some systematic training programs are quite extensive, whereas others are rather short and rudimentary. Whether the training program is complex or simple, developers must consider what to teach, whom to train, and how to train them.

Training Salespeople
To train their salespeople, companies sometimes employ the services of other organizations, such as Aon Consulting. Aon's REPeTrain™ is a web-delivered training program for salespeople.

Are your reps going upstream without a paddle?

With REPeTrain, Aon's new competency-based Web-delivered training program, you will equip your representatives with the knowledge and skills necessary to provide exceptional customer service.

Built on Aon's experience and expertise in the design and administration of outstanding training programs, REPeTrain, available in four industry versions, is a flexible, interactive and cost effective means of delivering targeted training modules to the desk tops of your representatives. Contact us today to find out how REPeTrain can help maximize performance excellence in your business.

e REP Train™

AON

www.asi-aon.com **1-800-837-HIRE**

A sales training program can concentrate on the company, its products, or selling methods. Training programs often cover all three. Such programs can be aimed at newly hired salespeople, experienced salespeople, or both. Training for experienced company salespeople usually emphasizes product information, although salespeople must also be informed about new selling techniques and changes in company plans, policies, and procedures. Ordinarily, new sales personnel require comprehensive training, whereas experienced personnel need both refresher courses on established products and training regarding new-product information.

Sales training may be done in the field, at educational institutions, in company facilities, or in more than one of these locations. Some firms train new employees before assigning them to a specific sales position. Others put them into the field immediately, providing formal training only after they have gained some experience. Training programs for new personnel can be as short as several days or as long as three years; some are even longer. Sales training for experienced personnel is often scheduled when sales activities are not too demanding. Because experienced salespeople usually need periodic retraining, a firm's sales management must determine the frequency, sequencing, and duration of these efforts.

Sales managers, as well as other salespeople, often engage in sales training, whether daily on the job or periodically during sales meetings. Salespeople sometimes receive training from technical specialists within their own organizations. In addition, a number of outside companies specialize in providing sales training programs. Materials for sales training programs range from videos, texts, online materials, manuals, and cases to programmed learning devices and audio- and videocassettes. Lectures, demonstrations, simulation exercises, and on-the-job training can all be effective teaching methods. Choice of methods and materials for a particular sales training program depends on type and number of trainees, program content and complexity, length and location, size of the training budget, number of teachers, and teacher preferences.

Compensating Salespeople

To develop and maintain a highly productive sales force, a business must formulate and administer a compensation plan that attracts, motivates, and retains the most effective individuals. The plan should give sales management the desired level of control and provide sales personnel with acceptable levels of income, freedom, and incentive. It should be flexible, equitable, easy to administer, and easy to understand. Good compensation programs facilitate and encourage proper treatment of customers. Obviously it is quite difficult to incorporate all of these requirements into a single program.

Developers of compensation programs must determine the general level of compensation required and the most desirable method of calculating it. In analyzing the required compensation level, sales management must ascertain a salesperson's value to the company on the basis of the tasks and responsibilities associated with the sales position. Sales managers may consider a number of factors, including salaries of other types of personnel in the firm, competitors' compensation plans, costs of sales force turnover, and nonsalary selling expenses. The average entry-level salesperson earns about $42,000 annually, whereas the average experienced salesperson (more than ten years) makes about $126,000 yearly.[5]

Sales compensation programs usually reimburse salespeople for selling expenses, provide some fringe benefits, and deliver the required compensation level. To achieve this, a firm may use one or more of three basic compensation methods: straight salary, straight commission, or a combination of salary and commission. In a **straight salary compensation plan,** salespeople are paid a specified amount per time period. This sum remains the same until they receive a pay increase or decrease. In a **straight commission compensation plan,** salespeople's compensation is determined solely by sales for a given period. A commission may be based on a single percentage of sales or on a sliding scale involving several sales levels and percentage rates. In a **combination compensation plan,** salespeople receive a fixed salary plus a commission based on sales volume. Some combination programs require

straight salary compensation plan Paying salespeople a specific amount per time period

straight commission compensation plan Paying salespeople according to the amount of their sales in a given time period

combination compensation plan Paying salespeople a fixed salary plus a commission based on sales volume

Table 19.1   Characteristics of Sales Force Compensation Methods

Compensation Method	Frequency of Use (%)*	When Especially Useful	Advantages	Disadvantages
Straight salary	17.5	Compensating new salespersons; firm moves into new sales territories that require developmental work; sales requiring lengthy presale and postsale services	Gives salesperson security; gives sales manager control over salespersons; easy to administer; yields more predictable selling expenses	Provides no incentive; necessitates closer supervision of salespersons; during sales declines, selling expenses remain constant
Straight commission	14.0	Highly aggressive selling is required; nonselling tasks are minimized; company uses contractors and part-timers	Provides maximum amount of incentive; by increasing commission rate, sales managers can encourage salespersons to sell certain items; selling expenses relate directly to sales resources	Salespersons have little financial security; sales manager has minimum control over sales force; may cause salespeople to give inadequate service to smaller accounts; selling costs less predictable
Combination	68.5	Sales territories have relatively similar sales potential; firm wishes to provide incentive but still control sales force activities	Provides certain level of financial security; provides some incentive; can move sales force efforts in profitable direction	Selling expenses less predictable; may be difficult to administer

*The figures are computed from *Dartnell's 30th Sales Force Compensation Survey,* Dartnell Corporation, Chicago, 1999.

Source: Charles Futrell, *Sales Management* (Ft. Worth, TX: Dryden Press), 2001, pp. 307–316.

that a salesperson exceed a certain sales level before earning a commission; others offer commissions for any level of sales.

Table 19.1 lists major characteristics of each sales force compensation method. Notice that the combination method is the most popular. When selecting a compensation method, sales management weighs the advantages and disadvantages listed in the table.

Motivating Salespeople

A sales manager should develop a systematic approach for motivating salespeople to be productive. Motivating should not be reserved for periods of sales decline. Effective sales force motivation is achieved through an organized set of activities performed continuously by the company's sales management.

Although financial compensation is an important incentive, motivational programs are needed to satisfy nonfinancial needs. Sales personnel, like other people, join organizations to satisfy personal needs and achieve personal goals. Sales managers must recognize salespeople's motives and goals and attempt to create an organizational climate that lets them satisfy personal needs. Recognition of individual goals is becoming more challenging as cultural diversity increases.

A sales manager can use a variety of motivational incentives other than financial compensation. Enjoyable working conditions, power and authority, job security, and opportunity to excel are effective motivators, as are company efforts to make sales jobs more productive and efficient.

Sales contests and other incentive programs can also be effective motivators. Sales contests can motivate salespeople to increase sales or add new accounts, promote special items, achieve greater volume per sales call, and cover territories more thoroughly. Some companies find such incentive programs powerful motivating tools

S N A P S H O T

Why good workers leave

Here are the most likely causes for good employees to quit, according to human resources executives.

41%
Limited advancement potential

25%
Lack of recognition

15%
Low salary/ benefits

Source: *USA Today,* 2000. Copyright 2000, *USA Today.* Reprinted with permission.

that marketing managers can use to achieve company goals. Properly designed incentive programs pay for themselves many times over. In fact, sales managers are relying on incentives more than ever. Recognition programs that acknowledge outstanding performance with symbolic awards, such as plaques, can be very effective when done in a peer setting. Other common awards include travel, merchandise, and cash. The advantages of a travel award are that it is a high-profile honor, can provide a unique experience that makes recipients feel special, and can build camaraderie among award-winning salespeople. However, recipients of travel awards may feel they already travel too much on the job. Also, the travel experience may not live up to expectations. The benefits of a cash award are that it is easy to administer, is almost always appreciated by recipients, and crosses all demographic barriers. However, cash has no visible trophy value and gives few "bragging rights." Also, the awardee may feel dissatisfied at receiving only a check. The benefits of awarding merchandise are that it has visible trophy value, recipients who are allowed to select the merchandise feel more control, and it can help build momentum for the sales force. The disadvantages of using merchandise include administrative complications and problems with perceived value on the part of recipients. Moreover, merchandise is simply less exciting than travel.[6]

Incentive Programs
Companies have access to numerous incentive programs focused on motivating salespeople.

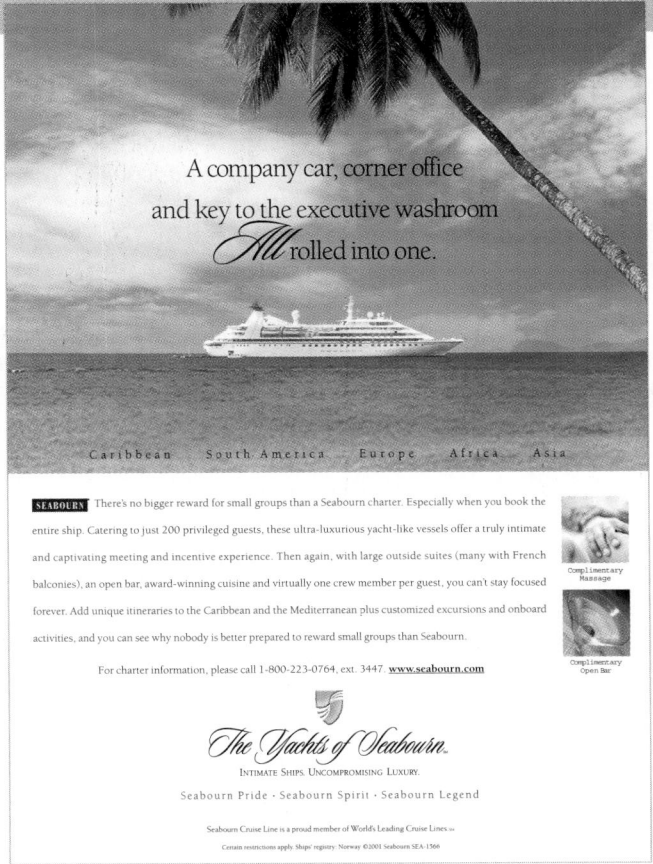

A company car, corner office and key to the executive washroom *All* rolled into one.

Caribbean   South America   Europe   Africa   Asia

SEABOURN There's no bigger reward for small groups than a Seabourn charter. Especially when you book the entire ship. Catering to just 200 privileged guests, these ultra-luxurious yacht-like vessels offer a truly intimate and captivating meeting and incentive experience. Then again, with large outside suites (many with French balconies), an open bar, award-winning cuisine and virtually one crew member per guest, you can't stay focused forever. Add unique itineraries to the Caribbean and the Mediterranean plus customized excursions and onboard activities, and you can see why nobody is better prepared to reward small groups than Seabourn.

For charter information, please call 1-800-223-0764, ext. 3447. www.seabourn.com

The Yachts of Seabourn
INTIMATE SHIPS. UNCOMPROMISING LUXURY.

Seabourn Pride · Seabourn Spirit · Seabourn Legend

Seabourn Cruise Line is a proud member of World's Leading Cruise Lines sm
Certain restrictions apply. Ships' registry: Norway. ©2001 Seabourn SEA-1566

They'll do anything for a *Super*Certificate™

There's no telling what they will do to earn a SuperCertificate from GiftCertificates.com. That's because a SuperCertificate lets them get just what they want – making it perfect for all of your incentive and customer acquisition programs.

See for yourself

DON'T WAIT! Order for the holidays now!

To place an order call **1-877-568-8404** or visit us online today at **www.GiftCertificates.com/adage**

GiftCertificates.com™
incentives • promotions • rewards

SuperCertificates are redeemable at GiftCertificates.com for original gift certificates from hundreds of the nation's most popular stores, restaurants and services including these and more.

Merchants subject to change.

Media Code: PR0033

Managing Sales Territories

The effectiveness of a sales force that must travel to customers is somewhat influenced by management's decisions regarding sales territories. When deciding on territories, sales managers must consider size, shape, routing, and scheduling.

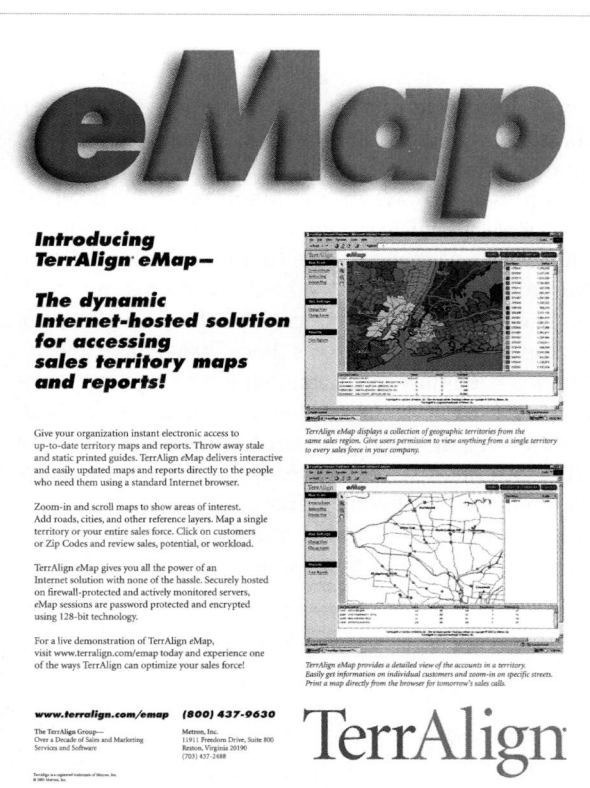

Introducing TerrAlign eMap—

The dynamic Internet-hosted solution for accessing sales territory maps and reports!

Give your organization instant electronic access to up-to-date territory maps and reports. Throw away stale and static printed guides. TerrAlign eMap delivers interactive and easily updated maps and reports directly to the people who need them using a standard Internet browser.

Zoom-in and scroll maps to show areas of interest. Add roads, cities, and other reference layers. Map a single territory or your entire sales force. Click on customers or Zip Codes and review sales, potential, or workload.

TerrAlign eMap gives you all the power of an Internet solution with none of the hassle. Securely hosted on firewall-protected and actively monitored servers, eMap sessions are password protected and encrypted using 128-bit technology.

For a live demonstration of TerrAlign eMap, visit www.terralign.com/emap today and experience one of the ways TerrAlign can optimize your sales force!

www.terralign.com/emap   (800) 437-9630

The TerrAlign Group—
Over a Decade of Sales and Marketing
Services and Software

Metron, Inc.
11911 Freedom Drive, Suite 800
Reston, Virginia 20190
(703) 437-2488

TerrAlign

TerrAlign eMap displays a collection of geographic territories from the same sales region. Give users permission to view anything from a single territory to every sales force in your company.

TerrAlign eMap provides a detailed view of the accounts in a territory. Easily get information on individual customers and zoom-in on specific streets. Print a map directly from the browser for tomorrow's sales calls.

Managing Sales Territories
At times, sales managers employ Internet-based tools, such as TerrAlign eMap, to help them manage sales territories.

Creating Sales Territories Several factors enter into the design of a sales territory's size and shape. First, sales managers must construct territories so that sales potential can be measured. Sales territories often consist of several geographic units, such as census tracts, cities, counties, or states, for which market data are obtainable. Sales managers usually try to create territories with similar sales potential or requiring about the same amount of work. If territories have equal sales potential, they will almost always be unequal in geographic size. Salespeople with larger territories have to work longer and harder to generate a certain sales volume. Conversely, if sales territories requiring equal amounts of work are created, sales potential for those territories will often vary. If sales personnel are partially or fully compensated through commissions, they will have unequal income potential. Many sales managers try to balance territorial workloads and earning potential by using differential commission rates. At times sales managers use commercial programs to help them balance sales territories. Although a sales manager seeks equity when developing and maintaining sales territories, some inequities always prevail.

A territory's size and shape should also help the sales force provide the best possible customer coverage and should minimize selling costs. Customer density and distribution are important factors.

Routing and Scheduling Salespeople The geographic size and shape of a sales territory are the most important factors affecting the routing and scheduling of sales calls. Next in importance are the number and distribution of customers within the territory, followed by sales call frequency and duration. Those in charge of routing and scheduling must consider the sequence in which customers are called on, specific roads or transportation schedules to be used, number of calls to be made in a given period, and time of day the calls will occur. In some firms, salespeople plan their own routes and schedules with little or no assistance from the sales manager; in other organizations, the sales manager draws up the routes and schedules. No matter who plans the routing and scheduling, the major goals should be to minimize salespeople's non-selling time (time spent traveling and waiting) and maximize their selling time. Planners should try to achieve these goals so that a salesperson's travel and lodging costs are held to a minimum.

Controlling and Evaluating Sales Force Performance

To control and evaluate sales force performance properly, sales management needs information. A sales manager cannot observe the field sales force daily and so relies on salespeople's call reports, customer feedback, and invoices. Call reports identify the customers called on and present detailed information about interaction with those clients. Traveling sales personnel often must file work schedules indicating where they plan to be during specific time periods.

Dimensions used to measure a salesperson's performance are determined largely by sales objectives, normally set by the sales manager. If an individual's sales objective is stated in terms of sales volume, that person should be evaluated on the basis of sales volume generated. Even if a salesperson is assigned a major objective, he or she is ordinarily expected to achieve several related objectives as well. Thus, salespeople are often judged along several dimensions. Sales managers evaluate many performance indicators, including average number of calls per day, average sales per customer, actual sales relative to sales potential, number of new-customer orders, average cost per call, and average gross profit per customer.

To evaluate a salesperson, a sales manager may compare one or more of these dimensions with predetermined performance standards. However, sales managers commonly compare a salesperson's performance with that of other employees operating under similar selling conditions or the salesperson's current performance with past performance. Sometimes management judges factors that have less direct bearing on sales performance, such as personal appearance and product knowledge.

After evaluating salespeople, sales managers take any needed corrective action to improve sales force performance. They may adjust performance standards, provide additional training, or try other motivational methods. Corrective action may demand comprehensive changes in the sales force.

The Nature of Sales Promotion

sales promotion An activity and/or material meant to induce resellers or salespeople to sell a product or consumers to buy it

Sales promotion is an activity or material, or both, that acts as a direct inducement, offering added value or incentive for the product, to resellers, salespeople, or consumers. It encompasses all promotional activities and materials other than personal selling, advertising, and public relations. In competitive markets, where products are very similar, sales promotion provides additional inducements that encourage product trial and purchase.

BUILDING CUSTOMER RELATIONSHIPS

Sales Promotion Builds Share for McDonald's

Buy a burger, get a toy. Toy giveaways are a major sales promotion weapon in McDonald's battle for fast-food market share. McDonald's has 13,000 U.S. restaurants, and its market share is approaching 43 percent. However, rival Burger King, with about 8,000 U.S. restaurants and nearly 22 percent of the market, is working hard to narrow the gap. To strengthen customer relationships in this high-stakes food fight, McDonald's is using a variety of promotional tools to target families as well as African American and Hispanic consumers.

Fast-food restaurants have long put toys in kids' meals to build traffic and encourage repeat visits from families. In recent years, however, the competition has gotten fiercer—and the budgets bigger—as the top chains develop promotional offers linked to new movies and hit television shows. Knowing that Disney films are generally big box-office draws for families, McDonald's signed a ten-year, multimillion-dollar agreement to be the only fast-food restaurant promoting Disney movies. Typically the chain's movie-related sales promotions include colorful store displays, free toys, and a contest, giving families an incentive to return to McDonald's again and again. The deal is paying off. Already four of the ten best-selling Happy Meals have featured Disney tie-ins such as toys from *Toy Story 2*. In addition, McDonald's is encouraging families to vary their food orders by tying specific menu items to movie and television promotions.

The family segment is just one of several market segments McDonald's has been targeting. Through research, the chain learned that African American and Hispanic consumers each account for 15 percent of its customer base. As a result, McDonald's has developed special promotional offers geared to these two segments. "McDonald's is doing bigger and better things to reach both African Americans and Hispanics with campaigns designed to be very specific to them," explains Mary Kay Eschbach, McDonald's U.S. media director. "Both communities are incredibly important to us."

One January, for example, McDonald's mounted a chainwide salute to Martin Luther King, followed by a February sweepstakes giving away a family vacation. In early fall, McDonald's promotional efforts carried an African American heritage theme. McDonald's has also been promoting its annual in-store Monopoly game and other promotions on the BET cable channel and website. To reach out to Hispanic consumers, McDonald's is airing a Spanish-language advertising campaign and spotlighting in-store promotions on Galavision. More sales promotion activities are ahead as McDonald's continues its battle to gain market share.

The use of sales promotion has risen dramatically over the last 20 years, primarily at the expense of advertising. This shift in how promotional dollars are used has occurred for several reasons. Heightened concerns about value have made customers more responsive to promotional offers, especially price promotions, coupons, and point-of-purchase displays. Because of their sheer size and access to scanner data, retailers have become much more powerful than manufacturers and are placing greater demands on them for sales promotion efforts that generate retail profits. Declines in brand loyalty have produced an environment in which sales promotions aimed at persuading customers to switch brands are more effective. Finally, the stronger emphasis placed on improving short-term performance results calls for greater use of sales promotion methods that yield quick (although perhaps short-lived) sales increases.[7]

An organization often uses sales promotion to facilitate personal selling, advertising, or both. Companies also use advertising and personal selling to support sales promotion activities. For example, marketers frequently use advertising to promote contests, free samples, and premiums. The most effective sales promotion efforts are highly interrelated with other promotional activities. Decisions regarding sales promotion often affect advertising and personal selling decisions, and vice versa.

Sales Promotion Opportunities and Limitations

Sales promotion can increase sales by providing extra purchasing incentives. Many opportunities exist to motivate consumers, resellers, and salespeople to take desired actions. Some kinds of sales promotion are designed specifically to stimulate resellers' demand and effectiveness, some are directed at increasing consumer demand, and some focus on both resellers and consumers. Regardless of the purpose, marketers must ensure that sales promotion objectives are consistent with the organization's overall objectives, as well as with its marketing and promotion objectives.

Although sales promotion can support brand image, excessive sales promotion efforts at price reduction—through coupons, for example—can negatively affect brand image. Indeed, in the future, brand advertising may become more important than sales promotion. Some firms that have shifted from brand advertising to sales promotion have lost market share. For instance, Minute Maid orange juice (owned by Coca-Cola Foods) experienced its most dramatic sales declines after shifting the majority of promotional spending to sales promotion while one of its major competitors, Tropicana, continued to focus on brand advertising. Tradeoffs exist between these two forms of promotion, and marketing managers must determine the right balance to achieve maximum promotional effectiveness.

Sales Promotion Methods

Most sales promotion methods can be grouped into consumer sales promotion and trade sales promotion. **Consumer sales promotion methods** encourage or stimulate consumers to patronize specific retail stores or try particular products. **Trade sales promotion methods** stimulate wholesalers and retailers to carry a producer's products and market those products more aggressively.

consumer sales promotion methods Ways of encouraging consumers to patronize specific stores or try particular products

trade sales promotion methods Ways of persuading wholesalers and retailers to carry a producer's products and market them aggressively

In deciding which sales promotion methods to use, marketers must take several factors into account. They must consider both product characteristics (size, weight, costs, durability, uses, features, and hazards) and target market characteristics (age, sex, income, location, density, usage rate, and shopping patterns). How products are distributed and the number and types of resellers may determine the type of method used. The competitive and legal environment may also influence the choice.

In this section we examine several consumer and trade sales promotion methods, including what they entail and what goals they can help marketers achieve.

Consumer Sales Promotion Methods

Consumer sales promotion methods initiated by retailers often aim to attract customers to specific locations, whereas those used by manufacturers generally introduce new products or promote established brands. In this section we discuss coupons, demonstrations, frequent-user incentives, point-of-purchase displays, free samples, money refunds and rebates, premiums, cents-off offers, consumer contests and games, and consumer sweepstakes.

coupons Written price reductions used to encourage consumers to buy a specific product

Coupons. **Coupons** reduce a product's price and are used to prompt customers to try new or established products, increase sales volume quickly, attract repeat purchasers, or introduce new package sizes or features. Savings may be deducted from the purchase price or offered as cash. For best results, the coupons should be easy to recognize and state the offer clearly. The nature of the product (seasonal demand for it, life cycle stage, frequency of purchase) is the prime consideration in setting up a coupon promotion.

Coupons are the most widely used consumer sales promotion technique. In 2000, manufacturers distributed more than 248 billion coupons, of which 4.5 billion were redeemed. Popular product categories for coupons include disposable diapers, paper products, pet treats, cheese, snacks, and household cleansers.[8]

Paper coupons are distributed on and in packages, through free-standing inserts (FSIs), in print advertising, and through direct mail. Electronic coupons are distributed online, via in-store kiosks, through shelf dispensers in stores, and at checkout counters.[9] When deciding on the distribution method for coupons, marketers should consider strategies and objectives, redemption rates, availability, circulation, and exclusivity. The coupon distribution and redemption arena has become very competitive. To draw customers to their stores, grocers double and sometimes even triple the value of customers' coupons.

Coupons offer several advantages. Print advertisements with coupons are often more effective at generating brand awareness than are print ads without coupons. Generally, the larger the coupon's cash offer, the better the recognition generated. Coupons reward present product users, win back former users, and encourage purchases in larger quantities. Because they are returned, coupons also let a manufacturer

Coupons
Coupons should be easily recognized and should state the offer clearly.

determine whether it reached the intended target market. The advantages of using electronic coupons over paper coupons include lower cost per redemption, greater targeting ability, improved data-gathering capabilities, and improved experimentation capabilities to determine optimal face values and expiration cycles.[10]

Drawbacks of coupon use include fraud and misredemption, which can be expensive for manufacturers. Another disadvantage, according to some experts, is that coupons are losing their value; because so many manufacturers offer them, consumers have learned not to buy without some incentive, whether it is a coupon, rebate, or refund. Furthermore, brand loyalty among heavy coupon users has diminished, and many consumers redeem coupons only for products they normally buy. It is believed that about three-fourths of coupons are redeemed by people already using the brand on the coupon. Thus, coupons have questionable success as an incentive for consumers to try a new brand or product. An additional problem with coupons is that stores often do not have enough of the coupon item in stock. This situation generates ill will toward both the store and the product.

Demonstrations.   **Demonstrations** are excellent attention getters. Manufacturers offer them temporarily to encourage trial use and purchase of a product or to show how a product works. Because labor costs can be extremely high, demonstrations are not used widely. They can be highly effective for promoting certain types of products, such as appliances, cosmetics, and cleaning supplies. Cosmetics marketers, such as Merle Norman and Clinique, sometimes offer potential customers "makeovers" to demonstrate product benefits and proper application.

demonstrations A sales promotion method manufacturers use temporarily to encourage trial use and purchase of a product or to show how a product works

Frequent-User Incentives.   Do you have a "Sub Club Card" from Subway? Many firms develop incentive programs to reward customers who engage in repeat (frequent) purchases. For example, most major airlines offer frequent-flier programs that reward customers who have flown a specified number of miles with free tickets for additional travel. Frequent-user incentives foster customer loyalty to a specific company or group of cooperating companies. They are favored by service businesses, such as airlines, auto rental agencies, and hotels. Hilton Hotels, for example, uses its Hilton Honors program to reward travelers who stay at its hotels with points redeemable for stays at Hilton hotels and travel adventures such as African safaris. To encourage members to try its Hampton Inn chain, the company created a special program awarding 1 million Hilton Honors points to one Hampton Inn guest every month.[11]

Point-of-Purchase Displays.   **Point-of-purchase (P-O-P) materials** include outdoor signs, window displays, counter pieces, display racks, and self-service cartons. Innovations in P-O-P displays include sniff-teasers, which give off a product's aroma in the store as consumers walk within a radius of four feet, and computerized interactive displays. These items, often supplied by producers, attract attention, inform customers, and encourage retailers to carry particular products. A retailer is likely to use point-of-purchase materials if they are attractive, informative, well constructed, and in harmony with the store's image.

point-of-purchase (P-O-P) materials Signs, window displays, display racks, and similar means used to attract customers

Free Samples.   Marketers use **free samples** to stimulate trial of a product, increase sales volume in the early stages of a product's life cycle, and obtain desirable distribution. Sampling is the most expensive sales promotion method because production and distribution—at local events, by mail or door-to-door delivery, online, in stores, and on packages—entail high costs. Many consumers prefer to get their samples by mail. In designing a free sample, marketers should consider factors such as seasonal demand for the product, market characteristics, and prior advertising. Free samples usually are not appropriate for slow-turnover products. Despite high costs, use of sampling is increasing. In a given year, almost three-fourths of consumer product companies may use sampling.

free samples Samples of a product given out to encourage trial and purchase

Distribution of free samples through websites such as StartSampling.com and FreeSamples.com is growing. Consumers choose the free samples they would like to receive and request delivery. The online company manages the packaging and distribution of the samples. NSI, manufacturer of coffee flavorings called Flavour Creations, used a StartSampling.com online sample program to promote its products and expand their distribution. The owner of NSI was very impressed with consumer response to the StartSampling campaign. He said, "We have never had a response like this. People liked our product and they called us and asked where they could buy it."[12]

money refunds A sales promotion technique offering consumers money when they mail in a proof of purchase, usually for multiple product purchases

rebates A sales promotion technique whereby a customer is sent a specific amount of money for purchasing a single product

Money Refunds and Rebates. With **money refunds,** consumers submit proof of purchase and are mailed a specific amount of money. Usually manufacturers demand multiple product purchases before consumers qualify for refunds. With **rebates,** the customer is sent a specified amount of money for making a single purchase. Money refunds, used primarily to promote trial use of a product, are relatively low in cost, but because they sometimes generate a low response rate, they have limited impact on sales.

One problem with money refunds and rebates is that many people perceive the redemption process as too complicated. Only about half of individuals who purchase rebated products actually apply for the rebates.[13] Consumers may also have negative

GLOBAL MARKETING

Global Marketers Put Sampling to Work

Sampling is a traditional sales promotion technique used by Lancôme and many other sophisticated marketers all over the world. But does this expensive tool work? According to a recent study by the Promotion Marketing Association, sampling produces incremental sales for both food and nonfood products, regardless of whether the samples are distributed in a store, through direct mail, in a newspaper, or during a special event. Lancôme, for example, which owns L'Oréal and other global brands, is a frequent and enthusiastic user of sampling. When the company launched its Miracle Homme men's fragrance in European markets, it distributed samples as scent strips mounted on magazine advertisements and in trial-size vials given to cosmetics customers in upscale department stores.

Experts offer these rules for effective sampling:

Select a specific and appropriate target audience. Just as advertisements need to be carefully targeted, so do samples. People attending a pet show are more likely to be interested in receiving dog food samples than people attending a boat show, for example. "Ask yourself whether the product matches the consumer segment," advises Brian Wansink, director of the Food and Brand Lab at the University of Illinois.

Clarify why sampling is being used. Marketers should determine the goal of their sampling program. Uses for sampling are include generating awareness and stimulating trial of a new or repositioned product, introducing an existing product to a new segment, protecting market share by reminding customers of an existing product's

benefits, and strengthening connections with key retailers.

Determine how, when, and where samples will be distributed. Marketers are becoming more imaginative in their choices of locations for sampling. Some candy manufacturers, for example, are offering samples to movie audiences and theme park attendees. In addition, a growing number of firms offering samples on their own websites or on special sampling sites in exchange for marketing data about consumer demographics and behavior.

Learn from previous sampling programs. Before launching a new sampling program, marketers should check the results of previous programs to find out what worked and what didn't. In some cases, marketers can improve results by making a small change in the program. For instance, a sampling program in which a free steak sauce sample was distributed with a recipe flyer increased sales more than the sauce sample alone.

Make it easy to buy. Giving away a coupon along with a sample is a good way to encourage customers to buy the product after trying the sample. Another idea is to have products available for purchase at the sampling location. The purpose is to smooth the way toward a purchase so customers can take action once they have received a sample.

perceptions of manufacturers' reasons for offering rebates. They may believe the products are new, untested, or haven't sold well. If these perceptions are not changed, rebate offers may actually degrade the image and desirability of the products.

premiums Items offered free or at a minimal cost as a bonus for purchasing a product

Premiums
Premiums are items offered free or at minimal cost as a bonus for purchasing a product. They are used to attract competitors' customers, introduce different sizes of established products, add variety to other promotional efforts, and stimulate consumer loyalty. Creativity is essential when using premiums; to stand out and achieve a significant number of redemptions, the premium must match both the target audience and the brand's image. Premiums must also be easily recognizable and desirable. Premiums are placed on or in packages and can also be distributed by retailers or through the mail. Examples include a service station giving a free carwash with a fill-up, a free toothbrush available with a tube of toothpaste, and a free plastic storage box given with the purchase of Kraft Cheese Singles.

cents-off offers Promotions that let buyers pay less than the regular price to encourage purchase

Cents-Off Offers.
With a **cents-off offer,** buyers pay a certain amount less than the regular price shown on the label or package. Similar to coupons, this method can be a strong incentive for trying products. It can stimulate product sales, yield short-lived sales increases, and promote products in off-seasons. It is an easy method to control and is often used for specific purposes. However, if used on an ongoing basis, cents-off offers reduce the price for customers who would buy at the regular price and may also cheapen a product's image. In addition, the method often requires special handling by retailers.

consumer contests and games Competitions for prizes used to generate retail traffic and increase exposure to promotional messages

Consumer Contests and Games.
In **consumer contests and games,** individuals compete for prizes based on analytical or creative skills. This method can be used to generate retail traffic and frequency of exposure to promotional messages. Marketers should exercise care in setting up a contest or game. Problems or errors may anger customers or even result in lawsuits. Contestants are usually more involved in consumer contests and games than in sweepstakes, even though total participation may be lower. Contests and games may be used in conjunction with other sales promotion methods, such as coupons.

Consumer Games
To win a trip to Hawaii or other prizes, Hershey encourages customers to look under the cap of special cow-shaped bottles of Hershey Syrup to find out if they have won.

PICK UP HERSHEY'S SYRUP. END UP IN HAWAII.

consumer sweepstakes
A sales promotion in which entrants submit their names for inclusion in a drawing for prizes

Consumer Sweepstakes.   Entrants in a **consumer sweepstakes** submit their names for inclusion in a drawing for prizes. Sweepstakes are used to stimulate sales and are sometimes teamed with other sales promotion methods. Sweepstakes are used more often than consumer contests and tend to attract a greater number of participants. Successful sweepstakes can generate widespread interest and short-term increases in sales or market share.

Trade Sales Promotion Methods

To encourage resellers, especially retailers, to carry their products and to promote them effectively, producers use sales promotion methods. These include buy-back allowances, buying allowances, scan-back allowances, count-and-recount, free merchandise, merchandise allowances, cooperative advertising, dealer listings, premium or push money, sales contests, and dealer loaders.

buy-back allowance A sum of money given to a reseller for each unit bought after an initial promotion deal is over

Buy-Back Allowances.   A **buy-back allowance** is a sum of money a producer gives to a reseller for each unit the reseller buys after an initial promotional deal is over. This method is a secondary incentive in which the total amount of money resellers receive is proportional to their purchases during an initial consumer promotional offer, such as a coupon offer. Buy-back allowances foster cooperation during an initial sales promotion effort and stimulate repurchase afterward. The main drawback of this method is expense.

buying allowance A temporary price reduction to resellers for purchasing specified quantities of a product

Buying Allowances.   A **buying allowance** is a temporary price reduction to resellers for purchasing specified quantities of a product. A soap producer, for example, might give retailers $1 for each case of soap purchased. Such offers may be an incentive to handle new products, achieve temporary price reductions, or stimulate purchase of items in larger than normal quantities. The buying allowance, which takes the form of money, yields profits to resellers and is simple and straightforward. There are no restrictions on how resellers use the money, which increases the method's effectiveness. One hazard of buying allowances is that customers will buy "forward," meaning buy large amounts that keep them supplied for many months. Another problem is that competition may match (or beat) the reduced price, which can lower profits for all sellers.

scan-back allowance A manufacturer's reward to retailers based on the number of pieces scanned

Scan-Back Allowances.   A **scan-back allowance** is a manufacturer's reward to retailers based on the number of pieces moved through their scanners during a specific time period. To participate in scan-back programs, retailers usually are expected to pass along savings to consumers through special pricing. Scan-backs are becoming widely used by manufacturers because they link trade spending directly to product movement at the retail level.

count-and-recount A producer's payment of a specific amount of money for each product unit moved from a reseller's warehouse in a given period

Count-and-Recount.   The **count-and-recount** method is based on a producer's payment of a specific amount of money for each product unit moved from a reseller's warehouse in a given time period. Units of a product are counted at the start of the promotion and again at the end to determine how many units have moved out of the warehouse. This method can reduce retail stockouts by moving inventory out of warehouses and can also clear distribution channels of obsolete products or packages and reduce warehouse inventories. The count-and-recount method may benefit a producer by decreasing resellers' inventories, making resellers more likely to place new orders. However, this method is often difficult to administer and may not appeal to resellers with small warehouses.

free merchandise A manufacturer's reward given to resellers for purchasing a stated quantity of products

Free Merchandise.   Manufacturers sometimes offer **free merchandise** to resellers that purchase a stated quantity of products. Occasionally free merchandise is used as payment for allowances provided through other sales promotion methods. To avoid handling and bookkeeping problems, the "free" merchandise usually takes the form of a reduced invoice.

merchandise allowance
A manufacturer's agreement to help resellers pay for special promotional efforts

Merchandise Allowances. A **merchandise allowance** is a manufacturer's agreement to pay resellers certain amounts of money for providing promotional efforts such as advertising or displays. This method is best suited to high-volume, high-profit, easily handled products. Its major drawback is that some retailers perform activities at a minimally acceptable level simply to obtain allowances. Before paying retailers, manufacturers usually verify their performance. Manufacturers hope that retailers' additional promotional efforts will yield substantial sales increases.

cooperative advertising
Sharing of media costs by manufacturer and retailer for advertising the manufacturer's products

Cooperative Advertising. **Cooperative advertising** is an arrangement whereby a manufacturer agrees to pay a certain amount of a retailer's media costs for advertising the manufacturer's products. The amount allowed is usually based on the quantities purchased. Before payment is made, a retailer must show proof that advertisements did appear. These payments give retailers additional funds for advertising. Some retailers exploit cooperative-advertising agreements by crowding too many products into one advertisement. Surprisingly, not all available cooperative-advertising dollars are used. Some retailers cannot afford to advertise; others can afford it but do not want to advertise. A large proportion of all cooperative-advertising dollars are spent on newspaper advertisements.

dealer listings Ads promoting a product and identifying retailers that sell it

Dealer Listings. **Dealer listings** are advertisements promoting a product and identifying participating retailers that sell the product. Dealer listings can influence retailers to carry the product, build traffic at the retail level, and encourage consumers to buy the product at participating dealers.

premium (push) money
Extra compensation to salespeople for pushing a line of goods

Premium (Push) Money. **Premium,** or **push, money** is additional compensation to salespeople by the manufacturer in order to push a line of goods. This method is appropriate when personal selling is an important part of the marketing effort; it is not effective for promoting products sold through self-service. The method often helps manufacturers obtain a commitment from the sales force, but it can be very expensive.

sales contest A means of motivating distributors, retailers, and salespeople by recognizing outstanding achievements

Sales Contests. A **sales contest** is designed to motivate distributors, retailers, and sales personnel by recognizing outstanding achievements. To be effective, this method must be equitable for all persons involved. One advantage is that it can achieve participation at all distribution levels. However, positive effects may be temporary, and prizes are usually expensive.

dealer loader A gift, often part of a display, offered to a retailer who purchases a specified quantity of merchandise

Dealer Loaders. A **dealer loader** is a gift to a retailer who purchases a specified quantity of merchandise. Often dealer loaders are used to obtain special display efforts from retailers by offering essential display parts as premiums. For example, a manufacturer might design a display that includes a sterling silver tray as a major component and give the tray to the retailer. Marketers use dealer loaders to obtain new distributors and to push larger quantities of goods.

Summary

Personal selling is the process of informing customers and persuading them to purchase products through paid personal communication in an exchange situation. The three general purposes of personal selling are finding prospects, persuading them to buy, and keeping customers satisfied.

Many salespeople, either consciously or unconsciously, move through a general selling process as they sell products. In prospecting, the salesperson develops a list of potential customers. Before contacting prospects, the salesperson conducts a preapproach that involves finding and analyzing information about prospects and their needs. The approach is the way in which a salesperson contacts potential customers. During the sales presentation, the salesperson must attract and hold the prospect's attention to stimulate interest in and desire for the product. If possible, the salesperson should handle objections as they arise. During the closing, the salesperson asks the prospect to buy the product or products. After a successful closing, the salesperson must follow up the sale.

In developing a sales force, marketing managers consider which types of salespeople will sell the firm's products most effectively. The three classifications of salespeople are order getters, order takers, and support personnel. Order getters inform both current customers and new prospects and persuade them to buy. Order takers seek repeat sales and fall into two categories: inside order takers and field order takers. Sales support personnel facilitate selling, but their duties usually extend beyond making sales. The three types of support personnel are missionary, trade, and technical salespeople.

Sales force management is an important determinant of a firm's success because the sales force is directly responsible for generating the organization's sales revenue. Major decision areas and activities are establishing sales force objectives; determining sales force size; recruiting, selecting, training, compensating, and motivating salespeople; managing sales territories; and controlling and evaluating sales force performance.

Sales objectives should be stated in precise, measurable terms and specify the time period and geographic areas involved. The size of the sales force must be adjusted occasionally because a firm's marketing plans change along with markets and forces in the marketing environment.

Recruiting and selecting salespeople involves attracting and choosing the right type of salesperson to maintain an effective sales force. When developing a training program, managers must consider a variety of dimensions, such as who should be trained, what should be taught, and how should training occur. Compensation of sales-

people involves formulating and administrating a compensation plan that attracts, motivates, and retains the right types of salespeople. Motivation of salespeople should allow the firm to attain high productivity. Managing sales territories focuses on such factors as size, shape, routing, and scheduling. To control and evaluate sales force performance, sales managers must use information obtained through salespeople's call reports, customer feedback, and invoices.

Sales promotion is an activity or a material (or both) that acts as a direct inducement, offering added value or incentive for the product to resellers, salespeople, or consumers. Marketers use sales promotion to identify and attract new customers, introduce new products, and increase reseller inventories. Sales promotion techniques fall into two general categories: consumer and trade. Consumer sales promotion methods encourage consumers to trade at specific stores or try a specific product. These sales promotion methods include coupons, demonstrations, frequent-user incentives, point-of-purchase displays, free samples, money refunds and rebates, premiums, cents-off offers, consumer contests and games, and consumer sweepstakes. Trade sales promotion techniques can motivate resellers to handle a manufacturer's products and market those products aggressively. These sales promotion techniques include buy-back allowances, buying allowances, scan-back allowances, count-and-recount, free merchandise, merchandise allowances, cooperative advertising, dealer listings, premium (or push) money, sales contests, and dealer loaders.

Important Terms

Personal selling
Prospecting
Approach
Closing
Order getter
Order taker
Support personnel
Missionary salesperson
Trade salesperson
Technical salesperson
Recruiting
Straight salary
  compensation plan
Straight commission
  compensation plan
Combination compensation
  plan
Sales promotion
Consumer sales promotion
  methods
Trade sales promotion
  methods
Coupons

Demonstrations
Point-of-purchase (P-O-P)
  materials
Free samples
Money refunds
Rebates
Premiums
Cents-off offers
Consumer contests and
  games
Consumer sweepstakes
Buy-back allowance
Buying allowance
Scan-back allowance
Count-and-recount
Free merchandise
Merchandise allowance
Cooperative advertising
Dealer listings
Premium (push) money
Sales contest
Dealer loader

Discussion and Review Questions

1. What is personal selling? How does personal selling differ from other types of promotional activities?
2. What are the primary purposes of personal selling?
3. Identify the elements of the personal selling process. Must a salesperson include all these elements when selling a product to a customer? Why or why not?
4. How does a salesperson find and evaluate prospects? Do you consider any of these methods to be ethically questionable? Explain.
5. Are order getters more aggressive or creative than order takers? Why or why not?
6. Identify several characteristics of effective sales objectives.
7. How should a sales manager establish criteria for selecting sales personnel? What do you think are the general characteristics of a good salesperson?
8. What major issues or questions should management consider when developing a training program for the sales force?
9. Explain the major advantages and disadvantages of the three basic methods of compensating salespeople. In general, which method would you prefer? Why?

10. What major factors should be taken into account when designing the size and shape of a sales territory?
11. How does a sales manager, who cannot be with each salesperson in the field on a daily basis, control the performance of sales personnel?
12. What is sales promotion? Why is it used?
13. For each of the following, identify and describe three techniques, and give several examples: (a) consumer sales promotion methods and (b) trade sales promotion methods.
14. What types of sales promotion methods have you observed recently? Comment on their effectiveness.

Application Questions

1. Briefly describe an experience you have had with a salesperson at a clothing store or an automobile dealership. Describe the steps used by the salesperson. Did the salesperson skip any steps? What did the salesperson do well? Not so well?
2. Refer to your answer to question 1. Would you describe the salesperson as an order getter, an order taker, or a support salesperson? Why? Did the salesperson perform more than one of these functions?
3. Leap Athletic Shoe, Inc., a newly formed company, is in the process of developing a sales strategy. Market research indicates sales management should segment the market into five regional territories. The sales potential for the North region is $1.2 million, for the West region $1 million, for the Central region $1.3 million, for the South Central region $1.1 million, and for the Southeast region $1 million. The firm wishes to maintain some control over the training and sales processes because of the unique features of its new product line, but Leap marketers realize the salespeople need to be fairly aggressive in their efforts to break into these markets. They would like to provide the incentive needed for the extra selling effort. What type of sales force compensation method would you recommend to Leap? Why?

4. Consumer sales promotions aim to increase the sales of a particular retail store or product. Identify a familiar type of retail store or product. Recommend at least three sales promotion methods that should be used to promote the store or product. Explain why you would use these methods.

5. Producers use trade sales promotions to encourage resellers to promote their products more effectively. Identify which method or methods of sales promotion a producer might use in the following situations, and explain why the method would be appropriate.
   a. A golf ball manufacturer wants to encourage retailers to add a new type of golf ball to current product offerings.
   b. A life insurance company wants to increase sales of its universal life products, which have been lagging recently (the company has little control over sales activities).
   c. A light bulb manufacturer with an overproduction of 100-watt bulbs wants to encourage its grocery store chain resellers to increase their bulb inventories.

Internet
Exercise & Resources

Visit **www.prideferrell.com** for resources to help you master the material in this chapter, plus materials that will help you expand your marketing knowledge, including: Internet exercise updates, ACE self-tests, hotlinks to companies featured in this chapter, and much more.

TerrAlign

TerrAlign offers consulting services and software products designed to help a firm maximize control and deployment of its field sales representatives. Review its website at

http://www.terralign.com

1. Identify three features of TerrAlign software that are likely to benefit salespeople.

2. Identify three features of TerrAlign software that are likely to benefit sales managers.

3. Why might field sales professionals object to the use of software from TerrAlign?

▢ VIDEO CASE 19.1
Selling Bicycles and More at Wheelworks

From tricycles to tandems, Wheelworks sells just about every kind of bicycle. Founded in the 1970s, this three-store chain in suburban Boston has been named one of the top ten in the United States for more than a decade. The sales floor at each Wheelworks location boasts dozens of LeMond, Cannondale, Trek, and other brand-name bicycles for mountain biking, triathlon, cyclocross, touring, fitness, and other cycling activities. The chain currently markets more than 10,000 bicycles and brings in $10.5 million in sales revenue every year, with a staff of 45 full-time employees plus 55 additional employees to handle seasonal sales spikes.

Wheelworks' salespeople are cycling enthusiasts who are extremely knowledgeable about the company's products and enjoy sharing what they know with customers. Some were recruited through referrals and personal contacts with store staff who participate in local cycling groups. Others were hired after replying to job openings posted on the Wheelworks website. New salespeople hired for the main store go through a formal training program. At the two branch stores, experienced salespeople act as mentors to new hires in an informal buddy system that supplements on-the-job training. All of the firm's salespeople have the opportunity to gain more product knowledge and ask questions when manufacturers' representatives visit. In addition, they can take classes to become certified in technical skills such as fitting bicycles.

Wheelworks doesn't believe in scripted sales pitches. Instead its salespeople focus on building relationships by asking questions, providing information, and making suggestions to match the right product to the right customer. Kurt Begemann, a competitive racer who sells at Wheelworks, says that "it's better to be seen as a teacher than to be seen as a salesperson." To keep their product knowledge updated, salespeople attend three to five in-store training clinics every month, each focusing on a particular product, product category, or manufacturer. From time to time, the sales manager appeals to his team's competitive spirit to spur higher closing rates as salespeople strive to match or exceed their colleagues' sales accomplishments.

Just as the salespeople work hard to match the right product to the right customer, Doug Shoemaker, the sales manager, works hard to match the right salesperson to the right customer. When a new Wheelworks customer begins browsing the sales floor, Shoemaker makes the initial approach, quickly sizes up the customer's needs and interests, and then brings in the salesperson he believes will work best with that customer. Even language poses no barrier, because staff members speak French, Italian, Spanish, and Chinese.

After a sale is closed, sales personnel add that customer's name and address to the firm's mailing list to receive announcements of upcoming special events and sales. The store also invites customers to bring their new bicycles back for a free tune-up after 30 days. This allows salespeople to follow up by checking on customer satisfaction and making any necessary adjustments.

Wheelworks sales personnel receive competitive retail wages and benefits such as health insurance coverage, vacation and sick pay, profit sharing, and store discounts. They are also rewarded with seasonal bonuses tied to the company's sales achievements rather than to individual sales records. Sales manager Shoemaker stresses that this compensation method gives his salespeople the freedom to sell

the right product for each customer's needs rather than trying to earn a special incentive by selling an item that's not right for the customer. The salespeople also prefer this compensation method. Salesperson Juliana Popper says Wheelworks customers "don't feel preyed upon" because they know the salespeople aren't trying to make more money by selling higher-priced bicycles.

Each salesperson sets goals for personal development as well as for store sales contributions. Store managers sit down to formally evaluate the performance of new salespeople six months after the salespeople are hired, and then on an annual basis. But sales personnel don't have to wait months to find out how they are doing. Because Wheelworks is not a huge organization, managers and peers constantly provide informal feedback and support. And salespeople who turn out to be

stronger or more interested in nonsales activities can easily transfer, because at Wheelworks everybody, from the repair technicians to the graphic designer, has an important role to play in the personal selling process.[14]

QUESTIONS FOR DISCUSSION

1. Which of the three types of sales force compensation methods does Wheelworks use? Should Wheelworks change to another method? Explain.
2. How does Wheelworks motivate sales personnel?
3. What type of salesperson is Kurt Begemann? Explain.
4. Evaluate Kurt Begemann's statement that "it's better to be seen as a teacher than to be seen as a salesperson."

CASE 19.2
Sales Promotion Puts the Fizz into Dr Pepper

How can a soft-drink company get its message across when its advertising budget is much smaller than the budgets of its deep-pocketed competitors? For Dr Pepper, pitted against Mountain Dew and Sprite in the noncola soft-drink category, the way to put the fizz into sales is through sales promotion. Dr Pepper has scored solid market share increases for more than a decade with creative sales promotion efforts targeted at light and occasional users. The purpose is to encourage these customers to purchase more rather than trying to get non–Dr Pepper drinkers to switch. The company also uses trade sales promotion methods to support both its bottlers and the retailers that carry its products.

Sports play an important role in Dr Pepper's sales promotion activities. The company sponsors the Washington Erving Motorsports' Ford Taurus racecar on the NASCAR circuit. Owned by former NFL great Joe Washington and former NBA star Julius "Dr. J" Erving, the car sports a bold Dr Pepper logo on its hood, visible to spectators and television viewers throughout each race. For a small fee, local bottlers can park the racecar at key retail sites to generate excitement for the brand.

In addition, Dr Pepper uses special sales promotion efforts during the annual Southeastern Conference championship football game, putting its logo on everything from T-shirts and cups to coolers

and banners. In one recent year, consumers were invited to win free game tickets by checking under the caps of specially marked Dr Pepper bottles. Ticket winners were then entered into a drawing for the $1 Million Pepper Pass Challenge, which invited a consumer to try throwing a 40-yard pass during halftime (the consolation prize was a check for $10,000). During the championship weekend, the company handed out 100,000 product samples. On the trade side, Dr Pepper supported this promotion by providing retailers with shelf labels, refrigerator case decorations, and display signs. Among the other sporting events around which Dr Pepper builds sales promotions are college golf tournaments and college football games. Retailers get involved by creating point-of-purchase displays touting the Dr Pepper promotion. The best displays earn store employees free tickets to the events or free merchandise.

Dr Pepper is a long-time sponsor of the Hispanic Heritage Awards, and it often creates special promotions linked to these awards. In one recent tie-in promotion, called *Pinta Sus Suenos*—Paint Your Dreams—the company invited Hispanic teenagers to compete by submitting their artwork. First prize was a trip for four to the Hispanic Heritage Awards ceremony in Washington, DC. Other winners received U.S. savings bonds, and their schools received grants to buy art supplies. In addition, Dr Pepper displayed the winning works on local billboards and on its website.

College students are a particular target for Dr Pepper. As the purveyor of the official soft drink of the Collegiate Players Tour, Dr Pepper can park its colorful van in a prominent place during the 16 golf tournaments played at U.S. colleges and country clubs during the summer months—a peak period for soft-drink consumption. In this way, the company reinforces brand awareness and encourages more purchases.

Although soft-drink companies have traditionally targeted students, sales promotion activities geared toward children have drawn fire in some areas. Critics worry that such promotional efforts encourage youngsters to drink too many soft drinks—an average of three cans daily, according to some studies. Not long ago, Dr Pepper was criticized for paying the Grapevine-Colleyville school district near Dallas to paint the Dr. Pepper logo on two school rooftops that airline passengers could see when passing overhead. The school district also received more than $3 million in exchange for making only Dr Pepper drinks available in its schools for the next decade. A spokesperson for the school district explained that such agreements are not new. "We've had exclusive bottling agreements for about twenty-five years in the state," she said. "The thing that is new is that instead of having each campus determine what bottler it wants to stock its soda machine, districts are saying, "We"ll make you a deal for all of our campuses, and in return we get some extra funding."'

Despite this controversy, Dr Pepper and its bottlers aim to be good corporate citizens, donating free products, logo merchandise, and money for many community events and fundraisers. For example, a Dr Pepper bottler recently teamed up with Wal-Mart to raise money for the Red Cross by sponsoring a country music charity concert in Nashville. As another example, the company and its bottlers raised more than $35,000 for the central Mississippi March of Dimes by sponsoring a golf tournament fundraiser.

Because retailers account for a good chunk of Dr Pepper's sales, the company supports its consumer sales promotion activities with a constant stream of trade sales promotion efforts that boost its products' point-of-purchase visibility. For example, a North Carolina store displayed 400 cases of Dr Pepper products as part of its Santa's Workshop exhibit. Thanks in part to this promotion, holiday sales of Dr Pepper rose 24 percent at that outlet.

Dr Pepper's website plays an integral role in the company's sales promotion efforts. In addition to inviting online entries to games and sweepstakes, the website allows visitors to download a variety of personal computer screensavers, each emblazoned with the Dr Pepper name and logo. The website provides a means of bringing sales promotion activities directly into the customer's home or office. As Dr Pepper's sales increases attest, properly targeted and well-designed sales promotions can help any company compete against much larger rivals.[15]

QUESTIONS FOR DISCUSSION
1. Identify the major sales promotion methods Dr Pepper uses.
2. Why does Dr Pepper use both trade and consumer sales promotion methods?
3. How would you recommend that Dr Pepper respond to those who believe sales promotion efforts should not be targeted at students younger than college age?
4. Which trade sales promotion methods do you think are most suitable for Dr Pepper? Explain your answer.

STRATEGIC CASE 5

The American Dairy Industry: Got Promotion?

A television commercial begins by panning a roomful of papers and artifacts about the notorious duel between Aaron Burr and Alexander Hamilton. At a table sits a man spreading peanut butter on a slice of bread. As he takes a big bite, the radio announces the day's random telephone trivia question, worth $10,000 to the person who answers correctly: "Who shot Alexander Hamilton in that famous duel?" The phone rings and, of course, the man knows the answer. However, thanks to his mouthful of peanut butter, the words come out sounding like "Awuh Bwuh." Frantically he tries to pour a glass of milk to wash down his sticky sandwich, but the carton is empty. The radio announcer hangs up. As a dial tone sounds and the scene fades, on the screen appears this phrase: "Got Milk?" In magazine advertisements and on billboards from New York to Hollywood, celebrities like Britney Spears and Pete Sampras proudly wear something mothers have been wiping off children's faces for centuries: milk mustaches. These examples of creative advertising for milk illustrate only a small portion of the American dairy industry's aggressive promotional program designed to increase milk consumption.

Dairy Promoters Struggle to Make Milk Popular

For generations, milk was synonymous with health and nutrition in the minds of Americans. What conveyed the all-American image more than the milkman delivering fresh milk at dawn or Mom pouring tall, cold glasses of milk to go with her children's after-school snack? Although these images may endure, U.S. milk consumption started declining in the 1960s, largely the result of increasing concern about healthier eating and the perception that milk contains large amounts of fat.

During the 1980s, national milk promoters tried to counter those perceptions with advertising that touted milk's healthy attributes. Fresh faces and wholesome beauties drank frothy glasses of milk and assured consumers, "Milk. It Does a Body Good." Research revealed the ads successfully heightened awareness of milk's healthy qualities and convinced many Americans that they should be drinking milk. However, although Americans agreed milk did a body good, each of them continued to drink about 16 fewer gallons of it every year. To counter the failure of past efforts, various organizations within the dairy industry—including the National Dairy Board, the American Dairy Association, the National Dairy Promotion and Research Board, the United Dairy Industry Association, the National Fluid Milk Processors' Association, and various state and local organizations—have banded together in an all-out effort to promote milk as the perfect drink for people of all ages.

Advertising Efforts

Because milk is generally not seen as a trendy drink, competing with soft drinks is bound to be a losing battle. Therefore, advertising agencies for the dairy industry decided to position milk as an accompaniment to foods that just aren't the same without it. The Got Milk? campaign was born because milk, not Diet Coke or Snapple, is the drink people want with brownies or breakfast cereal. A number of television spots kicked off the $72 million campaign, each one depicting the predicaments of people who need milk but don't have it on hand. A man with a mouthful of chocolate cake pounds on a vending machine that refuses to release a container of milk. A man who believes he has gone to heaven realizes he has gone in the other direction when he discovers that all the milk cartons in a giant refrigerator are empty. Although the campaign relies predominantly on television, it also uses billboards showing brownies, cookies, and peanut butter sandwiches missing big bites and the simple tag line "Got Milk?" These television spots and billboards never mention calcium, strong bones, or healthy skin.

The Got Milk? campaign has won many awards, including an Obie for excellence in outdoor advertising. Follow-up studies show that three months after the premiere of the Got Milk? campaign, consumption of milk in one 24-hour period rose 2 percent. Newer tie-in spots with Nestlé, General Mills, Nabisco, and Kraft focus on foods that people wouldn't think of eating without milk. For example, the long-suffering Trix Rabbit, who has tried all his animated life to steal Trix cereal, finally succeeds. The victory is hollow, however, because when he gets home, he finds he is out of milk.

Unlike the Got Milk? campaign, the dairy industry's $52 million milk mustache advertising campaign does focus on the health advantages of drinking skim and low-fat milk. Ads that run in major monthly magazines feature sports figures, musicians, movie stars, and television personalities wearing very noticeable milk mustaches. In slightly humorous ways, each ad highlights a particular health feature that milk provides and includes the tag line "Milk. What a surprise!"

Follow-up research reveals the milk mustache campaign is having an impact on how people perceive milk. In an independent nationwide survey, *USA Today* discovered that of the 523 women polled, 60 percent had seen the ads and 69 percent considered them effective. In addition, the number of respondents who believe milk is good after exercising rose 22 percent, and the number who believe milk is an adult drink rose 22 percent.

Encouraged by the campaign's success, the dairy industry has expanded the programs' target audience to include young adults. Ads in teen and men's magazines focus on getting people to substitute milk for water in preparing foods like soups and hot chocolate. Mustaches in those ads are colored instead of white. Newer ads, featuring the cartoon world's PowerPuff Girls and SpongeBob Squarepants with orange mustaches (for orange-flavored milk) and pink mustaches (for strawberry-flavored milk), are geared toward building milk consumption among school-age children.

Sales Promotion Efforts

To stimulate milk sales and reinforce its advertising message, the dairy industry developed several sales promotion efforts, including contests, sweepstakes, premiums, and rebates. The Milk Mustache Contest asked people to submit photos of themselves wearing milk mustaches. Prizes included cameras and film, with the winner's picture appearing in *Life* magazine. By sending in their answers to three "Test Your Milk Mustache IQ" questions, consumers entered a sweepstakes for a $500 health club membership. Chocolate milk drinkers could receive a premium of 15

free removable tattoos by sending in proofs of purchase from two gallons of chocolate milk or a self-liquidating premium of a cow puppet with proofs of purchase and $4.50. To receive a $13 rebate off the price of Reebok sports and fitness videos, milk drinkers simply submitted proof-of-purchase seals from milk cartons.

Public Relations Efforts

In addition to the extremely visible advertising campaigns and very successful sales promotion activities, the dairy industry conducts lower-profile but equally important public relations efforts. These campaigns keep milk in the spotlight and make it easier for people to learn about milk's positive health attributes. The milk mustache campaign generated a great deal of publicity, showing up on David Letterman's Top 10 list, as an answer on the "Jeopardy" game show, in Jay Leno's "Tonight Show" monologue, and as a story on the "Saturday Night Live" Weekend Update. When a character in an episode of Fox Broadcasting's family program "Party of Five" looked in the refrigerator and asked, "Got milk?" the resulting publicity augmented the national launch of the Got Milk? print and television campaign.

The dairy industry's public relations efforts also include organized events to generate news about milk and an extensive public education program. National Milk Mustache Week, officially proclaimed in major U.S. cities such as New York, Chicago, San Francisco, St. Louis, and Seattle, is a week-long celebration of milk's contribution to women's health. The Milk Mustache March, which takes place in New York City, also draws media attention. In addition, the milk industry has formed a promotional partnership with the National Basketball Association. Now NBA all-stars participate in Got Milk? promotions and NBA promotions are part of the Chocolate Milk Mustache Mobile Tour, an interactive exhibition that travels to 100 U.S. cities every year.

The industry's toll-free hotline, 1–800-WHY-MILK, provides information about milk ranging from nutritional data to recipes. Consumers who call in can listen to recorded messages on milk-related topics, get answers to specific questions from registered dieticians and nurses, and order free informative brochures such as *Trim with Skim; Milk, What a Surprise;* and *Milk Matters to Mothers-To-Be.* In its first year of operation, the toll-free milk line received 72,000 calls, and to date more than 7 million brochures have been distributed. The Why Milk? website (http://www.whymilk.com) also offers educational information and entertaining contests.

Got Results?

For years, Americans harbored a number of negative attitudes toward milk: milk is fatty; milk is a kid's drink; milk doesn't taste good; milk causes heart disease. Thanks to the American dairy industry's promotional efforts, these misconceptions are finally fading. For example, more young women believe milk is good for their health, and more people identify milk as a thirst-quenching drink after a workout.

Whether positive attitudes toward milk will translate into long-term increased milk consumption is not yet clear. In recent years, milk consumption has stopped declining and is even increasing among certain market segments. However, the executive director of the California Milk Processor Board emphasizes that although the industry's promotional efforts "basically stopped the hemorrhaging," they won't spur significant consumption increases "until the milk processors come out with a wider variety of new packages, products, and flavors."

QUESTIONS FOR DISCUSSION

1. What types of promotional objectives is the American dairy industry attempting to achieve?
2. Assess the dairy industry's approach of advertising milk as an indispensable accompaniment to foods that traditionally go with a glassful of milk, such as brownies and cereal.
3. Why have the milk mustache and Got Milk? campaigns generated significant publicity?
4. Do you believe the American dairy industry's current promotional efforts will increase long-term milk consumption? Explain your answer.

Pricing Decisions

I f an organization is to provide a satisfying marketing mix, the price must be acceptable to target market members. Pricing decisions can have numerous effects on other parts of the marketing mix. For example price can influence how customers perceive the product, what types of marketing institutions are used to distribute the product, and how the product is promoted. Chapter 20 discusses the importance of price and looks at some characteristics of price and nonprice competition. It explores fundamental concepts such as demand, elasticity, marginal analysis, and breakeven analysis. Then it examines the major factors that affect marketers' pricing decisions. Chapter 21 discusses six major stages in the process marketers use to establish prices.

20 Pricing Concepts

OBJECTIVES

- To understand the nature and importance of price
- To identify the characteristics of price and nonprice competition
- To explore demand curves and the price elasticity of demand
- To examine the relationships among demand, costs, and profits
- To describe key factors that may influence marketers' pricing decisions
- To consider issues affecting the pricing of products for business markets

Who is the world's leading personal computer manufacturer? IBM was the market leader during part of the 1980s and again in the early 1990s. Then Compaq took over the coveted rank of the world's number one PC maker, while up-and-coming rival Dell Computer used numerous effective marketing techniques to wrench the top slot away. After Compaq enjoyed seven years at the top, Dell pulled ahead to become the global market share leader in 2001. But the rankings could change again at any time, thanks to an ongoing PC price war. In the high-stakes world of PC marketing, a market share increase of even a fraction of a percentage point translates into hundreds of thousands of units sold. This is why Dell, Compaq, and Gateway are jockeying for position, using price competition to score market share gains.

Inside the PC Price War

Because Dell deals directly with most customers and makes PCs to order, its costs are generally lower than those of Compaq and Gateway, which allows Dell to be very price competitive. In its bid for higher market share, Dell has been steadily cutting its prices and adding new low-price entry-level models. Over one year, the average price of a Dell PC fell from $2,300 to $2,000, and it continues to drop. Dell maintains a separate sales force to call on business customers, who are a particular focus of Dell's reduced prices. Salespeople have fanned out across the country offering special pricing to companies that buy in volume. Some customers are switching to Dell, but some are using Dell's offers to negotiate lower pricing from competitors. Either way, customers are benefiting from the lower prices as the intense price competition continues. "This strategy is working," says Dell's co-president. "We are not anticipating pulling back on our aggressive stance."

Compaq has been forced to respond with its own price cuts to defend its market share and remain competitive. In turn, these price cuts have lowered Compaq's sales revenues and profit margins, even as worldwide PC demand grows more slowly than in previous years. So Compaq is taking a longer-term approach by refocusing its efforts on larger computers and servers for corporate customers, a more profitable market. "There's a lot of chatter about PC price wars, but chasing prices is a very short-term strategy, and we're chasing profitable growth," explains Compaq's CEO.

Gateway, which recently lost market share as Dell strengthened its leadership position, is determined to use the PC price war to its advantage. One recent advertising campaign used the slogan "PC Price War? Cool." The campaign put the spotlight on Gateway's promise to beat the advertised price of any major competitor. But competitive pricing parity may not be enough to propel Gateway into a higher market share position as the price war continues and customers become accustomed to paying ever-lower prices for ever-higher computing power.[1]

Dell uses pricing as a tool to compete against its major competitors. However, to compete, Dell's rivals also employ pricing as a major competitive tool. In some industries, there are firms that are very successful but don't have the lowest prices. The best price is not always the lowest price.

In this chapter, we focus first on the nature of price and its importance to marketers. We then consider some characteristics of price and nonprice competition. Next, we discuss several pricing-related concepts such as demand, elasticity, and break-even analysis. Then, we examine in some detail the numerous factors that can influence pricing decisions. Finally, we discuss selected issues related to the pricing of products for business markets.

The Nature of Price

The purpose of marketing is to facilitate satisfying exchange relationships between buyer and seller. **Price** is the value exchanged for products in a marketing exchange. In most marketing situations, the price is very evident and buyer and seller are aware of the amount of value each must give up to complete the exchange.[2] However, price does not always take the form of money paid. In fact, trading of products, or **barter,** is the oldest form of exchange. Money may or may not be involved.

price   Value exchanged for products in a marketing exchange

barter   The trading of products

Buyers' interest in price stems from their expectations about the usefulness of a product or the satisfaction they may derive from it. Because buyers have limited resources, they must allocate those resources to obtain the products they most desire. Buyers must decide whether the utility gained in an exchange is worth the buying power sacrificed. Almost anything of value—ideas, services, rights, and goods—can be assessed by a price. In our society, financial price is the measurement of value commonly used in exchanges.

Terms Used to Describe Price

Value can be expressed in different terms for different marketing situations. For instance, students pay *tuition* for a college education. Automobile insurance companies charge a *premium* for protection from the cost of injuries or repairs stemming from an automobile accident. An officer who stops you for speeding writes a ticket that requires you to pay a *fine.* A lawyer who defends you charges a *fee.* If you use a taxi, the driver charges a *fare.* A *toll* is charged for the use of bridges or toll roads. *Rent* is paid for the use of equipment or an apartment. A *commission* is remitted to a broker for the sale of real estate. *Dues* are paid for membership in a club or group. A *deposit* is made to hold or lay away merchandise. *Tips* help pay waitpersons for their services. *Interest* is charged for a loan, and *taxes* are paid for government services. Although price may be expressed in a variety of ways, its purpose is to quantify and express the value of the items in a marketing exchange.

The Importance of Price to Marketers

As pointed out in Chapter 11, developing a product may be a lengthy process. It takes time to plan promotion and to communicate benefits. Distribution usually requires a long-term commitment to dealers that will handle the product. Often price is the only thing a marketer can change quickly to respond to changes in demand or to actions of competitors. Under certain circumstances, however, the price variable may be relatively inflexible.

Price is a key element in the marketing mix because it relates directly to the generation of total revenue. The following equation is an important one for the entire organization:

$$\text{Profit} = \text{Total Revenue} - \text{Total Costs}$$

or

$$\text{Profits} = (\text{Price} \times \text{Quantity Sold}) - \text{Total Costs}$$

Prices affect an organization's profits in several ways because it is a key component of the profit equation and can be a major determinant of the quantities sold. Furthermore, total costs are influenced by quantities sold.

Because price has a psychological impact on customers, marketers can use it symbolically. By pricing high, they can emphasize the quality of a product and try to increase the prestige associated with its ownership. By lowering a price, marketers can emphasize a bargain and attract customers who go out of their way to save a small amount of money. Thus, as this chapter details, price can have strong effects on a firm's sales and profitability.

Price and Nonprice Competition

The competitive environment strongly influences the marketing mix decisions associated with a product. Pricing decisions are often made according to the price or nonprice competitive situation in a particular market. Price competition exists when consumers have difficulty distinguishing competitive offerings and marketers emphasize low prices. Nonprice competition involves a focus on marketing mix elements other than price.

Price Competition

price competition
Emphasizing price and matching or beating competitors' prices

When engaging in **price competition,** a marketer emphasizes price as an issue and matches or beats the prices of competitors. To compete effectively on a price basis, a firm should be the low-cost seller of the product. If all firms producing the same product charge the same price for it, the firm with the lowest costs is the most profitable. Firms that stress low price as a key marketing mix element tend to market standardized products. A seller competing on price may change prices frequently or at least must be willing and able to do so. For example, Best Buy, a retail consumer electronic leader, engages in price competition. To attain sales growth, Best Buy has had to reduce its prices.[3] Whenever competitors change their prices, the seller usually responds quickly and aggressively.

Price competition gives a marketer flexibility. Prices can be altered to account for changes in the firm's costs or in demand for the product. If competitors try to gain market share by cutting prices, an organization competing on a price basis can react quickly to such efforts. However, a major drawback of price competition is that competitors too have the flexibility to adjust prices. If they quickly match or beat a company's price cuts, a price war may ensue. For example, in 1999 Sprint announced a nighttime long-distance rate of 5 cents per minute. About a month later, MCI matched Sprint's rate, and within a few weeks after that, AT&T, due to reduced revenues, cut its long-distance charges to 7 cents a minute all day, every day, for a fee of $5.95 per month. On the day of AT&T's announcement, the stock prices for all three companies dropped significantly. These long-distance carriers do not focus on service, quality, or other nonprice dimensions

At $999 the days of black & white are numbered!

Minolta Co., Ltd., Osaka, Japan

MINOLTA-QMS introduces the magicolor® 2200 DeskLaser.
The first color laser for the price of a black & white! Including free networking!

Sharp, beautiful prints. High-speed output. By far the best color laser printer in its class. All for a price you're used to paying for a black-and-white laser printer—just **$999***.
So, if your colleagues bark for a new printer, point them to the magicolor 2200 DeskLaser. Just go to www.minolta-qms.com/a/2200dl/999.html for a dealer in your neighborhood, or call 1-800-435-0966.

FREE Color 4 Free

The magicolor 2200 DeskLaser
■ up to 5 color or 20 black & white pages per minute
■ 1200 dpi print resolution ■ Windows® Plug and Play
■ automatic two-sided printing (optional)

© 2001 MINOLTA-QMS, Inc. The MINOLTA-QMS logo and magicolor are trademarks of MINOLTA-QMS, Inc.
All other trademarks or registered trademarks are the property of their respective owners. *Estimated street price after mail-in rebate.
Actual reseller prices may vary. Rebate offer valid 1/15/01 – 9/30/01 or while promotional supplies last.

COMPUSA   amazon.com   buy.com   COMPUTERS 4 sure

MINOLTA QMS
The essentials of imaging

www.minolta-qms.com

Price Competition
Minolta-QMS competes on the basis of price regarding its 2200 DeskLaser color laser printer.

that might add value to their services. They compete mainly on the basis of price reductions, per-second call billing, and free calls.[4] Chronic price wars such as this one can substantially weaken organizations.

Nonprice Competition

nonprice competition
Emphasizing factors other than price to distinguish a product from competing brands

Nonprice competition occurs when a seller decides not to focus on price and instead emphasizes distinctive product features, service, product quality, promotion, packaging, or other factors to distinguish its product from competing brands. Thus, nonprice competition allows a company to increase its brand's unit sales through means other than changing the brand's price. A major advantage of nonprice competition is that a firm can build customer loyalty toward its brand. If customers prefer a brand because of nonprice factors, they may not be easily lured away by competing firms and brands. In contrast, when price is the primary reason customers buy a particular brand, a competitor is often able to attract these customers through price cuts. However, some surveys show that a fairly small proportion of customers base their purchase decisions solely on price.[5]

Nonprice competition is effective only under certain conditions. A company must be able to distinguish its brand through unique product features, higher product quality, promotion, packaging, or excellent customer service. Buyers not only must be able to perceive these distinguishing characteristics but must also view them as important. The distinguishing features that set a particular brand apart from competitors should be difficult, if not impossible, for competitors to imitate. Finally, the organization must extensively promote the distinguishing characteristics of the

BUILDING CUSTOMER RELATIONSHIPS

Do Low Prices Build e-Loyalty?

Throughout the Internet's short history, many e-businesses have come to believe that online customers are interested only in paying the lowest possible prices. Now that myth has been exploded by research showing that companies can more effectively strengthen e-loyalty and counteract price sensitivity by building trust and enhancing the customer's shopping experience.

When the consulting firm Bain & Company studied e-loyalty, it found that online shoppers are generally more interested in convenience than in price and tend to be loyal to sites that fulfill the promise of simplifying the buying process. Therefore, e-businesses need to build trust among new customers by projecting an image of reliability and responsiveness. In return, as customers learn to trust a site, they become willing to provide more personal information, make repeat purchases, and voluntarily refer new customers. Industrial supply firm Grainger, for example, provides a convenient search tool and knowledgeable phone representatives to help business customers find just the right products among the 1 million items available on its website. Customers spend less time searching for what they want, and they can check out quickly—time-saving benefits they value

more than paying the rock-bottom price for a particular product.

In another study, McKinsey & Company, a consulting firm, found that few online shoppers take the time to compare prices on every product they want to buy. In fact, 89 percent of book buyers and 84 percent of toy buyers actually buy at the first site they visit rather than clicking from site to site seeking the lowest price. As long as they perceive a site's prices to be within a reasonable range, customers will go ahead and make the purchase. What consumers consider a reasonable price range varies from product to product, however. McKinsey found that although e-businesses could raise prices up to 17 percent on brand name beauty products without losing customers, buyers balked at a price increase of less than 1 percent on certain financial services.

To avoid a backlash, e-businesses need to conduct ongoing research to analyze each segment's price sensitivity and to carefully test customer reaction before implementing price changes. With the right pricing and the right mix of trust and convenience, companies can attract new customers and strengthen e-loyalty year after year to build sales and profits.

brand to establish its superiority and set it apart from competitors in the minds of buyers.

Even a marketer that is competing on a nonprice basis cannot ignore competitors' prices. It must be aware of them and sometimes be prepared to price its brand near or slightly above competing brands. Therefore, price remains a crucial marketing mix component even in environments that call for nonprice competition.

Analysis of Demand

Determining the demand for a product is the responsibility of marketing managers, who are aided in this task by marketing researchers and forecasters. Marketing research and forecasting techniques yield estimates of sales potential, or the quantity of a product that could be sold during a specific period. These estimates are helpful in establishing the relationship between a product's price and the quantity demanded.

The Demand Curve

For most products, the quantity demanded goes up as the price goes down, and as the price goes up, the quantity demanded goes down. Intel, for example, knows that lowering prices boosts demand for its Pentium PC chips. By cutting the price of its sophisticated Pentium 4 chip from $795 to $519 in less than five months, Intel was able to keep sales growing even as the PC market suffered a slowdown.[6] Thus, an inverse relationship exists between price and quantity demanded. As long as the marketing environment and buyers' needs, ability (purchasing power), willingness, and authority to buy remain stable, this fundamental inverse relationship holds.

demand curve A graph of the quantity of products expected to be sold at various prices if other factors remain constant

Figure 20.1 illustrates the effect of one variable—price—on the quantity demanded. The classic **demand curve** (D_1) is a graph of the quantity of products expected to be sold at various prices if other factors remain constant.[7] It illustrates that as price falls, the quantity demanded usually rises. Demand depends on other factors in the marketing mix, including product quality, promotion, and distribution. An improvement in any of these factors may cause a shift to, say, demand curve D_2. In such a case, an increased quantity (Q_2) will be sold at the same price (P).

There are many types of demand, and not all conform to the classic demand curve shown in Figure 20.1. Prestige products, such as selected perfumes and jewelry, seem to sell better at high prices than at low ones. These products are desirable partly because their expense makes buyers feel elite. If the price fell drastically and many people owned these products, they would lose some of their appeal.

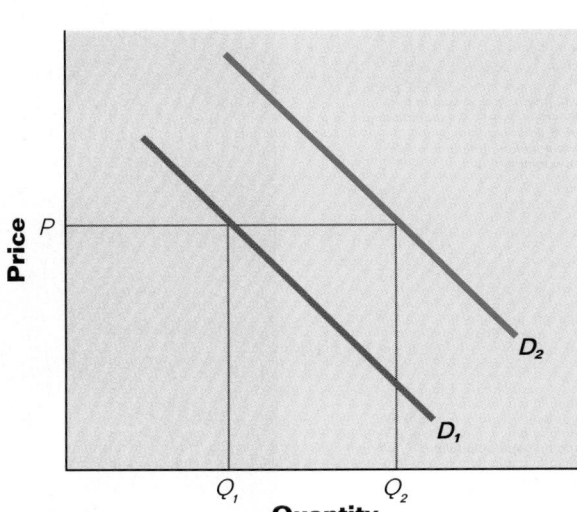

FIGURE 20.1
Demand Curve Illustrating the Price/Quantity Relationship and Increase in Demand

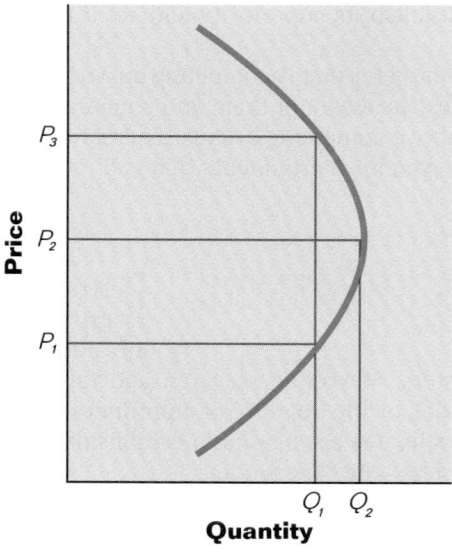

FIGURE 20.2
Demand Curve Illustrating the Relationship Between Price and Quantity for Prestige Products

The demand curve in Figure 20.2 shows the relationship between price and quantity demanded for prestige products. Quantity demanded is greater, not less, at higher prices. For a certain price range—from P_1 to P_2—the quantity demanded (Q_1) goes up to Q_2. After a certain point, however, raising the price backfires. If the price goes too high, the quantity demanded goes down. The figure shows that if the price is raised from P_2 to P_3, the quantity demanded goes back down from Q_2 to Q_1.

Prestige Products
This $8,500 television from Bang & Olufsen and the Steuben Hellenic Urn are examples of prestige products.

Demand Fluctuations

Changes in buyers' needs, variations in the effectiveness of other marketing mix variables, the presence of substitutes, and dynamic environmental factors can influence demand. Restaurants and utility companies experience large fluctuations in demand daily. Toy manufacturers, fireworks suppliers, and air-conditioning and heating contractors also face demand fluctuations because of the seasonal nature of their products. The demand for online services, whole milk, and fur coats has changed over the last few years. In some cases, demand fluctuations are predictable. It is no surprise to restaurants and utility company managers that demand fluctuates. However, changes in demand for other products may be less predictable, and this leads to problems for some companies. Other organizations anticipate demand fluctuations and develop new products and prices to meet consumers' changing needs.

Assessing Price Elasticity of Demand

Up to this point, we have seen how marketers identify the target market's evaluation of price and its ability to purchase and how they examine demand to learn whether price is related inversely or directly to quantity. The next step is to assess price elasticity of demand. **Price elasticity of demand** provides a measure of the sensitivity of demand to changes in price. It is formally defined as the percentage change in quantity demanded relative to a given percentage change in price (see Figure 20.3).[8] The percentage change in quantity demanded caused by a percentage change in price is much greater for elastic demand than for inelastic demand. For a product such as electricity, demand is relatively inelastic: when its price increases, say, from P_1 to P_2, quantity demanded goes down only a little, from Q_1 to Q_2. For products such as recreational vehicles, demand is relatively elastic: when price rises sharply, from P_1 to P_2, quantity demanded goes down a great deal, from Q_1 to Q_2.

If marketers can determine the price elasticity of demand, setting a price is much easier. By analyzing total revenues as prices change, marketers can determine whether a product is price elastic. Total revenue is price times quantity; thus, 10,000 rolls of wallpaper sold in one year at a price of $10 per roll equals $100,000 of total revenue. If

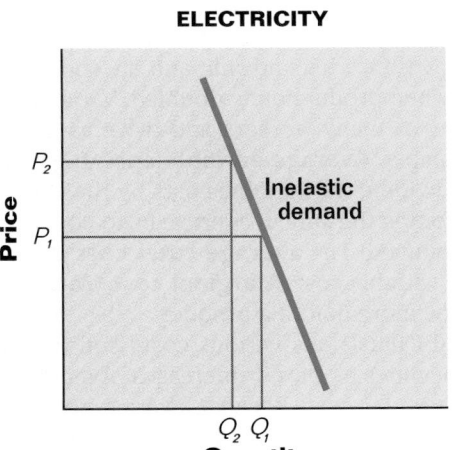

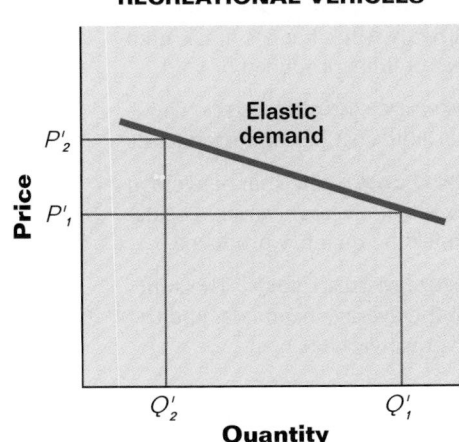

FIGURE 20.3
Elasticity of Demand

price elasticity of demand
A measure of the sensitivity of demand to changes in price

Source: *USA Today*, May 24, 2001, p. 1B. Copyright 2001, *USA Today*. Reprinted with permission.

demand is *elastic,* a change in price causes an opposite change in total revenue; an increase in price will decrease total revenue, and a decrease in price will increase total revenue. *Inelastic* demand results in a change in the same direction in total revenue. An increase in price will increase total revenue, and a decrease in price will decrease total revenue. The following formula determines the price elasticity of demand:

$$\text{Price Elasticity of Demand} = \frac{\%\ \text{Change in Quantity Demanded}}{\%\ \text{Change in Price}}$$

For example, if demand falls by 8 percent when a seller raises the price by 2 percent, the price elasticity of demand is −4 (the negative sign indicating the inverse relationship between price and demand). If demand falls by 2 percent when price is increased by 4 percent, elasticity is −1/2. The less elastic the demand, the more beneficial it is for the seller to raise the price. Products without readily available substitutes and for which consumers have strong needs (for example, electricity or appendectomies) usually have inelastic demand.

Marketers cannot base prices solely on elasticity considerations. They must also examine the costs associated with different sales volumes and evaluate what happens to profits.

Demand, Cost, and Profit Relationships

The analysis of demand, cost, and profit is important because customers are becoming less tolerant of price increases, forcing manufacturers to find new ways to control costs. In the past, many customers desired premium brands and were willing to pay extra for these products. Today customers pass up certain brand names if they can pay less without sacrificing quality. To stay in business, a company has to set prices that not only cover its costs but also meet customers' expectations. In this section we explore two approaches to understanding demand, cost, and profit relationships: marginal analysis and breakeven analysis.

Marginal Analysis

Marginal analysis examines what happens to a firm's costs and revenues when production (or sales volume) changes by one unit. Both production costs and revenues must be evaluated. To determine the costs of production, it is necessary to distinguish among several types of costs. **Fixed costs** do not vary with changes in the number of units produced or sold. For example, a wallpaper manufacturer's cost of renting a factory does not change because production increases from one to two shifts a day or because twice as much wallpaper is sold. Rent may go up, but not because the factory has doubled production or revenue. **Average fixed cost** is the fixed cost per unit produced and is calculated by dividing fixed costs by the number of units produced.

Variable costs vary directly with changes in the number of units produced or sold. The wages for a second shift and the cost of twice as much paper are extra costs that occur when production is doubled. Variable costs are usually constant per unit; that is, twice as many workers and twice as much material produce twice as many rolls of wallpaper. **Average variable cost,** the variable cost per unit produced, is calculated by dividing the variable costs by the number of units produced.

Total cost is the sum of average fixed costs and average variable costs times the quantity produced. The **average total cost** is the sum of the average fixed cost and the average variable cost. **Marginal cost (MC)** is the extra cost a firm incurs when it produces one more unit of a product.

Table 20.1 illustrates various costs and their relationships. Notice that average fixed cost declines as output increases. Average variable cost follows a U shape, as does average total cost. Because average total cost continues to fall after average variable cost begins to rise, its lowest point is at a higher level of output than that of average variable cost. Average total cost is lowest at 5 units at a cost of $22.00, whereas average variable cost is lowest at 3 units at a cost of $11.67. As Figure 20.4

fixed costs   Costs that do not vary with changes in the number of units produced or sold

average fixed cost   The fixed cost per unit produced

variable costs   Costs that vary directly with changes in the number of units produced or sold

average variable cost   The variable cost per unit produced

total cost   The sum of average fixed and average variable costs times the quantity produced

average total cost   The sum of the average fixed cost and the average variable cost

marginal cost (MC) The extra cost a firm incurs by producing one more unit of a product

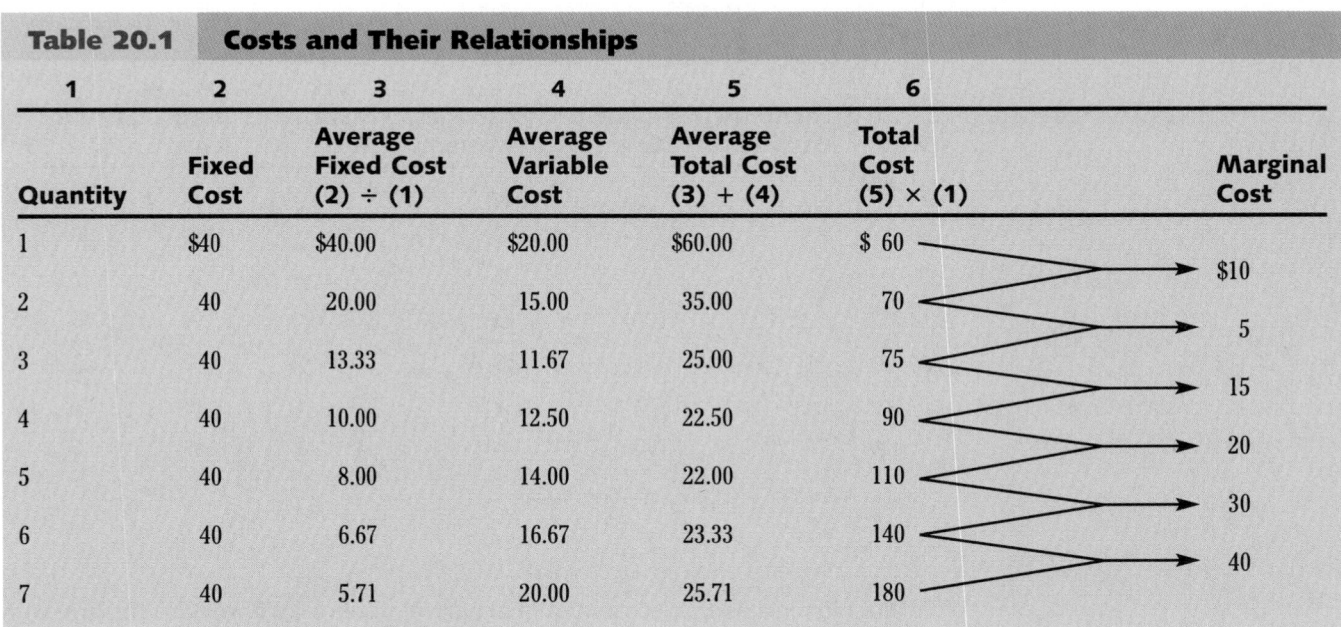

Table 20.1 Costs and Their Relationships

1 Quantity	2 Fixed Cost	3 Average Fixed Cost (2) ÷ (1)	4 Average Variable Cost	5 Average Total Cost (3) + (4)	6 Total Cost (5) × (1)	Marginal Cost
1	$40	$40.00	$20.00	$60.00	$ 60	
						$10
2	40	20.00	15.00	35.00	70	
						5
3	40	13.33	11.67	25.00	75	
						15
4	40	10.00	12.50	22.50	90	
						20
5	40	8.00	14.00	22.00	110	
						30
6	40	6.67	16.67	23.33	140	
						40
7	40	5.71	20.00	25.71	180	

shows, marginal cost equals average total cost at the latter's lowest level. In Table 20.1, this occurs between 5 and 6 units of production. Average total cost decreases as long as marginal cost is less than average total cost, and it increases when marginal cost rises above average total cost.

marginal revenue (MR) The change in total revenue resulting from the sale of an additional unit of a product

Marginal revenue (MR) is the change in total revenue that occurs when a firm sells an additional unit of a product. Figure 20.5 depicts marginal revenue and a demand curve. Most firms in the United States face downward-sloping demand curves for their products; in other words, they must lower their prices to sell additional units.

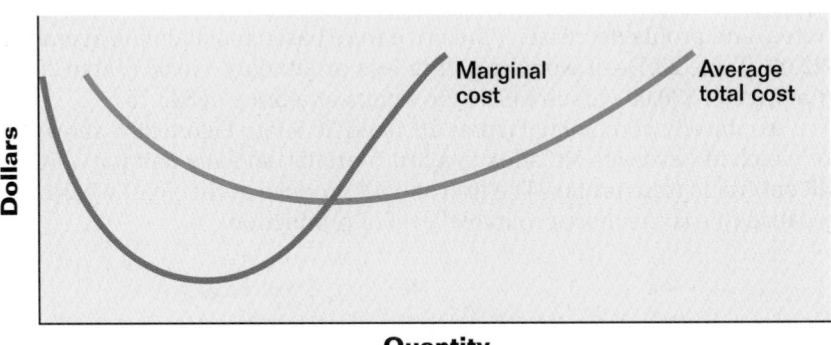

FIGURE 20.4
Typical Marginal Cost and Average Total Cost Relationship

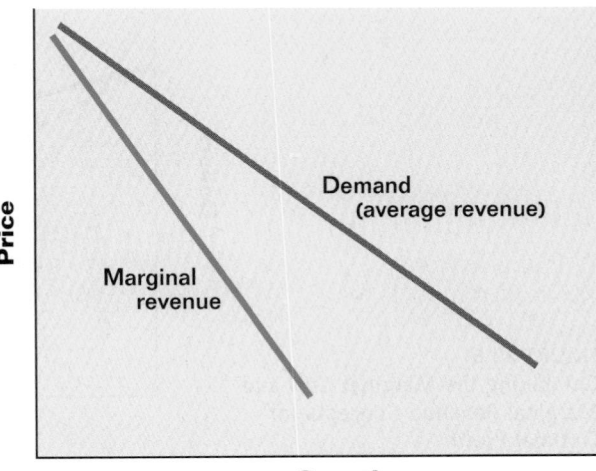

FIGURE 20.5
Typical Marginal Revenue and Average Revenue Relationship

Table 20.2		Marginal Analysis: Method of Obtaining Maximum Profit-Producing Price				
1	**2**	**3**	**4**	**5**	**6**	**7**
Price	**Quantity Sold**	**Total Revenue (1) × (2)**	**Marginal Revenue**	**Marginal Cost**	**Total Cost**	**Profit (3) − (6)**
$57.00	1	$ 57	$57	$ —	$ 60	−$ 3
55.00	2	110	53	10	70	40
39.00	3	117	7	5	75	42
33.75*	**4**	**135**	**15**	**15**	**90**	**45**
30.00	5	150	15	20	110	40
27.00	6	162	12	30	140	22
25.00	7	175	13	40	180	−5

* Boldface indicates the best price-profit combination.

This situation means that each additional unit of product sold provides the firm with less revenue than the previous unit sold. MR then becomes less than average revenue, as Figure 20.5 shows. Eventually MR reaches zero, and the sale of additional units actually hurts the firm.

However, before the firm can determine whether a unit makes a profit, it must know its cost, as well as its revenue, because profit equals revenue minus cost. If MR is a unit's addition to revenue and MC is a unit's addition to cost, MR minus MC tells us whether or not the unit is profitable. Table 20.2 illustrates the relationships among price, quantity sold, total revenue, marginal revenue, marginal cost, and total cost. It indicates where maximum profits are possible at various combinations of price and cost.

Profit is maximized where MC = MR (see Table 20.2). In this table, MC = MR at 4 units. The best price is $33.75, and the profit is $45.00. Up to this point, the additional revenue generated from an extra unit sold exceeds the additional total cost. Beyond this point, the additional cost of another unit sold exceeds the additional revenue generated, and profits decrease. If the price were based on minimum average total cost—$22.00 (Table 20.1)—it would result in less profit: only $40.00 (Table 20.2) for 5 units at a price of $30.00 versus $45.00 for 4 units at a price of $33.75.

Graphically combining Figures 20.4 and 20.5 into Figure 20.6 shows that any unit for which MR exceeds MC adds to a firm's profits, and any unit for which MC exceeds MR subtracts from profits. The firm should produce at the point where MR equals MC because this is the most profitable level of production.

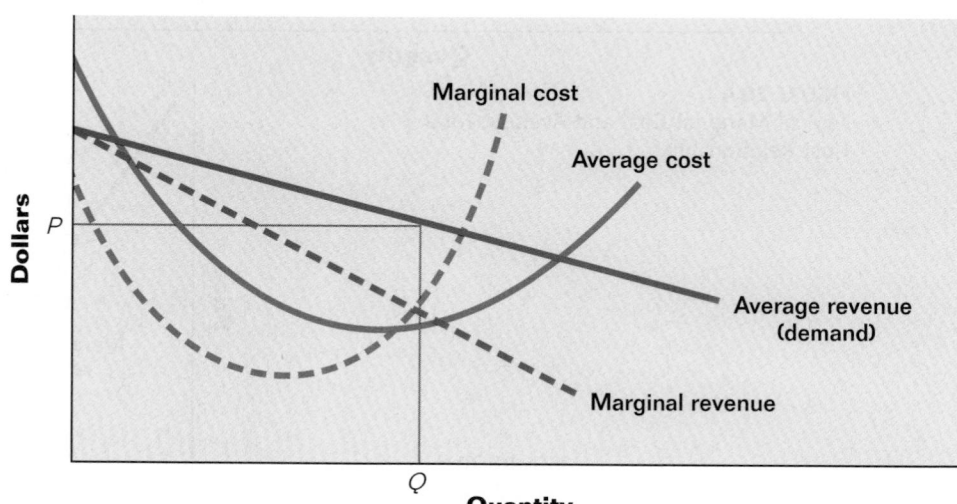

FIGURE 20.6
Combining the Marginal Cost and Marginal Revenue Concepts for Optimal Profit

This discussion of marginal analysis may give the false impression that pricing can be highly precise. If revenue (demand) and cost (supply) remained constant, prices could be set for maximum profits. In practice, however, cost and revenue change frequently. The competitive tactics of other firms or government action can quickly undermine a company's expectations of revenue. Thus, marginal analysis is only a model from which to work. It offers little help in pricing new products before costs and revenues are established. On the other hand, in setting prices of existing products, especially in competitive situations, most marketers can benefit by understanding the relationship between marginal cost and marginal revenue.

Breakeven Analysis

The point at which the costs of producing a product equal the revenue made from selling the product is the **breakeven point.** If a wallpaper manufacturer has total annual costs of $100,000 and sells $100,000 worth of wallpaper in the same year, the company has broken even.

Figure 20.7 illustrates the relationships among costs, revenue, profits, and losses involved in determining the breakeven point. Knowing the number of units necessary to break even is important in setting the price. If a product priced at $100 per unit has an average variable cost of $60 per unit, the contribution to fixed costs is $40. If total fixed costs are $120,000, the breakeven point in unit is determined as follows:

$$\text{Breakeven Point} = \frac{\text{Fixed Costs}}{\text{Per-Unit Contribution to Fixed Costs}}$$

$$= \frac{\text{Fixed Costs}}{\text{Price} - \text{Variable Costs}}$$

$$= \frac{\$120,000}{\$40}$$

$$= 3,000 \text{ Units}$$

To calculate the breakeven point in terms of dollar sales volume, multiply the breakeven point in units by the price per unit. In the preceding example, the breakeven point in terms of dollar sales volume is 3,000 (units) times $100, or $300,000.

To use breakeven analysis effectively, a marketer should determine the breakeven point for each of several alternative prices. This determination allows the marketer to compare the effects on total revenue, total costs, and the breakeven point for each price under consideration. Although this comparative analysis may not tell the marketer exactly what price to charge, it will identify highly undesirable price alternatives that should definitely be avoided.

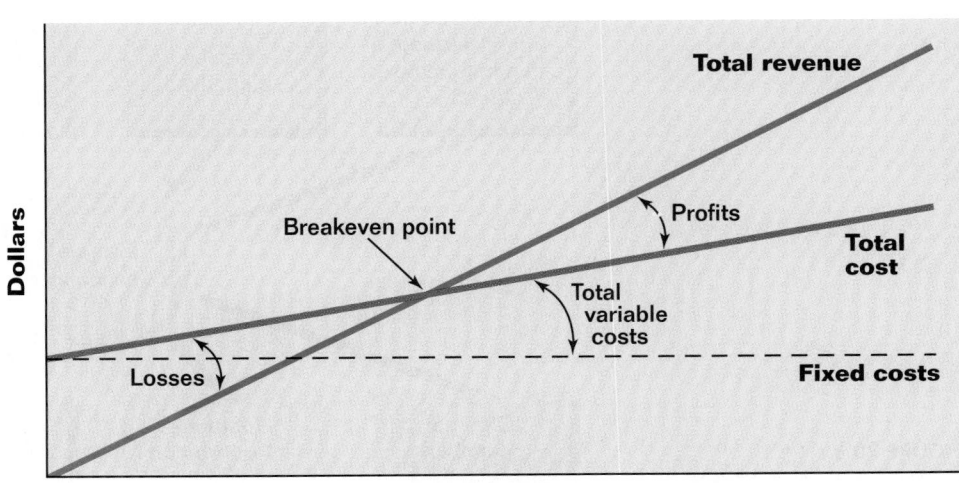

FIGURE 20.7
Determining the Breakeven Point

Breakeven analysis is simple and straightforward. It does assume, however, that the quantity demanded is basically fixed (inelastic) and that the major task in setting prices is to recover costs. It focuses more on how to break even than on how to achieve a pricing objective, such as percentage of market share or return on investment. Nonetheless, marketing managers can use this concept to determine whether a product will achieve at least a breakeven volume.

Factors Affecting Pricing Decisions

Pricing decisions can be complex because of the number of factors to be considered. Frequently there is considerable uncertainty about the reactions to price among buyers, channel members, and competitors. Price is also an important consideration in marketing planning, market analysis, and sales forecasting. It is a major issue when assessing a brand's position relative to competing brands. Most factors that affect pricing decisions can be grouped into one of the eight categories shown in Figure 20.8. In this section, we explore how each of these eight groups of factors enters into price decision making.

Organizational and Marketing Objectives

Marketers should set prices that are consistent with the organization's goals and mission. For example, a retailer trying to position itself as value oriented may wish to set prices that are quite reasonable relative to product quality. In this case, a marketer would not want to set premium prices on products but would strive to price products in line with this overall organizational goal.

Pricing decisions should also be compatible with the organization's marketing objectives. For instance, suppose one of a producer's marketing objectives is a 12 percent increase in unit sales by the end of the next year. Assuming buyers are price sensitive, increasing the price or setting a price above the average market price would not be in line with this objective.

Types of Pricing Objectives

The type of pricing objectives a marketer uses obviously has considerable bearing on the determination of prices. For example, an organization that uses pricing to increase its market share would likely set the brand's price below competing brands of similar quality to attract competitors' customers. A marketer sometimes uses temporary price reductions in the hope of gaining market share. If a business needs to raise cash quickly, it will likely use temporary price reductions such as sales, rebates, and special discounts. We examine pricing objectives in more detail in the next chapter.

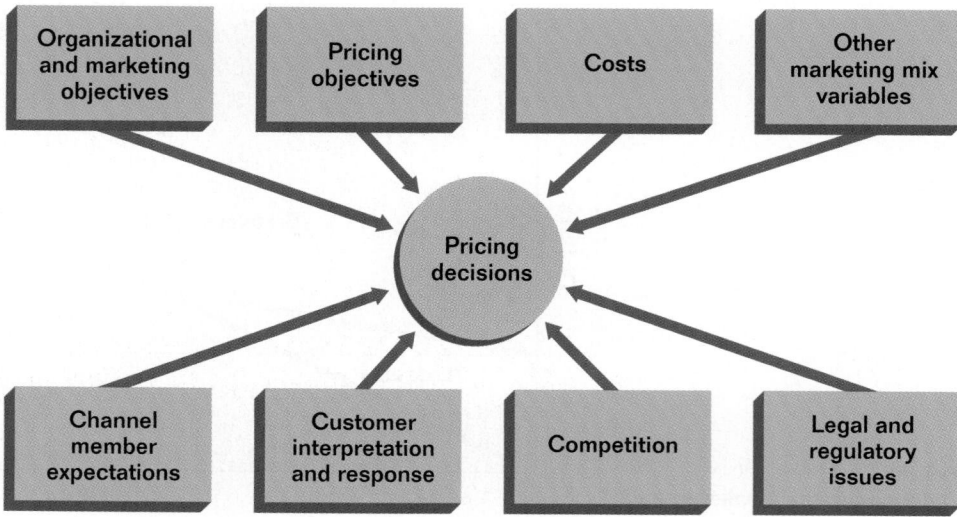

FIGURE 20.8
Factors That Affect Pricing Decisions

Cost as a Pricing Consideration
Through this advertisement, the Indianapolis ICE indicates that costs are considered when setting ticket prices.

Costs

Clearly, costs must be an issue when establishing price. A firm may temporarily sell products below cost to match competition, to generate cash flow, or even to increase market share, but in the long run it cannot survive by selling its products below cost. Even when a firm has a high-volume business, it cannot survive if each item is sold slightly below what it costs. A marketer should be careful to analyze all costs so that they can be included in the total cost associated with a product.

To maintain market share and revenue in an increasingly price-sensitive market, many marketers have concentrated on reducing costs. For example, Exxon Mobil, the world's largest corporation, constantly fights to lower the cost of finding and tapping new oil sources so it can keep its prices competitive and preserve profits. For this reason, the company has found ways to lower these costs from $4 to just 65 cents per barrel over the past 20 years.[9]

Labor-saving technologies, a focus on quality, and efficient manufacturing processes have brought productivity gains that translate into reduced costs and lower prices for customers. In an industry ravaged by labor concerns and monetary losses, Southwest Airlines has managed to stay one step ahead of its larger rivals. Southwest is the low-fare leader on more of the top 100 routes in the United States than the three largest airlines—American, Delta, and United. One reason for the Texas-based airline's success is its ability to control costs. Southwest's per-seat mile costs are somewhat less than those of its "big three" rivals.

Besides considering the costs associated with a particular product, marketers must take into account the costs the product shares with others in the product line. Products often share some costs, particularly the costs of research and development, production, and distribution. Most marketers view a product's cost as a minimum, or floor, below which the product cannot be priced.

Other Marketing Mix Variables

All marketing mix variables are highly interrelated. Pricing decisions can influence decisions and activities associated with product, distribution, and promotion variables. A product's price frequently affects the demand for that item. A high price, for instance, may result in low unit sales, which in turn may lead to higher production costs per unit. Conversely, lower per-unit production costs may result from a low price. For many products, buyers associate better product quality with a high price and poorer product quality with a low price. This perceived price/quality relationship influences customers' overall image of products or brands. Sony, for example, prices its television sets higher than average to help communicate that Sony television sets are high-quality electronic products. Consumers recognize the Sony brand name, its reputation for quality, and the prestige associated with buying Sony products. Individuals who associate quality with a high price are likely to purchase products with well-established and recognizable brand names.[10]

The price of a product is linked to several dimensions of its distribution. Premium-priced products are often marketed through selective or exclusive distribution; lower-priced products in the same product category may be sold through intensive distribution. For example, Cross pens are distributed through selective distribution and Bic pens through intensive distribution. When setting a price, the profit margins of marketing channel members, such as wholesalers and retailers, must be considered. Channel members must be adequately compensated for the functions they perform.

Price may determine how a product is promoted. Bargain prices are often included in advertisements. Premium prices are less likely to be advertised, though they are sometimes included in advertisements for upscale items such as luxury cars or fine jewelry. Higher-priced products are more likely than lower-priced ones to require per-

MARKETING CITIZENSHIP

Protecting Brand Name Drug Prices

Giving up a multibillion-dollar product isn't easy. Just ask the big pharmaceutical manufacturers, which stand to lose billions of dollars in sales when their patents expire on dozens of blockbuster brand name drugs over the next few years. But these drugs aren't going to disappear entirely from pharmacy shelves. A few hours after each patent expires, pharmacies will begin receiving shipments of lower-priced, nonbranded versions of the drugs produced by firms that specialize in generic drugs. With as much as $30 billion in brand name drug sales at stake, pharmaceutical firms are trying to extend patent protection as long as possible. For their part, the generic manufacturers and health care insurers are using a variety of legal techniques to increase competition and bring prices down.

Consider the battle over fluoxetine, an antidepression drug developed by Eli Lilly under the Prozac brand. Lilly introduced Prozac in 1987, and it quickly became the fourth-highest-selling drug in America, with annual sales close to $3 billion. Given the high cost of research and development, Lilly put a relatively high price tag on Prozac, charging about $2.50 per 20mg capsule. As Prozac's patent approached its expiration date, Lilly convinced the Food and Drug Administration (FDA) to extend the patent for six more months while the company conducted tests on an appropriate children's dosage. Meanwhile generic manufacturer Barr Laboratories sued and won the right to be the first to introduce a generic version of the most popular dosage. Experts say competition could bring down the retail price by at least 60 percent as additional generic versions become available.

Like Lilly, many drug firms file for last-minute patent extensions so they can enjoy a longer period of protection before generic competitors force prices down. Another technique they use is to fight the transition to nonprescription status. Wellpoint Health Networks, a managed care provider, recently asked the FDA to allow the anti-allergy drugs Allegra, Claritin, and Zyrtec to be sold over the counter. Wellpoint argues that the drugs have been proven safe and need not be sold by prescription, opening the way for cheaper, over-the-counter versions. The manufacturers oppose this switch, claiming more time is needed to assess drug safety.

Although an FDA advisory panel recommended the change, the FDA is still making up its mind, as Aventis continues to ring up $1 billion in annual sales from the sale of Allegra, Schering-Plough $3 billion from Claritin, and Pfizer $700 million from Zyrtec. Is it ethical for drug companies to keep charging customers high prices for branded drugs? Should stockholders benefit while customers pay high prices? More legal battles lie ahead as pharmaceutical firms fight to protect their biggest branded drugs.

sonal selling. Furthermore, the price structure can affect a salesperson's relationship with customers. A complex pricing structure takes longer to explain to customers, is more likely to confuse potential buyers, and may cause misunderstandings that result in long-term customer dissatisfaction. For example, the pricing structures of many airlines are complex and frequently confuse ticket sales agents and travelers alike.

Channel Member Expectations

When making price decisions, a producer must consider what members of the distribution channel expect. A channel member certainly expects to receive a profit for the functions it performs. The amount of profit expected depends on what the intermediary could make if it were handling a competing product instead. Also, the amount of time and the resources required to carry the product influence intermediaries' expectations.

Channel members often expect producers to give discounts for large orders and prompt payment. At times, resellers expect producers to provide several support activities such as sales training, service training, repair advisory service, cooperative advertising, sales promotions, and perhaps a program for returning unsold merchandise to the producer. These support activities clearly have associated costs that a producer must consider when determining prices.

Customers' Interpretation and Response

When making pricing decisions, marketers should be concerned with a vital question: How will our customers interpret our prices and respond to them? *Interpretation* in this context refers to what the price means or what it communicates to customers. Does the price mean "high quality" or "low quality," or "great deal," "fair price," or "rip-off"? Customer *response* refers to whether the price will move customers closer to the purchase of the product and the degree to which the price enhances their satisfaction with the purchase experience and with the product after purchase.

Customers' interpretation of and response to a price are to some degree determined by their assessment of what they receive compared with what they give up to make the purchase. In evaluating what they receive, customers will consider product attributes, benefits, advantages, disadvantages, the probability of using the product, and possibly the status associated with the product. In assessing the cost of the product, customers likely will consider its price, the amount of time and effort required to obtain it, and perhaps the resources required to maintain it after purchase.

At times customers interpret a higher price as higher product quality. They are especially likely to make this price-quality association when they cannot judge the quality of the product themselves. This is not always the case, however; whether price is equated with quality depends on the types of customers and products involved. Obviously, marketers that rely on customers making a price-quality association and that provide moderate- or low-quality products at high prices will be unable to build long-term customer relationships.

internal reference price
A price developed in the buyer's mind through experience with the product

external reference price
A comparison price provided by others

When interpreting and responding to prices, how do customers determine if the price is too high, too low, or about right? In general, they compare prices with internal or external reference prices. An **internal reference price** is a price developed in the buyer's mind through experience with the product. It is a belief that a product should cost approximately a certain amount. As consumers, our experiences have given each of us internal reference prices for a number of products. For example, most of us have a reasonable idea of how much to pay for a six-pack of soft drinks, a loaf of bread, or a gallon of milk. For the product categories with which we have less experience, we rely more heavily on external reference prices. An **external reference price** is a comparison price provided by others, such as retailers or manufacturers. For example, a retailer in an advertisement might state "while this product is sold for $100 elsewhere, our price is only $39.95." When attempting to establish a reference price in customers' minds by advertising a higher price against which to compare the company's real price, a marketer must make sure the higher price is realistic, because if it is

Value-Conscious and Price-Conscious Customers
By emphasizing both quality and price, this Dell advertisement is focused especially at value-conscious customers. The Buy.com advertisement emphasizes only price and thus is primarily aimed at price-conscious customers.

value conscious Concerned about price and quality of a product

price conscious Striving to pay low prices

prestige sensitive Drawn to products that signify prominence and status

not, customers will not use this price when establishing or altering their reference prices.[11] Customers' perceptions of prices are also influenced by their expectations about future price increases, by what they paid for the product recently, and by what they would like to pay for the product. Other factors affecting customers' perception of whether the price is right include time or financial constraints, the costs associated with searching for lower-priced products, and expectations that products will go on sale.

Buyers' perceptions of a product relative to competing products may allow the firm to set a price that differs significantly from rivals' prices. If the product is deemed superior to most of the competition, a premium price may be feasible. However, even products with superior quality can be overpriced. Strong brand loyalty sometimes provides the opportunity to charge a premium price. On the other hand, if buyers view a product less than favorably (though not extremely negatively), a lower price may generate sales.

In the context of price, buyers can be characterized according to their degree of value consciousness, price consciousness, and prestige sensitivity. Marketers who understand these characteristics are better able to set pricing objectives and policies. **Value-conscious** consumers are concerned about both price and quality of a product. **Price-conscious** individuals strive to pay low prices. **Prestige-sensitive** buyers focus on purchasing products that signify prominence and status.[12]

Competition

A marketer needs to know competitors' prices so it can adjust its own prices accordingly. This does not mean a company will necessarily match competitors' prices; it may set its price above or below theirs. However, for some organizations (such as airlines), matching competitors' prices is an important strategy for survival.

When adjusting prices, a marketer must assess how competitors will respond. Will competitors change their prices and, if so, will they raise or lower them? In Chapter 3, we described several types of competitive market structures. The structure that characterizes the industry to which a firm belongs affects the flexibility of

Pricing Decisions Are Affected by Competitors' Prices
Net2Phone card rates are affected by competitors' rates.

price setting. For example, because of reduced pricing regulation, firms in the telecommunications industry have moved from a monopolistic market structure to an oligopolistic one, which has resulted in significant price competition.

When an organization operates as a monopoly and is unregulated, it can set whatever prices the market will bear. However, the company may not price the product at the highest possible level to avoid government regulation or to penetrate a market by using a lower price. If the monopoly is regulated, it normally has less pricing flexibility; the regulatory body lets it set prices that generate a reasonable, but not excessive, return. A government-owned monopoly may price products below cost to make them accessible to people who otherwise could not afford them. Transit systems, for example, sometimes operate this way. However, government-owned monopolies sometimes charge higher prices to control demand. In some states with state-owned liquor stores, the price of liquor is higher than in states where liquor stores are not owned by a government body.

The automotive, and aircraft industries exemplify oligopolies, in which there are only a few sellers and the barriers to competitive entry are high. Companies in such industries can raise their prices, hoping competitors will do the same. When an organization cuts its price to gain a competitive edge, other companies are likely to follow suit. Thus, very little advantage is gained through price cuts in an oligopolistic market structure.

A market structure characterized by monopolistic competition has numerous sellers with product offerings that are differentiated by physical characteristics, features, quality, and brand images. The distinguishing characteristics of its product may allow a company to set a different price than its competitors. However, firms in a monopolistic competitive market structure are likely to practice nonprice competition, discussed earlier in this chapter.

Under conditions of perfect competition, many sellers exist. Buyers view all sellers' products as the same. All firms sell their products at the going market price, and buyers will not pay more than that. This type of market structure, then, gives a marketer no flexibility in setting prices. Farming, as an industry, has some characteristics of perfect competition. Farmers sell their products at the going market price. At times, for example, corn, soybean, and wheat growers have had bumper crops and been forced to sell them at depressed market prices.

Legal and Regulatory Issues

As discussed in Chapter 3, legal and regulatory issues influence pricing decisions. To curb inflation, the federal government can invoke price controls, freeze prices at certain levels, or determine the rates at which prices may be increased. In some states, regulatory agencies set prices on such products as insurance, dairy products, and liquor.

Many regulations and laws affect pricing decisions and activities. The Sherman Antitrust Act prohibits conspiracies to control prices, and in interpreting the act, courts have ruled that price fixing among firms in an industry is illegal. Marketers must refrain from fixing prices by developing independent pricing policies and setting prices in ways that do not even suggest collusion. Both the Federal Trade Commission Act and the Wheeler-Lea Act prohibit deceptive pricing. In establishing prices, marketers must guard against deceiving customers.

The Robinson-Patman Act has had a strong impact on pricing decisions. For various reasons, marketers may wish to sell the same type of product at different prices. Provisions in the Robinson-Patman Act, as well as those in the Clayton Act, limit the use of such price differentials. The practice of providing price differentials that tend to injure competition by giving one or more buyers a competitive advantage over other buyers is called **price discrimination** and is prohibited by law. However, not all price differentials are discriminatory. A marketer can use price differentials if they do not hinder competition, if they result from differences in the costs of selling or transportation to various customers, or if they arise because the firm has had to cut its price to a particular buyer to meet competitors' prices.

price discrimination
Providing price differentials that injure competition by giving one or more buyers a competitive advantage

Pricing for Business Markets

Business markets consist of individuals and organizations that purchase products for resale, for use in their own operations, or for producing other products. Establishing prices for this category of buyers sometimes differs from setting prices for consumers. Differences in the size of purchases, geographic factors, and transportation considerations require sellers to adjust prices. In this section, we discuss several issues unique to the pricing of business products, including discounts, geographic pricing, and transfer pricing.

Price Discounting

Producers commonly provide intermediaries with discounts, or reductions, from list prices. Although there are many types of discounts, they usually fall into one of five categories: trade, quantity, cash, seasonal, and allowance. Table 20.3 summarizes some reasons to use each type of discount and provides examples.

Table 20.3	Discounts Used for Business Markets	
Type	**Reasons for Use**	**Examples**
Trade (functional)	To attract and keep effective resellers by compensating them for performing certain functions, such as transportation, warehousing, selling, and providing credit	A college bookstore pays about one-third less for a new textbook than the retail price paid by a student.
Quantity	To encourage customers to buy large quantities when making purchases and, in the case of cumulative discounts, to encourage customer loyalty	Large department store chains purchase some women's apparel at lower prices than do individually owned specialty stores.
Cash	To reduce expenses associated with accounts receivable and collection by encouraging prompt payment of accounts	Numerous companies serving business markets allow a 2% discount if an account is paid within 10 days.
Seasonal	To allow a marketer to use resources more efficiently by stimulating sales during off-peak periods	Florida hotels provide companies holding national and regional sales meetings with deeply discounted accommodations during the summer months.
Allowance	In the case of a trade-in allowance, to assist the buyer in making the purchase and potentially earn a profit on the resale of used equipment; in the case of a promotional allowance, to ensure that dealers participate in advertising and sales support programs	A farm equipment dealer takes a farmer's used tractor as a trade-in on a new one. Nabisco pays a promotional allowance to a supermarket for setting up and maintaining a large, end-of-aisle display for a two-week period.

trade (functional) discount
A reduction off the list price given by a producer to an intermediary for performing certain functions

Trade Discounts.   A reduction off the list price given by a producer to an intermediary for performing certain functions is called a **trade,** or **functional, discount.** A trade discount is usually stated in terms of a percentage or series of percentages off the list price. Intermediaries are given trade discounts as compensation for performing various functions, such as selling, transporting, storing, final processing, and perhaps providing credit services. Although certain trade discounts are often a standard practice within an industry, discounts vary considerably among industries. It is important that a manufacturer provide a trade discount large enough to offset the intermediary's costs, plus a reasonable profit, to entice the reseller to carry the product.

quantity discounts
Deductions from list price for purchasing large quantities

Quantity Discounts.   Deductions from list price that reflect the economies of purchasing in large quantities are called **quantity discounts.** Quantity discounts are used to pass on to the buyer cost savings gained through economies of scale.

cumulative discounts
Quantity discounts aggregated over a stated period

Quantity discounts can be either cumulative or noncumulative. **Cumulative discounts** are quantity discounts aggregated over a stated time period. Purchases totaling $10,000 in a three-month period, for example, might entitle the buyer to a 5 percent, or $500, rebate. Such discounts are supposed to reflect economies in selling and to encourage the buyer to purchase from one seller. **Noncumulative discounts** are one-time reductions in prices based on the number of units purchased, the dollar value of the order, or the product mix purchased. Like cumulative discounts, these discounts should reflect some economies in selling or trade functions.

noncumulative discounts
One-time reductions in price based on specific factors

cash discount   A price reduction given to buyers for prompt payment or cash payment

Cash Discounts.   A **cash discount,** or price reduction, is given to a buyer for prompt payment or cash payment. Accounts receivable are an expense and a collection problem for many organizations. A policy to encourage prompt payment is a popular practice and sometimes a major concern in setting prices.

Discounts are based on cash payments or cash paid within a stated time. For example, "2/10 net 30" means that a 2 percent discount will be allowed if the account is paid within 10 days. If the buyer does not make payment within the 10-day period, the entire balance is due within 30 days without a discount. If the account is not paid within 30 days, interest may be charged.

seasonal discount   A price reduction given to buyers for purchasing goods or services out of season

Seasonal Discounts.   A price reduction to buyers who purchase goods or services out of season is a **seasonal discount.** These discounts let the seller maintain steadier production during the year. For example, automobile rental agencies offer seasonal discounts in winter and early spring to encourage firms to use automobiles during the slow months of the automobile rental business.

allowance   A concession in price to achieve a desired goal

Allowances.   Another type of reduction from the list price is an **allowance,** or a concession in price to achieve a desired goal. Trade-in allowances, for example, are price reductions granted for turning in a used item when purchasing a new one. Allowances help make the buyer better able to make the new purchase. This type of discount is popular in the aircraft industry. Another example is a promotional allowance, a price reduction granted to dealers for participating in advertising and sales support programs intended to increase sales of a particular item.

Geographic Pricing

geographic pricing
Reductions for transportation and other costs related to the physical distance between buyer and seller

F.O.B. factory   The price of the merchandise at the factory, before shipment

F.O.B. destination   A price indicating the producer is absorbing shipping costs

uniform geographic pricing
Charging all customers the same price, regardless of geographic location

zone pricing   Pricing based on transportation costs within major geographic zones

base-point pricing
Geographic pricing combining factory price and freight charges from the base point nearest the buyer

freight absorption pricing
Absorption of all or part of actual freight costs by the seller

Geographic pricing involves reductions for transportation costs or other costs associated with the physical distance between buyer and seller. Prices may be quoted as F.O.B. (free-on-board) factory or destination. An **F.O.B. factory** price indicates the price of the merchandise at the factory, before it is loaded onto the carrier, and thus excludes transportation costs. The buyer must pay for shipping. An **F.O.B. destination** price means the producer absorbs the costs of shipping the merchandise to the customer. This policy may be used to attract distant customers. Although F.O.B. pricing is an easy way to price products, it is sometimes difficult for marketers to administer, especially when a firm has a wide product mix or when customers are widely dispersed. Because customers will want to know about the most economical method of shipping, the seller must be informed about shipping rates.

To avoid the problems involved in charging different prices to each customer, **uniform geographic pricing,** sometimes called *postage-stamp pricing*, may be used. The same price is charged to all customers regardless of geographic location, and the price is based on average shipping costs for all customers. Gasoline, paper products, and office equipment are often priced on a uniform basis.

Zone pricing sets uniform prices for each of several major geographic zones; as the transportation costs across zones increase, so do the prices. For example, a Florida manufacturer's prices may be higher for buyers on the Pacific Coast and in Canada than for buyers in Georgia.

Base-point pricing is a geographic pricing policy that includes the price at the factory, plus freight charges from the base point nearest the buyer. This approach to pricing has virtually been abandoned because of its questionable legal status. The policy resulted in all buyers paying freight charges from one location, such as Detroit or Pittsburgh, regardless of where the product was manufactured.

When the seller absorbs all or part of the actual freight costs, **freight absorption pricing** is being used. The seller might choose this method because it wishes to do business with a particular customer or to get more business; more business will cause the average cost to fall and counterbalance the extra freight cost. This strategy is used to improve market penetration and to retain a hold in an increasingly competitive market.

Transfer Pricing

transfer pricing   Prices charged in sales between an organization's units

Transfer pricing occurs when one unit in an organization sells a product to another unit. The price is determined by one of the following methods.

Actual full cost: calculated by dividing all fixed and variable expenses for a period into the number of units produced

Standard full cost: calculated based on what it would cost to produce the goods at full plant capacity

Cost plus investment: calculated as full cost, plus the cost of a portion of the selling unit's assets used for internal needs

Market-based cost: calculated at the market price less a small discount to reflect the lack of sales effort and other expenses

The choice of transfer-pricing method depends on the company's management strategy and the nature of the units' interaction. An organization must also ensure that transfer pricing is fair to all units involved in the purchases.

Summary

Price is the value exchanged for products in marketing transactions. Price is not always money paid; barter, the trading of products, is the oldest form of exchange. Price is a key element in the marketing mix because it relates directly to the generation of total revenue. The profit factor can be determined mathematically by multiplying price by quantity sold to get total revenue and then subtracting total costs. Price is the only variable in the marketing mix that can be adjusted quickly and easily to respond to changes in the external environment.

A product offering can compete on either a price or a nonprice basis. Price competition emphasizes price as the product differential. Prices fluctuate frequently, and price competition among sellers is aggressive. Nonprice competition emphasizes product differentiation through distinctive features, service, product quality, or other factors. Establishing brand loyalty by using nonprice competition works best when the product can be physically differentiated and the customer can recognize these differences.

An organization must determine the demand for its product. The classic demand curve is a graph of the quantity of products expected to be sold at various prices if other factors hold constant. It illustrates that as price falls, the quantity demanded usually increases. However, for prestige products, there is a direct positive relationship between price and quantity demanded; demand increases as price increases. Next, price elasticity of demand—the percentage change in quantity demanded relative to a given percentage change in price—must be determined. If demand is elastic, a change in price causes an opposite change in total revenue. Inelastic demand results in a parallel change in total revenue when a product's price is changed.

Analysis of demand, cost, and profit relationships can be accomplished through marginal analysis or breakeven analysis. Marginal analysis examines what happens to a firm's costs and revenues when production (or sales volume) is changed by one unit. Marginal analysis combines the demand curve with the firm's costs to develop a price that yields maximum profit. Fixed costs do not vary with changes in the number of units produced or sold; average fixed cost is the fixed cost per unit produced. Variable costs vary directly with changes in the number of units produced or sold. Average variable cost is the variable cost per unit produced. Total cost is the sum of average fixed cost and average variable cost times the quantity produced. The optimal price is the point at which marginal cost (the cost associated with producing one more unit of the product) equals marginal revenue (the change in total revenue that occurs when one additional unit of the product is sold). Marginal analysis is only a model; it offers little help in pricing new products before costs and revenues are established.

Breakeven analysis—determining the number of units that must be sold to break even—is important in setting price. The point at which the costs of production equal the revenue from selling the product is the breakeven point. To use breakeven analysis effectively, a marketer should determine the breakeven point for each of several alternative prices. This determination makes it possible to compare the effects on total revenue, total costs, and the breakeven point for each price under consideration. However, this approach assumes that the quantity demanded is basically fixed and that the major task is to set prices to recover costs.

Eight factors enter into price decision making: organizational and marketing objectives, pricing objectives, costs, other marketing mix variables, channel member expectations, customer interpretation and response, competition, and legal and regulatory issues. When setting prices, marketers should make decisions consistent with the organization's goals and mission. Pricing objectives heavily influence price-setting decisions. Most marketers view a product's cost as the floor below which a product cannot be priced. Because of the interrelation among the marketing mix variables, price can affect product, promotion, and distribution decisions. The revenue channel members expect for their functions must also be considered when making price decisions.

Buyers' perceptions of price vary. Some consumer segments are sensitive to price, but others may not be. Thus, before determining price, a marketer needs to be aware of its importance to the target market. Knowledge of the prices charged for competing brands is essential so that the firm can adjust its prices relative to competitors. Government regulations and legislation influence pricing decisions. Several laws aim to enhance competition in the marketplace by outlawing price fixing and deceptive pricing. Legislation also restricts price differentials that can injure competition. Moreover, the government can invoke price controls to curb inflation.

Unlike consumers, business buyers purchase products for resale, for use in their own operations, or for producing other products. When adjusting prices, business sellers take into consideration the size of the purchase, geographic factors, and transportation requirements. Producers commonly provide discounts off list prices to intermediaries. The categories of discounts include trade, quantity, cash, seasonal, and allowance. A trade discount is a price reduction for performing such functions as storing, transporting, final processing, or providing credit services. If an intermediary purchases in large enough quantities, the producer gives a quantity discount, which can be either cumulative or noncumulative. A cash discount is a price reduction for prompt payment or payment in cash. Buyers who purchase goods or services out of season may be granted a seasonal discount. A final type of reduction from the list price is an allowance, such as a trade-in allowance.

Geographic pricing involves reductions for transportation costs or other costs associated with the physical distance between buyer and seller. A price quoted as F.O.B. factory means the buyer pays for shipping from the factory. An F.O.B. destination price means the producer pays for shipping; this is the easiest way to price products, but it is difficult for marketers to administer. When the seller charges a fixed average cost for transportation, it is using uniform geographic pricing. Zone prices are uniform within major geographic zones; they increase by zone as the transportation costs increase. With base-point pricing, prices are adjusted for shipping expenses incurred by the seller from the base point nearest the buyer. Freight absorption pricing occurs when a seller absorbs all or part of the freight costs.

Important Terms

Price	Quantity discounts
Barter	Cumulative discounts
Price competition	Noncumulative discounts
Nonprice competition	Cash discount
Demand curve	Seasonal discount
Price elasticity of demand	Allowance
Fixed costs	Geographic pricing
Average fixed cost	F.O.B. factory
Variable costs	F.O.B. destination
Average variable cost	Uniform geographic
Total cost	pricing
Average total cost	Zone pricing
Marginal cost (MC)	Base-point pricing
Marginal revenue (MR)	Freight absorption
Breakeven point	pricing
Internal reference price	Transfer pricing
External reference price	
Value conscious	
Price conscious	
Prestige sensitive	
Price discrimination	
Trade (functional) discount	

Discussion and Review Questions

1. Why are pricing decisions important to an organization?
2. Compare and contrast price and nonprice competition. Describe the conditions under which each form works best.
3. Why do most demand curves demonstrate an inverse relationship between price and quantity?
4. List the characteristics of products that have inelastic demand, and give several examples of such products.
5. Explain why optimal profits should occur when marginal cost equals marginal revenue.
6. Chambers Company has just gathered estimates for conducting a breakeven analysis for a new product. Variable costs are $7 a unit. The additional plant will cost $48,000. The new product will be charged $18,000 a year for its share of general overhead. Advertising expenditures will be $80,000, and $55,000 will be spent on distribution. If the product sells for $12, what is the breakeven point in units? What is the breakeven point in dollar sales volume?
7. In what ways do other marketing mix variables affect pricing decisions?
8. What types of expectations may channel members have about producers' prices? How might these expectations affect pricing decisions?
9. How do legal and regulatory forces influence pricing decisions?
10. Compare and contrast a trade discount and a quantity discount.
11. What is the reason for using the term *F.O.B.*?
12. What are the major methods used for transfer pricing?

Application Questions

1. Price competition is intense in the fast-food, air travel, and personal computer industries. Discuss a recent situation in which companies had to meet or beat a competitor's price in a price-competitive industry. Did you benefit from this situation? Did it change your perception of the companies and/or their products?
2. Customers' interpretations and responses regarding a product and its price are an important influence on marketers' pricing decisions. Perceptions of price are affected by the degree to which a customer is value conscious, price conscious, or prestige sensitive. Discuss how value consciousness, price consciousness, and prestige sensitivity influence the buying decision process for the following products:
   a. A new house
   b. Weekly groceries for a family of five
   c. An airline ticket
   d. A soft drink from a vending machine

Internet
Exercise & Resources

Autosite

Autosite offers car buyers a free, comprehensive website to find the invoice prices for almost all car models. The browser can also access a listing of all the latest new-car rebates and incentives. Visit this site at

www.autosite.com

1. Find the lowest-priced Lexus available today, and examine its features. Which Lexus dealer is closest to you?

2. If you wanted to purchase this Lexus, what are the lowest monthly payments you could make over the longest time period?

3. Is this free site more credible than a "pay" site? Why or why not?

VIDEO CASE 20.1
JetBlue's Flight Plan for Profitability

When David Neeleman sold his Utah-based airline to Southwest Airlines in 1994, he signed a contract agreeing not to compete in the air travel industry for five years. By 1999, the entrepreneur had created a new flight plan—and $160 million in financial backing—for his full-throttle return to the skies with a customer-friendly, low-fare airline called JetBlue.

CEO Neeleman and his management team decided to base the startup airline in New York City after they thoroughly analyzed the area's air travel patterns. "Essentially, New Yorkers were prisoners," explains John Owen, JetBlue's chief financial officer. "They had only low-quality, high-fare airlines to choose from. Their expectations were at [the] bottom."

New York travelers also had to contend with crowds and delays at nearby La Guardia Airport, unless they were willing to venture eight miles farther to fly from John F. Kennedy International Airport. Unlike some metropolitan airports, JFK was not a regional hub for major airlines or for low-fare carriers such as Southwest. Seizing an opportunity to trade off a slightly less convenient location for less competition and better on-time performance, Neeleman secured more than 70 takeoff and landing slots at JFK Airport, enough to accommodate JetBlue's projected growth through 2005.

Neeleman understands price is one of the top considerations for travelers. He therefore has sharpened his pencil to keep JetBlue's ticket prices highly competitive to attract vacationers as well as business travelers. Major carriers such as Delta typically quote dozens of fares between two locations, depending on time of day and other factors. By comparison, JetBlue's everyday pricing structure is far simpler and avoids complicated requirements such as Saturday-night stayovers. Neeleman says the fares are based on demand and JetBlue uses pricing to equalize the loads on the flights so no jet takes off empty while another is completely full. Thus, fares for Sunday-night flights tend to be higher because of higher demand, whereas Tuesday-night flights may be priced lower due to lower demand. Still, the CEO observes that JetBlue's highest fare generally undercuts the lowest fare of its competitors.

JetBlue's promotional fares are even lower. When inaugurating service between New York and California, the airline offered a one-way fare of $99, an unusually low price for a nonstop flight. Low fares definitely stimulate traffic, Neeleman says, and this helps JetBlue weather the turbulence of tough economic times and challenges such as the fall-off in air travel that occurred following the terrorist attacks on New York City and Washington, DC. Its flights have an average passenger load of 80 percent of full capacity, compared with an industry average load of 68.4 percent.

Neeleman and his team have made other decisions to set their startup apart from other new airline ventures. Whereas many new carriers buy used jets, JetBlue flies new, state-of-the-art Airbus A320 jets with seat-back personal video screens. Rather than squeeze in the maximum 180 seats that A320s can hold, JetBlue flies with only 162, which allows passengers more legroom. In addition, the jets are outfitted with roomier leather seats. Neeleman notes that leather costs twice as much but lasts twice as long. More important, passengers feel pampered when they sink into the leather seats and enjoy free satellite television programming, which also differentiates JetBlue from other low-fare airlines.

Another advantage of flying new jets is higher fuel efficiency. Because of their dual engines and weight, A320s can operate on 60 percent of the amount of fuel burned by an equivalent jet built decades before. As a result, Neeleman has not had to raise ticket prices to compensate for rising fuel costs even as the airline expands beyond the East Coast to western destinations such as Long Beach (California) and Seattle. In addition, because JetBlue's technicians work on only one type of jet, they become highly proficient at their maintenance tasks, which saves time and money. New jets come with a five-year warranty, so JetBlue has to budget only for routine maintenance service.

From its first day of operation, JetBlue has relied on Internet bookings to minimize sales costs. Travelers who buy tickets directly through the company's website (www.jetblue.com) get a special discount and are also eligible for online specials such as "Get It Together" fares designed for two people traveling together. By the airline's second year, it was selling 50 percent of its tickets over the Internet. JetBlue also set up a special web-based service to encourage travel agents to buy tickets for their customers online.

JetBlue's total costs equal about 6.5 cents per mile, well below the per-mile costs of most major competitors. In turn, the low cost structure allows Neeleman to keep ticket prices low while delivering a comfortable flying experience. His decision to fly from JFK Airport also means JetBlue's on-time record is generally better than that of the big airlines, another important consideration for business travelers and vacationers alike. Not surprisingly, JetBlue flew into profitability just months after its launch, and Neeleman aims to keep the airline's revenues and profits soaring in the future.[13]

QUESTIONS FOR DISCUSSION

1. In an industry where pricing has driven many firms out of business or into bankruptcy protection, why does JetBlue compete so successfully on the basis of price?
2. How does JetBlue use pricing to deal with demand fluctuations?
3. Is a businessperson's demand for air travel likely to be relatively elastic or inelastic? Is a vacationer's demand for air travel likely to be relatively elastic or inelastic?
4. What other factors related to pricing are most important to JetBlue's management when making pricing decisions?

CASE 20.2

Priceline.com Lets Online Customers Set Prices

Priceline.com, the original name-your-price website, has had a challenging few years. The site invites customers to name the price they are willing to pay for an airline ticket, a hotel room, a rental car, long-distance telephone service, a mortgage, or a new car or truck. In its first four months of operation, the company sold 40,000 airline tickets and continues to attract more than 1 million visitors a week. At peak times, it sells a ticket every 70 seconds to one of its 11 million registered customers.

However, Priceline only recently recorded its first profit since the company burst onto the Internet with much fanfare in 1998. Like other e-businesses, Priceline has employed a substantial promotional budget to build awareness and attract customers. The company has also been saddled with costs related to its withdrawal from ill-fated attempts to expand its product mix to include name-your-price groceries, gasoline, and insurance. On top of these challenges, Priceline is learning to deal with competition now that it is no longer the only name-your-price site on the Web.

Travel services remain Priceline's most popular offering. Unsold airline seats and hotel rooms are wasted; they cannot be stored in warehouses for later sale. Priceline.com, which provides an anonymous link between buyers and sellers, gives buyers an opportunity to pay a price they can afford and sellers the chance to reduce waste by accepting a buyer's offer. Since planes fly with more than 500,000 empty seats a day, waste and lost revenues are a major problem for airlines, and many are therefore cooperating with Priceline.com.

How does Priceline.com's airline ticket service work? Using the lowest available advance purchase fares as a guideline, customers go to the Priceline site, enter their destinations and travel dates, offer a price for a ticket, and type in their credit card numbers. Travel must begin in the United States, and customers must be flexible regarding the time of day they are willing to travel. However, destinations can be worldwide, and there are no blackout dates or advance purchase requirements. After receiving an offer, Priceline searches ticket availability on participating airlines. Within an hour or less (one day for international flights), Priceline lets the customer know whether his or her offer has been accepted, charges the credit card, and processes the tickets. Customers whose offers are rejected can try again. This web-based pricing system is so original that the U.S. Patent and Trademark Office granted Priceline a patent on the method.

Shopping at Priceline.com sounds easy and economical, and most of its customers agree. Critics, however, point out that Priceline's airline ticket service has some drawbacks. In addition to committing themselves to fly at hours that will not be specified until after their offers are accepted, customers must be willing to take flights that may include one or more stops or connections and possibly a long layover. Tickets are nonrefundable, cannot be changed, and earn no frequent flier miles. Some reporters who have tested Priceline's system complain that the airfares are not always the lowest available and conclude that the site works best for people who must fly on short notice and can't meet advance purchase requirements for lower fares.

Customers can also use Priceline to name their price for hotel rooms in major U.S. cities. First, they enter their destination, dates, number of rooms, desired quality level of the hotel (two, three, four, or five stars), and how much they are willing to pay per night. As with the airline ticket system, they have to provide a credit card number so Priceline can lock in the reservation if it finds accommodations that meet their criteria. Priceline searches its database of participating hotels for one with a rate at or below the customer's request, books the room, buys it from the hotel, and charges the customer $5 more than the price it paid. This Priceline service has become so popular that it is now growing much faster than the company's airline travel business. Customers are also reserving more rental cars, helping to boost Priceline's overall revenues and contributing to its profitability.

Although Priceline had no name-your-price competition in its early years, two other travel sites now offer variations on this pricing approach. Expedia, backed by Microsoft, offers Flight Price

Matcher, a service very similar to Priceline's—so similar, in fact, that Priceline sued for patent infringement (a settlement calls for Expedia to pay royalties to Priceline). Expedia customers don't find out which airline they are using or when their flights leave until their bids have been accepted, which takes up to 15 minutes. Hotwire.com, started by several major airlines, invites customers to bid on airline tickets, rental cars, and hotel rooms. Unlike Expedia and Priceline, Hotwire allows customers one hour to make a decision once they find out whether their price has been accepted, but they still don't learn all the details until they have agreed to the purchase.

Because travelers have become more savvy about searching out special Internet deals, online travel is experiencing tremendous growth. Priceline hopes its name-your-price strategy will prove irresistible to a large number of these price-sensitive travelers, bringing them to Priceline's site rather than to competing sites again and again.[14]

QUESTIONS FOR DISCUSSION

1. What effect do name-your-price sites seem to be having on demand for travel services? What are the implications for price elasticity of demand?
2. Does the pricing facilitated by Priceline.com result in price or nonprice competition?
3. What are the advantages and disadvantages of Priceline.com's pricing approach for buyers? For sellers?

Setting Prices

21

OBJECTIVES

- To understand the six major stages of the process used to establish prices
- To explore issues related to developing pricing objectives
- To understand the importance of identifying the target market's evaluation of price
- To examine how marketers analyze competitive prices
- To describe the bases used for setting prices
- To explain the different types of pricing strategies

Family Dollar Stores' Strategy Is Driven by Everyday Low Prices

The low-price appeal of Family Dollar Stores is evident in its name. This chain of 4,000-plus stores targets families with incomes of $25,000 or less who know the value of a dollar and want to stretch it as far as possible. Rather than hold an endless series of advertised price promotions on selected merchandise, Family Dollar has an everyday low price policy that encourages customers to shop more often and buy more products. Few items sell for more than $10, and because the shelves are filled with bargain-priced household supplies, customers return every time they run out of something.

Headquartered in Matthews, North Carolina, Family Dollar first spread its stores across the South before expanding northward into Pennsylvania, Ohio, Michigan, and New York. Half of its stores are located in towns with populations of less than 15,000, towns too small even for Wal-Mart. Yet Family Dollar has thrived by opening relatively small neighborhood stores—generally less than 8,000 square feet—where customers find shorter checkout lines and less parking congestion compared to much larger stores. The company also keeps costs low by concentrating stores in a specific area to gain economies of scale from shared distribution and management supervision. As chainwide sales approach $3.5 billion, the company continues to open hundreds of stores every year, including a growing number in urban locations abandoned by troubled retailers.

Family Dollar competes with a number of retail chains that also position themselves as low-price "dollar" stores. The largest competitor is Dollar General, which rings up $3.9 billion in annual sales through about 4,900 stores. Other competitors include Dollar Tree Stores, Bill's Dollar Stores, Dollar Discount Stores of America, and 99 Cents Only Stores. Family Dollar is also feeling some competitive pressure from Wal-Mart's Neighborhood Market stores, which are a fraction of the size of a typical Wal-Mart SuperCenter and are opening in some smaller communities.

For years, Family Dollar packed its stores with high-margin apparel products and shoes. A few years ago, however, management realized the company could increase repeat business by stocking more discounted soaps, paper products, and other "hardline" products. Today hardlines make up two-thirds of the merchandise assortment, and the retailer is enjoying higher sales and higher gross profits. Even when a recession slows sales in other retail sectors, Family Dollar's everyday low pricing policy keeps sales high. "We're basically a store that meets the recurring, everyday needs of the community we're going into," explains a Family Dollar vice president. "We sell things people need on an ongoing basis. We're not recession-proof. But we are recession-resistant."[1]

1 | Development of pricing objectives

2 | Assessment of target market's evaluation of price

3 | Evaluation of competitors' prices

4 | Selection of a basis for pricing

5 | Selection of a pricing strategy

6 | Determination of a specific price

FIGURE 21.1
Stages for Establishing Prices

Family Dollar Stores helps to position itself in customers' minds through its highly visible pricing strategy. Selecting a pricing strategy is one of the fundamental components in the process of setting prices. In this chapter, we examine six stages of a process marketers can use when setting prices. Figure 21.1 illustrates these stages. Stage 1 is the development of a pricing objective that is compatible with the organization's overall objectives and its marketing objectives. Stage 2 entails assessing the target market's evaluation of price. Stage 3 involves evaluating competitors' prices, which helps determine the role of price in the marketing strategy. Stage 4 involves choosing a basis for setting prices. Stage 5 is the selection of a pricing strategy, or the guidelines for using price in the marketing mix. Stage 6, determining the final price, depends on environmental forces and marketers' understanding and use of a systematic approach to establishing prices. These stages are not rigid steps that all marketers must follow; rather, they are guidelines that provide a logical sequence for establishing prices.

Development of Pricing Objectives

pricing objectives Goals that describe what a firm wants to achieve through pricing

Pricing objectives are goals that describe what a firm wants to achieve through pricing. Developing pricing objectives is an important task because pricing objectives form the basis for decisions about other stages of pricing. Thus, pricing objectives must be stated explicitly, and the statement should include the time frame for accomplishing them.

Marketers must make sure the pricing objectives are consistent with the organization's marketing objectives and with its overall objectives because pricing objectives influence decisions in many functional areas, including finance, accounting, and production. A marketer can use both short- and long-term pricing objectives and can employ one or multiple pricing objectives. For instance, a firm may wish to increase market share by 18 percent over the next three years, achieve a 15 percent return on investment, and promote an image of quality in the marketplace.

In this section, we examine some of the pricing objectives that companies might set for themselves. Table 21.1 shows the major pricing objectives and typical actions associated with them.

Table 21.1	Pricing Objectives and Typical Actions Taken to Achieve Them
Objective	**Possible Action**
Survival	Adjust price levels so the firm can increase sales volume to match organizational expenses
Profit	Identify price and cost levels that allow the firm to maximize profit
Return on investment	Identify price levels that enable the firm to yield targeted ROI
Market share	Adjust price levels so the firm can maintain or increase sales relative to competitors' sales
Cash flow	Set price levels to encourage rapid sales
Status quo	Identify price levels that help stabilize demand and sales
Product quality	Set prices to recover research and development expenditures and establish a high-quality image

Survival

A fundamental pricing objective is survival. Most organizations will tolerate difficulties such as short-run losses and internal upheaval if necessary for survival. Because price is a flexible variable, it is sometimes used to keep a company afloat by increasing sales volume to levels that match expenses. For example, a women's apparel retailer may run a three-day, 60 percent-off sale to generate enough cash to pay creditors, employees, and rent.

Profit

Although a business may claim its objective is to maximize profits for its owners, the objective of profit maximization is rarely operational because its achievement is difficult to measure. Because of this difficulty, profit objectives tend to be set at levels that the owners and top-level decision makers view as satisfactory. Specific profit objectives may be stated in terms of actual dollar amounts or in terms of a percentage of sales revenues. For example, the main pricing objective for Shoebuy.com, an online shoe retailer, is to return an overall 30 percent profit. To achieve this objective, the company minimizes costs by having a small work force and holding no inventory. Manufacturers ship directly to customers.[2]

Return on Investment

Pricing to attain a specified rate of return on the company's investment is a profit-related pricing objective. Most pricing objectives based on return on investment (ROI) are achieved by trial and error because not all cost and revenue data needed to project the return on investment are available when prices are set. General Motors uses ROI pricing objectives.

Market Share

Many firms establish pricing objectives to maintain or increase market share, a product's sales in relation to total industry sales. Airbus Industrie, the European aircraft manufacturer that is Boeing's major competitor, uses pricing as a strategic tool for expanding market share. By offering discounts of as much as 40 percent off the list price, Airbus increased its global share of the aircraft market from 21 percent to nearly 50 percent over the past five years.[3] Many firms recognize that high relative market shares often translate into higher profits. The Profit Impact of Market Strategies (PIMS) studies, conducted over the last 30 years have shown that both market share and product quality heavily influence profitability. Thus, marketers often use an increase in market share as a primary pricing objective.

Maintaining or increasing market share need not depend on growth in industry sales. Remember that an organization can increase its market share even if sales for the total industry are flat or decreasing. On the other hand, an organization's sales volume may increase while its market share decreases if the overall market is growing.

Market Share Pricing Objective
Teligent is attempting to gain market share and has set market share pricing objectives.

Cash Flow

Some organizations set prices so they can recover cash as quickly as possible. Financial managers understandably seek to quickly recover capital spent to develop products. This objective may have the support of a marketing manager who anticipates a short product life cycle.

Although it may be acceptable in some situations, the use of cash flow and recovery as an objective oversimplifies the value of price in contributing to profits. If this pricing objective results in high prices, competitors with lower prices may gain a large share of the market.

Status Quo

In some cases, an organization is in a favorable position and, desiring nothing more, may set an objective of status quo. Status quo objectives can focus on several dimensions, such as maintaining a certain market share, meeting (but not beating) competitors' prices, achieving price stability, and maintaining a favorable public image. A status quo pricing objective can reduce a firm's risks by helping to stabilize demand for its products. The use of status quo pricing objectives sometimes minimizes pricing as a competitive tool, leading to a climate of nonprice competition in an industry.

Product Quality

A company may have the objective of leading its industry in product quality. This goal normally dictates a high price to cover the high product quality and, in some instances, the high cost of research and development. For example, Mercedes-Benz cars are priced to reflect and emphasize high product quality. As previously mentioned, the PIMS studies have shown that both product quality and market share are good indicators of profitability. The products and brands that customers perceive to be of high quality are more likely to survive in a competitive marketplace. High quality usually enables a marketer to charge higher prices for the product. For example, by setting the price of the MACH3 razor at approximately 35 percent above the Sensor price, Gillette clearly communicates that the MACH3 is a high-quality product. The premium prices on Kate Spade handbags ($70 to $250) signal high product quality to customers.

Product Quality Pricing Objective
Gramophone produces high-quality products that are priced to communicate this level of quality.

Assessment of the Target Market's Evaluation of Price

Source: *USA Today,* June 4, 2001, p. 1B. Copyright 2001, *USA Today.* Reprinted with permission.

Despite the general assumption that price is a major issue for buyers, the importance of price depends on the type of product, the type of target market, and the purchase situation. For example, buyers are probably more sensitive to gasoline prices than to luggage prices. With respect to the type of target market, adults may have to pay more than children for certain products. The purchase situation also affects the buyer's view of price. Most moviegoers would never pay in other situations the prices charged for soft drinks, popcorn, and candy at movie concession stands. By assessing the target market's evaluation of price, a marketer is in a better position to know how much emphasis to put on price. Information about the target market's price evaluation may also help a marketer determine how far above the competition the firm can set its prices.

Because some consumers today are seeking less expensive products and shopping more selectively, some manufacturers and retailers are focusing on the value of their products. Value combines a product's price and quality attributes, which customers use to differentiate among competing brands. Consumers are looking for good deals on products that provide better value for their money. Understanding the importance of a product to customers, as well as their expectations about quality and value, helps marketers correctly assess the target market's evaluation of price.

Evaluation of Competitors' Prices

In most cases, marketers are in a better position to establish prices when they know the prices charged for competing brands. Learning competitors' prices may be a regular function of marketing research. Some grocery and department stores, for example, have full-time comparative shoppers who systematically collect data on prices. Companies may also purchase price lists, sometimes weekly, from syndicated marketing research services.

Finding out what prices competitors are charging is not always easy, especially in producer and reseller markets. Competitors' price lists are often closely guarded. Even if a marketer has access to competitors' price lists, these lists may not reflect the actual prices at which competitive products are sold because those prices may be established through negotiation.

Knowing the prices of competing brands can be very important for a marketer. Competitors' prices and the marketing mix variables they emphasize partly determine how important price will be to customers. A marketer in an industry in which price competition prevails needs competitive price information to ensure its prices are the same as, or lower than, competitors' prices.

In some instances, an organization's prices are designed to be slightly above competitors' prices to give its products an exclusive image. Alternately, another company may use price as a competitive tool and price its products below those of competitors. Category killers like Toys "R" Us and Home Depot have acquired large market shares through highly competitive pricing.

Selection of a Basis for Pricing

The three major dimensions on which prices can be based are cost, demand, and competition. The selection of the basis to use is affected by the type of product, the market structure of the industry, the brand's market share position relative to competing brands, and customer characteristics. In this section, we discuss each basis separately. However, when setting prices, an organization generally considers two or all three of these dimensions, even though one may be the primary dimension on which it bases prices. For example, if an organization is using cost as a basis for setting prices, marketers in that organization are also aware of and concerned about competitors' prices. If a company is using demand as a basis for pricing, those making pricing decisions still must consider costs and competitors' prices.

Cost-Based Pricing

cost-based pricing Adding a dollar amount or percentage to the cost of the product

With **cost-based pricing,** a dollar amount or percentage is added to the cost of the product. This approach thus involves calculations of desired profit margins. Cost-based pricing does not necessarily take into account the economic aspects of supply and demand, nor must it relate to just one pricing strategy or pricing objective. Cost-based pricing is straightforward and easy to implement. Two common forms of cost-based pricing are cost-plus and markup pricing.

cost-plus pricing Adding a specified dollar amount or percentage to the seller's cost

Cost-Plus Pricing.   In **cost-plus pricing,** the seller's costs are determined (usually during a project or after a project is completed), and then a specified dollar amount or percentage of the cost is added to the seller's cost to establish the price. When production costs are difficult to predict, cost-plus pricing is appropriate. Projects involving custom-made equipment and commercial construction are often priced by this technique. The government frequently uses such cost-based pricing in granting defense contracts. One pitfall for the buyer is that the seller may increase costs to establish a larger profit base. Furthermore, some costs, such as overhead, may be difficult to determine. In periods of rapid inflation, cost-plus pricing is popular, especially when the producer must use raw materials that are fluctuating in price. In industries in which cost-plus pricing is common and sellers have similar costs, price competition may not be especially intense.

markup pricing Adding to the cost of the product a predetermined percentage of that cost

Markup Pricing.   A common pricing approach among retailers is **markup pricing,** in which a product's price is derived by adding a predetermined percentage of the cost, called *markup,* to the cost of the product. Although the percentage markup in a retail store varies from one category of goods to another—35 percent of cost for hardware items and 100 percent of cost for greeting cards, for example—the same percentage often is used to determine the price on items within a single product category, and the percentage markup may be largely standardized across an industry at the retail level. Using a rigid percentage markup for a specific product category reduces pricing to a routine task that can be performed quickly.

Markup can be stated as a percentage of the cost or as a percentage of the selling price. The following example illustrates how percentage markups are determined and points out the differences in the two methods. Assume a retailer purchases a can of tuna at 45 cents, adds 15 cents to the cost, and then prices the tuna at 60 cents. Here are the figures:

$$\text{Markup as a Percentage of Cost} = \frac{\text{Markup}}{\text{Cost}}$$

$$= \frac{15}{45}$$

$$= 33.3\%$$

$$\text{Markup as a Percentage of Selling Price} = \frac{\text{Markup}}{\text{Selling Price}}$$

$$= \frac{15}{60}$$

$$= 25.0\%$$

Obviously, when discussing a percentage markup, it is important to know whether the markup is based on cost or selling price.

Markups normally reflect expectations about operating costs, risks, and stock turnovers. Wholesalers and manufacturers often suggest standard retail markups that are considered profitable. To the extent that retailers use similar markups for the same product category, price competition is reduced. In addition, using rigid markups is convenient and is the major reason retailers, which face numerous pricing decisions, favor this method.

Demand-Based Pricing

demand-based pricing
Pricing based on the level of demand for the product

Marketers sometimes base prices on the level of demand for the product. When **demand-based pricing** is used, customers pay a higher price when demand for the product is strong and a lower price when demand is weak. For example, hotels that otherwise attract numerous travelers often offer reduced rates during lower-demand periods. Some long-distance telephone companies, such as Sprint and AT&T, also use demand-based pricing by charging peak and off-peak rates. To use this pricing basis, a marketer must be able to estimate the amounts of a product consumers will demand at different prices. The marketer then chooses the price that generates the highest total revenue. Obviously, the effectiveness of demand-based pricing depends on the marketer's ability to estimate demand accurately.

Demand-Based Pricing
Vacation destinations often use demand-based pricing, as is the case with Vermont promoting the value of skiing midweek.

Competition-Based Pricing
These advertisements suggest that both of these organizations employ competition-based pricing.

Compared with cost-based pricing, demand-based pricing places a firm in a better position to reach higher profit levels, assuming buyers value the product at levels sufficiently above the product's cost.

Competition-Based Pricing

competition-based pricing
Pricing influenced primarily by competitors' prices

In **competition-based pricing,** an organization considers costs as secondary to competitors' prices. The importance of this method increases when competing products are relatively homogeneous and the organization is serving markets in which price is a key purchase consideration. A firm that uses competition-based pricing may choose to price below competitors' prices, above competitors' prices, or at the same level. Airlines use competition-based pricing, often charging identical fares on the same routes.

Although not all introductory marketing texts have exactly the same price, they do have similar prices. The price the bookstore paid to the publishing company for this textbook was determined on the basis of competitors' prices. Competition-based pricing can help a firm achieve the pricing objective of increasing sales or market share. Competition-based pricing may necessitate frequent price adjustments. For example, for many competitive airline routes, fares are adjusted often.

Selection of a Pricing Strategy

A pricing strategy is an approach or a course of action designed to achieve pricing and marketing objectives. Generally, pricing strategies help marketers solve the practical problems of establishing prices. Table 21.2 lists the most common pricing strategies, which we discuss in this section.

Table 21.2	Common Pricing Strategies
Differential Pricing	**Psychological Pricing**
Negotiated Pricing	Reference Pricing
Secondary-Market Pricing	Bundle Pricing
Periodic Discounting	Multiple-Unit Pricing
Random Discounting	Everyday Low Prices
	Odd-Even Pricing
New-Product Pricing	Customary Pricing
Price Skimming	Prestige Pricing
Penetration Pricing	
	Professional Pricing
Product-Line Pricing	
Captive Pricing	**Promotional Pricing**
Premium Pricing	Price Leaders
Bait Pricing	Special-Event Pricing
Price Lining	Comparison Discounting

Differential Pricing

An important issue in pricing decisions is whether to use a single price or different prices for the same product. Using a single price has several benefits. A primary advantage is simplicity. A single price is easily understood by both employees and customers, and since many salespeople and customers do not like having to negotiate a price, it reduces the chance of an adversarial relationship developing between marketer and customer. The use of a single price does create some challenges, however. If the single price is too high, a number of potential customers may be unable to afford the product. If it is too low, the organization loses revenue from those customers who would have paid more if the price had been higher.

differential pricing Charging different prices to different buyers for the same quality and quantity of product

Differential pricing means charging different prices to different buyers for the same quality and quantity of product. For differential pricing to be effective, the market must consist of multiple segments with different price sensitivities, and the method should be used in a way that avoids confusing or antagonizing customers. Customers paying the lower prices should not be able to resell the product to the individuals and organizations paying higher prices, unless that is the intention of the seller. Differential pricing can occur in several ways, including negotiated pricing, secondary-market discounting, periodic discounting, and random discounting.

negotiated pricing Establishing a final price through bargaining

Negotiated Pricing.   **Negotiated pricing** occurs when the final price is established through bargaining between seller and customer. Negotiated pricing occurs in a number of industries and at all levels of distribution. Even when there is a predetermined stated price or a price list, manufacturers, wholesalers, and retailers may still negotiate to establish the final sales price. Consumers commonly negotiate prices for houses, cars, and used equipment.

secondary-market pricing Setting one price for the primary target market and a different price for another market

Secondary-Market Pricing.   **Secondary-market pricing** means setting one price for the primary target market and a different price for another market. Often the price charged in the secondary market is lower. However, when the costs of serving a secondary market are higher than normal, secondary-market customers may have to pay a higher price. Examples of secondary markets include a geographically isolated domestic market, a market in a foreign country, and a segment willing to purchase a product during off-peak times. For example, during the early evening hours, some restaurants offer special "early-bird" prices; movie theaters offer senior-citizen discounts; and some textbooks and pharmaceutical products are sold for considerably less in certain foreign countries than in the United States. Secondary markets give an organization an opportunity to use excess capacity and to stabilize the allocation of resources.

periodic discounting
Temporary reduction of prices on a patterned or systematic basis

Periodic Discounting.   **Periodic discounting** is the temporary reduction of prices on a patterned or systematic basis. For example, many retailers have annual holiday sales. Some women's apparel stores have two seasonal sales each year: a winter sale in the last two weeks of January and a summer sale in the first two weeks of July. Automobile dealers regularly discount prices on current models when the next year's models are introduced. From the marketer's point of view, a major problem with periodic discounting is that because the discounts follow a pattern, customers can predict when the reductions will occur and may delay their purchases until they can take advantage of the lower prices.

random discounting
Temporary reduction of prices on an unsystematic basis

Random Discounting.   To alleviate the problem of customers knowing when discounting will occur, some organizations employ **random discounting;** that is, they temporarily reduce their prices on an unsystematic basis. When price reductions of a product occur randomly, current users of that brand are likely to be unable to predict when the reductions will occur and so will not delay their purchases. Marketers also use random discounting to attract new customers. For example, Lever Brothers may temporarily reduce the price of one of its bar soaps in the hope of attracting new customers.

GLOBAL MARKETING

De Beers Polishes Prestige Pricing

"A diamond is forever," but not a monopoly. De Beers, which rigidly controlled the world's diamond supply for decades, recently decided not to maintain monopoly pricing over its dominant but dwindling share of the market. Since the discovery of new diamond sources in North America, Australia, and Russia during the mid-1980s, the Switzerland-based company has seen its share of global diamond supplies shrink from nearly 90 to 63 percent. De Beers was indicted in 1994 for price fixing in the United States, and it knows European Union antitrust officials are concerned about companies that dominate their markets. Faced with these regulatory pressures and increased competition, De Beers is polishing a new prestige pricing approach for its diamond business.

The centerpiece is the Supplier of Choice program, intended to boost global diamond demand by helping producers, dealers, wholesalers, and retailers market branded gems at prestige prices. Participants in the Suppliers of Choice program benefit from De Beers's training and expertise, its proprietary marketing research, and its $170 million annual investment in diamond promotion. They are also allowed to use the new Forevermark symbol, which De Beers created to differentiate its diamonds from competing gems. Like the Intel Inside logo, the Forevermark aims to reassure buyers of the quality of the diamonds being marketed. This coordinated marketing program will strengthen relationships throughout the supply chain and help all participants achieve their pricing objectives. "We want people to say, 'While I can get diamonds from people other than De Beers, the package De Beers gives me is so valuable, I get a better return from them,'" says the company's chairperson.

In the past, De Beers rarely asked how its intermediaries planned to market the diamonds it supplied. Today, however, De Beers wants to be sure its products move through the strongest and most effective upscale channels. "I don't want diamonds to be discounted," explains Gary Ralfe, managing director of De Beers. "What is tantalizing is that at the luxury end—the famous blue box of Tiffany's—there are brands getting the margins and markups enjoyed in the luxury-goods business as a whole. We want to see stores pushing the preciousness of diamonds rather than treating them as a commodity you can discount."

www.coldwatercreek.com

"I click
I shop I find
the clothes
I love."

Now take
$15 off
your online
order of $75 or more

Simply enter WHA0909
at checkout. Applies to one online
order once, please cannot be combined
with other offers. Offer good through
December 31, 2001. Some not valid
at www.gallery.thecreek.com.

Questions? Call 1-800-510-2800

Coldwater Creek
Your kind of clothes. Online. All the time.

Irrespective of whether periodic discounting or random discounting is used, retailers often employ tensile pricing when putting products on sale. *Tensile pricing* refers to a broad statement about price reductions as opposed to detailing specific price discounts. Examples of tensile pricing would be statements such as "20 to 50% off," "up to 75% off," and "save 10% or more." Generally, using and advertising the tensile price that mentions only the maximum reduction (such as "up to 50% off") generates the highest customer response.[4]

New-Product Pricing

Setting the base price for a new product is a necessary part of formulating a marketing strategy. The base price is easily adjusted (in the absence of government price controls), and its establishment is one of the most fundamental decisions in the marketing mix. The base price can be set high to recover development costs quickly or to provide a reference point for developing discount prices to different market segments. When a marketer sets base prices, it also considers how quickly competitors will enter the market, whether they will mount a strong campaign on entry, and what effect their entry will have on the development of primary demand. Two strategies used in new-product pricing are price skimming and penetration pricing.

price skimming Charging the highest possible price that buyers who most desire the product will pay

Price Skimming.   **Price skimming** is charging the highest possible price that buyers who most desire the product will pay. This approach provides the most flexible introductory base price. Demand tends to be inelastic in the introductory stage of the product life cycle.

Price skimming can provide several benefits, especially when a product is in the introductory stage of its life cycle. A skimming policy can generate much-needed initial cash flows to help offset sizable developmental costs. When introducing a new model of camera, Polaroid initially uses a skimming price to defray large research and development costs. Price skimming protects the marketer from problems that arise when the price is set too low to cover costs. When a firm introduces a product, its production capacity may be limited. A skimming price can help keep demand consistent with the firm's production capabilities. The use of a skimming price may attract competition into an industry because the high price makes that type of business appear to be quite lucrative.

penetration pricing Setting prices below those of competing brands to penetrate a market and gain a significant market share quickly

Penetration Pricing.   In **penetration pricing,** prices are set below those of competing brands to penetrate a market and gain a large market share quickly. For example, when Hyundai introduced its all-new sports-utility vehicle, the Santa Fe, it used penetration pricing by pricing Santa Fe models approximately $10,000 below the prices of comparable competing brands.[5] This approach is less flexible for a marketer than price skimming because it is more difficult to raise a penetration price than to lower or discount a skimming price. It is not unusual for a firm to use a penetration price after having skimmed the market with a higher price.

Penetration pricing can be especially beneficial when a marketer suspects that competitors could enter the market easily. If penetration pricing allows the marketer to gain a large market share quickly, competitors may be discouraged from entering the market. In addition, entering a market may be less attractive to competitors when penetration pricing is used because the lower per-unit price results in lower per-unit profit; this may cause competitors to view the market as not being especially lucrative.

Product-Line Pricing

product-line pricing
Establishing and adjusting prices of multiple products within a product line

Rather than considering products on an item-by-item basis when determining pricing strategies, some marketers employ product-line pricing. **Product-line pricing** means establishing and adjusting the prices of multiple products within a product line. When marketers use product-line pricing, their goal is to maximize profits for an entire product line rather than focusing on the profitability of an individual product. Product-line pricing can provide marketers with flexibility in price setting. For example, marketers can set prices so that one product is quite profitable while another increases market share by virtue of having a lower price than competing products.

Net Sights

On the U.S. government Bureau of Labor Statistics' Consumer Price Index page (**http://www.bls.gov/cpi/home.htm**), visitors have access to an Inflation Calculator, news releases, and a plethora of information on the consumer price index. Information on this site illuminates some of the complexity involved in setting prices.

Before setting prices for a product line, marketers evaluate the relationship among the products in the line. When products in a line are complementary, sales increases in one item raise demand for other items. For instance, desktop printers and toner cartridges are complementary products. When products in a line function as substitutes for one another, buyers of one product in the line are unlikely to purchase one of the other products in the same line. In this case, marketers must be sensitive to how a price change for one of the brands may affect the demand not only for that brand but also for the substitute brands. For example, if decision makers at Procter & Gamble were considering a price change for Tide detergent, they would be concerned about how the price change might influence the sales of Cheer, Bold, and Gain.

When marketers employ product-line pricing, they have several strategies from which to choose. These include captive pricing, premium pricing, bait pricing, and price lining.

captive pricing   Pricing the basic product in a product line low while pricing related items at a higher level

Captive Pricing.   With **captive pricing,** the basic product in a product line is priced low, while the price on the items required to operate or enhance it may be higher. For example, a manufacturer of cameras and film may set the price of the cameras at a level low enough to attract customers but set the film price relatively high because to use the cameras, customers must continue to purchase film.

premium pricing   Pricing the highest-quality or most versatile products higher than other models in the product line

Premium Pricing.   **Premium pricing** is often used when a product line contains several versions of the same product; the highest-quality products or those with the most versatility are given the highest prices. Other products in the line are priced to appeal to price-sensitive shoppers or to those who seek product-specific features. Marketers that use a premium strategy often realize a significant portion of their profits from premium-priced products. Examples of product categories that commonly use premium pricing are small kitchen appliances, beer, ice cream, and cable television service.

bait pricing   Pricing an item in the product line low with the intention of selling a higher-priced item in the line

Bait Pricing.   To attract customers, marketers may put a low price on one item in the product line with the intention of selling a higher-priced item in the line; this strategy is known as **bait pricing.** For example, a computer retailer might advertise its lowest-priced computer model, hoping that when customers come to the store they will purchase a higher-priced one. This strategy can facilitate sales of a line's higher-priced products. As long as a retailer has sufficient quantities of the advertised low-priced

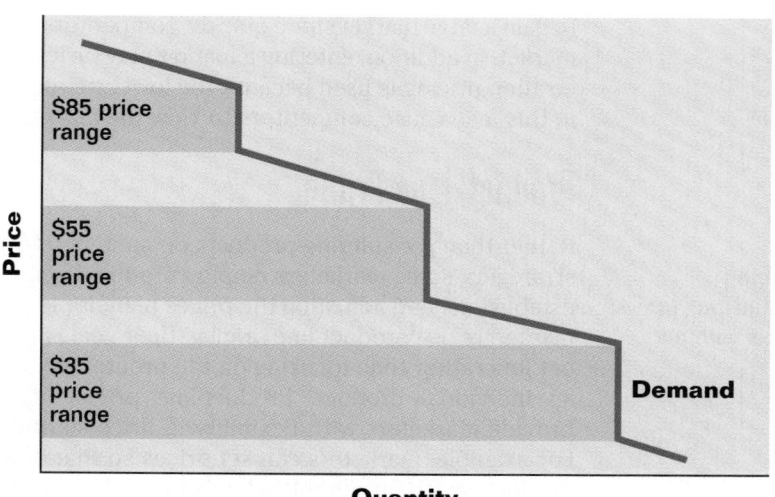

FIGURE 21.2
Price Lining

model available for sale, this strategy is considered acceptable. However, *bait and switch* is an activity in which retailers have no intention of selling the bait product; they use the low price merely to entice customers into the store to sell them higher-priced products. Bait and switch is considered unethical, and in some states it is illegal as well.

price lining Setting a limited number of prices for selected groups or lines of merchandise

Price Lining.   When an organization sets a limited number of prices for selected groups or lines of merchandise, it is using **price lining.** A retailer may have various styles and brands of similar-quality men's shirts that sell for $15 and another line of higher-quality shirts that sell for $22. Price lining simplifies customers' decision making by holding constant one key variable in the final selection of style and brand within a line.

The basic assumption in price lining is that the demand for various groups or sets of products is inelastic. If the prices are attractive, customers will concentrate their purchases without responding to slight changes in price. Thus, a women's dress shop that carries dresses priced at $85, $55, and $35 may not attract many more sales with a drop to, say, $83, $53, and $33. The "space" between the price of $85 and $55, however, can stir changes in consumer response. With price lining, the demand curve looks like a series of steps, as shown in Figure 21.2.

Psychological Pricing

psychological pricing Pricing that attempts to influence a customer's perception of price to make a product's price more attractive

Learning the price of a product is not always a pleasant experience for customers. It can sometimes be surprising (as at a movie concession stand) and sometimes downright horrifying; most of us have been afflicted with "sticker shock." **Psychological pricing** attempts to influence a customer's perception of price to make a product's price more attractive. In this section, we consider several forms of psychological pricing: reference pricing, bundle pricing, multiple-unit pricing, everyday low prices (EDLP), odd-even pricing, customary pricing, and prestige pricing.

reference pricing Pricing a product at a moderate level and positioning it next to a more expensive model or brand

Reference Pricing.   **Reference pricing** means pricing a product at a moderate level and positioning it next to a more expensive model or brand in the hope that the customer will use the higher price as an external reference price (i.e., a comparison price). Because of the comparison, the customer is expected to view the moderate price favorably. Reference pricing is based on the "isolation effect," meaning an alternative is less attractive when viewed by itself than when compared with other alternatives. When you go to Sears to buy a DVD player, a moderately priced DVD player

10 Days Wonder from $1,799 per person

Bundle Pricing
Travel- and tour-related products are sometimes priced using bundle pricing.

may appear especially attractive because it offers most of the important attributes of the more expensive alternatives on display and at a lower price. It is not unusual for an organization's moderately priced private brands to be positioned alongside more expensive, better-known manufacturer brands.

Bundle Pricing.

bundle pricing Packaging together two or more complementary products and selling them for a single price

Bundle pricing is packaging together two or more products, usually complementary ones, to be sold for a single price. To attract customers, the single price is usually considerably less than the sum of the prices of the individual products. The opportunity to buy the bundled combination of products in a single transaction may be of value to the customer as well. For example, Gateway Computers bundles a computer, software, and Internet service and makes the entire package available for a single monthly charge. Bundle pricing not only helps increase customer satisfaction, but by bundling slow-moving products with ones with higher turnover, an organization can stimulate sales and increase its revenues. Selling products as a package rather than individually may also result in cost savings. Bundle pricing is commonly used for banking and travel services, computers, and automobiles with option packages.

Multiple-Unit Pricing.

multiple-unit pricing
Packaging together two or more identical products and selling them for a single price

Multiple-unit pricing occurs when two or more identical products are packaged together and sold for a single price. This normally results in a lower per-unit price than the one regularly charged. Multiple-unit pricing is commonly used for twin packs of potato chips, four-packs of light bulbs, and six- and twelve-packs of soft drinks. Customers benefit from the cost saving and convenience this pricing strategy affords. A company may use multiple-unit pricing to attract new customers to its brand and, in some instances, to increase consumption of its brands. When customers buy in larger quantities, their consumption of the product may increase. For example, multiple-unit pricing may encourage a customer to buy larger quantities of snacks, which are likely to be consumed in higher volume at the point of consumption simply because they are available. However, this is not true for all products. For instance, greater availability at the point of consumption of light bulbs, bar soap, and table salt is not likely to increase usage.

Discount stores and especially warehouse clubs, such as Sam's Club, are major users of multiple-unit pricing. For certain products in these stores, customers receive significant per-unit price reductions when they buy packages containing multiple units of the same product, such as an eight-pack of canned tuna fish.

Everyday Low Prices (EDLP).   To reduce or eliminate the use of frequent short-term price reductions, some organizations use an approach referred to as **everyday low prices (EDLP).** With EDLP, a marketer sets a low price for its products on a consistent basis rather than setting higher prices and frequently discounting them. Everyday low prices, though not deeply discounted, are set far enough below competitors' prices to make customers feel confident they are receiving a fair price. EDLP is employed by retailers like Wal-Mart and manufacturers like Procter & Gamble. A company that uses EDLP benefits from reduced losses from frequent markdowns, greater stability in sales, and reduced promotional costs. For example, Family Dollar Stores changed its pricing strategy to EDLP. Just prior to the change, Family Dollar was printing and distributing 22 promotional price circulars a year. Now it prints and distributes only three promotional circulars a year, significantly reducing its promotion costs.[6]

A major problem with EDLP is that customers have mixed responses to it. Over the last several years, many marketers have "trained" customers to seek and to expect deeply discounted prices. In some product categories, such as apparel, finding the deepest discount has become almost a national consumer sport. Thus, failure to provide deep discounts can be a problem for certain marketers. In some instances, customers simply don't believe that everyday low prices are what marketers claim they are but are instead a marketing gimmick.

Odd-Even Pricing.   Through **odd-even pricing**—ending the price with certain numbers—marketers try to influence buyers' perceptions of the price or the product. Odd pricing assumes that more of a product will be sold at $99.95 than at $100. Supposedly, customers will think, or at least tell friends, that the product is a bargain—not $100, but $99 and change. Also, customers will supposedly think the store could have charged $100 but instead cut the price to the last cent, to $99.95. Some claim, too, that certain types of customers are more attracted by odd prices than by even ones. However, no substantial research findings support the notion that odd prices produce greater sales. Nonetheless, odd prices are far more common today than even prices.

Even prices are often used to give a product an exclusive or upscale image. An even price supposedly will influence a customer to view the product as being a high-quality, premium brand. A shirtmaker, for example, may print on a premium shirt package a suggested retail price of $42.00 instead of $41.95; the even price of the shirt is used to enhance its upscale image.

Customary Pricing.   In **customary pricing,** certain goods are priced primarily on the basis of tradition. Recent economic uncertainties have made most prices fluctuate fairly widely, but the classic example of the customary, or traditional, price is the price of a candy bar. For years, a candy bar cost 5 cents. A new candy bar would have had to be something very special to sell for more than a nickel. This price was so sacred that rather than change it, manufacturers increased or decreased the size of the candy bar itself as chocolate prices fluctuated. Today, of course, the nickel candy bar has disappeared. Yet most candy bars still sell at a consistent, but obviously higher, price. Thus, customary pricing remains the standard for this market.

Prestige Pricing.   In **prestige pricing,** prices are set at an artificially high level to convey prestige or a quality image. Prestige pricing is used especially when buyers associate a higher price with higher quality. Pharmacists report that some consumers complain when a prescription does not cost enough; apparently some consumers associate a drug's price with its potency. Typical product categories in which selected products are prestige priced include perfumes, liquor, jewelry, and cars. Porsche,

everyday low prices (EDLP) Setting a low price for products on a consistent basis

odd-even pricing Ending the price with certain numbers to influence buyers' perceptions of the price or product

customary pricing Pricing on the basis of tradition

prestige pricing Setting prices at an artificially high level to convey prestige or a quality image

for example, signals luxury and top performance by setting high prices for its cars, ranging from the $42,000 Boxster to the 911 Turbo at $111,000. As a result of its costs and use of prestige pricing, Porsche earns about $7,350 profit per car, whereas General Motors earns about $850 profit per car.[7] If producers that use prestige pricing lowered their prices dramatically, the new prices would be inconsistent with the perceived high-quality images of their products.

Professional Pricing

professional pricing Fees set by people with great skill or experience in a particular field

Professional pricing is used by people who have great skill or experience in a particular field. Professionals often believe their fees (prices) should not relate directly to the time and effort spent in specific cases; rather, a standard fee is charged regardless of the problems involved in performing the job. Some doctors' and lawyers' fees are prime examples: $55 for a checkup, $1,500 for an appendectomy, and $399 for a divorce. Other professionals set prices in other ways. Like other marketers, professionals have costs associated with facilities, labor, insurance, equipment, and supplies. Certainly, costs are considered when setting professional prices.

The concept of professional pricing carries the idea that professionals have an ethical responsibility not to overcharge customers. In some situations, a seller can charge customers a high price and continue to sell many units of the product. Medicine offers several examples. If a diabetic requires one insulin treatment per day to survive, the individual will buy that treatment whether its price is $1 or $10. In fact, the patient surely would purchase the treatment even if the price went higher. In these situations, sellers could charge exorbitant fees. Drug companies claim that despite their positions of strength in this regard, they charge ethical prices rather than what the market will bear.

price leaders Products priced below the usual markup, near cost, or below cost

special-event pricing Advertised sales or price cutting linked to a holiday, season, or event

Promotional Pricing

As an ingredient in the marketing mix, price is often coordinated with promotion. The two variables sometimes are so interrelated that the pricing policy is promotion oriented. Types of promotional pricing include price leaders, special-event pricing, and comparison discounting.

Price Leaders.   Sometimes a firm prices a few products below the usual markup, near cost, or below cost, which results in prices known as **price leaders.** This type of pricing is used most often in supermarkets and restaurants to attract customers by giving them especially low prices on a few items. Management hopes that sales of regularly priced products will more than offset the reduced revenues from the price leaders.

Special-Event Pricing.   To increase sales volume, many organizations coordinate price with advertising or sales promotions for seasonal or special situations. **Special-event pricing** involves advertised sales or price cutting linked to a holiday, season, or event. If the pricing

Special-Event Pricing
A number of organizations, especially retailers such as Sears, create special events and employ special event pricing.

Comparison Discounting
Filene's Basement compares its $99.99 leather jackets with comparable $179–$450 leather jackets sold by competitors.

objective is survival, special sales events may be designed to generate the necessary operating capital. Special-event pricing entails coordination of production, scheduling, storage, and physical distribution. Whenever a sales lag occurs, special-event pricing is an alternative that marketers should consider.

comparison discounting
Setting a price at a specific level and comparing it with a higher price

Comparison Discounting. **Comparison discounting** sets the price of a product at a specific level and simultaneously compares it with a higher price. The higher price may be the product's previous price, the price of a competing brand, the product's price at another retail outlet, or a manufacturer's suggested retail price. Customers may find comparative discounting informative, and it can have a significant impact on their purchases. However, overuse of comparison pricing may reduce customers' internal reference prices, meaning they no longer believe the higher price is the regular or normal price.[8]

Because this pricing strategy has on occasion led to deceptive pricing practices, the Federal Trade Commission has established guidelines for comparison discounting. If the higher price against which the comparison is made is the price formerly charged for the product, the seller must have made the previous price available to customers for a reasonable period of time. If the seller presents the higher price as the one charged by other retailers in the same trade area, it must be able to demonstrate that this claim is true. When the seller presents the higher price as the manufacturer's suggested retail price, the higher price must be similar to the price at which a reasonable proportion of the product was sold. Some manufacturers' suggested retail prices are so high that very few products are actually sold at those prices. In such cases, comparison discounting would be deceptive. An example of deceptive comparison discounting occurred when a major retailer sold 93 percent of its power tools on sale, with discounts ranging from 10 to 40 percent. The retailer's frequent price reductions meant that the tools sold at sale prices most of the year. Thus, comparisons with regular prices were deemed to be deceptive.

Determination of a Specific Price

A pricing strategy will yield a certain price. However, this price may need refinement to make it consistent with pricing practices in a particular market or industry.

Pricing strategies should help in setting a final price. If they are to do so, it is important for marketers to establish pricing objectives, have considerable knowledge about target market customers, and determine demand, price elasticity, costs, and competitive factors. Also, the way pricing is used in the marketing mix will affect the final price.

In the absence of government price controls, pricing remains a flexible and convenient way to adjust the marketing mix. The online brokerage arm of American Express, for example, sets prices on a sliding scale, depending on how much service support each customer uses. Customers who conduct all their securities trades without going through Amex employees pay lower prices than those who work with the firm's financial advisers to complete trades. As a result, American Express can provide the exact services each customer requires at an appropriate price.[9] In many situations, prices can be adjusted quickly—in a matter of minutes or over a few days. Such flexibility is unique to this component of the marketing mix.

TECH * KNOW

Using Software to Set Prices

One price does not fit all, as the major airlines have known for some time. American, Continental, and many other airlines routinely use sophisticated software to set the prices for specific products or customers based on moment-to-moment data about inventory, sales history, and other relevant variables. Experts estimate that companies can boost profits by at least 5 percent—and possibly as much as 100 percent—through the careful use of price-setting software.

Gymboree, JCPenney, and the Gap are three major retailers using software made by ProfitLogic to figure out the most effective markdown prices for moving old inventory. As a result, Gymboree not only clears out its inventory on time but has been able to boost its gross profit margins by 4 percent. An electronics retailer also uses this software to set prices on a regular basis, factoring in weekly sales information and other data. Online retailer Buy.com uses a competing software package from KhiMetrics to analyze each product's life cycle, sales history, and competitive situation in determining the most appropriate price. Other e-businesses use software to vary prices according to when and what a customer buys. Some programs even help e-businesses increase sales by offering special spur-of-the-moment pricing on

products that complement items already in a customer's shopping basket.

Companies break no U.S. laws when they price the same product differently for two consumers. However, marketers selling to businesses must comply with the Robinson-Patman Act, which requires sellers to avoid price discrimination when selling to buyers that compete with one another. "If I'm selling bread to Safeway at one price and to Albertson's at another price," says one legal expert, "that represents a Robinson-Patman issue, because sellers are under a general obligation to sell to competing buyers at nondiscriminatory terms."

Even when companies use software to set prices in a legal manner, they risk a backlash if consumers find out that the same product is selling at different price points. To avoid this problem, companies should inform customers of the factors that lead to price differences, such as seasonal demand, shipping choices, payment terms, and cost variations. Once customers understand that a seller is using objective criteria to guide its pricing, they are less likely to feel they have been treated unfairly.

Summary

The six stages in the process of setting prices are (1) developing pricing objectives, (2) assessing the target market's evaluation of price, (3) evaluating competitors' prices, (4) choosing a basis for pricing, (5) selecting a pricing strategy, and (6) determining a specific price.

Setting pricing objectives is critical because pricing objectives form a foundation on which the decisions of subsequent stages are based. Organizations may use numerous pricing objectives, including short-term and long-term ones, and different ones for different products and market segments. Pricing objectives are overall goals that describe the role of price in a firm's long-range plans. There are several major types of pricing objectives. The most fundamental pricing objective is the organization's survival. Price usually can be easily adjusted to increase sales volume or combat competition to help the organization stay alive. Profit objectives, which are usually stated in terms of sales dollar volume or percentage change, are normally set at a satisfactory level rather than at a level designed for profit maximization. A sales growth objective focuses on increasing the profit base by increasing sales volume. Pricing for return on investment (ROI) has a specified profit as its objective. A pricing objective to maintain or increase market share implies that market position is linked to success. Other types of pricing objectives include cash flow, status quo, and product quality. Assessing the target market's evaluation of price tells the marketer how much emphasis to place on price and may help determine how far above the competition the firm can set its prices. Understanding how important a product is to customers relative to other products, as well as customers' expectations of quality, helps marketers correctly assess the target market's evaluation of price.

A marketer needs to be aware of the prices charged for competing brands. This allows the firm to keep its prices in line with competitors' prices when nonprice competition is used. If a company uses price as a competitive tool, it can price its brand below competing brands.

The three major dimensions on which prices can be based are cost, demand, and competition. When using cost-based pricing, the firm determines price by adding a dollar amount or percentage to the cost of the product. Two common cost-based pricing methods are cost-plus and markup pricing. Demand-based pricing is based on the level of demand for the product. To use this method, a marketer must be able to estimate the amounts of a product that buyers will demand at different prices. Demand-based pricing results in a high price when demand for a product is strong and a low price when demand is weak. In the case of competition-based pricing, costs and revenues are secondary to competitors' prices.

A pricing strategy is an approach or a course of action designed to achieve pricing and marketing objectives. Pricing strategies help marketers solve the practical problems of establishing prices. The most common pricing strategies are differential pricing, new-product pricing, product-line pricing, psychological pricing, professional pricing, and promotional pricing.

When marketers employ differential pricing, they charge different buyers different prices for the same quality and quantity of products. Negotiated pricing, secondary-market discounting, periodic discounting, and random discounting are forms of differential pricing. Establishing the final price through bargaining between seller and customer is called negotiated pricing. Secondary-market pricing involves setting one price for the primary target market and a different price for another market; often the price charged in the secondary market is lower. Marketers employ a strategy of periodic discounting when they temporarily lower their prices on a patterned or systematic basis; the reason for the reduction may be a seasonal change, a model-year change, or a holiday. Random discounting occurs on an unsystematic basis.

Two strategies used in new-product pricing are price skimming and penetration pricing. With price skimming, the organization charges the highest price that buyers who most desire the product will pay. A penetration price is a low price designed to penetrate a market and gain a significant market share quickly.

Product-line pricing establishes and adjusts the prices of multiple products within a product line. This strategy includes captive pricing, in which the marketer prices the basic product in a product line low but prices related items at a higher level; premium pricing, in which prices on higher-quality or more versatile products are set higher than those on other models in the product line; bait pricing, in which the marketer tries to attract customers by pricing an item in the product line low with the intention of selling a higher-priced item in the line; and price lining, in which the organization sets a limited number of prices for selected groups or lines of merchandise. Organizations that employ price lining assume the demand for various groups of products is inelastic.

Psychological pricing attempts to influence customers' perceptions of price to make a product's price more attractive. In reference pricing, marketers price a product at a moderate level and position it next to a more expensive model or brand. Bundle pricing is packaging together two or more complementary products that are sold for a single price. In multiple-unit pricing, two or more identical products are packaged together and sold for a single price. To reduce or eliminate use of frequent short-term price reductions, some organizations employ everyday low pricing, setting a low price for products on a consistent basis. When employing odd-even pricing, marketers try to influence buyers' perceptions of the price or the product by ending the price with certain numbers. Customary pricing is based on traditional prices. With prestige pricing, prices are set at an artificially high level to convey prestige or a quality image.

Professional pricing is used by people who have great skill or experience in a particular field, therefore allowing them to set the price. This concept carries the idea that professionals have an ethical responsibility not to overcharge customers. As an ingredient in the marketing mix, price is often coordinated with promotion. The two variables are sometimes so interrelated that the pricing policy is promotion oriented. Promotional pricing includes price leaders, special-event pricing, and comparison discounting.

Special-event pricing involves advertised sales or price cutting linked to a holiday, season, or event. Marketers who use a comparison discounting strategy price a product at a specific level and compare it with a higher price.

Once a price is determined by using one or more pricing strategies, it will need to be refined to a final price consistent with the pricing practices in a particular market or industry.

Important Terms

Pricing objectives
Cost-based pricing
Cost-plus pricing
Markup pricing
Demand-based pricing
Competition-based pricing
Differential pricing
Negotiated pricing
Secondary-market pricing
Periodic discounting
Random discounting
Price skimming
Penetration pricing
Product-line pricing
Captive pricing
Premium pricing
Bait pricing
Price lining
Psychological pricing

Reference pricing
Bundle pricing
Multiple-unit pricing
Everyday low prices
 (EDLP)
Odd-even pricing
Customary pricing
Prestige pricing
Professional pricing
Price leaders
Special-event pricing
Comparison discounting

Discussion and Review Questions

1. Identify the six stages in the process of establishing prices.
2. How does a return on investment pricing objective differ from an objective of increasing market share?
3. Why must marketing objectives and pricing objectives be considered when making pricing decisions?
4. Why should a marketer be aware of competitors' prices?
5. What are the benefits of cost-based pricing?
6. Under what conditions is cost-plus pricing most appropriate?
7. A retailer purchases a can of soup for 24 cents and sells it for 36 cents. Calculate the markup as a percentage of cost and as a percentage of selling price.
8. What is differential pricing? In what ways can it be achieved?
9. For what type of products would price skimming be most appropriate? For what type of products would penetration pricing be more effective?

10. Describe bundle pricing and give three examples using different industries.
11. What are the advantages and disadvantages of using everyday low prices?
12. Why do customers associate price with quality? When should prestige pricing be used?
13. Are price leaders a realistic approach to pricing? Explain your answer.

Application Questions

1. Price skimming and penetration pricing are strategies commonly used to set the base price of a new product. Which strategy is more appropriate for the following products? Explain.
   a. Short airline flights between cities in Florida
   b. A DVD player
   c. A backpack or book bag with a lifetime warranty
   d. Season tickets for a newly franchised NBA basketball team
2. Price lining is used to set a limited number of prices for selected lines of merchandise. Visit a few local retail stores to find examples of price lining. For what types of products and stores is this practice most common? For what products and stores is price lining not typical or usable?
3. Professional pricing is used by people who have great skill in a particular field, such as doctors, lawyers, and business consultants. Find examples (advertisements, personal contacts) that reflect a professional-pricing policy. How is the price established? Are there any restrictions on the services performed at that price?
4. Organizations often use multiple pricing objectives. Locate an organization that uses several pricing objectives, and discuss how this approach influences the company's marketing mix decisions. Are some objectives oriented toward the short term and others toward the long term? How does the marketing environment influence these objectives?

Internet Exercise & Resources

VoiceStream

VoiceStream has attempted to position itself as a low-cost cellular phone service provider. A person can purchase a calling plan, a cellular phone, and phone accessories at its website. Visit the VoiceStream website at

www.voicestream.com

1. Determine the various nationwide rates available in Houston, Texas.

2. How many different calling plans are available in the Houston area?

3. What type of pricing strategy is VoiceStream using on its Houston rate plans?

VIDEO CASE 21.1
VIPdesk.com: At Your Service at a Reasonable Price

Imagine having a concierge on call to make restaurant reservations, obtain sports tickets, arrange for home repairs, or find that perfect gift—all at any hour of the day. MasterCard's platinum cardholders have immediate access to round-the-clock concierge services through VIPdesk, a web-based business headed by CEO Mary Naylor. VIPdesk evolved from Naylor's years of experience providing on-site concierge services for the employees of corporations in major office complexes around metropolitan Washington, DC. Recognizing the opportunity to cost effectively serve a wider corporate customer base through technology, Naylor established her first concierge website in 1996 and then upgraded it to VIPdesk in 2000.

Today VIPdesk specializes in handling concierge services for 10 million users in two segments of the U.S. business market. Companies like Van Kampen offer VIPdesk's services as a reward for outstanding employees. In addition, corporate clients like MasterCard, Citibank, Diner's Club, and America Online offer VIPdesk's services to select customers located all over the United States.

Naylor offers access to her concierge services in many ways. Users can search the VIPdesk website for information, initiate a live text chat with a concierge, send e-mail messages requesting assistance, have a telephone conversation with a concierge, access customized information via web-enabled cell phones, or contact a concierge via a handheld computer such as a Palm. Among the most common requests are help with travel arrangements, auto rentals, local entertainment options, last-minute theater and sports tickets, personal shopping, and other errands. No matter how users reach VIPdesk or what they request, they get fast, free, professional help. "In effect, what we provide to the customer is a virtual personal assistant," Naylor says.

For example, when MasterCard was planning the launch of its platinum World Card, management realized VIPdesk's high-tech but highly personalized service would be a good way to help member banks differentiate this product. Alice Droogan, vice president of Worldwide Cardholder Services, notes that VIPdesk's personalized services cost MasterCard "pennies a card, and as enhancements go, that's quite valuable." Seventeen financial institutions have begun using the service to attract new cardholders and reinforce cardholder loyalty. Although usage rates have been low in the first few years, Droogan sees demand increasing, especially for online access to concierge expertise.

MasterCard is particularly enthusiastic about VIPdesk's flexibility in responding to just about any request rather than simply offering a limited menu of preset options from which customers can choose. Although "most of the other companies we looked at were just basically travel assistance services," Droogan was impressed with VIPdesk's wider capabilities. Given the highly competitive environment in the credit card field, where MasterCard must battle Visa, American Express, Discover, and Diner's Club, VIPdesk is playing an important role because it helps MasterCard "support our initiatives to offer more services to our issuers," says Droogan.

When pricing her services, Naylor first looks at the number of employees or customers who will be covered under the contract. "Then we can look at how much usage we expect or how many requests will be placed from a population of a given size," she explains. Based on this information, she says she can "determine the level of staffing of concierges to handle all those requests." In addition to maintaining two call centers staffed with dozens of concierges, VIPdesk hires former hotel concierges to work part time from home during periods of peak demand. These part-timers also bring an in-depth knowledge of local resources they can tap to satisfy requests from callers in their area.

Estimating her costs allows Naylor to set a profitable price for servicing a company's employees or customers, ranging "anywhere from $25 a person a year to as low as 25 cents per person per year."

Instead of charging companies for each use of VIPdesk's services, she sets a flat annual fee. This means companies can set a definite budget for the expense rather than being billed different amounts every month if usage varies. This pricing approach is helping VIPdesk become profitable after only two years.

"A concierge customer can give financial institutions a competitive edge by decommoditizing its products and extending the relationship well beyond the core products to the everyday life of the customer," says Naylor. "It can cost less than a key chain or some token item that a corporation may give as a gift to a customer, and yet it keeps giving every day and keeps that brand identity in front of that end user."[10]

QUESTIONS FOR DISCUSSION

1. What pricing objectives does Mary Naylor seem to have set for VIPdesk?
2. When a bank offers VIPdesk's concierge services as part of the benefit package for a platinum MasterCard, what type of pricing strategy is it using?
3. What are some variable costs Mary Naylor must consider when pricing VIPdesk's concierge services?

CASE 21.2

Apple iMac: Byting into Pricing

One product brought Apple Computer back to profitability: the colorful and stylish iMac. Apple scored big in the 1980s with its Macintosh line of personal computers, which were hailed for their compact size and easy operating system. Then, in the 1990s, the company lost significant market share as competitors launched new Windows-based personal computers priced lower than the Macintosh. In a three-year period, Apple's share of the education market plummeted from 47 percent to just 27 percent. Its share of the consumer market for PCs also dropped during that period, falling from nearly 15 percent to a mere 5 percent.

By the time Apple was getting set to launch the iMac, it was playing catch-up in highly competitive markets that were growing by as much as 15 percent every year. As Apple's market share slipped, so did the retail space devoted to software titles for Apple computers, as well as the ranks of developers writing new programs for Apple products. Worse, the company was having profitability problems and posted hefty losses for six consecutive quarters.

Then came the sleek iMac, a computer designed to be plugged in and turned on right out of the box. The iMac has an integrated monitor unlike desktop Windows-based PCs, which have separate monitors that must be connected by cable to the main processing unit. The iMac also

sports a CD-ROM and a built-in modem for convenient access to the Internet. The product's simplicity appeals to first-time buyers, who are often intimidated by the complexity of Windows-based PCs. However, some experts have criticized the lack of a floppy-disk drive on the iMac. Some have also expressed concern that the factory-installed modem on the iMac runs at slower speeds than those available on competing PCs.

With the iMac, Apple also launched a new pricing strategy, putting a $1,299 price tag on the first models. "People are seeing the value at these prices, and our goal is to continue to lower prices on products like iMac," CEO Steven Jobs explained. "An iMac costs about as much as heating a New England home in the winter, a lot less than the cost of an automobile. We're not in the sweet spot totally, but we're getting there. For Apple, this is a pretty big step. Apple hasn't had a compelling product under $2,000 for the last several years."

The "sweet spot" of the PC market has been drifting downward to the under-$1,000 category. Major competitors such as IBM, Compaq, and Dell have been using basic models, low prices, and advertising to attract customers who want to buy PCs for family or home-office use. Just weeks after Compaq began offering a $699 Windows-based PC, IBM responded with a $599 PC. These low-priced products were sold without monitors, and they lacked the features prized by power users, such as the fastest chips and the largest hard-disk capacity.

Apple fought back with a $100 million multimedia campaign to boost consumer demand for the iMac and its other products, including PowerBook laptops. With the theme Think Different, the television and print ads did not rely on head-to-head comparisons of technical specifications the way ads for many competing products did, nor did they mention price. Instead Apple's ads reemphasized that Apple computers are different from and, by implication, better than other computers.

The company took a number of other steps to get back on the road toward profitability. In addition to slashing operating expenses by 32 percent, Apple changed the depth of its product mix. Reducing the number of different models in each product line allowed the company to lower produc-

tion and distribution costs. Apple also changed its distribution strategy by concentrating on only two wholesale distributors and two main retail chains. Finally, following the popular (and profitable) lead of Dell Computer, Apple began offering build-to-order computers sold directly to customers.

Combined with the new lower-pricing strategy, all these marketing mix changes gave Apple the leverage it needed to regain ground in the marketplace and reverse the downward trend in profitability. Before the iMac even hit store shelves, the company had 150,000 orders. Soon Apple introduced more powerful high-end models with larger hard-disk capacity and advanced features, with prices ranging up to $2,199. It also launched a low-end model selling for $899. In another smart move, the company began offering iMac buyers a choice of colors and patterns.

In the first three years iMacs were available, Apple sold 5 million units. Supported by the iMac, Apple's sales and profit margins improved dramatically, and the company has maintained its share of the education market. Just as important, the product's success has convinced more software developers to work on programs for Apple products. For example, Intuit, which makes Quicken personal finance software, had not planned to update its Macintosh version of the program. However, after Apple showed the iMac to company executives, Intuit decided to move ahead with a Quicken upgrade for the Macintosh. And more software means customers have more reason to consider iMac computers—and to buy one, if the price is right.[11]

QUESTIONS FOR DISCUSSION

1. What type(s) of pricing objectives did Apple set for its iMac computer?
2. Which new-product pricing approach did Apple use for the iMac? Explain your answer.
3. When setting the iMac's price at $1,299, was Apple using cost-based, demand-based, or competition-based pricing? Explain.
4. How effectively do you think Apple's $899 iMac will compete with low-end Windows-based PCs?

STRATEGIC CASE 6

Blockbuster Puts the Spotlight on Pricing

Blockbuster is the category killer of movie rental chains, with 7,800 stores in 28 countries and $5 billion in annual sales. Every minute of every day, the company rents nearly 1,500 movies—a total of 1 billion rentals over the course of a year. Headed by CEO John Antioco, Blockbuster wields enormous power because of its market leadership. In recent years, it has applied that power to influence some of the factors that govern movie rental pricing decisions.

Sharing Revenue with the Studios

Costs and product availability are two key factors in Blockbuster's pricing. For years, rental stores had to pay about $65 per new movie while studios delayed the sale of new videotape releases to consumers. Under this system, stores ordered only a few of each new title, which meant many customers were disappointed when they tried to rent a hot movie. Once the studios began selling the videotape through retail channels, rentals often dropped as some customers chose to buy their favorite movies.

By 1997, videotape rentals were barely growing, and Blockbuster's CEO was looking for a way to increase rental revenue. He struck a deal with the major U.S. movie studios to obtain a larger quantity of recent videotape releases, both hits and non-hits, at a much lower cost. With plenty of stock, Blockbuster could better satisfy the hordes of customers eager to rent movies for home viewing, especially during peak weekend and holiday periods. In exchange for paying less upfront, Antioco agreed to share 40 percent of the videotape rental fees with the studios, usually guaranteeing a minimum of $25 to $35 per movie. Thanks to this revenue-sharing arrangement, Blockbuster filled its store shelves, consumers had a wider choice of movies, and the studios received a steady source of income.

The Rise of DVDs and Online Reservations

Once DVDs became popular in the late 1990s, revenues and profits changed. DVD rentals grew quickly, accounting for nearly one-third of Blockbuster's rental sales within the first two years and half of its rental sales by the end of the third year. Although Blockbuster has set the same price for DVDs and videotape rentals—about $3.65—its costs differ for each. The company buys DVDs from the movie studios at $15 per disk. In contrast, it pays about $10, plus a portion of the rental fees, for each videotape. Because its cost is $1.20 per DVD rental transaction and $1.60 per videotape rental transaction, Blockbuster enjoys a better profit margin on DVD rentals.

With DVD rentals on the rise and Blockbuster's profits in a slump, CEO Antioco announced he wanted to end the revenue-sharing arrangement with studios that he had pioneered just a few years earlier. This announcement displeased the studios, which were deriving 15 percent of their sales from dealing with Blockbuster. Warner Home Video was the first to respond by setting a retail price of $22.98 for its *Swordfish* videotape release, a price low enough to encourage consumers to purchase rather than rent that movie. Meanwhile the MGM studio and the Hollywood Video retail chain set a precedent by negotiating a revenue-sharing deal on DVD rentals, an arrangement Blockbuster wanted very much to avoid.

Blockbuster is also taking advantage of Internet technology to allow customers to reserve movies and games online. Customers simply log on, identify their local Blockbuster store, and input their names, addresses, e-mail addresses, and credit card information. Then they can reserve up to nine titles at one time and receive an e-mail confirmation

within a few minutes. The local store will hold reserved items for pickup for up to two days. To encourage participation, Blockbuster is offering the first online rental free.

Legal and Regulatory Issues

In addition, Blockbuster faces legal and regulatory concerns over its approach to pricing. Independent videotape rental stores recently filed a class-action lawsuit charging Blockbuster and three movie studios (Paramount, Buena Vista, and Columbia TriStar) with price fixing and price discrimination. Although Blockbuster and the studios deny the charges, the suit is moving through the California court system.

On another legal front, Blockbuster has settled a class-action lawsuit brought by customers claiming they paid too much in late fees from 1992 to 2001. As part of the settlement, customers who filed claims were entitled to receive free rentals and coupons for rental discounts. Blockbuster informed customers of the terms of the settlement by posting notices on its website (http://www.blockbuster.com) and printing out notices on the receipts given to customers when they rented movies.

Boosting Loyalty, Fighting Competition

Blockbuster is also using pricing to support a promotion known as Blockbuster Rewards. For a special price of $9.95, customers can rent one dozen older movies and earn a free rental when they pay for five other rentals during a single month. This program not only rewards frequent renters for their loyalty but also increases demand for slower-renting movies.

Despite Blockbuster's dominance of the retail movie rental market, it faces a new source of competition from Internet-based challengers, such as Netflix, that specialize in DVD rentals. In its first three years of operation, Netflix attracted 300,000 online customers. Now the e-business rents 70,000 disks every day, building on its huge inventory and its unusual pricing approach. The company says it has more than ten times as many DVDs for rent than local Blockbuster stores. It has also negotiated

deals with several major studios to acquire large quantities of new DVD releases to meet higher demand. DVDs are both small and light enough to mail easily, and Netflix pays the postage both ways.

Instead of setting a per-rental price, Netflix charges each customer $20 per month for all DVD rentals. Customers are allowed to be in possession of three DVDs at any one time. As soon as they return their current rentals, they can request additional DVDs. Unlike Blockbuster, Netflix doesn't charge a late fee or set a due date on its rentals, counting on customers to watch and return movies quickly so they can get the most for their $20 charge. Customers may be able to watch ten or more movies in a month, depending on how quickly they view and return each DVD. CEO Reed Hastings describes the average Netflix customer as "someone who loves movies and hates Blockbuster. That's not everybody, but it is a large section of America and it crosses all kinds of demographics."

Battling back, Blockbuster designed a single-price promotional effort to accelerate rentals during the summer months. The promotion offered customers a Blockbuster Entertainment Pass for a flat $30 monthly fee, entitling them to one movie or game every day for 30 consecutive days. The pass was good only at the store where it was purchased, so it was a good way to build individual store traffic and stimulate impulse purchases of snacks and other nonmovie items displayed at the point of sale. Although Blockbuster officials are evaluating the results before deciding whether to run this program again, they are very aware of the need to react to online competitors who target their customers.

QUESTIONS FOR DISCUSSION

1. What are Blockbuster's primary pricing objectives?
2. Is Blockbuster relying on price or nonprice competition? Explain.
3. What type of pricing strategy does the Blockbuster Entertainment Pass represent?
4. Given Blockbuster's costs per transaction, evaluate the company's long-term use of the Blockbuster Entertainment Pass.

Implementation and Electronic Marketing

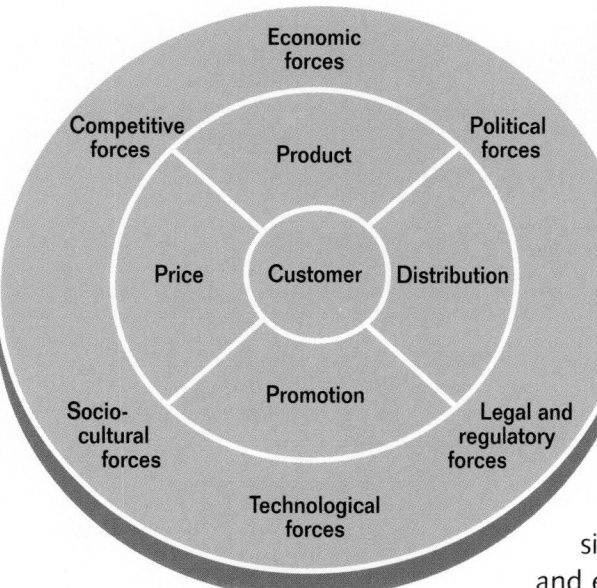

We have divided marketing into several sets of variables and discussed the decisions and activities associated with each variable. By now you should understand how to analyze marketing opportunities and how to identify the components of the marketing mix. Now we focus on how these components are implemented in a dynamic environment. Chapter 22 explores approaches to organizing a marketing unit, issues regarding strategy implementation, and techniques for controlling marketing strategies. Chapter 23 provides a framework for understanding the use of the Internet in marketing strategy. It offers insights about characteristics of the Internet and how marketing strategy can be implemented. Online Chapter 24 is an extension of Chapter 23, with the most up-to-date information and examples of electronic marketing.

22

Marketing Implementation and Control

OBJECTIVES

- To describe the marketing implementation process and the major approaches to marketing implementation

- To identify the components of the marketing implementation process

- To understand the role of the marketing unit in a firm's organizational structure

- To describe the alternatives for organizing a marketing unit

- To understand the control processes used in managing marketing strategies

- To explain how cost and sales analyses are used to evaluate the performance of marketing strategies

- To identify the major components of a marketing audit

German-based DaimlerBenz, best known for its Mercedes luxury automobiles, merged with Chrysler Corporation in 1998. Executives believed that combining Chrysler's marketing and design expertise with Mercedes' renowned engineering would create a very competitive firm that could develop vehicles to satisfy customers around the world. In the years following the merger, however, executives from the two firms found it difficult to trust each other and compromise, even on the simplest issues. During this period, more efficient firms, including Honda and Toyota, competed aggressively with similar vehicles and lower prices. Chrysler's sales began to decline, and by 2001 the American unit was hemorrhaging $2 billion a year and losing market share. Worse, except for the new Jeep Liberty sport-utility vehicle and the updated Dodge Ram pickup, Chrysler would not have a new vehicle ready before 2004.

Looking for a Turnaround at Chrysler

Dieter Zetsche, the new CEO of Chrysler Group, faced the difficult task of revitalizing the company. Zetsche quickly launched a three-year, $2.9 billion effort to make Chrysler more efficient in order to reduce costs and raise quality. He began by announcing 26,000 layoffs. He also demanded that Chrysler's suppliers immediately cut prices by 5 percent, saving Chrysler $2 billion a year, and agree to reduce prices by another 10 percent by 2003, producing an additional $4 billion in cost savings. The company also worked with suppliers to identify more efficient ways to build automotive parts. By simplifying the wiring in the Dodge Ram's taillights, for example, the company saved $4 million.

Although these changes helped Chrysler save millions, Zetsche realized that, in the long run, the company must improve its marketing and vehicle development processes to keep customers coming into dealer showrooms. He began by lowering base prices on many models in an effort to achieve balance between volume and profits. The base price of the 2002 Jeep Grand Cherokee, for example, was slashed by $2,000 to $25,000. To speed the product development process, Zetsche pulled together teams from across the company—design, engineering, manufacturing, purchasing, and marketing—to find ways to reduce waste and boost quality. Zetsche labeled this approach "disciplined pizzazz"—finding a balance between style and economy. To achieve this balance, he borrowed both engineering processes and parts from Chrysler's German parent. By 2004, an increasing number of Chrysler vehicles, including the Jeep Grand Cherokee and the Dodge Intrepid, will include Mercedes parts.

Chrysler also worked to strengthen the vehicle development process to develop new "must-have" models, such as the popular PT Cruiser, to compete against Ford and General Motors. Through its FastCar project, Chrysler can seamlessly coordinate the flow of information from six major information systems, allowing everyone in the firm to keep pace with changes to each new design and assess how changes will affect their own areas of responsibility. The ultimate goal of FastCar is to slash the time required to develop a new model, from design to mass manufacturing, to two years—about half the current industry standards.

To implement all these changes, Chrysler needs strong leadership. Although auto executives seldom speak at union gatherings, Zetsche addressed the United Auto Workers convention in 2001. He also makes a point of eating in the company cafeteria and regularly visiting with workers. He even pledged to shave his head if the Dodge Ram maintains its position at the top of the J. D. Power & Associates quality survey.[1]

To achieve its objectives, DaimlerChrysler must carefully implement its strategic plan. Even the best strategic plan will fail if poorly implemented. In this chapter we concentrate on how marketing strategies should be implemented and controlled. First, we explore several issues regarding implementation. We then focus on the marketing unit's position in the organization and the ways the unit itself can be organized. Next, we consider the basic components of the marketing control process and discuss the use of cost and sales analyses to evaluate the effectiveness of marketing strategies and measure the firm's performance. Finally, we describe a marketing audit.

The Marketing Implementation Process

Marketing implementation
The process of putting marketing strategies into action

intended strategy   The strategy the company decides on during the planning phase

realized strategy   The strategy that actually takes place

Marketing implementation is the process of putting marketing strategies into action. It is the "how?" of marketing strategy. Although implementation is often neglected in favor of strategic planning, the implementation process itself can determine whether a marketing strategy succeeds. Alberto-Culver, for example, has been quite successful in the hair and skin care markets with its Alberto VO5, Tresemmé, and St. Ives brands. By consistently revitalizing packaging, reformulating products, and, through its Sally Beauty Supply stores, acquiring wholesale distribution and exclusive licenses, the company continues to compete head on against Procter & Gamble, Unilever, and other large, multinational firms. Sales of Alberto-Culver's moderately priced products, distributed through food, drug, and mass merchants, have tripled over the past decade. Thus, Alberto-Culver has found success through a niche marketing strategy and strong implementation.[2]

An important aspect of the implementation process is understanding that marketing strategies almost always turn out differently than expected. In essence, all organizations have two types of strategy: intended strategy and realized strategy.[3] The **intended strategy** is the strategy the organization decided on during the planning phase and wants to use, whereas the **realized strategy** is the strategy that actually takes place. The difference between the two is often the result of how the intended strategy is implemented. The realized strategy, though not necessarily any better or worse than the intended strategy, often does not live up to planners' expectations.

Marketing Implementation
Teva's 16-year heritage of product innovation and successful marketing implementation has led to strong consumer loyalty.

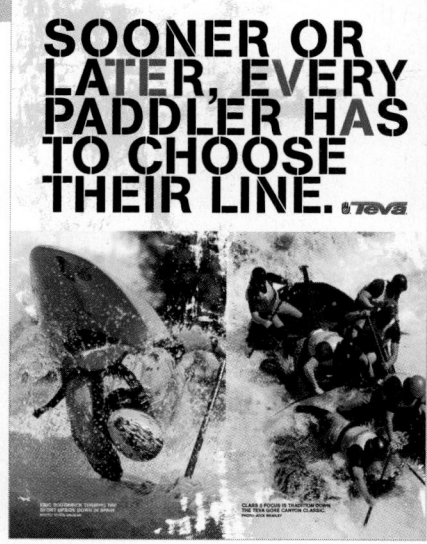

Problems in Implementing Marketing Activities

Why do marketing strategies sometimes turn out differently than expected? The most common reason is that managers fail to realize that marketing implementation is just as important as marketing strategy. The relationship between strategic planning and implementation creates a number of problems for managers when they plan implementation activities. Three of the most important problems are as follows:[4]

- *Marketing strategy and implementation are related.* Companies often assume that strategic planning always comes first, followed by implementation. In reality, marketing strategies and implementation should be planned simultaneously. The content of the marketing strategy determines how the strategy will be implemented. Likewise, implementation activities may require changes in the marketing strategy. Thus, it is important for marketing managers to understand that strategy and implementation are really two sides of the same coin.

- *Marketing strategy and implementation are constantly evolving.* Both strategy and implementation are affected by the marketing environment. Since the environment is constantly changing, both marketing strategy and implementation must remain flexible enough to adapt. The relationship between strategy and implementation is never fixed; it is always evolving to accommodate changes in customer needs, government regulation, or competition. For example, when Western Pacific Airlines began service from Colorado Springs, competitors like American and United moved to match Western Pacific's discount fares to the same destination cities. When Western Pacific went out of business, competitors responded by raising their fares, although they remain lower than before Western Pacific entered the picture.[5]

- *The responsibility for marketing strategy and implementation is separated.* This problem is often the biggest obstacle in implementing marketing strategies. Typically marketing strategies are developed by the top managers in an organization. However, the responsibility for implementing those strategies rests at the frontline, or customer-contact point, of the organization. This separation, shown in Figure 22.1, can impair implementation in two ways. First, because top managers are separated from the frontline, where the company

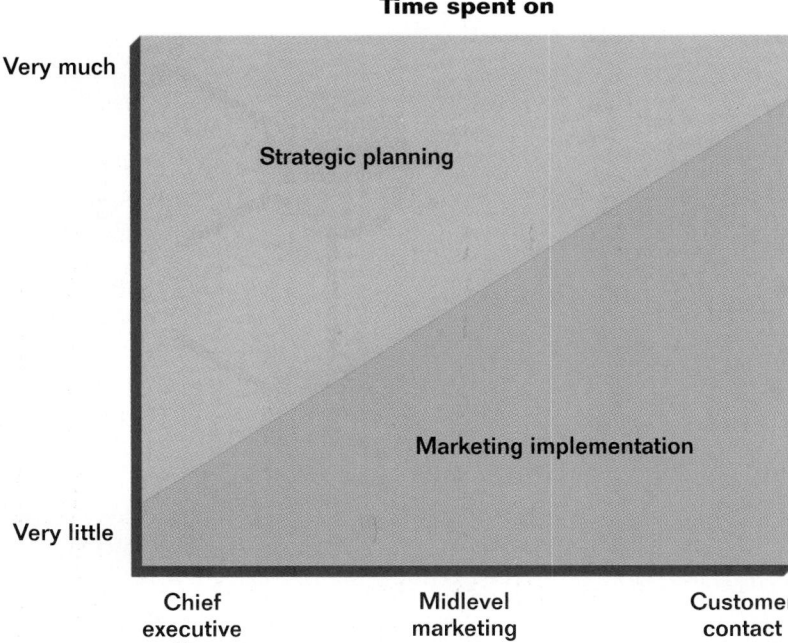

FIGURE 22.1
Separation of Strategic Planning and Marketing Implementation

Source: Figure adapted from *Marketing Strategy* by O. C. Ferrell, Michael Hartline, and George H. Lucas, Jr. Copyright © 2002 Harcourt Brace & Company. Reproduced by permission of the publisher.

interacts daily with customers, they may fail to grasp the unique problems associated with implementing marketing activities. Second, customer-contact managers and employees are often responsible for implementing strategies even if they had no voice in developing them. Consequently some customer-contact employees may lack motivation and commitment. We discuss the importance of employee motivation later in this chapter.

Components of Marketing Implementation

As Figure 22.2 shows, the implementation process has several components, all of which must mesh if implementation is to succeed. At the center of marketing implementation are shared goals and objectives. They occupy the central position because they draw the entire organization into a single, functioning unit, holding all components together to ensure successful marketing implementation. Goals may be simple statements of the company's objectives. Northwest Airlines, for example, has communicated to all levels of the organization its goal of on-time arrivals. On the other hand, the goals may be derived from mission statements that outline the organization's philosophy and direction. Without shared goals or objectives to hold the organization together, different parts of the firm may work at cross-purposes and limit the success of the overall organization.

The employee component of marketing implementation includes the functional area of human resources and such factors as the quality, skill, and diversity of the firm's work force. Ben & Jerry's Homemade understands the importance of satisfying both employees and suppliers. The company gives employees three free pints of its premium ice cream a day, and it supports 550 Vermont farming families owning more than 40,000 Holstein cows.[6] Issues like employee recruitment, selection, and training have great bearing on the implementation of marketing activities.[7] Organizations must design programs to recruit and select the right employees for the job. Through training and socialization programs, employees learn what is expected of them in implementing a marketing strategy.[8]

Closely linked to the employee component is leadership, the art of managing people. The leadership provided by the organization's managers and the performance of employees go hand in hand in the implementation process. How managers

FIGURE 22.2
Marketing Implementation

The
TJX
Companies, Inc.

is proud to encourage

DIVERSITY

amoung its

**Minority & Women
Suppliers**

TJX
THE TJX COMPANIES, INC.

T·K·MAXX   *Marshalls*   T·K·MAXX
W I N N E R S   *HomeGoods*   A.J.Wright

The Employee Component
The TJX Companies, Inc. acknowledges the importance of diversity.

communicate with employees and how they motivate them to implement a marketing strategy are important facets of leadership. Research suggests that marketing implementation may be more successful when leaders create an organizational culture characterized by open communication between employees and managers. This type of leadership creates a climate in which employees feel free to discuss their opinions and ideas about implementation tasks, and managers and employees trust each other.[9] We examine additional components of marketing implementation, including internal marketing, total quality management, marketing structure, and marketing control, as well as employee motivation and communication, later in this chapter.

Approaches to Marketing Implementation

Once they grasp the problems and recognize the components of marketing implementation, marketing managers can decide on an approach for implementing marketing activities. Just as organizations can achieve their goals by using different marketing strategies, they can implement their marketing strategies by using different approaches. In this section, we discuss two general approaches to marketing implementation: internal marketing and total quality management. Both approaches represent mindsets that marketing managers may adopt when organizing and planning marketing activities. These approaches are not mutually exclusive; indeed, many companies adopt both when designing marketing activities.

external customers
Individuals who patronize a business

internal customers
A company's employees

internal marketing
Coordinating internal exchanges between the firm and its employees to achieve successful external exchanges between the firm and its customers

Internal Marketing.   **External customers** are the individuals who patronize a business—the familiar definition of customers—whereas **internal customers** are the company's employees. For implementation to succeed, the needs of both groups of customers must be met. If internal customers are not satisfied, it is likely external customers will not be either. Thus, in addition to targeting marketing activities at external customers, a firm uses internal marketing to attract, motivate, and retain qualified internal customers by designing internal products (jobs) that satisfy their wants and needs. **Internal marketing** is a management philosophy that coordinates internal exchanges between the organization and its employees to achieve successful external exchanges between the organization and its customers.[10]

Generally speaking, internal marketing refers to the managerial actions necessary to make all members of the marketing organization understand and accept their respective roles in implementing the marketing strategy. This means everyone, from the president of the company down to the hourly workers on the shop floor, must understand the role they play in carrying out their jobs and implementing the marketing strategy. Ford Motor Company, for example, revised its employee performance evaluations to recognize "high achievers," "achievers," and "improvement required." To encourage trust and cohesion in serving customers, all categories qualify for bonuses and merit pay.[11] There is a relationship among satisfied employees, marketing orientation, and organizational performance.[12] In short, anyone invested in the firm, both marketers and those who perform other functions, must recognize the tenet of customer orientation and service that underlies the marketing concept. Internal customers may also include a firm's franchisees. Building Customer Relationships describes one firm's efforts to help its franchisees succeed and satisfy customers.

BUILDING CUSTOMER RELATIONSHIPS

Great Harvest Bread Company Grows Through Learning Relationships

Like a number of successful startups, Great Harvest Bread Company began in a garage, where Pete and Laura Wakeman baked bread to sell from a roadside stand in Durham, Connecticut, to put themselves through college. After graduation, the Wakemans moved to Great Falls, Montana, where they opened a Great Harvest Bread bakery in 1976. The venture proved so successful that friends and customers regularly inquired as to how they might open their own stores based on the Great Harvest Bread concept. So in 1978, the Wakemans sold their first Great Harvest Bread Company franchise. Today Great Harvest Bread Company, based in Dillon, Montana, oversees 137 franchised bakeries in 34 states that generate annual revenues of more than $60 million. The franchiser is committed to "baking the best bread and providing the best customer service around." This customer focus includes the company's relaxed, sharing relationships with its franchisees.

Unlike most franchise operations, Great Harvest doesn't require standardized procedures; instead it encourages innovation and fast learning. The basic principle underlying the company's growth is that "expansion comes from experimentation." Thus, new Great Harvest franchisees operate their bakeries as they see fit, although they may look to an operating manual that describes the best practices accumulated from established stores. The only condition Great Harvest imposes is that franchisees share what they learn with other franchisees. One idea shared among franchisees is the Baker for a Day program, in which participating stores open on Sundays and hand over the day's sales to a local charity.

In fact, Great Harvest believes that "owners make the best teachers." When Great Harvest grants a new franchise, the new owner attends a week-long training session at company headquarters on baking bread and running a small business. During training, an experienced franchise owner serves as a role model and offers examples to help the new owner get started. Following this training, the new franchise owner is expected to visit two established franchises in different parts of the country to observe how other franchisees operate.

To help its franchisees keep learning and improving, Great Harvest requires new stores to get a check-up visit from an experienced franchisee within six months of opening. The company pays for the visitor's travel expenses; it also covers half the expenses whenever one established owner visits another. In addition, Great Harvest maintains a companywide intranet, called the Breadboard, that serves as a storehouse for recipes and ideas about managing, marketing, promotions, and decorating. Eighty percent of Great Harvest's franchisees communicate regularly with one another through e-mail. The interaction between franchiser and franchisee and among franchisees helps the company keep growing and responding to its external customers' needs. As one franchisee says, "We stay in touch with the owners we met in Dillon and with the people we've visited. They're our best source for ideas."

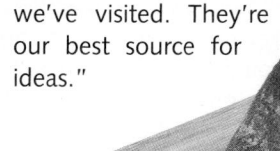

FIGURE 22.3
The Internal Marketing Framework
Source: Adapted from Nigel F. Piercy, *Market-Led Strategic Change,* Copyright © 1992, Butterworth-Heinemann Ltd., p. 371. Used with permission.

Customer orientation is fostered by training and education and by keeping the lines of communication open throughout the firm. Southwest Airlines, for example, sends new employees to training programs where they learn about the airline's playful culture and history, its demanding standards for customer service, and how to achieve these standards. Southwest's strong training program helps employees understand their role in satisfying the airline's customers and ensures they have the tools to do so.

Like external marketing activities, internal marketing may involve market segmentation, product development, research, distribution, and even public relations and sales promotion.[13] The internal marketing framework appears in Figure 22.3. As in external marketing, the marketing mix in internal marketing is designed to satisfy the needs of customers—in this case, both internal and external customers. For example, an organization may sponsor sales contests to inspire sales personnel to boost their selling efforts. This helps employees (and ultimately the company) to understand customers' needs and problems, teaches them valuable new skills, and heightens their enthusiasm for their regular jobs. In addition, many companies use planning sessions, workshops, letters, formal reports, and personal conversations to ensure employees comprehend the corporate mission, the organization's goals, and the marketing strategy. The ultimate results are more satisfied employees and improved customer relations.

Total Quality Management.   Quality has become a major concern in many organizations, particularly in light of intense foreign competition, more demanding customers, and poorer profit performance owing to reduced market share and higher costs. Over the last several years, many U.S. firms have lost the dominant, competitive positions they had held for decades. To regain a competitive edge, a number of firms have adopted a total quality management approach. **Total quality management (TQM)** is a philosophy that uniform commitment to quality in all areas of the organization will promote a culture that meets customers' perceptions of quality. It involves coordinating efforts to improve customer satisfaction, increase employee participation and empowerment, form and strengthen supplier partnerships, and facilitate an organizational culture of continuous quality improvement. Customer satisfaction can be improved through higher-quality products and better customer service such as reduced delivery times, faster responses to customer inquiries, and treatment of customers that shows caring on the company's part. Taco Bell, for example,

total quality management (TQM)   A philosophy that uniform commitment to quality in all areas of the organization will promote a culture that meets customers' perceptions of quality

Once Again, Ranked #1
Performing Global Network.

If you want to be a winner in today's business world, rely on a winner. Once again, SAVVIS' high-performance Intelligent IP Network™ is the #1 performing network in the world.* SAVVIS surpassed AT&T, Sprint, UUNet and Qwest, as well as 32 other service providers for this annual honor. And now that we've added intelligence to our #1 performing network, you can take advantage of an endless array of choices. Internet, Extranet, Intranet and E-commerce applications — configured any way you want — combined into one simple networking solution for your business. The truth is, SAVVIS earned the winner's cup, but the real winner is you.

SAVVIS

Intelligent IP Networking for Dynamic Companies™

www.savvis.net/trophy

1-866-4SAVVIS

© 2000 SAVVIS Communications. All rights reserved. All trademarks property of their respective owners.
* According to Keynote Systems, an independent auditor, as reported in Boardwatch Magazine's annual "Directory of Internet Service Providers."

Total Quality Management
Savvis provides a global networking service that is perceived as a market leader in quality.

following several quarters of declining sales, evaluated its overall marketing strategy and implementation and decided changes were necessary to address image and quality issues. Modeling the fast-food chain after rival Wendy's, the company planned to focus on cleaning up stores, improving the quality of key ingredients such as ground beef and steak, and adding grilled items. In addition, Taco Bell planned to limit the menu of items offered for less than $1 in favor of more large, pricier items. Abandoning its iconic chihuahua, the company also planned to update its image with a new ad campaign emphasizing quality.[14]

As a management philosophy, TQM relies heavily on the talents of employees to continually improve the quality of the organization's goods and services. TQM is founded on three basic principles: continuous quality improvement, empowered employees, and quality improvement teams.[15]

Continuous quality improvement. Continuous improvement of an organization's goods and services is built around the notion that quality is free; by contrast, *not* having high-quality goods and services can be very expensive, especially in terms of dissatisfied customers.[16] Continuous quality improvement requires more than simple quality control, or the screening out of bad products during production. Rather, continuous improvement means building quality from the very beginning—totally redesigning the product if necessary. It is a slow, long-term process of creating small improvements in quality. Companies that adopt TQM realize that the major advancements in quality result from an accumulation of these small improvements over time.

benchmarking Comparing the quality of the firm's goods, services, or processes with that of the best-performing competitors

A primary tool of the continuous improvement process is **benchmarking,** the measuring and evaluating of the quality of the organization's goods, services, or processes as compared with the quality produced by the best-performing companies in the industry.[17] Benchmarking lets the organization know where it stands competitively in its industry, thus giving it a goal to aim for over time. The design of the Ford Taurus attests to the value of benchmarking. By asking customers what they wanted in a car, Ford compiled a list of more than 400 desired features. Ford engineers then examined the best-selling cars in the industry, primarily foreign makes like the Honda Accord and Toyota Camry, to determine how the competition delivered each of these features. The result was an improved Taurus, which at one time was the best-selling car in America.

Empowered employees. Ultimately TQM succeeds or fails because of the efforts of the organization's employees. Thus, employee recruitment, selection, and training are critical to the success of marketing implementation. **Empowerment** gives customer-contact employees the authority and responsibility to make marketing decisions without seeking the approval of their supervisors.[18] Although employees at any level in an organization can be empowered to make decisions, empowerment is used most often at the frontline, where employees interact daily with customers.

empowerment Giving customer-contact employees authority and responsibility to make marketing decisions on their own

One characteristic of empowerment is that employees can perform their jobs the way they see fit, as long as their methods and outcomes are consistent with the organization's mission. However, empowering employees is successful only if the organization is guided by an overall corporate vision, shared goals, and a culture that supports the TQM effort.[19] Customer-contact employees often continue to maintain productivity levels (i.e., getting the tasks done) even while the quality of their work deteriorates. Providing control mechanisms that achieve desired quality standards can maintain productivity and quality.[20] For example, Ritz Carlton hotels give each customer-contact employee permission to take care of customer needs as he or she observes issues. A great deal of time, effort, and patience are needed to develop and sustain a quality-oriented culture in an organization.

Quality improvement teams. The idea behind the team approach is to get the best and brightest people with a wide variety of perspectives working together on a quality improvement issue. Team members are usually selected from a cross-section of jobs within the organization, as well as from among suppliers and customers. As we discussed in Chapter 15, suppliers can have a tremendous impact on the ability of a company to deliver quality products and services to its customers. Customers are included in quality improvement teams because they are in the best position to know what they and other customers want from the company.

Net Sights

In 1987, the U.S. Congress established the Malcolm Baldrige National Quality Award to recognize U.S. organizations for their achievements in quality and performance and to boost awareness about the importance of quality and performance in our competitive environment. The National Institute of Standards and Technology (NIST) may give up to three awards annually in each of five categories: manufacturing, service, small business, education, and health care. Recent winners include the Los Alamos National Bank, Ritz Carlton Hotel Company, KARLEE Company, and Dana Corporation's Spicer Driveshaft Division. To learn more about the criteria for the award and how it can help a firm focus on improving quality and motivate employees to achieve performance standards, visit **http://www.quality.nist.gov/**.

Total quality management can provide several benefits. Overall financial benefits include lower operating costs, higher returns on sales and investment, and an improved ability to use premium pricing rather than competitive pricing. Additional benefits include faster development of innovations, improved access to global markets, higher levels of customer retention, and an enhanced reputation.[21]

Putting the TQM philosophy into practice requires a substantial investment of time, effort, money, and patience on the part of the organization. However, companies that have the resources needed to implement TQM and the commitment of top management gain an effective means of achieving major competitive advantages within their industries.

Organizing Marketing Activities

The structure and relationships of a marketing unit, including lines of authority and responsibility that connect and coordinate individuals, strongly affect marketing activities. In this section, we look at the role of marketing within an organization and examine the major alternatives available for organizing a marketing unit.

The Role of Marketing in an Organization's Structure

As industries become more competitive both domestically and globally, marketing activities gain importance. Firms that truly adopt the marketing concept develop a distinct organizational culture: a culture based on a shared set of beliefs that makes the customer's needs the pivotal point of the firm's decisions about strategy and operations.[22] Instead of developing products in a vacuum and then trying to persuade customers to purchase them, companies using the marketing concept begin with an orientation toward their customers' needs and desires. Recreational Equipment, Inc. (REI), for example, gives customers a chance to try out sporting goods in conditions that approximate how the products will actually be used. Customers can try out hiking boots on a simulated hiking path with a variety of trail surfaces and inclines or test climbing gear on an indoor climbing wall. In addition, REI offers clinics to customers, such as "Rock Climbing Basics," "Basic Backpacking," and "REI's Outdoor School."[23]

As we discussed in Chapter 1, a marketing-oriented organization concentrates on discovering what buyers want and satisfying those wants in such a way that it achieves its objectives. Such a company has an organizational culture that effectively and efficiently produces a sustainable competitive advantage. It focuses on customer analysis, competitor analysis, and the integration of its resources to provide customer value and satisfaction, as well as long-term profits.[24] In Chapter 1, we also defined customer relationship management (CRM) as a concept that focuses on using this information about customers to develop marketing strategies that build and sustain desirable customer relationships. In today's competitive, global marketplace, it is essential to provide quality, value, and satisfaction to retain customers for the long term.[25]

If the marketing concept serves as a guiding philosophy, the marketing unit will be closely coordinated with other functional areas such as production, finance, and human resources. Marketing must interact with other departments in a number of key areas. It needs to work with manufacturing in determining the volume and variety of the company's products. Those in charge of production rely on marketers for accurate sales forecasts. Research and development departments depend heavily on information gathered by marketers about product features and benefits consumers desire. Decisions made by the physical distribution department hinge on information about the urgency of delivery schedules and cost/service tradeoffs. Information technology is often a crucial ingredient in effectively managing customer relationships, but successful CRM programs must include every department involved in customer relations. Many CRM programs' systems fail because marketing and sales personnel do not understand or effectively use the underlying technology.[26]

Customer Relationship Management
Avaya assists companies in expanding communication alternatives to meet business customers' needs. SalesLogix® is a fully integrated customer relationship management software suite encompassing sales, marketing, and support modules.

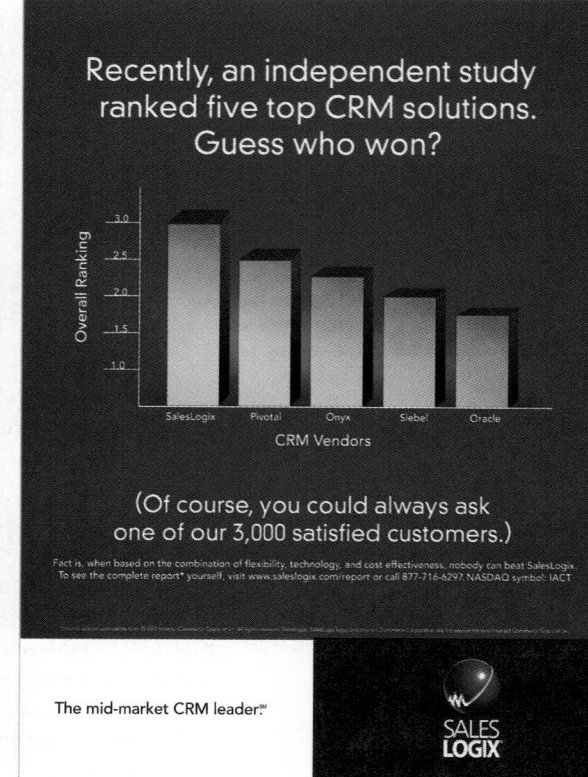

Alternatives for Organizing the Marketing Unit

How effectively a firm's marketing management can plan and implement marketing strategies also depends on how the marketing unit is organized. Effective organizational planning can give the firm a competitive advantage. The organizational structure of a marketing department establishes the authority relationships among marketing personnel and specifies who is responsible for making certain decisions and performing particular activities. This internal structure helps direct marketing activities.

One crucial decision regarding structural authority is centralization versus decentralization. In a **centralized organization,** top-level managers delegate very little authority to lower levels. In a **decentralized organization,** decision-making authority is delegated as far down the chain of command as possible. The decision to centralize or decentralize the organization directly affects marketing. Most traditional organizations are highly centralized. In these organizations, most, if not all, marketing decisions are made at the top levels. However, as organizations become more marketing oriented, centralized decision making proves somewhat ineffective. In these organizations, decentralized authority allows the company to respond to customer needs more quickly.

In organizing a marketing unit, managers divide the work into specific activities and delegate responsibility and authority for those activities to individuals in various positions within the unit. These positions include, for example, the sales manager, the research manager, and the advertising manager.

No single approach to organizing a marketing unit works equally well in all businesses. The best approach or approaches depends on the number and diversity of the firm's products, the characteristics and needs of the people in the target market, and many other factors. A marketing unit can be organized according to (1) functions, (2) products, (3) regions, or (4) types of customers. Firms often use some combination of these organizational approaches. Product features may dictate that the marketing unit be structured by products, whereas customer characteristics require that it be organized by geographic region or by types of customers. By using more than one type of structure, a flexible marketing unit can develop and implement marketing plans to match customers' needs precisely.

Organizing by Functions. Some marketing departments are organized by general marketing functions, such as marketing research, product development, distribution, sales, advertising, and customer relations. The personnel who direct these functions report directly to the top-level marketing executive. This structure is fairly common because it works well for some businesses with centralized marketing operations, such as Ford and General Motors. In more decentralized firms, such as grocery store chains, functional organization can cause serious coordination problems. However, the functional approach may suit a large, centralized company whose products and customers are neither numerous nor diverse.

Organizing by Products. An organization that produces and markets diverse products may find the functional approach inadequate. The decisions and problems related to a single marketing function for one product may be quite different from those related to the same marketing function for another product. As a result, businesses that produce diverse products sometimes organize their marketing units according to product groups. Organizing by product groups gives a firm the flexibility to develop special marketing mixes for different products. Procter & Gamble, like many firms in the consumer packaged goods industry, is organized by product group. One product manager oversees paper products, another oversees soap and cleaning products, and so on. Each group develops its own product plans, implements them, monitors the results, and takes corrective action as necessary. The product group manager may also draw on the resources of specialized staff in the company, such as the advertising, research, or distribution manager. Although organizing by products allows a company to remain flexible, this approach can be rather expensive unless efficient categories of products are grouped together to reduce duplication and improve coordination of product management.

centralized organization
A structure in which top management delegates little authority to levels below it

decentralized organization
A structure in which decision-making authority is delegated as far down the chain of command as possible

Organizing by Regions.   A large company that markets products nationally (or internationally) may organize its marketing activities by geographic regions. Managers of marketing functions for each region report to their regional marketing manager; all the regional marketing managers report directly to the executive marketing manager. Frito-Lay, for example, is organized into four regional divisions, allowing the company to get closer to its customers and respond more quickly and efficiently to regional competitors. This form of organization is especially effective for a firm whose customers' characteristics and needs vary greatly from one region to another. Firms that try to penetrate the national market intensively may divide regions into subregions.

Organizing by Types of Customers.   Sometimes a company's marketing unit is organized according to types of customers. This form of internal organization works well for a firm that has several groups of customers whose needs and problems differ significantly. For example, Bic may sell pens to large retail stores, wholesalers, and institutions. Retailers may want more rapid delivery of small shipments and more personal selling by the producer than do either wholesalers or institutional buyers. Because the marketing decisions and activities required for these two groups of customers differ considerably, the company may find it efficient to organize its marketing unit by types of customers.

In a marketing department organized by customer group, the marketing manager for each group directs all activities needed to market products to that specific group. The marketing managers report to the top-level marketing executive.

Implementing Marketing Activities

Through planning and organizing, marketing managers provide purpose, direction, and structure for marketing activities. Likewise, understanding the problems and elements of marketing implementation, as well as selecting an overall approach, sets the stage for the implementation of specific marketing activities. As we have stated before, people are ultimately responsible for implementing marketing strategy. Therefore, the effective implementation of any and all marketing activities depends on motivating marketing personnel, effectively communicating within the marketing unit, coordinating all marketing activities, and establishing a timetable for the completion of each marketing activity. Building Customer Relationships examines a feedback system that companies can use to motivate and communicate with marketing personnel.

Motivating Marketing Personnel

People work to satisfy physical, psychological, and social needs. To motivate marketing personnel, managers must discover their employees' needs and then develop motivational methods that will help employees satisfy those needs. It is crucial that the plan to motivate employees be fair, ethical, and well understood by employees. In addition, rewards to employees should be tied to organizational goals. In general, to

Motivating Employees
Blockbuster offers corporate incentive programs to help companies motivate their employees.

improve employee motivation, companies need to find out what workers think, how they feel, and what they want. Some of this information can be obtained from an employee attitude survey. A firm can motivate its workers by directly linking pay with performance, informing workers how their performance affects department and corporate results, following through with appropriate compensation, implementing a flexible benefits program, and adopting a participative management approach.[27] Motivation is also facilitated by informing employees about how their performance affects their own compensation. For example, Kmart underwent a two-year plan to improve supply chain management, inventory control, store appearance, technology, and customer service. To improve customer satisfaction at its 2,100 stores, Kmart asked employees to sign an eight-point customer service pledge that commits them to smiling at customers, offering to help anyone within ten feet, and keeping their aisles clean, clear, and stocked. To motivate employees to help the company achieve its goals, Kmart now gives employees whose stores are rated "excellent" a quarterly bonus; the company paid out more than $18 million in one recent quarter. The result: more than 56 percent of customers calling with feedback now rate their shopping experience as excellent, up from 40 percent when the program began.[28]

Besides tying rewards to organizational goals, managers should use a variety of other tools to motivate individuals. Selecting effective motivational tools has become

BUILDING CUSTOMER RELATIONSHIPS

Evaluating and Motivating Marketing Personnel with 360° Feedback

Although marketing is important in an organization's decision structure, marketing managers and customer-contact personnel set the stage for implementing specific marketing activities. Because people are ultimately responsible for implementation, it is vital that all marketing personnel receive communication and feedback to motivate them to achieve peak performance. It simply isn't possible for marketing managers to observe their employees in every situation. To build trust and develop individuals, multiple sources of feedback are important. One way to improve feedback is through the 360° review, which moves away from evaluating people on a daily basis to obtaining feedback from a variety of sources in order to improve understanding across coworkers, managers, and other employees responsible for marketing implementation.

A 360° evaluation emphasizes personal development. Its purpose is to help employees become better managers or to improve their performance by obtaining open feedback from them. This type of evaluation uses all contact or touch points, including customers. Trust and anonymity are used to ensure honest feedback. For example, at Autodesk, a software company, a feeling of trust and respect for all employees involved in the process prevails. Although reviews include direct quotes, the feedback is presented anonymously.

Implementing a 360° feedback review system requires the support of top management. Most compa-

nies that implement a 360° review program begin with one group of employees, usually at a senior level, to demonstrate commitment to the process. Once employees can observe how the process works, they usually understand the benefits and provide support. For example, Coach, which markets purses and leather accessories, launched a 360° review system that focused on store managers who had the potential for promotion to higher levels of management. The store managers picked their reviewers and, after the review process, developed an action plan documenting the steps needed to improve in particular areas, such as communication. To be successful, 360° feedback must include such action plans so employees can improve their skills.

Appropriate communication within the marketing unit can enhance morale and increase productivity. Marketing managers need to communicate with top management to guide marketing activities and integrate those activities with those of other departments or units within the organization. Failure to get along with senior executives can hinder implementation of marketing strategies. The 360° review provides full-circle, multi-source assessment across operating units; provides direction; and, hopefully, yields insights to help prevent poor implementation. Even customers can contribute to the review process. The 360° review can provide the feedback necessary to implement customer relationship management and achieve marketing objectives.

SNAPSHOT

Manners at work

Nearly one half of workers say workplace courtesy has declined over the past five years due to pressure to work more quickly and efficiently.

- 18% No change
- 2% Don't know
- 36% Increased
- 44% Decreased

Source: *USA Today*. www.usatoday.com/snapshot/money/2001-07-31-manners.htm. Copyright 2001, *USA Today*. Reprinted with permission.

more complex because of greater differences among workers in terms of race, ethnicity, gender, and age. Indeed, one of the most common forms of diversity in today's organizations is the diversity across generations of employees. Such differences broaden the range of individual value systems within an organization, which in turn calls for a more diverse set of motivational tools. For example, an employee might value autonomy or recognition more than a slight pay increase. Managers can reward employees not just with money and additional fringe benefits but also with such nonfinancial rewards as prestige or recognition, job autonomy, skill variety, task significance, increased feedback, or even a more relaxed dress code. It is crucial for management to show that it takes pride in its work force and to motivate employees to take pride in their company.

One problem for many organizations has been an increase in workplace rudeness. In a recent survey, 71 percent of workers reported they had experienced condescending or rude behavior on the job. A lack of civility in the workplace has been linked to anxiety and depression, as well as to reduced productivity and employee satisfaction. Civility issues should be addressed to motivate and satisfy marketing personnel and minimize unnecessary turnover.[29] Although such efforts may seem frivolous, they acknowledge employees' feelings and efforts and thereby boost morale and motivation.

Communicating Within the Marketing Unit

With good communication, marketing managers can motivate personnel and coordinate their efforts. Poor communication can harm morale and reduce productivity. Poor communication between managers and employees can be especially damaging in emotionally charged situations.

Marketing managers must be able to communicate with the firm's top management to ensure marketing activities are consistent with the company's overall goals. Communication with top-level executives keeps marketing managers aware of the company's overall plans and achievements. It also guides the marketing unit's activities and indicates how they are to be integrated with those of other departments, such as finance, production, or human resources, with whose management the marketing manager must also communicate to coordinate marketing efforts. For example, marketing personnel should work with the production staff to help design products that customers want. To direct marketing activities, marketing managers must communicate with marketing personnel at the operations level, such as sales and advertising personnel, researchers, wholesalers, retailers, and package designers. To improve efficiency and communication, Procter & Gamble uses a new software program that allows employees all over the world to collaborate, watch TV commercials, evaluate print ads, and receive supervisory approval for their work. The program also documents project stages, noting the time each takes and where slowdowns may be occurring. The software also helps new employees track their responsibilities. One employee estimated that projects were completed in 20 to 30 percent less time than normal.[30]

One of the most important types of communication in marketing is communication that flows upward from the frontline of the marketing unit to higher-level marketing managers. Customer-contact employees are in a unique position to understand customers' wants and needs. By taking steps to encourage upward communication, marketing managers can gain access to a rich source of information about what customers require, how well products are selling, whether marketing activities are working, and what problems are occurring in marketing implementation.[31] Upward communication also allows marketing managers to understand the problems and needs of employees. As we noted earlier, such communication is an important aspect of the internal marketing approach.

Training is a key part of communicating with marketing employees. Setting clear objectives and demonstrating that training adds value to the individual helps create a productive organizational climate. Through an effective training program, employees can learn, ask questions, and become accountable for marketing performance.[32] Communication is also facilitated by an information system within the marketing unit. The marketing information system (discussed in Chapter 6) should make it easy for marketing managers, sales managers, and sales personnel to communicate with one another. Marketers need an information system to support a variety of activities, such as planning, budgeting, sales analyses, performance evaluations, and report preparation. An information system should also expedite communications with other departments in the organization and minimize destructive interdepartmental competition for organizational resources.

Coordinating Marketing Activities

Because of job specialization and differences among marketing activities, marketing managers must synchronize individuals' actions to achieve marketing objectives. They must work closely with managers in research and development, production, finance, accounting, and human resources to ensure that marketing activities mesh with other functions of the firm. They must coordinate the activities of marketing staff within the firm and integrate those activities with the marketing efforts of external organizations—advertising agencies, resellers (wholesalers and retailers), researchers, and shippers, among others. Marketing managers can improve coordination by making each employee aware of how his or her job relates to others and how his or her actions contribute to the achievement of marketing objectives.

Establishing a Timetable for Implementation

Successful marketing implementation requires that employees know the specific activities for which they are responsible and the timetable for completing each activity. One company that is very good at establishing implementation timetables is Domino's Pizza. Every activity involved in creating and delivering a pizza, from taking the phone order to handing the pizza to the customer, has an employee who is responsible for its implementation. In addition, all employees know the specified time frame for completion of their activities.

Establishing an implementation timetable involves several steps: (1) identifying the activities to be performed, (2) determining the time required to complete each activity, (3) separating the activities to be performed in sequence from those to be performed simultaneously, (4) organizing the activities in the proper order, and (5) assigning responsibility for completing each activity to one or more employees, teams, or managers. Some activities must be performed before others, whereas others can be performed at the same time or later in the implementation process. Completing all implementation activities on schedule requires tight coordination among departments —marketing, production, advertising, sales, and so on. Pinpointing those implementation activities that can be performed simultaneously will greatly reduce the total amount of time needed to put a given marketing strategy into practice. Since scheduling is a complicated task, most organizations use sophisticated computer programs to plan the timing of marketing activities. Figure 22.4 is an example of an implementation timetable for a new product.

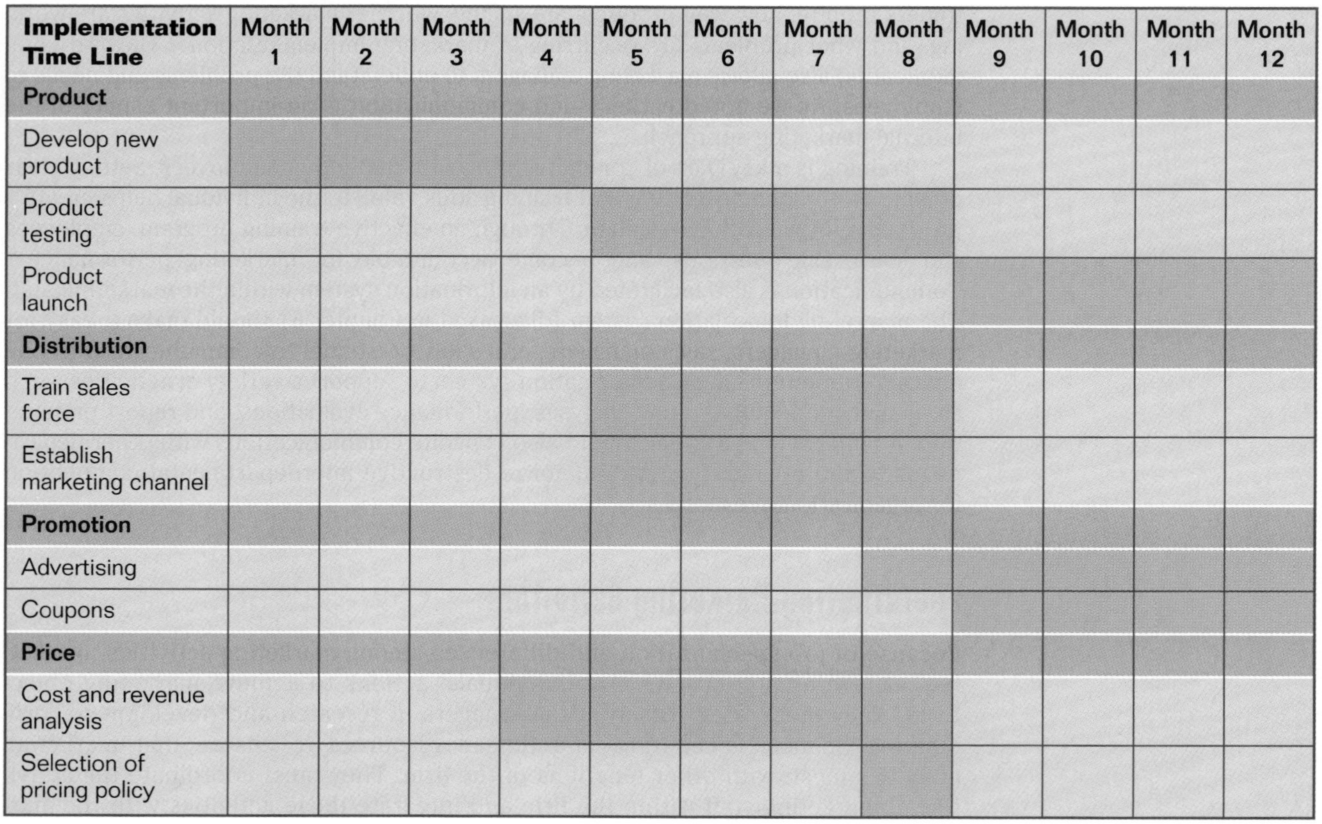

Implementation Time Line	Month 1	Month 2	Month 3	Month 4	Month 5	Month 6	Month 7	Month 8	Month 9	Month 10	Month 11	Month 12
Product												
Develop new product												
Product testing												
Product launch												
Distribution												
Train sales force												
Establish marketing channel												
Promotion												
Advertising												
Coupons												
Price												
Cost and revenue analysis												
Selection of pricing policy												

FIGURE 22.4
Example of an Implementation Timetable

Controlling Marketing Activities

To achieve both marketing and general organizational objectives, marketing managers must effectively control marketing efforts. The **marketing control process** consists of establishing performance standards, evaluating actual performance by comparing it with established standards, and reducing the differences between desired and actual performance.

Although the control function is a fundamental management activity, it has received little attention in marketing. Organizations have both formal and informal control systems. The formal marketing control process, as mentioned before, involves performance standards, evaluation of actual performance, and corrective action to remedy shortfalls (see Figure 22.5). The informal control process involves self-control, social or group control, and cultural control through acceptance of a firm's value system. Which type of control system dominates depends on the environmental context of the firm.[33] We now discuss these steps in the formal control process and consider the major problems they involve.

Establishing Performance Standards

Planning and controlling are closely linked because plans include statements about what is to be accomplished. For purposes of control, these statements function as performance standards. A **performance standard** is an expected level of performance against which actual performance can be compared. A performance standard might be a reduction of customers' complaints by 20 percent, a monthly sales quota of $150,000, or a 10 percent increase per month in new-customer accounts. Performance standards are also given in the form of budget accounts; that is, marketers are expected to achieve a certain objective without spending more than a given amount of

marketing control process
Establishing performance standards and trying to match actual performance to those standards

performance standard
An expected level of performance

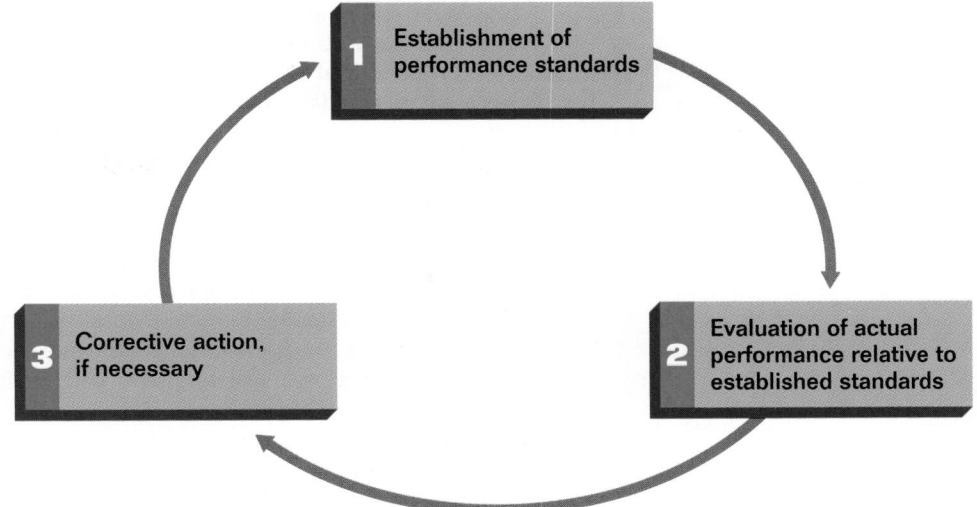

FIGURE 22.5
The Marketing Control Process

resources. As stated earlier, performance standards should be tied to organizational goals. General Motors, for example, has a goal of increasing the number of Saab automobiles sold from 130,000 to 250,000 by 2005. This standard will be supported with the introduction of a Saab sport-utility vehicle and an all-wheel drive version of the 9–5 sedan.[34] Performance standards can also relate to products or service quality. Achieving performance standards is becoming increasingly difficult as a shortage of high-quality service employees grows more severe.[35]

Evaluating Actual Performance

To compare actual performance with performance standards, marketing managers must know what employees within the company are doing and have information about the activities of external organizations that provide the firm with marketing assistance. Lexus, for example, evaluates its product and service level by how well it ranks on the J.D. Power & Associates Customer Satisfaction Survey. In 2000, Lexus ranked number one among all automakers, followed by Saturn, Cadillac, Infiniti, and Acura.[36] (We discuss specific methods for assessing actual performance later in this chapter.) Information is required about the activities of marketing personnel at the operations level and at various marketing management levels. Most businesses obtain marketing assistance from one or more external individuals or organizations, such as advertising agencies, intermediaries, marketing research firms, and consultants. To maximize benefits from external sources, a firm's marketing control process must monitor their activities. Although it may be difficult to obtain the necessary information, it is impossible to measure actual performance without it.

Evaluating Actual Performance
Deepak Sareen's TimeSheet Professional software package assists companies in evaluating how effectively employees are spending their time and money.

Records of actual performance are compared with performance standards to determine whether and how much of a discrepancy exists. For example, if General Motors determines that only 220,000 Saabs have been sold in 2005, a discrepancy exists because its goal for Saab was 250,000 vehicles sold annually.

Taking Corrective Action

Marketing managers have several options for reducing a discrepancy between established performance standards and actual performance. They can take steps to improve actual performance, reduce or totally change the performance standard, or do both. To improve actual performance, the marketing manager may have to use better methods of motivating marketing personnel or find more effective techniques for coordinating marketing efforts.

Performance standards are sometimes unrealistic when written, and changes in the marketing environment can make feasible goals unrealistic. For example, a company's annual sales goal may become unrealistic if several aggressive competitors enter the firm's market. In fact, changes in the marketing environment may dictate radical revisions in marketing strategy. Gillette, the parent company of Duracell, focused much of its promotional budget on a new technology producing a longer-life, superior battery in the Duracell Ultra. However, sales of Duracell batteries fell 11 percent and profits declined about 59 percent. To rejuvenate sales, Gillette planned to return to promoting the Duracell Coppertop with its first broadcast advertising campaign in four years, using a bee theme to demonstrate the hard-working nature of the Duracell battery. The company boosted spending by 40 percent for the $100 million campaign, which sought to position Duracell as the market leader among alkaline batteries.[37]

Problems in Controlling Marketing Activities

In their efforts to control marketing activities, marketing managers frequently run into several problems. Often the information required to control marketing activities is unavailable or is available only at a high cost. Even though marketing controls should be flexible enough to allow for environmental changes, the frequency, intensity, and unpredictability of such changes may hamper control. In addition, the time lag between marketing activities and their results limits a marketing manager's ability to measure the effectiveness of specific marketing activities. This is especially true for all advertising activities.

Because marketing and other business activities overlap, marketing managers cannot determine the precise costs of marketing activities. Without an accurate measure of marketing costs, it is difficult to know if the outcome of marketing activities is worth the expense. Finally, marketing control may be difficult because it is very hard to develop exact performance standards for marketing personnel.

Methods of Evaluating Performance

There are specific methods for assessing and improving the effectiveness of a marketing strategy. A marketer should state in the marketing plan what a marketing strategy is supposed to accomplish. These statements should set forth performance standards—usually in terms of profits, sales, costs, or communication standards—relating to such matters as brand recall. Actual performance should be measured in similar terms to facilitate comparisons. In this section, we consider three general ways to evaluate the actual performance of marketing strategies: sales analysis, marketing cost analysis, and the marketing audit.

Sales Analysis

sales analysis   Use of sales figures to evaluate a firm's current performance

Sales analysis uses sales figures to evaluate a firm's current performance. It is probably the most common method of evaluation because sales data partially reflect the target market's reactions to a marketing mix and often are readily available, at least in aggregate form.

Marketers use current sales data to monitor the impact of current marketing efforts. However, that information alone is not enough. To provide useful analyses, current sales data must be compared with forecasted sales, industry sales, specific competitors' sales, or the costs incurred to achieve the sales volume. For example, knowing that a specialty store attained a $600,000 sales volume this year does not tell management whether its marketing strategy has succeeded. However, if managers know expected sales were $550,000, they are in a better position to determine the effectiveness of the firm's marketing efforts. In addition, if they know the marketing costs needed to achieve the $600,000 volume were 12 percent less than budgeted, they are in an even better position to analyze their marketing strategy precisely.

Although sales may be measured in several ways, the basic unit of measurement is the sales transaction. A sales transaction results in an order for a specified quantity of the organization's product sold under specified terms by a particular salesperson or sales group on a certain date. Many organizations record these bits of information about their transactions. With such a record, a company can analyze sales in terms of dollar volume or market share.

Firms frequently use dollar volume in their sales analyses because the dollar is a common denominator of sales, costs, and profits. However, price increases and decreases affect total sales figures. This is especially true in the auto industry, where profit margins are being squeezed. Even though auto prices are increasing, customers are demanding rock-bottom prices and low lease rates on everything but the hottest-selling trucks.[38] If a company increased its prices by 10 percent this year and its sales volume is 10 percent greater than last year, it has not experienced any increase in unit sales. A marketing manager who uses dollar volume analysis should factor out the effects of price changes.

A firm's market share is the firm's sales of a product stated as a percentage of industry sales of that product. Market share analysis lets a company compare its marketing strategy with competitors' strategies. The primary reason for using market share analysis is to estimate whether sales changes have resulted from the firm's marketing strategy or from uncontrollable environmental forces. When a company's sales volume declines but its share of the market stays the same, the marketer can assume industry sales declined (because of some uncontrollable factors) and this decline was reflected in the firm's sales. However, if a company experiences a decline in both sales and market share, it should consider the possibility that its marketing strategy is not effective or was improperly implemented.

Even though market share analysis can be helpful in evaluating the performance of a marketing strategy, the user must interpret results cautiously. When attributing a sales decline to uncontrollable factors, a marketer must keep in mind that such factors do not affect all firms in the industry equally. Not all firms in an industry have the same objectives and strategies, and some change strategies from one year to the next. Changes in the strategies of one company can affect the market shares of one or all companies in that industry. For example, Campbell Soup Company split its North American operations into two divisions: soup and the remainder of Campbell's businesses (V-8 beverages and Pace and Prego sauces). This reorganization sought to refocus the company on the soup business to compete more effectively with Pillsbury's Progresso soup line even though the market for condensed soups has been declining over the past several years.[39] Within an industry, the entrance of new firms, the launch of new products by competing firms, or the demise of established products also affects a specific firm's market share, and market share analysts should attempt to account for these effects. KFC, for example, had to reevaluate its marketing strategies when McDonald's introduced its own fried chicken product.

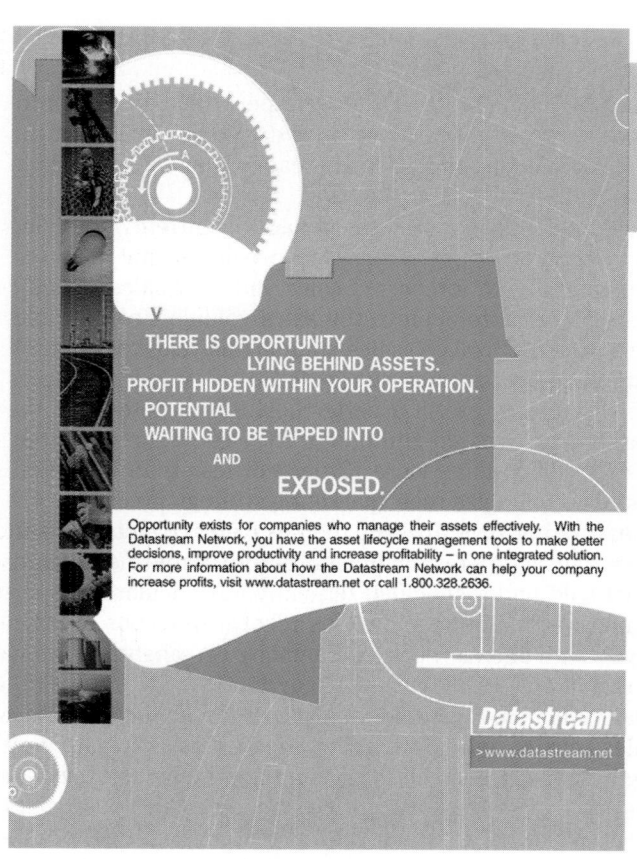

Marketing Cost Analysis

Although sales analysis is critical for evaluating the effectiveness of a marketing strategy, it gives only part of the picture. A marketing strategy that successfully generates sales may also be extremely costly. To get a complete picture, a firm must know the marketing costs associated with using a given strategy to achieve a certain sales level. **Marketing cost analysis** breaks down and classifies costs to determine which are associated with specific marketing activities. By comparing costs of previous marketing activities with results generated, a marketer can better allocate the firm's marketing resources in the future. Marketing cost analysis lets a company evaluate the effectiveness of marketing strategy by comparing sales achieved and costs incurred. By pinpointing exactly where a company is experiencing high costs, this form of analysis can help isolate profitable or unprofitable customer segments, products, and geographic areas.

marketing cost analysis
Breaking down and classifying costs to determine those that stem from specific marketing activities

fixed costs   Costs based on how money was actually spent

variable costs   Costs directly attributable to production and selling volume

traceable common costs
Costs allocated indirectly to the functions they support

nontraceable common costs
Costs assignable only on an arbitrary basis

full-cost approach   Including direct costs and both traceable and nontraceable common costs in the cost analysis

direct-cost approach
Including only direct costs and traceable common costs in the cost analysis

The task of determining marketing costs is often complex and difficult. Simply ascertaining the costs associated with marketing a product is rarely adequate. Marketers usually must determine the marketing costs of serving specific geographic areas, market segments, or even specific customers.

Four broad categories are used in marketing cost analysis: fixed costs, variable costs, traceable common costs, and nontraceable common costs. **Fixed costs,** such as rent, salaries, office supplies, and utilities, are based on how the money was actually spent. However, fixed costs often do not explain what marketing functions were performed using those funds. It does little good, for example, to know that $80,000 is spent for rent each year. The analyst has no way of knowing whether the money is spent for the rental of production, storage, or sales facilities. **Variable costs** are directly attributable to production and selling volume. For example, sales force salaries might be allocated to the cost of selling a specific product, selling in a certain geographic area, or selling to a particular customer. **Traceable common costs** can be allocated indirectly, using one or several criteria, to the functions they support. For example, if the firm spends $80,000 annually to rent space for production, storage, and selling, the rental costs of storage could be determined on the basis of cost per square foot used for storage. **Nontraceable common costs** cannot be assigned according to any logical criteria; they are assignable only on an arbitrary basis. Interest, taxes, and the salaries of top management are nontraceable common costs.

How costs are dealt with depends on whether the analyst uses a full-cost or a direct-cost approach. When a **full-cost approach** is used, cost analysis includes variable costs, traceable common costs, and nontraceable common costs. Proponents of this approach claim that if an accurate profit picture is desired, all costs must be included in the analysis. However, opponents point out that full costing does not yield actual costs because nontraceable common costs are determined by arbitrary criteria. With different criteria, the full-costing approach yields different results. A cost-conscious operating unit can be discouraged if numerous costs are assigned to it arbitrarily. To eliminate such problems, the **direct-cost approach,** which includes variable costs and traceable common costs but not nontraceable common costs, is used. However, critics of this approach say it is not accurate because it omits one cost category.

The Marketing Audit

marketing audit   A systematic examination of the marketing group's objectives, strategies, organization, and performance

A **marketing audit** is a systematic examination of the marketing group's objectives, strategies, organization, and performance. Its primary purpose is to identify weaknesses in ongoing marketing operations and plan improvements to correct these weaknesses. Like an accounting or a financial audit, a marketing audit should be conducted regularly instead of just when performance evaluation mechanisms show that the system is out of control. The marketing audit is not a control process to be used only during a crisis, though, of course, it can help a troubled business isolate problems and generate solutions. Marketing audits have become more difficult as organizations have merged and acquired other firms, thus gaining technology, world market share, new products, and distribution systems.

customer service audit
A comparison of the performance of specific customer service activities with service goals and standards

One specialized type of audit is the **customer service audit,** in which specific customer service activities are analyzed and service goals and standards are compared with actual performance.[40] Table 22.1 provides a typical outline for a customer service audit. Another type is the social audit, which helps a firm evaluate its social responsibility efforts (refer back to Table 4.5 on page 102). Specialized audits can also be performed for product development, pricing, sales, advertising, and other promotional activities. The scope of any audit depends on the costs involved, the target markets served, the structure of the marketing mix, and environmental conditions. The results of the audit can be used to reallocate marketing efforts and reexamine marketing opportunities.

The marketing audit should aid evaluation by doing the following:

1. Describing current activities and results related to sales, costs, prices, profits, and other performance feedback

2. Gathering information about customers, competition, and environmental developments that may affect the marketing strategy

3. Identifying opportunities and alternatives for improving the marketing strategy

4. Providing an overall database to use in evaluating the attainment of organizational goals and marketing objectives

Marketing audits can be performed internally or externally. An internal auditor may be a top-level marketing executive, a companywide auditing committee, or a manager from another office or functional area. Although more expensive, an audit by outside consultants is usually more effective because external auditors bring to the task more objectivity, more time for the audit, and greater experience.

There is no single set of procedures for all marketing audits. However, firms should adhere to several general guidelines. Audits are often based on a series of questionnaires administered to the firm's personnel; these questionnaires should be developed carefully to ensure the audit focuses on the right issues. Auditors should develop and follow a step-by-step plan to guarantee the audit is systematic. When interviewing personnel, the auditors should strive to talk with a diverse group of people from many parts of the company.

Although the concept of auditing implies an official examination of marketing activities, many organizations audit their marketing activities informally. Any attempt to verify operating results and compare them with standards can be considered an auditing activity. Many smaller firms probably would not use the word *audit,* but they do perform auditing activities.

Marketing audits can pose several problems. They can be expensive and time consuming, and selecting the auditors may be difficult if objective, qualified personnel are not available. Employees sometimes fear comprehensive evaluations, especially by outsiders, and in such cases marketing audits can be extremely disruptive.

Table 22.1	Dimensions of a Customer Service Audit

A. Identify Activities

1. What specific customer service activities does the company currently provide?
   Product related activities: repairs, maintenance, technical assistance
   Pricing related activities: credit, financing, billing
   Distribution related activities: delivery, installation, locations
   Promotion related activities: customer service phone lines, complaint handling

2. Are these customer services provided by our company or by outside contractors? If outside contractors provide these services, how are they performing?

3. What customer service activities do customers want or need?

B. Review Standard Procedures for Each Activity

1. Do written procedures (manuals) exist for each activity? If so, are these procedures (manuals) up-to-date?

2. What oral or unwritten procedures exist for each activity? Should these procedures be included in the written procedures, or should they be eliminated?

3. Do customer service personnel regularly interact with other functions to establish standard procedures for each activity?

C. Identify Performance Goals by Customer Service Activity

1. What specific, quantitative goals exist for each activity?

2. What qualitative goals exist for each activity?

3. How does each activity contribute to customer satisfaction with each marketing element (i.e., product, pricing, distribution, promotion)?

4. How does each activity contribute to the long-term success of the company?

D. Specify Performance Measures by Customer Service Activity

1. What are the internal, profit-based measures for each activity?

2. What are the internal, time-based measures for each activity?

3. How is performance monitored and evaluated internally by management?

4. How is performance monitored and evaluated externally by customers?

E. Review and Evaluate Customer Service Personnel

1. Are the company's current recruiting, selection, and retention efforts consistent with the customer service requirements established by customers?

2. What is the nature and content of our employee-training activities? Are these activities consistent with the customer service requirements established by customers?

3. How are customer service personnel supervised, evaluated, and rewarded? Are these procedures consistent with customer requirements?

4. What effect do employee evaluation and reward policies have on employee attitudes, satisfaction, and motivation?

F. Identify and Evaluate Customer Service Support Systems

1. Are the quality and accuracy of our customer service materials consistent with the image of our company and its products? (Examples: instruction manuals, brochures, form letters, etc.)

2. Are the quality and appearance of our physical facilities consistent with the image of our company and its products? (Examples: offices, furnishings, layout, etc.)

3. Are the quality and appearance of our customer service equipment consistent with the image of our company and its products? (Examples: repair tools, telephones, computers, delivery vehicles, etc.)

4. Are our record-keeping systems accurate? Is the information always readily available when it is needed? What technology could be acquired to enhance our record-keeping abilities (i.e., bar code scanners, portable computers)?

Source: Reprinted from Christopher H. Lovelock, *Services Marketing*, Second Edition. Copyright © 1991 Prentice-Hall, a division of Simon & Schuster, Inc. Used with permission.

Summary

Marketing implementation, the process of putting marketing strategies into action, is an important part of the marketing management process. To ensure effective implementation, marketing managers must consider why the intended marketing strategies do not always turn out as expected. Realized marketing strategies often differ from the intended strategies because of three implementation problems: marketing strategy and implementation are related, they are constantly evolving, and the responsibility for them is separated. Marketing managers must also consider other vital components of implementation—shared goals and objectives, employees, and leadership—to ensure proper implementation of marketing strategies.

Organizations often follow two major approaches to marketing implementation: internal marketing and total quality management (TQM). Internal marketing is a management philosophy that coordinates internal exchanges between the organization and its employees to achieve successful external exchanges between the organization and its customers. In this approach, all employees are considered internal customers. For implementation to be successful, the needs of both internal and external customers must be met. The TQM approach relies heavily on the talents of employees to continually improve the quality of the organization's goods and services. The three essentials of the TQM philosophy are continuous quality improvement, empowered employees, and quality improvement teams. One of TQM's primary tools is benchmarking, or measuring and evaluating the quality of the organization's goods, services, or processes in relation to the quality produced by the best-performing companies in the industry.

The organization of marketing activities involves the development of an internal structure for the marketing unit. The internal structure is the key to directing marketing activities. In a marketing-oriented organization, the focus is on finding out what buyers want and providing it in a way that lets the organization achieve its objectives. In a centralized organization, top-level managers delegate very little authority to lower levels. In a decentralized organization, decision-making authority is delegated as far down the chain of command as possible. The marketing unit can be organized by functions, products, regions, or types of customers. An organization may use only one approach or a combination.

Proper implementation of a marketing plan depends on the motivation of personnel who perform marketing activities, effective communication within the marketing unit, coordination of marketing activities, and establishment of a timetable for implementation. To motivate marketing personnel, managers must discover employees' needs and then develop motivational methods that will help employees satisfy those needs. A company's communication system should allow the marketing manager to communicate with high-level management, with managers of other functional areas in the firm, and with personnel involved in marketing activities both inside and outside the organization. Marketing managers should coordinate the activities of marketing personnel and integrate them with those in other areas of the company and with the marketing efforts of personnel in external organizations. Finally, successful marketing implementation requires that employees know the specific activities for which they are responsible and the timetable for completing each activity.

The marketing control process consists of establishing performance standards, evaluating actual performance by comparing it with established standards, and reducing the discrepancy between desired and actual performance. Performance standards, which are established in the planning process, are expected levels of performance with which actual performance can be compared. To evaluate actual performance, marketing managers must know what employees within the firm are doing and have information about the activities of external organizations that provide the firm with marketing assistance. When actual performance is compared with performance standards, marketers must determine whether a discrepancy exists and, if so, whether it requires corrective action such as changing the performance standards or improving actual performance.

The control of marketing activities is not a simple task. Problems encountered include environmental changes, time lags between marketing activities and their effects, and difficulty in determining the costs of marketing activities. In addition, it may be hard to develop performance standards.

Control of marketing strategy can be facilitated through sales and cost analyses. For the purpose of analysis, sales are usually measured in terms of either dollar volume or market share. To be effective, a sales analysis must compare current sales performance with forecasted company sales, industry sales, specific competitors' sales, or the costs incurred to generate the current sales volume.

Marketing cost analysis involves an examination of accounting records and fixed costs, variable costs, and traceable and nontraceable common costs. Such an analysis is often difficult because there may be no logical, clear-cut way to allocate fixed costs into functional accounts. The analyst may choose either full costing or direct costing.

A marketing audit is a systematic examination of the marketing group's objectives, strategies, organization, and performance. A marketing audit attempts to identify what a marketing unit is doing, evaluate the effectiveness of these activities, and recommend future marketing activities. The scope of a marketing audit can be very broad or very narrow. Some companies use specialized audits, such as a customer service audit, to address problems within specific marketing functions.

Important Terms

Marketing implementation	Fixed costs
Intended strategy	Variable costs
Realized strategy	Traceable common costs
External customers	Nontraceable common
Internal customers	costs
Internal marketing	Full-cost approach
Total quality management	Direct-cost approach
(TQM)	Marketing audit
Benchmarking	Customer service audit
Empowerment	
Centralized organization	
Decentralized organization	
Marketing control process	
Performance standard	
Sales analysis	
Marketing cost analysis	

Discussion and Review Questions

1. Why does an organization's intended strategy often differ from its realized strategy?
2. Discuss the three problems associated with implementing marketing activities. How are these problems related to the discrepancies between intended and realized marketing strategies?
3. What is internal marketing? Why is it important in implementing marketing strategies?
4. How does the total quality management approach relate to marketing implementation? For what types of marketing strategies might TQM be best suited?
5. What factors can be used to organize the decision-making authority of a marketing unit? Discuss the benefits of each type of organization.
6. Why might an organization use multiple bases for organizing its marketing unit?
7. Why is the motivation of marketing personnel important in implementing marketing plans?
8. How does communication help in implementing marketing plans?
9. What are the major steps of the marketing control process?

10. Discuss the major problems in controlling marketing activities.
11. What is a sales analysis? What makes it an effective control tool?
12. Identify and contrast two cost analysis methods.
13. How is the marketing audit used to control marketing program performance?

Application Questions

1. IBM has decentralized its product development and marketing operations to be more responsive to its customers. Explain to what degree and how you would decentralize the following types of businesses. Would you empower the customer-contact employees?
   a. Full-service restaurant
   b. Prestigious clothing store
   c. Automobile dealership
2. Marketing units may be organized according to functions, products, regions, or types of customers. Describe how you would organize the marketing units for the following:
   a. Toothpaste with whitener; toothpaste with extra-strong nicotine cleaners; toothpaste with bubble-gum flavor
   b. National line offering all types of winter and summer sports clothing for men and women
   c. Life insurance company that provides life, health, and disability insurance
3. Why would it be important to implement both an internal and an external marketing strategy for the following companies?
   a. McDonald's
   b. Ford Motor Company
   c. Hoover Vacuum
4. Assume you are the marketing manager for a small printing company in your city. Convince the owner of the company of the need for a customer service audit, and explain briefly what conducting the audit will involve. What benefits would you expect? How often would you suggest conducting the audit?

Internet Exercise & Resources

Lower Colorado River Authority

The Lower Colorado River Authority (LCRA) is a conservation and reclamation district created in 1934 by the Texas legislature to improve the quality of life in central Texas. The organization supplies electricity to many central Texans and water to numerous customers, including cities, municipal utility districts, and agricultural users. In addition to working to control floods in central Texas, the LCRA protects the quality of the lower Colorado River and its tributaries, provides parks and recreation facilities, helps water and waste-water utilities, and provides soil, energy, and water conservation programs. The organization's revenues come from its provision of services rather than from taxes. Learn more about this organization by exploring its website at

> **www.lcra.org**

1. Find the LCRA's mission statement. Judging from the activities its site describes, do you think the LCRA is fulfilling its mission?

2. How is the LCRA organized? Does this structure foster effective marketing implementation?

3. What plans does the LCRA have for implementing its marketing strategies in the future?

VIDEO CASE 22.1

The AOL Time Warner Merger

A unique combination of the world's most trusted brands, journalistic integrity, and Internet expertise resulted when America Online and Time Warner joined forces on January 11, 2001. Quickly labeled "the beginning of the end of old mass media," the merger has the potential to dramatically alter the competitive landscape in the information and entertainment industries. Combining the resources of these media giants should give the world's readers, viewers, and listeners greater access to a breathtaking array of choices and connections to the ever-expanding online universe. Investors should benefit from a projected extra $1 billion of pretax operating profits from the combined firms. For these benefits to be realized, however, AOL Time Warner must integrate the operations of two complex firms with hundreds of subsidiaries and establish a strategy for successful implementation and control to satisfy investors, customers, and partners.

The union of America Online and Time Warner represents the culmination of a series of mergers and acquisitions among numerous well-known media firms. Time, Inc., was incorporated in 1922 by Henry Luce and Briton Hadden; they published the

first issue of *Time* magazine the following year. In 1927 Warner Brothers, a separate company, released the first "talking" movie, *The Jazz Singer*. Over the following decades, these two firms grew independently by launching many new products, acquiring related companies, and building large audiences for their respective products. By the 1970s, entrepreneur Ted Turner had begun building his own media empire, Turner Broadcasting System, by launching or acquiring a number of sports franchises and television networks, most notably the Cable News Network (CNN). Finally, another entrepreneur, Steve Case, launched Quantum Computer Services in 1985; the service was later renamed America Online (AOL) and grew to become the nation's largest Internet content and service provider. Time acquired Warner Brothers in 1989 to create the world's largest media company, representing some of the most respected names in journalism, publishing, and music. Time Warner expanded this empire further when it merged with Turner Broadcasting System in 1996 and America Online in 2001. According to Jerry Levin, the firm's new CEO (on right in photo), "AOL Time Warner's

scale, scope, and reach will enable us to capitalize on the digital revolution that is shaping global media, entertainment, and communications on behalf of consumers worldwide."

To ensure the combined businesses perform to expectations, executives from both America Online and Time Warner participated in defining AOL Time Warner's mission "to become the world's most respected and valued company by connecting, informing, and entertaining people everywhere in innovative ways that will enrich their lives." They also specified a set of values for the firm: creativity, customer focus, agility, teamwork, integrity, diversity, and responsibility. For example, AOL Time Warner strives to expand customer experiences by creating value in people's lives through volunteerism, civic engagement, and providing appropriate information to ensure everyone can share in the benefits of the "information revolution" fostered by the growth of the Internet.

The ultimate goal of this created value is to serve as a legacy to be followed for years to come. The new corporation has organized into six operating units of subsidiaries, brands, products, and services. The Interactive Services and Properties unit includes America Online, the world's leading Internet service and content provider with more than 30 million subscribers. This unit also owns or operates AOL Services, AOL Anywhere, AOL International, AOL@School, CompuServe, Digital City, DMS, ICQ, iPlanet, MapQuest, Moviefone, Netscape, and AOL Music. The Networks unit con-

sists of the Home Box Office premium movie network and the Turner Broadcasting System; the latter owns many of the most recognized brands in entertainment and news, including TBS, TNT, the WB, the Cartoon Network, Turner Classic Movies, and CNN, as well as the Atlanta Braves, Atlanta Hawks, Atlanta Thrashers, and many international networks and businesses. The Publishing Unit includes the holdings of the former Time, Inc., which publishes more than 64 magazines—including *Time, Sports Illustrated, People, Fortune, Southern Living,* and *Sunset*—with more than 268 million readers. AOL Time Warner's Filmed Entertainment Unit includes many well-known film studios, such as Warner Brothers and New Line Cinema. The Music unit includes Warner Music Group. The company also owns the nation's largest cable television service provider, Time Warner Cable.

To capitalize on the synergies created by the brands and products these units own, AOL Time Warner has established a number of public policies to guide its decision makers in responding to a dynamic marketing environment. For example, the company has chosen to market itself as a responsible firm that recognizes and respects the privacy of its customers, especially online. The issue of online privacy has proven controversial as the Internet continues to revolutionize how consumers make purchases and marketers learn about customer buying habits. To demonstrate its ongoing support of personal privacy, AOL Time Warner has led private sector efforts to find ways to address public concerns about the safety and security of personal information while continuing to develop consumer-friendly marketing practices tailored to individual preferences and tastes. The company helped create the Direct Marketing Association's Privacy Promise, which requires explaining to consumers how personal information is used and what actions they can take to direct the use of personal information by marketers.

AOL Time Warner has taken similar steps with regard to the thousands of filmmakers, songwriters, artists, authors, and others whose creative works are now publicly available through the Internet. The company has made a commitment to protect the intellectual property of these individuals and groups by protecting copyrights and trademarks that safeguard those rights as well as ensure royalties for those works. The company is also developing protective technology and new business plans that will make the works available to everyone in every format on every device.

By specifying its position on significant public policy issues such as privacy and intellectual property, AOL Time Warner has communicated policies and standards for the performance of every subsidiary and individual within the firm. The company has established performance standards, which are tied to its organizational goal of adding value for customers and clients without compromising the worth of available information. These standards allow the firm to assess its performance through both internal and external sources and to take corrective action as necessary. As Steve Case, the firm's new chairperson (on left in photo), says, "Our brands, services, and technologies already touch hundreds of millions of people and, by closely integrating our assets, we will embed the AOL Time Warner experience more deeply into their everyday lives."[41]

QUESTIONS FOR DISCUSSION

1. Given the size and complexity of the operations of AOL Time Warner after the most recent merger, what problems might the firm encounter in implementing new marketing plans and strategies to achieve its goals?
2. How does AOL Time Warner appear to be organized? Assess how this structure will affect the organization's ability to implement and control its marketing activities.
3. How will AOL Time Warner's public policy positions help the firm implement and control its marketing plans? What other mechanisms has AOL Time Warner established to control its marketing activities?

CASE 22.2
Amtrak Rides into the Twenty-First Century

In 1971, the federal government created the National Railroad Passenger Corporation, better known as Amtrak, to manage the nation's intercity passenger rail service. Like the U.S. Postal Service, Amtrak operates as a quasi-public corporation. The company serves 500 communities in 45 states and operates more than 22,000 route miles. In 2000 it earned more than $1.2 billion in revenue from 22.5 million passengers, as well as $886 million in revenues from other services. But despite its effective monopoly in passenger rail service, Amtrak has yet to turn a profit, and it lost a record $994 million in 2000. Facing a congressional mandate to become self-sufficient by 2003, Amtrak is implementing a challenging new business plan to carry it into the twenty-first century. This plan includes the development and implementation of six key strategies: building a market-based network, delivering consistent quality service, revitalizing the Amtrak brand, operating a cost-effective business, leveraging public and private partnerships, and developing corridor services.

To implement the first strategy, building a marketing-oriented network, the company has conducted extensive marketing research to define consumer demand, identify growth opportunities, and increase its share of travel business within the United States. Using state-of-the-art forecasting and analytical tools, Amtrak identified opportunities to improve customer service, reduce costs, and increase revenues. Based on the results of this analysis, the company launched a new plan to strengthen and improve the performance of its national network by maximizing its most profitable routes.

To implement its second strategy, delivering consistent quality service, the company developed a service standards program to ensure reliable, high-quality service to boost customer loyalty and ridership. This initiative includes analyzing the "best practices" of other successful companies; providing customer service training for all employees; standardizing equipment, station planning, and maintenance practices; and starting an initiative to make all trains "right and ready." Amtrak is revamping its onboard services with new menus, more legroom, and tougher employee conduct standards. It is also sprucing up train stations, restoring trains, and adding new trains—including the Acela, the nation's first high-speed train, which can travel up to 150 miles per hour between Boston and Washington—to provide better, faster service. Perhaps most important, the company has introduced an unconditional service guarantee, the first in the national transportation industry. The guarantee grants a travel voucher for a free trip to customers who do not believe they received a safe, comfortable, and enjoyable travel experience. The program's ambitious goal is to achieve a satisfaction rate of 99.9 percent. Within a few months, the company had achieved a 99.6 percent satisfaction rate.

To implement the third strategy, revitalizing the Amtrak brand, the firm adopted a commercial approach to better define its product and position it competitively against other transportation companies. After determining that its brand identity was outdated, the company began extensive marketing research to update its corporate identity. Based on this research, Amtrak modernized its logo to reflect the positive aspects of train travel and began implementing a new brand identity that will cover all of Amtrak's products, including the new Acela high-speed trains.

Amtrak's fourth strategy, to operate a cost-effective business, required a number of changes as well. To implement this goal, managers examined accounts, policies, processes, organizational structures, and costs to identify areas with the potential for improved cost management. As a result, Amtrak has developed new accounting procedures to better track costs and emphasize to all employees the need to deliver quality services in a cost-effective manner.

Amtrak's fifth strategy involves working to identify commercial and investment partners to generate additional revenues to support basic rail services and maximize Amtrak's own investments. State and municipal governments have long supported specific Amtrak routes, and private entities have helped finance and develop Amtrak assets. These partnerships have been crucial to Amtrak's long-term capitalization, and the company must continue to maintain these relationships and identify potential new partners that can help the firm achieve its other strategic goals.

Amtrak's final strategy involves working with these partners to develop new rail corridors in the Midwest, California, the Pacific Northwest, and the Southeast; along the Gulf Coast; and in New York State. Amtrak's launch of the Acela high-speed service in the northeast corridor represents the start of this high-speed network. Through initiatives with state and municipal governments, a number of other high-speed services are in the planning phase.

To implement these strategies, Amtrak is making a number of investments to improve infrastructure, adopt new technologies, expand rail services, launch additional high-speed rail services, work with states and other partners to develop new rail corridors, and boost nonpassenger revenues (such as mail and express service). Amtrak has established a number of performance goals related to increasing ridership, offering new and more frequent passenger services based on market-driven demand, expanding mail and express businesses, and exploiting new commercial opportunities.

Will Amtrak's strategic plan help it achieve its congressionally mandated objective of self-sufficiency on schedule? The reality is that no passenger rail system in the world operates profitably and, compared to the subsidies lavished on European and Asian passenger rail systems, Amtrak operates on a shoestring budget. According to new chief executive George Warrington, "The key to Amtrak's long-term success depends on transforming the national passenger rail system into a more market-based system that delivers services that customers want and takes them to and from destinations of their choice."[42]

QUESTIONS FOR DISCUSSION

1. Are Amtrak's performance standards sufficiently related to its organizational goals? Are they realistic?
2. What role do sales and marketing cost analyses play in the implementation of Amtrak's strategic plan?
3. If properly implemented, will Amtrak's strategic plan ensure the firm achieves its ultimate goal of self-sufficiency? What factors could prevent the firm from achieving this goal?

Marketing on the Internet

23

OBJECTIVES

- To define **electronic marketing** and **electronic commerce** and recognize their increasing importance in strategic planning

- To understand the characteristics of electronic marketing—addressability, interactivity, memory, control, accessibility, and digitalization—and how they differentiate electronic marketing from traditional marketing activities

- To examine how the characteristics of electronic marketing affect marketing strategy

- To identify the legal and ethical considerations in electronic marketing

eBay Auctions Everything

One of the best-known Internet companies is eBay, whose stated mission is "to help practically anyone trade practically anything on earth." The leading online auction site has grown into a community of nearly 30 million registered users who can buy or sell literally anything, from automobiles, boats, and furniture to jewelry, musical instruments, electronics, and collectibles. Users can participate in the bidding on any of the more than 100,000 transactions completed every day. Unlike many high-tech "dot-com" companies, eBay has been profitable almost from the beginning. With more than $5 billion in merchandise transacted through its site, the online auctioneer accounts for about 85 percent of the online auction market. The company's revenues doubled to $431 million in 2000, and its 50 percent annual growth rate is expected to continue for the foreseeable future.

Why has eBay been so successful when so many other Internet startups have failed? Many people believe the company's success is due largely to the leadership of CEO Meg Whitman, ranked third on a recent *Fortune* list of the most powerful women in business. Whitman, who gained experience at Hasbro, FTD, Stride Rite, Disney, and Procter & Gamble before taking the reins at eBay, keeps the company focused on "big-picture" objectives and key priorities, such as keeping expenses down and building a world-class executive team to keep the company on its fast-growing, profitable pace. She expects to meet company objectives by making smart acquisition decisions; reaching new customers, including more corporate ones; and opening a fixed-price bazaar. Whitman believes her most valuable contribution to eBay's success is the development of a work ethic and an organizational culture that focuses on a fun, open, and trusting environment, which she hopes will help the firm achieve $3 billion in revenues by 2005.

Although eBay is known primarily for consumer-to-consumer auctions, many business organizations have discovered they can sell older equipment and excess inventory through eBay. Sun Microsystems and IBM, for example, have their own

pages within eBay's computer category from which they market products, primarily to small and midsize business customers.

To maintain customer confidence in auction transactions, eBay has taken numerous steps to avoid fraud. Although fraud occurs in only 1 out of 40,000 online trades (less than one-tenth of 1 percent), fraudulent activities generate negative publicity and ill will and could jeopardize the firm's reputation for quality transactions. The company modified its user agreement to permit the barring of any user from the auction site and established feedback forms that allow buyers and sellers to rate each other based on their experience. The company also offers escrow and credit card protection services, through Billpont.com and other providers, that reduce the potential for fraud.

By providing an easy-to-use site for consumers and businesses to buy and sell goods and remaining proactive, eBay has essentially become the poster child for a successful Internet venture. With strong leadership from Meg Whitman, Internet insiders believe the company will continue to serve as a model for electronic commerce.[1]

The phenomenal growth of the Internet presents exciting opportunities for marketers such as eBay to forge interactive relationships with consumers and business customers. The interactive nature of the Internet, particularly the World Wide Web, has made it possible to target markets more precisely and even reach markets that previously were inaccessible. It also facilitates supply chain management, allowing companies to network with manufacturers, wholesalers, retailers, suppliers, and outsource firms to serve customers more efficiently. Because of its ability to enhance the exchange of information between customer and marketer, the Internet has become an important component of many firms' marketing strategies—so important that many consider it marketing's new frontier.

We devote this chapter to exploring this new frontier. We begin by defining *electronic marketing* and exploring its context within marketing strategies. Next, we examine the characteristics that differentiate electronic marketing activities from traditional ones and explore how marketers are using the Internet strategically to build competitive advantage. Finally, we consider some of the ethical and legal implications that affect Internet marketing.

The Dynamic Nature of Electronic Marketing

A number of terms have been coined to describe marketing activities and commercial transactions on the Internet. One of the most popular terms is **electronic commerce** (or **e-commerce**), which has been defined as "the sharing of business information, maintaining business relationships, and conducting business transactions by means of telecommunications networks."[2] As Figure 23.1 shows, experts project that worldwide e-commerce will grow to $6.8 trillion by 2004.[3] Even the United States government engages in e-commerce activities, marketing everything from bonds and other financial instruments to oil-drilling leases and wild horses. The federal government had $3.6 billion in online sales in 2000, ranking it well ahead of even the most successful online retailers, including Amazon.com ($2.8 billion in sales) and eBay ($431 million in sales).[4]

electronic commerce (e-commerce) Sharing business information, maintaining business relationships, and conducting business transactions by means of telecommunications networks

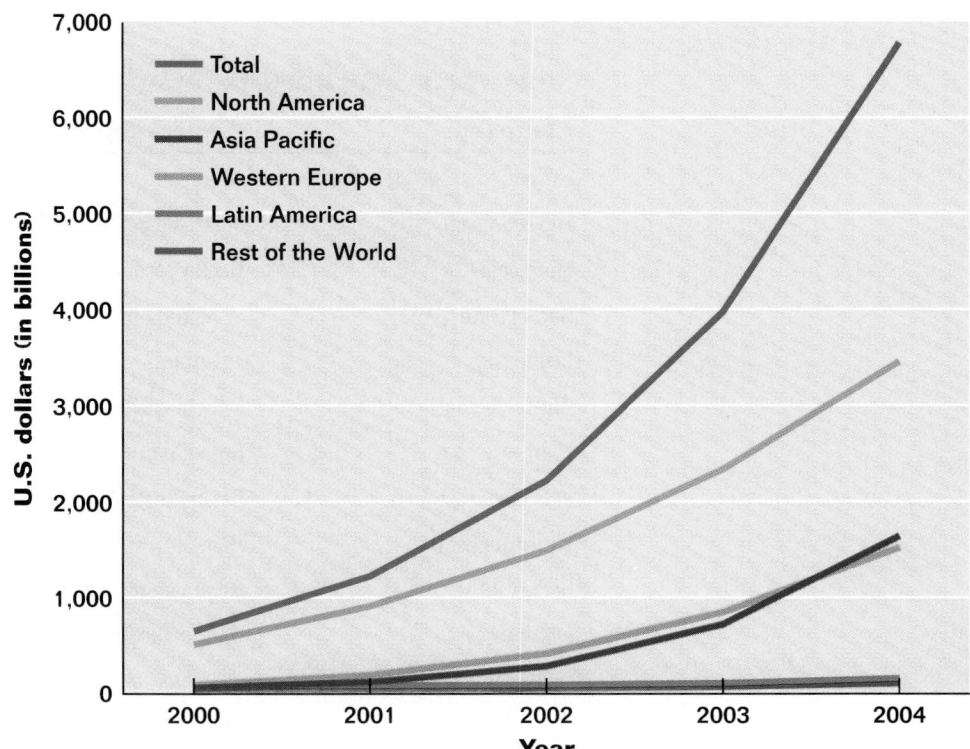

FIGURE 23.1
The Projected Growth of e-Commerce Worldwide

Source: Forrester Research, Inc. "Global eCommerce Approaches Hypergrowth," April 18, 2000, copyright (c) 2000. Reprinted by permission of Forrester Research, Inc.

electronic marketing (e-marketing) The strategic process of creating, distributing, promoting, and pricing products for targeted customers in the virtual environment of the Internet

In this chapter, we focus on how the Internet, especially the World Wide Web, relate to all aspects of marketing, including strategic planning. Thus, we use the term **electronic marketing** (or **e-marketing**) to refer to the strategic process of creating, distributing, promoting, and pricing products for targeted customers in the virtual environment of the Internet.

One of the most important benefits of e-marketing is the ability of marketers and customers to share information. Through company websites, consumers can learn about a firm's products, including features, specifications, and even prices. Many websites also provide feedback mechanisms through which customers can ask questions, voice complaints, indicate preferences, and otherwise communicate about their needs and desires. The Internet has changed the way marketers communicate and develop relationships not only with their customers but also with their employees and suppliers. Many companies use e-mail, groupware (software that allows people in different locations to access and work on the same file or document over the Internet), and videoconferencing to coordinate activities and communicate with employees. Because such technology facilitates and lowers the cost of communications, the Internet can contribute significantly to any industry or activity that depends on the flow of information, such as entertainment, health care, government services, education, travel services, and software.[5]

Telecommunications technology offers additional benefits to marketers, including rapid response expanded customer service capability (e.g., 24 hours a day, 7 days a week, or "24 × 7"), decreased operating costs, and reduced geographic barriers. Data networks have decreased cycle and decision times and permitted companies to treat customers more efficiently.[6] In today's fast-paced world, the ability to shop for books, clothes, and other merchandise at midnight, when traditional stores are usually closed, is a benefit for both buyers and sellers. The Internet allows even small firms to reduce the impact of geography on their operations. For example, Coastal Tool & Supply, a small power tool and supply store in Connecticut, has generated sales from around the world through its website.

Despite these benefits, many companies that chose to make the Internet the core of their marketing strategies—often called "dot-coms"—failed to earn profits or acquire sufficient resources to remain in business. Even Amazon.com, the world's leading online retailer, continues to struggle to earn a profit. Table 23.1 lists a sampling of failed Internet-based companies. In some cases, their brand names, once backed by

Table 23.1	A Dot-Com Graveyard
Company	**Primary Product**
eToys	Toys
FoodUSA.com	Meat and poultry exchange
More.com	Health products
Garden.com	Gardening products
Living.com	Furniture
BigWords.com	College textbooks
Hardware.com	Home improvement
Pets.com	Pet products
Furniture.com	Home furnishings
Beautyscene.com	Fashion and cosmetics
Auctions.com	Online auctions

Source: "Welcome to the Dot-Com Graveyard," *Upside Today*, www.upside.com/graveyard, Aug. 8, 2001.

Thanks to the Internet, you know it's flooding in Tasmania.

Why don't you know if this month's profit margins are under water?

know now.

You can know now with OutlookSoft's patented, web-based, budgeting, planning, reporting, and performance analysis software—*Everest*™. In fact, using *Everest's* portal-based architecture, every manager can create budgets that support the corporate strategy and every manager knows their personalized, up-to-the-minute performance compared to the plan . . . and more.

Shouldn't **you** know now?

Request a "Guide to Know Now Technologies" at **www.outlooksoft.com** or call **203.964.3100**.

OutlookSoft™

The Web Analytics Company™

Marketing Planning
OutlookSoft provides software for web-based marketing planning.

millions of promotional dollars, have been acquired by competitors that appreciate the strong brand equity these names represent. KB Toys, for example, purchased the name and inventory of defunct web retailer eToys.

Many dot-coms failed because they thought the only thing that mattered was brand awareness. In reality, however, Internet markets are more similar to traditional markets than they are different.[7] Thus, successful e-marketing strategies, like traditional marketing ones, depend on creating, distributing, promoting, and pricing products that customers need or want, not merely developing a brand name or reducing the costs associated with online transactions. In fact, traditional retailers continue to do quite well in some areas that many people thought the Internet would dominate just a few years ago. For example, although many marketers believed there would be a shift to buying cars online, experts predict that just 3 percent of all new cars will be sold through the Internet in 2003. Research suggests that online shoppers are very concerned about price, and a firm's profits can vanish quickly as competition drives prices down. Few consumers are willing to spend $30,000 online to purchase a new automobile. However, consumers are increasingly making car-buying decisions on the basis of information found online.[8]

Indeed, e-marketing has not changed all industries, although it has had more of an impact in some industries in which the costs of business and customer transactions are very high. For example, trading stock has become significantly easier and less expensive for customers who can go online and execute their own orders. Firms such as E*Trade and Charles Schwab have been innovators in this area, and traditional brokerage firms such as Merrill Lynch have had to introduce online trading for their customers to remain competitive. In many other industries, however, the impact of e-marketing may be incremental.

Communication remains a major element of any strategy to develop and manage long-term customer relationships. By providing multiple points of interactions with customers, including telephone, fax, e-mail, and personal contact, companies can personalize customer relationships.[9] Regardless of the medium through which communication occurs, customers should ultimately be the drivers of marketing strategy because they best understand what they want. Customer relationship management systems should ensure that marketers listen to customers to respond to their needs and concerns and build long-term relationships. The Internet can provide a valuable listening post and serve as a medium to manage customer relationships.[10] Online surveys, for example, provide immediate customer response inexpensively.[11] Experts suggest that most of the benefits of Internet marketing will stem from changes in marketing practices and the way organizations function. Given the crucial role of communication and information in marketing, the long-term impact of the Internet on economic growth could be substantial.[12]

Basic Characteristics of Electronic Marketing

Although e-marketing is similar to traditional marketing, it is helpful to understand the basic characteristics that distinguish this environment from the traditional marketing environment. These characteristics include addressability, interactivity, memory, control, accessibility, and digitalization.

Addressability

addressability A marketer's ability to identify customers before they make a purchase

The technology of the Internet makes it possible for visitors to a website to identify themselves and provide information about their product needs and wants before making a purchase. The ability of a marketer to identify customers before they make a purchase is called **addressability.** Many websites encourage visitors to register to maximize their use of the site or to gain access to premium areas; some even require it. Registration forms typically ask for basic information, such as name, e-mail address, age, and occupation, from which marketers can build user profiles to enhance their marketing efforts. CDNow, for example, asks music lovers to supply information about their listening tastes so the company can recommend new releases. Some websites even offer contests and prizes to encourage users to register. Marketers can also conduct surveys to learn more about the people who access their websites, offering prizes as motivation for participation.

Marketers have always been able to identify potential customers. Long before the advent of the World Wide Web, they were able to purchase databases or use sales personnel to develop lists of potential customers. However, these methods are not the most efficient way to target customers. They often limit marketers to targeting groups of homogeneous individuals or organizations, and because they are relatively expensive, they are used primarily for higher-priced products. Not until the widespread use

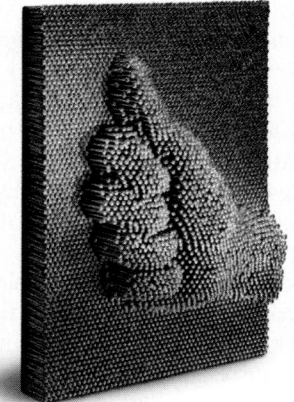

Addressability
Customized information sent daily to customers, such as the tax information provided by CCH, illustrates addressability.

of the Internet could mass marketers duplicate the capabilities of a sales force on a large scale at a relatively low cost.

Addressability represents the ultimate expression of the marketing concept. With the knowledge about individual customers garnered through the Web, marketers can tailor marketing mixes more precisely to target customers with narrow interests, such as recorded blues music or golf. Addressability also facilitates tracking website visits and online buying activity, which makes it easier for marketers to accumulate data about individual customers to enhance future marketing efforts. Amazon.com, for example, stores data about customers' purchases and uses that information to make recommendations the next time they visit the site.

cookie An identifying string of text stored on a website visitor's computer

Some website software can store a **cookie,** an identifying string of text, on a visitor's computer. Marketers use cookies to track how often a particular user visits the website, what he or she may look at while there, and in what sequence. Cookies also permit website visitors to customize services, such as virtual shopping carts, as well as the particular content they see when they log onto a webpage. CNN, for example, allows visitors to its website to create a custom news page tailored to their particular interests. The use of cookies to store customer information can be an ethical issue, however, depending on how the data are used. If a website owner can use cookies to link a visitor's interests to a name and address, that information could be sold to advertisers and other parties without the visitor's consent or even knowledge. The potential for misuse of cookies has made many consumers wary of this technology. Because technology allows access to large quantities of data about customers' use of websites, companies must carefully consider how the use of such information affects individuals' privacy, as we discuss in more detail later in this chapter.

Interactivity

interactivity The ability to allow customers to express their needs and wants directly to the firm in response to the firm's marketing communications

Another distinguishing characteristic of e-marketing is **interactivity,** which allows customers to express their needs and wants directly to a firm in response to its marketing communications. This means marketers can interact with prospective customers in real-time (or at least a close approximation of it). Of course, salespeople have always been able to do this, but at a much greater cost. The Web provides the advantages of a sales representative's presence, but with broader market coverage and at lower cost.

One implication of interactivity is that a firm's customers can also communicate with other customers (and noncustomers). For this reason, differences in the amount and type of information possessed by marketers and their customers are not as pronounced as in the past. One result is that the new- and used-car businesses have become considerably more competitive because buyers are coming into dealerships armed with more complete product and cost information obtained through comparison shopping on the Net. By providing information, ideas, and a context for interacting with other customers, e-marketers can enhance customers' interest and involvement with their products.

community A sense of group membership or feeling of belonging

Interactivity enables marketers to capitalize on the concept of community to help customers derive value from the firm's products and website. **Community** refers to a sense of group membership or feeling of belonging by individual members of a group.[13] One such community is Tripod, a website where Generation Xers can create their own webpages and chat or exchange messages on bulletin boards about topics ranging from cars and computers to health and careers. Much of the site's content has been developed by members of the Tripod community. Like many online communities, Tripod is free but requires members to register to access the site.[14] The success of websites like Tripod corroborates an analysis by *Business Week* suggesting that the most successful online marketers do not just duplicate existing businesses online but fully exploit the interactivity of the World Wide Web for the benefit of their customers. The most successful websites become "virtual communities" where "like-minded cybernauts congregate, swap information, buy something, and come back week after week."[15] They encourage visitors to "hang out" and contribute to the community (and see the website's advertising) instead of clicking elsewhere. Because

you can conduct surveys over the internet. or you can wait.

Online surveys are lightning fast. The response rate is higher. The information is richer and more qualitative. And now, you can do online surveys with a company that for nearly 40 years has been one of the most respected full-service research firms in the nation. So what are you waiting for? Contact us at info@InterFeedback.com, or give us a call. We'll give you something to be excited about.

InterFeedback.com
A service of Southeastern Institute of Research, Inc.
www.InterFeedback.com
800/807-8981

Interactivity
The Internet facilitates efficient customer feedback through online research and surveys like those conducted by InterFeedback.com.

such communities have well-defined demographics and common interests, they represent a valuable audience for advertisers, which typically generate the funds to maintain such sites.[16]

In business markets, many firms are using telecommunications technology, such as videoconferencing, to bring together representatives of the firm and its customers over the Internet. This capability reduces travel costs, saves time, and allows more frequent contact with the firm's customer base. Firms are also using web technology to bring sales force personnel in widely dispersed offices together with the home office for conferences, group discussions, and training sessions. Intranets, as discussed in Chapter 6, allow widespread employees to access internal marketing data, such as customer profiles and product inventory, to enhance the firm's marketing efforts. For example, Weyerhaeuser's intranet includes software that tracks inventory and compares prices, helping the company reduce the costs and time required to manufacture doors.[17]

Memory

memory The ability to access databases or data warehouses containing individual customer profiles and past purchase histories and to use these data in real-time to customize a marketing offer

Memory refers to a firm's ability to access databases or data warehouses containing individual customer profiles and past purchase histories and use these data in real-time to customize its marketing offer to a specific customer. Although companies have had database systems for many years, the information these systems contain did not become available on a real-time basis until fairly recently. Current software technology allows a marketer to identify a specific visitor to its website instantaneously, locate that customer's profile in its database, and then display the customer's past purchases or suggest new products based on past purchases while he or she is still visiting the site. For example, Bluefly, an online clothing retailer, asks visitors to provide their e-mail addresses, clothing preferences, brand preferences, and sizes so it can create a customized online catalog ("My Catalog") of clothing that matches the customer's specified preferences. The firm uses customer purchase profiles to manage its merchandise buying. Whenever it adds new clothing items to its inventory, it checks them against its database of customer preferences and, if it finds a match, alerts the individual in an e-mail message. Applying memory to large numbers of customers represents a significant advantage when a firm uses it to learn more about individual customers each time they visit the firm's website.

Control

control   Customers' ability to regulate the information they view and the rate and sequence of their exposure to that information

In the context of e-marketing, **control** refers to customers' ability to regulate the information they view as well as the rate and sequence of their exposure to that information. The Web is sometimes referred to as a *pull* medium because users determine what they view at websites; website operators' ability to control the content users look at and in what sequence is limited. In contrast, television can be characterized as a *push* medium because the broadcaster determines what the viewer sees once he or she has selected a particular channel. Both television and radio provide "limited exposure control" (you see or hear whatever is broadcast until you change the station). With the World Wide Web, users have a greater degree of control because they can click to another page within a given site, go to another site, or log off the system.

hypertext   Highlighted text that permits visitors to a website to jump from one point to other points on the site or to other websites

Most websites employ **hypertext,** defined as "text that branches and allows choices to the reader, best read at an interactive screen. As popularly conceived, this is a series of text chunks connected by links which offer the reader different pathways."[18] In other words, hypertext permits visitors to jump from one point in a website to other points or even to other websites. Different viewers may experience the same website in different ways, depending on the path of their progress through the content. Firms using hypertext in their marketing content have limited control over the sequence in which the viewer looks at the content.

For e-marketers, the primary implication of control is that attracting—and retaining—customers' attention is more difficult. Marketers have to work harder and more creatively to communicate the value of their websites clearly and quickly, or the viewer will lose interest and click to another site. With literally hundreds of millions of unique pages of content available to any web surfer, simply putting a website on the Internet does not guarantee anyone will visit it or make a purchase. Publicizing the website may require innovative promotional activities. For this reason, many firms pay millions of dollars to advertise their products or websites on high-traffic sites such as America Online (AOL). Because of AOL's growing status as a **portal** (a multiservice website that serves as a gateway to other websites), firms are eager to link to it and other such sites to help draw attention to their own sites. Indeed, consumers spend most of their time online on portal sites such as MSN and Yahoo!, checking e-mail, tracking stocks, and perusing news, sports, and weather.

portal   A multiservice website that serves as a gateway to other websites

Accessibility

accessibility   The ability to obtain information available on the Internet

An extraordinary amount of information is available on the Internet. The ability to obtain it is referred to as **accessibility.** Because customers can access in-depth information about competing products, prices, reviews, and so forth, they are much better informed about a firm's products and their relative value than ever before. Someone looking to buy a new truck, for example, can go to the websites of Ford, General Motors, and Dodge to compare the features of the Ford F-150, the GMC Sierra, and the Dodge Ram. The truck buyer can also access online magazines and pricing guides to get more specific information about product features, performance, and prices.

Accessibility also dramatically increases the competition for Internet users' attention. Without significant promotion, such as advertising on portals like America Online, MSN, Yahoo!, and other high-traffic sites, it is becoming increasingly difficult to attract a visitor's attention to a particular website. Consequently, e-marketers are having to become more creative and innovative to attract visitors to their sites. We look closer at promotion on the Web later in this chapter.

Another implication of accessibility is that the recognition power of brand names may become a more important competitive weapon for e-marketers. Because consumers have no tangible way to assess the benefits or quality of the escalating number of unknown brands promoted on the Web, they may prefer to stick with familiar brands to ensure they are getting quality. Many firms are therefore attempting to build brand recognition among online consumers. MasterCard International, for example, has modified its online marketing strategy from simply touting its credit card to providing online shoppers with security and service. It even grants a sort of

MasterCard "seal of approval," the Shop Smart seal, to e-commerce sites that use advanced security systems for credit card purchases. This tactic allows the company to post its well-known logo on the most popular online shopping sites, thus promoting its Internet image.[19]

Uniform Resource Locator (URL)　A website address

A related consideration is the recognition value of a firm's **Uniform Resource Locator (URL),** or website address. The first firm to register a particular URL gains the exclusive right to use that URL as its website address. Imagine the difficulty of promoting a website for Coca-Cola and being unable to use www.coke.com as a URL. As the number of websites proliferates, web surfers will find it increasingly difficult to learn or remember the URLs for various firms and products. A URL that doesn't match the brand or company name can represent a serious obstacle to new or first-time visitors looking for a particular product on the Web. Consider the URL eToys.com, first registered by a company of the same name. When Toys "R" Us set up a website sometime later, it was unable to use that URL for its cyberstore.[20] When eToys went out of business a few years later, the URL was acquired by competitor KB Toys.

Digitalization

digitalization　The ability to represent a product, or at least some of its benefits, as digital bits of information

Digitalization is the ability to represent a product, or at least some of its benefits, as digital bits of information. Digitalization allows marketers to use the Internet to distribute, promote, and sell those features apart from the physical item itself. FedEx, for example, has developed web-based software that allows consumers and business customers to track their own packages from starting point to destination.

Digitalization
The United States Postal Service used digitalization to create eBillPay.

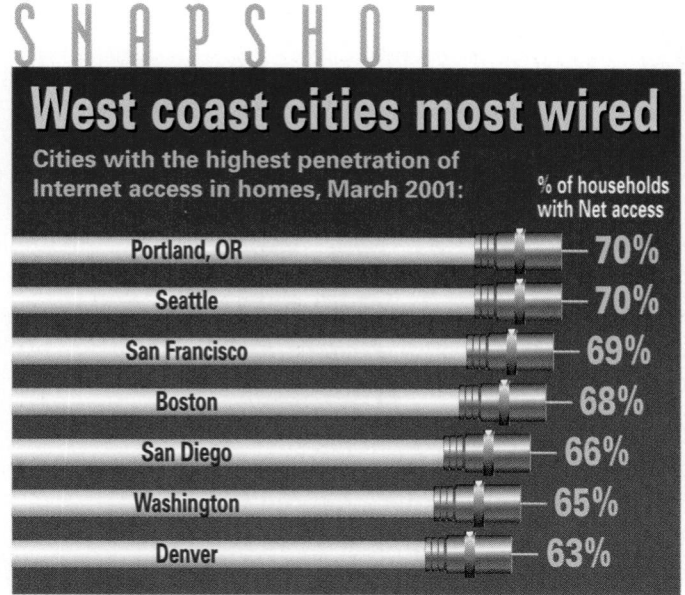

Distributed over the Web at very low cost, the online tracking system adds value to FedEx's delivery services. Digitalization can be enhanced for users who have broadband access to the Internet, because broadband's faster connections allow streaming audio and video and other new technologies. Nearly one-third of Internet users in the United States have broadband connections at home, work, or school,[21] although these users tend to be concentrated in the nation's leading urban areas.

In addition to providing distribution efficiencies, digitizing part of a product's features allows new combinations of features and services to be created quickly and inexpensively. For example, a service station that keeps a customer's history of automotive oil changes in a database can e-mail that customer when the next oil change is due and at the same time suggest other types of preventive maintenance, such as tire rotations or a tune-up. Digital features are easy to mix and match to meet the demands of individual customers.

e-Marketing Strategies

Now that we have examined some distinguishing characteristics of doing business on the Internet, it is time to consider how these characteristics affect marketing strategy. Marketing strategy involves identifying and analyzing a target market and creating a marketing mix to satisfy individuals in that market, regardless of whether those individuals are accessible online or through more traditional avenues. However, there are significant differences in how the marketing mix components are developed and combined into a marketing strategy in the electronic environment of the Web. As we continue this discussion, keep in mind that the Internet is a very dynamic environment, meaning e-marketing strategies may need to be modified frequently to keep pace.

Target Markets

Electronic marketing permits companies to target customers more precisely and accurately than ever before. The addressability, interactivity, and memory characteristics of e-marketing enable marketers to identify specific customers, establish interactive dialogs with them to learn their needs, and combine this information with their purchase histories to customize products to meet those needs. The ability to identify individual customers allows marketers to shift their focus from targeting groups of similar customers to increasing their share of an individual customer's purchases. Thus, the emphasis shifts from "share of market" to "share of customer." For example, Amazon.com stores and analyzes purchase data to better understand each customer's interests. Being able to learn more about each customer's needs and preferences helps Amazon.com improve its ability to satisfy individual customers and thereby increase sales to each customer. However, in shifting its perspective to "share of customer," a firm should ensure that individual target customers have the potential to do enough business with the firm to justify such specialized efforts. Indeed, one benefit arising from the addressability characteristic of e-marketing is that firms can track and analyze individual customers' purchases and identify the most profitable and loyal customers.

One characteristic of firms engaged in e-marketing is a renewed focus on relationship marketing by building customer loyalty and retaining customers—in other

Target Markets
Buzzsaw.com provides e-commerce and collaboration services for businesses in design and construction. CollegeClub.com targets the college student and is rated by Nielsen as #1 among all websites targeting 18 to 24 year olds.

words, on customer relationship management (CRM). As we noted in Chapter 1, CRM focuses on using information about customers to create marketing strategies that develop and sustain desirable customer relationships. This focus on customer relationship management is possible in e-marketing because of marketers' ability to target individual customers. This effort is enhanced over time as the customer invests more time and effort in "teaching" the firm what he or she wants. Commitment to the firm also increases the costs the customer would incur by switching to another company. Once a customer has learned to trade stocks online through Charles Schwab, for example, there is a cost of leaving to find a new brokerage firm; not only may another firm offer less service, but it also takes time to find a new firm and learn a new system. Any time a firm can learn more about its customers to improve the match between its marketing mix and the target customers' desires, it increases the perceived costs of switching to another firm.

There are a variety of ways to look at online target markets. A business-to-business aspect of e-marketing is automating a retailer's inventory orders from a supplier via computer—an electronic data interchange (EDI) activity that was available long before the World Wide Web came into widespread use. Booking flight reservations directly through an airline's website is a business-to-consumer aspect of e-marketing. Buying collectibles from other consumers through online auctions like eBay is still another aspect of e-marketing. Thus, e-marketing involves business-to-business, business-to-consumer, and even consumer-to-consumer dimensions. As with traditional marketing, some companies serve more than one market: mycounsel.com, for example, provides both business-to-business and business-to-consumer markets with legal services.

Business-to-Business (B2B) Marketing. The forces unleashed by the Internet are particularly important in business-to-business (B2B) relationships, where improving the quality, reliability, and timeliness of information reduces uncertainties. Ford Motor Company, for example, has a network that links 30,000 auto parts suppliers and Ford's 6,900 dealers. The company expects this system to reduce costs by $8.9 billion a year and generate approximately $3 million a year from fees charged for the use of the supplier network.[22] B2B transactions through the Internet are growing faster than any other area of e-marketing and now comprise one-fourth of all organizational transactions. Experts estimate that worldwide, online B2B transactions will increase to $8.5 trillion by 2005, up from $433 billion in 2000.[23] The number of firms engaged in B2B e-marketing is expected to continue accelerating at a rapid rate over the next few years. For example, Cisco Systems, which markets Internet infrastructure hardware, receives 68 percent of its orders online, and 70 percent of its service calls are resolved online. The company plans to link all of its contract manufacturers and key suppliers into an advanced web-based supply chain management system called eHUB, which speeds up the distribution of information about product demand to suppliers.[24]

> **Net Sights**
>
> Anything associated with the Internet seems to move at the speed of light; thus, statistics on Internet access and usage are obsolete almost as soon as they appear in print. One valuable source of up-to-date statistics for marketers is CyberAtlas (**http://cyberatlas.internet.com/**), which provides an easily accessible clearinghouse of Internet data from leading research firms such as Forrester Research, Jupiter Research, Gartner Dataquest, and Nielsen/NetRatings. The award-winning site offers the latest demographic and geographic, usage, and traffic statistics, as well as articles about Internet advertising, business-to-business markets, retailing, and more.

B2B marketing activities help companies adjust production in response to up-to-date information about demand. In addition, firms can shorten product development time and lower the costs of components and other supplies. Procter & Gamble has developed a B2B information-sharing network that facilitates collection and evaluation of new-product ideas from the firm's more than 110,000 employees.[25] The Covisint alliance among Ford, General Motors, DaimlerChrysler, Renault, Nissan, Oracle, and Commerce One makes parts from suppliers available through a competitive online auction, reducing months of negotiations into a single day. The goal of the alliance is to reduce the time needed to bring a new vehicle to market from 54 months to 18.[26] In many cases, companies are moving toward making most of their purchases online.[27]

Business-to-Consumer (B2C) Marketing. As you might expect, business-to-consumer (B2C) marketing involves marketing goods and services directly to consumers. Dell Computer is a leading B2C e-marketer that not only custom builds computers but also provides customer service online. Although as a share of retail sales B2C e-marketing is increasing, it still represents just 1 percent of all consumer purchases.[28] A majority of online consumers use the Internet to research potential product purchases, but most still prefer to make the actual purchase offline from a trusted retailer. Marketers therefore should consider the effect of such online "window shopping" when developing integrated marketing communications to ensure their promotional messages are consistent across all media, including website, catalogs, advertisements, and in-store promotions.[29] In the long run, consumer marketing will be enhanced by its ability to build strong customer relationships and obtain information that can help provide successful products.

Consumer-to-Consumer (C2C) Marketing. One market that is some-times overlooked is the consumer-to-consumer (C2C) market, where consumers market goods and services to one another. C2C marketing has become very popular thanks to eBay and other online auctions through which consumers can sell goods they no longer need or want, often for higher prices than they might receive through newspaper classified ads or garage sales. Some consumers have even turned their passion for trading online into successful businesses. For example, a collector of vintage guitars might find items in local markets, such as pawn shops, which he then sells for a higher price on eBay. The growing C2C market may threaten certain marketers if consumers find it more efficient to sell their books, CDs, and other used items through online auctions or other C2C venues.[30]

Product Considerations

The exponential growth of the Internet and the World Wide Web presents exciting opportunities for marketing products to both consumers and organizations. Computers and computer peripherals, industrial supplies, and packaged software are the leading business purchases online. Consumer products account for a small but growing percentage of Internet transactions, with securities trading, travel/tourism, and books among the largest consumer purchases.[31] Through e-marketing, companies can provide products, including goods, services, and ideas, that offer unique benefits and improve customer satisfaction.

The online marketing of goods such as computer hardware and software, books, videos/DVDs, CDs, toys, automobiles, and even groceries is accelerating rapidly. Dell Computer sold about $32 billion worth of computers and related software and hardware last year, about half of that amount through its website.[32] Autobytel has established an effective model for online auto sales by helping consumers find the best price on their preferred models and then arranging for local delivery. However, low profit margins due to customized deliveries have challenged the ability of firms to deliver tangible goods.

Some services can also be marketed online, perhaps even more successfully than goods. At Century 21's website, consumers can search for the home of their dreams anywhere in the United States, get information about mortgages and credit and tips on buying real estate, and learn about the company's relocation services. Charles Schwab is one of several online brokerage firms that offer online trading of stocks and bonds and provide quotes, news, research, planning, and other specialized services. Airlines are increasingly booking flights via their websites. Southwest Airlines, for example, booked more than $1.2 billion worth of airplane tickets online last year.[33]

Brand recognition is likely to become increasingly important in the marketing of services online. Recall from Chapter 13 that whereas goods have search qualities (tangible attributes such as engine size for cars, hard drive size for computers) that customers can evaluate before making a purchase, services tend to have experience qualities that buyers can assess only if they buy and use the product. Because it is difficult for customers to judge the quality of services before they purchase and use them, they often look for recognizable brand names as a means to ensure quality. Well-known brand names are even more likely to give a firm a competitive advantage online, given the huge number of websites and products available. Edmund's, for example, has established a reputation for accurate auto price, product feature, and road test information in its 30 years of publishing *Edmund's New Car Prices and Reviews* and other publications. Customers' trust in the accuracy of the information found on Edmund's website is a function of their past experience with the firm or their recognition of the brand.

The proliferation of information on the World Wide Web has itself spawned new services. Web search engines and directories such as Yahoo!, Google, Excite, Lycos, and Alta Vista are among the most heavily accessed sites on the Internet. Without these services, which track and index the vast quantity of information available on the Web, the task of finding something of interest would be tantamount to searching for the proverbial needle in a haystack. Many of these services, most notably Yahoo!, have evolved into portals by offering additional services, including news, weather, chat rooms, free e-mail accounts, and shopping.

Marketers have also created unique web-based services to target specific markets. GolfWeb, for example, provides links to 35,000 golf-related webpages, a virtual ProShop, and the opportunity to subscribe to special services such as handicapping and online games. Advertising, which accounts for 35 percent of GolfWeb's revenues, can therefore target precisely at this market niche.[34] Online city guides like Digital City, Yahoo! Local, and CitySearch are another popular new product. At CitySearch Nashville, for example, residents can find out about sporting events and recreation opportunities, movie listings and reviews, restaurants and other businesses, museums, news, and weather, and exchange views on local issues. Most major cities now have one or more such guides.

Even ideas have potential for success on the Internet. Web-based distance learning and educational programs are becoming increasingly popular. Corporate employee training is a $55 billion industry, and online training modules are growing rapidly. Additional ideas being marketed online include marriage and personal counseling; medical, tax, and legal advice; and even psychic services.

Distribution Considerations

The role of distribution is to make products available at the right time at the right place in the right quantities. Physical distribution is especially compatible with e-marketing. The ability to process orders electronically and increase the speed of communications via the Internet reduces inefficiencies, costs, and redundancies throughout the marketing channel. The interactivity of the Internet allows firms to develop close working relationships with members of their supply chain. For example, the website for CSX, one of the nation's largest shipping companies, permits General Motors, Home Depot, PepsiCo, and other customers to get price quotes, book shipments, and track the exact locations of their shipments.[35]

More firms are exploiting advances in information technology to synchronize the relationships between their manufacturing or product assembly and their customer contact operations. This increase in information sharing among various operations of the firm makes product customization easier to accomplish. Marketers can use their websites to query customers about their needs and then manufacture products that exactly fit those needs. Gateway and Dell, for example, help their customers build their own computers by asking them to specify what components to include; these firms then assemble and ship the customized product directly to the customer in a few days.

Granting suppliers access to customer transaction databases fosters better coordination. By observing electronically what a firm's customers are ordering, a supplier knows exactly when to ship the materials needed to meet demand, and the firm can keep less inventory on hand. This lowers distribution costs for the firm, allowing it to become more competitive. Wal-Mart, for example, exchanges data about inventory levels and product availability with Procter & Gamble and other manufacturers, thus creating partnerships that maximize opportunities for profits and competitive advantage for all members of Wal-Mart's supply chain.[36] Supply chain management is enhanced because the Internet provides the network necessary to optimize cooperation and communication.

B2B transactions in particular have benefited from the amount of organizational resources available to build technologically advanced networks among manufacturers and other members of the supply chain. The use of *extranets* (secure web-based networks that connect companies with their customers and suppliers) has facilitated coordination of physical distribution of products, order processing, and inventory management activities. For example, Weyerhaeuser's DoorBuilder intranet has been so successful that the manufacturer expanded it into an extranet to improve communications with suppliers and customers. Through Weyerhaeuser's extranet, builders, architects, and other customers can order a complete package of doors, frames, hardware, and stains from Weyerhaeuser's product list and vendors of related products.[37]

The development of business-to-business e-marketing infrastructures has made the distribution process more efficient, flexible, and less costly, thereby increasing customer satisfaction.

One of the most visible members of any marketing channel is the retailer, and the Internet is increasingly becoming a retail venue. The Internet provides an opportunity for marketers of everything from computers to travel reservations to encourage exchanges. Amazon.com, for example, sold almost $3 billion of books, CDs, DVDs and videos, toys, games, and electronics directly from its website in 2000.[38] Indeed, Amazon.com's success at marketing books online has been so phenomenal that a host of imitators have adopted its retailing model for everything from CDs to toys. Another retailing venture is online auctioneers, such as eBay and Haggle Online, which auction everything from fine wines and golf clubs to computer goods and electronics.

Promotion Considerations

The Internet is an interactive medium that can be used to inform, entertain, and persuade target markets to accept an organization's products. The accessibility of the Internet presents marketers with an exciting opportunity to expand and complement their traditional promotional efforts or to operate through the Internet exclusively. Many companies augment their TV and print advertising campaigns with web-based promotions. Both Kraft and Ragu, for example, have created websites with recipes and entertaining tips to help consumers get the most out of their products. Many movie studios have set up websites at which visitors can view clips of their latest releases, and television commercials for new movies often encourage viewers to visit these sites. In addition, some television networks have developed websites that offer viewing guides and additional content to enhance viewers' enjoyment. Some TV shows even have their own websites. Discovery Channel's "Your New House," for instance, has a website that provides building and remodeling tips, a mortgage calculator, floor plans, and links to hundreds of websites operated by manufacturers of building products, appliances, and fixtures. Even political parties use websites to promote their ideas and interact with voters, as illustrated in Global Marketing.

The characteristics of e-marketing make promotional efforts on the Internet significantly different than those using more traditional media. First, because Internet users can control what they see, customers who visit a firm's website are there because they chose to be, which implies they are interested in the firm's products and therefore may be more involved in the message and dialog provided by the firm. Second, the interactivity characteristic allows marketers to enter into dialogs with customers to learn more about their interests and needs. This information can then be used to tailor promotional messages to the individual customer. Finally, addressability can make marketing efforts directed at specific customers more effective. Indeed, direct marketing combined with effective analysis of customer databases may become one of e-marketing's most valuable promotional tools.

Ironically, however, the control and accessibility that characterize e-marketing combine to make it harder to attract the attention of potential customers. Consequently, websites that have clearly demonstrated their ability to generate traffic, such as portals like Yahoo!, MSN, and America Online, have become more valuable—and more expensive—for firms to work with. Accessibility means that as the number of pages available to web users increases, each individual website has to work harder to attract viewers.

Advertising and Publicity.   Advertising and publicity are probably the most visible promotion mix elements on the Web. Thousands of well-known firms, from Adidas to 3Com, have set up webpages to tout their products, circulate company information, post press releases, list job opportunities, and entertain, inform, and interact with customers. More and more companies are using the Web to present "infotainment," thereby fostering brand identity and loyalty and building long-term customer relationships.[39]

banner ads   Small, rectangular ads, static or animated, that typically appear at the top of a webpage

click-through rate   The percentage of ads that website visitors actually click on

keyword ads   Ads that relate to text or subject matter specified in a web search

button ads   Small ads, square or rectangular, bearing a corporate or brand name or logo and usually appearing at the bottom of a webpage

Marketers can also advertise their products on the websites of other organizations. You are most likely to encounter these in the form of **banner ads**—small, rectangular ads, static or animated, that typically appear at the top of a webpage. Clicking on a banner takes the visitor to the advertiser's site for more information. Many websites, including GolfWeb, Tripod, iVillage, and the Internet Movie Database, fund their sites through banners that advertise other firms' goods and services. Although banner ads account for 56 percent of all Internet advertising, their **click-through rate**—the percentage of ads website visitors actually click on—is less than 2 percent. Research suggests that more interactive banner ads generate higher click-through rates,[40] and, even when they don't, they can promote brand awareness.[41]

Using web search engines or indexes, you are likely to encounter **keyword ads,** which relate to text or subject matter specified in a web search. For example, if you search for the term *laptop* on Yahoo!, a banner ad for an IBM product pops up because the company has purchased the rights to that and many other terms on Yahoo! **Button ads** are small ads, square or rectangular in shape, bearing a corporate or brand name or logo; they usually appear at the bottom of a webpage. As with banner ads, clicking on the button takes the user directly to the advertiser's website. By clicking on button

GLOBAL MARKETING

Mexico's PRI Party Woos Younger Voters

On July 3, 2000, leaders of Mexico's powerful Partido Revolucionario Institucional (PRI) were shocked when voters elected opposition candidate Vincente Fox to be Mexico's new president instead of PRI candidate Francisco Labastida. Labastida was the first PRI candidate to lose a presidential election since the office was established in 1929. PRI candidates also lost other key races in the election, including the mayorship of Mexico City and the governorships of Guanajuanto and Morelos, and the PRI now shares power with other political parties in both of Mexico's legislative bodies. These losses effectively ended seven decades of political domination for the party.

To revitalize the PRI and bring back voters who abandoned the party in the 2000 election, party leaders realized they need to communicate that the PRI is no longer the same party many Mexicans have come to associate with decades of corruption and autocratic policies. Moreover, the PRI needed to find new ways to appeal to the 45 percent of Mexican voters between 18 and 30 years of age, a group who found Vincente Fox's message especially appealing. More than a decade before, Fox's Partido Acción Nacional (PAN) had established a special office to target young people, a strategy that may have led more than 70 percent of Mexico's college-age voters to support Fox in the 2000 election. The PRI had to develop its own strategies for reaching these crucial voters. As Adriana Delgado, PRI's press secretary, says, "We can't keep using the traditional methods, because they don't get us anywhere." Indeed, Delgado represents the type

of voter the PRI wants to attract: young, urban, and, increasingly, female.

To entice these voters, the PRI designated 50 percent of the seats at its next national convention for female delegates and one-third of the seats for members under age 30. The party promoted young activists and recorded a new jingle to the tune of a popular Cuban dance song. The PRI also turned to the World Wide Web to target new voters with a site that not only provides election news and information about its platform, issue positions, and programs but also offers pages targeted specifically to children, teenagers, and women.

In 2001, the party also launched a matchmaking service through its website. *"Encuentra el amor en el PRI"* ("Find love through the PRI"), promoted heavily with television ads, allows registered visitors to enter personal details and provide a photograph that other singles may view. Participants were also invited to meet one another at a gala at the party's headquarters in Mexico City. In just four months, more than 7,000 people registered to participate. The matchmaking web promotion has been criticized as a gimmick, and some participants even admitted they signed up not out of an interest in politics but to find a new love. However, as Delgado says, "We have to find the channels of communication that allow us to reach those Mexicans who turned their backs on us [in the 2000 election]." Party leaders will have to wait until the next presidential election in 2006 to see whether these channels have been successful.

ads for Netscape Navigator or Internet Explorer, which appear at the bottom of many webpages, users go directly to the site, where they can download the latest browser software.

pop-up ads   Large ads that open in a separate web browser window on top of the website being viewed

pop-under ads   Large ads that open in a new browser window underneath the currently viewed site

sponsorship ads   Ads that integrate companies' brands and products with the editorial content of certain websites

Pop-up ads are large ads that open in a separate web browser window on top of the webpage being viewed. Procter & Gamble, for example, has used pop-up ads for its Pantene shampoo on iVillage.com. When these ads open in a new browser window underneath the currently viewed site, they are called **pop-under ads.** Although pop-up and pop-under ads are 50 percent more likely to be noticed by web surfers, they are 100 percent more likely to be considered intrusive.[42]

Finally, **sponsorship ads,** sometimes called *advertorials,* integrate companies' brands and products with the editorial content of certain websites. More subtle than other web advertisements, sponsorship ads are intended to link the advertiser with the website's mission in the visitor's mind.[43] For instance, Martex, a sponsor of iVillage.com, has an advertorial on home decorating on that site.

Personal Selling and Sales Promotion.   Companies are also using the Internet to facilitate personal selling and sales promotion activities. The Internet can help salespeople do their jobs more effectively and efficiently, particularly in the prospecting and preapproach phases of the personal selling process. In fact, the Internet, e-mail, and notebook computers are among the high-tech tools most commonly used by salespeople. Of companies that have more than 100 salespeople, 80 percent are using notebook computers to link to their organization and customers. Heidelberg USA, which manufactures offset presses, uses a customer relationship management system that allows its global sales force to access critical customer and product information quickly. By linking customers, suppliers, and employees, this system has allowed Heidelberg to maximize customer relationships.[44]

Many marketers are promoting sales by offering buying incentives or adding value to their products online. For example, the website for Carter-Wallace, a consumer products company, offers visitors the opportunity to obtain free product samples. Many firms, including Johnson & Johnson and Eye Masters, have offered coupons through their websites or the sites they sponsor. In addition, many Internet sites, such as Val-Pak's, make coupons available online.

Promotion
Planters offers games and contests on its website.

Pricing Considerations

The Internet gives consumers access to more information about the costs and prices of products than was ever available before. For example, car shoppers can access many automakers' webpages, configure an ideal vehicle, and get instant feedback on its cost. They can also visit Edmund's and other websites to obtain pricing information on both new and used cars. They can then go to a car dealer armed with significantly more price-related information than in the past. The Internet not only helps customers with comparative shopping but also gives manufacturers that want to make price a key element in their marketing mix another opportunity to get pricing information to customers. Marketers can thus use the Internet to facilitate both price and nonprice competition.

Some organizations are implementing low-price policies through the Internet. One is Autobytel, a service that helps customers find the best deals on new cars and trucks. Autobytel helps a customer negotiate a final price, then contracts with a member dealer, who pays a fee to participate, to deliver the vehicle to a dealership near the customer. Most major airlines have websites that publicize their fares and, in some cases, offer lower prices to customers who are willing to wait to book their flights at the last moment. Northwest Airlines, for example, makes seats available over the Internet and gives customers a chance to save money by making travel arrangements online. Lower promotion costs on the Web may result in lower product prices. Mailing catalogs, for example, is very expensive, but if companies can replace paper catalogs with interactive ones on the Web, they may be able to pass the cost savings on to consumers in the form of lower prices, thereby gaining a competitive advantage.

Legal and Ethical Issues in e-Marketing

The Internet has evolved so rapidly that numerous new legal and ethical concerns have emerged, and these are being hotly debated both online and off. Among these concerns are personal privacy, unsolicited e-mail, and the misappropriation of copyrighted intellectual property.

One of the most significant privacy issues involves the personal information companies collect from website visitors. A Federal Trade Commission investigation found that about 93 percent of commercial websites collect at least one type of personally identifying information from visitors, and 57 percent gather some type of demographic information.[45] Cookies are the most common means of obtaining such information. Some people fear the collection of personal information from website users may violate users' privacy, especially if done without their knowledge. In fact, in a *Business Week*/Harris Poll survey, 65 percent of respondents indicated they are not willing to share personal and financial information about themselves online so that ads can be targeted to their tastes and interests.[46]

In response to privacy concerns, the FTC investigated how website operators gathered and use personal information. It found that just 14 percent of the sites surveyed reveal what they do with the personal information they collect.[47] Many in the industry are urging self-policing on this issue to head off potential regulation. One effort toward self-policing is the online privacy program developed by the BBBOnLine subsidiary of the Council of Better Business Bureaus (See Figure 23.2). The program awards a privacy seal to companies that clearly disclose to their website visitors what information they are collecting and how they are using it.[48] Marketing Citizenship on page 621 examines another online privacy initiative that is gaining in popularity.

Few laws specifically address personal privacy in the context of e-marketing, but the standards for acceptable marketing conduct implicit in other laws and regulations can generally be applied to e-marketing. Personal privacy is protected by the U.S. Constitution; various Supreme Court rulings; and laws such as the 1971 Fair Credit Reporting Act, the 1978 Right to Financial Privacy Act, and the 1974 Privacy Act, which deals with the release of government records. However, with few regulations on how

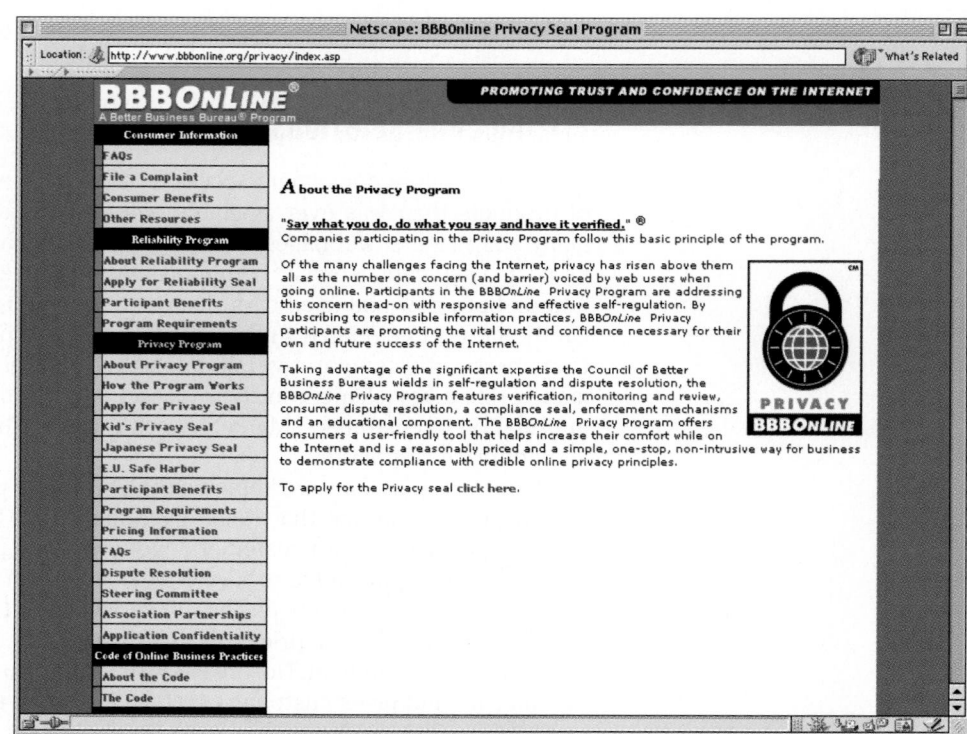

FIGURE 23.2
The BBBOnLine Privacy Program and Seal

businesses use information, companies can legally buy and sell information about customers to gain competitive advantage. Some have suggested that if personal data were treated as property, customers would have greater control over their use.

As we have pointed out, e-marketing differs from traditional marketing in that information on customers is far more accessible. Of particular concern is the collection of data from children. Concerns about protecting children's privacy were highlighted by a study reporting that two-thirds of children ages 10 to 17 would reveal their favorite online stores to receive a free gift, more than half would divulge their parents' favorite stores, and another quarter would disclose details about their parents' weekend activities. The study also found that many children would share information about the family car and the amount of their allowance. Note that this survey was conducted before the U.S. Children's Online Privacy Protection Act (COPPA) went into effect in 2000. That law prohibits website operators and Internet providers from seeking personal information from children under age 13 without parental consent.[49]

The most serious strides toward regulating privacy issues associated with e-marketing are emerging in Europe. The 1998 European Union Directive on Data Protection specifically requires companies that want to collect personal information to explain how the information will be used and to obtain the individual's permission. Companies must make customer data files available on request, just as U.S. credit reporting firms must grant customers access to their personal credit histories. The law also bars website operators from selling e-mail addresses and using cookies to track visitors' movements and preferences without first obtaining permission. Because of this legislation, no company may deliver personal information about EU citizens to countries whose privacy laws do not meet EU standards.[50] The directive may ultimately establish a precedent for Internet privacy that other nations emulate.

Ethical and Legal Issues
Some of the ethical issues facing Internet businesses revolve around privacy concerns for customers.

spam Unsolicited commercial e-mail

Spam, or unsolicited commercial e-mail (UCE), is likely to be the next target of government regulation in the United States. Many Internet users believe spam violates their privacy and steals their resources. Spam has been likened to receiving a direct-mail promotional piece with postage due. Some angry recipients of spam have even organized boycotts against companies that advertise in this manner. Other recipients, however, appreciate the opportunity to learn about new products. Most commercial online services (e.g., America Online) and Internet service providers offer their subscribers the option to filter out e-mail from certain Internet addresses that generate a large volume of spam. Nonetheless, the debate over spam is far from over, and legislation to regulate it is being considered on both the federal and state levels. Whatever the outcome, it will certainly affect the ability to use e-mail for marketing purposes.

The Internet has also created issues associated with intellectual property, the copyrighted or trademarked ideas and creative materials developed to solve problems, carry out applications, educate, and entertain others. Intellectual property losses in the United States total more than $11 billion a year in lost revenue from the illegal copying of computer programs, movies, compact discs, and books. This issue has become a global concern because of disparities in enforcement of laws throughout the world. For example, according to the International Intellectual Property Alliance, a

MARKETING CITIZENSHIP

TRUSTe: "Building a Web You Can Believe In"

TRUSTe is a nonprofit organization devoted to building global trust in the Internet by providing a standardized, third-party oversight privacy program that addresses the privacy concerns of consumers, website operators, and government officials. A cornerstone of the program is the "trustmark," which TRUSTe awards only to websites that adhere to its established privacy principles and agree to comply with its oversight and resolution process. Websites that display the trustmark must disclose their personal information collection and privacy policies in a straightforward privacy statement, generally via a link from the website. TRUSTe is supported by a network of corporate, industry, and nonprofit sponsors, including the Electronic Frontier Foundation (EFF), CommerceNet, America Online, Excite@Home, Microsoft, Novell, Symantec, and Verizon.

Internet users have a right to expect online privacy and a responsibility to exercise choice over how websites collect, use, and share personal information. The TRUSTe program was designed expressly to ensure that users' privacy is protected by fostering open disclosure and empowering users to make informed choices. Its established privacy principles embody fair information practices developed by the U.S. Department of Commerce, the Federal Trade Commission, and prominent industry-represented organizations and associations.

Obtaining a trustmark to display on a website involves several steps. The first step is the creation of a privacy statement and submission of a copy of the statement along with an application to TRUSTe. Next, the organization must read TRUSTe's license agreement and sign the two copies. TRUSTe then reviews the application, and if approved, signs both license agreements and returns them to the submitting organization. Finally, TRUSTe determines an annual fee based on the company's yearly revenue and grants permission to display a trustmark on the company's website.

Organizations that join the TRUSTe online seal program are leading the way in "building a Web you can believe in," where users can exchange information and conduct transactions, and websites can thrive and become profitable. Its members believe that creating an environment of mutual trust and openness will help keep the Internet a free, comfortable, and diverse community for everyone. TRUSTe's goals are to give online consumers control over their personal information, provide website operators with a standardized, cost-effective solution for addressing consumer anxiety about privacy issues while achieving their own business objectives, and demonstrate to government regulators that the industry can successfully regulate itself.

trade association, more than half of the business software used in Israel is pirated, costing U.S. companies roughly $170 million in one year.[51] The software industry estimates that worldwide piracy costs its companies roughly $12 billion every year.[52] The Digital Millennium Copyright Act (DMCA) was passed to protect copyrighted materials on the Internet.

Protecting trademarks can also be problematic. For example, some companies have discovered that another firm has registered a URL that duplicates or is very similar to their own trademarks. The "cyber-squatter" then attempts to sell the right to use the URL to the legal trademark owner. Companies such as Taco Bell, MTC, and KFC have paid thousands of dollars to gain control of domain names that match or parallel their company trademarks.[53] To help companies address this conflict, Congress

Table 23.2	American Marketing Association Code of Ethics for Marketing on the Internet

Preamble

The Internet, including online computer communications, has become increasingly important to marketers' activities, as they provide exchanges and access to markets worldwide. The ability to interact with stakeholders has created new marketing opportunities and risks that are not currently specifically addressed in the American Marketing Association Code of Ethics. The American Marketing Association Code of Ethics for Internet marketing provides additional guidance and direction for ethical responsibility in this dynamic area of marketing. The American Marketing Association is committed to ethical professional conduct and has adopted these principles for using the Internet, including online marketing activities utilizing network computers.

General Responsibilities

Internet marketers must assess the risks and take responsibility for the consequences of their activities. Internet marketers' professional conduct must be guided by:

1. Support of professional ethics to avoid harm by protecting the rights of privacy, ownership and access.

2. Adherence to all applicable laws and regulations with no use of Internet marketing that would be illegal, if conducted by mail, telephone, fax or other media.

3. Awareness of changes in regulations related to Internet marketing.

4. Effective communication to organizational members on risks and policies related to Internet marketing, when appropriate.

5. Organizational commitment to ethical Internet practices communicated to employees, customers and relevant stakeholders.

Privacy

Information collected from customers should be confidential and used only for expressed purposes. All data, especially confidential customer data, should be safeguarded against unauthorized access. The expressed wishes of others should be respected with regard to the receipt of unsolicited e-mail messages.

Ownership

Information obtained from the Internet sources should be properly authorized and documented. Information ownership should be safeguarded and respected. Marketers should respect the integrity and ownership of computer and network systems.

Access

Marketers should treat access to accounts, passwords, and other information as confidential, and only examine or disclose content when authorized by a responsible party. The integrity of others' information systems should be respected with regard to placement of information, advertising or messages.

Source: Reprinted by permission of the American Marketing Association.

passed the Federal Trademark Dilution Act of 1995, which gives trademark owners the right to protect their trademarks, prevents the use of trademark-protected entities, and requires the relinquishment of names that duplicate or closely parallel registered trademarks.

As the Internet continues to evolve, more legal and ethical issues will certainly arise. Recognizing this, the American Marketing Association has developed a Code of Ethics for Marketing on the Internet (see Table 23.2). Such self-regulatory policies may help head off government regulation of electronic marketing and commerce. Marketers and all other users of the Internet should make an effort to learn and abide by basic "netiquette" (Internet etiquette) to ensure they get the most out of the resources available on this growing medium. Fortunately, most marketers recognize the need for mutual respect and trust when communicating in any public medium. They know that doing so will allow them to maximize the tremendous opportunities the Internet offers to foster long-term relationships with customers.

Summary

Electronic commerce (e-commerce) refers to sharing business information, maintaining business relationships, and conducting business transactions by means of telecommunications networks. Electronic marketing (e-marketing) is the strategic process of creating, distributing, promoting, and pricing products for targeted customers in the virtual environment of the Internet. The Internet has changed the way marketers communicate and develop relationships with their customers, employees, and suppliers. Telecommunications technology offers marketers potential advantages such as rapid response, expanded customer service capability, reduced operating costs, and reduced geographic barriers. Despite these benefits, many Internet companies have failed because they did not realize Internet markets are more similar to traditional markets than they are different and thus require the same marketing principles.

Addressability is a marketer's ability to identify customers before they make a purchase. One way websites achieve addressability is through cookies, identifying strings of text placed on a visitor's computer. Interactivity allows customers to express their needs and wants directly to the firm in response to the firm's marketing communications. It also enables marketers to capitalize on the concept of community to help customers derive value from the use of the firm's products and websites. Memory refers to a firm's ability to access databases or data warehouses containing individual customer profiles and past purchase histories and to use these data in real-time to customize their marketing offer to specific customers. Control refers to customers' ability to regulate the information they view as well as the rate and sequence of their exposure to that information. Control is possible largely because of hypertext, which allows users to jump from one point in a website to another or to other websites. Accessibility refers to customers' ability to obtain information available on the Internet. This is enhanced by the recognition value of a firm's Uniform Resource Locator, or website address. Digitalization is the representation of a product, or at least some of its benefits, as digital bits of information.

The addressability, interactivity, and memory characteristics of e-marketing enable a marketer to identify specific customers, establish interactive dialogs with them to learn their needs, and combine this information with their purchase histories to customize products to meet their needs. Thus, e-marketers can focus on building customer loyalty and retaining customers. E-marketing involves business-to-business (B2B), business-to-consumer (B2C), and consumer-to-consumer (C2C) dimensions.

The growth of the Internet and the World Wide Web presents opportunities for marketing products (goods, services, and ideas) to both consumers and organizations. Brand recognition is likely to become increasingly important in the marketing of services online.

The ability to process orders electronically and to increase the speed of communications via the Internet reduces inefficiencies, costs, and redundancies throughout the marketing channel. It also speeds delivery time and improves customer service. More firms are exploiting advances in information technology to synchronize the relationships between their manufacturing or product assembly and their customer-contact operations. This increase in information sharing among various operations of the firm facilitates product customization. The use of extranets has facilitated coordination of physical distribution of products, order-processing, and inventory management activities. The Internet is increasingly becoming a retail venue.

Due to its interactive nature, the Internet can be used to inform, entertain, and persuade target markets to accept an organization's products. The accessibility of the Internet gives marketers an opportunity to expand and complement their traditional media promotional efforts. The characteristics of e-marketing make promotional efforts on the Internet significantly different than those using more traditional media. Advertising and publicity are probably the most visible promotion mix elements on the World Wide Web. Advertising most often occurs in the form of banner ads, keyword ads, button ads, pop-up and pop-under ads, and sponsorship ads. Companies are also using the Internet to facilitate personal selling and sales promotion activities.

The Internet gives consumers access to more information about the costs and prices of products than has ever been available before. Marketers can use the Internet to facilitate both price and nonprice competition. Some organizations are implementing low-price policies through the Internet.

The Internet has evolved so rapidly that numerous new legal and ethical concerns have emerged. One of the most controversial issues is personal privacy, especially the personal information companies collect from website visitors, often through the use of cookies. Additional issues relate to spam, or unsolicited commercial e-mail (UCE), and the misappropriation of copyrighted or trademarked intellectual property. More issues are likely to emerge as the Internet and e-marketing continue to evolve.

Important Terms

Electronic commerce (e-commerce)	Accessibility
Electronic marketing (e-marketing)	Uniform Resource Locator (URL)
Addressability	Digitalization
Cookie	Banner ads
Interactivity	Click-through rate
Community	Keyword ads
Memory	Button ads
Control	Pop-up ads
Hypertext	Pop-under ads
Portal	Sponsorship ads
	Spam

Discussion and Review Questions

1. What is electronic marketing? Explain the advantages telecommunications technology offers to marketers.
2. How does addressability differentiate e-marketing from the traditional marketing environment? How do marketers use cookies to achieve addressability?
3. Define *interactivity* and explain its significance. How can marketers exploit this characteristic to improve relations with customers?
4. How can marketers use the concept of community to add value to their products?
5. Memory gives marketers quick access to customers' purchase histories. How can a firm use this capability to customize its product offerings?
6. Explain the distinction between *push* and *pull* media. What is the significance of control in terms of using websites to market products?
7. Vast numbers of goods and services from many different countries are available on the Web. Do you think brand name recognition is more important in electronic marketing than in more traditional marketing environments? Why or why not?
8. What is the significance of digitalization?
9. How can marketers use relationship marketing to increase their customers' loyalty and perceived costs of switching to another firm?

10. How can marketers exploit the characteristics of the Internet to improve the product element of the marketing mix?
11. How is the Internet changing relations among supply chain members?
12. How do the characteristics of e-marketing affect the promotion element of the marketing mix?
13. A number of types of advertisements have evolved on the Internet. List, define, and provide an example of each type.
14. Electronic marketing has raised a number of ethical questions related to consumer privacy. How can cookies be misused? Should the government regulate the use of cookies by marketers?

Application Questions

1. Amazon.com is one of the Web's most recognizable marketers. Visit the company's site at www.amazon.com, and describe how the company adds value to its customers' buying experience.
2. Some products are better suited than others to electronic marketing activity. For example, Art.com specializes in selling art prints via its online store. The ability to display a variety of prints in many different categories gives customers a convenient and efficient way to search for art. On the other hand, GE has a website displaying its appliances, but customers must visit a retailer to actually purchase them. Visit www.art.com and www.geappliances.com, and compare how each firm uses the electronic environment of the Internet to enhance its marketing efforts.
3. Visit the website www.covisint.com and evaluate the nature of the business customers attracted. Who is the target audience for this business marketing site? Describe the types of firms that are currently doing business through this exchange. What other types of organizations might be attracted? Is it appropriate to sell any banner advertising on a site such as this? What other industries might benefit from developing similar e-marketing exchange hubs?

Internet
Exercise & Resources

Visit **www.prideferrell.com** for resources to help you master the material in this chapter, plus materials that will help you expand your marketing knowledge, including: Internet Exercise updates, ACE self-tests, hotlinks to companies featured in this chapter, and much more.

iVillage.com

iVillage is an example of an online community. Explore the content of this website at

www.ivillage.com

1. What target market can marketers access through this community?

2. How can marketers target this community to market their goods and services?

3. Based on your understanding of the characteristics of e-marketing, analyze the advertisements you observe on this website.

VIDEO CASE 23.1
4SURE.com Targets B2B Customers

Many companies that chose to make the Internet the core of their marketing strategies failed to earn profits or acquire sufficient resources to remain in business. Many early dot-coms, such as eToys, pets.com, garden.com, and hardware.com, found that high technology and a strong brand name were insufficient to guarantee success in the ultra-competitive and dynamic Internet market. In reality, Internet markets are far more similar to than different from traditional markets. Although many people thought the Internet would change the nature of business and marketing, successful Internet marketing has been credited primarily to opportunities to lower costs and increase efficiency. Indeed, companies that offer quality products that customers need or want through online transactions with improved convenience, service, and prices have found success.

One company that has succeeded in the dot-com arena is 4SURE.com, which rang up $200 million in sales in 2000. Founded in 1998 by Bruce Martin and Linwood Lacy, 4SURE.com markets technology products online primarily to business customers through two distinct websites: solutions4SURE.com and computers4SURE.com. Solutions4SURE.com caters to the needs of large businesses and of government and educational customers, while computers4SURE.com targets individuals and small office and home office (SOHO) customers. Both websites serve as online technology superstores featuring more than 60,000

brand name products, including computers, hardware, software, and supplies. Among the characteristics that distinguish these sites from competitors are a powerful search engine, fast checkout, the ability to pay with credit cards and wire transfers, and a bill-when-shipped policy.

4SURE.com is committed to offering customers an extensive selection of products at competitive prices with first-rate customer service. Its easy-to-navigate website is backed by well-trained, knowledgeable customer service representatives, hassle-free exchanges and returns, and guaranteed secure transactions. The company alerts customers about sale prices and new items via e-mail and provides technical customer service for more knowledgeable buyers. To foster a close working relationship with customer-contact personnel, the company has kept sales and customer service teams in-house. The firm even installed giant digital clocks to count down the time customers are kept on hold. The company is also linked electronically to all of its major distributors and partners, which include Compaq Computer and Sony Electronics. Although the company outsources much of its logistics needs, it has built its own warehouse to ensure that it can supply customers quickly—even overnight when necessary. By leveraging extensive relationships with manufacturers and suppliers, 4SURE.com grants customers the opportunity to "buy with confidence—guaranteed." To further reinforce business customers' confidence, the company's websites carry the TRUSTe trust-mark logo, as well as certifications from Bizrate.com, VeriSign, and the BBBOnline Reliability Program.

Thanks to the company's strong focus on customer service, computers4SURE.com has received three prestigious awards—from Bizrate.com, Gomez.com, and RatingWonders.com—for its site's product selection, ease of use, privacy policy, and customer support. Bizrate.com, which rates online stores on the basis of customer feedback, gave the computers4SURE.com site 4.5 stars out of a potential 5, the highest rating achieved by any company reviewed by that site. RatingWonders.com also gave computers4SURE.com a score of 4.5 out of 5. Upon receiving these awards, Bruce Martin, the firm's president and CEO, said, "We set out to provide the ultimate online shopping experience for our customers, and it's great to see that we're being recognized as a leader by not only industry experts, but those customers as well."

In 2001, 4SURE.com was acquired by Office Depot, the world's largest retailer of office products. Office Depot's own websites, including nine international sites, have already been recognized as industry leaders in the online retailing of office products. Office Depot hopes that 4SURE.com's brand name and success will help the firm reach new markets and achieve its goal of being the industry leader in providing knowledge, solutions, and products through multiple channels. According to Office Depot's CEO, Bruce Nelson, "This acquisition strategically positions Office Depot to grow in an online customer/product segment we have not successfully reached."[54]

QUESTIONS FOR DISCUSSION

1. How does 4SURE.com exploit the characteristics of electronic marketing to serve its customers? Which of these characteristics are most important to 4SURE.com's success?
2. Describe 4SURE.com's marketing mix. How does this mix differ from that of a more traditional, "brick-and-mortar" office supply store?
3. 4SURE.com has focused primarily on B2B markets, but it does market to consumers through its computers4SURE.com site. Assess this strategy in light of the firm's apparent success at a time when so many other dot-coms have failed.

CASE 23.2

Napster: Copyright Infringement or Technological Breakthrough?

Napster is an online service that allows computer users to share high-quality digital copies (MP3s) of music recordings via the Internet. The San Mateo–based company doesn't actually store the recordings on its own computers; rather, it provides an index of all the songs available on the computers of members currently logged onto the service. Napster therefore functions as a sort of clearinghouse that members can log onto, search by artist or song title, and identify where MP3s of interest are so they can download them from other users' hard drives. Napster has become one of the most popular sites on the Internet, claiming some 15 million users in little more than a year. Indeed, so many students were downloading songs from Napster that many universities were forced to block the site from their systems to regain bandwidth.

From the beginning, Napster's service has been almost as controversial as it has been popular. Barely a year after its launch, it was sued by the Recording Industry Association of America (RIAA), which represents major recording companies such as Universal Music, BMG, Sony Music, Warner Music Group, and EMI. The RIAA claimed that by allowing users to swap music recordings for free, Napster's service violated copyright laws. The RIAA also sought an injunction to stop the downloading of copyrighted songs owned by its members as well as damages for lost revenue. The RIAA argued that song swapping via Napster and similar firms has cost the music industry more than $300 million in lost sales. A few months after the RIAA lawsuit was filed, Metallica (a heavy-metal band) and rap star Dr. Dre filed separate lawsuits accusing Napster of copyright infringement and racketeering. Lars Ulrich, Metallica's drummer, told a Senate committee that Napster users are basically stealing from the band every time they download one of its songs.

On July 26, 2000, U.S. District Judge Marilyn Patel granted the RIAA's request for an injunction and ordered Napster to stop making copyrighted recordings available for download, which would have effectively shut down the service by pulling the plug on its most popular feature. However, on July 28, 2000, just nine hours before Napster would have had to shut down, the 9th Circuit Court of Appeals stayed that order, granting Napster a last-minute reprieve until the lawsuits could be tried in court.

In its battle with the RIAA, Napster turned to three past rulings on copyright infringement to support its defense: Sony Betamax, the 1992 Audio Home Recording Act, and the 1998 Digital Millennium Copyright Act. In the Sony Betamax case, the Motion Picture Association of America (MPAA) filed suit against Sony alleging that Sony's new video recording technology would unlock the door for widespread film production. Although a lower court found Sony guilty of copyright infringement, the U.S. Supreme Court overturned the decision, stating that a new technology must be "merely capable of substantial non-infringing uses in order to be protected by law." Because Napster's MP3 technology has legitimate uses, Napster argued that it should have the same protections as Sony.

Napster also sought to apply the 1992 Audio Home Recording Act (AHRA), which permits people to copy music for personal use. The law, enacted in response to the development of digital audiotape recorders, was passed before the Internet revolution. Napster supporters contended that the law applies to music downloads because the music being copied is for personal use, not redistribution for profit. Many others, however, including the U.S. Justice Department, disagreed because this act was based on digital audiotapes, not web music.

The 1998 Digital Millennium Copyright Act (DMCA) grants immunity to Internet service providers for the actions of their customers. Napster attorneys argued that the company has broad protection from copyright claims because it functions as a search engine rather than being directly involved in music swapping. However, according to the legal community, "Napster does not take the legal steps required of search engines in dealing with copyright violations."

Despite its claims, Napster was found guilty of direct infringement of the RIAA's musical recordings, and the ruling was upheld on appeal on February 12, 2001. The district court of appeals refuted all of Napster's defense tactics and ordered the company to stop allowing its millions of users to download and share copyrighted material without properly compensating the material's owners. The court determined the Audio Home Recording Act was irrelevant because it did not address the downloading of MP3 files or digital audio recording devices.

The court also rejected Napster's reliance on the Digital Millennium Copyright Act, stating simply that it does not include contributory infringers.

In response to the ruling, Hank Barry, CEO of Napster and Shawn Fanning, Napster's founder, (photo below) released statements to the public. They claimed they remain committed to finding an industry-supported solution to the controversy, such as a membership-based service. They also acknowledged negotiations with Bertelsmann AG to expand and improve Napster with the goal of prohibiting pirated music transfers and counting the number of song downloads in order to properly reimburse their artists.

A few days later, Napster offered $1 billion to the recording industry to settle the lawsuit. Under the proposal, $150 million would be paid annually for the first five years to Sony, Warner, BMG, EMI, and Universal, with $50 million allotted annually for independent labels. However, record industry executives refused Napster's proposal, claiming they were not willing to settle for anything less than shutting down Napster. To date, the service has not been shut down because doing so could violate the rights of artists who have given Napster permission to trade their music. However, the company was required to block all songs on a list of 5,000 provided by the RIAA.[55]

QUESTIONS FOR DISCUSSION

1. Based on the facts in the Napster case, who do you think should have control over intellectual property: the artists or distributors of their works? How did the legal system answer this question?
2. Can Napster's existence be defended on the basis of the idea that other online music services will take its place if it is forced to shut down?
3. While this case involves many issues, identify the characteristics of Napster's service that made it so successful. What can other dot-coms learn from Napster's success?

STRATEGIC CASE 7

DoubleClick Inc.

DoubleClick Inc. is an information revolution phenomenon. What began as an outgrowth of self-proclaimed computer "geeks" and savvy advertising agency executives has grown into a high-tech heavyweight providing advertising services and information about Internet users for advertisers, website operators, and other companies. The nature of its business has also put DoubleClick squarely in the center of a brewing controversy over Internet privacy. The company contends it is committed to protecting the privacy of all Internet users and helping to maintain the Internet as a free medium driven by highly targeted advertising. Consumer groups, however, see it differently, noting that DoubleClick's actions loom larger than its words regarding access to personal information.

Merging Silicon Alley and Madison Avenue

Like many entrepreneurs in recent years, Kevin O'Connor and Dwight Merriman recognized an opportunity to cash in on the growing popularity of the Internet. The two Atlanta-based engineers had observed the challenges facing niche-driven, subscription-based content websites attempting to compete with America Online's growing mass audience. They reasoned they could capitalize on the situation by creating a single network to bring together numerous online publications to create a critical mass of information. With the idea of multiple publications forming a larger online network, it became crucial to address a significant issue for these publications: advertising. After substantial research, O'Connor and Merriman decided the advertising rather than the publishing industry could be better served with such a network. Thus, they founded the DoubleClick Network in January 1996.

Although O'Connor and Merriman's engineering background helped them deal with the technology issues associated with their concept, it provided little insight into the sophisticated world of advertising. To address this issue, the startup formally merged with a division of ad agency Poppe Tyson. O'Connor believed a marriage of nerd and Madison Avenue cultures was possible because of a common bond: love of the Internet. The "offspring" of this union set up shop in the heart of Silicon Alley in New York City—the location, coincidentally, where some of New York's first advertising agencies sprang up a century ago.

Throwing Darts

Like traditional advertising agencies, DoubleClick's focus is to get the right advertisement to the right person at the right time. The difference between DoubleClick and offline ad agencies is the use of technology to track web-surfing activities more directly compared to older media such as magazines. Although a magazine publisher can detail the number of subscribers as well as the number of issues sold at newsstands, it lacks a clear picture as to which articles in a magazine issue have been read, by whom, and when. Online technology developed by DoubleClick, however, can monitor traffic to a given customer's website and identify specific articles selected. Moreover, DoubleClick can trail traffic to and from the website to establish a surfing portfolio of site visitors.

The heart of DoubleClick's technology is its DART (Dynamic Advertising Reporting and Targeting) system. DART works by reading 22 criteria regarding website visitors' actions, such as their cyber location and time of visit. This technology also leaves, often without the user's knowledge, a "cookie" on his or her computer. Cookies are simply bits of information sent to a web browser to be saved on the user's hard drive. Cookies are helpful for Internet users because they often contain important information, such as login information and user preferences, that makes return visits to subscription-based websites more manageable. Cookies are also useful for website operators because they may include additional information such as evidence of repeat visits or advertisements viewed. The information the cookie provides about website visitors' activities and interests helps DoubleClick tailor advertisements to specific users. However, because cookies do not collect personally identifiable information such as a user's name, mailing address, telephone number, or e-mail address, individual profiles are essentially anonymous. Instead of tracking an identifiable individual, then, cookies track users' digital footsteps.

The breadth and depth of information provided by DoubleClick quickly made it a valuable service provider to online advertisers trying to make advertising work on the Internet. By the end of its first year of business, DoubleClick had secured the business of 25 websites. Today the company places banner advertisements on more than 11,500 websites, generating more than $500 million in sales annually. This growth has allowed DoubleClick to command fees of 35 to 50 percent of advertising expenditures compared to the 15 percent fee structure charged by more traditional offline advertising agencies. The DoubleClick network also has the capability to add hundreds of thousands of anonymous consumer profiles per day. Thus, its technological capabilities make the company an increasingly attractive ad-servicing option.

Despite the phenomenal sales growth DoubleClick has achieved, executives believe the DART system offers further potential. In fact, DART technologies alone are expected to account for 50 percent of future revenues. However, those revenue expectations are not limited to just the DoubleClick network. The company is intent on servicing clients outside its own network and growing complementary businesses in the projected $11.3 billion (by 2003) ad-servicing business. Like traditional companies, DoubleClick has used its growing clout to develop and acquire important worldwide subsidiaries both on- and offline.

Among DoubleClick's most important acquisitions were Abacus Direct, an offline catalog database company, and Net-Gravity, Inc., a direct competitor. The idea behind the Abacus acquisition was the potential to merge the database company's personally identifiable offline buying habits with DoubleClick's nonpersonally identifiable online habits to provide even greater depth of consumer information to current and future clients. The trend toward collecting more personally identifiable information continued with DoubleClick's development of Flashbase, an automation tool that allows DoubleClick clients a means of collecting personal information by running contests and sweepstakes online. In addition, DoubleClick websites, such as www.NetDeals.com and www.IAF.net, collect personally identifiable information online. However, DoubleClick contends that it provides ways for consumers to limit communication only to prize- or deal-specific information. In other words, consumers are able to "opt out" of future communications not specific to the instance when and where they entered their personal data.

The Controversy

The only problem with these developments and acquisitions was that their intended use signaled a significant philosophical shift in the way DoubleClick had always done business. Specifically it created a drastic change in the company's consumer privacy position, a fact that consumer privacy groups and the Federal Trade Commission (FTC) did not take long to notice. According to Jason Catlett of Junkbusters, an Internet privacy activist, "Thousands of sites are ratting on you, so as soon as one gives you away, you're exposed on all of them. For years, [DoubleClick] has said [their services] don't identify you personally, and now they're admitting they are going to identify you."

Facing growing public concern, Kevin O'Connor defended the company's plans: "The merger with Abacus Direct, along with the recent closing of the NetGravity merger, will allow us to offer publishers and advertisers the most effective means of advertising online and offline." Kevin Ryan, DoubleClick's CEO, took it a step further: "What we continue to hear from consumers is that they'd like to be in a position to have better content, greater access for everyone in the United States, and they would love it all to be free and advertising-served." Ryan pointed out that the Internet is driven by advertising and advertising companies need to know their substantial investments are being spent in the best way possible—that is, targeted to the right audience or individual. Without more accurate information, Ryan asserted, much of the free content on the Internet would no longer be free.

DoubleClick's posted privacy policy states that online users are given *notice* about the data collection and the *choice* not to participate or to opt out. However, Internet users must read carefully to understand that granting permission, or failing to deny permission, at even one DoubleClick- or Abacus-serviced website allows the company to select personal information across all sites. Consequently the Center for Democracy and Technology (CDT), a Washington-based watchdog organization, launched a hard-line campaign against DoubleClick. The campaign centered around a "Websit" under the slogan "I Will Not Be

Targeted," where users can opt out of DoubleClick's profiling activities. According to Deirdre Mulligan, CDT's staff counsel, "You may have already been double-crossed by DoubleClick or you may be next in line. In either case, if you care about your privacy and want to surf the Web without your every move being recorded in a giant database connected to your name, it's time to opt-out."

The CDT campaign was just one challenge DoubleClick faced as public concerns about Internet privacy escalated. A California woman brought a lawsuit against DoubleClick alleging the company had unlawfully obtained and sold her private personal information. Media critics labeled DoubleClick a "Big Brother" that passed on information about employees' Internet surfing behavior on to their employers. Attorneys general in Michigan and New York launched investigations into DoubleClick's business practices. One of the most publicized challenges was the Electronic Privacy Information Center (EPIC) complaint filed with the FTC regarding DoubleClick's profiling practices. The complaint led to a full-scale investigation of DoubleClick's business practices by the federal watchdog. EPIC and similar privacy groups prefer an opt-in mechanism as opposed to DoubleClick's current opt-out platform. EPIC executive director Marc Rotenberg said, "Several years ago, DoubleClick said it would not collect personally identifiable information and keep anonymous profiles. Privacy experts applauded that approach." But as a result of the Abacus merger, "DoubleClick has changed its mind and they're trying to convince users they should accept that [new] model."

DoubleClick attempted to defuse the growing controversy by announcing a program to protect consumers it tracks online. The program included a major newspaper campaign, 50 million banner ads directing consumers to the privacy rights information and education site PrivacyChoices (www.privacychoices.org/), the appointment of a chief privacy officer, the hiring of an external accounting firm to conduct privacy audits, and the establishment of an advisory board. The board in particular was less than well received. Calling the board a "facade," Jeffrey Chester, executive director of the Center of Media Education, said, "This is a public relations ploy to ward off federal and state scrutiny." The center and other privacy organizations expressed dismay that the advisory board had no true privacy advocates and, worse, included a DoubleClick customer; moreover, that customer advocated technologies called "Web bugs" or "clear-gifs" that some consider even more intrusive than cookies. These sentiments prompted O'Connor to state, "It is clear from these discussions that I made a mis-

take by planning to merge names with anonymous user activity across websites in the absence of government and industry privacy standards."

Another attempt to regain consumer goodwill is DoubleClick's participation in the Responsible Electronic Communication Alliance (RECA), along with 15 of the nation's leading online marketers. The purpose of the RECA is to give consumers greater choice and notice regarding their online activities. To identify companies that subscribe to the RECA's proposed standards, the alliance is developing a "seal of approval" program in the spirit of *Good Housekeeping*. According to Christopher Wolf, RECA president, "Our ultimate goal is to phase in a set of firm standards on privacy, notice, access, and choice."

A New Era
In early 2001, the Federal Trade Commission announced it had completed its investigation of DoubleClick. In a letter to the company, the commission said, "It appears to staff that DoubleClick never used or disclosed consumers' PII [personally identifiable information] for purposes other than those disclosed in its privacy policy." However, the FTC also warned that its decision should not "be construed as a determination that a violation may not have occurred" and reserved the right to take further action. Needless to say, privacy advocates were not happy with the announcement. EPIC, for example, contends that the FTC never addressed its allegations. DoubleClick CEO Kevin Ryan, however, believes the company has been vindicated: "We felt from the beginning that our privacy policy and practices are solid. We never felt there was any substantial problem with them." Although the storm seems to have quieted for now, Internet consumers, privacy advocates, and government officials will be watching DoubleClick closely, and the issue of Internet privacy will almost certainly persist.

QUESTIONS FOR DISCUSSION
1. Why did DoubleClick's decision to merge Abacus Direct's database of personally identifiable offline buying habits with DoubleClick's nonpersonally identifiable online habits upset privacy advocates and arouse the attention of federal and state officials?
2. How do the services DoubleClick provides facilitate e-marketing? What characteristics of e-marketing contribute to DoubleClick's strategy?
3. Assess DoubleClick's growth strategy. What steps could or should DoubleClick take to address concerns about personal privacy protection in implementing this strategy?

e-Marketing   www.prideferrell.com   24

The Internet is changing design and implementation of marketing strategies. This dynamic technology provides marketers with efficient, powerful methods of designing, promoting, and distributing products, conducting research, and gathering market information. Chapter 24 has been developed to complement Chapter 23 by providing the most current statistics about usage patterns and emerging trends in e-marketing. In addition, up-to-date strategies are provided to illustrate the best practices in e-marketing.

Chapter 24 is updated on a regular basis to stay current with this dynamic area of marketing.

Chapter 24 is located at http://www.prideferrell.com. This unique site serves as a forum for students to explore how the Internet is changing marketing. In addition to Chapter 24, the website contains **Internet Exercises** and **Summaries** for Chapters 1 through 23; a **Resource Center,** with links to marketing organizations, publications, and other information sources; **Self-Tests;** a **Glossary** of key terms; **Marketing Plan Worksheets;** and more.

Through Chapter 24 and the other tools on the website we hope to help track the evolution of online marketing and practice *as it is happening.*

APPENDIX A
Careers in Marketing

Changes in the Workplace

Between one-fourth and one-third of the civilian work force in the United States is employed in marketing-related jobs. Although the field offers a multitude of diverse career opportunities, the number of positions in each area varies. For example, millions of workers are employed in many facets of sales, but relatively few people work in public relations and marketing research.

Many nonbusiness organizations now recognize that they perform marketing activities. For that reason, the number of marketing positions in government agencies, hospitals, charitable and religious groups, educational institutions, and similar organizations is increasing. Nonprofit organizations today are competitive and better managed, with job growth rates often matching those of private-sector firms. Another area ripe with opportunities is the World Wide Web. The federal government makes more sales to consumers online than even Amazon.com. With so many businesses setting up websites, demand will rise for people who have the skills to develop and design marketing strategies for the Web.

When searching for a job, you might want to consider the many alternatives outside the traditional large corporation. Within the last five years, companies with more than 500 employees have shed more than 5 million jobs through downsizing, reorganizations, and mergers. However, job losses in larger companies have been more than offset by gains in smaller businesses employing fewer than 500 employees. In recent years, two-thirds of new jobs were created by new companies with fewer than 25 workers, and most were in firms employing fewer than ten.[1]

Many workers outplaced from large corporations are choosing an entrepreneurial path, creating even more new opportunities for first-time job seekers. Even some of those who have secure managerial positions are leaving corporations and heading to smaller companies, toward greater responsibility and autonomy. The traditional career path used to be graduation from college, then a job with a large corporation, and a climb up the ladder to management. This pattern has changed, however. Today people are more likely to experience a career path of sideways "gigs" rather than sequential steps up a corporate ladder.

Career Choices Are Major Life Choices

Many people think career planning begins with an up-to-date résumé and a job interview.[2] In reality, it begins long before you prepare your résumé. It starts with *you* and what you want to become. In some ways, you have been preparing for a career ever since you started school. Everything you have experienced during your lifetime you can use as a resource to help you define your career goals. Since you will likely spend more time at work than at any other single place during your lifetime, it makes sense to spend that time doing something you enjoy. Unfortunately, some people just work at a *job* because they need money to survive. Other people choose a *career* because of their interests and talents or commitment to a particular profession. Whether you are looking for a job or a career, you should examine your priorities.

Personal Factors Influencing Career Choices

Before choosing a career, you need to consider what motivates you and what skills you can offer an employer. The following questions may help you define what you consider important in life.

1. *What types of activities do you enjoy?* Although most people know what they enjoy in a general way, a number of interest inventories exist. By helping you determine specific interests and activities, these inventories can help you land a job that will lead to a satisfying career. In some cases, it may be sufficient just to list the activities you enjoy, along with those you dislike. Watch for patterns that may influence your career choices.

2. *What do you do best?* All jobs and all careers require employees to be able to "do something." It is extremely important to assess what you do best. Be honest with yourself about your ability to succeed in a specific job. It may help to make a list of your strongest job-related skills. Also, try looking at your skills from an employer's perspective: What can you do that an employer would be willing to pay for?

3. *What kind of education will you need?* The amount of education you need is determined by the type of career you choose. In some careers, it is impossible to get an entry-level position without at least a college degree. In other careers, technical or hands-on skills may also be important. Generally, more education increases your potential earning power.

4. *Where do you want to live?* When you enter the job market, you may want to move to a different part of the country. According to the Bureau of Labor Statistics, the western and southern sections of the United States will experience the greatest population increase between now and 2005; the population in the Midwest will stay about the same, whereas the Northeast's population will decrease slightly. These population changes will affect job prospects in each region. Before entering the job market, some people think they will be free to move any place they want, whereas others want to reside in only one specific area. In reality, successful job applicants must be willing to go where the jobs are.

Job Search Activities

When people begin to search for a job, they often turn first to the classified ads in their local newspaper. Those ads are an important source of information about jobs in a particular area, but they are only one source. Many other sources can lead to employment and a satisfying career. Because there is a wealth of information about career planning, you should be selective in both the type and the amount of information you use to guide your job search.

The library, a traditional job-hunting tool, has been joined in recent years by the Internet. Both the library and the Internet are sources of everything from classified newspaper ads and government job listings to detailed information on individual companies and industries. You can use either to research an area of employment or a particular company that interests you. In addition, the Internet allows you to check electronic bulletin boards for current job information, exchange ideas with other job seekers through online discussion groups or e-mail, and get career advice from professional counselors. You can also create your own webpage to inform prospective employers of your qualifications. You may even have a job interview online. Many companies use their websites to post job openings, accept applications, and interview candidates.

As you start your job search, you may find the following websites helpful. (Addresses of additional career-related websites appear in the Pride/Ferrell Learning Center.)

America's Job Bank: www.ajb.dni.us
This massive site contains information on nearly 250,000 jobs. Listings come from 1,800 state employment offices around the country and represent every line of work, from professional and technical to blue-collar, and from entry level on up.

CareerPath.com: www.careerpath.com
This site features classified employment ads from 21 major newspapers, including the *New York Times,* the *Washington Post,* the *Chicago Tribune,* the *Los Angeles Times,* and the *Boston Globe,* as well as from some smaller newspapers.

Hoover's Online: www.hoovers.com
Hoover's offers a variety of job search tools, including information on potential employers and links to sites that post job openings.

The Monster Board: www.monster.com
The Monster Board carries hundreds of job listings and offers links to related sites, such as company home pages and sites with information about job fairs.

Federal jobs: www.fedworld.gov/jobs/jobsearch.html
If you are interested in working for a government agency, this site lists positions all across the country. You can limit your search to specific states or do a general cross-country search for job openings.

Other web addresses for job seekers include:

www.careers-in-marketing.com

www.marketingjobs.com

www.starthere.com/jobs

www.careermag.com

www.careermosaic.com

www.espan.com

www.occ.com

www.boldfacejobs.com

www.salary.com

More websites can be accessed at the www.prideferrell.com Student Career Center.

In addition to the library and the Internet, the following sources can be of great help when trying to find the "perfect job":

1. *Campus placement offices.* Colleges and universities have placement offices staffed by trained personnel specialists. In most cases, these offices serve as clearinghouses for career information. The staff may also be able to give you guidance on how to create your résumé and prepare for a job interview.

2. *Professional sources and networks.* A network is a group of people—friends, relatives, and professionals—who are in a position to exchange information, including information about job openings. According to many job applicants, networking is one of the best sources of career information and job leads. Start with as many people as you can think of to establish your network. (The Internet can be very useful in this regard.) Contact these people and ask specific questions about job opportunities they may be aware of. Also, ask each individual to introduce or refer you to someone else who may be able to help you in your job search.

3. *Private employment agencies.* Private employment agencies charge a fee for helping people find jobs. Typical fees can be as high as 15 to 20 percent of an employee's first-year salary. The fee may be paid by the employer or the employee. Like campus placement offices, private employment agencies provide career counseling, help create résumés, and provide preparation for job interviews. Before you use a private employment agency, be sure you understand the terms of any contract or agreement you sign. Above all, make sure you know who is responsible for paying the agency's fee.

4. *State employment agencies.* The local office of your state employment agency is a source of information about job openings in your immediate area. Some job applicants are reluctant to use state agencies because most jobs available through them are for semiskilled or unskilled workers. From a practical standpoint though, it can't hurt to consult state employment agencies. They will have information about some professional and managerial positions available in your area, and you will not be charged a fee if you obtain a job through one of these agencies.

Many people want a job immediately and are discouraged at the thought that an occupational search can take months. But people seeking entry-level jobs should expect their job search to take considerable time. Of course, the state of the economy and whether or not employers are hiring can shorten or extend a job search.

During a job search, you should use the same work habits that effective employees use on the job. When searching for a job, resist the temptation to "take the day off." Instead, make a master list of the activities you want to accomplish each day. If necessary, force yourself to make contacts, do job research, or schedule interviews that might lead to job opportunities. (In fact, many job applicants look at the job hunt as their actual job and "work" full time at it until they find the job they want.) Above all, realize that an occupational search requires patience and perseverance. According to many successful applicants, perseverance may be the job hunter's most valuable trait.

Planning and Preparation

The key to landing the job you want is planning and preparation—and planning begins with goals. In particular, it is important to determine your *personal* goals, to decide on the role your career will play in reaching those goals and then develop your career goals. Once you know where you are going, you can devise a reasonable plan for getting there.

The time to begin planning is as early as possible. You must, of course, satisfy the educational requirements for the occupational area you desire. Early planning will give you the opportunity to do so. But some of the people with whom you will compete for the better jobs will also be fully prepared. Can you do more? Company recruiters say the following factors give job candidates a definite advantage:

● *Work experience.* You can get valuable work experience in cooperative work/school programs, during summer vacations, or in part-time jobs during the school year. Experience in your chosen occupational area carries the most weight, but even unrelated work experience is useful.

● *The ability to communicate well.* Verbal and written communications skills are increasingly important in all aspects of business. Yours will be tested in your letters to recruiters, in your résumé, and in interviews. You will use these same communication skills throughout your career.

● *Clear and realistic job and career goals.* Recruiters feel most comfortable with candidates who know where they are headed and why they are applying for a specific job.

Again, starting early will allow you to establish well-defined goals, sharpen your communication skills (through elective courses, if necessary), and obtain solid work experience. To develop your own personal career plan go to www.prideferrell.com student site and access the Student Career Center. There you will find personal career plan worksheets.

The Résumé

An effective résumé is one of the keys to being considered for a good job. Because your résumé states your qualifications, experiences, education, and career goals, a

LORRAINE MILLER
2212 WEST WILLOW
PHOENIX, AZ 12345
(416) 862-9169

EDUCATION: B.A. Arizona State University, 2002, Marketing, achieved a 3.4 on a 4.0 scale throughout college

POSITION DESIRED: Product manager with an international firm providing future career development at the executive level

QUALIFICATIONS:

- Communicates well with individuals to achieve a common goal
- Handles tasks efficiently and in a timely manner
- Understands advertising sales, management, marketing research, packaging, pricing, distribution, and warehousing
- Coordinates many activities at one time
- Receives and carries out assigned tasks or directives
- Writes complete status or research reports

EXPERIENCES:

- Assistant Editor of college paper
- Treasurer of the American Marketing Association (student chapter)
- Internship with 3-Cs Advertising, Berkeley, CA
- Student Assistantship with Dr. Steve Green, Professor of Marketing, Arizona State University
- Solo cross-Canada canoe trek, summer 2001

WORK RECORD:

2001–Present	Blythe and Co., Inc.	
	—Junior Advertising Account Executive	
1999–2000	Student Assistant for Dr. Steve Green	
	—Research Assistant	
1998–1999	The Men	
	—Retail sales and consumer relations	
1996–1998	Farmer	
	—Helped operate relative's blueberry farm in Michigan for three summers	

FIGURE A.1   **A Résumé Targeted at a Specific Position**

potential employer can use it to assess your compatibility with the job requirements. The résumé should be accurate and current.

In preparing a résumé, it helps to think of it as an advertisement. Envision yourself as a product and the company, particularly the person or persons doing the hiring, as your customer. To interest the customer in buying the product—hiring you—your résumé must communicate information about your qualities and indicate how you can satisfy the customer's needs—that is, how you can help the company achieve its objectives. The information in the résumé should persuade the organization to take a closer look at you by calling you in for an interview.

To be effective, the résumé should be targeted at a specific position, as Figure A.1 shows. This document is only one example of an acceptable résumé. The job target section is specific and leads directly to the applicant's qualifications for the job. The qualifications section details capabilities—what the applicant can do—and also shows that the applicant has an understanding of the job's requirements. Skills and strengths that relate to the specific job should be emphasized. The achievement section ("Experiences" in Figure A.1) indicates success at accomplishing tasks or goals on the job and at school. The work experience section in Figure A.1 includes an unusual listing, which might pique the interest of an interviewer: "helped operate relative's blueberry farm in Michigan for three summers." That is something that could help launch an interview discussion. It tends to incite rather than satisfy curiosity, thus inviting further inquiry.

Another type of résumé is the chronological résumé, which lists work experience and educational history in order by date. This type of résumé is useful for those just entering the job market because it helps to highlight education and work experience. In some cases, education is more important than unrelated work experience because it indicates the career direction you desire despite the work experience you have thus far.

Common suggestions for improving résumés include deleting useless or outdated information, improving organization, using professional printing and typing, listing duties (not accomplishments), maintaining grammatical perfection, and avoiding an overly elaborate or fancy format.[3] Keep in mind that the person who will look at your résumé may have to look through hundreds in the course of the day in addition to handling other duties. Consequently it is important to keep your résumé short (one page is best, never more than two), concise, and neat. Moreover, you want your résumé to be distinctive so it will stand out from all the others.

In addition to having the proper format and content, a résumé should be easy to read. It is best to use only one or two kinds of type and plain, white paper. When a résumé is sent to a large company, several copies may be made and distributed. Textured, gray, or colored paper may make a good impression on the first person who sees the résumé, but it will not reproduce well for the others, who will see only a poor copy. You should also proofread your résumé with care. Typos and misspellings will grab attention—the wrong kind.

Along with the résumé itself, always be sure to submit a cover letter. In the letter, you can convey a bit more than is included in your résumé and send a message that expresses your interest and enthusiasm about the organization and the job.

The Job Interview

Your résumé and cover letter are, in essence, an introduction. The deciding factor in the hiring process is the interview (or several interviews) with representatives of the firm. It is through the interview that the firm gets to know you and your qualifications. At the same time, the interview gives you a chance to learn about the firm.

Here again, preparation is the key to success. Research the firm before your first interview. Learn all you can about its products, its subsidiaries, the markets in which it operates, its history, the locations of its facilities, and so on. If possible, obtain and read the firm's most recent annual report. Be prepared to ask questions about the firm and the opportunities it offers. Interviewers welcome such questions. They expect you to be interested enough to spend some time thinking about your potential relationship with their firm.

Also, prepare to respond to questions the interviewer may ask. Table A.1 lists typical interview questions that job applicants often find difficult to answer. But don't expect interviewers to stick to the list given in the table or to the items appearing in your résumé. They will be interested in anything that helps them decide what kind of person and worker you are.

Make sure you are on time for your interview and are dressed and groomed in a businesslike manner. Interviewers take note of punctuality and appearance just as they do of other personal qualities. Have a copy of your résumé with you, even if you already sent one to the firm. You may also want to bring a copy of your course transcript and letters of recommendation. If you plan to furnish interviewers with the names and addresses of references rather than with letters of recommendation, make sure you have your references' permission to do so.

Consider the interview itself as a two-way conversation rather than a question-and-answer session. Volunteer any information that is relevant to the interviewer's questions. If an important point is skipped in the discussion, don't hesitate to bring it

Table A.1	Interview Questions Job Applicants Often Find Difficult to Answer

1. Tell me about yourself.

2. What do you know about our organization?

3. What can you do for us? Why should we hire you?

4. What qualifications do you have that make you feel you will be successful in your field?

5. What have you learned from the jobs you've held?

6. If you could write your own ticket, what would be your ideal job?

7. What are your special skills, and where did you acquire them?

8. Have you had any special accomplishments in your lifetime that you are particularly proud of?

9. Why did you leave your most recent job?

10. How do you spend your spare time? What are your hobbies?

11. What are your strengths and weaknesses?

12. Discuss five major accomplishments.

13. What kind of boss would you like? Why?

14. If you could spend a day with someone you've known or known of, who would it be?

15. What personality characteristics seem to rub you the wrong way?

16. How do you show your anger? What type of things make you angry?

17. With what type of person do you spend the majority of your time?

Source: Adapted from The *Ultimate Job Hunter's Guidebook,* 3rd ed. by Susan D. Greene and Melanie C. L. Martel. Copyright © 2001 by Houghton Mifflin Company.

up. Be yourself, but emphasize your strengths. Good eye contact and posture are important, too. They should come naturally if you take an active part in the interview. At the conclusion of the interview, thank the recruiter for taking the time to see you.

In most cases, the first interview is used to *screen* applicants, or choose those who are best qualified. These applicants are then given a second interview and perhaps a third, usually with one or more department heads. If the job requires relocation to a different area, applicants may be invited there for these later interviews. After the interviewing process is complete, applicants are told when to expect a hiring decision.

After the Interview

Attention to common courtesy is important as a follow-up to your interview. You should send a brief note of thanks to the interviewer and give it as much care as you did your résumé. A short, typewritten letter is preferred to a handwritten note or card. Avoid not only typos but also overconfident statements such as "I look forward to helping you make Universal Industries successful over the next decade." Even in the thank-you letter, it is important to show team spirit and professionalism, as well as convey proper enthusiasm. Everything you say and do reflects on you as a candidate.

After the Hire

Clearly, performing well in a job has always been a crucial factor in keeping a position. In a tight economy and job market, however, a person's attitude, as well as his or her performance, counts greatly. People in their first jobs can commit costly political blunders by being insensitive to their environments. Politics in the business world includes how you react to your boss, how you react to your coworkers, and your general demeanor. Here are a few rules to live by:

1. *Don't bypass your boss.* One major blunder an employee can make is to go over the boss's head to resolve a problem. This is especially hazardous in a bureaucratic organization. You should become aware of the generally accepted chain of command and, when problems occur, follow that protocol, beginning with your immediate superior. No boss likes to look incompetent, and making him or her appear so is sure to crush or hamper a budding career. However, there may be exceptions to this rule in emergency situations. It would be advantageous for you to discuss with your supervisor what to do in an emergency, before an emergency occurs.[4]

2. *Don't criticize your boss.* Adhering to the old adage "praise in public and criticize in private" will keep you out of the line of retaliatory fire. A more sensible and productive alternative is to present the critical commentary to your boss in a diplomatic way during a private session.

3. *Don't show disloyalty.* If dissatisfied with the position, a new employee may start a fresh job search, within or outside the organization. However, it is not advisable to begin a publicized search within the company for another position unless you have held your current job for some time. Careful attention to the political climate in the organization should help you determine how soon to start a new job campaign and how public it may be. In any case, it is not a good idea to publicize that you are looking outside the company for a new position.

4. *Don't be a naysayer.* Employees are expected to become part of the organizational team and to work together with others. Behaviors to avoid, especially if you are a new employee, include being critical of others; refusing to support others' projects; always playing devil's advocate; refusing to help others when a crisis occurs; and complaining all the time, even about such matters as the poor quality of the food in the cafeteria, the crowded parking lot, or the temperature in the office.

5. *Learn to correct mistakes appropriately.* No one likes to admit having made a mistake, but one of the most important political skills you can acquire is minimizing the impact of a blunder. It is usually advantageous to correct the damage as soon as possible to avoid further problems. Some suggestions: be the first to break the bad news to your boss; avoid being defensive; stay poised and don't panic; and have solutions ready for fixing the blunder.[5]

Types of Marketing Careers

In considering marketing as a career, the first step is to evaluate broad categories of career opportunities in the areas of marketing research, sales, industrial buying, public relations, distribution management, product management, advertising, retail management, and direct marketing. Keep in mind that the categories described here are not all-inclusive and that each encompasses hundreds of marketing jobs.

Marketing Research

Clearly, marketing research and information systems are vital aspects of marketing decision making. Marketing researchers survey customers to determine their habits, preferences, and aspirations. The information about buyers and environmental forces that research and information systems provide improves a marketer's ability to understand the dynamics of the marketplace and make effective decisions.

Marketing research firms are usually employed by a client organization such as a provider of goods or services, a nonbusiness organization, a research consulting firm, or an advertising agency. The activities performed include concept testing, product testing, package testing, advertising testing, test-market research, and new-product research.

Marketing researchers gather and analyze data relating to specific problems. A researcher may be involved in one or several stages of research, depending on the size of the project, the organization of the research unit, and the researcher's experience. Marketing research trainees in large organizations usually perform a considerable amount of clerical work, such as compiling secondary data from the firm's accounting and sales records and from periodicals, government publications, syndicated data services, the Internet, and unpublished sources. A junior analyst may edit and code questionnaires or tabulate survey results. Trainees may also participate in gathering primary data through mail and telephone surveys, personal interviews, and observation. As a marketing researcher gains experience, he or she may become involved in defining problems and developing research questions; designing research procedures; and analyzing, interpreting, and reporting findings. Exceptional personnel may assume responsibility for entire research projects.

Although most employers consider a bachelor's degree sufficient qualification for a marketing research trainee, many specialized positions require a graduate degree in business administration, statistics, or other related fields. Today trainees are more likely to have a marketing or statistics degree than a liberal arts degree. Courses in statistics, information technology, psychology, sociology, communications, economics, and technical writing are valuable preparation for a career in marketing research.

The Bureau of Labor Statistics indicates that marketing research provides abundant employment opportunities, especially for applicants with graduate training in marketing research, statistics, economics, and the social sciences. Generally, the value of information gathered by marketing information and research systems becomes more important as competition increases, thus expanding the opportunities for prospective marketing research personnel.

The major career paths in marketing research are with independent marketing research agencies/data suppliers and marketing research departments in advertising agencies and other businesses. In a company in which marketing research plays a key role, the researcher is often a member of the marketing strategy team. Surveying or interviewing customers is the heart of the marketing research firm's activities. A statistician selects the sample to be surveyed, analysts design the questionnaire and synthesize the gathered data into a final report, data processors tabulate the data, and the research director controls and coordinates all these activities so that each project is completed to the client's satisfaction.

Salaries in marketing research depend on the type, size, and location of the firm, as well as the nature of the position. Overall, salaries of marketing researchers have increased slightly during the last few years. However, the specific position within the marketing research field determines the percentage of fluctuation.[6] Generally, starting salaries are somewhat higher and promotions somewhat slower than in other occupations requiring similar training. The typical salary for a market analyst is $24,000 to $50,000; a marketing research director can earn $75,000 to $200,000.[7]

Sales

Millions of people earn a living through personal selling. Chapter 19 defined personal selling as paid personal communication that attempts to inform customers and persuade them to purchase products in an exchange situation. Although this definition describes the general nature of sales positions, individual selling jobs vary enormously with respect to the types of businesses and products involved, the educational background and skills required, and the specific activities sales personnel perform. Because the work is so varied, it offers numerous career opportunities for people with a wide range of qualifications, interests, and goals. The two types of career opportunities we discuss relate to business-to-business sales.

Sales Positions in Wholesaling.   Wholesalers buy products intended for resale, for use in making other products, and for general business operations and sell them directly to business markets. Wholesalers thus provide services to both retailers and producers. They can help match producers' products to retailers' needs and provide services that save producers time, money, and resources. Some activities a sales representative for a wholesaling firm is likely to engage in include planning and negotiating transactions; assisting customers with sales, advertising, sales promotion, and publicity; facilitating transportation and storage; providing customers with inventory control and data processing assistance; establishing prices; and giving customers technical, managerial, and merchandising assistance.

The background needed by wholesale personnel depends on the nature of the product handled. A sales representative for a drug wholesaler, for example, needs extensive technical training and product knowledge, and may have a degree in chemistry, biology, or pharmacology. A wholesaler of standard office supplies, on the other hand, may find it more important for its sales staff to be familiar with various brands, suppliers, and prices than to have technical knowledge about the products. A person just entering the wholesaling field may begin as a sales trainee or hold a nonselling job that provides experience with inventory, prices, discounts, and the firm's customers. A college graduate usually enters a wholesaler's sales force directly. Competent salespeople also transfer from manufacturer and retail sales positions.

The number of sales positions in wholesaling is expected to grow about as rapidly as the average for all occupations. Earnings for wholesale personnel vary widely because commissions often make up a large proportion of their incomes.

Sales Positions in Manufacturing. A manufacturer's sales personnel sell the firm's products to wholesalers, retailers, and industrial buyers; they thus perform many of the same activities as a wholesaler's representatives. As in wholesaling, educational requirements for a sales position depend largely on the type and complexity of the products and markets. Manufacturers of nontechnical products usually hire college graduates who have a liberal arts or business degree and train them so they become knowledgeable about the firm's products, prices, and customers. Manufacturers of highly technical products generally prefer applicants who have degrees in fields associated with the particular industry and market.

Sales positions in manufacturing are expected to increase at an average rate. Manufacturers' sales personnel are well compensated and earn above-average salaries; most are paid a combination of salary and commission. Commissions vary according to the salesperson's efforts, abilities, and sales territory, as well as the type of products sold. Annual salary and/or commission for sales positions range from $50,000 to $100,000 for a sales manager and $36,000 to $75,000 for a field salesperson. A sales trainee would start at about $35,000 in business sales positions.

Industrial Buying

Industrial buyers, or purchasing agents, are responsible for maintaining an adequate supply of the goods and services an organization requires for its operations. In general, industrial buyers purchase all items needed for direct use in producing other products and for use in day-to-day operations. Industrial buyers in large firms often specialize in purchasing a single, specific class of products—for example, all petroleum-based lubricants. In smaller organizations, buyers may be responsible for many different categories of purchases, including raw materials, component parts, office supplies, and operating services.

An industrial buyer's main job is to select suppliers that offer the best quality, service, and price. When the products to be purchased are standardized, buyers may base their purchasing decisions on suppliers' descriptions of their offerings in catalogs and trade journals. Buyers who purchase highly homogeneous products often meet with salespeople to examine samples and observe demonstrations. Sometimes buyers must inspect the actual product before purchasing it; in other cases, they invite suppliers to bid on large orders. Buyers who purchase equipment made to specifications often deal directly with manufacturers. After choosing a supplier and placing an order, an industrial buyer usually must trace the shipment to ensure on-time delivery. Sometimes the buyer is also responsible for receiving and inspecting an order and authorizing payment to the shipper.

Training requirements for a career in industrial buying relate to the needs of the firm and the types of products purchased. A manufacturer of heavy machinery may prefer an applicant who has a background in engineering. A service company, on the other hand, may recruit liberal arts majors. Although not generally required, a college degree is becoming increasingly important for industrial buyers who wish to advance to management positions.

Employment prospects for industrial buyers are expected to increase faster than average. Opportunities will be excellent for individuals with a master's degree in business administration or a bachelor's degree in engineering, science, or business administration. Companies that manufacture heavy equipment, computer equipment, and communications equipment will need buyers with technical backgrounds.

Public Relations

Public relations encompasses a broad set of communication activities designed to create and maintain favorable relations between an organization and its stakeholders—customers, employees, stockholders, government officials, and society in general. Public relations specialists help clients create the image, issue, or message they wish to present and communicate it to the appropriate audience. According to the Public Relations Society of America, about 120,000 people work in public relations in the United States. Half the billings of the nation's 4,000 public relations agencies and firms come from Chicago and New York. The highest starting salaries can also be found there. Communication is basic to all public relations programs. To communicate effectively, public relations practitioners must first gather data about the firm's stakeholders to assess their needs, identify problems, formulate recommendations, implement new plans, and evaluate current activities.

Public relations personnel disseminate large amounts of information to the organization's stakeholders. Written communication is the most versatile tool of public relations; thus, good writing skills are essential. Public relations practitioners must be adept at writing for a variety of media and audiences. It is not unusual for a person in public relations to prepare reports, news releases, speeches, broadcast scripts, technical manuals, employee publications, shareholder reports, and other communications aimed at both organizational personnel and external groups. In addition, a public relations practitioner needs a thorough knowledge of the production techniques used in preparing various communications. Public relations personnel also establish distribution channels for the organization's publicity. They must have a thorough understanding of the various media, their areas of specialization, the characteristics of their target audiences, and their policies regarding publicity. Anyone who hopes to succeed in public relations must develop close working relationships with numerous media personnel to enlist their interest in disseminating an organization's communications.

A college education combined with writing or media-related experience is the best preparation for a career in public relations. Most beginners have a college degree in journalism, communications, or public relations, but some employers prefer a business background. Courses in journalism, business administration, marketing, creative writing, psychology, sociology, political science, economics, advertising, English, and public speaking are recommended. Some employers ask applicants to present a portfolio of published articles, scripts written for television or radio programs, slide presentations, and other work samples. Other agencies require written tests that include such tasks as writing sample press releases. Manufacturing firms, public utilities, transportation and insurance companies, and trade and professional associations are the largest employers of public relations personnel. In addition, sizable numbers of public relations personnel work for health-related organizations, government agencies, educational institutions, museums, and religious and service groups.

Although some larger companies provide extensive formal training for new personnel, most new public relations employees learn on the job. Beginners usually perform routine tasks such as maintaining files about company activities and searching secondary data sources for information to be used in publicity materials. More experienced employees write press releases, speeches, and articles and help plan public relations campaigns.

Employment opportunities in public relations are expected to increase faster than the average for all occupations. One caveat is in order, however: competition for beginning jobs is keen. The prospects are best for applicants who have solid academic preparation and some media experience. Abilities that differentiate candidates, such as an understanding of information technology, are becoming increasingly important. Public relations account executives received $30,000 to $50,000. Public relations agency managers earn in the $45,000 to $60,000 range.

Distribution Management

A distribution manager arranges for transportation of goods within firms and through marketing channels. Transportation is an essential distribution activity that permits a firm to create time and place utility for its products. It is the distribution manager's job to analyze various transportation modes and select the combination that minimizes cost and transit time while providing acceptable levels of reliability, capability, accessibility, and security.

To accomplish this task, a distribution manager performs many activities. First, the individual must choose one or a combination of transportation modes from the five major modes available: railroads, trucks, waterways, airways, and pipelines. The distribution manager must then select the specific routes the goods will travel and the particular carriers to be used, weighing such factors as freight classifications and regulations, freight charges, time schedules, shipment sizes, and loss and damage ratios. In addition, this person may be responsible for preparing shipping documents, tracing shipments, handling loss and damage claims, keeping records of freight rates, and monitoring changes in government regulations and transportation technology.

Distribution management employs relatively few people and is expected to grow about as fast as the average for all occupations in the near future. Manufacturing firms are the largest employers of distribution managers, although some distribution managers work for wholesalers, retail stores, and consulting firms. Salaries of experienced distribution managers vary but generally are much higher than the average for all nonsupervisory personnel. Entry-level positions are diverse, ranging from inventory control and traffic scheduling to operations or distribution management. Inventory management is an area of great opportunity because of increasing global competition. While salaries in the distribution field vary depending on the position and information technology skill requirements, entry salaries are in the $35,000 to $45,000 range.

Most employers of distribution managers prefer to hire graduates of technical programs or people who have completed courses in transportation, logistics, distribution management, economics, statistics, computer science, management, marketing, and commercial law. A successful distribution manager must be adept at handling technical data and be able to interpret and communicate highly technical information.

Product Management

The product manager occupies a staff position and is responsible for the success or failure of a product line. Product managers coordinate most of the activities required to market a product. However, because they hold a staff position, they have relatively little actual authority over marketing personnel. Even so, they take on a large amount of responsibility and typically are paid quite well relative to other marketing employees. Being a product manager can be rewarding both financially and psychologically, but it can also be frustrating because of the disparity between responsibility and authority.

A product manager should have a general knowledge of advertising, transportation modes, inventory control, selling and sales management, sales promotion, marketing research, packaging, pricing, and warehousing. The individual must be knowledgeable enough to communicate effectively with personnel in these functional areas and to make suggestions and help assess alternatives when major decisions are being made.

Product managers usually need college training in an area of business administration. A master's degree is helpful, although a person usually does not become a product manager directly out of school. Frequently several years of selling and sales management experience are prerequisites for a product

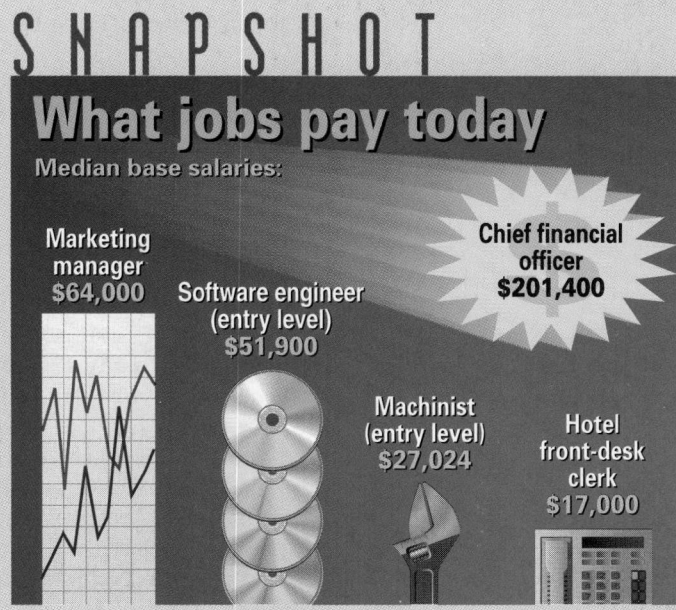

SNAPSHOT

What jobs pay today
Median base salaries:

Marketing manager
$64,000

Software engineer (entry level)
$51,900

Chief financial officer
$201,400

Machinist (entry level)
$27,024

Hotel front-desk clerk
$17,000

Source: *USA Today*, July 24, 2001, p. 1B. Copyright 2001, *USA Today*. Reprinted with permission.

management position, which often is a major step in the career path of top-level marketing executives. Product managers can earn $60,000 to $120,000, while an assistant product manager starts at about $40,000.[8]

Advertising

Advertising pervades our daily lives. Business and nonbusiness organizations use advertising in many ways and for many reasons. Advertising clearly needs individuals with diverse skills to fill a variety of jobs. Creativity, imagination, artistic talent, and expertise in expression and persuasion are important for copywriters, artists, and account executives. Sales and managerial abilities are vital to the success of advertising managers, media buyers, and production managers. Research directors must have a solid understanding of research techniques and human behavior. A related occupation is an advertising salesperson, who sells newspaper, television, radio, or magazine advertising to advertisers.

Advertising professionals disagree on the most beneficial educational background for a career in advertising. Most employers prefer college graduates. Some employers seek individuals with degrees in advertising, journalism, or business; others prefer graduates with broad liberal arts backgrounds. Still other employers rank relevant work experience above educational background.

"Advertisers look for generalists," says a staff executive of the American Association of Advertising Agencies, "thus, there are just as many economics or general liberal arts majors as M.B.A.'s." Common entry-level positions in an advertising agency are found in the traffic department, account service (account coordinator), or in the media department (media assistant). Starting salaries in these positions are often quite low, but to gain experience in the advertising industry, employees must work their way up in the system. Assistant account executives start at $25,000, while a typical account executive earns $30,000 to $50,000. Copywriters earn $30,000 to $50,000 a year.[9]

A variety of organizations employ advertising personnel. Although advertising agencies are perhaps the most visible and glamorous employers, many manufacturing firms, retail stores, banks, utility companies, and professional and trade associations maintain advertising departments. Advertising jobs are also available with television and radio stations, newspapers, and magazines. Other businesses that employ advertising personnel include printers, art studios, letter shops, and package design firms.

Specific advertising jobs include advertising manager, account executive, research director, copywriter, media specialist, and production manager.

About 59 percent of advertising employees are between 25 and 44 years of age compared to 51 percent of all workers in the U.S. economy. Employment opportunities in advertising are expected to increase faster than the average of all occupations through 2008.[10]

Retail Management

Although a career in retailing may begin in sales, there is more to retailing than simply selling. Many retail personnel occupy management positions. Besides managing the sales force, they focus on selecting and ordering merchandise, promotional activities, inventory control, customer credit operations, accounting, personnel, and store security.

How retail stores are organized varies. In many large department stores, retail management personnel rarely engage in actual selling to customers; these duties are performed by retail salespeople. However, other types of retail organizations may require management personnel to perform selling activities from time to time.

Large retail stores offer a variety of management positions, including assistant buyers, buyers, department managers, section managers, store managers, division managers, regional managers, and vice president of merchandising. The following list describes the general duties of four of these positions; the precise nature of these duties may vary from one retail organization to another.

A section manager coordinates inventory and promotions and interacts with buyers, salespeople, and ultimate consumers. The manager performs merchandising, labor relations, and managerial activities and can usually expect to work more than a 40-hour workweek.

The buyer's task is more focused. This fast-paced occupation involves much travel and pressure, and the need to be open-minded with respect to new, potentially successful items.

The regional manager coordinates the activities of several stores within a given area, usually monitoring and supporting sales, promotions, and general procedures.

The vice president of merchandising has a broad scope of managerial responsibility and reports to the organization's president.

Most retail organizations hire college graduates, put them through management training programs, and then place them directly in management positions. They frequently hire candidates with backgrounds in liberal arts or business administration. Sales positions and retail management positions offer the greatest employment opportunities for marketing students.

Retail management positions can be exciting and challenging. Competent, ambitious individuals often assume a great deal of responsibility very quickly and advance rapidly. However, a retail manager's job is physically demanding and sometimes entails long working hours. In addition, managers employed by large chain stores may be required to move frequently during their early years with the company. Nonetheless, positions in retail management often offer the chance to excel and gain promotion. Growth in retailing, which is expected to accompany the growth in population, is likely to create substantial opportunities during the next ten years. While a trainee may start in the $30,000 to $40,000 range, a store manager can earn from $50,000 to $200,000 depending on the size of the store.

Direct Marketing

One of the most dynamic areas in marketing is direct marketing, in which the seller uses one or more direct media (telephone, mail, print, or television) to solicit a response. The telephone is a major vehicle for selling many consumer products. Telemarketing is direct selling to customers using a variety of technological improvements in telecommunications. Direct-mail catalogs appeal to such market segments as working women and people who find going to retail stores difficult or inconvenient. Newspapers and magazines offer great opportunity, particularly in special market segments. *Golf Digest,* for example, is obviously a good medium for selling golfing equipment. Cable television provides many opportunities for selling directly to consumers. Home shopping channels, for instance, have been very successful. The Internet offers numerous direct marketing opportunities.

The most important asset in direct marketing is experience. Employers often look to other industries to locate experienced professionals. This preference means that if you can get an entry-level position in direct marketing, you will have an advantage in developing a career.

Jobs in direct marketing include buyers, such as department store buyers, who select goods for catalog, telephone, or direct-mail sales. Catalog managers develop marketing strategies for each new catalog that goes into the mail. Research/mail-list management involves developing lists of products that will sell in direct marketing and lists of names of consumers who are likely to respond to a direct-mail effort. Order fulfillment managers direct the shipment of products once they are sold. Direct marketing's effectiveness is enhanced by periodic analysis of advertising and communications at all phases of contact with the consumer. Direct marketing involves all aspects of marketing decision making. Most positions in direct marketing involve planning and market analysis. Some direct marketing jobs involve the use of databases that include customer information, sales history, and other tracking data. A database manager might receive a salary of $60,000 to $100,000. A telemarketing director in business-to-business sales could receive a salary of $60,000 to $75,000.

e-Marketing and Customer Relationship Management

Today only about 1 percent of all retail sales are conducted on the Internet. Business-to-business transactions are expected to reach almost $9 trillion by 2005, up from $433 billion in 2000.[12] One characteristic of firms engaged in e-marketing is a renewed focus on relationship marketing by building customer loyalty and retaining customers—in other words, on customer relationship management (CRM). This focus on CRM is possible because of e-marketers' ability to target individual customers. This effort is enhanced over time as the customer invests more time and effort in "teaching" the firms what he or she wants.

Opportunities exist to combine information technology expertise with marketing knowledge. By providing an integrated communication system of websites, fax, telephone, and personal contacts, marketers can personalize customer relationships. Careers exist for individuals who can integrate the Internet as a touch point with customers as part of effective customer relationship management. Many Internet-only companies ("dot-coms") failed because they were overly focused on brand awareness and did not understand an integrated marketing strategy.

The use of laptops, cellular phones, e-mail, voice mail, and other devices is necessary to maintain customer relationships and allow purchases on the Internet. A variety of jobs exist for marketers who have integrated technology into their work and job skills. Job titles include e-marketing manager, customer relationship manager, and e-services manager, as well as jobs in dot-coms.

Salaries in this emerging area depend on technical expertise and experience. For example, a CRM customer service manager receives a salary in the $40,000 to $45,000 range. Database managers receive higher salaries of approximately $60,000 to $90,000. With five years of experience in e-marketing, individuals that are responsible for online product offerings can earn from $50,000 to $85,000.

APPENDIX B
Financial Analysis in Marketing*

Our discussion in this book focuses more on fundamental concepts and decisions in marketing than on financial details. However, marketers must understand the basic components of financial analyses if they are to explain and defend their decisions. In fact, they must be familiar with certain financial analyses to reach good decisions in the first place. To control and evaluate marketing activities, they must understand the income statement and what it says about the operations of their organization. They also need to be acquainted with performance ratios, which compare current operating results with past results and with results in the industry at large. We examine the income statement and some performance ratios in the first part of this appendix. In the last part, we discuss price calculations as the basis of price adjustments. Marketers are likely to use all these areas of financial analysis at various times to support their decisions and make necessary adjustments in their operations.

The Income Statement

The income, or operating, statement presents the financial results of an organization's operations over a certain period. The statement summarizes revenues earned and expenses incurred by a profit center, whether a department, a brand, a product line, a division, or the entire firm. The income statement presents the firm's net profit or net loss for a month, quarter, or year.

Table B.1 is a simplified income statement for Stoneham Auto Supplies, a fictitious retail store. The owners of the store, Rose Costa and Nick Schultz, see that net sales of $250,000 are decreased by the cost of goods sold and by other business expenses to yield a net income of $83,000. Of course, these figures are only highlights of the complete income statement, which appears in Table B.2.

The income statement can be used in several ways to improve the management of a business. First, it enables an owner or manager to compare actual results with budgets for various parts of the statement. For example, Rose and Nick see that the total amount of merchandise sold (gross sales) is $260,000. Customers returned merchandise or received allowances (price reductions) totaling $10,000. Suppose the budgeted amount was only $9,000. By checking the tickets for sales returns and allowances, the owners can determine why these events occurred and whether the $10,000 figure could be lowered by adjusting the marketing mix.

Table B.1	Simplified Income Statement for a Retailer
Stoneham Auto Supplies **Income Statement for the Year Ended December 31, 2002**	
Net Sales	$250,000
Cost of Goods Sold	45,000
Gross Margin	$205,000
Expenses	122,000
Net Income	$ 83,000

* We gratefully acknowledge the assistance of Jim L. Grimm, Professor of Marketing, Illinois State University, in writing this appendix.

Table B.2   Income Statement for a Retailer

Stoneham Auto Supplies
Income Statement for the Year Ended December 31, 2002

Gross Sales			$260,000
Less: Sales returns and allowances			$ 10,000
Net Sales			$250,000
Cost of Goods Sold			
Inventory, January 1, 2002 (at cost)		$48,000	
Purchases	$51,000		
Less: Purchase discounts	4,000		
Net purchases	$47,000		
Plus: Freight-in	2,000		
Net cost of delivered purchases		$49,000	
Cost of goods available for sale		$97,000	
Less: Inventory, December 31, 2002			
(at cost)		52,000	
Cost of goods sold			$ 45,000
Gross Margin			$205,000
Expenses			
Selling expenses			
Sales salaries and commissions	$32,000		
Advertising	16,000		
Sales promotions	3,000		
Delivery	2,000		
Total selling expenses		$53,000	
Administrative expenses			
Administrative salaries	$20,000		
Office salaries	20,000		
Office supplies	2,000		
Miscellaneous	1,000		
Total administrative expenses		$43,000	
General expenses			
Rent	$14,000		
Utilities	7,000		
Bad debts	1,000		
Miscellaneous (local taxes, insurance, interest, depreciation)	4,000		
Total general expenses		$26,000	
Total expenses			$ 122,000
Net Income			$ 83,000

After subtracting returns and allowances from gross sales, Rose and Nick can determine net sales, the amount the firm has available to pay its expenses. They are pleased with this figure because it is higher than their sales target of $240,000.

A major expense for most companies that sell goods (as opposed to services) is the cost of goods sold. For Stoneham Auto Supplies, it amounts to 18 percent of net sales. Other expenses are treated in various ways by different companies. In our example, they are broken down into standard categories of selling expenses, administrative expenses, and general expenses.

The income statement shows that for Stoneham Auto Supplies, the cost of goods sold was $45,000. This figure was derived in the following way. First, the statement shows that merchandise in the amount of $51,000 was purchased during the year. In paying the invoices associated with these inventory additions, purchase (cash) discounts of $4,000 were earned, resulting in net purchases of $47,000. Special requests for selected merchandise throughout the year resulted in $2,000 in freight charges, which increased the net cost of delivered purchases to $49,000. When this amount is added to the beginning inventory of $48,000, the cost of goods available for sale during 2002 totals $97,000. However, the records indicate that the value of inventory at the end of the year was $52,000. Because this amount was not sold, the cost of goods that were sold during the year was $45,000.

Rose and Nick observe that the total value of their inventory increased by 8.3 percent during the year:

$$\frac{\$52,000 - \$48,000}{\$48,000} = \frac{\$4,000}{\$48,000} = \frac{1}{12} = .0825, \text{ or } 8.3\%$$

Further analysis is needed to determine whether this increase is desirable or undesirable. (Note that the income statement provides no details concerning the composition of the inventory held on December 31; other records supply this information.) If Nick and Rose determine that inventory on December 31 is excessive, they can implement appropriate marketing action.

Gross margin is the difference between net sales and cost of goods sold. Gross margin reflects the markup on products and is the amount available to pay all other expenses and provide a return to the owners. Stoneham Auto Supplies had a gross margin of $205,000:

Net sales	$250,000
Cost of goods sold	− 45,000
Gross margin	$205,000

Stoneham's expenses (other than cost of goods sold) during 2002 totaled $122,000. Observe that $53,000, or slightly more than 43 percent of the total, constituted direct selling expenses:

$$\frac{\$53,000 \text{ selling expenses}}{\$122,000 \text{ total expenses}} = .434, \text{ or } 43\%$$

The business employs three salespeople (one full time) and pays competitive wages. The selling expenses are similar to those in the previous year, but Nick and Rose wonder whether more advertising is necessary because the value of inventory increased by more than 8 percent during the year.

The administrative and general expenses are essential for operating the business. A comparison of these expenses with trade statistics for similar businesses indicates that the figures are in line with industry amounts.

Net income, or net profit, is the amount of gross margin remaining after deducting expenses. Stoneham Auto Supplies earned a net profit of $83,000 for the fiscal year ending December 31, 2002. Note that net income on this statement is figured before payment of state and federal income taxes.

Income statements for intermediaries and for businesses that provide services follow the same general format as that shown for Stoneham Auto Supplies in Table B.2. The income statement for a manufacturer, however, is somewhat different in that the "purchases" portion is replaced by "cost of goods manufactured." Table B.3 shows the entire Cost of Goods Sold section for a manufacturer, including cost of goods manufactured. In other respects, income statements for retailers and manufacturers are similar.

Performance Ratios

Rose and Nick's assessment of how well their business did during fiscal year 2002 can be improved through use of analytical ratios. Such ratios enable a manager to compare the results for the current year with data from previous years and industry statistics. However, comparisons of the current income statement with income statements and industry statistics from other years are not very meaningful because

Table B.3	Cost of Goods Sold for a Manufacturer

ABC Manufacturing
Income Statement for the Year Ended December 31, 2002

Cost of Goods Sold				$ 50,000
Finished goods inventory				
January 1, 2002				
Cost of goods manufactured				
Work-in-process inventory,				
January 1, 2002			$ 20,000	
Raw materials inventory,				
January 1, 2002	$ 40,000			
Net cost of delivered				
purchases	$240,000			
Cost of goods available				
for use	$280,000			
Less: Raw materials				
inventory,				
December 31, 2002	42,000			
Cost of goods placed in				
production		$238,000		
Direct labor		32,000		
Manufacturing overhead				
Indirect labor	$ 12,000			
Supervisory salaries	10,000			
Operating supplies	6,000			
Depreciation	12,000			
Utilities	$ 10,000			
Total manufacturing overhead		$ 50,000		
Total manufacturing costs			$320,000	
Total work-in-process			$340,000	
Less: Work-in-process				
inventory,				
December 31, 2002			22,000	
Cost of Goods Manufactured				$318,000
				$368,000
Cost of Goods Available for Sale				
Less: Finished goods inventory,				
December 31, 2002				48,000
Cost of Goods Sold				**$320,000**

factors like inflation are not accounted for when comparing dollar amounts. More meaningful comparisons can be made by converting these figures to a percentage of net sales, as this section shows.

The first analytical ratios we discuss, the operating ratios, are based on the net sales figure from the income statement.

Operating Ratios

Operating ratios express items on the income, or operating, statement as percentages of net sales. The first step is to convert the income statement into percentages of net sales, as illustrated in Table B.4.

Table B.4 Income Statement Components as Percentages of Net Sales

Stoneham Auto Supplies
Income Statement as a Percentage of Net Sales for the Year Ended December 31, 2002

			Percentage of Net Sales
Gross Sales			103.8%
Less: Sales returns and allowances			3.8
Net Sales			100.0%
Cost of Goods Sold			
Inventory, January 1, 2002 (at cost)		19.2%	
Purchases	20.4%		
Less: Purchase discounts	1.6		
Net purchases	18.8%		
Plus: Freight-in	0.8		
Net cost of delivered purchases		19.6	
Cost of goods available for sale		38.8%	
Less: Inventory, December 31, 2002 (at cost)		20.8	
Cost of goods sold			18.0
Gross Margin			82.0%
Expenses			
Selling expenses			
Sales salaries and commissions	12.8%		
Advertising	6.4		
Sales promotions	1.2		
Delivery	0.8		
Total selling expenses		21.2%	
Administrative expenses			
Administrative salaries	8.0%		
Office salaries	8.0		
Office supplies	0.8		
Miscellaneous	0.4		
Total administrative expenses		17.2%	
General expenses			
Rent	5.6%		
Utilities	2.8		
Bad debts	0.4		
Miscellaneous	1.6		
Total general expenses		10.4%	
Total expenses			48.8
Net Income			**33.2%**

After making this conversion, the manager looks at several key operating ratios: two profitability ratios (the gross margin ratio and the net income ratio) and the operating expense ratio.

For Stoneham Auto Supplies, these ratios are determined as follows (see Tables B.2 and B.4 for supporting data):

$$\text{Gross margin ratio} = \frac{\text{Gross margin}}{\text{Net sales}} = \frac{\$205{,}000}{\$250{,}000} = 82\%$$

$$\text{Net income ratio} = \frac{\text{Net income}}{\text{Net sales}} = \frac{\$83{,}000}{\$250{,}000} = 33.2\%$$

$$\text{Operating expenses ratio} = \frac{\text{Total expense}}{\text{Net sales}} = \frac{\$122{,}000}{\$250{,}000} = 48.8\%$$

The gross margin ratio indicates the percentage of each sales dollar available to cover operating expenses and achieve profit objectives. The net income ratio indicates the percentage of each sales dollar that is classified as earnings (profit) before payment of income taxes. The operating expense ratio indicates the percentage of each dollar needed to cover operating expenses.

If Nick and Rose believe the operating expense ratio is higher than historical data and industry standards, they can analyze each operating expense ratio in Table B.4 to determine which expenses are too high and then take corrective action.

After reviewing several key operating ratios, Nick and Rose, like many managers, will probably want to analyze all the items on the income statement. By doing so, they can determine whether the 8 percent increase in the value of their inventory was necessary.

Inventory Turnover Rate

The inventory turnover rate, or stockturn rate, is an analytical ratio that can be used to answer the question, "Is the inventory level appropriate for this business?" The inventory turnover rate indicates the number of times an inventory is sold (turns over) during one year. To be useful, this figure must be compared with historical turnover rates and industry rates.

The inventory turnover rate is computed (based on cost) as follows:

$$\text{Inventory turnover} = \frac{\text{Cost of goods sold}}{\text{Average inventory at cost}}$$

Rose and Nick would calculate the turnover rate from Table B.2 as follows:

$$\frac{\text{Cost of goods sold}}{\text{Average inventory at cost}} = \frac{\$45{,}000}{\$50{,}000} = 0.9 \text{ times}\%$$

Their inventory turnover is less than once per year (0.9 times). Industry averages for competitive firms are 2.8 times. This figure convinces Rose and Nick that their investment in inventory is too large and they need to reduce their inventory.

Return on Investment

Return on investment (ROI) is a ratio that indicates management's efficiency in generating sales and profits from the total amount invested in the firm. For Stoneham Auto Supplies, the ROI is 41.5 percent, which compares well with competing businesses.

We use figures from two different financial statements to arrive at ROI. The income statement, already discussed, gives us net income. The balance sheet, which states the firm's assets and liabilities at a given point in time, provides the figure for total assets (or investment) in the firm.

The basic formula for ROI is

$$\text{ROI} = \frac{\text{Net income}}{\text{Total investment}}$$

For Stoneham Auto Supplies, net income is $83,000 (see Table B.2). If total investment (taken from the balance sheet for December 31, 2002) is $200,000, then

$$\text{ROI} = \frac{\$83,000}{\$200,000} = 0.415, \text{ or } 41.5\%$$

The ROI formula can be expanded to isolate the impact of capital turnover and the operating income ratio separately. Capital turnover is a measure of net sales per dollar of investment; the ratio is figured by dividing net sales by total investment. For Stoneham Auto Supplies,

$$\text{Capital turnover} = \frac{\text{Net sales}}{\text{Total investment}} = \frac{\$250,000}{\$200,000} = 1.25$$

ROI is equal to capital turnover times the net income ratio. The expanded formula for Stoneham Auto Supplies is

$$\text{ROI} = \frac{\text{Net sales}}{\text{Total investment}} \times \frac{\text{Net income}}{\text{Net sales}}$$

$$= \frac{\$250,000}{\$200,000} \times \frac{\$83,000}{\$250,000}$$

$$= (1.25)(33.2\%) = 41.5\%$$

Price Calculations

An important step in setting prices is selecting a basis for pricing, as discussed in Chapter 21. The systematic use of markups, markdowns, and various conversion formulas helps in calculating the selling price and evaluating the effects of various prices.

Markups

As indicated in the text, markup is the difference between the selling price and the cost of the item; that is, selling price equals cost plus markup. The markup must cover cost and contribute to profit; thus, markup is similar to gross margin on the income statement.

Markup can be calculated on either cost or selling price as follows:

$$\frac{\text{Markup as percentage}}{\text{of cost}} = \frac{\text{Amount added to cost}}{\text{Cost}} = \frac{\text{Dollar markup}}{\text{Cost}}$$

$$\frac{\text{Markup as percentage}}{\text{of selling price}} = \frac{\text{Amount added to cost}}{\text{Selling price}} = \frac{\text{Dollar markup}}{\text{Selling price}}$$

Retailers tend to calculate the markup percentage on selling price.

To review the use of these markup formulas, assume an item costs $10 and the markup is $5:

$$\text{Selling price} = \text{Cost} + \text{Markup}$$
$$\$15 = \$10 + \$5$$

Thus,

$$\text{Markup percentage on cost} = \frac{\$5}{\$10} = 50\%$$

$$\text{Markup percentage on selling price} = \frac{\$5}{\$15} = 33\tfrac{1}{3}\%$$

It is necessary to know the base (cost or selling price) to use markup pricing effectively. Markup percentage on cost will always exceed markup percentage on price, given the same dollar markup, as long as selling price exceeds cost.

On occasion, we may need to convert markup on cost to markup on selling price, or vice versa. The conversion formulas are

$$\text{Markup percentage on selling price} = \frac{\text{Markup percentage on cost}}{100\% + \text{Markup percentage on cost}}$$

$$\text{Markup percentage on cost} = \frac{\text{Markup percentage on selling price}}{100\% - \text{Markup percentage on selling price}}$$

For example, if the markup percentage on cost is 33 1/3 percent, the markup percentage on selling price is

$$\frac{33\frac{1}{3}\%}{100\% + 33\frac{1}{3}\%} = \frac{33\frac{1}{3}\%}{133\frac{1}{3}\%} = 25\%$$

If the markup percentage on selling price is 40 percent, the corresponding percentage on cost is as follows:

$$\frac{40\%}{100\% - 40\%} = \frac{40\%}{60\%} = 66\frac{2}{3}\%$$

Finally, we can show how to determine selling price if we know the cost of the item and the markup percentage on selling price. Assume an item costs $36 and the usual markup percentage on selling price is 40 percent. Remember that selling price equals markup plus cost. Thus, if

$$100\% = 40\% \text{ of selling price} + \text{Cost}$$

then,

$$60\% \text{ of selling price} = \text{Cost}$$

In our example, cost equals $36. Therefore,

$$0.6X = \$36$$

$$X = \frac{\$36}{0.6}$$

$$\text{Selling price} = \$60$$

Alternatively, the markup percentage could be converted to a cost basis as follows:

$$\frac{40\%}{100\% - 40\%} = 66\frac{2}{3}\%$$

The computed selling price would then be as follows:

$$\text{Selling price} = 66\frac{2}{3}\%(\text{Cost}) + \text{Cost}$$
$$= 66\frac{2}{3}\% \ (\$36) + \$36$$
$$= \$24 + \$36 = \$60$$

If you keep in mind the basic formula—selling price equals cost plus markup—you will find these calculations straightforward.

Markdowns

Markdowns are price reductions a retailer makes on merchandise. Markdowns may be useful on items that are damaged, priced too high, or selected for a special sales event. The income statement does not express markdowns directly because the change in price is made before the sale takes place. Therefore, separate records of markdowns would be needed to evaluate the performance of various buyers and departments.

The markdown ratio (percentage) is calculated as follows:

$$\text{Markdown percentage} = \frac{\text{Dollar markdowns}}{\text{Net sales in dollars}}$$

In analyzing their inventory, Nick and Rose discover three special automobile jacks that have gone unsold for several months. They decide to reduce the price of each item from $25 to $20. Subsequently, these items are sold. The markdown percentage for these three items is

$$\text{Markdown percentage} = \frac{3(\$5)}{3(\$20)} = \frac{\$15}{\$60} = 25\%$$

Net sales, however, include all units of this product sold during the period, not just those marked down. If ten of these items were already sold at $25 each, in addition to the three items sold at $20, the overall markdown percentage would be

$$\text{Markdown percentage} = \frac{3(\$5)}{10(\$25) + 3(\$20)}$$

$$= \frac{\$15}{\$250 + \$60} = \frac{\$15}{\$310} = 4.8\%$$

Sales allowances are also a reduction in price. Thus, the markdown percentage should include any sales allowances. It would be computed as follows:

$$\text{Markdown percentage} = \frac{\text{Dollar markdowns} + \text{Dollar allowances}}{\text{Net sales in dollars}}$$

Discussion and Review Questions

1. How does a manufacturer's income statement differ from a retailer's income statement?
2. Use the following information to answer questions a through c:

TEA Company
Fiscal year ended June 30, 2002

Net sales	$500,000
Cost of goods sold	300,000
Net income	50,000
Average inventory at cost	100,000
Total assets (total investment)	200,000

a. What is the inventory turnover rate for TEA Company? From what sources will the marketing manager determine the significance of the inventory turnover rate?

b. What is the capital turnover ratio? What is the net income ratio? What is the return on investment (ROI)?

c. How many dollars of sales did each dollar of investment produce for TEA Company?

3. Product A has a markup percentage on cost of 40 percent. What is the markup percentage on selling price?

4. Product B has a markup percentage on selling price of 30 percent. What is the markup percentage on cost?

5. Product C has a cost of $60 and a usual markup percentage of 25 percent on selling price. What price should be placed on this item?

6. Apex Appliance Company sells 20 units of product Q for $100 each and 10 units for $80 each. What is the markdown percentage for product Q?

APPENDIX C Sample Marketing Plan

This sample marketing plan for a hypothetical company illustrates how the marketing planning process described in Chapter 2 might be implemented. If you are asked to create a marketing plan, this model may be a helpful guide, along with the concepts in Chapter 2.

1 The Executive Summary, one of the most frequently read components of a marketing plan, is a synopsis of the marketing plan. Although it does not provide detailed information, it does present an overview of the plan so readers can identify key issues pertaining to their roles in the planning and implementation processes. Although this is the first section in a marketing plan, it is usually written last.

2 The Environmental Analysis presents information regarding the organization's current situation with respect to the marketing environment, the current target market(s), and the firm's current marketing objectives and performance.

3 This section of the environmental analysis considers relevant external environmental forces such as competitive, economic, political, legal and regulatory, technological, and sociocultural forces.

Star Software, Inc. Marketing Plan

1 I. EXECUTIVE SUMMARY

Star Software, Inc., is a small, family-owned corporation in the first year of a transition from first-generation to second-generation leadership. Star Software sells custom-made calendar programs and related items to about 400 businesses, which use the software mainly for promotion. Star's 18 employees face scheduling challenges, as Star's business is highly seasonal, with its greatest demand during October, November, and December. In other months, the equipment and staff are sometimes idle. A major challenge facing Star Software is how to increase profits and make better use of its resources during the off-season.

An evaluation of the company's internal strengths and weaknesses and external opportunities and threats served as the foundation for this strategic analysis and marketing plan. The plan focuses on the company's growth strategy, suggesting ways in which it can build on existing customer relationships, and on the development of new products and/or services targeted to specific customer niches. Since Star Software markets a product used primarily as a promotional tool by its clients, it currently is considered a business-to-business marketer.

2 II. ENVIRONMENTAL ANALYSIS

Founded as a commercial printing company, Star Software, Inc., has evolved into a marketer of high-quality, custom-made calendar software and related business-to-business specialty items. In the mid-1960s, Bob McLemore purchased the company and, through his full-time commitment, turned it into a very successful family-run operation. In the near future, McLemore's 37-year-old son, Jonathan, will take over as Star Software's president and allow the elder McLemore to scale back his involvement.

3 A. *The Marketing Environment*

1. *Competitive forces.* The competition in the specialty advertising industry is very strong on a local and regional basis but somewhat weak nationally. Sales figures for the industry as a whole are difficult to obtain since very little business is conducted on a national scale.

   The competition within the calendar industry is strong in the paper segment and weak in the software-based segment. Currently paper calendars hold a dominant market share of approximately 90 percent; however, the software-

1

based segment is growing rapidly. The 10 percent market share held by software-based calendars is divided among many different firms. Star Software, which holds 30 percent of the software-based calendar market, is the only company that markets a software-based calendar on a national basis. As software-based calendars become more popular, additional competition is expected to enter the market.

2. *Economic forces.* Nationwide, many companies have reduced their overall promotion budgets as they face the need to cut expenses. However, most of these reductions have occurred in the budgets for mass media advertising (television, magazines, newspapers). While overall promotion budgets are shrinking, many companies are diverting a larger percentage of their budgets to sales promotion and specialty advertising. This trend is expected to continue as a weak, slow-growth economy forces most companies to focus more on the "value" they receive from their promotion dollar. Specialty advertising, such as can be done with a software-based calendar, provides this value.

3. *Political forces.* There are no expected political influences or events that could affect the operations of Star Software.

4. *Legal and regulatory forces.* In recent years, more attention has been paid to "junk mail." A large percentage of specialty advertising products are distributed by mail, and some of these products are considered "junk." Although this label is attached to the type of products Star Software makes, the problem of junk mail falls on the clients of Star Software and not on the company itself. While legislation may be introduced to curb the tide of advertising delivered through the mail, the fact that more companies are diverting their promotion dollars to specialty advertising indicates that most companies do not fear the potential for increased legislation.

5. *Technological forces.* A major emerging technological trend involves personal information managers (PIMs), or personal digital assistants (PDAs). A PDA is a handheld device, similar in size to a large calculator, that can store a wide variety of information, including personal notes, addresses, and a calendar. Some PDAs even have the ability to fax letters via microwave communication. As this trend continues, current software-based calendar products may have to be adapted to match the new technology.

6. *Sociocultural forces.* In today's society, consumers have less time for work or leisure. The hallmarks of today's successful products are convenience and ease of use. In short, if the product does not save time and is not easy to use, consumers will simply ignore it. Software-based calendars fit this consumer need quite well. A software-based calendar also fits in with other societal trends: a move to a paperless society, the need to automate repetitive tasks, and the growing dependence on computers, for example.

4 The analysis of current target markets assesses demographic, geographic, psychographic, and product usage characteristics of the target markets. It also assesses the current needs of each of the firm's target markets, anticipated changes in those needs, and how well the organization's current products are meeting those needs.

5 A company must set marketing objectives, measure performance against those objectives, and then take corrective action if needed.

4 *B. Target Market(s)*

By focusing on commitment to service and quality, Star Software has effectively implemented a niche differentiation strategy in a somewhat diverse marketplace. Its ability to differentiate its product has contributed to superior annual returns. Its target market consists of manufacturers or manufacturing divisions of large corporations that move their products through dealers, distributors, or brokers. Its most profitable product is a software program for a PC-based calendar, which can be tailored to meet client needs by means of artwork, logos, and text. Clients use this calendar software as a promotional tool, providing a disk to their customers as an advertising premium. The calendar software is not produced for resale.

The calendar software began as an ancillary product to Star's commercial printing business. However, due to the proliferation of PCs and the growth in technology, the computer calendar soon became more profitable for Star than its wall and desktop paper calendars. This led to the sale of the commercial printing plant and equipment to employees. Star Software has maintained a long-term relationship with these former employees, who have added capabilities to reproduce computer disks and whose company serves as Star's primary supplier of finished goods. Star's staff focuses on the further development and marketing of the software.

C. Current Marketing Objectives and Performance

Star Software's sales representatives call on potential clients and, using a template demonstration disk, help them create a calendar concept. Once the sale has been finalized, Star completes the concept, including design, copywriting, and customization of the demonstration disk. Specifications are then sent to the supplier, located about a thousand miles away, where the disks are produced. Perhaps what most differentiates Star from its competitors is its high level of service. Disks can be shipped to any location the buyer specifies. Since product development and customization of this type can require significant amounts of time and effort, particularly during the product's first year, Star deliberately pursues a strategy of steady, managed growth.

Star Software markets its products on a company-specific basis. It has an approximate 90 percent annual reorder rate and an average customer-reorder relationship of about eight years. The first year in dealing with a new customer is the most stressful and time consuming for Star's salespeople and product developers. The subsequent years are faster and significantly more profitable.

5 The company is currently debt free except for the mortgage on its facility. However, about 80 percent of its accounts receivable are billed during the last three months of the calendar year. Seasonal account billings, along with the added travel of its sales staff during the peak season, pose a special challenge to the company.

3

The need for cash to fund operations in the meantime makes it necessary for the company to borrow significant amounts of money to cover the period until customer billing occurs.

Star Software's marketing objectives include increases in both revenues and profits of approximately 10 percent over the previous year. Revenues should exceed $4 million, and profits are expected to reach $1.3 million.

III. SWOT ANALYSIS

6 Strengths are competitive advantages or core competencies that give the organization an advantage in meeting the needs of its customers.

6 A. Strengths

1. Star Software's product differentiation strategy is the result of a strong marketing orientation, commitment to high quality, and customization of products and support services.

2. There is little turnover among employees who are well compensated and liked by customers. The relatively small size of the staff promotes camaraderie with coworkers and clients, and fosters communication and quick response to clients' needs.

3. A long-term relationship with the primary supplier has resulted in shared knowledge of the product's requirements, adherence to quality standards, and a common vision throughout the development and production process.

4. The high percentage of reorder business suggests a satisfied customer base, as well as positive word-of-mouth communication, which generates some 30 percent of new business each year.

7 Weaknesses are limitations a firm has in developing or implementing a marketing strategy.

7 B. Weaknesses

1. The highly centralized management hierarchy (the McLemores) and lack of managerial backup may impede creativity and growth. Too few people hold too much knowledge.

2. Despite the successful, long-term relationship with the supplier, single-sourcing could make Star Software vulnerable in the event of a natural disaster, strike, or dissolution of the current supplier. Contingency plans for suppliers should be considered.

3. The seasonal nature of the product line creates bottlenecks in productivity and cash flow, places excessive stress on personnel, and strains the facilities.

4. Both the product line and the client base lack diversification. Dependence on current reorder rates could breed complacency, invite competition, or create a

4

false sense of customer satisfaction. The development of a product that would make the software calendar obsolete would probably put Star out of business.

5. While the small size of the staff fosters camaraderie, it also impedes growth and new-business development.

6. Star Software is reactive rather than assertive in its marketing efforts because of its heavy reliance on positive word-of-mouth communication for obtaining new business.

7. Star's current facilities are crowded. There is little room for additional employees or new equipment.

8

Opportunities are favorable conditions in the environment that could yield rewards for an organization if acted on properly.

8 C. Opportunities

1. Advertising expenditures in the United States exceed $132 billion annually. More than $25 billion of this is spent on direct-mail advertising, and another $20 billion is spent on specialty advertising. The potential for Star Software's growth is significant in this market.

2. Technological advances have not only freed up time for Americans and brought greater efficiency but also have increased the amount of stress in their fast-paced lives. Personal computers have become commonplace, and personal information managers have gained popularity.

3. As U.S. companies look for ways to develop customer relationships rather than just close sales, reminders of this relationship could come in the form of acceptable premiums or gifts that are useful to the customer.

4. Computer-based calendars are easily distributed nationally and globally. The globalization of business creates an opportunity to establish new client relationships in foreign markets.

9

Threats are conditions or barriers that may prevent the organization from reaching its objectives.

9 D. Threats

1. Reengineering, right-sizing, and outsourcing trends in management may alter traditional channel relationships with brokers, dealers, and distributors or eliminate them altogether.

2. Calendars are basically a generic product. The technology, knowledge, and equipment required to produce such an item, even a computer-based one, are minimal. The possible entry of new competitors is a significant threat.

3. Theft of trade secrets and software piracy through unauthorized copying are difficult to control.

5

4. Specialty advertising through promotional items relies on gadgetry and ideas that are new and different. As a result, product life cycles may be quite short.

5. Single-sourcing can be detrimental or even fatal to a company if the buyer-supplier relationship is damaged or if the supplying company has financial difficulty.

6. Competition from traditional paper calendars and other promotional items is strong.

(10) **E. Matching Strengths to Opportunities/
Converting Weaknesses and Threats**

1. The acceptance of technological advances and the desire to control time create a potential need for a computer-based calendar.

2. Star Software has more opportunity for business growth during its peak season than it can presently handle because of resource (human and capital) constraints.

3. Star Software must modify its management hierarchy, empowering its employees through a more decentralized marketing organization.

4. Star Software should discuss future growth strategies with its supplier and develop contingency plans to deal with unforeseen events. Possible satellite facilities in other geographic locations should be explored.

5. Star Software should consider diversifying its product line to satisfy new market niches and develop nonseasonal products.

6. Star Software should consider surveying its current customers and its customers' clients to gain a better understanding of their changing needs and desires.

(11) **IV. MARKETING OBJECTIVES**

Star Software, Inc., is in the business of helping other companies market their products and/or services. Besides formulating a marketing-oriented and customer-focused mission statement, Star Software should establish an objective to achieve cumulative growth in net profit of at least 50 percent over the next five years. At least half of this 50 percent growth should come from new, nonmanufacturing customers and from products that are nonseasonal or that are generally delivered in the off-peak period of the calendar cycle.

10 During the development of a marketing plan, marketers attempt to match internal strengths to external opportunities. In addition, they try to convert internal weaknesses into strengths and external threats into opportunities.

11 The development of marketing objectives is based on environmental analysis, SWOT analysis, the firm's overall corporate objectives, and the organization's resources. For each objective, this section should answer the question, "What is the specific and measurable outcome and time frame for completing this objective?"

To accomplish its marketing objectives, Star Software should develop benchmarks to measure progress. Regular reviews of these objectives will provide feedback and possible corrective actions on a timely basis. The major marketing objective is to gain a better understanding of the needs and satisfaction of current customers. Since Star Software is benefiting from a 90 percent reorder rate, it must be satisfying its current customers. Star could use the knowledge of its successes with current clients to market to new customers. To capitalize on its success with current clients, benchmarks should be established to learn how Star can improve the products it now offers through knowledge of its clients' needs and specific opportunities for new product offerings. These benchmarks should be determined through marketing research and Star's marketing information system.

Another objective should be to analyze the billing cycle Star now uses to determine if there are ways to bill accounts receivable in a more evenly distributed manner throughout the year. Alternatively, repeat customers might be willing to place orders at off-peak cycles in return for discounts or added customer services.

Star Software also should create new products that can utilize its current equipment, technology, and knowledge base. It should conduct simple research and analyses of similar products or product lines with an eye toward developing specialty advertising products that are software based but not necessarily calendar related.

V. MARKETING STRATEGIES

(12) A. Target Market(s)

Target market 1: Large manufacturers or stand-alone manufacturing divisions of large corporations with extensive broker, dealer, or distributor networks

> *Example:* An agricultural chemical producer, such as Dow Chemical, distributes its products to numerous rural "feed and seed" dealers. Customizing calendars with Chicago Board of Trade futures or USDA agricultural report dates would be beneficial to these potential clients.

Target market 2: Nonmanufacturing, nonindustrial segments of the business-to-business market with extensive customer networks, such as banks, medical services, or financial planners

> *Example:* Various sporting goods manufacturers distribute to specialty shop dealers. Calendars could be customized to the particular sport, such as golf (with PGA, Virginia Slims, or other tour dates), running (with various national marathon dates), or bowling (with national tour dates).

12 The marketing plan clearly specifies and describes the target market(s) toward which the organization will aim its marketing efforts. The difference between this section and the earlier section covering target markets is that the earlier section deals with present target markets, whereas this section looks at future target markets.

Target market 3:   Direct consumer markets for brands with successful licensing arrangements for consumer products, such as Coca-Cola

> *Example:* Products with major brand recognition and fan club membership, such as Harley-Davidson motorcycles or the Bloomington Gold Corvette Association, could provide additional markets for customized computer calendars. Brands with licensing agreements for consumer products could provide a market for consumer computer calendars in addition to the specialty advertising product, which would be marketed to the manufacturer/dealer.

Target market 4:   Industry associations that regularly hold or sponsor trade shows, meetings, conferences, or conventions

> *Example:* National associations, such as the National Dairy Association or the American Marketing Association, frequently host meetings or annual conventions. Customized calendars could be developed for any of these groups.

13 **B. *Marketing Mix***

> **13** Though the marketing mix section in this plan is abbreviated, this component should provide considerable details regarding each element of the marketing mix: product, price, distribution, and promotion.

1. *Products.* Star Software markets not only calendar software but also the service of specialty advertising to its clients. Star's intangible attributes are its ability to meet or exceed customer expectations consistently, its speed in responding to customers' demands, and its anticipation of new customer needs. Intangible attributes are difficult for competitors to copy, thereby giving Star Software a competitive advantage.

2. *Price.* Star Software provides a high-quality specialty advertising product customized to its clients' needs. The value of this product and service is reflected in its premium price. Star should be sensitive to the price elasticity of its product and overall consumer demand.

3. *Distribution.* Star Software uses direct marketing. Since its product is compact, lightweight, and nonperishable, it can be shipped from a central location direct to the client via United Parcel Service, FedEx, or the U.S. Postal Service. The fact that Star can ship to multiple locations for each customer is an asset in selling its products.

4. *Promotion.* Since 90 percent of Star's customers reorder each year, the bulk of promotional expenditures should focus on new product offerings through direct-mail advertising and trade journals or specialty publications. Any remaining promotional dollars could be directed to personal selling (in the form of sales performance bonuses) of current and new products.

8

VI. MARKETING IMPLEMENTATION

14 ### A. Marketing Organization

14 This section of the marketing plan details how the firm will be organized—by functions, products, regions, or types of customers—to implement its marketing strategies. It also indicates where decision-making authority will rest within the marketing unit.

Because Star's current and future products require extensive customization to match clients' needs, it is necessary to organize the marketing function by customer groups. This will allow Star to focus its marketing efforts exclusively on the needs and specifications of each target customer segment. Star's marketing efforts will be organized around the following customer groups: (1) manufacturing group; (2) non-manufacturing, business-to-business group; (3) consumer product licensing group; and (4) industry associations group. Each group will be headed by a sales manager who will report to the marketing director (these positions must be created). Each group is responsible for the marketing of Star's products within that customer segment. In addition, each group will have full decision-making authority. This represents a shift from the current highly centralized management hierarchy. Frontline salespeople will be empowered to make decisions that will better satisfy Star's clients.

These changes in marketing organization will enable Star Software to be more creative and flexible in meeting customers' needs. Likewise, these changes will overcome the current lack of diversification in Star's product lines and client base. Finally, this new marketing organization will give Star a better opportunity to monitor the activities of competitors.

15 ### B. Activities, Responsibility, and Timetables for Completion

15 This component of the marketing plan outlines the specific activities required to implement the marketing plan, who is responsible for performing these activities, and when these activities should be accomplished based on a specified schedule.

All implementation activities are to begin at the start of the next fiscal year on April 1. Unless specified, all activities are the responsibility of Star Software's next president, Jonathan McLemore.

- On April 1, create four sales manager positions and the position of marketing director. The marketing director will serve as project leader of a new business analysis team, to be composed of nine employees from a variety of positions within the company.

- By April 15, assign three members of the analysis team to each of the following projects: (1) research potential new product offerings and clients, (2) analyze the current billing cycle and billing practices, and (3) design a customer survey project. The marketing director is responsible.

- By June 30, the three project groups will report the results of their analyses. The full business analysis team will review all recommendations.

- By July 31, develop a marketing information system to monitor client reorder patterns and customer satisfaction.

- By July 31, implement any changes in billing practices as recommended by the business analysis team.

- By July 31, make initial contact with new potential clients for the current product line. Each sales manager is responsible.

- By August 31, develop a plan for one new product offering along with an analysis of its potential customers. The business analysis team is responsible.

- By August 31, finalize a customer satisfaction survey for current clients. In addition, the company will contact those customers who did not reorder for the 2001 product year to discuss their concerns. The marketing director is responsible.

- By January, implement the customer satisfaction survey with a random sample of 20 percent of current clients who reordered for the 2001 product year. The marketing director is responsible.

- By February, implement a new product offering, advertising to current customers and to a sample of potential clients. The business analysis team is responsible.

- By March, analyze and report the results of all customer satisfaction surveys and evaluate the new product offering. The marketing director is responsible.

- Reestablish the objectives of the business analysis team for the next fiscal year. The marketing director is responsible.

(16) VII. EVALUATION AND CONTROL

A. Performance Standards and Financial Controls

A comparison of the financial expenditures with the plan goals will be included in the project report. The following performance standards and financial controls are suggested:

- The total budget for the billing analysis, new-product research, and the customer survey will be equal to 60 percent of the annual promotional budget for the coming year.

- The breakdown of the budget within the project will be a 20 percent allocation to the billing cycle study, a 30 percent allocation to the customer survey and marketing information system development, and a 50 percent allocation to new-business development and new-product implementation.

- Each project team is responsible for reporting all financial expenditures, including personnel salaries and direct expenses, for their segment of the project. A standardized reporting form will be developed and provided by the marketing director.

16 This section details how the results of the marketing plan will be measured and evaluated. The control portion of this section includes the types of actions the firm can take to reduce the differences between the planned and the actual performance.

10

- The marketing director is responsible for adherence to the project budget and will report overages to the company president on a weekly basis. The marketing director also is responsible for any redirection of budget dollars, as required for each project of the business analysis team.

- Any new product offering will be evaluated on a quarterly basis to determine its profitability. Product development expenses will be distributed over a two-year period, by calendar quarters, and will be compared with gross income generated during the same period.

B. Monitoring Procedures

To analyze the effectiveness of Star Software's marketing plan, it is necessary to compare its actual performance with plan objectives. To facilitate this analysis, monitoring procedures should be developed for the various activities required to bring the marketing plan to fruition. These procedures include, but are not limited to, the following:

- A project management concept will be used to evaluate the implementation of the marketing plan by establishing time requirements, human resource needs, and financial or budgetary expenditures.

- A perpetual comparison of actual and planned activities will be conducted on a monthly basis for the first year and on a quarterly basis after the initial implementation phase. The business analysis team, including the marketing director, will report their comparison of actual and planned outcomes directly to the company president.

- Each project team is responsible for determining what changes must be made in procedures, product focus, or operations as a result of the studies conducted in its area.

Glossary

Accessibility   The ability to obtain the information available on the Internet. (23)

Accessory equipment   Equipment used in production or office activities; does not become a part of the final physical product. (10)

Addressability   A marketer's ability to identify customers before they make a purchase. (23)

Advertising   A paid form of nonpersonal communication about an organization and/or its products that is transmitted to a target audience through a mass medium. (18)

Advertising appropriation   The total amount of money a marketer allocates for advertising for a specific time period. (18)

Advertising campaign   The creation and execution of a series of advertisements to communicate with a particular target audience. (18)

Advertising platform   The basic issues or selling points that an advertiser wishes to include in the advertising campaign. (18)

Advocacy advertising   A form of advertising promoting a company's position on a public issue. (18)

Aesthetic modification   Changing the sensory appeal of a product by altering its taste, texture, sound, smell, or visual characteristics. (11)

Agents   Functional intermediaries representing buyers or sellers on a permanent basis. (15)

Aided recall test   A posttest method of evaluating the effectiveness of advertising in which respondents are asked to identify advertisements they have seen recently; they are shown a list of products, brands, company names, or trademarks to jog their memory. (18)

Allowance   A concession in price to achieve a desired goal. (20)

APEC   An alliance that promotes open trade and economic and technical cooperation among member nations throughout the world. (5)

Approach   The manner in which a salesperson contacts a potential customer. (19)

Arbitrary approach   A method for determining the advertising appropriation in which a high-level executive states how much the firm should spend on advertising for a certain time period. (18)

Artwork   The illustration in an advertisement and layout of the advertisement's components. (18)

Atmospherics   The physical elements in a store's design that appeal to consumers' emotions and encourage buying. (16)

Attitude   An individual's enduring evaluation, feelings, and behavioral tendencies toward an object or idea. (8)

Attitude scale   A means of measuring consumer attitudes, usually consisting of a series of adjectives, phrases, or sentences about an object; respondents are asked to indicate the intensity of their feelings toward the object by reacting to the statements in a certain way. (8)

Automatic vending   The use of machines to dispense products selected by customers when they insert money. (16)

Average fixed cost   The fixed cost per unit produced; calculated by dividing fixed costs by number of units produced. (20)

Average total cost   The sum of average fixed cost and average variable cost. (20)

Average variable cost   The variable cost per unit produced; calculated by dividing variable cost by number of units produced. (20)

Bait pricing   Pricing an item low with the intention of selling a higher-priced item in the same product line. (21)

Balance of trade   The difference in value between a nation's exports and its imports. (5)

Banner ads   Small, rectangular ads, static or animated, that typically appear at the top of a webpage. (23)

Barter   The trading of products. (20)

Base-point pricing   A geographic pricing policy that includes the price at the factory, plus freight charges from the base point nearest the buyer. (20)

Benchmarking   The measurement and evaluation of the quality of an organization's goods, services, or processes as compared with the best-performing companies in the industry. (22)

Benefit segmentation   The division of a market according to benefits that customers want from the product. (7)

Better Business Bureau   A local, nongovernmental regulatory agency, supported by local businesses, that aids in settling problems between specific business firms and customers. (3)

Brand   A name, term, symbol, design, or combination of these that identifies a seller's products and differentiates them from competitors' products. (12)

Brand competitors   Firms that market products with similar features, benefits, and prices to the same customers. (3)

Brand equity   The marketing and financial value associated with a brand's strength in the market, including actual proprietary brand assets, brand name awareness, brand loyalty, perceived brand quality, and brand associations. (12)

Brand-extension branding   A type of branding in which a firm uses one of its existing brand names as part of a brand for an improved or new product that is usually in the same product category as the existing brand. (12)

Brand insistence   The strongest degree of brand loyalty, in which a customer prefers a specific brand so strongly that he or she will accept no substitute. (12)

Brand licensing   An agreement by which a company permits another organization to use its brand on products for a licensing fee. (12)

Brand loyalty   A customer's favorable attitude toward a brand and likelihood of consistent purchase. (12)

Brand manager A type of product manager responsible for a single brand. (9, 11)

Brand mark The element of a brand, such as a symbol or design, that cannot be spoken. (12)

Brand name The part of a brand that can be spoken, including letters, words, and numbers. (12)

Brand preference A degree of customer loyalty in which a customer prefers one brand to competitive offerings and will purchase the brand if it is available but will accept substitutes if it is not. (12)

Brand recognition Awareness that a brand exists and can be a purchase alternative. (12)

Breakdown approach A general approach for measuring company sales potential based on a general economic forecast and the market sales potential derived from it; the company sales potential is based on the general economic forecast and the estimated market sales potential. (7)

Breakeven point The point at which the costs of producing a product equal the revenue made from selling the product. (20)

Brokers Functional intermediaries that bring buyers and sellers together temporarily and help negotiate exchanges. (15)

Buildup approach A general approach to measuring company sales potential in which the analyst initially estimates how much the average purchaser of a product will buy in a specified time period and then multiplies that amount by the number of potential buyers; estimates are calculated by individual geographic areas. (7)

Bundle pricing Packaging two or more usually complementary products together for a single price. (21)

Business analysis An analysis providing a tentative sketch of a product's compatibility in the marketplace, including its potential profitability. (11)

Business (organizational) buying behavior The purchase behavior of producers, government units, institutions, and resellers; also called *industrial buying behavior*. (9)

Business cycle Fluctuations in the economy following a general pattern of prosperity, recession, depression, and recovery. (3)

Business (industrial) market Individuals or groups that purchase a specific kind of product for resale, direct use in producing other products, or use in general daily operations. (7, 9)

Business products Products bought to use in a firm's operations, to sell, or to make other products. (10)

Business services Intangible products an organization uses in its operations, such as financial products or legal services. (10)

Business-to-business buying behavior *See* Business buying behavior.

Business-to-business markets Markets consisting of individuals, groups, or organizations that purchase specific kinds of products for resale, for direct use in producing other products, or for use in day-to-day operations; also called *organizational markets*. (7)

Button ads Small ads, square or rectangular, bearing a corporate or brand name or logo and usually appearing at the bottom of a webpage. (23)

Buy-back allowance A sum of money given to a reseller for each unit bought after an initial promotion deal is over. (19)

Buying allowance A temporary price reduction to resellers for purchasing specified quantities of a product. (19)

Buying behavior The decision processes and acts of people involved in buying and using products. (8)

Buying center The group of people within an organization who make business purchase decisions; these people take part in the purchase decision process as users, influencers, buyers, deciders, and gatekeepers. (9)

Buying power Resources, such as money, goods, and services, that can be traded in an exchange situation. (3)

Captioned photograph A photograph with a brief description that explains the picture's content. (18)

Captive pricing Pricing the basic product in a product line low but pricing related items higher. (21)

Cash-and-carry wholesalers Limited-service wholesalers whose customers pay cash and furnish transportation. (15)

Cash discount A price reduction to the buyer for prompt payment or cash payment. (20)

Catalog marketing A type of marketing in which an organization provides a catalog from which customers make selections and place orders by mail, telephone, or the Internet. (16)

Catalog showroom A form of warehouse showroom in which consumers shop from a catalog and buy the products at a warehouse. (16)

Category killer A large specialty store that concentrates on a major product category and competes on the basis of low prices and product availability. (16)

Causal research Research in which it is assumed that a particular variable X causes a variable Y. (6)

Cause-related marketing Linking a firm's products to a particular social cause on an ongoing or short-term basis. (4)

Centralized organization An organization in which top-level managers delegate very little authority to lower levels. (22)

Cents-off offer A sales promotion device for established products whereby buyers receive a certain amount off the regular price shown on the label or package. (19)

Channel capacity The limit on the volume of information that a communication channel can handle effectively. (17)

Channel captain The dominant member of a marketing channel or supply chain. (14)

Channel of distribution *See* Marketing channel.

Channel power The ability of one channel member to influence another channel member's goal achievement. (14)

Click-through rate The percentage of ads that website visitors actually click on. (23)

Client-based relationships Interactions that result in satisfied customers who use a service repeatedly over time. (13)

Client publics The direct consumers of the product of a nonbusiness organization; for example, the client public of a university is its student body. (13)

Closing The part of the selling process in which the salesperson asks the prospect to buy the product. (19)

Co-branding The use of two or more brands on one product. (12)

Codes of conduct Formalized rules and standards that describe what a company expects of its employees. (4)

Coding process The process by which a meaning is placed into a series of signs that represents ideas; also called *encoding*. (17)

Cognitive dissonance Doubts that may occur shortly after the purchase of a product when the buyer questions whether or not he or she made the right decision. (8)

Combination compensation plan A plan by which salespeople are paid a fixed salary and a commission based on sales volume. (19)

Commercialization A phase of new-product development in which plans for full-scale manufacturing and marketing must be refined and settled and budgets for the product prepared. (11)

Commission merchants Agents that receive goods on consignment and negotiate sales in large markets. (15)

Communication A sharing of meaning through the transmission of information. (17)

Community A sense of group membership or feeling of belonging by individual group members. (23)

Community shopping centers Shopping centers that include one or two department stores and some specialty stores, as well as convenience stores, which serve several neighborhoods and draw consumers who cannot find desired products in neighborhood shopping centers. (16)

Company sales potential The maximum percentage of market potential that an individual firm within an industry can expect to obtain for a specific product. (7)

Comparative advertising Advertising that compares two or more identified brands in the same general product class in terms of one or more specific product characteristics. (18)

Comparison discounting Pricing a product at a specific level and comparing it to a higher price. (21)

Competition Organizations marketing products that are similar to or can be substituted for a marketer's products in the same geographic area. (3)

Competition-based pricing A pricing method in which an organization considers costs and revenues secondary to competitors' prices. (21)

Competition-matching approach A method of ascertaining the advertising appropriation in which an advertiser tries to match a major competitor's appropriations in absolute dollars or in using the same percentage of sales for advertising. (18)

Competitive advantage The result of a company's matching a core competency to the opportunities it has discovered in the marketplace. (2)

Competitive advertising Advertising that points out a brand's uses, features, and advantages that benefit consumers but may not be available in competing brands. (18)

Component parts Finished items ready for assembly or products that need little processing before assembly and become a part of the physical product. (10)

Concentrated targeting strategy A market segmentation strategy in which an organization directs its marketing efforts toward a single market segment through one marketing mix. (7)

Concept testing The stage in the product development process in which initial buying intentions and attitudes regarding a product are determined by presenting a written or oral description of the product to a sample of potential buyers and obtaining their responses. (11)

Consideration set A group of brands in a product category that a buyer views as alternatives for possible purchase. (8)

Consistency of quality The ability of a product to provide the same level of quality over time. (11)

Consumer buying behavior Buying behavior of people who purchase products for personal or household use and not for business purposes. (8)

Consumer buying decision process A five-stage purchase decision process that includes problem recognition, information search, evaluation of alternatives, purchase, and postpurchase evaluation. (8)

Consumer contests and games Sales promotion devices for established products based on the analytical or creative skill of contestants. (19)

Consumerism Organized efforts by individuals, groups, and organizations seeking to protect consumers' rights. (3)

Consumer jury A panel used to pretest advertisements; consists of a number of actual or potential buyers of the product to be advertised. (18)

Consumer market Purchasers and/or household members who intend to consume or benefit from the purchased products and do not buy products for the main purpose of making profits. (7)

Consumer products Products purchased for the ultimate satisfaction of personal and family needs. (10)

Consumer sales promotion methods A category of sales promotion techniques that encourages or stimulates customers to patronize a specific retail store or to try and/or purchase a particular product. (19)

Consumer socialization The process through which a person acquires the knowledge and skills to function as a consumer. (8)

Consumer sweepstakes A sales promotion device for established products in which entrants submit their names for inclusion in a drawing for prizes. (19)

Contract manufacturing The practice of hiring a foreign firm to produce a designated volume of a firm's product to specification; the final product carries the domestic firm's name. (5)

Control Customers' ability to regulate the information they view as well as the rate and sequence of their exposure to that information. (23)

Convenience products Relatively inexpensive, frequently purchased items that buyers want to exert only minimal effort to obtain. (10)

Cookie An identifying string of text stored on a website visitor's computer that allows the sender to track website usage. (23)

Cooperative advertising An arrangement in which a manufacturer agrees to pay a certain amount of a retailer's media costs for advertising the manufacturer's products. (19)

Copy The verbal portion of advertisements; includes headlines, subheadlines, body copy, and signature. (18)

Core competencies Things a firm does extremely well, which sometimes give the firm a competitive advantage. (2)

Corporate culture *See* Organizational culture.

Corporate strategy A strategy that determines the means for utilizing resources in the areas of production, finance, research and development, human resources, and marketing to reach the organization's goals. (2)

Cost-based pricing   A pricing policy in which a firm determines price by adding a dollar amount or percentage to the cost of the product. (21)

Cost comparison indicator   Allows an advertiser to compare the costs of several vehicles within a specific medium relative to the number of people reached by each vehicle. (18)

Cost-plus pricing   A form of pricing in which the seller's costs are determined and then a specified dollar amount or percentage of the cost is added to the seller's cost to set the price. (21)

Count-and-recount   A sales promotion method based on payment of a specific amount for each product unit moved from a reseller's warehouse in a given period of time. (19)

Coupons   A product sales promotion technique used to reduce a product's price and prompt trial of a new or improved product, increase sales volume quickly, attract repeat purchasers, or introduce new package sizes or features. (19)

Credence qualities   Qualities of services that cannot be assessed even after purchase and consumption. (13)

Culture   The accumulation of values, knowledge, beliefs, customs, objects, and concepts that a society uses to cope with its environment and passes on to future generations. (8)

Cumulative discount   A quantity discount that is aggregated over a stated period of time. (20)

Customary pricing   A type of psychological pricing in which certain goods are priced primarily on the basis of tradition. (21)

Customer(s)   The purchaser(s) of the products that organizations develop, promote, distribute, and price. (1)

Customer contact   The level of interaction between service provider and customer necessary to deliver the service. (13)

Customer forecasting survey   The technique of asking customers what types and quantities of products they intend to buy during a specific period in order to predict the sales level for that period. (7)

Customer relationship management (CRM)   Using information about customers to create marketing strategies that develop and sustain desirable customer relationships. (1)

Customer service audit   A specialized audit in which specific consumer service activities are analyzed and service goals and standards are compared to actual performance. (22)

Customer services   Anything a company provides in addition to the product that adds value and builds relationships with customers. (11)

Cycle analysis   A method of predicting sales by analyzing sales figures for a period of three to five years to ascertain whether sales fluctuate in a consistent, periodic manner. (7)

Cycle time   The time it takes to complete a process. (15)

Database   A collection of information arranged for easy access and retrieval. (6)

Dealer brand   *See* Private distributor brand.

Dealer listing   An advertisement that promotes a product and identifies the names of participating retailers that sell the product. (19)

Dealer loader   A gift, often part of a display, given to a retailer purchasing a specified quantity of merchandise. (19)

Decentralized organization   An organization in which decision-making authority is delegated as far down the chain of command as possible. (22)

Decline stage   The stage in a product's life cycle in which sales fall rapidly. (10)

Decoding process   The stage in the communication process in which signs are converted into concepts and ideas. (17)

Delphi technique   A procedure in which experts create initial forecasts, submit them to the company for averaging, and have the results returned to them so that they can make individual refined forecasts. (7)

Demand-based pricing   A pricing policy based on the level of demand for the product, resulting in a higher price for the product when demand is strong and a lower price when demand is weak. (21)

Demand curve   A graph showing the relationship between price and quantity demanded. (20)

Demonstrations   A sales promotion method manufacturers use temporarily to encourage trial use and purchase of the product or to show how the product works. (19)

Department stores   Large retail organizations characterized by wide product mixes and organized into separate departments to facilitate marketing efforts and internal management. (16)

Depression   A stage of the business cycle during which unemployment is extremely high, wages are very low, total disposable income is at a minimum, and consumers lack confidence in the economy. (3)

Depth of product mix   The average number of different products offered to buyers in a firm's product lines. (10)

Derived demand   A characteristic of business demand that arises because industrial demand stems from the demand for consumer products. (9)

Descriptive research   Research conducted to clarify the characteristics of certain phenomena to solve a particular problem. (6)

Differential pricing   Charging different prices to different buyers for the same quantity of product. (21)

Differentiated targeting strategy   A targeting strategy in which an organization directs its marketing efforts at two or more segments by developing a marketing mix for each segment. (7)

Digitalization   The representation of a product, or at least some of its benefits, as digital bits of information, or using the Internet to distribute, promote, and sell product features apart from the physical item itself. (23)

Direct-cost approach   An approach to determining marketing costs in which cost analysis includes variable costs and traceable common costs but not nontraceable common costs. (22)

Direct marketing   The use of the telephone and nonpersonal media to introduce products to consumers, who can then purchase them by mail, telephone, or the Internet. (15)

Direct ownership   A situation in which a company owns subsidiaries or other facilities overseas. (5)

Direct-response marketing   A type of marketing that occurs when a retailer advertises a product and makes it available through mail or telephone orders. (16)

Direct selling   The marketing of products to ultimate consumers through face-to-face sales presentations at home or in the workplace. (16)

Discount stores Self-service, general-merchandise stores offering brand name and private brand products at low prices. (16)

Discretionary income Disposable income available for spending and saving after an individual has purchased the basic necessities of food, clothing, and shelter. (3)

Disposable income The amount of money left after payment of taxes. (3)

Distribution The activities that make products available to customers when and where they want to purchase them. (14)

Distribution centers Large, centralized warehouses that receive goods from factories and suppliers, regroup the goods into orders, and ship the orders to customers quickly, with the focus on movement of goods rather than storage. (15)

Diversified growth Growth that occurs when new products are developed to be sold in new markets. (2)

Drop shippers Limited-service wholesalers that take title to products and negotiate sales but never actually take possession of products; also known as *desk jobbers*. (15)

Dual distribution The use of two or more channels to distribute the same product to the same target market. (14)

Dumping Selling products at unfairly low prices. (5)

Early adopters Individuals who choose new products carefully and are viewed by individuals in the early majority, late majority, and laggard categories as being "the people to check with." (10)

Early majority Individuals who adopt a new product just prior to the average person; they are deliberate and cautious in trying new products. (10)

Electronic commerce (e-commerce) The sharing of business information, maintenance of business relationships, and conduct of business transactions by means of telecommunications networks. (23)

Electronic data interchange (EDI) A means of integrating order processing with production, inventory, accounting, and transportation. (15)

Electronic marketing (e-marketing) The strategic process of creating, distributing, promoting, and pricing products for targeted customers in the virtual environment of the Internet. (23)

Embargo Government suspension of trade of a particular product or within a given country. (5)

Empowerment Giving frontline employees the authority and responsibility to make marketing decisions without seeking the approval of their supervisors. (22)

Encoding *See* Coding process.

Environmental analysis The process of assessing and interpreting the information gathered through environmental scanning. (3)

Environmental scanning The process of collecting information about the forces in the marketing environment. (3)

Ethical issue An identifiable problem, situation, or opportunity requiring an individual or organization to choose from among several actions that must be evaluated as right or wrong, ethical or unethical. (4)

European Union An alliance that promotes trade among its member countries in Europe. (5)

Evaluative criteria Objective and subjective characteristics that are important to a buyer and used to evaluate a consideration set. (8)

Everyday low prices (EDLP) Pricing products low on a consistent basis. (21)

Exchange The provision or transfer of goods, services, or ideas in return for something of value. (1)

Exchange controls Restrictions on the amount of a particular currency that can be bought or sold. (5)

Exclusive dealing A situation in which a manufacturer forbids an intermediary to carry products of competing manufacturers. (14)

Exclusive distribution Using a single outlet in a fairly large geographic area to distribute a product. (14)

Executive judgment A sales forecasting method based on the intuition of one or more executives. (7)

Experience qualities Qualities of services that can be assessed only after purchase and consumption (taste, satisfaction, courtesy, and the like). (13)

Experiment A research method that attempts to maintain certain variables while measuring the effects of experimental variables. (6)

Expert forecasting survey Preparation of the sales forecast by experts outside the firm, such as economists, management consultants, advertising executives, or college professors. (7)

Exploratory research Research conducted to gather more information about a problem or make a tentative hypothesis more specific. (6)

Exporting The sale of products to foreign markets. (5)

Extended problem solving A type of consumer problem-solving process used when unfamiliar, expensive, or infrequently bought products are purchased. (8)

External customers The individuals who patronize a business. (22)

External reference price A comparison price provided by others. (20)

External search The process of seeking information from sources other than one's memory. (8)

Family branding A policy of branding all of a firm's products with the same name or at least part of the name. (12)

Family packaging A policy in an organization that all packages are to be similar or are to include one common element of the design. (12)

Feature article A form of publicity, up to three thousand words long, that is usually prepared for a specific publication. (18)

Federal Trade Commission (FTC) A government agency that regulates a variety of business practices and curbs false advertising, misleading pricing, and deceptive packaging and labeling. (3)

Feedback The receiver's response to a decoded message. (17)

Fixed costs Costs that do not vary with changes in the number of units produced or sold; costs allocated on the basis of how money was actually spent, such as rent, salaries, office supplies, and utilities. (20, 22)

F.O.B. (free-on-board) destination Part of a price quotation used to indicate who must pay shipping charges. With F.O.B. destination price, the producer absorbs the costs of shipping the merchandise to the customer. (20)

F.O.B. (free-on-board) factory Part of a price quotation used to indicate who must pay shipping charges. F.O.B.

factory price indicates the price of the merchandise at the factory, before it is loaded onto the carrier vehicle; the buyer pays for shipping. (20)

Focus-group interview   A research method involving observation of group interaction when members are exposed to an idea or concept. (6)

Franchising   An arrangement in which a supplier (franchiser) grants a dealer (franchisee) the right to sell products in exchange for some type of consideration. (5, 16)

Free merchandise   A sales promotion method aimed at retailers whereby free merchandise is offered to resellers that purchase a stated quantity of product. (19)

Free samples   A new-product sales promotion technique that marketers use to stimulate trial of a product, increase sales volume in early stages of the product's life cycle, or obtain desirable distribution. (19)

Freight absorption pricing   Pricing for a particular customer or geographical area whereby the seller absorbs all or part of the actual freight costs. (20)

Freight forwarders   Businesses that consolidate shipments from several organizations into efficient lot sizes. (15)

Full-cost approach   An approach to determining marketing costs in which cost analysis includes variable, traceable common costs and nontraceable common costs. (22)

Full-service wholesalers   Marketing intermediaries providing the widest range of wholesaling functions. (15)

Functional discount   *See* Trade discount.

Functional middlemen   Intermediaries that negotiate purchases and expedite sales for a fee but do not take title to products. (15)

Functional modification   A change that affects a product's versatility, effectiveness, convenience, or safety, usually requiring the redesign of one or more parts of the product. (11)

GATT   *See* General Agreement on Tariffs and Trade.

General Agreement on Tariffs and Trade (GATT)   International marketing negotiations to reduce worldwide tariffs and increase trade. (5)

General-merchandise retailer   A retail establishment that offers a variety of product lines that are stocked in depth. (16)

General-merchandise wholesalers   Full-service wholesalers with a wide product mix but limited depth within product lines. (15)

General publics   The indirect consumers of the product of a nonbusiness organization; for instance, the general public of a university includes alumni, trustees, parents of students, and other groups. (13)

Generic brands   Brands that indicate only the product category (such as *aluminum foil*), not the company name and other identifying terms. (12)

Generic competitors   Firms that provide very different products that solve the same problem or satisfy the same basic customer need. (3)

Geodemographic segmentation   A method of market segmentation that divides people into zip code areas and smaller neighborhood units based on lifestyle information. (7)

Geographic pricing   A form of pricing that involves reductions for transportation costs or other costs associated with the physical distance between buyer and seller. (20)

Globalization   The development of marketing strategies as though the entire world (or regions of it) were a single entity. (5)

Good   A tangible item. (10)

Government markets   Markets made up of federal, state, county, and local governments, spending billions of dollars annually for goods and services to support their internal operations and provide such products as defense, energy, and education. (9)

Green marketing   Development, pricing, promotion, and distribution of products that do not harm the natural environment. (4)

Gross domestic product (GDP)   Overall measure of a nation's economic standing in terms of the market value of the total output of goods and services produced in that nation for a given period of time. (5)

Growth stage   The product life cycle stage in which sales rise rapidly; profits reach a peak and then start to decline. (10)

Heterogeneity   Variation from one service to another or in the service provided by a single individual from day to day and from customer to customer. (13)

Heterogeneous market   A market made up of individuals with diverse needs for products in a specific product class. (7)

Homogeneous market   A type of market in which a large proportion of customers have similar needs for a product. (7)

Horizontal channel integration   Combining institutions at the same level of operation under one management. (14)

Hypermarkets   Stores that combine supermarket and discount store shopping in one location. (16)

Hypertext   Highlighted text that permits visitors to a website to jump from one point to other points on the site or to other websites. (23)

Hypothesis   An informed guess or assumption about a certain problem or set of circumstances. (6)

Idea   A concept, philosophy, image, or issue. (10)

Idea generation   The search by businesses and other organizations for product ideas that help them achieve their objectives. (11)

Illustrations   Photographs, drawings, graphs, charts, and tables used to encourage an audience to read or watch an advertisement. (18)

Importing   The purchase of products from a foreign source. (5)

Import tariff   Any duty levied by a nation on goods bought outside its borders and brought in. (5)

Impulse buying   An unplanned buying behavior that involves a powerful, persistent urge to buy something immediately. (8)

Income   The amount of money received through wages, rents, investments, pensions, and subsidy payments for a given period. (3)

Individual branding   A branding policy in which each product is given a different name. (12)

Industrial distributor   An independent business organization that takes title to industrial products and carries inventories. (14)

Inelastic demand A type of demand in which a price increase or decrease will not significantly affect the quantity demanded. (9)

Information inputs Sensations received through sense organs. (8)

In-home (door-to-door) interview A personal interview that takes place in the respondent's home. (6)

Innovators The first consumers to adopt a new product; they enjoy trying new products and tend to be venturesome. (10)

Input-output data A type of information, sometimes used in conjunction with the Standard Industrial Classification system, based on the assumption that the output or sales of one industry are the input or purchases of other industries. (9)

Inseparability A condition in which the consumer frequently is directly involved in the production process because services normally are produced at the same time they are consumed. (13)

Installations Facilities and nonportable major equipment. (10)

Institutional advertising A form of advertising promoting organizational images, ideas, and political issues. (18)

Institutional markets Markets that consist of organizations with charitable, educational, community, or other nonbusiness goals. (9)

Intangibility A characteristic of services: they cannot be seen, touched, tasted, or smelled, nor can they be possessed. (13)

Integrated marketing communications The coordination of promotional elements and other marketing efforts. (17)

Intended strategy In implementing marketing strategies, the strategy the organization decided on during the planning phase and wants to use. (22)

Intensive distribution Using all available outlets to distribute a product. (14)

Intensive growth Growth that occurs when current products and current markets have the potential for increasing sales. (2)

Interactivity The ability to allow customers to express their needs and wants directly to the firm in response to the firm's marketing communications. (23)

Intermodal transportation Combining and coordinating two or more modes of transportation. (15)

Internal customers The employees of a company. (22)

Internal marketing A management philosophy that coordinates internal exchanges between the organization and its employees to better achieve successful external exchanges between the organization and its customers. (22)

Internal reference price The price in the buyer's mind developed through experience with the product. (20)

Internal search An aspect of an information search in which buyers first search their memories for information about products that might solve their problem. (8)

International marketing Developing and performing marketing activities across national boundaries. (5)

Introduction stage The stage in a product's life cycle beginning at a product's first appearance in the marketplace, when sales are zero and profits are negative. (10)

Inventory management Developing and maintaining adequate assortments of products to meet customers' needs. (15)

Joint demand A characteristic of industrial demand that occurs when two or more items are used in combination to produce a product. (9)

Joint venture A partnership between a domestic firm and a foreign firm and/or government. (5)

Just-in-time (JIT) Making products and materials arrive just as they are needed for use in production or for resale. (15)

Keyword ads Ads that relate to text or subject matter specified in a web search. (23)

Kinesic communication Communication through body movement. (17)

Labeling Providing identifying, promotional, or other information on package labels. (12)

Laggards The last consumers to adopt a new product; they are oriented toward the past and suspicious of new products. (10)

Late majority People who are quite skeptical of new products but eventually adopt them because of economic necessity or social pressure. (10)

Layout The physical arrangement of the illustration, headline, subheadline, body copy, and signature of an advertisement. (18)

Learning A change in an individual's behavior caused by information and experience. (8)

Level of involvement The intensity of interest and importance that an individual places on a product. (8)

Level of quality The amount of quality a product possesses. (9, 11)

Licensing An alternative to direct investment that requires a licensee to pay commissions or royalties on sales or supplies used in manufacturing. (5)

Lifestyle An individual's pattern of living expressed through activities, interests, and opinions. (7)

Limited-line wholesalers Full-service wholesalers that carry only a few product lines but offer an extensive assortment of products within those lines. (15)

Limited problem solving A type of consumer problem-solving process employed when buying products occasionally and when information about an unfamiliar brand in a familiar product category is needed. (8)

Limited-service wholesalers Intermediaries that provide some services and specialize in a few functions. (15)

Line extension A product that is closely related to existing products in the line but meets different customer needs. (11)

Mail-order wholesalers Limited-service wholesalers that sell products through catalogs. (15)

Mail survey A questionnaire sent to respondents, who are encouraged to complete and return it. (6)

Manufacturer brands Brands initiated by a producer that make it possible for the producer to be identified with its product at the point of purchase. (12)

Manufacturers' agents Independent intermediaries who represent more than one seller and offer complete product lines. (15)

Marginal cost (MC) The cost associated with producing one more unit of a product. (20)

Marginal revenue (MR) The change in total revenue that occurs after an additional unit of a product is sold. (20)

Market A group of individuals and/or organizations that have needs for products in a product class and have the ability, willingness, and authority to purchase those products. (2, 7)

Market density The number of potential customers within a unit of land area, such as a square mile. (7)

Market-growth/market-share matrix A strategy planning tool based on the philosophy that a product's market growth rate and market share are important considerations in determining its marketing strategy. (2)

Marketing The process of creating, distributing, promoting, and pricing goods, services, and ideas to facilitate satisfying exchange relationships with customers in a dynamic environment. (1)

Marketing audit A systematic examination of the marketing group's objectives, strategies, organization, and performance. (22)

Marketing channel A group of individuals and organizations that direct the flow of products to customers; also called *channel of distribution* or *distribution channel.* (14)

Marketing citizenship The adoption of a strategic focus for fulfilling the economic, legal, ethical, and philanthropic social responsibilities expected by stakeholders. (4)

Marketing concept A managerial philosophy that an organization should try to satisfy customers' needs through a coordinated set of activities that also allows the organization to achieve its goals. (1)

Marketing control process A process that consists of establishing performance standards, evaluating actual performance by comparing it with established standards, and reducing the differences between desired and actual performance. (22)

Marketing cost analysis Breaking down and classifying costs to determine which are associated with specific marketing activities. (22)

Marketing decision support system (MDSS) Customized computer software that aids marketing managers in decision making. (6)

Marketing environment The competitive, economic, political, legal and regulatory, technological, and sociocultural forces that surround the customer and affect the marketing mix. (1)

Marketing ethics Principles and standards that define acceptable conduct in marketing as determined by various stakeholders. (4)

Marketing implementation The process of putting marketing strategies into action. (22)

Marketing information system (MIS) A framework for the management and structuring of information gathered regularly from sources inside and outside an organization. (6)

Marketing intermediary A middleman linking producers to other intermediaries or ultimate consumers through contractual arrangements or through the purchase and resale of products. (14)

Marketing management The process of planning, organizing, implementing, and controlling marketing activities to facilitate exchanges effectively and efficiently. (1)

Marketing mix Four marketing activities—product, distribution, promotion, and pricing—that a firm can control to meet the needs of customers within its target market. (1)

Marketing objective A statement of what is to be accomplished through marketing activities. (2)

Marketing orientation An organization committed to researching and responding to customer needs. (1)

Marketing plan A written document that specifies an organization's resources, objectives, marketing strategy, and implementation and control efforts planned for use in marketing a specific product or product group. (2)

Marketing planning A systematic process of assessing marketing opportunities and resources, determining marketing objectives, defining marketing strategies, and establishing guidelines for implementation and control of the marketing program. (2)

Marketing research The systematic design, collection, interpretation, and reporting of information to help marketers solve specific marketing problems or take advantage of marketing opportunities. (6)

Marketing strategy A plan of action for analyzing a target market and developing a marketing mix to meet the needs of that market. (2)

Market manager A person responsible for the marketing activities necessary to serve a particular group or class of customers. (11)

Market opportunity A combination of circumstances and timing that permits an organization to take action to reach a particular target market. (2)

Market potential The total amount of a product for all firms in an industry that customers will purchase within a specified period at a specific level of industrywide marketing activity. (7)

Market segment A group of individuals, groups, or organizations sharing one or more characteristics that make them have relatively similar product needs. (7)

Market segmentation The process of dividing a total market into groups of people or organizations with relatively similar product needs to enable marketers to design a marketing mix that more precisely matches the needs of consumers in a selected segment. (7)

Market share The percentage of a market that buys a specific product from a particular company. (2)

Market test A stage of new-product development that involves making a product available to buyers in one or more test areas and measuring purchases and consumer responses to promotion, price, and distribution efforts. (7)

Markup pricing A pricing method in which the price is derived by adding a predetermined percentage of the cost to the cost of the product. (21)

Maslow's hierarchy of needs The five levels of needs that humans seek to satisfy, from the most to least important. (8)

Materials handling Physical handling of products. (15)

Maturity stage A stage in the product life cycle in which the sales curve peaks and starts to decline as profits continue to fall. (10)

Media plan A plan that sets forth the exact media vehicles to be used for advertisements and the dates and times the advertisements are to appear. (18)

Medium of transmission The medium that carries the coded message from the source to the receiver or audience. (17)

Megacarriers Freight transportation companies providing several methods of shipment. (15)

Memory The ability to access databases containing individual customer profiles and past purchase histories and to use these data in real-time to customize a marketing offer. (23)

Merchandise allowance A sales promotion method aimed at retailers; consists of a manufacturer's agreement to pay resellers certain amounts of money for providing special promotional efforts, such as setting up and maintaining a display. (19)

Merchant wholesalers Independently owned businesses that take title to goods, assume ownership risks, and buy and resell products to business or retail customers. (15)

MERCOSUR An alliance that promotes the free circulation of goods, services, and production factors, and has a common external tariff and commercial policy among member nations in South America. (5)

Micromarketing An approach to market segmentation in which organizations focus precise marketing efforts on very small geographic markets. (7)

Missionary salesperson A support salesperson, usually employed by a manufacturer, who assists the producer's customers in selling to their own customers. (19)

Mission statement A long-term view, or vision, of what the organization wants to become. (2)

Modified rebuy purchase A type of business purchase in which a new-task purchase is changed the second or third time, or the requirements associated with a straight rebuy purchase are modified. (9)

Money refunds Sales promotion techniques in which the producer mails a consumer a specific amount of money when proof of purchase is established. (19)

Monopolistic competition A competitive structure in which a firm with many potential competitors attempts to develop a marketing strategy to differentiate its product. (3)

Monopoly A competitive structure in which a firm offers a product that has no close substitutes, making that organization the sole source of supply. (3)

Motive An internal energizing force that directs a person's behavior toward satisfying needs or achieving goals. (8)

MRO supplies An alternative term for supplies; supplies can be divided into maintenance, repair, and operating (or overhaul) items. (10)

Multinational enterprise A firm with operations or subsidiaries in many countries. (5)

Multiple sourcing An organization's decision to use several suppliers. (9)

Multiple-unit pricing Packaging two or more of the same products together for sale at a single price. (21)

NAFTA *See* North American Free Trade Agreement.

NAICS *See* North American Industry Classification System.

National Advertising Review Board (NARB) A self-regulatory unit that considers cases in which an advertiser challenges issues raised by the National Advertising Division (an arm of the Council of Better Business Bureaus) about an advertisement. (3)

Negotiated pricing Establishing a final price through bargaining between seller and customer. (21)

Neighborhood shopping centers Shopping centers that usually consist of several small convenience and specialty stores and serve consumers living within ten minutes' driving time from the center. (16)

New-product development process A process consisting of seven phases: idea generation, screening, concept testing, business analysis, product development, test marketing, and commercialization. (11)

News release A form of publicity that is usually a single page of typewritten copy containing fewer than 300 words. (18)

New-task purchase An initial purchase by an organization of an item to be used to perform a new job or solve a new problem. (9)

Noise Anything that reduces the clarity and accuracy of communication. (17)

Noncumulative discount A one-time price reduction based on the number of units purchased, the size of the order, or the product combination purchased. (20)

Nonprice competition A policy in which a seller elects not to focus on price and instead emphasizes distinctive product features, service, product quality, promotion, packaging, or other factors to distinguish its product from competing brands. (20)

Nonprobability sampling A sampling technique in which there is no way to calculate the likelihood that a specific element of the population being studied will be chosen. (6)

Nonprofit marketing Marketing activities conducted by individuals and organizations to achieve some goal other than ordinary business goals such as profit, market share, or return on investment. (13)

Nonstore retailing The selling of products outside the confines of a retail facility. (16)

Nontraceable common costs Costs that cannot be assigned to any specific function according to any logical criteria and thus are assignable only on an arbitrary basis. (22)

North American Free Trade Agreement (NAFTA) An alliance that merges Canada, the United States, and Mexico into a single market. (5)

North American Industry Classification System (NAICS) A system for classifying industries that will generate comparable statistics among the United States, Canada, and Mexico. (9)

Objective-and-task approach An approach to determining the advertising appropriation: marketers determine the objectives a campaign is to achieve and then ascertain the tasks required to accomplish those objectives; the costs of all tasks are added to ascertain the total appropriation. (18)

Odd-even pricing A type of psychological pricing that assumes that more of a product will be sold at $99.99 than at $100.00, indicating that an odd price is more appealing than an even price to customers. (21)

Off-price retailers Stores that buy manufacturers' seconds, overruns, returns, and off-season merchandise for resale to consumers at deep discounts. (16)

Oligopoly   A competitive structure in which a few sellers control the supply of a large proportion of a product. (3)

Online retailing   Retailing that makes products available between buyers and sellers through computer connections. (16)

Online survey   A research method in which respondents answer a questionnaire via e-mail or on a website. (6)

On-site computer interview   A variation of the shopping mall intercept interview in which respondents complete a self-administered questionnaire displayed on a computer monitor. (6)

Opinion leader   The member of a reference group who provides information about a specific sphere of interest to reference group participants seeking information. (8)

Opportunities   Favorable conditions in the environment that could produce rewards for the organization if acted on properly. (2)

Opportunity cost   The value of the benefit given up by selecting one alternative over another. (13)

Order getter   A salesperson who increases the firm's sales by selling to new customers and by increasing sales to present customers. (19)

Order processing   The receipt and transmission of sales order information in the physical distribution process. (15)

Order taker   A salesperson who primarily seeks repeat sales. (19)

Organizational (corporate) culture   A set of values, beliefs, goals, norms, and rituals that members of an organization share. (4)

Outsourcing   The contracting of physical distribution tasks to third parties who do not have managerial authority within the marketing channel. (15)

Patronage motives   Motives that influence where a person purchases products on a regular basis. (8)

Penetration pricing   Pricing below the prices of competing brands; designed to penetrate a market and gain a significant market share quickly. (21)

Percent-of-sales approach   A method for establishing the advertising appropriation whereby marketers multiply a firm's past sales, forecasted sales, or a combination of the two by a standard percentage based on what the firm traditionally has spent on advertising and on the industry average. (18)

Perception   The process by which an individual selects, organizes, and interprets information inputs to create a meaningful picture of the world. (8)

Performance standard   An expected level of performance against which actual performance can be compared. (22)

Periodic discounting   The temporary lowering of prices on a patterned or systematic basis. (21)

Perishability   A condition where, because of simultaneous production and consumption, unused capacity to produce services in one time period cannot be stockpiled or inventoried for future time periods. (13)

Personal interview survey   A face-to-face interview that allows in-depth interviewing, probing, follow-up questions, or psychological tests. (6)

Personality   A set of internal traits and distinctive behavioral tendencies that result in consistent patterns of behavior in certain situations. (8)

Personal selling   Personal, paid communication that attempts to inform customers and persuade them to purchase products in an exchange situation. (19)

Physical distribution   The activities used to move products from producers to consumers and other end users. (15)

Pioneer advertising   A type of advertising that stimulates demand for a product by informing people about the product's features, uses, and benefits. (18)

Pioneer promotion   A type of promotion that informs potential customers about a product: what it is, what it does, how it can be used, and where it can be purchased. (17)

Point-of-purchase (P-O-P) materials   A sales promotion method that uses such items as outside signs, window displays, and display racks to attract attention, inform customers, and encourage retailers to carry particular products. (19)

Population   All elements, units, or individuals that are of interest to researchers for a specific study. (6)

Pop-under ads   Large ads that open in a new browser window underneath the currently viewed site. (23)

Pop-up ads   Large ads that open in a separate web browser window on top of the website being viewed. (23)

Portal   A multiservice website that serves as a gateway to other websites. (23)

Posttest   An evaluation of advertising effectiveness after the campaign. (18)

Premium (push) money   Extra compensation to salespeople for pushing a line of goods. (19)

Premium pricing   Pricing higher-quality or more versatile products higher than other models in the product line. (21)

Premiums   Items that are offered free or at a minimum cost as a bonus for purchasing a product. (19)

Press conference   A meeting used to announce major news events. (18)

Prestige pricing   Setting prices at a high level to facilitate a prestige or quality image. (21)

Prestige sensitive   A characteristic of buyers who purchase products that signify prominence and status. (20)

Pretest   Evaluation of an advertisement before it is actually used. (18)

Price   The value that is exchanged for products in a marketing transaction. (20)

Price competition   A policy whereby a marketer emphasizes price as an issue and matches or beats the prices of competitors. (20)

Price conscious   A characteristic of buyers who strive to pay low prices. (20)

Price discrimination   A policy of charging some buyers lower prices than other buyers, giving those paying less a competitive advantage. (20)

Price elasticity of demand   A measure of the sensitivity of demand to changes in price. (20)

Price leaders   Products sold at less than cost to increase sales of regular merchandise. (21)

Price lining   A form of psychological pricing in which an organization sets a limited number of prices for selected lines of products. (21)

Price skimming   Charging the highest possible price that buyers who most desire the product will pay. (21)

Glossary

G-11

Pricing objectives   Goals that describe the role of price in an organization's long-range plans. (21)

Primary data   Data observed and recorded or collected directly from respondents. (6)

Primary demand   Demand for a product category rather than for a specific brand of product. (17)

Private brand   *See* Private distributor brand.

Private distributor brand   A brand that is initiated and owned by a reseller; also called *private brand, store brand,* or *dealer brand.* (12)

Private warehouses   Facilities operated by companies for storing and shipping their own products. (16)

Probability sampling   A sampling technique in which every element in the population being studied has a known chance of being selected for study. (6)

Process materials   Materials used directly in the production of other products; unlike component parts, they are not readily identifiable. (10)

Producer markets   Markets consisting of individuals and business organizations that purchase products for the purpose of making a profit by using them in their operations. (9)

Product   A good, service, and/or idea received in an exchange. (1, 10)

Product adoption process   The five-stage process of buyer acceptance of a product: awareness, interest, evaluation, trial, and adoption. (10)

Product advertising   Advertising that promotes the uses, features, and benefits of products. (18)

Product competitors   Firms that compete in the same product class but have products with different features, benefits, and prices. (3)

Product deletion   The process of eliminating a product from the product mix when it no longer satisfies a sufficient number of customers. (11)

Product design   How a product is conceived, planned, and produced. (11)

Product development   The phase in which the firm finds out if producing the product is feasible and cost-effective. (11)

Product differentiation   The process of creating and designing products so that consumers perceive them as different from competing products. (11)

Product features   Specific design characteristics allowing a product to perform certain tasks. (11)

Product item   A specific version of a product that can be designated as a distinct offering among an organization's products. (10)

Product life cycle   The course of product development, consisting of four major stages: introduction, growth, maturity, and decline. As a product moves through these stages, the strategies relating to competition, pricing, promotion, distribution, and market information must be evaluated and possibly changed. (10)

Product line   A group of closely related products that are considered a unit because of marketing, technical, or end-use considerations. (10)

Product-line pricing   The establishing and adjusting prices of multiple products within a product line. (21)

Product manager   A person who holds a staff position in a multiproduct company and is responsible for a product, a product line, or several distinct products that are considered an interrelated group. (11)

Product mix   The composite of products that an organization makes available to customers. (10)

Product modification   Changing one or more of a product's characteristics. (11)

Product positioning   The decisions and activities that are directed toward trying to create and maintain the firm's intended product concept in customers' minds. (11)

Professional pricing   Pricing used by persons who have great skills or experience in a particular field or activity, indicating that a price should not relate directly to the time and involvement in a specific case; rather, a standard fee is charged regardless of the problems involved in performing the job. (21)

Promotion   The communication with individuals, groups, or organizations to directly or indirectly facilitate exchanges by influencing audience members to accept an organization's products. (17)

Promotion mix   The specific combination of promotional methods an organization uses for a particular product. (17)

Prospecting   Developing a list of potential customers for personal selling purposes. (19)

Prosperity   A stage of the business cycle characterized by low unemployment and relatively high total income, which together cause buying power to be high (provided the inflation rate stays low). (3)

Proxemic communication   A subtle form of interpersonal communication used in face-to-face interactions when either party varies the physical distance that separates them. (17)

Psychological influences   Factors that operate within individuals to partially determine their general behavior and thus influence their behavior as consumers. (8)

Psychological pricing   Pricing that attempts to influence a customer's perception of price to make a product's price more attractive. (21)

Publicity   Nonpersonal communication in news story form, regarding an organization and/or its products, that is transmitted through a mass medium at no charge. (18)

Public relations   A broad set of communication activities used to create and maintain favorable relations between the organization and its stakeholders. (18)

Public warehouses   Organizations that rent storage and related physical distribution facilities. (16)

Pull policy   Promotion of a product directly to consumers with the intention of developing strong consumer demand. (17)

Purchasing power   *See* Buying power.

Pure competition   A competitive structure characterized by a large number of sellers, not one of which could significantly influence price or supply. (3)

Push policy   The promotion of a product only to the next institution down the marketing channel. (17)

Quality   The overall characteristics of a product that allow it to perform as expected in satisfying customer needs. (11)

Quality modification   A change that relates to a product's dependability and durability and is generally executed by alterations in the materials or production process used. (11)

Copyright © Houghton Mifflin Company. All rights reserved.

Quantity discount   Deductions from list price that reflect the economies of purchasing in large quantities. (20)

Quota   A limit set on the amount of goods an importing company will accept for certain product categories in a specific period of time. (5)

Quota sampling   Nonprobability sampling in which the final choice of respondents is left to the interviewers. (6)

Random discounting   Temporarily reducing a regular-priced product using an unsystematic time schedule. (21)

Random factor analysis   A method of predicting sales whereby an attempt is made to attribute erratic sales variations to random, nonrecurrent events, such as a regional power failure or a natural disaster. (7)

Random sampling   A type of sampling in which all units in a population have an equal chance of appearing in the sample. (6)

Raw materials   Basic materials that become part of a physical product; obtained from mines, farms, forests, oceans, and recycled solid wastes. (10)

Realized strategy   In implementing marketing strategies, the strategy that actually takes place. (22)

Rebates   Sales promotion techniques in which the producer mails a consumer a specified amount of money for making a single purchase. (19)

Receiver   The individual, group, or organization that decodes a coded message. (17)

Recession   A stage of the business cycle during which unemployment rises and total buying power declines, stifling both consumer and business spending. (3)

Reciprocity   A practice unique to organizational sales in which two organizations agree to buy from each other. (9)

Recognition test   A posttest method of evaluating the effectiveness of advertising; individual respondents are shown the actual advertisement and asked whether they recognize it. (18)

Recovery   A stage of the business cycle during which the economy moves from depression or recession toward prosperity. (3)

Recruiting   A process by which the sales manager develops a list of applicants for sales positions. (19)

Reference group   Any group that positively or negatively affects a person's values, attitudes, or behavior. (8)

Reference pricing   The pricing of a product at a moderate level and positioning it next to a more expensive model or brand. (21)

Regional issues   Versions of a magazine that differ across geographic regions and in which a publisher can vary the advertisements and editorial content. (18)

Regional shopping center   A type of shopping center that usually has the largest department stores, the widest product mix, and the deepest product lines of all shopping centers in an area. (16)

Regression analysis   A method of predicting sales whereby a forecaster attempts to find a relationship between past sales and one or more independent variables, such as population or income. (7)

Reinforcement advertising   An advertisement attempting to assure current users that they have made the right choice and telling them how to get the most satisfaction from the product. (18)

Reliability   A condition existing when use of a research technique produces almost identical results in successive repeated trials. (6)

Reminder advertising   Advertising used to remind consumers that an established brand is still around and has certain uses, characteristics, and benefits. (18)

Research design   An overall plan for obtaining the information needed to address a research problem or issue. (6)

Reseller markets   Markets consisting of intermediaries, such as wholesalers and retailers, that buy finished goods for profit. (9)

Retailer   An organization that purchases products for the purpose of reselling them to ultimate consumers. (16)

Retailing   Transactions in which the buyer intends to consume the product through personal, family, or household use. (16)

Retail positioning   Identifying an unserved or underserved market segment and serving it through a strategy that distinguishes the retailer from others in the minds of consumers in that segment. (16)

Role   A set of actions and activities that a person in a particular position is supposed to perform based on the expectations of both the individual and the people surrounding him or her. (8)

Routinized response behavior   A consumer problem-solving process used when buying frequently purchased, low-cost items that require very little search and decision effort. (8)

Sales analysis   The use of sales figures to evaluate a firm's current performance. (22)

Sales branches   Manufacturer-owned intermediaries that sell products and provide support services to the manufacturer's sales force. (15)

Sales contest   A sales promotion method used to motivate distributors, retailers, and sales personnel through recognition of outstanding achievements. (19)

Sales force forecasting survey   Estimation by a firm's sales force of the anticipated sales in their territories for a specified period. (7)

Sales forecast   The amount of a product a company expects to sell during a specific period at a specified level of marketing activities. (7)

Sales offices   Manufacturer-owned operations that provide services normally associated with agents. (15)

Sales promotion   An activity and/or material that acts as a direct inducement to resellers, salespeople, or consumers; offers added value or incentive to buy or sell the product. (19)

Sample   A limited number of units chosen to represent the characteristics of a total population. (6)

Sampling   The process of selecting representative units from a total population. (6)

Scan-back allowance   A reward given by manufacturers to retailers based on the number of pieces scanned. (19)

Scrambled merchandising   The addition of unrelated products and product lines to an existing product mix, particularly fast-moving items that can be sold in large volume. (16)

Screening   A stage in the product development process in which the ideas that do not match organizational objectives are rejected and those with the greatest potential are selected for further development. (11)

Search qualities Tangible attributes that can be viewed prior to purchase. (13)

Seasonal analysis A method of predicting sales whereby an analyst studies daily, weekly, or monthly sales figures to evaluate the degree to which seasonal factors, such as climate and holiday activities, influence sales. (7)

Seasonal discount A price reduction that sellers give buyers who purchase goods or services out of season; these discounts allow the seller to maintain steadier production during the year. (20)

Secondary data Data compiled inside or outside the organization for some purpose other than the current investigation. (6)

Secondary-market pricing Setting a price, for use in another market, that is different from the price charged in the primary market. (21)

Segmentation variables Dimensions or characteristics of individuals, groups, or organizations that are used to divide a market into segments. (7)

Selective demand Demand for a specific brand. (17)

Selective distortion The changing or twisting of currently received information that occurs when a person receives information inconsistent with his or her feelings or beliefs. (8)

Selective distribution Using only some available outlets to distribute a product. (14)

Selective exposure The process of selecting some inputs to be exposed to our awareness while ignoring many others. (8)

Selective retention Remembering information inputs that support personal feelings and beliefs and forgetting inputs that do not. (8)

Self-concept One's own perception or view of oneself. (8)

Selling agents Intermediaries that market a whole product line or a manufacturer's entire output. (15)

Service An intangible result of the application of human and mechanical efforts to people or objects. (10, 13)

Service heterogeneity *See* Heterogeneity.

Service inseparability *See* Inseparability.

Service intangibility *See* Intangibility.

Service perishability *See* Perishability.

Service quality Customers' perceptions of how well a service meets or exceeds their expectations. (13)

Shopping mall intercept interviews A research method that involves interviewing a percentage of people passing by "intercept" points in a mall. (6)

Shopping products Items for which buyers are willing to put forth considerable effort in planning and making purchases. (10)

Single-source data Information provided by a single firm on household demographics, purchases, television viewing behavior, and responses to promotions like coupons and free samples. (6)

Situational influences Influences resulting from circumstances, time, and location that affect the consumer buying decision process. (8)

Social class An open aggregate of people with similar social ranking. (8)

Social influences The forces other people exert on one's buying behavior. (8)

Social responsibility An organization's obligation to maximize its positive impact and minimize its negative impact on society. (4)

Sociocultural forces The influences in a society and its culture(s) that change people's attitudes, beliefs, norms, customs, and lifestyles. (3)

Socioeconomic factors *See* Demographic factors.

Sole sourcing An organization's decision to use only one supplier. (9)

Source A person, group, or organization with a meaning that it intends and attempts to share with a receiver or an audience. (17)

Spam Unsolicited commercial e-mail. (23)

Special-event pricing Advertised sales or price cutting to increase revenue or lower costs. (21)

Specialty-line wholesalers Full-service wholesalers that carry only a single product line or a few items within a product line. (15)

Specialty products Items that possess one or more unique characteristics that a significant group of buyers is willing to expend considerable effort to obtain. (10)

Sponsorship ads Ads that integrate companies' brands and products with the editorial content of certain websites. (23)

Stakeholders Constituents who have a "stake" or claim on some aspect of a company's products, operations, markets, industry, and outcomes. (4)

Standard Industrial Classification (SIC) System A system developed by the federal government for classifying business organizations based on what the firm primarily produces; also classifies selected economic characteristics of commercial, financial, and service organizations; uses code numbers to classify firms in different industries. (9)

Statistical interpretation An interpretation that focuses on what is typical or what deviates from the average and so indicates how widely respondents vary and how they are distributed in relation to the variable being measured. (6)

Store brand *See* Private distributor brand.

Storyboard A blueprint used by technical personnel to produce a television commercial; combines the copy with the visual material to show the sequence of major scenes in the commercial. (18)

Straight commission compensation plan A plan in which a salesperson's compensation is determined solely by the amount of his or her sales for a given time period. (19)

Straight rebuy purchase A type of business purchase in which a buyer purchases the same products routinely under approximately the same terms of sale. (9)

Straight salary compensation plan A plan in which salespeople are paid a specified amount per time period. (19)

Strategic alliance A partnership formed to create competitive advantage on a worldwide basis. (5)

Strategic business unit (SBU) A division, product line, or other profit center within a parent company that sells a distinct set of products and/or services to an identifiable group of customers and competes against a well-defined set of competitors. (2)

Strategic channel alliance A marketing channel that distributes the products of one organization through the marketing channels of another. (14)

Strategic philanthropy   The synergistic use of an organization's core competencies and resources to address key stakeholders' interests and achieve both organizational and social benefits. (4)

Strategic planning   The process of establishing an organizational mission and formulating goals, corporate strategy, marketing objectives, marketing strategy, and a marketing plan. (2)

Strategic window   A temporary period of optimal fit between the key requirements of a market and the particular capabilities of a firm competing in that market. (2)

Stratified sampling   A type of sampling in which the population of interest is divided into groups according to a common characteristic or attribute and a probability sample is then conducted within each group. (6)

Strengths   Competitive advantages or core competencies that give the firm an advantage in meeting the needs of its target markets. (2)

Styling   The physical appearance of the product. (11)

Subculture   A group of individuals who have similar values and behavior patterns that differ from those of other groups; usually based on geographic regions or human characteristics, such as age or ethnic background. (8)

Supermarkets   Large, self-service stores that carry complete lines of food products and some nonfood products. (16)

Superstores   Giant retail outlets that carry food and nonfood products found in supermarkets, as well as most routinely purchased consumer products. (16)

Supply chain management   Long-term partnerships among marketing channel members working together to reduce inefficiencies, costs, and redundancies to satisfy customers. (14)

Support personnel   Members of the sales staff who facilitate selling but usually are not involved only with making sales. (19)

Sustainable competitive advantage   An advantage that the competition cannot copy. (2)

SWOT analysis   An assessment of an organization's strengths, weaknesses, opportunities, and threats. (2)

Tactile communication   Interpersonal communication through touching. (17)

Target audience   The group of people at which advertisements are aimed. (18)

Target market   A specific group of customers on whose needs and wants a company focuses its marketing efforts. (1)

Target public   A group of people who have an interest in or a concern about an organization, a product, or a social cause. (13)

Technical salesperson   A support salesperson who directs efforts toward the organization's current customers by providing technical assistance in system design, product application, product characteristics, or installation. (19)

Technology   The application of knowledge and tools to solve problems and perform tasks more efficiently. (3)

Technology assessment   A procedure for anticipating the effects of new products and processes on a firm's operation, other business organizations, and society. (3)

Telemarketing   The performance of marketing-related activities by telephone. (16)

Telephone depth interview   An interview that combines the traditional focus group's ability to probe with the confidentiality provided by a telephone survey. (6)

Telephone surveys   The soliciting of respondents' answers to a questionnaire over the telephone, with the answers written down by the interviewer. (6)

Television home shopping   A form of selling in which products are presented to television viewers, who can buy them by calling a toll-free number and paying with a credit card. (16)

Test marketing   A limited introduction of a product in areas chosen to represent the intended market to determine prospective buyers' reactions to various parts of a marketing mix. (11)

Threats   Conditions or barriers that may prevent the firm from reaching its objectives. (2)

Time series analysis   A forecasting method that uses the firm's historical sales data to discover patterns in the firm's sales volume over time. (7)

Total budget competitors   Firms that compete for the limited financial resources of the same customers. (3)

Total cost   The sum of average fixed and average variable costs times the quantity produced. (20)

Total quality management (TQM)   A philosophy that uniform commitment to quality in all areas of the organization will promote a culture that meets customers' perceptions of quality. (22)

Traceable common costs   Costs that can be allocated indirectly, using one or several criteria, to the functions they support. (22)

Trade (functional) discount   A reduction off the list price a producer gives to an intermediary for performing certain functions. (20)

Trademark   A legal designation indicating the owner has exclusive use of a brand or part of a brand and others are prohibited by law from using it. (12)

Trade name   The legal name of an organization rather than the name of a specific product. (12)

Trade salesperson   A type of salesperson not strictly classified as support personnel because he or she takes orders as well. (19)

Trade sales promotion methods   A category of sales promotion techniques that stimulate wholesalers and retailers to carry a producer's products and market these products more aggressively. (19)

Trading company   A company that links buyers and sellers in different countries but is not involved in manufacturing or owning assets related to manufacturing. (5)

Traditional specialty retailers   Stores that carry a narrow product mix with deep product lines. (16)

Transfer pricing   A type of pricing used when one unit in a company sells a product to another unit. (20)

Transportation   Moving a product from where it is made to where it is purchased and used, thus adding time and place utility to the product. (15)

Trend analysis   An analysis that focuses on aggregate sales data, such as the company's annual sales figures, over a period of many years to determine whether annual sales are generally rising, falling, or staying about the same. (7)

Truck wholesalers   Limited-service wholesalers that transport products directly to customers for inspection and selection; also known as *truck jobbers* or *wagon jobbers*. (15)

Tying agreement A practice requiring a channel member to buy other products from a supplier besides the one it wants. (14)

Unaided recall test A posttest method of evaluating the effectiveness of advertising; respondents are asked to identify advertisements they have seen recently but are not shown any clues to help them remember. (18)

Undifferentiated targeting strategy A targeting strategy in which an organization defines an entire market for a particular product as its target market and designs a single marketing mix directed at that market. (7)

Uniform geographic pricing A type of pricing, sometimes called "postage-stamp price," that results in fixed average transportation; used to avoid the problems involved in charging different prices to each customer. (20)

Uniform Resource Locator (URL) A website address. (23)

Universal product code (UPC) A series of thick and thin lines read by an electronic scanner to identify the product and provide inventory and pricing information. (12)

Unsought products Products purchased because of a sudden need that must be solved (e.g., emergency automobile repairs), products of which customers are unaware, and products that people do not necessarily think of purchasing. (10)

Validity A condition existing when a research method measures what it is supposed to measure, rather than something else. (6)

Value analysis An evaluation of each component of a potential purchase, including quality, design, or materials, to acquire the most cost-effective product. (9)

Value conscious Concern about price and quality aspects of a product. (20)

Variable costs Costs directly attributable to production and selling volume; costs that vary directly with changes in the number of units produced or sold. (20, 22)

Vending *See* Automatic vending.

Vendor analysis A formal, systematic evaluation of current and potential vendors. (9)

Venture team An organizational unit established to create entirely new products that may be aimed at new markets. (11)

Vertical channel integration Combining two or more stages of the marketing channel under one management. (14)

Vertical marketing system (VMS) A marketing channel in which channel activities are coordinated or managed by a single channel member to achieve efficient, low-cost distribution aimed at satisfying target market customers. (14)

Warehouse clubs Large-scale, members-only establishments that combine features of cash-and-carry wholesaling with discount retailing. (16)

Warehouse showrooms Retail facilities in large, low-cost buildings with large on-premises inventories and minimal services. (16)

Warehousing Designing and operating facilities for storing and moving goods. (15)

Weaknesses Any limitations that a company faces in developing or implementing a marketing strategy. (2)

Wealth The accumulation of past income, natural resources, and financial resources. (3)

Wheel of retailing A hypothesis holding that new retailers usually enter the market as low-status, low-margin, low-price operators but eventually evolve into high-cost, high-price merchants. (16)

Wholesaler An individual or organization that facilitates and expedites wholesale transactions. (15)

Wholesaling All transactions in which products are bought for resale, for making other products, or for general business use. (15)

Width of product mix The number of product lines a company offers. (10)

Willingness to spend An inclination to buy because of expected satisfaction from a product as well as the ability to buy. (3)

World Trade Organization (WTO) An entity that promotes free trade among member nations by eliminating trade barriers and educating individuals, companies, and governments about trade rules around the world. (5)

Zone pricing Regional prices that vary for major geographic zones as the transportation costs increase. (20)

Box Sources

CHAPTER 1

Page 6: Richard C. Morais, "Listen Up, Sucker," *Forbes,* Jan. 8, 2001, p. 212; Daniel Woolls, "Spanish Firm's Lollipops Have International Flavor," *Mobile Register,* May 6, 2001, p. 3F. *Page 14:* Fred Crawford, "Speaking the Language of the Consumer," *Chain Store Age,* Dec. 2000, pp. 119–128; Lorrie Grant, "Home Depot Sales Soar," *USA Today,* Aug. 15, 2001, p. B1; *Home Depot 2000 Annual Report;* Patricia Sellers, "Exit the Builder, Enter the Repairman," *Fortune,* Mar. 2001, pp. 86–88.

CHAPTER 2

Page 38: Joann S. Lublin, "Fountain-Pen Fashions: Try 5,072 Diamonds or Abe Lincoln's DNA," *The Wall Street Journal,* August 24, 2001, pp. A1, A4; Airline International, www.airlineintl.com/html/abraham_lincoln. html, Aug. 28, 2001. *Page 47:* Dan Mitchell, "A Microsofty Goes Bowling . . . and Winds up Buying the League," *Business 2.0,* Jan. 2001, www.business2.com/articles/mag/0,1640,14443,FF.html; Professional Bowlers Association, www.pba.com, June 27, 2001; Lyle Zikes, "The PBA Goes Digital," *Bowling Digest,* Aug. 2000, via findarticles.com; Hilary Cassidy, "Miller Angles to Be Bowling Kingpin, Pennzoil Gets Out the ESPN Vote," *Brandweek,* Jan. 22, 2001, p. 22.

CHAPTER 3

Page 58: Bruce Einhorn, Manjeet Kripalani, and Pete Engardio, "India 3.0," *Business Week,* Feb. 26, 2001, pp. 44–46; "Infosys Technologies Ltd," India Infoline.com, May 29, 2001, www.indiainfoline.com/comp/ infy/290501.html; Kala Rao, "US Downturn Slows Outsourcing Stars," *Euromoney,* May 2001, pp. 130–134; Tata Steel, www.tata.com, June 27, 2001; Wipro Technologies, www.wipro.com, June 27, 2001. *Page 68:* Mike France, "The Litigation Machine," *Business Week,* Jan. 29, 2001, pp. 116–118; Richard Willing, "Lawsuits Follow Growth Curve of Wal-Mart," *USA Today,* Aug. 14, 2001, pp. A1, A2. Wal-Mart Stores, Inc., www.walmart.com, Aug. 28, 2001.

CHAPTER 4

Page 88: "About Us," WorldWise, Inc., www.worldwise.com/whoweare2. html, June 28, 2001; Mika Edwards, "WorldWise Turns Recycled Materials into New Products," *Marin Independent Journal,* May 18, 2001; Thea Singer, "Can Business Still Save the World?" *Inc.,* Apr. 2001, pp. 58–71. *Page 93:* "Alaska's Black Water: Cruise Ship Dumping Sparks Regulators' Interests," ABCNews, Dec. 2, 1999, http://abcnews.go. com/sections/travel/DailyNews/cruiseships991202.html; Sharon L. Crenson, "Spills Tarnish Cruise Ships' 'Love Boat' Image," CNN, Apr. 9, 2001, www.cnn.com/; "Cruise Line Pays Alaska $3.5 Million for Dumping Violations," Fox News Online, Jan. 14, 2000, www.foxmarketwire.com/ wires/0114/f_ap_0114_65.sml; Charles Fishman, "Fantastic Voyage," *Fast Company,* Mar. 2000, pp. 169–186; Royal Caribbean Cruise Lines, *1998 Environmental Report,* www.royalcaribbean.com/environment98/intro. html, June 26, 2001.

CHAPTER 5

Page 114: "Heinz Annual Report Celebrates Innovation," *Business Wire,* Aug. 3, 2001, www.businesswire.com; "Heinz Ketchup Gets Funky with New Purple EZ Squirt," *Business Wire,* July 30, 2001, www.businesswire. com; Heinz 2000 Annual Report. *Page 123:* Bill Spindle, "Universal Tweaks Its Osaka Park to Meet Tastes of Japanese Patrons," *The Wall Street Journal Interactive,* Mar. 22, 2001, http://interactive.wsj.com; "Universal Studios Brings Tinseltown to Japan," *The Times of India,* Apr. 1, 2001, www.indiatimes.com/toit/01wrap5.htm; "Universal Studios in Largest Japanese Project Financing," *International Financial Law Review,* Jan. 2000, p. 9; "Welcome to Movie World: Universal Studios Comes to Japan," Japan Information Network, Mar. 9, 2001, www. jinjapan.org/trends/honbun/tj010309.html.

STRATEGIC CASE 1

Page 136: "Baseball Weekly Hits Record Circulation," *PR Newswire,* Apr. 13, 1998, p. 413; "Circulation Slide for Newspapers," *Editor & Publisher,* May 10, 1997, p. 3; "Company Profile," Gannett Inc., www.gannett.com, Sep. 5, 2001; R. Cook, "Gannett Hits Heights in Print but Falls Short of TV Stardom," *Campaign,* Jan. 17, 1997, p. 24; R. Curtis, "Introducing Your New *USA Today,*" *USA Today,* Apr. 3, 2000, p. 27A; J. Duscha, "Satisfying Advertiser Position Demands Now Easier," *NewsInc,* Sep. 13, 1999; Gannett Company, Inc., 1997 annual report; Gannett Company, Inc., 1999 annual report; Gannett Company, Inc., 2000 annual report; Gannett Company, Inc., 1996 Form 10-K (on file with the Securities and Exchange Commission); "Giving Samples Made Easy Through *USA Today* from Shampoo to CDs," *NewsInc,* June 22, 1998; K. Jurgensen, "Quick Response; Paper Chase: *USA Today* Editor Sees Shifts in How Information Is Generated and Delivered to Readers," *Advertising Age,* Feb. 14, 2000, p. S6; K. Jurgensen, *USA Today's* New Look Designed for Readers," *USA Today,* Apr. 3, 2000, p. 1A; A. M. Kerwin, "Daily Paper's Circulation Woes Persist into '97," *Advertising Age,* May 12, 1997, p. 26; P. Long, "After Long Career, *USA Today* Founder Al Neuharth Is Ready for More," *Knight-Ridder/Tribune Business News,* Apr. 28, 1999; J. McCartney, "*USA Today* Grows Up," *American Journalism Review,* Sep. 1997, p. 19; B. Miller, "*USA Today,* Gannett to Launch *USA Today Live,*" *Television & Cable,* Feb. 8, 2000; T. Noah, "At Least It's Free, Right?" *U.S. News & World Report,* Dec. 2, 1996, p. 60; N. Paul, "McWeb Site: *USA Today* Online," *Searcher,* May 1999, p. 58; M. L. Stein, "Don't Sweat, the Internet Says *USA Today's* Curley," *Editor & Publisher,* Aug. 22, 1998, p. 40; M. Stone, *USA Today Online* Listens to Its Logs," *Editor & Publisher,* Aug. 7, 1999, p. 66; J. Strupp, "Accuracy Is the Aim," *Editor & Publisher,* May 1, 2000, p. 9; J. Strupp, "*USA Today* Ads Go Page One," *Editor and Publisher,* May 8, 1999, p. 40; "Where Are Newspapers Headed?" *Editor and Publisher,* June 28, 1997; R. Tedesco, "Internet Profit Sites Elusive," *Broadcasting & Cable,* Nov. 17, 1997, p. 74; "*USA Today:* A Case Study," prepared by M. Condry, R. Dailey, F. Gasquet, M. Holladay, A. Johnson, S. Menzer, and J. Miller, University of Memphis, 1997; "*USA Today* Launches New Life Section Friday Format," *PR Newswire,* Mar. 16, 1998, p. 316; "*USA Today* Launches Online Classifieds Area and 17 New Marketplace Partnerships," *Business Wire,* Apr. 15, 1997; "*USA Today* Launches Pay-Per-View Archives Service," *Business Wire,* Jan. 5, 1998; "*USA Today Online* Launches Real Time Survey System," *Business Wire,* Feb. 18, 1998; *USA Today* Press Kit, 1997, Gannett Company, Inc.; "*USA Today* Sells Page One Advertising Space," *PR Newswire,* May 5, 1999, p. 3517; I. Wada, "*USA Today* Marketplace Signs Up Six for On-Line Services," *Travel Weekly,* Apr. 28, 1997, p. 44. Geoffrey Lantos, Stonehill College, prepared this case for classroom discussion rather than to illustrate either effective or ineffective handling of an administrative situation. Cheryl Anne Molchan, Stonehill College, and James G. Maxham, Louisiana State University, provided research assistance on earlier versions.

CHAPTER 6

Page 153: Gerry Khermouch, "Consumers in the Mist," *Business Week,* Feb. 26, 2001, pp. 92, 94; Kendra Parker, "How Do You Like Your Beef?" *American Demographics,* Jan. 2000, www.americandemographics.com/; Sharon Walsh, "Corporate Anthropology: Dirt-Free Research," CNN.com, May 23, 2001, www.cnn.com. *Page 176:* Mannie Jackson, "Bringing a Dying Brand Back to Life," *Harvard Business Review,* May 2001, pp. 53–61; Hal Mattern, "Back on the Ball," *Arizona Republic,* Nov. 5, 2000, pp. D1, D3; Erik Brady, "Hoop Troupe Gets Serious," *USA Today,* Nov. 10, 2000, p. 3C; John Morell, "Jackson Discusses Popularity, Future of Harlem Globetrotters," *Amusement Business,* Nov. 6, 2000, p. 11; *Page 158:* Dawn Barrs, "Tailor Made," *Profit Magazine,* Nov. 1998, p. 108; "An Introduction to Data Mining," The Data Mine, www.andypryke.com/

university/dm_docs/dm_intro.html, Aug. 16, 2001; Peter R. Peacock, "Data Mining in Marketing: Part I," *Marketing Management,* Winter 1998, pp. 9–18; Peter R. Peacock, "Data Mining in Marketing: Part II," *Marketing Management,* Spring 1998, pp. 15–24; Srikumar S. Rao, "Diaper-Beer Syndrome," *Forbes,* Apr. 6, 1998, pp. 128–130.

CHAPTER 7

Page 181: Kemba Johnson, "Forget Football," *American Demographics,* Feb. 2001, pp. 34–36; David Ronfeldt, "Social Science at 190 MPH on NASCAR's Biggest Superspeedways," *FirstMonday,* Feb. 7, 2000, www.firstmonday.dk/issues/issue5_2/ronfeldt/; Lee Spencer, "NASCAR Broadcasts Will Be Familiar," *The Sporting News,* Jan. 13, 2001, www.msnbc.com/news/515972.asp?cp1=1.

CHAPTER 8

Page 204: Emily Nelson, "On the Right Scent: Beauty Sites Have Gotten a Total Makeover," *The Wall Street Journal,* Feb. 12, 2001, pp. R18+; Alison Stein Wellner, "Beauty in Distress," *American Demographics,* January 2001, pp. 62–64. *Page 207:* Brad Stone, "Busting the Web Bandits," *Newsweek,* July 16, 2001, p. 55; Rebecca Gardyn, "Toplines: Penny for Your Thoughts," *American Demographics,* Sep. 2000, pp. 8–9; "Crime and Punishment," *Money,* June 1, 2001, p. 24; "Tackling the High Cost of Theft," *Chain Store Age Executive,* June 2001, pp. 108+.

CHAPTER 9

Page 228: Don Steinberg, "Jet-Set Service," *Smart Business,* June 2001, pp. 84–85; Steve Hamm, "An Eagle Eye on Customers," *Business Week,* Feb. 21, 2000, pp. 66–76; Michael Grebb, "Behavioral Science," *Business 2.0,* Mar. 2000, pp. 112–114; "Permaboss.com's Streaming Video Solution Reduces Sales Cycle by 30 Percent," *Business 2.0,* May 14, 2001, http://business2.com/whatworks/entry/1,1981,2404,FF.html; Joseph Rosenbloom, "Midnight Express," *Inc.,* July 2001, pp. 76–79. *Page 235:* P. Daukantas, "Peace Packs Will Carry IT to Third World," *Government Computer News,* Feb. 5, 2001, p. 5; David Kirkpatrick, "Looking for Profits in Poverty," *Fortune,* Feb. 5, 2001, pp. 174, 176; "HP Expands Position in India," Hewlett-Packard news release, Apr. 24, 2001, http://www.hp.com/e-inclusion/en/news/india2.html.

STRATEGIC CASE 2

Page 244: Anthony Lazarus, "USR Wants to Be Your Co-Pilot," CNet News.com, Mar. 19, 1997, www.news.com/News/Item/0,4,8665,00.html?st.cn.nws.rl.ne, Jan. 13, 1999; Suruchi Mohan, "PalmPilot Leads the Pack," *Computerworld,* Nov. 27, 1997, www.computerworld.com/home/print9497.nsf/all/SL47ROBOT16FB, Jan. 13, 1999; Stephanie Miles, "PalmPilot In, Newton Out," CNet News.com, Feb. 27, 1998, www.news.com/News/Item/0,4,19551,00.html?st.cn.nws.rl.ne, Jan. 13, 1999; Deborah Radcliff, "The Undesktop," *Computerworld,* May 4, 1998, www.computerworld.com/home/print.nsf/all/9805447B2, Jan. 13, 1999; Pat Dillon, "The Next Small Thing," *Fast Company,* June/July 1998, pp. 97–110; Melanie Warner, "A Much Anticipated Sequel: Silicon Valley Awaits Palm Creators' New Project," *Fortune,* Jan. 11, 1999, www.pathfinder.com/fortune, Jan. 18, 1999; "Reading the Palm Market Right," *Business Week,* Jan. 11, 1999, p. 95; "Palm Future," ZDNet Products, Jan. 13, 1999, www.zdnet.com/products/stories/reviews/0,4161,2186825,00.ht ml, Jan. 19, 1999; Cliff Edwards, "Palm's Market Starts to Melt in Its Hands," *Business Week,* June 4, 2001, p. 42; Robert Strohmeyer, "Palms Away," *Smart Business,* June 2001, pp. 40, 42; John Simons, "Has Palm Lost Its Grip?" *Fortune,* May 28, 2001, pp. 104–108; Reed Stevenson, "Stage Being Set for Wireless PDA Battle in Japan," *Yahoo! Finance,* Feb. 14, 2001, http://biz.yahoo.com/rf/010214/t7898_2.html.

CHAPTER 10

Page 260: Daniel Howes, "Caddy Faces Acid Test in Europe," *The Detroit News,* Apr. 15, 2001; Joe Miller, "Can GM Jump-Start Cadillac?" *The Detroit News,* Apr. 15, 2001, pp. 1A, 10A; Joe Miller, "Crowded Premium Market Heats Up," *The Detroit News,* Apr. 15, 2001, p. 1C; Joe Miller, "Luxury Brand's Ads Play on Heritage," *The Detroit News,* Apr. 15, 2001, p. 11A; Joe Miller, "New Factory Signals Faith in Cadillac," *The Detroit*

News, Apr. 15, 2001, pp. 1C, 4C; Keith Naughton, "Fixing Cadillac," *Newsweek,* May 28, 2001, pp. 36–37. *Page 265:* Diana Ayton-Shenker, "Newman's Own Gives Additional $18,000 to Save Texas Shakespeare Festival," *Free Expression Network,* press release, Apr. 11, 2000, www.freeexpression.org/newswire/0411_2000.htm; Newman's Own, www.newmansown.com, Feb. 24, 2001; "Newman's Own and *George* Magazine Announce Corporate Hero Award," *Philanthropy News Digest,* Apr. 22, 1998, http://fdncenter.org/pnd/19980422/002053.html; Rudi Williams, "Newman's Own Posts Awards for Quality of Life Programs," American Forces Information Services, www.defenselink.mil/news/Feb2000/n02092000_20002084.html, July 6, 2001.

CHAPTER 11

Page 275: Earle Eldridge, "Pickups Get Women's Touch," *USA Today,* June 13, 2001, p. 1B; "Women Truck Designers: A Traditionally Male-Dominated Industry," About.com, http://4wheeldrive.about.com/library/weekly/aa062101a.htm, Sep. 10, 2001; "Women Truck Designers: The Women Behind the Scenes," About.com, http://4wheeldrive.about.com/library/weekly/aa062101b.htm, Sep. 10, 2001. *Page 284:* Bernice Kanner, "The Weaver," *Chief Executive,* June 2000, www.findarticles.com; Longaberger Company, www.longaberger.com, Sep. 19, 2001.

CHAPTER 12

Page 305: Elana Harris, "Boot Camp for Marketers," *Sales & Marketing Management,* Feb. 2001, p. 88; David M. Ewalt, "3Com Axes Consumer Line, More Jobs," March 26, 2001, p. 36; "3Com Corporation," *Hoover's Handbook of American Business 2001* (Austin, TX: Hoovers Business Press, 2001), pp. 64–65; "3Com's Claflin Outlines Strategies to Build Brand at National Advertisers Annual Conference," 3Com news release, Oct. 16, 2000, http://3com.com/news/releases/pr00/oct1600a.html. *Page 308:* Paul A. Greenberg, "Online Toy Shops Already in Holiday Spirit," *E-Commerce Times,* June 13, 2001, http://www.ecommercetimes.com/perl/story/?id=11163; Keith Regan, "Babiesrus.com to Get Amazon Treatment," *E-Commerce Times,* May 22, 2001, http://www.ecommercetimes.com/perl/story/9918.html; Jennifer Gilbert, "When Brands Get Burned," *Business 2.0,* Jan. 23, 2001, pp. 62–65.

CHAPTER 13

Page 327: Meredith Wadman, "So You Want a Girl?" *Fortune,* Feb. 19, 2001, pp. 174–182; Tom Frederickson, "Clinics Offering Gender Selection with Fertilization," *Crain's New York Business,* Dec. 11, 2000, p. 16. *Page 331:* Andy Patrizio, "Home-Grown CRM," *Insurance and Technology,* Feb. 2001, pp. 49–50; "Banks Integrate Channels to Support One-to-One Marketing," *Retail Delivery News,* Apr. 28, 1999; Mary E. Thyfault, "Customer Service Drives Upgrade," *Information Week,* Oct. 5, 1998, p. 52; F. W. Timmerman, Jr., "ECHO System Helps USAA Listen—and Respond—to Customer Feedback," *Journal of Retail Banking Services,* Summer 1998, pp. 29–33.

STRATEGIC CASE 3

Page 347: Deborah Adamson, "Trouble in Toyland," CBS Marketwatch, Mar. 8, 2000, http://cbs.marketwatch.com/; Lisa Bannon, "Hi, Barbie! I'm Samantha. Can I Boost Your Sales?" *The Wall Street Journal,* June 16, 1998, pp. B1, B3; Lisa Bannon, "Let's Play Makeover Barbie," *The Wall Street Journal,* Feb. 17, 2000, p. B2; "Barbie Site a Hit with Consumers, Marketers," *Youth Markets Alert,* Dec. 7, 1997; Karen Benezra, "Toymakers & Animated Friends Take Heroic Steps Toward Girls," *Brandweek,* Feb. 20, 1995, p. 9; Adam Bryant, "Mattel CEO Jill Barad and a Toyshop That Doesn't Forget to Play," *The New York Times,* Oct. 11, 1998, p. C8; Larry Carlat, "Queen of the Aisles," *Brandweek,* Feb. 12, 1996, pp. 20–22, 24, 26; Bill Duryea, "Barbie-holics: They're Devoted to the Doll," *St. Petersburg Times,* Aug. 7, 1998, p. B1; Kathleen Grassel, "Barbie Around the World," *New Renaissance,* Apr. 1999, pp. 33–88; Gary Hoover, Alta Campbell, and Patrick J. Spains, eds., *Hoover's Handbook of American Business* (Austin, TX: Reference Press, 1995), pp. 732–734; Nancy J. Kim, "Barbie Gets an Image Makeover," *Puget Sound Business Journal,* Mar. 15, 1999, p. 17; "Margin Magic: Collectibles," *Discount Store News,* Feb. 9, 1998, p. 63; Mattel, www.mattel.com, Sep. 24, 2001; "Mattel Celebrates the Birthday of the Barbie Doll with the Launch of

Barbie.com for Girls," Mattel press release, www.prnewswire.com, Mar. 9, 1998; "Mattel to Consider Book Publishing after Purchase of Pleasant Company," *BP Report,* June 22, 1998; Pamela Sherrid, "Troubles in BarbieLand," *U.S. News & World Report,* Jan. 17, 2000, pp. 47–48; Karen Springen, "Hi There, Dollface. You Look Like Someone We Know," *Newsweek,* Nov. 16, 1998, p. 14; Elizabeth Stephenson, "Mattel Dolls Up Barbie for Adult Collectors," *Advertising Age,* Oct. 9, 1995, p. 44; Michael White, "Barbie Will Lose Some Curves When Mattel Modernizes Icon," *Detroit News,* Nov. 18, 1997, p. E32; Sue Zeidler, "Mattel Finds Famous Friends for Barbie," Reuters, Jan. 20, 1999.

CHAPTER 14

Page 356: "Barnes & Noble Implements i2 Solutions to Increase Distribution Center Efficiencies Nationwide," *Canadian Corporate News,* May 8, 2001, http://www.comtextnews.com; "Barnes & Noble Selects Retek to Support Supply Chain Planning and Optimization," Barnes & Noble news release, Jan. 10, 2001, http://www.prnewswire.com; Herb Greenberg, "Dead Mall Walking," *Fortune,* May 1, 2000, p. 304; Tom Andel, "Logistics@Barnesandnoble.com," *Material Handling Management,* Jan. 2000, p. 39; "Mezzanines Help Support Store and Web Demand," *Material Handling Management,* Jan. 2000, p. 14SCF. *Page 360:* "Office Depot's E-Diva," *Business Week,* Aug. 6, 2001, pp. EB22+; David Stires, "Office Depot Finds an E-Business That Works," *Fortune,* Feb. 19, 2001, p. 232.

CHAPTER 15

Page 383: David Arnold, "Seven Rules of International Distribution," *Harvard Business Review,* Nov.–Dec. 2000, pp. 131–137; "23 of the World's Leading Companies Join Commerce One in Incorporating the Global Trading Web Association," *M2 Presswire,* Aug. 15, 2000, http://www.presswire.net. *Page 392:* Jeff Stacklin, "Online Transport Firm to Fly on Its Own," *Crain's Cleveland Business,* Mar. 5, 2001, p. 28; Kristin S. Krause, "Messenger Service," *Traffic World,* Dec. 11, 2000, pp. 37–38; Candace Goforth, "Akron, Ohio–Based Shipping Firm Takes FedEx Name," *Akron Beacon Journal,* Jan. 20, 2000; Victoria Reynolds Harrow, "King of the Road," *Inside Business,* Nov. 1999.

CHAPTER 16

Page 404: Liz Evans, "Web Kiosks: Here to Stay?" *Sporting Goods Business,* Feb. 12, 2001, p. 16; "Shakeout Seen in E-Commerce Players," *Los Angeles Times,* Apr. 12, 2000, part C, p. 3; Janet Ginsburg, "Extreme Retailing," *Business Week,* Dec. 20, 1999, pp. 120–128; Joshua Macht, "Mortar Combat," *Inc. Tech 1999,* no. 3, pp. 102–110. *Page 413:* Hazel Ward, "Tesco Lays Firm Foundations for Winning the Online War," *Computer Weekly,* June 21, 2001, p. 20; Miranda James, "UK Alone in Europe over Preference for Using Credit Cards to Pay for E-Shopping," *New Media Age,* June 14, 2001, p. 18; "E-Strategy Brief: Seven-Eleven, Over the Counter E-Commerce," *The Economist,* May 26, 2001, pp. 77–78; John Fetto, "Global Shopping Spree," *American Demographics,* Oct. 2000, pp. 14–18.

STRATEGIC CASE 4

Page 428: Andrew Backover, "Bass Pro Shops Signs Grapevine Superstore Deal," *Fort Worth Star-Telegram,* Oct. 7, 1997, p. 1; Eddie Bass, "Renovations Add More Retail Space," *Springfield News-Leader,* Dec. 1, 1997, p. 11; Bass Pro Shops, "Outdoor World," promotional pamphlet C1-670, n.d.; Bass Pro Shops, "The Outdoor World Showroom," *Springfield News-Leader,* Special Advertising Supplement, Aug. 20, 1989, p. 1; Bass Pro Shops, "Welcome to Outdoor World," promotional pamphlet, CL-902, n.d.; "Bass Pro Shops: An RV/Fishing Venue," *RV Business,* July 1996, pp. 34, 41–42; Robert E. Carr, "Bass Pro Challenges Vendor Price Policies," *Sporting Goods Business,* Feb. 1994, p. 8; Paul Flemming, "Civic Park Tops List of Tax Beneficiaries," *Springfield Business Journal,* Jan. 26, 1998, p. 1; Michael Grunwald, "Megamall Sells Stimulation," *Boston Globe,* Dec. 9, 1997, p. 1A; Matt Hiebert, "Restaurant Offers More Than Delicious Food," *Springfield News-Leader,* Special Advertising Supplement, Aug. 20, 1989, p. 6; Steve Koehler, "A New Zenith for Bass Pro," *Springfield News-Leader,* Jan. 16, 1997, p. 1A; Jeff Kurowski, "Bass Pro Shops Goes to Illinois, Texas," *Boating Industry,* Sep. 1996, p. 16; Kate Marymount, "Hemingway's Makes Debut with Flavor," *Springfield News-Leader,* pr. 24, 1987, p. 1C; Kathleen O'Dell, "Bass Pro Plans Big

Renovation," *Springfield News-Leader,* Jan. 6, 1988, pp. 1A, 10A; Kathleen O'Dell, "Old Sea Tales: Bass Pro Barbershop Cuts Hairs with Nautical Flair," *Springfield News-Leader,* Oct. 1, 1987, pp. 6B, 8B; John Rogers, "State Conservation Department Pledges $2.5 Million Toward Wildlife Museum," *St. Louis Post-Dispatch,* Dec. 19, 1997, p. 6C; Dan Sewell, "After the Strike: UPS Tries to Recoup Losses," *Commercial Appeal,* Aug. 21, 1997, p. B8; "Wildlife Museum Backers Seek Millions from Public," *St. Louis Post-Dispatch,* May 3, 1997, p. 18; David Nicklaus, "Bass Pro Shops Prepares to Open First Store in St. Louis Area," *St. Louis Post-Dispatch,* Aug. 11, 2001, http://www.postnet.com; Bass Pro Shops Capsule, *Hoover's Online,* http://www.hooversonline.com; "Bass Pro Wins Top Design Honors," *Chain Store Age Executive,* Feb. 2000, p. 2RSOY; "In the Beginning . . ." Bass Pro Media Kit, http://www.basspro.com.

CHAPTER 17

Page 435: Michelle Wirth Fellman, "Cause Marketing Takes a Strategic Turn," *Marketing News,* Apr. 26, 1999, p. 4; Timberland, www.timberland. com, (accessed) Feb. 24, 2001. *Page 445:* Kim Cross, "Jean Therapy," *Business 2.com,* Jan. 2001, pp. 70–75; Sandra Dolbow, "New Spots Sing the Praises of Buddy Lee," *Brandweek,* Jun. 4, 2001, via www. findarticles.com; "FAQ," Lee Jeans, www.leejeans.com, (accessed) Sep. 26, 2001.

CHAPTER 18

Page 467: Beth Snyder Bulik, "Who Wants To Use AT&T?" *Business 2.0,* July 10, 2001, pp. 30–31; Michael McCarthy, "Digital Ads Show Up in Unexpected Places," *USA Today,* June 19, 2001, http://www.usatoday. com; Joanne Weintraub, "Products Play Big Roles in Plots—Whether You Know It Or Not," *Dallas Morning News,* June 9, 2001, p. 4C; Becky Ebenkamp, "Return to Peyton Placement," *Brandweek,* June 4, 2001, p. S10. *Page 474:* John Fetto, "Toplines: Where's the Lovin'?" *American Demographics,* February 2001, pp. 10–11. "Defining Sex," *Traffic World,* January 8, 2001, p. 47; David Goetzel, "Virgin's Ads Lack Chastity," *Advertising Age,* December 18, 2000, p. 8; Pete Millard, "Sex-pack," *The Business Journal-Milwaukee,* December 8, 2000, p. 1.

CHAPTER 19

Page 501: Kate MacArthur, "New Tastes Offers Sampling of McD's Marketing Strategy," *Crain's Chicago Business,* February 5, 2001, p. 32; Amy Zuber, "McD-Disney Marketing Alliances Grow with Burger Invasion Concept's Debut," *Nation's Restaurant News,* January 22, 2001, p. 4; Kate MacArthur, "Burger Giants Dig Up Dinos for Summer Movie Tie-Ins," *Advertising Age,* April 17, 2000, p. 3; "Segmenting the Message," *Adweek Eastern Edition,* April 17, 2000, p. 20. *Page 505:* Jennifer Weil, "Lancome: A Miracle for Men," *WWD,* July 6, 2001, p. 4; Brian Wansink, "Listening to the Consumer," *Brandweek,* May 7, 2001, p. 14; "Where Do We Go from Here," *Brandweek,* May 7, 2001, p. 13.

STRATEGIC CASE 5

Page 514: "California Processors Vote To Continue 'Got Milk?' " *Adweek,* March 26, 2001, p. 5; "Colorful Campaign Set To Create Cool Milk," *Selling To Kids,* March 21, 2001; "Got NBA? Milk Becomes an Official Promotional Partner of the NBA," *Business Wire,* October 30, 2000, http://www.businesswire.com; "Milk Does a Body Good, but Ads Do the Industry Even Better," *USA Today,* June 14, 2000, p. 7B; Jeff Manning, "How the Udder Beverage Aims to Steal Share," *Beverage World,* January 15, 1998, pp. 115–116; National Fluid Milk Processor Promotion Board press kit.

CHAPTER 20

Page 522: Keith Regan, "Harnessing the Power of Online Pricing," *E-Commerce Times,* March 22, 2001, http://www.ecommercetimes.com/ perl/story/?id=8370#story-start; Frederick F. Reichheld and Phil Schefter, "E-Loyalty: Your Secret Weapon on the Web," *Harvard Business Review,* July–August 2000, pp. 105–113. *Page 532:* Rea Blakey, "Barr Labs Sparked Prozac Decision," *CNN.com,* August 2, 2001, http://www.cnn. com/2001/HEALTH/08/02/blakey.debrief.otsc; "FDA Approves 'Generic Prozac' For Sale," *CNN.com,* August 2, 2001, http://www.cnn.com/ 2001/health/08/02/prozac.barr.0904; John Greenwald, "Rx for Nosebleed Prices," *Time,* May 21, 2001, pp. 42–43; "Allergy Drugs Deemed Safe,"

CNNfn.com, May 11, 2001, http://cnnfn.cnn.com/2001/05/11/companies/allergy_drugs/index.htm.

CHAPTER 21

Page 555: Nicholas Stein, "A New Cut on an Old Monopoly," *Fortune,* February 19, 2001, pp. 186–209; Neil Behrmann and Robert Block, "De Beers To Abandon Monopoly, Aim at New Role in Diamonds," *Wall Street Journal,* July 13, 2000, pp. A20+. *Page 563:* Michael Menduno, "Priced to Perfection," *Business 2.0,* March 6, 2001, pp. 40–41; Joy LePree Anderson, "Variations on Variable Pricing," Office.com, January 2000, http://www.office.com.

STRATEGIC CASE 6

Page 569: John Gorham, "The Player," *Forbes,* September 3, 2001, p. 60; Scott Hettrick, "Studios Wage War on Vidtailers," *Variety,* August 13, 2001, p. 9; Paul Sweeting, "Antioco Takes Pause on Studio Rev-Sharing," *Video Business,* July 30, 2001, p. 1; Paul Sweeting, "Sweeting: No Time To Share," *Video Business,* July 30, 2001, p. 12; Wendy Wilson, "Blockbuster, Studios Deny Price Fixing," *Video Business,* July 16, 2001, p. 4; Warren Epstein, "Blockbuster Settlement Could Mean Free Flicks," *Gazette/Colorado Springs,* June 26, 2001, http://www.gazette.com; "Blockbuster Company Capsule," *Hoovers Online,* http://www.hoovers.com; Tom Mainelli, "Three Minutes With Netflix CEO Reed Hastings," *PCWorld.com,* June 8, 2001, http://www.pcworld.com/news/article/0,aid,51463,00.asp; "A Rental a Day," *Video Business,* June 4, 2001, p. 21; Leslie Limbo, "Blockbuster Unveils Online Rentals in Denver," *Denver Business Journal,* May 25, 2001, p. 11A; Paul Sweeting, "DVD Rentals Boost Big Blue," *Video Business,* April 23, 2001, p. 4; Herschell Gordon Lewis, "A Blockbuster of a Marketing Mistake," *Direct,* November 1, 2000, p. 200.

CHAPTER 22

Page 578: Great Harvest Bread Company, www.greatharvest.com/, (accessed) Oct. 4, 2001; Heath Row, "Great Harvest's Recipe for Growth," *Fast Company,* Dec. 1998, pp. 46–48; Michael S. Hopkins, "Zen and the Art of the Self-Managing Company," *Inc.,* Nov. 1, 2000, http://www.inc.com/incmagazine/article/1,,ART20904_CNT53,00.html. *Page 585:* Steve Watkins, "Ever Wanted to Review the Boss? 360-Degree Feedback Gains Favor," *Investor's Business Daily,* Aug. 10, 2001, p. A1; Steve Watkins, "Top Companies Take Action Fast When Time Arrives to Fire Execs," *Investor's Business Daily,* Aug. 22, 2001, p. A1.

CHAPTER 23

Page 617: "Historic Mexican Election Sweeps Long-Ruling PRI Party from Power," CNN, Jul. 3, 2000, www.cnn.com/2000/WORLD/americas/07/03/mexico.elections.04/index.html; Marion Lloyd, "Mexico's PRI Tries to Attract Youths with Its 'Love' Web Site," *The Austin American-Statesman,* Aug. 12, 2001, www.austin360.com/statesman/; Partido Revolucionario Institucional, www.pri.org.mx/, Aug. 14, 2001. *Page 621:* TRUSTe, www.truste.org, Aug. 14, 2001.

STRATEGIC CASE 7

Page 628: Eryn Brown, "The Silicon Alley Heart of Internet Advertising," *Fortune,* Dec. 6, 1999, pp. 166–67; Lynn Burke, "A DoubleClick Smokescreen?" *WiredNews,* May 23, 2000, www.wirednews.com/news/print/0,1294,36404,00.html; "Company Profile: Key Facts," *The Wall Street Journal,* http://interactive.wsj.com, (accessed) Oct. 12, 2001; Tom Conroy and Rob Sheffield, "Hot Marketing Geek," *Rolling Stone,* Aug. 20, 1998, p. 80; "Crisis Control @ DoubleClick," *Privacy Times,* Feb. 18, 2000, www.privacytimes.com/New Webstories/doubleclick_priv_2_23.htm; "DoubleClick Accused of Double-Dealing Double-Cross," *News Bytes News Network,* Feb. 2, 2000, www.newsbytes.com; "DoubleClick Completes $1.8 Bil Abacus Direct Buyout," *News Bytes News Network,* Nov. 30, 1999, www.newsbytes.com; "DoubleClick Outlines Five-step Privacy Initiative," *News Bytes News Network,* Feb. 15, 2000, www.newsbytes.com; "Double-Click's Reprieve," *Marketing News,* Feb. 16, 2001, p. 48; "Double-Click Rolls Out Better Method for Ad Tracking," MSN MoneyCentral, http://news.moneycentral.msn.com/, (accessed) Mar. 5, 2001; "DoubleClick Tracks Online Movements," *News Bytes News Network,* Jan. 26, 2000, www.newsbytes.com (originally reported by *USA Today,* www.usatoday.com); "eCompany 40," *eCompany,* Apr. 2001, p. 147; Jane Hodges, "DoubleClick Takes Standalone Route for Targeting Tools," *Advertising Age,* Dec. 16, 1996, p. 32; "I Will Not Be Targeted," Center for Democracy and Technology, http://www.cdt.org/action/doubleclick.shtml; Chris Oakes, "DoubleClick Plan Falls Short," *WiredNews,* Feb. 14, 2000, www.wirednews.com/news/print/0,1294,34337,00.html; Chris O'Brien, "DoubleClick Sets Off Privacy Firestorm," *San Jose Mercury News,* Feb. 26, 2000, www.mercurycenter.com/business/top/042517.htm; "Online Marketing Coalition Announces Proposals for Internet Privacy Guidelines," *MSN MoneyCentral,* Sep. 25, 2000, http://news.moneycentral.msn.com/; "Privacy Choices," DoubleClick, Inc., http://www.privacychoices.org/, (accessed) Oct. 12, 2001; "Privacy Policy," DoubleClick Inc., http://www.doubleclick.net/, (accessed) Oct. 12, 2001; "Privacy Standards Proposed," *MSNBC,* Sep. 25, 2000, www.msnbc.com/news/467212.asp; Randall Rothenberg, "An Advertising Power, but Just What Does DoubleClick Do?" *The New York Times: E-Commerce Special Section,* 1999, www.nytimes.com/library/tech/99/09/biztech/technology/22roth.html; Allen Wan and William Spain, "FTC Ends DoubleClick Investigation," CBS MarketWatch.com, Jan. 23, 2001, www.aolpf.marketwatch.com/pf/archive/20010123/news/current/dclk.asp. Case contributed by Tracy Suter, Oklahoma State University.

Notes

CHAPTER 1

1. Byron Acohido, "Microsoft Bets on Xbox Success, But Some Skeptical," *USA Today,* Apr. 24, 2001, p. 6B; Brian Bremner, "Microsoft Vs. Sony: Mortal Combat," *Business Week Online,* Apr. 3, 2001, www.businessweek.com; N'Gai Croal, "Game Wars 5.0," *Newsweek,* May 28, 2001, pp. 65–66; Alan Hughes, "Activision: Pulling the Joystick into High Gear," *Business Week Online,* Mar. 13, 2001, www.businessweek.com; "Nintendo to Use New Game Boy to Fight Against Sony, Microsoft," Bloomberg Newswire, Apr. 30, 2001, via America Online; Chris Taylor, "The Battle of Seattle," *Time,* May 21, 2001, pp. 58–59; "Video-Game Industry Sales Rise 18% in First Quarter, Report Says," Bloomberg Newswire, May 11, 2001, via America Online.
2. Greg Winter, "Pepsi Looks to a New Drink to Jolt Soda Sales," *The New York Times,* May 1, 2001, http://partners. nytimes.com.
3. "Letter to Shareholders," *McDonald's 2000 Annual Report,* www.McDonalds.com, May 20, 2001.
4. Great Southern Sauce Company, www.greatsauce.com, June 1, 2001.
5. David Goetzl, "Schering-Plough Hopes for Hit with Piazza Spots," *Advertising Age,* May 3, 2001, www.adage.com.
6. Shelly K. Schwartz, "Do Big Boxes Stack Up?" CNNfn, May 3, 2001, www.cnn.com.
7. Thurston Hatcher, "Health Advocates Back Coke's New School Policy," CNN, Mar. 15, 2001, www.cnn.com.
8. "AT Rewards," AirTran, www.airtran.com, May 11, 2001.
9. Ajay K. Kohli and Bernard J. Jaworski, "Market Orientation: The Construct, Research Propositions, and Managerial Implications," *Journal of Marketing,* Apr. 1990, pp. 1–18.
10. Ibid.
11. Dottie Enrico, "M&M's Candies Singing the Blues," *USA Today,* Sept. 5, 1995, p. B1.
12. Alan Grant and Leonard Schlesinger, "Realize Your Customers' Full Profit Potential," *Harvard Business Review,* Sept./Oct. 1995, p. 59.
13. Jagdish N. Sheth and Rajendras Sisodia, "More than Ever Before, Marketing Is under Fire to Account for What It Spends," *Marketing Management,* Fall 1995, pp. 13–14.
14. Lynette Ryals and Adrian Payne, "Customer Relationship Management in Financial Services: Towards Information-Enabled Relationship Marketing," *Journal of Strategic Marketing,* Mar. 2001, p. 3.
15. "2000 Worldwide Case Volume by Region," *Coca-Cola 2000 Annual Report,* www.cocacola.com, May 11, 2001.
16. O. C. Ferrell, Michael Hartline, and George Lucas, *Marketing Strategy* (Ft. Worth, TX: Dryden, 2002), p. 97.
17. Werner J. Reinartz and V. Kumar, "On the Profitability of Long-Life Customers in a Noncontractual Setting: An Empirical Investigation and Implications for Marketing," *Journal of Marketing,* Oct. 2000, pp. 17–35.
18. Libby Estell, "This Call Center Accelerates Sales," *Sales & Marketing Management,* Feb. 1999, p. 72.
19. Jerry Wind and Arvind Rangaswamy, "Customization: The Next Revolution in Mass Customization," *Journal of Interactive Marketing,* Winter 2001, pp. 13+.
20. Ryals and Payne, "Customer Relationship Management in Financial Services," pp. 3–27.
21. Alan Brown, "How Amazon.com Sells," *eCompany,* June 2001, p. 114.

22. Ferrell, Hartline, and Lucas, *Marketing Strategy,* pp. 102–103.
23. Jamie Smith, "Put Out the Word," *Marketing News,* May 7, 2001, pp. 6, 8.
24. "Total Giving Reaches $190.16 Billion as Charitable Contributions Increase $15.80 Billion in 1999," AAFRC press release, May 24, 2000, www.aafrc.org/News.htm.
25. Michael J. Mondel, "Rethinking the Internet," *Business Week,* Mar. 21, 2001, p. 118.
26. Karen DeYoung and Bill Brubaker, "Bristol-Myers Cuts Cost of AIDS Drugs in Most of Africa," *The Austin American-Statesman,* Mar. 15, 2001, www.austin360.com/statesman/.
27. Sources: Cara Beardi, "Harte-Hanks Teams with Xchange," *Advertising Age,* Feb. 15, 2001, www.adage.com; Cara Beardi, "Harte-Hanks to Use E-Dialog E-mail Tools," *Advertising Age,* June 12, 2001, www.adage.com; Melissa Campanelli, "The Sports Authority Picks Harte-Hanks for CRM Services," *DMNews,* Feb. 15, 2001, www.dmnews.com; personal interview with Chet Dalzell, Harte-Hanks director of public relations, June 18, 2001; Harte-Hanks, www.harte-hanks.com, Sep. 4, 2001; "Harte-Hanks Wins Web Assignment for Celebrex," *Advertising Age,* Dec. 7, 2000, www.adage.com; Beth Negus Viveiros, "Image Isn't Everything, But It Is an Important Part of the Mix," *Direct Listline,* May 15, 2001, http://industryclick. com/magazinearticle.asp?releaseid=6302&magazinearticleid= 102091&siteid=2&magazineid=151.
28. Sources: Stephen Franklin, "Ward Masterstroke Was Catalog; Stores Didn't Keep Up," *The Austin American-Statesman,* Jan. 2, 2001, pp. D1, D3; "Montgomery Ward Closing Its Doors," KOIN, Dec. 29, 2000, www.channel6000. com/sh/news/stories/nat-news-20001228-133211.html; "Wards Files for Chapter 11," CNNFN, Dec. 28, 2000, www.cnnfn.com.

CHAPTER 2

1. Sources: Robert Berner, "Can Procter & Gamble Clean Up Its Act?" *Business Week,* Mar. 12, 2001, pp. 80–83; "Our History Making Brand," Kimberly-Clark, www.scottbrand.com/history/, Apr. 2, 2001; "We've Got Answers to Frequently Asked Questions," Kimberly-Clark, www.scottbrand.com/faqs/, Apr. 2, 2001.
2. O. C. Ferrell, Michael D. Hartline, and George H. Lucas, Jr., *Marketing Strategy* (Ft. Worth, Tex.: Dryden, 2002), p. 2.
3. Ibid.
4. Lloyd C. Harris and Emmanuel Ogbonna, "Strategic Human Resource Management, Market Orientation, and Organizational Performance," *Journal of Business Research,* Feb. 2001, pp. 157–166.
5. Elliot Matz and Ajay K. Kohli, "Reducing Marketing's Conflict with Other Functions: The Differential Effects of Integrating Mechanisms," *Journal of the Academy of Marketing Science,* 28, no. 4 (2000), pp. 479–492.
6. David Kiley, "Huge Losses Could Jeopardize Future of GM's Saturn," *USA Today,* Apr. 24, 2001, p. B1.
7. Ibid.
8. Ferrell, Hartline, and Lucas, *Marketing Strategy,* p. 31.
9. Lea Goldman, "Red-Hot Chili's," *Forbes,* Jan. 8, 2001, pp. 134–136.
10. Derek F. Abell, "Strategic Windows," *Journal of Marketing,* July 1978, p. 21.
11. "Is Your Company's Bottom Line Taking a Hit?" www.prnewswire.com, May 29, 1998.

12. "Our Mission," Celestial Seasonings, www.celestialseasonings.com/whoweare/corporatehistory/mission.jhtml, Jun. 6, 2001.

13. Christopher Palmeri, "Mattel: Up the Hill Minus Jill," *Business Week,* Apr. 9, 2001, pp. 53–54.

14. Jeff Green and David Welch, "Jaguar May Find It's a Jungle Out There," *Business Week,* Mar. 26, 2001, p. 62.

15. Andrew Campbell, Michael Goold, and Marcus Alexander, "Corporate Strategy: The Quest for Parenting Advantage," *Harvard Business Review,* Mar./Apr. 1995, pp. 120–132.

16. Cliff Edwards, "No Cartwheels for Handspring," *Business Week,* Apr. 2, 2001, pp. 56–58.

17. Joseph P. Guiltinan and Gordon W. Paul, *Marketing Management: Strategies and Programs* (New York: McGraw-Hill, 1991), p. 43.

18. George S. Day, "Diagnosing the Product Portfolio," *Journal of Marketing,* Apr. 1977, pp. 30–31.

19. Berner, "Can Procter & Gamble Clean Up Its Act?"

20. "Coca-Cola Buying Mad River Traders," Associated Press via America Online, May 14, 2001.

21. Roger A. Kerin, Vijay Majahan, and P. Rajan Varadarajan, *Contemporary Perspectives on Strategic Marketing Planning* (Boston: Allyn & Bacon, 1990).

22. Berner, "Can Procter & Gamble Clean Up Its Act?"

23. G. Tomas, M. Hult, David W. Cravens, and Jagdish Sheth, "Competitive Advantage in the Global Marketplace: A Focus on Marketing Strategy," *Journal of Business Research,* Jan. 2001, pp. 1–3.

24. Kelly Barron, "Culture Gap," *Forbes,* Mar. 19, 2001, p. 62.

25. "Hewlett-Packard Takes Gateway's Place at OfficeMax," Reuters Newswire via America Online, May 14, 2001.

26. Lorrie Grant, "Coach Bags Old Ideas," *USA Today,* Apr. 24, 2001, p. 3B.

27. Christian Homburg, John P. Workman, and Ove Jensen, "Fundamental Changes in Marketing Organization: The Movement Toward a Customer-Focused Organizational Structure," *Academy of Marketing Science,* Fall 2000, pp. 459–478.

28. "On-line Music," *USA Today,* June 12, 1998, p. B1.

29. Rajdeep Grewal and Patriya Tansuhaj, "The Chain of Effects from Brand Trust and Brand Affect to Brand Performance: The Role of Brand Loyalty," *Journal of Marketing,* Apr. 2001, pp. 67–80.

30. Kathleen Kerwin, "Carmakers May Be Flooding the Engine," *Business Week,* May 18, 1998, p. 43.

31. Robert J. Dolan, "How Do You Know When the Price Is Right?" *Harvard Business Review,* Sept./Oct. 1995, pp. 174–183.

32. Ronald D. Michman, "Linking Futuristics with Marketing Planning, Forecasting, and Strategy," *Journal of Consumer Marketing,* Summer 1984, pp. 17, 23.

33. Hemant C. Sashittal and Avan R. Jassawalla, "Marketing Implementation in Smaller Organizations: Definition, Framework, and Propositional Inventory," *Academy of Marketing Science,* Winter, 2001, pp. 50–69.

34. Ferrell, Hartline, and Lucas, *Marketing Strategy,* p. 20.

35. James U. McNeal, "Kids' Markets," *American Demographics,* Apr. 1998, p. 39.

36. Larry Light and David Greising, "Litigation: The Choice of a New Generation," *Business Week,* May 25, 1998, p. 42.

37. Ferrell, Hartline, and Lucas, *Marketing Strategy,* p. 61.

38. Douglas Bowman and Hubert Gatignon, "Determinants of Competitor Response Time to a New Product Introduction," *Journal of Marketing Research,* Feb. 1995, pp. 42–53.

39. Kevin T. Higgins, "Never Ending Journey," *Marketing Management,* Spring 1997, p. 6.

40. Sashittal and Jassawalla, "Marketing Implementation in Smaller Organizations."

41. Sources: "About Buzzsaw.com," Buzzsaw.com, www.buzzsaw.com/content/about/about.asp, Sep. 4, 2001; "Autodesk Completes Buzzsaw Acquisition, Augmenting Its Building Industry Strategy with Leading Online Collaboration and Printing Solutions," Buzzsaw.com press release, Aug. 28, 2001, www.buzzsaw.com/content/about/press_releases/01_08_28-acquisition.asp; "Autodesk Signs Definitive Agreement to Purchase Buzzsaw.com, the Leading Provider of Online Collaboration Services and Printing Applications to the Building Industry," Buzzsaw.com press release, July 10, 2001, www.buzzsaw.com/content/about/press_releases/01_07_10-Autodesk.asp; Jonathan Burton, "Bricks and Mortar on the Web," *Chief Executive,* Apr. 2001, via www.findarticles.com/cf_0/m4070/2001_April/74524564/p1/article.jhtml?term=Buzzsaw; "Buzzsaw.com Recognized as Market Leader in Engineering News-Record," Buzzsaw.com press release, June 20, 2001, www.buzzsaw.com/content/about/press_releases/01_06_19-ENRSurvey.asp; Erich Luening, "Can Construction Industry Rise to Online Challenge?" *c/net News,* Aug. 9, 2000, www.cnet.com/news/0-1007-200-2467593.html; Mark Roberti, "Cutting Construction Chaos," *Industry Standard,* June 11, 2001, via www.findarticles.com/cf_0/m0HWW/23_4/75669920/p1/article.jhtml?term=Buzzsaw.

42. Sources: Kristine Breese, "First Saturn Day: Diary of a Dealer," *Advertising Age,* Oct. 29, 1990; Rich Ceppos, "Saturn—Finally, It's Here, But Is It Good Enough?" *Car and Driver,* Nov. 1990, pp. 132–138; Stuart Elliott, "Campaign Takes Aim at Heartstrings," *USA Today,* Nov. 1, 1990, pp. 1B, 2B; Bob Garfield, "Down-to-Earth Ads Give Saturn an Underrated Liftoff," *Advertising Age,* Oct. 29, 1990, p. 68; General Motors, www.gm.com/, Aug. 30, 2001; James R. Healey, "Saturn, Day One: Business Is Brisk," *USA Today,* Oct. 26, 1990, pp. 1B, 2B; James R. Healey, "Saturn Demand Delivers Excitement to Dealers," *USA Today,* Nov. 5, 1990, p. B1; J. D. Power & Associates, www.jdpa.com/, Aug. 30, 2001; Kathleen Kerwin and Keith Naughton, "A Different Kind of Saturn," *Business Week,* July 5, 1999, p. 28; Barbara Lippert, "It's a Saturn Morning in America," *Adweek,* Oct. 15, 1990, p. 67; Micheline Maynard, "Fulfilling Buyers' Wishes, Saturn's Well Runs Dry," *USA Today,* Aug. 18, 1992, p. B1; Michelle Maynard, "Sales Slump Forces Saturn to Cut Production," *USA Today,* Jan. 21, 1998, p. B1; Robyn Meredith, "As Sales Fall, Saturn Workers to Vote on Ditching Contract," *The [Memphis] Commercial Appeal,* Mar. 8, 1998, pp. C1, C3; Ian P. Murphy, "Charged Up: Electric Cars Get Jolt of Marketing," *Marketing News,* Aug. 18, 1997, pp. 1, 7; Saturn, www.saturnbp.com/, Aug. 30, 2001; "Saturn Debuts 'Lightship' as Cornerstone of Promotional Plan for New VUE Sport-Utility," Saturn, press release, June 27, 2001, www.saturnbp.com/company/news_and_events/press_releases/?id=22; "Saturn Puts Hopes in Wagon Revival for New L-Series," *The Wall Street Journal,* Aug. 20, 1999, p. A6; Raymond Serafin, "Saturn's Goal: To B Worthy," *Advertising Age,* Nov. 5, 1990, p. 21; Raymond Serafin, "The Saturn Story," *Advertising Age,* Nov. 16, 1992, pp. 1, 13, 16; Raymond Serafin and Patricia Strand, "Saturn People Star in First Campaign," *Advertising Age,* Aug. 27, 1990, pp. 1, 38; Alex Taylor III, "GM's Over-the-Hill Gang," *Fortune,* Aug. 20, 2001, www.fortune.com; Alex Taylor III, "Wrong Turn at Saturn," *Fortune,* July 24, 2000, www.fortune.com; Neal Templin and Joseph B. White, "GM's Saturn in Early Orbit, Intrigues Buyers," *The Wall Street Journal,* Oct. 25, 1990, pp. B1, B6; James B. Treece, "Here Comes GM's Saturn," *Business Week,* Apr. 9, 1990, pp. 56–62; "23 More Dealers Open Doors to Saturn Buyers," *USA Today,* Nov. 15, 1990, p. 6B; David Welch, "Running Rings Around Saturn," *Business Week,* Feb. 21, 2000, pp. 114–118; David Welch, with Christine N. Tierney and Chester Dawson, "GM Tries to Show Who's Boss," *Business Week,* Mar. 12, 2001,

www.businessweek.com/magazine./content/01_11/b3723157. htm; Phil West, "Saturn Corp. Rings Up First Profitable Month," *The Commercial Appeal,* June 11, 1993, p. B2; Gregory L. White, "As GM Courts the Net, Struggling Saturn Line Exposes Rusty Spots," *The Wall Street Journal,* July 11, 2000, p. A1; Gregory L. White, "GM's Saturn Unit Temporarily Closes Plants on Slow Sales, Launch Problems," *The Wall Street Journal,* Jan. 7, 2000, p. A4; Gregory L. White, "Saturn Expands Brand in New Campaign," *The Wall Street Journal,* June 28, 1999, p. B8; Joseph B. White and Melinda Grenier Guiles, "Rough Launch," *The Wall Street Journal,* July 9, 1990, pp. A1, A12; Cindy Wolff, "First Saturn Here Runs Jag Off Road," *The Commercial Appeal,* Oct. 26, 1990, pp. A1, A12; David Woodruff, with James B. Treece, Sunita Wadekar Bhargava, and Karen Lowry Miller, "Saturn: GM Finally Has a Real Winner, But Success Is Bringing a Fresh Batch of Problems," *Business Week,* Aug. 17, 1992, pp. 86–91; Mark Yost and Joseph B. White, "GM to Invest $1.5 Billion in Saturn Unit," *The Wall Street Journal,* Apr. 26, 2000, p. A4.

CHAPTER 3

1. Sources: "About FedEx," FedEx, www.fedex.com/us/about/, June 18, 2001; "FedEx Finds an Overnight Partner," *Business Week Online,* Jan. 22, 2001, www.businessweek.com; Tom Jacobs, "FedEx and Postal Service in $7 Billion Deal," *The Motley Fool,* Jan. 11, 2001, http://aolsnapshot.fool.com/news/breakfast/2001/breakfast010111.html; Nicole Maestri, "FedEx in $7 Billion Alliance with USPS," CBS Marketwatch.com, Jan. 10, 2001, http://www.aolpf.marketwatch.com/.

2. P. Varadarajan, Terry Clark, and William M. Pride, "Controlling the Uncontrollable: Managing Your Market Environment," *Sloan Management Review,* Winter 1992, pp. 39–47.

3. Christine Koberg, Julie A. Chesley, and Kurt A. Heppard, "Adaptive Latitude: Environment, Organization, and Individual Influences," *Journal of Business Research,* 50, no. 3 (2000), pp. 259–272.

4. O. C. Ferrell, Michael D. Hartline, and George H. Lucas, Jr., *Marketing Strategy* (Ft. Worth, Tex.: Dryden, 2002), p. 37.

5. Ibid.

6. Rodolfo Vazquez, Maria Leticia Santos, and Luis Ignacio Álvarez, "Market Orientation, Innovation and Competitive Strategies in Industrial Firms," *Journal of Strategic Marketing,* Mar. 2001, pp. 69–90.

7. Eberhard Stickel, "Uncertainty Reduction in a Competitive Environment," *Journal of Business Research,* 51, no. 3 (2001), pp. 169–177.

8. Jennifer Gilbert and Jane Hodges, "Bear Opportunities," *Business 2.0,* Apr. 17, 2001, pp. 52–55.

9. Paula Lyon Andruss, "Staying in the Game: Turning an Economic Dip into Opportunity," *Marketing News,* May 7, 2001, pp. 1, 9.

10. Bureau of the Census, *Statistical Abstract of the United States, 2000* (Washington DC: Government Printing Office, 2001), p. 467.

11. Patrick Barta and Anne Marie Chaker, "Consumers Voice Rising Dissatisfaction with Companies," *The Wall Street Journal,* May 21, 2001, p. A2.

12. Debbie Thorne McAlister, Linda Ferrell, and O. C. Ferrell, *Business and Society: A Strategic Approach to Corporate Citizenship* (Boston: Houghton Mifflin, 2003); Don Corney, Amy Borrus, and Jay Greene, "Microsoft's All Out Counterattack," *Business Week,* May 15, 2000, pp. 103–106.

13. Mary Lou Steptoe, "Sherman Tank," *Journal of Business Strategy,* Jan./Feb. 1994, p. 12.

14. "U.S. Company to Plead Guilty and Pay Fine for Its Role in an International Price-Fixing Conspiracy," U.S. Department of Justice, press release, Mar. 15, 2001, www.usdoj.gov/opa/pr/2001/March/109at.htm.

15. "Survey: Kids Disclose Private Details Online," CNN, May 17, 2000, www.cnn.com.

16. "Marketers of 'The Enforma System' Settle FTC Charges of Deceptive Advertising for Their Weight Loss Product," Federal Trade Commission, Apr. 26, 2000, www.ftc.gov/opa/2000/04/enforma.htm.

17. David A. Balto, "Emerging Antitrust Issues in Electronic Commerce," *Journal of Public Policy & Marketing,* Fall 2000, pp. 277–286.

18. Jennifer Rewick, "Connecticut Attorney General Launches Probe of Priceline.com After Complaints," *The Wall Street Journal,* Oct. 2, 2000, p. B16.

19. "NAD Asks Kal Kan to Modify Advertising for Whiskas Homestyle Favorite Cat Food: Kal Kan Appeals Decision to the NARB," Better Business Bureau, May 18, 2000, www.nadreview.org/nad00/0504.asp.

20. Ibid.

21. "Telework America 2000: Research Results," International Telework Association and Council, www.telecommute.org/twa2000/research_results_summary.shtml, Apr. 10, 2001.

22. McAlister, Ferrell, and Ferrell, *Business and Society.*

23. Ibid.

24. Dana James, "Broadband Horizons," *Marketing News,* Mar. 13, 2000, pp. 1, 9.

25. Steven Rosenbush, "Broadband: What Happened?" *Business Week,* June 11, 2001, pp. 38–41.

26. McAlister, Ferrell, and Ferrell, *Business and Society.*

27. Vladimir Zwass, "Electronic Commerce: Structures and Issues," *International Journal of Electronic Commerce,* Fall 2000, pp. 3–23.

28. "Covisint Parts Exchange Officially Opens for Business," Bloomberg Newswire, Dec. 11, 2000, via AOL.

29. "Hard-Core Internet Sales," *Business Week Online,* Mar. 9, 2000, www.businessweek.com.

30. Michael J. Mondel, "Rethinking the Internet," *Business Week,* Mar. 21, 2001, p. 118; McAlister, Ferrell, and Ferrell, *Business and Society.*

31. Nicholas Negroponte, "Will Everything Be Digital?" *Time,* June 19, 2000.

32. "Novell Extends Net Services to the Mobile Internet," Novell, press release, Sep. 11, 2000, www.novell.com/news/press/archive/2000/09/pr00092.html.

33. Negroponte, "Will Everything Be Digital?"

34. Bureau of the Census, *Statistical Abstract of the United States,* p. 15.

35. Ibid., pp. 51, 55.

36. Ibid., p. 14.

37. Ibid., p. 9.

38. Ibid., p. 12.

39. Eduardo Porter, "Hispanic Marketers Try to Push Ad Spending Aimed at Latinos," *The Wall Street Journal,* Apr. 24, 2001, http://interactive.wsj.com.

40. Robert Sharoff, "Diversity in the Mainstream," *Marketing News,* May 21, 2001, pp. 1, 13.

41. Porter, "Hispanic Marketers."

42. Marcia Mogelonsky, "Food on Demand," *American Demographics,* Jan. 1998, www.marketingtools.com/publicationsad/index.html.

43. Sources: "America Online Announces New Organization to Integrate Netscape and Extend Industry Leadership," Netscape press release, Mar. 24, 1999, http://home.netscape.com/newsref/pr/newsrelease747.html; "Direct Testimony of Jim Barskdale," MSNBC, www.msnbc.com/news/206739.asp, Sep. 4, 2001; Gwendolyn Mariano, "Netscape Unveils Online Magazine," *c/net News,* May 23, 2001, http://news.cnet.com/

news/0-1005-200-601743.html; "Netscape," *Business Now,* http://www.batv.com, Sep. 5, 2001; Stephen H. Wildstrom, "A Nimbler Netscape Navigator," *Business Week Online,* Aug. 24, 2001, www.businessweek.com/bwdaily/dnflash/aug2001/nf20010824_557.htm.

44. Sources: Christopher Barr, "The Justice Department's Lawsuit Against Microsoft," C/Net, www.cnet.com/content/voices/Barr/012698/ss01.html, July 13, 1998; Charles Bierbauer, "What's Next in Microsoft Case?" CNN, June 28, 2001, www.cnn.com; Ted Bridis, "More Accusations Hit Microsoft," *Denver Post,* Oct. 23, 1998, sec. B; Rebecca Buckman, "Go Figure: In Valuing a Split Microsoft, Analysts Offer a Wide Range of Numbers," *The Wall Street Journal,* May 2, 2000, pp. C1, C3; Rebecca Buckman, "Looking Through Microsoft's Window; On the Firm's Sprawling Campus, It's Almost Business as Usual as Talk of Breakup Brews," *The Wall Street Journal,* May 1, 2000, pp. B1, B10; Dan Check, "The Case Against Microsoft," CompuServe, http://ourworld.compuserve.com/homepages/spazz/mspaper.htm, Spring 1996; Don Clark and Ted Bridis, "Creating Two Behemoths? Company Bets Appeals Court Will Overturn Jackson, Making Any Remedy Moot," *The Wall Street Journal,* Apr. 28, 2000, pp. B1, B4; Tim Clark, "Go Away," http://ne2.news.com/News/Item/0,4,2076,00.html, Aug. 7, 1996; "Company Research, Briefing Books," *The Wall Street Journal,* http://interactive.wsj.com, Mar. 12, 2001; Paul Davidson, "Expert's View May Influence Ruling," *USA Today,* Feb. 2, 2000, p. B1; Paul Davidson, "Microsoft Awaits a New Hand; Executives Expert Appeals Judges to Be More Amenable," *USA Today,* June 8, 2000, pp. B1, B2; Paul Davidson, "Microsoft Responds to Judge's Findings," *USA Today,* Jan. 19, 2000, p. B1; Paul Davidson, "Microsoft Split Ordered; Appeal Could Go Directly to Supreme Court," *USA Today,* June 8, 2000, p. A1; Dana Gardner, "Java Is an Unleashed Force of Nature, Says JavaOne Panel," *InfoWorld Electric,* Mar. 26, 1998, www.infoworld.com/cgi-bin/displayStory.pl?980326.ehjavapanel.htm; "Feud Heats Up," http://ne2.news.com/SpecialFeature...d/0,6,2216_2,00.html'st.ne.ni.prev, July 13, 1998; Bill Gates and Steve Ballmer, "To Our Customers, Partners and Shareholders," *USA Today,* Apr. 5, 2000, p. B7; Lee Gomes and Rebecca Buckman, "Creating Two Behemoths? Microsoft Split Might Not Be Much Help for Competitors and Could Harm Consumer," *The Wall Street Journal,* Apr. 28, 2000, p. B1; Dan Goodin, "New Microsoft Java Flaws Alleged," C/Net, July 9, 1998, http://news.cnet.com/news/0-1003-200-331044.html; John Harwood and David Bank, "CyberSpectacle: Senate Meets Electronic Elite," *The Wall Street Journal,* Mar. 4, 1998, pp. B1, B13; "International Design for Office 2000," Microsoft Corp., www.microsoft.com/Office/ORK/2000Journ/LangPack.htm, Sep. 28, 2000; Edward Iwata and John Swartz, "Bill Gates Won't Be Dethroned So Easily; Software King—and His Myth—to Survive on Iron Will, Talent," *USA Today,* June 8, 2000, p. B3; Margaret A. Jacobs, "Injunction Looms as Showdown for Microsoft," *The Wall Street Journal,* May 20, 1998, pp. B1, B6; "Java Contract Lawsuit Update," Microsoft Corp., http://msdn.microsoft.com/visualj/lawsuitruling.asp, Sep. 28, 2000; Eun-Kyung Kim, "Microsoft Court Gets Lesson on Monopolies," *The [Fort Collins] Coloradoan,* Nov. 20, 1998, p. B2; Malcolm Maclachlan, "New Lawsuit Is Over Java, Sun Says," *TechWeb,* May 12, 1998; Malcolm Maclachlan, "Sun Attacks an Embattled Microsoft," *TechWeb,* May 14, 1998, www.techweb.com/wire/story/msftdoj/TWB19980514S0002; Malcolm Maclachlan, "Sun Targets Microsoft: Software Maker Says Windows 98 Must Be Java Compatible," *TechWeb,* May 12, 1998, www.techweb.com/news/story/TWB19980512S0012; Kevin Maney, "Microsoft's Uncertain Future Rattles Investors; Justice Must Make Recommendation; Breakup Possible," *USA*

Today, Apr. 25, 2000, p. B1; Michael J. Martinez, "Microsoft Buys Time to Retool," *The Coloradoan,* Sep. 27, 2000, pp. A1, A2; Richard B. McKenzie, *Trust on Trial; How the Microsoft Case Is Reframing the Rules of Competition* (Cambridge, MA: Perseus Publishing, 2000); Patrick McMahon, "Stoic Staffers Shake Heads, Return to Work," *USA Today,* June 8, 2000, p. B3; "Microsoft Antitrust Ruling," Court TV, www.courttv.com/legaldocs/cyberlaw/mseruling.html, Feb. 13, 2001; "Microsoft Asks Court to Limit Gates Disposition," Yahoo Daily News, http://dailynews.yahoo.com/headlines/politics/story.html/s=z/reuters/980805/politics/stories/microsoft_1.html; "Microsoft Corporate Information. What We Do," Microsoft Corp., www.microsoft.com/mscorp/, Mar. 8, 2001); "Microsoft Files Summary Judgment Motions in Caldera Lawsuit," Microsoft Corp. press release, Feb. 12, 1999, www.microsoft.com/PressPass/press/1999/Feb99/Calderapr.asp; "Microsoft: What's Next?" CNN, June 29, 2001, www.cnn.com; Michael Moeller, "Amended Complaint: Microsoft Wants Access to 'Highly Confidential' Documents," *PC Week Online,* Aug. 4, 1998; "Notice Regarding Java Lawsuit Ruling; Notice to Customers," Microsoft Corp., http://msdn.microsoft.com/visualj/statement.asp, Sep. 28, 2000; Robert O'Brien, "Kodak, Lexmark Lead Decline as Profit Warnings Hurt Stocks," *The Wall Street Journal,* Sep. 27, 2000, p. C2; Tim O'Brien, "Explaining the Microsoft Ruling," CNN, Aug. 17, 2001, www.cnn.com; Lisa Picarille, "Microsoft, Sun Postpone Java Hearing," *TechWeb,* July 7, 1998, www.techweb.com/wire/story/TWB19980707S0001; Jared Sandberg, "Bring on the Chopping Block," *Newsweek,* May 8, 2000, pp. 34–35; Jared Sandberg, "Microsoft's Six Fatal Errors," *Newsweek,* June 19, 2000, pp. 23–27; Julie Schmit, "Tech Industry's Direction Hangs in Balance," *USA Today,* Oct. 16, 1998, p. 3B; Jon Swartz, "Microsoft Split Ordered; Will Breakup Help or Hurt Consumers?" *USA Today,* June 8, 2000, pp. A1, A2; Bob Trott and David Pendery, "Allchin E-Mail Adds to Microsoft's Legal Woes"; Geri Coleman Tucker and Will Rodger, "Facing Breakup, Gates to Take Case to People; Microsoft Says Don't Punish Success," *USA Today,* May 1, 2000, pp. B1, B2; U.S. Justice Department and State Attorneys General, "Statement by Microsoft Corporation," www.microsoft.com/presspass.doj.7-28formalresponse.htm, Aug. 3, 1998; John R. Wilke and David Bank, "Microsoft's Chief Concedes Hardball Tactics," *The Wall Street Journal,* Mar. 4, 1998, pp. B1, B13; Nick Wingfield, "Net Assault," http://ne2.news.com/News/Item/0,4,1940,00.html, July 25, 1996; Nick Wingfield and Tim Clark, "Dirty," http://ne2.news.com/News/Item/0,4,2072,00.html, Aug. 7, 1996; Aaron Zitner, "Feds Assail Gates," *Denver Post,* Oct. 30, 1998, sec. C. This case was prepared by Robyn Smith for the purpose of classroom discussion rather than to illustrate either effective or ineffective handling of an administrative situation.

CHAPTER 4

1. Sources: Jim Carlton, "Norway's Tomra Redefines Recycling with Bright, Clean, Accessible Kiosks," *The Wall Street Journal,* Mar. 6, 2001, http://interactive.wsj.com; "News" Tomra, www.tomra.as/PM/777599.html, June 13, 2001; Robinson Shaw, "Recycling Centers Pay Handsome Dividends," Environmental News Network, Apr. 14, 2000, www.enn.com/enn-news-archive/2000/04/04142000/replanet_12005.asp; "Tomra," Tomra, www.tomra.no/tomra.htm, Jun. 21, 2001.

2. "Growth in Piracy Reverses Trend," *The Star Tribune,* May 28, 2001, p. D7.

3. Yuri Kageyama, "Mitsubishi Motors Says Massive Defect Cover-ups Were Intentional," *The Boston Globe,* Aug. 22, 2000, www.boston.com/; Yuri Kageyama, "Mitsubishi Motors Says Massive Defect Cover-ups Were Intentional," *SF Gate,* Aug. 22, 2000, www.sfgate.com/.

4. "About Avon," Avon, www.avoncompany.com/about/, Jun. 21, 2001; "The Avon Breast Cancer Crusade," Avon, www.avoncompany.com/women/avoncrusade/, Jun. 21, 2001.

5. Isabelle Maignan and O. C. Ferrell, "Antecedents and Benefits of Corporate Citizenship: An Investigation of French Businesses," *Journal of Business Research,* 51, no. 1 (2001), pp. 37–51.

6. Debbie Thorne, Linda Ferrell, and O. C. Ferrell, *Business and Society: A Strategic Approach to Corporate Citizenship* (Boston: Houghton Mifflin, 2002).

7. B&Q, www.diy.com/, Apr. 16, 2001.

8. Archie Carroll, "The Pyramid of Corporate Social Responsibility: Toward the Moral Management of Organizational Stakeholders," *Business Horizons,* July/Aug. 1991, p. 42.

9. Thea Singer, "Can Business Still Save the World?" *Inc.,* Apr. 2001, pp. 58–71.

10. Debbie Thorne LeClair, O. C. Ferrell, and John P. Fraedrich, *Integrity Management: A Guide to Legal and Ethical Issues in the Workplace* (Tampa, FL: University of Tampa Press, 1998), pp. 139–140.

11. Robert Manor, "Corporate Spy Case Unfolds in Lawsuit," *Chicago Tribune,* Apr. 8, 2001, www.chicagotribune.com/business/businessnews/article/0,2669,2-51039,FF.html.

12. "Total Giving Reaches $203.45 Billion as Charitable Contributions Increase 6.6 Percent in 2000," AAFRC, press release, May 23, 2001, www.aafrc.org/press3.html.

13. Minette E. Drumwright and Patrick E. Murphy, "Corporate Societal Marketing," in Paul N. Bloom and Gregory T. Gundlach, eds., *Handbook of Marketing and Society* (Thousand Oaks, CA: Sage, 2001), pp. 162–183.

14. The Hitachi Foundation, www.hitachi.org/, June 21, 2001.

15. Thorne, Ferrell, and Ferrell, *Business and Society.*

16. Ibid.

17. Alan K. Reichert, Marion S. Webb, and Edward G. Thomas, "Corporate Support for Ethical and Environmental Policies: A Financial Management Perspective," *Journal of Business Ethics,* 25 (2000), pp. 53–64.

18. Jeffrey Ball, "GM to Produce Hybrid Trucks, Buses in Scramble to Build 'Green' Vehicles," *The Wall Street Journal,* Aug. 3, 2000, p. A4.

19. Thorne, Ferrell, and Ferrell, *Business and Society.*

20. "Saving the Forest for the Trees," *Business Week,* Nov. 20, 2000, pp. 62–63.

21. Jim Carlton, "Chiquita to Take Part in Environmental Program," *The Wall Street Journal,* Nov. 16, 2000, p. A3.

22. Paul Hawken and William McDonough, "Seven Steps to Doing Good Business," *Inc.,* Nov. 1993, pp. 79–90.

23. Peter J. Gallanis, "Community Support Is a Powerful Tool," *DSN Retailing Today,* July 24, 2000, pp. 57, 71.

24. New Belgium Brewing Company, www.newbelgium.com/n_vibe.shtml, June 21, 2000.

25. Thorne, Ferrell, and Ferrell, *Business and Society.*

26. *Business Ethics,* Jan./Feb. 1995, p. 13.

27. "Dealers Gear Up for Massive Tire Recall," *The Pantagraph,* May 24, 2001, p. C1.

28. "Ford's Finance Unit Is Accused of Charging Higher Rates to Blacks," *The Wall Street Journal,* Nov. 2, 2000, p. B20.

29. Gisele Durham, "Study Finds Lying, Cheating in Teens," AOL News, Oct. 16, 2000.

30. Peggy H. Cunningham and O. C. Ferrell, "The Influence of Role Stress on Unethical Behavior by Personnel Involved in the Marketing Research Process" (working paper, Queens University, Ont., 1998), p. 35.

31. Joseph W. Weiss, *Business Ethics: A Managerial, Stakeholder Approach* (Belmont, CA: Wadsworth, 1994), p. 13.

32. Ethics Resource Center, *The Ethics Resource Center's 2000 National Business Ethics Survey: How Employees Perceive Ethics at Work* (Washington, DC: Ethics Resource Center, 2000), p. 85.

33. O. C. Ferrell, Larry G. Gresham, and John Fraedrich, "A Synthesis of Ethical Decision Models for Marketing," *Journal of Macromarketing,* Fall 1989, pp. 58–59.

34. Barry J. Babin, James S. Boles, and Donald P. Robin, "Representing the Perceived Ethical Work Climate Among Marketing Employees," *Journal of the Academy of Marketing Science,* 28, no. 3 (2000), pp. 345–358.

35. Ethics Resource Center, *2000 National Business Ethics Survey,* p. 38.

36. Ferrell, Gresham, and Fraedrich, "A Synthesis of Ethical Decision Models."

37. Lawrence B. Chonko and Shelby D. Hunt, "Ethics and Marketing Management: A Retrospective and Prospective Commentary," *Journal of Business Research,* 50, no. 3 (2000), pp. 235–244.

38. Linda K. Trevino and Stuart Youngblood, "Bad Apples in Bad Barrels: A Causal Analysis of Ethical Decision Making Behavior," *Journal of Applied Psychology,* 75, no. 4 (1990), pp. 378–385.

39. Gene R. Laczniak and Patrick E. Murphy, *Ethical Marketing Decisions: The Higher Road* (Boston: Allyn & Bacon, 1993), p. 14.

40. "Industry Social Responsibility Statement," American Apparel Manufacturers Association, www.americanapparel.org/AAMA_Social_Responsibility.html, June 21, 2001; "WRAP Principles," Worldwide Responsible Apparel Production, www.wrapapparel.org/infosite2/index.htm, June 21, 2001.

41. "Anatomy of an Ethics Office," *Business Ethics,* Sep./Oct. and Nov./Dec. 1999, p. 14.

42. Thorne, Ferrell, and Ferrell, *Business and Society.*

43. Edward Petry, "Six Myths about the Corporate Ethics Office," *Ethikos,* Mar./Apr. 1998, p. 4.

44. Sir Adrian Cadbury, "Ethical Managers Make Their Own Rules," *Harvard Business Review,* Sept./Oct. 1987, p. 33.

45. O. C. Ferrell, Michael D. Hartline, George H. Lucas, Jr., and David J. Luck, *Marketing Strategy* (Ft. Worth, TX: Dryden, 1999), p. 169.

46. Isabelle Maignan, "Antecedents and Benefits of Corporate Citizenship: A Comparison of U.S. and French Businesses" (Ph.D. dissertation, University of Memphis, 1997).

47. Kurschner, "5 Ways Ethical Busine$$ Creates Fatter Profit$," pp. 20–23.

48. Margaret A. Stroup, Ralph L. Newbert, and Jerry W. Anderson, Jr., "Doing Good, Doing Better: Two Views of Social Responsibility," *Business Horizons,* Mar./Apr. 1987, p. 23.

49. Ferrell et al., *Marketing Strategy,* p. 170.

50. Sources: Peter Asmus, "Goodbye Coal, Hello Wind," *Business Ethics,* July/Aug. 1999, pp. 10–11; Robert Baun, "What's in a Name? Ask the Makers of Fat Tire," *The [Fort Collins] Coloradoan,* Oct. 8, 2000, pp. E1, E3; Rachel Brand, "Colorado Breweries Bring Home 12 Medals in Festival," *Rocky Mountain [Denver] News,* www.insidedenver.com/news/1008beer6.shtml, Nov. 6, 2000; Stevi Deter, "Fat Tire Amber Ale," The Net Net, www.thenetnet.com/reviews/fat.html, Mar. 5, 2001; DirtWorld.com, www.dirtworld.com/races/Colorado_race745.htm, Nov. 6, 2000; Robert F. Dwyer and John F. Tanner, Jr., *Business Marketing* (Burr Ridge, IL: Irwin McGraw-Hill, 1999), p. 104; "Fat Tire Amber Ale," *Achwiegut (The Guide to Austrian Beer),* www.austrianbeer.com/beer/b000688.shtml, Mar. 5, 2001; Del I. Hawkins, Roger J. Best, and

Kenneth A. Coney, *Consumer Behavior: Building Marketing Strategy,* 8th ed. (Burr Ridge, IL: Irwin McGraw-Hill, 2001); David Kemp, Tour Connoisseur, New Belgium Brewing Company, personal interview by Nikole Haiar, Nov. 21, 2000; New Belgium Brewing Company, Ft. Collins, CO, www.newbelgium.com, Mar. 5, 2001; New Belgium Brewing Company Tour by Nikole Haiar, Nov. 20, 2000; Dan Rabin, "New Belgium Pours It on for Bike Riders," *Celebrator Beer News,* www.celebrator.com/9808/rabin.html, Mar. 5, 2001. This case was prepared by Nikole Haiar for classroom discussion rather than to illustrate either effective or ineffective handling of an administrative, ethical, or legal decision by management.

51. Sources: Timothy Aeppel, "Firestone Milestone Brings on Dilemma," *The Wall Street Journal,* Aug. 18, 2000, p. B8; Bridgestone/Firestone, www.firestone.com, Aug. 30, 2001; Lauren Comander, "Firestone Tires Shipped from Japan to Boost Supply," *Chicago Tribune,* Aug. 23, 2000, pp. 1, 2; "Consumer Advisory: Potentially Dangerous Tires," *Fox Market News,* Sep. 1, 2000, http://foxmarketwire.com/090100/tiredeaths_list.sml; Claudia H. Deutsch, "Where Rubber Meets the Road; Recall of Firestone Tires Is Aimed at Damage Control," *The New York Times,* http://archives.nytimes.com, Aug. 21, 2000; Melita Marie Garza, Lauren Comander, and Patrick Cole, "Problems at Tire Plant Alleged," *Chicago Tribune,* Aug. 20, 2000, pp. 1, 10; Milo Geyelin and Timothy Aeppel, "For Firestone, Tire Trial Is Mixed Victory," *The Wall Street Journal,* Aug. 27, 2001, pp. A3, A4; Lori Grant, "More Retailers Pull 3 Firestone Tires from Stock," *USA Today,* Aug. 7, 2000, p. 1B; James R. Healey, "What You Don't Know About Your Tires," *USA Today,* Aug. 11, 2000, p. B1; David Kiley, "Bridgestone Exec Will Speak to Congress," *The [Fort Collins] Coloradoan,* Aug. 30, 2000, p. D7; Kathryn Kranhold and Erin White, "The Perils and Potential Rewards of Crisis Management for Firestone," *The Wall Street Journal,* Sep. 8, 2000, pp. B1, B4; Robert Guy Matthews, "How the Rubber Meets the Road," *The Wall Street Journal,* Sep. 8, 2000, pp. B1, B4; Jayne O'Donnell, "Transportation Travels Bumpy Road," *USA Today,* July 18, 2001, p. 3B; Stephen Power, "Update Needed for Tire Rules, Activists Argue," *The Wall Street Journal,* Sep. 8, 2000, pp. B1, B4; Stephen Power and Clare Ansberry, "Bridgestone/Firestone Says It Made 'Bad Tires,' " *The Wall Street Journal,* Sep. 13, 2000, pp. A3, A6; Robert L. Simison, "For Ford CEO Nasser, Damage Control Is the New 'Job One,' " *The Wall Street Journal,* Sep. 11, 2000, pp. A1, A8; Calvin Sims, "A Takeover with Problems for Japanese Tire Maker," *The New York Times,* http://archives.nytimes.com, Aug. 21, 2000; Devon Spurgeon, "State Farm Researcher's Sleuthing Helped Prompt Firestone Recall," *The Wall Street Journal,* Sep. 1, 2000, pp. B1, B6; Jason Szip, "Firestone's Japanese Parent Hit Again," *Fox Market Wire,* Sep. 1, 2000, http://foxmarketwire.com/090100/tirestrike_side2.sml; Bill Vlasic, "Anatomy of a Crisis," *The Coloradoan,* Sep. 4, 2000, pp. C1, C2. This case was prepared by Dana Schubert and O. C. Ferrell for classroom discussion rather than to illustrate either effective or ineffective handling of an administrative situation.

CHAPTER 5

1. Sources: "And the Grammy Nominees Are . . .", *USA Today,* Jan. 4, 2001, www.usatoday.com/; "List of Latin Grammy Award Winners," *USA Today,* Sep. 14, 2000, www.usatoday.com/; Bruce Orwell, "Grooming of Colombian Pop Star Shows Shift in Gears for U.S. Culture Machine," *The Wall Street Journal Interactive,* Feb. 13, 2001, http://interactive.wsj.com; "Shakira: Colombia's Pop Daughter Hits Big Time," *CNN,* Sep. 6, 2000, www.cnn.com.

2. "WTO Secretariat Releases 2001 Annual Report," World Trade Organization, press release, May 23, 2001, www.wto.org/ english/news_e/pres01_e/pr226_e.htm; "Growth Rate of World Merchandise Trade Expected to Double in 2000, According to Latest Report by WTO Secretariat," World Trade Organization, press release, Nov. 30, 2000, www.wto.org/english/news_e/ pres00_e/pr200_e.htm.

3. "Go Global," *Business 2.0,* May 2000, p. 179; "McDonald's Announces Changes to the Global Management Team," McDonald's, press release, May 1, 2001, www.mcdonald.com/ corporate/press/corporate/2001/05012001/05012001.html.

4. Nick Bromell, "Yahoo France," *Fortune,* Oct. 16, 2000, p. 246.

5. "Product Pitfalls Proliferate in Global Cultural Maze," *The Wall Street Journal,* May 14, 2001, p. B11.

6. Ibid.

7. Ibid.

8. Jeffrey G. Blodgett, Long-Chuan Lu, Gregory M. Rose, and Scott J. Vitell, "Ethical Sensitivity to Stakeholder Interests: A Cross-Cultural Comparison," *Journal of the Academy of Marketing Science,* 29, no. 2 (2001), pp. 190–202.

9. Nigel G.G. Campbell, John L. Graham, Alain Jolibert, and Hans Gunther Messner, "Marketing Negotiations in France, Germany, the United Kingdom, and the United States," *Journal of Marketing,* Apr. 1988, pp. 49–62.

10. Brian Mark Hawrysh and Judith Lynne Zaichkowsky, "Cultural Approaches to Negotiations: Understanding the Japanese," *International Marketing Review,* 7, no. 2 (1990), pp. 28–42.

11. Zeynep Gürhan-Canli and Durairaj Maheswaran, "Cultural Variations in Country of Origin Effects," *Journal of Marketing Research,* Aug. 2000, pp. 309–317.

12. Joseph Albright and Marcia Kunstel, "Schlotzsky's First China Opening Less Than Red-Hot," *Austin American-Statesman,* www.austin360.com, May 27, 1998.

13. Dave Izraeli and Mark S. Schwartz, "What We Can Learn from the Federal Sentencing Guidelines for Organizational Ethics," *Journal of Business Ethics,* July 1998, pp. 9–10.

14. "International Accounts Data: Trade in Goods and Services: Tables," Bureau of Economic Analysis, www.bea.doc.gov/bea/di/tradgs-d.htm, June 20, 2001.

15. Bureau of the Census, *Statistical Abstract of the United States, 2000* (Washington, DC: Government Printing Office, 2001), pp. 822–824, 832.

16. Earl Naumann and Douglas J. Lincoln, "Non-Tariff Barriers and Entry Strategy Alternatives: Strategic Marketing Implications," *Journal of Small Business Management,* Apr. 1991, pp. 60–70.

17. Charles R. Taylor, George R. Franke, and Michael L. Maynard, "Attitudes Toward Direct Marketing and Its Regulation: A Comparison of the United States and Japan," *Journal of Public Policy & Marketing,* Fall 2000, pp. 228–237.

18. "European Consumers Getting Comfortable with Online Channel," CyberAtlas, July 6, 2001, http://cyberatlas.internet.com/big_picture/geographics/article/0,,5911_794321,00.html.

19. "Japan's Online Population," CyberAtlas, Apr. 25, 2001, http://cyberatlas.internet.com/big_picture/geographics/article/0,,5911_752061,00.html.; "China's Online Population," Cyber Atlas, Apr. 25, 2001, http://cyberatlas.internet.com/ big_picture/geographics/article/0,,5911_752081,00.html.

20. Jim Rohwer, "China's Coming Telecom Battle," *Fortune,* Nov. 27, 2000, p. 209.

21. Louisa Kasdon Sidell, "The Economics of Inclusion," *Continental,* Apr. 2001, pp. 64–67.

22. Bureau of the Census, *Statistical Abstract,* pp. 822–824, 832.

23. "U.S. Trade Balance with Canada," U.S. Bureau of the Census, www.census.gov/foreign-trade/balance/c1220.html, June 20, 2001.

24. William C. Symonds, "Meanwhile, to the North, NAFTA Is a Smash," *Business Week,* Feb. 27, 1995, p. 66.

25. Bureau of the Census, *Statistical Abstract,* pp. 822–824, 832; Cheryl Farr Leas, "The Big Boom," *Continental,* Apr. 2001, pp. 85–94.

26. Leas, "The Big Boom," pp. 85–94.

27. "European Union Embarks on Expansion," CNN, www.cnn.com/SPECIALS/2000/eurounion/story/enlarge/, July 3, 2001.

28. "The Single Currency," CNN, www.cnn.com/SPECIALS/2000/eurounion/story/currency/, July 3, 2001.

29. Eric G. Fribert, "1992: Moves Europeans Are Making," *Harvard Business Review,* May/June 1989, p. 89.

30. "Mercosur Web Site," U.S. Department of Commerce, International Trade Administration, http://www.mac.doc.gov/ola/mercosur/index.htm, July 3, 2001; Mercosur, www.mercosur.org, July 3, 2001; Mercosur.com, www.mercosur.com, July 3, 2001.

31. Asia-Pacific Economic Cooperation, www.apecsec.org.sg/, July 5, 2001.

32. Dexter Roberts, with Joyce Barnathan and Robert J. Dowling, "Now, It's Reform or Bust," *Business Week,* Apr. 6, 1998, p. 54.

33. Pamela Yatsko, "Knocking Out the Knockoffs," *Fortune,* Oct. 2, 2000, pp. 213–218.

34. "U.S. Trade Balance with China," U.S. Bureau of the Census, www.census.gov/foreign-trade/balance/c5700.html, June 20, 2001.

35. "What Is the WTO," World Trade Organization, www.wto.org/, June 29, 2001.

36. Pradeep Tyagi, "Export Behavior of Small Business Firms in Developing Economies: Evidence from the Indian Market," *Marketing Management Journal,* Fall/Winter 2000, pp. 12–20.

37. Berrin Dosoglu-Guner, "How Do Exporters and Non-Exporters View Their 'Country of Origin' Image Abroad?" *Marketing Management Journal,* Fall/Winter 2000, pp. 21–27.

38. Farok J. Contractor and Sumit K. Kundu, "Franchising versus Company-Run Operations: Model Choice in the Global Hotel Sector," *Journal of International Marketing,* Nov. 1997, pp. 28–53.

39. Andrew Kupfer, "How to Be a Global Manager," *Fortune,* Mar. 14, 1988, pp. 52–58.

40. Kathryn Rudie Harrigan, "Joint Ventures and Competitive Advantage," *Strategic Management Journal,* May 1988, pp. 141–158.

41. Margaret H. Cunningham, "Marketing's New Frontier: International Strategic Alliances" (working paper, Queens University, Ont., 1998).

42. William Q. Judge and Joel A. Ryman, "The Shared Leadership Challenge in Strategic Alliances: Lessons from the U.S. Healthcare Industry," *Academy of Management Executive,* May 2001, pp. 71–79.

43. Ibid.

44. Leslie Gornstein, "Retailers Cater to Growing U.S. Hispanic Population," *Pensacola News Journal,* June 17, 2001, p. 4B.

45. Jagdish N. Sheth, "From International to Integrated Marketing," *Journal of Business Research,* Jan. 2001, pp. 5–9.

46. Theodore Levitt, "The Globalization of Markets," *Harvard Business Review,* May/June 1983, p. 92.

47. Deborah Owens, Timothy Wilkinson, and Bruce Keillor, "A Comparison of Product Attributes in a Cross-Cultural/Cross-National Context," *Marketing Management Journal,* Fall/Winter 2000, pp. 1–11.

48. Anil K. Gupta and Vijay Govindarajan, "Converting Global Presence into Global Competitive Advantage," *Academy of Management Executive,* May 2001, pp. 45–58.

49. Sources: Houghton Mifflin video, *Global Growth: The Subway Story;* Subway, "Jared's Statistics," Subway, www.subway.com/society/foj/jared_stats.htm, Aug. 13, 2001;

"Man Loses 245 Pounds Eating Nothing But SUBWAY® Sandwiches," Subway, Dec. 2000, www.subway.com/society/public_rel/pcr_press/011101pr.htm; "Subway® Restaurants Announces Opening of First Location in Croatia," Subway, June 2001, www.subway.com/society/public_rel/pcr_press/062501.htm; "Subway® Restaurants Announces Opening of First Location in France," Subway, June 2001, www.subway.com/society/public_rel/pcr_press/070301.htm; "Subway® Restaurants Announces Opening of First Location in Oman," Subway, Feb. 2001, www.subway.com/society/public_rel/pcr_press/020701bpr.htm; "Subway® Restaurants Announces Opening of 300th Australian Location," Subway, Feb. 2001, www.subway.com/society/public_rel/pcr_press/022101bpr.htm; "Subway® Restaurants Reach the 15,000 Mark Worldwide," Subway, Apr. 2001, www.subway.com/society/public_rel/pcr_press/043001pr.htm; Subway Student and Educator Resource Guide, www.subway.com/sub1/student_ed/, Aug. 13, 2001.

50. Sources: Dat'l Do-It World Wide Headquarters, www.datl-doit.com/, Aug. 29, 2001; Susanna P. Barton, "Chip Selling Tough, and That's No Bull," *Jacksonville Business Journal,* Sep. 27, 1996, p. 1; "Florida Company Cashing in on Hot Pepper Craze," *Chattanooga Free Press,* June 18, 1995; Jan Norris, "The Pepper Cult," *Palm Beach Post,* July 28, 1994; Steven Wolcott, "Hotter Is Better at Dat'l Do-It in St. Augustine," *Jacksonville Business Journal,* Jan. 21, 1994, p. 1–1.

CHAPTER 6

1. Sources: Emily Nelson, "P&G Checks Out Real Life," *The Wall Street Journal,* May 17, 2000, pp. B1, B4; "National Poll Finds Home-Cooked Meal Retains Its Appeal But Appetite for Dish Washing Wanes," Cascade Complete, www.cascadecomplete.com/cascadeCorner/surveyRes.html, June 4, 2001.

2. Rebecca Gardyn, "VIPs (Very Important Pets)," *American Demographics,* Mar. 2001, www.demographics.com.

3. "Pizza Hut (R) Studies Effects of 'Pizza Deprivation' on College and High School Students," PRNewswire, via AmericaOnline, May 30, 2001.

4. Jacquelyn S. Thomas, "A Methodology for Linking Custom Acquisition to Customer Retention," *Journal of Marketing Research,* May 2001, pp. 262–268.

5. "We Know Who Our Customers Are," Lowe's 2000 annual report, p. 9.

6. "Shoppers' Bizarre," *Marketing News,* Aug. 3, 1998, p. 2.

7. Jeffrey M. Humphrey, "Minority Buying Power," Selig Center for Economic Growth, University of Georgia, reported in *Marketing News,* July 2, 2001, p. 17.

8. Vikas Mittal and Wagner A. Kamakura, "Satisfaction, Repurchase Intent, and Repurchase Behavior: Investigating the Moderating Effects of Customer Characteristics," *Journal of Marketing Research,* Feb. 2001, pp. 131–142.

9. "Internal Secondary Market Research," Small Business Owner's Toolkit, www.lycos.com/business/cch/guidebook.html?lpv=1&docNumber=P03_3020, June 23, 2001.

10. Amy Merrick, "New Population Data Will Help Marketers Pitch Their Products," *The Wall Street Journal,* Feb. 14, 2001, http://interactive.wsj.com/.

11. "External Secondary Market Research," CCH Business Owner's Toolkit, www.lycos.com/business/cch/guidebook.html?lpv=1&docNumber=P03_3011, June 23, 2001.

12. Martha Farnsworth Riche, "Who Says Yes?" *American Demographics,* Feb. 1987, p. 8.

13. Peter S. Tuckel and Harry W. O'Neill, "Call Waiting," *Marketing Research,* Spring 1995, p. 8.

14. Martin Opperman, "E-mail Surveys—Potentials and Pitfalls," *Marketing Research,* Summer 1995, pp. 29, 32.

15. Leonardo Felson, "Netting Limitations: Online Researchers' New Tactics for Tough Audiences," *Marketing News,* Feb. 26, 2001, www.ama.org/pubs/.

16. Alissa Quart, "Ol' College Pry," *Business 2.0,* Apr. 3, 2001.

17. Cynthia Webster, "Consumers' Attitudes toward Data Collection Methods, in *Marketing: Toward the 21st Century,* ed. Robert L. King (Atlanta: Proceedings of the Southern Marketing Association, Nov. 1991), p. 221.

18. Peter DePaulo, "Sample Size for Qualitative Research," *Quirk's Marketing Research Review,* Dec. 2000, www.quirks.com.

19. Barbara Allan, "The Benefits of Telephone Depth Sessions," *Quirk's Marketing Research Review,* Dec. 2000, www.quirks.com.

20. Jagdip Singh, Roy D. Howell, and Gary K. Rhoads, "Adaptive Designs for Likert-Type Data: An Approach for Implementing Marketing Surveys," *Journal of Marketing Research,* Aug. 1990, pp. 304–321.

21. Alison Stein Wellner, "Research on a Shoestring," *American Demographics,* Apr. 2001, www.americandemographics.com.

22. Richard G. Barlow, "Today's Loyalty Leaders Won't Last," *Marketing News,* May 12, 2001, p. 13.

23. "Marketing Campaigns Impact on Consumer Habits," *The Guardian,* Nov. 15, 2000, www.society.guardian.co.uk/.

24. Eunkyu Lee, Michael Y. Hu, and Rex S. Toh, "Are Consumer Survey Results Distorted? Systematic Impact of Behavioral Frequency and Duration on Survey Response Errors," *Journal of Marketing Research,* Feb. 2000, pp. 125–133.

25. Judy Strauss and Donna J. Hill, "Consumer Complaints by E-mail: An Exploratory Investigation of Corporate Responses and Customer Reactions," *Journal of Interactive Marketing,* Winter 2001, pp. 63–73.

26. Laurence N. Goal, "High Technology Data Collection for Measurement and Testing," *Marketing Research,* Mar. 1992, pp. 29–38.

27. Philip Hans Franses, "How Nobel-Worthy Economics Relates to Databases," *Marketing News,* Mar. 12, 2001, p. 14.

28. Kathleen Cholewka, "Tiered CRM: Serving Pip-Squeaks to VIPs," *Sales & Marketing Management,* Apr. 2001, pp. 25–26.

29. Merrick, "New Population Data."

30. Alison L. Sprout, "The Internet inside Your Company," *Fortune,* Nov. 27, 1995, pp. 161–168.

31. Joseph Rydholm, "A Global Perspective: Syndicated Survey Monitors Airline Performance Around the World," *Quirk's Marketing Research Review,* Nov. 2000, www.quirks.com/.

32. "Top 50 U.S. Research Organizations," *Marketing News,* June 4, 2001, p. H4.

33. Lambeth Hochwald, "Are You Smart Enough to Sell Globally?" *Sales & Marketing Management,* July 1998, pp. 52–56.

34. Ibid.

35. Sources: "Key Facts," *The Wall Street Journal,* http://interactive.wsj.com, Sep. 7, 2001; "On-Line Purchases of Consumer Packaged Goods on the Rise" (study by Information Resources, Inc.), *DSN Retailing Today,* June 4, 2001, www.findarticles.com/cf_0/m0FNP/11_40/75452753/p1/article.jhtml?term=%22Information+Resources%22; "Overview," Information Resources, Inc., www.infores.com/public/us/aboutiri/default.htm, Sep. 3, 2001.

36. Sources: Patrick Goldstein, "Untangling the Web of Teen Trends," *Los Angeles Times,* Nov. 21, 2000, www.Look-look.com/looklook/html/Test_Drive_Press_LA_Times2.html; Sarah Moore, "On Your Markets," *Working Woman,* Feb. 2001, p. 26; Michael Quintanilla and Marian Lu, "The Very Latest in Hanging out at the Mall," *Los Angeles Times,* July 28, 2000, www.Look-look.com/looklook/html/Test_Drive_Press_LA_Times.html; "Who We Are," Look-Look.com, www.look-look.com, Aug. 29, 2001.

CHAPTER 7

1. Sources: Sheree R. Curry, "Wireless Trend Taking Hold," *Advertising Age,* June 25, 2001, pp. S2+; "Guessing Game," *Telephony,* June 25, 2001, p. 14; "Nokia Keeps Eye on 40%," *Wireless Week,* May 7, 2001, p. 1; Todd Wasserman, "Nokia, Ericsson, Moto Call Up New Movie Roles," *Brandweek,* April 2, 2001, p. 10; Matthew Grimm, "Cutting the Cord," *American Demographics,* Jan. 2001, pp. 66–67; Stephen Baker, "Nokia's Costly Stumble," *Business Week,* Aug. 14, 2000, pp. 42+.

2. Jeff Green, "The Toy-Train Company That Thinks It Can," *Business Week,* Dec. 4, 2000, pp. 64–69.

3. Service Corporation International, http://www.hoovers.com.

4. Chester Dawson, "Young, Funky, Hip . . . Toyota?" *Business Week,* Apr. 23, 2001, p. 58.

5. James U. McNeal, *Kids Marketing: Myths and Realities* (Ithaca, NY: Paramount Market Publishing, 1999), p. 29.

6. Bureau of the Census, *Statistical Abstract of the United States 2000,* p. 16.

7. J. D. Mosley-Matchett, "Marketers: There's a Feminine Side to the Web," *Marketing News,* Feb. 16, 1998, p. 6.

8. Charles L. P. Fairweather, "Mr. Goodwrench Meets His Match," *New York Times,* March 11, 2001, sec. 3, p. 4.

9. Yuri Radzievsky, "Untapped Markets: Ethnics in the U.S.," *Advertising Age,* June 21, 1993.

10. Ann Therese Palmer, "What's Hot: Take Five, Elsie," *Business Week,* Apr. 9, 2001, p. 8.

11. Joseph T. Plummer, "The Concept and Application of Life Style Segmentation," *Journal of Marketing,* Jan. 1974, p. 33.

12. Rebecca Piirto Heath, "You Can Buy a Thrill: Chasing the Ultimate Rush," *American Demographics,* June 1997, pp. 47–51.

13. Philip Kotler, *Marketing Management: Analysis, Planning, Implementation, and Control,* 7th ed. (Englewood Cliffs, NJ: Prentice Hall, 2000), pp. 118–119.

14. Charles W. Chase, Jr., "Selecting the Appropriate Forecasting Method," *Journal of Business Forecasting,* Fall 1997, pp. 2, 23, 28–29.

15. Sources: Eve Epstein, "Dot-Com Brokerage Exploits a Market Niche," *InfoWorld,* Jan. 8, 2001, pp. 34+; "Broker Cuts Fees, Adds New Payment Plan," *Financial Net News,* Dec. 18, 2000, p. 2; "BuyandHold.com First to Introduce the Virtual Direct Stock Purchase Plan," *PR Newswire,* Apr. 25, 2000, www.prnewswire.com; John P. Mello, Jr., "Going Direct," *CFO,* Oct. 2000, p. 22; "BuyandHold.com Introduces New Pricing Options," *PR Newswire,* Nov. 6, 2000, www.prnewswire.com; BuyandHold.com website, www.buyandhold.com.

16. Sources: Jake Holden, "High-Tech Take-Out," *American Demographics,* Oct. 1998, pp. 16, 18; Kitty Kevin, "A Golden Age for Meal Solutions: LifeSource Nutrition Solutions' Line of Nutritionally Balanced Meals," *Food Processing,* Oct. 1998, pp. 37+; "New Ventures," www.agewave.com/agewave/lifesource.html, Nov. 30, 1998; John Hale, LifeSource COO, personal communication with author, Dec. 4, 1998. "LifeSpring Acquires Dr. McDougall's Right Foods Inc.," LifeSpring news release, April 9, 2001, http://www.homenutrition.com; "Home Is Where the Heart-healthy Diet Is," American Heart Association, April 10, 2000, http://www.americanheart.org/whats_news/AHA_News_Releases/04-10-00_2-comment.html.

CHAPTER 8

1. Sources: Amy Zuber, "McD Addresses Investor Unease with Management Changes, New Brands," *Nation's Restaurant News,* May 28, 2001, pp. 1+; "Open-Door Policy," *Restaurants & Institutions,* May 15, 2001, p. 20; "Feel-Good Fast Food," *American Demographics,* Oct. 2000, pp. 66–67; "McSmarter," *Advertising Age,* Apr. 9, 2001, p. 16; Ramona Dzinkowski, "McDonald's Europe," *Strategic Finance,* May 2001, pp. 25+.

2. "First Source for Car Shoppers in Online Households," *USA Today* Snapshot, November 16, 2001, http://www.usatoday.com/snapshot.

3. Russell W. Belk, "Situational Variables and Consumer Behavior," *Journal of Consumer Research,* Dec. 1975, pp. 157–164.

4. Joan Oleck, "Dieting: More Fun with a Buddy?" *Business Week,* Apr. 23, 2001, p. 16.

5. Joann Muller, "Kmart's Bright Idea," *Business Week,* Apr. 9, 2001, pp. 50–51.

6. Laura Q. Hughes and Alice Z. Cuneo, "Lowe's Retools Image in Push Toward Women," *Advertising Age,* February 26, 2001, http://www.adage.com/news_and_features/features/20010226/article7.html.

7. Casey Keller, "So Far, It's Easy Being Green," *New York Times,* Oct. 22, 2000, sec. 3, p. 2.

8. David Pilla, "Insurers' Marketing Efforts Target Minority Groups," A.M. Best Newswire, Dec. 1, 2000.

9. Laurie Freeman, "Cereal Marketers Find Sweet Tooth," *Advertising Age,* Nov. 20, 2000, p. S4.

10. Alison Stein Wellner, "Every Day's a Holiday," *American Demographics,* Dec. 2000, pp. 62–65.

11. "Kmart Marketing: Urban/Ethnic Strategy Remains Pillar of Competitive Advantage," *Dsn Retailing Today,* Mar. 5, 2001, pp. 44–46.

12. Becky Ebenkamp, "Year of the Rat Pack?" *Brandweek,* Nov. 27, 2000.

13. Sharon Nelton, "Building an Empire One Smile at a Time," *Success,* Sep. 2000, pp. 34+; Brad Patten, "Teddy Bear Bonanza Run by Sweetheart of a System," *Washington Business Journal,* Feb. 4, 2000, p. 53; Marilyn Vise, "Corporate Culture: Build-A-Bear Workshop," *St. Louis Business Journal,* May 7, 2001, http://stlouis.bcentral.com/stlouis/stories/2001/05/07/focus11.html.

14. Sources: "Around Town: The Susan G. Komen Breast Cancer Foundation," www2ford.com/display.asp?story=133, Jan. 5, 1999; Bob Black, "No Letup in Demand for Trucks," *Chicago Sun-Times,* Feb. 7, 1997, p. 45; Daniel Howes, "GM: Automaker with a Cause," *Detroit News,* June 22, 1997, p. D3; Patrick Barrett, "Who's in the Driver's Seat?" *Marketing* (Aug. 14, 1997), www.dbu.texshare.edu/ovidweb/ovidwebb...&ST=6&R=8&totalCIT=12&D=infoz&S=15, Dec. 1, 1998; "Ford Focuses on Women, Minorities," *Orlando Sentinel,* Aug. 28, 1997, p. F13; Elena Scotti, "Born to Be Mild, or Wild?" *Brandweek,* Mar. 16, 1998, pp. 22–23; "Automotive Overview," *Women Consumers, '98 Highlights,* About Women, Inc., 1998, p. 4; Katherine Yung, "Hot Lexus Sport-Ute Wins over Drivers," *Detroit News,* Aug. 4, 1998, p. B1; "Women Cyclists Convene in North Carolina," Subaru press release, Sept. 25, 1998, www.subaru.com/corporate_newsroom/press_release/pr_98/09_25_women_cyclists.html, Jan. 6, 1999; Keith Bradsher, "Light Trucks Exceed Cars in U.S. Sales," *New York Times,* Dec. 4, 1998, p. C4; "Acura Presents Local Events," www.acura.com/presents/aplocal.html, Jan. 5, 1999; "The 'Masters' of Women's Professional Golf," www.toyota.com/events/dinashore_golf.html, Jan. 5, 1999; "General Motors Presents More Than Half a Million Dollars to the National Alliance of Breast Cancer Organizations," General Motors press release, Oct. 21, 1997, www.gm.com/about/community/pink/pressrelease.html, Jan. 5, 1999; "Women's Day Planned at Auto Show," DaimlerChrysler News Release, Jan. 5, 1999, www1.daimlerchrysler.com/news/daily/index_e.html; "1999 Sneak Preview," Julie Cantwell, "Diet, Exercise, and Subaru," *Automotive News,* May 28, 2001, p. 23; "Chevrolet, Michelle Kwan Reward 10 College-Bound Female Athletes with Scholarships," General Motors news release, June 27, 2001, http://www.gm.com/company/gmability/philanthropy/news/kwan_062701.html; Josh Max, "Road Test," *New York Daily News Online,* Feb. 24, 2001, http://www.nydailynews.com/2001-02-24/New_York_Now/Cityscape/a-100962.asp.

CHAPTER 9

1. Sources: "Sodexho Marriott Puts a Little ZIP into a Customer-Profile Program," *Nation's Restaurant News,* Apr. 30, 2001, p. 20; "Foodservice Industry," *SBI Market Profile,* June 5, 2001, www.marketresearch.com; "Foodservice Provider Compares Remodeled University Dining Hall to Fine Restaurant," *Nation's Restaurant News,* Feb. 26, 2001, p. 18; David J. Lipke, "You Are What You Eat," *American Demographics,* Oct. 2000, pp. 42–45.

2. Bureau of the Census, *Statistical Abstract of the United States* (Washington, DC: Government Printing Office, 2000), p. 543.

3. Ibid., pp. 543–544.

4. Ibid., p. 342.

5. Ibid., p. 297.

6. "A Talk with SBA's Subcontractor of the Year," http://www.smallbusinessdepot.com/success/subcontractor.html, May 26, 2000.

7. Michael A. Verespej, "Sitting Pretty," *Industry Week,* Mar. 5, 2001, http://www.industryweek.com.

8. Moin Uddin, "Loyalty Programs: The Ultimate Gift," *Dsn Retailing Today,* Mar. 5, 2001, p. 12.

9. Frederick E. Webster, Jr., and Yoram Wind, "A General Model for Understanding Organizational Buyer Behavior," *Marketing Management,* Winter/Spring 1996, pp. 52–57.

10. Robert D. McWilliams, Earl Naumann, and Stan Scott, "Determining Buying Center Size," *Industrial Marketing Management* 21 (1992), pp. 43–49.

11. Suzanne Sabrosk, "NAICS Codes: A New Classification System for a New Economy," *Technology Information,* Nov. 2000, p. 18.

12. Sources: Antony Adshead, "Big Three Battle over Slowing Database Market," *Computer Weekly,* June 7, 2001, p. 44; Jennifer Couzin, "A Hospital for the Digital Age," *Industry Standard,* Mar. 26, 2001, www.thestandard.com; Adrian Slywotzky, "Four Lessons from Larry," *Fortune,* Mar. 5, 2001, pp. 178, 180; Heather Harreld, "Oracle Looks to a 'Services-as-Software' Role," *InfoWorld,* Feb. 26, 2001, pp. 10+; Paula Rooney, "Oracle Pushes E-Integration," *CRN,* Feb. 26, 2001, pp. 10+; Elizabeth Corcoran, "Oracle: Walking the Talk," *Forbes,* Jan. 8, 2001, pp. 120+; Joseph C. Panettieri and Ed Sperling, "Can Oracle Keep Its Upper Hand?" *Smart Reseller,* Mar. 6, 2000, pp. 24+; Aaron Ricadela and Rick Whiting, "Back to Data Basics," *InformationWeek,* Oct. 2, 2000, pp. 22+.

13. Sources: Alessandra Bianchi, "Without You, I'm Nothing," *Inc.,* Nov. 1998, pp. 50–58; "About Jo's Candies," www.joscandies.com/about.html, Nov. 23, 1998; Tom King, Jo's Candies CEO, personal communication with author, Dec. 1998.

CHAPTER 10

1. Sources: Julie Gordon, "King of Kites," *The Coloradoan,* May 13, 2001, pp. E1, E4; Windy Conditions Kite Systems, http://www.flagkites.com/index.shtml, Sep. 13, 2001.

2. James Champy, "New Products or New Processes?" *Sales & Marketing Management,* May 2001, pp. 30–32.

3. Earle Eldridge, "Bentley Gets Buyers' Hearts Racing," *USA Today,* May 21, 2001, p. 3B.

4. Emily Nelson, "Too Many Choices," *The Wall Street Journal,* Apr. 20, 2001, pp. B1, B4.

5. William P. Putsis, Jr., and Barry L. Bayus, "An Empirical Analysis of Firms' Product Line Decisions," *Journal of Marketing Research,* Feb. 2001, pp. 110–118.

6. Nelson, "Too Many Choices."

7. Brian A. Lukas and O. C. Ferrell, "The Effect of Market Orientation on Product Innovation," *Journal of the Academy of Marketing Science,* Feb. 2000, pp. 239–247.

8. Paul Davidson, "AOL Prepares to Grab Net Users from Europe's Phone Titans," *USA Today,* May 21, 2001, p. 3B.
9. O. C. Ferrell, Michael Hartline, and George Lucas, *Marketing Strategy* (Ft. Worth, TX: Dryden, 2002), p. 116.
10. Matthew Swibel, "Spin Cycle," *Forbes,* Apr. 2, 2001, p. 118.
11. Nelson, "Too Many Choices."
12. Ferrell, Hartline, and Lucas, *Marketing Strategy.* p. 117.
13. Adapted from Everett M. Rogers, *Diffusion of Innovations* (New York: Macmillan, 1962), pp. 81–86.
14. Ibid., pp. 247–250.
15. Gerald Tellis and Peter Golder, "First to Market, First to Fail? Real Causes of Enduring Market Leadership," *Sloan Management Review,* Winter 1996, pp. 65–75.
16. Susan Casey, "Object-Oriented: Everything I Ever Needed to Know about Business I Learned in the Frozen Food Aisle," *eCompany,* Oct. 2000, www.ecompany.com.
17. Ibid.
18. Louis Lavelle, "What Campbell's New Chief Needs to Know," *Business Week,* June 25, 2001, p. 60.
19. Sources: Byron Acohido, "Microsoft Bets on Xbox Success, but Some Skeptical," *USA Today,* Apr. 24, 2001, p. 6B; Brian Bremner, "Microsoft vs. Sony: Mortal Combat," *Business Week Online,* Apr. 3, 2001, www.businessweek.com; N'Gai Croal, "Game Wars 5.0," *Newsweek,* May 28, 2001, pp. 65–66; Alan Hughes, "Activision: Pulling the Joystick into High Gear," *Business Week Online,* Mar. 13, 2001, www.businessweek.com; "Nintendo to Use New Game Boy to Fight Against Sony, Microsoft," *Bloomberg Newswire,* Apr. 30, 2001, via America Online; Chris Taylor, "The Battle of Seattle," *Time,* May 21, 2001, pp. 58–59; Khanh T. L. Tran, "Video-Game Sales Advance on PlayStation 2 Availability," *MSNBC,* July 25, 2001, www.msnbc.com; "Video-Game Industry Sales Rise 18% in First Quarter, Report Says," *Bloomberg Newswire,* May 11, 2001, via America Online.
20. Sources: John Beauge, "New Process Used to Make Bicycles," *[Harrisburg, Penn.] Evening News,* June 5, 1995, p. 3; Judith Crown, "Zell & Co. Peddling Schwinn," *Crain's Chicago Business,* May 12, 1991, p. 1; Scott M. Davis, "Great Brands Continue to Find Relevance," *Brandweek Online,* Apr. 16, 2001, www.findarticles.com; Roy Furchgott, "Retro Bikes with '90s Pizzazz," *Business Week,* May 19, 1997, p. 143; Elana Ashanti Jefferson, "Michigan Firm Buys Schwinn," *Denver Post,* Aug. 14, 1997, p. B1; Jan Larson, "The Bicycle Market," *American Demographics,* Mar. 1995, pp. 42–43, 46–48, 50; Laura Loro, "Schwinn Aims to Be a Big Wheel Again," *Advertising Age,* Jan. 2, 1995, p. 4; Patrick McGeehan, "Biking Icon Wants to Lose Training Wheels," *USA Today,* Aug. 8, 1995, p. 1B; "Pacific Cycle Acquires Schwinn/GT," Pacific Cycle press release, Sep. 10, 2001, www.mongoose.com:80/mongoose/press_detail.asp?releaseid=15&mscssid=7NBS7FS3TF409KTLLAGV6EKWB1K92FCB; Andy Pargh, "Pedal Back in Time with New Retro-Bikes," *Design News,* May 19, 1997, p. 134; "Questor Buys Schwinn, Hopes for Revival of Brand," *USA Today,* Aug. 14, 1997; Jerd Smith, "Acquisition Gives Schwinn Muscle," *Rocky Mountain News,* Aug. 14, 1997, pp. 1B, 20B; "Schwinn/GT Corporation Sells Cycling and Fitness Divisions," Schwinn, press release, Sep. 12, 2001, www.schwinn.com/news/index.html?nid=49; "Schwinn/GT Corporation to Sell Cycling Division to Huffy Corporation," Schwinn press release, July 16, 2001, www.schwinn.com/news/index.html?nid=48.

CHAPTER 11
1. Sources: "Campbell Board Approves Major Investment Plan," Campbell Soup Company press release, July 27, 2001, www.shareholder.com/campbell/news/20010727-51511.htm; Gerry Khermouch, "What Campbell's New Chief Needs to Do Now," *Business Week,* June 25, 2001, p. 60; Sonia Reyes, "Back to the Drawing Board," *Brandweek,* Apr. 30, 2001, pp. 20–26, 42; Sonia Reyes, "Strategy: IBP Heats Up $20M for 1st National Brand," *Brandweek,* May 14, 2001, pp. 10–11, 42.
2. Jean Halliday, "Hyundai to Unveil a Sporty Elantra," *Advertising Age,* June 4, 2001, p. 13.
3. Ibid.
4. Chung K. Kim, Anne M. Lavack, and Margo Smith, "Consumer Evaluation of Vertical Brand Extensions and Core Brands," *Journal of Business Research,* Mar. 2001, pp. 211–222.
5. Halliday, "Hyundai to Unveil a Sporty Elantra."
6. Kim B. Clark and Takahiro Fujimoto, "The Power of Product Integrity," *Harvard Business Review,* Nov./Dec. 1990, pp. 108–118.
7. Lisa Robinson, "Caller ID Add-Ons Screen Out Unidentified Callers," Reuters Newswire, via AOL, July 11, 2001.
8. Robert M. McMath, "When Cold Coffee Gets Iced," *American Demographics,* Mar. 1997, p. 60.
9. Lee G. Cooper, "Strategic Marketing Planning for Radically New Products," *Journal of Marketing,* Jan. 2000, pp. 1–16.
10. Lisa C. Troy, David M. Szymanski, and P. Rajan Varadarajan, "Generating New Product Ideas: An Initial Investigation of the Role of Market Information and Organizational Characteristics," *Journal of the Academy of Marketing Science,* Jan. 2001, pp. 89–101.
11. John Grossman, "The Idea Guru," *Inc.,* May 2001, pp. 32–41.
12. Aric Rindfleisch and Christine Moorman, "The Acquisition and Utilization of Information in New Product Alliances: A Strength-of-Ties Perspective," *Journal of Marketing,* Apr. 2001, pp. 1–18.
13. Jack Neff, "White Bread, USA," *Advertising Age,* July 9, 2001, pp. 1, 12.
14. Douglas Robson, "Nike: Just Do . . . Something," *Business Week,* via AOL, July 2, 2001.
15. Hillary Chura, "A-B Readies Test of Energy Drink to Rival Red Bull," *Advertising Age,* www.adage.com, July 18, 2001.
16. Barry L. Bayus, Sanjay Jain, and Ambar G. Rao, "Truth or Consequences: An Analysis of Vaporware and New Product Announcements," *Journal of Marketing Research,* Feb. 2001, pp. 3–13.
17. "P&G Ends Test of Impress Plastic Wrap," *Advertising Age,* www.adage.com, July 18, 2001.
18. "P&G to Launch Hair Care for Men," *Advertising Age,* www.adage.com, July 18, 2001.
19. Faye Rice, "How to Deal with Tougher Customers," *Fortune,* Dec. 3, 1990, pp. 39–48.
20. Sal Marino, "Is 'Good Enough' Good Enough?" *IW,* Feb. 3, 1997, p. 22.
21. Shelly M. Reese, "Suitcase Savvy," *American Demographics,* June 1995, p. 58.
22. Adapted from Michael Levy and Barton A. Weitz, *Retailing Management* (Burr Ridge, IL: Irwin/McGraw-Hill, 1998), p. 570.
23. Doug Young, "U.S. Hotels Make Headway into Online Booking," Reuters Newswire, via AOL, June 22, 2001.
24. Patrick Barta and Anne Marie Chaker, "Consumers Voice Rising Dissatisfaction with Companies," *The Wall Street Journal,* May 21, 2001, p. A2.
25. Mike Drummond, "Customer Service Woes," *Business 2.0,* June 4, 2001, www.business2.com/marketing/2001/06/service_woes.html.
26. Pamela Sebastian Ridge, "Chico's Scores Big with Its Nonjudgmental Sizes," *The Wall Street Journal,* Mar. 8, 2001, pp. B1, B4.
27. Terry Lefton, "Widening the Expressway," *Brandweek,* Sep. 7, 1998, pp. 33–35, 38.

28. Jack Neff, "White Clouds Could Bring Rain on P&G," *Advertising Age,* July 2, 2001, p. 4.

29. Rajesh Sethi, "New Product Quality and Product Development Teams," *Journal of Marketing,* Apr. 2000, pp. 1–14.

30. Sources: "Olive Oil-Cosmetics and Soaps," The Olive Oil Source, www.oliveoilsource.com/cosmetics.htm, Sep. 7, 2001; Jean Patteson, "Olive Oil, Essences Are Being Poured into Beauty Products," *The Morning Call,* Aug. 3, 2001, www.mcall.com/html/news/am_mag/d_pg001oliveoil.htm; Pamela Sauer, "A Makeover for Personal Care and Cosmetics," *Chemical Market Reporter,* May 14, 2001, www.findarticles.com.

31. Sources: "Cuba Gooding, Jr. Stars in New Pepsi ONE Commercials," PRNewswire, www.prnewswire.com, Oct. 15, 1998; Nikhil Deogun, "Beverages: New Sweetener—Pepsi Pounces, Coke Ponders," *The Wall Street Journal,* July 1, 1998, p. B1; Nikhil Deogun, "Marketing: PepsiCo Draws New Battle Plan to Fight Coke," *The Wall Street Journal,* Jan. 27, 1998, p. B1; Nikhil Deogun, "Pepsi Takes Aim at Coke with New One-Calorie Drink," *The Wall Street Journal,* Oct. 5, 1998, p. B4; Denise Gellene, "Advertising and Marketing: Ad Reviews—Pepsi Hopes Ads Help Show Them the Money," *The Los Angeles Times,* Oct. 22, 1998, p. C6; Bruce Horovitz, "One-Calorie Product May Spell Sweet Success," *USA Today,* Oct. 6, 1998, pp. 1A, 1B; Theresa Howard, "It's B-a-a-ack!!" *Brandweek Online,* Mar. 20, 2000, www.findarticles.com; Theresa Howard, "The Next Hot Celebrity Diet," *Brandweek Online,* Apr. 10, 2000, www.findarticles.com; Louise Kramer, "Pepsi-Cola Puts Hopes, Dreams, $$, into Pepsi One," *Advertising Age,* Oct. 5, 1998, p. 16; Kevin O'Rourke, "Diet Sodas Quench Sales of Carbonated Beverages," *Drug Store News,* May 22, 2000, findarticles.com; "Pepsi Launches Breakthrough Product: Pepsi One," PepsiCo press release, June 30, 1998; Lucas Sloane, "Pepsi One," *Mediaweek,* July 6, 1998, p. 36.

CHAPTER 12

1. Sources: Douglas Robson, "Just Do . . . Something," *Business Week,* July 2, 2001, pp. 70–71; "Tiger Tees Off for Nike with New Signature Logo," *Brandweek,* June 11, 2000, p. 14; Elisa Williams, "Swoosh Suits," *Forbes,* Apr. 16, 2001, p. 62; Louise Lee, "Take Our Swoosh, Please," *Business Week,* February 21, 2000, p. 128.

2. Peter D. Bennett, ed., *Dictionary of Marketing Terms* (Chicago: American Marketing Association, 1995), p. 27.

3. U.S. Patent and Trademark Office, telephone interview, Apr. 17, 2001; David J. Lipke, "Pledge of Allegiance," *American Demographics,* Nov. 2000, pp. 40–42.

4. Lipke, "Pledge of Allegiance."

5. David A. Aaker, *Managing Brand Equity: Capitalizing on the Value of a Brand Name* (New York: Free Press, 1991), pp. 16–17.

6. Paul Davidson and Theresa Howard, "FTC Could Try to Block Pepsi-Quaker Merger," *USA Today,* May 10, 2001, p. 1B.

7. Alice Z. Cueno, "Private Label Line Anchors Millers Outpost Re-Launch," *Advertising Age,* May 7, 2001, p. 8.

8. Private Label Manufacturers Association, *PLMA's 2001 Private Label Yearbook,* p. 7.

9. "British Retailing: Chemistry Upset," *The Economist,* February 24, 2001, p. 68.

10. Marcel Corstjens and Rajiv Lal, "Building Store Loyalty Through Store Brands," *Journal of Marketing Research,* August 2000, pp. 281–291.

11. Gerry Khermouch, "Triarc's Smooth Move," *Brandweek,* June 22, 1998, pp. 26–31.

12. Leonard Berry, Edwin E. Leikowith, and Terry Clark, "In Services, What's in a Name?" *Harvard Business Review,* Sep./Oct. 1988, pp. 2–4.

13. Dorothy Cohen, "Trademark Strategy," *Journal of Marketing,* Jan. 1986, p. 63.

14. Chiranjev Kohli and Rajheesh Suri, "Brand Names That Work: A Study of the Effectiveness of Different Brand Names," *Marketing Management Journal,* Fall/Winter 2000, pp. 112–120.

15. U.S. Trademark Association, "Trademark Stylesheet," no.1A.

16. Dorothy Cohen, "Trademark Strategy Revisited," *Journal of Marketing,* July 1991, pp. 46–59.

17. Suzanne Bidlake, "Unilever's Leaner Lineup to Get $1.6 Bil Spending Boost," *Advertising Age,* February 2000; "Unilever Unveils 'Big Hit' Innovations, Brand Cull Progress," *Advertising Age,* Feb. 9, 2001, http://www.adage.com.

18. Vicki R. Lane, "The Impact of Ad Repetition and Ad Content on Consumer Perceptions of Incongruent Extensions," *Journal of Marketing,* Apr. 2000, pp. 80–91.

19. David Breitkopf, "Airline Co-Brand Cards Reach for New Heights," *American Banker,* Dec. 12, 2000, p. 1.

20. Cara Beardi, "Photo Op, Nike Pair Up for Footwear Line," *Advertising Age,* Apr. 2, 2001, p. 8.

21. Christopher Palmeri, "Mattel: Up the Hill Minus Jill," *Business Week,* Apr. 9, 2001, pp. 53–54.

22. Bob Vavra, "The Game of the Name," *Supermarket Business,* Mar. 15, 2001, pp. 45–56.

23. Thomas J. Madden, Kelly Hewett, and Martin S. Roth, "Managing Images in Different Cultures: A Cross-National Study of Color Meanings and Preferences," *Journal of International Marketing,* Winter 2000, p. 90.

24. Stephanie Thompson, "Nestlé Gives Mate Update in New Package, Ad Effort," *Advertising Age,* Sep. 18, 2000, p. 8.

25. "FDA Proposed New Rules for GM Foods," *Chemical Market Reporter,* Jan. 29, 2001, p. 7.

26. Federal Trade Commission, www.ftc.gov, May 16, 2001.

27. Sources: Harry Cline, "Premium Wine in Screw-Top," *Western Farm Press,* July 15, 2000, pp. 9+; "PlumpJack Winery Owners Gordon Getty, Bill Getty, and Gavin Newsom Announce First Screw Cap Closures for Luxury Wine," *Business Wire,* June 5, 2000, http://www.businesswire.com.

28. Sources: Greg Gatlin, "Branding Becomes Gem of an Idea," *Boston Herald,* Feb. 11, 2001, p. 31; Rodney Ho, "Brand-Name Diamonds: A Cut Above?" *The Wall Street Journal,* June 1, 1998, pp. B1–B2; Samantha T. Smith, "A Cut Above the Rest," *Boston Business Journal,* Jan. 16, 1998, p. 1; "Brand Slam," *Modern Jeweler,* May 1998, pp. 51–52, 54, 56, 58; Di-Star Ltd. press kit.

CHAPTER 13

1. Sources: Arline Bleecker, "Booking Shore Excursions Is a Breeze with Royal Caribbean," *Orlando Sentinel,* June 25, 2001, http://www.orlandosentinel.com; Richard Friese, "Setting the Pace," *Travel Agent,* Apr. 23, 2001, pp. 16+; Matthew Grimm, "Anchors Aweigh," *American Demographics,* Mar. 2001, pp. 74–75; Jane Wooldridge, "Royal Caribbean's Explorer: Twin Sister with a Twist," *Knight-Ridder News Service,* Jan. 29, 2001, http://www.herald.com; Hillary Chura and David Goetzl, "Royal Caribbean Christens New Baby Boomer Effort," *Advertising Age,* Jan. 17, 2000, p. 3.

2. Leonard L. Berry and A. Parasuraman, *Marketing Services: Competing through Quality* (New York: Free Press, 1991), p. 5.

3. Michael Levy and Barton A. Weitz, *Retailing Management* (Burr Ridge, IL: McGraw-Hill/Irwin, 2001), p. 585.

4. Herschol N. Chait, Shawn M. Carraher, and M. Ronald Buckley, "Measuring Service Orientation with Biodata," *Journal of Managerial Issues,* Spring 2000, pp. 109–120.

5. The information in this section is based on K. Douglas Hoffman and John E. G. Bateson, *Essentials of Services Marketing* (Ft. Worth, TX: Dryden Press, 1997), pp. 25–38; and Valarie A. Zeithaml, A. Parasuraman, and Leonard L. Berry,

Delivering Quality Service: Balancing Customer Perceptions and Expectations (New York: Free Press, 1990).

6. J. Paul Peter and James H. Donnelly, *A Preface to Marketing Management* (Burr Ridge, IL: McGraw-Hill/Irwin, 2000), p. 203.

7. Michael D. Hartline and O. C. Ferrell, "Service Quality Implementation: The Effects of Organizational Socialization and Managerial Actions of Customer Contact Employee Behavior," *Marketing Science Institute Working Paper Series,* no. 93-122 (Cambridge, MA: Marketing Science Institute, 1993).

8. Kathy Mulady, "Retail Notebook: Activists Drawn to Starbucks Spotlight?" *Seattle Post-Intelligence Reporter,* Mar. 17, 2001.

9. Richard B. Chase and Sriram Dasu, "Want to Perfect Your Company's Service? Use Behavioral Science," *Harvard Business Review,* June 2001, pp. 78-84.

10. Elizabeth Blakey, "Ameritrade—the Symbol of Net Brokerage Shakeout?" *E-Commerce Times,* Apr. 24, 2001, http://www.ecommercetimes.com/perl/printer/9214/.

11. Susan Greco, "Fanatics!" *Inc.,* Apr. 2001, pp. 36-48.

12. Jack Neff and Suzanne Bidlake, "P&G, Unilever Aim to Take Customers to the Cleaners," *Advertising Age,* Feb. 12, 2001, http://www.adage.com/news and features/features/20010212/article3.html.

13. Zeithaml, Parasuraman, and Berry, *Delivering Quality Service.*

14. Valarie A. Zeithaml, "How Consumer Evaluation Processes Differ between Goods and Services," in *Marketing of Services,* ed. James H. Donnelly and William R. George (Chicago: American Marketing Association, 1981), pp. 186-190.

15. A. Parasuraman, Leonard L. Berry, and Valarie A. Zeithaml, "An Empirical Examination of Relationships in an Extended Service Quality Model," *Marketing Science Institute Working Paper Series,* no. 90-112 (Cambridge, MA: Marketing Science Institute, 1990), p. 29.

16. Valarie A. Zeithaml, Leonard L. Berry, and A. Parasuraman, "Communication and Control Processes in the Delivery of Service Quality," *Journal of Marketing,* Apr. 1988, pp. 35-48.

17. Valarie A. Zeithaml, Leonard L. Berry, and A. Parasuraman, "The Nature and Determinants of Customer Expectations of Service," *Journal of the Academy of Marketing Science,* Winter 1993, pp. 1-12.

18. Linda Himelstein, " 'Room Service, Send Up a Techie,' " *Business Week,* Apr. 9, 2001, p. 10.

19. Philip Kotler, "Marketing for Nonprofit Organizations, 2nd ed. (Englewood Cliffs, NJ: Prentice-Hall, 1982), p. 37.

20. Ibid.

21. Sources: Emily Thornton, " 'Reengineering' at Merrill Lynch," *Business Week,* Aug. 6, 2001, p. 31; "W-Technologies and Merrill Lynch Direct to Showcase 'Merrill Mobile' At Gartner Group's Internet and E-Commerce Expo," *Business Wire,* Mar. 29, 2001, www.businesswire.com; "Full-Service Brokers," *Financial Net News,* Feb. 12, 2001, p. 9; Peter Edmonston, "Merrill Lynch Analysts Get Their Closeups," *The Wall Street Journal,* Jan. 24, 2001, p. C20; Brooke Southall, "Merrill On-Line Push Suffering from Benign Neglect," *Crain's New York Business,* Nov. 6, 2000, pp. 22+; "Merrill Lynch & Co.," *Hoover's Handbook of American Business 2001* (Austin, TX: Hoover's Business Press, 2001), pp. 956-957.

22. Sources: Kate Fitzgerald, "Senior Tour Hits the Mall," *Advertising Age,* July 16, 2001, p. 41; Gerry Romano, "Feeling Groovy? Join AARP," *Association Management,* Feb. 2001, pp. 32+; David J. Lipke, "Fountain of Youth," *American Demographics,* Sep. 2000, pp. 37-40.

CHAPTER 14

1. Sources: Constance Loizos, "Polo Ponies Up to the Web," *Business 2.0,* Feb. 20, 2001, pp. 4-5; Peter Braunstein, "Ralph's

Media Empire," *Women's Wear Daily,* Dec. 18, 2000, p. 18B; Catherine Curan, "Fashion Retail's Spin on the Web; Store Sales Displaced by Net Sales?" *Crain's New York Business,* Dec. 11, 2000, p. 3; "Polo Ralph Lauren Launches Polo.com, Its Luxury Designer E-Commerce Web Site," Polo Ralph Lauren news release, Nov. 9, 2000, http://www.prnewswire.com.

2. Chester Dawson, "Machete Time," *Business Week,* Apr. 9, 2001, pp. 42-44.

3. Shane McLaughlin, "Using Supply-Chain Technology to Create Competitive Advantage," *Inc.,* www.inc.com, Mar. 17, 1998.

4. Cliff Edwards, "No Cartwheels for Handspring," *Business Week,* Apr. 2, 2001, pp. 56-58.

5. Lester E. Goodman and Paul A. Dion, "The Determinants of Commitment in the Distributor-Manufacturer Relationship," *Industrial Marketing Management,* Apr. 2001, pp. 287-300.

6. "Estee Lauder Sees Dept. Stores as Smaller Portion of Its Business," *Forbes,* February 28, 2001, http://www.forbes.com/newswire/2001/02/28/rtrl94332.html.

7. Leo Aspinwall, "The Marketing Characteristics of Goods," in *Four Marketing Theories* (Boulder: University of Colorado Press, 1961), pp. 27-32.

8. Tony Seideman, "Get with the Program," *Inbound Logistics,* Sep. 1998, p. 29.

9. Wroe Alderson, *Dynamic Marketing Behavior* (Homewood, IL: Irwin, 1965), p. 239.

10. Seideman, "Get with the Program," p. 31.

11. Jonathan D. Hibbard, Nirmalya Kumar, and Louis W. Stern, "Examining the Impact of Destructive Acts in Marketing Channel Relationships," *Journal of Marketing Research,* Feb. 2001, pp. 45-61.

12. Anne T. Coughlan, Erin Anderson, Louis W. Stern, and Adel I. El-Ansary, *Marketing Channels* (Upper Saddle River, NJ: Prentice-Hall, 2001), pp. 368-369.

13. Sources: "Top Retailers Strengthen Relationship with CommercialWare," CommercialWare news release, Jan. 16, 2001, http://www.businesswire.com; Cheryl Rosen, "Software Bridges Disconnect Gap on Orders, Deliveries," *Information Week,* Oct. 2, 2000, p. 30; James Christie, "CommercialWare Staples Up a Deal," *Red Herring,* June 29, 2000, http://www.redherring.com; Maria Seminerio, "J. Jill Tries E-Biz on for Size," *E-Week,* Nov. 6, 2000, http://www.zdnet.com/eweek/stories/general/0,11011,2647802.html.

14. Sources: "Grainger Retreats, Closes Material Logic," *Industrial Distribution,* June 2001, p. 19; James P. Miller, "Firm to Close Its Troubled Chicago-Area 'E-Procurement' Business," *Chicago Tribune,* Apr. 24, 2001, http://www.chicago.tribune.com; Alan Earls, "Valuing Exchanges," *Industrial Distribution,* Sep. 2000, p. E15; "W. W. Grainger," *Hoover's Online,* http://www.hoovers.com, August 8, 2001; "W. W. Grainger," *Hoover's Handbook of American Business 2001* (Austin, TX: Hoover's Business Press, 2001), pp. 1550-1551.

CHAPTER 15

1. Sources: Owen Thomas, "Direct Sales Force: Homestore.com," *E-Company,* Mar. 2001, p. 132; "Homestore.com, Inc. Reports Eighth Consecutive Quarter of Strong Results," Homestore.com news release, July 25, 2001, http://www.homestore.com; Laurie Freeman, "Branding Hits Home," *Advertising Age,* Nov. 6, 2000, p. S46; Christopher Palmeri, "The Architect of Homestore.com," *Business Week,* July 10, 2000, pp. 180-184.

2. Bureau of the Census, *Statistical Abstract of the United States* (Washington, DC: Government Printing Office, 2000), p. 543.

3. *Hoover's Handbook of American Business 2001* (Austin, TX: Hoover's Business Press, 2001), p. 656.

4. Ibid., p. 1442.

5. Mark Del Franco, Shawn Ferriolo, and Lisa Santo, "Benchmark 2001 Operations," *Catalog Age,* Mar. 15, 2001, pp. 50–54.

6. "How Federated Stays a Leader," *Inbound Logistics,* Aug. 2000, p. 36.

7. Margaret L. Williams and Mark N. Frolick, "The Evolution of EDI for Competitive Advantage: The FedEx Case," *Information Systems Management,* Spring 2001, pp. 47–53.

8. Anne T. Coughlan, Erin Anderson, Louis W. Stern, and Adel I. El-Ansary, *Marketing Channels* (Upper Saddle River, NJ: Prentice-Hall, 2001), p. 510.

9. "How Federated Stays a Leader," p. 36.

10. "Low Inventory, High Expectations," *Inbound Logistics,* June 2000, pp. 36–42.

11. Anne Stuart, "Express Delivery," *Inc. Tech 2001,* Mar. 15, 2001, pp. 54–56.

12. Sources: "Quick International Courier Launches QuickOnline, Knowledge Management Tool Delivers Extremely Urgent and First-Flight-Out Transportation Solutions Through Internet," Quick International Courier news release, Apr. 18, 2001, http://www.quickintl.com; Margaret Allen, "Quick's Delivery Service Moving at Rapid Pace," *Dallas Business Journal,* Jan. 28, 2000, p. 24; Ken Cottrill, "Electronic Runway," *Traffic World,* Sep. 4, 2000, p. 28.

13. Sources: "World-Class Merchandising Model Leverages Global Synergies," *DSN Retailing Today,* June 2001, p. 15; "Trucking Company to Expand to Accommodate Wal-Mart," *Capital District Business Review,* May 7, 2001, p. 8; Liz Parks, "Wal-Mart Gets Onboard Early with Collaborative Planning," *Drug Store News,* Feb. 19, 2001, p. 14; Jean Kinsey, "A Faster, Leaner Supply Chain: New Uses of Information Technology," *American Journal of Agricultural Economics,* Nov. 15, 2000, pp. 1123+; Alorie Gilbert, "Retail's Super Supply Chains— Wal-Mart Inks Deal to Roll Out Private Trading Hub; Kmart Readies an Overhaul of Its Planning Systems," *InformationWeek,* Oct. 16, 2000, p. 22; "U.S. Operations," Wal-Mart, n.d., http://www.walmartstores.com; "Wal-Mart Fuels Expansion at M.S. Carriers," *Memphis Business Journal,* July 28, 2000, p. 3.

CHAPTER 16

1. Sources: David Koenig, "Internet Shines for Retailer," *Bryan-College Station Eagle,* Mar. 18, 2001, pp. A7–A9; Stephanie Anderson Forest, "Can an Outsider Fix J.C. Penney?" *Business Week,* Feb. 12, 2001, pp. 56–58; Dan Scheraga, "Penney's Net Advantage," *Chain Store Age,* Sep. 2000, pp. 114–118.

2. Bureau of the Census, *Statistical Abstract of the United States* (Washington, DC: Government Printing Office, 2000), pp. 543–544.

3. Roger O. Crockett, "Chat Me Up . . . Please," *Business Week,* Mar. 19, 2001, p. EB10.

4. Robert Scally, "New Measures, New Markets Up Ante in Club Game," *Dsn Retailing Today,* June 5, 2000, pp. 141–142.

5. "Ikea Finds New Living Rooms to Conquer," *International Herald Tribune,* July 30, 1998, p. 13.

6. Jeffrey Arlan, "Retailers Jockeyed for $180 Billion in 2000 Sales: Who Are the Winners?" *Dsn Retailing Today,* Feb. 5, 2001, pp. A6–A8.

7. "Economic Impact: US Direct Marketing Today Executive Summary," Direct Marketing Association, www.dma.org.

8. Jill Hecht Maxwell, "Sit! Stay! Make Money! Good Company," *Inc. Tech 2001,* Mar. 15, 2001, pp. 42–44.

9. "Fear of the Internet," *Chain Store Age Executive,* Apr. 2001, p. 18.

10. "Two Out of Three Web Users Plan to Buy Online," *New Media Age,* Dec. 21, 2000, p. 42.

11. Todd Wasserman, "Kodak Rages in Favor of the Machines," *Brandweek,* Feb. 26, 2001, p. 6.

12. "ABCs of Franchising," International Franchise Association, www.franchise.org.

13. Nora Ganim Barnes, "As the Mall Falls: Is Mall Entertainment Too Little, Too Late?" *Marketing Advances in the New Millennium,* Proceedings of the Society for Marketing Advances, 2000, pp. 51–54.

14. "McDonald's New McCafé," *CNNfn.com,* Mar. 23, 2001, http://cnnfn.cnn.com/2001/03/23/companies/wires/mcdonalds wg/.

15. Richard F. Yalch and Eric R. Spangenberg, "The Effects of Music in a Retail Setting on Real and Perceived Shopping Times," *Journal of Business Research,* Aug. 2000, pp. 139–147.

16. Stephen Brown, "The Wheel of Retailing: Past and Future," *Journal of Retailing,* Summer 1990, pp. 143–149.

17. Sources: Nora Macaluso, "1-800-Flowers Lifted by Holiday Sales," *E-Commerce Times,* Jan. 24, 2001, http://www.ecommercetimes.com; Paul Miller, "1-800-Flowers.com Plays Up Nonfloral Items," *Catalog Age,* Jan. 2001, p. 6; "1-800-Flowers Blossoms on the Wireless Web with 2Roam," *Business Wire,* Mar. 20, 2001, http://www.businesswire.com; Marty Jerome, "E-Commerce," *Ziff Davis Smart Business for the New Economy,* Dec. 1, 2000, pp. 104+; Ken Burke and Chris McCann, "Ask the Experts," *Catalog Age,* Aug. 2000, p. 1S5; Jeff Sweat, "The Well-Rounded Customer," *InformationWeek,* Apr. 10, 2000, pp. 44+; Stephen Boey, "1-800-Flowers.com Seeks Partners to Expand," *Business Times (Malaysia),* Feb. 15, 2000; "Company Overview," 1-800-Flowers.com website.

18. Sources: R. Michelle Breyer, "All-Natural Capitalist," *Austin American-Statesman,* May 10, 1998, pp. A1, A8; "Children of the Earth Go Corporate," *Austin American-Statesman,* May 10, 1998, p. A10; "Labor Practices Draw Praise and Pickets," *Austin American-Statesman,* May 10, 1998, p. A10; Joseph Serwach, "With Large Chains and Specialty Stores Looking to Expand Their Markets, Detroit Becomes a Grocery Battleground," *Crain's Detroit Business,* Dec. 11, 2000, p. 3; "Whole Foods Market Takes Manhattan . . . Naturally by Opening New York City's Largest Natural Supermarket," Whole Foods Market news release, Feb. 15, 2001, http://bizyahoo.com/prnews/010115/ny_tx_whole.html; "Natural Supermarket Whole Foods Abandons Internet Strategy," *Food & Drink Weekly,* June 26, 2000, p. 2.

CHAPTER 17

1. Hemelgarn Racing, www.hemelgarnracing.com/, (accessed) Aug. 28, 2001; Ron Hemelgarn, personal interview with author, May 26, 2001; "Tae-Bo Creator Looks to Change Shape of Racing Through Sponsorship of Hemelgarn Racing," Indy Racing League, Mar. 17, 1999, www.indyracingleague.com; "Sports Marketing," in O. C. Ferrell, Michael D. Hartline, and George H. Lucas, Jr., *Marketing Strategy* (Ft. Worth, TX: Dryden, 2001), http://www.harcourtcollege.com/marketing/ferrell/student/reading/sports.html.

2. Vanessa O'Connell, "Advertisers Turn to Touting Themselves," *The Wall Street Journal,* Apr. 17, 2001, p. B4.

3. Rebecca Gardyn, "Swap Meet: Customers Are Willing to Exchange Personal Information for Personalized Products," *American Demographics,* July 2001, pp. 51–55.

4. Ibid.

5. Chad Terhune, "Wood Folks Hope for 'Got Milk' Success," *The Wall Street Journal,* Feb. 9, 2001, p. B7.

6. Erin White, "Word of Mouth Makes Nike Slip-On Sneakers Take Off," *The Wall Street Journal,* June 7, 2001, pp. B1, B4.

7. In case you do not read Chinese, the message, prepared by Chih Kang Wang, says, "In the factory we make cosmetics, and in the store we sell hope."

8. Shimp, *Advertising,* p. 105.

9. Judy A. Wagner, Noreen M. Klein, and Janet E. Keith, "Selling Strategies: The Effects of Suggesting a Decision Structure to Novice and Expert Buyers," *Journal of the Academy of Marketing Science,* 29, no. 3 (2001); pp. 289–306.

10. Sandra Yin, "Making a Healthy Choice," *American Demographics,* July 2001, pp. 40–42.

11. John S. McClenahen, "How Can You Possibly Say That?" *Industry Week,* July 17, 1995, pp. 17–19.

12. Ibid.

13. Bruce Horovitz, "Color Them Beautiful—and Visible," *USA Today,* May 2, 2001, pp. B1, B2.

14. David M. Szymanski, "Modality and Offering Effects in Sales Presentations for a Good Versus a Service," *Journal of the Academy of Marketing Science,* 29, no. 2 (2001), pp. 179–189.

15. Sally Beatty, "Advance Sales of Children's Ads Slacken," *The Wall Street Journal,* May 11, 2001, p. B8.

16. O'Connell, "Advertisers Turn to Touting Themselves," p. B4.

17. Michael McCarthy, "$250M Ad Campaign Aims to Hit Homer," *USA Today,* Apr. 3, 2001, p. 3B.

18. Reshma Kapadia, "AOL Internet Service Members Surpass 30 Million," Reuters Newswire, via AOL, June 25, 2001.

19. Libby Estell, "This Call Center Accelerates Sales," *Sales & Marketing Management,* Feb. 1999, p. 72.

20. Karen Lundegaard, "Car Crash Ads May Lose Impact," *The Detroit News,* Apr. 15, 2001, p. C1.

21. *Time,* www.time-planner.com/planner2001/home.html, July 19, 2001.

22. Vicki R. Lane, "The Impact of Ad Repetition and Ad Content on Consumer Perceptions of Incongruent Extensions," *Journal of Marketing,* Apr. 2000, pp. 80–91.

23. "Got Milk," National Fluid Milk Processor Promotion Board, www.whymilk.com, July 19, 2001.

24. Scott B. MacKenzie, Philip M. Podsakoff, and Gregory A. Rich, "Transformational and Transactional Leadership and Salesperson Performance," *Journal of the Academy of Marketing Science,* 29, no. 2 (2001), pp. 115–134.

25. Ken Grant, David W. Cravens, George S. Low, and William C. Moncrief, "The Role of Satisfaction with Territory Design on the Motivation, Attitudes, and Work Outcomes of Salespeople," *Journal of the Academy of Marketing Science,* 29, no. 2 (2001), pp. 165–178.

26. "Sears Links Appliances to Olympics," *Advertising Age,* www.adage.com, July 19, 2001.

27. John J. Burnett, *Promotion Management* (Boston: Houghton Mifflin, 1993), p. 7.

28. "Toyota Readies Promotion with Hardware Chain," *Advertising Age,* www.adage.com, Apr. 5, 2001.

29. Jack Neff, "Clorox Gives in on Glad, Hikes Trade Promotion," *Advertising Age,* www.adage.com, July 19, 2001.

30. Gerry Khermouch and Jeff Green, "Buzz Marketing," *Business Week,* July 30, 2001, pp. 50–51.

31. Greg Winter, "Pepsi Looks to a New Drink to Jolt Soda Sales," *New York Times,* May 1, 2001, http://www.partners.nytimes.com.

32. Michael McCarthy, "Recent Crop of Sneaky Ads Backfire," *USA Today,* July 17, 2001, p. 3B.

33. Abraham H. Maslow, *Motivation and Personality* (New York: Harper and Row, 1954).

34. Ira Teinowitz and Keith J. Kelly, "PM Fires Up Warning over Tobacco Ad Limits," *Advertising Age,* Nov. 20, 1995, pp. 3, 23.

35. Sources: Brainshark, www.brainshark.com, (accessed) Sep. 12, 2001; "Brainshark Expands the Reach of Online Communications," Brainshark, press release, June 13, 2001, www.brainshark.com/news_events/releases/pr061301a.html; "Brainshark Makes a Big Splash with Customers, Partners,

and Investors in 2000; Positive Momentum Positions Rich-Media Web Communications Provider as Market Leader," *Business Wire,* Jan. 24, 2001, via www.findarticles.com; "Brainshark Unveils Solution to Improve Sales and Marketing Effectiveness," *Business Wire,* Dec. 5, 2000, via www.findarticles.com; Sharky, "Taking the Bite Out of Online Presentations," *Computerworld,* June 26, 2000, www.computerworld.com/.

36. Sources: "APPMA Survey Finds Pet Ownership Continues Growth Trend in U.S.; Trade Group's Biennial Study Reports More Than 63 Million Households Include Animal Companions," *Business Wire,* May 1, 2001, via www.findarticles.com; Rebecca Gardyn, "VIPs (Very Important Pets)," *American Demographics,* March 2001, www.demographics.com; Christie Brown, "Pooper-Scooper Dooper," *Forbes,* Feb. 13, 1995, pp. 78–81; "Key Facts: PETsMART," *The Wall Street Journal,* http://www.interactive.wsj.com, (accessed) Sep. 26, 2001; Julie Liesse, "Superstores Add Bite to Pet Market's Bark," *Advertising Age,* Apr. 25, 1994, p. 42; Ryan Matthews, "Pet Projects," Progressive Grocer, Jul. 1995, pp. 69–70; Jerry Minkoff, "Perking Up Pet Supplies," *Discount Merchandiser,* Jul. 1995, pp. 30–32; Marcia Mogelonsky, "Reigning Cats and Dogs," *American Demographics,* Apr. 1995, pp. 30–32; "No 1 Still Leads Pack, Despite Flat Sales," *DSN Retailing Today,* Aug. 7, 2000, via www.findarticles.com; "Pet Consolidation in Offing," *Discount Stores News,* Mar. 21, 1994, pp. 3, 46; PETsMART 2000 Annual Report, www.irconnect.com/petm/pages/areport.html, (accessed) Sep. 26, 2001; PETsMART, www.petsmart.com, (accessed) Sep. 26, 2001; PETsMART, company video; Marguerite Smith, "The New World of Health Care for Your Pet," *Money,* Apr. 1994, pp. 144–158; R. Lee Sullivan, "Puppy Love," *Forbes,* Dec. 20, 1993, pp. 138–142; Tim Triplett, "Superstores Tap into Bond Between Owners and Pets," *Marketing News,* Apr. 25, 1994, pp. 1–2.

CHAPTER 18

1. Based on information from Kate MacArthur, "McDonald's," *Advertising Age,* August 6, 2001, p. S4; Abbey Klaassen, "Nike," *Advertising Age,* August 6, 2001, p. S4; Sarah J. Heim, "Pepsi Previews TV Spot on Web Prior To On-Air Debut," *Adweek Southwest,* July 16, 2001, p. 7; Devin Leonard, "Madison Ave. Fights Back," *Fortune,* February 5, 2001, pp. 150–154.

2. "100 Leaders by U.S. Advertising Spending," *Advertising Age,* Sep. 28, 1998, p. 52.

3. Tobi Elkin, "Handspring Handheld Goes High Fashion," *Advertising Age,* Mar. 16, 2001, www.adage.com/news_and_features/features/20010316/article2.html.

4. William F. Arens, *Contemporary Advertising* (Burr Ridge, IL: Irwin/McGraw-Hill, 1999), p. 378.

5. Tobi Elkin, "64% Respond to Wireless Ads in Market Test," *Advertising Age,* Mar. 8, 2001, www.adage.com/news_and_features/features/20010308/article3.html.

6. George E. Belch and Michael A. Belch, *Advertising and Promotion* (Burr Ridge, IL: Irwin/McGraw-Hill, 2001), pp. 576–577.

7. Thea Singer, "Can Business Still Save the World?" *Inc.,* Apr. 30, 2001, pp. 58–71.

8. "UPS Holds Official Status at Daytona International Speedway," *Business Wire,* Feb. 15, 2001, p. 2260.

9. Belch and Belch, *Advertising and Promotion,* p. 598.

10. Sources: Keith Regan, "Report: Financial Services Firms Top Web Advertisers," *E-Commerce Times,* August 7, 2001, www.ecommercetimes.com/perl/story/12591.html; Richard Linnett and Wayne Friedman, "No Gain: Super Bowl Ad Pricing Is Flat," *Advertising Age,* January 15, 2001, http://adage.com/news_and_features/features/20010115/article5.html; Jennifer Gilbert, "Running On Empty," *Advertising Age,* 2000,

http://adage.com/i20/srmain.html; "There's No Escaping the Dot.Com Ad Blitz," *ZDNet.com U.K.,* 1999, http://www.zdnet.co.uk/news/1999/47/ns-11785.html; "The Net Goes Guerilla," 1999, http://www.zdnet.co.uk/news/1999/47/ns-11783.html.
11. Sources: Dan Carney, "Outreach, Microsoft Style," *Business Week,* July 23, 2001, p. 47; William O'Neal, "Behold the Xbox!" *Computer Gaming World,* March 1, 2001, p. 118; Rick Tetzeli and David Kirkpatrick, "America Loves Microsoft," *Fortune,* Feb. 1998, pp. 80+; Steve Hamm, " 'I'm Humble, I'm Respectful,' " *Business Week,* Feb. 9, 1998, pp. 40–42; Greg Miller and Leslie Helm, "Microsoft Plans Stealth Media Blitz," *Los Angeles Times,* Apr. 10, 1998, p. A1; Thomas W. Haines, "Lesson Plan: Microsoft Hits the Hallways, because Today's Fifth-Grader Is Tomorrow's Software Buyer," *Seattle Times,* Apr. 12, 1998, p. F1; Bradley Johnson, "Microsoft Eyes Ads in Antitrust Struggle with Justice Dept.," *Advertising Age,* Apr. 13, 1998, p. 39; David Bank and John Simons, "Microsoft Is on Defensive over Media Strategy," *The Wall Street Journal,* Apr. 13, 1998, p. B8; Amy Cortese, "Emperor of High Tech, Sultan of Spin," *Business Week,* May 18, 1998, p. 37; Geoffrey James, "Image Making at Mighty Microsoft," *Upside,* June 1998, pp. 81–86; Susan B. Garland, "A Tough Sell, but Not Impossible," *Business Week,* Jan. 18, 1999, p. 44; and Mike France and Susan B. Garland, "Microsoft: The View at Halftime," *Business Week,* Jan. 25, 1999, pp. 78–82.

CHAPTER 19
1. Based on information from Betsy Cummings, "Welcome to the Real Whirled," *Sales & Marketing Management,* February 2001, pp. 87–88; Rekha Balu, "Whirlpool Gets Real With Customers," *Fast Company,* December 1999, pp. 74, 76; "Whirlpool Corporation in 2000," Whirlpool corporate description, http://www.whirlpoolcorp.com; "Whirlpool Corporation," *Hoover's Online,* n.d., http://www.hoovers.com.
2. "What a Sales Call Costs," *Sales & Marketing Management,* Sep. 2000, p. 80.
3. Dan Brekke, "What You Don't Know Can Hurt You," *Smart Business,* Mar. 2001, pp. 64–74.
4. Sarah Lorge, "The Best Way to Prospect," *Sales & Marketing Management,* Jan. 1998, p. 80.
5. Andy Cohen, "2001 Salary Survey," *Sales & Marketing Management,* May 2001, pp. 47–50.
6. Nora Wood, "What Motivates Best?" *Sales & Marketing Management,* Sep. 1998, pp. 71–78.
7. George E. Belch and Michael A. Belch, *Advertising and Promotion* (Burr Ridge, IL: Irwin/McGraw-Hill, 2001), pp. 526–532.
8. Kate Fitzgerald, "Coupons 2000: Volume Down, Value Up," *Advertising Age,* Mar. 12, 2001, www.adage.com.
9. Arthur L. Porter, "Direct Mail's Lessons for Electronic Couponers," *Marketing Management Journal,* Spring/Summer 2000, pp. 107–115.
10. Arthur L. Porter, "Direct Mail's Lessons for Electronic Couponers," *Marketing Management Journal,* Spring/Summer 2000, pp. 107–115.
11. "Hotels Plan Deals to Lure Cost-Conscious Travelers," *Promo,* Apr. 11, 2001, http://www.marketingclick.com.
12. Karen J. Bannan, "Freebies in Cyberspace: Online Companies Let Consumers Pick the Samples They Want Mailed to Them," *The Wall Street Journal,* Nov. 27, 2000, p. 10.
13. Janet Singleton, "Mail-in Rebates Aren't Worth the Trouble for Most Customers," *Denver Post,* May 6, 2001, p. D08.
14. Sources: Based on a personal interview with Deborah Bernard of Wheelworks, August 22, 2001; "Motivating the Sales Force at Wheelworks" video.

15. Sources: "Soft Drink Sales Increased 0.5% in 2000 According to Beverage Marketing Corporation," *Business Wire,* February 15, 2001, http://www.businesswire.com; Laurie Russo, "Takin' It To the Streets," *Beverage World,* November 15, 2000; Jordan Mackay, "The Fight Over Soft Drinks in the Public Schools Fizzes Up in Texas," *Texas Monthly,* December 1998, p. 30; Theresa Howard, "Brand Builders: Strategy: The Pepper Paradigm," *Brandweek,* November 2, 1998, pp. 24, 28; "Third Quarter Ad Spending Up 8.8%," http://www.cmr.com, February 1, 1999.

CHAPTER 20
1. Based on information from Rebecca Sausner, "Dell Pegs New PC Price Point Below $600," *E-Commerce Times,* June 4, 2001, http://www.ecommercetimes.com/perl/story/10240.html; Tim McDonald, "Gateway Takes Offensive in PC Price War," *E-Commerce Times,* May 31, 2001, http://www.ecommercetimes.com/perl/story/10140.html; Leah Beth Ward, "Dell Vows To Persist With Price Strategy: Firm Says Cuts Led To Market Share Gains," *Dallas Morning News,* May 18, 2001, p. 1D; Tim McDonald, "Dell Beats Out Compaq For First Time," *E-Commerce Times,* April 20, 2001, http://www.ecommercetimes.com/perl/story/9120.html; Ken Popovich, "PC Price Wars Begin To Shake Loyalties—Dell, Compaq Battle For Users By Slashing Prices," *eWeek,* April 30, 2001, p. 1; Martin Veitch, "Compaq Builds Corporate Line To Challenge IBM in Enterprise," *IT Week,* February 19, 2001, p. 22.
2. Donald Lichtenstein, Nancy M. Ridgway, and Richard G. Netemeyer, "Price Perceptions and Consumer Shopping Behavior: A Field Study," *Journal of Marketing Research,* May 1993, pp. 234–245.
3. "Broadcast of New Vision Gets Mixed Reception from the Street," *Dsn Retailing Today,* Jan. 2001, p. 16.
4. Akshay R. Rao, Mark E. Bergen, and Scott Davis, "How to Fight a Price War," *Harvard Business Review,* Mar./Apr. 2000, pp. 107–116.
5. David Aaker and Erich Joachimsthaler, "An Alternative to Price Competition," *American Demographics,* Sep. 2000, p. 11.
6. Cliff Edwards, "Intel Inside the War Room," *Business Week,* Apr. 30, 2001, p. 40.
7. Peter D. Bennett, *Dictionary of Marketing Terms* (Chicago: American Marketing Association, 1995), p. 79.
8. Ibid., p. 215.
9. Anthony Bianco, "Exxon Unleashed," *Business Week,* Apr. 9, 2001, pp. 58–70.
10. Lichtenstein, Ridgway, and Netemeyer, "Price Perceptions."
11. Bruce L. Alford and Brian T. Engelland, "Advertised Reference Price Effects on Consumer Price Estimates, Value Perception, and Search Intention," *Journal of Business Research,* May 2000, pp. 93–100.
12. Lichtenstein, Ridgway, and Netemeyer, "Price Perceptions."
13. Sources: J. K. Dineen, "JetBlue Offering $99 Nonstop Coast-To-Coast Flights," *New York Daily News,* August 15, 2001, http://www.nydailynews.com; "Blue Skies: Is JetBlue the Next Great Airline—Or Just a Little Too Good To Be True?" *Time,* July 30, 2001, pp. 24+; Darren Shannon, "Three of a Kind," *Travel Agent,* July 23, 2001, pp. 60+.
14. Sources: Maryann Keller, "Inside Priceline's Sausage Factory," *Fortune,* September 3, 2001, p. 42; Greg Dalton, "Priceline Is Finally on the Ascent," *Industry Standard,* July 31, 2001, http://www.thestandard.com/article/0,1902,28394,00.html; Clare Saliba, "Priceline, Expedia End Patent Flap," *E-Commerce Times,* January 10, 2001, http://ecommercetimes.com/perl/story/?id=6605; Jay Walker, "What Price Brand Loyalty?" *Marketing Week,* June 29, 2000, p. 53.

CHAPTER 21

1. Based on information from "Family Dollar To Join S&P 500," *Business Journal of Charlotte,* July 31, 2001, http://charlotte.bcentral.com/charlotte/stories/2001/07/30/daily23.html; Adelia Cellini Linecker, "Family Dollar Uses 'Hardline' Stance to Get a Leg Up in Discount Battles," *Investor's Daily Business,* May 23, 2001, p. 1; Tim Schooley, "Discounter Finds Plenty To Like Here," *Pittsburgh Business Times,* May 18, 2001, p. 3; Ken Clark, "Where the Dollar Is King," *Chain Store Age Executive,* February 2001, p. 35.

2. Christopher Caggiano, "E-tailing by the Numbers," *Inc. Tech 2001,* Mar. 15, 2001, pp. 46–49.

3. Stanley Holmes, "Rumble over Tokyo," *Business Week,* Apr. 2, 2001, pp. 80–81.

4. Marla Royne Stafford and Thomas F. Stafford, "The Effectiveness of Tensile Pricing Tactics in the Advertising of Services," *The Journal of Advertising,* Summer 2000, pp. 45–56.

5. "Hyundai Redefines Value Among V-6 Powered SUVs with the Introduction of the All-New Santa Fe," Hyundai press release, Sep. 18, 2000.

6. Adulla Cellini Linecker, "Family Dollar Store Uses 'Hardline' Stance to Get a Leg Up in Discount Battles," *Investor's Daily Business,* May 23, 2001, p. A1.

7. Alex Taylor III, "Can You Believe Porsche Is Putting Its Badge on This Car?" *Fortune,* Feb. 19, 2001, pp. 168–172.

8. Bruce L. Alford and Brian T. Engelland, "Advertised Reference Price Effects on Consumer Price Estimates, Value Perception, and Search Intention," *Journal of Business Research,* May 2000, pp. 93–100.

9. Nigel Cox, "Amex Charges Ahead," *Smart Business,* Apr. 2001, pp. 123–128.

10. Sources: Maria Bruno, "Winning Customers: Concierge Services," *Bank Technology News,* July 2001, http://www.electronicbanker.com/btn/articles/btnjul01-6.shtml#top; "VIPdesk Expands Web-Based Personal Assistant Service To Wireless Devices," VIPdesk news release, June 25, 2001, http://www.vipdesk.com; Terry Brock, "The Internet Is Not About Dot-Coms," *Business Journal of Milwaukee,* February 16, 2001, p. 14; VIPdesk video; "Online Concierge Service Secures Funding," *Business Wire,* January 20, 2000, http://www.businesswire.com.

11. Sources: "IDC Report Shows Apple Is the Leader in K-12 Education," Apple news release, July 17, 2001, http://www.apple.com; "iMacs Indicate Apple's Unique Strength," *New Straits Times,* May 10, 2001; Philip Michaels, "Just Another Pretty Face?" *Macworld,* May 2001, p. 22; Penelope Patsuris, "Apple Is More Than the iMac," *Forbes,* January 13, 1999, http://www.forbes.com/tool/html/99/jan/0113/mu5.htm; Stephen H. Wildstrom, "Where Wintel Fears To Tread," *Business Week,* September 14, 1998, p. 19; Ira Sager and Peter Burrows, "Back To the Future at Apple," *Business Week,* May 25, 1998, http://www.businessweek.com.

CHAPTER 22

1. Sources: William J. Holstein, "DaimlerChrysler's Net Designs," *Business2.com,* Apr. 17, 2001, pp. 26 +; Robyn Meredith, "The Anti-Iacocca," *Forbes,* Aug. 20, 2001, pp. 50–54; Joann Muller, with Christine Tierney, "Can This Man Save Chrysler?" *Business Week,* Sep. 17, 2001, pp. 86–94.

2. Robin M. Grugal, "Alberto Sculpts Out Market Niche in Fighting Big Guns of Hair Care," *Investor's Daily Business,* July 17, 2001, p. A1.

3. O. C. Ferrell, Michael Hartline, and George Lucas, *Marketing Strategy* (Ft. Worth, TX: Dryden, 2002), p. 179.

4. Ibid., pp. 179–180.

5. David Field, "New Airlines' Cut Rates Could Be Too Good to Keep Flying," *USA Today,* Oct. 27, 1998, p. 3B.

6. Nicholas Roe, "Ben & Jerry Create Ice-Cream Flavors That the World Adores," *[London] Sunday Express,* July 8, 2001, p. 81.

7. Myron Glassman and Bruce McAfee, "Integrating the Personnel and Marketing Functions: The Challenge of the 1990s," *Business Horizons,* May/June 1992, pp. 52–59.

8. Michael D. Hartline and O. C. Ferrell, "Service Quality Implementation: The Effects of Organizational Socialization and Managerial Actions on the Behaviors of Customer-Contact Employees," *Marketing Science Institute Working Paper Series,* no. 93–122 (Cambridge, MA: Marketing Science Institute, 1993), pp. 36–40.

9. O. C. Ferrell, Michael D. Hartline, George H. Lucas, Jr., and David Luck, *Marketing Strategy* (Ft. Worth, TX: Dryden, 1999), pp. 135–136.

10. Adapted from Nigel F. Piercy, *Market-Led Strategic Change* (Newton, MA: Butterworth-Heinemann, 1992), pp. 374–385.

11. David Kiley and Del Jones, "Ford Alters Worker Evaluation Process," *USA Today,* July 11, 2001, p. B1.

12. Lloyd C. Harris and Emmanuel Ogbonna, "Strategic Human Resource Management, Market Orientation, and Organizational Performance," *Journal of Business Research,* Feb. 2001, pp. 157–166.

13. Sybil F. Stershic, "Internal Marketing Campaign Reinforces Service Goals," *Marketing News,* July 31, 1998, p. 11.

14. Jennifer Ordonez, "Taco Bell Chief Has New Tactic: Be Like Wendy's," *The Wall Street Journal,* Feb. 23, 2001, p. B1.

15. Adapted from Joseph R. Jablonski, *Implementing Total Quality Management* (Albuquerque, NM: Technical Management Consortium, 1990).

16. Philip B. Crosby, *Quality Is Free: The Art of Making Quality Certain* (New York: McGraw-Hill, 1979), pp. 9–10.

17. Piercy, *Market-Led Strategic Change.*

18. Kenneth W. Thomas and Betty A. Velthouse, "Cognitive Elements of Empowerment: An 'Interpretive' Model of Intrinsic Task Motivation," *Academy of Management Review,* Oct. 1990, pp. 666–681.

19. Hartline and Ferrell, "Service Quality Implementation."

20. Jagdip Singh, "Performance Productivity and Quality of Frontline Employees in Service Organizations," *Journal of Marketing,* Apr. 2000, pp. 15–34.

21. Fred Steingraber, "Total Quality Management: A New Look at a Basic Issue," *Vital Speeches of the Day,* May 1990, pp. 415–416.

22. Rohit Deshpande and Frederick E. Webster, Jr., "Organizational Culture and Marketing: Defining the Research Agenda," *Journal of Marketing,* Jan. 1989, pp. 3–15.

23. REI, www.rei.com, July 20, 2001.

24. Ajay K. Kohli and Bernard J. Jaworski, "Marketing Orientation: The Construct, Research Propositions, and Managerial Implications," *Journal of Marketing,* Apr. 1990, pp. 1–18.

25. Ferrell, Hartline, and Lucas, *Marketing Strategy,* p. 95.

26. Kathleen Cholewka, "CRM: Lose the Hype and Strategize," *Sales & Marketing Management,* June 2001, pp. 27–28.

27. David C. Jones, "Motivation the Catalyst in Profit Formula," *National Underwriter,* July 13, 1987, pp. 10, 13.

28. Lorrie Grant, "CEO Rigs Up Plan to Restore Kmart," *USA Today,* June 27, 2001, p. 3B.

29. Marilyn Elias, "Rudeness Poisoning Workplace, Study Says," *Pensacola News Journal,* June 17, 2001, p. B1.

30. Emily Nelson, "P&G Moves to Set Up a System to Share Employee Know-How," *The Wall Street Journal,* Jan. 23, 2001, p. B6.

31. Hartline and Ferrell, "Service Quality Implementation," pp. 36–48.

32. Gloria Lau, "A Training Program Should Zero in on What Your Staffers Must Know," *Investor's Business Daily,* June 18, 2001, p. A1.

33. Bernard J. Jaworski, "Toward a Theory of Marketing Control: Environmental Context, Control Types, and Consequences," *Journal of Marketing,* July 1988, pp. 23–39.

34. David Welch, Christine N. Tierney, and Chester Dawson, "GM Tries to Show Who's Boss," *Business Week Online,* Mar. 12, 2001, www.businessweek.com.

35. Richard A. Melcher, "Industry Outlook 1996: Business Services," *Business Week,* Jan. 8, 1996, p. 107.

36. "J. D. Powers & Associates Reports: Lexus Continues as Top Provider in Dealer Service Customer Satisfaction," J. D. Powers & Associates press release, July 11, 2001, www.jdpa.com/presspass/pr/pressrelease.asp?ID=127.

37. Brad Dorfman, "Gillette Q2 Operating Profits Drop 59 Pct," Reuters Newswire, via AOL, July 20, 2001; "Duracell Launches New Advertising Campaign for Duracell Coppertop Batteries; 'Bees' Spot Demonstrates Battery's Long-Lasting, Hard-Working Qualities," Gillette Company press release, June 26, 2001, www.gillette.com/pressroom/portablepower.asp; "Duracell Relaunches Duracell Coppertop Batteries with $100 Million Strategic Initiative; Enhanced Copper & Black Battery Technologies Will Deliver 'Quality That Lasts,' " Gillette Company press release, Mar. 28, 2001, www.gillette.com/pressroom/portablepower.asp.

38. Kathleen Kerwin and Keith Naughton, "Cruise Control?" *Business Week,* Jan. 8, 1996, pp. 82–83.

39. "Campbell Soup Splitting Operations into Two Units," *Advertising Age,* Apr. 16, 2001, www.adage.com.

40. Christopher H. Lovelock, *Services Marketing,* 2d ed. (Englewood Cliffs, NJ: Prentice-Hall, 1991), p. 270.

41. Sources: "About Us," AOL Time Warner, www.aoltw.com, (accessed) Oct. 5, 2001; "America Online Reorganizes to Lead Next Chapter of Internet's Growth," AOL Time Warner, press release, Aug. 21, 2001, http://media.aoltimewarner.com/media/press_view.cfm?release_num=55252126; "AOL Time Warner to Create New TV Networks Group under Time Warner Broadcasting Umbrella, Including Basic Cable Networks and the WB Broadcast Network," AOL Time Warner, press release, Mar. 6, 2001, http://media.aoltimewarner.com/media/press_view.cfm?release_num=50252312; Neil Hickey, "Coping with Mega-Mergers," *Columbia Journalism Review,* Mar./Apr. 2000, www.cjr.org/year/00/2/aoltw.asp; "AOL/Time Warner Coverage," BATV, video, www.batv.com, (accessed) Oct. 5, 2001; and "America Online and Time Warner Complete Merger to Create AOL Time Warner," AOL Time Warner, press release, Jan. 11, 2001, www.aoltimewarner.com/media/press_view.cfm?release_num=50252141.

42. Sources: "Amtrak, at 30, Faces Old Problems But New Urgency," CNN, Apr. 30, 2001, www.cnn.com; "Amtrak Facts," Amtrak, www.amtrak.com/about/amtrakfacts.html, (accessed) Aug. 14, 2001; "Amtrak Looks for New Ways to Make Money," CNN, Jul. 13, 2001, www.cnn.com; "Amtrak's Money-Making Efforts," CNN, Jul. 13, 2001, www.cnn.com; "Amtrak's Strategic Business Plan Fiscal Year 1999–2002," Amtrak, www.amtrak.com/news/pr/hilites.html, (accessed) Feb. 24, 1999; "Building a Commercial Enterprise (FY01-05 Financial Plan Update): Investing in the Future of Passenger Rail," Amtrak, http://www.amtrak.com/press/businessplan-copy.html, (accessed) Aug. 14, 2001; Lisa Gubernick and Daniel Machalaba, "Travelers Take to the Rails, But Find Service Is Spotty," *The Wall Street Journal,* Sep. 26, 2001, http://interactive.wsj.com/; Daniel Machalaba, "Fast Trains, Local Beer Mark Makeover Effort at Amtrak," *The Wall Street Journal,* Jan. 27, 1999, interactive.wsj.com.

CHAPTER 23

1. Sources: Karen Bannan, "Sole Survivor," *Sales & Marketing Management,* July 2001, pp. 36–41; "Company Overview," eBay, http://pages.ebay.com/community/aboutebay/overview/index.html, July 11, 2001; Robert Goff, "Ebay's Cop," *Forbes,* June 25, 2001, p. 42; Robert D. Hof, "Online Extra: Q&A with eBay's Meg Whitman," *Business Week Online,* May 14, 2001, www.businessweek.com; Julia King, "Web Sites Crack Down on Fraud," *Computerworld,* Sep. 13, 1999, p. 1113; Chuck Lenatti, "Auction Mania," *Upside,* July 11, 1999, pp. 84–92; Ellen Messmer, "Ebay Acts to Curtail Internet Fraud," *Network World,* July 24, 2000, pp. 31, 34; "Most Powerful Women," *Fortune,* www.fortune.com, Aug. 8, 2001; Jon Swartz, " 'E' in eBay Might Stand for Expansion," *USA Today,* Mar. 28, 2001, www.usatoday.com; Eric Young, "Ebay Says Fixed-Price Bazaar Will Open Next Quarter," *The Standard,* May 25, 2001, www.thestandard.com.

2. Vladimir Zwass, "Electronic Commerce: Structures and Issues," *International Journal of Electronic Commerce,* Fall 1996, pp. 3–23.

3. "Internet Commerce," Forrester Research, www.forrester.com/ER/Press/ForrFind/0,1768,0,00.html, Aug. 6, 2001.

4. D. Ian Hopper, "U.S. Government Outpaces Retailers in Internet Sales," *The Coloradoan,* May 30, 2001, p. D7.

5. Michael J. Mandel and Robert D. Hof, "Rethinking the Internet," *Business Week,* Mar. 26, 2001, pp. 116–122.

6. Michael Totty, "The Researcher," *The Wall Street Journal,* July 16, 2001, p. R20.

7. David W. Stewart and Qin Zhao, "Internet Marketing, Business Models, and Public Policy," *Journal of Public Policy & Marketing,* Fall 2000, pp. 287–296.

8. Totty, "The Researcher."

9. Venky Shankar, "Multiple Touch Point Marketing," American Marketing Association Faculty Consortium on Electronic Commerce, Texas A&M University, July 14–17, 2001.

10. David Pottruck and Terry Peace, "Listening to Customers in the Electronic Age," *Fortune,* May 2000, www.business2.com/articles/mag/0,1640,7700,00.html.

11. Mark McMaster, "E-marketing: Poll Vault," *Sales & Marketing Management,* Aug. 2001, p. 25.

12. Mandel and Hof, "Rethinking the Internet," p. 118.

13. Jon Mark Giese, "Place Without Space, Identity Without Body: The Role of Cooperative Narrative in Community and Identity Formation in a Text-Based Electronic Community," unpublished dissertation, Pennsylvania State University, 1996.

14. Robert D. Hof, with Seanna Browder and Peter Elstrom, "Internet Communities," *Business Week,* May 5, 1997, pp. 64–80.

15. Kathy Rebello, with Larry Armstrong and Amy Cortese, "Making Money on the Net," *Business Week,* Sep. 23, 1996, pp. 104–118.

16. Hof, "Internet Communities."

17. Bill Richards, "A Total Overhaul," *The Wall Street Journal,* Dec. 7, 1998, interactive.wsj.com.

18. George P. Landow, *Hypertext 2.0: The Convergence of Contemporary Critical Theory and Technology* (Baltimore: The John Hopkins University Press, 1997).

19. Ellen Neuborne, with Robert D. Hof, "Branding on the Net," *Business Week,* Nov. 9, 1998, pp. 76–86.

20. Joshua Macht, "Upstarts: Toy Seller Plays Internet Hard Ball," *Inc.,* Oct. 1998, p. 18.

21. "Nearly One-Third of American Internet Users Have Access to Broadband According to Arbitron and Coleman Study; Majority of Broadband Users Connected Through Work," *Business Wire,* via AOL, June 21, 2001.

22. Kathleen Kerwin and Marcia Stepanek, "At Ford, E-Commerce Is Job 1," *Business Week,* Feb. 28, 2000, pp. 74–78.

23. Gartner, Inc., "Economic Downturn Slows B2B Commerce," CyberAtlas, Mar. 21, 2001, http://cyberatlas.internet.com/markets/b2b/article/0,,10091_719571,00.html.

24. Mandel and Hof, "Rethinking the Internet," p. 121.

25. Kerwin and Stepanek, "At Ford," p. 74.
26. "Covisint Parts Exchange Officially Opens for Business," Bloomberg Newswire, Dec. 11, 2000, via AOL.
27. Alan Greenspan, remarks to the Economic Club of New York, Jan. 13, 2000, Federal Reserve Board, www.federalreserve.gov/boarddocs/speeches/2000/200001132.htm.
28. Kerwin and Stepanek, "At Ford," p. 74.
29. "Web Influences Offline Purchases, Especially Among Teens," CyberAtlas, July 18, 2001, http://cyberatlas.internet.com/markets/retailing/article/0,,6061_804141,00.html#table.
30. Adapted from Judy Strauss and Raymond Frost, *EMarketing,* 2nd ed. (Upper Saddle River, NJ: Prentice-Hall, 2001).
31. Industry Standard, as reported in John W. Munsell, "How to Increase Sales and Develop Customer Relationships on the Web," presentation to American Marketing Association, Nov. 20, 1998.
32. "Company Facts," Dell, www.dell.com, Aug. 8, 2001.
33. Tessa Romita, "Sky's the Limit for Airlines Online," *Business2.0,* Jan. 23, 2001.
34. Rebello, "Making Money on the Net."
35. George Anders, "Click and Buy: Why—and Where—Internet Commerce Is Succeeding," *The Wall Street Journal,* Dec. 7, 1998, interactive.wsj.com.
36. Tony Seideman, "Get with the Program," *Inbound Logistics,* Sep. 1998, pp. 28–34.
37. Richards, "A Total Overhaul."
38. "About Amazon.com," Amazon.com, www.amazon.com, Aug. 8, 2001.
39. Gary Welz, "The Ad Game," *Internet World,* July 1996, pp. 50–57.
40. Robbin Zeff, "Five Easy Questions: Free Liquor!! Money!! The Secrets of Eternal Youth!!" *Business2.0,* Sep. 2000, www.business2.com.
41. "Banners Can Brand, Honestly, They Can," CyberAtlas, July 12, 2001, http://cyberatlas.internet.com/markets/advertising/article/0,1323,5941_800091,00.html.
42. "Pop-up Internet Ads: More Eyeballs—and More Frowns," Statistical Research, press release, May 3, 2001, http://www.statisticalresearch.com/press/pr050301.htm.
43. Linda Himelstein, with Ellen Neuborne and Paul M. Eng, "Web Ads Start to Click," *Business Week,* Oct. 6, 1997, pp. 128–138.
44. Ginger Conlon, "Plug and Play," *Sales & Marketing Management,* Dec. 1998, p. 65.
45. Edward C. Baig, "Progress in Online Privacy, But Critics Say Not Enough," *Business Week Online,* May 13, 1999, www.businessweek.com.
46. Keith H. Hammonds, *"Business Week*/Harris Poll: A Lot of Looking, Not Much Buying—Yet," *Business Week,* Oct. 6, 1997, p. 140.
47. Nick Wingfield, "A Marketer's Dream: The Internet Promises to Give Companies a Wealth of Invaluable Data about Their Customers. So Why Hasn't It?" *The Wall Street Journal,* Dec. 7, 1998, interactive.wsj.com.
48. "About the Privacy Program," BBBOnLine, www.BBBOnLine.org/privacy/index.asp, Aug. 8, 2001.
49. "Survey: Kids Disclose Private Details Online," CNN, May 17, 2000, www.cnn.com.
50. "European Union Directive on Privacy," E-Center for Business Ethics, Nov. 1, 1999, www.e-businessethics.com/privacy.eud.htm.
51. David G. McDonough, ". . . But Can the WTO Really Sock It to Software Pirates?" *Business Week Online,* Mar. 9, 1999, www.businessweek.com.
52. Stephen H. Wildstrom, "Can Microsoft Stamp Out Piracy?" *Business Week Online,* Oct. 2, 2000, www.businessweek.com.
53. William T. Neese and Charles R. McManis, "Summary Brief: Law, Ethics and the Internet: How Recent Federal Trademark Law Prohibits a Remedy Against Cyber-squatters," Proceedings from the Society of Marketing Advances, Nov. 4–7, 1998.
54. Sources: Computers4SURE.com, www.computers4sure.com, (accessed) Oct. 10, 2001; "Computers4SURE.com Awarded Three Prominent Industry Web Site Awards," PRNewswire, Oct. 25, 1999, via www.findarticles.com; "Engage Enabling Technologies: Ad Management Solutions with AdBureau and AdManager," Engage, Inc., case study, www.engage.com/au/solutions/cs_solutions_shop4sure.cfm, (accessed) Sep. 19, 2001; David Jastrow, "Attacking the B2B Market," Computer Reseller News, www.crn.com/sections/special/estars/estars.asp?ArticleID=15761, (accessed) Sep. 20, 2001; "Office Depot Announces Acquisition of Computers4Sure.com and Solutions4Sure.com," 4SURE.com, press release, Jul. 9, 2001, www.computers4sure.com/static/releaseOfficeDepot.asp; "Shopping4SURE.com," BATV, video, www.batv.com, (accessed) Sep. 20, 2001; "Shopping4SURE.com, the Award Winning On-line Retailer, Chooses ICC's B2B Fulfillment Solution," Internet Commerce Corporation, press release, Dec. 15, 1999, www.icc.net/aboutICC/ICCnews/pressReleases/1215299.html; Solutions4SURE.com, www.solutions4sure.com, (accessed) Oct. 10, 2001.
55. Sources: "Bigger Battle Brewing: Napster-RIAA Court Case Becoming Goliath Vs. Goliath," www.sfgate.com, (accessed) Sep. 18, 2000; Don Clark and Martin Peers, "Can the Record Industry Beat Free Web Music?" *The Wall Street Journal,* Jun. 20, 2000, p. B1; Amy Doan, "MP3.com Loses Big in Copyright Case," *Forbes,* Sep. 6, 2000, www.forbes.com; "Early Birth on Web for Latest Offspring," www.smh.com.au/news, (accessed) Sep. 19, 2000; Jack Ewing, "A New Net Powerhouse?" *Business Week,* Nov. 13, 2000, pp. 46–52; "Federal Court Sets October Trial Date for Napster Case," CNN Aug. 29, 2000, www.cnn.com; Lee Gomes, "Judge Orders Napster to Stop Downloads of Copyrighted Music," *The Wall Street Journal Interactive,* July 27, 2000, http://interactive.wsj.com/; Lee Gomes, "Napster, Fighting for Survival, to Make Case Before Appeals Panel," *The Wall Street Journal,* Oct. 2, 2000, p. B24; Lee Gomes, "Napster Ruling May Be Just the Overture," *The Wall Street Journal,* Jul. 28, 2000; Lee Gomes, "Think Music Moguls Don't Like Sharing? Try Copying Software," *The Wall Street Journal,* Aug. 14, 2000, p. B1; Lee Gomes, "When Its Own Assets Are Involved, Napster Is No Fan of Sharing," *The Wall Street Journal,* Jul. 26, 2000, pp. A1, A10; Ron Harris, "Heavy Metal Thunder," ABC News, www.abcnews.go/com, (accessed) Sep. 25, 2000; "How VCRs May Help Napster's Legal Fight," *The Standard,* www.thestandard.com/article, (accessed) Jul. 24, 2000; Margarita Lenk, "Our Music: Can We Mutually Support the Artist and the Business?" Colorado State University; Carolyn Duffy Marsan, "Is Rock and Roll Bad for Your Net?" CNN, Feb. 15, 2000, www.cnn.com; Anna Wilde Mathews, "Sampling Free Music Over the Internet Often Leads to Sale," *The Wall Street Journal,* Jun. 15, 2000, pp. A3, A12; Anna Wilde Mathews, "Web Music Isn't Just for Kids," *The Wall Street Journal,* Sep. 26, 2000, p. B1; Walter S. Mossberg, "Behind the Lawsuit: Napster Offers Model for Music Distribution," *The Wall Street Journal,* May 11, 2000, p. B1; "Napster and Recording Association to Face off in Court," CNN, July 26, 2000, www.cnn.com; "Napster Defends Its Song Technology," MSNBC, July 3, 2000, www.msnbc.com; "Napster: Downloading Music for Free Is Legal," C|net, http://news.cnet.com/news, (accessed) Jul. 3, 2000; "Napster Grows Up," www.redherring.com/industries, (accessed) Mar. 10, 2000; "Napster, Inc., Response to Ninth Circuit Court of Appeals Ruling on the U.S. District Court Injunction in A&M, Inc. v. Napster," Feb. 12, 2001, www.napster.com/pressroom/pr/010212.html; "Napster Not Trying Hard Enough, Judge Warns," Fox News, Apr. 11, 2001,

www.foxnews.com/story/0,2933,5497,00.html; "Napster Vs. the Record Stores," Salon.com, www.salon.com/business/feature, (accessed) Aug. 7, 2000; "Napster Wins Reprieve; Next Move Up to Recording Industry," CNN, Jul. 28, 2000, www.cnn.com; Martin Peers, "Survey Studies Napster's Spread on Campuses," *The Wall Street Journal,* May 5, 2000, p. B8; Martin Peers and Lee Gomes, "Music CD Sales Suffer in Stores Near 'Wired' Colleges, Study Says," *The Wall Street Journal,* Jun. 13, 2000, p. A4; Martin Peers and Ron Harris, "Napster Offers $1 Billion to Settle Copyright Suit," *The [Memphis] Commercial Appeal,* Jan. 2, 2001, pp. C1, C6; "Recording Industry and Online Music Services Battle Over Copyright Laws," CNN, May 16, 2000, www.cnn.com; "Stats Speak Kindly of Napster," *The Standard,* www.thestandard.com, (accessed) Jul. 21, 2000; "Study: Napster Boosts CD Sales," ZDNet, www.zdnet.com, (accessed) Jul. 21, 2000; "University to Lift Napster Ban," C|net, Mar. 23, 2000, http://news.cnet.com.

APPENDIX A
1. Jean Koretz, "Where the New Jobs Are," *Business Week,* Mar. 20, 1995, p. 24.

2. This section and the three that follow are adapted from William M. Pride, Robert J. Hughes, and Jack R. Kapoor, *Business* (Boston: Houghton Mifflin, 2002), pp. A1–A9.
3. Sal Divita, "Resume Writing Requires Proper Strategy," *Marketing News,* July 3, 1995, p. 6.
4. Andrew J. DuBrin, "Deadly Political Sins," *Wall Street Journal's Managing Your Career,* Fall 1993, pp. 11–13.
5. Ibid.
6. Cyndee Miller, "Marketing Research Salaries Up a Bit, but Layoffs Take Toll," *Marketing News,* June 19, 1995, p. 1.
7. Market research—salaries: http://www.careers-in-marketing.com/mrsal.htm, Aug. 8, 2001.
8. Product management—salaries: http://www.careers-in-marketing.com/pmsal.htm, Aug. 8, 2001.
9. Advertising—significant points: http://www.bls.gov/oco/cg/cgs030.htm, Aug. 8, 2001.
10. Advertising and public relations—salaries: http://www.careers-in-marketing.com/adsal.htm, Aug. 8, 2001.
11. Gartner, Inc., "Economic Downturn Slows B2B Commerce," CyberAtlas, Mar. 21, 2001, http://cyberatlas.internet.com/markets/b2b/article/0,,10091_719571,00.html.

CREDITS

CHAPTER 1:   **Page 3:** Carol Lundeen. **Page 5:** Reprinted with permission of Target Corporation. **Page 6:** © Copyright 2003, PhotoDisc, Inc. **Page 8:** The Martin Agency, Richmond, VA/Photo by Karl Steinbrenner. **Page 11:** Courtesy of Bose Corporation. **Page 14:** © Copyright 2003, PhotoDisc, Inc. **Page 16:** COVAD Communications. **Page 19 (left):** Courtesy of Accenture. **(right):** Courtesy of Handspring Inc. **Page 20:** Reprinted with permission of the Massachusetts Society for the Prevention of Cruelty to Animals (617) 524-7400. **Page 25:** Gary C. Caskey/Reuters/TimePix.
CHAPTER 2:   **Page 28:** © Copyright 2003, PhotoDisc, Inc. **Page 31:** Courtesy of Leo Burnett USA, Inc. Photo by Tim Simmons. **Page 32:** Reproduced with permission of Southwest Airlines, Inc. **Page 34 (left):** © Reebok International Ltd. **(right):** Datek OnLine. **Page 37:** © 2001 BMW of North America, LLC. Used with permission. The BMW name and logo are registered trademarks. **Page 43:** The Eagle Symbol is a registered trademark of the United States Postal Service. © 2001 United States Postal Service. **Page 46 (left):** Reprinted with permission of AT&T. Photo by David Leach. **(right):** Courtesy of Autolite. Reprinted with permission of Arnold Worldwide. Photo by Jim Sloane. **Page 47:** © Copyright 2003, PhotoDisc, Inc. **Page 51:** © Copyright 2003, PhotoDisc, Inc.
CHAPTER 3:   **Page 56:** Reuters/Fred Prouse/TimePix. **Page 59:** American Honda Motor Co., Inc. **Page 60 (left and right):** Courtesy of the Procter & Gamble Co. Used by permission. **Page 65 (left and right):** Courtesy of the Centers for Disease Control. **Page 67:** Reprinted with permission of Mercedes-Benz USA, LLC, A DaimlerChrysler Company. **Page 68:** © Copyright 2003, PhotoDisc, Inc. **Page 71:** Courtesy of PG&E Corporation. **Page 73:** Used by permission of Sony Electronics, Inc. **Page 76 (top and bottom):** Reproduced courtesy of AARP. **Page 80:** © Copyright 2003, PhotoDisc, Inc.
CHAPTER 4:   **Page 84:** © Copyright 2003, PhotoDisc, Inc. **Page 87:** Courtesy of Ford Motor Company. **Page 88:** © Copyright 2003, PhotoDisc, Inc. **Page 89:** Carol Lundeen.

Page 91 (top): Courtesy of The Nature Conservancy. Photo by Ron Semrod. **Page 91 (left):** Reprinted with permission of DTE Energy and Jankowski Co. **(right):** Reprinted with permission of the European Commission (http://europa.eu.int). **Page 92:** Courtesy of Environmental Defense. **Page 94:** Reprinted with permission of Weyerhaeuser. **Page 101:** Reprinted with permission of Business Ethics, PO Box 8439, Minneapolis, MN 55408, 612-879-0695, www.business-ethics.com. **Page 103 (left):** American Airlines, Inc. **(right):** Merck & Co. **Page 109:** © Copyright 2003, PhotoDisc, Inc.
CHAPTER 5:   **Page 112:** © Copyright 2003, PhotoDisc, Inc. **Page 113:** Reprinted with permission of Palm, Inc./Courtesy AKQA Advertising. **Page 115:** Used by permission of Uniscape. Photo by Getty Images. **Page 117 (left):** Courtesy of Ernst & Young. **(right):** Courtesy of Xporta. Reprinted with permission of YAD2M Creative, photo: GerryEllis.com. **Page 120:** Reprinted with permission of Vastera. **Page 123:** © Copyright 2003, PhotoDisc, Inc. **Page 124 (left and right):** Courtesy of AeroMexico Airlines. **Page 126 (left):** Reprinted with permission of BellSouth Advertising and Publishing Corporation. **(right):** Courtesy of UPS. **Page 130:** Courtesy of Sandor Marketing Group Inc. and WorldFinder Corp. **Page 134:** © Copyright 2003, PhotoDisc, Inc.
STRATEGIC CASE 1:   **Page 137:** © Copyright 2003, PhotoDisc, Inc.
CHAPTER 6:   **Page 141:** © Copyright 2003, PhotoDisc, Inc. **Page 142 (left):** Courtesy of Pine Company. **(right):** JRP Marketing Research, Inc. **Page 148:** Courtesy of Walker Information. **Page 150 (left):** Courtesy of RDD, Inc./Reprinted with permission by KnollGroup, Portland, Oregon. **(right):** Courtesy of Fieldwork, Inc. **Page 154:** Triversity, Inc. Reprinted with permission. **Page 157 (left):** Courtesy of Harris Interactive, Inc. **(right):** Reprinted with permission of LexisNexis. **Page 158:** © Copyright 2003, PhotoDisc, Inc. **Page 160:** Reprinted with permission of Common Knowledge Research Services, Dallas, Texas. **Page 162:** Courtesy of International Survey Research. **Page 166:** © Copyright 2003, PhotoDisc, Inc.

CHAPTER 7:   **Page 168:** © Copyright 2003, PhotoDisc, Inc. **Page 170 (left):** Reprinted by permission of Benjamin Moore & Co. **(right):** Corbis Images. **Page 173 (left and right):** Courtesy of A.T. Cross. **Page 176:** © Copyright 2003, PhotoDisc, Inc. **Page 177 (top):** Reprinted with permission of Planet Propaganda, Inc. **(bottom):** Courtesy of Dorfman Jewels—Boston, MA. **Page 179:** Courtesy of SAAB Cars of America. **Page 182:** © Simms Fishing Products, 2001. **Page 187:** Courtesy of State Farm VP Management Corp. Photo by Peter Zander. **Page 194:** © Copyright 2003, PhotoDisc, Inc.

CHAPTER 8:   **Page 196:** Felicia Martinez/PhotoEdit, Inc. **Page 198 (left):** Reprinted with permission of the Colgate-Palmolive Company, Inc. **(right):** Courtesy of Toyota Motor Sales, Inc., USA. **Page 199 (left and right):** Courtesy of Delta Carbona LP. **Page 201:** The Hoover Company. **Page 203:** M.C. Escher's "Sky and Water 1." © 2001 Cordon Art B.V.—Baarn-Holland. All rights reserved. **Page 204:** © Copyright 2003, PhotoDisc, Inc. **Page 209:** Reprinted with permission of Steve Madden, Ltd. and Butch Belaire. **Page 210:** Courtesy of Allen-Edmonds Shoe Corporation. **Page 215:** Mark Richards/PhotoEdit, Inc. **Page 219:** © Copyright 2003, PhotoDisc, Inc.

CHAPTER 9:   **Page 222:** © Copyright 2003, PhotoDisc, Inc. **Page 224 (left):** Courtesy of Baldor Electric Company. **(right):** Courtesy Engelhard Corporation. **Page 225:** © 2001 BIC Corporation. **Page 227:** © 2001 Hertz System, Inc. Hertz is a registered service mark and trademark of Hertz System, Inc. Photo by Getty Images. **Page 229:** Courtesy of General Motors Corporation. **Page 230:** © Neopost, Inc. Neopost and Simply Postage are registered trademarks of Neopost, Inc. **Page 233:** Courtesy of GERS Retail Systems. **Page 234:** Courtesy of State Farm Insurance Companies. **Page 235:** © Copyright 2003, PhotoDisc, Inc. **Page 242:** © Copyright 2003, PhotoDisc, Inc.

STRATEGIC CASE 2:   **Page 245:** Bonnie Kamin/PhotoEdit.

CHAPTER 10:   **Page 249:** Courtesy of Windy Conditions Kites. **Page 250 (left):** © Office of National Drug Control Policy/Partnership for a Drug-Free America. **(right):** Courtesy of the Centers for Disease Control. **Page 252:** © Graff Jewelers. **Page 254 (left):** Courtesy of Autodesk. **(right):** Courtesy of Salesforce.com. **Page 255 (left and right):** Reprinted with permission of Royal Jewelers. **Page 257:** Courtesy of Johnson & Johnson. **Page 259 (left and right):** ™/® "M&M's," "M," and the "M&M's" Characters *The Green Ones," "Feel the Charge," "M&M's Mores"* are registered trademarks of Mars, Incorporated and its affiliates. All are used with permission. Mars, Incorporated is not associated with the Houghton Mifflin Company or Pride/Ferrell, the authors. Advertisements printed with permission of Mars, Incorporated. **Page 260:** Michael Newman/PhotoEdit. **Page 262:** ™/® "*Snickers Cruncher, Hungry? Crunch This*" is a registered trademark of Mars, Incorporated and its affiliates. All are used with permission. Mars, Incorporated is not affiliated with Houghton Mifflin Company or Pride/Ferrell, the authors. Advertisements printed with permission of Mars, Incorporated. **Page 269:** © Copyright 2003, PhotoDisc, Inc. CHAPTER 11:   **Page 272:** © Copyright 2003, PhotoDisc, Inc. **Page 273:** *"Taste the Rainbow, Skittles"* is a registered trademark of Mars, Incorporated and its affiliates. All are used with permission. Mars, Incorporated is not affiliated with

Houghton Mifflin Company or Pride/Ferrell, the authors. Advertisements printed with permission of Mars, Incorporated. **Page 274:** Courtesy of Warner-Lambert, a Pfizer Company. **Page 276 (left):** Reprinted with permission of the TORO Company. **(right):** Courtesy of S.C. Johnson & Sons. **Page 280:** The Procter & Gamble Co. Used by permission. **Page 283:** Courtesy of Century 21 Real Estate Corporation. **Page 284:** © Copyright 2003, PhotoDisc, Inc. **Page 285:** Reprinted with permission of DANNON. **Page 286:** Courtesy of Audi of America, Inc. **Page 288 (left and right):** Courtesy of Wheaties Energy Crunch™ and General Mills, Inc. **Page 293:** © Copyright 2003, PhotoDisc, Inc.

CHAPTER 12:   **Page 296:** Will Hart/PhotoEdit. **Page 297:** Reprinted with permission of Swiss Army Brands, Inc. **Page 299:** Courtesy of Del Monte Fresh Produce. **Page 302:** Tony Freeman/Photo Edit. **Page 304:** Reprinted with permission of HireCheck, Inc.–St. Petersburg, FL. **Page 305:** David Young-Wolff/PhotoEdit. **Page 307:** Courtesy of Pro-Line International, Inc. **Page 309:** Courtesy of Marriott International. **Page 310:** Reprinted with permission of PACTIV Corporation. **Page 311:** Reprinted with permission of Vitro Packaging, Inc. **Page 313:** Courtesy of Evian. Photo © Steve Hellerstein. **Page 315:** Reprinted with permission of Heinz North America. **Page 318:** © Copyright 2003, PhotoDisc, Inc.

CHAPTER 13:   **Page 322:** © Copyright 2003, PhotoDisc, Inc. **Page 324:** Courtesy of Four Seasons Hotels & Resorts. **Page 326:** Reprinted with permission of Hawaiian Airlines, Inc. **Page 327:** © Copyright 2003, PhotoDisc, Inc. **Page 328 (left):** Courtesy Emory Healthcare. **(right):** © 2001 Kinko's Inc. All Rights Reserved. **Page 330:** Reprinted with permission of State Farm Insurance. **Page 333:** Carol Lundeen. **Page 336:** Courtesy of Pacific Bell. **Page 338:** Courtesy of Hotjobs.com. **Page 339 (left):** Reprinted with permission from Bethany College. **(right):** Courtesy of the National Bone Health Campaign. **Page 341:** Courtesy of The Waikiki Aquarium. **Page 344:** Ryan McVay/PhotoEdit.

STRATEGIC CASE 3:   **Page 347:** Carol Lundeen.

CHAPTER 14:   **Page 351:** © Copyright 2003, PhotoDisc, Inc. **Page 355:** Courtesy of Frontstep. **Page 359:** Reprinted with permission of Pioneer-Standard Electronics. **Page 360:** © Copyright 2003, PhotoDisc, Inc. **Page 361:** Courtesy Hershey Foods Corporation. **Page 362 (left):** Courtesy of Brown Cow Yogurt. **(right):** Reprinted with permission of HUMMER. **Page 364:** Courtesy Chevrolet Motor Division. **Page 367:** Reprinted with permission of StreetFlyers. **Page 372:** Comstock KLIPS.

CHAPTER 15:   **Page 374:** © Copyright 2003, PhotoDisc, Inc. **Page 376:** Reprinted with permission of TTI and TYCO Electronics. **Page 383:** © Copyright 2003, PhotoDisc, Inc. **Page 385 (left and right):** Reprinted with permission of BAX Global. **Page 387 (left):** Courtesy of iSolve Incorporated. **(right):** Courtesy of Manugistics. **Page 388:** Reprinted with permission of the Raymond Corp. **Page 391 (left):** Courtesy of Roadway Express. **(right):** Courtesy of American Freightways, Inc. **Page 393:** Reprinted with permission of Virgin Atlantic Cargo/Russell J. Varano, Jr. **Page 395:** Courtesy of R.O.E. Logistics. **Page 400:** © Copyright 2003, PhotoDisc, Inc.

CHAPTER 16:   **Page 402:** © Copyright 2003, PhotoDisc, Inc. **Page 405:** Reprinted with permission of Saks Fifth Ave. **Page 406 (left):** Courtesy of Wal-Mart Stores, Inc. **(right):**

Photographer Stephen Wilkes. Courtesy of Kmart Corporation. **Page 408:** David Young-Wolff/PhotoEdit. **Page 409:** Carol Lundeen. **Page 412:** © Lands' End, Inc. Used with permission. **Page 413:** © Copyright 2003, PhotoDisc, Inc. **Page 415:** Reprinted with permission of Wendy's International, Inc. **Page 418 (left):** Courtesy of Copley Place. **(right):** Reprinted with permission of Ram Management Co. and Kittery Commercial Associates. **Page 420 (top left):** Retail Planning Associates. **(bottom right):** David Young-Wolff/PhotoEdit. **Page 425:** © Copyright 2003, PhotoDisc, Inc.

STRATEGIC CASE 4:   **Pages 428, 429:** © Copyright 2003, PhotoDisc, Inc.

CHAPTER 17:   **Page 433:** © Indianapolis Motor Speedway. **Page 436:** Crayola, chevron, and serpentine designs are registered trademarks. The Power of Creativity It Starts Here and the rainbow/swash are trademarks of Binney & Smith, used with permission. **Page 440:** Chick-fil-A, Inc. © 2001. **Page 441:** © *This Old House* Magazine. **Page 443:** © The Keebler Company. **Page 445:** Houghton Mifflin/School Division. **Page 451:** Carol Lundeen. **Page 453:** © California Department of Health Services. **Page 457:** © Copyright 2003, PhotoDisc, Inc.

CHAPTER 18:   **Page 460:** Carol Lundeen. **Page 462:** Coca-Cola gave unprecedented permission to the American Advertising Federation (AAF) to modify their logo for use in the "Great Brands" campaign. This integrated communications program was launched by AAF to reinforce the essential strategic importance of advertising to C-level executives. To date, other participating brands are Sunkist, Energizer, Budweiser, Intel, and Altoids. Reprinted with permission of the AAF. **Page 464 (left):** Courtesy of Toyota Motor Manufacturing North America, Inc. **(right):** Reprinted with permission of Neutrogena Corp. **Page 467:** © Copyright 2003, PhotoDisc, Inc. **Page 468:** Reprinted with permission of Lifetime Productions, Inc. **Page 469 (left and right):** Courtesy of Target Corp. **Page 472:** Copyright © General Motors Corp., used with permission. **Page 473:** Reprinted with permission of Hill, Holliday, Connors, Cosmopolus, and AutoNation. **Page 475:** Courtesy of Decision Analyst, Inc. **Page 477:** Courtesy of Cahan & Associates. **Page 478:** Reprinted with permission of The Children's Museum Boston. **Page 484:** Reuters New Media, Inc./CORBIS.

CHAPTER 19:   **Page 488:** © Copyright 2003, PhotoDisc, Inc. **Page 490:** © Salesnet. **Page 491 (left):** © InFocus Corporation. **(right):** © 2001 Sanyo Presentation Technologies. **Page 495:** © Deploy Solutions. **Page 496:** ASI Solutions. **Page 499 (left):** reprinted with permission of Seabourn Cruise Line. **(right):** Reprinted with permission of GiftCertificates.com. **Page 500:** Courtesy of the TerrAlign Group, Metron, Inc., (800) 437-9603. **Page 503:** © Duracell. **Page 505:** © Comstock KLIPS. **Page 506:** Reprinted with permission by Hershey Foods Corporation. **Page 511:** © Copyright 2003, PhotoDisc, Inc.

STRATEGIC CASE 5:   **Page 515:** © Copyright 2003, PhotoDisc, Inc.

CHAPTER 20:   **Page 519** © Copyright 2003, PhotoDisc, Inc. **Page 521:** Reprinted with permission of Minolta-QMS. **Page 524 (left):** Reprinted with permission of Bang & Olufsen Newbury Street, Boston. **(right):** Courtesy of Corning Incorporated. **Page 531:** Reprinted with permission of Indianapolis Ice. **Page 532:** © Copyright 2003, PhotoDisc, Inc. **Page 534 (left):** Courtesy of Dell Computer Corporation. **(right):** Reprinted with permission of Buy.com. **Page 535:** Courtesy of Net2Phone. **Page 543:** © Copyright 2003, PhotoDisc, Inc.

CHAPTER 21:   **Page 546:** © Copyright 2003, PhotoDisc, Inc. **Page 548:** reprinted with permission of Teligent. **Page 549:** Courtesy of the Campbell Group, Baltimore. **Page 552:** Reprinted with permission of Vermont Ski Areas. **Page 553 (left):** Courtesy of Microsoft. **(right):** Courtesy of Quantum Corp. **Page 555:** © Copyright 2003, PhotoDisc, Inc. **Page 556:** Reprinted with permission of Coldwater Creek. **Page 559 (left):** Courtesy of Swain Tours, Air New Zealand, and Tourism New Zealand. **(right):** Reprinted with permission of CITYPASS, Inc. **Page 561:** Courtesy of Sears Roebuck & Company. **Page 562:** Reprinted with permission of Filene's Basement. Illustrated by Kurt Limpkins. **Page 567:** Mark Richards/PhotoEdit.

STRATEGIC CASE 6:   **Page 569:** Bill Aron/PhotoEdit.

CHAPTER 22:   **Page 573:** M. Vazquez–MVT/AFP/CORBIS. **Page 574:** Reprinted with permission of TEVA and the Frank Creative Workgroup. Creative Director: David Karstad; Art Director; Matt Lindaur; Photography: Jock Bradley, Rippin' Productions. **Page 577:** Reprinted with permission of the TJX Companies. **Page 578:** © Copyright 2003, PhotoDisc, Inc. **Page 580:** Reprinted with permission of Savvis Communications. **Page 582 (left):** Courtesy of Avaya. **(right):** Reprinted with permission of SalesLogix. **Page 584:** BLOCKBUSTER name, design and related marks are trademarks of Blockbuster, Inc. © 2001 Blockbuster, Inc. All rights reserved. **Page 589:** Courtesy of Deepak Sareen Associates. **Page 592:** Courtesy of Datastream Systems, Inc. **Page 598:** Stan Honda/AFP/CORBIS #FT0025617.

CHAPTER 23:   **Page 602:** © Copyright 2003, PhotoDisc, Inc. **Page 605:** Reprinted with permission of OutlookSoft Corporation. **Page 606:** Copyrighted by and reprinted with permission from CCH Incorporated. **Page 608:** Courtesy of InterFeedback.com. **Page 610:** Reprinted with permission of the U.S. Postal Service. **Page 612 (left):** Reprinted with permission of Autodesk, Inc. **(right):** Courtesy of CollegeClub.com, a division of Student Advantage, Inc. All rights reserved. **Page 618:** Carol Lundeen. **Page 620:** © TimePix. **Page 621:** © Copyright 2003, PhotoDisc, Inc. **Page 627:** David Scull/AFP/CORBIS.

STRATEGIC CASE 7:   **Page 629:** Tim Alt © Digital Art/CORBIS.

Name Index

Aaker, David A., 300(illus.), G30, G34
Abell, Derek F., G20
Agarwal, Rohit, 371
Aguilera, Christina, 112
Alderson, Wroe, G31
Alexander, Marcus, G21
Alford, Bruce L., G34, G35
Allan, Barbara, G27
Allchin, Jim, 82
Allen, Diane, 275
Allen, Paul G., 81
Alvarez, Luis Ignacio, G22
Andel, Tom, G18
Anderson, Erin, G31, G32
Anderson, Jerry W., Jr., G24
Andreessen, Marc, 79
Andruss, Paula Lyon, G22
Ansoff, H. I., 36(illus.)
Antioco, John, 569
Arens, William F., 471(table), G33
Arlan, Jeffery, G32
Arnold, David, G18
Asmus, Peter, G24
Aspinwall, Leo, G31

Babin, Barry J., G24
Balto, David A., G22
Bannan, Karen, G36
Barksdale, James, 80
Barlow, Richard G., G27
Barnes, Nora Ganim, G32
Barrett, Patrick, G28
Barrs, Dawn, G16
Barry, Hank, 627
Bateson, John E. G., 329(table), G30
Bayus, Barry L., G28, G29
Beardi, Cara, G20, G30
Begemann, Kurt, 511
Belch, George E., 471(table), G33, G34
Belch, Michael A., 471(table), G33, G34
Belk, Russell W., G28
Bell, Martin L., 289(illus.)
Benezra, Karen, G17
Bennett, Peter D., G30, G34
Beretzky, Steve, 109
Bergen, Mark E., G34
Berry, Leonard L., 329(table),
     335(table), 337(illus.), G30, G31
Best, Roger J., G24
Bidlake, Suzanne, G30, G31
Blank, Arthur, 14
Blodgett, Jeffrey G., G25
Bloom, Paul N., G24
Boles, James S., G24
Bowman, Douglas, G21

Braunstein, Peter, G31
Breen, Peter E., 192
Breese, Kristine, G21
Breitkopf, David, G30
Brennan, Bernard F., 26
Brown, Alan, G20
Brown, Stephen, G32
Bruno, Maria, G35
Buck, Peter, 133
Buckley, M. Ronald, G30
Burke, Ken, G32
Burnett, John J., G33
Burr, Aaron, 514
Burton, Jonathan, G21
Bush, George W., 143

Cadbury, Sir Adrian, G24
Campanelli, Melissa, G20
Campbell, Andrew, G21
Campbell, Nigel G. G., G25
Cantwell, Julie, G28
Carlat, Larry, G17
Carr, Robert E., G18
Carraher, Shawn M., G30
Carroll, Archie B., 86(illus.), G24
Carter, Vince, 460
Case, Steve, 80, 597, 599
Cassidy, Hillary, G16
Catlett, Jason, 629
Chait, Herschol N., G30
Champy, James, G28
Chaplin, Charlie, 123
Chase, Charles W., Jr., G27
Chase, Richard B., 330, G31
Chesley, Julie A., G22
Chester, Jeffrey, 630
Cholewka, Kathleen, G27, G35
Chonko, Lawrence B., G24
Chura, Hillary, G29, G30
Claflin, Bruce, 305
Clark, Brian, 488
Clark, Jim, 79
Clark, Ken, G35
Clark, Kim B., G29
Clark, Maxine, 218–219
Clark, Terry, G22, G30
Claybrook, Joan, 109
Coe, Renny, 404
Coen, Robert J., 466(table)
Cohen, Andy, G34
Cohen, Dorothy, G30
Coleman, Richard P., 212, 213(table)
Condry, M., G16
Coney, Kenneth A., G25
Conlon, Ginger, G37

Conover, John, 318, 319
Contractor, Farok J., G26
Cook, R., G16
Cooper, Lee G., G29
Corstjens, Marcel, G30
Cottrill, Ken, G32
Coughlan, Anne T., G31, G32
Couric, Katie, 134
Cravens, David W., G21, G33
Crawford, Fred, G16
Crosby, Philip B., G35
Cross, Sandra, G18
Crown, Judith, G29
Cueno, Alice Z., G30
Cummings, Betsy, G34
Cuneo, Alice Z., G28
Cunningham, Margaret H., G24, G26
Curan, Catherine, G31
Curry, Sheree R., G27

Dailey, R., G16
Dalzell, Chet, 24
Dasu, Sriram, 330, G31
Davis, Scott M., G29, G34
Day, George S., G21
Delgado, Adriana, 617
DeLuca, Fred, 133
DeMann, Freddy, 112
DePaulo, Peter, G27
Deshpande, Rohit, G35
Dillon, Pat, G17
Dion, Paul A., G31
Divita, Sal, G38
Dolan, Robert J., G21
Dolbow, Sandra, G18
Donnelly, James H., G31
Doolittle, Sid, 26
Dosoglu-Guner, Berrin, G26
Dougherty, Janice, 457
Dougherty, Jim, 457
Dow, Randy, 371
Dr. Dre, 626
Droogan, Alice, 566–567
Drumwright, Minette E., G24
Dubinsky, Donna, 245
DuBrin, Andrew J., G38
Duffy, William E., 356
Duscha, J., G16
Dwyer, Robert F., G24
Dykman, Robert, 371
Dzinkowski, Ramona, G27

Earls, Alan, G31
Ebenkamp, Becky, G18, G28
Edgar, David, 108

I-2   Name Index

Organization Index

Subject Index

Inelastic demand, 231
Information inputs, 203
Information search in consumer buy-
ing decision process, 200
In-home (door-to-door) interviews,
151
Innovative packaging, 313
Innovators, 263
Input-output data, 237
Inseparability of service production
and consumption, 325
Inside order takers, 493
Inside transit, 470–471(table)
Inspection as business buying
method, 229
Installations, 253
Institutional advertising, 461
Institutional markets, 226
Intangibility of services, 324–325,
325(illus.)
Integrated marketing communications,
432–454. *See also* Promotion;
Promotion mix
nature of, 434–436
Intended strategy, 574
Intensive distribution, 361–362
Intensive growth, 36
Interactivity in electronic marketing,
607–608
Interest, 520
Intermodal transportation, 394
Internal customers, 577
Internal marketing, 577–579, 579(illus.)
Internal search in consumer buying
decision process, 200
International marketing environment,
114–120
economic forces in, 117–118,
119(table)
ethics in, 116–117
legal forces in, 119
political forces in, 119
sociocultural forces in, 115–116,
116(table)
technological forces in, 119–120
Internet, 159(table), 159–160. *See also*
Electronic marketing (e-marketing); e-marketing strategies;
Internet; Technology; Websites
as advertising medium,
470–471(table)
Interviews for survey research,
151–152
Introduction stage of product life
cycle, 257
Inventory management, 386–387
Inventory turnover rate, B6
Involvement, levels of
in consumer buying process, 197
in international marketing,
125(illus.), 125–129

Issue definition for marketing
research, 143–144

JIT (just-in-time) approach, 387
Jobbers, 377–379, 378(illus.)
Job interviews, A6–A7, A7(table)
Jobs. *See* Careers
Job searches, A2–A4
Joint demand, 231
Joint ventures in international market-
ing, 128
Just-in-time (JIT) approach, 387

Keyword ads, 617
Kinesic communication, 444

Labeling, 314–316
Laggards, 264
Lanham Act (1946), 66(table), 67
Late majority, 264
Layout of advertisements, 474
Leadership of channels, 364
Learning in consumer buying decision
process, 206–207
Legal issues
in electronic marketing, 619–623,
620(illus.), 622(table)
in international marketing environ-
ment, 119
pricing and, 535–536
Legislation, 64, 66(table), 66–71
consumer protection, 66(table), 67
encouraging compliance with, 67–69
procompetitive, 66(table), 67
Levels of quality, 283
Licensing in international marketing,
127
Lifestyle in consumer buying decision
process, 209
Limited-line wholesalers, 378
Limited problem solving, 197–198
Limited-service wholesalers, 378–379
Line extensions, 273–274
Load flexibility, 394
Lobbying, 65
Logistics. *See* Physical distribution

Magazines as advertising medium,
470–471(table)
Magnuson-Moss Warranty Act (1975),
66(table)
Mail-order wholesalers, 379
Mail surveys, 148–149
Manufacturer brands, 301
Manufacturers' agents, 380–381
Manufacturers' sales branches and
offices, 381–382
Manufacturers' wholesalers, 381–382
Manufacturing, sales positions in,
A10
Maquiladoras, 121

Marginal analysis, 526–529, 527(illus.),
527(table), 528(illus.), 528(table)
Marginal cost (MC), 526–527,
527(illus.), 528(illus.), 528(table)
Marginal revenue (MR), 527(illus.),
527–528, 528(illus.), 528(table)
Markdowns, B8–B9
Market(s), 169–170
business. *See* Business markets
defined, 35
requirements of, 169
target. *See* Market segmentation;
Target markets
types of, 169–170
Market-based cost method for price
determination, 538
Market coverage, intensity of, 361–363
Market density, 180
Market-growth/market-share matrix,
35(illus.), 35–36
Marketing, defined, 4
Marketing audits, 593, 594(table)
Marketing careers. *See* Careers
Marketing channels, 352(table),
352–361
for business products, 358(illus.),
358–360
for consumer products, 357(illus.),
357–358
exchange efficiencies facilitated by,
353–354, 354(illus.)
expectations of members of, pricing
and, 533
legal issues related to, 367–368
multiple, 360–361
strategic channel alliances and, 361
supply chain management and. *See*
Supply chain management
utility created by, 353
Marketing citizenship, 85
brand name protection and, 532
cause branding and, 435
environmental responsibility and,
88, 93
legal issues and, 68
secure websites and, 621
sex-selection services and, 327
unethical consumer behavior and,
207
unplanned success and, 265
Marketing communications. *See*
Integrated marketing communications; Promotion; Promotion mix
Marketing concept, 11–13
evolution of, 12(illus.), 12–13
implementing, 13
Marketing control process, 588–590,
589(illus.)
corrective action for, 590
evaluating actual performance in,
589–590

Technology, 72–74. *See also* Electronic marketing (e-marketing); e-marketing strategies; Internet; Websites
 adoption and use of, 73(illus.), 73–74
 brick-and-mortar versus online retailing and, 404
 business buying behavior and, 228
 databases and, 157–159
 data mining and, 158
 guerrilla marketing and, 445
 impact of, 72–73
 in international marketing environment, 119–120
 Internet and, 159(table), 159–160
 linking multiple marketing channels and, 360
 management information systems and, 156
 marketing decision support systems and, 159
 marketing strategy and, 47
 marketing's use of, 20
 online co-branding and, 308
 online information sources and, 159(table), 159–160
 software for price setting and, 563
 television advertising and, 467
 web-based cosmetic retailing and, 204
Technology assessment, 74
Telemarketing, 412
Telephone Consumer Protection Act (1991), 66(table)
Telephone depth interviews, 151
Telephone surveys, 149–150
Television as advertising medium, 470–471(table)
Television home shopping, 412–413
Tensile pricing, 556
Test marketing in new-product development process, 279–281, 281(table)
Threats in SWOT analysis, 44
Time series analysis for sales forecasting, 189

Timetables for marketing implementation, 587, 588(illus.)
Tips, 520
Tolls, 520
Total budget competitors, 60
Total cost, 526
Total quality management (TQM), 579–581
Traceable common costs, 592
Trade discounts, 537
Trademark(s), 297
Trademark Counterfeiting Act (1980), 66(table)
Trademark Law Revision Act (1988), 66(table)
Trade names, 297
Trade salespeople, 494
Trade sales promotion methods, 502, 507–508
Trading companies, 127
Traditional specialty retailers, 409–410
Training of salespeople, 496–497
Transfer pricing, 538
Transportation, 390–395
 coordinating, 394–395
 modes of, 390(illus.), 390–394, 391(table)
Trend analysis for sales forecasting, 189
Trucking, 391 and *table,* 393(table)
Truck wholesalers, 379
Tuition, 520
Tying agreements, 368

UCE (unsolicited commercial e-mail), 621
Unaided recall tests, 476
Undifferentiated targeting strategy, 171–172
Uniform geographic pricing, 538
Uniform Resource Locators (URLs), 610
U.S. Sentencing Commission, 68
Unit loading, 388
Universal product codes (UPCs), 314
Unsolicited commercial e-mail (UCE), 621
Unsought products, 253

URLs (Uniform Resource Locators), 610
Usage rate, 387
Utility, creation by marketing channels, 353

Validity, 145
Value, marketing driven by, 15–17
Value analysis, 234
Value-conscious consumers, 534
Variable costs, 526, 592
Vending, automatic, 414
Vendor analysis, 234
Venture teams, 290
Vertical channel integration, 366
Vertical marketing systems (VMSs), 366
Viral marketing, 448

Warehouse clubs, 405(table), 407–408
Warehouse showrooms, 405(table), 408
Warehousing, 388–390
Waterways, 391(table), 392, 393(table)
Weaknesses in SWOT analysis, 44
Wealth, 63
Websites
 CEO Express, 36
 for this textbook, 20
 of U.S. Census Bureau, 75
Wheeler-Lea Act (1938), 66(table), 535
Wheel of retailing, 421–422, 422(illus.)
Wholesalers, 375(table), 375–382
 agents and brokers, 379–381, 380(illus.), 380(table)
 manufacturers' sales branches and offices, 381–382
 merchant, 377–379, 378(illus.)
 services provided by, 376–377
Wholesaling, sales positions in, A9–A10
Width of product mix, 255(illus.), 255–256
Willingness to spend, 64 and *illus.*
World Trade Organization (WTO), 125

Zone of tolerance, 336
Zone pricing, 538

Leading the Way with a Complete Package of Support Materials!

For Students

Student Website. The Marketing Learning Center at www.prideferrell.com includes Chapter 24, e-Marketing; the end-of-chapter Internet exercises with links (updated as necessary) to the assigned sites; ACE online self-tests; a resource list linking to numerous sites with authoritative marketing information; links to the companies highlighted in the text's boxes and cases; an online glossary, chapter summaries, and flashcards for review; marketing plan worksheets; career-related information; and more.

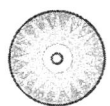

Real Deal UpGrade CD. This self-study tool includes information and exercises on improving time management, reading, note taking, and test taking skills, plus interactive self-tests for every chapter in the book.

Study Guide. This book helps students review and integrate key marketing concepts. The *Study Guide* contains different questions from those in the online study aids and *Real Deal UpGrade* CD, and includes chapter outlines as well as matching, true/false, multiple-choice, and mini-case sample test items with answers.

For Instructors

Instructor's Website. This password-protected site includes valuable tools to help instructors design and teach the course. The contents include sample syllabi; downloadable PowerPoint® slides and Word files from the *Instructor's Resource Manual*; new role-play exercises; and suggested answers to questions on the student site. NEW: *Who Wants to Be an "A" Student?* A fun, easy-to-use, interactive in-class game written in PowerPoint®, which reinforces key concepts and terminology and has been shown to increase student performance.

PowerPoint® Slide Presentations. These files, available on the instructor's website, contain over 25 slides per chapter, provide complete lectures based on the learning objectives, and include key figures from the text as well as new illustrations. Instructors can use these presentation as is, or may edit, delete, and add to them to suit their specific class needs.